# THE BEST 331 COLLEGES

# THE PRINCETON REVIEW

# THE BEST 331 COLLEGES

## 2002 Edition

By Robert Franek
Tom Meltzer
Roy Opochinski
Eric Owens
Tara Bray

Random House, Inc.
New York
www.review.com

Princeton Review Publishing, L.L.C.
2315 Broadway
New York, NY  10024
E-mail: comments@review.com

ISBN 0-375-76201-9
ISSN 1093-9679

Editors: Robert Franek and Erik Olson

Manufactured in the United States of America on partially recycled paper.

9  8  7  6  5  4  3  2  1

2002 Edition

The Independent Education Consultants Association Recognizes The Princeton Review as a valuable resource for high school and college students applying to college and graduate school.

# FOREWORD

Every year, over two million high school graduates go to college. To make sure they end up at the *right* school, they spend several billion dollars on the admissions process. This money pays for countless admissions officers and counselors, a bunch of standardized tests (and preparation for them), and many books similar to—but not as good as—this one.

It's so expensive because most admissions professionals have a thing about being in control. As a group, colleges resist almost every attempt to standardize or otherwise simplify the process. Admissions officers want you to believe that every admissions decision that they render occurs within systems of weights, measures, and deliberations that are far too complex for you to comprehend. They shudder at the notion of having to respond to students and their parents in down-to-earth language that might reveal the arbitrary nature of a huge percentage of the admissions and denials that they issue during each cycle. That would be admitting that good luck and circumstance play a major part in many successful applications. So, in flight from public accountability, they make the process a lot more mysterious than it needs to be.

Even the most straightforward colleges hide the information you would want to know about the way they'll evaluate your application: What grades and SATs are they looking for? Do their reported SAT averages include minority students, athletes, and legacies (kids whose parents went to their school)? Exactly how much do extracurricular activities count? What percentage of the aid that they give out is in loans and what percentage is in grants?

We couldn't get answers to these questions from many colleges. In fact, we couldn't get answers to *any* questions from some schools. Others who supplied this information to us for earlier editions of this guide have since decided that they never should have in the first place. After all, knowledge is power.

Colleges seem to have the time and money to create beautiful brochures that generally show that all college classes are held under a tree on a beautiful day. Why not just tell you what sort of students they're looking for, and what factors they'll use to consider your application?

Until the schools demystify the admissions process, this book is your best bet. It's not a phone book containing every fact about every college in the country. And it's not a memoir written by a few graduates describing their favorite dining halls or professors. We've given you the facts you'll need to apply to the few hundred best schools in the country. And enough information about them—which we gathered from hundreds of counselors and admissions officers and tens of thousands of students—to help you make a smart decision about going there.

One note: We don't talk a lot about majors. This is because most high school students really don't know what they want to major in—and the ones who do almost always change their minds by the beginning of junior year. Choosing a school because of the reputation of a single department is often a terrible idea.

As complicated and difficult as the admissions process is, we think you'll love college itself—especially at the schools listed in this book.

Good luck in your search.

*John Katzman*
*June 2001*

# ACKNOWLEDGMENTS

In the past I thought it would be impossible to assemble such a stellar team of authors, editors, data collectors, and designers as is needed to create a superior work of this nature, but again with this year's edition of *The Best 331 Colleges*, the impossible has happened. There are many people to thank for their dedication, attention to detail, and clear focus on providing an indispensable guide that gives students the chance to learn from the real experts, the current students at these 331 colleges. Through each player's participation in the preparation of this book, we have again successfully provided an uncompromising look into the true nature of each school profiled. I am without question pleased with the outcome.

A special thank you goes to our authors, Tom Meltzer, Eric Owens, Tara Bray, and Roy Opochinski for their dedication in sifting through thousands of surveys to impart the essence of each school in three paragraphs! Special thanks must go to Erik Olson, Guidebook Editor, for his ability and willingness to jump right into this project. He gave clear direction to all authors on the voice and sensibilities of The Princeton Review. Erik is without question our guardian and gatekeeper, and the venerable watchdog of our SPICE ideals.

In addition, thanks goes to Kristin Campbell, a veteran of guidebook and Web publications, for steering me in the right direction, no matter what the question. Thanks go to the entire guidebook staff, and special thanks to Amy Kinney for her shepherding of each survey collected for this publication. Amy is, in my eyes, a master of protocol and a talented liaison on par with a UN hostage negotiator. She is a true asset and I will miss her next year. My continued thanks goes to our data collection staff for their successful efforts in collecting and accurately representing the statistical data that appear with each school profiled: Brian Flumen, Kevin McDonough, Jenny Fallon, Julie Mandelbaum, Yojaira Cordero, and Michelene Rhymer.

Indeed, my gratitude goes to Chris Wujciak for his insight regarding data collection and representation, and the math behind our master lists. I respect his unwavering ability to address nearly any question I had regarding this publication. Chris, again I am in your debt.

The enormity of this project and its deadline constraints could not have been realized without the quiet presence of our production team; I am in the debt of two more pros: Julieanna Lambert and Scott Harris. Their unwavering ability to remain focused throughout the production of this project inspires and impresses me daily. Indeed, this year was extra special, for Scott Harris and his wife Sarah welcomed the newest member of their family, Miles, into the world! Even in the wake of this joyous news, Scott and Julieanna were still able to keep this book on track.

Last, thanks to our part-time production team of talented Deweys: Michael Palumbo, Omar Islam, Thatcher Goodwin, Jose Cordero, and Alex Simon. Your efforts are noble and always appreciated.

Again, to all who worked hard on this publication, thank you for your efforts, they do not go unnoticed.

*Robert Franek*
*Director of Guidebook Publications*
*and Associate Producer*

# CONTENTS

**DOONESBURY**                                                 By Garry Trudeau

# PART 1

# INTRODUCTION

# A Parent's Guide to the College Search: Why It Ought To Be An Enjoyable Year

*By Dan Lundquist, Dean of Admissions; and Peter Blankman, Director of Public Relations; Union College, Schenectady, NY. Reprinted with their permission from the Union College brochure of the same name.*

There are some 3,500 colleges and universities in the United States, and by the time you leave your son or daughter at new student orientation, you may feel that you've seen every one of them—or at least received mail from most of them!

We hope that by sharing a college's perspective, we can shed some light on the search process and help you understand it better. We hope these "educated insights" will help you approach the process in the most positive and productive way.

The college search process ought to be a positive, educational experience in itself, not just something to be "survived." At this point—the bridge between high school and college, adolescence and young adulthood—students have a remarkable range of options in front of them, and it's a shame when the excitement of this situation becomes anxiety.

While there's no sure-fire way to eliminate anxiety, we believe proper planning, combined with a realistic and appropriate attitude, can go a long way toward minimizing anxiety.

And that's a laudable goal in itself.

## Getting started

The college search needn't be that overwhelming—not if you start early, plan ahead, and take things one step at a time.

No question, you're facing a big change in your family's life. So how do you find a compass? How do you begin to sort through all the information and begin to make some choices that will make sense for you and your child?

There are a couple of first steps. One is to take a self-inventory. You and your child should ask yourselves realistic, sometimes tough, person-centered questions about interests, skills, values, and aspirations. Soon it will be appropriate to begin thinking about externally oriented issues like college size, location, and cost. And it's okay to admit that trepidation and uncertainty exist, even among "veteran" families.

Alongside the self-inventory is the gathering of objective information about colleges themselves—the kind of details that will help you narrow that list from 3,500 to perhaps a handful. This can be daunting. One of the overwhelming aspects of the college search is that there's so much information available. Sometimes it's hard to distinguish between what is and what isn't valuable.

One of the resources that too often is not used properly is your school counseling office. Nearly everything you need to start doing some preliminary sorting is here—an experienced college counseling staff, publications from colleges, guidebooks of all kinds, and electronic databases.

Along with the experiences of friends—students and adults—your own child's "instincts" are also resources to draw on. These anecdotal resources should not drive the search process, but you should feel free to start the preliminary list of colleges with some sentimental favorites.

As a goal begins to come into focus, sometimes working backward from that goal makes great sense. If your goal is to get to a small, liberal arts college in the Northeast, for example, start with a group of schools and work backward, applying increasingly personal, student-oriented questions to make distinctions and winnow the list.

## Let the student lead

It's important that the student take the lead in thinking critically to get down to the shortlist. Ultimately a student who's been spoon-fed is the one who's going to be disappointed in college when he or she discovers that other people's interests and values drove the college search.

One of your best strategies is to ask questions, keep your eyes open, and evaluate information and impressions. In the end, it's a question and answer process between family and college, parent and child.

Determining the fit between student and college depends on how you want to define the outcome of your child's college education. If you want to define it vocationally, you might look purely at statistics. To the extent that cost will be a factor, you will need to research tuition prices and/or financial aid policies. And if you want to define it as an academic, intellectual, personal, and cultural experience—and you are attuned to those values and clues that give you insights into a college's "character"—then your child's college years will be all the richer for that.

## No such thing as a perfect fit

Happily, for most students there is no one perfect fit. In fact, against the backdrop of so many fine options, your child certainly has the talent and flexibility to succeed at a number of colleges. Strange as it may sound now, some of the students who turn out the happiest, in fact, are the ones who thought they had lost the "admissions sweepstakes" at the end of their senior year. Hence the old college counseling truism: The vast majority of students are at their first-choice college by Halloween of their first year.

Even though your child could be happy at a number of colleges, you still have to focus the search. Rankings, objective data, and reputation are necessary, but not sufficient, to judge the correctness of the fit between the individual and institution.

In short, it's time to hit the road.

## Make those visits

Visiting a college is really the only way you're going to get a sense of the reality or the personality of the place—its strengths, its surprises, its life in and outside the classroom. From the time you first walk on campus, you will start picking up messages, from the quality of the facilities to the friendliness of the students to the physical care of the campus grounds.

A prospective student ought to ask, "Can I see myself here?" Look at the students; look at the announcements on the bulletin boards; feel comfortable asking questions about any issue, from housing and campus safety to graduate school placement. Try to get a handle on the tone of the campus, what the students care about and pay attention to, and help your child compare that with her needs and "comfort zone."

The same goes for an interview. Treat it as a conversation, not an inquisition. Who does well in an interview? A relaxed student armed with good questions and ready to speak articulately about his interests and aspirations.

Will you get straight answers to your questions? In the overwhelming number of cases, yes. Sure, we're recruiters—salespeople—but we're also counselors. We want to enroll students who are going to be happy at our college. Maybe that's one reason we're an admissions office, not a rejection office. An overarching goal of ours is that the college search process be a positive educational experience in itself.

## The "heart" quotient

A lot of people do a great job with the analytical part of the search, but they leave out the heart component, if you will. They are transfer students in the making!

When students are asked how they came to choose Union, they almost always cite the "smart," cognitive factors, such as academic program, size, and post-graduate placement.

That's fine. But we always discover that, as they narrowed it down, the answers come much more from the heart and describe how they felt when they first visited campus, or how much they liked the students and professors they met. If someone doesn't have a reasonable measure of that "heart" quotient, then college's general educational value, as a total experience, is going to be lessened.

## How we choose

At a certain point this whole process becomes more of an art than a science for you.

It's the same for us.

We have a parallel, shared process and goal. You are choosing a college, we are selecting students, and our goal—the best "match"—is the same.

Just like you, we begin by looking at the objective criteria (grades, quality of courses, and test scores) to see if there is an initial fit between your son or daughter and our college.

And like your college search, assembling a class is not a purely objective process. We want to bring together young men and women who have enough in common so that they're going to be good roommates, study partners, and friends, and support each other as they take the "prudent risks" that are an important part of the educational experience. We also want enough differences so they're going to educate each other in some subtle ways. That's the richness of a residential, undergraduate college.

Being a selective college means having a large enough applicant pool to select the students we think will be appropriate for our institution. It's important for parents to understand that at selective colleges the process is going to be just that—selective. And it is important to acknowledge that selective judgements based upon subjective evaluations are, to some extent, going to be "unfair." Coming to terms with that reality early on will help put any disappointments, if they come, into perspective later on.

## A good rule of thumb

From the start of the process, you should keep this thought in mind:

What is a realistic pool for my child?

Most counselors are going to recommend that you have four schools that look likely, have a reach or two (based on the objective data), and have a sure bet or two. That rule of thumb has been around all these decades because it's based on experience and realism.

## A positive experience

We hope that some of these comments help you approach the college search process from a positive, productive perspective. College counselors—admissions officers, recruiters, and guidance personnel—believe that it ought to be an enjoyable, educational experience, one guided by concerns for what's best for the student at this pivotal point between late adolescence and young adulthood.

Assaying one's options at this time of life ought to be exciting and fun—at least most of the time. It's true that choosing a college is a serious business, but that does not mean one must be deadly serious about it.

Best wishes, good luck, and don't forget, Halloween is just around the corner!

*For the past twenty years Dan Lundquist has worked at small, liberal arts colleges and Ivy League universities. He is now vice president of admissions at Union College in Schenectady, NY.*

*A former reporter, Peter Blankman has been director of communications at Union College since 1981.*

# APPLYING TO COLLEGE VIA ELECTRONIC APPLICATION

Just a few years ago, it was popular opinion that electronic college applications were an impossibility. Today, colleges across the country are scrambling to make electronic versions of their applications available to students over the Internet. The Princeton Review's Review.com has proven to be the leading electronic application service provider for students and colleges nationwide.

Review.com allows you to search through our database of more than 1,600 colleges. You can search by more than thirty categories, including location, major, average test scores, and student services to build a personalized list of colleges. Once you have a preliminary list, you can view detailed information on each one, and for some even fill out an exact duplicate of each college's application, complete with logos and graphics. The best part is you only have to type in your basic information one time. Review.com then automatically populates each form for you. Once the application is complete, just print out the form and submit the application directly to the school's admissions office.

## Looking for Colleges Online

The Princeton Review offers a variety of services to help you gather information about colleges and learn more about the admissions process.

**Search:** Review.com's search engine is the most sophisticated college search tool available on the Internet. To use it, select the things that are important to you in choosing a college—everything from average SAT scores to Greek representation. The result is a list of the schools that match your needs and a wealth of detailed information about each, including, in many cases, the inside word from students about their schools' faculty, workload, social life, sports, and more. Each profile includes a link to the college's website.

**College Admissions Discussion:** Share your college admissions experiences and get expert advice from Princeton Review moderators. It's the most popular college admissions discussion area on the Internet.

**Majors:** Review.com's brand new resource with three ways to search for everything you'd want to know about college majors. From our suggested high school preparation to the average starting salary for each major, you'll find all the information you need to wisely choose a major that fits your goals and personality.

**Counselor-O-Matic:** Get a sense of your chance of admission at schools in which you are interested. Start by completing your profile, and then find out if counselor-o-matic thinks you're a shoo-in or out of your league.

*APPLY!* **at Review.com:** Access hundreds of college-specific admissions applications, including everything from instructions to financial aid forms, as well as teacher recommendations and counselor reports. Our application system lets you enter personal information just once—common information automatically appears in each application you choose. Complete each application by viewing it on the screen and tabbing through to fill in the blanks. Finally, print and mail applications to the college in the traditional manner. It's the easiest and most popular way to complete college applications anywhere!

The Princeton Review can be reached on the World Wide Web at www.review.com.

# How We Produce This Book

When we first began work on this project in 1991, there was a void in the world of college guides (hard to believe, but true!). No one publication provided prospective college students with in-depth statistical data from the colleges on admission, financial aid, student body demographics, and academics, as well as narrative descriptions of college academic and social life on each campus based on the opinions of the very students who attend them. Thus *Best Colleges* was born. There wasn't then—and there still isn't now—any other college guide like this one.

The differences start right on the cover with the name—*The Best 331 Colleges*. Why not *The Best 300 Colleges*? Or just *The Best Colleges*? And how did we arrive at 331? Well, to be honest, the original plan back at the beginning was to produce a guide entitled *The Best 300 Colleges*. An initial list of colleges to be included was compiled, and the authors got to work arranging for on-campus student surveys to be conducted. Since student feedback is such an integral part of the individual college entries and several other aspects of the guide, it was absolutely imperative that every campus intended for inclusion be surveyed by academic year's end. Alas, Mother Nature and other forces kept our surveyors off of many campuses that year, and a number of colleges could not be included in the first edition. Thus it was simply called *The Best Colleges*, sans number.

The guide enjoyed some early success, but it really needed a number in its title in order to help position it in relation to other guides on the shelves of your friendly neighborhood book superstore. The second edition was referred to as *The Best 286 Colleges*, and it's all history from there.

To determine which colleges and universities are included in *The Best Colleges*, we have avoided using any sort of mathematical calculations or formulas. The initial list was built through consultation with a variety of expert sources, including fifty independent educational consultants from throughout the nation. From that point, new institutions have been added annually; a few have been dropped. A careful review of the guide will reveal a wide representation of colleges geographically, large and small, public and private, historically black colleges and universities, science and technology-focused institutions, nontraditional colleges, highly selective and virtually open-door admissions profiles, great buys and the wildly expensive. All are institutions well worth considering; though not every college included will appeal to every student, this guide represents our version of the cream of the crop—comprising less than 10 percent of all colleges in the nation—and our best 331.

In addition to closely monitoring the statistical data we collect, we meet with dozens of admissions officers and college presidents annually, and keep abreast of college news 24-7 throughout each year. As a result, we are able to maintain a working list of colleges to consider adding to or deleting from the guide for each subsequent edition. Any college we consider adding to the guide must agree to allow anonymous student surveys to be completed on campus; it is difficulty with this issue alone that explains why the United States Air Force Academy was conspicuously absent from *Best Colleges* for many years, while West Point and Annapolis were (and still are) included in the guide. We tried to survey there for three editions before we finally succeeded; it always deserved to be included in the guide—but only if and when it would allow student anonymity in response to our survey. We're very psyched that they're finally a part of our guide.

Hundreds of thousands of students in total have been surveyed on the various campuses that comprise the best 331. Each annual edition includes information based on the opinions of nearly 60,000 students; we've surveyed anywhere from all twenty-six men at Deep Springs College in the California desert to several hundred collegians at places like Florida State University and the University of Michigan. It's a mammoth undertaking, and we're always looking for ways to get an even bigger and better response.

So how do we do it? Early on we surveyed at all of the included colleges and universities on our own, marshalling resources through our network of dozens of Princeton Review offices nationwide. Once we'd gone through a few editions, we switched to a two-to-three-year cycle for revisiting each campus. (The reality is that, unless there's been some grand upheaval at a campus, we've found that there's little change in student opinion from one year to the next.) Thus, each year we now survey on approximately 100–125 campuses. Colleges that wish to be resurveyed prior to their regular survey cycle are accommodated with an earlier visit if at all possible.

All colleges and universities we plan to visit are notified through established campus contacts that we wish to arrange a survey; we depend upon these contacts for assistance in identifying common, high-traffic areas on-campus in which to survey, and to help us make any necessary arrangements as required by campus policies. At colleges in the New York metropolitan area (we call it home), we most often send our own team to conduct the typically half-day surveys; at colleges that are further afield, we seek the assistance of our institutional contacts in hiring current students to conduct the surveys if at all possible.

The survey itself is extensive, divided into four fundamental sections—"About Yourself," "Your School's Academics/Administration," "Students," and "Life at Your School"—that collectively include seventy-four questions. We ask about everything imaginable, from "how many out-of-class hours do you spend studying each day?" to "how widely used is beer?" and other mind-altering substances. Most questions are multiple-response in nature, but six offer students the opportunity to expand on their answers with narrative responses. These narrative responses are the sources for the student quotes that appear throughout each entry in *Best Colleges*.

Once the surveys have been completed and the responses stored in our database, each college is given a grade point average (GPA) for its students' answers to each individual multiple-response question. It is these GPAs that enable us to compare student opinions from college to college, and to gauge which aspects of the complete experience at each college rate highest and lowest according to the institution's own students. Once we have this information in hand, we write the individual college entries. Student quotes expressed within the entries are not chosen for their extreme nature, humor, or singular perspective—in all cases the intention is that they represent closely the sentiments expressed by the majority of survey respondents from the college or that they illustrate one side or another of a mixed bag of student opinion, in which case one should also find a counterpoint within the text. And, of course, if they accomplish this *and* are noteworthy for their humor or erudition, they'll definitely make it into the guide.

The entries in general seek to accomplish that which a college admissions viewbook by its very nature can never really hope to achieve—to provide a (relatively) uncensored view of life at a particular college, and acknowledge that even the best of the best of America's 3,500 or so colleges have their drawbacks. Though some college administrators find this book hard to accept, most have come to recognize that college officials no longer enjoy the luxury of controlling every word that students hear or read about their institutions and that the age of consumerism in the college search process is here to stay.

Our survey is qualitative and anecdotal rather than quantitative and scientific. While this approach sometimes means we blow a result—such as when we surveyed at Stephens College during the week the administration was debating the abolition of women's studies as a major at that small women's college and (*surprise!*) the survey results indicated an unhappy student body—most of our results are confirmed by feedback we get from alums, current students, counselors, and prospective students who visit the campuses. In order to help guard against the likelihood that we produce an entry that's way off the mark for any particular college, we send administrators at each school a copy of the entry we intend to publish prior to its actual publication date, with ample opportunity to respond with corrections, comments, and/or outright objections. In every case in which we receive a reply, we take careful steps to insure that we review their suggestions and make appropriate changes when warranted.

Far more important than what college administrators think is what YOU think. Take our information on colleges as you should take information from all sources—as input that reflects the values and opinions of others, which may be helpful to you as you *form your own opinions* about the colleges you're considering. This guide is not an end point from which you should cull your list of colleges to apply to without referencing any other source or visiting any of the colleges covered here. Rather, it's a starting point, a tool that can help you to probe the surface and get a sense of the college experience. You simply must do your own investigation and develop your own list of best colleges. Only then will this book be the useful tool that it is intended to be.

# HOW THIS BOOK IS ORGANIZED

Each of the colleges and universities listed in this book has its own two-page spread. To make it easier to find information about the schools of your choice, we've used the same format for every school. Look at the sample pages below:

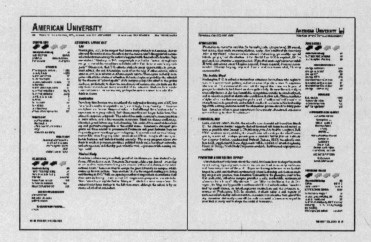

Each spread has nine major components. First, at the very top of the spread you will see the school's address, telephone, and fax numbers for the admissions office, the telephone number for the financial aid office, and the school's web site and/or Email address. Second, there are two "sidebars" (the narrow columns on the outside of each page, which consist mainly of statistics) divided into the categories of Campus Life, Academics, Admissions, and Financial Facts. Third, there are four headings in the main body text or "write-up" called Students Speak Out, Admissions, Financial Aid, and From the Admissions Office. Here's what each part contains:

## The Sidebars

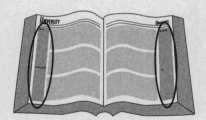

The sidebars contain various statistics culled either from our own online surveys and from questionnaires sent to the schools. Keep in mind that not every category will appear for every school, since in some cases the information is not reported or not applicable.

Here is what each heading tells you:

### Quality of Life Rating

How happy students are with their lives outside the classroom. This rating is given on a scale of one to four arrows. One arrow is the equivalent of a grade of 60 to 69; two are equivalent to a grade of 70 to 79; three are equivalent to a grade of 80 to 89; and four are equivalent to a grade of 90 to 100. The ratings were determined using the results from our surveys. We weighed several factors, including students' overall happiness, the beauty, safety, and location of the campus, comfort of dorms, food quality, and ease in dealing with the administration. Note that even if a school's rating is in the low 60s, it does not mean that the quality of life is horrible—there are no "failing" schools. A low ranking just means that the school placed low compared with others in *Best 331 Colleges*. This individual rating places each college on a continuum for purposes of comparing all colleges within this edition only. Though similar, these ratings are not intended to be compared directly to those within any prior edition, as our ratings computations are refined and change somewhat annually.

### Type of school

Whether the school is public or private.

### Affiliation

Any religious order with which the school is affiliated.

### Environment

Whether the campus is located in an urban, suburban, or rural setting.

### Total undergrad enrollment

The total number of undergraduates who attend the school.

### "% male/female" through "# countries represented"

The demographic breakdown of the full-time undergraduate student body and what percentages of the student body live on campus, belong to Greek organizations, and, finally, the number of countries represented by the student body.

### Survey Says

Summarizes the results of our survey. This list shows what the students we surveyed felt unusually strongly about, both positively and negatively, at their schools (see the end of the introduction for a more detailed explanation of items on the list).

## Academic Rating

On a scale of one to four arrows, how hard students work at the school and how much they get back for their efforts. The ratings are determined based on results from our surveys of students and administrators. Factors weighed included how many hours students studied and the quality of students the school attracts; we also considered students' assessments of their professors' abilities and helpfulness. This individual rating places each college on a continuum for purposes of comparing all colleges within this edition only. Though similar, these ratings are not intended to be compared directly to those within any prior edition, as our ratings computations are refined and change somewhat annually.

## Calendar

The school's schedule of academic terms. A "semester" schedule has two long terms, usually starting in September and January. A "trimester" schedule has three terms, one usually beginning before Christmas and two after. A "quarterly" schedule has four terms, which go by very quickly: the entire term, including exams, usually lasts only nine or ten weeks. A "4-1-4" schedule is like a semester schedule, but with a month-long term in between the fall and spring semesters. When a school's academic calendar doesn't match any of these traditional schedules we note that by saying "other." For schools that have "other" as their calendar, it is best to call the admissions office for details.

## Student/faculty ratio

The ratio of full-time undergraduate instructional faculty members to all undergraduates.

## Profs interesting rating

Based on the answers given in our survey in response to the question, "In general, how good are your instructors as teachers?"

## Profs accessible rating

Based on the answers given in our survey in response to the question, "In general, how accessible are your instructors outside the classroom?"

## % profs teaching UG courses

Largely self-explanatory; this category eliminates any faculty whose focus is solely on research.

## % classes taught by TAs

Many universities that offer graduate programs use graduate students as teaching assistants (TAs). They teach undergraduate courses, primarily at the introductory level. This category reports on the percentage of classes that are taught by TAs instead of regular faculty.

## Average lab size; Average regular class size

College-reported figures on class size averages for introductory courses, laboratory courses, and regular courses.

## Most Popular Majors

The three most popular majors at the school.

## Admissions Rating

How competitive admission is at the school, on a scale of one to four arrows. This rating is determined by several factors, including the class rank of entering freshmen, test scores, and percentage of applicants accepted. By incorporating all these factors, our competitiveness rating adjusts for "self-selecting" applicant pools. Swarthmore, for example, has a very high competitiveness rating, even though it admits a surprisingly large proportion of its applicants. Swarthmore's applicant pool is self-selecting; that is, nearly all the school's applicants are exceptional students. This individual rating places each college on a continuum for purposes of comparing all colleges within this edition only. Though similar, these ratings are not intended to be compared directly to those within any prior edition, as our ratings computations are refined and change somewhat annually.

## % of applicants accepted

The percentage of applicants to which the school offered admission.

## % of acceptees attending

The percentage of those who were accepted who eventually enrolled.

## # accepting a place on wait list

The number of students who decided to take a place on the wait list when offered this option.

## % admitted from wait list

The percent of applicants who opted to take a place on the wait list and were subsequently offered admission. These figures will vary tremendously from college to college, and should be a consideration when deciding whether to accept a place on a college's wait list.

## # of early decision applicants

The number of students who applied under the college's early decision or early action plan.

## % accepted early decision

The percent of early decision or early action applicants who were admitted under this plan. By nature of these plans, the vast majority who are admitted wind up enrolling. (See the early decision/action description that follows in this section for more detail.)

## Range/Average SAT Verbal, Range/Average SAT Math, Range/Average ACT Composite

The average or middle 50 percent of test scores for entering freshmen. When specific averages are not available, we report scores using middle 50 percent ranges provided by the school. Don't be discouraged from applying to the school of your choice even if your combined SAT scores are 80 or even 120 points below the average, because you may still have a chance of getting in. Remember that many schools emphasize other aspects of your application (e.g., your grades, how good a match you make with the school) more heavily than test scores.

## Minimum TOEFL

The minimum test score necessary for entering freshmen who are required to take the TOEFL (Test of English as a Foreign Language). Most schools will require all international students or non-native English speakers to take the TOEFL in order to be considered for admission.

## Average HS GPA

We report this on a scale of 1–4 (occasionally colleges report averages on a 100 scale, in which case we report those figures). This is one of the key factors in college admissions. Be sure to keep your GPA as high as possible straight through until graduation from high school.

## % graduated top 10%, top 25%, top 50% of class

Of those students for whom class rank was reported, the percentage of entering freshmen who ranked in the top tenth, quarter, and half of their high school classes.

## Early decision/action deadlines

The deadline for submission of application materials under the early decision or early action plan. Early decision is generally for students for whom the school is a first choice. The applicant commits to attending the school if admitted; in return, the school renders an early decision, usually in December or January. If accepted, the applicant doesn't have to spend the time and money applying to other schools. In most cases, students may apply for early decision to only one school. Early action is similar to early decision, but less binding; applicants need not commit to attending the school and in some cases may apply early action to more than one school. The school, in turn, may not render a decision, choosing to defer the applicant to the regular admissions pool. Each school's guidelines are a little different, and some colleges offer more than one early decision cycle; it's a good idea to call and get full details if you plan to pursue one of these options.

### Early decision, early action, priority, and regular admission deadlines

The dates by which all materials must be postmarked (we'd suggest "received in the office") in order to be considered for admission under each particular admissions option/cycle for admission for the fall term.

### Early decision, early action, priority, and regular admission notification

The dates by which you can expect a decision on your application under each admissions option/cycle.

### Nonfall registration

Some schools will allow applicants or transfers to matriculate at times other than the fall term—the traditional beginning of the academic calendar year. Other schools will only allow you to register for classes if you can begin in the fall term. A simple "yes" or "no" in this category indicates the school's policy on nonfall registration.

### Applicants also look at

These lists were formulated with data from our on-campus surveys and information solicited directly from the colleges. We asked students to list all the schools to which they applied and those at which they were accepted. Schools they named most often appear in these three lists. When students consistently rejected a school in favor of the featured school, that school appears under "and rarely prefer"; schools that split applicants on a relatively even basis with the featured school appear under "and sometimes prefer"; schools that students usually chose over the featured school appear under "and often prefer." For example, students in our survey who are accepted at both Princeton and the University of Pennsylvania generally choose Princeton. Therefore, on Princeton's feature page, UPenn appears in the "and rarely prefer" category (because students rarely preferred UPenn to Princeton), and on UPenn's feature page, Princeton appears in the "and often prefer" category (because students often prefer Princeton to UPenn). Admissions officers are given the opportunity to annually review and suggest alterations to these lists for their schools.

### Financial Aid Rating

Based on their survey responses, students' satisfaction with the financial aid they receive. Again, this is on a scale of one to four arrows. This individual rating places each college on a continuum for purposes of comparing all colleges within this edition only. Though similar, these ratings are not intended to be compared directly to those within any prior edition, as our ratings computations are refined and change somewhat annually.

### Tuition, In-state tuition

The tuition at the school, or for public colleges, for a resident of the school's state. Usually much lower than out-of-state tuition for state-supported public schools.

### In-district tuition

Some public colleges have three basic levels of tuition charges: in-state, out-of-state, and in-district. Where applicable, in-district tuition charges apply to students who are from the region surrounding the college regardless of state boundaries. Such plans are typically worked out through agreements between bordering states, and occur in rare instances.

### Out-of-state tuition

For public colleges, the tuition for a nonresident of the school's state. This entry appears only for public colleges, since tuition at private colleges is generally the same regardless of state of residence.

### Room & board

Estimated room and board costs.

### Books and supplies

Estimated annual cost of necessary textbooks and/or supplies.

### % frosh receiving aid

According to the school's financial aid department, the percentage of all freshmen who received need-based aid.

### % UG receiving aid

According to the school's financial aid department, the percentage of all undergrads who receive need-based financial aid.

### Avg frosh grant

The average grant or scholarship value.

### Avg frosh loan

The average amount of loan.

# THE WRITE-UP

## Students Speak Out

This section summarizes the results of the surveys we distributed to students at the school. It also incorporates statistics provided by the schools themselves. It is divided into three subheadings: Academics, Life, and Student Body. The Academics section reports how hard students work and how satisfied they are with the education they are getting. It also tells you which academic departments 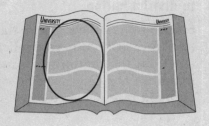 our respondents rated favorably. The Life section describes life outside the classroom and addresses questions ranging from "How nice is the campus?" and "How comfortable are the dorms?" to "How popular are fraternities and sororities?" The Student Body section tells you about what type of student the school traditionally attracts and how the students view the level of interaction between various groups, including those of different ethnic origins.

All quotes in these sections are from students' essay responses to our surveys except, where noted, when we cite an area college counselor. **We choose quotes based on the accuracy with which they reflect our survey results.** Those students who wrote entertaining but nonrepresentative essays will find excerpts of their work in part three of the book, a section titled "My Roommate's Feet Really Stink."

## Admissions

This section tells you what aspects of your application are most important to the 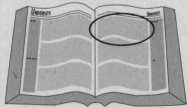 school's admissions officers. It also lists the high school curricular prerequisites for applicants, which standardized tests (if any) are required, and special information about the school's admissions process (e.g., Do minority students and legacies, for example, receive special consideration? Are there any unusual application requirements for applicants to special programs?).

## The Inside Word

This section contains our own insights into each school's admissions process.

## Financial Aid

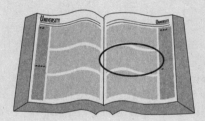

This section summarizes the financial aid process at the school: What forms you need and what types of merit-based aid and loans are available. Information about need-based aid is contained in the financial aid sidebar. While this section includes specific deadline dates for submission of materials as reported by the colleges, we strongly encourage students seeking financial aid to file all forms—federal, state, and institutional—as soon as they become available. In the world of financial aid, the early birds almost always get the best worms (provided, of course, that they're eligible for a meal!).

## From the Admissions Office

This section contains text supplied by the colleges in response to our invitation that they use this space to "speak directly to the readers of our guide." For schools that did not respond, we excerpted an appropriate passage from the school's catalog, website, or admissions literature.

# SURVEY SAYS

Our Survey Says list, located in the Campus Life sidebar on each school's two-page spread, is based entirely on the results of our on-campus surveys. In other words, the items on this list are based on the opinions of the students we surveyed at those schools (*not* on any numerical analysis of library size, endowment, etc.). Items are defined as those that are unusually popular or unpopular on a campus. Some of the terms that appear on the list are not entirely self-explanatory; these terms are defined below.

**Different students interact:** We asked students whether students from different class and ethnic backgrounds interacted frequently and easily. When students' collective response is "yes," the heading "different students interact" appears on the list. When student response indicates there are not many interactions between different students from different class and ethnic backgrounds, the heading "students are cliquish" appears on the list.

**Cheating:** We asked students how prevalent cheating is at their school. If students reported cheating to be rare, "no one cheats" shows up on the list.

**Students are happy:** This category reflects student responses to the question "Overall, how happy are you with your school?"

**Profs teach upper-level classes or TAs teach upper-level classes:** At some large universities, you'll continue to be taught by teaching assistants even in your upper-level courses. It is safe to assume that when "TAs teach upper-level courses" appears on the list, TAs also teach a disproportionate number of intro courses as well.

**Religion:** We asked students how religious they are. Their responses are reflected in this category.

**Diverse student body:** We asked students whether their student body is made up of ethnic groups. This category reflects their answers to this question. This heading shows up as "diversity lacking on campus" or "ethnic diversity on campus."

**Town-gown relations:** We asked students whether they got along with local residents; their answers are reflected by this category.

If you have any questions, comments, or suggestions, please contact us at Princeton Review Publishing, 2315 Broadway, New York, NY 10024, or e-mail us at comments@review.com. We appreciate your input and want to make our books as useful to you as they can be.

# GLOSSARY

**ACT:** Like the SAT I but less tricky. Many schools accept either SAT or ACT scores; if you consistently get blown away by the SAT, you might want to consider taking the ACT instead.

**College-prep curriculum:** 16 to 18 academic credits (each credit equals a full year of a high school course), usually including: 4 years of English, 3 to 4 years of social studies, and at least 2 years each of science, mathematics, and foreign language.

**Core curriculum:** Students at schools with core curricula must take a number of required courses, usually in such subjects as world history, western civilization, writing skills, and fundamental math and science.

**CSS/Financial Aid PROFILE:** The College Scholarship Service PROFILE. An optional financial aid form required by some colleges in addition to the FAFSA.

**Distribution requirements:** Students at schools with distribution requirements must take a number of courses in various subject areas, such as foreign language, humanities, natural science, and social science. Distribution requirements do not specify which courses you must take, only which types of courses.

**FAFSA:** The Free Application for Federal Student Aid. Schools are required by law to accept the FAFSA; some require that applicants complete at least one other form (usually a CSS/Financial Aid PROFILE or the college's own form) to be considered for financial aid.

**4-1-4:** A type of academic schedule. It's like a semester schedule, but with a short semester (usually one month long) between the two semesters. Most schools offer internship programs or nontraditional studies during the short semester.

**GDI:** "Goddamned independents," a term frequently used by students in fraternities and sororities to describe those not in fraternities and sororities.

**Greek system, Greeks:** Fraternities and sororities.

**Humanities:** These include such disciplines as art history, drama, English, foreign languages, music, philosophy, and religion.

**Merit-based grant:** A scholarship (not necessarily full) given to students because of some special talent or attribute. Artists, athletes, community leaders, and geniuses are typical recipients.

**Natural sciences:** These include such disciplines as astronomy, biology, chemistry, genetics, geology, mathematics, physics, and zoology.

**Need-based grant:** A scholarship (not necessarily full) given to students because they would otherwise be unable to afford college. Student need is determined on the basis of the FAFSA. Some schools also require the CSS Profile and/or institutional applications.

**P.C.:** Politically correct—a genuine buzzword on campuses today. It signifies either (1) an enlightened awareness of how society rewards certain members and punishes others solely on the basis of class, ethnicity, and gender; or (2) an unrelenting, humorless hypersensitivity on all issues even remotely related to class, ethnicity, and gender.

**Priority deadline:** Some schools will list a deadline for admission and/or financial aid as a "priority deadline," meaning that while they will accept applications after that date, all applications received prior to the deadline are assured of getting the most thorough, in some instances potentially more generous, appraisal possible.

**RA:** Residence assistant (or residential advisor). Someone, usually an upperclassman or graduate student, who supervises a floor or section of a dorm, usually in return for free room and board. RAs are responsible for enforcing the drinking and noise rules.

**SAT I:** A college entrance exam required by many schools; some schools will accept either the ACT or the SAT I.

**SAT II: Subject Tests:** Subject-specific exams administered by the Educational Testing Service (the SAT people). These tests are required by some, but not all, admissions offices. English Writing and Math Level I or IIc are the tests most frequently required.

**Social sciences:** These include such disciplines as anthropology, economics, geography, history, international studies, political science, psychology, and sociology.

**TA:** Teaching assistant. Most often a graduate student, a TA will often teach discussion sections of large lectures. At some schools, TAs and graduate students teach a large number of introductory-level and even some upper-level courses. At smaller schools, professors generally do all the teaching.

**Work-study:** A government-funded financial aid program that provides assistance to financial aid recipients in return for work in the school's library, labs, etc.

# ABOUT THOSE COLLEGE RANKINGS

We've shed some light on how we produce the entries, ratings, and rankings that make up *Best Colleges*, as well as a sense of why we publish the guide; now we'd like to discuss how to use the information that we've compiled—specifically the rankings.

Perhaps no single element of our guide to *The Best 331 Colleges* gets more attention than the front section entitled "Schools Ranked By Category." Since it's become an annual subject addressed by the media, and subsequently college presidents, admission directors, public relations officers, students, and their parents, we want to share our own thoughts about it with the students and parents who have chosen this guide.

The "Schools Ranked By Category" section of *Best Colleges* includes sixty-four different rankings. (One of these rankings focuses on a single institution, Deep Springs College, the only two-year college ever included in the guide. Deep Springs is assigned its own "Honor Roll" list that includes all categories in which it placed highly, thus eliminating perpetual "apples and oranges" comparisons between it and the four-year colleges in the rankings.) All of the rankings are broad-based in their intent, designed to generally illustrate environmental considerations at the colleges across a wide variety of categories.

Sixty-one of these lists are based entirely on either individual questions from our student surveys or are compiled from responses to several student survey questions. The other three lists include computations based on both student survey responses and statistical data provided by the colleges. Each list, even those entitled in a somewhat tongue-in-cheek manner, covers one of many aspects of a college's character that can be helpful in deciding if it's the right or wrong place for an individual student.

The rankings are often misconstrued; many in the media and general public think that The Princeton Review annually deems colleges "party schools" or places where the "students never stop studying." Actually, the rankings are based directly upon what students on each campus tell us about their college. Besides inquiring about where else they applied for admission, we ask them only about the college they're attending. No students are asked to rate other colleges comparatively in terms of any of the items the lists rank. And compound rankings are just that—compound calculations based on responses to multiple questions. There's no individual "party school" question on the survey.

In case you haven't heard by now, the party school ranking draws lots of attention every year. It's even been the subject of a *Doonesbury* cartoon. Calls, e-mail, and letters begin to arrive in our offices as soon as the first word of our rankings hits the media. Some contacts are from students who complain that their college didn't make the list, while others are from those who are irate because their college did. A *Washington Post* writer challenged WVU's number-one ranking in the 1998 edition as undeserved, contending that it's nothing like the good old days when he attended the university. Local media have touted the fact that nearby colleges didn't make the list when they aren't even in the guide in the first place, and thus were not surveyed at all. Many incorrectly assume that an institution that shows up on the party school ranking is a lousy college to attend—when the basic premise of the guide is to highlight colleges that The Princeton Review feels are among the top 10 percent of colleges and universities in the U.S.

*Best Colleges* begins with the best as its basis. Rankings that are among the less flattering of the sixty-two categories are not lists of bad schools—colleges on all of these lists are still among the best in the nation. This holds equally true for those on the party school list in particular. Remember our earlier comments about these rankings reflecting environmental considerations; broad categorizations of the college experience on each campus. Even schools placed at the top of the party school list are excellent places to pursue one's college career, and offer not only an exuberant social atmosphere but also a wide range of high-quality academic programs, as does every college or university that has ever appeared on this list in *Best Colleges*.

With few notable exceptions, no one should make the mistake of assuming that the colleges and universities that don't show up on the party school rankings are in any way insulated from the influences of alcohol and drugs on their student bodies and campuses. While a student who has little self-discipline or is easily led might be best off on a campus with a more distinctly academic emphasis, a glance at the news of the past academic year reveals that such considerations aren't often useful benchmarks.

The gaps aren't large in this regard, and tragedy is not exclusive. A Harvard University study has revealed that 86 percent of college fraternity residents and 44 percent of undergraduates in general binge drink (consume five or more alcoholic beverages in one sitting). These facts are sobering, as they should be. Fingers can be pointed in many directions as concerns campus drinking and partying. "Dry campus" policies drive drinking off-campus, make it even more dangerous, and only exacerbate the problem by removing any opportunity to influence student behavior in this regard. If you're going off campus to drink, don't drive back drunk—get a designated driver. Wherever you're going to drink, do it safely, smartly, responsibly, and within the law. Don't let a peer situation (fraternity rush, etc.) put you in jeopardy—it's simply not worth it. Don't use alcohol or drugs as a badge of your coolness—there's not much of a fine line between someone who's socially engaging and someone who's totally disengaging because s/he's performed a chemically enabled auto-lobotomy. Lastly, don't simply take responsibility for yourself; remember to keep an eye on your friends, and never leave them passed out and alone.

Some critics contend that The Princeton Review glorifies drinking and partying with these rankings; we submit that we glorify important information for students preparing to make one of the biggest choices they'll ever make in their lives. What could be more useful to students choosing a college than the opinions of current college students about their campuses? College is an incredible growth experience, one that covers a significant portion of the full spectrum of life's lessons. It's much more than classrooms, books, and professors—it's a complete experience that you're bound never to forget. College—there's nothing like it.

# PART 2

# Schools Ranked by Category

One of the great things about a multiple-choice survey is that the results give you lots of numbers. We wanted to present those numbers to you in a fun and informative way; hence, the following rankings of schools in sixty-three categories. In the following lists, the top twenty schools in each category are listed in descending order. Remember, of course, that our survey included only students at *The Best 331 Colleges*, and that all schools appearing on negative lists have many assets that counterbalance their various deficiencies.

Although these lists are presented mostly for fun, they can be used to help you clarify some of the choices you have to make in picking the right college. As you read through them, focus on those categories that are important to you: Do you want to go to a school where discussion takes up most of the class time? Would you prefer only to be lectured to? Do you care? Do you want to go to a school where students party nonstop? Or would you rather go somewhere with a subdued social scene? By looking through these lists, you should be able to get a good idea of what are and are not important considerations to you.

We've broken the rankings down into nine categories: Academics; Administration; Quality of Life; Politics; Demographics; Social Life; Extracurriculars; Parties; Schools by Type. Under each list heading, we tell you the survey question or assessment that we used to tabulate the list. For the Schools by Type rankings, we combined student responses to several questions to determine whether a school was a "jock" school, a "party" school, and so on. These lists have changed considerably since the first edition of this book, as we have had time to rethink what truly defines a school's character. For instance, we now factor students' answers to the question "How many hours a day do you study?" into our party-school calibrations. After all, as some of our readers have pointed out, at some schools students drink and do drugs to relieve the stress of their demanding curricula. And, in some cases, statistical data reported by the colleges is also factored in.

Be aware that all of these lists are based on our survey results. Therefore, they do not reflect our opinions, nor do they perfectly reflect reality; that is to say, we can't tell you at which schools registration is actually the biggest hassle. What we can tell you is at which school students are most pissed off about registration hassles. Our feeling is that students' self-perceptions are quite valuable. After all, what better way is there to judge a school than by how its students feel about it?

## ACADEMICS

### Best Overall Academic Experience For Undergraduates
*Based on The Princeton Review ACADEMIC RATING*

1. Princeton University
2. Amherst College
3. Harvard College
4. United States Air Force Academy
5. United States Coast Guard Academy
6. Swarthmore College
7. Williams College
8. California Institute of Technology
9. Massachusetts Institute of Technology
10. Dartmouth College
11. Rice University
12. Haverford College
13. Smith College
14. Carleton College
15. Pomona College
16. Harvey Mudd College
17. Davidson College
18. Duke University
19. Stanford University
20. United States Naval Academy

### The Toughest to Get Into
*Based on The Princeton Review ADMISSIONS RATING*

1. Cooper Union
2. Harvard College
3. Princeton University
4. Stanford University
5. United States Air Force Academy
6. United States Military Academy
7. United States Naval Academy
8. Columbia University
9. Yale University
10. Amherst College
11. Brown University
12. Dartmouth College
13. Williams College
14. Massachusetts Institute of Technology
15. Duke University
16. University of Pennsylvania
17. Swarthmore College
18. Bates College
19. Georgetown University
20. University of Notre Dame

**Your college.**
*All the sordid details.*
*We want them.*
survey.review.com

## Their Students Never Stop Studying
*How many out-of-class hours do you spend studying each day?*

1. Massachusetts Institute of Technology
2. United States Coast Guard Academy
3. California Institute of Technology
4. Georgia Institute of Technology
5. Rice University
6. Carnegie Mellon University
7. United States Naval Academy
8. Swarthmore College
9. Grinnell College
10. Amherst College
11. Princeton University
12. Santa Clara University
13. Harvard College
14. Davidson College
15. Middlebury College
16. Brandeis University
17. Whitman College
18. Northwestern University
19. Wake Forest University
20. Bryn Mawr College

## Their Students (Almost) Never Study
*How many out-of-class hours do you spend studying each day?*

1. University of Alabama—Tuscaloosa
2. University of Georgia
3. University of California—Santa Cruz
4. Ohio State University—Columbus
5. Saint Bonaventure University
6. University of Mississippi
7. University of California—Los Angeles
8. Louisiana State University—Baton Rouge
9. University of Rhode Island
10. Florida State University
11. University of Tennessee—Knoxville
12. University of California—Irvine
13. University of Montana—Missoula
14. University of Colorado—Boulder
15. Pepperdine University
16. Arizona State University
17. University of Florida
18. Ohio University—Athens
19. University of Hawaii—Manoa
20. Seton Hall University

## Professors Bring Material to Life
*Are your instructors good teachers?*

1. Smith College
2. Haverford College
3. Columbia University
4. New York University
5. Babson College

6. Johns Hopkins University
7. DePauw University
8. Tufts University
9. Wabash College
10. Emerson College
11. Rollins College
12. Pitzer College
13. Kenyon College
14. Colorado College
15. Millsaps College
16. Villanova University
17. Boston University
18. Harvard College
19. Georgetown University
20. Catholic University of America

## Professors Suck All Life From Materials
*Are your instructors good teachers?*

1. Miami University
2. State University of New York at Buffalo
3. Binghamton University (SUNY)
4. Ohio State University—Columbus
5. Clemson University
6. University of Toronto
7. Hofstra University
8. University of Michigan—Ann Arbor
9. University of California—Los Angeles
10. New Jersey Institute of Technology
11. Georgia Institute of Technology
12. St. Lawrence University
13. Stevens Institute of Technology
14. TCU
15. Beloit College
16. Muhlenberg College
17. State University of New York at Stony Brook
18. University of Idaho
19. University of California—Riverside
20. Warren Wilson College

## Professors Make Themselves Accessible
*Are your instructors accessible outside the classroom?*

1. United States Naval Academy
2. United States Coast Guard Academy
3. College of the Atlantic
4. Tufts University
5. United States Military Academy
6. Saint Bonaventure University
7. Rensselaer Polytechnic Institute
8. Colorado School of Mines
9. The Evergreen State College
10. Haverford College
11. Austin College
12. University of Miami
13. Bowdoin College
14. Stetson University
15. Morehouse College

16. Carleton College
17. University of Connecticut
18. Pitzer College
19. University of Minnesota—Twin Cities
20. University of Texas—Austin

## Professors Make Themselves Scarce
*Are your instructors accessible outside the classroom?*

1. University of North Dakota
2. Florida State University
3. State University of New York at Buffalo
4. University of Maryland, Baltimore County
5. Sonoma State University
6. Northeastern University
7. California Institute of Technology
8. Syracuse University
9. Arizona State University
10. University of California—Irvine
11. City University of New York—Hunter College
12. New Jersey Institute of Technology
13. University of Minnesota—Twin Cities
14. Louisiana State University—Baton Rouge
15. Georgia Institute of Technology
16. Hofstra University
17. Florida A&M University
18. University of Hawaii—Manoa
19. Illinois Institute of Technology
20. City University of New York—Queens College

## Class Discussions Encouraged
*How much of your overall class time is devoted to discussion as opposed to lectures?*

1. Wofford College
2. Georgetown University
3. Drew University
4. Colorado School of Mines
5. Macalester College
6. Wells College
7. Occidental College
8. College of St. Benedict/St. John's University
9. Rice University
10. Kenyon College
11. Sarah Lawrence College
12. Denison University
13. Carleton College
14. Boston College
15. Gustavus Adolphus College
16. Stetson University
17. Hobart and William Smith Colleges
18. Trinity College (CT)
19. Clark University
20. Calvin College

## Class Discussions Rare
*How much of your overall class time is devoted to discussion as opposed to lectures?*

1. University of Wyoming
2. University of Toronto
3. University of Georgia
4. University of Idaho
5. University of Indiana—Bloomington
6. Iowa State University
7. University of Arkansas—Fayetteville
8. McGill University
9. University of Nevada—Las Vegas
10. Illinois Institute of Technology
11. University of California—San Diego
12. University of Minnesota—Twin Cities
13. Arizona State University
14. University of Delaware
15. University of Maryland, Baltimore County
16. Pennsylvania State University—University Park
17. University of Iowa
18. Clarkson University
19. Virginia Tech
20. California Polytechnic State University—San Luis Obispo

## Teaching Assistants Teach Too Many Upper-Level Courses

1. University of Alabama—Tuscaloosa
2. Louisiana State University—Baton Rouge
3. Ohio State University—Columbus
4. University of California—Los Angeles
5. University of Florida
6. University of Arkansas—Fayetteville
7. University of Mississippi
8. University of Delaware
9. Indiana University—Bloomington
10. University of Illinois at Urbana-Champaign
11. University of New Mexico
12. Arizona State University
13. Michigan State University
14. State University of New York at Buffalo
15. University of Iowa
16. University of Missouri—Rolla
17. University of Tennessee—Knoxville
18. University of Georgia
19. University of Connecticut
20. Binghamton University (SUNY)

## Great Libraries
*Based on students' assessment of library facilities*

1. University of Virginia
2. New York University
3. Johns Hopkins University
4. University of Notre Dame
5. Yale University
6. Harvard College
7. University of Michigan—Ann Arbor
8. Smith College
9. Haverford College
10. Hamilton College
11. Mount Holyoke College
12. Pomona University
13. University of Toronto
14. Southern Methodist University
15. Knox College
16. Baylor University
17. Skidmore College
18. Tufts University
19. Boston University
20. Georgetown University

## This is a Library?
*Based on students' assessment of library facilities*

1. Florida State University
2. Catawba College
3. Rollins College
4. Miami University
5. Indiana University of Pennsylvania
6. Hollins University
7. University of North Dakota
8. Muhlenberg College
9. Middlebury College
10. St. Lawrence University
11. Seton Hall University
12. Catholic University of America
13. Wheaton College (IL)
14. University of California—Riverside
15. University of Nevada—Las Vegas
16. Morehouse College
17. University of California—Los Angeles
18. Hanover College
19. University of Tennessee
20. Spelman College

## Students Happy with Financial Aid
*Based on The Princeton Review FINANCIAL AID RATING*

1. Lake Forest College
2. Oglethorpe University
3. Ripon College
4. Knox College
5. Wofford College
6. University of Puget Sound
7. Agnes Scott College
8. Warren Wilson College
9. Hollins University
10. Catawba College
11. California Institute of Technology
12. Lawrence University
13. Hobart and William Smith Colleges
14. Birmingham Southern College
15. Ursinus College
16. Centenary College of Louisiana
17. Goddard College
18. Susquehanna University
19. Sweet Briar College
20. Guilford College

## Students Dissatisfied with Financial Aid
*Based on The Princeton Review FINANCIAL AID RATING*

1. Hofstra University
2. University of Hawaii—Manoa
3. University of California—San Diego
4. University of Minnesota—Twin Cities
5. Hampton University
6. North Carolina State University
7. University of North Dakota
8. George Mason University
9. Drexel University
10. College of the Holy Cross
11. College of William and Mary
12. Howard University
13. Binghamton University (SUNY)
14. University of California—Santa Barbara
15. State University of New York at Albany
16. University of Iowa
17. Columbia University
18. Boston College
19. Temple University
20. The College of New Jersey

## School Runs Like Butter
*Overall, how smoothly is your school run?*

1. Harvard College
2. University of Virginia
3. Middlebury College
4. Haverford College
5. Trinity College
6. College of the Atlantic
7. Millsaps College
8. United States Naval Academy
9. Williams College
10. Carleton College
11. Hamilton College
12. United States Air Force Academy
13. TCU
14. Colorado College

15. Boston College
16. Villanova University
17. Pomona College
18. Massachusetts Institute of Technology
19. Wheaton College (IL)
20. Davidson College

## Long Lines and Red Tape
*Overall, how smoothly is your school run?*

1. University of Massachusetts—Amherst
2. Boston University
3. California Institute of Technology
4. City University of New York—
   Hunter College
5. State University of New York at Stony Brook
6. Spelman College
7. Temple University
8. Rutgers University—Rutgers College
9. University of Connecticut
10. Hofstra University
11. Hampton University
12. Stevens Institute of Technology
13. Florida A&M University
14. University of Tennessee—Knoxville
15. City University of New York—
    Queens College
16. University of California—San Diego
17. Seton Hall University
18. University of Kentucky
19. University of Arkansas—Fayetteville
20. University of Delaware

## QUALITY OF LIFE

## Happy Students
*Overall, how happy are you?*

1. Pomona College
2. St. Lawrence University
3. Bard College
4. Wabash College
5. Saint Bonaventure University
6. College of the Atlantic
7. Tufts University
8. Vassar College
9. Washington and Lee University
10. Wells College
11. Pepperdine University
12. University of Richmond
13. Villanova University
14. Boston College
15. Coe College
16. Columbia University
17. Boston University
18. Pitzer College
19. Whitman College
20. DePaul University

## Least Happy Students
*Overall, how happy are you?*

1. State University of New York at Buffalo
2. University of Missouri—Rolla
3. Temple University
4. City University of New York—
   Queens College
5. Clarkson University
6. Spelman College
7. Colorado School of Mines
8. Hofstra University
9. University of Arkansas—Fayetteville
10. University of Connecticut
11. Seton Hall University
12. New Jersey Institute of Technology
13. University of California—Riverside
14. University of Toronto
15. Ohio Wesleyan University
16. Guilford College
17. Syracuse University
18. Rensselaer Polytechnic Institute
19. Loyola Marymount University
20. University of Idaho

## Beautiful Campus
*Based on students' rating of campus beauty*

1. Mount Holyoke College
2. Bryn Mawr College
3. University of Richmond
4. Stanford University
5. University of California—Santa Barbara
6. University of the Pacific
7. Haverford College
8. Susquehanna University
9. Colby College
10. Bowdoin College
11. Sweet Briar College
12. Swarthmore College
13. University of the South
14. Williams College
15. College of the Holy Cross
16. Georgetown University
17. Drew University
18. Ithaca College
19. Washington and Lee University
20. Randolph-Macon Woman's College

## Campus is Tiny, Unsightly, or Both
*Based on students' rating of campus beauty*

1. State University of New York at Stony Brook
2. Rochester Institute of Technology
3. Duquesne University
4. Golden Gate University
5. California Polytechnic State University
6. Drexel University
7. University of Dallas

8. Seton Hall University
9. Tuskegee University
10. Illinois Institute of Technology
11. State University of New York at Albany
12. State University of New York at Buffalo
13. Binghamton University (SUNY)
14. University of California—Riverside
15. North Carolina State University
16. University of Maryland, Baltimore County
17. University of Idaho
18. Tufts University
19. Case Western Reserve University
20. University of Massachusetts—Amherst

## Great Food
*Based on students' rating of campus food*

1. Wheaton College (IL)
2. Washington University
3. College of the Atlantic
4. Colby College
5. Dickinson College
6. Bowdoin College
7. American University
8. Cornell University
9. Brown University
10. Boston University
11. Emerson College
12. Bates College
13. Randolph-Macon Woman's College
14. Columbia University
15. Bennington College
16. Villanova University
17. Bryn Mawr College
18. Rutgers University—Rutgers College
19. Albertson College
20. Trinity College

## Is IT Food?
*Based on students' rating of campus food*

1. Saint Bonaventure University
2. Colorado School of Mines
3. Fordham University
4. Tuskegee University
5. University of Texas—Austin
6. Oglethorpe University
7. Hampton University
8. University of Arkansas—Fayetteville
9. The Evergreen State College
10. Westminster College
11. Catawba College
12. University of North Dakota
13. University of Montana—Missoula
14. New Jersey Institute of Technology
15. University of Idaho
16. University of California—Riverside
17. Swarthmore College

18. Hiram College
19. Saint Louis University
20. Stevens Institute of Technology

## Dorms Like Palaces
*Based on students' rating of dorm comfort*

1. Bryn Mawr College
2. Sarah Lawrence College
3. Randolph-Macon Woman's College
4. Mount Holyoke College
5. Washington and Lee University
6. Swarthmore College
7. Grinnell College
8. Smith College
9. California Institute of Technology
10. Davidson College
11. Wellesley College
12. Haverford College
13. Reed College
14. Carleton College
15. Rhodes College
16. Middlebury College
17. Bennington College
18. Marlboro College
19. Wells College
20. Boston University

## Dorms Like Dungeons
*Based on students' rating of dorm comfort*

1. State University of New York at Buffalo
2. California Polytechnic State University—San Luis Obispo
3. University of Montana—Missoula
4. University of Georgia
5. University of Florida
6. Florida A&M University
7. State University of New York at Stony Brook
8. Rutgers University—Rutgers College
9. University of Washington
10. University of California—San Diego
11. University of Connecticut
12. Auburn University
13. Clemson University
14. Georgia Institute of Technology
15. City University of New York—Hunter College
16. Brigham Young University
17. Hofstra University
18. Beloit College
19. Gustavus Adolphus College
20. Ripon College

## Best Quality of Life
*Based on The Princeton Review's QUALITY OF LIFE RATING*

1. University of Richmond
2. Harvard College
3. University of California—Santa Cruz
4. Dartmouth College
5. Brigham Young University
6. Goddard College
7. University of California—Santa Barbara
8. Smith College
9. Davidson College
10. Georgetown University
11. Mount Holyoke College
12. Rhodes College
13. Agnes Scott College
14. Eckerd College
15. Trinity University
16. Florida State University
17. Haverford College
18. Macalester College
19. Washington and Lee University
20. Claremont McKenna College

## POLITICS

## Students Most Nostalgic for Ronald Reagan
*Based on students' assessment of their personal political views*

1. University of Dallas
2. Louisiana State University—Baton Rouge
3. Villanova University
4. Lehigh University
5. Wheaton College (IL)
6. Samford University
7. Hamilton College
8. Colgate University
9. Grove City College
10. Southern Methodist University
11. Wabash College
12. Baylor University
13. Pepperdine University
14. Wofford College
15. Vanderbilt University
16. Illinois Wesleyan University
17. Randolph-Macon College
18. United States Naval Academy
19. Ohio Wesleyan University
20. Auburn University

**Your school.**
*Virtue and vice.*
*Tell us.*
*survey.review.com*

## Students Most Nostalgic for Bill Clinton
*Based on students' assessment of their personal political views*

1. Lewis & Clark College
2. New York University
3. Drew University
4. Sarah Lawrence College
5. Reed College
6. Grinnell College
7. Vassar College
8. Bard College
9. Warren Wilson College
10. Wesleyan University
11. Hampshire College
12. Smith College
13. Clark University
14. Macalester College
15. Knox College
16. Bennington College
17. Guilford College
18. Barnard College
19. Eugene Lang College
20. Carleton College

## Most Politically Active
*How popular are political/activist groups?*

1. New York University
2. Bard College
3. Simon's Rock College of Bard
4. Georgetown University
5. Warren Wilson College
6. Tufts University
7. Swarthmore College
8. The Evergreen State College
9. Hampshire College
10. Syracuse University
11. Mount Holyoke College
12. Earlham College
13. Oberlin College
14. George Washington University
15. Furman University
16. St. Lawrence University
17. Calvin College
18. Pitzer College
19. Vassar College
20. Lewis & Clark College

## Election? What Election?
*How popular are political/activist groups?*

1. Carnegie Mellon University
2. California Institute of Technology
3. University of Missouri—Rolla
4. University of California—Riverside
5. Rose-Hulman Institute of Technology
6. Lehigh University

7. University of Idaho
8. TCU
9. University of the Pacific
10. Colorado School of Mines
11. Samford University
12. Scripps College
13. Wofford College
14. Austin College
15. Rollins College
16. Babson College
17. Bennington College
18. Rensselaer Polytechnic Institute
19. Saint Bonaventure University
20. The College of New Jersey

## DEMOGRAPHICS

### Diverse Student Population
*Is your student body made up of diverse social and ethnic types?*

1. Boston University
2. New York University
3. Temple University
4. Columbia University
5. Massachusetts Institute of Technology
6. University of Maryland, Baltimore County
7. Seton Hall University
8. Carnegie Mellon University
9. University of Miami
10. University of California—Berkeley
11. Clark University
12. DePaul University
13. Bard College
14. Rose-Hulman Institute of Technology
15. California Institute of Technology
16. Brown University
17. Mount Holyoke College
18. Rutgers University—Rutgers College
19. Cornell University
20. Occidental College

### Homogeneous Student Population
*Is your student body made up of diverse social and ethnic types?*

1. Boston College
2. Trinity College
3. Reed College
4. Gettysburg College
5. Fairfield University
6. Colgate University
7. Grove City College
8. Washington and Lee University
9. Indiana University of Pennsylvania
10. Bucknell University
11. Saint Bonaventure University

12. Whitman College
13. University of Vermont
14. University of Notre Dame
15. University of Richmond
16. Lehigh University
17. Hanover College
18. Hamilton College
19. Hampden-Sydney College
20. Westminster College (PA)

### Students from Different Backgrounds Interact
*Do different types of students (black/white, rich/poor) interact frequently and easily?*

1. Boston University
2. California Institute of Technology
3. Carnegie Mellon University
4. St. Lawrence University
5. Florida State University
6. Seton Hall University
7. Syracuse University
8. TCU
9. Temple University
10. Bard College
11. Babson College
12. Harvard College
13. Pitzer College
14. Swarthmore College
15. Mount Holyoke College
16. University of California—Berkeley
17. University of Miami
18. University of Arizona
19. United States Coast Guard Academy
20. New York University

### Little Race/Class Interaction
*Do different types of students (black/white, rich/poor) interact frequently and easily?*

1. Bennington College
2. Colorado School of Mines
3. Austin College
4. The Evergreen State College
5. Tufts University
6. Saint Bonaventure University
7. Emory University
8. Trinity College
9. University of Idaho
10. University of California—Santa Barbara
11. University of Pittsburgh—Pittsburgh
12. Haverford College
13. Grinnell College
14. Miami University
15. Lehigh University
16. Denison University
17. Knox College
18. University of Notre Dame
19. Colorado College
20. Villanova University

## Gay Community Accepted
*Is there very little discrimination against homosexuals?*

1. Smith College
2. New York University
3. Drew University
4. Wesleyan University
5. Colby College
6. Simon's Rock College of Bard
7. Connecticut College
8. Pitzer College
9. Reed College
10. Vassar College
11. Sarah Lawrence
12. Wells College
13. Boston University
14. Barnard College
15. Whitman College
16. University of California—Berkeley
17. Lewis & Clark College
18. Grinnell College
19. Mount Holyoke College
20. Marlboro College

## Alternative Lifestyles Not an Alternative
*Is there very little discrimination against homosexuals?*

1. Duke University
2. Boston College
3. Seton Hall University
4. Wheaton College (IL)
5. University of Notre Dame
6. Grove City College
7. University of Connecticut
8. Brigham Young University
9. College of the Holy Cross
10. University of Dallas
11. Austin College
12. Johns Hopkins University
13. Miami University
14. Rice University
15. Denison University
16. Wofford College
17. Knox College
18. Hampton University
19. Southern Methodist University
20. Hanover College

## Students Pray on a Regular Basis
*Are students very religious?*

1. Wheaton College (IL)
2. Brigham Young University
3. Grove City College
4. Samford University
5. Pepperdine University
6. Calvin College
7. Loyola Marymount University

8. University of Dallas
9. Baylor University
10. Unites States Coast Guard Academy
11. St. Olaf College
12. Furman University
13. Gustavus Adolphus College
14. Villanova University
15. Valparaiso University
16. University of Notre Dame
17. DePauw University
18. Fisk University
19. Birmingham Southern College
20. Creighton University

## Students Ignore God on a Regular Basis
*Are students very religious?*

1. Macalester College
2. Lewis & Clark College
3. Wesleyan University
4. Pitzer College
5. Colby College
6. Bard College
7. Vassar College
8. Reed College
9. Connecticut College
10. Colorado College
11. Muhlenberg College
12. Grinnell College
13. Hampshire College
14. Guilford College
15. Drew University
16. Cooper Union
17. Bowdoin College
18. Simon's Rock College of Bard
19. University of California—Santa Cruz
20. Bates College

# SOCIAL LIFE

## Great College Towns
*Based on students' assessment of the surrounding city or town*

1. Georgetown University
2. Emory University
3. Boston University
4. Cooper Union
5. New York University
6. Emerson College
7. University of Georgia
8. University of California—Berkeley
9. Tulane University
10. University of Michigan—Ann Arbor
11. American University
12. DePaul University
13. McGill University

14. University of Wisconsin—Madison
15. University of Chicago
16. Stevens Institute of Technology
17. University of Miami
18. University of California—Los Angeles
19. Johns Hopkins University
20. Temple University

## More to Do on Campus
*Based on students' assessment of the surrounding city or town*

1. Syracuse University
2. Georgia Institute of Technology
3. Tufts University
4. Bennington College
5. St. Lawrence University
6. University of Maine
7. Clark University
8. Seton Hall University
9. The College of New Jersey
10. Susquehanna University
11. Louisiana State University—Baton Rouge
12. Hanover College
13. Centre College
14. University of Wyoming
15. Rensselaer Polytechnic Institute
16. Villanova University
17. University of Colorado—Boulder
18. University of Mississippi
19. University of Connecticut
20. Siena College

## Town-Gown Relations are Good
*Do students get along well with members of the local community?*

1. Wells College
2. Wheaton College (IL)
3. Emerson College
4. Mount Holyoke College
5. United States Coast Guard Academy
6. Albertson College
7. Ohio Wesleyan University
8. Rensselaer Polytechnic Institute
9. Carnegie Mellon University
10. Scripps College
11. Smith College
12. Earlham College
13. St. Olaf College
14. DePaul University
15. Amherst College
16. University of Arizona
17. Drew University
18. Rice University
19. Millsaps College
20. University of New Hampshire

## Town-Gown Relations are Strained
*Do students get along well with members of the local community?*

1. Babson College
2. Fairfield University
3. College of the Atlantic
4. Sarah Lawrence College
5. Bennington College
6. Villanova University
7. University of Idaho
8. University of the Pacific
9. Beloit College
10. Vassar College
11. The College of New Jersey
12. Tufts University
13. Simon's Rock College of Bard
14. Lehigh University
15. Lafayette College
16. Colorado College
17. University of California—Santa Barbara
18. TCU
19. Connecticut College
20. Austin College

## EXTRACURRICULARS

## Students Pack the Stadiums
*How popular are intercollegiate sports?*

1. Pennsylvania State University—University Park
2. University of Michigan—Ann Arbor
3. Duke University
4. University of North Carolina—Chapel Hill
5. Florida State University
6. Michigan State University
7. University of Arizona
8. Texas A&M University—College Station
9. Syracuse University
10. University of Southern California
11. University of Notre Dame
12. University of Oklahoma
13. University of Georgia
14. University of Miami
15. Wake Forest University
16. University of Nebraska—Lincoln
17. University of Alabama—Tuscaloosa
18. University of Colorado—Boulder
19. University of Tennessee—Knoxville
20. University of Florida

## Intercollegiate Sports Unpopular or Nonexistent
*How popular are intercollegiate sports?*

1. Bennington College
2. Emerson College
3. Cooper Union
4. Oberlin College
5. Bard College
6. Goddard College
7. Golden Gate College
8. Sarah Lawrence College
9. St. John's College (NM)
10. Marlboro College
11. Emory University
12. California Institute of Technology
13. The Evergreen State College
14. New College of the University of South Florida
15. St. John's College (MD)
16. Fordham University
17. Reed College
18. Whitman College
19. Illinois Institute of Technology
20. Scripps College

## Everyone Plays Intramural Sports
*How popular are intramural sports?*

1. Williams College
2. Auburn University
3. Massachusetts Institute of Technology
4. University of Notre Dame
5. Wake Forest University
6. Pennsylvania State University—University Park
7. Trinity College
8. Colgate University
9. University of Michigan—Ann Arbor
10. Grove City College
11. University of Arizona
12. St. John's College (MD)
13. Whitman College
14. University of Wisconsin—Madison
15. University of Alabama—Tuscaloosa
16. University of Florida
17. Florida State University
18. Hanover College
19. Rice University
20. University of Arkansas—Fayetteville

## Nobody Plays Intramural Sports
*How popular are intramural sports?*

1. Cooper Union
2. Reed College
3. Emerson College
4. Marlboro College

5. Scripps College
6. Bryn Mawr College
7. Babson College
8. Goddard College
9. Guilford College
10. Eugene Lang College
11. The Evergreen State College
12. New College of the University of South Florida
13. Fordham University
14. Bennington College
15. Stephens College
16. Columbia University
17. New York University
18. Simon's Rock College of Bard
19. Spelman College
20. Sarah Lawrence College

## Great College Radio Station
*How popular is the radio station?*

1. Fordham University
2. Emerson College
3. Louisiana State University—Baton Rouge
4. Union College
5. Florida State University
6. Franklin & Marshall College
7. Saint Bonaventure University
8. DePauw University
9. Goddard College
10. Skidmore College
11. Boston University
12. Vassar College
13. Bennington College
14. Whitman College
15. University of Chicago
16. Hamilton College
17. Seton Hall University
18. Rice University
19. Brown University
20. Earlham College

## College Newspaper Gets Read
*How popular is the newspaper?*

1. University of Pennsylvania
2. Tufts University
3. Arizona State University
4. University of North Carolina—Chapel Hill
5. University of Florida
6. University of Maryland—College Park
7. Emerson College
8. Syracuse University
9. University of Minnesota—Twin Cities
10. Wabash College
11. University of Washington
12. University of Massachusetts—Amherst
13. Pennsylvania State University—University Park

14. University of Kansas
15. New York University
16. Temple University
17. Northwestern University
18. University of Arizona
19. University of Georgia
20. Boston University

## College Theater is Big
*How popular are theater groups?*

1. Emerson College
2. Ithaca College
3. Brown University
4. St. Olaf College
5. Boston University
6. New York University
7. Whitman College
8. Hendrix College
9. Sarah Lawrence College
10. Albertson College
11. Worcester Polytechnic Institute
12. Vassar College
13. Hampshire College
14. Goddard College
15. Middlebury College
16. Carnegie Mellon University
17. Guilford College
18. Drew University
19. Bowdoin College
20. Fairfield University

## PARTIES

## Lots of Beer
*How widely used is beer?*

1. University of Tennessee—Knoxville
2. University of California—Santa Cruz
3. Lehigh University
4. University of New Hampshire
5. University of Texas—Austin
6. Louisiana State University—Baton Rouge
7. Duke University
8. Dartmouth College
9. Union College
10. Florida State University
11. Trinity College
12. Seton Hall University
13. Saint Bonaventure University
14. Tulane University
15. New York University
16. University of Colorado—Boulder
17. Ohio State University—Columbus
18. University of Wisconsin—Madison

**Your school.**
*You're the expert.*
*Prognosis?*
*survey.review.com*

19. University of Florida
20. Muhlenberg College

## Got Milk?
*How widely used is beer?*

1. Brigham Young University
2. College of the Ozarks
3. Wesleyan College
4. Cooper Union
5. Mount Holyoke College
6. United States Military Academy
7. Golden Gate University
8. Wheaton College (IL)
9. Samford University
10. Morehouse College
11. New Jersey Institute of Technology
12. Pitzer College
13. California Institute of Technology
14. Calvin College
15. Randolph-Macon Woman's College
16. Spelman College
17. Fisk University
18. Wellesley College
19. Howard University
20. Bryn Mawr College

## Lots of Hard Liquor
*How widely used is hard liquor?*

1. University of Wisconsin—Madison
2. University of Alabama—Tuscaloosa
3. University of Vermont
4. Tulane University
5. Florida State University
6. Colgate University
7. University of Tennessee—Knoxville
8. University of Colorado—Boulder
9. Louisiana State University—Baton Rouge
10. University of California—Santa Barbara
11. Southern Methodist University
12. Randolph-Macon College
13. Loyola University New Orleans
14. Washington and Lee University
15. University of California—Santa Cruz
16. Saint Bonaventure University
17. Bucknell University
18. Seton Hall University
19. Lafayette College
20. Vanderbilt University

## Scotch and Soda, Hold the Scotch
*How widely used is hard liquor?*

1. Brigham Young University
2. California Institute of Technology
3. Calvin College
4. Cooper Union
5. Simmons College

6. Haverford College
7. Wheaton College (IL)
8. Mount Holyoke College
9. Grove City College
10. Simon's Rock College of Bard
11. Bryn Mawr College
12. Samford University
13. United States Air Force Academy
14. Morehouse College
15. Fisk University
16. United States Coast Guard Academy
17. Wesleyan College
18. Wellesley College
19. Spelman College
20. Golden Gate University

## Reefer Madness
*How widely used is marijuana?*

1. New York University
2. University of Colorado—Boulder
3. University of New Hampshire
4. University of Oregon
5. Colorado College
6. University of California—Santa Cruz
7. University of Wisconsin—Madison
8. Oberlin College
9. Lehigh University
10. Skidmore College
11. Bard College
12. Warren Wilson College
13. Reed College
14. University of Tennessee—Knoxville
15. Guilford College
16. Goddard College
17. Lewis & Clark College
18. Smith College
19. Trinity College
20. Pitzer College

## Don't Inhale
*How widely used is marijuana?*

1. Brigham Young University
2. Furman University
3. Wheaton College (IL)
4. California Institute of Technology
5. Samford University
6. Wells College
7. College of the Ozarks
8. Centenary College of Louisiana
9. Grove City College
10. Montana Tech of the University of Montana
11. Morehouse College
12. University of Notre Dame
13. Creighton University
14. Claremont McKenna College
15. United States Naval Academy

16. Rose-Hulman Institute of Technology
17. Fairfield University
18. Sweet Briar College
19. University of Dallas
20. Wellesley College

## Major Frat and Sorority Scene
*How popular are fraternities/sororities?*

1. Washington and Lee University
2. DePauw University
3. Centre College
4. Pennsylvania State University—University Park
5. University of Michigan—Ann Arbor
6. Michigan State University
7. Ohio University—Athens
8. University of Alabama—Tuscaloosa
9. Florida State University
10. University of Texas—Austin
11. Louisiana State University—Baton Rouge
12. University of Colorado—Boulder
13. University of Florida
14. University of Tennessee—Knoxville
15. University of Georgia
16. Lafayette College
17. Vanderbilt University
18. University of Mississippi
19. Colgate University
20. Southern Methodist University

## SCHOOL BY TYPE

## Party Schools
*Based on a combination of survey questions concerning the use of alcohol and drugs, hours of study each day, and the popularity of the Greek system*

1. University of Tennessee—Knoxville
2. Louisiana State University—Baton Rouge
3. University of California—Santa Cruz
4. Florida State University
5. University of Colorado—Boulder
6. University of Alabama—Tuscaloosa
7. Saint Bonaventure University
8. Ohio State University—Columbus
9. University of Wisconsin—Madison
10. University of Florida
11. University of New Hampshire
12. University of Georgia
13. University of Texas—Austin
14. Tulane University
15. Lehigh University
16. New York University
17. Colgate University
18. University of Vermont
19. Southern Methodist University
20. University of California—Santa Barbara

## Stone-Cold Sober Schools

*Based on a combination of survey questions concerning the use of alcohol and drugs, hours of study each day, and the popularity of the Greek system*

1. Brigham Young University
2. Wheaton College (IL)
3. California Institute of Technology
4. United States Naval Academy
5. United States Coast Guard Academy
6. Cooper Union
7. United States Air Force Academy
8. Haverford College
9. College of the Ozarks
10. Calvin College
11. Mount Holyoke College
12. Wellesley College
13. Illinois Institute of Technology
14. Rose-Hulman Institute of Technology
15. Colorado School of Mines
16. Golden Gate University
17. Wells College
18. Simmons College
19. United States Military Academy
20. Grove City College

## Jock Schools

*Based on a combination of survey questions concerning intercollegiate and intramural sports, the popularity of the Greek system, theater, and cigarettes*

1. Pennsylvania State University—University Park
2. University of Michigan—Ann Arbor
3. Michigan State University
4. University of Notre Dame
5. University of Arizona
6. Florida State University
7. Syracuse University
8. University of Florida
9. Duke University
10. University of Oklahoma
11. University of North Carolina—Chapel Hill
12. University of Georgia
13. University of Iowa
14. University of Alabama—Tuscaloosa
15. Texas A&M University—College Station
16. Baylor University
17. Villanova University
18. University of Nebraska—Lincoln
19. University of Oregon
20. Washington State University

## Dodge-Ball Targets

*Based on a combination of survey questions concerning intercollegiate and intramural sports, the popularity of the Greek system, theater, and cigarettes*

1. Cooper Union
2. Emerson College
3. Reed College
4. The Evergreen State College
5. Oberlin College
6. Hampshire College
7. Smith College
8. New York University
9. Swarthmore College
10. Bard College
11. Eugene Lang College
12. Connecticut College
13. Occidental College
14. Bennington College
15. Goddard College
16. Golden Gate University
17. Bryn Mawr College
18. Clark University
19. New College of the University of South Florida
20. Hollins University

## Future Rotarians and Daughters of the American Revolution

*Based on a combination of survey questions concerning political persuasion, the use of marijuana and hallucinogens, the prevalence of religion, the popularity of student government, and the students' level of acceptance of the gay community on campus*

1. United States Coast Guard Academy
2. Fairfield University
3. Miami University
4. Brigham Young University
5. University of Notre Dame
6. Boston College
7. Creighton University
8. College of the Holy Cross
9. Wheaton College (IL)
10. Grove City College
11. Claremont McKenna College
12. Providence College
13. University of Dallas
14. Furman University
15. TCU
16. Villanova University
17. Sweet Briar College
18. Auburn University
19. Baylor University
20. Samford University

## Birkenstock-Wearing, Tree-Hugging, Clove-Smoking Vegetarians

*Based on a combination of survey questions concerning political persuasion, the use of marijuana and hallucinogens, the prevalence of religion, the popularity of student government, and the students' level of acceptance of the gay community on campus*

1. Hampshire College
2. Warren Wilson College
3. Smith College
4. Reed College
5. Bard College
6. Haverford College
7. Sarah Lawrence College
8. Bennington College
9. Whitman College
10. Guilford College
11. College of the Atlantic
12. Pitzer College
13. Grinnell College
14. Clark University
15. Pomona College
16. Vassar College
17. Marlboro College
18. Lewis & Clark College
19. Mount Holyoke College
20. Macalester College

## Deep Springs Honor Roll

*Since Deep Springs is a two-year college — the only one of its kind in The Best 331 Colleges — we've decided to remove it from the body of our individual rankings in order to avoid comparing "apples and oranges." Instead we've created this "honor roll," which includes all categories in which Deep Springs ranks high (or low, as it were) among the best colleges*

Beautiful Campus
Best Overall Academic Experience for
    Undergraduates
Dodge-Ball Targets
Don't Inhale
Election? What Election?
Gay Community Accepted
Got Milk?
Great Food on Campus
Happy Students
Professors Bring Material to Life
Professors Make Themselves Accessible
School Runs Like Butter
Scotch and Soda, Hold the Scotch
Stone Cold Sober Schools
Students from Different Backgrounds Interact
Students Most Nostalgic for George McGovern
The Toughest to Get Into
Their Students Never Stop Studying
This is a Library?

# PART 3

# THE BEST
# 331 COLLEGES

# AGNES SCOTT COLLEGE

141 EAST COLLEGE AVENUE, ATLANTA, GA 30030-3797 • ADMISSIONS: 800-868-8602 • FAX: 404-471-6414

## CAMPUS LIFE

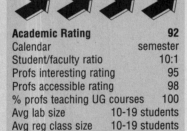

**Quality of Life Rating**    **91**
| | |
|---|---|
| Type of school | private |
| Affiliation | Presbyterian |
| Environment | urban |

### STUDENTS
| | |
|---|---|
| Total undergrad enrollment | 892 |
| % from out of state | 49 |
| % from public high school | 79 |
| % live on campus | 89 |
| % African American | 21 |
| % Asian | 5 |
| % Caucasian | 64 |
| % Hispanic | 4 |
| % international | 4 |

### SURVEY SAYS . . .
*Dorms are like palaces*
*Campus easy to get around*
*No one cheats*
*Beautiful campus*
*Students love Atlanta*
*Very little drug use*
*No one plays intramural sports*
*Very little hard liquor*
*Very little beer drinking*

## ACADEMICS

**Academic Rating**    **92**
| | |
|---|---|
| Calendar | semester |
| Student/faculty ratio | 10:1 |
| Profs interesting rating | 95 |
| Profs accessible rating | 98 |
| % profs teaching UG courses | 100 |
| Avg lab size | 10-19 students |
| Avg reg class size | 10-19 students |

### MOST POPULAR MAJORS
psychology
economics (and business)
English

## STUDENTS SPEAK OUT

### Academics

Students come to Agnes Scott College to enjoy a first-rate education in a homey, southern atmosphere. Few leave disappointed, thanks largely to a dedicated faculty, a caring administration, and a well-loved honor code. Students report that "the faculty, professors, and students get along so well that many of our closest friends tend to be not only students but also teachers and faculty. The overall academic experience of Agnes Scott is wonderful." Because the school is so small, "one of the best aspects of our school is easy access to everyone in power. We can always get an appointment with anyone from our professor to the dean to the president of the college. They are interested in our input and in answering our questions." Students also brag about their "strong honor code, the backbone for our trusting community." As at many small schools, course selection can be a problem. "Many classes are only offered once every two years and some never offered at all (even though they're listed in the catalog)!" complains one student. Students may cross-register at 19 other area colleges and universities, which broadens their academic options.

### Life

Social life on the Agnes Scott campus, students agree, is subdued. "Because it is an all-women's liberal arts college," explains one, "the life at my school is so much different than the life at a coed university. The school is mainly academic, and we don't have many social activities or parties. For fun, we go to Georgia Tech or to Buckhead (the area of Atlanta with a lot of clubs)." Some see the upside to this situation; writes one such undergrad, "Life at Agnes Scott is well balanced. We have tons of social activities planned for the students every week. Still, I know several people, including myself, go to Georgia Tech and/or Emory two or three times a week. The Scottie girls usually have fun with the frat boys." Others are less pleased, reporting that "for fun, we get the hell off campus. There's NOTHING to do here. I was hoping with a big, brand-new student center that might change, but there's nothing for entertainment in the student center besides a lame 'Cyber Café' (more accurately a computer lab) and a couple new eating places that all serve the same food." Fortunately, the school is "in the Atlanta area so there is always something to do. For the most part we go shopping and out to eat." Adds one student, "Being in Decatur is okay, but Atlanta is 15 minutes away. Atlanta may in fact be the greatest college town in the U.S. We go to the theater, the movies, bars and clubs (tons of those)." Students also note that "the warm, mild weather is nice and our campus is pretty and peaceful . . . . We're on the wrong side of the tracks and crime (though not against ASC students for the most part) abounds in our neighborhood."

### Student Body

Agnes Scott undergrads "are generally from Georgia or Florida." Students share at least one other common bond: writes one student, "My fellow students are largely rich—I mean, yearly summer trips to Europe—and mostly supported by their parents. Those who aren't are noticeably in the minority." Students warn that "since it's so small, there's a lot of gossip here and catty behavior. Sometimes, we all come together to cheer on Agnes Scott (like during Black Cat weekend), but generally we're a pretty cliquey bunch." Also, most agree that "although we have a relatively large African American population, the whites and the blacks generally do not interact. Even in class, there is a noticeable black half and a white half. In all fairness, no one seems to be eager to branch out, so it's a mutual thing."

FINANCIAL AID: 404-471-6395 • E-MAIL: ADMISSION@AGNESSCOTT.EDU • WEBSITE: WWW.AGNESSCOTT.EDU

## ADMISSIONS

*Very important* academic and nonacademic factors considered by the admissions office include secondary school record, standardized test scores, class rank, essay, recommendations, talent/ability, and character/personal qualities. *Important* factors considered include extracurricular activities, volunteer work, and work experience. *Other* factors considered include interview, alumnae relations, geography, state residency, and minority status. Factors *not* considered include religious affiliation. SAT I or ACT required. TOEFL required of all international applicants. High school diploma is required and GED is accepted. *High school units required/recommended:* 16 total required; 16 total recommended; 4 English recommended, 3 math recommended, 2 science recommended, 2 foreign language recommended, 2 social studies recommended.

### The Inside Word

Women's colleges are enjoying a renaissance of late and to top it off, Agnes Scott has always been a great choice for strong students. Don't be deceived by the college's generous admission rate—we're talking about a small applicant pool of well-qualified candidates, and one of the best small liberal arts colleges to be found anywhere. Look for greater selectivity as the college recruits students from further afield and application totals continue to increase at top women's colleges. The admissions process can't get any more personalized than it is at Agnes Scott—every candidate is assigned her own specific admission advisor, who works with the student throughout the process.

## FINANCIAL AID

*Students should submit:* FAFSA, institution's own financial aid form, state aid form, noncustodial (divorced/separated) parent's statement, business/farm supplement and PROFILE for Early Decision applicants. Priority filing deadline is February 15. Regular filing deadline is May 1. The Princeton Review suggests that all financial aid forms be submitted as soon as possible after January 1. *Need-based scholarships/grants offered:* Pell, SEOG, state scholarships/grants, private scholarships, and the school's own gift aid. *Loan aid offered:* FFEL Subsidized Stafford, FFEL Unsubsidized Stafford, FFEL PLUS, college/university loans from institutional funds, and Achiever. Institutional employment available. Federal Work-Study Program available. Applicants will be notified of awards on a rolling basis beginning on or about March 1. Off-campus job opportunities are excellent.

## FROM THE ADMISSIONS OFFICE

"Agnes Scott's size offers many advantages. Students can look forward to individual attention from professors and stimulating classroom discussions with women ranked among the top students in their secondary schools. The Atlanta area provides students with numerous career and educational opportunities, including cross registration with local colleges and universities and internships with national and international businesses. Agnes Scott guarantees internship opportunities for all students. The college also has a strong commitment to global education, as evidenced by their having five consecutive Fulbright Scholars in the past few years and ranking among the top 30 colleges for study abroad participation. Students are encouraged to arrange a campus visit to take a first-hand look at the academic program, residential life, and student and alumnae accomplishments."

## ADMISSIONS

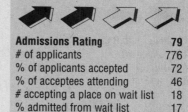

| | |
|---|---|
| Admissions Rating | 79 |
| # of applicants | 776 |
| % of applicants accepted | 72 |
| % of acceptees attending | 46 |
| # accepting a place on wait list | 18 |
| % admitted from wait list | 17 |
| # of early decision applicants | 39 |
| % accepted early decision | 74 |

### FRESHMAN PROFILE

| | |
|---|---|
| Range SAT Verbal | 560-680 |
| Average SAT Verbal | 612 |
| Range SAT Math | 530-640 |
| Average SAT Math | 586 |
| Range ACT Composite | 25-30 |
| Average ACT Composite | 27 |
| Minimum TOEFL | 600 |
| Average HS GPA | 3.7 |
| % graduated top 10% of class | 53 |
| % graduated top 25% of class | 80 |
| % graduated top 50% of class | 98 |

### DEADLINES

| | |
|---|---|
| Early decision | 11/15 |
| Early decision notification | 12/15 |
| Regular admission | 3/1 |
| Nonfall registration? | yes |

### APPLICANTS ALSO LOOK AT

**AND OFTEN PREFER**
U. Georgia
Emory
**AND SOMETIMES PREFER**
Randolph-Macon Woman's
Smith
Rhodes
Hollins
Sweet Briar
**AND RARELY PREFER**
UNC—Chapel Hill

### FINANCIAL FACTS

| | |
|---|---|
| Financial Aid Rating | 87 |
| Tuition | $16,600 |
| Room & board | $6,900 |
| Books and supplies | $700 |
| Required fees | $145 |
| % frosh receiving aid | 72 |
| % undergrads receiving aid | 68 |
| Avg frosh grant | $13,832 |
| Avg frosh loan | $2,625 |

# ALBERTSON COLLEGE

2112 CLEVELAND BOULEVARD, CALDWELL, ID 83605 • ADMISSIONS: 208-459-5305 • FAX: 208-459-5757

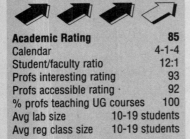
## STUDENTS SPEAK OUT

### Academics

"Challenging classes," a "strong reputation," and "overall high standards" make for "vigorous" academics at Albertson College of Idaho, a "wonderful" little dynamo of a liberal arts college that gets rave reviews from its students. Albertson offers "small classes," "lots of personal attention," and a very active, six-week intersession between semesters that affords a variety of opportunities to study in locales far afield from Idaho and to participate in a range of cultural and academic activities on campus. The "extraordinarily personable" professors at ACI are "passionate about what they do" and "adept" at showing students "different ways to think and different ways to approach issues." Profs also "really take the time to get to know you as a person," says a sophomore. "The professors here are the school," agrees a political science major. "I can't reiterate this enough!" The administration is a little more of a mixed bag, but in general the bigwigs are "immediately responsive and easily contacted." Students say Albertson's curriculum is "rigid, whatever your major happens to be." A "good percentage of graduates go to medical school," and ACI's "highly respected academic programs" have also produced six Rhodes Scholars, two governors, Academy Award and Pulitzer Prize winners, a co-discoverer of vitamin B-12, and the guy who invented the method used to freeze french fries.

### Life

"Some of the most active and involved students on the planet" are right here on Albertson's "beautiful" campus, where "extracurriculars are almost overwhelming." Frats are reportedly popular, as are "pool, movies, free air hockey," and intercollegiate and intramural sports. "Intellectual" and "philosophical" debates are another popular pastime, and "religious discussions are never far away." Albertson's food service, on the other hand, is definitely a point of contention, and several students here tell us it "needs improvement," but, they are working on it. ACI's campus also boasts an international center, a center for performing and fine arts, and a unique Early Leadership Identification Program that provides new students who show leadership capabilities with a wide range of opportunities to broaden and enhance these talents. Off campus, the Great Outdoors offers a wealth of "tremendous recreation possibilities" including whitewater rafting, hiking, skiing, fishing, camping, and "snowboarding during the winter months." Students can also "fly-fish, trap shoot, and shoot archery," all within an hour of campus. The surrounding town of Caldwell, a small community located a few minutes from Boise, is nothing to write home about, and "getting out" is occasionally "necessary."

### Student Body

"Everyone knows your name" at Albertson, where the "friendly, open, and accepting" students are "outgoing," "generally relaxed," and "very kind." Sure, a few are "grumpy and inconsiderate" but, "with the exception of the odd psycho," most "everyone is talented and interesting in their own way." The "overachievers" at ACI "study way too much," though, and they are "extremely competitive" and "a bit manic, perhaps due to caffeine-induced insomnia," speculates a first-year student. Politically, students at Albertson "tend to be conservative," and they predict that they are "people who will be rich" in the future. The majority hail from Idaho, Washington, Oregon, and nearby large, square states in the Pacific Northwest.

FINANCIAL AID: 208-459-5308 • E-MAIL: ADMISSION@ALBERTSON.EDU • WEBSITE: WWW.ALBERTSON.EDU

## ADMISSIONS

*Very important* academic and nonacademic factors considered by the admissions committee include class rank, secondary school record, and standardized test scores. *Important* factors considered include character/personal qualities, interview, recommendations, and talent/ability. *Other* factors considered include alumni/ae relation, essays, extracurricular activities, state residency, volunteer work, and work experience. Factors *not* considered include geography. SAT I or ACT required. TOEFL required of all international applicants. High school diploma is required and GED is accepted. *High school units required/recommended:* 4 English recommended, 4 math recommended, 4 science recommended, 4 foreign language recommended, 4 social studies recommended.

### The Inside Word

Albertson's widely open doors are a quirk of location. The college offers a challenging, high-quality academic program best suited to those who are intellectually curious and serious about their studies; the high admission rate simply makes applying relatively stress-free. (Note: For now, enrollment is on the rise. If Albertson were closer to the nation's population centers, admission would no doubt be far more selective.) As it is, the admissions committee is no less thorough than those at the highly selective level; its makeup consists of several deans and directors, as well as faculty members. Students seeking to attend a small college in a rural setting owe it to themselves to take a look. The admissions office points out that "although this college has a rolling admissions policy, it is to the applicant's advantage to apply by February 15 in order to be eligible for many scholarships."

## FINANCIAL AID

*Students should submit:* FAFSA and institution's own financial aid form. The Princeton Review suggests that all financial aid forms be submitted as soon as possible after January 1. *Need-based scholarships/grants offered:* Pell, SEOG, state scholarships/grants, private scholarships, and the school's own gift aid. *Loan aid offered:* FFEL Subsidized Stafford, FFEL Unsubsidized Stafford, FFEL PLUS, Federal Perkins, and alternative loans. Institutional employment available. Federal Work-Study Program available. Applicants will be notified of awards on or about April 1. Off-campus job opportunities are good.

## FROM THE ADMISSIONS OFFICE

"While the mission of Albertson College is traditional in that it remains committed to the teaching of the liberal arts, many of the approaches to accomplishing this goal are unique. Within the campus community is the creativity to create classroom opportunities for students that span the globe—both technologically and geographically. Here, students are just as apt to attend a biology class on campus as they are to hike in the nearby Owyhee or Sawtooth Mountains to carry out field research. And during the college's six-week winter term, more than 30 percent of the students are emailing friends and family from such locales as Australia, Israel, France, Ireland, England, Peru, or Mexico while taking part in faculty-led, multidisciplinary trips. Students are invited to visit the campus and the admissions counselors, either in person or by the website at www.albertson.edu."

### ADMISSIONS

| Admissions Rating | 80 |
| --- | --- |
| # of applicants | 669 |
| % of applicants accepted | 97 |
| % of acceptees attending | 39 |

| FRESHMAN PROFILE | |
| --- | --- |
| Range SAT Verbal | 500-650 |
| Average SAT Verbal | 573 |
| Range SAT Math | 500-630 |
| Average SAT Math | 569 |
| Range ACT Composite | 22-28 |
| Average ACT Composite | 25 |
| Minimum TOEFL | 550 |
| Average HS GPA | 3.5 |
| % graduated top 10% of class | 31 |
| % graduated top 25% of class | 64 |

| DEADLINES | |
| --- | --- |
| Priority admission deadline | 2/15 |
| Regular admission | 6/1 |
| Nonfall registration? | yes |

### FINANCIAL FACTS

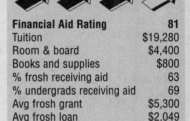

| Financial Aid Rating | 81 |
| --- | --- |
| Tuition | $19,280 |
| Room & board | $4,400 |
| Books and supplies | $800 |
| % frosh receiving aid | 63 |
| % undergrads receiving aid | 69 |
| Avg frosh grant | $5,300 |
| Avg frosh loan | $2,049 |

# ALBION COLLEGE

611 EAST PORTER, ALBION, MI 49224 • ADMISSIONS: 800-858-6770 • FAX: 517-629-0569

## STUDENTS SPEAK OUT

### Academics

Small and private Albion College is an expensive, Methodist-affiliated college in Michigan that boasts "great teacher-student relations," "great liberal arts education," and "a very positive" academic environment. "On a scale of 1 to 10," Albion "is an 8," according to a junior here. "The teachers are always available and you can really get to know your profs outside of class," asserts a Spanish major. "You can tell they enjoy their area of expertise." Classes are small and generally engaging. "Dressing up like a clown for Halloween" and "trips to breweries for economics classes" are just a few of the stunts professors here pull to keep students interested. The administration is more of a mixed bag. Some administrators are "easily approachable" while others are "a pain." One of Albion's strengths is its freshman seminars for first-year students. Albion also boasts five very fancy-sounding institutes: Gerstacker Liberal Arts Institute for Professional Management, Institute for the Study of the Environment, Shurmur Education Institute, the nation's first Gerald R. Ford Institute for Public Policy and Service, and the Liberal Arts Institute for Pre-Medical and Health Care Studies. The Ford Institute "combines course work in public service and a semester-long, full-time internship." The Gerstacker Institute provides a liberal arts foundation, training in business and management, internships galore in big cities (especially Detroit and Chicago), and its grads are "good recruiting fodder for many companies."

### Life

"Life at school is about studying during the week, with a Wednesday party break," of course, "then partying on the weekends," explains a sophomore. "Greek life is big" on Albion's "small, accessible campus"—too big for some students' tastes. "Frat parties are the main social outlet" and some students say the quality of life is "not very good unless you drink" because the surrounding town is "dead," the academics are "stressful," and there is little to do. Other, more optimistic students say "you have to be creative to have fun" here. "We are a school that knows how to do homework and balance a social life," explains one student. There are "a decent variety of activities for a small school," including "lectures, concerts, and movies." Students also "go for walks, play video games," "hang out in the TV lounge" "play Euchre," and "go to sporting events" (especially football games, as Albion's Division III team is perennially competitive). When they want to get off campus, nearby Ann Arbor provides big school fun, and the campus is roughly an hour from Detroit. There is also the annual City Service Day, when "students beautify the land around the college community and around campus" by cleaning area parks and repairing homes of the needy and elderly.

### Student Body

Adding all manner of diversity to this campus of mostly white, Protestant, in-state students "would be a major improvement." As things stand, "most" students come from Michigan and "are very similar in tastes, dress, and overall philosophies." There are a few "rich snobs" and some "crazy party guys" here, and "students who are in sororities and fraternities basically talk to other people in their fraternities and sororities," discloses a sophomore. "Non-Greeks basically talk to other non-Greeks." Albion students describe themselves as "goal-oriented, studious, and socially inclined" as well as "fun" and "easy to get along with." Albion students are also "almost all abnormally friendly" and share a strong "sense of community." They are "the nicest people I have ever met," swears one student. "They are willing to do anything for you, anytime, anywhere." Thanks to the school's small size, "you can pretty much see people you know all over the place," according to one student. "I think this is a great plus." It's a minus, though, in the sense that privacy is severely limited, and gossip is pretty rampant on campus. Sometimes, "the rumors bring you down."

FINANCIAL AID: 517-629-0440 • E-MAIL: ADMISSIONS@ALBION.EDU • WEBSITE: WWW.ALBION.EDU

## ADMISSIONS

*Very important* academic and nonacademic factors considered by the admissions committee include character/personal qualities, extracurricular activities, and secondary school record. *Important* factors considered include essays, interview, recommendations, standardized test scores, talent/ability, volunteer work, and work experience. *Other* factors considered include class rank. Factors *not* considered include alumni/ae relation, geography, minority status, religious affiliation/commitment, and state residency. SAT I or ACT required. TOEFL required of all international applicants. High school diploma is required and GED is accepted. *High school units required/recommended:* 4 English recommended, 4 math recommended, 4 science recommended, 3 foreign language recommended, 2 social studies recommended, 2 history recommended.

### The Inside Word

Albion's approach to admissions is typical of many small colleges. Despite a very high admit rate, candidates can expect to undergo a thorough review, as matchmaking plays a strong part in the evaluation process here. Your personal side and extracurricular involvements count a great deal when an admissions committee is engaged in community building. Though the college is on a rolling admission schedule, we encourage you to apply early in order to have the best shot at both admission and financial aid. Albion will waive the application fee for candidates who apply online.

## FINANCIAL AID

*Students should submit:* FAFSA. The Princeton Review suggests that all financial aid forms be submitted as soon as possible after January 1. *Need-based scholarships/grants offered:* Pell, SEOG, state scholarships/grants, private scholarships, and the school's own gift aid. *Loan aid offered:* Direct Subsidized Stafford, Direct Unsubsidized Stafford, FFEL Subsidized Stafford, FFEL Unsubsidized Stafford, FFEL PLUS, Federal Perkins, and state. Institutional employment available. Federal Work-Study Program available. Applicants will be notified of awards on a rolling basis beginning on or about March 15. Off-campus job opportunities are good.

## FROM THE ADMISSIONS OFFICE

Albion was the first private college in Michigan to have a chapter of Phi Beta Kappa, the oldest national honor society, founded in 1776. Albion's heavily endowed professional institutes in environmental science, public policy and service, professional management, pre-medical and healthcare studies, honors and education offer world-class internships and study abroad opportunities. Albion is among the top 85 private, liberal arts colleges for the number of alumni who are corporate executives, including top executives and CEOs of *Newsweek,* the Lahey Clinic (MA), PricewaterhouseCoopers, Dow Corning, the NCAA, NYNEX, and the Federal Accounting Standards Board (FASB). Albion's graduate school placement rates at 98 percent for law, 96 percent for dental and 89 percent for medical schools, including Harvard, Michigan, Columbia, Northwestern, Notre Dame, Vanderbilt, and Wisconsin. Albion was the top award winner at the 2001 Michigan Campus Compact, which includes public and private schools in Michigan committed to service and volunteerism. The long list of campus organizations includes Model United Nations, Fellowship of Christian Athletes, Canoe Club, Black Student Alliance, Equestrian Club, Medievalist Society, Ecological Awareness Club, and fraternity and sorority service organizations. Of particular note is Albion's athletics program, where in addition to dominating Division III football, women's soccer, and men's and women's golf and swimming, five varsity teams have earned the highest grade-point average in the MIAA conference, NCAA Division III, or any division nationwide."

## ADMISSIONS

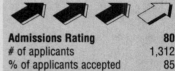

| | |
|---|---|
| Admissions Rating | 80 |
| # of applicants | 1,312 |
| % of applicants accepted | 85 |
| % of acceptees attending | 36 |
| # of early decision applicants | 55 |
| % accepted early decision | 95 |

### FRESHMAN PROFILE

| | |
|---|---|
| Range SAT Verbal | 510-620 |
| Average SAT Verbal | 569 |
| Range SAT Math | 520-650 |
| Average SAT Math | 587 |
| Range ACT Composite | 23-28 |
| Average ACT Composite | 25 |
| Minimum TOEFL | 550 |
| Average HS GPA | 3.5 |
| % graduated top 10% of class | 32 |
| % graduated top 25% of class | 73 |
| % graduated top 50% of class | 94 |

### DEADLINES

| | |
|---|---|
| Early decision | 11/15 |
| Early decision notification | 12/15 |
| Regular admission | 4/1 |
| Nonfall registration? | yes |

### APPLICANTS ALSO LOOK AT
#### AND OFTEN PREFER
U. Michigan
#### AND SOMETIMES PREFER
Kalamazoo College
Hope College
Alma College
Michigan State
Denison
#### AND RARELY PREFER
Western Michigan
Central Michigan

### FINANCIAL FACTS

| | |
|---|---|
| Financial Aid Rating | 83 |
| Tuition | $19,390 |
| Room & board | $5,604 |
| Books and supplies | $600 |
| Required fees | $188 |
| % frosh receiving aid | 63 |
| % undergrads receiving aid | 62 |
| Avg frosh grant | $13,112 |
| Avg frosh loan | $3,386 |

# ALFRED UNIVERSITY

ALUMNI HALL, ONE SAXON DRIVE, ALFRED, NY 14802-1205 • ADMISSIONS: 607-871-2115 • FAX: 607-871-2198

## CAMPUS LIFE

**Quality of Life Rating**    **75**
| | |
|---|---|
| Type of school | private |
| Affiliation | none |
| Environment | rural |

### STUDENTS
| | |
|---|---|
| Total undergrad enrollment | 2,085 |
| % male/female | 48/52 |
| % from out of state | 37 |
| % from public high school | 83 |
| % live on campus | 65 |
| % in (# of) fraternities | 18 (8) |
| % in (# of) sororities | 11 (4) |
| % African American | 4 |
| % Asian | 2 |
| % Caucasian | 91 |
| % Hispanic | 4 |
| % international | 2 |

### SURVEY SAYS . . .
*Lots of beer drinking*
*Students aren't religious*
*Campus easy to get around*
*High cost of living*
*Theater is unpopular*
*Class discussions encouraged*
*Lousy off-campus food*
*Political activism is (almost) nonexistent*
*(Almost) no one listens to college radio*

## ACADEMICS

**Academic Rating**    **79**
| | |
|---|---|
| Calendar | semester |
| Student/faculty ratio | 12:1 |
| Profs interesting rating | 92 |
| Profs accessible rating | 93 |
| % profs teaching UG courses | 100 |
| Avg lab size | 10-19 students |
| Avg reg class size | 10-19 students |

### MOST POPULAR MAJORS
ceramic engineering
art and design
business administration

## STUDENTS SPEAK OUT

### Academics

Alfred University, a school renowned for its ceramics and glassworks programs, provides a "stimulating and rewarding" academic experience. What makes Alfred unique is that it isn't only an art school. Students speak highly of the English and business departments and point out that science courses are quite challenging. The "brilliant" professors "know you on a first-name basis" and "are often available for help in a class. One-on-one sessions with professors are often available." Class sizes are small and TAs are uncommon. One first-year student writes, "I am a freshman and have already been to two of my professors' homes for dinner." The administration is "friendly" and "quite approachable." They are "willing to discuss any situation that might arise." Some students note that they would like to see more professors in order "to increase the diversity of classes." Several transfer students are extremely fond of Alfred: "Compared to my previous school, this is heaven." Students note that the computer and library facilities need improvement, as does the food. On-campus parking also needs to be expanded. A junior English major summarizes Alfred University thusly: "Alfred University is a wonderful institution. The buildings are nice-looking, the professors are knowledgeable, and the students are brilliant."

### Life

AU's location in a "small, rural town in upstate New York"—two hours away from both Buffalo and Rochester—doesn't inspire its students. "If you expect to have a thrill a minute, then this may not be the best place for you." Still, students say, "there is fun. You just have to find it." The university is aware that students don't have many entertainment options in the surrounding area, and so "they try to plan events for us." Students rent movies or go to Alfred's on-campus movie theater. Though students are concerned about their studies, "there is usually a frat party going on Tuesday through Saturday nights." Students also go to "the one or two bars in town." Those who partake in winter sports appreciate the campus' proximity to the nearby mountains.

### Student Body

Students looking for a diverse population won't find one at Alfred. "The students are mostly white kids from the East Coast who grew up in upper-middle-class families." Another student adds, "A large number of students have never encountered someone of a different ethnic background." The university's lack of diversity bothers many students. "The white kids mainly hang out with white kids, while black [kids] hang out with black [kids]." The same student adds that a certain sorority won't accept nonwhites into its house. Alfred's small size—about 2,200 undergrads—means that students get to know their peers. "They are a great bunch of people," though "they are sometimes clique-ish." The art students are regarded as the most outgoing. "People mingle freely with ideas, are very friendly, and varied in their dress, interests, and opinions." At the same time, she points out that while "the art school is liberal . . . the school [itself] is rural and in a conservative area."

FINANCIAL AID: 607-871-2159 • E-MAIL: ADMWWW@ALFRED.EDU • WEBSITE: WWW.ALFRED.EDU

## ADMISSIONS

*Very important* academic and nonacademic factors considered by the admissions committee include character/personal qualities, class rank, extracurricular activities, recommendations, and secondary school record. *Important* factors considered include essays and standardized test scores. *Other* factors considered include interview, talent/ability, volunteer work, and work experience. Factors *not* considered include alumni/ae relation, geography, minority status, religious affiliation/commitment, and state residency. SAT I or ACT required; SAT II recommended. High school diploma is required and GED is accepted. *High school units required/recommended:* 16 total required; 4 English required, 2 math required, 3 math recommended, 2 science required, 3 science recommended, 2 foreign language recommended, 3 social studies required, 4 social studies recommended. A portfolio is required of all applicants to the School of Art and Design. *The admissions office says:* "Each application is read by the counselor who travels and recruits in the applicant's geographic area. The counselor is then familiar with the strengths and characteristics of the applicant's high school and can be better prepared to evaluate the compatibility between the applicant and the institution."

### The Inside Word

There's no questioning the high quality of academics at Alfred, especially in their internationally known ceramics program. Still, the university's general lack of name recognition and relatively isolated campus directly affect both the applicant pool and the number of admitted students who enroll, and thus keeps selectivity relatively low for a school of its caliber. (The exception is clearly in ceramic arts, where candidates will face a very rigorous review.) If you're a back-to-nature type looking for a challenging academic environment, Alfred could be just what the doctor ordered. And if you're a standout academically, you may find that they're generous with financial aid, too—they are serious about competing for good students.

## FINANCIAL AID

*Students should submit:* FAFSA, institution's own financial aid form, state aid form, noncustodial (divorced/separated) parent's statement, and business/farm supplement. There is no regular filing deadline. The Princeton Review suggests that all financial aid forms be submitted as soon as possible after January 1. *Need-based scholarships/grants offered:* Pell, SEOG, state scholarships/grants, private scholarships, and the school's own gift aid. *Loan aid offered:* FFEL Subsidized Stafford, FFEL Unsubsidized Stafford, FFEL PLUS, Federal Perkins, and college/university loans from institutional funds. Institutional employment available. Federal Work-Study Program available. Applicants will be notified of awards on a rolling basis beginning on or about February 1. Off-campus job opportunities are good.

## FROM THE ADMISSIONS OFFICE

"The admissions process at Alfred University is the foundation for the personal attention that a student can expect from this institution. Each applicant is evaluated individually and can expect genuine, personal attention at Alfred University."

### ADMISSIONS

| | |
|---|---|
| Admissions Rating | 77 |
| # of applicants | 1,942 |
| % of applicants accepted | 76 |
| % of acceptees attending | 34 |
| # of early decision applicants | 44 |
| % accepted early decision | 98 |

### FRESHMAN PROFILE

| | |
|---|---|
| Range SAT Verbal | 500-610 |
| Range SAT Math | 500-610 |
| Range ACT Composite | 23-27 |
| Minimum TOEFL | 550 |
| % graduated top 10% of class | 19 |
| % graduated top 25% of class | 45 |
| % graduated top 50% of class | 80 |

### DEADLINES

| | |
|---|---|
| Early decision | 12/1 |
| Early decision notification | 12/15 |
| Priority admission deadline | 2/1 |
| Nonfall registration? | yes |

### APPLICANTS ALSO LOOK AT

**AND OFTEN PREFER**
SUNY Geneseo

**AND SOMETIMES PREFER**
SUNY Buffalo
SUNY Albany
U. Rochester
Syracuse

**AND RARELY PREFER**
Clarkson U.
RIT
U. Mass—Amherst

### FINANCIAL FACTS

| | |
|---|---|
| Financial Aid Rating | 83 |
| Tuition (Freshmen) | $18,498 |
| Avg frosh loan | $3,200 |

# ALLEGHENY COLLEGE

OFFICE OF ADMISSIONS, ALLEGHENY COLLEGE, MEADVILLE, PA 16335 • ADMISSIONS: 814-332-4351 • FAX: 814-337-0431

## CAMPUS LIFE

| **Quality of Life Rating** | **75** |
|---|---|
| Type of school | private |
| Affiliation | Methodist |
| Environment | rural |

### STUDENTS

| | |
|---|---|
| Total undergrad enrollment | 1,904 |
| % male/female | 48/52 |
| % from out of state | 35 |
| % from public high school | 85 |
| % live on campus | 75 |
| % in (# of) fraternities | 25 (4) |
| % in (# of) sororities | 28 (4) |
| % African American | 2 |
| % Asian | 1 |
| % Caucasian | 94 |
| % Hispanic | 1 |
| % Native American | 1 |
| % international | 1 |
| # of countries represented | 15 |

### SURVEY SAYS . . .

*Athletic facilities are great*
*Frats and sororities dominate social scene*
*Classes are small*
*Student publications are ignored*
*Library needs improving*
*Lousy food on campus*
*Political activism is (almost) nonexistent*
*Lousy off-campus food*
*Diversity lacking on campus*

## ACADEMICS

| **Academic Rating** | **82** |
|---|---|
| Calendar | semester |
| Student/faculty ratio | 14:1 |
| Profs interesting rating | 73 |
| Profs accessible rating | 85 |
| % profs teaching UG courses | 100 |
| Avg lab size | 10-19 students |
| Avg reg class size | 10-19 students |

### MOST POPULAR MAJORS

psychology
biology
economics

## STUDENTS SPEAK OUT

### Academics

Allegheny College tailors its programs to the needs of the highly motivated student. The academic demands here are great, students agree, but the rewards for those who can handle the workload are just as great. "This place is very competitive. Many people double major, and classes can get rough," notes one student. Another adds, "Allegheny is very difficult, but since there is nothing to do in Meadville except watch the rain, snow, or sleet, we have plenty of time to study." But, while the workload is "large and difficult," it is also "definitely worth it." As one student explains, "The academic experience is what you make of it. There are no easy courses, but professors are more than willing to help. You can only get out of Allegheny what you put in. If you honestly do your best, you can leave Allegheny with an awesome education and experience." The academic intensity is eased somewhat by the school's "very friendly atmosphere. This is consistent across professors, administrators, and students." Professors are "innovative and interesting in their teaching styles" and "very available outside the classroom and often invite students into their homes for informal gatherings. I've played baseball with my freshman advisor and been invited to Thanksgiving dinner by another professor." Allegheny keeps class sizes small, which "helps get everyone involved." Students approve; as one typical respondent sums up, "I've found the right school: strong academics, the personal attention I want, great facilities, and friendships that will last a lifetime. I love it here."

### Life

Allegheny's rigorous academics translate into a campus experience that "is typically very stressful. The coursework is challenging and it takes a lot of time and effort to get good grades, which is the goal of most students. There aren't a whole lot of options for fun on the weekend, except parties off campus." Options are limited by the school's setting: the town of Meadville "is very uncultured and downright painfully boring." Another student adds, "The only exciting things in Meadville are bowling and Wal-Mart. Fortunately the campus makes its own fun, so you don't have to leave." On-campus organizations keep students busy with "different types of concerts, and other things like sales in the Campus Center that are pretty fun. They also have movies every Wednesday." Students also note that "drinking, football, and pop culture rule." Regarding drinking, students identify themselves as "a very intelligent group of people that loves being intoxicated." Students tell us that "for fun we drive to a nearby larger city." The drive to Pittsburgh or Cleveland, the two closest large cities, takes about an hour and a half.

### Student Body

Like many small, expensive, private schools, Allegheny has a hard time attracting a sizable minority population, leading students to observe that "the campus is very homogeneous as to types of students, and sometimes it seems everyone just thinks and acts the same way." For those who don't fit the "WASPy, upper-middle-class suburbanite," "real conservative" mold, the administration does work hard to be responsive to diversity issues. Overall, Allegheny is a "friendly, comfortable campus. When you walk down the street, most everyone says 'hi' and smiles." Others may find themselves feeling a little isolated at times.

FINANCIAL AID: 800-835-7780 • E-MAIL: ADMISS@ADMIN.ALLEG.EDU • WEBSITE: WWW.ALLEG.EDU

## ADMISSIONS

*Very important* academic and nonacademic factors considered by the admissions committee include class rank, secondary school record, and standardized test scores. *Important* factors considered include character/personal qualities, extracurricular activities, interview, and recommendations. *Other* factors considered include essays, geography, minority status, talent/ability, volunteer work, alumi/ae relation, and work experience. Factors *not* considered include religious affiliation/commitment and state residency. SAT I required or ACT and SAT II recommended. TOEFL required of all international applicants. High school diploma is required and GED is accepted. *High school units required/recommended:* 16 total required; 4 English required, 3 math required, 3 science required, 2 foreign language required, 3 social studies required, 1 elective required.

### The Inside Word

Don't be deceived by the fairly high admit rate here—Allegheny draws a strong pool of academically well-qualified applicants, and candidate evaluation here is rigorous and personalized. The admissions staff strongly recommends campus visits and interviews; students who visit the campus prior to Allegheny's application deadline receive application fee waivers. Given the highly personalized nature of candidate evaluation here, we'd suggest both the visit and taking the most challenging courses in high school in order to be as competitive in the applicant pool as possible.

## FINANCIAL AID

*Students should submit:* FAFSA and federal income tax form (for verification). Regular filing deadline is February 15. The Princeton Review suggests that all financial aid forms be submitted as soon as possible after January 1. *Need-based scholarships/grants offered:* Pell, SEOG, state scholarships/grants, private scholarships, and the school's own gift aid. *Loan aid offered:* FFEL, Subsidized Stafford, FFEL Unsubsidized Stafford, FFEL PLUS, Federal Perkins, and state loans. Institutional employment available. Federal Work-Study Program available. Applicants will be notified of awards on or about April 1. Off-campus job opportunities are good.

## FROM THE ADMISSIONS OFFICE

"At Allegheny, students learn to 'think outside.' While we value and maintain the traditional hallmarks of an excellent education—small classes, low student-faculty ratio, strong majors—we also believe that the classroom is just the starting point for your education. You have to take what you've learned in the classroom out into the world. Allegheny is constantly devising new ways for you to do just that: Through research, internships, community service, and leadership programs, Allegheny gives you unexpected opportunities for learning and growth. The outcome is the knowledge and know-how employers and graduate schools demand. If you expect more out of life, expect more from your college—visit Allegheny and find out how much more we offer."

### ADMISSIONS

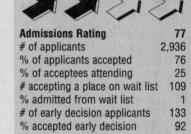

| | |
|---|---|
| Admissions Rating | 77 |
| # of applicants | 2,936 |
| % of applicants accepted | 76 |
| % of acceptees attending | 25 |
| # accepting a place on wait list | 109 |
| % admitted from wait list | 1 |
| # of early decision applicants | 133 |
| % accepted early decision | 92 |

### FRESHMAN PROFILE

| | |
|---|---|
| Range SAT Verbal | 560-650 |
| Average SAT Verbal | 603 |
| Range SAT Math | 560-650 |
| Average SAT Math | 601 |
| Range ACT Composite | 23-27 |
| Average ACT Composite | 25 |
| Minimum TOEFL | 550 |
| Average HS GPA | 3.7 |
| % graduated top 10% of class | 41 |
| % graduated top 25% of class | 75 |
| % graduated top 50% of class | 95 |

### DEADLINES

| | |
|---|---|
| Early decision | 1/15 |
| Early decision notification | 10/15 |
| Regular admission | 2/15 |
| Nonfall registration? | yes |

### FINANCIAL FACTS

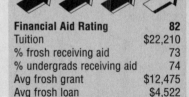

| | |
|---|---|
| Financial Aid Rating | 82 |
| Tuition | $22,210 |
| % frosh receiving aid | 73 |
| % undergrads receiving aid | 74 |
| Avg frosh grant | $12,475 |
| Avg frosh loan | $4,522 |

# AMERICAN UNIVERSITY

4400 MASSACHUSETTS AVE, NW, WASHINGTON, DC 20016-8001 • ADMISSIONS: 202-885-6000 • FAX: 202-885-1025

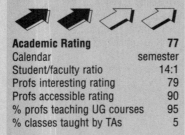

## CAMPUS LIFE

| | |
|---|---|
| **Quality of Life Rating** | **78** |
| Type of school | private |
| Affiliation | Methodist |
| Environment | urban |

### STUDENTS

| | |
|---|---|
| Total undergrad enrollment | 5,705 |
| % male/female | 39/61 |
| % from out of state | 75 |
| % from public high school | 60 |
| % live on campus | 59 |
| % in (# of) fraternities | 15 (9) |
| % in (# of) sororities | 18 (10) |
| % African American | 8 |
| % Asian | 4 |
| % Caucasian | 56 |
| % Hispanic | 6 |
| % international | 14 |

### SURVEY SAYS . . .

*Great food on campus*
*Beautiful campus*
*No one cheats*
*Campus feels safe*
*Campus easy to get around*
*Students are not very happy*
*Student government is unpopular*
*Students are cliquish*
*Students aren't religious*
*Very little beer drinking*

## ACADEMICS

| | |
|---|---|
| **Academic Rating** | **77** |
| Calendar | semester |
| Student/faculty ratio | 14:1 |
| Profs interesting rating | 79 |
| Profs accessible rating | 90 |
| % profs teaching UG courses | 95 |
| % classes taught by TAs | 5 |

### MOST POPULAR MAJORS
international studies
political science
business administration

## STUDENTS SPEAK OUT
### Academics

"Challenging but not overwhelming" American University, a "finishing school for future lawyers and politicians," boasts tremendous resources (thanks to its Washington, D.C., location) and strong programs in pre-law and international relations. The School of Communication shines as well; its students have instant, inside-the-Beltway access to the biggest kahunas on the national and international political scene. AU's professors are generally "helpful and inspiring," and most are "extremely knowledgeable in their fields." However, while there are plenty of "accessible" and "devoted" instructors here who "really care about teaching," students tell us there are some "horrible" teachers as well. Beyond the classroom, AU's "well-staffed Career Center" is on the ball. Internships galore are available "in government and business," and a unique cooperative education program allows students to gain valuable work experience and earn credit while working at government offices, political think tanks, and broadcast networks. Unfortunately, "registration is awful," the school "spends too much money on gardening," and students sometimes feel awash in a sea of "red tape" because "administrative offices do not communicate well enough with each other." As a result, "it seems like everything has to be done twice." Good luck if "you want to find a book" at the "extremely outdated" library. All in all, though, "the overall experience is quite enjoyable" at AU. "I am a transfer student," reveals a senior, "and AU is a hell of a lot better than a state school."

### Life

"Life is good" on this campus, located in a nice, safe residential area of the District of Columbia. American conspicuously "lacks a traditional college atmosphere," though, and student life often has "little to do with school." AU "basically shuts down on the weekends" because "most people take advantage of the city for nightlife, food, leisure, and friends," explains a senior. "It is a great asset." The nation's capital offers ample opportunities for "clubbing, drinking, networking" as well as "movies, bowling, ice skating," and "some good restaurants in the area." There's also the White House, Kennedy Center, the Smithsonian, and Dupont Circle, and many students head over to the Georgetown area of the District to socialize. On and around campus, the "recreation facilities are horrible," and there is "not a lot of partying" save for "good old frat parties," and students who have pledged fraternities and sororities tell us that it "adds to social life" tremendously. For incoming students, AU has an optional program called the Freshman Service Experience. Students who sign up volunteer to move in early to do community experience projects. While meeting other students and learning about campus, these students teach English, work in soup kitchens, paint the streets, and generally do a lot of good.

### Student Body

Eureka! "I transferred from a small liberal arts college looking to find more diversity, and I have to say I found it," says a sophomore. Indeed, AU's culture is a real "melting pot" and "students come here from all over with very diverse backgrounds so you can learn a lot." Cliques are abundant, though, as "students usually stick to their own groups." Consequently, "it's really hard to meet people," warns a senior. Many students at American "seem to come from very well-to-do families." Some of the international students here are "unbelievably wealthy and disconnected," and there is definitely a contingent of "rich snots who give the impression they have money to burn." Also, "most students are incredibly unattractive but dressed to the hilt," observes a style-conscious sophomore. On the plus side, "no one is nerdy." Not surprisingly given AU's location, the students here also describe themselves as "goal-oriented," "very politically aware," and "interested in activism." The political slant on campus is somewhat "liberal," and students gripe that something about the place seems to make them "rehash political arguments on a daily basis."

FINANCIAL AID: 202-885-6100 • E-MAIL: AFA@AMERICAN.EDU • WEBSITE: WWW.AMERICAN.EDU

## ADMISSIONS

*Very important* academic and nonacademic factors considered by the admissions committee include secondary school record and standard test scores. *Important* factors considered include essays, recommendations, interview, extracurricular activities, and talent and ability. *Other* factors considered include alumni/ae relation, character/personal qualities, class rank, geography, minority status, volunteer work, and work experience. Factors *not* considered include religious affiliation/commitment and state residency. SAT I or ACT required. High school diploma is required and GED is accepted. *High school units required/recommended:* 16 total required; 4 English required, 3 math required, 4 math recommended, 3 science required, 2 science lab recommended, 2 foreign language required, 2 social studies recommended.

### The Inside Word

Washington, D.C., is indeed a tremendous attraction for students who aspire to careers in government, politics, and other areas of public service. Georgetown skims most of the cream of the crop off the top of this considerable pool of prospective students, but American does quite nicely. Because the university is nationally known it also has formidable competition outside its own backyard, and as a result its yield of admits who enroll is on the low side. This necessitates a higher admit rate than one might expect at a school with considerable academic strength and an impressively credentialed faculty. If you're an active leadership type with a strong academic record the admissions process should be fairly painless—American offers a great opportunity for a quality educational experience without having to plead for admission.

## FINANCIAL AID

*Students should submit:* FAFSA and institution's own financial aid form. Regular filing deadline is March 1. The Princeton Review suggests that all financial aid forms be submitted as soon as possible after January 1. *Need-based scholarships/grants offered:* Federal Pell Grant, Federal SEOG, some state grants, private scholarships, and the school's own gift aid. *Loan aid offered:* Direct Subsidized Stafford, Direct Unsubsidized Stafford, Direct PLUS, Federal Perkins, and college/university loans from institutional funds. Institutional employment available. Federal Work-Study Program available. Applicants will be notified of awards on or about April 1. Off-campus job opportunities are excellent.

## FROM THE ADMISSIONS OFFICE

"Our students not only learn about the world, but also learn how to shape the world by interacting regularly with decision makers and leaders in every profession and from every corner of the world. If you are looking to be academically challenged in a rich multicultural environment where leadership and decision making are put into practice, then American University is the place you want to be. Our residential, urban campus provides a safe, comfortable environment where students from all 50 states and over 140 countries live and work. Our expert, teaching faculty provide a well-rounded liberal arts education characterized by small classes, an interdisciplinary curriculum, and the extensive resources of Washington, D.C. In addition, students enjoy a rich variety of professional internship opportunities throughout the city. American University offers all the tools you need to become an expert in your field of study and to shape the world of tomorrow."

## ADMISSIONS

| | |
|---|---|
| Admissions Rating | 82 |
| # of applicants | 8,501 |
| % of applicants accepted | 72 |
| % of acceptees attending | 21 |
| # accepting a place on wait list | 282 |
| % admitted from wait list | 14 |
| # of early decision applicants | 324 |
| % accepted early decision | 80 |

### FRESHMAN PROFILE

| | |
|---|---|
| Range SAT Verbal | 550-650 |
| Average SAT Verbal | 599 |
| Range SAT Math | 550-640 |
| Average SAT Math | 592 |
| Range ACT Composite | 23-29 |
| Average ACT Composite | 26 |
| Average HS GPA | 3.2 |
| % graduated top 10% of class | 28 |
| % graduated top 25% of class | 70 |
| % graduated top 50% of class | 92 |

### DEADLINES

| | |
|---|---|
| Early decision | 11/15 |
| Early decision notification | 12/31 |
| Regular admission | 2/1 |
| Regular notification | 4/1 |
| Nonfall registration? | yes |

### APPLICANTS ALSO LOOK AT

**AND OFTEN PREFER**
Georgetown U.
UNC—Chapel Hill
Northwestern U.
Emory, Boston U.

**AND SOMETIMES PREFER**
Catholic U., Dickinson
Boston Coll.
George Washington
U. Maryland, Coll. Park

**AND RARELY PREFER**
U. Delaware
Loyola Marymount

### FINANCIAL FACTS

| | |
|---|---|
| Financial Aid Rating | 74 |
| Tuition | $21,144 |
| Room & board | $8,372 |
| Books and supplies | $450 |
| Required fees | $255 |
| % frosh receiving aid | 62 |
| % undergrads receiving aid | 64 |
| Avg frosh grant | $13,028 |
| Avg frosh loan | $2,921 |

# AMHERST COLLEGE

CAMPUS BOX 2231, PO BOX 5000, AMHERST, MA 01002 • ADMISSIONS: 413-542-2328 • FAX: 413-542-2040

## CAMPUS LIFE

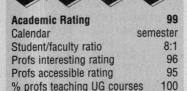

| Quality of Life Rating | 88 |
|---|---|
| Type of school | private |
| Affiliation | none |
| Environment | rural |

### STUDENTS

| | |
|---|---|
| Total undergrad enrollment | 1,682 |
| % male/female | 52/48 |
| % from out of state | 86 |
| % from public high school | 56 |
| % live on campus | 98 |
| % African American | 8 |
| % Asian | 12 |
| % Caucasian | 55 |
| % Hispanic | 7 |
| % international | 4 |
| # of countries represented | 30 |

### SURVEY SAYS . . .

*Campus easy to get around*
*Registration is a breeze*
*Students are happy*
*Dorms are like palaces*
*No one cheats*
*Very little hard liquor*
*Very little drug use*
*Students aren't religious*
*Lousy food on campus*
*Student publications are ignored*

## ACADEMICS

| Academic Rating | 99 |
|---|---|
| Calendar | semester |
| Student/faculty ratio | 8:1 |
| Profs interesting rating | 96 |
| Profs accessible rating | 95 |
| % profs teaching UG courses | 100 |
| Avg lab size | 10-19 students |
| Avg reg class size | 10-19 students |

### MOST POPULAR MAJORS
English
economics
political science

## STUDENTS SPEAK OUT

### Academics

Small classes, great professors, as much academic freedom as students are willing to grab, and a beautiful campus; no wonder students say, "I could not, in my wildest dreams, imagine an environment better suited for a young adult to grow intellectually than Amherst College." Excellent professors dedicated to undergraduate teaching lie at the heart of the Amherst experience. "Professors make it their business to get to know students and show an interest in them," writes one undergrad. "They are very supportive." Recounts another, "When I wrote my math professor a panic-filled e-mail the night before a test, he called me to help at one in the morning." The administration aggressively encourages close student-teacher relationships, sponsoring "a program [that allows] students to take professors out to dinner and thus extend the educational realm beyond the classroom." Amherst's open curriculum means students "take every course by choice, not because it is required" and can easily "create [their] own interdisciplinary major." Classes are small and selection is limited, so classes close quickly. However, "while on paper it may seem [difficult] to get into classes, Amherst students take the words 'course closed' as a challenge. Here, the administration and many professors encourage us to whine and grovel to get what we want out of our academics. The rules are written so that anyone can be an exception." When students tire of their own college community, it is easy to take a class or audition for a play at one of the other four schools in the Five College Consortium (UMass—Amherst, Smith, Hampshire, and Mount Holyoke). The Five College system, according to students, "gives you all the opportunities of a large university, without any of the drawbacks."

### Life

According to most students, "Social life at Amherst isn't varied. Mostly it's either parties with lots of alcohol or else just hanging out with your group of friends and talking. But most people seem satisfied with this, and there are a few alternative social events for those who aren't." For fun, students "watch a lot of movies sponsored by campus groups, dance, and go out to dinner with friends." They also attend TAP, a.k.a. The Amherst Party, a regular campuswide blowout held in upper-class dorms. TAP "is huge here, as is drinking. But it's not as if drinking is mandatory for having a good time or fitting in." As an alternative, "some of the substance-free dorms run 'anti-parties' every Saturday in response to TAP." Otherwise, students engage in "lots of preppy activities, e.g. sailing, fencing, and crew"; take advantage of "the Five College system, which brings an endless stream of stuff to do to the Valley"; or just hang out in their amazing dorms. They do not, as a rule, since "dating is difficult at a school this small. Most people either randomly hook up on Saturdays or are in long-term relationships." When the campus social scene grows stifling, they head to the close-by fraternities of UMass.

### Student Body

Despite a minority population that is uncommonly large among New England private schools, Amherst students still complain that "this is not a very diverse school, and a lot of people don't make efforts to be friends with different kinds of people." Even the more generous undergrads qualify their praise, pointing out that "this school is more diverse than your average bear, but since it's in New England it's still pretty whitewashed." Students "get along very well" and appreciate the fact that their classmates are "very smart, somewhat intimidating, but great company." There are, notes one student, "lots of extremely talented students," and "many fun late-night discussions." Some warn that "too much political correctness is our biggest problem. Lots of complaining about nonexistent problems."

FINANCIAL AID: 413-542-2296 • E-MAIL: ADMISSIONS@AMHERST.EDU • WEBSITE: WWW.AMHERST.EDU

## ADMISSIONS

*Very important* academic and nonacademic factors considered by the admissions committee include character/personal qualities, essays, extracurricular activities, recommendations, secondary school record, standardized test scores, and talent/ability. *Important* factors considered include alumni/ae relation, class rank, volunteer work, and work experience. *Other* factors considered include geography, minority status, and state residency. Factors *not* considered include interview and religious affiliation/commitment. SAT I or ACT required; 3 SAT IIs also required. TOEFL, ELPT (SAT II English Language Proficiency Test), MELAB, or APIEL required for applicants whose first or primary language is not English. High school diploma is required and GED is accepted. *High school units required/recommended:* 20 total recommended; 4 English recommended, 4 math recommended, 3 science recommended, 1 science lab recommended, 4 foreign language recommended, 2 social studies recommended, 2 history recommended.

### The Inside Word

Despite an up-and-down fluctuation in application totals at most highly selective colleges over the past couple of years, Amherst remains a popular choice and very competitive. You've got to be a strong match all-around, and given their formidable applicant pool, it's very important that you make your case as direct as possible. If you're a special-interest candidate such as a legacy or recruited athlete, you may get a bit of a break from the admissions committee, but you'll still need to show sound academic capabilities and potential. Those without such links have a tougher task. On top of taking the toughest courses available to them and performing at the highest of their abilities, they must be strong writers who demonstrate that they are intellectually curious self-starters who will contribute to the community and profit from the experience. In other words, you've got to have a strong profile and a very convincing application in order to get admitted.

## FINANCIAL AID

*Students should submit:* FAFSA, CSS/Financial Aid PROFILE, noncustodial (divorced/separated) parent's statement, and business/farm supplement. Regular filing deadline is February 1. The Princeton Review suggests that all financial aid forms be submitted as soon as possible after January 1. *Need-based scholarships/grants offered:* Pell, SEOG, state scholarships/grants, private scholarships, and the school's own gift aid. *Loan aid offered:* Direct Subsidized Stafford, Direct Unsubsidized Stafford, Direct PLUS, Federal Perkins, and college/university loans from institutional funds. Institutional employment available. Federal Work-Study Program available. Applicants will be notified of awards on or about April 5. Off-campus job opportunities are good.

## FROM THE ADMISSIONS OFFICE

"Amherst College looks, above all, for men and women of intellectual promise who have demonstrated qualities of mind and character that will enable them to take full advantage of the college's curriculum. . . . Admission decisions aim to select from among the many qualified applicants those possessing the intellectual talent, mental discipline, and imagination that will allow them most fully to benefit from the curriculum and contribute to the life of the college and of society. Whatever the form of academic experience—lecture course, seminar, conference, studio, laboratory, independent study at various levels—intellectual competence and awareness of problems and methods are the goals of the Amherst program, rather than the direct preparation for a profession."

### ADMISSIONS

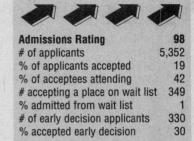

| | |
|---|---|
| Admissions Rating | 98 |
| # of applicants | 5,352 |
| % of applicants accepted | 19 |
| % of acceptees attending | 42 |
| # accepting a place on wait list | 349 |
| % admitted from wait list | 1 |
| # of early decision applicants | 330 |
| % accepted early decision | 30 |

#### FRESHMAN PROFILE

| | |
|---|---|
| Range SAT Verbal | 650-760 |
| Average SAT Verbal | 702 |
| Range SAT Math | 650-740 |
| Average SAT Math | 696 |
| Range ACT Composite | 28-32 |
| Average ACT Composite | 30 |
| Minimum TOEFL | 600 |
| % graduated top 10% of class | 84 |
| % graduated top 25% of class | 96 |
| % graduated top 50% of class | 99 |

#### DEADLINES

| | |
|---|---|
| Early decision | 11/15 |
| Early decision notification | 12/15 |
| Regular admission | 12/31 |
| Regular notification | 4/5 |

#### APPLICANTS ALSO LOOK AT
**AND OFTEN PREFER**
Harvard
Princeton
Yale
**AND SOMETIMES PREFER**
Brown
Williams
Stanford
Dartmouth
**AND RARELY PREFER**
U. Virginia
Vassar
Tufts

### FINANCIAL FACTS

| | |
|---|---|
| Financial Aid Rating | 84 |
| Tuition | $25,600 |
| % frosh receiving aid | 49 |
| % undergrads receiving aid | 43 |
| Avg frosh grant | $23,605 |
| Avg frosh loan | $2,624 |

# ARIZONA STATE UNIVERSITY

PO Box 870112, Tempe, AZ 85287-0112 • Admissions: 480-965-7788 • Fax: 480-965-3610

## CAMPUS LIFE

| | |
|---|---|
| Quality of Life Rating | 77 |
| Type of school | public |
| Affiliation | none |
| Environment | suburban |

### STUDENTS

| | |
|---|---|
| Total undergrad enrollment | 33,985 |
| % male/female | 48/52 |
| % from out of state | 23 |
| % live on campus | 16 |
| % in (# of) fraternities | 9 (23) |
| % in (# of) sororities | 8 (18) |
| % African American | 3 |
| % Asian | 5 |
| % Caucasian | 74 |
| % Hispanic | 11 |
| % Native American | 2 |
| % international | 3 |
| # of countries represented | 124 |

### SURVEY SAYS . . .

*Students love Tempe, AZ*
*Athletic facilities are great*
*Everyone loves the Sun Devils*
*Popular college radio*
*Great library*
*Ethnic diversity on campus*
*Student publications are popular*
*Large classes*
*Lots of TAs teach upper-level courses*
*Dorms are like dungeons*

## ACADEMICS

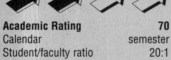

| | |
|---|---|
| Academic Rating | 70 |
| Calendar | semester |
| Student/faculty ratio | 20:1 |
| Profs interesting rating | 87 |
| Profs accessible rating | 87 |
| % profs teaching UG courses | 75 |
| Avg lab size | 20-29 students |
| Avg reg class size | 20-29 students |

### MOST POPULAR MAJORS
business
psychology
communication

## STUDENTS SPEAK OUT

### Academics

"Walking to class in sunshine is great!" writes a first year. Indeed, among those surveyed, "temperature" and "weather" were some of the top reasons listed for choosing this huge (40,000 grad and undergrad combined) Pac-10 school located in Tempe, Arizona (quickly followed by "tuition, beer, parties, girls"—and in that order). This isn't to say ASU is only known for its sun-drenched, beer-soaked, bare-naked partying. A serious-minded senior argues: "There's a lot of people who complain that this is a party school. College is what you make of it. If you want to study, you can. If you want to party, you can. Thankfully, I've managed to balance the two." It's a sentiment that's echoed again and again. With its academic tutoring resources, relatively low cost, proximity to Phoenix industry, and strong programs (architecture, psychology, business administration, and the Walter Cronkite School of Journalism), Arizona State is a school with plenty of opportunities for an education—if, perhaps, a few more opportunities to have a good time. As with any school of its size, hassles with preregistration, overcrowded classes, inadequate facilities (especially the school's computer networking), and "too many teaching assistants" can lead to frustration. Still, say most, "at ASU professors care very much and they want students to succeed." As at any school, "There's a marked difference between mere professors and educators," concludes a junior. "All the people I learned from were the latter."

### Life

A first-year waxes profound: "Life is awesome here. Can't beat life in the sun." Tongue-tied from a bit too much of ASU's legendary partying? Perhaps. After all, Tempe's reputation as "extremely social" and "an excellent college town" is hard to live down. "The downtown area is spectacular," writes a freshman. "Lots of fun stuff to do. Lots of cool festivals, and, being close to Phoenix, many big musicians have concerts nearby." Of course, everyone's got a different pace, and ASU's size and diversity seems to be able to accommodate most. A junior describes her typical day: "People think about going to class, grades, studying, friends, relationships, parties, etc. We watch movies and TV, we exercise, [and] go out. We write, read, etc." So many people around all the time can put a strain on the facilities, and ASU's dorms bear witness to decades of wear. "Dorms here are essentially low-rent apartments in every sense of the word," gripes a sophomore. Still, when a first-year's only complaint is "more shade (it's really hot)," things can't be all bad.

### Student Body

"Lots of working out, tanning, dieting, highlighting, and plastic surgery. And everyone always seems to be on a cell phone." Is it all just a bunch of "Barbies & Kens," as one sick-of-it senior claims? We like this upperclassman's take on things: "Like any other place where there's a huge group of people, you learn patience. Sometimes people are really cool, sometimes they aren't." While some members of ASU's student body have been accused of "apathy" and of having a "safety-don't-talk-to-me bubble" around them, "many are ambitious and generally nice." A freshman concludes, "College is a slice of life. You run into everyone and every style of personality." Indeed, cultural, ethnic, and economic diversity is one of ASU's biggest strengths. An upbeat sophomore notes, "Students interact with a variety of others on a daily basis. There is more diversity here than anywhere else I have been."

## ADMISSIONS

*Very important* academic and nonacademic factors considered by the admissions committee include class rank, secondary school record, and standardized test scores. *Important* factors considered include state residency. *Other* factors considered include essays, recommendations, extracurricular activities, interviews, and talent/ability. Factors *not* considered include religious affiliation/commitment. SAT I or ACT required. TOEFL required of all international applicants. High school diploma is required and GED is accepted. *High school units required/recommended:* 16 total recommended; 4 English recommended, 4 math recommended, 3 science recommended, 2 foreign language recommended, 2 social studies recommended, 1 fine art recommended.

### The Inside Word

A college preparatory curriculum and solid grades should lead to hassle-free admission. ASU uses a formula and cutoff admission process. Candidates who don't fill the bill through the formula can appeal their denial and submit additional information for consideration.

## FINANCIAL AID

*Students should submit:* FAFSA. There is no regular filing deadline. The Princeton Review suggests that all financial aid forms be submitted as soon as possible after January 1. *Need-based scholarships/grants offered:* Pell, SEOG, state scholarships/grants, private scholarships, the school's own gift aid, and Federal Nursing. *Loan aid offered:* Direct Subsidized Stafford, Direct Unsubsidized Stafford, Direct PLUS, FFEL PLUS, and Federal Perkins. Institutional employment available. Federal Work-Study Program available. Applicants will be notified of awards on a rolling basis beginning on or about March 15. Off-campus job opportunities are good.

## FROM THE ADMISSIONS OFFICE

"ASU is a place where students from all 50 states and abroad come together to live and study in one of the nation's premier collegiate environments. Situated in Tempe, ASU boasts a physical setting and climate second to none. ASU offers more than 150 academic programs of study leading to the BS and BA in eight undergraduate colleges and one school. Many of these programs have received national recognition for their quality of teaching, innovative curricula, and outstanding facilities. ASU's Honors College, the only Honors College in the Southwest that spans all academic disciplines, provides unique and challenging experiences for its students and was recently named one of eight 'best buys' in honors education by *Money* magazine."

## ADMISSIONS

| | |
|---|---:|
| **Admissions Rating** | **76** |
| # of applicants | 18,247 |
| % of applicants accepted | 77 |
| % of acceptees attending | 43 |

### FRESHMAN PROFILE

| | |
|---|---:|
| Range SAT Verbal | 480-600 |
| Average SAT Verbal | 538 |
| Range SAT Math | 490-610 |
| Average SAT Math | 552 |
| Range ACT Composite | 20-26 |
| Average ACT Composite | 23 |
| Minimum TOEFL | 500 |
| Average HS GPA | 3.3 |
| % graduated top 10% of class | 26 |
| % graduated top 25% of class | 52 |
| % graduated top 50% of class | 82 |

### DEADLINES

| | |
|---|---:|
| Priority admission deadline | 4/15 |
| Nonfall registration? | yes |

### APPLICANTS ALSO LOOK AT

**AND OFTEN PREFER**
UCLA
U. Colorado—Boulder

**AND SOMETIMES PREFER**
U. Southern Cal
BYU
UC—Irvine
U. Arizona

**AND RARELY PREFER**
San Diego State
Northern Arizona

## FINANCIAL FACTS

| | |
|---|---:|
| **Financial Aid Rating** | **74** |
| In-state tuition | $2,272 |
| Out-of-state tuition | $9,728 |
| Room & board | $5,240 |
| Books and supplies | $700 |
| Required fees | $74 |
| % frosh receiving aid | 34 |
| % undergrads receiving aid | 43 |
| Avg frosh grant | $4,562 |
| Avg frosh loan | $3,359 |

# AUBURN UNIVERSITY

202 MARY MARTIN HALL, AUBURN, AL 36849-5149 • ADMISSIONS: 334-844-4080 • FAX: 334-844-6179

## CAMPUS LIFE

| Quality of Life Rating | 75 |
|---|---|
| Type of school | public |
| Affiliation | none |
| Environment | suburban |

### STUDENTS

| | |
|---|---|
| Total undergrad enrollment | 18,326 |
| % male/female | 52/48 |
| % from out of state | 31 |
| % from public high school | 86 |
| % live on campus | 16 |
| % in (# of) fraternities | 21 (28) |
| % in (# of) sororities | 35 (19) |
| % African American | 7 |
| % Asian | 1 |
| % Caucasian | 90 |
| % Hispanic | 1 |
| % international | 1 |
| # of countries represented | 89 |

### SURVEY SAYS . . .

*Everyone loves the Tigers*
*Frats and sororities dominate social scene*
*(Almost) everyone plays intramural sports*
*Great library*
*Students love Auburn, AL*
*Students get along with local community*
*Student publications are popular*
*Students are very religious*
*Large classes*
*Theater is unpopular*

## ACADEMICS

| Academic Rating | 72 |
|---|---|
| Calendar | semester |
| Student/faculty ratio | 16:1 |
| Profs interesting rating | 89 |
| Profs accessible rating | 91 |
| % profs teaching UG courses | 98 |
| % classes taught by TAs | 10 |
| Avg lab size | 10-19 students |
| Avg reg class size | 20-29 students |

### MOST POPULAR MAJORS
business
engineering
education

## STUDENTS SPEAK OUT

### Academics

When asked why she chose Auburn University, a land-grant institution located in the heart of Alabama, a sophomore explains, "The Blue and the Orange flows in my veins!" Strong on "people, atmosphere, education, and spirit," traditional, pragmatic Auburn inspires devotion among its undergrads, who are proud of the school's "great reputation" and "opportunity for advancement." Students must complete a core program of math, science, social science, fine arts, literature, and writing before they head off into one of 11 specialized schools (especially good are agricultural studies and agricultural engineering, veterinary medicine, engineering, architecture, nursing, and pharmacology). Classes are usually deemed "challenging, worthwhile, and fun," and profs are given high marks for teaching style and accessibility. "They are seriously interested in our education and personal lives," notes a junior. The administration, however, while considered "ambitious" in its quest to improve Auburn's program, has received flak in recent years for raising tuition. A senior sums up: "Auburn was great until proration hit. Now everything is expensive! Auburn has the potential to be one of the top schools. But as long as one trustee is running things . . . it won't happen."

### Life

A positive, symbiotic relationship between "town and gown" is one of the best aspects of life at Auburn; notes a junior, "The town of Auburn supports the university—which makes for a good college town setting and a friendly and safe atmosphere." "There's a great campus and community spirit," adds a senior. "You feel safe here." School spirit, too, runs high at Auburn, especially during football season. Regularly producing professional players, the Tigers provide a good rallying point for the students. Student government is also popular—a senior writes that "it's pretty political here." Despite their dissatisfaction with the current board of trustees, Auburn students find time to enjoy themselves on their "beautiful" campus. Greek life is popular, claiming about a quarter of the student body. Students more into "clubbing and bands" can also drive to Montgomery (about an hour away) or Atlanta (90 minutes).

### Student Body

"It's all about learning about yourself," writes a first-year, and the Auburn community seems to be uniquely suited to helping its undergrads achieve that goal. Maybe too suited. "Most people do not want to leave after graduation," writes a senior. While the school attracts a student body drawn mostly by the university's reputation of Southern traditionalism, and despite its mostly southern, white constituency, people are "warm" and "diverse," and "friendly smiles and faces are easily found." In recent years, Auburn's reputation and relatively low public tuition have enticed more out-of-state students, fueling a sense of its own growing potential as a high-caliber public institution.

FINANCIAL AID: 334-844-4367 • E-MAIL: ADMISSIONS@AUBURN.EDU • WEBSITE: WWW.AUBURN.EDU

## ADMISSIONS

*Very important* academic and nonacademic factors considered by the admissions committee include standardized test scores and secondary school record. *Important* factors considered include state residency. *Other* factors considered include alumni/ae relation, geography, minority status, and talent/ability. Factors *not* considered include class rank, essays, recommendations, character/personal qualities, extracurricular activities, interview, religious affiliation/commitment, volunteer work, and work experience. SAT I or ACT required. TOEFL required of all international applicants. High school diploma is required and GED is accepted. *High school units recommended:* 15 total recommended; 4 English recommended, 3 math recommended, 3 science recommended, 2 science lab recommended, 1 foreign language recommended, 4 social studies recommended, 2 history recommended.

### The Inside Word

Auburn is another "follow the numbers" admission institution—if you have what they require, you're in with little sweat.

## FINANCIAL AID

*Students should submit:* FAFSA and institution's own financial aid form. There is no regular filing deadline. The Princeton Review suggests that all financial aid forms be submitted as soon as possible after January 1. *Need-based scholarships/grants offered:* Pell and SEOG. *Loan aid offered:* Direct Subsidized Stafford, Direct Unsubsidized Stafford, Direct PLUS, Federal Perkins, and college/university loans from institutional funds. Institutional employment available. Federal Work-Study Program available. Off-campus job opportunities are good.

## FROM THE ADMISSIONS OFFICE

"Auburn University is a comprehensive land-grant university serving Alabama and the nation. The university is especially charged with the responsibility of enhancing the economic, social, and cultural development of the state through its instruction, research, and extension programs. In all of these programs the university is committed to the pursuit of excellence. The university assumes an obligation to provide an environment of learning in which the individual and society are enriched by the discovery, preservation, transmission, and application of knowledge; in which students grow intellectually as they study and do research under the guidance of competent faculty; and in which the faculty develop professionally and contribute fully to the intellectual life of the institution, community, and state. This obligation unites Auburn University's continuing commitment to its land-grant traditions and the institution's role as a dynamic and complex comprehensive university."

## ADMISSIONS

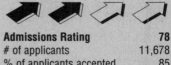

| | |
|---|---|
| Admissions Rating | 78 |
| # of applicants | 11,678 |
| % of applicants accepted | 85 |
| % of acceptees attending | 39 |
| # accepting a place on wait list | 459 |
| % admitted from wait list | 5 |

### FRESHMAN PROFILE

| | |
|---|---|
| Range SAT Verbal | 500-590 |
| Average SAT Verbal | 546 |
| Range SAT Math | 510-610 |
| Average SAT Math | 563 |
| Range ACT Composite | 21-26 |
| Average ACT Composite | 24 |
| Minimum TOEFL | 550 |
| Average HS GPA | 3.3 |
| % graduated top 10% of class | 24 |
| % graduated top 25% of class | 54 |
| % graduated top 50% of class | 81 |

### DEADLINES

| | |
|---|---|
| Regular admission | 8/1 |
| Nonfall registration? | yes |

### APPLICANTS ALSO LOOK AT
**AND OFTEN PREFER**
Florida State
University of Georgia
Mississippi State
U. Tenn—Knoxville
University of Florida
**AND SOMETIMES PREFER**
U. Mississippi
Georgia Tech
**AND RARELY PREFER**
U. Alabama

## FINANCIAL FACTS

| | |
|---|---|
| Financial Aid Rating | 76 |
| In-state tuition | $3,050 |
| Out-of-state tuition | $9,150 |
| Books and supplies | $900 |
| Required fees | $104 |
| % frosh receiving aid | 49 |
| % undergrads receiving aid | 60 |
| Avg frosh grant | $6,449 |
| Avg frosh loan | $2,960 |

# AUSTIN COLLEGE

900 NORTH GRAND AVENUE, SUITE 6N, SHERMAN, TX 75090-4440 • ADMISSIONS: 903-813-3000 • FAX: 903-813-3198

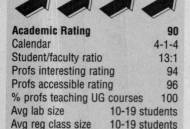
## STUDENTS SPEAK OUT
### Academics

Austin College is "a great liberal arts school" with "superb" academics located in a "yawner of a town" in the suburbs north of Dallas. While a required, three-course, interdisciplinary at AC called the Heritage of Western Culture program is lavishly praised by some students and thoroughly panned by others, just about everyone loves its 4-1-4 calendar (two semesters with a middle session that allows students to pursue independent courses of study), especially "January term." Students tell us that January term offers four "once-in-a-lifetime opportunities" to "do whatever in the hell you want academically." AC also boasts an "excellent pre-med program" and strong departments in biology, chemistry, political science/international relations, education, and business. "Classes are hard" but the "eccentric," "approachable and friendly" professors are "great motivators" who are "very knowledgeable in their fields" and "care about helping you learn." They "love what they do and want the students to understand why" and "they give out their phone numbers and even (in some cases) directions to their houses," beams a first-year student. "The accessibility you have to professors is great," agrees a sophomore. "It is not unusual to eat lunch with faculty or have a 'sidewalk chat' with the president of the college." Unfortunately, the administration as a whole "is not with it," especially the registrar's office. Class selection is reportedly limited at AC, and "if you ever wanted to be in a circus," quips a psychology major, "class registration at Austin is the place to be."

### Life

"Life is good at AC," according to a junior, this despite a "repetitive party scene," a campus that is "somewhat lacking as far as activities," but the 41-acre lake campus offers a cool alternative for students who take advantage of it. The fact is that students do "a lot of studying." For fun, the industrious students here often "socialize in the library" or, if all else fails, "a lot of friends just get together to hang out and talk for hours in the dorms." On the weekends, "drinking is quite popular" and there are "lots of parties," thanks mostly to a Greek system that is "very unlike the stereotypical fraternities and sororities" because "all Greek organizations are local." Beyond the Austin College campus, students can "go shopping at the local mall," to the movies, or "to local bars." They can't do much else, though, because "the surrounding town" of Sherman "has few entertainment opportunities." Consequently, "you have to go to Dallas to do anything." Luckily, the lights of Dallas are "only a 50-minute drive," not far by Texas standards. "Big D" offers clubs and plenty of culture for students who need to get away. One popular off-campus activity among AC students is eating out, but we hear that students are staying on campus to enjoy the local fare at their new dining hall.

### Student Body

At "relaxed, laid back," and relatively "diverse" Austin College, there are "long-haired hippies" mingling with "right-wing conservatives" and "a lot of weird people." AC also has its fair share of students "from white, middle-class America" who "have no clue about life outside the shelter of Daddy's Money." Everyone "is really friendly," though. "It's like *Cheers* here," claims a junior. "Everybody knows your name" and "it is extremely rare to walk across campus without being blasted with hellos." Of course, since "everybody knows or has heard of everyone else," it's nearly "impossible to enjoy comfortable anonymity" on this tiny campus. The "highly competitive" and "very intellectual" students here describe themselves as "religious," "mostly bright people" who "definitely have academics as their first priority." They are "very accepting and open-minded" as well, and "nobody takes themselves too seriously." Upper-class students "offer good advice" as well. "Greeks and non-Greeks interact great," which is pretty rare, but AC can be "a lot like high school" in that there are some "exclusive" cliques.

FINANCIAL AID: 903-813-2900 • E-MAIL: ADMISSION@AUSTINC.EDU • WEBSITE: WWW.AUSTINC.EDU

## ADMISSIONS

*Very important* academic and nonacademic factors considered by the admissions committee include secondary school record. *Important* factors considered include class rank, standardized test scores, and talent/ability. *Other* factors considered include character/personal qualities, essays, extracurricular activities, geography, interview, recommendations, volunteer work, and work experience. Factors *not* considered include minority status, religious affiliation/commitment, and state residency. SAT I or ACT required. TOEFL required of all international applicants. High school diploma is required and GED is accepted. *High school units required/recommended:* 15 total required; 4 English required, 3 math required, 3 science required, 2 science lab required, 2 foreign language required, 3 social studies required, 1 elective required.

### The Inside Word

Austin continues to be a prize find among lesser-known colleges, but it isn't as much of a secret anymore. Freshman enrollment saw a major surge last year, which could translate into a somewhat tougher admissions committee. The college's emphasis on academic quality and its very sincere approach to recruitment of students has paid off handsomely. Efforts to increase minority representation on campus have been a big success—few small colleges have as impressive a level of diversity. Out-of-state students will continue to be appealing to the admissions committee, as their number is still rather low.

## FINANCIAL AID

*Students should submit:* FAFSA and institution's own financial aid form. The Princeton Review suggests that all financial aid forms be submitted as soon as possible after January 1. *Need-based scholarships/grants offered:* Pell, SEOG, state scholarships/grants, private scholarships and the school's own gift aid. *Loan aid offered:* Federal Subsidized Stafford, Federal Unsubsidized Stafford, Federal PLUS, Federal Perkins, state, and college/university loans from institutional funds. Institutional employment available. Federal Work-Study Program available. Applicants will be notified of awards on a rolling basis beginning on or about March 1. Off-campus job opportunities are good.

## FROM THE ADMISSIONS OFFICE

"Austin College's 81,000-square-foot Robert J. and Mary Wright Campus Center opened in the spring of 2000. 'A campus center is an extension of our home,' said student body president Judson Richardson at the dedication ceremony. 'It is our living room, our kitchen, and our social and entertainment center. But this is so much more. It is our town hall . . . our gathering place. It is an extension of the student community.' At the heart of the facility a two-story living room forms a hub, surrounded by the snack bar, post office, bookstore, and game room. The facility also houses the campus dining room, student organization offices, a large banquet room, meeting rooms, and a reception gallery, as well as offices for the Student Affairs staff.

"The college has only recently completed renovations of all residence halls and construction of the Jordan Family Language House where students of French, German, Japanese, and Spanish leave their English at the door to learn practical aspects of language and culture. Other projects underway scheduled for completion in 2000: Jerry Apple Stadium (football), and a fitness center which will feature a huge pavilion with the latest cardiovascular and weight training equipment, locker rooms, training rooms, and more!"

### ADMISSIONS

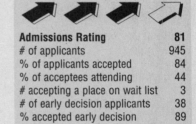

| | |
|---|---|
| Admissions Rating | 81 |
| # of applicants | 945 |
| % of applicants accepted | 84 |
| % of acceptees attending | 44 |
| # accepting a place on wait list | 3 |
| # of early decision applicants | 38 |
| % accepted early decision | 89 |

#### FRESHMAN PROFILE

| | |
|---|---|
| Range SAT Verbal | 560-660 |
| Average SAT Verbal | 610 |
| Range SAT Math | 560-660 |
| Average SAT Math | 611 |
| Range ACT Composite | 25-28 |
| Average ACT Composite | 27 |
| Minimum TOEFL | 550 |
| % graduated top 10% of class | 47 |
| % graduated top 25% of class | 78 |
| % graduated top 50% of class | 94 |

#### DEADLINES

| | |
|---|---|
| Early decision | 12/1 |
| Early decision notification | 1/10 |
| Priority admission deadline | 3/1 |
| Regular admission | 8/15 |
| Nonfall registration? | yes |

#### APPLICANTS ALSO LOOK AT
**AND OFTEN PREFER**
Rice
Trinity U.
U. Texas—Austin
**AND SOMETIMES PREFER**
Southwestern
Baylor
Texas A&M
SMU

### FINANCIAL FACTS

| | |
|---|---|
| Financial Aid Rating | 88 |
| Tuition | $15,838 |
| Room & board | $6,187 |
| Books and supplies | $800 |
| Required fees | $125 |
| % frosh receiving aid | 62 |
| % undergrads receiving aid | 62 |
| Avg frosh grant | $9,433 |
| Avg frosh loan | $3,080 |

# BABSON COLLEGE

MUSTARD HALL, BABSON PARK, MA 02457-0310 • ADMISSIONS: 800-488-3696 • FAX: 781-239-4006

## CAMPUS LIFE

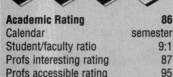

| Quality of Life Rating | 88 |
|---|---|
| Type of school | private |
| Affiliation | none |
| Environment | suburban |

### STUDENTS

| | |
|---|---|
| Total undergrad enrollment | 1,751 |
| % male/female | 60/40 |
| % from out of state | 50 |
| % from public high school | 52 |
| % live on campus | 85 |
| % in (# of) fraternities | 9 (3) |
| % in (# of) sororities | 10 (2) |
| % African American | 2 |
| % Asian | 7 |
| % Caucasian | 73 |
| % Hispanic | 3 |
| % international | 20 |
| # of countries represented | 73 |

### SURVEY SAYS . . .

Beautiful campus
Great computer facilities
Campus easy to get around
Great library
Campus feels safe
Diversity lacking on campus
Student publications are ignored
(Almost) no one listens to college
radio
Political activism is (almost)
nonexistent

## ACADEMICS

| Academic Rating | 86 |
|---|---|
| Calendar | semester |
| Student/faculty ratio | 9:1 |
| Profs interesting rating | 87 |
| Profs accessible rating | 95 |
| % profs teaching UG courses | 100 |
| Avg lab size | 10-19 students |
| Avg reg class size | 26 students |

### MOST POPULAR MAJORS
business management
entrepreneurship
accounting

## STUDENTS SPEAK OUT

### Academics

It's all about the "real world" and "networking" at "rigorous," career-oriented Babson College, "an intensely difficult" little enclave near Boston where "serious studying" is the norm and "the workload can be overwhelming at times." Students assure us that the effort pays off handsomely, though. Babson, they say, is the "top business school in the country," complete with unparalleled "connections to the business world." However, as a well-rounded business education is pretty much the only alternative here, students warn: "If you don't like business, don't come here." If you do like business, the "hands-on" curriculum—complete with "unique real-life case studies"—will reportedly prepare you "for the business world" like no other. Babson's highly praised, compulsory entrepreneurship program requires all students to work in teams to start and operate their own businesses with—get this—seed money supplied by the college. At the end of the academic year, teams either donate their profits to their favorite charities or learn how to file for bankruptcy. Also, the faculty is "very knowledgeable," and most professors are "accomplished business people" who "know about business because they came from owning one or working in one." Many are "excited about their subjects" as well. Others, unfortunately, are "a tad boring."

### Life

"During the week, there isn't much free time" for students on this "small, beautiful," suburban campus. The food is more than edible and the dorms are comfortable, but the social life is nothing to write home about. This is not necessarily for lack of trying on behalf of the administration. School-sponsored events here include the *Jeopardy*-style Babson Bowl; September Stomp, a series of events like Big Wheel races with cash prizes for winning teams; and the traditional Midnight Breakfast during finals each semester, at which the deans and faculty members cook and serve students a full breakfast. The Babson Dance Ensemble and Babson Players are student-run and quite good as well. Still, "the campus is dead a lot." There are parties but "on-campus recreation is limited" and "many kids go to Boston to get away," which is—happily—"just around the corner." "It is expensive to go into Boston," especially if you do not own a car but, students advise, "you must go." In Beantown, students tell us they "go clubbing, [and] to the movies," and generally pursue its countless charms.

### Student Body

"If you come with a cell phone," promises a first-year student at Babson, "You'll fit right in. If not, you can buy one on campus." The commerce-savvy students here are "not too friendly," perhaps because they are "very busy, stressed, and tired." The average Babson student here is "very conservative" and "many come from very wealthy" backgrounds. "Some are very materialistic," concedes one student. "Since it is a business school, we all have a common goal of getting rich." Indeed, Babson students tell us they "dream about making millions" and being "millionaire CEOs in 20 years." Students "mostly get along," according to a sophomore. "There are definitely separate cliques," including a large contingent of international students, most of whom "keep themselves separated from the Americans." Almost 20 percent of the undergraduates are from outside the United States. There is "a lot of toleration," though, and Babson's environment is "highly interactive." Minority representation here is pretty low.

FINANCIAL AID: 781-239-4219 • E-MAIL: UGRADADMISSION@BABSON.EDU • WEBSITE: WWW.BABSON.EDU

## ADMISSIONS

*Very important* academic and nonacademic factors considered by the admissions committee include character/personal qualities and secondary school record. *Important* factors considered include essays, extracurricular activities, interview, recommendations, standardized test scores, and talent/ability. *Other* factors considered include alumni/ae relation, class rank, geography, minority status, volunteer work, and work experience. Factors *not* considered include religious affiliation/commitment and state residency. SAT I or ACT required. TOEFL not required of all international applicants. High school diploma is required and GED is accepted. *High school units required/recommended:* 16 total required; 17 total recommended; 4 English required, 4 math required, 2 science required, 3 science recommended, 1 science lab required, 3 science lab recommended, 3 foreign language recommended, 2 social studies required, 3 elective required.

### The Inside Word

Minority representation, including that of women, remains low, which makes for a very advantageous situation for such candidates. Legacies are also well accommodated by Babson's committee. In this age of corporate "downsizing" it has become much more commonplace for students to pursue college programs that lead directly to career paths, and Babson has benefited handsomely from this trend. When this trend and the college's fine reputation are combined, the result is a relatively challenging admissions process despite a relatively modest freshman academic profile. On top of this, the college is also recruiting further afield than in the past. Be wary of overconfidence when applying.

## FINANCIAL AID

*Students should submit:* FAFSA, CSS/Financial Aid PROFILE, noncustodial (divorced/separated) parent's statement, business/farm supplement, and tax returns. Regular filing deadline is February 15. The Princeton Review suggests that all financial aid forms be submitted as soon as possible after January 1. *Need-based scholarships/grants offered:* Pell, SEOG, state scholarships/grants, private scholarships, and the school's own gift aid. *Loan aid offered:* FFEL Subsidized Stafford, FFEL Unsubsidized Stafford, FFEL PLUS, Federal Perkins, state, and college/university loans from institutional funds. Institutional employment available. Federal Work-Study Program available. Applicants will be notified of awards on or about April 1. Off-campus job opportunities are excellent.

## FROM THE ADMISSIONS OFFICE

"In addition to theoretical knowledge, Babson College is dedicated to providing its students with hands-on business experience. The Foundation Management Experience (FME) and Management Consulting Field Experience (MCFE) are two prime examples of this commitment. During the FME, all freshmen are placed into groups of 30 and actually create their own businesses that they operate until the end of the academic year. The profits of each FME business are then donated to the charity of each group's choice.

"MCFE offers upperclassmen the unique and exciting opportunity to work as actual consultants for private companies and/or nonprofit organizations in small groups of three to five. Students receive academic credit for their work as well as invaluable experience in the field of consulting. FME and MCFE are just two of the ways Babson strives to produce business leaders with both theoretical knowledge and practical experience."

## ADMISSIONS

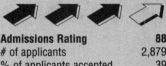

| Admissions Rating | 88 |
|---|---|
| # of applicants | 2,879 |
| % of applicants accepted | 39 |
| % of acceptees attending | 40 |
| # accepting a place on wait list | 391 |
| % admitted from wait list | 0 |
| # of early decision applicants | 175 |
| % accepted early decision | 31 |

### FRESHMAN PROFILE

| | |
|---|---|
| Range SAT Verbal | 530-610 |
| Range SAT Math | 590-680 |
| Minimum TOEFL | 550 |
| % graduated top 10% of class | 38 |
| % graduated top 25% of class | 81 |
| % graduated top 50% of class | 99 |

### DEADLINES

| | |
|---|---|
| Early decision | 12/1 |
| Early decision notification | 1/1 |
| Regular admission | 2/1 |
| Regular notification | 4/1 |
| Nonfall registration? | no |

### APPLICANTS ALSO LOOK AT

**AND OFTEN PREFER**
U. Penn
Georgetown U.
NYU
Tufts

**AND SOMETIMES PREFER**
George Washington
Boston Coll.
Boston U.

**AND RARELY PREFER**
Bentley
Providence
U. New Hampshire
U. Conn
U. Mass—Amherst
Bryant

## FINANCIAL FACTS

| Financial Aid Rating | 78 |
|---|---|
| Tuition | $24,544 |
| Room & board | $9,226 |
| Books and supplies | $658 |
| % frosh receiving aid | 41 |
| % undergrads receiving aid | 40 |
| Avg frosh grant | $13,094 |
| Avg frosh loan | $2,867 |

# BARD COLLEGE

OFFICE OF ADMISSIONS, ANNANDALE-ON-HUDSON, NY 12504 • ADMISSIONS: 914-758-7472 • FAX: 914-758-5208

## CAMPUS LIFE

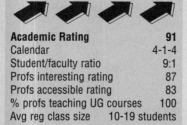

| Quality of Life Rating | 81 |
|---|---|
| Type of school | private |
| Affiliation | none |
| Environment | rural |

### STUDENTS

| | |
|---|---|
| Total undergrad enrollment | 1,342 |
| % male/female | 46/54 |
| % from out of state | 76 |
| % from public high school | 60 |
| % live on campus | 82 |
| % African American | 2 |
| % Asian | 3 |
| % Caucasian | 91 |
| % Hispanic | 4 |
| % international | 6 |

### SURVEY SAYS . . .

*Theater is hot*
*Political activism is hot*
*Popular college radio*
*(Almost) everyone smokes*
*Students don't like Annandale-on-Hudson, NY*
*Intercollegiate sports unpopular or nonexistent*
*Students don't get along with local community*
*Student government is unpopular*
*Athletic facilities need improving*
*Students aren't religious*

## ACADEMICS

| Academic Rating | 91 |
|---|---|
| Calendar | 4-1-4 |
| Student/faculty ratio | 9:1 |
| Profs interesting rating | 87 |
| Profs accessible rating | 83 |
| % profs teaching UG courses | 100 |
| Avg reg class size | 10-19 students |

### MOST POPULAR MAJORS

literature
studio arts
area studies

## STUDENTS SPEAK OUT

### Academics

A sophomore tells us that, true to its motto, "Bard College is—I swear to God—a place to think. I'm learning more than I ever have in my whole life and finally gaining some understanding about why the world is the way it is." The "highly self-motivated" students in this "rich academic environment" receive substantial individual attention from "extremely supportive" and "incredible" professors. Writes one student, "The professors in general are amazing. They're what Bard is all about." Adds another, "Even the celebrity profs are incredibly helpful and make themselves available." All students must complete a Senior Project (a thesis-type paper or other original work) to graduate; warns one, "I'm a senior, so I work on my senior project. For fun, I work on it some more. Sometimes I sleep. As a senior, it's really tough to have school and a job and do anything else." Even so, many describe this experience as "absolutely the most valuable part of a Bard education." The school's progressive Excellence and Equal Cost Program, which makes Bard available to top students at a state-school price, is another asset. As for the administration, students have mixed feelings. Notes one, "The red tape at Bard would boggle the mind, but if you actually go and talk to administrators and deans, you'll find yourself getting things done a lot faster than it may first appear." Administrators make themselves easily accessible to students; as one explains, "You can even make an appointment with the president to just chat. I think it's great how they encourage deans to teach classes." Sums up one student, "You can take from Bard whatever you want. If you don't want to work hard, you can find ways to pull it off and still graduate. But if you are interested in something, you'll find professors who will share your passion and who will kick your ass until you excel."

### Life

A decidedly artsy bent to the student body, coupled with Bard's remote location, results in a lot of creative extracurricular activity. For example, "Students really get into theme parties—Drag Race and pseudo-proms with lounge music. We like costumes." Still, creativity takes the students only so far. Explains one student, "Bard is located in East Nowhere, USA. I suppose that means that academics and friendship should be particularly strong, but that's not necessarily so. People generally drink or go away to have fun. Go figure." Adds another, "If you plan it, they will come. Because Bard is so isolated, most any campus event is crowded. If they were to show *The Adventures of Milo and Otis*, it would probably be packed." To put it another way, "It gets really boring here sometimes." Fortunately, "There are hourly shuttles to villages nearby, and you can go to NYC for the weekend." Most students who don't split for New York (or Boston) spend their weekends on their "gorgeous" campus "out in the boonies."

### Student Body

The Bard campus can be an unusually chilly place, and it's not just because of the weather. "People don't smile at each other here," explains one student. "May be the cold, may be the stress . . . " Another qualifies this observation, noting that "Bard students seem particularly cold in passing, but aren't necessarily so if you stop to talk to them." Students admit that most among them are lost in their own worlds, reporting that "people are pretty self-absorbed, but we are supportive of each others' self-absorption." Still, all and all, students coexist fairly well. Despite feelings that the college "is very cliquish," "there is no antagonism between groups" and "everybody gets along most of the time." However, the predominantly leftist student body sometimes creates an atmosphere "so militantly P.C. that it occasionally resembles a fascist state," at least according to one undergrad.

FINANCIAL AID: 914-758-7526 • E-MAIL: ADMISSION@BARD.EDU • WEBSITE: WWW.BARD.EDU

## ADMISSIONS

*Very important* academic and nonacademic factors considered by the admissions committee include character/personal qualities, class rank, essays, recommendations, and secondary school record. *Important* factors considered include extracurricular activities and talent/ability. *Other* factors considered include standardized test scores, alumni/ae relation, geography, interview, minority status, volunteer work, and work experience. Factors *not* considered include religious affiliation/commitment and state residency. TOEFL required of all international applicants. High school diploma is required and GED is accepted. *High school units recommended:* 4 English, 4 math, 4 science, 4 foreign language, 4 social studies, 4 history.

### The Inside Word

Applicants tend to be cerebral sorts. Bard is highly selective, but it's the match that counts more than having the right numerical profile.

## FINANCIAL AID

*Students should submit:* FAFSA, CSS/Financial Aid PROFILE. The Princeton Review suggests that all financial aid forms be submitted as soon as possible after January 1. *Need-based scholarships/grants offered:* Pell, SEOG, state scholarships/grants, private scholarships, and the school's own gift aid. *Loan aid offered:* FFEL Subsidized Stafford, FFEL Unsubsidized Stafford, FFEL PLUS, Federal Perkins, and college/university loans from institutional funds (for international students only). Institutional employment available. Federal Work-Study Program available. Applicants will be notified of awards on or about April 1. Off-campus job opportunities are fair.

## FROM THE ADMISSIONS OFFICE

"Bard is well known for its programs in literature, languages, and the arts; those in the sciences and mathematics are not as well known. Almost all our math and science graduates pursue graduate or professional studies; 70 percent of our applicants to medical and health professional schools are accepted.

"A new alliance with Rockefeller University, the renowned graduate scientific research institution, will expand our program and give Bardians access to Rockefeller's professors and laboratories. Bard students will have reserved places in Rockefeller's Summer Research Fellows Program and, in fall 2000, will be offered a special weekly seminar on human disease.

"We encourage students with an interest in the sciences or mathematics, or those who would like to combine these studies with the arts and the humanities, to look closely at Bard."

## ADMISSIONS

| | |
|---|---|
| Admissions Rating | 93 |
| # of applicants | 2,741 |
| % of applicants accepted | 48 |
| % of acceptees attending | 27 |
| # accepting a place on wait list | 75 |
| % admitted from wait list | 13 |

### FRESHMAN PROFILE

| | |
|---|---|
| Range SAT Verbal | 550-700 |
| Range SAT Math | 540-670 |
| Minimum TOEFL | 600 |
| Average HS GPA | 3.5 |
| % graduated top 10% of class | 60 |
| % graduated top 25% of class | 95 |
| % graduated top 50% of class | 100 |

### DEADLINES

| | |
|---|---|
| Regular admission | 1/15 |
| Regular notification | 4/15 |
| Nonfall registration? | yes |

### APPLICANTS ALSO LOOK AT

**AND OFTEN PREFER**
Amherst
Yale
Harvard
Brown

**AND SOMETIMES PREFER**
Reed
Boston U.
Vassar
Oberlin
NYU

**AND RARELY PREFER**
Hampshire
Skidmore
Macalester
Ithaca
Sarah Lawrence

## FINANCIAL FACTS

| | |
|---|---|
| Financial Aid Rating | 85 |
| Tuition | $25,620 |
| Room & board | $7,742 |
| Books and supplies | $700 |
| Required fees | $550 |
| % frosh receiving aid | 57 |
| % undergrads receiving aid | 60 |
| Avg frosh grant | $18,500 |
| Avg frosh loan | $3,500 |

# BARNARD COLLEGE

3009 BROADWAY, NEW YORK, NY 10027 • ADMISSIONS: 212-854-2014 • FAX: 212-854-6220

## CAMPUS LIFE

| | |
|---|---|
| **Quality of Life Rating** | **89** |
| Type of school | private |
| Affiliation | none |
| Environment | urban |

### STUDENTS

| | |
|---|---|
| Total undergrad enrollment | 2,290 |
| % from out of state | 63 |
| % from public high school | 55 |
| % live on campus | 88 |
| % African American | 5 |
| % Asian | 22 |
| % Caucasian | 64 |
| % Hispanic | 6 |
| % international | 3 |
| # of countries represented | 30 |

### SURVEY SAYS . . .

*Students love New York, NY*
*Political activism is hot*
*Great off-campus food*
*(Almost) everyone smokes*
*Campus feels safe*
*Ethnic diversity on campus*
*Intercollegiate sports unpopular or*
*nonexistent*
*Very little beer drinking*
*No one plays intramural sports*
*Students are very religious*

## ACADEMICS

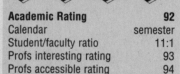

| | |
|---|---|
| **Academic Rating** | **92** |
| Calendar | semester |
| Student/faculty ratio | 11:1 |
| Profs interesting rating | 93 |
| Profs accessible rating | 94 |
| % profs teaching UG courses | 100 |
| Avg lab size | under 10 students |
| Avg reg class size | 10-19 students |

### MOST POPULAR MAJORS
English
psychology
economics

## STUDENTS SPEAK OUT
### Academics

The women of Barnard College describe their "very safe and beautiful campus" located in Manhattan as "a big university with a small college atmosphere" only minutes from everything the capital of the world offers. Right across the street is Columbia University, which offers a wealth of Ivy League educational opportunities to Barnard students who can enroll in any course offered there. At Barnard, the "small and intimate" classes are "very time consuming." Students must complete many requirements, including a foreign language sequence and a first-year seminar aimed at "intellectual inquiry and discourse." Barnard's "captivating" professors "are really into teaching" and "really, really care," relates one student. "Each student gets a real, full-fledged professor as her personal academic advisor." Students across the street should be so lucky. One student boasts, "My seminar class at Barnard was 14 people and, by the end of it, the prof was showing us pictures of her kids." Not all Barnard classes are as small, though, and bigger ones can be "really easy and boring." But in most classes the faculty "expects a lot," and then some. The administration here is "helpful," but sometimes "lacking in diplomatic skills." On the plus side, "Career Counseling really helps you look for jobs."

### Life

Some students say Barnard's campus provides a "small-school atmosphere without the small-school claustrophobia." Others say "the dorm life sucks." Overall, the athletic facilities and the food on campus fare poorly in our survey. The dating scene here is plagued by the competition between Barnard and Columbia women; between the two undergraduate populations, women substantially outnumber men. Basically, "if you are looking for a college like in the movies, this is not the place to go," advises a junior. "This is a school that teaches about life and reality, not how to do keg stands." The women of Barnard don't spend much free time on Barnard's "four-acre" campus. "New York City shapes your college life" here, explains one student. Barnard is "like a room of one's own, but with subways." Though "people work hard" during the week, "on weekends, most everyone is clubbing or going to a party." Students say the Big Apple is "the mecca of arts, music, and entertainment" and, hands down, "the best city to spend your college years in. It's exhilarating." And expensive. Though "museums, coffee houses, poetry reading downtown, and off-off-off- Broadway plays for $5" can be had on the cheap, most students admit that having a good time here costs "a lot of money."

### Student Body

"It takes a certain kind of woman to go to an all-female college in the middle of New York City," observes a sophomore. Students describe themselves as "extremely ambitious, independent," and "politically conscious" feminists who are "chic, sophisticated, and very New York." The college's student population is "very diverse," although "there is not a lot of interaction between social groups." "There's a lot of brain power at this school, but I don't think that Barnard women would be able to work together in problem-solving situations," maintains one student. Given the highly accomplished ranks of Barnard's alumnae, we're inclined to disagree, and think that perhaps another student sums up the student body more accurately when she writes that "students at Barnard are individuals." Barnard women "want to make a difference" and assure us that they "will be very successful."

FINANCIAL AID: 212-854-2154 • E-MAIL: ADMISSIONS@BARNARD.EDU • WEBSITE: WWW.BARNARD.EDU

## ADMISSIONS

*Very important* academic and nonacademic factors considered by the admissions committee include character/personal qualities and secondary school record. *Important* factors considered include essays, recommendations, standardized test scores, and talent/ability. *Other* factors considered include alumni/ae relation, class rank, extracurricular activities, interview, minority status, volunteer work, and work experience. Factors *not* considered include geography, religious affiliation/commitment, state residency, and financial need. TOEFL required of all international applicants. *High school units required/recommended:* 16 total recommended; 4 English recommended, 3 math recommended, 2 science recommended, 3 foreign language recommended, 1 social studies recommended, 1 history recommended, 1 elective recommended. *The admissions office says:* "Every application is read two times by admissions officers and all decisions are made by a committee. No formulas are used in the selection process. We attract women who are independent in spirit, who want to be in New York City for the richness and opportunities it provides, and who describe themselves as 'serious.'"

### The Inside Word

As at many top colleges, early decision applications have increased at Barnard—despite the fact that admissions standards are virtually the same as for their regular admissions cycle. The college's admissions staff is open and accessible, which is not always the case at highly selective colleges with as long and impressive a tradition of excellence. The admissions committee's expectations are high, but their attitude reflects a true interest in who you are and what's on your mind. Students have a much better experience throughout the admissions process when treated with sincerity and respect—perhaps this is why Barnard continues to attract and enroll some of the best students in the country.

## FINANCIAL AID

*Students should submit:* institution's own financial aid form, parents' and individual and corporate and\or partnership federal income tax returns. Regular filing deadline is February 1. The Princeton Review suggests that all financial aid forms be submitted as soon as possible after January 1. *Need-based scholarships/grants offered:* Pell, SEOG, state scholarships/grants, private scholarships, the school's own gift aid, and New York Higher Eduactional Opportunity Program. *Loan aid offered:* FFEL Subsidized Stafford, FFEL Unsubsidized Stafford, FFEL PLUS, Federal Perkins, state, and college/university loans from institutional funds. Institutional employment available. Federal Work-Study Program available. Applicants will be notified of awards on or about April 1. Off-campus job opportunities are excellent.

## FROM THE ADMISSIONS OFFICE

"Barnard College, a small, distinguished liberal arts college for women that is affiliated with Columbia University, and located in the heart of New York City. The College enrolls women from all over the United States, Puerto Rico, and the Caribbean. Thirty countries, including France, England, Hong Kong, and Greece, are also represented in the student body. Students pursue their academic studies in over 35 majors, and are able to cross-register at Columbia University."

## ADMISSIONS

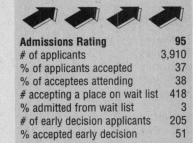

| | |
|---|---:|
| Admissions Rating | 95 |
| # of applicants | 3,910 |
| % of applicants accepted | 37 |
| % of acceptees attending | 38 |
| # accepting a place on wait list | 418 |
| % admitted from wait list | 3 |
| # of early decision applicants | 205 |
| % accepted early decision | 51 |

### FRESHMAN PROFILE

| | |
|---|---:|
| Range SAT Verbal | 620-710 |
| Average SAT Verbal | 661 |
| Range SAT Math | 610-700 |
| Average SAT Math | 652 |
| Range ACT Composite | 26-30 |
| Average ACT Composite | 28 |
| Minimum TOEFL | 600 |
| Average HS GPA | 3.8 |
| % graduated top 10% of class | 78 |
| % graduated top 25% of class | 97 |
| % graduated top 50% of class | 100 |

### DEADLINES

| | |
|---|---:|
| Early decision | 11/15 |
| Early decision notification | 12/15 |
| Regular admission | 1/15 |
| Regular notification | 4/1 |
| Nonfall registration? | yes |

### APPLICANTS ALSO LOOK AT

**AND OFTEN PREFER**
Yale, Columbia
Brown, Stanford

**AND SOMETIMES PREFER**
Dartmouth, U. Penn
Georgetown U., Brandeis U.
U. Michigan—Ann Arbor

**AND RARELY PREFER**
NYU, George Washington
Boston Coll., Boston U.
Binghamton U.

### FINANCIAL FACTS

| | |
|---|---:|
| Financial Aid Rating | 75 |
| Tuition | $22,940 |
| Room & board | $9,650 |
| Books and supplies | $800 |
| Required fees | $1,090 |
| % frosh receiving aid | 41 |
| % undergrads receiving aid | 46 |
| Avg frosh grant | $20,007 |
| Avg frosh loan | $2,625 |

# BATES COLLEGE

23 CAMPUS AVENUE, LEWISTON, ME 04240-9917 • ADMISSIONS: 207-786-6000 • FAX: 207-786-6025

## CAMPUS LIFE

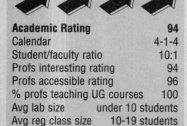

| Quality of Life Rating | **84** |
|---|---|
| Type of school | private |
| Affiliation | none |
| Environment | suburban |

### STUDENTS

| | |
|---|---|
| Total undergrad enrollment | 1,694 |
| % male/female | 48/52 |
| % from out of state | 89 |
| % from public high school | 63 |
| % live on campus | 93 |
| % African American | 2 |
| % Asian | 4 |
| % Caucasian | 88 |
| % Hispanic | 1 |
| % international | 4 |
| # of countries represented | 56 |

### SURVEY SAYS . . .

*Great food on campus*
*Dorms are like palaces*
*Everyone loves the Bobcats*
*Students don't get along with local community*
*No one cheats*
*Low cost of living*
*Students don't like Lewiston, ME*

## ACADEMICS

| Academic Rating | **94** |
|---|---|
| Calendar | 4-1-4 |
| Student/faculty ratio | 10:1 |
| Profs interesting rating | 94 |
| Profs accessible rating | 96 |
| % profs teaching UG courses | 100 |
| Avg lab size | under 10 students |
| Avg reg class size | 10-19 students |

### MOST POPULAR MAJORS

political science
economics
biology

## STUDENTS SPEAK OUT

### Academics

If you were to give us a nickel for every time a Bates College student tells us "this school is great; I just love it" or "I have had such a positive experience here" or something along those lines, we could probably stop updating this book every year and retire to a nice island in the South Pacific. Bates is a "small, intimate" liberal arts college that follows a 4-4-1 calendar. There is a fall and a winter semester, then a "Short Term" in May that provides students with opportunities to study less traditional topics, or to study or intern off campus. Bates offers an academic atmosphere conducive to learning. "The faculty is fabulous," but "the work here is hard." The "dedicated and enthusiastic" professors here are notoriously difficult graders, and all students must complete a thesis or a comprehensive exam in their major to graduate. "The thesis thing really blows," warns a senior, "but you do learn a lot." Administratively, Bates is the picture of stability—since 1855 they've had only six presidents and only two budgets in the red. When problems arise, the "professors and administrators are very approachable," according to a first-year student. "Whenever I need help I can usually count on it."

### Life

Bates is located in "a quiet, residential area" of Lewiston, Maine, about 140 miles north of Boston. Thanks to the academic workload, "the library is packed" during the week. On weekends, "there is really not much to do off campus." On campus "there is usually a good mix of big keggers, smaller parties," and "parties with themes." Nostalgic upper-class students say "the social environment isn't as good as it used to be" thanks to a new, "more strict alcohol policy" but most agree that the social scene still "revolves around drinking." Beyond the party scene, "participation in sports, clubs, and especially student organizations is strongly encouraged within the school." Popular diversions include trips to nearby Freeport, "skiing, and sporting events on Saturdays." A first-year student tells us that "the hardest part is choosing which great thing you are going to do. If you love to be involved, this is the place to be." Students here praise the food and the dormitories (some of which are Victorian houses). Huge houses nearby are also affordable options for off-campus living.

### Student Body

The "outgoing, active, and friendly" students here describe themselves as "kind and easy to talk to." They are "outdoorsy jocks" who are "open-minded, athletic, and intelligent" and they "keep North Face and J.Crew in business." There are "lots of new-age hippies and mountain people" here, as well as "many self-righteous preps" and "multitudes of wanna-be crunchies." Bates students characterize themselves as "particularly interested in social and political issues" and back up their contention with "some activism on campus," mostly of the left-wing variety. "Most students are from well-off families and students who aren't from wealthy families are not necessarily discriminated against, but the difference in atmosphere is there," observes a sophomore. The population is "very homogeneous"—"whiter than a sugar factory," according to one student—"but personalities are really diverse." Bates draws most of its students from New England. Only about 10 percent of the students are natives of Maine.

# BATES COLLEGE

## ADMISSIONS

*Very important* academic and nonacademic factors considered by the admissions committee include character/personal qualities, class rank, essays, recommendations, and secondary school record. *Important* factors considered include alumni/ae relation, extracurricular activities, geography, minority status, talent/ability, and volunteer work. *Other* factors considered include interview, standardized test scores, and work experience. Factors *not* considered include religious affiliation/commitment and state residency. TOEFL required of all international applicants. High school diploma is required and GED is not accepted. *High school units required/recommended:* 4 English required, 3 math required, 4 math recommended, 2 science required, 3 science recommended, 1 science lab required, 3 foreign language required, 4 foreign language recommended, 1 social studies required, 1 social studies recommended, 2 history required, 2 history recommended.

### The Inside Word

With or without test scores, the admissions office here will weed out weak students showing little or no intellectual curiosity. Students with high SAT scores should always submit them. If you are curious about Bates, it is important to have solid grades in challenging courses; without them, you are not a viable candidate for admission. Tough competition for students between the College and its New England peers has intensified greatly over the past couple of years; Bates is holding its own. It remains a top choice among its applicants, and as a result selectivity is on the rise.

## FINANCIAL AID

*Students should submit:* FAFSA, CSS/Financial Aid PROFILE, noncustodial (divorced/separated) parent's statement, and business/farm supplement. Regular filing deadline is January 15. The Princeton Review suggests that all financial aid forms be submitted as soon as possible after January 1. *Need-based scholarships/grants offered:* Pell, SEOG, state scholarships/grants, private scholarships, and the school's own gift aid. *Loan aid offered:* FFEL Subsidized Stafford, FFEL Unsubsidized Stafford, FFEL PLUS, Federal Perkin,s and college/university loans from institutional funds. Institutional employment available. Federal Work-Study Program available. Applicants will be notified of awards on or about March 31. Off-campus job opportunities are good.

## FROM THE ADMISSIONS OFFICE

"The people on the Bates admissions staff read your applications carefully, several times. We get to know you from that reading. Your high school record and the quality of your writing are particularly important. We strongly encourage a personal interview, either on campus or with an alumni representative."

## ADMISSIONS

| | |
|---|---|
| Admissions Rating | 97 |
| # of applicants | 4,240 |
| % of applicants accepted | 29 |
| % of acceptees attending | 38 |
| # accepting a place on wait list | 350 |
| # of early decision applicants | 352 |
| % accepted early decision | 44 |

### FRESHMAN PROFILE

| | |
|---|---|
| Range SAT Verbal | 620-710 |
| Average SAT Verbal | 660 |
| Range SAT Math | 630-700 |
| Average SAT Math | 670 |
| % graduated top 10% of class | 56 |
| % graduated top 25% of class | 94 |
| % graduated top 50% of class | 100 |

### DEADLINES

| | |
|---|---|
| Regular admission | 1/15 |
| Regular notification | 3/31 |
| Nonfall registration? | yes |

### APPLICANTS ALSO LOOK AT

**AND OFTEN PREFER**
Amherst
Wesleyan U.
Tufts
Williams
Bowdoin

**AND SOMETIMES PREFER**
Middlebury
U. Vermont
Colby
Colgate

## FINANCIAL FACTS

| | |
|---|---|
| Financial Aid Rating | 74 |
| Tuition | $32,650 |
| Books and supplies | $1,750 |
| % frosh receiving aid | 40 |
| % undergrads receiving aid | 45 |
| Avg frosh grant | $17,206 |
| Avg frosh loan | $3,060 |

# BAYLOR UNIVERSITY

PO Box 97056, Waco, TX 76798-7056 • Admissions: 254-710-3435 • Fax: 254-710-3436

## CAMPUS LIFE

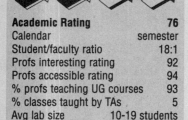

| Quality of Life Rating | 74 |
|---|---|
| Type of school | private |
| Affiliation | Baptist |
| Environment | suburban |

### STUDENTS

| | |
|---|---|
| Total undergrad enrollment | 11,806 |
| % male/female | 42/58 |
| % from out of state | 17 |
| % live on campus | 30 |
| % in (# of) fraternities | 20 (18) |
| % in (# of) sororities | 26 (15) |
| % African American | 6 |
| % Asian | 5 |
| % Caucasian | 78 |
| % Hispanic | 7 |
| % Native American | 1 |
| % international | 2 |

### SURVEY SAYS . . .

*Frats and sororities dominate social scene*
*Very little drug use*
*(Almost) everyone plays intramural sports*
*Lots of conservatives on campus*
*Diversity lacking on campus*
*Students are very religious*
*Students don't like Waco, TX*
*Very little hard liquor*
*Very little beer drinking*
*(Almost) no one smokes*

## ACADEMICS

| Academic Rating | 76 |
|---|---|
| Calendar | semester |
| Student/faculty ratio | 18:1 |
| Profs interesting rating | 92 |
| Profs accessible rating | 94 |
| % profs teaching UG courses | 93 |
| % classes taught by TAs | 5 |
| Avg lab size | 10-19 students |
| Avg reg class size | 20-29 students |

### MOST POPULAR MAJORS

management information systems
teacher education
business marketing

## STUDENTS SPEAK OUT

### Academics

For students seeking a solid education built on a Christian foundation, Baylor is an excellent choice. Explains one student, "It's wonderful to be able to ask your teacher about how something relates to religion without worrying that if they mention God they'll be fired." Of particular note is the "excellent" Baylor Interdisciplinary Core (BIC), which admits only 200 freshmen each year. The BIC replaces Baylor's traditional requirements with a 41-credit sequence covering world culture, natural and social sciences, mathematics, health, rhetoric, and the Bible, with particular emphasis on the interconnectedness of these disciplines. As home to six undergraduate divisions (including excellent schools of business, nursing, and education), Baylor provides students access to numerous career paths. Writes one student, "While not as bureaucratic as big state schools, Baylor still has just as many options available to its students." Prospective students are forewarned that, while better than state schools, Baylor's administration is hardly streamlined; rather, "'Red tape' and 'wrong line' are such common phrases at Baylor that even the squirrels on campus understand their meaning." Students praise their professors, especially for their accessibility. Notes one, "The relationships students are able to form with professors here are remarkable. The faculty is very service-minded and willing to go out of their way to assist students."

### Life

The Baylor administration is "very controlling of alcohol, student life, and fraternities." To get an idea of what the environment here is like, all you need to know is that Baylor had prohibited dancing at school functions until 1996. One student theorizes that Baylor's paternalistic attitude probably stems from the fact that "some people come from sheltered childhoods and strict homes, so when they get freedom in college, they go crazy." Baylor's Greek system is "huge," so much so that students outside the system complain that there is "too much emphasis on Greek life. If you don't feel that it's for you, good luck finding things to do." As a result, "many students leave town on the weekend." Still others report that "outings, dances, and a multitude of special events are available every day" and that "many students enjoy frequenting the many area clubs and pool halls, while others choose to socialize through local church college groups." Also, there are always "tons of Bible studies and Christian activities to get involved in." The town of Waco "isn't too happening" but "is well located, very central. There is quite a bit to do in Dallas and Austin."

### Student Body

Sums up one student, "Baylor is a very Southern Baptist school with lots of rich preppy white kids that you'd love to hate, but for the most part they're so nice that you can't!" Our respondents describe their classmates as the type of folks who "think about God's plan for their lives, who they're going to take to their next formal, and what they are going to order this month from Harolds." Although cordial, students are also "very cliquish. Different groups do not interact very well. Those that are able to join Greek social clubs do not get along well with others." Several minority students tell us about their sense of isolation among the Baylor student body. Writes one black student, "I do not understand why black and white students do not mingle. I had many more white friends in high school. Baylor's minority enrollment has increased from 12 percent to over 21 percent over the last seven years."

FINANCIAL AID: 254-710-2611 • E-MAIL: ADMISSIONS_SERV_OFFICE@BAYLOR.EDU • WEBSITE: WWW.BAYLOR.EDU

## ADMISSIONS

*Very important* academic and nonacademic factors considered by the admissions committee include character/personal qualities, interview, recommendations, and secondary school record. *Important* factors considered include alumni/ae relation, class rank, essays, extracurricular activities, minority status, standardized test scores, talent/ability, and volunteer work. *Other* factors considered include geography, religious affiliation/commitment, and work experience. Factors *not* considered include state residency. SAT I or ACT required. TOEFL required of all international applicants. High school diploma is required and GED is accepted. *High school units required/recommended:* 4 English required, 3 math required, 4 math recommended, 2 science lab required, 3 science lab recommended, 2 foreign language required, 3 foreign language recommended, 2 history required, 2 elective required.

### The Inside Word

A largely self-selected applicant pool and the need for a fairly large freshman class each year makes for a high admit rate. If your values reflect those of the community at Baylor, the chances are you will be offered admission.

## FINANCIAL AID

*Students should submit:* FAFSA. The Princeton Review suggests that all financial aid forms be submitted as soon as possible after January 1. *Need-based scholarships/grants offered:* Pell, SEOG, state scholarships/grants, private scholarships, and the school's own gift aid. *Loan aid offered:* FFEL Subsidized Stafford, FFEL Unsubsidized Stafford, FFEL PLUS, Federal Perkins, Federal Nursing, state, and college/university loans from institutional funds. Institutional employment available. Federal Work-Study Program available. Applicants will be notified of awards on a rolling basis beginning on or about March 1. Off-campus job opportunities are excellent.

## FROM THE ADMISSIONS OFFICE

"Baylor University, chartered by the Republic of Texas in 1845, is one of the world's major academic church-related institutions providing liberal arts and professional education in a Christian environment. Baylor's student body comes from all 50 states and 79 foreign countries. The university's number of National Merit Scholars places it in the top 1 percent of all colleges nationwide. . . . In addition, the Templeton Foundation has repeatedly named Baylor as one of America's top character-building colleges. Professors teach 93 percent of all courses; the student/faculty ratio is 18 to 1, and the typical class numbers 35. There are 162 bachelor's programs and 72 master's programs as well as numerous doctoral, professional, and specialist programs. More than 225 student organizations provide opportunities for social, intellectual, physical, spiritual, and professional development. One of the most inexpensive major private universities in the country, Baylor is consistently ranked by national organizations as one of the best buys in higher education. Take a closer look. . . . There is a place for you at Baylor."

## ADMISSIONS

| | |
|---|---|
| Admissions Rating | 81 |
| # of applicants | 7,011 |
| % of applicants accepted | 84 |
| % of acceptees attending | 48 |

### FRESHMAN PROFILE

| | |
|---|---|
| Range SAT Verbal | 530-630 |
| Range SAT Math | 550-650 |
| Range ACT Composite | 22-27 |
| Minimum TOEFL | 540 |
| % graduated top 10% of class | 38 |
| % graduated top 25% of class | 65 |
| % graduated top 50% of class | 92 |

### DEADLINES

| | |
|---|---|
| Priority admission deadline | 3/1 |
| Nonfall registration? | yes |

### APPLICANTS ALSO LOOK AT

**AND OFTEN PREFER**
Texas A&M
U. Texas—Austin
**AND SOMETIMES PREFER**
U. Oklahoma
SMU
TCU
**AND RARELY PREFER**
Austin
Southwestern
Trinity U.

## FINANCIAL FACTS

| | |
|---|---|
| Financial Aid Rating | 72 |
| Tuition | $11,370 |
| Room & board | $5,327 |
| Books and supplies | $1,256 |
| Required fees | $1,384 |
| % frosh receiving aid | 40 |
| % undergrads receiving aid | 44 |

# BELLARMINE UNIVERSITY

2001 NEWBURG ROAD, LOUISVILLE, KY 40205 • ADMISSIONS: 502-452-8131 • FAX: 502-452-8002

## CAMPUS LIFE

| | |
|---|---|
| **Quality of Life Rating** | **77** |
| Type of school | private |
| Affiliation | Roman Catholic |
| Environment | suburban |

### STUDENTS

| | |
|---|---|
| Total undergrad enrollment | 2,175 |
| % male/female | 36/64 |
| % from out of state | 31 |
| % from public high school | 50 |
| % live on campus | 37 |
| % in (# of) fraternities | 3 (2) |
| % in (# of) sororities | 3 (1) |
| % African American | 3 |
| % Asian | 1 |
| % Caucasian | 94 |
| % Hispanic | 1 |
| % international | 1 |
| # of countries represented | 21 |

### SURVEY SAYS . . .

*Students love Louisville, KY*
*Student publications are popular*
*Diverse students interact*
*Lots of liberals*
*Theater is unpopular*
*Very small frat/sorority scene*
*Library needs improving*
*Lousy off-campus food*

## ACADEMICS

| | |
|---|---|
| **Academic Rating** | **76** |
| Calendar | semester |
| Student/faculty ratio | 14:1 |
| Profs interesting rating | 78 |
| Profs accessible rating | 77 |
| % profs teaching UG courses | 98 |
| Avg reg class size | 20-29 students |

### MOST POPULAR MAJORS
nursing
business administration
accounting

## STUDENTS SPEAK OUT
### Academics

For the undergraduates at Bellarmine University, it's all about personal attention. "Bellarmine has really fulfilled my expectations in its concern for students," explains one student. "Professors, faculty, and administrators all strive to give the best education to each student as an individual. It is this ultimate learning environment that makes Bellarmine a wonderful college." Notes another, "Bellarmine is the ideal place if you are looking for personal attention. The professors are easy to get along with and are extremely knowledgeable. The sense of community makes one feel at home, even if home is a thousand miles away." All this support from faculty and administration helps somewhat to lighten the difficult workload. Writes one student, "It has been very tough with all the work assigned. My professors are very nice, but they really expect a lot from us." Studies here begin with intro courses and distribution (General Education) requirements, then proceed to major study. "Our Gen Ed requirements allows students to try different things without falling behind," says one student. Summing up the Bellarmine experience, one student cites "excellent professors, and an emphasis on discussion and critical thinking. We're taught to create our own ideas, not repeat old ones."

### Life

A small, Catholic liberal arts university, Bellarmine is home to a quiet, friendly academic community. Campus life, Bellarmine students readily concede, is a little slow. There's "not much to do at this school on weekends with the exception of going off campus and partying," agree many. Even those who disagree portray a social scene that is more quaint than exciting. "There is always something to be done—studying, homework, tae kwon do, laundry, or hanging out," as one student describes it. Some cite the lack of athletics as a drawback to the school spirit and would like to see an upgrade in the athletic facilities. Still, academics keep most plenty busy, and for distraction there is always Louisville, a Southern burg replete with cafes, tattoo parlors, restaurants, and clubs. Says one student, "Life at school is busy, busy, busy. Louisville nightlife is so tempting that I have to make myself stay home and study for at least three days a week." Louisville is also home to an excellent arts center and, of course, the first leg of thoroughbred racing's Triple Crown, the Kentucky Derby.

### Student Body

Bellarmine draws the vast majority of its student body from the surrounding area, resulting in a fairly homogeneous group. "Most of the students," observes one among them, "are upper-middle-class conservatives." Many are pre-professional majors (e.g., nursing, business, psychology) who "are looking toward graduate school in the future" and take an accordingly businesslike approach to their studies. One student writes, "People here are career-oriented. They attend Bellarmine to get an excellent education and a job in their chosen field." Although "cliques abound . . . there is a good vibe on campus." One student tells us, "The foreign exchange students tend to stay together, but everyone for the most part is friendly." Adds another, "Overall, students on this campus are friendly. They wave, smile, and say 'hi,' even if they don't know you."

FINANCIAL AID: 502-452-8124 • E-MAIL: ADMISSIONS@BELLARMINE.EDU • WEBSITE: WWW.BELLARMINE.EDU

## ADMISSIONS

*Very important* academic and nonacademic factors considered by the admissions committee include secondary school record and standardized test scores. *Important* factors considered include character/personal qualities, class rank, extracurricular activities, talent/ability, alumni/ae relation, interview, minority status, volunteer work, and work experience. Factors *not* considered include geography and state residency. SAT I or ACT required. TOEFL required of all international applicants. High school diploma is required and GED is accepted. *High school units required/recommended:* 4 English required, 3 math required, 4 math recommended, 2 science required, 3 science recommended, 2 social studies required, 2 foreign language required. *The admissions office says:* "An audition is required for all music program applicants."

### The Inside Word

Bellarmine's admissions process follows the typical small liberal arts college approach fairly closely—solid grades, test scores, and course selection from high school combined with a broad complement of extracurriculars generally will add up to an admit. The applicant pool is very regional here; students who hail from outside the university's normal markets may benefit from the appeal that their relative scarcity brings to their candidacies.

## FINANCIAL AID

*Students should submit:* FAFSA. Priority filing deadline is March 1. The Princeton Review suggests that all financial aid forms be submitted as soon as possible after January 1. *Need-based scholarships/grants offered:* Pell, SEOG, state scholarships/grants, and the school's own gift aid. *Loan aid offered:* FFEL Subsidized Stafford, FFEL Unsubsidized Stafford, FFEL PLUS, Federal Perkins and college/university loans from institutional funds. Institutional employment available. Federal Work-Study Program available. Applicants will be notified of awards on a rolling basis beginning on or about April 1. Off-campus job opportunities are excellent.

## FROM THE ADMISSIONS OFFICE

"A wealth of opportunity awaits you on our 120-acre campus nestled in one of Louisville's most desirable neighborhoods. Here you'll have the chance to learn from an outstanding faculty deeply committed to teaching. Our small class size makes getting to know your professors and classmates easy, while providing a stimulating learning environment. Many students also take advantage of international study in nearly 50 countries through the university's foreign exchange program."

### ADMISSIONS

| | |
|---|---|
| Admissions Rating | 74 |
| # of applicants | 974 |
| % of applicants accepted | 87 |
| % of acceptees attending | 39 |

**FRESHMAN PROFILE**

| | |
|---|---|
| Range SAT Verbal | 500-600 |
| Average SAT Verbal | 576 |
| Range SAT Math | 490-620 |
| Average SAT Math | 576 |
| Range ACT Composite | 22-26 |
| Average ACT Composite | 24 |
| Minimum TOEFL | 550 |
| Average HS GPA | 3.5 |
| % graduated top 10% of class | 28 |
| % graduated top 25% of class | 55 |
| % graduated top 50% of class | 79 |

**DEADLINES**

| | |
|---|---|
| Priority admission deadline | 1/15 |
| Regular admission | 8/15 |
| Nonfall registration? | yes |

**APPLICANTS ALSO LOOK AT
AND SOMETIMES PREFER**
U. Louisville
Hanover
Transylvania
Miami U.

**AND RARELY PREFER**
Ohio U.
Ohio State U.—Columbus
U. Dayton
U. Kentucky
Indiana U.—Bloomington

### FINANCIAL FACTS

| | |
|---|---|
| Financial Aid Rating | 82 |
| Tuition | $13,590 |
| Room & board | $4,160 |
| Books and supplies | $750 |
| Required fees | $170 |
| % frosh receiving aid | 63 |
| Avg frosh grant | $4,742 |
| Avg frosh loan | $2,894 |

# BELOIT COLLEGE

700 COLLEGE STREET, BELOIT, WI 53511 • ADMISSIONS: 608-363-2500 • FAX: 608-363-2075

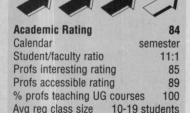

## CAMPUS LIFE

**Quality of Life Rating** **80**
| | |
|---|---|
| Type of school | private |
| Affiliation | none |
| Environment | urban |

### STUDENTS
| | |
|---|---|
| Total undergrad enrollment | 1,254 |
| % male/female | 42/58 |
| % from out of state | 75 |
| % from public high school | 80 |
| % live on campus | 93 |
| % in (# of) fraternities | 16 (3) |
| % in (# of) sororities | 8 (2) |
| % African American | 4 |
| % Asian | 4 |
| % Caucasian | 77 |
| % Hispanic | 4 |
| % international | 10 |

### SURVEY SAYS . . .
*Classes are small*
*Students don't get along with local community*
*Students aren't religious*
*(Almost) everyone smokes*
*Great food on campus*
*Campus difficult to get around*
*Lousy off-campus food*
*Students don't like Beloit, WI*

## ACADEMICS

**Academic Rating** **84**
| | |
|---|---|
| Calendar | semester |
| Student/faculty ratio | 11:1 |
| Profs interesting rating | 85 |
| Profs accessible rating | 89 |
| % profs teaching UG courses | 100 |
| Avg reg class size | 10-19 students |

### MOST POPULAR MAJORS
anthropology
English
biology

## STUDENTS SPEAK OUT
### Academics

"Invent yourself" is the philosophy and the unofficial motto of Beloit College, "a small, liberal, liberal arts school" located on the Wisconsin-Illinois border. The Beloit approach to learning "stresses the importance of students' taking charge of their lives and their academics. The administration is excellent about supporting student endeavors." Says one undergrad, "It is a very hands-on education." Beloit's size affords students many opportunities that simply aren't as readily accessible at larger schools. Students here regularly hold art exhibits, intern at campus museums, and design, direct, and star in plays. A hallmark Beloit experience is Student Symposium, which occurs each spring: For an entire day, students and faculty ditch classes to view student projects displayed all across campus. Students give the "very demanding" academic experience here solid marks, singling out the English, biochemistry, economics, and geology departments as particularly praiseworthy. In nearly all departments, Beloit students sing the praises of their professors. Writes one, "Professors are one of the best parts of the school. I call all my professors by their first name. They always have time to talk about anything. You're a real person to them." Students develop relationships with their professors that extend well beyond the classroom. "I've done everything with my professors," relates a senior, "from serious academic discourse to beer-drinking to weekend fishing trips." The Beloit administration provides an "excellent support network. Faculty and administration are amazing: they'll go out of their way to accommodate you." One senior sums up his experience at Beloit as "excellent. I came here to get first-hand attention from professors and administrators, and what I have received is more than I could have imagined."

### Life

For most students, social life at Beloit begins and ends within the campus gates. Explains one undergrad, "Life at Beloit is all about what is termed the 'Beloit Bubble,' and whether or not you choose to live inside or outside the Bubble. People on campus who are concerned about the outside world have the opportunity to become involved. But for the rest of us, we have plenty of fun just living in our own happy Bubble." On a typical Beloit weekend, "people get drunk and party. There are a lot of theme parties, where you dress up. Everyone gets into them; it's cool." Warns one student, "If you are not careful you will party your way out of this school." During the week, students "bowl, go to plays, listen to speeches," and take advantage of the "tons of opportunities to get involved with the school. Many are involved with clubs, sports, and organizations that they love." What students don't do is venture off campus to take in the sights of downtown Beloit, since "the town has little to offer by way of social activity." When students decide they need to get away, "the only thing to do is drive to Madison or Chicago." While this life suits most, a few succumb to "a lot of drinking, the result of boredom." One student's prescription for 'Beloit Bubble Syndrome': "Having a car can be vital to maintaining sanity."

### Student Body

Beloit's "diverse, both ethnically and politically," student body enjoys "a very intimate community feeling, at times verging on incestuous. By the same token, it creates a very strong bond of intimacy." Students regard themselves as "good folks, many with working-class backgrounds because of the generous financial aid," although a few warn that "the student body is getting preppier and preppier." This preppy onslaught notwithstanding, the prevailing mood at Beloit is funky and free-thinking, just as it has been in the past. Students here are "crazy, creative," and "very individualized. They like to express themselves in colorful ways." For example: "pink hair and pierced faces." If you come here, "be prepared for some pretty strange people." Like many small schools, "Beloit is one big gossip ring made up of people who claim they would 'never do that.'"

FINANCIAL AID: 608-363-2500 • E-MAIL: ADMISS@BELOIT.EDU • WEBSITE: WWW.BELOIT.EDU

## ADMISSIONS

*Very important* academic and nonacademic factors considered by the admissions committee include secondary school record. *Important* factors considered include character/personal qualities, essays, extracurricular activities, and standardized test scores. *Other* factors considered include alumni/ae relation, minority status, recommendations, talent/ability, volunteer work, and work experience. Factors *not* considered include geography, interview, religious affiliation/commitment, and state residency. SAT I or ACT required. TOEFL required of all international applicants. High school diploma is required and GED is not accepted. *High school units required/recommended:* 18 total recommended; 4 English recommended, 3 math recommended, 3 science recommended, 1 science lab recommended, 2 foreign language recommended, 3 social studies recommended, 3 elective recommended. *The admissions office says:* "In application review, we are conscious that as much can be learned from failure as success, and that quantitative results are never adequate measures of human character. We believe each student is an individual; as such, each application is reviewed in a holistic manner—one at a time."

### The Inside Word

Beloit expects to find evidence of sensitivity and thoughtfulness in successful candidates. There is tough competition for students among colleges in the Midwest, which gives those Beloit applicants who don't show consistent strength a bit of a break.

## FINANCIAL AID

*Students should submit:* FAFSA, noncustodial (divorced/separated) parent's statement, and Beloit College Financial Aid Application. There is no regular filing deadline. The Princeton Review suggests that all financial aid forms be submitted as soon as possible after January 1. *Need-based scholarships/grants offered:* private scholarships and the school's own gift aid. *Loan aid offered:* FFEL Subsidized Stafford, FFEL Unsubsidized Stafford, FFEL PLUS, Federal Perkins, and college/university loans from institutional funds. Institutional employment available. Federal Work-Study Program available. Applicants will be notified of awards on a rolling basis beginning on or about March 1. Off-campus job opportunities are fair.

## FROM THE ADMISSIONS OFFICE

"While Beloit students clearly understand the connection between college and career, they are more apt to value learning for its own sake than for the competitive advantage that it will afford them in the workplace. As a result, Beloit students adhere strongly to the concept than an educational institution, in order to be true to its own nature, must imply and provide a context in which a free exchange of ideas can take place. This precept is embodied in the mentoring relationship that takes place between professor and student and the dynamic, participatory nature of the classroom experience."

## ADMISSIONS

| | |
|---|---|
| Admissions Rating | 79 |
| # of applicants | 1,478 |
| % of applicants accepted | 67 |
| % of acceptees attending | 31 |

### FRESHMAN PROFILE

| | |
|---|---|
| Range SAT Verbal | 580-680 |
| Average SAT Verbal | 630 |
| Range SAT Math | 540-640 |
| Average SAT Math | 600 |
| Range ACT Composite | 24-29 |
| Average ACT Composite | 27 |
| Minimum TOEFL | 525 |
| Average HS GPA | 3.5 |
| % graduated top 10% of class | 30 |
| % graduated top 25% of class | 56 |
| % graduated top 50% of class | 91 |

### DEADLINES

| | |
|---|---|
| Priority admission deadline | 2/1 |
| Early decision | 11/15 |
| Early decision notification | 12/15 |

### APPLICANTS ALSO LOOK AT

#### AND OFTEN PREFER
Carleton
Macalester
Lawrence
Grinnell
Oberlin

#### AND SOMETIMES PREFER
Colorado Coll.
Wooster
Kenyon
U. Illinois—Urbana-Champaign
U. Madison

#### AND RARELY PREFER
Knox
Ripon
Northwestern U.
Lewis & Clark
Gustavus Adolphus

## FINANCIAL FACTS

| | |
|---|---|
| Financial Aid Rating | 90 |
| Tuition | $22,184 |
| Room & board | $5,078 |
| Books and supplies | $350 |
| Required fees | $220 |
| % frosh receiving aid | 80 |
| % undergrads receiving aid | 83 |
| Avg frosh grant | $12,688 |
| Avg frosh loan | $3,507 |

# BENNINGTON COLLEGE

OFFICE OF ADMISSIONS, BENNINGTON, VT 05201 • ADMISSIONS: 802-440-4312 • FAX: 802-440-4320

## CAMPUS LIFE

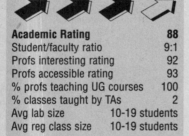

| | |
|---|---|
| **Quality of Life Rating** | **81** |
| Type of school | private |
| Affiliation | none |
| Environment | rural |

### STUDENTS

| | |
|---|---|
| Total undergrad enrollment | 545 |
| % from out of state | 94 |
| % live on campus | 98 |
| % African American | 2 |
| % Asian | 2 |
| % Caucasian | 79 |
| % Hispanic | 2 |
| % international | 8 |

### SURVEY SAYS . . .
*Popular college radio*
*Great food on campus*
*Dorms are like palaces*
*Theater is hot*
*No one plays intramural sports*
*Students aren't religious*

## ACADEMICS

| | |
|---|---|
| **Academic Rating** | **88** |
| Student/faculty ratio | 9:1 |
| Profs interesting rating | 92 |
| Profs accessible rating | 93 |
| % profs teaching UG courses | 100 |
| % classes taught by TAs | 2 |
| Avg lab size | 10-19 students |
| Avg reg class size | 10-19 students |

### MOST POPULAR MAJORS
interdisciplinary studies
literature/language
visual arts

## STUDENTS SPEAK OUT
### Academics

Bennington College prides itself on its longest-standing tradition: its commitment to nontraditional education. Unlike the vast majority of undergraduate programs, Bennington makes few curricular requirements of its students and encourages all to design their own academic programs. Explains one student, "We don't have required courses; we prefer to learn over getting good grades—in fact, grades don't even exist. We get written evaluations instead." Within this framework of independence, however, students receive a tremendous amount of supervision. Notes one, "Any student-initiated project or class is supported by the faculty but also receives harsh constructive criticism." Adds another, "I'm in my second year here and I have five one-on-one tutorials. Where else can you get that?" The end result of this approach is that "more than almost any other school, Bennington works for those students who make it work. For those of us who take the time to get to know our professors, approach administrators, set up tutorials, and initiate independent projects, Bennington becomes everything we could possibly want from a school. The resources are available to do anything you want. Unfortunately, many students here don't realize that and wind up with a mediocre education." Bennington's small size fosters a close relationship between students and faculty. Professors "are for the most part excellent. They have a wealth of knowledge in their fields and are highly approachable. I call all of my professors by their first names and have ample opportunity to discuss events outside of class with them, especially soccer! They ALL seem to love English football!" Similarly, administrators "are welcoming and willing to hear you," although some students complain that "they don't always heed your advice and don't communicate well enough with each other and with the student body as a whole."

### Life

Students agree: There is no escaping the effect of Bennington's size on the community's social life. Bennington is a tiny college in a tiny town. Most students live, eat, and do all their socializing on campus. The result is a homey, family-like atmosphere that can, at times, become oppressive (especially in the dead of winter, when Benningtonians are frequently snowbound). Students overcome their claustrophobia by staying very busy; explains one, "There's always something going on here on weeknights and weekends, from poetry readings to theme parties, from plays to dance performances, from art exhibits to lectures. There's never a dull moment!" Bennington undergrads love dressing up for their near-weekly theme parties. However, it's the arts (theater, film, poetry, art shows) that really drive the social life here. As one student remarks, "I didn't believe the guidebook crap about how students 'make their own fun,' but it's true. There are readings, shows, dances, and house parties every weekend." As in all parts of the world, life gets better when winter lifts. Writes one student, "When the weather breaks in the spring, everyone goes outside. People study outside, classes are held outside . . . it is glorious."

### Student Body

The diminutive student body at Bennington is "diverse, not racially but in terms of personalities." One student describes the population as "a strange mix of people who are very motivated to work hard and others who do nothing but party. Likewise, we are a mix of extremely intelligent people and complete morons. Miraculously, we all get along together pretty well." Women far outnumber men, and as a result "whenever Bennington girls go to parties at other schools they frighten people. We know how to have a good time and our horrid ratio (two-to-one female-to-male) has made us strong, independent, self-confident, and intimidating. We are a crazy breed." The artistic bias of the population led one student to remark that "I am a scientist at this school, but here I am known as 'The Scientist.' This is both a commentary on the popularity of science here and the ability to create an impact in such a small place."

# BENNINGTON COLLEGE

## ADMISSIONS

*Very important* academic and nonacademic factors considered by the admissions committee include secondary school record. *Important* factors considered include class rank and standardized test scores. *Other* factors considered include alumni/ae relation, character/personal qualities, essays, extracurricular activities, interview, recommendations, talent/ability, volunteer work, and work experience. Factors *not* considered include geography, minority status, religious affiliation/commitment, and state residency. SAT I or ACT required. TOEFL required of all international applicants. High school diploma is required and GED is accepted. *High school units required/recommended:* 20 total required; 21 total recommended; 4 English required, 3 math required, 3 science required, 3 science lab required, 2 foreign language required, 3 foreign language recommended, 3 social studies required, 3 social studies recommended, 5 elective required. *The admissions office says:* "We do not evaluate the applications with a 'standard formula.' The Committee spends considerable time with the applicant by requiring interviews and giving close scrutiny to essays and recommendations. It is a process that resists formulas and subdivisions."

### The Inside Word

For intellectually curious students Bennington can be a godsend, but for those who lack self-motivation it can represent a sidetracking of progress toward a degree. Campus controversy regarding the refocusing of academic offerings and faculty retrenchment has yet to fade years after the fact, but most students who were enrolled when things were different than they are today have either graduated or moved on. Admissions standards remain rigorous and enrollment is on an upswing. Candidates will encounter a thorough review process that places great emphasis on matchmaking, which means that strong essays and solid interviews are a must. Intellectual types whose high school grades are inconsistent with their potential will find an opportunity for forgiveness here if they can write well and demonstrate self-awareness and a capacity to thrive in the college's self-driven environment. Minority students are rarities in the applicant pool, and thus enjoy "most-favored candidate" status—provided they fit Bennington's profile.

## FINANCIAL AID

*Students should submit:* FAFSA, institution's own financial aid form, noncustodial (divorced/separated) parent's statement, student and parent federal tax returns, and W-2s. The Princeton Review suggests that all financial aid forms be submitted as soon as possible after January 1. *Loan aid offered:* FFEL Subsidized Stafford, FFEL Unsubsidized Stafford, FFEL PLUS, college/university loans from institutional funds, and GATE loans. Institutional employment available. Federal Work-Study Program available. Applicants will be notified of awards on a rolling basis beginning on or about February 25. Off-campus job opportunities are fair.

## FROM THE ADMISSIONS OFFICE

"Bennington is designed for students with the motivation and maturity to give shape to their own academic lives. It invites you not merely to study the subject you are learning but to put into practice, to act, to compose, to write, to do science: to make the choices through which you become an educated person. Faculty guide the process, but students make it their own at every stage, leaving Bennington prepared to think and create for themselves."

## ADMISSIONS

| | |
|---|---|
| Admissions Rating | 83 |
| # of applicants | 678 |
| % of applicants accepted | 70 |
| % of acceptees attending | 34 |
| # of early decision applicants | 36 |
| % accepted early decision | 75 |

### FRESHMAN PROFILE

| | |
|---|---|
| Range SAT Verbal | 580-690 |
| Average SAT Verbal | 638 |
| Range SAT Math | 530-630 |
| Average SAT Math | 575 |
| Minimum TOEFL | 550 |
| Average HS GPA | 3.5 |
| % graduated top 10% of class | 52 |
| % graduated top 25% of class | 61 |
| % graduated top 50% of class | 97 |

### DEADLINES

| | |
|---|---|
| Early decision | 11/15 |
| Early decision notification | 12/15 |
| Regular admission | 1/1 |
| Nonfall registration? | yes |

### APPLICANTS ALSO LOOK AT

**AND OFTEN PREFER**
Vassar
Smith
Bard
Swarthmore

**AND SOMETIMES PREFER**
Boston Coll.
U. Vermont
Sarah Lawrence
Hampshire
NYU

**AND RARELY PREFER**
U. New Hampshire
U. Conn

## FINANCIAL FACTS

| | |
|---|---|
| Financial Aid Rating | 82 |
| Tuition | $24,450 |
| Room & board | $6,350 |
| Books and supplies | $1,900 |
| Required fees | $500 |
| % frosh receiving aid | 69 |
| % undergrads receiving aid | 75 |
| Avg frosh grant | $16,730 |
| Avg frosh loan | $4,030 |

# BENTLEY COLLEGE

175 FOREST STREET, WALTHAM, MA 02452-4705 • ADMISSIONS: 781-891-2244 • FAX: 781-891-3414

## CAMPUS LIFE

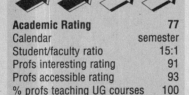

| Quality of Life Rating | 79 |
| --- | --- |
| Type of school | private |
| Affiliation | none |
| Environment | suburban |

### STUDENTS
| | |
| --- | --- |
| Total undergrad enrollment | 4,316 |
| % male/female | 56/44 |
| % from out of state | 35 |
| % from public high school | 76 |
| % live on campus | 75 |
| % African American | 3 |
| % Asian | 8 |
| % Caucasian | 73 |
| % Hispanic | 3 |
| % international | 8 |
| # of countries represented | 61 |

### SURVEY SAYS . . .
*Musical organizations aren't popular*
*Classes are small*
*Great computer facilities*
*Students aren't religious*
*Ethnic diversity on campus*
*Theater is unpopular*

## ACADEMICS

| Academic Rating | 77 |
| --- | --- |
| Calendar | semester |
| Student/faculty ratio | 15:1 |
| Profs interesting rating | 91 |
| Profs accessible rating | 93 |
| % profs teaching UG courses | 100 |
| Avg reg class size | 20-25 students |

### MOST POPULAR MAJORS
finance
management
accountancy

## STUDENTS SPEAK OUT
### Academics
A primary focus of the educational process at Bentley College is preparing students for life in the business world. As one student writes, "people, technology, and business—that's what Bentley is about." Many undergraduates affirm that the on-campus trading floor drew them to Bentley. The college's 57-station trading floor is one of only a handful of such real-time trading floor facilities in the U.S. A NASDAQ stock market Premier Partner, Bentley's facility has live data feed from Bloomberg, Reuters, and Dow Jones, among others. Students frequently describe the school's technological and business resources as one of its major strengths. Of course, good technology is not enough to prepare prospective businesspeople. The students save their highest compliments for their professors. "They are all pretty much down to earth," one student writes, and another comments that "the professors are like our best friends. They are there when you need them." When describing professors, a favorite adjective of undergrads is "accessible." Writes one typical student, "All of the professors are extremely helpful and accessible." Classes and seminars are relatively small, which helps to increase student-faculty intimacy. "Because of the small size of our school, it is easy to develop a relationship outside of class between the students and teachers that is comfortable and very helpful." Most students are not as fond of Bentley's administrators, asserting that "it is virtually impossible to get things changed." In general, students believe that the school prepares them well for life after graduation. One muses that Bentley "builds a strong business foundation that will last for a lifetime."

### Life
Bentley is located in the small Massachusetts town of Waltham, but because of the school's proximity to Boston (about 20 minutes via a free shuttle), students "can always go there and have a good time." Many especially enjoy Boston's active club scene. Students describe the campus as beautiful and quiet, though many add that there is an obvious lack of school spirit, and "not nearly enough support is given to the sports teams or organizations on campus." According to one morose student, "fun at Bentley consists of sitting in a room and drinking." Still, other students believe that the active Greek life "keeps the campus busy with activities, charities, and parties" that allow them "to meet a lot of people and [enjoy] good times." However you slice it, drinking is a popular activity, and people "party every weekend through Monday." Students agree that the food at Bentley is less than satisfying, and cite the need for improved on-campus parking and cleaner, better-looking dormitories. However, undergrads praise the feeling of safety that they have while on campus and the new Student Center (opening January 2002) will provide a better space for students. Overall, student sentiment about life on campus was perhaps best summarized by the student who told us "Bentley is definitely a fun school with a big party scene," but one which also provides "a very good academic foundation."

### Student Body
Though its technologically advanced business curriculum has gained national attention, Bentley remains a college that primarily attracts students from the Northeast. Students lean towards political conservatism, which isn't surprising considering that approximately three-quarters of the students come from New England. Many students list the student body's lack of diversity as one of Bentley's major weaknesses, saying undergrads tend to be very "cliquey, depending on what ethnicity you are." Others write that "everyone is pretty much white, preppy, and rich" and "if you can't afford all A&E and AF, then you won't interact with anyone." Still, most students agree that the campus is very friendly and that students should have "no problem making friends." One student told us, "the people are very nice." International students are not only accepted, but well respected. "The students [at Bentley] are very similar in nature. They all have a really competitive nature," one student wrote, but manage to remain "friendly."

FINANCIAL AID: 781-891-3441 • E-MAIL: UGADMISSION@BENTLEY.EDU • WEBSITE: WWW.BENTLEY.EDU

## ADMISSIONS

*Very important* academic and nonacademic factors considered by the admissions committee include secondary school record. *Important* factors considered include character/personal qualities, class rank, essays, extracurricular activities, interview, minority status, recommendations, standardized test scores and talent/ability. *Other* factors considered include alumni/ae relation, geography, volunteer work and work experience. Factors *not* considered include religious affiliation/commitment and state residency. SAT I or ACT required. TOEFL required of all international applicants. High school diploma is required and GED is accepted. *High school units required/recommended:* 16 total required; 22 total recommended; 4 English required, 3 math required, 4 math recommended, 2 science required, 3 science recommended, 1 science lab required, 2 science lab recommended, 2 foreign language required, 2 social studies required, 1 history required, 2 history recommended, 1 elective required, 3 elective recommended.

### The Inside Word

If you're a solid "B" student there's little challenge to encounter in the admissions process here. The College's appealing greater Boston location and career-oriented academic strengths account for a sizable applicant pool and the moderate selectivity that it enjoys.

## FINANCIAL AID

*Students should submit:* FAFSA, CSS/Financial Aid PROFILE, noncustodial (divorced/separated) parent's statement, and business/farm supplement. Regular filing deadline is February 1. The Princeton Review suggests that all financial aid forms be submitted as soon as possible after January 1. *Need-based scholarships/grants offered:* Pell, SEOG, state scholarships/grants, private scholarships, and the school's own gift aid. *Loan aid offered:* Federal Perkins and state. Institutional employment available. Federal Work-Study Program available. Applicants will be notified of awards on a rolling basis beginning on or about March 25. Off-campus job opportunities are excellent.

## FROM THE ADMISSIONS OFFICE

"Bentley College combines the look and feel of a small New England college and the resources of the largest business school in the region. Students learn in an environment that integrates information with a broad business and arts and sciences curriculum. More than one-third of students' courses must be taken in the arts and sciences. From there, they choose to go deep in a business specialty or pursue a comprehensive business program or liberal arts field of study, such as international studies or law. They may also choose to pursue a five-year combined program leading to both a bachelor's and master's degree. Bentley's hands-on, high-tech learning facilities are among the first of their kind in higher education. A financial trading room combines cutting-edge technology and real-time data to let students explore key financial concepts simulated in stock trading sessions. In the Center for Marketing Technologies, undergraduates learn the latest strategies in marketing and advertising. And the Accounting Center for Electronic Learning and Business Measurement is an available resource for anyone taking an accounting course. Every classroom in the new Smith Academic Technology Center is equipped to handle the latest technologies as they come onto the market. Through the Bentley Mobile Computing Program, all Bentley freshmen receive a network-ready laptop computer, fully loaded with software, with an automatic 'trade-up' policy after two years. More than 90 student groups, 22 varsity teams in Division I and II, and extensive intramural and recreational sports programs energize campus life. Boston, just 10 miles from campus, and Cambridge, a regular trip on the Bentley shuttle, are great resources for internships and jobs."

## ADMISSIONS

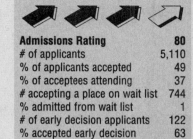

| | |
|---|---|
| Admissions Rating | 80 |
| # of applicants | 5,110 |
| % of applicants accepted | 49 |
| % of acceptees attending | 37 |
| # accepting a place on wait list | 744 |
| % admitted from wait list | 1 |
| # of early decision applicants | 122 |
| % accepted early decision | 63 |

### FRESHMAN PROFILE

| | |
|---|---|
| Range SAT Verbal | 490-580 |
| Average SAT Verbal | 542 |
| Range SAT Math | 540-630 |
| Average SAT Math | 588 |
| Range ACT Composite | 22-26 |
| Minimum TOEFL | 550 |
| % graduated top 10% of class | 22 |
| % graduated top 25% of class | 60 |
| % graduated top 50% of class | 95 |

### DEADLINES

| | |
|---|---|
| Early decision | 12/1 |
| Early decision notification | 12/28 |
| Regular admission | 2/1 |
| Regular notification | 4/1 |
| Nonfall registration? | yes |

### APPLICANTS ALSO LOOK AT

**AND OFTEN PREFER**
Babson
Boston Coll.
Boston U.

**AND SOMETIMES PREFER**
Providence College
Northeastern U.
U. Mass—Amherst
U. New Hampshire
Fairfield

**AND RARELY PREFER**
Bryant

### FINANCIAL FACTS

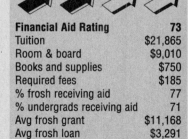

| | |
|---|---|
| Financial Aid Rating | 73 |
| Tuition | $21,865 |
| Room & board | $9,010 |
| Books and supplies | $750 |
| Required fees | $185 |
| % frosh receiving aid | 77 |
| % undergrads receiving aid | 71 |
| Avg frosh grant | $11,168 |
| Avg frosh loan | $3,291 |

# BIRMINGHAM-SOUTHERN COLLEGE

900 ARKADELPHIA ROAD, BIRMINGHAM, AL 35254 • ADMISSIONS: 205-226-4686 • FAX: 205-226-3074

## CAMPUS LIFE

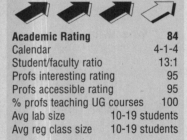

| | |
|---|---|
| **Quality of Life Rating** | **86** |
| Type of school | private |
| Affiliation | Methodist |
| Environment | urban |

### STUDENTS

| | |
|---|---|
| Total undergrad enrollment | 1,453 |
| % male/female | 40/60 |
| % from out of state | 23 |
| % African American | 12 |
| % Asian | 4 |
| % Caucasian | 83 |
| % Native American | 1 |
| % international | 1 |

### SURVEY SAYS . . .
*Theater is hot*
*Frats and sororities dominate social scene*
*Athletic facilities are great*
*Campus feels safe*
*Students love Birmingham, AL*
*Students are very religious*
*Students get along with local community*
*Political activism is (almost) nonexistent*

## ACADEMICS

| | |
|---|---|
| **Academic Rating** | **84** |
| Calendar | 4-1-4 |
| Student/faculty ratio | 13:1 |
| Profs interesting rating | 95 |
| Profs accessible rating | 95 |
| % profs teaching UG courses | 100 |
| Avg lab size | 10-19 students |
| Avg reg class size | 10-19 students |

### MOST POPULAR MAJORS
business administration
biology
English

## STUDENTS SPEAK OUT

### Academics

Birmingham-Southern College is a top-flight small liberal arts school that is also strong in undergraduate business and management. Business-minded students, who make up roughly one-third of the student body, benefit from BSC's wide-ranging set of distribution requirements in the humanities and social sciences; these requirements may, in fact, play a large role in the high acceptance rate BSC students enjoy at MBA programs. Pre-medical sciences and education are also popular, high-quality majors here. Students warn, "The academic experience at BSC is intense at the least. The parties are happening, but academic excellence is first priority for everyone." The demands are great, but so are the returns; as one student tells us, "This school provides students with opportunities they wouldn't get at bigger schools. That sounds like something straight out of the viewbook, I know, but it's true; I've had several chances to work closely with professors." Professors "are dedicated to teaching, and seldom are upper-level courses taught by adjunct faculty. Professors are also readily available outside of class." One student notes, "The faculty make the school. Teaching is consistently strong. Professors are available and easily accessible for help with a class or special projects. It is not uncommon for faculty to have students over for dinner on Greenboro Road, which is 'Faculty Row.'"

### Life

With well over half its students pledging a Greek house, BSC is one of the nation's most Greek-dominated campuses. Students sum up the situation simply: "Fraternity parties tend to dominate the social landscape at BSC." Another writes, "The Greek mixers are very popular, probably due to the themes such as Country Club, Road Warriors, and Dazed 'n' Confused." Those few non-Greeks who attend BSC are, fortunately, welcome at most Greek events and parties. Still there are detractors who tell us that "Greek life is too big—the administration mixes rush in with orientation to rope students in. The truth is, life is great here as an independent. Don't let them fool you! The city of Birmingham is fun—concerts, restaurants, theater (there's a Shakespeare Festival in Montgomery). Plus, there are road trips to the beach, the Smoky Mountains, etc." Few students take advantage of what Birmingham offers, however; writes one student, "The campus is fairly contained. People seldom go off campus." This inertia is partly due to students' satisfaction with the on-campus social scene. When fun parties and all your friends are nearby, why go anywhere else? It's also due in part to students' commitment to their studies; explains one student, "Campus life mostly consists of studying as a first priority. Recreational activities vary from throwing the Frisbee in the courtyard to competitive online computer games."

### Student Body

BSC students readily admit, "This is a very conservative liberal arts school. Lots of rich white kids. They don't allow room for much diversity." Another agrees, "We are a pretty homogeneous bunch. There is a strange mix of intellectual life with old-style Greek life on this small campus. It's possible to immerse yourself in one or the other or both." Both comments, characteristic of many we receive, seemingly ignore a relatively large African American population—for a predominantly white private school, that is. A small student body makes for a homey atmosphere enhanced by the region's traditional hospitality and good manners. As one student puts it, "You know who almost everyone is. Even if you don't know someone, they'll often smile and wave as you pass."

FINANCIAL AID: 205-226-4688 • E-MAIL: ADMISSIONS@BSC.EDU • WEBSITE: WWW.BSC.EDU

## ADMISSIONS

*Very important* academic and nonacademic factors considered by the admissions committee include class rank and secondary school record. *Important* factors considered include character/personal qualities, essays, recommendations, standardized test scores, and talent/ability. *Other* factors considered include alumni/ae relation, extracurricular activities, geography, interview, minority status, state residency, volunteer work, and work experience. Factors *not* considered include religious affiliation/commitment. SAT I or ACT required. TOEFL required of all international applicants. High school diploma is required and GED is accepted. *High school units required/recommended:* 19 total required; 4 English required, 3 math required, 3 science required, 3 science lab required, 3 foreign language required, 2 social studies required, 1 history required, 2 elective required.

### The Inside Word

Birmingham-Southern's lack of widespread national recognition by students and parents results in a small applicant pool, the majority of whom are admitted. Most of the admits are looking for a quality southern college, recognize a good situation here, and decide to enroll. Our impression is that few regret their decision. In a reflection of the entire administration, the admissions staff is truly personal and very helpful to prospective students.

## FINANCIAL AID

*Students should submit:* FAFSA. There is no regular filing deadline. The Princeton Review suggests that all financial aid forms be submitted as soon as possible after January 1. *Need-based scholarships/grants offered:* Pell, SEOG, state scholarships/grants, private scholarships, and the school's own gift aid. *Loan aid offered:* FFEL Subsidized Stafford, FFEL Unsubsidized Stafford, FFEL PLUS, Federal Perkins, college/university loans from institutional funds, and Alternative. Institutional employment available. Federal Work-Study Program available. Applicants will be notified of awards on a rolling basis beginning on or about March 1. Off-campus job opportunities are excellent.

## FROM THE ADMISSIONS OFFICE

"Respected publishers continue to recognize Birmingham-Southern College as one of the top-ranked liberal arts colleges in the nation. One guide highlights our small classes and the fact that we still assign each student a 'faculty-cum-mentor,' to assure individualized attention to our students. One notable aspect of our academic calendar is our January interim term, a four-week period in which students can participate in special projects in close collaboration with faculty members, either on or off campus. One dimension of Birmingham-Southern's moral focus is the commitment to volunteerism. In fact, former President George Bush visited the campus to present our Conservancy group with one of his 'Points of Light' volunteer service awards. The Center for Leadership Studies assists students in realizing their leadership potential by combining the academic study of leadership with significant community service."

## ADMISSIONS

| Admissions Rating | 81 |
| --- | --- |
| # of applicants | 867 |
| % of applicants accepted | 95 |
| % of acceptees attending | 41 |

### FRESHMAN PROFILE

| | |
| --- | --- |
| Range SAT Verbal | 540-660 |
| Average SAT Verbal | 598 |
| Range SAT Math | 530-640 |
| Average SAT Math | 588 |
| Range ACT Composite | 23-29 |
| Average ACT Composite | 26 |
| Minimum TOEFL | 500 |
| Average HS GPA | 3.3 |
| % graduated top 10% of class | 34 |
| % graduated top 25% of class | 60 |
| % graduated top 50% of class | 89 |

### DEADLINES

| | |
| --- | --- |
| Priority admission deadline | 1/15 |
| Nonfall registration? | yes |

### APPLICANTS ALSO LOOK AT

**AND OFTEN PREFER**
Vanderbilt
Rhodes

**AND SOMETIMES PREFER**
Samford
U. Alabama
U. Auburn
U. of the South
Furman

**AND RARELY PREFER**
LSU—Baton Rouge
Tulane

## FINANCIAL FACTS

| Financial Aid Rating | 89 |
| --- | --- |
| Tuition | $15,170 |
| Room & board | $5,460 |
| Books and supplies | $500 |
| Required fees | $328 |
| % frosh receiving aid | 43 |
| % undergrads receiving aid | 34 |
| Avg frosh grant | $5,129 |
| Avg frosh loan | $2,517 |

# BOSTON COLLEGE

140 COMMONWEALTH AVENUE, DEVLIN HALL 208, CHESTNUT HILL, MA 02467-3809 • ADMISSIONS: 617-552-3100 • FAX: 617-552-0798

## CAMPUS LIFE

| Quality of Life Rating | **76** |
| --- | --- |
| Type of school | private |
| Affiliation | Roman Catholic |
| Environment | suburban |

### STUDENTS

| | |
| --- | --- |
| Total undergrad enrollment | 8,930 |
| % male/female | 48/52 |
| % from out of state | 73 |
| % from public high school | 59 |
| % live on campus | 76 |
| % African American | 5 |
| % Asian | 8 |
| % Caucasian | 74 |
| % Hispanic | 6 |
| % international | 2 |
| # of countries represented | 100 |

### SURVEY SAYS . . .

*Lots of classroom discussion*
*Students love Chestnut Hill, MA*
*Great on campus food*
*Everyone loves the Eagles*
*Political activism is hot*
*Students are cliquish*
*Student publications are ignored*
*(Almost) no one listens to college*
*radio*

## ACADEMICS

| Academic Rating | **91** |
| --- | --- |
| Calendar | semester |
| Student/faculty ratio | 13:1 |
| Profs interesting rating | 88 |
| Profs accessible rating | 88 |
| % profs teaching UG courses | 100 |
| Avg lab size | 10-19 students |
| Avg reg class size | 10-19 students |

### MOST POPULAR MAJORS
communication/English
finance
psychology

## STUDENTS SPEAK OUT

### Academics

To those unacquainted with the school, the name "Boston College" evokes the image of a tiny liberal arts school tucked away in Cambridge. This image couldn't be more inaccurate: Boston College, which is neither a college (it's a university) nor in Boston (it's in Chestnut Hill), is a large Jesuit school whose greatest strengths lie in its schools of business, nursing, and education. In all academic areas, BC pursues the Jesuit ideals of developing the intellect and serving the community. The Jesuit spirit is particularly evident in the school's optional PULSE program, which allows students to combine courses in philosophy and ethics with community service in order to "address the relationship of self and society, the nature of community, the mystery of suffering, and the practical difficulties of developing a just society." Other optional course sequences, such as Perspectives on Western Culture and the Faith, Peace, and Justice Program, provide students with the opportunity to concentrate a sizable part of their undergraduate study on global social, philosophical, and theological questions. One drawback of BC is its size; students here complain that professors are often inaccessible. However, online registration gets high marks.

### Life

Boston College was at one time considered a party school, but times change, and the results of our survey indicate that BC has moved along. Students here report an average amount of beer and drug consumption: BC students aren't teetotalers, but neither are they the party animals they once were. The campus is officially dry, but students say that local bars that will serve them can be found ("A fake ID is key!" reports one student). BC has no fraternities or sororities, but the lack of a Greek system doesn't limit the number of parties, which are plentiful during weekends. Intercollegiate and intramural sports are popular on-campus activities, and many students become involved in community-service-oriented organizations. Downtown Boston, with its vital, college-oriented night life, is only 20 minutes away by car or public transportation.

### Student Body

Despite a relatively large minority population, BC students consider themselves more alike than different. For example, one student inaccurately reports, "People here are all white, Irish-Catholic, beer-drinking clones and are damn proud of it, too." Agrees another, "People think BC is very homogeneous, but you come here because you want to be around people like yourself." Perhaps this misconception arises from the large Catholic population and the fact that "BC is a very cliquish place. As a result, you have to be extremely dynamic in order to make the most of it."

## ADMISSIONS

*Very important* academic and nonacademic factors considered by the admissions committee include class rank and secondary school record. *Important* factors considered include alumni/ae relation, character/personal qualities, extracurricular activities, interview, minority status, recommendations, talent/ability, and volunteer work. *Other* factors considered include essays, geography, standardized test scores, state residency, and work experience. Factors *not* considered include religious affiliation/commitment. TOEFL required of all international applicants. High school diploma is required and GED is accepted. *High school units required/recommended:* 16 total required; 21 total recommended; 4 English required, 3 math required, 4 math recommended, 3 science required, 4 science recommended, 3 science lab required, 4 science lab recommended, 2 foreign language required, 4 foreign language recommended, 1 social studies required, 3 history required, 4 history recommended. *The admissions office says:* "Boston College seeks a student body with a diversity of talents, attitudes, backgrounds, and interests to produce a vital community atmosphere. As a Jesuit institution, Boston College also chooses responsible and concerned students who are interested in the ideals of commitment and service to others."

### The Inside Word

While applications to BC in general have increased over the past couple of years, early action applications have risen more dramatically. Standards remain high, and we more than recommend a strong college-preparatory curriculum in high school—it's a must in order to have a shot. With a large percentage of its students coming from Catholic high schools such applicants are treated well, but there is little room for relaxation in the process. Applicants need to show strong SAT and SAT II scores, but keep the tests in perspective—BC is interested in the whole package.

## FINANCIAL AID

*Students should submit:* FAFSA, CSS/Financial Aid PROFILE, noncustodial (divorced/separated) parent's statement, and business/farm supplement. The Princeton Review suggests that all financial aid forms be submitted as soon as possible after January 1. *Need-based scholarships/grants offered:* Pell, SEOG, state scholarships/grants, private scholarships, and the school's own gift aid. *Loan aid offered:* FFEL Subsidized Stafford, FFEL Unsubsidized Stafford, FFEL PLUS, Federal Perkins, Federal Nursing, and state. Institutional employment available. Federal Work-Study Program available. Applicants will be notified of awards on or about the first week in April. Off-campus job opportunities are good.

## FROM THE ADMISSIONS OFFICE

"Boston College students enjoy the quiet, suburban atmosphere of Chestnut Hill, with easy access to the cultural and historical richness of Boston. Junior Year Abroad and Scholar of the College Program offer students flexibility within the curriculum. Facilities opened in the past 10 years include: the Merkert Chemistry Center, a new dorm and dining hall facility, and a new library. Fifteen Presidential Scholars enroll in each freshman class with a half-tuition scholarship irrespective of need, and funding is available to meet full demonstrated need. These students, selected from the top 1 percent of the Early Action applicant pool, participate in the most rewarding intellectual experience offered at the university."

## ADMISSIONS

| | |
|---|---|
| Admissions Rating | 95 |
| # of applicants | 20,743 |
| % of applicants accepted | 32 |
| % of acceptees attending | 34 |

### FRESHMAN PROFILE

| | |
|---|---|
| Range SAT Verbal | 600-690 |
| Range SAT Math | 600-690 |
| Minimum TOEFL | 550 |
| % graduated top 10% of class | 62 |
| % graduated top 25% of class | 91 |
| % graduated top 50% of class | 100 |

### DEADLINES

| | |
|---|---|
| Regular admission | 1/15 |
| Regular notification | 4/15 |
| Nonfall registration? | yes |

### APPLICANTS ALSO LOOK AT

**AND OFTEN PREFER**
Georgetown U.
Notre Dame

**AND SOMETIMES PREFER**
Villanova
Holy Cross
Boston U.
Syracuse
Fairfield

**AND RARELY PREFER**
U. Vermont
U. Conn
U. New Hampshire

## FINANCIAL FACTS

| | |
|---|---|
| Financial Aid Rating | 74 |
| Tuition | $24,050 |
| Books and supplies | $600 |
| Required fees | $700 |
| % frosh receiving aid | 47 |
| % undergrads receiving aid | 47 |
| Avg frosh grant | $13,934 |
| Avg frosh loan | $3,459 |

# BOSTON UNIVERSITY

121 BAY STATE ROAD, BOSTON, MA 02215 • ADMISSIONS: 617-353-2300 • FAX: 617-353-9695

## CAMPUS LIFE

**Quality of Life Rating** **79**
Type of school                     private
Affiliation                          none
Environment                         urban

### STUDENTS
Total undergrad enrollment   17,819
% male/female                   41/59
% from out of state                75
% from public high school          72
% live on campus                   66
% in (# of) fraternities         3 (9)
% in (# of) sororities           4 (9)
% African American                  3
% Asian                             4
% Caucasian                        65
% Hispanic                          5
% international                     8
# of countries represented        100

### SURVEY SAYS . . .
*Students love Boston, MA
Very little drug use
Lousy food on campus
Great off-campus food
Class discussions are rare
Ethnic diversity on campus
Unattractive campus
Large classes
Very small frat/sorority scene
Athletic facilities need improving*

## ACADEMICS

**Academic Rating** **89**
Calendar                        semester
Student/faculty ratio              14:1
Profs interesting rating             88
Profs accessible rating              91
% profs teaching UG courses          80
% classes taught by TAs              13
Avg lab size            20-29 students
Avg reg class size      10-19 students

### MOST POPULAR MAJORS
social sciences
communications
management

## STUDENTS SPEAK OUT
### Academics
Whether they love the school or simply love to hate it, students at BU know how to communicate their beliefs. On the quality of teaching: "Come here and have any life path available to you," writes a first year, "and brilliant, energetic, enthusiastic professors ready to give you the equivalent knowledge of a Ferrari to drive down it." Sound too good to be true? A sophomore puts it into perspective: "I guess the professors here are like those at any university. Some have been wicked funny, awe inspiring, and life changing. Of course there are also a fair share of pompous, misogynistic jerks—but that's why BU has such a great system for dropping classes." Also, "the school's administration resembles a small dictatorship of some Central American country," quips a sophomore. "It is rash, volatile, and hopefully it won't last long." Yet some appreciate the "generally well-run" nature of the school itself. As for the school's large size, one junior remarks, "BU is a large university that may appear overwhelming to a freshman just beginning; however, BU is actually a collection of tiny schools that make up one large institution. Each individual school looks after their individual students, making sure they are not just another number." Not so, counters a sage senior: "If you want individual attention, you need to seek it. Professors (and everyone, really) are receptive if you approach them, but since this is a big school with big classes, they won't seek you out." Most students seem to like the school's deep coffers—financial aid awards are often generous and widespread. Unfortunately, the money doesn't seem to trickle down to the physical plant: a fairly spread-out, urban school, Boston University seems to suffer in the eyes of its students from a lack of a central, well-maintained campus. Writes a senior, "It would be nice to have a campus . . . or at least a patch of shrubs."

### Life
While some students view the strictly enforced rules on alcohol, drugs, and guest visitation as providing a safe haven, others, like this sophomore, find the school's strict dorm regulations infantilizing and unnecessarily harsh: "The guest policy creates a type of environment not conducive to socializing or feeling laid-back. We live in a dictatorship!" Still, students at BU seem to get through; as a sophomore describes it, "During the week, students are very focused on class work and courses, but on the weekends, their mindset is completely different. All thoughts lean toward parties, sex, clubs, and alcohol. In short, good old-fashioned college fun." And for those not in the mood for body shots and early morning walks of shame, there's always Boston, "one of the best college towns in the country." Why go to BU? An answer from a particularly expressive senior: "The BU experience goes way beyond the classroom. Just in the last month, I've gone to see the Phantom of the Opera, gone skiing in Vermont, and gone to the Fogg Museum at Harvard. Its location is BU's greatest strength."

### Student Body
It might seem incredible that such a large and opinionated student body gets along as well as they do. Writes one junior, "Generally students are unique and independent and encourage healthy competition and collaboration on projects. They are easy to get along with." So it's just like the cast of *Friends* but on a really big scale? Well . . . not quite, according to a sophomore. "There are, of course, a few cliques on campus composed of students who obviously skipped the day in preschool when they taught 'How to Get Along With Others and Not Be a Eurotrashy Snot.'" Ouch. Fortunately, in a large school there's bound to be someone to click with. How does a typical BUer feel about his or her fellow students? We like this answer: "How should I know?" asks a first year. "Out of 15,000 undergraduates [sic] I have seen about 2,000, spoken to about 500, and hung around with 50." Really good odds, we'd say.

FINANCIAL AID: 617-353-2965 • E-MAIL: ADMISSIONS@BU.EDU • WEBSITE: WWW.BU.EDU

## ADMISSIONS

*Very important* academic and nonacademic factors considered by the admissions committee include character/personal qualities, secondary school record, and talent/ability. *Important* factors considered include class rank, essays, extracurricular activities, and recommendations. *Other* factors considered include alumni/ae relation, geography, interview, minority status, standardized test scores, state residency, volunteer work, and work experience. Factors *not* considered include religious affiliation/commitment. SAT I or ACT required. TOEFL required of all applicants for whom English is not their first language. High school diploma is required and GED is accepted. *High school units required/recommended:* 16 total required; 4 English required, 3 math required, 3 science required, 2 foreign language required, 3 history/social studies required. *The admissions office says:* "BU does recommend a rigorous college preparatory curriculum, including a full complement of math, science, and foreign language courses. "

### The Inside Word

Boston is one of the nation's most popular college towns, and BU benefits tremendously. The university's last few entering classes have been chock-full of high-caliber students; despite a general decline in applications at colleges in the Northeast it will continue to be competitive to gain admission to BU, as applications keep a steady upward trend and entering class size is kept in check. Those who aren't up to traditional standards are sometimes referred to the less selective College of General Studies, which allows students to continue on to other divisions of the university once they prove themselves academically—but standards here are rising.

## FINANCIAL AID

*Students should submit:* FAFSA, CSS/Financial Aid PROFILE, state aid form, noncustodial (divorced/separated) parent's statement, and business/farm supplement. The Princeton Review suggests that all financial aid forms be submitted as soon as possible after January 1. *Need-based scholarships/grants offered:* Pell, SEOG, state scholarships/grants, private scholarships, and the school's own gift aid. *Loan aid offered:* Direct Subsidized Stafford, Direct Unsubsidized Stafford, Direct PLUS, Federal Perkins, and state. Institutional employment available. Federal Work-Study Program available. Applicants will be notified of awards on a rolling basis between March 15 and April 15. Off-campus job opportunities are excellent.

## FROM THE ADMISSIONS OFFICE

"The spirit of Boston University is in the possibilities. With more than 250 major and minor concentrations led by a faculty dedicated to the art of teaching, the university's academic opportunities are nearly unrivaled among American institutions of higher learning. Beyond the classroom, Boston University students—who come from all 50 states and more than 100 foreign countries—may choose to participate in any of the more than 400 student organizations, from environmental groups to intramural ice broomball teams. Students find abundant opportunities for growth and enjoyment not only in the city of Boston but in cities throughout the world where Boston University students study and work."

## ADMISSIONS

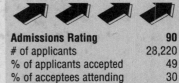

| Admissions Rating | 90 |
|---|---|
| # of applicants | 28,220 |
| % of applicants accepted | 49 |
| % of acceptees attending | 30 |
| # accepting a place on wait list | 974 |
| % admitted from wait list | 23 |
| # of early decision applicants | 450 |
| % accepted early decision | 20 |

### FRESHMAN PROFILE

| | |
|---|---|
| Range SAT Verbal | 600-680 |
| Average SAT Verbal | 639 |
| Range SAT Math | 610-690 |
| Average SAT Math | 645 |
| Range ACT Composite | 26-30 |
| Average ACT Composite | 28 |
| Minimum TOEFL | 215 |
| Average HS GPA | 3.5 |
| % graduated top 10% of class | 57 |
| % graduated top 25% of class | 93 |
| % graduated top 50% of class | 99 |

### DEADLINES

| | |
|---|---|
| Early decision | 11/1 |
| Early decision notification | 12/15 |
| Regular admission | 1/1 |
| Nonfall registration? | yes |

### APPLICANTS ALSO LOOK AT
### AND OFTEN PREFER
Harvard, Pennsylvania
Cornell U., Boston Coll.
Georgetown U.
### AND SOMETIMES PREFER
NYU
U. Mass—Amherst
Northeastern U.
Binghamton U., Notre Dame
### AND RARELY PREFER
U. New Hampshire
Syracuse, RIT
Rutgers U.—Rutgers Coll.

## FINANCIAL FACTS

| Financial Aid Rating | 74 |
|---|---|
| Tuition | $25,872 |
| Room & board | $8,750 |
| Books and supplies | $670 |
| Required fees | $356 |
| % frosh receiving aid | 69 |
| % undergrads receiving aid | 65 |
| Avg frosh grant | $17,720 |
| Avg frosh loan | $3,677 |

# BOWDOIN COLLEGE

5000 COLLEGE STATION, BRUNSWICK, ME 04011-8441 • ADMISSIONS: 207-725-3100 • FAX: 207-725-3101

## CAMPUS LIFE

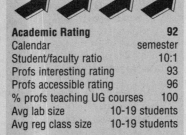

| Quality of Life Rating | 88 |
|---|---|
| Type of school | private |
| Affiliation | none |
| Environment | suburban |

### STUDENTS

| | |
|---|---|
| Total undergrad enrollment | 1,609 |
| % male/female | 49/51 |
| % from out of state | 86 |
| % from public high school | 55 |
| % live on campus | 87 |
| % African American | 2 |
| % Asian | 7 |
| % Caucasian | 80 |
| % Hispanic | 3 |
| % international | 3 |
| # of countries represented | 32 |

### SURVEY SAYS . . .

*Great food on campus*
*Everyone loves the Polar Bears*
*Very little drug use*
*Athletic facilities are great*
*(Almost) no one smokes*
*Low cost of living*

## ACADEMICS

| Academic Rating | 92 |
|---|---|
| Calendar | semester |
| Student/faculty ratio | 10:1 |
| Profs interesting rating | 93 |
| Profs accessible rating | 96 |
| % profs teaching UG courses | 100 |
| Avg lab size | 10-19 students |
| Avg reg class size | 10-19 students |

### MOST POPULAR MAJORS
government/legal studies
economics
biology

## STUDENTS SPEAK OUT

### Academics

"Independence," "freedom," and "self-motivation" are words Bowdoin College students frequently associate with their undergraduate experience. Perhaps it has something to do with the size and location of the campus itself—a few miles from the coast of southern Maine (and its islands, lakes, and wilderness), tiny but highly selective Bowdoin prides itself on its "Walden Pond" atmosphere and challenges its students to, like Thoreau, find their own way. Notes one senior, "You are encouraged to explore all sorts of academic areas, and once you find something you love, you can run with it." Bowdoin's campus is, according to its students, "unbeatable." Remodeled buildings, "pretty good housing—especially for first years," and some of the best college food around all make Joe and Jane College's quest for knowledge a little more, well, comfortable. Professors are, for the most part, accessible (Brunswick is a small town—they can't go far) and full of encouragement. Writes another senior, "Professors are excellent. We've had them over to our house for dinner." Unfortunately, students also note that the "whale of a bureaucracy" at Bowdoin can make retaining such teaching excellence difficult. A savvy junior describes the situation as such: "Great professors, but the school's rush to determine whether to tenure or not leaves their status uncertain and hurries, regrettably, some good ones away."

### Life

As one would expect, a major aspect of Bowdoin's social life revolves around—you guessed it—the great outdoors. "There are great opportunities for getting outside," writes a senior. "With the Bowdoin Outing Club you can spend the weekend skiiing, camping, hiking, snowshoeing, rock climbing, hanging out at the Outing Club's cabin drinking hot chocolate all weekend." Athletics, too, seem to draw the campus together, whether it's "hockey on the town commons," playing on the rugby team and in other club sports, or watching Bowdoin continue an eons-old rivalry with nearby Colby College during one of their "especially insane" hockey matches. Of course, not everyone is thrilled about all this huffing and puffing in the name of good, clean fun; one junior makes it plain that "athletics and personal fitness activities are a little too popular." In terms of nightlife, there seems to be only a few options at Bowdoin, and most of those involve drinking. Though the administration and the recently transformed "social house" system (sororities and fraternities were banned a few years ago) try to promote non-alcoholic programming such as concerts, dances, and performances, many students stick close to the keg. "I drink for fun," writes a senior, and while one student's soused state might not speak for everyone, at least one first-year agrees: "There's a lot of drinking here."

### Student Body

"Everyone here is interesting," says a first year. "We can talk about girls on TV and China's foreign policy as it relates to European trade in the same moment." Another freshman provides a living example of Bowdoin's reputation for turning out aware and independent yet community-minded thinkers and doers: "I am an athlete, don't smoke, and voted Republican. I live next to a kid who smokes, listens to Phish, voted for Nader, and we are now best friends." Too bad much of Bowdoin's diversity is limited to political parties and smoking habits. Another freshman weighs in about what is increasingly seen as a major drawback to an otherwise excellent college experience: "Good thing this campus is traditionally liberal and open minded," she writes. "Otherwise, we would be confused with a white pride meeting." It's a negative the school's administration has not overlooked, and according to students, is working hard to change. "Only recently is Bowdoin attempting to push away from the stale, prep-school boy's attitude that it previously held. Yet the effort is commendable and noticeable." Besides, jokes a sophomore, "It turns out that white, New England prep-school kids are pretty nice. Who knew?"

FINANCIAL AID: 207-725-3273 • E-MAIL: ADMISSIONS@HENRY.BOWDOIN.EDU • WEBSITE: WWW.BOWDOIN.EDU

## ADMISSIONS

*Very important* academic and nonacademic factors considered by the admissions committee include secondary school record, character/personal qualities, class rank, essays, minority status, and recommendations. *Important* factors considered include extracurricular activities, talent/ability, alumni/ae relation, geography, and volunteer work. *Other* factors considered include standardized test scores, interview, and work experiences. TOEFL required of all international applicants. *High school units required/recommended:* 20 total recommended; 4 English recommended, 4 math recommended, 4 science recommended, 3 science lab recommended, 4 foreign language recommended, 4 social studies recommended. *The admissions office says:* "The admissions committee focuses a great deal of its attention on each candidate's academic record, intellectual interests, and overall ability to thrive in a challenging academic environment. To enhance the educational scope and stimulation of the Bowdoin community, special consideration is given to applicants who represent a culture, region, or background that will contribute to the diversity of the college. Added consideration is also given to candidates who have demonstrated talents in leadership, communication, social service, and other fields that will contribute to campus life."

### The Inside Word

This is one of the 20 or so most selective colleges in the country. Virtually everyone who applies is well qualified academically, which means criteria besides grades and test scores become critically important in candidate review. Who you are, what you think, where you are from, and why you are interested in Bowdoin are the sorts of things that will determine whether you get in, provided you meet their high academic standards.

## FINANCIAL AID

*Students should submit:* FAFSA, institution's own financial aid form, CSS/Financial Aid PROFILE, noncustodial (divorced/separated) parent's statement, and business/farm supplement. The Princeton Review suggests that all financial aid forms be submitted as soon as possible after January 1. *Need-based scholarships/grants offered:* Pell, SEOG, state scholarships/grants, private scholarships, and the school's own gift aid. *Loan aid offered:* FFEL Subsidized Stafford, FFEL Unsubsidized Stafford, FFEL PLUS, Federal Perkins, state, and college/university loans from institutional funds. Institutional employment available. Federal Work-Study Program available. Applicants will be notified of awards on or about April 5. Off-campus job opportunities are fair.

## FROM THE ADMISSIONS OFFICE

"At Bowdoin, each year a student activities budget of more than $450,000 is spent on events ranging from performances by bands, comedians, and novelty acts to scavenger hunts, dances, film series, and community services events. An additional $160,000 is available to bring lectures and concerts to campus. Performers who have appeared at Bowdoin recently include The Roots, Ben Folds Five, Guster, Paula Poundstone, and Keb' Mo'. Speakers have included Carl Bernstein, George Will, and Spike Lee. The college has more than 90 active student organizations. About 70 percent of students participate in community services during their time at Bowdoin, and the college's many volunteer programs allow students to interact with the Brunswick community. Club and intramural sports and the Outing Club enable students to get involved in physical fitness without having to be star athletes. For those without cars, the college provides shuttle rides to nearby malls and movie theaters as well as Freeport and Portland. Bowdoin is determined to be a place that nurtures people from diverse backgrounds. The number of students of color on campus increases each year, and Bowdoin is working to ensure that diversity also includes students from varied economic backgrounds, from different parts of the country, and with divergent political and religious identities and academic interests."

### ADMISSIONS

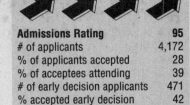

| | |
|---|---|
| Admissions Rating | 95 |
| # of applicants | 4,172 |
| % of applicants accepted | 28 |
| % of acceptees attending | 39 |
| # of early decision applicants | 471 |
| % accepted early decision | 42 |

### FRESHMAN PROFILE

| | |
|---|---|
| Range SAT Verbal | 640-720 |
| Average SAT Verbal | 680 |
| Range SAT Math | 650-710 |
| Average SAT Math | 680 |
| Minimum TOEFL | 600 |
| % graduated top 10% of class | 75 |
| % graduated top 25% of class | 93 |
| % graduated top 50% of class | 99 |

### DEADLINES

| | |
|---|---|
| Early decision | 11/15 |
| Early decision notification | 12/30 |
| Regular admission | 1/1 |
| Regular notification | 4/5 |

### APPLICANTS ALSO LOOK AT
### AND OFTEN PREFER
Brown
Dartmouth
Harvard
Williams
Middlebury
### AND SOMETIMES PREFER
Princeton
Cornell U.
Bates
Colby
Wesleyan U.

### FINANCIAL FACTS

| | |
|---|---|
| Financial Aid Rating | 74 |
| Tuition | $26,700 |
| Room & board | $7,000 |
| Books and supplies | $830 |
| Required fees | $580 |
| % frosh receiving aid | 42 |
| % undergrads receiving aid | 41 |
| Avg frosh grant | $18,291 |
| Avg frosh loan | $3,104 |

# BRADLEY UNIVERSITY

1501 WEST BRADLEY AVENUE, PEORIA, IL 61625 • ADMISSIONS: 309-677-1000 • FAX: 309-677-2797

## CAMPUS LIFE

| Quality of Life Rating | 75 |
| --- | --- |
| Type of school | private |
| Affiliation | none |
| Environment | urban |

### STUDENTS

| | |
| --- | --- |
| Total undergrad enrollment | 5,116 |
| % male/female | 46/54 |
| % from out of state | 15 |
| % from public high school | 76 |
| % live on campus | 66 |
| % in (# of) fraternities | 34 (19) |
| % in (# of) sororities | 31 (11) |
| % African American | 5 |
| % Asian | 2 |
| % Caucasian | 87 |
| % Hispanic | 2 |
| % international | 2 |
| # of countries represented | 35 |

### SURVEY SAYS . . .

*Frats and sororities dominate social scene*
*(Almost) everyone smokes*
*Popular college radio*
*Hard liquor is popular*
*Lots of beer drinking*
*Athletic facilities need improving*
*Library needs improving*
*Students don't like Peoria, IL*
*Lousy food on campus*

## ACADEMICS

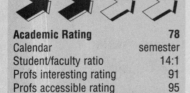

| Academic Rating | 78 |
| --- | --- |
| Calendar | semester |
| Student/faculty ratio | 14:1 |
| Profs interesting rating | 91 |
| Profs accessible rating | 95 |
| % profs teaching UG courses | 100 |
| Avg reg class size | 20-29 students |

### MOST POPULAR MAJORS
communications
elementary education
mechanical engineering

## STUDENTS SPEAK OUT
### Academics

Career-oriented undergraduates seeking the intimacy of a small college and the resources of a research institution might want to consider Bradley University. With just under 5,000 undergrads and nearly 1,000 grad students, Bradley is small enough to allow personal interaction between students and professors and big enough to offer more than 90 academic and pre-professional majors in five undergraduate colleges. Many who attend agree that "Bradley is the perfect size. The smaller school atmosphere has allowed me to get more involved in campus." Indicative of the level of intimacy here is the fact that "many professors include their home number on the syllabus so we can contact them. One even said we could call until 1 A.M. because they're on a college schedule, but after that to wait until the next day." The business, chemistry, and engineering departments all receive high marks here, and liberal arts faculty members have their advocates as well. Professors generally "are good. With small schools, the classes are small and close-knit, but class variety is limited. The trade-off is good, though." The administration gets mixed reviews; explains one student, "Academically, Bradley is run very well. But in the area of nonacademics, the administration needs to be more open." Writes another, "Administrators seem willing to hear students' questions but not necessarily as willing to do anything about them." Other student complaints center on the library ("out of date") and technology services. All in all, though, the students tell us that they're happy with the "memorable" and "excellent" academic experience that Bradley offers. "I love Bradley University," beams one sophomore. "I have never regretted my decision [to attend] at all."

### Life

Students describe a "laid-back," midwestern vibe permeating the "self-contained" and "pretty campus" at Bradley University. For some, especially those outside the Greek system, it's a little too laid back. Explains one student, "Bradley is a good school if you don't care about a social life." Those within Greek society, however, find plenty to fill their extracurricular hours. "Social life is somewhat Greek-oriented," concedes one frat member. Adds another student, "If you don't like Greek parties you are kind of screwed." For the alternatively inclined, "art parties are pretty hip, or you could go to local rock shows. Local bars are also popular." For all others, the school provides a few activities "specifically designed to get everyone on campus involved," but for the most part, students find few distractions enticing them from their studies. The gym facilities, a potential source of diversion, "need serious improvement." To make matters worse, most students agree that Peoria "is boring." On the positive side, it is "easy, quick, and convenient to get to and from class" at Bradley, especially considering the size of the undergraduate population. Also, brand new dorms are soon to be available for upperclassmen; in just a few years you'll be living in really swank digs.

### Student Body

"Most people are either athletes or Greeks" at Bradley, where the "atmosphere is on the conservative side, not so open to activism." However, "people are friendly for the most part," writes one student, and others further characterize their classmates as "outgoing," "courteous," "wealthy, educated," and "slightly motivated." Because the student body is small, "everyone knows everyone else [by the beginning of senior year], which can be a good thing or a bad thing." Some students say self-imposed racial and ethnic segregation is "obvious," but others feel that tolerance and unity are hallmarks here. "Bradley is like a family," coos a junior. "People from all different backgrounds are constantly interacting."

FINANCIAL AID: 309-677-3089 • E-MAIL: ADMISSIONS@BRADLEY.EDU • WEBSITE: WWW.BRADLEY.EDU

## ADMISSIONS

*Very important* academic and nonacademic factors considered by the admissions committee include essays, extracurricular activities, secondary school record, standardized test scores, volunteer work, and work experience. *Important* factors considered include talent/ability. *Other* factors considered include alumni/ae relation, character/personal qualities, and state residency. Factors *not* considered include class rank, geography, interview, minority status, recommendations, and religious affiliation/commitment. SAT I or ACT required. TOEFL required of all international applicants. High school diploma is required and GED is accepted. *High school units required/recommended:* 4 English required, 4 math recommended, 3 science recommended, 2 foreign language recommended, 3 social studies recommended.

## The Inside Word

Though students come here from far and wide, Bradley is best known within the Midwest and its reach is primarily regional. As a result, the admission process at Bradley is not super competitive; combined with solid academic quality and a broad range of offerings, this makes Bradley a worthwhile choice for those seeking to attend a strong school without running a grueling admissions gauntlet.

## FINANCIAL AID

*Students should submit:* FAFSA. The Princeton Review suggests that all financial aid forms be submitted as soon as possible after January 1. *Need-based scholarships/grants offered:* Pell, SEOG, state scholarships/grants, private scholarships, and the school's own gift aid. *Loan aid offered:* Direct Subsidized Stafford, Direct Unsubsidized Stafford, Direct PLUS, Federal Perkins, Federal Nursing, and college/university loans from institutional funds. Institutional employment available. Federal Work-Study Program available. Applicants will be notified of awards on a rolling basis. Off-campus job opportunities are good.

## FROM THE ADMISSIONS OFFICE

"Does the size of a college make a difference? Bradley's 5,000 undergraduates and 1,000 graduates think so. They like the opportunities, choices, and technologies of a larger university and the quality, personal attention, and challenge of a small, private college. Bradley's size makes so many things possible—recognition instead of anonymity, accessibility instead of bureaucracy, and academic choices instead of limits. Bradley students choose from more than 90 programs of study in the Foster College of Business Administration, Slane College of Communications and Fine Arts, College of Education and Health Sciences, College of Engineering and Technology, and Liberal Arts and Sciences. Clearly, size does make a difference."

## ADMISSIONS

| | | | |
|---|---|---|---|
| Admissions Rating | | | 76 |
| # of applicants | | | 4,821 |
| % of applicants accepted | | | 79 |
| % of acceptees attending | | | 28 |
| # accepting a place on wait list | | | 143 |
| % admitted from wait list | | | 64 |

### FRESHMAN PROFILE

| | |
|---|---|
| Average SAT Verbal | 590 |
| Average SAT Math | 610 |
| Range ACT Composite | 23-28 |
| Average ACT Composite | 25 |
| Minimum TOEFL | 500 |
| % graduated top 10% of class | 29 |
| % graduated top 25% of class | 60 |
| % graduated top 50% of class | 88 |

### DEADLINES

| | |
|---|---|
| Priority admission deadline | 3/1 |
| Regular admission | rolling |
| Regular notification | rolling |
| Nonfall registration? | yes |

## FINANCIAL FACTS

| | |
|---|---|
| Financial Aid Rating | 81 |
| Tuition | $14,500 |
| Room & board | $5,460 |
| Books and supplies | $500 |
| Required fees | $80 |
| % frosh receiving aid | 63 |
| % undergrads receiving aid | 72 |
| Avg frosh grant | $8,132 |
| Avg frosh loan | $3,672 |

# BRANDEIS UNIVERSITY

415 SOUTH ST., MS003, WALTHAM, MA 02454 • ADMISSIONS: 781-736-3500 • FAX: 781-736-3536

## STUDENTS SPEAK OUT
### Academics

Students who choose Brandeis expect both university-caliber facilities and a small-college experience. For the most part, they feel they get what they came for. "I love the fact that my school feels like a college, yet has so many resources," writes one undergrad. Muses another, "The school is large enough that it isn't stifling, but small enough that it is homey." Only a few complain that "Brandeis tries to be both a small liberal arts school and a research university. I think in trying to be both it succeeds at neither." Typical of a progressive university, "Brandeis has a continued commitment to improving the school. It is constantly reinventing itself." Students warn that "academics are tough and there's not much getting around it. Especially for pre-meds (computer science and biology students also complain of ultra-heavy workloads), things can get really stressful at times. However, the professors are very accessible and the advising, both peer and academic, is great." Economics, English, life sciences, theater arts, and Near Eastern and Jewish studies ("One of the best departments in the country!" raves one student) are among the many excellent majors here. Brandeis's core curriculum (math, science, humanities, and foreign language), which takes at least two semesters to complete, "makes sure we get a broad-based education." Students say the "wonderful professors" are "some of the biggest characters I've ever met" and are "genuinely concerned with the academic interests of their students." The administration "keeps the school running quite well, but they seem out of touch with the students." Among students' chief complaints: "We could really use a 24-hour study area year-round. Often I have to go to BC or MIT to study."

### Life

Brandeis has long been known as a low-key campus, but things are gradually changing. "Social life at Brandeis has slowly been improving since my freshman year," reports one senior. Popular happenings include "the fall weekend, called 'Louie, Louie,' and the spring weekend, 'Bronstein,' " as well as the "The Less You Wear, the Less You Pay" dance, which students deem "very entertaining." Also, "volunteer groups are very popular here and so are student-run theater and a cappella groups," and "the opportunities to join clubs and associations are terrific." Fraternity members say that, though frats are underground, they "try to remain active [even though] the administration does a pretty good job of suppressing our existence and badmouthing us to each year's incoming freshmen." Despite all these options, though, many students still choose to seek entertainment off campus. "Brandeis students tend to fall into two groups: on- and off-campus socializers," points out one undergrad. "Some spend all their time on campus doing various activities and seem to forget about the outside world. Others spend all their time in town (Waltham) or in Boston, stepping foot on campus only for class." An on-campus commuter rail takes students into downtown Boston in a scant half hour. Boston has "so much to offer," but "most things tend to close early."

### Student Body

Because Jewish students make up about half the population here, "Brandeis has a reputation for being a solely Jewish school, but in the two months I've been here I've found an amazing[ly diverse] group of friends, and everyone is more than willing to talk about their differences and explain their beliefs. That's one of the main things I love about this place: the lack of intolerance." Efforts to create a more diverse student body appear to be working. Explains one undergrad, "This place may have a 'Jew U' feel, but it's weakening as the student body diversifies . . . it's not the shtetl it used to be." Politically, "Brandeis is for people who are leaning to the left." Students "are politically active and working for social justice and awareness. It's an amazing place to be when we rally for recycling, GLBT issues, abortion rights, whatever." They also "tend to be highly opinionated . . . and passionate about causes." Don't expect the sports teams to win any major championships, though, since "everyone here is someone in your high school PE class that was completely ostracized."

FINANCIAL AID: 781-736-3700 • E-MAIL: SENDINFO@BRANDEIS.EDU • WEBSITE: WWW.BRANDEIS.EDU

## ADMISSIONS

*Very important* academic and nonacademic factors considered by the admissions committee include secondary school record. *Important* factors considered include class rank and standardized test scores. *Other* factors considered include alumni/ae relation, character/personal qualities, essays, extracurricular activities, geography, interview, minority status, recommendations, state residency, talent/ability, volunteer work, and work experience. Factors *not* considered include religious affiliation/commitment. TOEFL required of all international applicants. High school diploma is required and GED is accepted. *High school units recommended:* 12 total required; 15 total recommended; 4 English recommended, 3 math recommended, 1 science recommended, 3 foreign language recommended, 1 social studies recommended.

### The Inside Word

While the university has a reputation for quality, the low yield of admits who actually choose to attend Brandeis results in a higher acceptance rate than one might expect. Weak students will still find it difficult to gain admission. The option of submitting ACT scores instead of SAT and SAT II: Subject Test scores should be the hands-down choice of any candidate who doesn't have to take SAT IIs for any other reason.

## FINANCIAL AID

*Students should submit:* FAFSA, CSS/Financial Aid PROFILE, noncustodial (divorced/separated) parent's statement, and business/farm supplement. The Princeton Review suggests that all financial aid forms be submitted as soon as possible after January 1. *Need-based scholarships/grants offered:* Pell, SEOG, state scholarships/grants, private scholarships, and the school's own gift aid. *Loan aid offered:* Direct Subsidized Stafford, Direct Unsubsidized Stafford, Direct PLUS, Federal Perkins, state, and college/university loans from institutional funds. Institutional employment available. Federal Work-Study Program available. Applicants will be notified of awards on or about April 1. Off-campus job opportunities are excellent.

## FROM THE ADMISSIONS OFFICE

"Brandeis's top-ranked faculty focuses on teaching undergraduates and is accessible to students during classes, during office hours, and even at home. Students become involved in cutting-edge faculty research at the Volen Center for Complex Systems—studying the brain's cognitive process—and throughout the university. Brandeis has an ideal location on the commuter rail nine miles west of Boston; state-of-the-art sports facilities; and internships that complement interests in law, medicine, government, finance, the media, public service, and the arts. Brandeis offers broad renewable financial aid for domestic and international students, including both need- and merit-based scholarships that cover up to 75 percent of tuition."

## ADMISSIONS

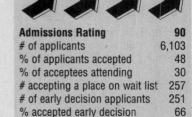

| | |
|---|---|
| Admissions Rating | 90 |
| # of applicants | 6,103 |
| % of applicants accepted | 48 |
| % of acceptees attending | 30 |
| # accepting a place on wait list | 257 |
| # of early decision applicants | 251 |
| % accepted early decision | 66 |

### FRESHMAN PROFILE

| | |
|---|---|
| Range SAT Verbal | 610-710 |
| Average SAT Verbal | 660 |
| Range SAT Math | 610-710 |
| Average SAT Math | 660 |
| Minimum TOEFL | 600 |
| Average HS GPA | 3.5 |
| % graduated top 10% of class | 61 |
| % graduated top 25% of class | 94 |
| % graduated top 50% of class | 100 |

### DEADLINES

| | |
|---|---|
| Early decision | 1/1 |
| Early decision notification | 2/1 |
| Regular admission | 1/31 |
| Regular notification | 4/15 |
| Nonfall registration? | yes |

### APPLICANTS ALSO LOOK AT
#### AND OFTEN PREFER
Cornell U.
Columbia
U. Penn
Brown
Amherst
#### AND SOMETIMES PREFER
Union Coll. (NY)
Tufts
Barnard
#### AND RARELY PREFER
Binghamton U.
Boston U.
Clark

### FINANCIAL FACTS

| | |
|---|---|
| Financial Aid Rating | 74 |
| Tuition | $25,392 |
| Room & board | $7,189 |
| Books and supplies | $500 |
| Required fees | $774 |
| % frosh receiving aid | 49 |
| % undergrads receiving aid | 50 |
| Avg frosh grant | $13,668 |
| Avg frosh loan | $3,599 |

# BRIGHAM YOUNG UNIVERSITY

A-183 ASB, Provo, UT 84602-1110 • Admissions: 801-378-2507 • Fax: 801-378-4264

## CAMPUS LIFE

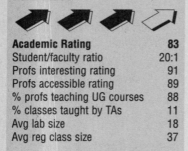

**Quality of Life Rating**     **92**
Type of school     private
Affiliation    Church of Jesus Christ of
Latter-day Saints
Environment     urban

### STUDENTS
Total undergrad enrollment    29,688
% male/female     48/52
% from out of state     71
% live on campus     20
% Asian     3
% Caucasian     91
% Hispanic     3
% Native American     1
% other     3
# of countries represented    108

### SURVEY SAYS . . .
*Very little drug use*
*Everyone loves the Cougars*
*Great food on campus*
*Lots of conservatives on campus*
*(Almost) everyone plays intramural sports*
*Very little beer drinking*
*(Almost) no one smokes*
*Very little hard liquor*
*Students are very religious*

## ACADEMICS

**Academic Rating**     **83**
Student/faculty ratio     20:1
Profs interesting rating     91
Profs accessible rating     89
% profs teaching UG courses     88
% classes taught by TAs     11
Avg lab size     18
Avg reg class size     37

### MOST POPULAR MAJORS
business management
family sciences
zoology

## STUDENTS SPEAK OUT
### Academics

The Church of Jesus Christ of Latter-day Saints is the lifeblood of affordable, "rigorous," and "academically demanding" Brigham Young University, where students enjoy a "one-of-a-kind academic and religious" experience. Tolerably broad curriculum requirements include a handful of general education courses as well as seven religious education courses. Though students tell us the enormous general education requirements "suck," they appreciate the "spiritual atmosphere" created by the emphasis on Mormonism and faith in general. "I love the way the professors incorporate religion into academics," says a theater major. "We have prayers in the classroom." In addition, students say BYU's "very accomplished" professors "know their stuff and do an excellent job teaching it," though some are "arrogant" and "seem to see teaching as secondary to their research and publishing responsibilities." Most professors here "really want you to learn," though, and they certainly push you to do it. Consequently, "studying requires a great amount of time," and virtually everyone here is "extremely serious" about academics. This huge private school is not a great place if you hate "red tape," though. "You have to visit 10 different offices to get anything done," gripes a senior.

### Life

Here in the "dull" but "nice" "Happy Valley" of Provo, students are annoyed by perpetual campus construction and a dearth of parking, but they cherish the "welcoming, uplifting," and "clean" "moral atmosphere" here—"the spirit of BYU." Every student must live according to an honor code, which prohibits the use of drugs, including alcohol, tobacco, and, yes, even caffeine. "People know how to have fun without getting high or smashed," says a sophomore. It's all "good, clean fun" and "Christian values" at BYU. After all, "who needs drugs or alcohol when you have Mormons?" Students say "there are always constructive events and activities" on and near campus. "There are tons of dances" as well as "movies, bowling, arcades," and intramural sports. "Great outdoor activities" including "hiking, climbing, biking" and skiing are also big. Most students attend church regularly (a requirement for all Mormon students) and devote themselves to volunteer work and church-related missionary activities. When BYU students aren't busy studying or swearing off vices, they're reportedly thinking, "When will I find my eternal mate?" In fact, so many students come to BYU looking for Mr. or Ms. Right that it has earned the nicknames "B-Y-Woo" and "the happy Mormon Marriage Hunting Grounds." As a first-year student observes, "dating and courtship are very important aspects of life." Everyone here from the administration on down goes "to great lengths to make sure you feel guilty if you graduate without being married."

### Student Body

A whopping 99 percent of the "tremendously homogenous" students at BYU belong to the Mormon Church, and there is a "common religious bond" here that the "straight arrow" students relish. "I appreciate being able to include God in a discussion and not being thought of as extreme for it," relates a sophomore. The thousands of students who "worked so hard to be here" because of their religious beliefs would agree with this sentiment. Many of the students we talked to didn't even apply anywhere else; it was BYU or bust. These "friendly and hardworking" students are "serious about education" and "eager to serve one another and the community." However, BYU students often come from "very sheltered" backgrounds, and can be "closed-minded," especially when it comes to nonconformity. "If you fit the 'norm,' students are very nice," says a senior. "Any variation is scorned, mocked, feared, or reported." And the ultrapositive, "friendly" attitude can seem mildly bizarre to outsiders. "You can't go anywhere without having someone hold a door open for you," exclaims a Georgia native. "It drives me crazy. Why can't I have some exposure to weirdo stalkers or something?"

FINANCIAL AID: 801-378-4104 • E-MAIL: ADMISSIONS@BYU.EDU • WEBSITE: WWW.BYU.EDU

## ADMISSIONS

*Very important* academic and nonacademic factors considered by the admissions committee include an ecclesiastical recommendation, secondary school record, and standardized test scores. *Important* factors considered include essays, demonstrated service, leadership, special talents, and other creative endeavors. *Other* factors considered include character/personal qualities, extracurricular activities, geography, minority status, recommendations, and work experience. Factors *not* considered include religious affiliation/commitment, state residency, alumni/ae relation, and class rank. ACT required. TOEFL required of all international applicants. High school diploma is required and GED is accepted. *High school units recommended:* 15-16 total; 4 English, 3 or 4 math, 2 to 3 lab science, 3 foreign language, and 2 history. *The admissions office says:* "Applicants must meet published application deadlines to be considered. Our applicants have agreed to abide by the University 'Code of Honor' and 'Dress and Grooming' guidelines prior to enrolling."

### The Inside Word

Despite the high acceptance rate, this is a rigorous application process that will quickly and efficiently eliminate candidates who make a poor match. Most eliminate themselves by not applying to begin with, as the matchmaking places the greatest weight on the ideological fit.

## FINANCIAL AID

The Princeton Review suggests that all financial aid forms be submitted as soon as possible after January 1. *Need-based scholarships/grants offered:* Pell, SEOG, state scholarships/grants, private scholarships, the school's own gift aid, and Federal Nursing. *Loan aid offered:* FFEL Subsidized Stafford, FFEL Unsubsidized Stafford, FFEL PLUS, Federal Perkins, and Federal Nursing. Federal Work-Study Program available. Off-campus job opportunities are good.

## FROM THE ADMISSIONS OFFICE

"The mission of Brigham Young University—founded, supported, and guided by the Church of Jesus Christ of Latter-day Saints—is to assist individuals in their quest for perfection and eternal life. That assistance should provide a period of intensive learning in a stimulating setting where a commitment to excellence is expected and the full realization of human potential is pursued. All instruction, programs, and services at BYU, including a wide variety of extracurricular experiences, should make their own contribution toward the balanced development of the total person. Such a broadly prepared individual will not only be capable of meeting personal challenge and change but will also bring strength to others in the tasks of home and family life, social relationships, civic duty, and service to mankind."

## ADMISSIONS

| | |
|---|---|
| Admissions Rating | 87 |
| # of applicants | 7,267 |
| % of applicants accepted | 74 |
| % of acceptees attending | 80 |

### FRESHMAN PROFILE

| | |
|---|---|
| Range ACT Composite | 25-29 |
| Average ACT Composite | 28 |
| Minimum TOEFL | 500 |
| Average HS GPA | 3.8 |
| % graduated top 10% of class | 54 |
| % graduated top 25% of class | 88 |
| % graduated top 50% of class | 98 |

### DEADLINES

| | |
|---|---|
| Regular admission | 2/15 |
| Nonfall registration? | yes |

### APPLICANTS ALSO LOOK AT
#### AND OFTEN PREFER
U. Utah
Utah State
Utah Valley State Coll.
#### AND RARELY PREFER
Boston U.
U. Texas—Austin
UC—Berkeley
U. Michigan—Ann Arbor
U. Washington

## FINANCIAL FACTS

| | |
|---|---|
| Financial Aid Rating | 88 |
| Comprehensive tuition | $7,590 |
| Tuition | $2,940 |
| Room & board | $4,650 |
| Books and supplies | $1,080 |
| % frosh receiving aid | 28 |
| % undergrads receiving aid | 35 |
| Avg frosh grant | $2,278 |
| Avg frosh loan | $2,809 |

# BROWN UNIVERSITY

BOX 1876, 45 PROSPECT STREET, PROVIDENCE, RI 02912 • ADMISSIONS: 401-863-2378 • FAX: 401-863-9300

## CAMPUS LIFE

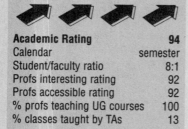

| | |
|---|---|
| **Quality of Life Rating** | **88** |
| Type of school | private |
| Affiliation | none |
| Environment | urban |

### STUDENTS

| | |
|---|---|
| Total undergrad enrollment | 6,029 |
| % male/female | 47/53 |
| % from out of state | 96 |
| % from public high school | 60 |
| % live on campus | 85 |
| % in (# of) fraternities | 11 (10) |
| % in (# of) sororities | 9 (3) |
| % African American | 7 |
| % Asian | 16 |
| % Caucasian | 60 |
| % Hispanic | 7 |
| % Native American | 1 |
| % international | 7 |
| # of countries represented | 72 |

### SURVEY SAYS . . .

*Political activism is hot*
*Students aren't religious*
*Great off-campus food*
*Class discussions are rare*
*Ethnic diversity on campus*
*Intercollegiate sports unpopular or nonexistent*

## ACADEMICS

| | |
|---|---|
| **Academic Rating** | **94** |
| Calendar | semester |
| Student/faculty ratio | 8:1 |
| Profs interesting rating | 92 |
| Profs accessible rating | 92 |
| % profs teaching UG courses | 100 |
| % classes taught by TAs | 13 |

### MOST POPULAR MAJORS
biology
economics
international relations

## STUDENTS SPEAK OUT

### Academics

The current trend in undergraduate education is toward more structured curricula and increased requirements for graduation. In this regard—and perhaps only in this regard—popular Brown University remains defiantly unfashionable. Brown's New Curriculum imposes no course requirements on undergrads. Furthermore, it includes an unusually lenient grading system that allows students to choose between ABC/No Credit (wherein grades below C do not appear on students' transcripts) and Pass/No Credit (essentially Pass/Fail without the Fail option). Writes one student, "Brown is definitely the school for those who want an active role in their education. Students are given an immense amount of freedom and there are amazing resources and teachers at one's disposal. It does, however, take initiative on the students' part." One benefit of the system is that "students are self-driven, yet the academic atmosphere is relaxed. Competition between students is practically nonexistent." Some complain, however, that "the New Curriculum is a cop-out for professors to forego their responsibilities toward students. They never reach out until you fail." Despite the apparent laxity of Brown's policies, "This school is tough, but it's worth it. My teachers love students, teaching, and their field. My overall experience has been great. Every class can rock if you put in the effort. It's almost impossible to do all of the work for all of your classes, though. It's all about selective slacking for survival." Professors, who "are generally open and available outside of class," will make "incredible research opportunities" available to students who seek them out.

### Life

Brown's high-profile, Ivy League status means "life on campus is pretty stressful. People are busy and very active in student organizations. People are excited but usually highly stressed. Fun includes a huge range of things—not just drinking." Brown provides "tons of activities on campus," including " frat parties and nonfrat parties, cultural shows, excellent theater and music groups, foreign flicks, lectures, sporting events, diverse interest groups, etc. You don't really have to leave campus." Another student agrees, "Most social life revolves around the campus and on-campus parties. There are also some clubs downtown and a budding music scene. You can do this or just chill with friends." Brown's long-standing reputation as a hotbed of political activism is the subject of some debate among students. Some tell us that "Brown isn't as politically correct as people think. There's a small percentage of people who are really frenzied, but the rest of us are pretty laid back, if not annoyed by the outspoken minority." Another points out that "many activist groups are present on campus, although not to the extent that we are stereotyped for."

### Student Body

The consensus among Brown students is that "the student body is amazingly diverse, but groups with different backgrounds tend to remain segregated from each other." Students also acknowledge that they are, as a group, "very wealthy." One student notes, "I think classism is a big issue here." Still, the vast majority of our respondents express deep admiration for their classmates and satisfaction with their choice of schools: "I've never felt more comfortable with my peers than at Brown." Students also describe their classmates as "overachievers, but they compete against themselves, not each other."

# BROWN UNIVERSITY

## ADMISSIONS

*Very important* academic and nonacademic factors considered by the admissions committee include secondary school record. *Important* factors considered include character/personal qualities, class rank, minority status, standardized test scores, state residency, talent/ability, and volunteer work. *Other* factors considered include alumni/ae relation, essays, extracurricular activities, geography, interview, recommendations, and work experience. Factors *not* considered include religious affiliation/commitment. TOEFL required of all international applicants. High school diploma is required and GED is not accepted. *High school units required/recommended:* 4 English required, 3 math recommended, 3 science recommended, 3 foreign language recommended, 3 social studies recommended, 3 history recommended.

### The Inside Word

The cream of just about every crop applies to Brown. Gaining admission requires more than just a superior academic profile from high school. Some candidates, such as the sons and daughters of Brown graduates (who are admitted at virtually double the usual acceptance rate), have a better chance for admission than most others. Minority students benefit from some courtship, particularly once admitted. Ivies like to share the wealth and distribute offers of admission across a wide range of constituencies. Candidates from states that are overrepresented in the applicant pool, such as New York, have to be particularly distinguished in order to have the best chance at admission. So do those who attend high schools with many seniors applying to Brown, as it is rare for more than two or three students from any one school to be offered admission.

## FINANCIAL AID

*Students should submit:* FAFSA, CSS/Financial Aid PROFILE, noncustodial (divorced/separated) parent's statement, and business/farm supplement. Regular filing deadline is February 1. The Princeton Review suggests that all financial aid forms be submitted as soon as possible after January 1. *Need-based scholarships/grants offered:* Pell, SEOG, state scholarships/grants, private scholarships, and the school's own gift aid. *Loan aid offered:* Direct Subsidized Stafford, Direct Unsubsidized Stafford, Direct PLUS, Federal Perkins, state, and college/university loans from institutional funds. Institutional employment available. Federal Work-Study Program available. Applicants will be notified of awards on or about April 1. Off-campus job opportunities are good.

## FROM THE ADMISSIONS OFFICE

"It is our pleasure to introduce you to a unique and wonderful learning place: Brown University. Brown was founded in 1764 and is a private, coeducational, Ivy League university in which the intellectual development of undergraduate students is fostered by a dedicated faculty on a traditional New England campus."

## ADMISSIONS

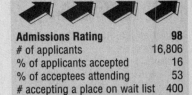

| Admissions Rating | 98 |
|---|---|
| # of applicants | 16,806 |
| % of applicants accepted | 16 |
| % of acceptees attending | 53 |
| # accepting a place on wait list | 400 |
| % admitted from wait list | 48 |

### FRESHMAN PROFILE

| | |
|---|---|
| Range SAT Verbal | 640-750 |
| Average SAT Verbal | 690 |
| Range SAT Math | 650-740 |
| Average SAT Math | 690 |
| Range ACT Composite | 27-32 |
| Average ACT Composite | 29 |
| Minimum TOEFL | 600 |
| % graduated top 10% of class | 87 |
| % graduated top 25% of class | 97 |
| % graduated top 50% of class | 100 |

### DEADLINES

| | |
|---|---|
| Regular admission | 1/1 |
| Regular notification | 4/1 |
| Nonfall registration? | yes |

### APPLICANTS ALSO LOOK AT
**AND OFTEN PREFER**
Harvard
Princeton
Yale
Stanford
**AND SOMETIMES PREFER**
Swarthmore
Amherst
Williams
Smith
**AND RARELY PREFER**
Tufts
Georgetown U.
Bowdoin
Oberlin

### FINANCIAL FACTS

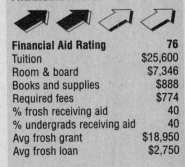

| Financial Aid Rating | 76 |
|---|---|
| Tuition | $25,600 |
| Room & board | $7,346 |
| Books and supplies | $888 |
| Required fees | $774 |
| % frosh receiving aid | 40 |
| % undergrads receiving aid | 40 |
| Avg frosh grant | $18,950 |
| Avg frosh loan | $2,750 |

# BRYN MAWR COLLEGE

101 NORTH MERION AVENUE, BRYN MAWR, PA 19010-2899 • ADMISSIONS: 610-526-5152 • FAX: 610-526-7471

## CAMPUS LIFE

**Quality of Life Rating**    **86**
Type of school    private
Affiliation    none
Environment    suburban

### STUDENTS
Total undergrad enrollment    1,358
% male/female    1/99
% from out of state    72
% from public high school    73
% live on campus    91
% African American    4
% Asian    18
% Caucasian    75
% Hispanic    3
% international    7
# of countries represented    44

### SURVEY SAYS . . .
*Theater is hot*
*No one cheats*
*Great food on campus*
*Dorms are like palaces*
*Campus feels safe*
*Very little beer drinking*
*No one plays intramural sports*
*Very little hard liquor*
*Intercollegiate sports unpopular or nonexistent*

## ACADEMICS

**Academic Rating**    **93**
Calendar    semester
Student/faculty ratio    9:1
Profs interesting rating    95
Profs accessible rating    97
% profs teaching UG courses    100
Avg lab size    10-19 students
Avg reg class size    10-19 students

### MOST POPULAR MAJORS
English
history
chemistry

## STUDENTS SPEAK OUT

### Academics

"If you want a fantastic education with lots of personal attention, come to Bryn Mawr," advises a political science major. However, "you'd better know what you are getting into." The "intimate" atmosphere of this "stellar" and "distinct women's community" is "very academically focused" and "social life always has to come after academics." The core curriculum is "rigid," required seminars are "the bane of every student's existence," and the "intense" workload here is the stuff of legend. A highly praised honor code allows each student to schedule her own exams, though, and "Mawrters" can also take courses at nearby Haverford, Swarthmore, and the University of Pennsylvania. Also, unlike most colleges, the administration at Bryn Mawr "is usually effective" (except for the "terrifying" registrar) and "able to pull strings in unusual situations." Students gripe, though, that they "wait in line way too often—for food, registration, at the campus post office. The school could easily accommodate its students but instead has a love affair with bureaucracy and paperwork." There are no complaints, however, about the "amazing, brilliant, accessible" professors here. They "engage students in lively discussions, whether it's a class in biology or classical archaeology," and they are "always willing to work with you after class." A first-year student seems to have had a representative academic experience: "I came to Bryn Mawr with a dread of chemistry. My experience in high school was awful. However, the chemistry professors here are so dedicated, friendly, and are such good teachers that I'm thinking about majoring in it."

### Life

Students say Bryn Mawr is a combination of "a work camp, a cult, and a summer camp" that is "disconnected from the outside world." In fact, "it sometimes can be difficult to pull students out of the library." "This is not a party school," to say the very least. "For fun, people talk—about everything," explains one student. They "discuss philosophy in coffeehouses and hang out in bookstores" and "sit in the halls of the dorms and do problem sets, labs, whatever." "Hall acrobatics" and "wrestling" are also commonplace in the dorms. "Schoolwork is always at the center" of Mawrters' lives, though, and "this makes having fun somewhat difficult because you're always thinking about it." Students still "make an effort to have a social life." On weekends, "there's an exodus" to the coed social scenes at nearby Haverford and Swarthmore, and Philadelphia is close by as well. On campus, "there are a few organizations trying to rescue some obscure activist in China" and Mawrters frequently attend cultural events. In addition, the school "tries to have special events" ("but they're often nerdy guitar players or puppeteers") and a series of splendid campus traditions keeps students entertained. "On any given weekend, I'll balance two papers, a bunch of parties, a couple of rehearsals, and a trip to Philadelphia's Chinatown for the best dim sum ever," relates a typical Bryn Mawr student.

### Student Body

The "incredibly driven" women at Bryn Mawr are definitely not at a loss of adjectives to describe themselves. They are "motivated to the point of collapse" and they "eat, think, and dream whatever it is they are studying." They are "unrelenting" and "very serious about their academic work" and themselves. "There's a major guilt complex about not working in order to have a good time. It's like the plague," says a junior. "You will not find drifters or perpetual students here. Mawrters are going places." They are "too uptight and stressed," though, as well as "overworked and tired," not to mention "arrogant," "pretentious, and annoying." "Most seem to have a problem with everything they possibly can," observes one student. A few are "obnoxious vegans" and nearly all are politically active liberals. "The intelligent outcast girls" at Bryn Mawr can also be "quirky," "amicable, fun, and just eccentric enough to make life interesting." They are "feisty, independent, poised, and confident"—"the most outgoing and fun people in the world." Many are "extremely friendly" and there is "a very high level of respect for one another's ideas, beliefs, and personal dignity" on this "very diverse" campus.

FINANCIAL AID: 610-526-5245 • E-MAIL: ADMISSIONS@BRYNMAWR.EDU • WEBSITE: WWW.BRYNMAWR.EDU

## ADMISSIONS

*Very important* academic and nonacademic factors considered by the admissions committee include essays, extracurricular activities, recommendations, secondary school record, and standardized test scores. *Important* factors considered include interview. *Other* factors considered include alumni/ae relation, character/personal qualities, class rank, talent/ability, volunteer work, and work experience. Factors *not* considered include geography, minority status, religious affiliation/commitment, and state residency. TOEFL required of all international applicants. High school diploma is required and GED is accepted. *High school units required/recommended:* 16 total required; 20 total recommended; 4 English required, 3 math required, 4 math recommended, 2 science required, 3 science recommended, 2 science lab required, 3 science lab recommended, 2 foreign language required, 4 foreign language recommended, 2 social studies required, 2 history required, 1 elective required.

### The Inside Word

Do not be deceived by Bryn Mawr's admit rate; its student body is among the best in the nation academically. Outstanding preparation for graduate study draws an applicant pool that is well prepared and intellectually curious. The admissions committee includes eight faculty members and four seniors. Each applicant is reviewed by four readers, including at least one faculty member and one student.

## FINANCIAL AID

*Students should submit:* FAFSA, CSS/Financial Aid PROFILE, noncustodial (divorced/separated) parent's statement, and business/farm supplement. Regular filing deadline is January 15. The Princeton Review suggests that all financial aid forms be submitted as soon as possible after January 1. *Need-based scholarships/grants offered:* Pell, SEOG, state scholarships/grants, private scholarships, and the school's own gift aid. *Loan aid offered:* FFEL Subsidized Stafford, FFEL Unsubsidized Stafford, FFEL PLUS, Federal Perkins, college/university loans from institutional funds, and Teri Loans. Institutional employment available. Federal Work-Study Program available. Applicants will be notified of awards on or about April 1. Off-campus job opportunities are good.

## FROM THE ADMISSIONS OFFICE

"Prepare to be surprised. One wouldn't ordinarily assume that a small institution could offer as diverse a range of opportunities as many large universities, or that some of the residence halls at a women's college would be coeducational, or that a campus looking like the English countryside could exist within 20 minutes of downtown Philadelphia. But Bryn Mawr is not an ordinary institution. Bryn Mawr was founded in 1885 to extend to women the opportunity for rigorous academic training, including the study of Greek, mathematics, and philosophy, that was then available only to men. Being small, it could offer a kind of attention to the needs and concerns of its students that large universities could not. Being new and somewhat arrogant, it could challenge educational convention whenever that seemed important. Those traditions continue, and Bryn Mawr is today very much a demanding and caring place where both ideas and individuals matter very much."

## ADMISSIONS

| | |
|---|---|
| Admissions Rating | 92 |
| # of applicants | 1,596 |
| % of applicants accepted | 59 |
| % of acceptees attending | 35 |
| # accepting a place on wait list | 94 |
| % admitted from wait list | 28 |
| # of early decision applicants | 132 |
| % accepted early decision | 64 |

### FRESHMAN PROFILE

| | |
|---|---|
| Range SAT Verbal | 620-710 |
| Average SAT Verbal | 665 |
| Range SAT Math | 590-680 |
| Average SAT Math | 636 |
| Range ACT Composite | 26-31 |
| Average ACT Composite | 29 |
| Minimum TOEFL | 600 |
| % graduated top 10% of class | 60 |
| % graduated top 25% of class | 93 |
| % graduated top 50% of class | 100 |

### DEADLINES

| | |
|---|---|
| Early decision | 11/15 |
| Early decision notification | 12/15 |
| Regular admission | 1/15 |
| Regular notification | 4/15 |

### APPLICANTS ALSO LOOK AT
**AND OFTEN PREFER**
Brown
Yale
Princeton
**AND SOMETIMES PREFER**
Wellesley
Swarthmore
Smith
Mount Holyoke
Vassar
**AND RARELY PREFER**
Haverford
Oberlin

### FINANCIAL FACTS

| | |
|---|---|
| Financial Aid Rating | 76 |
| Tuition | $22,730 |
| Room & board | $8,100 |
| Books and supplies | $1,400 |
| Required fees | $630 |
| % frosh receiving aid | 58 |
| % undergrads receiving aid | 59 |
| Avg frosh grant | $16,226 |
| Avg frosh loan | $1,294 |

# BUCKNELL UNIVERSITY

FREAS HALL, LEWISBURG, PA 17837 • ADMISSIONS: 570-577-1101 • FAX: 570-577-3538

## CAMPUS LIFE

**Quality of Life Rating**    **89**
Type of school    private
Affiliation    none
Environment    rural

### STUDENTS

| | |
|---|---|
| Total undergrad enrollment | 3,426 |
| % male/female | 52/48 |
| % from out of state | 66 |
| % from public high school | 71 |
| % live on campus | 87 |
| % in (# of) fraternities | 39 (13) |
| % in (# of) sororities | 44 (7) |
| % African American | 3 |
| % Asian | 5 |
| % Caucasian | 86 |
| % Hispanic | 3 |
| % international | 2 |
| # of countries represented | 32 |

### SURVEY SAYS . . .

*Frats and sororities dominate social
scene
Great food on campus
Great library
Low cost of living
Diversity lacking on campus*

## ACADEMICS

**Academic Rating**    **89**
Calendar    semester
Student/faculty ratio    12:1
Profs interesting rating    94
Profs accessible rating    97
% profs teaching UG courses    100
Avg lab size    10-19 students
Avg reg class size    10-19 students

### MOST POPULAR MAJORS
business administration
economics
biology

## STUDENTS SPEAK OUT
### Academics

Engineering, science, and business are among the top drawing cards at Bucknell University, where tomorrow's leaders (and the sons and daughters of today's leaders) enjoy a great faculty, up-to-date facilities, and—perhaps most important to students—"a great reputation. Everyone that goes here has worked hard in their life to actually make it here, so you know that they are smart." Professors here "are unbelievably enthusiastic and genuinely care about their students." Administrators receive similarly high praise. Reports one student, "I have eaten meals with school administrators. They are very accessible. If I ever need to speak with a dean, I never have to wait more than a couple of minutes even if I show up without an appointment." All of these institutional assets help students handle the "challenging" academic environment at Bucknell, which is definitely not for the faint at heart. "The workload is tough," warns one student, and competition for good grades is stiff.

### Life

On Bucknell's "gorgeous" campus, most agree that "the Greek system is everything. It's a great place to party and drink for free. The parties are loud and crazy, and everyone basically gets drunk and hooks up." This helps make up for the fact that "there is not much to do in this area." Some warn that "the Greek stuff makes our school cliquey. It also makes dating a rare thing. Sororities are usually fun, except during rush, which is miserable. You are basically judged based on a short first impression. . . . A lot of girls cry during the process." For those adverse to Greek life or crying, "Bucknell is really good at having events on the weekends that people who do not want to participate in Greek life can attend. There are always movies being shown or comedians or musical entertainment." Adds one student, "Bucknell really tries to bring in programs that would be attractive for students to participate in." As far as hometown Lewisburg is concerned, "it's a quaint Victorian-style town, but it's rather lacking as far as activities go. There aren't really any stores of interest in town other than the CVS and grocery store. This makes it hard on freshman, since no cars are permitted first year. There is a mall, a Wal-Mart, and a K-mart in the area, but none are within walking distance." Reports one student, "The school needs to improve the relations between students and the town; there have been problems with off-campus houses and parties disrupting" members of the community.

### Student Body

A homogeneous, upper-crust student body has always been part of Bucknell's reputation. According to students, that reputation is justified. Writes one student, "Everyone here is pretty much the same. You wear J.Crew and Abercrombie, you join a frat or sorority, you have a stylish and conservative haircut. It sounds scary, but it really isn't." Jokes one undergrad, "It's kind of irritating that everyone here is so incredibly attractive, although you get used to it. Actually, I'm not complaining. It's weird to go home, though, and realize that in the real world not every girl is a size two and has long, blonde hair." Students are comfortable with their classmates, reporting that "most of the kids at Bucknell are nice. It's not the most intellectual school on the face of the planet, but the kids are friendly, 'good kids.'"

FINANCIAL AID: 570-577-1331 • E-MAIL: ADMISSIONS@BUCKNELL.EDU • WEBSITE: WWW.BUCKNELL.EDU

## ADMISSIONS

*Very important* academic and nonacademic factors considered by the admissions committee include secondary school record and standardized test scores. *Important* factors considered include alumni/ae relation, character/personal qualities, class rank, extracurricular activities, recommendations, talent/ability, volunteer work, and work experience. *Other* factors considered include essays, interview, and minority status. Factors *not* considered include geography, religious affiliation/commitment and state residency. SAT I or ACT required, SAT I preferred. TOEFL required of all international applicants. High school diploma is required and GED is accepted. *High school units required/recommended:* 16 total required; 4 English required, 3 math required, 2 science required, 1 science lab required, 2 foreign language required, 3 social studies required. *The admissions office says:* "At Bucknell, each applicant has every piece of his or her credentials read and evaluated by professional staff. It is a personal, hands-on process, one that is not driven by a formula or indices, but one that attempts to assess an individual's capability for becoming a productive and contributing member of the Bucknell community."

### The Inside Word

Each application is read by two admissions officers. If you are serious about attending Bucknell and have strong grades and test scores, there is little to get in your way. Still, overconfidence or a so-so match can throw a wrench in the plans of some; recent trends show larger numbers on the university's wait list and a track record of increased competitiveness for admission.

## FINANCIAL AID

*Students should submit:* FAFSA, CSS/Financial Aid PROFILE, noncustodial (divorced/separated) parent's statement, and business/farm supplement. Regular filing deadline is January 1. The Princeton Review suggests that all financial aid forms be submitted as soon as possible after January 1. *Need-based scholarships/grants offered:* Pell, SEOG, state scholarships/grants, private scholarships, and the school's own gift aid. *Loan aid offered:* FFEL Subsidized Stafford, FFEL Unsubsidized Stafford, FFEL PLUS, and Federal Perkins. Institutional employment available. Federal Work-Study Program available. Applicants will be notified of awards on or about April 10. Off-campus job opportunities are poor.

## FROM THE ADMISSIONS OFFICE

"Bucknell offers a unique learning environment and is one of a few primarily undergraduate colleges that offers the opportunity to investigate both the human and technical aspects of life in the 21st century. A major curricular revision was implemented by the faculty in 1993. All students enrolling in the College of Arts and Sciences will complete a first-year foundation seminar; distributional requirements which include four humanities courses, two social science courses, and three courses in natural science and mathematics; broadened perspectives for the 21st century consisting of one course each in natural and fabricated worlds and on human diversity; departmental, college, or interdepartmental majors; and a capstone seminar or experience during the senior year. Bucknell also requires all students to complete three writing emphasis courses."

## ADMISSIONS

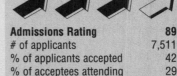

| | |
|---|---|
| Admissions Rating | 89 |
| # of applicants | 7,511 |
| % of applicants accepted | 42 |
| % of acceptees attending | 29 |
| # accepting a place on wait list | 910 |
| % admitted from wait list | 2 |
| # of early decision applicants | 591 |
| % accepted early decision | 52 |

### FRESHMAN PROFILE

| | |
|---|---|
| Range SAT Verbal | 580-660 |
| Average SAT Verbal | 622 |
| Range SAT Math | 620-690 |
| Average SAT Math | 653 |
| Range ACT Composite | 26-30 |
| Minimum TOEFL | 550 |
| % graduated top 10% of class | 58 |
| % graduated top 50% of class | 99 |

### DEADLINES

| | |
|---|---|
| Early decision | 11/15 |
| Early decision notification | 12/15 |
| Regular admission | 1/1 |
| Regular notification | 4/1 |

### APPLICANTS ALSO LOOK AT

**AND OFTEN PREFER**
Cornell U.
Middlebury
Duke
Dartmouth

**AND SOMETIMES PREFER**
Boston Coll.
Colgate
Villanova
Penn State—Univ. Park
Lehigh

**AND RARELY PREFER**
Lafayette

### FINANCIAL FACTS

| | |
|---|---|
| Financial Aid Rating | 74 |
| Tuition | $25,144 |
| Room & board | $5,761 |
| Books and supplies | $750 |
| Required fees | $191 |
| % frosh receiving aid | 45 |
| % undergrads receiving aid | 52 |
| Avg frosh grant | $19,024 |
| Avg frosh loan | $3,191 |

# CALIFORNIA INSTITUTE OF TECHNOLOGY

1200 EAST CALIFONIA BOULEVARD, PASÁDENA, CA 91125 • ADMISSIONS: 626-395-6341 • FAX: 626-683-3026

## CAMPUS LIFE

**Quality of Life Rating**     **76**
Type of school     private
Affiliation     none
Environment     suburban

### STUDENTS

| | |
|---|---|
| Total undergrad enrollment | 929 |
| % male/female | 68/32 |
| % from out of state | 60 |
| % from public high school | 70 |
| % live on campus | 87 |
| % African American | 1 |
| % Asian | 25 |
| % Caucasian | 58 |
| % Hispanic | 6 |
| % international | 9 |

### SURVEY SAYS . . .

*Class discussions are rare*
*Great food on campus*
*Students get along with local community*
*Diverse students interact*
*Student publications are ignored*
*Campus difficult to get around*
*Beautiful campus*
*Students aren't religious*

## ACADEMICS

**Academic Rating**     **95**
Calendar     quarter
Student/faculty ratio     3:1
Profs interesting rating     68
Profs accessible rating     70
Avg lab size     10-19 students
Avg reg class size     10-19 students

### MOST POPULAR MAJORS
engineering/applied science
biology
electrical engineering

## STUDENTS SPEAK OUT
### Academics

Students at the California Institute of Technology brag that their school offers "the best programs for science and technology in the country" and, unlike many similarly proud undergrads at other institutions, they may just be right. Certainly Caltech boasts an impressive faculty, one that could allow a student to boast that he's "had lunch with no fewer than three Nobel laureates. People here are really accessible; you can pretty much wander into anyone's office." Access to all this brilliance, world-class facilities, and a "suicidal (yet effective) work-load" constitute Caltech's formula for greatness. An excellent teaching faculty, alas, is not part of the equation. Professors "are great researchers and horrible teachers" who "give vaguely coherent lectures, then let us learn the material from the homework and tests." Instruction isn't uniformly obtuse: "Half the pro-fessors know the material too well to teach it, but the other half remember the joy of learning and care enough about their students to make every lecture worth waking up for at 8 A.M." Elaborates one student, "Typically, the CORE courses are poorly taught by very good professors. The professors in the upper-division classes are much better teachers, and the classes are smaller, which also helps." The workload at Caltech increases as the instruction improves; writes one stu-dent, "The freshman academic load is bearable, almost easy, but it gets harder every year. Students are encouraged to do homework in groups, which makes the most difficult homework sets much more bearable." The school works hard to help students deal with the academic pressure. First-year classes are Pass/Fail and "instead of strict rules and policies, people at Caltech follow an Honor Code. It gives students a lot of privileges such as take-home exams, collaboration on homework, and access to master keys."

### Life

Life at Caltech is defined by the workload, which "is ludicrously intense. Unlike anything else anywhere, at least eight hours of study a day. I love it." Most stu-dents arrive at Caltech a little on the eccentric side, but even those who don't find the academic pressure pushing them in that direction. "Some guy filled his room with string and now lives in a spider's web," reports one student matter-of-factly. For fun, students report that "building things and taking them apart again is good, aside from some of the safety hazards posed by having half-assembled Wheels O' Death and flaming bits of former objets d'art filling the courtyard." Students also "build things, then burn them or blow them up" and "freeze stuff with liquid nitrogen." "We try to pack as much fun into as little time as possible (not because we want to but because we have to)," explains a sophomore. Caltech's world-renowned pranks like "turning the library into a lighted Christmas tree" and "filling professors' offices with lime gelatin on their birthdays" are perennially popular. Sports are also widely enjoyed and are open to any student. The unique "half dorm/half frat" housing system is "great! House members are like one big (sometimes dysfunctional) family." After a "shopping week," students are matched up with houses that fit their personal-ities. "Caltech is a weird, wacky, wonderful place," sums up one student.

### Student Body

How smart are the students of Caltech? "We might have the only flag football team in which the total IQ of the players is greater than their total weight," opines one undergrad. "Be prepared to change from number one to average," warns another. Students here "tend to be linear thinkers with little interest in the humani-ties. It can be a shock to go back into the real world and realize that not everyone thinks like you do." Tech undergrads "come from many different backgrounds" and share "a strong sense of community." Students have "lots of bizarre talents," although according to some, social grace is not among them; "Most of them are brilliant," writes one student, "but highly socially inept." Responding to a ques-tion about areas in which the school might improve, one undergrad suggests: "The admissions committee could let some normal people in."

# CALIFORNIA INSTITUTE OF TECHNOLOGY

FINANCIAL AID: 626-395-6280 • E-MAIL: UGADMISSIONS@CALTECH.EDU • WEBSITE: WWW.ADMISSIONS.CALTECH.EDU

## ADMISSIONS

*Very important* academic and nonacademic factors considered by the admissions committee include secondary school record and character/personal qualities. *Important* factors considered include recommendations, standardized test scores, essay, extracurricular activities, and talent/ability. *Other* factors considered include volunteer work and work experience. Factors *not* considered include interview, alumni/ae relation, geographical residence, state residency, religious affiliation, and minority status. SAT I and SAT II required. *High school units required/recommended:* 13 total required; 19 total recommended; 4 English required, 3 math required, 3 science required, 3 science lab required. *The admissions office says:* "Because we are so small, our admissions process is very individualized—every application is reviewed several times and discussed in small committees, so we get to know every applicant very well."

### The Inside Word

A mere glance at Caltech's freshman profile can discourage all but the most self-confident of high school seniors. It should. The impact of grades and test scores on the admissions process is minimized significantly when virtually every freshman was in the top fifth of his or her high school class and has a 1400 SAT. The admissions office isn't kidding when they emphasize the personal side of their criteria. Six students are on the admissions committee; every file is read at least twice. The process is all about matchmaking, and the Tech staff is very interested in getting to know you. Don't apply unless you have more than high numbers to offer.

## FINANCIAL AID

The Princeton Review suggests that all financial aid forms be submitted as soon as possible after January 1. *Need-based scholarships/grants offered:* Pell, SEOG, state scholarships/grants, private scholarships, the school's own gift aid and Federal Nursing. *Loan aid offered:* FFEL Subsidized Stafford, FFEL Unsubsidized Stafford, FFEL PLUS, Federal Perkins, and Federal Nursing. Institutional employment available. Federal Work-Study Program available. Off-campus job opportunities are excellent.

## FROM THE ADMISSIONS OFFICE

"Admission to the freshman class is based on many factors—some quantifiable, some not. What you say in your application is important! And, because we don't interview students for admission, your letters of recommendation are weighed heavily. High school academic performance is very important, as is a demonstrated interest in math, science, and/or engineering. We are also interested in your character, maturity, and motivation. We are very proud of the process we use to select each freshman class. It's very individual, it has great integrity, and we believe it serves all the students who apply. If you have any questions about the process or about Caltech in general, write us a letter or give us a call. We'd like to hear from you!"

## ADMISSIONS

| | |
|---|---|
| **Admissions Rating** | **98** |
| # of applicants | 3,515 |
| % of applicants accepted | 13 |
| % of acceptees attending | 43 |
| # accepting a place on wait list | 90 |
| % admitted from wait list | 42 |

### FRESHMAN PROFILE

| | |
|---|---|
| Range SAT Verbal | 690-780 |
| Average SAT Verbal | 727 |
| Range SAT Math | 760-800 |
| Average SAT Math | 776 |
| % graduated top 10% of class | 98 |

### DEADLINES

| | |
|---|---|
| Regular admission | 1/1 |
| Regular notification | 4/1 |

### APPLICANTS ALSO LOOK AT
#### AND OFTEN PREFER
Stanford
Harvard
Princeton
#### AND SOMETIMES PREFER
MIT
UC—Berkeley
Harvey Mudd
Georgia Tech.
RPI
#### AND RARELY PREFER
Virginia Poly. Inst.

## FINANCIAL FACTS

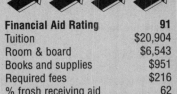

| | |
|---|---|
| **Financial Aid Rating** | **91** |
| Tuition | $20,904 |
| Room & board | $6,543 |
| Books and supplies | $951 |
| Required fees | $216 |
| % frosh receiving aid | 62 |
| % undergrads receiving aid | 67 |
| Avg frosh grant | $20,453 |
| Avg frosh loan | $3,383 |

# CALIF. POLYTECHNIC STATE U.—SAN LUIS OBISPO

1 GRAND AVENUE, SAN LUIS OBISPO, CA 93407 • ADMISSIONS: 805-756-2311 • FAX: 805-756-5400

## CAMPUS LIFE

**Quality of Life Rating** 83
Type of school public
Affiliation none
Environment suburban

### STUDENTS
Total undergrad enrollment 15,867
% male/female 56/44
% from out of state 4
% from public high school 91
% live on campus 18
% in (# of) fraternities 6 (25)
% in (# of) sororities 4 (10)
% African American 1
% Asian 11
% Caucasian 59
% Hispanic 11
% Native American 1
% international 1

### SURVEY SAYS . . .
*Very little drug use*
*Students love San Luis Obispo, CA*
*Athletic facilities are great*
*Class discussions are rare*
*Campus difficult to get around*
*Dorms are like dungeons*
*Registration is a pain*
*Lousy food on campus*
*Unattractive campus*
*Diversity lacking on campus*

## ACADEMICS

**Academic Rating** 77
Calendar quarter
Student/faculty ratio 20:1
Profs interesting rating 88
Profs accessible rating 90
Avg lab size 10-19 students
Avg reg class size 20-29 students

### MOST POPULAR MAJORS
business
agribusiness
mechanical engineering

## STUDENTS SPEAK OUT
### Academics

"Cal Poly says it's really hands on, and it is." Students learn processes by doing, which gives them "a very good idea about the major they're studying." This real-world experience helps students a great deal when they graduate. The University encourages students to pursue co-op and internship opportunities. "Cal Poly grads get the job first because they know how to do it." Some students believe that the general education classes are "too broad and mostly boring." Also, some students have a difficult time getting into required, entry-level math and English courses that fill up quickly. The school operates on a quarterly calendar, and students quickly learn that they cannot fall behind in their studies. "There is so much information that the teachers want to go over, one lecture missed could be one entire chapter missed." The faculty is highly respected. "Most of the professors are here because they want to teach you," one student says. They are very accessible and not only go over theory but also explain how it relates to real-world experiences. Students' opinions about the administration are mixed. While some say that the "administration does a good job at involving students in decisions," others say that certain members of the administration are rarely seen. "I have been here for two years and I have yet to actually see our university president," one skeptical student said. On campus, the running joke is "that he doesn't really exist, or maybe he died years ago, and they've left his body in the house."

### Life

"It's the classic college life," writes one student. "Go to school through the day and when the sun goes down, the drinking starts up." Fraternities and private houses often host large parties. For students over the age of 21, "the night life in San Luis Obispo is pretty good." On Thursday night, the Farmers' Market downtown is the place to be. Life at Cal Poly is laid back. The beautiful California weather combined with the university's location 15 minutes from the beach means that students take part in many outdoor activities. The nearby ocean "attracts a lot of surfers to San Luis Obispo." In addition, students enjoy having bonfires and partying on the beach. Hiking and rock climbing are other popular activities, and the ski club takes an annual week-long trip. Though students are not politically active, they do get down socially. Many volunteer with Habitat for Humanity, and the frats are especially active participants. ("Must be something about hammers and jocks," one student quips.) "On campus and in the surrounding area, you can go to the movies, go kayaking, go to the beach, build a computer, go clubbing, go camping, or shear some sheep." On- and off-campus housing is "very hard to find," and "what is available is expensive." Also, "the food stinks," and on-campus buildings are old and "need more windows."

### Student Body

More than 80 percent of Cal Poly students live off campus, which means that students don't get to know each other. " . . . You must join a club or an organization" if you want to make friends, according to one student. And students tend to befriend other students in their respective majors. Cal Poly students are very laid back and some are apathetic as regards the classroom. "There is a general trend for students here not to think for themselves, which means they're always smiling and easy to get along with." People are "very respectful of differences," though some of the on-campus religious groups "like to tell everyone else how awful they are." One student comments that most of the people in the "huge" Christian club on campus "are in it to hook up with people who believe in God." There is little diversity and "too much fraternity and right-wing religious activity." One student advises, "This is white-bread university. If you want to be surrounded by diverse people with diverse ideas, go somewhere else."

# CALIFORNIA POLYTECHNIC STATE UNIVERSITY—SAN LUIS OBISPO

FINANCIAL AID: 805-756-2927 • E-MAIL: ADMISSIONS@CALPOLY.EDU • WEBSITE: WWW.CALPOLY.EDU

## ADMISSIONS

*Very important* academic and nonacademic factors considered by the admissions committee include character/personal qualities and secondary school record. *Important* factors considered include extracurricular activities, recommendations, standardized test scores, and talent/ability. *Other* factors considered include alumni/ae relation, class rank, essays, interview, minority status, volunteer work, and work experience. Factors *not* considered include geography, religious affiliation/commitment, and state residency. SAT I or ACT required. TOEFL required of all international applicants. High school diploma is required and GED is accepted. *High school units required/recommended:* 16 total required; 18 total recommended. *The admissions office says:* "California Polytech uses the following formula to determine whether a candidate is admitted: Multiply your high school GPA (on a 0 to 4 scale, add one point to your grade in each honors-level course) by 800 plus your combined SAT score. If you took the ACT, multiply your GPA by 200 and add 10 times your ACT composite score. The cutoffs for California residents are 2800 (SAT) or 694 (ACT); for non-residents, the cutoffs are 3402 (SAT) or 842 (ACT). Required high school curriculum: English, 4 years; mathematics, 3 years (including algebra I and II and geometry); foreign language, 2 years; lab science, U.S. history, art, 1 year each; academic electives, 3 years total."

### The Inside Word

While it's tough to get admitted, Cal Poly doesn't spend much time on frills in the admissions process. Satisfy the formulas or else! As with all California public institutions, the banning of affirmative action will continue to roil the application process for the near future.

## FINANCIAL AID

*Students should submit:* FAFSA and institution's own financial aid form. Regular filing deadline is June 30. The Princeton Review suggests that all financial aid forms be submitted as soon as possible after January 1. *Need-based scholarships/grants offered:* Pell, SEOG, state scholarships/grants, private scholarships, and the school's own gift aid. *Loan aid offered:* FFEL Subsidized Stafford, FFEL Unsubsidized Stafford, FFEL PLUS, Federal Perkins, and college/university loans from institutional funds. Institutional employment available. Federal Work-Study Program available. Applicants will be notified of awards on or about April 15. Off-campus job opportunities are good.

## FROM THE ADMISSIONS OFFICE

"From row crops to computers, Cal Poly believes the best way for someone to learn something is to do it. That's been the school's philosophy since it began. Learn by doing, the university calls it. Cal Poly students gain invaluable first-hand experience both on campus and off. On-campus opportunities such as the daily student-run newspaper and real-world agricultural enterprise projects make hands-on learning a daily reality, not just a catch phrase. Off-campus work with government agencies and major national corporations for both academic credit and a salary is available through various programs that include the largest Cooperative Education Program in the western United States. With its approach to education and success in applying it, Cal Poly has built a solid statewide and national reputation."

## ADMISSIONS

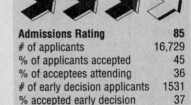

| | |
|---|---:|
| Admissions Rating | 85 |
| # of applicants | 16,729 |
| % of applicants accepted | 45 |
| % of acceptees attending | 36 |
| # of early decision applicants | 1531 |
| % accepted early decision | 37 |

### FRESHMAN PROFILE

| | |
|---|---:|
| Range SAT Verbal | 510-620 |
| Average SAT Verbal | 532 |
| Range SAT Math | 550-660 |
| Average SAT Math | 569 |
| Range ACT Composite | 22-27 |
| Average ACT Composite | 23 |
| Minimum TOEFL | 550 |
| Average HS GPA | 3.6 |
| % graduated top 10% of class | 38 |
| % graduated top 25% of class | 73 |
| % graduated top 50% of class | 94 |

### DEADLINES

| | |
|---|---:|
| Early decision | 10/31 |
| Early decision notification | 12/15 |
| Regular admission | 11/30 |
| Nonfall registration? | yes |

### APPLICANTS ALSO LOOK AT
### AND SOMETIMES PREFER
UC—Berkeley
UC—Santa Cruz
UCLA
UC—Santa Barbara
UC—Davis
### AND RARELY PREFER
U. Pacific

## FINANCIAL FACTS

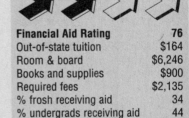

| | |
|---|---:|
| Financial Aid Rating | 76 |
| Out-of-state tuition | $164 |
| Room & board | $6,246 |
| Books and supplies | $900 |
| Required fees | $2,135 |
| % frosh receiving aid | 34 |
| % undergrads receiving aid | 44 |

# CALVIN COLLEGE

3201 BURTON STREET, SE, GRAND RAPIDS, MI 49546 • ADMISSIONS: 616-957-6106 • FAX: 616-957-6777

## CAMPUS LIFE

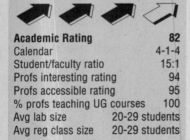

**Quality of Life Rating**     **90**
Type of school     private
Environment     suburban

### STUDENTS

Total undergrad enrollment     4,263
% male/female     45/55
% from out of state     42
% from public high school     46
% live on campus     56
% African American     1
% Asian     2
% Caucasian     93
% Hispanic     1
% international     7

### SURVEY SAYS . . .
*Very little drug use*
*Lots of conservatives on campus*
*Class discussions are rare*
*Classes are small*
*Very small frat/sorority scene*
*Very little beer drinking*
*Very little hard liquor*
*Students are very religious*
*Musical organizations are hot*
*Diversity lacking on campus*

## ACADEMICS

**Academic Rating**     **82**
Calendar     4-1-4
Student/faculty ratio     15:1
Profs interesting rating     94
Profs accessible rating     95
% profs teaching UG courses     100
Avg lab size     20-29 students
Avg reg class size     20-29 students

### MOST POPULAR MAJORS
elementary education
business
English

## STUDENTS SPEAK OUT
### Academics
There is a definite "emphasis on Christian values" at "rigorous" and "uniquely Christian" Calvin College. Students here describe their college as "an academically strong school in the Midwest" with a "strong religious foundation" that "prepares students to serve God." While "it's not hard to get in," according to a junior, "it's hard to stay." The "challenging" but "very rewarding" academics here center around an intensive, western-oriented core curriculum (13 courses that require students to demonstrate competence in the liberal arts, sciences, and math, as well as spoken rhetoric, writing, a foreign language, and physical education). Students seem to appreciate the idea of "the core," though several complain that it makes the course load "too heavy." Calvin's "often entertaining and subversive" professors are "dedicated and passionate about their work" and they "know their material." They also "require a lot of work" and are "sometimes not too sensitive" to students who don't know the material as well as they do, but students unabashedly call their profs "some of the best professors in the country with a Christian worldview." A devout senior explains, "The school's mission is equipping students to be agents, models, and witnesses of God's peace. This is a place where you can really grow in your faith without being smothered by in-your-face theology." While virtually all students at Calvin report that "financial aid is excellent," some complain that the administration is "too caught up in" religious tradition and bemoan its "burgeoning bureaucracy."

### Life
"People at Calvin drink a lot of coffee" and "spend a good amount of time studying." When they close their books, the "blissful" students at Calvin indulge in the "great, relaxed Christian atmosphere" and enjoy "a very strong sense of community." A few students do "keg stands" here, as at most college campuses, but most "find new and original things to do instead of drinking themselves into oblivion." Sometimes, students simply "sit around and discuss issues of theology." Social life "often revolves around" the residence halls, especially for underclassmen, who "have fierce loyalty toward their dorms." "Dances, banquets, and floor dates" are all the rage. In general, "there are a lot of campus activities" and "tons of opportunities to get involved"—"almost too many," given the academic workload. "Swing dancing," "free movies in the lecture hall," "worship nights," "singing hymns, " and "hay rides" are all enjoyed by Calvin students. There are also "many concerts on campus" at "a fantastic concert venue," including recent shows by Wilco, Branford Marsalis, Jars of Clay, and Ziggy Marley. Although some students complain that "Grand Rapids isn't much of a city," students do manage to venture off campus on occasion. When they do, they hit the "dance clubs and bars," or go out for "karaoke," "bowling," "IHL hockey," and other substance-free merriment. After hours, strict visitation rules keep hanky-panky between students of the opposite sex to a minimum.

### Student Body
"Many of my fellow students don't have to think," quips a junior. "Their future is predestined." Such is life at this Christian Reformed school, where the "one thing that holds everyone together is Jesus." Without a doubt, the "academically driven" multitudes at Calvin are "focused on spiritual matters" and they take their faith very seriously. Students here are also "very cliquey," and there are "definitely different groups" on campus. There are "the drinkers," the "stone cold sober" folks, the "ultra-religious" types, the "shallow airheads," the "deeply troubled visionaries," the "Abercrombie and J.Crew people," the "Target gals," and the people who "come to get married." Most are "very sheltered" and come from "conservative, Republican, Dutch, Christian backgrounds." Very few are homosexual. Calvin students describe themselves as "a wonderful group" of "very friendly and likable," "tall, blonde, and blue-eyed" people. To be sure, "Calvin is not a very diverse community," though, according to one student, "it tries to be."

FINANCIAL AID: 616-957-6134 • E-MAIL: ADMISSIONS@CALVIN.EDU • WEBSITE: WWW.CALVIN.EDU

## ADMISSIONS

*Very important* academic and nonacademic factors considered by the admissions committee include character/personal qualities, essays, recommendations, secondary school record, and standardized test scores. *Important* factors considered include class rank and extracurricular activities. *Other* factors considered include alumni/ae relation, minority status, talent/ability, volunteer work, and work experience. Factors *not* considered include geography, religious affiliation/commitment, and state residency. SAT I or ACT required, ACT preferred. TOEFL required of all international applicants. High school diploma is required and GED is accepted. *High school units required/recommended:* 17 total recommended; 4 English recommended, 4 math recommended, 2 science recommended, 3 social studies recommended, 4 elective recommended. *The admissions office says:* "One essay question asks applicants to interact with the faith perspective that lies at the heart of Calvin's curriculum."

### The Inside Word

Calvin's applicant pool is highly self-selected and small. Nearly all candidates get in, and over half choose to enroll. The freshman academic profile is fairly solid, but making a good match with the college philosophically is much more important for gaining admission than anything else.

## FINANCIAL AID

*Students should submit:* FAFSA and institution's own financial aid form. The Princeton Review suggests that all financial aid forms be submitted as soon as possible after January 1. *Need-based scholarships/grants offered:* Pell, SEOG, state scholarships/grants, private scholarships, and the school's own gift aid. *Loan aid offered:* Direct Subsidized Stafford, Direct Unsubsidized Stafford, Direct PLUS, Federal Perkins, and state. Institutional employment available. Federal Work-Study Program available. Applicants will be notified of awards on a rolling basis beginning on or about March 20. Off-campus job opportunities are excellent.

## FROM THE ADMISSIONS OFFICE

"Calvin is one of North America's largest and oldest Christian colleges. Our graduates have an outstanding record for career placement, and an impressive number of students pursue graduate studies. We encourage students to question, to examine, and to make their own decisions. Our 4-1-4 calendar, with its one-month Interim Term, offers opportunities for intensive studies here and abroad. Over 80 percent of our professors hold the highest degree in their field, and our student/professor ratio is 15:1. We seek to live by the foundational principles of our faith heritage: the sovereignty of God, the Lordship of Jesus Christ, the goal of individual service, and the wonder of God's grace."

## ADMISSIONS

| | |
|---|---|
| Admissions Rating | 78 |
| # of applicants | 1,870 |
| % of applicants accepted | 99 |
| % of acceptees attending | 57 |

### FRESHMAN PROFILE

| | |
|---|---|
| Range SAT Verbal | 540-650 |
| Average SAT Verbal | 594 |
| Range SAT Math | 530-670 |
| Average SAT Math | 597 |
| Range ACT Composite | 23-29 |
| Average ACT Composite | 26 |
| Minimum TOEFL | 550 |
| Average HS GPA | 3.5 |
| % graduated top 10% of class | 30 |
| % graduated top 25% of class | 56 |
| % graduated top 50% of class | 82 |

### DEADLINES

| | |
|---|---|
| Regular admission | 8/15 |
| Nonfall registration? | yes |

### APPLICANTS ALSO LOOK AT

**AND OFTEN PREFER**
Hope
**AND SOMETIMES PREFER**
U. Michigan—Ann Arbor
Wheaton Coll. (IL)
Grand Valley State
**AND RARELY PREFER**
Michigan Tech.
Michigan State

## FINANCIAL FACTS

| | |
|---|---|
| Financial Aid Rating | 87 |
| Tuition | $14,870 |
| Room & board | $5,180 |
| Books and supplies | $600 |
| % frosh receiving aid | 66 |
| % undergrads receiving aid | 64 |
| Avg frosh grant | $6,000 |
| Avg frosh loan | $3,000 |

# CARLETON COLLEGE

100 SOUTH COLLEGE STREET, NORTHFIELD, MN 55057 • ADMISSIONS: 507-646-4190 • FAX: 507-646-4526

## CAMPUS LIFE

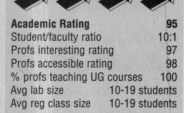

| Quality of Life Rating | 87 |
|---|---|
| Type of school | private |
| Affiliation | none |
| Environment | rural |

### STUDENTS

| | |
|---|---|
| Total undergrad enrollment | 1,936 |
| % male/female | 48/52 |
| % from out of state | 77 |
| % from public high school | 76 |
| % live on campus | 89 |
| % African American | 3 |
| % Asian | 8 |
| % Caucasian | 85 |
| % Hispanic | 4 |
| % international | 2 |

### SURVEY SAYS . . .

*(Almost) everyone plays intramural
sports
No one cheats
Students aren't religious
Lab facilities need improving
Great computer facilities
Theater is hot
(Almost) no one smokes
Musical organizations are hot*

## ACADEMICS

| Academic Rating | 95 |
|---|---|
| Student/faculty ratio | 10:1 |
| Profs interesting rating | 97 |
| Profs accessible rating | 98 |
| % profs teaching UG courses | 100 |
| Avg lab size | 10-19 students |
| Avg reg class size | 10-19 students |

### MOST POPULAR MAJORS
biology
English
economics

## STUDENTS SPEAK OUT

### Academics

"Academics are the central pillar of most students' lives here, and rightly so." Carleton College is a truly excellent liberal arts school. "This is the result of the highly qualified people that attend this institution," writes one student. Indeed, its student body is one of the most academically accomplished in the country, but the faculty can also take some credit for making Carleton special. One student explains, "Even in the intro classes the professors try to convey the liberal arts experience—how different disciplines fit together and what makes their own scholarly activities important to them." The professors are "engaging," "accessible," and "caring," going out of their way to make the student comfortable by hosting potluck dinners and handing out their home phone numbers. An English student says simply, "Professors here are teachers, not writers." The administration gets high marks from the students in terms of ease of registration and campus policy. "The administration treats us like adults," writes one student. Carleton's only problem might be with its reputation, or lack thereof, outside its region. But this is bound to change, as its virtues continue to draw the driven-to-learn student. This junior is full of praise: "Carleton has the integrity, drive, and pride of any great eastern school mixed with the charming, casual, friendly atmosphere of the small-town Midwest."

### Life

Carleton College is located in Northfield, in the middle of rural Minnesota. "Just survive the winters, and you'll love this place," insists one student. Students must entertain themselves ("Northfield is not a metropolis, so you've got to be creative"), even though the college makes every effort to sponsor events like movies, concerts, plays, and dances. This student explains one particularly popular pastime: "Traying is a winter tradition—sliding down snow-covered hills on cafeteria trays." And the students seem resigned to make the best of the art of conversation: "Other nights it's watching the fish swim in your room and hanging out with friends." Athletics are important at Carleton, whether it's organized meets or pick-up games of basketball. As this student writes, "Sports, either intercollegiate or intramural, give people a break from the everyday academic life and serve as an outlet for built-up energy." Many of the students mentioned dorm parties ("I love dorm life—minus the food") as a highlight, and the college has a very lenient policy with regard to alcohol. But it seems as if the students respect the responsibility given them and don't take advantage of this freedom. One student says, "Students who prefer to have fun without alcohol are accepted just as well as they would be if they were drinkers." The students at Carleton take academics very seriously, but there appears to be a good blend. As this senior majoring in history writes, "Light-hearted as well as serious pursuits engage most students."

### Student Body

Despite being a geographically diverse bunch, "the students resist cliques" according to many Carleton students. Three-quarters of the student body are white (and many of these from middle-upper-class backgrounds), but acceptance is a way of life at Carleton ("We are, in a word, 'respectful'"). The wealthy students have a tendency to "act poor." As one student comments, "The rich students dress the 'poorest' but the Birkenstocks give them away." Politically the campus is liberal although the level of commitment is negligible: "Political activism is virtually nonexistent."

# CARLETON COLLEGE

FINANCIAL AID: 507-646-4190 • E-MAIL: ADMISSIONS@ACS.CARLETON.EDU • WEBSITE: WWW.CARLETON.EDU

## ADMISSIONS

*Very important* academic and nonacademic factors considered by the admissions committee include class rank, secondary school record, and standardized test scores. *Important* factors considered include essays, extracurricular activities, recommendations, and talent/ability. *Other* factors considered include alumni/ae relation, character/personal qualities, interview, volunteer work, and work experience. Factors *not* considered include geography, minority status, religious affiliation/commitment, and state residency. SAT I or ACT required; SAT II recommended. TOEFL required of all international applicants. High school diploma is required and GED is accepted. *High school units required/recommended:* 19 total recommended; 4 English recommended, 4 math recommended, 4 science recommended, 3 foreign language recommended, 2 social studies recommended, 1 history recommended, 1 elective recommended. *The admissions office says:* "Of importance [in the admissions process] are superior academic achievement; personal qualities and interests; participation in extracurricular activities; and potential for development as a student and a graduate of the college."

### The Inside Word

Admission to Carleton would be even more difficult if the college had more name recognition. Current applicants should be grateful for this, because standards are already rigorous. Only severe competition with the best liberal arts colleges in the country prevents an even lower admit rate.

## FINANCIAL AID

*Students should submit:* CSS/Financial Aid PROFILE and noncustodial (divorced/separated) parent's statement. Regular filing deadline is February 15. The Princeton Review suggests that all financial aid forms be submitted as soon as possible after January 1. *Need-based scholarships/grants offered:* Pell, SEOG, state scholarships/grants, and the school's own gift aid. *Loan aid offered:* FFEL Subsidized Stafford, FFEL Unsubsidized Stafford, FFEL PLUS, Federal Perkins, state, college/university loans from institutional funds, and Minnesota SELF Loan program. Institutional employment available. Federal Work-Study Program available. Applicants will be notified of awards on or about April 15. Off-campus job opportunities are good.

## FROM THE ADMISSIONS OFFICE

"Carleton, a residential, coeducational liberal arts college, is located about 35 miles south of Minneapolis–St. Paul. More than 80 percent of those entering as freshmen graduate within four years, and nearly 90 percent in five years. About 75 percent enter graduate or professional school within five years of graduation. Carleton ranks first of all liberal arts colleges in the number of its graduates who earned PhDs in each of the laboratory sciences during the years 1986–1995, and ranks second in the total number who earned PhDs in all fields."

## ADMISSIONS

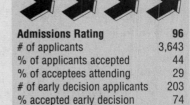

| | |
|---|---|
| Admissions Rating | 96 |
| # of applicants | 3,643 |
| % of applicants accepted | 44 |
| % of acceptees attending | 29 |
| # of early decision applicants | 203 |
| % accepted early decision | 74 |

### FRESHMAN PROFILE

| | |
|---|---|
| Range SAT Verbal | 640-750 |
| Range SAT Math | 640-720 |
| Range ACT Composite | 28-32 |
| Minimum TOEFL | 600 |
| % graduated top 10% of class | 68 |
| % graduated top 25% of class | 92 |
| % graduated top 50% of class | 99 |

### DEADLINES

| | |
|---|---|
| Early decision | 11/15 |
| Early decision notification | 12/15 |
| Regular admission | 1/15 |
| Regular notification | 4/15 |

### APPLICANTS ALSO LOOK AT
**AND OFTEN PREFER**
Stanford
Harvard
Brown
Swarthmore
Willaims
**AND SOMETIMES PREFER**
Pomona
Northwestern U.
Haverford
Wesleyan U.
Grinnell
**AND RARELY PREFER**
Macalester
Washington U.
Oberlin

### FINANCIAL FACTS

| | |
|---|---|
| Financial Aid Rating | 80 |
| Tuition | $24,420 |
| Room & board | $4,950 |
| Books and supplies | $600 |
| Required fees | $150 |
| % frosh receiving aid | 50 |
| % undergrads receiving aid | 51 |
| Avg frosh grant | $15,862 |
| Avg frosh loan | $3,673 |

# CARNEGIE MELLON UNIVERSITY

5000 FORBES AVENUE, PITTSBURGH, PA 15213 • ADMISSIONS: 412-268-2082 • FAX: 412-268-7838

## CAMPUS LIFE

**Quality of Life Rating**    **79**
| | |
|---|---|
| Type of school | private |
| Affiliation | none |
| Environment | urban |

### STUDENTS
| | |
|---|---|
| Total undergrad enrollment | 5,106 |
| % male/female | 64/36 |
| % from out of state | 69 |
| % live on campus | 74 |
| % in (# of) fraternities | 12 (13) |
| % in (# of) sororities | 8 (5) |
| % African American | 3 |
| % Asian | 20 |
| % Caucasian | 44 |
| % Hispanic | 5 |
| % Native American | 1 |
| % international | 10 |
| # of countries represented | 54 |

### SURVEY SAYS . . .
*Great computer facilities*
*Diverse students interact*
*Popular college radio*
*Student publications are popular*
*Ethnic diversity on campus*
*Theater is hot*
*Intercollegiate sports unpopular or nonexistent*
*Lab facilities need improving*
*Campus difficult to get around*
*Students aren't religious*

## ACADEMICS

**Academic Rating**    **88**
| | |
|---|---|
| Calendar | semester |
| Student/faculty ratio | 10:1 |
| Profs interesting rating | 71 |
| Profs accessible rating | 68 |
| Avg lab size | 20-29 students |
| Avg reg class size | 10-19 students |

### MOST POPULAR MAJORS
business administration
electrical and computer engineering
computer science

## STUDENTS SPEAK OUT
### Academics
With excellent programs in engineering, fine arts, and computer science—along with reputable and popular offerings in drama, architecture, business administration, the humanities, social sciences, and the pure sciences—Carnegie Mellon offers a virtual cornucopia of academic options to undergraduates. Says one student, "Carnegie Mellon is a school with tons of opportunities and even more paths to reach them." In nearly all areas, the workload is extremely tough; explains one student, "I study more than I eat and sleep. I actually feel guilty if I go a day without studying (including Saturdays and holidays)." Another identifies the school's defining trait as "a lot of work. People come here to work, and they do not leave disappointed." Professors here receive mixed grades; some students brag that "nearly all of them have open-door policies if you need help," while others complain that "my professors are all doing research or other outside projects that seem more important to them than teaching a boring intro class." Even with hard-to-reach profs, though, students find that "walking a couple of blocks out of my way to a professor's off-campus office does wonders for my grades! They like to see your effort and are very helpful in explaining errors." Computer and lab facilities at Carnegie Mellon are excellent ("There are more computers here than people"), and the school recently completed a new 240,000-square-foot university center containing recreational, athletic, dining, meeting, student activity, and lounge spaces for the campus community.

### Life
Within the parameters of its grinding academic demands, Carnegie Mellon manages to host a reasonably active undergraduate social scene. Students explain that part of the rigor of intense study is knowing when to take a break and let off steam. For this purpose, "Fraternities are fairly popular, as are intramural sports." Enthusiasm for the frequent $1 on-campus movies is high, as it is for performances by such campus groups as the No Parking Players comedy improv troupe. For the most part, however, students seek entertainment beyond campus in Pittsburgh, a city that has grown substantially more cosmopolitan in recent years. "I love going shopping in Shadyside, checking out the nightlife downtown, going to a cheap bistro to eat in Squirrel Hill, or hitting the Pitt frats in Oakland," enthuses one student. Notes another, "Our school is in a convenient area. There are a couple of bars, etc. and we have free bus passage to get anywhere around the city." As in past years, "dining services here earn two 'thumbs down.'"

### Student Body
Carnegie Mellon is a school where "incredibly intelligent engineer types" rub shoulders with "flamboyant drama majors," who can't help running into "fraternity partiers," who stumble over "the rest of us quiet, studious types." Carnegie Mellon students are also a demographically diverse bunch; notes one student, "We have so many ethnicities and differences of sexual orientation on campus, I can honestly claim to be a minority: I'm a straight white female!" One undergrad assesses the situation this way: "The students are a strange bunch. They seem to get along, but as in high school, there are lots of cliques. A lot of kids here are socially inept." Most here are extremely hardworking; as one explains, "My friends and I were discussing this today—no matter how studious and nerdy we try to be (in order to feel like good students and get good grades), there's always someone who can out-nerd us. Just go to a computer cluster on a Friday night and you'll understand."

FINANCIAL AID: 412-268-2068 • E-MAIL: UNDERGRADUATE-ADMISSIONS@ANDREW.CMU.EDU • WEBSITE: WWW.CMU.EDU

## ADMISSIONS

*Very important* academic and nonacademic factors considered by the admission committee include secondary school record, extracurricular activities, recommendations, standardized test scores, and volunteer work. *Important* factors considered include class rank, character/personal qualities, and essays. *Other* factors considered include alumni/ae relation, talent/ability, and work experience. Interviews are not required, but are recommended. Factors *not* considered are geography, minority status, religious affiliation/commitment, and state residency. SAT I or ACT required of all applicants. SAT II requirements vary by college. TOEFL required of all international applicants. High school diploma is required and GED is accepted. High school units required/recommended vary by college, but typically: 20 total recommended; 4 English recommended, 4 math recommended, 4 science recommended, 3 science lab recommended, 2 foreign language recommended, 4 social studies recommended.

### The Inside Word

The Office of Admission reports that it uses "no cutoffs, no formulas" in assessing its applicant pool. Don't get too excited—that doesn't necessarily mean that applicants are looked at in a more personal fashion. Applications have seesawed here over the past couple of years, and to temper the effects of a decline in application totals on selectivity CMU maintains a huge wait list. A very low yield of admits who enroll keeps selectivity moderate, but you've got to have strong numbers to gain admission.

## FINANCIAL AID

*Students should submit:* FAFSA, institution's own financial aid form, parents' tax forms and W-2 forms, and student's tax form. Regular filing deadline is February 15. The Princeton Review suggests that all financial aid forms be submitted as soon as possible after January 1. *Need-based scholarships/grants offered:* Pell, SEOG, state scholarships/grants, private scholarships, and the school's own gift aid. *Loan aid offered:* FFEL Subsidized Stafford, FFEL Unsubsidized Stafford, FFEL PLUS and Federal Perkins. Institutional employment available. Federal Work-Study Program available. Applicants will be notified of awards on a rolling basis. Off-campus job opportunities are good.

## FROM THE ADMISSIONS OFFICE

"Carnegie Mellon is a private, coeducational university with approximately 5,100 undergraduates, 3,300 graduate students, and 778 full-time faculty members. The University's 103-acre campus is located in the Oakland area of Pittsburgh, five miles from downtown. The University is composed of seven colleges: the Carnegie Institute of Technology (engineering); the College of Fine Arts; the College of Humanities and Social Sciences (combining liberal arts education with professional specializations); the Graduate School of Industrial Administration (undergraduate business and industrial management); the Mellon College of Science; the School of Computer Science; and the H. Hohn Heina III School of Public Policy and Management."

## ADMISSIONS

| | |
|---|---|
| Admissions Rating | 91 |
| # of applicants | 14,621 |
| % of applicants accepted | 36 |
| % of acceptees attending | 25 |
| # accepting a place on wait list | 690 |
| % admitted from wait list | 12 |
| # of early decision applicants | 196 |
| % accepted early decision | 41 |

### FRESHMAN PROFILE

| | |
|---|---|
| Range SAT Verbal | 600-750 |
| Average SAT Verbal | 649 |
| Range SAT Math | 680-800 |
| Average SAT Math | 713 |
| Range ACT Composite | 27-32 |
| Average ACT Composite | 29 |
| Minimum TOEFL | 600 |
| Average HS GPA | 3.6 |
| % graduated top 10% of class | 72 |
| % graduated top 25% of class | 94 |
| % graduated top 50% of class | 99 |

### DEADLINES

| | |
|---|---|
| Early decision | 11/1–11/15 |
| Early decision notification | 1/15 |
| Regular admission | 12/15–1/1 |
| Regular notification | 4/15 |

### APPLICANTS ALSO LOOK AT

**AND OFTEN PREFER**
Cornell U.
Tufts
U. Penn

**AND SOMETIMES PREFER**
Case Western Reserve
Washington U.

**AND RARELY PREFER**
U. Pittsburgh
Boston U.
Syracuse
Penn State—Univ. Park

## FINANCIAL FACTS

| | |
|---|---|
| Financial Aid Rating | 82 |
| Tuition | $23,820 |
| Room & board | $7,264 |
| Books and supplies | $865 |
| Required fees | $202 |
| % frosh receiving aid | 47 |
| % undergrads receiving aid | 54 |
| Avg frosh grant | $13,712 |
| Avg frosh loan | $3,211 |

# CASE WESTERN RESERVE UNIVERSITY

103 TOMLINSON HALL, 10900 EUCLID AVENUE, CLEVELAND, OH 44106-7055 • ADMISSIONS: 216-368-4450 • FAX: 216-368-5111

## CAMPUS LIFE

| | |
|---|---|
| **Quality of Life Rating** | **68** |
| Type of school | private |
| Affiliation | none |
| Environment | urban |

### STUDENTS

| | |
|---|---|
| Total undergrad enrollment | 3,434 |
| % male/female | 61/39 |
| % from out of state | 40 |
| % from public high school | 70 |
| % live on campus | 73 |
| % in (# of) fraternities | 32 (18) |
| % in (# of) sororities | 16 (5) |
| % African American | 5 |
| % Asian | 14 |
| % Caucasian | 76 |
| % Hispanic | 2 |
| % international | 3 |
| # of countries represented | 95 |

### SURVEY SAYS . . .
Great library
Class discussions are rare
Students love Cleveland, OH
Students don't get along with local community
Great computer facilities
Ethnic diversity on campus
Unattractive campus
Campus difficult to get around
Intercollegiate sports unpopular or nonexistent
Registration is a pain

## ACADEMICS

| | |
|---|---|
| **Academic Rating** | **78** |
| Calendar | semester |
| Student/faculty ratio | 8:1 |
| Profs interesting rating | 85 |
| Profs accessible rating | 89 |
| % profs teaching UG courses | 55 |
| % classes taught by TAs | 5 |
| Avg lab size | 20-29 students |
| Avg reg class size | 10-19 students |

### MOST POPULAR MAJORS
biology
computer engineering
psychology

## STUDENTS SPEAK OUT
### Academics
Cleveland is the home of not only the Rock and Roll Hall of Fame and the reborn NFL Browns but also Case Western Reserve University. Formed by the union of Western Reserve University (a traditional liberal arts college) and the Case Institute of Technology (an engineering and physical sciences college), CWRU offers many "strong departments" and "great research opportunities." Not surprising at a place with such a strong technical orientation, the workload is intense. Some undergraduates mention that they spend much of their time teaching themselves ("A lot of professors are here for research and not for teaching"), while others report that their professors are "amazing teachers and researchers." Case undergrads love the small class size and the fact that many classes are taught by professors and not TAs. With respect to the administration, however, the students are less supportive: "The education is excellent, but this school does not run efficiently." Specifically, Case students would love to see a "better registration" process. The administration has complied; there is a new online registration system. Facilities, a sore point with many students in previous surveys we've conducted, are in upgrade mode; the university recently completed a new library and is getting started on a new home for their school of management designed by one of the world's top architects. CWRU's high price tag prompts a few students to suggest that the university could stand to "improve financial aid."

### Life
Given the very distinct division of its population between the liberal arts and engineering, Case Western is like two separate schools sharing a single campus. Coupled with the prevalence of techno-types on campus, this division affects the social scene because "you sometimes feel left out if you're not a part of" the engineering side of the university. On the other hand, perhaps the liberal arts minority doesn't realize that the grass isn't necessarily greener on the other side. According to a sophomore mechanical engineering major who turned down Vanderbilt, Swarthmore, and Georgia Tech to enroll at CWRU, "If you wonder where engineers learn how to not have social lives, this is the place. . . . Study, study, study—get the picture?" Even so, many survey respondents share the sentiment expressed by the respondent who tells us that CWRU's greatest strength is the "large amounts of social geeks that seem truly happy here." "School and life are what you make of them, and there are plenty of us that go out, party, and have fun." And truly, there is a lot to do, including "lots of student-run organizations." Also, "Fraternity parties and the movies are very popular." Many of the students warn that "you really need a car" in order to appreciate all that Cleveland has to offer. The "campus is surrounded by clubs, museums, parks, and malls." But trying to find a date at Case "is like finding decent food on campus." But from the point of view of this junior studying biology, the "influx of women nursing students has changed the dating scene for the better."

### Student Body
Case's large minority population comprises a far larger percentage of its student body than at most universities in the country. The majority of these minorities are Asian, and CWRU also boasts a large international population. "The student body is very diverse. There are many minority/cultural groups" sponsoring events on campus that "many [other] students attend." One student classifies CWRU students as "very studious, serious, diverse, and conservative." Another uses a more colloquial classification system: "There are three types of people here: hardcore nerds; geniuses by day, drunks by night; and the rarest of the three, the somewhat normal person." Maybe we're overdoing it, but so many students emphasize the point that we've just got to close with a quote from one student who writes, "Are you a geek? Proud of it? Come here!" However, the *Wall Street Journal* recently cited CWRU as "not as geeky as it used to be."

FINANCIAL AID: 216-368-4530 • E-MAIL: ADMISSION@PO.CWRU.EDU • WEBSITE: WWW.CWRU.EDU

## ADMISSIONS

*Very important* academic and nonacademic factors considered by the admissions committee include secondary school record and standardized test scores. *Important* factors considered include character/personal qualities, essays, extracurricular activities, interview, and talent/ability. *Other* factors considered include alumni/ae relation, class rank, minority status, recommendations, volunteer work, and work experience. Factors *not* considered include geography, religious affiliation/commitment, and state residency. SAT I or ACT required; SAT II recommended. TOEFL required of all international applicants. High school diploma is required and GED is accepted. *High school units required/recommended:* 16 total required; 4 English required, 3 math required, 3 science required, 2 science lab required, 2 foreign language required, 3 social studies required. *The admissions office says:* "Rather than require students to apply to a specific school, CWRU admits its students to the university without regard to intended major (with the exception of the nursing program, which limits undergraduate enrollment). A student can keep options open during the admissions process and, if admitted based on overall academic performance and promise, choose to begin study in any area."

### The Inside Word

Case Western faces tough competition, and they handle it very well. The university received a record number of applications last year, and as a result it's quite a bit tougher to get admitted. Even if you solidly meet the academic profile, don't be complacent—Case's freshman profile reflects well on the academic preparedness of its candidates, and due to their good fortune they've got an opportunity to be significantly more choosy about who gets an offer.

## FINANCIAL AID

*Students should submit:* FAFSA, CSS/Financial Aid PROFILE, noncustodial (divorced/separated) parent's statement, business/farm supplement, and parent and student income tax returns and W-2 forms. Regular filing deadline is April 15. The Princeton Review suggests that all financial aid forms be submitted as soon as possible after January 1. *Need-based scholarships/grants offered:* Pell, SEOG, state scholarships/grants, private scholarships, and the school's own gift aid. *Loan aid offered:* Direct Subsidized Stafford, Direct Unsubsidized Stafford, FFEL PLUS, Federal Perkins, Federal Nursing, state, and college/university loans from institutional funds. Institutional employment available. Federal Work-Study Program available. Applicants will be notified of awards on a rolling basis beginning on or about March 15. Off-campus job opportunities are good.

## FROM THE ADMISSIONS OFFICE

"CWRU's note to you is not self-promoting. We would rather use this space to send a simple message: To thine own self be true. Filter the word-of-mouth, the slick guidebook ratings, and flattering college-generated literature through your own sense of what will work for you. Read no further in this guidebook if you haven't already taken thoughtful stock of your own needs. If you know yourself well, then have the confidence to look beyond the surface impressions and discover how less glamorous or well-known colleges may very well meet your individual needs."

### ADMISSIONS

| | |
|---|---|
| Admissions Rating | 84 |
| # of applicants | 4,760 |
| % of applicants accepted | 71 |
| % of acceptees attending | 25 |
| # accepting a place on wait list | 350 |
| % admitted from wait list | 17 |

### FRESHMAN PROFILE

| | |
|---|---|
| Range SAT Verbal | 600-710 |
| Range SAT Math | 640-740 |
| Range ACT Composite | 27-32 |
| Minimum TOEFL | 550 |
| % graduated top 10% of class | 71 |
| % graduated top 25% of class | 91 |
| % graduated top 50% of class | 98 |

### DEADLINES

| | |
|---|---|
| Early decision | 1/1 |
| Regular admission | 2/1 |
| Regular notification | 4/1 |
| Nonfall registration? | yes |

### APPLICANTS ALSO LOOK AT

**AND OFTEN PREFER**
Northwestern U.
Carnegie Mellon
U. Michigan—Ann Arbor

**AND SOMETIMES PREFER**
Washington U.
Boston U.

**AND RARELY PREFER**
Ohio State U.—Columbus
Purdue U.—West Lafayette
Penn State—Univ. Park

### FINANCIAL FACTS

| | |
|---|---|
| Financial Aid Rating | 78 |
| Tuition | $21,000 |
| Room & board | $6,250 |
| Books and supplies | $750 |
| Required fees | $168 |
| % frosh receiving aid | 57 |
| % undergrads receiving aid | 58 |

# CATAWBA COLLEGE

2300 WEST INNES STREET, SALISBURY, NC 28144 • ADMISSIONS: 704-637-4402 • FAX: 704-637-4222

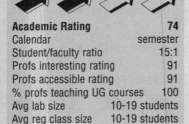

## CAMPUS LIFE

**Quality of Life Rating**     **72**
Type of school     private
Affiliation     United Church of Christ
Environment     suburban

### STUDENTS
Total undergrad enrollment     1,195
% male/female     50/50
% from out of state     39
% live on campus     55
% African American     14
% Asian     1
% Caucasian     83
% Hispanic     1
% international     2

### SURVEY SAYS . . .
*Theater is hot*
*Student publications are ignored*
*Everyone loves the Indians*
*Classes are small*
*(Almost) everyone smokes*
*Lousy food on campus*
*Political activism is (almost)*
*nonexistent*
*Library needs improving*

## ACADEMICS

**Academic Rating**     **74**
Calendar     semester
Student/faculty ratio     15:1
Profs interesting rating     91
Profs accessible rating     91
% profs teaching UG courses     100
Avg lab size     10-19 students
Avg reg class size     10-19 students

### MOST POPULAR MAJORS
business
communication arts
elementary education

## STUDENTS SPEAK OUT

### Academics

How does a small regional liberal arts college distinguish itself among hundreds of other similar schools around the nation? For Catawba College, specialization is the answer. In the areas of performance arts, sports medicine, and physical education, Catawba has established itself as a leader. That's not to say that these are Catawba's only strengths: business, education, and communications are among the school's other rock-solid departments, and students brag that their alma mater is "a great school for athletics and theater arts." A new Environmental Science building, soon to be completed, suggests Catawba's commitment to bolstering its offerings in the sciences. In all departments, teaching skill and accessibility are paramount. Students tell us that "professors go above and beyond what can be expected of them. They become your friends." Writes another student, "The professors in our program are extremely informative and willing to do just about anything to help us out." Our respondents are also happy to report that "the small classes are good and students get a lot of personal attention." The administration is similarly "very accessible and willing to listen to student concerns."

### Life

Students describe campus life at Catawba as low-key. Part of the problem lies in the town of Salisbury, "a small town with not much to do." Writes one student, "You really have to make your own fun at Catawba. The surrounding town is very quiet and modest. For fun you can throw parties, have get-togethers, watch movies, attend the few campus events, or have a study group." The campus itself is rarely dormant; one student explains, "We have a free program every night: a comedian, a band, something like that." Adds another, "If you want to get involved, Catawba is an easy place to do that. Being in clubs makes campus much more fun." An astounding one-third of all students participate in intercollegiate sports. Still, there are those who feel that "activities for students could use some improvement." When small-town, small-campus life becomes too confining, students "go on road trips to the mountains, which are two hours away, or to the beach (four and a half hours away)."

### Student Body

As at many Christian schools, Catawba attracts a student body that is, on the whole, more religious than its counterparts at nondenominational schools. We're not talking fanatics, but rather the subtle, ever-present religiosity typical in much of the South. More prevalent is the cliquishness. Writes one undergrad, "Students here are very nice, but it's very high schoolish and cliquish." Another points out that "of course you have your cliques, but all in all students are friendly, easygoing, and sociable. As of yet I haven't heard of any brawls." Students subdivide most often by major, and there is a pervasive sense that students in performing arts and sports consider themselves better than others. "We have three types of students: theater majors, sports people (jocks and athletic trainers), and other. I happen to be an 'other' so it's not ideal. If you're not one of them, they don't talk to you." A theater major agreed: "Because I'm a theater student there isn't anyone that I talk to outside of the department, and vice versa."

FINANCIAL AID: 704-637-4416 • E-MAIL: ADMISSION@CATAWBA.EDU • WEBSITE: WWW.CATAWBA.EDU

## ADMISSIONS

*Very important* academic and nonacademic factors considered by the admissions committee include secondary school record. *Important* factors considered include alumni/ae relation, character/personal qualities, class rank, essays, extracurricular activities, recommendations, standardized test scores, talent/ability, volunteer work, and work experience. *Other* factors considered include interview, minority status, and religious affiliation/commitment. Factors *not* considered include geography and state residency. SAT I or ACT required, SAT I preferred. TOEFL required of all international applicants. High school diploma is required and GED is accepted. *High school units required/recommended:* 16 total recommended; 4 English recommended, 3 math recommended, 2 science recommended, 2 science lab recommended, 2 foreign language recommended, 2 social studies recommended.

### The Inside Word

Catawba's applicant pool is mainly from the Southeast, which tends to give candidates from far afield some extra appeal. There is serious competition for students among similar colleges in this neck of the woods, and the admissions staff here has to work hard to bring in the freshman class each year. They succeed because they are truly friendly and personal in their dealings with students and their families, and the college seems to have carved a worthwhile niche for itself amid the myriad choices available in the area.

## FINANCIAL AID

*Students should submit:* FAFSA. There is no regular filing deadline. The Princeton Review suggests that all financial aid forms be submitted as soon as possible after January 1. *Need-based scholarships/grants offered:* Pell, SEOG, state scholarships/grants, private scholarships, and the school's own gift aid. *Loan aid offered:* Direct Subsidized Stafford, Direct Unsubsidized Stafford, Direct PLUS, FFEL Subsidized Stafford, FFEL Unsubsidized Stafford, FFEL PLUS, Federal Perkins, and college/university loans from institutional funds. Institutional employment available. Federal Work-Study Program available. Applicants will be notified of awards on a rolling basis beginning on or about February 15. Off-campus job opportunities are excellent.

## FROM THE ADMISSIONS OFFICE

"Perhaps one of Catawba's greatest assets is location, location, location. The town of Salisbury (www.ol.salisbury.no.us) is a small city of 26,000 people, a leader in the historic preservation movement, and a place with a rare wealth of opportunities in the arts. The town embraces the college, and vice versa. Catawba College has just significantly upgraded the computer technology made available to students. A fiber-optic loop has been completed, and our three computer labs are equipped with 486 and Pentium chip computers, many of which have sound cards and 10-watt speakers. The library has also been electronically upgraded with the addition of the same online system used by the Museum of Natural History."

## ADMISSIONS

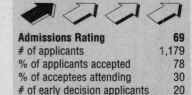

| | |
|---|---|
| Admissions Rating | 69 |
| # of applicants | 1,179 |
| % of applicants accepted | 78 |
| % of acceptees attending | 30 |
| # of early decision applicants | 20 |
| % accepted early decision | 75 |

### FRESHMAN PROFILE

| | |
|---|---|
| Range SAT Verbal | 423-583 |
| Average SAT Verbal | 488 |
| Range SAT Math | 420-585 |
| Average SAT Math | 494 |
| Average ACT Composite | 20 |
| Minimum TOEFL | 525 |
| Average HS GPA | 3.0 |
| % graduated top 10% of class | 7 |
| % graduated top 25% of class | 24 |
| % graduated top 50% of class | 54 |

### DEADLINES

| | |
|---|---|
| Early decision | 12/1 |
| Early decision notification | 2/16 |
| Nonfall registration? | yes |

### APPLICANTS ALSO LOOK AT AND SOMETIMES PREFER

UNC—Chapel Hill
UNC—Charlotte

### AND RARELY PREFER

UNC—Wilmington
UNC—Greensboro
North Carolina State
Elon
Appalachian State

## FINANCIAL FACTS

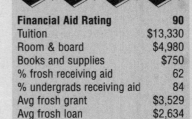

| | |
|---|---|
| Financial Aid Rating | 90 |
| Tuition | $13,330 |
| Room & board | $4,980 |
| Books and supplies | $750 |
| % frosh receiving aid | 62 |
| % undergrads receiving aid | 84 |
| Avg frosh grant | $3,529 |
| Avg frosh loan | $2,634 |

# CATHOLIC UNIVERSITY OF AMERICA

CARDINAL STATION, WASHINGTON, DC 20064 • ADMISSIONS: 202-319-5305 • FAX: 202-319-6533

## CAMPUS LIFE

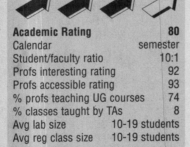

| Quality of Life Rating | 80 |
|---|---|
| Type of school | private |
| Affiliation | Roman Catholic |
| Environment | urban |

### STUDENTS

| | |
|---|---|
| Total undergrad enrollment | 2,609 |
| % male/female | 46/54 |
| % from out of state | 92 |
| % from public high school | 39 |
| % live on campus | 58 |
| % in (# of) fraternities | 1 (2) |
| % in (# of) sororities | 1 (2) |
| % African American | 8 |
| % Asian | 4 |
| % Caucasian | 76 |
| % Hispanic | 4 |
| % international | 3 |
| # of countries represented | 31 |

### SURVEY SAYS . . .

*Very little drug use*
*Classes are small*
*Diversity lacking on campus*
*Registration is a breeze*
*Very small frat/sorority scene*
*Library needs improving*
*Lousy food on campus*
*No one plays intramural sports*
*Dorms are like dungeons*

## ACADEMICS

| Academic Rating | 80 |
|---|---|
| Calendar | semester |
| Student/faculty ratio | 10:1 |
| Profs interesting rating | 92 |
| Profs accessible rating | 93 |
| % profs teaching UG courses | 74 |
| % classes taught by TAs | 8 |
| Avg lab size | 10-19 students |
| Avg reg class size | 10-19 students |

### MOST POPULAR MAJORS
architecture
business & economics
nursing

## STUDENTS SPEAK OUT

### Academics

In Washington, D.C., a city known for its prestigious academic institutions, students seeking a quality education sometimes overlook the Catholic University of America. Some might be discouraged by the fact that the university is—surprise!—overwhelmingly populated by students who have Catholic backgrounds and are politically conservative to boot. Those who eliminate Catholic from their list of potential schools might miss out on a place where "professors know [students] by name" and the "faculty is extremely accessible." Catholic students praise the "great and available professors truly committed to a student's learning." The only university in the United States with a papal charter, it isn't surprising that the religion department earns high marks from many students, one senior writing, "My experience as a religion major has convinced me that this department is the best in the country. Where else can students have [this kind of] access to faculty members . . . even for an e-mail discussion at 3 A.M.?" The theater, nursing, and biology departments are touted by undergraduates, and many cite the quality of the music department as the primary reason they decided to attend Catholic. Meanwhile, the modern language departments need improvement, and many students wish that more classes were offered each semester and complain that the library could stand some improvement. Also, students are just plain unhappy with the university's administrators. One junior grumbles that "the administration treats us as if we cannot think for ourselves. Unless our parents call or are people of the cloth, we are not taken seriously." Despite students' dislike of the administration, most describe Catholic in a very positive light. "An education at Catholic University will last a lifetime," writes one student. "The doors opened by the professors here are amazing."

### Life

Though they cite Catholic as having "perhaps the most boring campus life this side of a veterans' hospital," most students agree that the university's proximity to the center of town (eight minutes by Metro) was a deciding factor in their decision to attend Catholic because "D.C. is full of things to do." The world-famous museums, shops, and clubs easily counterbalanced a "slow" campus life. One student explains, "The city offers a great club scene, and there's always something going on downtown." The school's strict alcohol policies cause most students to "depend on the city for night fun." One student points out that age is rarely a factor for those looking for a good time in the immediate neighborhood surrounding Catholic: "If you have a good fake ID, your weekends will be rockin'." Undergrads report they have concerns for their safety and note that campus/community relations are quite strained. They also mention that the food, housing, and athletic facilities need significant improvement. "We're working out on ancient machines," writes one student. Though many students point out that there are not enough on-campus activities, most agree that Catholic's campus ministry, which sponsors some events, is "very strong and growing," and "provides great support." Overall, the unique opportunities provided by living in Washington, D.C., and the "beautiful" campus more than outweigh the concerns that most students have about the lack of on-campus social activities.

### Student Body

Most students agree that homogeny in the student body is Catholic's biggest weakness. However, most say that while "the lack of diversity here is very disappointing," the majority of the students are "friendly and approachable." Many also point to a lack of school spirit as another shortcoming. It results, writes one student, from the fact that "many kids are here because it was their backup school, and they are not as excited about being [at Catholic]." Despite the religious affiliation of the university, students do not feel smothered by religion. While many students speak of an abundance of cliques, most say "people here generally get along. There is a fairly friendly atmosphere on campus."

## ADMISSIONS

*Very important* academic and nonacademic factors considered by the admissions committee include class rank and secondary school record. *Important* factors considered include recommendations, standardized test scores, state residency, and talent/ability. *Other* factors considered include alumni/ae relation, character/personal qualities, essays, extracurricular activities, interview, minority status, volunteer work, and work experience. Factors *not* considered include geography and religious affiliation/commitment. SAT I or ACT required; SAT II recommended and required for placement in the School of Arts and Sciences. TOEFL required of all international applicants. High school diploma is required and GED is accepted. *High school units required/recommended:* 17 total recommended; 4 English recommended, 3 math recommended, 3 science recommended, 1 science lab recommended, 2 foreign language recommended, 4 social studies recommended, 1 elective recommended. *The admissions office says:* "We are looking for a well-rounded student [who demonstrates a] balance of academics, activities, and community service." CUA also notes that "students are evaluated on the basis of the whole application package."

### The Inside Word

This is not the place to try radical approaches to completing your admissions application: smooth sailing for solid students and even friendlier for candidates from distant states or unique high schools.

## FINANCIAL AID

*Students should submit:* FAFSA and CSS/Financial Aid PROFILE. The Princeton Review suggests that all financial aid forms be submitted as soon as possible after January 1. *Need-based scholarships/grants offered:* Pell. *Loan aid offered:* Direct Subsidized Stafford, Direct Unsubsidized Stafford, and Federal Perkins. Institutional employment available. Federal Work-Study Program available. Off-campus job opportunities are excellent.

## FROM THE ADMISSIONS OFFICE

"The Catholic University of America's friendly atmosphere, rigorous academic programs, and emphasis on time-honored values attract students from most states and more than 100 foreign countries. Its 144-acre, tree-lined campus is 10 minutes from the nation's capital. Distinguished as the national university of the Catholic Church in the United States, CUA is the only institution of higher education established by the U.S. Catholic bishops. Students from all religious traditions are welcome. CUA offers undergraduate degrees in more than 50 major areas. With Capitol Hill and The Smithsonian Institution minutes away via the Metrorail rapid transit system, students enjoy a residential campus in an exciting city of historical monuments, theaters, ethnic restaurants, and parks."

## ADMISSIONS

| Admissions Rating | 85 |
| --- | --- |
| # of applicants | 3,117 |
| % of applicants accepted | 87 |
| % of acceptees attending | 20 |

### FRESHMAN PROFILE

| | |
| --- | --- |
| Range SAT Verbal | 540-640 |
| Range SAT Math | 520-630 |
| Range ACT Composite | 22-29 |
| Minimum TOEFL | 550 |
| Average HS GPA | 3.4 |
| % graduated top 10% of class | 24 |
| % graduated top 25% of class | 54 |
| % graduated top 50% of class | 86 |

### DEADLINES

| | |
| --- | --- |
| Priority admission deadline | 11/15 |
| Regular admission | 2/15 |
| Regular notification | 3/20 |
| Nonfall registration? | yes |

### APPLICANTS ALSO LOOK AT
#### AND OFTEN PREFER
Notre Dame
U. Virginia
Boston Coll.
Georgetown U.
#### AND SOMETIMES PREFER
Holy Cross
William and Mary
Villanova
Loyola Coll. (MD)
U. Scranton
#### AND RARELY PREFER
American
Fordham
LaSalle U.
George Washington

## FINANCIAL FACTS

| Financial Aid Rating | 77 |
| --- | --- |
| Tuition | $20,050 |
| Room & board | $8,382 |
| Books and supplies | $1,000 |
| Required fees | $900 |
| % frosh receiving aid | 89 |
| % undergrads receiving aid | 88 |
| Avg frosh grant | $13,573 |
| Avg frosh loan | $3,341 |

# CENTENARY COLLEGE OF LOUISIANA

PO BOX 41188, SHREVEPORT, LA 71134-1188 • ADMISSIONS: 318-869-5131 • FAX: 318-869-5005

## CAMPUS LIFE

**Quality of Life Rating** 77
Type of school private
Affiliation Methodist
Environment suburban

### STUDENTS
| | |
|---|---|
| Total undergrad enrollment | 858 |
| % male/female | 39/61 |
| % from out of state | 38 |
| % live on campus | 61 |
| % in (# of) fraternities | 8 (4) |
| % in (# of) sororities | 17 (2) |
| % African American | 5 |
| % Asian | 1 |
| % Caucasian | 86 |
| % Hispanic | 3 |
| % Native American | 1 |
| % international | 2 |
| # of countries represented | 10 |

### SURVEY SAYS . . .
Frats and sororities dominate social scene
Very little drug use
Classes are small
Student government is popular
(Almost) everyone plays intramural sports
Musical organizations are hot
Theater is popular
(Almost) no one listens to college radio
Students get along with local community
Class discussions encouraged

## ACADEMICS

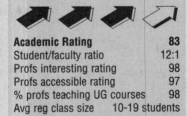

**Academic Rating** 83
Student/faculty ratio 12:1
Profs interesting rating 98
Profs accessible rating 97
% profs teaching UG courses 98
Avg reg class size 10-19 students

### MOST POPULAR MAJORS
business
sociology
biology

## STUDENTS SPEAK OUT

### Academics

The students of Centenary College, "a private, affordable liberal arts college" affiliated with the Methodist Church, grow most passionate about their school when discussing the relationships they forge with faculty and administrators. "The interaction with professors is great," writes one. "Same with the administration. Students are invited to participate in the governance of the school. I've even traded e-mails with the Provost of the college." Says another, "Walking across campus, it is not uncommon to hear several professors and instructors ask you about your day. This makes you feel special." Such touches are reinforced by small class sizes and ample personal attention from a "supportive and accomplished" faculty. "The professors are the heart and soul of this institution," a junior writes. "They're available almost anytime they are not teaching another class." Professors teach all classes and have been known to invite entire classes "to their homes for movie nights and crawfish boils." A "high rate of acceptance into medical school," exceptional classroom facilities, and "an incredible music faculty" draw further praise from students. Most say their school is run smoothly as well, but some disagree. Says a dissenter, "I wonder how anything gets done with so many committees." Centenary's traditional approach to a "classical" college education includes a number of distribution requirements across the humanities and sciences, an integrated full-year course called First Year Experience, and Honor Code.

### Life

Students agree that the social scene at Centenary is pretty much a one-horse town. "Social life sucks unless you're a Greek," explains one student. "The age limit—21—pretty much kills any fun." Writes another, "For 17- to 20-year-olds, life at Centenary focuses on campus and the fraternity houses are the place to be. However, as senior year approaches, academics fill the spotlight. More nightlife opportunities become available, too." Many undergrads feel trapped on campus, complaining that "Shreveport is scary, especially because Centenary is in the middle of a ghetto." Still, life at Centenary isn't all frat parties and cowering on campus. "If you are coming to college to experience culture and reasonable amounts of partying, Centenary is for you. The students here can let it all out on Friday, yet go to an opera on Saturday—and enjoy it." Centenary also requires all first-year and sophomore students to live on campus and participate in the meal plan. The only way to get out of this is to get married. One student comments that the enforced living scenario inspires "a true feeling of community. You don't go unnoticed."

### Student Body

The largely affluent student body of Centenary maintains an uneasy state of equilibrium, neither friendly nor hostile. Some students contend that the atmosphere would be better if "the gap between fraternities with one another and with the total non-Greek student body" could be bridged. "All the sorority girls and frat guys talk only to each other." It's the kind of place where students routinely opine about their peers: "Everyone seems friendly, but some are not, once you get to know them better." Although some claim that Centenary "has more and more diversity each year," the population is still "very homogenous."

FINANCIAL AID: 318-869-5137 • E-MAIL: ADMISSIONS@CENTENARY.EDU • WEBSITE: WWW.CENTENARY.EDU

## ADMISSIONS

*Very important* academic and nonacademic factors considered by the admissions committee include character/personal qualities, recommendations, religious affiliation/commitment, secondary school record, standardized test scores, and talent/ability. *Important* factors considered include alumni/ae relation, class rank, essays, extracurricular activities, interview, minority status, and volunteer work. *Other* factors considered include work experience. Factors *not* considered include geography and state residency. SAT I or ACT required. TOEFL required of all international applicants. High school diploma is required and GED is accepted. *High school units required/recommended:* 14 total required; 18 total recommended; 4 English required, 3 math required, 4 math recommended, 2 science required, 3 science recommended, 2 science lab required, 3 science lab recommended, 2 foreign language required, 3 foreign language recommended, 3 social studies required, 4 social studies recommended.

### The Inside Word

Centenary has a very small applicant pool, and thus has to admit the vast majority in order to meet its freshman enrollment goals. Its reputation, though regional, is quite solid, and the college does a good job of enrolling its admits. A very friendly and efficient admissions office no doubt contributes to such success.

## FINANCIAL AID

*Students should submit:* FAFSA by February 15th, the college's priority deadline. The Princeton Review suggests that all financial aid forms be submitted as soon as possible after January 1. *Need-based scholarships/grants offered:* Pell, SEOG, state scholarships/grants, private scholarships and the school's own gift aid. *Loan aid offered:* FFEL Subsidized Stafford, FFEL Unsubsidized Stafford, FFEL PLUS, and Federal Perkins. Institutional employment available. Federal Work-Study Program available. Applicants will be notified of awards on or about March 15. Off-campus job opportunities are excellent.

## FROM THE ADMISSIONS OFFICE

"Centenary students work closely with a gifted faculty and inquisitive peers. Small classes and interactive learning keep our students coming back after class to ask that extra question . . . or working a little longer to produce their very best. Our students were the leaders of their schools and communities. We know college should not be an end to their activities, but a furthering of their experiences. Centenary College provides ample and varied opportunities to further leadership experiences in an atmosphere of integrity and honesty encouraged by the Honor Code. Our students come for experiential learning through our service-learning program. They participate in a global classroom through our intercultural and study abroad programs. They develop their career paths with the help of dedicated faculty, staff, and internship mentors. Come visit Centenary College, get the facts, and find out if we are best for you."

## ADMISSIONS

| | |
|---|---|
| Admissions Rating | 75 |
| # of applicants | 549 |
| % of applicants accepted | 89 |
| % of acceptees attending | 47 |

### FRESHMAN PROFILE

| | |
|---|---|
| Range SAT Verbal | 480-620 |
| Range SAT Math | 490-610 |
| Range ACT Composite | 22-27 |
| Average ACT Composite | 25 |
| Minimum TOEFL | 550 |
| % graduated top 10% of class | 29 |
| % graduated top 25% of class | 54 |
| % graduated top 50% of class | 80 |

### DEADLINES

| | |
|---|---|
| Early decision | 12/1 |
| Early decision notification | 1/1 |
| Priority admission deadline | 2/15 |
| Regular notification | 3/15 |
| Nonfall registration? | yes |

### APPLICANTS ALSO LOOK AT
#### AND OFTEN PREFER
Tulane
Trinity U.
#### AND SOMETIMES PREFER
LSU—Baton Rouge
U. New Orleans
U. Southwestern Louisiana
Millsaps
Austin
#### AND RARELY PREFER
TCU
SMU

### FINANCIAL FACTS

| | |
|---|---|
| Financial Aid Rating | 88 |
| Tuition | $15,400 |
| Room & board | $4,800 |
| Books and supplies | $850 |
| Required fees | $400 |
| % frosh receiving aid | 95 |
| % undergrads receiving aid | 95 |

## CAMPUS LIFE

| | |
|---|---|
| **Quality of Life Rating** | **75** |
| Type of school | private |
| Affiliation | Presbyterian |
| Environment | suburban |

### STUDENTS

| | |
|---|---|
| Total undergrad enrollment | 1,055 |
| % male/female | 47/53 |
| % from out of state | 31 |
| % from public high school | 79 |
| % live on campus | 96 |
| % in (# of) fraternities | 57 (6) |
| % in (# of) sororities | 65 (4) |
| % African American | 3 |
| % Asian | 1 |
| % Caucasian | 95 |
| % international | 1 |
| # of countries represented | 12 |

### SURVEY SAYS . . .
Theater is hot
Frats and sororities dominate social
scene
No one cheats
Campus feels safe
Athletic facilities need improving
Diversity lacking on campus
Low cost of living
Lousy off-campus food
Diverse students interact

## ACADEMICS

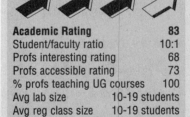

| | |
|---|---|
| **Academic Rating** | **83** |
| Student/faculty ratio | 10:1 |
| Profs interesting rating | 68 |
| Profs accessible rating | 73 |
| % profs teaching UG courses | 100 |
| Avg lab size | 10-19 students |
| Avg reg class size | 10-19 students |

### MOST POPULAR MAJORS
economics and English
history
government

## STUDENTS SPEAK OUT

### Academics

Founded in 1819, small, "prestigious" Centre College is one of America's oldest colleges and, according to Centre students, one of its best. Students here go so far as to call it "the Harvard of the South." Oh, that Harvard could be as affordable as Centre, which boasts a tremendously "low price," thanks in part to remarkably generous donations from rabidly loyal alumni. The curriculum here strongly emphasizes the liberal arts. "Centre teaches the skills of critical thinking, public speaking, and thoughtful writing," explains a history major. The "rigorous liberal arts curriculum works to develop the whole individual." It's no walk in the park, though. "Numerous papers, presentations, and exams" make courses "extremely challenging" and "stressful." Profs at Centre "not only present material in a lively, interesting way, but they challenge you to think critically and work hard." But students absolutely love them for it. They say their "supportive, well-informed, and amiable" professors "live to teach." Also, "personal attention" is the norm here. The "very dedicated" professors "care so much for their students, we often study at their homes," claims a first-year student. And "they expect you to walk in and see them" in their offices. Though the "unfair" registration process could be improved, the administration receives high praise as well. Administrators know most students "by name, and it is always a joy to interact with them." In a nutshell, students say Centre offers an "unrivaled" experience. "I knew it was the place for me and I haven't doubted it since," crows a sophomore. "I feel confident that I will leave here very employable and very well educated."

### Life

Though the Bluegrass Region surrounding Danville is "one of the most beautiful areas on the planet," the town itself "is not a happening place." Though it did host the 2000 vice presidential debate; it was jumpin' that night, no doubt. While "Centre makes a concentrated effort to bring the world" to the "scenic" campus "by bringing in Broadway plays and musicians like the Royal Philharmonic Orchestra," "Wal-Mart is the cultural highlight" of Danville. Nevertheless, students call their college's home "the prototypical college town" because it is "built around the activities" of the school. Social life here is, "as a rule, Greek," and it tends to be cyclical. "Everybody studies during the week" but the weekends are reserved for letting off steam. One student observes that "Danville is a dry city but Centre is a drowning campus on weekends." It's possible to "get drunk every weekend at frat parties" here. While it's also possible to "have fun without drinking," students warn that "you have to be willing to tolerate those who do." When the party scene gets old, students can trek to nearby Lexington "for recreation," to "go to the mall," or just "to get away." Pilgrimages to "Rupp Arena" (home to University of Kentucky basketball) are also big. Students gripe that the athletic facilities need improvement, and say the food isn't very good, though the cafeteria staff is reportedly one of the most sociable in the nation.

### Student Body

Just over 1,050 "friendly, supportive," and "just plain swell" students attend Centre. They are "career-oriented and highly motivated individuals" who are "genuinely interested in getting a good education." Many "aspire to continue their education" at graduate and professional schools. In the meantime, some are "raging alcoholics." Students say they are "gossipy," but they "get along with each other," as "southern hospitality" permeates the tiny campus. While some students contend that the students at Centre "come from very different backgrounds, from very rich to dirt poor," others argue that they are "spoiled, white middle-class people" who are "ignorant of the advantages over others they enjoy in life." It's definitely a bit on the "homogenous" side. "I think Centre could greatly benefit from a more culturally diverse and larger student body," suggests a junior. These complaints aside, "nowhere else is there a group of people so interested in achieving scholastically and yet so ready to have fun at a moment's notice."

FINANCIAL AID: 859-238-5365 • E-MAIL: ADMISSION@CENTRE.EDU • WEBSITE: WWW.CENTRE.EDU

## ADMISSIONS

*Very important* academic and nonacademic factors considered by the admissions committee include class rank, essays, secondary school record, and standardized test scores. *Important* factors considered include character/personal qualities, extracurricular activities, interview, and recommendations. *Other* factors considered include alumni/ae relation, talent/ability, and volunteer work. Factors *not* considered include geography, minority status, religious affiliation/commitment, state residency, and work experience. SAT I or ACT required. TOEFL required of all international applicants. *High school units required/recommended:* 16 total required; 20 total recommended; 4 English required, 4 math required, 3 science required, 4 science recommended, 2 science lab required, 2 foreign language required, 1 social studies required, 2 social studies recommended, 2 history required, 2 elective recommended.

### The Inside Word

Centre's small but very capable student body reflects solid academic preparation from high school, and it's no surprise that this is exactly what the admissions committee expects from applicants. If you're ranked in the top quarter of your graduating class and have taken challenging courses throughout your high school career, you should have smooth sailing through the admissions process. Those who rank below the top quarter or who have inconsistent academic backgrounds will find entrance here more difficult, and may benefit from an interview.

## FINANCIAL AID

*Students should submit:* FAFSA and institution's own financial aid form. Regular filing deadline is March 1. The Princeton Review suggests that all financial aid forms be submitted as soon as possible after January 1. *Need-based scholarships/grants offered:* Pell, SEOG, state scholarships/grants, private scholarships, and the school's own gift aid. *Loan aid offered:* FFEL Subsidized Stafford, FFEL Unsubsidized Stafford, FFEL PLUS, Federal Perkins, and college/university loans from institutional funds. Institutional employment available. Federal Work-Study Program available. Applicants will be notified of awards on or about April 1. Off-campus job opportunities are fair.

## FROM THE ADMISSIONS OFFICE

"'What's different about Centre?' The extraordinary advantages it provides. For example: national top 50 academic reputation; great opportunities for leadership development; global experience (among the nation's top 20 in study-abroad percentage); 'majors' advantages (create your own or 'do two'); personalized education with great advising (one-to-one from day one); and exposure to the world's best and most interesting (internationally known artists and scholars, the 2000 U.S. Vice Presidential Debate on campus).

"These kinds of benefits produce extraordinary results. For example: entrance to top graduate and professional schools (Harvard, Johns Hopkins, MIT, Oxford, Yale); the most prestigious post-graduate scholarships (Rhodes—our most recent in the class of 2000—Fulbright, Truman, Goldwater); and interesting and rewarding jobs (within nine months of graduation, 95 percent of graduates are either employed or engaged in advanced study.)

"How do alumni respond to the advantages Centre gave them? They express their customer satisfaction by leading the U.S. in their percentage of annual financial support.

"P.S. We also have a pretty good deal for students on the world-class entertainment (Willie Nelson, *STOMP*, Yo-Yo Ma) featured at our Norton Arts Center—it's free."

## ADMISSIONS

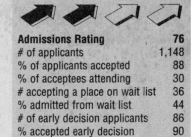

| | |
|---|---|
| Admissions Rating | 76 |
| # of applicants | 1,148 |
| % of applicants accepted | 88 |
| % of acceptees attending | 30 |
| # accepting a place on wait list | 36 |
| % admitted from wait list | 44 |
| # of early decision applicants | 86 |
| % accepted early decision | 90 |

### FRESHMAN PROFILE

| | |
|---|---|
| Range SAT Verbal | 560-660 |
| Average SAT Verbal | 619 |
| Range SAT Math | 540-640 |
| Average SAT Math | 603 |
| Range ACT Composite | 24-29 |
| Average ACT Composite | 27 |
| Minimum TOEFL | 580 |
| Average HS GPA | 3.8 |
| % graduated top 10% of class | 51 |
| % graduated top 25% of class | 80 |
| % graduated top 50% of class | 97 |

### DEADLINES

| | |
|---|---|
| Early decision | 11/15 |
| Early decision notification | 12/15 |
| Regular admission | 2/1 |
| Regular notification | 3/1 |

### APPLICANTS ALSO LOOK AT
**AND OFTEN PREFER**
Washington and Lee
Davidson
**AND SOMETIMES PREFER**
Rhodes
Sewanee
Kenyon
Furman
**AND RARELY PREFER**
Kentucky
Louisville

## FINANCIAL FACTS

| | |
|---|---|
| Financial Aid Rating | 74 |
| Tuition | $18,000 |
| Room & board | $6,000 |
| Books and supplies | $700 |
| % frosh receiving aid | 63 |
| % undergrads receiving aid | 59 |
| Avg frosh grant | $13,000 |
| Avg frosh loan | $2,600 |

# CITY UNIV. OF NY—HUNTER COLLEGE

695 PARK AVENUE, NEW YORK, NY 10021 • ADMISSIONS: 212-772-4000 • FAX: 212-650-3336

## CAMPUS LIFE

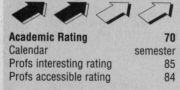

**Quality of Life Rating**    **69**
Type of school    public
Affiliation    none
Environment    urban

### STUDENTS

| | |
|---|---|
| Total undergrad enrollment | 15,422 |
| % male/female | 30/70 |
| % from out of state | 3 |
| % from public high school | 60 |
| % live on campus | 1 |
| % in (# of) fraternities | 2 (2) |
| % in (# of) sororities | 1 (2) |
| % African American | 21 |
| % Asian | 15 |
| % Caucasian | 39 |
| % Hispanic | 24 |
| % international | 6 |

### SURVEY SAYS . . .

*Ethnic diversity on campus*
*Political activism is hot*
*Everyone loves New York, NY*
*Different students interact*
*Lots of classroom discussion*
*Very little beer drinking*
*Very little hard liquor*
*Students are not very happy*

## ACADEMICS

**Academic Rating**    **70**
Calendar    semester
Profs interesting rating    85
Profs accessible rating    84

### MOST POPULAR MAJORS
psychology
English
sociology

## STUDENTS SPEAK OUT
### Academics

For many New York residents, Hunter College is the answer to the nagging question, "How in the world can I afford a college education?" With a solid reputation in the natural sciences, health sciences, social work, and English, Hunter offers not only a college degree but also one well regarded in academic circles, all at a price that's relatively easy on the bank account. Of course, because the school places a strong emphasis on keeping tuition and fees low, students enjoy few frills along with their learning experience. One student explains that as "with all city schools there are so many students, and sometimes getting exactly what you want is tough, but I think Hunter College does a good job trying to help students in times of need." Administrative issues are the most frustrating here. Writes one student, "It is very difficult to get information. You're always sent to another person. When you finish, you are back at the initial person." Another writes, "Classes are at times crowded and hard to get into. Nevertheless, it is possible to speak to professors and get individual attention if you are really interested." While "some profs are really good," others "need more training, and they need to be encouraged to spend time outside the classroom with their students." The honors program here is reportedly "very good."

### Life

Hunter is almost exclusively a commuter college. Even the school's few residents live away from campus, in a dormitory two miles south of the school. All others live in apartments scattered across New York's five boroughs, to which they return immediately after classes let out. Accordingly, there is "very little social life at Hunter. Everyone works and studies." Says one student, "Nothing active goes on. I try to get around and hear about social events, but it is usually a drag." Student organizations, intercollegiate and intramural sports, and campus theater help fill the void somewhat, but for most students extracurriculars take place off campus in the city that never sleeps. "New York is the best! The activities don't stop!" explains one enthusiastic student. Hunter's East Side location is close to art galleries, high-end fashion shops, and Central Park ("great for warm weather" and not nearly as dangerous as the movies make it out to be) and also provides easy subway access to Wall Street, Greenwich Village, Yankee Stadium, the Bronx Zoo, and any of a thousand other fabulous destinations. The campus itself, however, a four-building complex between Lexington and Park Avenues, "needs some serious updating."

### Student Body

Hunter's student body is among the nation's most racially varied, with African American, Asian, Latino, and Caucasian populations nearly in parity. "It would be impossible to have a more diverse student body," sums up one student. Diversity also manifests itself in students' attitudes. "Hunter is a melting pot of the highly intelligent and the extreme slacker," writes one undergrad. And another notes, "There is a scene here for any type, whether it be religious, studious, political, or stoned." Politically, student opinion ranges from the middle-of-the-road to the left, with very few students admitting to conservatism. Students are also "acutely aware of social, political, and cultural situations in general." With a large nontraditional population and little campus housing, students rarely see each other except in classes or at the library. Explains one, "Hunter students work. They are not, in the usual sense, college students. They live in the real world, not in an isolated, artificial social environment."

# CITY UNIVERSITY OF NEW YORK—HUNTER COLLEGE

FINANCIAL AID: 212-772-4820 • E-MAIL: ADMISSIONS@HUNTER.CUNY.EDU • WEBSITE: WWW.HUNTER.CUNY.EDU

## ADMISSIONS

*Very important* academic factors considered by the admission committee include secondary school record. *Important* factors include standardized test scores. Factors *not* considered include class rank, recommendations, essays, interview, extracurricular activities, talent/ability, character/personal qualities, alumni/ae relation, geographical residence, state residency, minority status, religious affiliation/commitment, volunteer work, and work experience. SAT I or ACT required. TOEFL required of all international applicants. High School diploma is required and GED is accepted. *High school units recommended:* 16 total recommended; 4 English, 3 math, 2 science lab, 2 foreign language, 4 social studies, and 1 visual and performing arts.

### The Inside Word

Nothing personal here; applications are processed through CUNY's enormous central processing center. Follow the numbers—and be sure to have followed the updated high school curriculum requirements—and gain admission. Looking ahead, expect admissions requirements throughout CUNY to continue to reflect heightened concern with academic preparedness. Hunter will no doubt continue to be among the most demanding CUNY units.

## FINANCIAL AID

*Students should submit:* FAFSA and state aid form. There is no regular filing deadline. The Princeton Review suggests that all financial aid forms be submitted as soon as possible after January 1. *Need-based scholarships/grants offered:* Pell, SEOG, state scholarships/grants, private scholarships, and the school's own gift aid. *Loan aid offered:* Direct Subsidized Stafford, Direct Unsubsidized Stafford, Direct PLUS, and Federal Perkins. Institutional employment available. Federal Work-Study Program available. Applicants will be notified of awards on a rolling basis. Off-campus job opportunities are good.

## FROM THE ADMISSIONS OFFICE

"Located in the heart of Manhattan, Hunter offers students the stimulating learning environment and career-building opportunities you might expect from a college that's been a part of the world's most exciting city since 1870. The largest college in the City University of New York and one of America's most ethnically diverse, Hunter pulses with energy. Its schools, including Arts and Sciences, Education, and the Health Professions, provide an affordable, first-rate education (it is no coincidence that 61 percent of Hunter students were accepted to medical school—the national acceptance rate is 36 percent). Undergraduates have extraordinary opportunities to conduct high-level research under renowned faculty, and many opt for credit-bearing internships in such exciting fields as media, the arts, and finance. Qualified students also benefit from Hunter's participation in the Research Centers in Minority Institutions Program, the prestigious Andrew W. Mellon Minority Undergraduate Program, and many other passports to professional success. The most academically gifted freshmen may be considered for the Hunter Honors Scholars Program, which emphasizes small classes with personalized mentoring by the most outstanding faculty and independent study options."

## ADMISSIONS

| | |
|---|---|
| Admissions Rating | 78 |
| # of applicants | 6,714 |
| % of applicants accepted | 53 |
| % of acceptees attending | 46 |

### FRESHMAN PROFILE

| | |
|---|---|
| Range SAT Verbal | 430-540 |
| Average SAT Verbal | 488 |
| Range SAT Math | 440-540 |
| Average SAT Math | 496 |
| Minimum TOEFL | 500 |
| Average HS GPA | 2.8 |
| % graduated top 10% of class | 10 |
| % graduated top 25% of class | 45 |
| % graduated top 50% of class | 73 |

### DEADLINES

| | |
|---|---|
| Regular admission | 12/1 |
| Regular notification | rolling |
| Nonfall registration? | yes |

### APPLICANTS ALSO LOOK AT AND OFTEN PREFER
CUNY Queens
NYU
### AND SOMETIMES PREFER
Fordham
Iona
SUNY Stony Brook

## FINANCIAL FACTS

| | |
|---|---|
| Financial Aid Rating | 74 |
| In-state tuition | $3,200 |
| Out-of-state tuition | $6,800 |
| Room & board | $1,890 |
| Books and supplies | $500 |
| Required fees | $150 |
| % frosh receiving aid | 81 |
| % undergrads receiving aid | 66 |
| Avg frosh grant | $4,200 |
| Avg frosh loan | $2,600 |

# CITY UNIV. OF NY—QUEENS COLLEGE

65-30 KISSENA BLVD., FLUSHING, NY 11367 • ADMISSIONS: 718-997-5000 • FAX: 718-997-5617

## CAMPUS LIFE

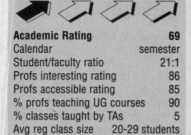

**Quality of Life Rating**          **67**
Type of school                      public
Affiliation                         none
Environment                         urban

### STUDENTS

| | |
|---|---|
| Total undergrad enrollment | 10,964 |
| % male/female | 37/63 |
| % from out of state | 1 |
| % from public high school | 67 |
| % in (# of) fraternities | 1 (2) |
| % in (# of) sororities | 1 (2) |
| % African American | 8 |
| % Asian | 15 |
| % Caucasian | 40 |
| % Hispanic | 14 |
| % international | 4 |

### SURVEY SAYS . . .
*Ethnic diversity on campus*
*Political activism is hot*
*Different students interact*
*Students love Flushing, NY*
*Lots of classroom discussion*
*Campus difficult to get around*
*Very little drug use*
*Unattractive campus*
*Lousy food on campus*
*Students are cliquish*

## ACADEMICS

| | |
|---|---|
| **Academic Rating** | **69** |
| Calendar | semester |
| Student/faculty ratio | 21:1 |
| Profs interesting rating | 86 |
| Profs accessible rating | 85 |
| % profs teaching UG courses | 90 |
| % classes taught by TAs | 5 |
| Avg reg class size | 20-29 students |

### MOST POPULAR MAJORS
sociology
accounting
psychology

## STUDENTS SPEAK OUT

### Academics

For many New York residents, Queens College offers the best opportunity for an excellent education at cut-rate prices. Explains one student, "The realities of academic life here are top-notch. I have studied and conducted independent research with world-class professors who are eager to devote much time to helping outstanding students achieve their fullest potential. Scholarships and study abroad opportunities abound here." Queens offers honors programs in the humanities, business, and the liberal arts, and the mathematical and natural sciences, which provide enhanced learning opportunities for excellent students. No Queens student, however, can avoid a bureaucracy that "is ridiculously confusing. All the running around should earn us 'frequent campus mileage.'" Many also expressed frustration over CUNY's financial status, complaining that "continuous budget cuts are destroying the CUNY system." Dealing with the CUNY bureaucracy, and the anxiety that ensues, is the trade-off students make for an affordable education. For most, it is a worthwhile tradeoff because it nets them an education that is "very good overall."

### Life

Because Queens College is a commuter school (QC has no dorms at all), campus life pretty much begins and ends during the day. Writes one student, "This is not a social campus because everyone commutes. You generally become friendly with those in your major, people you constantly have classes with." A few students do take apartments in Flushing; those that do enjoy the nearby Italian, Chinese, and Korean shopping and dining. Extracurricular activities here revolve around "lots of student organizations." Explains one student, "Campus clubs have a lot of activities." Adds another, "The doors to club offices are always open, so people make the rounds of the Student Union, visiting friends as they please. There are always free concerts at the music school during free hour." Students enjoy the fact that "professors like 'doing lunch' with their students; it alleviates a lot of the academic pressure for us." Unlike other CUNY schools such as Hunter and Baruch, Queens has an actual campus, which is "very safe" and "nice and pretty" despite an odd, sometimes clashing variety of architectural styles.

### Student Body

The borough of Queens is the residence of choice for many of New York City's immigrant groups. The Queens College student body reflects the international flavor of its home; the school's promotional material boasts that 67 different native languages are spoken on campus. The student body also accurately mirrors New York's democratic leanings, with over 40 percent of students identifying themselves as left-of-center politically. Minority students constitute nearly half the student body. Many students work their way through school here; they are "a hard-working bunch. Most are not well-off financially but are determined to better their lives through education."

FINANCIAL AID: 718-997-5101 • E-MAIL: ADMISSIONS@QC.EDU • WEBSITE: WWW.QC.EDU

## ADMISSIONS

*Very important* academic and nonacademic factors considered by the admissions committee include secondary school record. *Important* factors considered include standardized test scores and talent/ability. *Other* factors considered include class rank, essays, and recommendations. Factors *not* considered include alumni/ae relation, character/personal qualities, extracurricular activities, geography, interview, minority status, religious affiliation/commitment, state residency, volunteer work, and work experience. SAT I or ACT required, SAT I preferred; SAT II also recommended. TOEFL also required of all international applicants. High school diploma is required and GED is accepted. *High school units required/recommended:* 4 English required, 3 math required, 4 math recommended, 2 science required, 3 science recommended, 2 science lab required, 3 foreign language required, 2 social science required. *The admissions office says:* "Queens College seeks to admit freshmen who have completed a strong academic program in high school with a B+ average. Admission is based on a variety of factors, including grade point average, the academic program, and test scores. Those applying to the SEEK (Search for Education, Elevation, and Knowledge) program need not meet those requirements. SEEK 'helps economically and educationally disadvantaged students,' and provides those students with 'intensive academic services' (possibly including a stipend for educational expenses). Apply by January 15."

### The Inside Word

Applicants to Queens follow the usual CUNY application procedures, which have gotten tougher with the implementation of updated high school curriculum requirements. Candidates for the Aaron Copeland School of Music must also successfully pass through a rigorous audition process. CUNY admissions requirements are currently undergoing close scrutiny; beware of the possibility of further changes.

## FINANCIAL AID

*Students should submit:* FAFSA, CSS/Financial Aid PROFILE, and state aid form. There is no regular filing deadline. The Princeton Review suggests that all financial aid forms be submitted as soon as possible after January 1. *Need-based scholarships/grants offered:* Pell, SEOG, state scholarships/grants, and private scholarships. *Loan aid offered:* Direct Subsidized Stafford, Direct Unsubsidized Stafford, Direct PLUS, and Federal Perkins. Institutional employment available. Federal Work-Study Program available. Applicants will be notified of awards on a rolling basis beginning on or about April 15. Off-campus job opportunities are good.

## FROM THE ADMISSIONS OFFICE

"Applicants to Queens follow the usual CUNY application procedures, which have gotten tougher with the implementation of updated high school curriculum requirements. Candidates for the Aaron Copeland School of Music must also successfully pass through a rigorous audition process. CUNY admissions requirements are currently undergoing close scrutiny; beware of the possibility of further changes."

### ADMISSIONS

| | |
|---|---|
| Admissions Rating | 73 |
| # of applicants | 4,630 |
| % of applicants accepted | 56 |
| % of acceptees attending | 37 |

#### FRESHMAN PROFILE

| | |
|---|---|
| Range SAT Verbal | 450-565 |
| Average SAT Verbal | 506 |
| Range SAT Math | 480-590 |
| Average SAT Math | 536 |
| Minimum TOEFL | 500 |
| Average HS GPA | 3.1 |

#### DEADLINES

| | |
|---|---|
| Regular admission | 1/1 |
| Nonfall registration? | yes |

#### APPLICANTS ALSO LOOK AT AND OFTEN PREFER

CUNY Hunter
St. John's U. (NY)
Hofstra

#### AND SOMETIMES PREFER

Fordham
SUNY Albany
Binghamton U.
SUNY Buffalo
SUNY Stony Brook

### FINANCIAL FACTS

| | |
|---|---|
| Financial Aid Rating | 76 |
| In-state tuition | $3,200 |
| Out-of-state tuition | $6,800 |
| Required fees | $193 |
| % frosh receiving aid | 49 |
| % undergrads receiving aid | 38 |
| Avg frosh grant | $3,500 |
| Avg frosh loan | $2,500 |

# CLAREMONT McKENNA COLLEGE

890 COLUMBIA AVENUE, CLAREMONT, CA 91711 • ADMISSIONS: 909-621-8088 • FAX: 909-621-8516

## CAMPUS LIFE

| | |
|---|---|
| **Quality of Life Rating** | **92** |
| Type of school | private |
| Affiliation | none |
| Environment | suburban |

### STUDENTS

| | |
|---|---|
| Total undergrad enrollment | 2,005 |
| % male/female | 29/71 |
| % from out of state | 40 |
| % from public high school | 70 |
| % live on campus | 95 |
| % African American | 5 |
| % Asian | 17 |
| % Caucasian | 66 |
| % Hispanic | 12 |
| % international | 1 |

### SURVEY SAYS . . .

*Dorms are like palaces*
*Political activism is hot*
*Student government is popular*
*Lab facilities need improving*
*School is well run*
*(Almost) no one smokes*
*Diverse students interact*
*Student publications are popular*

## ACADEMICS

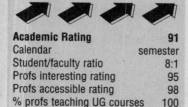

| | |
|---|---|
| **Academic Rating** | **91** |
| Calendar | semester |
| Student/faculty ratio | 8:1 |
| Profs interesting rating | 95 |
| Profs accessible rating | 98 |
| % profs teaching UG courses | 100 |

### MOST POPULAR MAJORS

economics
government
psychology

## STUDENTS SPEAK OUT

### Academics

"You can't beat the academics" at "small" Claremont McKenna, a "fun, tough, challenging, demanding, and rewarding" liberal arts college. "Conveniently located" in sunny southern California, CMC consistently churns out "pragmatic, marketable" grads who "will be leaders in the next millenium." CMC offers a slew of academic opportunities: "internships, innovative classes, study abroad," and some of the most respected research institutes in the country. It is "what East Coast Ivy League schools used to be," explains one student, "a tight-knit community of intellectuals," the "best professors in the nation," and "a financial aid office that rocks the world." Popular majors here include "economics, government econ, and more econ," as well as a "wonderful" pre-med program. The "engaging, interesting," and "unbelievable faculty" is composed of "extremely approachable, very intelligent, and personable" professors who "spend hours every week with students one-on-one." Tremendous library and computer facilities, "seamless registration," and "approachable, down-to-earth" administration also draw kudos. "I somewhat regretted CMC's small size until one day, my history professor called me because she noticed I wasn't registered for her class," explains an awestruck first-year student. "'But don't worry,' she says, 'I called Jane (the registrar) and told her you would come and register.' It blew me away."

### Life

Though it's "good for the occasional cup of coffee," Claremont is "entirely useless" otherwise. Also, there is "no dating scene" here. Nevertheless, students are "having a wonderful time," thank you very much. "The five-college cluster" of CMC, Pomona, Scripps, Harvey Mudd, and a central graduate school offers a "laid-back atmosphere" and a wealth of activities. The wildly popular Athenaeum provides "interesting" and "world-renowned" speakers on "everything from politics to music and great gourmet food." In addition, "there is always something to get involved in," from planned activities (including the Night in Vienna Dinner and Monte Carlo Night—"the big Homecoming and gambling formal") to political activism of all stripes. You can also "go to the beach" or "watch asteroids." Student government is "huge" (and genuinely powerful) as well, and "lots of people are into sports." Drinking and "outrageous parties" are also enormously popular at CMC. "The administration loves us so much," exclaims a sophomore, "they give us a $125,000 beer budget. Now that's love." CMC also provides housing options for its students who choose a substance-free lifestyle. Despite all the on-campus perks, the actual city of Claremont mainly consists of "boutiques and pricey restaurants." "Don't go to school in a town without public transportation if you don't have a car," advises a first-year student wise beyond her years. "The club scene" of Los Angeles is "rather close" as is San Diego.

### Student Body

"Claremont McKenna is what happens when you put a bunch of overachievers together in a quaint setting rich with a tradition of achievement." The campus is rife with "intelligent and witty" people and there are "many deep conversations to be had." The "socially outgoing and academically driven" students here are "friendly," "hardworking," "smart, funny, and well adjusted." Many are "preppy yuppies-in-the-making" who are "out to make as much money as possible." "One student I know watches the 'Greed is Good' speech from the movie *Wall Street* to brighten his day," relates a first-year student. Over one-third of CMC's ambitious students are minorities, and the diversity provides for regular "clashes" of politics. "The bell curve distribution of ideologies ensures a healthy dose of good-natured arguments," says a senior. Stereotypes "abound" at CMC, and there are "very concrete cliques"—the "North Quad partiers versus the South Quad Studiers" rivalry is "quite amazing"—but overall, students call their "very cohesive community" a place where "there is very little animosity or competitiveness."

FINANCIAL AID: 909-621-8356 • E-MAIL: ADMISSION@MCKENNA.EDU • WEBSITE: WWW.CLAREMONTMCKENNA.EDU

## ADMISSIONS

*Very important* academic and nonacademic factors considered by the admissions committee include secondary school record. *Important* factors considered include class rank, essays, recommendations, and standardized test scores. *Other* factors considered include alumni/ae relation, character/personal qualities, extracurricular activities, geography, interview, minority status, state residency, talent/ability, volunteer work, and work experience. Factors *not* considered include religious affiliation/commitment. SAT I or ACT required, SAT I preferred. TOEFL required of all international applicants. High school diploma is required and GED is accepted. *High school units required/recommended:* 16 total required; 4 English required, 3 math required, 2 science required, 2 science lab required, 2 foreign language required, 2 social studies required, 3 elective required. *The admissions office says:* "Because of the nature of CMC, we place extra emphasis on leadership ability/potential and extracurricular involvement. Our students typically have strong interpersonal skills. They also rate high in self-confidence, assertiveness, and motivation."

### The Inside Word

Although applicants have to possess solid academic qualifications in order to gain admission to Claremont McKenna, the importance of making a good match should not be underestimated. Colleges of such small size and selectivity devote much more energy to determining whether the candidate as an individual fits than they do to whether a candidate has the appropriate test scores.

## FINANCIAL AID

*Students should submit:* FAFSA and CSS/Financial Aid PROFILE. Regular filing deadline is February 1. The Princeton Review suggests that all financial aid forms be submitted as soon as possible after January 1. *Need-based scholarships/grants offered:* Pell, SEOG, state scholarships/grants, private scholarships, and the school's own gift aid. *Loan aid offered:* Direct Subsidized Stafford, Direct Unsubsidized Stafford, Direct PLUS, Federal Perkins, and college/university loans from institutional funds. Institutional employment available. Federal Work-Study Program available. Applicants will be notified of awards on or about April 1. Off-campus job opportunities are excellent.

## FROM THE ADMISSIONS OFFICE

"CMC's mission is clear: to educate students for meaningful lives and responsible leadership in business, government, and the professions. While many other colleges champion either a traditional liberal arts education with emphasis on intellectual breadth or training that stresses acquisition of technical skills, CMC offers a clear alternative. Instead of dividing the liberal arts and working world into separate realms, education at CMC is rooted in the interplay between the world of ideas and the world of events. By combining the intellectual breadth of liberal arts with the more pragmatic concerns of public affairs, CMC students gain the vision, skills, and values necessary for leadership in all sectors of society."

## ADMISSIONS

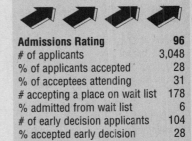

| | |
|---|---|
| Admissions Rating | 96 |
| # of applicants | 3,048 |
| % of applicants accepted | 28 |
| % of acceptees attending | 31 |
| # accepting a place on wait list | 178 |
| % admitted from wait list | 6 |
| # of early decision applicants | 104 |
| % accepted early decision | 28 |

### FRESHMAN PROFILE

| | |
|---|---|
| Range SAT Verbal | 650-730 |
| Average SAT Verbal | 700 |
| Range SAT Math | 660-740 |
| Average SAT Math | 700 |
| Range ACT Composite | 27-31 |
| Average ACT Composite | 30 |
| Minimum TOEFL | 600 |
| Average HS GPA | 3.9 |
| % graduated top 10% of class | 82 |
| % graduated top 25% of class | 95 |
| % graduated top 50% of class | 100 |

### DEADLINES

| | |
|---|---|
| Early decision | 11/15 |
| Early decision notification | 12/15 |
| Regular admission | 1/2 |
| Regular notification | 4/1 |
| Nonfall registration? | yes |

### APPLICANTS ALSO LOOK AT
**AND OFTEN PREFER**
Stanford
Georgetown U.
**AND SOMETIMES PREFER**
Pomona
UC—Berkeley
UCLA
**AND RARELY PREFER**
UC—San Diego
UC—Davis
UC—Irvine

## FINANCIAL FACTS

| | |
|---|---|
| Financial Aid Rating | 83 |
| Tuition | $20,390 |
| Room & board | $7,272 |
| Books and supplies | $750 |
| Required fees | $190 |
| % frosh receiving aid | 56 |
| % undergrads receiving aid | 60 |
| Avg frosh grant | $16,261 |
| Avg frosh loan | $3,000 |

# CLARK UNIVERSITY

950 MAIN STREET, WORCESTER, MA 01610 • ADMISSIONS: 508-793-7431 • FAX: 508-793-8821

## CAMPUS LIFE

| Quality of Life Rating | 69 |
|---|---|
| Type of school | private |
| Affiliation | none |
| Environment | urban |

### STUDENTS

| | |
|---|---|
| Total undergrad enrollment | 2,124 |
| % male/female | 41/59 |
| % from out of state | 60 |
| % from public high school | 70 |
| % live on campus | 71 |
| % African American | 4 |
| % Asian | 4 |
| % Caucasian | 72 |
| % Hispanic | 3 |
| % international | 9 |
| # of countries represented | 62 |

### SURVEY SAYS . . .
*Theater is hot*
*(Almost) everyone smokes*
*Students aren't religious*
*Students don't get along with local community*
*Ethnic diversity on campus*
*Students don't like Worcester, MA*
*Lousy food on campus*

## ACADEMICS

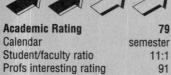

| Academic Rating | 79 |
|---|---|
| Calendar | semester |
| Student/faculty ratio | 11:1 |
| Profs interesting rating | 91 |
| Profs accessible rating | 91 |
| % profs teaching UG courses | 100 |
| % classes taught by TAs | 1 |
| Avg lab size | 10-19 students |
| Avg reg class size | 10-19 students |

### MOST POPULAR MAJORS
psychology
government and international relations
biology

## STUDENTS SPEAK OUT
### Academics

The "individualists" at "small and comfortable" Clark University frequently cite personal autonomy as their school's greatest attribute. "Clark's the kind of place individuals come to contribute themselves to education and college life." The "fair and caring" professors here are "great with very few exceptions." Clark profs are "very enthusiastic about their subjects and more than willing to help you outside of the classroom" and they "make every effort to get to know" their students. "My professors are all extremely nice. No matter how hard I try to hate them, I just can't," relates a first-year student. Clark is a "world-class" research university in many ways as well (which is rare for a small, private school). Undergrads here are able to participate to an unusually large degree in "interesting research." Some students, though, bemoan a "lack of communication" that often prevents them from knowing just what research the faculty is conducting. While some Clarkies complain that administrators "don't have a clue," they have created a handful of commendable programs. Clark originated the first "Fifth-Year Free Program" in the United States, which allows "qualified students" to attend for five years at the bargain-basement price of four and "receive a bachelor's and master's degree." Obviously, students in the program save a bundle in tuition. Clark is also a member of the Worcester Consortium, which allows undergraduates to take courses at any of nine other schools in the area.

### Life

"Clark means well, but if you want an active social life, this is not the place," advises a sophomore. "If you want to study a lot, Clark's your place." Students say their safe campus is "pretty," though certainly not spectacular, but it's a lot more attractive than the surrounding town of Worcester (pronounced "Woostah"). Though "Worcester is no cultural nirvana," it offers "great thrift stores" and "great ethnic restaurants" (which is a good thing because the cafeteria food is mediocre at best). "Many people go to bars and movies" off campus as well. But for college students, Worcester's appeal is severely limited. "Our recreation is what we make of it," explains a junior. "The open atmosphere lets you do what you want without being harassed." "Social life revolves around get-togethers and sometimes parties" but "the lack of fun, safe, and popular establishments leaves weekends open to mostly drinking and drug use." Students can also "go to the gym," "watch TV with friends," and "hang out in somebody's room" engrossed in late-night discussions. There's a pretty big international student population, and "cultural clubs throw parties" reasonably often. In addition, "campus activities can be cheesy but they're not bad." Best of all, Boston is only 40 miles away and is easily accessible by bus.

### Student Body

"There are two types of students here," discloses a senior, "the wealthy ones whose parents sent them to Clark to make them look good and the poor ones who Clark pays to go here to make the school look good." It works out to be a pretty diverse crew in terms of "race, spiritual beliefs, hobbies," and just about everything else. In fact, to say "Clark boasts about having one of the most diverse student populations around" is "an understatement." "If you spend five minutes on the Campus Green you might see basketball players walk by, then two tattooed, green-haired people," explains a freshman. "After two months here, it won't strike you as odd." You will see students who are apathetic, others who are "happy and amiable," and still others who "sweat coolness from their pores." You will also see "a high percentage of international students"—"friendly, interesting people" from "all over the world." Best of all, you will see "a lot of interaction between ethnic groups." Though "there is still cliquishness," students here are "very open to the individuality" of others and, as a rule, "Clarkies all get along." Sums up one student, "Although there is a lot of diversity, there is a definite sense of community within the university."

FINANCIAL AID: 508-793-7478 • E-MAIL: ADMISSIONS@CLARKU.EDU • WEBSITE: WWW.CLARKU.EDU

## ADMISSIONS

*Very important* academic and nonacademic factors considered by the admissions committee include class rank, essays, and secondary school record. *Important* factors considered include alumni/ae relation, character/personal qualities, extracurricular activities, interview, recommendations, standardized test scores, and talent/ability. *Other* factors considered include geography, minority status, volunteer work, and work experience. Factors *not* considered include religious affiliation/commitment and state residency. SAT I or ACT required; SAT II also required. TOEFL required of all international applicants. High school diploma is required and GED is accepted. *High school units required/recommended:* 16 total required; 4 English required, 3 math required, 4 math recommended, 2 science required, 3 science recommended. *The admissions office says:* "If a student plans to major in math or science, three or more years of math and science courses are strongly recommended."

### The Inside Word

Clark is surrounded by formidable competitors, and its selectivity suffers because of it. Most "B" students will encounter little difficulty gaining admission. Given the university's solid academic environment and access to other member colleges in the Worcester Consortium, it can be a terrific choice for students who are not up to the ultra-competitive admission expectations of "top-tier" universities.

## FINANCIAL AID

*Students should submit:* FAFSA and CSS/Financial Aid PROFILE. The Princeton Review suggests that all financial aid forms be submitted as soon as possible after January 1. *Need-based scholarships/grants offered:* Pell, SEOG, state scholarships/grants, and the school's own gift aid. *Loan aid offered:* FFEL Subsidized Stafford, FFEL Unsubsidized Stafford, FFEL PLUS, Federal Perkins, state, and college/university loans from institutional funds. Institutional employment available. Applicants will be notified of awards on or about March 31. Off-campus job opportunities are good.

## FROM THE ADMISSIONS OFFICE

"At Clark University, you are respected for challenging convention, for trying out new ideas and skills, and for inspiring new ways of thinking. You learn how social change is made, and you get to be a part of it. Individual development is nurtured by a dedicated faculty who encourages hands-on learning. Founded in 1887, Clark is home to students from more than 90 countries and 48 states."

## ADMISSIONS

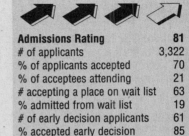

| | |
|---|---|
| Admissions Rating | 81 |
| # of applicants | 3,322 |
| % of applicants accepted | 70 |
| % of acceptees attending | 21 |
| # accepting a place on wait list | 63 |
| % admitted from wait list | 19 |
| # of early decision applicants | 61 |
| % accepted early decision | 85 |

### FRESHMAN PROFILE

| | |
|---|---|
| Range SAT Verbal | 540-650 |
| Average SAT Verbal | 590 |
| Range SAT Math | 530-640 |
| Average SAT Math | 584 |
| Range ACT Composite | 23-28 |
| Average ACT Composite | 25 |
| Minimum TOEFL | 550 |
| Average HS GPA | 3.3 |
| % graduated top 10% of class | 29 |
| % graduated top 25% of class | 63 |
| % graduated top 50% of class | 95 |

### DEADLINES

| | |
|---|---|
| Early decision | 11/15 |
| Early decision notification | 12/15 |
| Regular admission | 2/1 |
| Regular notification | 4/1 |
| Nonfall registration? | yes |

### APPLICANTS ALSO LOOK AT

**AND OFTEN PREFER**
Tufts, Boston Coll.
Brandeis, Vassar
**AND SOMETIMES PREFER**
Connecticut Coll.
Syracuse
U. New Hampshire
Skidmore
U. Mass—Amherst
**AND RARELY PREFER**
Wheaton Coll. (MA)

### FINANCIAL FACTS

| | |
|---|---|
| Financial Aid Rating | 77 |
| Tuition | $23,300 |
| Room & board | $4,350 |
| Books and supplies | $600 |
| Required fees | $220 |
| % frosh receiving aid | 63 |
| % undergrads receiving aid | 62 |
| Avg frosh grant | $12,626 |
| Avg frosh loan | $4,440 |

# CLARKSON UNIVERSITY

Box 5605, Potsdam, NY 13699 • Admissions: 315-268-6479 • Fax: 315-268-7647

## CAMPUS LIFE

**Quality of Life Rating**    71
Type of school    private
Affiliation    none
Environment    rural

### STUDENTS
Total undergrad enrollment    2,539
% male/female    73/27
% from out of state    26
% from public high school    90
% live on campus    80
% in (# of) fraternities    11 (11)
% in (# of) sororities    16 (3)
% African American    3
% Asian    3
% Caucasian    89
% Hispanic    1
% Native American    1
% international    4

### SURVEY SAYS . . .
Musical organizations aren't popular
Class discussions are rare
Diversity lacking on campus
Student publications are ignored
Students aren't religious
Theater is unpopular
Library needs improving
Large classes
Political activism is (almost) nonexistent
Students are not very happy

## ACADEMICS

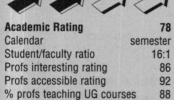

**Academic Rating**    78
Calendar    semester
Student/faculty ratio    16:1
Profs interesting rating    86
Profs accessible rating    92
% profs teaching UG courses    88
% classes taught by TAs    1
Avg lab size    20-29 students
Avg reg class size    20-29 students

### MOST POPULAR MAJORS
mechanical engineering
electrical and computer engineering
civil engineering

## STUDENTS SPEAK OUT
### Academics
"Clarkson University, the engineering school with a heart," might well serve as a slogan for this small upstate New York institution. "The professors really care about us as people, not just as students," report students here. "Getting hold of your department head is often easier than getting hold of your roommate," says one. "Most of my friends at other schools complain about their classes being taught by teaching assistants who do not 'know' their material," relates another student. "We don't have that problem." Unlike many engineering schools, "The level of competitiveness here is very low. It's not a fight to see who is the best; it's more of a 'let's all get through this together' kind of thing." Students cite the "small classes, great faculty, and laboratories" as additional academic strengths. On the downside, students complain that the library is not up to par and that some of the caring professors here "speak with heavy accents, making them hard to understand." One student laments the fact that the university is "always on the cutting edge of technology," but "so few courses take advantage of the high-tech resources."

### Life
Things are quiet in Potsdam, an isolated town in the farthest reaches of upstate New York that bills itself as "a unique Victorian village." How quiet? Writes one student, "We usually go to the P&C late at night because it is the only place open after 10 P.M. That is the time when students are just starting to come out for personal enjoyment, and everything is closed." Winters are long and cold here, and the bleakness can be discouraging for newcomers. One senior tells us, "Almost everyone I've talked to says that during the first year he wanted to transfer out, but by the time he graduated he thought Clarkson was the best and was happy he stayed. Clarkson, and even Potsdam, grows on you." Counters a junior, "After my four years are over I will not return." Winter sports, especially hockey and skiing, are very popular among students, although one student wryly observes, "For fun we try to ski around campus in the snow, but Campus Safety must feel that we should be smoking weed, because they're stricter about the skiing than about the pot smoking." Otherwise, students entertain themselves as do most other small-town college students. "Fraternity life and the bars are the things to do!" explains one student. Younger students take advantage of Canada's 18-year-old drinking age by "going up to Canada to go to nightclubs. Potsdam is a very boring town if you're under 21."

### Student Body
The "mostly homogenous population" of Clarkson hails primarily from New York and neighboring northeastern states. Most are white and "tend to stay with their own type, ignoring different races, sexual orientations, etc." Consequently, minority students can feel a little out of place. Complains one student, Clarkson undergrads "have small-town, upstate New York mentalities. There are lots of 'brains' but very few intellectuals." Others disagree, opining that "We mix laid-back spirit with intellectual maturity." The "people here don't think they're above anyone else," says another student. "That's what's so great about them." Nearly all students who are not engineers study business and management; pre-meds also contribute a small share to the student body. As at most engineering schools, students feel that Clarkson needs "more women."

FINANCIAL AID: 315-268-7699 • E-MAIL: ADMISSIONS@CLARKSON.EDU • WEBSITE: WWW.CLARKSON.EDU

## ADMISSIONS

*Very important* academic and nonacademic factors considered by the admissions committee include secondary school record. *Important* factors considered include character/personal qualities, class rank, essays, extracurricular activities, interview, recommendations, standardized test scores, and talent/ability. *Other* factors considered include alumni/ae relation, geography, minority status, volunteer work, and work experience. Factors *not* considered include religious affiliation/commitment and state residency. SAT I or ACT required. TOEFL required of all international applicants. High school diploma is required and GED is accepted. *High school units required/recommended:* 16 total recommended; 4 English recommended, 3 math recommended, 2 science recommended, 2 science lab recommended, 3 foreign language recommended, 2 social studies recommended, 2 history recommended, 2 elective recommended. *The admissions office says:* "We do not use cutoffs, but rather evaluate the overall match between student and Clarkson. Throughout the process, we are accessible to the students, their family, and their guidance counselor."

### The Inside Word

Clarkson's acceptance rate is too high for solid applicants to lose much sleep about gaining admission. Serious candidates should interview anyway. If you are particularly solid and really want to come here, it could help you get some scholarship money. Women and minorities will encounter an especially friendly admissions committee.

## FINANCIAL AID

*Students should submit:* FAFSA and state aid form. The Princeton Review suggests that all financial aid forms be submitted as soon as possible after January 1. *Need-based scholarships/grants offered:* Pell, SEOG, state scholarships/grants, private scholarships, and the school's own gift aid. *Loan aid offered:* Direct Subsidized Stafford, Direct Unsubsidized Stafford, Direct PLUS, Federal Perkins, college/university loans from institutional funds, and Gate. Institutional employment available. Federal Work-Study Program available. Applicants will be notified of awards on or about March 23. Off-campus job opportunities are fair.

## FROM THE ADMISSIONS OFFICE

"Clarkson is a blend of vivid contrasts—high-powered academics in a cooperative, friendly community; technically oriented students who enjoy people; a unique location that serves as gateway to all kinds of outdoor recreation and to social and cultural activities of four colleges within a 10-mile radius. Our students are described as smart, hardworking, outgoing, energized, fun-loving, and team players. Our academic programs are rigorous, relevant, flexible, and nationally respected. Our teachers are demanding, approachable, concerned, accomplished, and inspiring. Clarkson alumni, students, and faculty share an exceptionally solid bond and the lifetime benefits that come from an active, global network of personal and professional ties."

## ADMISSIONS

| | |
|---|---|
| Admissions Rating | 81 |
| # of applicants | 2,416 |
| % of applicants accepted | 83 |
| % of acceptees attending | 32 |
| # accepting a place on wait list | 30 |
| % admitted from wait list | 33 |
| # of early decision applicants | 201 |
| % accepted early decision | 71 |

### FRESHMAN PROFILE

| | |
|---|---|
| Range SAT Verbal | 520-620 |
| Average SAT Verbal | 570 |
| Range SAT Math | 570-660 |
| Average SAT Math | 615 |
| Minimum TOEFL | 500 |
| Average HS GPA | 3.4 |
| % graduated top 10% of class | 40 |
| % graduated top 25% of class | 70 |
| % graduated top 50% of class | 95 |

### DEADLINES

| | |
|---|---|
| Early decision | 12/1 |
| Early decision notification | 12/30 |
| Priority admission deadline | 2/1 |
| Regular admission | 3/15 |
| Nonfall registration? | yes |

### APPLICANTS ALSO LOOK AT

**AND OFTEN PREFER**
RIT
SUNY at Buffalo
RPI
U. Vermont
Penn State—Univ. Park

**AND SOMETIMES PREFER**
Worcester Poly.
U. Connecticut
U. Rochester
Alfred
Lehigh

**AND RARELY PREFER**
Syracuse

### FINANCIAL FACTS

| | |
|---|---|
| Financial Aid Rating | 74 |
| Tuition | $21,400 |
| Room & board | $8,084 |
| Books and supplies | $900 |
| Required fees | $400 |
| % frosh receiving aid | 83 |
| % undergrads receiving aid | 82 |
| Avg frosh grant | $11,571 |
| Avg frosh loan | $5,413 |

# CLEMSON UNIVERSITY

105 SIKES HALL, BOX 345124, CLEMSON, SC 29634-5124 • ADMISSIONS: 864-656-2287 • FAX: 864-656-2464

## Academics

Situated in the foothills of the Blue Ridge Mountains, Clemson University is a popular school for South Carolina students looking for a quality, in-state education. One sophomore writes, "You get a sound education in a friendly and helpful environment." Sounds sweet, doesn't it? Students rave about the "easy- going" classroom atmosphere, and professors are universally beloved for their accessibility. "My professors are very easy to talk to and are open to ideas and complaints or whenever I need help," a first-year beams. A senior travel and tourism major confirms that "most of the professors are good. They usually care about any problems you may be having with classes." Occasionally, though, one runs into a prof who is "mean and makes you cry." Professors are a part of campus life, both in and out of class. "I have seen lots of instructors out mixing with the students. They seem very eager to play an active part in the development of students' lives," one English major notes. Students remark that the workload is not often challenging enough and say that they would like more classes and majors to be offered. Class registration could use at least some tweaking, and if not that, a major overhaul.

## Life

Life at Clemson revolves around the school's football team, a posse with a storied heritage. Saturdays in the fall are dedicated to following the exploits of the Tigers. When not rooting for the home team at "Death Valley," students go downtown on the weekends. Springtime at Clemson means afternoons spitting sunflower seeds while watching the baseball team beat up on ACC rivals. Students also play an active role in on-campus religious organizations. Clemson is a big movie-watching campus, too, perhaps because there is close to "nothing to do" off campus. Post-game parties are a popular diversion, and fraternities play a large role in students' social lives. Clemson's "beautiful" geographic location allows students to pursue outdoor recreational activities, such as skiing, hiking, and camping. Don't look to get blown away by the fare on or off campus, though. Life at Clemson: "This is a good place to be. The only requirement is that you must like the color orange."

## Student Body

Clemson students are "friendly and outgoing." As one junior notes, "Everyone seems to be willing to make you at home." A sophomore adds, "I have never had a problem with any other student." If you are looking for a liberal student body, though, look elsewhere. Most of Clemson's students hail from South Carolina and are religious and politically conservative. Prime ground for Pat Robertson, baby. There are few minorities on campus and many students note the lack of on-campus diversity, but they shrug it off with a smile. How could anyone harp for long about anything when students all feel like "we are family"?

FINANCIAL AID: 864-656-2280 • E-MAIL: CUADMISSIONS@CLEMSON.EDU • WEBSITE: WWW.CLEMSON.EDU

## ADMISSIONS

*Very important* academic and nonacademic factors considered by the admissions committee include secondary school record. *Important* factors considered include class rank, extracurricular activities, standardized test scores, and talent/ability. *Other* factors considered include alumni/ae relation, character/personal qualities, essays, interview, minority status, recommendations, and volunteer work. Factors *not* considered include geography, religious affiliation/commitment, state residency, and work experience. SAT I or ACT required, SAT I preferred. TOEFL required of all international applicants. High school diploma is required and GED is accepted. *High school units required/recommended:* 19 total required; 4 English required, 3 math required, 4 math recommended, 3 science required, 3 science lab required, 2 foreign language required, 3 foreign language recommended, 2 social studies required, 1 history required, 2 elective required. *The admissions office says:* "Candidates for the College of Architecture should present a portfolio for review by the faculty early in the candidate's senior year."

### The Inside Word

Admission by formula. Out-of-state students are in abundance; such applicants will find little difference in admissions standards from those for state residents.

## FINANCIAL AID

*Students should submit:* FAFSA. The Princeton Review suggests that all financial aid forms be submitted as soon as possible after January 1. *Need-based scholarships/grants offered:* Pell, SEOG, state scholarships/grants, private scholarships, the school's own gift aid, and Federal Nursing. *Loan aid offered:* Direct PLUS, FFEL Subsidized Stafford, FFEL Unsubsidized Stafford, FFEL PLUS, Federal Perkins, state, and college/university loans from institutional funds. Institutional employment available. Federal Work-Study Program available. Applicants will be notified of awards on a rolling basis beginning on or about April 1. Off-campus job opportunities are good.

## FROM THE ADMISSIONS OFFICE

"Clemson University is a comprehensive land-grant university with approximately 16,000 students. Noted for its academic excellence, Clemson offers over 70 undergraduate degree programs in five academic colleges. Programs such as Calhoun College, the Honors Program, and study abroad are available to outstanding students. The campus is situated in the foothills of the Blue Ridge Mountains, with numerous outdoor opportunities available for students. Clemson has over 250 clubs and organizations, and the spirit that our students show for the university is unparalleled. Students should apply early in the fall, as the entering class closes earlier each year."

## ADMISSIONS

| Admissions Rating | 82 |
|---|---|
| # of applicants | 10,472 |
| % of applicants accepted | 64 |
| % of acceptees attending | 45 |
| # accepting a place on wait list | 295 |
| % admitted from wait list | 43 |

### FRESHMAN PROFILE

| | |
|---|---|
| Range SAT Verbal | 525-620 |
| Average SAT Verbal | 575 |
| Range SAT Math | 555-640 |
| Average SAT Math | 597 |
| Range ACT Composite | 23-27 |
| Average ACT Composite | 25 |
| Minimum TOEFL | 550 |
| Average HS GPA | 3.6 |
| % graduated top 10% of class | 37 |
| % graduated top 25% of class | 70 |
| % graduated top 50% of class | 96 |

### DEADLINES

| | |
|---|---|
| Regular admission | 5/1 |
| Regular notification | rolling |
| Nonfall registration? | yes |

### APPLICANTS ALSO LOOK AT

**AND OFTEN PREFER**
UNC—Chapel Hill
Duke
U. Georgia

**AND SOMETIMES PREFER**
Furman
James Madison
U. South Carolina, Columbia
Wake Forest
Vanderbilt

**AND RARELY PREFER**
U. Florida
Auburn U.

### FINANCIAL FACTS

| Financial Aid Rating | 75 |
|---|---|
| In-state tuition | $3,280 |
| Out-of-state tuition | $9,266 |
| Room & board | $4,122 |
| Books and supplies | $712 |
| Required fees | $190 |
| % frosh receiving aid | 36 |
| % undergrads receiving aid | 34 |
| Avg frosh grant | $4,357 |
| Avg frosh loan | $3,673 |

# COE COLLEGE

1220 FIRST AVENUE NE, CEDAR RAPIDS, IA 52402 • ADMISSIONS: 319-399-8500 • FAX: 319-399-8816

## CAMPUS LIFE

| Quality of Life Rating | 75 |
|---|---|
| Type of school | private |
| Affiliation | Presbyterian |
| Environment | urban |

### STUDENTS

| | |
|---|---|
| Total undergrad enrollment | 1,256 |
| % male/female | 45/55 |
| % from out of state | 40 |
| % from public high school | 88 |
| % live on campus | 84 |
| % in (# of) fraternities | 24 (4) |
| % in (# of) sororities | 18 (3) |
| % African American | 2 |
| % Asian | 1 |
| % Caucasian | 92 |
| % Hispanic | 1 |
| % international | 4 |

### SURVEY SAYS . . .

Classes are small
Athletic facilities are great
Great library
Registration is a breeze
Everyone loves the Kohawks
Musical organizations are hot
Student publications are popular
Diverse students interact
(Almost) no one listens to college
radio

## ACADEMICS

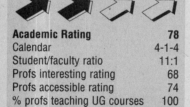

| Academic Rating | 78 |
|---|---|
| Calendar | 4-1-4 |
| Student/faculty ratio | 11:1 |
| Profs interesting rating | 68 |
| Profs accessible rating | 74 |
| % profs teaching UG courses | 100 |
| Avg reg class size | 10-19 students |

### MOST POPULAR MAJORS
business
biology
psychology

## STUDENTS SPEAK OUT

### Academics

"Amidst the corn, there lies Coe—a great place to be for education, friendship, and overall maturity." That's how one undergrad describes the academic experience at this small, prestigious liberal arts school in eastern Iowa. Coe's curriculum includes a rigorous set of prerequisites; between general education requirements, major studies, and a mandatory junior-year internship, nearly two-thirds of the credits necessary for graduation are prescribed by the school. Discussing the curriculum, one student notes that "Coe has some hoops you have to jump through, but people are willing to work with you," while another realizes that "Coe is all about figuring out that what you learn in classes is less important than working out how they fit together. Classes are small and discussion-based, and their materials spill out into the cafeteria, the quad, the dorms . . . class is never just class: class is life." Students praise both professors and administrators, pointing out that "The faculty, staff, and administrators are wonderful. The personal attention and friendly atmosphere create a great environment for learning." A typical anecdote: "Professors go out of their way to further your education. In one of my chemistry classes, we asked what happens to a person in space. Our professor brought in a vacuum tank and marshmallows to illustrate the property—that is dedication to teaching." Summing up her experience at Coe, one student tells us, "I've been through many trials and tribulations concerning Coe. It's been a love/hate relationship. Still, I've never regretted my choice because the opportunities available to me here have been incredible, beneficial, and helpful."

### Life

Students report that a pleasant but subdued social scene predominates at Coe. For fun, undergrads "take advantage of activities offered at the college such as balls, dances, fun programs, etc." Many students go Greek, explaining that "Fraternities are active, friendly, and useful," but also pointing out that "Life here is balanced between studies and parties." "If you're not a partygoer, you're still accepted. If you don't drink, you're not shunned. People here accept others' choices." The "clean and safe" campus is "great" and "is being expanded, which will make it even better. It makes Coe have its own community within the city." Beyond the campus lies Coe's hometown of Cedar Rapids, which continues to serve the Midwest as a manufacturing center ("Everything here is great, except for the smell from the city"), although high-tech industries have recently moved into the area and are slowly transforming the regional economy. Students enjoy this city of 150,000, writing that "Cedar Rapids has a lot of culture, considering its location. It has a symphony, community theaters, museums, shopping, and movies."

### Student Body

Attending a school with a total minority population of less than 100, Coe students recognize that "Our diversity is not racial, it's social. It's impossible not to fit in, from artsy to jock. This aura of camaraderie is noticeable and valued." Coe, like its home state of Iowa, is an oasis of liberalism in the mostly conservative Midwest ("This campus is very liberal and people are very open and friendly," notes one student). Like many small liberal arts schools, "Coe has an extremely close-knit community because of its size."

FINANCIAL AID: 319-399-8540 • E-MAIL: ADMISSION@COE.EDU • WEBSITE: WWW.COE.EDU

## ADMISSIONS

*Very important* academic and nonacademic factors considered by the admissions committee include character/personal qualities, extracurricular activities, secondary school record, standardized test scores, and talent/ability. *Important* factors considered include class rank, essays, recommendations, and volunteer work. *Other* factors considered include alumni/ae relation, interview, minority status and work experience. Factors *not* considered include geography, religious affiliation/commitment, and state residency. SAT I or ACT required. TOEFL required of all international applicants. High school diploma is required and GED is accepted. *High school units required/recommended:* 32 total recommended; 4 English recommended, 4 math recommended, 4 science recommended, 2 science lab recommended, 4 foreign language recommended, 4 social studies recommended, 10 elective recommended.

### The Inside Word

Coe's admissions process places a very high level of importance on your numbers. Candidates who don't have at least a 2.75 high school GPA and at least a 22 on the ACT may find tough going with the admissions committee. As is true of nearly all small liberal arts colleges, Coe conducts a thorough application review that also considers your personal background and involvements, but an emerging national reputation enables them to keep their focus upon academic achievement as the primary gatekeeper.

## FINANCIAL AID

Students should submit: FAFSA. Regular filing deadline is March 1. The Princeton Review suggests that all financial aid forms be submitted as soon as possible after January 1. Need-based scholarships/grants offered: Pell, SEOG, state scholarships/grants, private scholarships, and the school's own gift aid. Loan aid offered: Direct Subsidized Stafford, Direct Unsubsidized Stafford, Direct PLUS, Federal Perkins, and college/university loans from institutional funds. Institutional employment available. Federal Work-Study Program available. Applicants will be notified of awards on a rolling basis beginning on or about February 15. Off-campus job opportunities are excellent.

## FROM THE ADMISSIONS OFFICE

"A Coe education begins to pay off right away. In fact, 98 percent of last year's graduating class was either working or in graduate school within six months of graduation. One reason our graduates do so well is Coe's hands-on requirement, which can be satisfied through an internship, research, practicum, or study abroad. One student lived with a Costa Rican family while she studied the effects of selective logging on rain forest organisms. Others have interned at places like Warner Brothers in Los Angeles and the Chicago Board of Trade. Still others combine travel with an internship or student teaching for an unforgettable off-campus experience. Coe College is one of the few private liberal arts institutions in the country to require hands-on learning for graduation."

---

## ADMISSIONS

| | |
|---|---:|
| **Admissions Rating** | 82 |
| # of applicants | 1,095 |
| % of applicants accepted | 81 |
| % of acceptees attending | 32 |

### FRESHMAN PROFILE

| | |
|---|---:|
| Range SAT Verbal | 530-630 |
| Average SAT Verbal | 585 |
| Range SAT Math | 520-630 |
| Average SAT Math | 575 |
| Range ACT Composite | 22-27 |
| Average ACT Composite | 25 |
| Minimum TOEFL | 500 |
| Average HS GPA | 3.6 |
| % graduated top 10% of class | 27 |
| % graduated top 25% of class | 59 |
| % graduated top 50% of class | 93 |

### DEADLINES

| | |
|---|---:|
| Priority admission deadline | 12/15 |
| Regular admission | 3/1 |
| Regular notification | 3/15 |
| Nonfall registration? | yes |

### APPLICANTS ALSO LOOK AT AND SOMETIMES PREFER

Macalester
Beloit
Grinnell
Cornell College
U. Iowa

## FINANCIAL FACTS

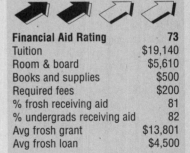

| | |
|---|---:|
| **Financial Aid Rating** | 73 |
| Tuition | $19,140 |
| Room & board | $5,610 |
| Books and supplies | $500 |
| Required fees | $200 |
| % frosh receiving aid | 81 |
| % undergrads receiving aid | 82 |
| Avg frosh grant | $13,801 |
| Avg frosh loan | $4,500 |

# COLBY COLLEGE

4800 MAYFLOWER HILL, WATERVILLE, ME 04901-8848 • ADMISSIONS: 207-872-3168 • FAX: 207-872-3474

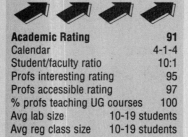
## STUDENTS SPEAK OUT

### Academics

An intimate, prestigious, liberal arts college tucked away in a "superb location in the Maine woods not far from civilization," Colby College offers a challenging but manageable undergraduate experience to its small student population. Undergrads report that all the support mechanisms necessary for success in college are in place here. Writes one, "I was intimidated at first by the whole idea of college, but after my first day of classes freshman year, my fears were soon assuaged. My professors were real pros and made otherwise very complex and involved material accessible to the students. At the end of my first semester, I was even asked to be a professor's research assistant." Another explains, "It is a very intimate, personal, inspiring, and wonderful relationship between professors and students. They're always there for you, ready and willing to ease any personal or academic stresses you are under." Not surprisingly, students grow attached to this friendly place. "I consider Colby my home and cannot imagine leaving this community behind," reflects a senior. "Colby has honestly been the most wonderful academic and social experience that I have ever experienced." Unique programs here include "Jan Plan," a short semester that allows students to study nontraditional subjects or intern during the month of January.

### Life

Combine a large group of college-age kids and a beautiful, remote, bucolic location and what you get is "summer camp with alcohol. Camp Colby is totally awesome." Students here love the beauty, food, and facilities and are no less than gushy about other kids and professors. Although many students "drink for fun," those who opt for a substance-free social life say "chem-free fun" is readily available as well, especially in the "chem-free" dorms. In addition, "the range of theatre productions, concerts, lectures, and sporting events is incredible." Colby is "a very athletic school" where there are "opportunities for every level of athlete." Outdoor sports are popular year-round, particularly throughout the winter. "Lots of snow. Need I say more?" writes one student. "It's fun, though, [since] the weather provides lots of outdoor activities." As for the school's location, students let us in on "the best thing about Waterville, Maine—local Karaoke night at the pub in town. We love getting drunk with the Mainahs and doing our little song and dance." Not surprisingly, then, students tend to stay on campus. Fortunately, "life can easily be contained entirely on campus and you will never be bored. There is always something fun going on." Even so, there are those who feel that "we need to integrate students into the surrounding community more, i.e. with more community service projects. We don't have enough contact with locals."

### Student Body

Colby undergrads are the first to admit that a diverse population is not one of the school's strengths. "We need to attract kids from a wider range of economic backgrounds," complains one undergrad. However, a current sophomore is quick to point out that while "a portion [of the students] are rich, religious, white snobs, the rest are wonderfully adjusting, friendly, and diverse in ideas and beliefs." Students can be "a little too cliquey, but if you catch people on an individual basis, they are usually friendly." Another student agrees, writing, "Everyone here is very approachable. We pride ourselves on it." Students describe their peers as "outgoing and always looking for a good time," though they do admit to being "focused on what is important to them only." As a result, "20 percent of the students here participate in 80 percent of the activities."

FINANCIAL AID: 207-872-3168 • E-MAIL: ADMISSIONS@COLBY.EDU • WEBSITE: WWW.COLBY.EDU

## ADMISSIONS

*Very important* academic and nonacademic factors considered by the admissions committee include class rank, secondary school record, essay, and character/personal qualities. *Important* factors considered include standardized test scores, recommendations, talent/ability, extracurricular activities, and minority status. *Other* factors considered include interview, alumni/ae relation, geography, state residence, volunteer work, and work experience. Factors *not* considered include religious affiliation/commitment. *High school units recommended:* 16 total recommended; 4 English recommended, 3 mathematics recommended, 3 foreign language recommended, 2 science recommended (of which 2 should be labs), 2 social studies OR history recommended, 2 academic electives recommended.

### The Inside Word

Colby continues to be both very selective and successful in converting admits to enrollees, which makes for a perpetually challenging admissions process.

## FINANCIAL AID

*Students should submit:* FAFSA and Institutional Financial Aid Supplement and either CSS/Financial Aid PROFILE or institutional form. Regular filing deadline is February 1. The Princeton Review suggests that all financial aid forms be submitted as soon as possible after January 1. *Need-based scholarships/grants offered:* Pell, SEOG, state scholarships/grants, private scholarships, and the school's own gift aid. *Loan aid offered:* Direct Subsidized Stafford, Direct Unsubsidized Stafford, Direct PLUS, Federal Perkins, state and college/university loans from institutional funds. Institutional employment available. Federal Work-Study Program available. Applicants will be notified of awards on or about April 1. Off-campus job opportunities are fair.

## FROM THE ADMISSIONS OFFICE

"Set on a hilltop overlooking the Kennebec River valley, Colby is 15 miles from the state capital and halfway between Maine's two largest cities, which are easily accessible on nearby Interstate 95. Colby's 714-acre campus ranks among the nation's most beautiful, and it provides a stunning environment for the college's rigorous academic programs and rich intellectual life. Colby's tradition of liberal arts learning dates to 1813, and the college has a long-standing commitment to innovation, one example being the Jan Plan for independent or focused study and internship opportunities. Colby has one of the most ambitious study abroad programs, and two thirds of all students study abroad during their four years. The faculty's commitment to teaching and to close interaction with students, both in and out of the classroom, consistently wins praise from students and alumni. Colby is recognized as a leader in the use of undergraduate research in teaching and for its organizations providing activities and leadership opportunities for men and women with varied interests; there is a lively interest among students in political and social activism and volunteer work. Students are directly involved in college governance and serving with faculty members on official college committees up to and including the board of trustees."

## ADMISSIONS

| Admissions Rating | 95 |
|---|---|
| # of applicants | 3,907 |
| % of applicants accepted | 37 |
| % of acceptees attending | 33 |
| # accepting a place on wait list | 224 |
| # of early decision applicants | 379 |
| % accepted early decision | 43 |

### FRESHMAN PROFILE

| | |
|---|---|
| Range SAT Verbal | 630-700 |
| Average SAT Verbal | 660 |
| Range SAT Math | 620-690 |
| Average SAT Math | 660 |
| Range ACT Composite | 27-31 |
| Average ACT Composite | 29 |
| Minimum TOEFL | 600 |
| % graduated top 10% of class | 64 |
| % graduated top 25% of class | 91 |
| % graduated top 50% of class | 99 |

### DEADLINES

| | |
|---|---|
| Early decision | 11/15 |
| Early decision notification | 12/15 |
| Regular admission | 1/15 |
| Regular notification | 4/1 |
| Nonfall registration? | yes |

### APPLICANTS ALSO LOOK AT

**AND OFTEN PREFER**
Bowdoin
Dartmouth
Williams
Brown
Middlebury

**AND SOMETIMES PREFER**
Colgate
Boston Coll.
Bates
Holy Cross

**AND RARELY PREFER**
Trinity
U. New Hampshire
Hamilton
U. Vermont

### FINANCIAL FACTS

| Financial Aid Rating | 73 |
|---|---|
| Books and supplies | $550 |
| % frosh receiving aid | 40 |
| % undergrads receiving aid | 36 |
| Avg frosh grant | $16,700 |
| Avg frosh loan | $3,300 |

# COLGATE UNIVERSITY

13 OAK DRIVE, HAMILTON, NY 13346 • ADMISSIONS: 315-228-7401 • FAX: 315-228-7544

## CAMPUS LIFE

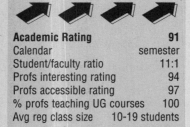

| Quality of Life Rating | 86 |
|---|---|
| Type of school | private |
| Affiliation | none |
| Environment | rural |

### STUDENTS

| | |
|---|---|
| Total undergrad enrollment | 2,773 |
| % male/female | 49/51 |
| % from out of state | 68 |
| % from public high school | 64 |
| % live on campus | 88 |
| % in (# of) fraternities | 39 (8) |
| % in (# of) sororities | 33 (4) |
| % African American | 5 |
| % Asian | 5 |
| % Caucasian | 86 |
| % Hispanic | 4 |
| % Native American | 1 |
| % international | 2 |
| # of countries represented | 29 |

### SURVEY SAYS . . .

*Frats and sororities dominate social
scene
Everyone loves the Red Raiders
Diversity lacking on campus
(Almost) everyone plays intramural
sports
Athletic facilities are great
Students don't like Hamilton, NY
Lousy off-campus food
Theater is unpopular
Class discussions encouraged*

## ACACEMICS

| Academic Rating | 91 |
|---|---|
| Calendar | semester |
| Student/faculty ratio | 11:1 |
| Profs interesting rating | 94 |
| Profs accessible rating | 97 |
| % profs teaching UG courses | 100 |
| Avg reg class size | 10-19 students |

### MOST POPULAR MAJORS

economics
English
history

## STUDENTS SPEAK OUT

### Academics

How warm and fuzzy do Colgate undergrads feel about their school? Writes one typical student, "Colgate is one big family: Your peers are your siblings, your professors are your friends, and the administrators are your parents." While students appreciate the school's stellar academic reputation, what they enjoy most is the caring atmosphere that accompanies it. "All of the professors are at the top of their fields," notes one undergrad, "but what makes the academic experience here superior to many other schools in this tier is their wonderful teaching abilities, personableness, and approachability." Explains another student, "All of the professors are extremely accessible both in class and out. Plus, the few teaching assistants actually assist instead of acting as substitutes for real professors." Enhancing the intimacy is the fact that "classes are small enough that you are able to form good working relationships with the faculty." Colgate isn't simply about professor interaction, though: "There is a lot of technology integration in the classroom" along with "great research opportunities and great study abroad programs." All Colgate students must complete core courses, "and even these are, for the most part, stimulating, although the upper-level classes are what people enjoy [most]." For ambitious students, opportunities for independent study are readily available.

### Life

"A lot of people view Colgate as a party school," explains one undergrad, "and it is, to a degree. However, it's more than just that. Given Colgate's rural location, the school works to bring the city to us. There are usually more events on weekends than just frat parties." Still, the parties—and the local bars—seem to attract most of the attention. "There's a lot of bar hopping and frat parties, although the administration is trying to get rid of those," writes one student. "Basically, there is a drinking scene here." Another summed up the situation neatly by saying, "There are four bars in town, one for each night of the weekend." Students party hard because they feel the community outside of campus "sucks. We are in the middle of nowhere!" Some consider that little more than a weak excuse. Writes one, "Hamilton is a pretty lazy town where there's not much to do. Nevertheless, Colgate provides a myriad of on- and off-campus activities for students. Though a majority of students party, there are always other options available." Athletics and outdoor activities are extremely popular: "Everybody runs here," and "when weather complies, the campus is bustling with outdoor activity. Almost everyone is involved in sports, clubs, and intramurals." A recently constructed indoor rock climbing wall provides a chance for outdoorsy fun even when the weather isn't cooperative. Undergraduates rank their campus among the nation's most beautiful, beaming that "this is what I had in mind when I anticipated coming to college—snow-covered trees and big limestone buildings." When they grow tired of the beauty, "there is civilization to go to if you're willing to drive for an hour. If you stay here there are frats to go to. If you don't like frats, you'd better find parties elsewhere."

### Student Body

"There are three kinds of students at Colgate," writes one undergraduate. "Those who are brilliant and can party all night, not study, and ace an exam; those who spend a lot of time at the library doing work; and those who put in some effort and get good or OK grades but don't really care." It is not unlikely that students from each type belong to the "big fraternity/sorority population from the white upper-middle class." They are extremely bright, but not "bookworm types," nor the kind to offer unsolicited opinions in class. Rather, they are the sort of folks whose "survival vocabulary" consists of "'Oh, my God!' 'Whatever!' and 'Sha!'" Not surprisingly, the campus "is an orgy of khaki and button-downs."

# COLGATE UNIVERSITY

FINANCIAL AID: 315-228-7431 • E-MAIL: ADMISSION@MAIL.COLGATE.EDU • WEBSITE: WWW.COLGATE.EDU

## ADMISSIONS

*Very important* academic and nonacademic factors considered by the admissions committee include secondary school record. *Important* factors considered include recommendations and standardized test scores. *Other* factors considered include alumni/ae relation, essays, character/personal qualities, class rank, extracurricular activities, minority status, talent/ability, and volunteer work. Factors *not* considered include geography, interview, religious affiliation/commitment, state residency, and work experience. TOEFL required of all international applicants. High school diploma is required and GED is accepted. *High school units required/recommended:* 16 total required; 18 total recommended; 4 English required, 1 math required, 1 science required, 1 social studies required, 1 history required, 8 elective required.

### The Inside Word

Like many colleges, Colgate caters to some well-developed special interests. Athletes, minorities, and legacies (the children of alums) are among the most special of interests and benefit from more favorable consideration than applicants without particular distinction. Students without a solid, consistent academic record, beware—the University's wait list leans toward jumbo size.

## FINANCIAL AID

*Students should submit:* FAFSA, CSS/Financial Aid PROFILE, noncustodial (divorced/separated) parent's statement, and business/farm supplement. Regular filing deadline is February 1. The Princeton Review suggests that all financial aid forms be submitted as soon as possible after January 1. *Need-based scholarships/grants offered:* Pell, SEOG, state scholarships/grants, and the school's own gift aid. *Loan aid offered:* FFEL Subsidized Stafford, FFEL Unsubsidized Stafford, FFEL PLUS, and Federal Perkins. Institutional employment available. Federal Work-Study Program available. Applicants will be notified of awards on or about April 1. Off-campus job opportunities are good.

## FROM THE ADMISSIONS OFFICE

"When the Roper Organization asked graduates from 1980 to 1992, 'What most influenced your decision to attend Colgate,' the key factor—cited on 90 percent of their responses—was academic reputation. Asked 'how well Colgate measured up to your expectations academically,' 97 percent of those same graduates responded positively. Students and faculty alike are drawn to Colgate by the quality of its academic programs. Faculty initiative has given the college a rich mix of learning opportunities that includes general education, 50 academic concentrations, and a wealth of off-campus study groups in the United States and abroad. But there is more to Colgate than academic life, including more than 100 student organizations, athletics and recreation at all levels, and a full complement of living options set within a campus described as one of the most beautiful in the country. For students in search of a busy and varied campus life, Colgate is a place to learn and grow."

## ADMISSIONS

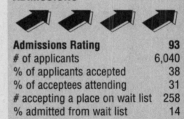

| | |
|---|---:|
| Admissions Rating | 93 |
| # of applicants | 6,040 |
| % of applicants accepted | 38 |
| % of acceptees attending | 31 |
| # accepting a place on wait list | 258 |
| % admitted from wait list | 14 |
| # of early decision applicants | 459 |
| % accepted early decision | 52 |

### FRESHMAN PROFILE

| | |
|---|---:|
| Range SAT Verbal | 620-690 |
| Average SAT Verbal | 650 |
| Range SAT Math | 630-700 |
| Average SAT Math | 670 |
| Range ACT Composite | 26-30 |
| Average ACT Composite | 28 |
| Minimum TOEFL | 600 |
| Average HS GPA | 3.4 |
| % graduated top 10% of class | 58 |
| % graduated top 25% of class | 86 |
| % graduated top 50% of class | 99 |

### DEADLINES

| | |
|---|---:|
| Early decision | 11/15 |
| Early decision notification | 12/15 |
| Regular admission | 1/15 |
| Regular notification | 4/1 |

### APPLICANTS ALSO LOOK AT

**AND OFTEN PREFER**
Williams
Dartmouth
Cornell U., Duke
Middlebury

**AND SOMETIMES PREFER**
Boston U.
Boston Coll.
Colby, Tufts

**AND RARELY PREFER**
Hamilton, Lehigh
Lafayette
Bucknell

### FINANCIAL FACTS

| | |
|---|---:|
| Financial Aid Rating | 74 |
| Tuition | $25,565 |
| Room & board | $6,330 |
| Books and supplies | $620 |
| Required fees | $175 |
| % frosh receiving aid | 36 |
| % undergrads receiving aid | 58 |
| Avg frosh grant | $20,295 |
| Avg frosh loan | $2,625 |

# THE COLLEGE OF NEW JERSEY

PO Box 7718, Ewing, NJ 08628-0718 • Admissions: 609-771-2131 • Fax: 609-637-5174

## CAMPUS LIFE

| Quality of Life Rating | 84 |
|---|---|
| Type of school | public |
| Affiliation | none |
| Environment | suburban |

### STUDENTS

| | |
|---|---|
| Total undergrad enrollment | 6,008 |
| % male/female | 41/59 |
| % from out of state | 5 |
| % from public high school | 65 |
| % live on campus | 63 |
| % in (# of) fraternities | 17 (13) |
| % in (# of) sororities | 17 (13) |
| % African American | 6 |
| % Asian | 5 |
| % Caucasian | 75 |
| % Hispanic | 5 |

### SURVEY SAYS . . .

Campus easy to get around
Beautiful campus
Campus feels safe
Athletic facilities are great
Great computer facilities
Student publications are ignored
Political activism is (almost)
nonexistent
Lousy food on campus
Students aren't religious
Students don't get along with local
community

## ACADEMICS

| Academic Rating | 84 |
|---|---|
| Calendar | semester |
| Student/faculty ratio | 14:1 |
| Profs interesting rating | 72 |
| Profs accessible rating | 92 |
| % profs teaching UG courses | 95 |
| Avg lab size | 20-29 students |
| Avg reg class size | 20-29 students |

### MOST POPULAR MAJORS

biology
elementary education
English

## STUDENTS SPEAK OUT

### Academics

In a region where sky-high tuition rates are common, the College of New Jersey (known until 1996 as Trenton State College) offers a solid academic alternative at a very reasonable price. Competitive admissions and strong departments in the sciences, education, and business allow TCNJ to provide many with a "first-rate education for very little money." Students enjoy the fact that "classes are pretty small and the campus is small, so though it's a public college, it feels like a private school." They are less sanguine about the wide assortment of general education requirements in math, science, and humanities courses. Writes one typical student, "My main complaint is with the Gen. Ed. program. I haven't gotten anything out of the required courses." Professors receive mixed notices as well: "Overall, teachers are decent. Most speak English fluently. The math department, though, leaves something to be desired, but computer science, women's studies, music, psych, and many other areas have a stock of good teachers." Still, "There are a lot of teachers who could use a class on how to express what they are trying to teach better, but they will help you to the best of their ability. Their doors are always open and if not, then you can get a tutor." Administrators, on the other hand, "need to establish a better connection to the academic and student body." For those prepared for an extra challenge, the school's Honors Program allows the school's best students a high degree of autonomy in designing their studies.

### Life

Students don't come to TCNJ for the social life. It's a good thing, because while the campus offers a plethora of academic opportunities, social events here are few and far between. As one student explains, "Social activities at my school are very limited. The campus is very isolated. There is nothing within walking distance with the exception of a 7-11. Even the fraternity and sorority houses are not in walking distance. Without a car, you are helpless." During the week, "You have to look hard for organizations to participate in. It is easy to not get involved at this school." On weekends, "everyone goes home . . . because there's nothing to do." Tuesday night is an exception to the doldrums as it is quickly becoming the traditional party night, with events at fraternities or parties in students' dorm rooms. Ewing doesn't provide much help, as it "definitely isn't a college town." Other student complaints center on the lack of parking, the dearth of student housing, and the poor quality of on-campus food. On the plus side, "the campus is beautiful," and Trenton is a good departure point for nearby major cities. New York City is "a train ride away," and students often "go to Princeton for the weekend for a change of pace." Philadelphia is also easily reached by train.

### Student Body

The "bright" students of TCNJ ("mostly nerds go here") hail predominantly from the Garden State, and many choose to come here "because it's close to home." Since "most students are from the same areas," there tend to be many "high-school style cliques" and "not much mingling between them." Notes one, "The students at this school are very clique-oriented. Most students form groups and separate off. There is no spirit of commonality." Although the population here is ethnically diverse, students "tend to separate into their ethnic groups, creating a segregated atmosphere." Still, "fellow students are very respectful of differences and very kind to each other."

# THE COLLEGE OF NEW JERSEY

FINANCIAL AID: 609-771-2211 • E-MAIL: ADMISS@VM.TCNJ.EDU • WEBSITE: WWW.TCNJ.EDU

## ADMISSIONS

*Very important* academic and nonacademic factors considered by the admissions committee include interview and secondary school record. *Important* factors considered include character/personal qualities, class rank, essays, extracurricular activities, recommendations, standardized test scores, talent/ability, and volunteer work. *Other* factors considered include alumni/ae relation, geography, and work experience. Factors *not* considered include minority status, religious affiliation/commitment, and state residency. SAT I required. TOEFL required of all international applicants. High school diploma is required and GED is accepted. *High school units required/recommended:* 16 total required; 4 English required, 3 math required, 2 science required, 2 science lab required, 2 foreign language required, 2 history required.

### The Inside Word

A new name and new-found visibility have given a boost to the applicant pool at The College of New Jersey, but selectivity remains at about the level it has been for the past few years. Since the pool is somewhat better than in prior years, this still translates into a stronger entering class.

## FINANCIAL AID

*Students should submit:* FAFSA. Regular filing deadline is June 1. The Princeton Review suggests that all financial aid forms be submitted as soon as possible after January 1. *Need-based scholarships/grants offered:* Pell, SEOG, state scholarships/grants, private scholarships, the school's own gift aid, and Federal Nursing. *Loan aid offered:* Direct Subsidized Stafford, Direct Unsubsidized Stafford, Direct PLUS, Federal Perkins, Federal Nursing, and state. Institutional employment available. Federal Work-Study Program available. Applicants will be notified of awards on a rolling basis beginning on or about April 1. Off-campus job opportunities are good.

## FROM THE ADMISSIONS OFFICE

"Twin lakes form the border of the The College of New Jersey campus, which is set on 289 acres of wooded and landscaped grounds in suburban Ewing Township, New Jersey. TCNJ offers more than 40 baccalaureate degree programs in the arts, sciences, business, engineering, and nursing. The campus is residential, with more than half of the full-time students housed on campus. Classes are small and are all taught by faculty members: there are no graduate teaching assistants. The college is strongly committed to retaining and graduating the students it enrolls. This commitment is reflected in the high return rate of entering students, which has consistently been over 90 percent for the past five years."

## ADMISSIONS

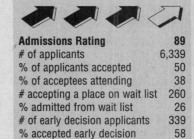

| | |
|---|---:|
| Admissions Rating | 89 |
| # of applicants | 6,339 |
| % of applicants accepted | 50 |
| % of acceptees attending | 38 |
| # accepting a place on wait list | 260 |
| % admitted from wait list | 26 |
| # of early decision applicants | 339 |
| % accepted early decision | 58 |

### FRESHMAN PROFILE

| | |
|---|---:|
| Range SAT Verbal | 570-660 |
| Average SAT Verbal | 610 |
| Range SAT Math | 590-680 |
| Average SAT Math | 627 |
| Minimum TOEFL | 550 |
| % graduated top 10% of class | 63 |
| % graduated top 25% of class | 93 |
| % graduated top 50% of class | 99 |

### DEADLINES

| | |
|---|---:|
| Early decision | 11/15 |
| Early decision notification | 12/15 |
| Regular admission | 2/15 |
| Nonfall registration? | yes |

### APPLICANTS ALSO LOOK AT
### AND OFTEN PREFER
Rutgers U.
### AND SOMETIMES PREFER
Villanova
U. Delaware
Boston Coll.
Drew
Seton Hall
### AND RARELY PREFER
Rider
Syracuse
Muhlenberg
Monmouth U. (NJ)

## FINANCIAL FACTS

| | |
|---|---:|
| Financial Aid Rating | 74 |
| In-state tuition | $4,654 |
| Out-of-state tuition | $8,127 |
| Room & board | $6,504 |
| Books and supplies | $700 |
| Required fees | $1,337 |
| % frosh receiving aid | 77 |
| % undergrads receiving aid | 70 |
| Avg frosh grant | $7,000 |
| Avg frosh loan | $5,000 |

# COLLEGE OF SAINT BENEDICT/SAINT JOHN'S UNIVERSITY

PO Box 7155, Collegeville, MN 56321-7155 • Admissions: 320-363-2196 • Fax: 320-363-3206

## CAMPUS LIFE

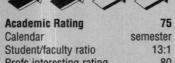

| | |
|---|---|
| **Quality of Life Rating** | **75** |
| Type of school | private |
| Affiliation | Roman Catholic |
| Environment | rural |

### STUDENTS

| | |
|---|---|
| Total undergrad enrollment | 3,904 |
| % male/female | 48/52 |
| % from out of state | 13 |
| % from public high school | 77 |
| % live on campus | 80 |
| % Asian | 2 |
| % Caucasian | 94 |
| % Hispanic | 1 |
| % international | 3 |
| # of countries represented | 34 |

### SURVEY SAYS . . .
*Great food on campus*
*Athletic facilities are great*
*Ethnic diversity lacking on campus*
*(Almost) everyone plays intramural sports*
*Students pack the stadium*
*Theater is unpopular*
*Students are very religious*
*Students get along with local community*
*Low cost of living*

## ACACADEMICS

| | |
|---|---|
| **Academic Rating** | **75** |
| Calendar | semester |
| Student/faculty ratio | 13:1 |
| Profs interesting rating | 80 |
| Profs accessible rating | 80 |
| % profs teaching UG courses | 100 |
| Avg lab size | 10-19 students |
| Avg reg class size | 10-19 students |

### MOST POPULAR MAJORS
business management
communication
psychology

## STUDENTS SPEAK OUT

### Academics

Ninety miles northwest of Minnesota's Twin Cities lay the twin campuses of the all-women's College of Saint Benedict and the all-men's Saint John's University. The two schools forged their partnership in 1964 in an effort to "take the best of what women's, men's, and co-ed colleges offer and combine them in a way you won't find at another pair of colleges in the nation." According to students, CSB/SJU more than meets the challenge it initially set for itself. Writes one, "Our school is more than a school. It's tradition, family, beauty, and presence all rolled into a tiny backwoods campus. You can't help but fall in love with the place, everything from the people to the profs." Agrees another, "Community is the greatest strength" of CSB/SJU. Students are particularly pleased at the way in which the curriculum here stresses critical thinking. Writes one, "Not only do you learn about skills for a major, you learn a better, open, and more knowledgeable way of thinking and applying it to real-life situations." Professors receive rave reviews, with undergrads gushing that "some of the profs are real gems. They're great teachers, some even friends, who would bend over backwards to make sure you learn what you have to know, and do their best to let you enjoy it." Adds another, "Several of my professors have become close friends of mine. They really get involved with the students on a personal level. Saint John's has great academics, and I feel it comes directly from the attitudes of the professors."

### Life

The gorgeous natural setting of CSB/SJU sets the tone for many student pastimes. Writes one student, "Saint John's is nestled on 2,400 acres of woodland that's surrounded by five lakes. The outdoor activities available are virtually unrivaled by any other college." To facilitate students' passion for the outdoors, the school has "a place on campus called the Outdoor Leadership Center, which rents out equipment to students (e.g., camping equipment, cross-country skis, rollerblades, and snowshoes)." Students also participate in "a wide range of athletics and intramural activities." For entertainment, "the school brings many things onto campus for us to do, such as musical performers, movies, and dances. Since these are all free, there are many great, cheap ways to have fun." Writes one student, "There is truly something for everyone. For those who like to party, you can find one just about every night of the week. For those who like to sit back and relax all week, you can do that too—it's really nice to do by Lake Sag at St. John's." The fact that the two campuses are about five miles apart seems to have little effect on social life; the two schools coordinate events through the Joint Events Council. And, "when there isn't anything going on here, Minneapolis is only an hour away. . . . When the serenity gets [to be] too much for you, the hustle and bustle of big city life is in reach. I have yet to be bored here."

### Student Body

The student body of CSB/SJU "is basically a bunch of white suburban kids from Minnesota and a bunch of white farm kids from Minnesota mixed together, and a few international students mainly from the Bahamas and a few out-of-state students thrown in to spice things up a bit." Students are "friendly, motivated, and courteous. Most people get along and socialize with many people." Reports one student, "It's not uncommon to say 'hello' to people you don't even know." Another points out that "there are a number of students here that do come from wealthy backgrounds, so sometimes it's tough for myself and others from not-so-wealthy backgrounds to see so many nice cars and people wearing Abercrombie. The students are in no way separated by money or what they wear, though. Everyone gets along very well."

# COLLEGE OF SAINT BENEDICT/SAINT JOHN'S UNIVERSITY

FINANCIAL AID: 320-363-3664 • E-MAIL: ADMISSIONS@CSBSJU.EDU • WEBSITE: WWW.CSBSJU.EDU

## ADMISSIONS

*Very important* academic and nonacademic factors considered by the admissions committee include class rank, essays, secondary school record, and standardized test scores. *Important* factors considered include alumni/ae relation, character/personal qualities, extracurricular activities, geography, interview, minority status, religious affiliation/commitment, state residency, talent/ability, volunteer work, and work experience. *Other* factors considered include recommendations. SAT I or ACT required. TOEFL required of all international applicants. High school diploma is required and GED is accepted. *High school units required/recommended:* 17 total recommended; 4 English required, 3 math required, 2 science required, 2 science lab required, 2 foreign language recommended, 2 social studies required, 4 elective recommended.

### The Inside Word

Though Saint John's University and the College of Saint Benedict have combined most of their efforts and operations on campus, admission remains distinct. Women must apply to the College of Saint Benedict and men to Saint John's. Since it is a joint admissions office, both are seeking exactly the same qualities in their students; in addition to solid academic records from high school, much attention is paid to the match a student makes with the schools. Candidates can expect their personal side to receive thorough evaluation within the admissions processes here.

## FINANCIAL AID

*Students should submit:* FAFSA, institution's own financial aid form, and federal tax returns. Priority filing deadline is February 1. The Princeton Review suggests that all financial aid forms be submitted as soon as possible after January 1. *Need-based scholarships/grants offered:* Pell, SEOG, state scholarships/grants, private scholarships, and the school's own gift aid. *Loan aid offered:* Subsidized Stafford, Unsubsidized Stafford, PLUS, Federal Perkins, state, Student Education Loan Fund (SELF) GOAL, Norwest Collegiate, Choice, Voyager, and GAP. Institution employment available. Federal Work-Study Program available. Applicants will be notified of awards on a rolling basis beginning on or about March 1. Off-campus job opportunities are good.

## FROM THE ADMISSIONS OFFICE

"CSB/SJU believes that a student's hard work in high school deserves recognition—that's why renewable scholarships such as the Regents'/Trustees' (worth $34,000 over four years); the President's (worth from $22,000 to $30,000 over four years); and the Dean's (worth from $12,000 to $20,000 over four years) are awarded competitively based on the student's past academic achievement, college entrance test scores, and demonstrated leadership and service. Excellence in Diversity, Leadership, and Service Scholarships (worth up to $20,000 over four years) are awarded to students who have promoted diversity in their leadership and service work. Performing and Fine Arts Scholarships (worth up to $8,000 over four years) are awarded to students who have participated in and excelled in art, music, or theater in high school. Approximately 90 percent of the students currently attending the colleges receive financial assistance; many receive both scholarship and need-based assistance."

## ADMISSIONS

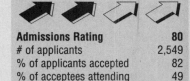

| | |
|---|---|
| Admissions Rating | 80 |
| # of applicants | 2,549 |
| % of applicants accepted | 82 |
| % of acceptees attending | 49 |

### FRESHMAN PROFILE

| | |
|---|---|
| Range SAT Verbal | 510-630 |
| Average SAT Verbal | 572 |
| Range SAT Math | 540-650 |
| Average SAT Math | 595 |
| Range ACT Composite | 22-28 |
| Average ACT Composite | 25 |
| Minimum TOEFL | 500 |
| Average HS GPA | 3.6 |
| % graduated top 10% of class | 33 |
| % graduated top 25% of class | 67 |
| % graduated top 50% of class | 94 |

### DEADLINES

| | |
|---|---|
| Priority admission deadline | 2/1 |
| Nonfall registration? | yes |

### FINANCIAL FACTS

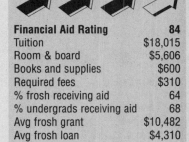

| | |
|---|---|
| Financial Aid Rating | 84 |
| Tuition | $18,015 |
| Room & board | $5,606 |
| Books and supplies | $600 |
| Required fees | $310 |
| % frosh receiving aid | 64 |
| % undergrads receiving aid | 68 |
| Avg frosh grant | $10,482 |
| Avg frosh loan | $4,310 |

# COLLEGE OF THE ATLANTIC

105 EDEN STREET, BAR HARBOR, ME 04609 • ADMISSIONS: 800-528-0025 • FAX: 207-288-4126

## CAMPUS LIFE

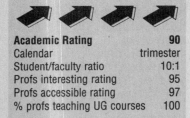

| | |
|---|---|
| **Quality of Life Rating** | **90** |
| Type of school | private |
| Affiliation | none |
| Environment | rural |

### STUDENTS

| | |
|---|---|
| Total undergrad enrollment | 278 |
| % male/female | 36/64 |
| % from out of state | 83 |
| % from public high school | 62 |
| % live on campus | 40 |
| % Caucasian | 93 |
| % international | 5 |
| # of countries represented | 9 |

### SURVEY SAYS . . .

*Beautiful campus*
*Campus easy to get around*
*Campus feels safe*
*Theater is hot*
*No one cheats*
*Intercollegiate sports unpopular or nonexistent*
*Students are cliquish*
*No one plays intramural sports*

## ACACEMICS

| | |
|---|---|
| **Academic Rating** | **90** |
| Calendar | trimester |
| Student/faculty ratio | 10:1 |
| Profs interesting rating | 95 |
| Profs accessible rating | 97 |
| % profs teaching UG courses | 100 |

### MOST POPULAR MAJORS

human ecology
marine biology
arts and design

## STUDENTS SPEAK OUT

### Academics

What with a campus smack-dab on the beach and "really small classes" that are, by all accounts, "amazing," students at College of the Atlantic compare spending four years on this intimate campus to "spending time at an intellectual spa." The "hands-on, interactive" course work at COA is divided into three 10-week terms. The curriculum is largely "self-guided" and students can design plenty of different variations into their majors, but students study an interdisciplinary integrated program known as Human Ecolgy. What exactly is Human Ecology, you ask? It's the understanding of the relationships between we humans and our natural, social, and technological environments. COA students praise their "wonderful" professors for being "very reliable and always willing to help." The instructors "make the school" and they are the "best-educated hippies in the world." The administration receives high marks as well. "The president eats with the rest of us," says one student. Says another: "This is the only school I know of where you can walk into the president's office—unannounced, no appointment—and say, 'Hey, Steve, what do you think of this?'" As far as complaints go, departments are tiny and registration continues to be far and away the biggest nuisance. Due to COA's rise in popularity, classes have both grown in size and become somewhat harder to obtain in recent years.

### Life

COA's small, oceanfront campus is nestled in Maine's rocky coastline on beautiful Mount Desert Island in the town of Bar Harbor, Maine, "as far away as you can get in the continental United States." The scenery is spectacular and "you can't beat the view," especially from the first-rate dining hall. Students swear that "everywhere is beautiful here," though. One even calls this campus "the greatest place on earth." Not surprisingly, "outdoor activities" are abundant. COA's location allows students to take advantage of the numerous resources offered by the Atlantic Ocean and nearby Acadia National Park. Students "hike, ski," "play in the snow and the leaves," and, basically, "do anything that involves being outside." They play soccer by day and "hide-and-seek at night." They "swim naked in the Atlantic." Also, "there's a killer rope swing on campus." Winters at COA are "very cold and long, but they are very conducive to study," which is a good thing. Entertainment options are obviously somewhat limited, but students say they manage. When the arctic air moves in, students at COA "play guitar, drum, cook dinner together," "watch movies, play Nintendo, and engage in deep philosophical conversations."

### Student Body

There are very few minority students at COA, a "hippie school" if ever there was one, and, needless to say, the student body is quite liberal. This paradise for the "environmentally conscious" attracts a "a very crunchy crowd" indeed. "I get tired of being constantly subjected to the music of Phish and the Grateful Dead blaring from every corner," gripes a first-year student. "Luckily, "you get desensitized" fairly quickly. Just about everyone is white, "atheist," and "leftist" here, and students say they spend a lot of time "thinking about what's going on locally, nationally, and internationally." Many students are vegetarians and a few are aggressively opposed to meat consumption as well. Everyone is "super-nice" and "easy to get along with," though, and the atmosphere is "pretty laid back." Students describe themselves as "fun, caring," and "compassionate."

FINANCIAL AID: 207-288-5015 • E-MAIL: INQUIRY@ECOLOGY.COA.EDU • WEBSITE: WWW.COA.EDU

## ADMISSIONS

*Very important* academic and nonacademic factors considered by the admissions committee include character/personal qualities, essays, extracurricular activities, interview, recommendations, and secondary school record. *Important* factors considered include class rank, talent/ability, volunteer work, and work experience. *Other* factors considered include standardized test scores. Factors *not* considered include alumni/ae relation, geography, minority status, religious affiliation/commitment, and state residency. TOEFL required of all international applicants. High school diploma is required and GED is accepted. *High school units required/recommended:* 15 total required; 17 total recommended; 4 English required, 4 math required, 3 science required, 4 science recommended, 2 science lab required, 2 foreign language recommended, 2 social studies required, 1 history required, 2 elective recommended. *The admissions office says:* "[The admissions process] is intentionally personal—we do not quantify our applicants in any way [and] we place a strong emphasis on writing throughout the admissions process."

### The Inside Word

COA's academic emphasis results in a highly self-selected applicant pool. Fortunately for the college, its focus on human ecology strikes a chord that is timely in its appeal to students. Enrolling here is definitely opting to take an atypical path to higher education. Admissions evaluations emphasize what's on your mind over what's on your transcript, which makes thoughtful essays and an interview musts for serious candidates. It also makes the admissions process a refreshing experience in the relatively uniform world of college admission. The admissions committee includes a few current students who have full voting rights as members.

## FINANCIAL AID

*Students should submit:* FAFSA, institution's own financial aid form, noncustodial (divorced/separated) parent's statement, and business/farm supplement. Regular filing deadline is February 15. The Princeton Review suggests that all financial aid forms be submitted as soon as possible after January 1. *Need-based scholarships/grants offered:* Pell, private scholarships, and the school's own gift aid. *Loan aid offered:* Direct Subsidized Stafford, Direct Unsubsidized Stafford, Direct PLUS, and Federal Perkins. Institutional employment available. Federal Work-Study Program available. Off-campus job opportunities are good.

## FROM THE ADMISSIONS OFFICE

"College of the Atlantic was created two decades ago at a time when it was becoming evident that conventional education was inadequate for citizenship in our increasingly complex and technical society. The growing interdependence of environmental and social issues and the limitations of academic specialization demand a wider vision. COA's founders created a pioneering institution dedicated to the interdisciplinary study of human ecology, a college in which students overcome narrow points of view and integrate knowledge across traditional academic lines."

### ADMISSIONS

| | |
|---|---|
| Admissions Rating | 85 |
| # of applicants | 251 |
| % of applicants accepted | 76 |
| % of acceptees attending | 47 |
| # of early decision applicants | 38 |
| % accepted early decision | 73 |

#### FRESHMAN PROFILE

| | |
|---|---|
| Average SAT Verbal | 617 |
| Average SAT Math | 600 |
| Average ACT Composite | 28 |
| Minimum TOEFL | 550 |
| Average HS GPA | 3.7 |
| % graduated top 10% of class | 28 |
| % graduated top 25% of class | 78 |
| % graduated top 50% of class | 98 |

#### DEADLINES

| | |
|---|---|
| Early decision | 12/1 |
| Early decision notification | 12/15 |
| Regular admission | 3/1 |
| Regular notification | 4/1 |
| Nonfall registration? | yes |

#### APPLICANTS ALSO LOOK AT
#### AND OFTEN PREFER
Bowdoin
Colby
Colorado Coll.
#### AND SOMETIMES PREFER
Bates
Bard
Marlboro
Hampshire
Cornell U.
#### AND RARELY PREFER
Oberlin
U. Maine—Orono
Mount Holyoke

### FINANCIAL FACTS

| | |
|---|---|
| Financial Aid Rating | 87 |
| Tuition | $21,138 |
| Room & board | $5,710 |
| Books and supplies | $500 |
| Required fees | $246 |
| % frosh receiving aid | 78 |
| % undergrads receiving aid | 76 |
| Avg frosh grant | $8,640 |
| Avg frosh loan | $2,625 |

# COLLEGE OF THE HOLY CROSS

ADMISSIONS OFFICE, 1 COLLEGE STREET, WORCESTER, MA 01610-2395 • ADMISSIONS: 508-793-2443 • FAX: 508-793-3888

## CAMPUS LIFE

**Quality of Life Rating**     **83**
Type of school     private
Affiliation     Roman Catholic
Environment     suburban

### STUDENTS
| | |
|---|---|
| Total undergrad enrollment | 2,826 |
| % male/female | 47/53 |
| % from out of state | 67 |
| % from public high school | 48 |
| % live on campus | 81 |
| % African American | 3 |
| % Asian | 3 |
| % Caucasian | 80 |
| % Hispanic | 5 |
| % international | 1 |
| # of countries represented | 19 |

### SURVEY SAYS . . .
*Diversity lacking on campus*
*Beautiful campus*
*Student publications are popular*
*Lots of beer drinking*
*Dorms are like palaces*
*Very small frat/sorority scene*
*Students don't like Worcester, MA*
*Lab facilities need improving*
*Athletic facilities need improving*
*Library needs improving*
*Students are cliquish*

## ACADEMICS

**Academic Rating**     **93**
| | |
|---|---|
| Calendar | semester |
| Student/faculty ratio | 12:1 |
| Profs interesting rating | 94 |
| Profs accessible rating | 93 |
| % profs teaching UG courses | 100 |
| Avg lab size | 10-19 students |
| Avg reg class size | 20-29 students |

### MOST POPULAR MAJORS
biology
English
political science

## STUDENTS SPEAK OUT

### Academics

The College of the Holy Cross is a "quality" bastion of liberal arts in New England with "fabulous" academics and a distinctively Catholic atmosphere. The "always available," "dedicated," and "very helpful" professors here "love to teach and it shows." "Often, if you miss a class, a professor will call to see if you are feeling well," and students are generally "in awe" of the faculty's "commitment and their passion for their respective disciplines." However, "they'll work you until you drop" and the "huge" amount of homework here (nearly four hours a day) is, by all accounts, "perfectly ridiculous." "Harvard is tougher to get into but Holy Cross is tougher academically," alleges a junior here. "Papers, papers, papers. That's what this school is about. I think everyone I know here has had at least one nervous breakdown at 3:00 A.M." Grading is also "difficult" and, not surprisingly, it's "easy to feel overwhelmed." Nevertheless, "it goes without saying that you will always give 110 percent" because "the professors expect no less." The reverence that students share for the faculty does not extend to the very businesslike administration, which "lacks a soul," is "as bureaucratic as Washington, D.C.," and is often "too worried about image." Also, "registration is somewhat a pain." These qualms aside, a degree from Holy Cross is well-regarded. About one-fourth of HC grads proceed directly to graduate school and a solid and loyal network of alumni provides a boost to those who opt immediately for the real world.

### Life

"Beer and studying"—that's Holy Cross in a nutshell. "People drink here. That's what they do for fun," explains a sophomore. Holy Cross is "more of a drinking school than a party school. The parties generally aren't that cool, or they get broken up within five minutes. It's more like getting drunk in your room." While weekends are largely devoted to boozing (and, of course, Sunday Mass), weekday diversions include intramural and intercollegiate sports as well numerous campus events. "They have different activities almost every night of the week," observes a sophomore, including "comedians, dances, plays, and movies." Off campus, "Worcester is the farthest thing from a college town" and "townies resent" HC students. "Boston and Providence are close enough" if "you are looking for a getaway." The "beauty of the campus is breathtaking," though, and most students don't stray from it too often, despite the "absolutely heinous" food and the fact that there are "way too many stairs to climb." While students here admit that they "tend to complain about a lot of things," they also admit that "no one would want to be anywhere else." Our survey results tend to bear this claim out: For all their griping, Holy Cross students rate themselves as extremely happy.

### Student Body

The "very outgoing, hardworking, and open-minded" students at Holy Cross say they are "men and women in the Jesuit tradition." They are "overworked, ambitious," "competitive but not cutthroat," as well as "bitter, stressed, and drunk." "Intelligent," too, and perhaps a bit "snobby." The campus is like "a walking J.Crew catalog—not that there's anything wrong with that." HC students "always dress up for class" and "many come from affluent families and are oftentimes oblivious to the working world." About 80 percent of Holy Cross students are white, and the minority population is pretty evenly divided among Asians, Hispanics, and African Americans, so each individual minority population is small. While a few students say Holy Cross is "a glorified high school," most contend that this place offers something more profound. "Our strength is in our community spirit and commonality of purpose. We share the same goals," explains one wistful student. "People form very close ties and you really get a sense of belonging and community here. People work hard, but also they are there for one another."

FINANCIAL AID: 508-793-2265 • E-MAIL: ADMISSIONS@HOLYCROSS.EDU • WEBSITE: WWW.HOLYCROSS.EDU

## ADMISSIONS

*Very important* academic and nonacademic factors considered by the admissions committee include character/personal qualities, interview, recommendations, secondary school record, and standardized test scores. *Important* factors considered include class rank and essays. *Other* factors considered include extracurricular activities, minority status, talent/ability, volunteer work, and work experience, alumni/ae relation, and geography. Factors *not* considered include religious affiliation/commitment, and ability to pay the cost of attendance. SAT I or ACT required; SAT II also required. TOEFL required of all international applicants. High school diploma is required and GED is accepted. *High school units required/recommended:* 16 total required; 4 English required, 3 math required, 2 science required, 1 science lab required, 2 foreign language required, 1 history required, 3 elective required. *The admissions office says:* "The Holy Cross admissions process is distinguished by the presence of a rolling Early Decision option; the ability to admit the class without regard to family finances; recognition of the applicants' energy and time commitment beyond the classroom."

### The Inside Word

The applicant pool at Holy Cross is strong; students are well advised to take the most challenging courses available to them in secondary school. Everyone faces fairly close scrutiny here, but as is the case virtually everywhere, the College does have its particular interests. The admissions committee takes good care of candidates from the many Catholic high schools that are the source of dozens of solid applicants each year.

## FINANCIAL AID

*Students should submit:* FAFSA, CSS/Financial Aid PROFILE, noncustodial (divorced/separated) parent's statement, and business/farm supplement. Regular filing deadline is February 1. The Princeton Review suggests that all financial aid forms be submitted as soon as possible after January 1. *Need-based scholarships/grants offered:* Pell, SEOG, state scholarships/grants, private scholarships, and the school's own gift aid. *Loan aid offered:* Direct Subsidized Stafford, Direct Unsubsidized Stafford, Direct PLUS, Federal Perkins, and MEFA. Institutional employment available. Federal Work-Study Program available. Applicants will be notified of awards on or about April 3. Off-campus job opportunities are good.

## FROM THE ADMISSIONS OFFICE

"When applying to Holy Cross, two areas deserve particular attention. First, the essay should be developed thoughtfully, with correct language and syntax in mind. That essay reflects for the Board of Admissions how you think and how you can express yourself. Second, activity beyond the classroom should be clearly defined. Since Holy Cross is 2,800 students, the chance for involvement/participation is exceptional. The Board reviews many applications for academically qualified students. A key difference in being accepted is the extent to which a candidate participates in-depth beyond the classroom—don't be modest; define who you are."

### ADMISSIONS

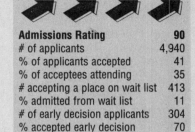

| | |
|---|---|
| Admissions Rating | 90 |
| # of applicants | 4,940 |
| % of applicants accepted | 41 |
| % of acceptees attending | 35 |
| # accepting a place on wait list | 413 |
| % admitted from wait list | 11 |
| # of early decision applicants | 304 |
| % accepted early decision | 70 |

### FRESHMAN PROFILE

| | |
|---|---|
| Range SAT Verbal | 570-650 |
| Average SAT Verbal | 626 |
| Range SAT Math | 580-670 |
| Average SAT Math | 623 |
| Minimum TOEFL | 550 |
| % graduated top 10% of class | 59 |
| % graduated top 50% of class | 99 |

### DEADLINES

| | |
|---|---|
| Early decision | 12/15 |
| Early decision notification | 2/15 |
| Regular admission | 1/15 |
| Regular notification | 4/1 |
| Nonfall registration? | yes |

### APPLICANTS ALSO LOOK AT
**AND OFTEN PREFER**
Dartmouth
Georgetown U.
Notre Dame
Boston Coll.
Tufts
**AND SOMETIMES PREFER**
Bowdoin
Colgate
Villanova
Providence
U. Mass—Amherst
**AND RARELY PREFER**
Fairfield

### FINANCIAL FACTS

| | |
|---|---|
| Financial Aid Rating | 71 |
| Tuition | $24,600 |
| Room & board | $7,760 |
| Books and supplies | $400 |
| Required fees | $420 |
| % frosh receiving aid | 51 |
| % undergrads receiving aid | 50 |
| Avg frosh grant | $12,438 |
| Avg frosh loan | $4,603 |

# COLLEGE OF THE OZARKS

OFFICE OF ADMISSIONS, POINT LOOKOUT, MO 65726 • ADMISSIONS: 417-334-6411 • FAX: 417-335-2618

## CAMPUS LIFE

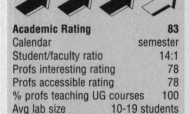

| Quality of Life Rating | 75 |
|---|---|
| Type of school | private |
| Affiliation | Presbyterian |
| Environment | rural |

### STUDENTS

| | |
|---|---|
| Total undergrad enrollment | 1,388 |
| % male/female | 44/56 |
| % from out of state | 33 |
| % live on campus | 84 |
| % Asian | 1 |
| % Caucasian | 96 |
| % Hispanic | 1 |
| % Native American | 1 |
| % international | 3 |

### SURVEY SAYS . . .

*Very little drug use*
*Lots of conservatives on campus*
*Classes are small*
*Students love Point Lookout, MO*
*Beautiful campus*
*Very little beer drinking*
*Very little hard liquor*
*(Almost) no one smokes*
*Political activism is (almost)*
*nonexistent*

## ACADEMICS

| Academic Rating | 83 |
|---|---|
| Calendar | semester |
| Student/faculty ratio | 14:1 |
| Profs interesting rating | 78 |
| Profs accessible rating | 78 |
| % profs teaching UG courses | 100 |
| Avg lab size | 10-19 students |
| Avg reg class size | 10-19 students |

### MOST POPULAR MAJORS

education
business
agriculture

## STUDENTS SPEAK OUT

### Academics

Tucked into the southwest corner of Missouri just this side of Branson (the Disney World of country music) lies one of the more unusual options in American higher education—Hard Work U., officially known as the College of the Ozarks. C of O was founded in 1906 "for the purpose of providing a Christian education for youth of both sexes, especially those found worthy but who are without sufficient means to procure such training." It's one of six colleges in the country that emphasizes offering educational opportunities to needy students in exchange for work in on-campus jobs. (The others are Berea, Alice Lloyd, Blackburn, Goddard, and Warren Wilson.) Financial need is considered during admissions evaluations, and they don't call it Hard Work U. for nothing: "Hard Work U. will work you hard," both academically and physically. Most students here consider it "a special school where you can obtain a free education and develop every aspect of your future, from spiritual values to academic excellence." Still, many feel that along with the "free" ride comes some pretty demanding expectations that go far beyond some labor. "It also is a college with morals and values that not many schools seem to have anymore." This is no joke, folks—C of O is clearly for those who are enthusiastic Christians who are ready to toe the line, including mandatory attendance at "convocations and seven chapels per semester." If you fit the bill, this place can provide a fabulous academic and personal growth experience. "The professors at C of O truly care about their students," and "it is very easy to contact any of the faculty or staff. Most of them know you by name." Academic offerings cover most of the liberal arts, as well as agriculturally oriented programs, aviation, and hotel and restaurant management. The "campus is beautiful," but labs and "computer facilities need help" in the eyes of many students. Some items of interest here are the Ralph Foster Museum, which houses the 1921 Oldsmobile from the original *Beverly Hillbillies* television series, and the fruitcake kitchen, where students bake nearly 40,000 fruitcakes annually.

### Life

It doesn't take a genius to realize that "College of the Ozarks is not the place for anyone who wants to drink their way through undergrad." According to many respondents, "College of the Ozarks has too many rules and restrictions. Campus gates close at 1:00 every night; opposite sexes are allowed in campus dorms for only three hours on one night a semester; no smoking on campus; if you are caught by a school official with alcohol outside of school (even if you are over 21) you will be kicked out . . . and many [administrators] are very discriminative against the students who dress alternative or portray themselves in their own ways. One student highlighted his hair and had to shave it off." Nonetheless, "student life is full of fun, spiritual, character-building activities." "Whether it's movie night, sporting events, a swing dance, or a concert, there's never a dull moment . . . especially if you're involved in a club, choir, or other group." The work commitment here takes care of about 15 hours worth of time per week, and "many students also have jobs in Branson." Though Branson doesn't exactly cater to the college crowd, "students get in free" to many shows, or at least get in "at a discount rate." "The downside is dealing with tourists!" Other popular pursuits are "outdoor things, like biking, hiking, swimming, fishing, and such."

### Student Body

Because the school was founded on Christian principles there are some very religious students here. Others are here because this was the only place they could afford." "This is a pretty diverse campus, with people from Africa, Brazil, Arkansas, California, and other places—it makes for an interesting college life. I'm glad to say that we all pretty much get along." Though they hail from far and wide, most have their roots in small-town America. "People here are great. I don't know if it's because we're in the Ozarks or what, but this is the friendliest place I've ever been to."

FINANCIAL AID: 417-334-6411 EXT. 4290 • E-MAIL: ADMISS4@COFO.EDU • WEBSITE: WWW.COFO.EDU

## ADMISSIONS

*Very important* academic and nonacademic factors considered by the admissions committee include character/personal qualities, essays, extracurricular activities, interview, secondary school record, and talent/ability. *Important factors* considered include alumni/ae relation, class rank, standardized test scores, volunteer work, and work experience. *Other factors* considered include geography, minority status, recommendations, religious affiliation/commitment, and state residency. SAT I or ACT required, ACT preferred. TOEFL required of all international applicants. High school diploma is required and GED is accepted. *High school units required/recommended:* 24 total recommended; 4 English recommended, 3 math recommended, 3 science recommended, 1 science lab recommended, 2 foreign language recommended, 2 social studies recommended, 2 history recommended.

### The Inside Word

The highly unusual nature of the College of the Ozarks translates directly into its admissions process. Because of the school's very purpose, providing educational opportunities to those with great financial need, one of the main qualifiers for admission is exactly that—demonstrated financial need. Despite not being a household word, Ozarks attracts enough interest to keep its admit rate consistently low from year to year. To be sure, the admissions process is competitive, but it's more important to be a good fit for the college philosophically and financially than it is to be an academic wizard. If you're a hard worker all around, you're just what they're looking for.

## FINANCIAL AID

*Students should submit:* FAFSA. There is no regular filing deadline. Priority filing deadline is March 15. The Princeton Review suggests that all financial aid forms be submitted as soon as possible after January 1. *Need-based scholarships/grants offered:* Pell, SEOG, state scholarships/grants, private scholarships, and the school's own gift aid. Institutional employment available. Applicants will be notified of awards on or about July 1. Off-campus job opportunities are excellent.

## FROM THE ADMISSIONS OFFICE

"College of the Ozarks is unique because of its no-tuition, work-study program, but also because it strives to educate the head, the heart, and the hands. At C of O, there are high expectations of students—the College stresses character development as well as study and work. An education from 'Hard Work U.' offers many opportunities, not the least of which is the chance to graduate debt-free. Life at C of O isn't all hard work and no play, however. There are many opportunities for fun. The nearby resort town of Branson, Missouri, offers ample opportunities for recreation and summer employment, and Table Rock Lake, only a few miles away, is a terrific spot to swim, sun, and relax. Numerous on-campus activities such as Mudfest, Luau Night, dances, and holiday parties give students lots of chances for fun without leaving the college. At 'Hard Work U.,' we work hard, but we know how to have fun, too."

## ADMISSIONS

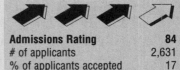

| | |
|---|---|
| Admissions Rating | 84 |
| # of applicants | 2,631 |
| % of applicants accepted | 17 |
| % of acceptees attending | 85 |

### FRESHMAN PROFILE

| | |
|---|---|
| Range ACT Composite | 18-25 |
| Average ACT Composite | 22 |
| Minimum TOEFL | 550 |
| Average HS GPA | 3.4 |
| % graduated top 10% of class | 17 |
| % graduated top 25% of class | 45 |
| % graduated top 50% of class | 84 |

### DEADLINES

| | |
|---|---|
| Priority admission deadline | 2/15 |
| Regular admission | 8/20 |
| Regular notification | rolling |
| Nonfall registration? | yes |

### APPLICANTS ALSO LOOK AT

**AND OFTEN PREFER**
Southwest Missouri State
Missouri Southern State

**AND SOMETIMES PREFER**
Drury College
Southeast Missouri State
Southwest Baptist U.

**AND RARELY PREFER**
Arkansas State
Ozarks Technical College

## FINANCIAL FACTS

| | |
|---|---|
| Financial Aid Rating | 88 |
| Room & board | $2,500 |
| Books and supplies | $600 |
| Required fees | $175 |
| % frosh receiving aid | 90 |
| % undergrads receiving aid | 90 |
| Avg frosh grant | $9,976 |

# COLLEGE OF WILLIAM AND MARY

PO BOX 8795, WILLIAMSBURG, VA 23187-8795 • ADMISSIONS: 757-221-4223 • FAX: 757-221-1242

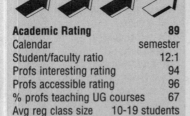
## STUDENTS SPEAK OUT

### Academics

Looking for a small public university with a big reputation (considered by some to be the most "prestigious" and "competitive" in the country), excellent location, and a down-to-earth attitude? William and Mary might just be your answer. Its students are certainly aware of this traditional liberal arts college's strengths and express them with intelligence and ease: "William and Mary is an undiscovered gem," writes one student. "It is an excellent undergraduate institution: small, but big enough to not limit you." Adds another, "At William and Mary, you get out of a class exactly what you put in. It's called self-determination. So, really, the school itself doesn't set the standards; we do." Listing the honor code, small class size, and rigorous academic standards as being among the college's greatest assets, students also appreciate its accessible, student-focused faculty, noting that at William and Mary, "we have professors who can make classes of 50 and more feel personal." One sophomore likes the fact that teachers "reward excellence and not competency with A's," while another appreciates "the option of being able to get to know the professors on a personal level." And though "the administration is a tad clueless," they also "listen to students the best that they can"—which presumably includes the issues surrounding financial aid, a popular gripe among William and Mary undergrads. "It's the best school for the money," comments a junior—with one caveat: You have to be a Virginia resident to take advantage of its state-school price tag. Basically, it comes down to one's feeling about a place, and the zeitgeist at William and Mary seems to be summed up best by a freshman: "Good times, guys. Good times."

### Life

"Intimate," "warm," and "tightly knit" are words often used to describe William and Mary's fairly well-developed social scene. According to a sophomore, it's the "size of the school" that "permits students to get involved in campus life." Writes another, "There is always something going on at William and Mary. It's easy to make friends and easy to be involved in activities. You can be as active as you want—there are a lot of opportunities." Some students might say that social life is somewhat skewed toward "fraternity parties and the brotherhood," however. There are lots of parties on weekends, and "delis [basically bars across the street from campus] are very fun to go to and hang out at." Williamsburg doesn't receive rave reviews. Writes one student, "Being far-ish from any major metropolitan area, cultural activities (concerts, museums, etc.) are rather rare." Still, while Williamsburg "doesn't have much," a trip to D.C. is worth the drive. Athletics are also a big draw; by one student's reckoning, "About 80 percent of the students participate in some kind of sport." Alas, "the meal plan is a rip-off," and while the colonial-style campus is scenic and lovely, parking seems to be a huge hassle (and impossible for first and second years). But hey—when the biggest complaint about a school is "more parking, better food, more hot boys," it can't be that bad.

### Student Body

In keeping with William and Mary's down-to-earth vibe, students at the school characterize their peers as "real" and "friendly," with "no fake attitudes and phoniness." Writes a sophomore, "Most everyone is approachable and genuinely concerned for others." Adds another, "Students are interesting and have neat stories—basically the same socioeconomic status but different life experiences." Of course not everyone is down with the group thing; a sophomore points out that "most students come from middle-class white backgrounds so the student body is too homogenous in attitudes/perspectives. Many are therefore unoriginal and boring." Still, a strong sense of community seems to be one of W&M's greatest strengths, even if it means getting through the hard times together. Jokes a junior, "Though half of the students are probably depressed, there exists an undeniable spirit of solidarity among them."

# COLLEGE OF WILLIAM AND MARY

FINANCIAL AID: 757-221-2420 EXT. 4290 • E-MAIL: ADMISS@FACSTAFF.WM.EDU • WEBSITE: WWW.WM.EDU

## ADMISSIONS

*Very important* academic and nonacademic factors considered by the admissions committee include secondary school record and state residency. *Important* factors considered include alumni/ae relation, class rank, essays, extracurricular activities, minority status, and standardized test scores. *Other* factors considered include character/personal qualities, geography, recommendations, talent/ability, and volunteer work. Factors *not* considered include interview, religious affiliation/commitment, and work experience. SAT I or ACT required; SAT II recommended. TOEFL required of all international applicants. *High school units required/recommended:* 4 English recommended, 4 math recommended, 4 science recommended, 3 science lab recommended, 4 foreign language recommended, 4 social studies recommended. *The admissions office says:* "[We have] two differently selective pools: in-state students—very competitive; out-of-state students—highly competitive. Special consideration is given to alumni children and athletes."

### The Inside Word

The volume of applications at William and Mary is extremely high; thus admission is ultra-competitive. Only very strong students from out of state should apply. The large applicant pool necessitates a rapid-fire candidate evaluation process; each admissions officer reads roughly 100 application folders per day during the peak review season. But this is one admissions committee that moves fast without sacrificing a thorough review. There probably isn't a tougher public college admissions committee in the country.

## FINANCIAL AID

*Students should submit:* FAFSA. Regular filing deadline is March 15. Priority filing deadline is February 15. The Princeton Review suggests that all financial aid forms be submitted as soon as possible after January 1. *Need-based scholarships/grants offered:* Pell, SEOG, state scholarships/grants, private scholarships, and the school's own gift aid. *Loan aid offered:* Subsidized Stafford, Unsubsidized Stafford, PLUS, and Federal Perkins. Institution employment available. Federal Work-Study Program available. Applicants will be notified of awards on or about April 1. Off-campus job opportunities are good.

## FROM THE ADMISSIONS OFFICE

"If you are an academicaly strong, involved student looking for a challenge in a great campus community, William and Mary may well be the place for you. Every year, students are drawn from all parts of the United States and dozens of foreign countries by the excellence of the undergraduate experience, the beauty of the campus and its surroundings, the size and residential character of the student body, and the history and traditions of the country's second oldest college. Our 1,200-acre campus, with its own woods and lake, offers life in the outdoors that complements opportunities in sports, the arts, service activities, Greek life, and just plain hanging out around campus or taking a break (in another century) in Colonial Williamsburg."

## ADMISSIONS

| Admissions Rating | 94 |
| --- | --- |
| # of applicants | 8,129 |
| % of applicants accepted | 41 |
| % of acceptees attending | 41 |
| # accepting a place on wait list | 735 |
| % admitted from wait list | 4 |
| # of early decision applicants | 736 |
| % accepted early decision | 63 |

### FRESHMAN PROFILE

| | |
| --- | --- |
| Range SAT Verbal | 620-710 |
| Average SAT Verbal | 663 |
| Range SAT Math | 610-700 |
| Average SAT Math | 654 |
| Range ACT Composite | 29-32 |
| Average ACT Composite | 31 |
| Minimum TOEFL | 600 |
| Average HS GPA | 4.0 |
| % graduated top 10% of class | 79 |
| % graduated top 25% of class | 97 |
| % graduated top 50% of class | 100 |

### DEADLINES

| | |
| --- | --- |
| Early decision | 11/1 |
| Early decision notification | 12/1 |
| Regular admission | 1/5 |
| Regular notification | 4/1 |
| Nonfall registration? | yes |

### APPLICANTS ALSO LOOK AT
### AND OFTEN PREFER
U. Virginia
Georgetown U.
Williams
Duke
Dartmouth
### AND SOMETIMES PREFER
Wake Forest
Randolph-Macon Woman's
Washington and Lee
Johns Hopkins
Rice
### AND RARELY PREFER
James Madison
U. Richmond
George Mason

### FINANCIAL FACTS

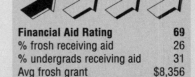

| Financial Aid Rating | 69 |
| --- | --- |
| % frosh receiving aid | 26 |
| % undergrads receiving aid | 31 |
| Avg frosh grant | $8,356 |
| Avg frosh loan | $2,417 |

# COLLEGE OF WOOSTER

1189 BEALL AVENUE, WOOSTER, OH 44691 • ADMISSIONS: 800-877-9905 • FAX: 330-263-2621

## CAMPUS LIFE

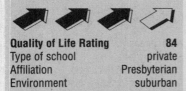

| Quality of Life Rating | 84 |
|---|---|
| Type of school | private |
| Affiliation | Presbyterian |
| Environment | suburban |

### STUDENTS

| | |
|---|---|
| Total undergrad enrollment | 1,837 |
| % male/female | 47/53 |
| % from out of state | 45 |
| % from public high school | 75 |
| % live on campus | 95 |
| % in (# of) fraternities | 15 (4) |
| % in (# of) sororities | 12 (6) |
| % African American | 4 |
| % Asian | 2 |
| % Caucasian | 91 |
| % Hispanic | 1 |
| % international | 8 |

### SURVEY SAYS . . .

Classes are small
Great computer facilities
Great library
Lots of beer drinking
Student government is unpopular
Registration is a pain
Low cost of living
Theater is unpopular
Musical organizations are hot

## ACADEMICS

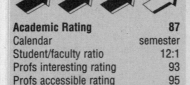

| Academic Rating | 87 |
|---|---|
| Calendar | semester |
| Student/faculty ratio | 12:1 |
| Profs interesting rating | 93 |
| Profs accessible rating | 95 |
| % profs teaching UG courses | 100 |
| Avg lab size | 10-19 students |
| Avg reg class size | 10-19 students |

### MOST POPULAR MAJORS

history
English
biology

## STUDENTS SPEAK OUT

### Academics

Like the hallmark of its curriculum—the independent study program—the College of Wooster seems intent on nurturing students into self-reliance. From the initial freshman seminar designed to foster critical thinking and writing skills, the Wooster curriculum is geared toward preparing students for their senior-year independent project. Fully integrated major requirements force students to master both content and methodology in their chosen fields of study before confronting the difficult but rewarding Independent Study (referred to by all on campus simply as "I.S."). Throughout, students are guided by professors who "are always willing to help you fully understand what is going on while they also force you to think for yourself." Writes one senior, "The independent study program, which has seniors research and write a thesis in the area of their major, scares the begeebers out of many students, but it allows students to work closely with professors and to examine something which is truly of interest to the student. It is the most difficult and yet the best aspect of education at Wooster." Student satisfaction levels at Wooster are high: "Professors are very accessible and genuinely concerned with their students. In the freshman first-year seminar class, professors sometimes invite you to their house for study sessions as a group". "Classes are small, and the relationships that can develop are special and long-lasting." Their only gripe: "The registration process is horrendous. It is arena-style lotto. Things need to be changed."

### Life

Wooster undergraduates report an active campus-based extracurricular life. Writes one, "There are a lot of things to do on weekends. The Student Activities Board is really active." Another elaborates that "the Student Activities Board provides a wide variety of social events, which help to make the campus active in a rather boring town. There are almost always parties, comedians, bands, films, and other activities going on. Having a bar/club on campus helps social life." Wooster football, complete with a marching band "wearing full Scottish military uniforms and a bagpipe corps," is also very popular. All this activity makes up for the fact that "the town of Wooster is basically devoid of all entertainment. A trip to the local Wal-Mart is one of the most exciting things I've done since I've been here. So you have to really work hard to entertain yourself at Wooster." Agrees another student, "The town is dead. There is nothing to do here: everything closes at 5. At least Akron is only 45 minutes, Cleveland an hour, and Columbus an hour and a half by car." Some students complain that "the Greeks control much of the social life, and there's a lot of drinking both on campus and off," but most agree that "people are generally happy."

### Student Body

While acknowledging that Wooster's minority population is rather small, most students seem to agree that "the campus seems pretty diverse for a small liberal arts school in the middle of Ohio. There are a wide range of students here, from my neighbor who is in the 'skater' culture to the jocks." Students report a lesser degree of cliquishness than do their counterparts at other small schools. "The people here for the most part are nice. I mean you do have your little groups, but people intermingle and get along fine." Wooster students also note that "people spend a lot of time working for causes they believe in: ecology, social activism, etc."

FINANCIAL AID: 800-877-3688 • E-MAIL: ADMISSIONS@WOOSTER.EDU • WEBSITE: WWW.WOOSTER.EDU

## ADMISSIONS

*Very important* academic and nonacademic factors considered by the admissions committee include class rank and secondary school record. *Important* factors considered include character/personal qualities, essays, recommendations, standardized test scores, and talent/ability. *Other* factors considered include alumni/ae relation, extracurricular activities, geography, interview, minority status, state residency, volunteer work, and work experience. Factors *not* considered include religious affiliation/commitment. SAT I or ACT required. TOEFL required of all international applicants. High school diploma is required and GED is accepted. *High school units required/recommended:* 16 total recommended; 4 English recommended, 3 math required, 3 science recommended, 2 science lab recommended, 2 foreign language recommended, 2 social studies recommended, 1 history recommended, 1 elective recommended.

### The Inside Word

Wooster has a solid academic reputation and holds its own against formidable competition for students with many national-caliber liberal arts colleges. Applicants should not take the admissions process lightly because candidate evaluations are very thorough and personal.

## FINANCIAL AID

*Students should submit:* FAFSA, institution's own financial aid form, CSS/Financial Aid PROFILE, and noncustodial (divorced/separated) parent's statement. There is no regular filing deadline. The Princeton Review suggests that all financial aid forms be submitted as soon as possible after January 1. *Need-based scholarships/grants offered:* Pell, SEOG, state scholarships/grants, private scholarships, and the school's own gift aid. *Loan aid offered:* Direct Subsidized Stafford, Direct Unsubsidized Stafford, Direct PLUS, Federal Perkins, and college/university loans from institutional funds. Institutional employment available. Federal Work-Study Program available. Applicants will be notified of awards on or about April 1. Off-campus job opportunities are good.

## FROM THE ADMISSIONS OFFICE

"At The College of Wooster, our mission is to graduate educated, not merely trained, people; to produce responsible, independent thinkers, rather than specialists in any given field. Our commitment to independence is especially evident in I.S., the college's distinctive program in which every senior works one-to-one with a faculty mentor to complete a project in the major. I.S. comes from 'independent study,' but, in reality, it is an intellectual collaboration of the highest order and permits every student the freedom to pursue something in which he or she is passionately interested. I.S. is the centerpiece of an innovative curriculum. More than just the project itself, the culture that sustains I.S.—and, in turn, is sustained by I.S.—is an extraordinary college culture. The same attitudes of student initiative, openness, flexibility, and individual support enrich every aspect of Wooster's vital residential college life."

## ADMISSIONS

| | |
|---|---|
| Admissions Rating | 78 |
| # of applicants | 2,305 |
| % of applicants accepted | 74 |
| % of acceptees attending | 29 |
| # accepting a place on wait list | 27 |
| % admitted from wait list | 74 |
| # of early decision applicants | 67 |
| % accepted early decision | 84 |

### FRESHMAN PROFILE

| | |
|---|---|
| Range SAT Verbal | 530-640 |
| Range SAT Math | 530-640 |
| Range ACT Composite | 23-28 |
| Minimum TOEFL | 550 |
| Average HS GPA | 3.5 |
| % graduated top 10% of class | 36 |
| % graduated top 25% of class | 66 |
| % graduated top 50% of class | 93 |

### DEADLINES

| | |
|---|---|
| Early decision | 12/1 |
| Early decision notification | 12/15 |
| Regular admission | 2/15 |
| Regular notification | 4/1 |
| Nonfall registration? | yes |

### APPLICANTS ALSO LOOK AT

**AND OFTEN PREFER**
Middlebury
DePauw U.
St. Olaf
Lawrence U.
Wittenberg U.

**AND SOMETIMES PREFER**
Ohio U.
Smith, Grinnell
Ohio Wesleyan U.
Kenyon

**AND RARELY PREFER**
Denison U.
Case Western Reserve U.
Dickinson
Penn State—Univ. Park

### FINANCIAL FACTS

| | |
|---|---|
| Financial Aid Rating | 86 |
| Tuition | $22,430 |
| Room & board | $5,920 |
| Books and supplies | $700 |
| % frosh receiving aid | 71 |
| % undergrads receiving aid | 65 |
| Avg frosh grant | $13,225 |
| Avg frosh loan | $3,084 |

# COLORADO COLLEGE

14 EAST CACHE LA POUDRE STREET, COLORADO SPRINGS, CO 80903 • ADMISSIONS: 719-389-6344 • FAX: 719-389-6816

## CAMPUS LIFE

| **Quality of Life Rating** | **85** |
|---|---|
| Type of school | private |
| Affiliation | none |
| Environment | urban |

### STUDENTS

| | |
|---|---|
| Total undergrad enrollment | 1,919 |
| % male/female | 46/54 |
| % from out of state | 69 |
| % from public high school | 72 |
| % live on campus | 67 |
| % in (# of) fraternities | 16 (3) |
| % in (# of) sororities | 16 (3) |
| % African American | 2 |
| % Asian | 4 |
| % Caucasian | 78 |
| % Hispanic | 5 |
| % Native American | 1 |
| % international | 2 |

### SURVEY SAYS . . .

*Campus easy to get around*
*Beautiful campus*
*Campus feels safe*
*Lab facilities are great*
*Great off-campus food*
*Very small frat/sorority scene*
*Student publications are ignored*
*Student government is unpopular*
*(Almost) no one smokes*

## ACADEMICS

| **Academic Rating** | **88** |
|---|---|
| Student/faculty ratio | 12:1 |
| Profs interesting rating | 92 |
| Profs accessible rating | 95 |
| % profs teaching UG courses | 100 |
| Avg reg class size | 10-19 students |

### MOST POPULAR MAJORS
biology
English
economics

## STUDENTS SPEAK OUT
### Academics

Colorado College "definitely embodies the liberal arts tradition," but in a unique form. Here's how: CC breaks up its academic year into three-and-a-half-week blocks ("the block plan") during which students concentrate on a single course. At the end of each block, a four-day "block break" lets students cleanse their minds before starting the next class. Undergraduates write that "most professors know the block plan and teach it really well, few are out-of-this-world amazing and even fewer are horrible," and caution prospective students that "the block plan is good for some people, but bad for others." Complains one who definitely falls into the latter camp, "The block plan is just TOO intense! Lots of nervous breakdowns. Ten-page papers from one day to the next—AAUGH! It's easy to pass your class, but hard to get a good grade. I can't believe I'm filling this survey in right now; I have two books to read and a six-page paper due tomorrow." The block plan is reportedly excellent for humanities and social sciences, but "the intensity of sciences is unbelievable," warns a biochemistry major. When the system works, it's because the "very accessible profs" serve as "catalysts of learning. They don't ingrain things in our minds, they make us think and challenge us to push ourselves."

### Life

Because "the Block Plan controls all aspects of your life," students agree that "block breaks are the best things ever invented." An art major explains: "You cram for three and a half weeks, then go snowboarding, skiing, rock climbing, or traveling for five days and thoroughly abuse yourself." The mountain surroundings provide plenty of opportunities for "camping in summer, skiing in winter." Opines one student, "Colorado is one of the most beautiful places to live, learn, and play. Having Pike's Peak as the backdrop to the things you learn and what you become is amazing." "Everyone here plays sports" and enjoys attending sporting events as well, "especially hockey games." Campus life "is wonderful if you get involved in things. Performance groups here are a great experience. People are open to do most anything." All the same, "Weekends are sometimes hard because the parties are all the same." Writes one undergrad, "Parties on campus are a nice release but they get old. Going to cafes, movies, and Denver are alternatives, but the usual stand-by is getting drunk." There are also "lots of drugs," at least among some circles. The school's hometown of Colorado Springs has the reputation of being "very military, right-wing, and Christian. The resistance the CC population feels from the city population acts as a unifying force in crazy ways."

### Student Body

CC's undergrads describe themselves as "a mere liberal slice of carrot in the conservative stew of Colorado Springs, but we are also a stew in and of ourselves: 'veggies,' 'med-heads,' etc. There are juicy opportunities and unique flavors to be had!" For those who aren't conversant in stew metaphors, we'll translate: Students here are "groovy, mellow, outdoorsy types" who count among their number "lots of rich New England students trying to pass as hippies," "Trustafarian ski bums," and "a large crunchy contingent, most of whom want to do away with electricity, yet spend most of their time skiing at Vail." "A fairly large lesbian community" and "a lot of 'out' gays—this is not a homophobic campus :-)" also figure into the mix. Some students complain that "there is a lot of politically correct bull, especially with students who like to let everyone know how cool they feel about being different." Sums up one student: "I've met some wonderful people here but also some absolute losers, pot-smoking, Phish-listening rich hippies who don't take advantage of this place."

FINANCIAL AID: 719-389-6651 • E-MAIL: ADMISSION@COLORADOCOLLEGE.EDU • WEBSITE: WWW.COLORADOCOLLEGE.EDU

## ADMISSIONS

*Very important* academic and nonacademic factors considered by the admissions committee include essays and secondary school record. *Important* factors considered include extracurricular activities and recommendations. *Other* factors considered include test scores, character/personal qualities, minority status, talent/ability, alumni/ae relation, class rank, geography, volunteer work, and work experience. Factors *not* considered include religious affiliation/commitment and state residency. SAT I or ACT required. TOEFL required of all international applicants. *High school units required/recommended:* 4 English required, 3 math required, 4 math recommended, 3 science required, 4 science recommended, 2 science lab required, 2 foreign language required, 4 foreign language recommended, 2 social studies required, 4 social studies recommended, 1 elective required. *The admissions office says:* "CC seeks students who demonstrate academic excellence, uncommon talents and interests, and a commitment to the idea of a liberal arts education. Economic and geographic diversity and the potential for making significant contributions to the college community are also factors considered for admission."

### The Inside Word

Colorado is seeking thinkers with personality. This makes for an admissions process that gives more credit to the match a candidate makes than simply to good numbers. Tough high school courses are nonetheless a strong factor in admission. The college is a rarity—an institution that admits that geography plays a part in admissions. Minority recruitment is improving, but needs to play an even bigger part. Students who view Colorado College as a safety, beware—the admissions committee employs a policy of denying candidates who, though strong academically, demonstrate little real interest in attending.

## FINANCIAL AID

*Students should submit:* FAFSA, CSS/Financial Aid PROFILE, and noncustodial (divorced/separated) parent's statement. Regular filing deadline is February 15. The Princeton Review suggests that all financial aid forms be submitted as soon as possible after January 1. *Need-based scholarships/grants offered:* Pell, SEOG, state scholarships/grants, and private scholarships. *Loan aid offered:* FFEL Subsidized Stafford, FFEL Unsubsidized Stafford, FFEL PLUS, and Federal Perkins. Institutional employment available. Federal Work-Study Program available. Applicants will be notified of awards on or about March 25. Off-campus job opportunities are good.

## FROM THE ADMISSIONS OFFICE

"Students enter Colorado College for the opportunity to study intensely in small learning communities. Groups of students work closely with one another and faculty in discussion-based classes and hands-on labs. CC encourages a well-rounded education, combining the academic rigor of an honors college with rich programs in athletics, community service, student government, the arts, and more. The college encourages students to push themselves academically, and many continue their studies at the best graduate and professional schools in the nation. CC is a great choice for field study and for international study (CC ranks fourth nationally in the number of students studying abroad). CC also takes advantage of its location, using it's Baca campus in the San Luis Valley and the mountain cabin for a variety of classes. Its location at the base of the Rockies makes CC a great choice for students who enjoy backpacking, hiking, climbing, and skiing."

## ADMISSIONS

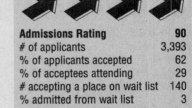

| | |
|---|---:|
| Admissions Rating | 90 |
| # of applicants | 3,393 |
| % of applicants accepted | 62 |
| % of acceptees attending | 29 |
| # accepting a place on wait list | 140 |
| % admitted from wait list | 3 |

### FRESHMAN PROFILE

| | |
|---|---:|
| Range SAT Verbal | 590-660 |
| Average SAT Verbal | 630 |
| Range SAT Math | 580-660 |
| Average SAT Math | 631 |
| Range ACT Composite | 26-29 |
| Average ACT Composite | 27 |
| Minimum TOEFL | 550 |
| % graduated top 10% of class | 50 |
| % graduated top 25% of class | 83 |
| % graduated top 50% of class | 98 |

### DEADLINES

| | |
|---|---:|
| Regular admission | 1/15 |
| Regular notification | 4/1 |
| Nonfall registration? | yes |

### APPLICANTS ALSO LOOK AT
### AND OFTEN PREFER
Stanford
Dartmouth
Carleton
Middlebury
### AND SOMETIMES PREFER
Macalester
Reed
Occidental
Grinnell
U. Colorado—Boulder
### AND RARELY PREFER
U. Vermont
Kenyon
Lewis & Clark Coll.

## FINANCIAL FACTS

| | |
|---|---:|
| Financial Aid Rating | 83 |
| Tuition | $24,528 |
| Room & board | $6,064 |
| Books and supplies | $900 |
| Required fees | $365 |
| % frosh receiving aid | 48 |
| % undergrads receiving aid | 45 |
| Avg frosh grant | $17,926 |
| Avg frosh loan | $2,839 |

# COLORADO SCHOOL OF MINES

WEAVER TOWERS, 1811 ELM STREET, GOLDEN, CO 80401-1842 • ADMISSIONS: 303-273-3220 • FAX: 303-273-3509

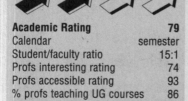
## STUDENTS SPEAK OUT

### Academics

For Colorado residents interested in engineering, math, and mineral sciences, it is difficult to ignore the bargain offered by the state-run Colorado School of Mines. There are a few select engineering programs out there with more prestigious reputations, but many fewer that can offer the same cost/benefit ratio as CSM. In fact, even out-of-state students should find the school's tuition—about 60 percent of what students at MIT pay—a genuine bargain. Not that students don't pay in other ways; the coin of the realm, in this regard, is sweat. "Most of us do homework seven days a week," says a junior. "This school is hard. You can't comprehend, out there, what that means. They test you two levels of comprehension above what they teach you, but if you can do it, the education you get is unbelievable." Particularly demanding is the core curriculum, a prescribed set of first-year courses called the Engineering Practices Introductory Course Sequence (EPICS). "I wish the classes weren't chosen for you your first year," moans one freshman. The intensity level, if anything, heightens when students turn to major studies. "In my department the faculty seems to be out to get you. In beginning-level courses, they want to weed you out, causing the students not to want to help each other," explains one chemical engineer. Adds an organic chemistry major, "They push you 'til you scream, then cram even more down your throat and enjoy every minute of it." Still, "There are some professors who truly care about their students," and there's always the pot of gold at the end of the rainbow: According to CSM, nearly 90 percent of its graduates are placed in jobs or graduate programs by graduation day, and the administration projects a 95 percent placement within six months. "The best thing about this school is the cooperation with industry. The career placement center has a very high placement rate. With their help, I was able to get a summer job at a precious metals refinery in South Africa," explains one student.

### Life

Needless to say, the workload at CSM precludes a conventional college social life. A first-year student explains: "This school is for engineers only. If you are unsure if you want to be an engineer, go somewhere else." For fun, many students "do math" and surf their idle hours away on the Internet. Making matters worse is the dearth of entertainment opportunities in Golden. Writes one engineer, "For fun, there isn't a whole lot to do. The town shuts down at 9:00 P.M. For fun, I try to leave the town." However, we do hear that both the town and CSM have tried to implement more social activities. Denver and Boulder, both 20 minutes away by car, are the chosen destinations of most road-trippers. Closer to home, CSM's Greek scene "is sometimes fun when it is going on." The tiny population of women here seem to find 'going Greek' particularly rewarding; reports one, "Being active in the Greek community is one of the best decisions I ever made. Having a network of close female friends is so valuable at a male-dominated engineering school." For others, "Athletics are the way to go for the social Diggers, computer games for the more introverted Diggers." The natural beauty of the surroundings is certainly a plus and, of course, "the area is great for hiking and skiing." According to one student, "Snowboarding is also a good stress reliever."

### Student Body

Students at this "quite conservative" school may be "social misfits" but as one student told us, "I've met some of the coolest people at CSM." "There are a lot of introverted people here who like to study for fun on Friday and Saturday nights," explains one "willing to try anything cool" person, "but then there are those who go to Coors Lab religiously and have fun." Minority representation is relatively sparse but the student population "seems diverse due to the large international student population." The school is predominantly male; notes one woman, "Life is weird in a 3-to-1 male-female setting."

FINANCIAL AID: 303-273-3301 • E-MAIL: ADMIT@MINES.EDU • WEBSITE: WWW.MINES.EDU

## ADMISSIONS

*Very important* academic and nonacademic factors considered by the admissions committee include secondary school record and standardized test scores. *Important* factors considered include talent/ability. *Other* factors considered include class rank, extracurricular activities, interview, and recommendations. Factors *not* considered include alumni/ae relation, character/personal qualities, essays, geography, religious affiliation/commitment, state residency, volunteer work, and work experience. SAT I or ACT required. TOEFL required of all international applicants. High school diploma is required and GED is accepted. *High school units required/recommended:* 15 total required; 4 English required, 3 math required, 4 math recommended, 2 science required, 3 science recommended, 2 science lab required, 3 science lab recommended, 2 foreign language required, 3 foreign language recommended, 2 social studies required, 2 elective required. *The admissions office says:* "While we are selective, we also try to be low-key, personable, and straightforward about the business of college admissions. We also are willing to take a chance with the unusual student (the one that doesn't fit the standard mold). The typical CSM student is directed, motivated, hardworking, and decent. They care about and take pride in themselves and the school."

### The Inside Word

Although the admissions process is rigorous and straightforward in its focus on the academic, the admissions staff is more personable than at most technically oriented schools. Minorities and women are in demand.

## FINANCIAL AID

*Students should submit:* FAFSA. There is no regular filing deadline. The Princeton Review suggests that all financial aid forms be submitted as soon as possible after January 1. *Need-based scholarships/grants offered:* Pell, SEOG, state scholarships/grants, private scholarships, and the school's own gift aid. *Loan aid offered:* Direct Subsidized Stafford, Direct Unsubsidized Stafford, Direct PLUS, Federal Perkins, state, and college/university loans from institutional funds. Institutional employment available. Federal Work-Study Program available. Applicants will be notified of awards on a rolling basis beginning on or about April 1. Off-campus job opportunities are good.

## FROM THE ADMISSIONS OFFICE

"CSM is a uniquely western school, not a typical college or university located in the West. The social environment is informal and friendly, and the academic environment is competitive but not cutthroat. Founded as a school of mining and geology, today we do much more. Nearly 40 percent of our students major in our broad-based, interdisciplinary, nontraditional engineering program, which offers course concentrations in civil, electrical, and mechanical engineering. Another 20 percent are studying chemical engineering. Our fastest growing area is mathematics and computer sciences."

## ADMISSIONS

| Admissions Rating | 86 |
| --- | --- |
| # of applicants | 1,943 |
| % of applicants accepted | 81 |
| % of acceptees attending | 40 |

### FRESHMAN PROFILE

| | |
| --- | --- |
| Range SAT Verbal | 530-650 |
| Average SAT Verbal | 590 |
| Range SAT Math | 600-700 |
| Average SAT Math | 650 |
| Range ACT Composite | 25-30 |
| Average ACT Composite | 28 |
| Minimum TOEFL | 550 |
| Average HS GPA | 3.8 |
| % graduated top 10% of class | 56 |
| % graduated top 25% of class | 90 |
| % graduated top 50% of class | 100 |

### DEADLINES

| | |
| --- | --- |
| Priority admission deadline | 4/15 |
| Regular admission | 6/1 |
| Nonfall registration? | yes |

### APPLICANTS ALSO LOOK AT
#### AND OFTEN PREFER
Carnegie Mellon
U. Colorado—Boulder
Rice
Texas A & M
Colorado Coll.
#### AND SOMETIMES PREFER
U. Missouri—Rolla
Colorado State
U. Texas—Austin
U. Denver
#### AND RARELY PREFER
U. Northern Colorado
Rose-Hulman

## FINANCIAL FACTS

| Financial Aid Rating | 79 |
| --- | --- |
| In-state tuition | $4,750 |
| Out-of-state tuition | $15,304 |
| Room & board | $4,900 |
| Books and supplies | $1,100 |
| Required fees | $662 |
| % frosh receiving aid | 74 |
| % undergrads receiving aid | 74 |
| Avg frosh grant | $4,240 |
| Avg frosh loan | $4,240 |

# COLUMBIA UNIVERSITY

535 WEST 116TH STREET, NEW YORK, NY 10027 • ADMISSIONS: 212-854-2521 • FAX: 212-894-1209

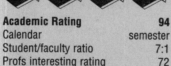
## STUDENTS SPEAK OUT

### Academics

Columbia University holds one major trump card in its battle against Princeton, Yale, Dartmouth, and the other members of the Ivy League: location. Students agree that, among CU's many assets, New York City is tops. "I believe that being in New York makes this the most well-rounded education anywhere," notes one student succinctly. Other drawing cards include world-class programs in engineering ("Engineering will challenge everything you know and believe in, every way you act, and absolutely every thought you have"), pre-medicine, pre-business, the liberal arts, and screenwriting. Then, of course, there's the much-vaunted core curriculum, a two-year sequence of survey courses in western culture. Enthuses one student, "The core curriculum changed my life. It taught me to love and appreciate the western canon, that it was mine to inherit." Another notes that the core, which most students complete by the end of sophomore year, sets the tone for all Columbia course work: "Columbia is all about discussion in its core curriculum and its discussion sections and seminars. Students who come here should be prepared to spar in debate in the classroom." They should also be prepared to fend for themselves, because "Columbia is a haven for the self-motivated. No one's going to hold your hand." Students "have to work and seek out the good professors, but if you put in the effort to find them, it's more than worth it." They also must prepare to do battle with "the brutal bureaucracy. . . . If you're not assertive and self-sufficient, it can be easy to get lost in the proverbial shuffle." Students agree that Columbia, like its hometown, is "a place that teaches you to sink or swim."

### Life

As a rule of thumb, student activity on any college campus is inversely proportional to the amount of leisure opportunity available in the school's hometown. With New York City waiting just outside CU's front gate, it should come as no surprise that most Columbia undergrads seek entertainment beyond the confines of campus. Points out one student, "It's great going to school in NYC—it's safe, it's exciting, and you never run out of things to do." Students take full advantage of the benefits of their location, especially on the weekends, when "the student body splits up into tiny cliques and flows into every nook and cranny of the city. Either that or they study." Any way you slice it, "Life for Columbia students doesn't revolve around Columbia," which suits most students just fine. "Whether it's going to a Broadway show," writes one student, "going to Little Italy for dinner, Flushing for karaoke, or to Soho for shopping, I can definitely say that my life here is just great." Campus life centers around dorms; libraries; the small cafes, restaurants, and bars on Broadway; and the steps in front of the administration building, where students hang out for hours on end, weather permitting. The Greek scene is subdued; "Columbia is neither pro-Greek or anti-Greek. It's more like a pro-'Greek party' school. Fraternities are filled with people who were dead set against them in high school." After years in the Ivy League basement, CU's sports teams are finally on the upswing; points out one student, "Though our teams are still remembered for 'The Streak' (45 straight football losses), our teams are better now and school spirit is growing."

### Student Body

New York City, a large endowment, and a long tradition of diversity help attract a wide array of races and classes to Columbia. Writes one student, "I think the diversity of Columbia is its best attribute. I've gotten the chance to meet and befriend people from a wide variety of backgrounds." Many, however, note that while "diversity is the name of the game—there are over 150 different student groups on campus—they don't really interact too much." CU undergrads are typically "bright, know a lot about current events, and care about their community. They are very serious but not always competitive, which is good." Some note wryly that "Columbia is a great school that attracts smart people: the downside of having such smart people is that they notice when things aren't perfect and whine about it," adding, "many students complain about Columbia" constantly.

# COLUMBIA UNIVERSITY

## ADMISSIONS

*Very important* academic and nonacademic factors considered by the admissions committee include class rank, secondary school record, and standardized test scores. *Important* factors considered include essays and recommendations. *Other* factors considered include alumni/ae relation, character/personal qualities, extracurricular activities, geography, talent/ability, volunteer work, and work experience. Factors *not* considered include interview, minority status, religious affiliation/commitment, and state residency. SAT I or ACT required; SAT II also required. TOEFL required of all international applicants. *High school units required/recommended:* 16 total required; 4 English required, 2 math required, 2 science required, 2 foreign language required, 2 social studies required, 4 elective required. *The admissions office says:* "Columbia seeks to attract candidates from a variety of backgrounds. It is misleading, therefore, to take a list or ranking of admissions criteria as definitive; it is safe to say, however, that a student's academic record (rigor of program and grades received) is the single most important factor in the admissions decision."

### The Inside Word

Columbia's application increases continue to outpace the rest of the Ivy League, and as a result the University keeps moving higher up in the Ivy pecking order. Crime is down in New York City, the football team wins (while still in baby-blue uniforms, no less!), and Columbia has become even more appealing. It's less selective than the absolute cream of the Ivy crop, but offers the advantage of being a bit more open and frank in discussing the admissions process with students, parents, and counselors—refreshing amid the typical shrouds of Ivy mystique.

## FINANCIAL AID

*Students should submit:* FAFSA, institution's own financial aid form, noncustodial parent's statement, business/farm supplement. Regular filing deadline is January 1. The Princeton Review suggests that all financial aid forms be submitted as soon as possible after January 1. *Need-based scholarships/grants offered:* Pell, SEOG, state scholarships/grants, private scholarships, and the school's own gift aid, and Federal Nursing. *Loan aid offered:* Subsidized Stafford, Unsubsidized Stafford, PLUS, Federal Perkins, Federal Nursing, state, and the school's own loans. Institutional employment available. Federal Work-Study Program available. Applicants will be notified of awards on or about April 1. Off-campus job opportunities are excellent.

## FROM THE ADMISSIONS OFFICE

"Located in the world's most international city, Columbia University offers a diverse student body a solid and broad liberal arts curriculum foundation coupled with more advanced study in specific departments."

---

## ADMISSIONS

| | |
|---|---:|
| **Admissions Rating** | **98** |
| # of applicants | 13,013 |
| % of applicants accepted | 13 |
| % of acceptees attending | 56 |
| # accepting a place on wait list | 900 |
| # of early decision applicants | 1158 |
| % accepted early decision | 37 |

### FRESHMAN PROFILE

| | |
|---|---:|
| Range SAT Verbal | 650-760 |
| Average SAT Verbal | 701 |
| Range SAT Math | 650-740 |
| Average SAT Math | 693 |
| Minimum TOEFL | 600 |
| % graduated top 10% of class | 83 |
| % graduated top 25% of class | 97 |
| % graduated top 50% of class | 100 |

### DEADLINES

| | |
|---|---:|
| Early decision | 11/1 |
| Early decision notification | 12/15 |
| Regular admission | 1/1 |
| Regular notification | 4/1 |

### APPLICANTS ALSO LOOK AT AND OFTEN PREFER

Harvard
Yale
Princeton
Stanford
Duke

### AND SOMETIMES PREFER

Brown
U. Penn
Dartmouth
Tufts

### AND RARELY PREFER

Wesleyan U.
Binghamton U.
Vassar
Barnard

## FINANCIAL FACTS

| | |
|---|---:|
| **Financial Aid Rating** | **72** |
| Tuition | $25,044 |
| Room & board | $7,966 |
| Books and supplies | $800 |
| Required fees | $878 |
| % frosh receiving aid | 46 |
| % undergrads receiving aid | 45 |
| Avg frosh grant | $18,662 |
| Avg frosh loan | $2,445 |

# CONNECTICUT COLLEGE

270 MOHEGAN AVENUE, NEW LONDON, CT 06320 • ADMISSIONS: 860-439-2200 • FAX: 860-439-4301

## CAMPUS LIFE

| | |
|---|---|
| **Quality of Life Rating** | **78** |
| Type of school | private |
| Affiliation | none |
| Environment | suburban |

### STUDENTS

| | |
|---|---|
| Total undergrad enrollment | 1,814 |
| % male/female | 43/57 |
| % from out of state | 85 |
| % from public high school | 51 |
| % live on campus | 98 |
| % African American | 3 |
| % Asian | 3 |
| % Caucasian | 82 |
| % Hispanic | 3 |
| % international | 8 |
| # of countries represented | 60 |

### SURVEY SAYS . . .
*Theater is hot*
*Students don't get along with local community*
*No one cheats*
*Political activism is hot*
*Students aren't religious*
*Class discussions encouraged*
*(Almost) no one listens to college radio*

## ACADEMICS

| | |
|---|---|
| **Academic Rating** | **85** |
| Calendar | semester |
| Student/faculty ratio | 11:1 |
| Profs interesting rating | 93 |
| Profs accessible rating | 95 |
| % profs teaching UG courses | 100 |
| Avg lab size | 10-19 students |
| Avg reg class size | 10-19 students |

### MOST POPULAR MAJORS
psychology
English
biology

## STUDENTS SPEAK OUT
### Academics

Variety—as in "variety of options"—is the watchword at Connecticut College. The small student body reaps the benefits of "the fact that such diverse departments are strong. Arts, drama, and dance attract a certain type of student, philosophy and psychology another, and a strong athletic department attracts yet another type." However, CC is truly a liberal arts school of the first order, with most students distributed in the arts, hard sciences, history, and the social sciences. Students in all departments report favorably on both faculty and administrators: "Teachers are caring people and most are ready and willing to help you if you are having trouble." Says one student, "Professors are not only available for communication, but rather expect it." "The student-faculty bond is the strongest I've seen," concurs another satisfied student. Students happily report that "most administrators are very available and more than willing to help you." CC's heavy workload includes a broad-based set of core requirements, which guarantee students will have to study literature, history, and the hard sciences prior to graduation. Explains one respondent, "This school puts tons of responsibility on you. Professors aren't going to get you out of bed, but they will help you if you ask for it."

### Life

Students dispute the quality of life at CC. Those who find social life here as enriching as academic life tell us that "there is always a lot to do. The campus has movies and information meetings on a regular basis," and there are "lots of opportunities for student involvement." Students participate enthusiastically in intramural sports and regularly attend the school's Division III sporting events. For the community-minded, "The school has some great volunteer programs." Still, a vocal segment of the population claims that "life at school isn't too great." The school's blue-collar hometown, New London, is "not very accepting of college students." New York City and Boston are great, but at about two hours away by car, they're a bit too far to facilitate regular getaways. Despite the number, it is clear that "alcohol becomes an integral part of fun for most of the students." One satisfied student sums it up by telling us that "people complain about the monotony of social life: drinking, dances, et cetera . . . but it's what you make if it. A lot of people drink, but I don't and I still have a blast."

### Student Body

The availability of financial aid notwithstanding, the high cost of attending CC tends to limit the diversity of the student body. Notes one student, "Most of the people here are prep school kids. . . . As a public school student I feel a bit out of place." Another puts it even more succinctly: "I wish there were more diversity. This is a white, rich-kid school." Some students find diversity beneath the superficial similarities, explaining that "the student body at first seems very homogeneous—middle class, white, WASPy. It takes a lot of time to locate all the interesting and unusual people. They tend to be hidden in the woodwork." Another puts it this way: "Our campus is not too ethnically diverse, but it is very personality diverse!"

FINANCIAL AID: 860-439-2200 • E-MAIL: ADMIT@CONNCOLL.EDU • WEBSITE: WWW.CONNCOLL.EDU

## ADMISSIONS

*Very important* academic and nonacademic factors considered by the admissions committee include character/personal qualities and class rank. *Important* factors include essays, extracurricular activities, and standardized test scores. *Other* factors considered include alumni/ae relation, geography, interview, talent/ability, work experience, and diversity. Factors *not* considered include religious affiliation. TOEFL required of all international applicants. High school diploma is required and GED is accepted. *High school units required/recommended:* 16 total recommended; 4 English recommended, 3 math recommended, 3 science recommended, 3 foreign language recommended, 3 social studies recommended. *The admissions office says:* "We spend a lot of time looking at each applicant as an individual, evaluating qualities and accomplishments within the context of each one's academic and personal environment. We look for students whose achievements have been characterized by stretch—going beyond the minimums and demonstrating real enthusiasm for learning in all its forms. And we look for each applicant's potential for success in our environment, that of a creative and flexible liberal arts curriculum and a diverse and involved student body."

### The Inside Word

Late in 1994, Connecticut became the most recent college to drop the SAT I as a requirement for admission, citing the overemphasis that the test receives from the media and, in turn, students. The college is judicious about keeping their acceptance rate as low as possible. Candidates undergo a rigorous review of their credentials, and should be strong students in order to be competitive. Still, the college's competition for students is formidable.

## FINANCIAL AID

*Students should submit:* FAFSA, CSS/Financial Aid PROFILE, noncustodial (divorced/separated) parent's statement, and business/farm supplement. Regular filing deadline is January 15. The Princeton Review suggests that all financial aid forms be submitted as soon as possible after January 1. *Need-based scholarships/grants offered:* Pell, SEOG, state scholarships/grants, and the school's own gift aid. *Loan aid offered:* FFEL Subsidized Stafford, FFEL Unsubsidized Stafford, FFEL PLUS, Federal Perkins, and college/university loans from institutional funds. Institutional employment available. Federal Work-Study Program available. Applicants will be notified of awards on or about April 1. Off-campus job opportunities are good.

## FROM THE ADMISSIONS OFFICE

"Distinguishing characteristics of the diverse student body at this small, highly selective college are honor and tolerance. Student leadership is pronounced in all aspects of the college's administration from exclusive jurisdiction of the honor code and dorm life to active representation on the president's academic and administrative cabinets. Differences of opinion are respected and celebrated as legitimate avenues to new understanding. Students come to Connecticut College seeking opportunities for independence and initiative and find them in abundance."

## ADMISSIONS

| | |
|---|---|
| Admissions Rating | 91 |
| # of applicants | 4,423 |
| % of applicants accepted | 32 |
| % of acceptees attending | 33 |
| # accepting a place on wait list | 298 |
| % admitted from wait list | 2 |

### FRESHMAN PROFILE

| | |
|---|---|
| Average SAT Verbal | 680 |
| Average SAT Math | 670 |
| Average ACT Composite | 28 |
| Minimum TOEFL | 600 |
| % graduated top 10% of class | 64 |
| % graduated top 20% of class | 86 |
| % graduated top 50% of class | 100 |

### DEADLINES

| | |
|---|---|
| Early decision | 11/15 |
| Early decision notification | 12/15 |
| Regular admission | 1/1 |
| Regular notification | 4/1 |

### APPLICANTS ALSO LOOK AT
**AND OFTEN PREFER**
Middlebury
Colby
Boston College
Vassar
Bates
**AND SOMETIMES PREFER**
Tufts
Williams
Colorado State
Haverford
Wellesley
**AND RARELY PREFER**
U. Connecticut
Dickinson

### FINANCIAL FACTS

| | |
|---|---|
| Financial Aid Rating | 74 |
| Books and supplies | $600 |
| % frosh receiving aid | 43 |
| % undergrads receiving aid | 46 |
| Avg frosh grant | $17,171 |
| Avg frosh loan | $2,682 |

# COOPER UNION

30 COOPER SQUARE, NEW YORK, NY 10003 • ADMISSIONS: 212-353-4120 • FAX: 212-353-4342

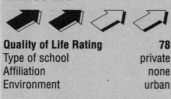
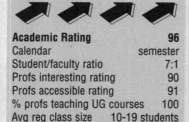
## STUDENTS SPEAK OUT

### Academics

Every student at the "prestigious" Cooper Union for the Advancement of Science and Art receives a full-tuition scholarship. The only catch is that students may only major in art, architecture, or engineering. It's an unbelievably good deal, considering Cooper's "incredible reputation" as "the best engineering undergraduate school on the East Coast." Students praise the "rigorous" and "unparalleled academics" here, though the process sometimes resembles "boot camp," and there is a meager allotment of good grades. "Unless you are a genius or super-lucky, you've got to work really hard to do well," discloses a junior. "So many of us try so hard to just do okay in our classes." Some of the "acclaimed" and "very dedicated" professors at Cooper are "the best in the city." They "challenge the students" and make themselves "very accessible outside of class." However, a good chunk of the faculty is merely "above average" and still others are "really awful." Though they are "extremely smart," some profs "just don't have what it takes to be good teachers." Also, many "don't understand how much work they assign and how much other teachers assign," suspects a chemical engineering major. Consequently, students spend endless hours in the library, and much of what they learn is apparently self-taught. "Whether they're good or bad, the professors are characters," according to a first-year student. They are "the kind of people it's fun to do impressions of." A "bit of a bureaucracy problem" notwithstanding, students have few complaints about the Cooper administration, as "students get the attention they need" and "interaction with administrators and deans is commonplace."

### Life

"Since we live in New York, we can do all kinds of things," attests a chemical engineering major. Situated as Cooper is "on the edge of Manhattan's East Village," students can "go to clubs, restaurants, the parks, and each other's apartments where, unlike at many dorms," they have "crazy parties." There are also "art museums, comedy clubs, gyms," and "great" shopping, but opportunities to "utilize Manhattan" are rare. Cooper Union is an "essentially academic" experience, so "no one gets out much." Students tell us that talk of "fun" and "life at Cooper" is "an oxymoron." "Computer games and surfing the Net" are favorite pastimes, and intramural sports are also big. "Fraternities provide the campus with a social life," but there is certainly no wild frat scene. Also, "the dating scene is horrible at Cooper," confides a sophomore. "I have never seen so many sexually frustrated men." In a nutshell, students here "study a lot." There is "little time for social life" because students "concentrate on school" for the bulk of their waking hours. As a result, Cooper is not for everyone. If an "insane workload" is not your bag, this place can seem "devoid of anything the least bit enjoyable," cautions a tormented sophomore. "If you're okay with having excellent technical facilities at your disposal but few social resources," though, "Cooper is for you."

### Student Body

At Cooper, first-year students "are normal," while "the seniors are weird," prompting one first-year to ask, "What happens over four years?" Well, "everyone at Cooper is really smart, but coming here humbles everyone," speculates a sophomore. The "independent" and "strange but likable" students here describe themselves as "the smartest, weirdest people in the world." These "smart students with low averages" are also "very intelligent and Bohemian," not to mention "extremely creative and self-motivated." Some are "very down-to-earth," while others are "freaks" or "boring and overly competitive," and most admit to being "workaholics who reject the thought of having fun." Though "the students in each of the schools—art, architecture, and engineering—have limited interaction," Cooper maintains a "tightly knit community" of "generally helpful" peers. "I think people are really nice to each other because they're all overworked," concludes one student. They are "good people in need of sleep."

FINANCIAL AID: 212-353-4130 • E-MAIL: ADMISSIONS@COOPER.EDU • WEBSITE: WWW.COOPER.EDU

## ADMISSIONS

*Very important* academic and nonacademic factors considered by the admissions committee include essays, recommendations, standardized test scores, and secondary school record. *Important* factors considered include extracurricular activities. *Other* factors considered include talent/ability and volunteer work. Factors *not* considered include alumni/ae relation, geography, minority status, religious affiliation/commitment, state residency, and work experience. SAT I or ACT required, SAT I preferred. TOEFL required of all international applicants. High school diploma is required and GED is accepted. *High school units required/recommended:* 4 English recommended, 3 math recommended, 2 science recommended, 2 foreign language recommended, 2 social studies recommended, 2 history recommended, 3 elective recommended. *The admissions office says:* "We concentrate very heavily on the importance of an appropriate match—we are so focused, there must be a demonstrated passion for the profession—you can't simply change majors here."

### The Inside Word

It is ultra-tough to gain admission to Cooper Union, and will only get tougher. Loads of people apply here, and national publicity and the addition of dorms have brought even more candidates to the pool. Not only do students need to have top academic accomplishments but they also need to be a good fit for Cooper's offbeat milieu.

## FINANCIAL AID

*Students should submit:* FAFSA, CSS/Financial Aid PROFILE, and state aid form. Regular filing deadline is May 1. The Princeton Review suggests that all financial aid forms be submitted as soon as possible after January 1. *Need-based scholarships/grants offered:* Pell, SEOG, state scholarships/grants, private scholarships, and the school's own gift aid. *Loan aid offered:* FFEL Subsidized Stafford, FFEL Unsubsidized Stafford, FFEL PLUS, Federal Perkins, and college/university loans from institutional funds. Institutional employment available. Federal Work-Study Program available. Applicants will be notified of awards on or about June 1. Off-campus job opportunities are excellent. All students receive a full-tuition scholarship.

## FROM THE ADMISSIONS OFFICE

"Each of the three schools, architecture, art, and engineering, adheres strongly to preparation for its profession and is committed to a problem-solving philosophy of education in a unique, scholarship environment. A rigorous curriculum and group projects reinforce this unique atmosphere in higher education and contribute to a strong sense of community and identity in each school. With McSorley's Ale House and the Joseph Papp Public Theater nearby, Cooper Union remains at the heart of the city's tradition of free speech, enlightenment, and entertainment. Cooper's Great Hall has hosted national leaders, from Abraham Lincoln to Booker T. Washington, from Mark Twain to Samuel Gompers, from Susan B. Anthony to Betty Friedan, and more recently, President Bill Clinton."

### ADMISSIONS

| | |
|---|---|
| Admissions Rating | 99 |
| # of applicants | 2,216 |
| % of applicants accepted | 13 |
| % of acceptees attending | 64 |
| # accepting a place on wait list | 43 |
| # of early decision applicants | 213 |
| % accepted early decision | 24 |

#### FRESHMAN PROFILE

| | |
|---|---|
| Range SAT Verbal | 600-720 |
| Average SAT Verbal | 680 |
| Range SAT Math | 670-740 |
| Average SAT Math | 700 |
| Minimum TOEFL | 600 |
| Average HS GPA | 3.2 |
| % graduated top 10% of class | 80 |
| % graduated top 25% of class | 100 |

#### DEADLINES

| | |
|---|---|
| Early decision | 12/1 |
| Early decision notification | 12/23 |
| Regular admission | 1/1 |
| Regular notification | 4/1 |

#### APPLICANTS ALSO LOOK AT AND OFTEN PREFER

Cornell U.
UC—Berkeley
NYU
Columbia
MIT

#### AND SOMETIMES PREFER

Harvey Mudd
Georgia Tech.
RIT

### FINANCIAL FACTS

| | |
|---|---|
| Financial Aid Rating | 80 |
| Tuition | $8,300 |
| Room & board | $10,000 |
| Books and supplies | $1,350 |
| Required fees | $500 |
| % frosh receiving aid | 100 |
| % undergrads receiving aid | 100 |
| Avg frosh grant | $12,247 |
| Avg frosh loan | $2,519 |

Look into your future with Counselor-o-Matic at *www.review.com*.

# CORNELL COLLEGE

600 FIRST STREET WEST, MOUNT VERNON, IA 52341-1098 • ADMISSIONS: 319-895-4477 • FAX: 319-895-4451

## CAMPUS LIFE

| | |
|---|---|
| **Quality of Life Rating** | **75** |
| Type of school | private |
| Affiliation | Methodist |
| Environment | rural |

### STUDENTS

| | |
|---|---|
| Total undergrad enrollment | 987 |
| % male/female | 41/59 |
| % from out of state | 69 |
| % from public high school | 90 |
| % live on campus | 89 |
| % in (# of) fraternities | 32 (7) |
| % in (# of) sororities | 32 (7) |
| % African American | 3 |
| % Asian | 1 |
| % Caucasian | 90 |
| % Hispanic | 2 |
| % Native American | 1 |
| % international | 2 |

### SURVEY SAYS . . .

*Classes are small*
*Student publications are ignored*
*Registration is a breeze*
*Students aren't religious*
*Campus easy to get around*
*Intercollegiate sports unpopular or nonexistent*
*Theater is unpopular*
*Lousy off-campus food*
*Class discussions encouraged*

## ACADEMICS

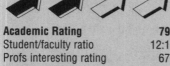

| | |
|---|---|
| **Academic Rating** | **79** |
| Student/faculty ratio | 12:1 |
| Profs interesting rating | 67 |
| Profs accessible rating | 79 |
| % profs teaching UG courses | 100 |
| Avg reg class size | 10-19 students |

### MOST POPULAR MAJORS
psychology
economics and business
secondary education

## STUDENTS SPEAK OUT
### Academics
Looking for an innovative and demanding approach to academics? You might consider Cornell College's "One-Course-at-a-Time," also commonly referred to as the "term." Under the term, students immerse themselves in a single course for three and a half weeks, complete a final exam, take a few days' breather, then start the whole process over again. The system, offered by only two other undergraduate programs in the U.S., meets with student approval. Writes one, "The [term] allows one to devote all of his/her attention to a single course." Adds another, "I like the [term]—taking four finals at once seems insane to me! It's all about immersion." Students warn, however, that the term leaves absolutely no time for slacking off. With the term, explains one, "you have to show up every day and do your work. If you need help you can get it, and you'll have to if you're going to get anything above a 1.0 grade point average." Fortunately, "the professors here . . . are, for the most part, caring individuals. They want us to succeed." Students complain, however, that there are "too many 'rent-a-profs.' We need more full-time faculty." Administrators receive high marks for facilitating academic flexibility: "You can do what you want to here. If you want to be a triple major in biology, philosophy, and psychology, the administration makes it possible." Sums up one student, "Cornell College provides a community for a small group of students to learn, socialize, and develop. Overall, the individual makes Cornell what they want it to be."

### Life
"Cornell is a small school in a small town," warns one undergrad. While some see Mount Vernon as "a lovely town with parks, a coffeehouse, and bars," others are less charitable, describing it as "a small farm town. There is one stoplight. We all go to the bar and hang out although we don't always drink." Because "there aren't any museums or theaters in town, one needs a car to go to Iowa City or Cedar Rapids to get some culture." Within the confines of campus, "Life can be extremely exciting if you get involved. If you don't, life can get pretty lonely on the hilltop." Most students agree, "Social life is an important part of campus. For fun we go to the coffee bar, shopping, movies, outdoor activities, or to the bars and to parties." Others point out a fringe benefit of the Block Plan: "With all students on a very similar schedule, it is easy to interact and meet almost everyone. Friendships are easy to come by." While there are no national fraternities at Cornell, local "social groups" fulfill the same function and "dominate the social scene." The school also has 19 intercollegiate sports teams. They go to the nationals every year!" Students caution prospectives to bring plenty of warm clothing to Mount Vernon, telling us that "the Cornell campus is beautiful in the snow. And it usually snows a lot!"

### Student Body
Most Cornell students are "very friendly," "down-home Middle Westerners. They're generally good people, but of course there are [some token Bible Beaters.] We try to ignore them." They, in turn, try to ignore the school's left-leaning majority, complaining that "this college is a bit too P.C. Someone always seems to get pissed off at a comment that isn't the least bit offensive." Overall, however, students report a high level of happiness with Cornell, a foolproof indicator that student interrelations are peaceful. Students warn that, because of the small student body, Cornell can get a little claustrophobic, but also note that "if you want to be a big fish in a very small pond, this is the place to do it."

FINANCIAL AID: 319-895-4216 • E-MAIL: ADMISSIONS@CORNELL-IOWA.EDU • WEBSITE: WWW.CORNELL-IOWA.EDU

## ADMISSIONS

*Very important* academic and nonacademic factors considered by the admissions committee include secondary school record. *Important* factors considered include class rank, essays, and standardized test scores. *Other* factors considered include character/personal qualities, extracurricular activities, minority status, recommendations, talent/ability, volunteer work, and work experience. Factors *not* considered include interview and religious affiliation/commitment. SAT I or ACT required. TOEFL required of all international applicants. High school diploma is required and GED is accepted. *High school units required/recommended:* 4 English required, 3 math required, 4 math recommended, 3 science required, 4 science recommended, 2 science lab required, 2 foreign language required, 4 foreign language recommended, 2 social studies required, 2 history required, 2 elective required.

### The Inside Word

Given Cornell's relatively unique approach to study, it's no surprise that the admissions committee here focuses attention on both academic and personal strengths. Cornell's small, highly self-selected applicant pool is chock-full of students with solid self-awareness, motivation, and discipline. Pay particular attention to offering evidence of challenging academic course work and solid achievement on your high school record. Strong writers can do much for themselves under admissions circumstances such as these.

## FINANCIAL AID

*Students should submit:* FAFSA and institution's own financial aid form. The Princeton Review suggests that all financial aid forms be submitted as soon as possible after January 1. *Need-based scholarships/grants offered:* Pell, SEOG, state scholarships/grants, private scholarships, and the school's own gift aid. *Loan aid offered:* FFEL Subsidized Stafford, FFEL Unsubsidized Stafford, FFEL PLUS, Federal Perkins, college/university loans from institutional funds, McElroy Loan, Sherman Loan, and United Methodist Loan. Institutional employment available. Federal Work-Study Program available. Applicants will be notified of awards on a rolling basis beginning on or about March 15. Off-campus job opportunities are fair.

## FROM THE ADMISSIONS OFFICE

"Cornell College is unique in U.S. higher education in the combination of these five points of distinction: liberal arts in a small-school setting; an active residential community; the One-Course-at-a-Time (OCAAT) framework; an emphasis on leadership and service; and pride of place. Founded in 1853, Cornell is associated with the Methodist Church. The 129-acre hilltop campus with its mix of 41 historic and contemporary buildings is listed as a Historic District on the National Register of Historic Places, the only U.S. campus with this distinction. Within the framework of the traditional liberal arts, Cornell offers students a distinctive way to learn. Under the OCAAT academic calendar, students study only one subject for a three-and-a-half-week term, devoting all their efforts to that course. Students take eight courses per year and a ninth term may be used for additional course work, employment, vacation, internships, or special study. Cornell is one of only three colleges in the nation to offer this approach to education, which intensifies the academic experience and opens a rich array of unique educational opportunities."

### ADMISSIONS

| | |
|---|---|
| Admissions Rating | 79 |
| # of applicants | 1,095 |
| % of applicants accepted | 74 |
| % of acceptees attending | 33 |
| # of early decision applicants | 79 |
| % accepted early decision | 92 |

### FRESHMAN PROFILE

| | |
|---|---|
| Range SAT Verbal | 530-650 |
| Average SAT Verbal | 595 |
| Range SAT Math | 540-640 |
| Average SAT Math | 594 |
| Range ACT Composite | 22-28 |
| Average ACT Composite | 25 |
| Minimum TOEFL | 500 |
| Average HS GPA | 3.5 |
| % graduated top 10% of class | 25 |
| % graduated top 25% of class | 55 |
| % graduated top 50% of class | 86 |

### DEADLINES

| | |
|---|---|
| Regular admission | rolling |
| Nonfall registration? | yes |

### FINANCIAL FACTS

| | |
|---|---|
| Financial Aid Rating | 84 |
| Tuition | $20,090 |
| Room & board | $5,600 |
| Books and supplies | $920 |
| Required fees | $160 |
| % frosh receiving aid | 80 |
| % undergrads receiving aid | 85 |
| Avg frosh grant | $7,715 |
| Avg frosh loan | $3,605 |

# CORNELL UNIVERSITY

410 Thurston Avenue, Ithaca, NY 14850 • Admissions: 607-255-5241 • Fax: 607-255-0659

## CAMPUS LIFE

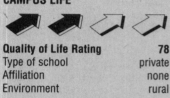

| | |
|---|---|
| **Quality of Life Rating** | **78** |
| Type of school | private |
| Affiliation | none |
| Environment | rural |

### STUDENTS

| | |
|---|---|
| Total undergrad enrollment | 13,590 |
| % from out of state | 55 |
| % live on campus | 62 |
| % in (# of) fraternities | 25 (41) |
| % in (# of) sororities | 20 (18) |
| % African American | 5 |
| % Asian | 18 |
| % Caucasian | 66 |
| % Hispanic | 6 |
| % Native American | 1 |
| % international | 7 |
| # of countries represented | 81 |

### SURVEY SAYS . . .

*Great food on campus*
*Frats and sororities dominate social scene*
*Great library*
*Class discussions are rare*
*Beautiful campus*
*Large classes*
*Campus difficult to get around*
*Ethnic diversity on campus*
*Student publications are popular*
*Musical organizations are hot*

## ACADEMICS

| | |
|---|---|
| **Academic Rating** | **94** |
| Calendar | semester |
| Student/faculty ratio | 11:1 |
| Profs interesting rating | 88 |
| Profs accessible rating | 90 |
| % profs teaching UG courses | 100 |
| Avg lab size | 10-19 students |
| Avg reg class size | 10-19 students |

### MOST POPULAR MAJORS
economics/business
biological sciences
computer science

## STUDENTS SPEAK OUT
### Academics

Ivy League member Cornell boasts a catalog of over 4,000 undergraduate courses, and a top notch faculty to boot. One student boasts "Profs are friendly and approachable." Classes at Cornell are a combination of lectures and sections. Professors teach lectures, and TAs teach sections. And "it's always a pleasant surprise when a TA can speak English." Professor accessibility is also good; as one student notes, "most will give you their home number for extra assistance." Most students agree with this sentiment. The hotel school earns high marks from students. And while students have positive feelings about their professors, their opinion of the administration is nearly unanimous. Cornell is "not called 'The Big Red Tape' for nothing." Bear Access, Cornell's computer-based class registration system, "is a nightmare the day classes go open for registration." Switching courses is also a difficult process, and students who attempt to do so find themselves "run[ning] all over campus to accomplish anything." Students complain that the advising system is weak, and "advisors really have no idea what their advisees need to have accomplished for graduation." Supplemental costs are a major sticking point. "Cornell loves to charge fees for whatever it can—Internet, using the gym, buses, parking, cable, many gym classes, printing. You name it, it ain't free." "The general feeling at Cornell is that the undergrads pay for the grad students."

### Life

Cornell students work hard all week and "party hard on the weekends." Ithaca is a small but cool town; however, the Greek system corners "the Saturday night entertainment market." The university's mandatory catering rules require all frat parties to be catered by companies "who card people as they come in and give them drinking or nondrinking color-coded wristbands." However, for every "sanctioned" party, there are other unsanctioned parties that "have no qualms about serving alcohol to minors." Some students say that those who don't drink "feel a little bit left out in the cold at times." One student shrugs, "So far, the assumption that students at Ivy League schools drink heavily to ease the pressure of the academic load has proven true." Students enjoy "swimming in the gorges during the summer, traying (on dining hall trays) down the slope during the winter, and going to the mega-grocery store at 2 A.M." Collegetown, which adjoins the campus, "is full of bars, clubs, and cheap eateries with great food." Students also go to the movies in town and take advantage of the many skiing and snowboarding opportunities. Cornell hockey is also extremely popular, and the rink is sold out every year.

### Student Body

Cornell's population is "friendly" and "very diverse, not only ethnically, but also in terms of individual personalities, activities, and goals." One student describes his peers as "typical Ivy League students mostly: upper-middle-class suburban kids who have probably never worked in their lives." Different groups of students "tend to interact mostly with members of their own groups." Still, "students for the most part are friendly and open-minded. Pretty much anything goes here." Some complain that their classmates are "cut-throat," especially in the hard sciences, and that engineering students "are hard to get along with."

# CORNELL UNIVERSITY

FINANCIAL AID: 607-255-5145 • E-MAIL: ADMISSIONS@CORNELL.EDU • WEBSITE: WWW.CORNELL.EDU

## ADMISSIONS

*Very important* academic and nonacademic factors considered by the admissions committee include secondary school record. *Important* factors considered include character/personal qualities, class rank, extracurricular activities, interview, and talent/ability. *Other* factors considered include alumni/ae relation, essays, geography, recommendations, standardized test scores, state residency, volunteer work, work experience, and racial/ethnic status. Factors *not* considered include religious affiliation/commitment. SAT I or ACT required. TOEFL required of all international applicants. *High school units required/recommended:* 4 English recommended, 3 math recommended, 3 science recommended, 3 foreign language recommended, 3 social studies recommended.

### The Inside Word

Cornell is the largest of the Ivies, and its admissions operation is a reflection of the fairly grand scale of the institution: complex and somewhat intimidating. Candidates should not expect contact with admissions to reveal much in the way of helpful insights on the admissions process, as the university seems to prefer to keep things close to the vest. Only applicants with top accomplishments, academic or otherwise, will be viable candidates. The university is a very positive place for minorities, and the public status presents a value that's hard to beat.

## FINANCIAL AID

*Students should submit:* FAFSA, CSS/Financial Aid PROFILE, noncustodial (divorced/separated) parent's statement, business/farm supplement, and Alien Registration Card. Regular filing deadline is February 14. The Princeton Review suggests that all financial aid forms be submitted as soon as possible after January 1. *Need-based scholarships/grants offered:* Pell, SEOG, state scholarships/grants, private scholarships, and the school's own gift aid. *Loan aid offered:* Direct Subsidized Stafford, Direct Unsubsidized Stafford, Direct PLUS, Federal Perkins, college/university loans from institutional funds, and Key Bank alternative loan. Institutional employment available. Federal Work-Study Program available. Applicants will be notified of awards on or about April 1. Off-campus job opportunities are good.

## FROM THE ADMISSIONS OFFICE

"The admissions process at Cornell University reflects the personality of the institution. When students apply to Cornell, they must apply to one of the seven undergraduate colleges. Applications are reviewed within each undergraduate college by individuals who know the college well. Life at Cornell is a blend of college-focused and University activities, and Cornell students participate at both the college and University level. Cornell students can take classes in any of the seven undergraduate colleges and they participate in one of the largest extracurricular/athletics programs in the Ivy League. Prospective students are encouraged to examine the range of opportunities, both academic and extracurricular, at Cornell. Within this great institution, there is a wealth of possibilities."

## ADMISSIONS

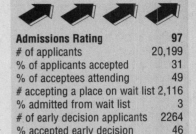

| | |
|---|---|
| Admissions Rating | 97 |
| # of applicants | 20,199 |
| % of applicants accepted | 31 |
| % of acceptees attending | 49 |
| # accepting a place on wait list | 2,116 |
| % admitted from wait list | 3 |
| # of early decision applicants | 2264 |
| % accepted early decision | 46 |

### FRESHMAN PROFILE

| | |
|---|---|
| Range SAT Verbal | 620-710 |
| Average SAT Verbal | 660 |
| Range SAT Math | 650-750 |
| Average SAT Math | 700 |
| Average ACT Composite | 29 |
| Minimum TOEFL | 550 |
| % graduated top 10% of class | 82 |
| % graduated top 25% of class | 94 |
| % graduated top 50% of class | 100 |

### DEADLINES

| | |
|---|---|
| Early decision | 11/10 |
| Early decision notification | 12/15 |
| Regular admission | 1/1 |
| Regular notification | 4/1 |
| Nonfall registration? | yes |

### APPLICANTS ALSO LOOK AT
#### AND OFTEN PREFER
Harvard
Yale
Princeton, Brown
Dartmouth
#### AND SOMETIMES PREFER
U. Penn
Wesleyan U.
Williams
Amherst
#### AND RARELY PREFER
U. Mass—Amherst
U. Rochester
Purdue U.—West Lafayette

### FINANCIAL FACTS

| | |
|---|---|
| Financial Aid Rating | 78 |
| Tuition | $24,760 |
| Room & board | $8,086 |
| Books and supplies | $590 |
| Required fees | $92 |
| % frosh receiving aid | 47 |
| % undergrads receiving aid | 49 |
| Avg frosh grant | $15,000 |
| Avg frosh loan | $5,500 |

# CREIGHTON UNIVERSITY

2500 CALIFORNIA PLAZA, OMAHA, NE 68178 • ADMISSIONS: 402-280-2703 • FAX: 402-280-2685

## CAMPUS LIFE

| Quality of Life Rating | 85 |
|---|---|
| Type of school | private |
| Affiliation | Roman Catholic |
| Environment | urban |

### STUDENTS

| | |
|---|---|
| Total undergrad enrollment | 3,765 |
| % male/female | 41/59 |
| % from out of state | 54 |
| % from public high school | 64 |
| % live on campus | 47 |
| % in (# of) fraternities | 28 (5) |
| % in (# of) sororities | 31 (5) |
| % African American | 5 |
| % Asian | 10 |
| % Caucasian | 78 |
| % Hispanic | 5 |
| % Native American | 1 |
| % international | 4 |

### SURVEY SAYS . . .

*Theater is hot*
*Frats and sororities dominate social scene*
*Very little drug use*
*Popular college radio*
*Musical organizations aren't popular*
*Students are very religious*
*Ethnic diversity on campus*
*Students get along with local community*
*Diverse students interact*
*Lousy food on campus*

## ACADEMICS

| Academic Rating | 82 |
|---|---|
| Calendar | semester |
| Student/faculty ratio | 14:1 |
| Profs interesting rating | 92 |
| Profs accessible rating | 93 |
| % profs teaching UG courses | 100 |
| Avg lab size | 10-19 students |
| Avg reg class size | 10-19 students |

### MOST POPULAR MAJORS
biology
finance
psychology

## STUDENTS SPEAK OUT
### Academics

Creighton University is a "small, personable" Jesuit school in Nebraska with an "excellent reputation," "hard" tests, and "too much homework." Once students complete a sweeping set of liberal arts core requirements (accounting for over one-third of the courses they take), a substantial percentage flock to the "tough" health-related programs. Solid programs in business administration are also a big draw. Creighton's "very caring and extremely dedicated" professors are "genuinely concerned about their students." However, not all are cut from the same cloth; "some professors are easy and others are like root canals with no anesthetic." Profs also differ in teaching ability. Some "always take the time to make sure students are learning and understand the material." Others are "not approachable" and "seem to desire draining all creativity and happiness" from the subject matter. "It is possible," though, "to have at least one professor a semester you will recommend to all your friends." Creighton has "less bureaucracy than most schools" and, though the administration doesn't receive rave reviews, students are mostly satisfied with the way their school is run. "I can't think of another university whose president is on campus conversing with students almost every day," conjectures one student. About the only complaint is that the campus in general "could be more modernized." "Very few people do not like Creighton," sums up a sophomore. "Most people are extremely happy" with the "grand educational experience" available here.

### Life

"Grades are everything" on Creighton's "small" and "beautiful" campus, "with beer coming a close second." Indeed, "beer is abundant" here, and students routinely "drink for fun." A "very popular" Greek system keeps the party scene humming. Beyond the frats, dorm life is "typically noisy" and "requires you to invent the fun." Luckily, students here are very inventive. Everything from "floor dinners to pumpkin-carving parties" to "playing 18 holes of golf on the floors" of the residence halls is fair game. Watching movies and "just hanging out" are favorite pastimes, and "going grocery shopping is even considered a good time." Students are divided about the merits of Omaha. There is the griping "not much to do in Omaha" faction and the carefree "there are lots of things to do in Omaha" crowd. Pro-Omaha students "get off campus once a week at least" to "go dancing" or to catch a sporting event. They also take advantage of the active dating scene here or just dine with friends at one of Omaha's many "exceptional restaurants." When all else fails, "there are always the riverboat casinos." Most students agree that there is a lack of school spirit on campus. However, while some say there's "not much school unity," others brag about the "real community atmosphere."

### Student Body

Creighton's undergraduates describe themselves as "motivated," "ethically grounded," "warm, cheerful, and caring." They are a "very welcoming and friendly" "intelligent group of people" who "care about each other" and "want to work hard and change the world." Many are devout Catholics who tend to be "conservative" politically, and don't tend to stray too far from conventional norms of behavior. Others are "rich brats" who "worry too much about grades" and "always whine about the school and the curriculum," especially the "disrespectful, grade-grubbing pre-meds." Though one Texas native observes that students here "all get along," others detect "a big tension between fraternity people and non-fraternity people." Homogeneity on campus is also a problem for some students. "Creighton needs some more diverse characters," pleads a junior, "people to spice up the campus and give it some flavor."

FINANCIAL AID: 402-280-2731 • E-MAIL: ADMISSIONS@CREIGHTON.EDU • WEBSITE: WWW.CREIGHTON.EDU

## ADMISSIONS

*Very important* academic and nonacademic factors considered by the admissions committee include character/personal qualities, class rank, essays, extracurricular activities, recommendations, and secondary school record. *Important* factors considered include standardized test scores. *Other* factors considered include alumni/ae relation, geography, interview, state residency, talent/ability, volunteer work, and work experience. Factors *not* considered include minority status and religious affiliation/commitment. SAT I or ACT required, SAT I recommended. TOEFL required of all international applicants. High school diploma is required and GED is accepted. *High school units required/recommended:* 12 total recommended; 4 English recommended, 3 math recommended, 3 science recommended, 2 science lab recommended, 2 foreign language recommended, 3 social studies recommended, 3 history recommended.

### The Inside Word

In this world of literal translation, even colleges and universities with admit rates that are higher than Creighton's refer to themselves as selective. While it should not be particularly difficult to get in, some applicants don't. The fact that the university places little weight on essays or interviews and gives greater weight to letters of recommendation is a peculiar twist that denies applicants a real voice in the process.

## FINANCIAL AID

*Students should submit:* FAFSA and institution's own financial aid form. The Princeton Review suggests that all financial aid forms be submitted as soon as possible after January 1. *Need-based scholarships/grants offered:* Pell, SEOG, state scholarships/grants, and the school's own gift aid. *Loan aid offered:* FFEL Subsidized Stafford, FFEL Unsubsidized Stafford, FFEL PLUS, Federal Perkins, Federal Nursing, and college/university loans from institutional funds. Institutional employment available. Federal Work-Study Program available. Applicants will be notified of awards on a rolling basis beginning on or about March 1. Off-campus job opportunities are excellent.

## FROM THE ADMISSIONS OFFICE

"An unusually high percentage (nearly one-third) of the freshmen class each year at Creighton considers itself pre-professional, hoping to eventually gain entry to the professional programs of medicine, dentistry, pharmacy, occupational therapy, physical therapy, and law. The competitiveness of these programs, coupled with the substantial financial investment involved in choosing a quality, private undergraduate education, might indicate that Creighton students are, indeed, motivated to succeed. Beyond academic excellence, we would say the single most identifiable characteristic of a Creighton education is the value-centered approach to study. No matter what the student's major, he or she will always feel the influence of the Jesuit tradition on campus, encouraging students to examine the moral as well as the factual dimension of issues."

## ADMISSIONS

| | |
|---|---|
| Admissions Rating | 73 |
| # of applicants | 3,239 |
| % of applicants accepted | 89 |
| % of acceptees attending | 31 |

### FRESHMAN PROFILE

| | |
|---|---|
| Range SAT Verbal | 520-630 |
| Average SAT Verbal | 574 |
| Range SAT Math | 530-640 |
| Average SAT Math | 582 |
| Range ACT Composite | 23-28 |
| Average ACT Composite | 26 |
| Minimum TOEFL | 525 |
| Average HS GPA | 3.7 |
| % graduated top 10% of class | 38 |
| % graduated top 25% of class | 68 |
| % graduated top 50% of class | 91 |

### DEADLINES

| | |
|---|---|
| Regular admission | 8/1 |
| Nonfall registration? | yes |

### APPLICANTS ALSO LOOK AT
**AND OFTEN PREFER**
Iowa State
Notre Dame
U. Colorado—Boulder
**AND SOMETIMES PREFER**
U. Iowa
Marquette
DePaul
**AND RARELY PREFER**
U. Wisconsin—Madison

## FINANCIAL FACTS

| | |
|---|---|
| Financial Aid Rating | 80 |
| Tuition | $16,500 |
| Room & board | $6,170 |
| Books and supplies | $800 |
| Required fees | $636 |
| % frosh receiving aid | 51 |
| % undergrads receiving aid | 46 |
| Avg frosh grant | $5,745 |
| Avg frosh loan | $4,285 |

# DARTMOUTH COLLEGE

6016 McNutt Hall, Hanover, NH 03755 • Admissions: 603-646-2875 • Fax: 603-646-1216

## CAMPUS LIFE

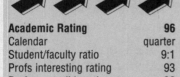

| Quality of Life Rating | 95 |
|---|---|
| Type of school | private |
| Affiliation | none |
| Environment | rural |

### STUDENTS
| | |
|---|---|
| Total undergrad enrollment | 4,057 |
| % male/female | 52/48 |
| % from out of state | 97 |
| % from public high school | 62 |
| % live on campus | 87 |
| % in (# of) fraternities | 40 (17) |
| % in (# of) sororities | 34 (9) |
| % African American | 6 |
| % Asian | 10 |
| % Caucasian | 60 |
| % Hispanic | 6 |
| % Native American | 2 |
| % international | 4 |

### SURVEY SAYS . . .
Frats and sororities dominate social scene
Great food on campus
Everyone loves the Big Green
Great computer facilities
Campus feels safe
(Almost) no one smokes
Musical organizations are hot
Theater is unpopular
Student publications are popular
(Almost) no one listens to college radio

## ACACEMICS

| Academic Rating | 96 |
|---|---|
| Calendar | quarter |
| Student/faculty ratio | 9:1 |
| Profs interesting rating | 93 |
| Profs accessible rating | 96 |
| % profs teaching UG courses | 100 |
| Avg lab size | 10-19 students |
| Avg reg class size | 10-19 students |

### MOST POPULAR MAJORS
economics
government
English

## STUDENTS SPEAK OUT
### Academics
There are few schools in North America that can boast the combination of world-class academics and beautiful location that Dartmouth College offers its students. This Ivy-League institution, tucked away in Hanover, New Hampshire, is the home of wonderful, caring professors, who are committed to the academic needs of their students. A sophomore German major speaks for the majority of students when he writes, "I love Dartmouth because it offers world-class professors who are there because they love to teach." Professors are always accessible, thanks to the Blitz—the campus Internet network—and many students note that they have been invited to their professors' houses for dinner. Students would like too see more study space on campus, though. While the professors are beloved, students don't feel quite the same way about the "draconian" administration. One student writes that the administration "thinks of this school as an advanced placement version of Disney World. You pay, and we hold your hand and kick you out when the park closes." A disheartened senior adds, "Dartmouth's administration has made every effort to destroy a wonderful school. They are attempting to turn Dartmouth into another cookie cutter example of a bland, lifeless university." A more glass-half-full type sophomore provides a little better marketing copy: "Dartmouth's academic experience is unbeatable because it unites a small liberal arts school with all the resources of a top university."

### Life
A senior government major reports the concerns of many students: "Students aren't particularly happy with the current administration's attempt to change social life on campus." A history major adds, "The administration likes establishing social guidelines for students even when they [the guidelines] are most often counter to desires or needs." The source of the administration's concerns is the active Greek life, since "frats are the entire social scene." Still, one first-year teetotaler points out, "I was pleasantly surprised to find that [my being such] was not a problem at Dartmouth." Beer pong is one of the most popular intramural sports. A sophomore summarizes campus life: "Dartmouth is the only school that can provide an Ivy League education, the benefits of a small college town, and the cultural and social aspects of a large city without big-city problems." A senior government major asks, "Where else could you attend classes in the morning, spend your afternoons fencing, hiking, or building a snowman, and spend your evenings relaxing with your friends at a coffee house?" While fraternities play a big role in having fun, there are fair amounts of other weekend options. Outdoor activities are a popular recreational alternative in this "beautiful, intimate, and friendly environment." Students hike the Appalachian Trail, play golf, ice skate on local ponds, and ski. One senior engineering major quips, "Sometimes I think Dartmouth has a double role of college and country club."

### Student Body
Students genuinely appreciate and respect their peers. Though Dartmouth students work hard, they aren't "cut-throat," as some believe all Ivy Leaguers are. A sophomore beams, "I am continuously surprised at how accomplished, mature, friendly, and fascinating my fellow students are." Despite administration efforts to diversify the student population, it consists of "a standard mix of marginal, pretentious, and extremely intelligent students." A disappointed senior psychology major writes, "There is not very much mixing of racial groups on this campus," and an Asian student adds, "People of different races sit apart from [each] other in [the] food court." Also, a senior computer science major says, "This school is very apathetic in terms of activism and politics. People here come from very privileged backgrounds and so they don't really care about much, except for drinking, academics, and athletics." All in all, students are "cheerful," and "the college is fun, vibrant, and beautiful."

FINANCIAL AID: 603-646-2451 • E-MAIL: ADMISSIONS.OFFICE@DARTMOUTH.EDU • WEBSITE: WWW.DARTMOUTH.EDU

## ADMISSIONS

*Very important* academic and nonacademic factors considered by the admissions committee include alumni/ae relation, minority status, secondary school record, and state residency. *Important* factors considered include character/personal qualities, class rank, essays, extracurricular activities, recommendations, standardized test scores, and talent/ability. *Other* factors considered include geography, volunteer work, and work experience. Factors *not* considered include interview and religious affiliation/commitment. SAT I or ACT required; SAT II also required. TOEFL required of all international applicants. *High school units required/recommended:* 18 total required; 4 English required, 3 math required, 3 science required, 2 science lab required, 2 foreign language required, 3 foreign language recommended, 2 social studies required, 2 history required. *The admissions office says:* "Admissions to Dartmouth is highly selective. The competition for admission is a function of both the number of applicants as well as their outstanding credentials. A large and well-qualified applicant pool offers Dartmouth the opportunity to enroll a freshman class that is not only very capable but also broad in the variety of backgrounds, talents, and interests represented."

### The Inside Word

Applications for the class of 2004 were down slightly less than 1 percent from the previous year's totals, but that certainly doesn't make this small-town Ivy any less selective in choosing who gets offered a coveted spot in the class. As is the case with those who apply to any of the Ivies or other highly selective colleges, candidates to Dartmouth are up against (or benefit from) many institutional interests that go unmentioned in discussions of appropriate qualifications for admission. This makes an already stressful process even more so for most candidates.

## FINANCIAL AID

*Students should submit:* FAFSA, CSS/Financial Aid PROFILE, noncustodial (divorced/separated) parent's statement, and business/farm supplement. The Princeton Review suggests that all financial aid forms be submitted as soon as possible after January 1. *Need-based scholarships/grants offered:* Pell, SEOG, state scholarships/grants, and the school's own gift aid. *Loan aid offered:* FFEL Subsidized Stafford, FFEL Unsubsidized Stafford, FFEL PLUS, Federal Perkins, and college/university loans from institutional funds. Institutional employment available. Federal Work-Study Program available. Applicants will be notified of awards on or about April 15. Off-campus job opportunities are excellent.

## FROM THE ADMISSIONS OFFICE

"Today Dartmouth's mission is to endow its students with the knowledge and wisdom needed to make creative and positive contributions to society. The college brings together a breadth of cultures, traditions, and ideas to create a campus that is alive with ongoing debate and exploration. The educational value of such discourse cannot be underestimated. From student-initiated round-table discussions that attempt to make sense of world events to the late-night philosophizing in a dormitory lounge, Dartmouth students take advantage of their opportunities to learn from each other. The unique benefits of sharing in this interchange are accompanied by a great sense of responsibility. Each individual's commitment to the Principles of Community ensures the vitality of this learning environment."

## ADMISSIONS

| | |
|---|---:|
| Admissions Rating | 98 |
| # of applicants | 10,188 |
| % of applicants accepted | 21 |
| % of acceptees attending | 50 |
| # accepting a place on wait list | 500 |
| # of early decision applicants | 1091 |
| % accepted early decision | 38 |

### FRESHMAN PROFILE

| | |
|---|---:|
| Range SAT Verbal | 660-760 |
| Average SAT Verbal | 708 |
| Range SAT Math | 670-760 |
| Average SAT Math | 713 |
| Range ACT Composite | 29-33 |
| Minimum TOEFL | 580 |
| % graduated top 10% of class | 86 |
| % graduated top 25% of class | 98 |
| % graduated top 50% of class | 100 |

### DEADLINES

| | |
|---|---:|
| Early decision | 11/1 |
| Early decision notification | 12/15 |
| Regular admission | 1/1 |
| Regular notification | 4/10 |

### APPLICANTS ALSO LOOK AT
### AND OFTEN PREFER
Harvard
Princeton
Yale
Stanford
### AND SOMETIMES PREFER
Brown
MIT
Amherst
Williams
### AND RARELY PREFER
U. Penn
Cornell U.
Northwestern U.
Middlebury

## FINANCIAL FACTS

| | |
|---|---:|
| Financial Aid Rating | 74 |
| Tuition | $25,497 |
| Room & board | $7,557 |
| Books and supplies | $810 |
| Required fees | $266 |
| % frosh receiving aid | 44 |
| % undergrads receiving aid | 48 |
| Avg frosh grant | $19,760 |
| Avg frosh loan | $3,849 |

# DAVIDSON COLLEGE

PO Box 1737, Davidson, NC 28036-1719 • Admissions: 704-894-2230 • Fax: 704-894-2016

## CAMPUS LIFE

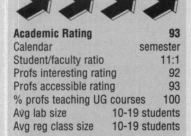

| | |
|---|---|
| **Quality of Life Rating** | **87** |
| Type of school | private |
| Affiliation | Presbyterian |
| Environment | suburban |

### STUDENTS

| | |
|---|---|
| Total undergrad enrollment | 1,679 |
| % male/female | 50/50 |
| % from out of state | 81 |
| % from public high school | 51 |
| % live on campus | 94 |
| % in (# of) fraternities | 48 (7) |
| % African American | 6 |
| % Asian | 3 |
| % Caucasian | 89 |
| % Hispanic | 2 |
| % international | 4 |
| # of countries represented | 33 |

### SURVEY SAYS . . .
*No one cheats*
*Student publications are popular*
*Everyone loves the Wildcats*
*Students are happy*
*Student government is popular*
*Lab facilities need improving*
*Athletic facilities need improving*
*Diversity lacking on campus*

## ACADEMICS

| | |
|---|---|
| **Academic Rating** | **93** |
| Calendar | semester |
| Student/faculty ratio | 11:1 |
| Profs interesting rating | 92 |
| Profs accessible rating | 93 |
| % profs teaching UG courses | 100 |
| Avg lab size | 10-19 students |
| Avg reg class size | 10-19 students |

### MOST POPULAR MAJORS
biology
history
English

## STUDENTS SPEAK OUT

### Academics

Davidson undergrads overwhelmingly agree that, true to the school's reputation, "the workload is significant at Davidson. There is no such thing as an easy course here." Why would anyone choose a school knowing that "academics are intense, and the amount of work assigned is often too cumbersome"? Explains one student, "The strong and brave of heart survive at Davidson. While about 50 percent of the people in the Southeast know about Davidson, it truly lives up to its reputation as the 'Princeton of the South.' The academics are rigorous, but the doors Davidson opens are worthwhile." Helping students cope with their difficult studies are an "administration and amazing faculty [who] strive to support every effort in and out of the classroom." Professors here "are eager to help you anytime. You can call them at home if you have any concerns or questions about the course." Notes one undergraduate, "Profs I've never met will introduce themselves in the hall because they heard of a paper I'm writing for another professor, and want to offer their help." Recounts another, "I never thought this would happen in college . . . but I walked by the president's office late one night. He was in there, and I stuck my head in and waved, and he called me in just to chat for about 20 minutes. I think that's a testament to the accessibility of administration and faculty here." Students also love the school's Honor Code, which allows for self-scheduled exams. Writes one student, "Most campuses have some version of the Honor Code, but it is rarely taken as seriously as it is here. I have yet to see any cheating, both because the students respect the code and because they are motivated to learn on their own."

### Life

"Studying," notes one student, "is by far the premier activity at this school." Still, Davidson undergrads manage to make time for a decent slate of extracurricular activities. So, "after working hard all week, many students party on the weekends. Partying is not the only weekend activity, though; some students go to Charlotte to see plays, go shopping, see an art show or a concert, or just to hang in the city." On campus, many feel that "the weekend social scene is Patterson Court [fraternity row]. If you don't want to be around alcohol during the weekend party scene, find some good friends to socialize with." Others, however, note that "while Patterson Court and the College Union provide many social outlets, the quintessential Davidson College experience is an intimate group of friends going out to dinner, heading to Charlotte, etc." Also, "People are really into sports [Davidson is one of the smallest Division I sports schools in the nation], getting involved in community volunteer organizations, and other campus organizations." "People always say 'we work hard and play hard,'" explains one undergrad, "and it's true. But the most amazing thing about this campus is that, in between the working and playing, people get involved! Most of us have lists of extracurriculars a mile long. People here are always doing something productive. I think that's how our campus can have all the activities and groups we have—overinvolvement." And since Davidson is in North Carolina, "the weather is picture-perfect."

### Student Body

On this "Ford Explorer and Volvo campus," students "work hard with the intention of making a lot of money." The mix of "Southern aristocrats" and "Bible-beating young Republicans" with "a large liberal minority" encourages "constant interchanges of ideas." Reports one student, "Religion is very widely talked about. There are two factions: those who party and those who go to church." Undergrads regard their peers as "a very friendly student population. People generally mix well, and since everyone has a heavy workload, there is a certain level of respect maintained among all." Points out one student, "On the one hand, Davidson is a homogeneous population of mostly white, Christian students, but on the other hand, I've never met such interesting and intelligent students as I have at Davidson."

FINANCIAL AID: 704-892-2232 • E-MAIL: ADMISSION@DAVIDSON.EDU • WEBSITE: WWW.DAVIDSON.EDU

## ADMISSIONS

*Very important* academic and nonacademic factors considered by the admissions committee include secondary school record. *Important* factors considered include class rank and standardized test scores. *Other* factors considered include recommendations. Factors *not* considered include alumni/ae relation, character/personal qualities, essays, extracurricular activities, geography, interview, minority status, religious affiliation/commitment, state residency, talent/ability, volunteer work, and work experience. SAT I or ACT required; SAT II recommended. TOEFL required of all international applicants. High school diploma is required and GED is not accepted. *High school units required/recommended:* 15 total required; 18 total recommended; 4 English required, 3 math required, 4 math recommended, 2 science required, 3 science recommended, 2 science lab required, 3 science lab recommended, 2 foreign language required, 3 foreign language recommended, 1 social studies required, 1 history required, 2 elective required. *The admissions office says:* "These are minimum requirements. Additional course work is recommended. Candidates must take a minimum of four academic courses each year in secondary school with five per year as 'standard.'"

### The Inside Word

Even though Davidson is little known outside the South, harbor no illusions regarding ease of admission. Getting in is every bit as tough as staying in, because an amazingly high percentage of those who are admitted choose to attend. Look for admission to become even more difficult as the college's name recognition increases.

## FINANCIAL AID

*Students should submit:* FAFSA, CSS/Financial Aid PROFILE, noncustodial (divorced/separated) parent's statement, and business/farm supplement. The Princeton Review suggests that all financial aid forms be submitted as soon as possible after January 1. *Need-based scholarships/grants offered:* Pell, SEOG, state scholarships/grants, private scholarships, the school's own gift aid, and need-linked special talent scholarship. *Loan aid offered:* FFEL Subsidized Stafford, FFEL Unsubsidized Stafford, FFEL PLUS, Federal Perkins, and alternative loans. Institutional employment available. Federal Work-Study Program available. Off-campus job opportunities are good.

## FROM THE ADMISSIONS OFFICE

"Davidson College is one of the nation's premier academic institutions, a college of the liberal arts and sciences respected for its intellectual vigor, the high quality of its faculty and students, and the achievements of its alumni. It is distinguished by its strong honor system, close interaction between professors and students, an environment that encourages both intellectual growth and community service, and a commitment to international education. Davidson places great value on student participation in extracurricular activities, intercollegiate athletics, and intramural sports. The college has a strong regional identity, which includes traditions of civility and mutual respect, and has historic ties to the Presbyterian Church."

### ADMISSIONS

| | |
|---|---:|
| Admissions Rating | 97 |
| # of applicants | 3,142 |
| % of applicants accepted | 36 |
| % of acceptees attending | 41 |
| # of early decision applicants | 344 |
| % accepted early decision | 54 |

#### FRESHMAN PROFILE

| | |
|---|---:|
| Range SAT Verbal | 620-710 |
| Average SAT Verbal | 659 |
| Range SAT Math | 620-710 |
| Average SAT Math | 663 |
| Range ACT Composite | 28-31 |
| Average ACT Composite | 29 |
| Minimum TOEFL | 600 |
| % graduated top 10% of class | 75 |
| % graduated top 25% of class | 95 |
| % graduated top 50% of class | 100 |

#### DEADLINES

| | |
|---|---:|
| Early decision 1 | 11/15 |
| Early decision 2 | 1/2 |
| Early decision notification | 12/15 |
| Regular admission | 1/2 |
| Regular notification | 4/1 |

#### APPLICANTS ALSO LOOK AT

**AND OFTEN PREFER**
Dartmouth, Duke
UNC—Chapel Hill

**AND SOMETIMES PREFER**
Emory
William and Mary
Wake Forest
Virginia
U. of the South

**AND RARELY PREFER**
Rhodes
North Carolina State
Vanderbilt
Wofford, Furman

### FINANCIAL FACTS

| | |
|---|---:|
| Financial Aid Rating | 83 |
| Tuition | $22,873 |
| Room & board | $6,571 |
| Books and supplies | $900 |
| Required fees | $222 |
| % frosh receiving aid | 30 |
| % undergrads receiving aid | 31 |
| Avg frosh grant | $14,000 |
| Avg frosh loan | $2,500 |

# DEEP SPRINGS COLLEGE

APPLICATION COMMITTEE, BOX 45001, DYER, NV 89010 • ADMISSIONS: 760-872-2000 • FAX: 760-872-4466

## CAMPUS LIFE

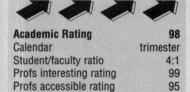

| Quality of Life Rating | 92 |
|---|---|
| Type of school | private |
| Affiliation | none |
| Environment | rural |

### STUDENTS

| Total undergrad enrollment | 26 |
|---|---|
| % from out of state | 77 |
| % live on campus | 100 |

### SURVEY SAYS . . .

Student government
Great library
Very little drug use
Lab facilities are great
Student government is popular
Very little beer drinking
Intercollegiate sports unpopular or
nonexistent
Very little hard liquor

## ACADEMICS

| Academic Rating | 98 |
|---|---|
| Calendar | trimester |
| Student/faculty ratio | 4:1 |
| Profs interesting rating | 99 |
| Profs accessible rating | 95 |
| % profs teaching UG courses | 100 |
| Avg reg class size | 5-10 students |

## STUDENTS SPEAK OUT

### Academics

Men seeking a challenging, unconventional educational experience: Welcome to Nirvana. Located on a remote desert ranch, Deep Springs College furnishes its students (all two dozen or so) with an intense two-year education that includes not only academics but mandatory ranch work and self-governance as well. Here's how it works: Students attend small discussion-oriented classes in the morning, then spend afternoons working unglamorous jobs (such as ditch-digger and general laborer), during which class discussions often continue. According to the school, the labor program is not a way for students to pay tuition or teach skills. Rather, it exists to help students develop self-discipline, self-reliance, and an awareness of their responsibilities to their communities. Students play a significant role in all aspects of their school's day-to-day operations. Administrative duties include screening prospective students, deciding what classes will be offered, and making recommendations for future professors. "Administration is a really misleading word," writes one student, "when you know everyone you live with as well as we do here. 'A problem with administration' means talking about something over dinner. Academics are the same way. Students come here to learn, not to impress anyone." Writes another, "We spend a lot of time and effort reviewing dozens of potential applicants for next year's faculty, but it's well worth it." Faculty members are usually teachers who "are on sabbatical from elsewhere or have experience teaching at some of the best universities in the world." Notes one student, "Usually Deep Springs hosts four to six teachers. With such a small faculty, and given that the turnover rate is almost every four months, we can suffer a year of lunatics followed by a year of masters." Once their two years in the desert are up, students transfer to the nation's top schools.

### Life

The word *Spartan* fairly describes daily life at Deep Springs. Students here forsake television, women, drugs, alcohol, and human contact with anyone outside "The Valley" for a rigorous liberal arts education, plenty of manual labor, coffee and cigarettes, and cattle. The schedule is rigorous; explains one student, "I forget what having free time is like. I spend about six hours a week not working, sleeping, or eating. But those six hours are usually great. Horseback riding, mountain climbing, rock climbing, biking, hiking, basketball, movies, and jamming fill what little time I can afford." Recreational activities "tend to be very simple: a game of Frisbee on the circle, a breakneck gallop across the sage, climbing in the Sierras, a Nietzsche reading group culminating in Dionysian revel, a long walk under a starry sky. Simple, but good!" The nearest town is 30 miles away, school is virtually year-round ("we don't get many holidays off"), and students may not leave campus, except for family or medical emergencies. The surrounding area, luckily, is gorgeous and quite amenable to skiers and hikers, thus providing at least some diversion. To be sure, this school is not for everyone, but "if pushing yourself mentally, physically, and spiritually is fun for you, then Deep Springs is your place." And rest assured, you will leave here with marketable skills; as one student notes, "Every college should have a backhoe so that students can get some real work done."

### Student Body

What sort of man attends Deep Springs College? "Students here range from the brilliant to the merely intelligent. Conversations with students here have taught me more than any class ever will," says one student. "Imagine Pat Buchanan, Wavy Gravy, and the nice boy next door forced to unite under the banner of 'service' and 'idealism' for two years. That's Deep Springs social culture," explains another. Deep Springs provides full scholarships for all students, so economic background is no barrier to acceptance here. Students agree that the close quarters "make friends out of polar opposites. I know I wouldn't have made friends with some of these people outside in the real world, but here at Deep Springs we can be best friends."

FINANCIAL AID: 760-872-2000 • E-MAIL: APCOM@DEEPSPRINGS.EDU • WEBSITE: WWW.DEEPSPRINGS.EDU

## ADMISSIONS

*Very important* academic and nonacademic factors considered by the admissions committee include character/personal qualities, essays, and interview. *Important* factors considered include class rank, extracurricular activities, secondary school record, volunteer work, and work experience. *Other* factors considered include minority status, recommendations, religious affiliation/commitment, standardized test scores, and talent/ability. Factors *not* considered include alumni/ae relation, geography, and state residency. SAT I or ACT required. *The admissions office says:* "Our admissions process is the most intense in the country. Finalists write seven essays and undergo a two-hour-long intensive interview. All applicants accepted for the second stage must travel to Deep Springs for a three-day visit. The deadline for the first stage of the application process is November 15, so don't be caught off-guard."

### The Inside Word

There is no admissions staff at Deep Springs. Along with faculty, students make up the admissions committee. There is likely to be no more rigorous, personal, or refreshing an admissions process to be found in U.S. higher education. This place requires serious commitment, and only the strong survive. Thorough self-assessment is a must before applying.

## FINANCIAL AID

All students admitted to Deep Springs receive full room, board, and tuition scholarships.

## FROM THE ADMISSIONS OFFICE

"Founded in 1917, Deep Springs College lies isolated in a high desert valley of California, 30 miles from the nearest town. Its enrollment is limited to 26 students, each of whom receives a full scholarship valued at over $40,000 per year, covering tuition, room, and board. The students engage in a rigorous academic program, govern themselves, and participate in the operation of the cattle and alfalfa ranch, which is owned by the school. After two or three years, they transfer to other schools to complete their studies. Students regularly transfer to Berkeley, Cornell, Harvard, and Yale. Students make up 8 of the 10 members of the applications committee."

## ADMISSIONS

| | |
|---|---|
| Admissions Rating | 99 |
| # of applicants | 95 |
| % of applicants accepted | 13 |
| % of acceptees attending | 92 |
| # accepting a place on wait list | 3 |
| % admitted from wait list | 8 |

### FRESHMAN PROFILE

| | |
|---|---|
| Average SAT Verbal | 736 |
| Average SAT Math | 720 |
| Average HS GPA | 3.9 |
| % graduated top 10% of class | 90 |
| % graduated top 50% of class | 100 |

### DEADLINES

| | |
|---|---|
| Regular admission | 11/15 |
| Regular notification | 4/7 |

### APPLICANTS ALSO LOOK AT AND SOMETIMES PREFER

Harvard
Yale
U. Chicago
UC—Berkeley
Swarthmore

## FINANCIAL FACTS

| | |
|---|---|
| Financial Aid Rating | 99 |
| Books and supplies | $1,200 |
| Avg frosh grant | $40,000 |

# DENISON UNIVERSITY

Box H, Granville, OH 43023 • Admissions: 740-587-6276 • Fax: 740-587-6306

## CAMPUS LIFE

| Quality of Life Rating | 75 |
|---|---|
| Type of school | private |
| Affiliation | none |
| Environment | suburban |

### STUDENTS

| | |
|---|---|
| Total undergrad enrollment | 2,108 |
| % male/female | 43/57 |
| % from out of state | 55 |
| % from public high school | 71 |
| % live on campus | 98 |
| % in (# of) fraternities | 33 (9) |
| % in (# of) sororities | 46 (9) |
| % African American | 6 |
| % Asian | 2 |
| % Caucasian | 88 |
| % Hispanic | 2 |
| % international | 4 |
| # of countries represented | 29 |

### SURVEY SAYS . . .
*Frats and sororities dominate social scene*
*Diversity lacking on campus*
*Athletic facilities are great*
*Students are cliquish*
*Classes are small*
*Theater is unpopular*
*Lousy off-campus food*
*Class discussions encouraged*
*Low cost of living*

## ACADEMICS

| Academic Rating | 80 |
|---|---|
| Calendar | semester |
| Student/faculty ratio | 11:1 |
| Profs interesting rating | 93 |
| Profs accessible rating | 96 |
| % profs teaching UG courses | 100 |
| Avg lab size | 10-19 students |
| Avg reg class size | 10-19 students |

### MOST POPULAR MAJORS
economics
psychology
English

## STUDENTS SPEAK OUT
### Academics

No, this is not your father's Denison, as students frequently made us aware. "It's more challenging and more fulfilling than I would have ever dreamed," writes one student. "It's a love/hate relationship because I know I could have gone somewhere easier and got all A's and made it to med school coasting, but then I would have missed out on the great academic experience Denison offers." Agrees another, "Academically, it has become more challenging each year due to the school's increasing population of strongly academic students. The rise in standards for Denison students has motivated and made my friends and me proud." Students appreciate the attentiveness and dedication of the DU faculty; writes one undergrad, "Although I have had my doubts about attending Denison, I cannot discount the superior education I have received. The faculty is engaging, interesting, and concerned about their students. Feedback flows, and help is almost always obtainable. The professors expect a lot of you, and you work hard trying not to disappoint them." Another praises the teaching methods here, explaining that "through classes based more on discussion than lecture, I have witnessed students growing not just objectively, but becoming better thinkers, and therefore better people." The administration is similarly "top notch. Not only are they accessible, but they have given me the impression that they are very interested in the well-being of students at this institution." Popular majors at Denison include English, economics, psychology, and biology. For those studying the latter, Denison offers The Polly Anderson Field Station at the Biological Reserve, and has its own planetarium for stargazers in Olin Science Hall.

### Life

Life at Denison "is pretty relaxed. Most people seem to get their work done before having fun." Writes one student, "Movies are the staple entertainment. But backing that up is the occasional spur-of-the-moment shopping trip. In general my free time is spent sitting in a friends room laughing the day away." Students also enjoy a wide assortment of campus organizations and "activities, concerts, comedians, etc." Hometown Granville "is very small, not conducive to college students, and does not have much activity. It is a nice town though, with a few good places to eat. You have to make your own fun at Denison." Adds another student, "There is little to do off campus. Granville is not very welcoming to university students, and there is no off-campus housing allowed. The occasional house party is a big deal." Despite efforts to curb partying, "drinking is one of the most popular activities." On weekends "a lot of students make the short 30-minute commute to Columbus to enjoy the city's night-life."

### Student Body

As in previous surveys, Denison undergrads note an incremental improvement in the school's demographic makeup this year. "Although our student body is predominantly white, our minority population is growing each and every year, heightening Denison's diversity. I notice on campus that most people interact with each other regardless of gender or other minority status. I feel that the campus is gradually—but surely—becoming more diverse and open-minded." Students regard classmates as "generally very friendly" and appreciate the fact that "although Denison is a small school with approximately 2,400 undergrad[s], there seems to be a group for everyone." They also note that "there is a strong separation between people who like to party and people who don't party at all, and due to [more demanding] admission standards, the latter is becoming dominant."

FINANCIAL AID: 740-587-6279 • E-MAIL: ADMISSIONS@DENISON.EDU • WEBSITE: WWW.DENISON.EDU

## ADMISSIONS

*Very important* academic and nonacademic factors considered by the admissions committee include essays and secondary school record. *Important* factors considered include character/personal qualities, recommendations, and standardized test scores. *Other* factors considered include alumni/ae relation, class rank, extracurricular activities, geography, interview, minority status, state residency, talent/ability, volunteer work, and work experience. Factors *not* considered include religious affiliation/commitment. SAT I or ACT required. TOEFL required of all international applicants. High school diploma is required and GED is accepted. *High school units required/recommended:* 19 total required; 4 English recommended, 4 math recommended, 4 science recommended, 3 foreign language recommended, 2 social studies recommended, 1 history recommended, 1 elective recommended. *The admissions office says:* "The quality of your academic performance and your GPA in your junior and senior years are the most important factors. Important also is the quality, rather than the quantity, of your extracurricular accomplishments."

### The Inside Word

Applicants who are statistically below Denison's freshman profile should proceed with caution. One of the simplest ways for a university to promote a reputation as an increasingly selective institution is to begin to cut off the bottom of the applicant pool. Only lack of success against heavy competition for students prevents Denison from being more aggressive in this regard.

## FINANCIAL AID

*Students should submit:* FAFSA. There is no regular filing deadline. The Princeton Review suggests that all financial aid forms be submitted as soon as possible after January 1. *Need-based scholarships/grants offered:* Pell, SEOG, state scholarships/grants, private scholarships, and the school's own gift aid. *Loan aid offered:* Direct Subsidized Stafford, Direct Unsubsidized Stafford, Direct PLUS, Federal Perkins, and college/university loans from institutional funds. Institutional employment available. Federal Work-Study Program available. Applicants will be notified of awards on a rolling basis beginning on or about April 1. Off-campus job opportunities are fair.

## FROM THE ADMISSIONS OFFICE

"Denison is a college that can point with pride to its success in enrolling and retaining bright, diverse, and well-balanced students who are being taught to become effective leaders in the 21st century. This year, 50 percent of our first-year students were in the top 10 percent of their high school graduating class, their average SAT scores have risen above 1200—an increase of some 40 points over the last five years—15 percent of the class is multicultural, and 95 percent of our student body is receiving some type of financial assistance. Our First-Year Program focuses on helping students make a successful transition from high school to college, and the small classes and accessibility of faculty assure students the opportunity to interact closely with their professors and fellow students. We care about our students, and the loyalty of our 24,000 alumni proves that the Denison experience is one that lasts for a lifetime."

## ADMISSIONS

| | |
|---|---|
| Admissions Rating | 81 |
| # of applicants | 3,017 |
| % of applicants accepted | 68 |
| % of acceptees attending | 32 |
| # accepting a place on wait list | 247 |
| # of early decision applicants | 80 |
| % accepted early decision | 79 |

### FRESHMAN PROFILE

| | |
|---|---|
| Range SAT Verbal | 560-660 |
| Average SAT Verbal | 606 |
| Range SAT Math | 560-660 |
| Average SAT Math | 610 |
| Range ACT Composite | 24-29 |
| Average ACT Composite | 26 |
| Minimum TOEFL | 550 |
| Average HS GPA | 3.5 |
| % graduated top 10% of class | 50 |
| % graduated top 25% of class | 76 |
| % graduated top 50% of class | 99 |

### DEADLINES

| | |
|---|---|
| Early decision I | 11/15 |
| Early decision notification | 12/1 |
| Priority admission deadline | 1/1 |
| Regular admission | 2/1 |
| Regular notification | 4/1 |
| Nonfall registration? | yes |

### APPLICANTS ALSO LOOK AT

**AND OFTEN PREFER**
Northwestern U., Miami U.
Kenyon, DePauw

**AND SOMETIMES PREFER**
Wittenberg
Ohio State U.—Columbus
Ohio Wesleyan
Dickinson, Vanderbilt

**AND RARELY PREFER**
Skidmore
Hobart & William Smith

## FINANCIAL FACTS

| | |
|---|---|
| Financial Aid Rating | 77 |
| Tuition | $21,710 |
| Room & board | $6,300 |
| Books and supplies | $600 |
| Required fees | $500 |
| % frosh receiving aid | 48 |
| % undergrads receiving aid | 48 |
| Avg frosh grant | $10,862 |
| Avg frosh loan | $4,625 |

# DePaul University

1 East Jackson Boulevard, Chicago, IL 60604-2287 • Admissions: 312-362-8300 • Fax: 312-362-5749

## CAMPUS LIFE

| | |
|---|---|
| **Quality of Life Rating** | **78** |
| Type of school | private |
| Affiliation | Roman Catholic |
| Environment | urban |

### STUDENTS

| | |
|---|---|
| Total undergrad enrollment | 12,436 |
| % male/female | 41/59 |
| % from out of state | 14 |
| % from public high school | 68 |
| % live on campus | 21 |
| % in (# of) fraternities | 6 (9) |
| % in (# of) sororities | 7 (8) |
| % African American | 12 |
| % Asian | 9 |
| % Caucasian | 59 |
| % Hispanic | 13 |
| % international | 2 |
| # of countries represented | 85 |

### SURVEY SAYS . . .

*Students love Chicago, IL*
*Dorms are like palaces*
*Great food on campus*
*Campus feels safe*
*Great off-campus food*
*Ethnic diversity on campus*
*Students get along with local community*
*Diverse students interact*
*Very little beer drinking*
*Very little hard liquor*

## ACADEMICS

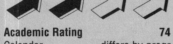

| | |
|---|---|
| **Academic Rating** | **74** |
| Calendar | differs by progr |
| Student/faculty ratio | 15:1 |
| Profs interesting rating | 88 |
| Profs accessible rating | 89 |
| Avg lab size | 10-19 students |
| Avg reg class size | 20-29 students |

### MOST POPULAR MAJORS

business management
liberal arts/humanities
computer sciences

## STUDENTS SPEAK OUT

### Academics

A Catholic university with strengths in business, computer science, and pre-professional programs, DePaul University is the choice of many who crave the prestige and one-on-one interaction of a top private school but can't afford a super-elite institution. DePaul is divided into two campuses: one in Chicago's downtown "Loop," the other in uptown Lincoln Park. The downtown campus caters to business and computer science students, while Lincoln Park is home to the liberal arts, music, education, and DePaul's world-renowned drama department. Students get plenty of bang for their buck on either campus, which explains why most are so sanguine about their school. According to our respondents, "Professors are overflowing with knowledge and always extremely accessible. I would have no qualms about placing my academic experience at DePaul in the same league as our nation's most prestigious universities." Adds another, "Professors are great. They even know you outside of class on a first-name basis. There are 25 or less students in each class." Similarly, the administration "is near flawless, establishing DePaul as a well-oiled machine," according to one political science major.

### Life

With its large commuter population, DePaul lacks the community base on which most schools build their extracurricular life. Add the lure of Chicago, one of the nation's top urban centers, and you begin to understand why there's not a whole lot happening on the DePaul campus once classes end. Students don't seem to mind, explaining that "the best part of DePaul is not the school itself, but rather the area surrounding the school. Anything you want to do is a block or two away." Adds another student, "Life in Chicago is great. The city has so much to offer: museums, theaters, and restaurants. In the summertime, going to the lake is the best." DePaul's few residents are housed on the Lincoln Park campus in a young, fun Chicago neighborhood. They supplement their off-campus activities with clubs, internships, and Greek life. Notes one student, "There is a club here for everyone," including ethnic, race-, and gender-based support groups, sports and games clubs, community service organizations, campus government, and hobby groups.

### Student Body

Like many Catholic schools, DePaul does a good job of keeping tuition and fees down, and as a result attracts a wider variety of low- and middle-income students, among them many minorities. Students "get along" but don't see much of each other, since "most are commuter students who care little about social interaction within the student body." Among residents, "you have the jocks, the theater majors, and the Greeks," explains one undergraduate. "They only hang out with one another and they only get along when they are all drunk." Politically the DePaul campus is sedate: "Life at this school is far detached from important worldly issues," explains one undergrad. "Students are generally more concerned about their clothes or the party they are going to than political or social issues."

FINANCIAL AID: 312-362-8091 • E-MAIL: ADMITDPU@WPPOST.DEPAUL.EDU • WEBSITE: WWW.DEPAUL.EDU

## ADMISSIONS

*Very important* academic and nonacademic factors considered by the admissions committee include secondary school record, volunteer work, and character/personal qualities. *Important* factors considered include class rank, standardized test scores, recommendations, extracurricular activities, work experience, and minority status. *Other* factors considered include essay, interview, particular talent/ability, alumni/ae relation, and geographical residence. SAT I or ACT required. TOEFL required of all international applicants. High school diploma is required and GED is accepted. *High school units required/recommended:* 16 total recommended; 4 English recommended, 3 math recommended, 3 science recommended, 3 foreign language recommended, 3 social studies recommended. *The admissions office says:* "No cutoffs or formulas are used in considering applicants. A student's total academic record and extracurricular or co-curricular activities are considered."

### The Inside Word

Applicants to DePaul will find the admissions staff is genuinely committed to helping students. Candidates whose academic qualifications fall below normally acceptable levels are reviewed for other evidence of potential for success. The Latino student presence on campus has begun to increase significantly, due in large part to the university's major commitment to active involvement in the National Hispanic Institute, an organization that works with top Hispanic students from junior high through college.

## FINANCIAL AID

*Students should submit:* FAFSA . Regular filing deadline is May 1. The Princeton Review suggests that all financial aid forms be submitted as soon as possible after January 1. *Need-based scholarships/grants offered:* Pell, SEOG, state scholarships/grants, private scholarships, and the school's own gift aid. *Loan aid offered:* Federal Direct Student Loan Program (Direct Loan), Direct Subsidized Stafford, Direct Unsubsidized Stafford, Direct PLUS, and Federal Perkins. Institutional employment available. Federal Work-Study Program available. Applicants will be notified of awards on a rolling basis beginning on or about February 15. Off-campus job opportunities are excellent.

## FROM THE ADMISSIONS OFFICE

"Founded by the Vincentian Order in 1898, DePaul is the second largest Catholic university in the country, including two main campuses: The Lincoln Park campus, located amid one of Chicago's most exciting neighborhoods— filled with century-old brownstone homes, theaters, cafes, clubs, and shops— is home to DePaul's College of Liberal Arts & Sciences, the School of Education, the Theatre School, and the School of Music, as well as residence halls and academic and recreational facilities. The focal point of this campus is a new library with its soaring three-story reading room that overlooks a landscaped quad. The Loop campus, located in Chicago's downtown—a world-class center for business, government, law, and culture—is home to DePaul's College of Commerce, the Law School, and the School of Computer Science and Information Systems."

## ADMISSIONS

| Admissions Rating | 77 |
| --- | --- |
| # of applicants | 8,076 |
| % of applicants accepted | 73 |
| % of acceptees attending | 33 |
| # accepting a place on wait list | 135 |
| % admitted from wait list | 74 |

### FRESHMAN PROFILE

| | |
| --- | --- |
| Range SAT Verbal | 510-610 |
| Average SAT Verbal | 560 |
| Range SAT Math | 500-610 |
| Average SAT Math | 555 |
| Range ACT Composite | 21-26 |
| Average ACT Composite | 24 |
| Minimum TOEFL | 550 |
| Average HS GPA | 3.3 |
| % graduated top 10% of class | 18 |
| % graduated top 25% of class | 41 |
| % graduated top 50% of class | 68 |

### DEADLINES

| | |
| --- | --- |
| Priority admission deadline | 2/1 |
| Nonfall registration? | yes |

### APPLICANTS ALSO LOOK AT
### AND OFTEN PREFER
Northwestern U.
U. Chicago
Illinois Tech.
Northeastern
Notre Dame
### AND SOMETIMES PREFER
U. Illinois—Urbana-Champaign
Loyola U. of Chicago
Boston U.
Indiana U.—Bloomington
### AND RARELY PREFER
Purdue U.—West Lafayette

## FINANCIAL FACTS

| Financial Aid Rating | 78 |
| --- | --- |
| Tuition | $15,390 |
| Room & board | $6,675 |
| Books and supplies | $900 |
| Required fees | $30 |
| % frosh receiving aid | 64 |
| % undergrads receiving aid | 77 |
| Avg frosh grant | $8,600 |
| Avg frosh loan | $3,500 |

# DePauw University

101 E. Seminary, Greencastle, IN 46135 • Admissions: 765-658-4006 • Fax: 765-658-4007

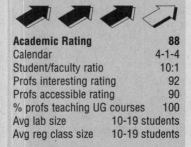
## STUDENTS SPEAK OUT

### Academics

Students come to DePauw seeking a creative yet conservative approach to undergraduate education, presented by a capable and supportive faculty. By and large, most find what they come looking for, especially in the "great school of music," social sciences, media studies, and literature. Chief among DePauw's innovations is the Winter Term, a month-long session during which students can pursue "many outstanding opportunities to do things you can't do in the classroom." Winter Term allows students to undertake "internships and undergraduate research opportunities that are unparalleled." Dedicated instructors greatly enhance the Winter Term experience. Recounts one undergrad, "Professors are awesome, so accessible. I went on a trip for Winter Term with my Latin professor and had a blast. Professors here are your friends as well as teachers." Students also appreciate the fact that "class sizes are very small, yielding great personal relationships with the professors." The administration, however, is not well regarded, with many students complaining that "administrators just seem concerned with the image DePauw projects to the outside world."

### Life

How students feel about social life at DePauw depends primarily on how they feel about the Greek system, which "definitely dominates the social scene." Warns one student, "If you're not into Greek life, don't come here! That's where everything is at here!" For some, "It's fine because it's free beer and a nice place to party. The majority of students stay on campus and hit the four local bars on weekends." Others find it oppressive and divisive. Making matters worse is the lack of alternative activities in hometown Greencastle, "the armpit of the earth. There is NOTHING to do here!" Given the situation, it is unsurprising that drinking "is a major pastime, perpetuated by the exclusive, gender-discriminatory Greek system." "For fun," one independent admits, "we leave town." Not all students paint such a bleak picture, though; writes one, "As an independent, I have no problem staying entertained. DePauw offers a lot of opportunities. Since it is a small school, it is very easy to become involved in all the different activities." Many participate in community service, either "through their church or through the campus ministries center." According to students, "The level of volunteer involvement with the community is amazing."

### Student Body

DePauw undergrads describe a Balkanized student body, one "divided ethnically, socially, and financially." Some blame the situation on the Greeks; writes one student, "The Greek system categorizes students into a fixed mold. Often, the Greek students only converse with and befriend students in their house." Others see it as a class issue, noting that "most students here are very upper-crust. They have very definite opinions and stereotypes about our classes, and therefore tend not to mix well with others." To others still, it's racial: "The African Americans hang out with the African Americans, Hispanics with Hispanics, international students with other international students, and everyone else in whatever fraternity or sorority they joined." Politically and socially conservative, students draw such vitriolic epithets as "uncreative" and "pompous" from classmates. Is there an upside? Notes one student, "A lot of people have a 'face' they put on, but once you get to know them, they shed it."

FINANCIAL AID: 765-658-4030 • E-MAIL: ADMISSIONS@DEPAUW.EDU • WEBSITE: WWW.DEPAUW.EDU

## ADMISSIONS

*Very important* academic and nonacademic factors considered by the admissions committee include class rank, interview, secondary school record, and standardized test scores. *Important* factors considered include character/personal qualities, essays, extracurricular activities, recommendations, talent/ability, and work experience. *Other* factors considered include alumni/ae relation and volunteer work. Factors *not* considered include geography, minority status, religious affiliation/commitment and state residency. SAT I or ACT required. TOEFL and SAT required of all international applicants. High school diploma is required and GED is accepted. *High school units required/recommended:* 16 total recommended; 4 English recommended, 3 math recommended, 3 science recommended, 3 science lab recommended, 3 foreign language recommended. *The admissions office says:* "We set no arbitrary cutoff for GPA, class rank, or SAT I/ACT test scores. The admission committee evaluates each candidate individually, seeking evidence of strong academic achievement and motivation, maturity, extracurricular involvement, and potential for growth.

### The Inside Word

Students considering DePauw should not be deceived by the university's high acceptance rate. The impressive freshman profile indicates a high level of self-selection in the applicant pool.

## FINANCIAL AID

*Students should submit:* FAFSA and institution's own financial aid form. Regular filing deadline is February 15. The Princeton Review suggests that all financial aid forms be submitted as soon as possible after January 1. *Need-based scholarships/grants offered:* Pell, SEOG, state scholarships/grants, private scholarships, and the school's own gift aid. *Loan aid offered:* FFEL Subsidized Stafford, FFEL Unsubsidized Stafford, FFEL PLUS, Federal Perkins, college/university loans from institutional funds, and alternative loans. Institutional employment available. Federal Work-Study Program available. Applicants will be notified of awards on a rolling basis beginning on or about March 21. Off-campus job opportunities are fair.

## FROM THE ADMISSIONS OFFICE

"DePauw University is nationally recognized for intellectual and experiential challenge that links liberal arts education with life's work, preparing graduates for uncommon professional success, service to others, and personal fulfillment. DePauw graduates count among their ranks a Nobel laureate, a vice president and U.S. Congressman, Pulitzer Prize and Newberry Award authors, and a number of CEOs and humanitarian leaders. Our students demonstrate a love for learning, a willingness to serve others, the reason and judgement to lead, an interest in engaging worlds and cultures unknown to them, the courage to question their assumptions, and a strong commitment to community. Pre-professional and career exploration are encouraged through Winter Term, when more than 700 students pursue their own off-campus internships. This represents more students in experiential learning opportunities than at any other liberal arts college in the nation. Other innovative programs include Honor Scholars, Management Fellows, Media Fellows, and Science Research Fellows, affording selected students additional seminar and internship opportunities."

## ADMISSIONS

| | |
|---|---|
| Admissions Rating | 85 |
| # of applicants | 2,996 |
| % of applicants accepted | 61 |
| % of acceptees attending | 33 |
| # accepting a place on wait list | 30 |
| % admitted from wait list | 50 |
| # of early decision applicants | 31 |
| % accepted early decision | 94 |

### FRESHMAN PROFILE

| | |
|---|---|
| Range SAT Verbal | 530-640 |
| Range SAT Math | 530-640 |
| Range ACT Composite | 24-29 |
| Minimum TOEFL | 560 |
| Average HS GPA | 3.6 |
| % graduated top 10% of class | 49 |
| % graduated top 25% of class | 81 |
| % graduated top 50% of class | 99 |

### DEADLINES

| | |
|---|---|
| Early decision | 11/1 |
| Early decision notification | 1/1 |
| Priority admission deadline | 12/1 |
| Regular admission | 2/1 |
| Regular notification | 4/1 |
| Nonfall registration? | yes |

### APPLICANTS ALSO LOOK AT

**AND OFTEN PREFER**
Notre Dame
Indiana U.—Bloomington
Northwestern U.
Vanderbuilt U., Washington U.

**AND SOMETIMES PREFER**
Miami Univ.
Rhodes
Denison
Butler, Purdue

**AND RARELY PREFER**
Illinois Wesleyan
Centre College
Xavier, Trinity Univ.

### FINANCIAL FACTS

| | |
|---|---|
| Financial Aid Rating | 87 |
| Tuition | $21,100 |
| Room & board | $6,500 |
| Books and supplies | $550 |
| Required fees | $320 |
| % frosh receiving aid | 59 |
| % undergrads receiving aid | 54 |
| Avg frosh grant | $17,150 |
| Avg frosh loan | $2,917 |

# DICKINSON COLLEGE

PO Box 1773, Carlisle, PA 17013-2896 • Admissions: 717-245-1231 • Fax: 717-245-1442

## CAMPUS LIFE

| | |
|---|---|
| **Quality of Life Rating** | **81** |
| Type of school | private |
| Affiliation | none |
| Environment | suburban |

### STUDENTS

| | |
|---|---|
| Total undergrad enrollment | 2,115 |
| % male/female | 39/61 |
| % from out of state | 57 |
| % from public high school | 71 |
| % live on campus | 92 |
| % in (# of) fraternities | 25 (8) |
| % in (# of) sororities | 27 (5) |
| % African American | 1 |
| % Asian | 3 |
| % Caucasian | 94 |
| % Hispanic | 2 |
| % international | 1 |
| # of countries represented | 18 |

### SURVEY SAYS . . .

Frats and sororities dominate social scene
Great food on campus
Diversity lacking on campus
Students don't get along with local community
Campus easy to get around
Students don't like Carlisle, PA
Low cost of living
Class discussions encouraged

## ACADEMICS

| | |
|---|---|
| **Academic Rating** | **86** |
| Calendar | semester |
| Student/faculty ratio | 12:1 |
| Profs interesting rating | 94 |
| Profs accessible rating | 96 |
| % profs teaching UG courses | 100 |
| Avg lab size | 10-19 students |
| Avg reg class size | 10-19 students |

### MOST POPULAR MAJORS
political science
psychology
history

## STUDENTS SPEAK OUT

### Academics

There's a good reason that most Dickinson students have little trouble adapting to their new home. "This college is almost exactly like being in high school," explains one undergrad. "There are small classes, understanding professors, and almost everyone knows the majority of other students on campus." Notes another, "Dickinson has a great community atmosphere. It's great to see the president and other administrators all over campus interacting with the students." Students speak glowingly of the administration, but they save their highest praise for the faculty. "Teachers here are active on campus and extremely concerned with the academic and social well-being of the individual student," writes one student. Adds another, "Half of the student-faculty interaction at Dickinson goes on outside the classroom. Professors are your teachers and your friends, your mentors and your equals." Students are so satisfied with their instruction that they stop resenting the tremendous workload here . . . eventually. "When you get over the feeling that all professors are out to ruin your life, you realize that professors here are extremely personable and even more helpful," observes one caustic respondent. Students even appreciate the core curriculum here, frequently a sore subject on other campuses. "The best thing about Dickinson's academic program is the requirements," says one student. "Seriously. They force you to open your mind and experience things you otherwise wouldn't." Summing up the Dickinson experience, one students explains that "it's great attending a small college because options are plentiful and one doesn't get lost in the numbers."

### Life

A small school in a small town, Dickinson provides students with a homey environment that can, at times, "get stifling. You work, eat, sleep, party, and attend classes with the same people. There isn't much variety on this tiny campus in this tiny town." Those who adapt best to the setting are usually self-starters. "Make sure a small school is what you're looking for before you come here," warns one undergrad. "You really have to plunge yourself into activities and get to know the people here if you want to be happy." Fortunately, students report a recent increase in on-campus extracurricular opportunities. "This year there are a lot more activities," reports one student. "In the past there was very little to do outside of the frats." Writes another, "There's a fair variety of activities such as comedians, laser tag, movies, and dances every weekend. They try to always have something going on, but it's hard to please everyone." Still, although "there is an incredible amount to do on campus . . . most people only go to the frat parties." As at most schools, the active Greek scene means an increased focus on alcohol, both pro and con. "There is too much irresponsible drinking on campus," complains one undergrad. Counters another, "The alcohol policy sucks here—too strict. And the negative stereotypes of Greek life are impossible to escape." Beyond campus lies the rural town of Carlisle, where there is "not much to do." Worse still, "The relationship between students and locals is terrible."

### Student Body

Dickinson's student body is composed of predominantly white and middle- to upper-middle-class students. "Most Dickinsonians are pretty boys and girls with J.Crew outfits," writes one student. "I wish it was as diverse as they said it would be in the admissions viewbook," bemoans a disgruntled junior. Explains another, "Dickinson attracts students mainly from Pennsylvania and the East Coast, so it isn't really that diverse." The undergraduate population has grown more politically active in recent years, leading one student to report that "we aren't a campus that identifies with *Animal House*, contrary to popular opinion. We are active academically, socially, and athletically. We are a campus of movers and shakers" and another to complain that "there is much 'in your face' liberalism here."

FINANCIAL AID: 717-245-1308 • E-MAIL: ADMIT@DICKINSON.EDU • WEBSITE: WWW.DICKINSON.EDU

## ADMISSIONS

*Very important* academic and nonacademic factors considered by the admissions committee include secondary school record, extracurricular activities, talent/ability, minority status, and volunteer work. *Important* factors considered include class rank, recommendations, standardized test scores, alumni/ae relation, and work experience. *Other* factors considered include essays, interview, character/personal qualities, geography, and state residency. Factors *not* considered include religion affiliation/commitment. SAT I/SAT II recommended. TOEFL required of all international applicants. High school diploma is required and GED is accepted. *High school units required/recommended:* 16 total required; 4 English required, 3 math required, 3 science required, 2 science lab required, 2 foreign language required, 2 social studies required, 2 elective required.

### The Inside Word

Dickinson's admissions process is typical of most small, conservative liberal arts colleges. The best candidates for such a place are those with solid grades and broad extracurricular involvement—the stereotypical "well-rounded student." Those who dance to the beat of a different drummer aren't likely to fit well here. Admissions selectivity is kept in check by a strong group of competitor colleges that fight tooth and nail for their cross-applicants.

## FINANCIAL AID

*Students should submit:* FAFSA, CSS/Financial Aid PROFILE, noncustodial (divorced/separated) parent's statement, and business/farm supplement. The Princeton Review suggests that all financial aid forms be submitted as soon as possible after January 1. *Need-based scholarships/grants offered:* Pell, SEOG, state scholarships/grants, private scholarships and the school's own gift aid. *Loan aid offered:* FFEL Subsidized Stafford, FFEL Unsubsidized Stafford, FFEL PLUS, Federal Perkins, and college/university loans from institutional funds. Institutional employment available. Federal Work-Study Program available. Applicants will be notified of awards in late March. Off-campus job opportunities are good.

## FROM THE ADMISSIONS OFFICE

"Dickinson's curriculum may be classified as traditional liberal arts characterized by considerable flexibility and diversity. There is a pattern of distribution to courses (not a core curriculum), which offers a great deal of choice. One of the special features is the Freshman Seminar Program, a distinctive vehicle of transition. There are over 35 seminars from which to choose; seminar participants are often housed together; in most cases, seminar instructors are also faculty advisers to the students; and the seminar is the first class, starting during orientation. Also, some introductory science and math courses are taught by the innovative workshop method, eliminating lecture and traditional labs in favor of a hands-on computer format. Dickinson has 12 centers in 12 countries, and 80 percent of the students will participate in these or other programs abroad at some point in their college careers."

## ADMISSIONS

| | |
|---|---|
| Admissions Rating | 81 |
| # of applicants | 3,801 |
| % of applicants accepted | 64 |
| % of acceptees attending | 24 |
| # accepting a place on wait list | 160 |
| % admitted from wait list | 24 |
| # of early decision applicants | 174 |
| % accepted early decision | 61 |

### FRESHMAN PROFILE

| | |
|---|---|
| Range SAT Verbal | 570-660 |
| Average SAT Verbal | 614 |
| Range SAT Math | 560-650 |
| Average SAT Math | 602 |
| Average ACT Composite | 26 |
| Minimum TOEFL | 550 |
| % graduated top 10% of class | 50 |
| % graduated top 25% of class | 78 |
| % graduated top 50% of class | 97 |

### DEADLINES

| | |
|---|---|
| Early decision | 11/15 |
| Early decision notification | 12/15 |
| Regular admission | 2/1 |
| Regular notification | 3/31 |
| Nonfall registration? | yes |

### APPLICANTS ALSO LOOK AT

**AND OFTEN PREFER**
Cornell U.
Georgetown U.
Swarthmore
Middlebury

**AND SOMETIMES PREFER**
Bucknell
Franklin & Marshall
Gettysburg, Lafayette
Connecticut Coll.

**AND RARELY PREFER**
Fairfield
Rutgers U.—Rutgers Coll.

### FINANCIAL FACTS

| | |
|---|---|
| Financial Aid Rating | 74 |
| Tuition | $25,250 |
| Room & board | $6,725 |
| Books and supplies | $750 |
| Required fees | $235 |
| % frosh receiving aid | 54 |
| % undergrads receiving aid | 63 |
| Avg frosh grant | $14,350 |
| Avg frosh loan | $4,260 |

# DREW UNIVERSITY

36 MADISON AVENUE, MADISON, NJ 07940-1493 • ADMISSIONS: 973-408-3739 • FAX: 973-408-3068

## STUDENTS SPEAK OUT

### Academics

Though the administration at Drew University sometimes suffers from "Ivy League envy," students here universally praise the school for its "excellent" academic quality. "Just about every department has someone who is well respected in their field," chirps a sophomore. The "encouraging" and "very accessible" professors "sincerely care and want you to do well." Deans teach courses along with the faculty here, as does President Thomas Kean, a former two-term governor of New Jersey. "Professors truly care and go out of their way to help you with class work, finding internships, and planning for life" after graduation. Students say most profs are "good teachers" to boot, though a few are on the "eccentric" side and others "get really boring." Thanks to its uniquely "ideal location" just "baby steps" from New York City and in the thick of dozens of huge corporate headquarters and research centers in suburban New Jersey, Drew boasts a "tremendous variety" of internship opportunities. In addition, Drew is among the most "technologically integrated" liberal arts schools. Drew was the very first liberal arts school to give a computer to every first-year student, and the laptop first-years receive today is a real stunner. Complaints about academics are few here, except when it comes to red tape. Many offices at Drew "don't communicate with each other," which rankles students to no end. Students also gripe that the variety of course offerings at Drew is very limited, and some classes are offered too sporadically.

### Life

Drew's wooded campus offers "beautiful scenery," a "small-school atmosphere," and an "astoundingly large number of squirrels running, mating, and eating everywhere." Unfortunately, students tell us their social lives are much less gratifying. "Drew gets awfully quiet sometimes," despite attempts to provide entertainment (recent concerts on campus include Jewel, Blues Traveler, and Bob Dylan). "You definitely have to make your own fun here," concedes a first-year student, especially "after the thrill of comedians and magicians wears off." "There are things to do, but they don't come get you from your room." Indeed, Drew students do manage to find interesting diversions. "On an average night you could find people at a party, working on a play, smoking pot and watching *The Simpsons*, or planning a march for women. And I'm not kidding," declares a senior. "I could be found doing any of those things." Though "alcohol is present" at Drew, "there is no oppressive party atmosphere." There is also no Greek system. There are "theme houses" instead, "where people with common interests can live together." Students applaud the set-up. "The people who like fall-down drunk weekends aren't hampered by the lack of fraternities," says a contented sophomore. "For those less inclined to be conformist, the lack of fraternities is a big help to social life." Besides occasional boredom, students also complain about the "bad" food and the ho-hum surrounding town of Madison. Students looking for more oddities can retreat to the eternal "excitement" of New York City, a mere "50-minute train ride" away.

### Student Body

Though "there are a lot of weirdos here" as well as "rich kid burn-outs who didn't get into their first choice, (not to mention the 2000 *Jeopardy!* College Champion) " a senior assures us that Drew students are "more or less good-natured." Most students at Drew are also "always friendly," but "very cliquish." While some students charge that their peers are "lazy and unable to articulate beliefs," not to mention "apathetic and often small-minded," others retort that Drew students are "independent and open-minded." Either way, geographic diversity is somewhat sparse. However, the university has made good progress in recruiting minority students and students from high schools outside New Jersey. Still, "it would be great to have more people from outside the northern New Jersey area," suggests a New Hampshire native.

# DREW UNIVERSITY

FINANCIAL AID: 973-408-3112 • E-MAIL: CADM@DREW.EDU • WEBSITE: WWW.DREW.EDU

## ADMISSIONS

*Very important* academic and nonacademic factors considered by the admissions committee include essays, extracurricular activities, and secondary school record. *Important* factors considered include character/personal qualities, recommendations, and standardized test scores. *Other* factors considered include alumni/ae relation, class rank, geography, minority status, talent/ability, volunteer work, and work experience. Factors *not* considered include interview, religious affiliation/commitment, and state residency. SAT I or ACT required, SAT I preferred. TOEFL required of all international applicants. *High school units required/recommended:* 4 English required, 3 math required, 4 math recommended, 3 science required, 4 science recommended, 3 science lab required, 4 science lab recommended, 4 foreign language required, 2 social studies required, 3 social studies recommended, 2 history required, 3 history recommended. *The admissions office says:* "The university is interested in the student as an individual—the special strengths, talents, and extracurricular activities of each applicant are considered. Rank in the highest quarter of the secondary school class is desirable."

### The Inside Word

Drew suffers greatly from the annual mass exodus of New Jersey's college-age residents and a lack of recognition by others. Application totals have increased slightly, but the university must begin to enroll more of its admitted students before any significant change in selectivity will occur. This makes Drew a great choice for solid students, and easier to get into than it should be given its quality.

## FINANCIAL AID

*Students should submit:* FAFSA and CSS/Financial Aid PROFILE. Regular filing deadline is March 1. The Princeton Review suggests that all financial aid forms be submitted as soon as possible after January 1. *Need-based scholarships/grants offered:* Pell, SEOG, state scholarships/grants, private scholarships, and the school's own gift aid. *Loan aid offered:* FFEL Subsidized Stafford, FFEL Unsubsidized Stafford, FFEL PLUS, Federal Perkins, and state. Institutional employment available. Federal Work-Study Program available. Off-campus job opportunities are excellent.

## FROM THE ADMISSIONS OFFICE

"At Drew, great teachers are transforming the undergraduate learning experience. With a commitment to teaching, Drew professors have made educating undergraduates their top priority. With a spirit of innovation, they have brought the most advanced technology and distinctive modes of experiential learning into the Drew classroom. The result is a stimulating and challenging education that connects the traditional liberal arts and sciences to the workplace and to the world."

## ADMISSIONS

| | |
|---|---|
| Admissions Rating | 87 |
| # of applicants | 2,545 |
| % of applicants accepted | 71 |
| % of acceptees attending | 23 |
| # of early decision applicants | 43 |
| % accepted early decision | 91 |

### FRESHMAN PROFILE

| | |
|---|---|
| Range SAT Verbal | 560-670 |
| Average SAT Verbal | 617 |
| Range SAT Math | 550-650 |
| Average SAT Math | 604 |
| Minimum TOEFL | 550 |
| % graduated top 10% of class | 42 |
| % graduated top 25% of class | 72 |
| % graduated top 50% of class | 92 |

### DEADLINES

| | |
|---|---|
| Early decision | 12/1 |
| Early decision notification | 12/24 |
| Regular admission | 2/15 |
| Regular notification | 3/20 |
| Nonfall registration? | yes |

### APPLICANTS ALSO LOOK AT AND SOMETIMES PREFER

George Washington
Penn State—Univ. Park
Fairfield
U. Rochester
Franklin & Marshall

### AND RARELY PREFER

Rutgers U.—Rutgers Coll.
Hofstra
SUNY Purchase

### FINANCIAL FACTS
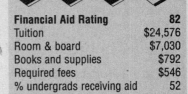

| | |
|---|---|
| Financial Aid Rating | 82 |
| Tuition | $24,576 |
| Room & board | $7,030 |
| Books and supplies | $792 |
| Required fees | $546 |
| % undergrads receiving aid | 52 |
| Avg frosh loan | $11,412 |

# DREXEL UNIVERSITY

3141 CHESTNUT STREET, PHILADELPHIA, PA 19104 • ADMISSIONS: 215-895-2400 • FAX: 215-895-5939

## STUDENTS SPEAK OUT
### Academics

Drexel University is known for its co-op program, which adds an extra year to an undergraduate education, and provides three half-year internships with companies in and around the Philadelphia area. The co-op program "is the best part of Drexel." Some students complain that the course work is "unchallenging," and that while some of the professors are good, others are not. The university employs some foreign professors, and students grumble about the difficulty understanding many of them. Classes often get canceled, and students find that it is difficult to get into required classes because not enough sections are offered.

Students gush about the wireless system that enables a student anywhere on campus to connect to the Internet via a T1 connection. They note, however, that the $5 million system allows faculty to post "assignments, study guides, notes, and exam times and locations for each class." Many believe that the engineering and hotel management departments are among the university's best. While students have mixed feelings about the quality of a Drexel education, they agree that "the Drexel Shaft," perpetrated by the administration, "is running the school into the ground." Students believe that "they accept too many students, have no place to house them, and spend too much time recruiting new students and not enough time keeping current students satisfied." The prevailing attitude amongst the administration is that the students are "customers." Administrative offices "are not coordinated with each other, and if you want something done, you have to do it yourself." The administrative problems begin at the top levels; student issues are "only cared about . . . if they were going to do it anyway."

### Life

Students love the fact that Drexel is located only five blocks away from Center City, Philadelphia. The City of Brotherly Love offers numerous cultural opportunities, from the museums and art galleries, to the city's four professional sports franchises, to the fantastic zoo. National music acts perform in town every night in venues of varying size. "It may be because we have an inner-city campus, but this whole East Coast urban feeling kind of creates this feeling of a hectic, nonstop lifestyle," writes one student. "Everyone is either working hard or playing hard. There's no such thing as relaxing and doing nothing." There are plenty of nightclubs and bars in the area, and students often attend frat parties and visit the neighboring University of Pennsylvania. Undergrads spend much of their time studying and praise the quality of the school newspaper. A significant number of students work off campus, and their prolonged absence diminishes school spirit.

### Student Body

Drexel students describe their peers as "apathetic" but "friendly and diverse," claiming "everyone gets along because there is a common bitterness against the school's administration." International students are valued for the different views that they bring to the university. Though certain groups "tend to stick together, I don't think they try to discriminate." Still, the "Drexel Shaft" is a "bond that ties us together." Another student adds, "We bond in our utter hatred of the Drexel empire." The Greek system also brings students together.

FINANCIAL AID: 215-895-2535 • E-MAIL: ENROLL@DREXEL.EDU • WEBSITE: WWW.DREXEL.EDU

## ADMISSIONS

*Very important* academic and nonacademic factors considered by the admissions committee include character/personal qualities, secondary school record, volunteer work, and work experience. *Important* factors considered include class rank, essays, recommendations, and standardized test scores. *Other* factors considered include alumni/ae relation, extracurricular activities, interview, minority status, and talent/ability. Factors *not* considered include religious affiliation/commitment and state residency. SAT I or ACT required, SAT I preferred. TOEFL required of all international applicants. High school diploma is required and GED is accepted. *High school units required/recommended:* 16 total required; 4 English required, 2 math required, 3 math recommended, 2 science required, 1 science lab required, 2 foreign language required, 3 social studies required, 3 history recommended, 4 elective required. *The admissions office says:* "Drexel students are very motivated and desire knowledge with a real-world application. Drexel's education is fast-paced and requires students to stay on top of their work."

### The Inside Word

Drexel's distinct nature creates a high level of self-selection in the applicant pool, and most decent students are admitted.

## FINANCIAL AID

*Students should submit:* FAFSA. The Princeton Review suggests that all financial aid forms be submitted as soon as possible after January 1. *Need-based scholarships/grants offered:* Pell, SEOG, state scholarships/grants, private scholarships, the school's own gift aid, and United Negro College Fund. *Loan aid offered:* FFEL Subsidized Stafford, FFEL Unsubsidized Stafford, FFEL PLUS, Federal Perkins, and college/university loans from institutional funds. Institutional employment available. Federal Work-Study Program available. Applicants will be notified of awards on a rolling basis beginning on or about April 1. Off-campus job opportunities are excellent.

## FROM THE ADMISSIONS OFFICE

"Drexel made history in 1983 when it became the first university to mandate that all students must have personal access to a microcomputer. This tradition of leadership in integrating state-of-the-art technologies into a Drexel education continued when, in early 1998, Drexel inaugurated the first totally wireless library in the nation. Beginning this fall, Drexel will again make history by becoming the nation's first major university to offer completely wireless Internet access across the entire campus.

"Our students will be able to access the Internet and Drexel's comprehensive system of information networks from anywhere on campus using a laptop computer in a fully wireless environment. Drexel students will be the first in the U.S. to enjoy the best of both worlds—a campus network ranked by Yahoo! Internet Life magazine's 'most wired' survey as number one in Philadelphia and among the top 20 nationwide, and an all-wireless environment where it's easy to access the network at any time and from any place on campus."

## ADMISSIONS

| | |
|---|---|
| Admissions Rating | 77 |
| # of applicants | 8,663 |
| % of applicants accepted | 78 |
| % of acceptees attending | 34 |

### FRESHMAN PROFILE

| | |
|---|---|
| Range SAT Verbal | 500-610 |
| Average SAT Verbal | 550 |
| Range SAT Math | 530-640 |
| Average SAT Math | 590 |
| Minimum TOEFL | 550 |
| Average HS GPA | 3.1 |
| % graduated top 10% of class | 22 |
| % graduated top 25% of class | 50 |
| % graduated top 50% of class | 85 |

### DEADLINES

| | |
|---|---|
| Regular admission | 3/1 |
| Nonfall registration? | yes |

### APPLICANTS ALSO LOOK AT

**AND OFTEN PREFER**
American
Boston U.
U. Delaware

**AND SOMETIMES PREFER**
U. Maryland—Coll. Park
Temple
LaSalle
Lehigh
Penn State—Univ. Park
Villanova

### FINANCIAL FACTS

| | |
|---|---|
| Financial Aid Rating | 72 |
| Tuition | $16,644 |
| Room & board | $8,705 |
| Books and supplies | $620 |
| Required fees | $980 |
| % frosh receiving aid | 67 |
| % undergrads receiving aid | 65 |

# DUKE UNIVERSITY

2138 CAMPUS DRIVE, DURHAM, NC 27708 • ADMISSIONS: 919-684-3214 • FAX: 919-681-8941

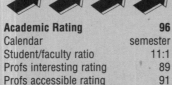
## STUDENTS SPEAK OUT

### Academics

There's no shortage of pride at Duke University, even when expressing criticism. Where else would a student complain that "the administration is trying to turn this place into Harvard, which it should not be, because as we are now, this is a better place to go to college"? We seriously doubt that Duke administrators are trying to develop a tradition of rotten basketball (go Crimson!), but they are hard at work building an academic powerhouse that can hold its own against any other. Duke is one of the nation's most competitive universities; it boasts incredible resources, a beautiful campus, outstanding faculty, and an academic program that is rigorous but not backbreaking. "Duke strikes a great balance between superior academics and an active student life"; students here spend much less time at the books than their counterparts at many top colleges. At the undergraduate level, Duke has two divisions: Trinity College of Arts and Sciences and the School of Engineering. Political science, economics, history, and engineering are favorite majors at this largely pre-professional student body. Though Duke is a major research university with world-class graduate programs, students report that their professors are "brilliant teachers and not just researchers," "amazingly inspirational," and "wonderful if you take advantage of them." It's no exception for engineers: "It's really easy to meet with the assistant dean . . . really, really helpful." Many feel alienated from the central administration, describing it as "out of touch." About 40 percent of the students go on to grad school immediately after graduation.

### Life

Duke's two beautiful campuses, separated by a mile of woodland, boast Gothic architecture, sprawling lawns, and a real Arthurian forest. (A shuttle bus carries students between the campuses.) "Durham, North Carolina, is not a college town at all, so unless you have a car to go to nearby UNC—Chapel Hill, you must be prepared to seek out things to do on campus." Hoards of Duke students find release via their first love, Blue Devils basketball. "Basketball is crazy fun. You can't camp out a month to get into a game and end up not loving it." "Camp" isn't talking figuratively. The perennial national championship contending men's basketball team is so popular that it's spawned Krzyzewskiville, whose namesake is Mike Krzyzewski, Duke's basketball coach. It's a tent city formed each season on the grounds outside Cameron Indoor Stadium by students hoping to get tickets to big games. "The only time we really have school pride is in Cameron—then we go crazy." Outside of basketball, the "social life revolves around the Greek system." "Weekends can get boring for independents." Despite the administration's institution of stricter alcohol policies, "there are still parties . . . but things are much more closed and drinking has been forced behind closed doors." It's still prevalent enough for some students to wish for more "fun activities that don't involve drinking on campus."

### Student Body

"Duke has the image of a preppy rich-kid school, and for the most part it's true." Students here are generally "very conservative" and "dress as if they have just stepped out of the pages of a J.Crew catalog. [I'm] not sure if people come here and conform or if they are already like that to begin with." "The student body is too homogeneous—racially, socioeconomically, politically, ideologically." Duke is working on diversity—more proactively than many other schools. Nevertheless, progress is slow. "There is a diverse ethnic make-up," but race relations could stand improvement.

# DUKE UNIVERSITY

FINANCIAL AID: 919-684-6225 • E-MAIL: UNDERGRAD-ADMISSIONS@DUKE.EDU • WEBSITE: WWW.DUKE.EDU

## ADMISSIONS

*Very important* academic and nonacademic factors considered by the admissions committee include class rank, essays, recommendations, and secondary school record. *Important* factors considered include extracurricular activities, interview, standardized test scores, and talent/ability. *Other* factors considered include character/personal qualities, geography, minority status, volunteer work and work, experience. Factors *not* considered include alumni/ae relation, religious affiliation/commitment, and state residency. SAT I or ACT required. TOEFL required of all international applicants. High school diploma is required and GED is not accepted. *High school units required/recommended:* 19 total required; 4 English required, 3 math required, 3 science required, 1 science lab required, 2 foreign language required, 3 social studies required, 4 elective required. *The admissions office says:* "Every application is reviewed by two or more readers before the candidate is presented to the full admissions committee. Candidates are rated on a one-to-five scale (with five as the highest rating) in six different categories: quality of the academic program, performance in secondary school course work, recommendations, personal qualities, performance in standardized tests, and quality of the essays. While applicants are reviewed by the admissions committee by school and by region, there are no school or regional quotas."

### The Inside Word

The way in which Duke discusses its candidate-review process should be a basic model for all schools to use in their literature. Just about all highly selective admissions committees use rating systems similar to the one described above, but few are willing to publicly discuss them.

## FINANCIAL AID

*Students should submit:* FAFSA, CSS/Financial Aid PROFILE, noncustodial (divorced/separated) parent's statement, business/farm supplement, and parent and student income tax returns. Regular filing deadline is February 1. The Princeton Review suggests that all financial aid forms be submitted as soon as possible after January 1. *Need-based scholarships/grants offered:* Pell, SEOG, state scholarships/grants, private scholarships, and the school's own gift aid. *Loan aid offered:* FFEL Subsidized Stafford, FFEL Unsubsidized Stafford, FFEL PLUS, Federal Perkins, and college/university loans from institutional funds. Institutional employment available. Federal Work-Study Program available. Applicants will be notified of awards on or about April 1. Off-campus job opportunities are good.

## FROM THE ADMISSIONS OFFICE

"Duke University offers an interesting mix of tradition and innovation, undergraduate college and major research university, southern hospitality and international presence, and athletic prowess and academic excellence. Students come to Duke from all over the United States and the world and from a range of racial, ethnic, and socioeconomic backgrounds. They enjoy contact with a world-class faculty through small classes and independent study. More than 40 majors are available in the arts and sciences and engineering; students may also design their own curriculum through Program II. Certificate programs are available in a number of interdisciplinary areas. Special academic opportunities include FOCUS programs and seminars for first-year students, study abroad, study at the Duke Marine Laboratory and Duke Primate Center, the Duke in New York and Duke in Los Angeles arts programs, and an exchange program with Howard University. While admission to Duke is highly selective, applications are evaluated without regard to financial need and the university pledges to meet 100 percent of the demonstrated need of all admitted students."

## ADMISSIONS

| | |
|---|---|
| Admissions Rating | 98 |
| # of applicants | 13,986 |
| % of applicants accepted | 26 |
| % of acceptees attending | 43 |
| # accepting a place on wait list | 890 |
| % admitted from wait list | 8 |
| # of early decision applicants | 1365 |
| % accepted early decision | 38 |

### FRESHMAN PROFILE

| | |
|---|---|
| Range SAT Verbal | 640-740 |
| Range SAT Math | 660-760 |
| Range ACT Composite | 28-33 |
| Average ACT Composite | 30 |
| % graduated top 10% of class | 86 |
| % graduated top 25% of class | 98 |
| % graduated top 50% of class | 100 |

### DEADLINES

| | |
|---|---|
| Early decision | 11/1 |
| Early decision notification | 12/15 |
| Regular admission | 1/2 |
| Regular notification | 4/15 |

### APPLICANTS ALSO LOOK AT AND OFTEN PREFER

Princeton
Harvard
Stanford
Yale

### AND SOMETIMES PREFER

Brown
U. Virginia
UNC—Chapel Hill
Cornell
Penn

### AND RARELY PREFER

Johns Hopkins
U. Michigan—Ann Arbor
Vanderbilt
Northwestern U.
Georgetown U.

### FINANCIAL FACTS

| | |
|---|---|
| Financial Aid Rating | 74 |
| Tuition | $26,000 |
| Room & board | $7,628 |
| Books and supplies | $740 |
| Required fees | $768 |
| % frosh receiving aid | 37 |
| % undergrads receiving aid | 38 |
| Avg frosh grant | $7,190 |
| Avg frosh loan | $3,522 |

# DUQUESNE UNIVERSITY

600 FORBES AVENUE, PITTSBURGH, PA 15282 • ADMISSIONS: 412-396-5000 • FAX: 412-396-5644

## CAMPUS LIFE

**Quality of Life Rating**      **72**
Type of school      private
Affiliation      Roman Catholic
Environment      urban

### STUDENTS
Total undergrad enrollment    5,499
% male/female    42/58
% from out of state    19
% from public high school    86
% live on campus    50
% in (# of) fraternities    14 (10)
% in (# of) sororities    14 (10)
% African American    4
% Asian    2
% Caucasian    80
% Hispanic    2
% international    3
# of countries represented    111

### SURVEY SAYS . . .
*Students love Pittsburgh, PA*
*Very little drug use*
*Great off-campus food*
*Student publications are ignored*
*High cost of living*
*Political activism is (almost)*
*nonexistent*
*Student government is unpopular*
*Dorms are like dungeons*
*Students get along with local*
*community*

## ACADEMICS

**Academic Rating**      **72**
Calendar      semester
Student/faculty ratio      15:1
Profs interesting rating      90
Profs accessible rating      93
% profs teaching UG courses      98
% classes taught by TAs      1
Avg lab size    10-19 students
Avg reg class size    20-29 students

### MOST POPULAR MAJORS
psycholoy
accounting
elementary special education

## STUDENTS SPEAK OUT
### Academics

Duquesne University students are satisfied with the education they receive. They are very career-oriented and believe that a Duquesne education prepares them for life after college. Students adore their instructors, and few classes—if any—are taught by TAs. A secondary education major writes, "I believe Duquesne University has an excellent staff who are always willing to assist the students as much as they can." A sophomore accounting major adds, "All of [my professors] have been willing to help outside of class." Professors keep classes interesting, comments one psychology major. Another student declares, "When I first came to college, I thought everything was going to be up to me. I was very surprised at how much my professors at Duquesne University are willing to help me." The administration fares just as well with Duquesne's students. "This school's administration [is] very thoughtful and caring. They will always be there when you need them," an athletic training major says. The administration is "available at convenient times to help answer any questions we may have," a special education major says. This wouldn't be The Best 331 Colleges without at least one student gripe, and for Duquesne students it's that Duquesne is too expensive. Also, while the university "offers great learning and research opportunities, even for undergrads," students believe that the library and research centers need improvement.

### Life

Duquesne is located in Pittsburgh, and students take advantage of the city's many cultural diversions. Students enjoy "both the benefits of a small campus and the opportunities of city life." Many of the university's students are commuters, and many residential students often go home on the weekend. Those who remain on campus tell us that campus life is only "satisfactory" because the place is a seeming ghostown from Friday through Sunday. Those who live on campus spend their weeknights studying and going to downtown clubs and enjoying late-night, on-campus movies on the weekends. "Life at school is fun. I feel very safe and comfortable on campus, despite the fact that we are located in the city," one biology major comments. Commuting students rave about the commuter center, where many activities go down. Parties at neighboring universities, such as the University of Pittsburgh and Carnegie Mellon, offer extra-campus amusement. The symphony is another popular distraction, as are the numerous coffee shops on the city's south side. Students say that the food and dorms need improvement ("fix the heating and cooling systems"), and they complain about the dorm policies that are "way too strict about visitors."

### Student Body

Duquesne is a Roman Catholic institution, one where students are extremely committed to volunteer work and to helping their fellow students. "You can always find someone willing to lend a helping hand," writes one biology major. Though some students mention that the campus lacks diversity, most agree that "everyone here is friendly and they seem to get along." Students mention that cliques are prevalent on campus. Nevertheless, you'll hear many students say, "I've met the best friends of my life at this campus." Oh yeah, and "everyone smokes except about 5 percent of the students." Commuter students have little interaction with those who live on campus full-time.

FINANCIAL AID: 412-396-6607 • E-MAIL: ADMISSIONS@DUQ.EDU • WEBSITE: WWW.DUQ.EDU

## ADMISSIONS

*Very important* academic and nonacademic factors considered by the admissions committee include character/personal qualities, extracurricular activities, secondary school record, and standardized test scores. *Important* factors considered include class rank and recommendations. *Other* factors considered include alumni/ae relation, essays, geography, minority status, state residency, talent/ability, volunteer work, and work experience. Factors *not* considered include interview and religious affiliation/commitment. SAT I or ACT required. High school diploma is required and GED is accepted. *High school units required/recommended:* 18 total recommended; 4 English recommended, 4 math recommended, 4 science recommended, 4 science lab recommended, 3 foreign language recommended, 3 social studies recommended. *The admissions office says:* "[We have] rolling admissions. We have a strong bond with many high schools and take the counselors' recommendation very seriously."

### The Inside Word

With such a high admit rate, the admissions process should create little anxiety in all but the weakest candidates.

## FINANCIAL AID

*Students should submit:* FAFSA and institution's own financial aid form. Regular filing deadline is May 1. The Princeton Review suggests that all financial aid forms be submitted as soon as possible after January 1. *Need-based scholarships/grants offered:* Pell, SEOG, state scholarships/grants, private scholarships, and the school's own gift aid. *Loan aid offered:* FFEL Subsidized Stafford, FFEL Unsubsidized Stafford, FFEL PLUS, Federal Perkins, Federal Nursing, and college/university loans from institutional funds. Institutional employment available. Federal Work-Study Program available. Applicants will be notified of awards on a rolling basis beginning on or about March 1. Off-campus job opportunities are excellent.

## FROM THE ADMISSIONS OFFICE

"Duquesne University was founded in 1878 by the Holy Ghost Fathers. Although it is a private, Roman Catholic institution, Duquesne is proud of its ecumenical reputation, and almost half of the student body is non-Catholic. The total University enrollment is 9,742. Duquesne University's attractive and secluded campus is set on a 43-acre hilltop ('the bluff') overlooking the large corporate metropolis of Pittsburgh's Golden Triangle. It offers a wide variety of educational opportunities, from the liberal arts to modern professional training. Duquesne is a medium-size university striving to offer personal attention to its students while having the versatility and opportunities of a true university. A deep sense of tradition is combined with innovation and flexibility to make the Duquesne experience both challenging and rewarding. The Palumbo Convocation/Recreation Complex features a 6,300-seat arena, home court to the University's Division I basketball teams; racquetball and handball courts; weight rooms; and saunas. Extracurricular activities are recognized as an essential part of college life, complementing academics in the process of total student development. Students are involved in nearly 100 university-sponsored activities, and Duquesne's location gives students the opportunity to enjoy sports and cultural events both on campus and citywide. There are five residence halls with the capacity to house 2,779 students."

## ADMISSIONS

| | |
|---|---|
| Admissions Rating | 76 |
| # of applicants | 3,776 |
| % of applicants accepted | 84 |
| % of acceptees attending | 40 |
| # accepting a place on wait list | 20 |
| % admitted from wait list | 100 |
| # of early decision applicants | 197 |
| % accepted early decision | 88 |

### FRESHMAN PROFILE

| | |
|---|---|
| Range SAT Verbal | 530-650 |
| Average SAT Verbal | 590 |
| Range SAT Math | 540-650 |
| Average SAT Math | 595 |
| Range ACT Composite | 21-26 |
| Average ACT Composite | 23 |
| Average HS GPA | 3.4 |
| % graduated top 10% of class | 44 |
| % graduated top 25% of class | 80 |
| % graduated top 50% of class | 97 |

### DEADLINES

| | |
|---|---|
| Early decision | 11/1 |
| Early decision notification | 12/15 |
| Priority admission deadline | 11/1 |
| Regular admission | 7/1 |
| Nonfall registration? | yes |

### APPLICANTS ALSO LOOK AT

**AND OFTEN PREFER**
Penn State—Univ. Park
**AND SOMETIMES PREFER**
Ohio State—Columbus
Marquette
**AND RARELY PREFER**
U. Pittsburgh

### FINANCIAL FACTS

| | |
|---|---|
| Financial Aid Rating | 75 |
| Tuition | $15,169 |
| Room & board | $6,504 |
| Books and supplies | $400 |
| Required fees | $1,351 |
| % frosh receiving aid | 66 |
| % undergrads receiving aid | 64 |
| Avg frosh grant | $7,665 |
| Avg frosh loan | $1,998 |

# EARLHAM COLLEGE

801 NATIONAL ROAD WEST, RICHMOND, IN 47374 • ADMISSIONS: 765-983-1600 • FAX: 765-983-1560

## CAMPUS LIFE

| **Quality of Life Rating** | **79** |
|---|---|
| Type of school | private |
| Affiliation | Quaker |
| Environment | suburban |

### STUDENTS

| | |
|---|---|
| Total undergrad enrollment | 1,104 |
| % male/female | 44/56 |
| % from out of state | 67 |
| % from public high school | 72 |
| % live on campus | 88 |
| % African American | 10 |
| % Asian | 2 |
| % Caucasian | 80 |
| % Hispanic | 2 |
| % international | 4 |
| # of countries represented | 25 |

### SURVEY SAYS . . .
*Political activism is hot*
*Students don't get along with local community*
*Student publications are popular*
*Campus easy to get around*
*Popular college radio*
*Athletic facilities are great*
*Lousy off-campus food*
*Great library*
*Students don't like Richmond, IN*

## ACADEMICS

| **Academic Rating** | **89** |
|---|---|
| Calendar | semester |
| Student/faculty ratio | 12:1 |
| Profs interesting rating | 93 |
| Profs accessible rating | 93 |
| % profs teaching UG courses | 100 |
| Avg lab size | 20-29 students |
| Avg reg class size | 10-19 students |

### MOST POPULAR MAJORS
biology
psychology
English

## STUDENTS SPEAK OUT
### Academics

At "small" Earlham College, where students address professors, administrators, "and even the president" by their first names, you'll find "Quaker principles," a "happy, healthy environment," and academics that are "difficult but worth it." Just about everybody here is "extremely accessible, which was driven home to me when I was in a program at another university," explains a senior. "I wanted to meet with the program's director and I was informed that I needed an appointment several days in advance. It was a strange change from Earlham, where I can just pop my head into a prof's or an administrator's office for help or simply a chat." Earlhamites generally give their "engaging," "brilliant," and otherwise "really incredible" instructors ringing endorsements. "The lectures are entertaining," professors are "willing to help outside of class," and "they are, for the most part, dedicated to the learning process and very much here for the students," asserts a music major. Earlham boasts a highly acclaimed library and solid computer resources as well. "Classes in popular majors can be overcrowded," though, and students tell us that support for the arts is "downright pathetic." "Fine arts are currently neglected for athletics and the biology department," gripes a junior.

### Life

"Life takes place almost entirely" on Earlham's "beautiful 600-acre" wooded campus. In addition to being "very busy with class work," students here are awhirl with extracurricular activities. "It's easy to get involved in 20 things that interest you," says a senior. Options include a student-run farm, a "very popular" gospel choir, the "swing dancing club," and "fascinating discussions on public discourse." "Almost everyone has work-study," and students often "watch movies" or dine out. "There's a chance you may go on a date, but not a big chance." "Alcohol and drugs are readily available, but only if you want to be part of it," according to a junior. In fact, "lots of 'party people' get bored," cautions a first-year student, "but if you are up for conversation, you can't miss." Earlhamites "hang out at the coffeehouse" and "in each other's rooms a lot," and it is reportedly "very easy to spark political, social, spiritual, or intellectual debates" here. Political activism—virtually entirely of the left-wing variety—is also widely embraced. If sports and physical fitness are your bag, be sure to check out the brand-spanking-new fitness center. You can also cheer on the nationally ranked men's soccer team or take a joyride at the Equestrian Center. Off campus, "there is nothing to do" and definite friction exists between students and the "hicks in town." Students who need a breather can "take trips to" the greener social pastures of Indianapolis, Chicago, and Dayton.

### Student Body

Earlham's "admissions department must be psychic." Students insist there's no other way to explain the yearly influx of "very reflective," "offbeat," "radically liberal," and "politically active" students who "refuse to be 'typed.'" The "quirky" and "wonderful people" on this campus also describe themselves as "friendly, tolerant, and charitable." They are also "self-righteous," "overcommitted, and broke," and there is a notable contingent of "granola-munching, shower-hating hippies." "Almost every student is neurotic," too. "But we're all civil," promises one student. Without a doubt, there is "a strong sense of community" on campus. Disagreements are "peaceful," as the Quaker tradition exerts a strong influence. "If there is ever a problem," Earlham students "will readily sit down and discuss it for hours," according to a sarcastic junior. Because the student population is relatively small, "social circles overlap, so you meet a huge variety of people." However, "some have a hard time accepting people into their cliques."

FINANCIAL AID: 765-983-1217 • E-MAIL: ADMISSION@EARLHAM.EDU • WEBSITE: WWW.EARLHAM.EDU

## ADMISSIONS

*Very important* academic and nonacademic factors considered by the admissions committee include essays, recommendations, secondary school record, character/personal qualities, and minority status. *Important* factors considered include standardized test scores, extracurricular activities, interview, talent/ability, and volunteer work. *Other* factors considered include class rank, alumni/ae relation, geography, religious affiliation/commitment, state residency, and work experience. SAT I or ACT required, SAT I preferred. TOEFL required of all international applicants. High school diploma is required and GED is accepted. *High school units required/recommended:* 15 total required; 4 English required, 3 math required, 4 math recommended, 2 science required, 3 recommended, 2 foreign language required, 3 foreign language recommended, 1 social studies required, 1 history required, 2 electives required, 8 electives recommended.

### The Inside Word

Like most colleges with a Friends affiliation, Earlham has a sincere interest in the person it admits. Essays and interviews carry virtually as much weight as the numbers. Quakers, minorities, legacies, and state residents receive special consideration in the admissions process, but special consideration is what this place is really all about. Earlham deserves a much higher national public awareness level than it has. Hopefully, this entry will help.

## FINANCIAL AID

*Students should submit:* FAFSA and institution's own financial aid form. The Princeton Review suggests that all financial aid forms be submitted as soon as possible after January 1. *Need-based scholarships/grants offered:* Pell, SEOG, state scholarships/grants and the school's own gift aid. *Loan aid offered:* Direct Subsidized Stafford, Direct Unsubsidized Stafford, Direct PLUS, Federal Perkins, and college/university loans from institutional funds. Institutional employment available. Federal Work-Study Program available. Applicants will be notified of awards on or about April 1. Off-campus job opportunities are good.

## FROM THE ADMISSIONS OFFICE

"The world is full of people with good intentions. What it needs is people with the intellect, the vision, the skills, and the energy to back up their good intentions. It needs people who are able to make a difference. Although only a few students identify themselves as Quakers, Earlham retains those humanistic values of its tradition that have relevance to students of all backgrounds."

## ADMISSIONS

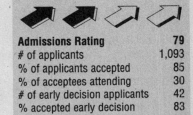

| Admissions Rating | 79 |
| --- | --- |
| # of applicants | 1,093 |
| % of applicants accepted | 85 |
| % of acceptees attending | 30 |
| # of early decision applicants | 42 |
| % accepted early decision | 83 |

### FRESHMAN PROFILE

| | |
| --- | --- |
| Range SAT Verbal | 560-680 |
| Average SAT Verbal | 620 |
| Range SAT Math | 510-640 |
| Average SAT Math | 590 |
| Range ACT Composite | 23-29 |
| Average ACT Composite | 26 |
| Minimum TOEFL | 550 |
| Average HS GPA | 3.4 |
| % graduated top 10% of class | 25 |
| % graduated top 25% of class | 53 |
| % graduated top 50% of class | 87 |

### DEADLINES

| | |
| --- | --- |
| Early decision | 12/1 |
| Early decision notification | 12/15 |
| Regular admission | 2/15 |
| Regular notification | 3/15 |
| Nonfall registration? | yes |

### APPLICANTS ALSO LOOK AT

**AND OFTEN PREFER**
Macalester
Kenyon

**AND SOMETIMES PREFER**
Oberlin
Vassar
Guilford
Carleton

**AND RARELY PREFER**
Antioch

## FINANCIAL FACTS

| Financial Aid Rating | 88 |
| --- | --- |
| Tuition | $20,480 |
| Room & board | $4,936 |
| Books and supplies | $550 |
| Required fees | $590 |
| % frosh receiving aid | 73 |
| % undergrads receiving aid | 66 |
| Avg frosh grant | $11,202 |
| Avg frosh loan | $3,531 |

# ECKERD COLLEGE

4200 54TH AVENUE SOUTH, ST. PETERSBURG, FL 33711 • ADMISSIONS: 727-864-8331 • FAX: 727-866-2304

## CAMPUS LIFE

| Quality of Life Rating | 86 |
|---|---|
| Type of school | private |
| Affiliation | Presbyterian |
| Environment | suburban |

### STUDENTS

| | |
|---|---|
| Total undergrad enrollment | 1,572 |
| % male/female | 45/55 |
| % from out of state | 69 |
| % from public high school | 80 |
| % live on campus | 71 |
| % African American | 3 |
| % Asian | 2 |
| % Caucasian | 88 |
| % Hispanic | 4 |
| % international | 11 |

### SURVEY SAYS . . .
Students are happy
Different students interact
Registration is a breeze
Lots of beer drinking
(Almost) everyone smokes
Library needs improving
Lousy food on campus
Very small frat/sorority scene
Student publications are ignored
Very little drug use

## ACADEMICS

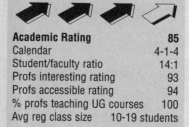

| Academic Rating | 85 |
|---|---|
| Calendar | 4-1-4 |
| Student/faculty ratio | 14:1 |
| Profs interesting rating | 93 |
| Profs accessible rating | 94 |
| % profs teaching UG courses | 100 |
| Avg reg class size | 10-19 students |

### MOST POPULAR MAJORS
international business
marine science
environmental studies (policy)

## STUDENTS SPEAK OUT
### Academics
Adding an entirely new meaning to the phrase "good learning environment," Eckerd College offers a solid liberal arts education in the idyllic setting of Florida's Gulf Coast. Given the easy access to water in almost any direction, it's no surprise that the marine and environmental sciences are Eckerd's strongest academic offerings. Students come from all over the nation and abroad to take advantage of the college's superb marine facilities and programs, often choosing Eckerd over better-known and more selective colleges and universities. Other academic strengths are in pre-professional studies, most notably business and management. Perhaps due to these strengths, "the opportunities for student research are phenomenal for an undergraduate institution." Though not as popular with students as the college would like it to be, the innovative Academy of Senior Professionals also presents outstanding opportunities for learning that are atypical of the college experience. The Academy brings retired professionals of varied persuasions to campus to serve as "mentors in residence" for an extended stay. Students speak highly of their faculty and visiting teachers, reporting that "the professors here really know their subjects and most have worked in their fields before coming to teach . . . . They are very helpful in and out of the classroom, always available for questions." Student satisfaction with the EC experience is tempered only in feelings expressed about the administration, which range from quite favorable to very critical—about normal for college students.

### Life
Campus life at Eckerd has quieted considerably since the school recently began aggressively enforcing the law against underage drinking. Reports a typical undergrad, "People complain about the social life on campus a lot. It's a really small campus and there are no fraternities or sororities, so there's really not much to do here on the weekends. Also, the drinking policies are pretty harsh, although the student government is working on changing this." Another adds, "Campus social life is nonexistent because of the new alcohol policy. It sucks! I only go off campus to hang out. It used to be really fun, one of the reasons I actually came here. Now we can't even have a beer at a barbecue!" Quite a few students point out, however, that "the beach is nearby, and a major city (Tampa) is within a half an hour." Students give a big thumbs-up to the beach and everything that goes with it: "I love this school because of the waterfront program. We can go sailing, canoeing, or swimming whenever we want for free." No doubt the beach contributes to the feeling of some that "life at Eckerd is pretty laid back," and "students are typically detached from reality. They live in their own country-club style. We rarely have student rallies in reaction to current events." Furthermore, Eckerd's small size makes it easy to get involved. It's "a great place for student leadership possibilities." Sports are very popular, as Eckerd has been quite successful in NCAA Division II basketball, baseball, and women's cross-country.

### Student Body
The EC student body includes a "strange mix, quite a few hippie types mixed with jock types and a sprinkling of hardworking overachievers." Many feel that "the size of the EC community, coupled with the fact that we don't have a Greek system, lends a real sense of community bonding and social strength." Some, however, point out that "there are a lot of students from families with a lot of money, so at times they can seem in general to be a bit close-minded and unaccepting of other types of people. Of course, not the entire school is like this, and there are a lot of really great smart people here." Another adds that "even though there is a good deal of ethnic diversity, there seems to be very little socioeconomic diversity." Ethnic diversity comes primarily in the form of a large international student body.

FINANCIAL AID: 727-864-8334 • E-MAIL: ADMISSIONS@ECKERD.EDU • WEBSITE: WWW.ECKERD.EDU

## ADMISSIONS

*Very important* academic and nonacademic factors considered by the admissions committee include essays, interview, secondary school record, and standardized test scores. *Important* factors considered include character/personal qualities, class rank, extracurricular activities, and recommendations. *Other* factors considered include alumni/ae relation, geography, minority status, talent/ability, volunteer work, and work experience. Factors *not* considered include religious affiliation/commitment and state residency. SAT I or ACT required; SAT II recommended. TOEFL required of all international applicants. High school diploma is required and GED is accepted. *High school units required/recommended:* 18 total recommended; 4 English recommended, 4 math recommended, 3 science recommended, 2 foreign language recommended, 3 social studies recommended. *The admissions office says:* "We do everything we can to personalize the admissions process, to be helping professionals, and to assess the personal qualities of our applicants. Eckerd students tend to have a strong inclination toward community volunteer service, and a strong commitment to improve environmental quality."

### The Inside Word

Budding marine biologists are by far the strongest students at Eckerd. They make up a significant percentage of the college's total applicant pool and do much to provide for a more impressive freshman profile. Applications totals have made significant strides over the past two years.

## FINANCIAL AID

*Students should submit:* FAFSA. The Princeton Review suggests that all financial aid forms be submitted as soon as possible after January 1. *Need-based scholarships/grants offered:* Pell, SEOG, state scholarships/grants, private scholarships, and the school's own gift aid. *Loan aid offered:* FFEL Subsidized Stafford, FFEL Unsubsidized Stafford, FFEL PLUS, Federal Perkins, and college/university loans from institutional funds. Institutional employment available. Federal Work-Study Program available. Applicants will be notified of awards on a rolling basis beginning on or about January 1. Off-campus job opportunities are excellent.

## FROM THE ADMISSIONS OFFICE

"Eckerd's diverse student body comes from 49 states and 62 countries. In this international setting, the majors of international relations and international business are very popular. Close to 70 percent of our graduates spend at least one term studying abroad. The beautiful, waterfront campus is a perfect location for the study of marine science and environmental studies. We characterize Eckerd students as competent givers because of their extensive involvement in the life of the campus and their many volunteer service contributions to the local environment and the St. Petersburg community. The Academy of Senior Professionals draws to campus distinguished persons who have retired from fields our students aspire to enter. Academy members, such as the late novelist James Michener, Nobel Prize winner Elie Wiesel, and noted Black historian John Hope Franklin enrich classes and offer valuable counsel for career and life planning."

## ADMISSIONS

| | |
|---|---|
| Admissions Rating | 78 |
| # of applicants | 1,948 |
| % of applicants accepted | 73 |
| % of acceptees attending | 30 |
| # accepting a place on wait list | 92 |
| % admitted from wait list | 12 |

### FRESHMAN PROFILE

| | |
|---|---|
| Range SAT Verbal | 520-630 |
| Average SAT Verbal | 580 |
| Range SAT Math | 520-640 |
| Average SAT Math | 572 |
| Range ACT Composite | 22-28 |
| Average ACT Composite | 26 |
| Minimum TOEFL | 550 |
| Average HS GPA | 3.1 |
| % graduated top 10% of class | 30 |
| % graduated top 25% of class | 61 |
| % graduated top 50% of class | 91 |

### DEADLINES

| | |
|---|---|
| Priority admission deadline | 2/15 |
| Nonfall registration? | yes |

### APPLICANTS ALSO LOOK AT AND OFTEN PREFER

Rollins
U. Florida
U. South Florida

### AND SOMETIMES PREFER

Stetson
U. Miami
Florida State

## FINANCIAL FACTS

| | |
|---|---|
| Financial Aid Rating | 89 |
| Tuition | $18,565 |
| Room & board | $5,110 |
| Books and supplies | $890 |
| Required fees | $220 |
| % frosh receiving aid | 59 |
| % undergrads receiving aid | 57 |
| Avg frosh grant | $11,000 |
| Avg frosh loan | $3,500 |

# EMERSON COLLEGE

120 BOYLSTON STREET, BOSTON, MA 02116-4624 • ADMISSIONS: 617-824-8600 • FAX: 617-824-8609

## CAMPUS LIFE

| Quality of Life Rating | 78 |
| --- | --- |
| Type of school | private |
| Affiliation | none |
| Environment | urban |

### STUDENTS

| | |
| --- | --- |
| Total undergrad enrollment | 3,168 |
| % male/female | 42/58 |
| % from out of state | 35 |
| % from public high school | 76 |
| % live on campus | 52 |
| % African American | 2 |
| % Asian | 2 |
| % Caucasian | 86 |
| % Hispanic | 2 |
| % international | 6 |
| # of countries represented | 67 |

### SURVEY SAYS . . .

Great food on campus
Great library
Lab facilities are great
Great computer facilities
Beautiful campus
Theater is hot
Student government is unpopular
Student publications are ignored
Everyone listens to college radio
Very little beer drinking

## ACADEMICS

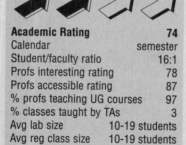

| Academic Rating | 74 |
| --- | --- |
| Calendar | semester |
| Student/faculty ratio | 16:1 |
| Profs interesting rating | 78 |
| Profs accessible rating | 87 |
| % profs teaching UG courses | 97 |
| % classes taught by TAs | 3 |
| Avg lab size | 10-19 students |
| Avg reg class size | 10-19 students |

### MOST POPULAR MAJORS

visual and media arts
performing arts
communications

## STUDENTS SPEAK OUT

### Academics

"The resources are vast and available" at "funky, offbeat" Emerson College, one of the nation's only four-year colleges devoted exclusively to the study of communications and performing arts. Emersonians tell us they have access to "excellent" computers, "good facilities," and a tremendous internship program, with hundreds of positions in Boston, Los Angeles, and other locations across the country and in Europe. Emerson also boasts "great, knowledgeable professors who don't drag on with theory" and who are "always available and willing to go the extra mile" for their passionate students. "Our teachers are, for the most part, struggling artists and writers themselves," notes a writing major. "This makes them especially sympathetic." However, there are also "teachers who don't know how to teach," and "some of the classes are a waste of time." And "there's too much work." Though Emerson is "not a study school" and "there isn't much book work," the "mostly hands-on" academic life here nevertheless "gets stressful," what with the massive amounts of time consumed by projects and internships. Emerson's administration is "good about allowing for creativity in planning a curriculum" but bad about a lot of other things. "Red tape is," unfortunately, "everywhere" and "communication among offices is poor for a communications school." Overall, though, "school is fun," according to a satisfied senior. "You come to Emerson to prepare for a career in something you love to do."

### Life

In "one word," life at Emerson is "busy." What with "10 billion opportunities," students tell us "the danger here isn't boredom; it's doing too much." Emersonians "may not spend as many hours as a Harvard student hitting the books," but they "get a level of hands-on experience not matched by any other school" and spend a great deal of time "in the video lab editing projects or in rehearsals." "Kids here work 30 to 40 hours per week at real jobs," emphasizes a junior. "Emerson will give you the opportunity to graduate not only with a degree but with a resume." Students are also able to establish "lots of professional contacts" by the time they get their diplomas. Not surprisingly, "social life centers around the arts" and around Boston, America's Great College Town. Emerson is "located in the heart of" Beantown, near Fenway Park, the theater district, and Copley Square. "Living across from Boston Common and the Public Garden is great," and the backdrop provides "a cool, mellow city scene." For the most part, "there's no real campus life. Students go out and do their own thing." Theaters, concerts, clubs, museums, "fabulous restaurants," "pubs," and unparalleled "cultural opportunities" abound. Drug use is more prevalent than drinking here, with marijuana as the opiate of choice, and "everyone—I mean everyone—parties," asserts one student. "That's the reality of college life in Boston." On campus, Emerson has one of the premier college radio stations on the planet.

### Student Body

"Picture the strange kid in high school who was really artsy, a little edgy, and had a strange fashion sense. Imagine an entire campus of them and you've got Emerson," says a sophomore. "If you are homosexual, have dyed hair, multiple piercings, and [/or] a creative side, it is the perfect place." Students here range from merely "fairly strange" to "fruity, artsy, atheist, freaky people." You'll find the "brooding, chain-smoking" crowd, "obnoxious theater majors," "zany, artsy types, crazy individualists," and "every color of hair." In fact, "if you don't have your eyebrow pierced, you're in the minority." Though some students here are "sickeningly pretentious," and "everyone wants to be seen in lights," students say theirs is a "very friendly, open environment," "full of creative energy and a solid work ethic." Emersonians are also "very career-oriented" and "enthusiastic about what they are doing." Most "spend every free second rehearsing a monologue, shooting a film, or writing the next Great American Novel." As far as ethnic diversity, "the school prides itself on cultural diversity and a diverse student body but it's 90 percent white," according to a perceptive first-year student.

# EMERSON COLLEGE

FINANCIAL AID: 617-824-8655 • E-MAIL: ADMISSION@EMERSON.EDU • WEBSITE: WWW.EMERSON.EDU

## ADMISSIONS

*Very important* academic and nonacademic factors considered by the admissions committee include secondary school record and standardized test scores. *Important* factors considered include character/personal qualities, essay, recommendations, and class rank. *Other* factors considered include extracurricular activities, minority status, talent/ability, alumni/ae relation, volunteer work and work experience. Factors *not* considered include interview, geography, and religious affiliation/commitment. SAT I or ACT required. Candidates for programs affered by the Department of Performing Arts may be required to audition, interview, or submit a portfolio, resume, or essay. TOEFL required of all international applicants. High school diploma or GED is accepted. *High school units required/recommended:* 16 total required; 20 total recommended; 4 English recommended, 3 math recommended, 3 science recommended, 3 foreign language recommended, 4 elective recommended. *The admissions office says:* "particular attention should be paid to the required admission essay. The ability to communicate ideas coherently in words is an important skill across the college's curriculum."

### The Inside Word

Being in Boston does more for Emerson's selectivity than do rigorous admissions standards.

## FINANCIAL AID

*Students should submit:* FAFSA, institution's own financial aid form, and CSS /Financial Aid PROFILE. Regular filing deadline is March 1. The Princeton Review suggests that all financial aid forms be submitted as soon as possible after January 1. *Need-based scholarships/grants offered:* Pell, SEOG, state scholarships/grants, private scholarships, and the school's own gift aid. *Loan aid offered:* Direct Subsidized Stafford, Direct Unsubsidized Stafford, Direct PLUS, Federal Perkins and state. Institution employment available. Federal Work-Study Program available. Applicants will be notified of awards on or about April 1. Off-campus job opportunities are good.

## FROM THE ADMISSIONS OFFICE

"Founded in 1880 Emerson is one of the premier colleges in the United States for the study of communication and the performing arts. Students may choose from over 20 undergraduate majors and 12 graduate programs supported by state-of-the-art facilities and a nationally renowned faculty. The campus is home to WERS 88.9 FM, the oldest noncommercial radio station in New England; the 850-seat Emerson Majestic Theatre; and *Ploughshares*, the literary journal for new writing. A new 11-story performance and production center is currently under construction, slated to open in 2002.

"Located on Boston Common in the heart of the city's Theatre District, the campus is walking distance from the Massachusetts State House, historic Freedom Trial, Newbury Street shops, financial district, and numerous restaraunts and museums. Emerson's 2,700 undergraduate and 800 graduate students come from over 60 countries and 45 U.S. states and territories. There are more than 50 student orginizations and performance groups, 10 NCAA Division III intercollegiate teams, student publications, and honor societies. The college also sponsors programs in Los Angeles, Kasteel Well (The Netherlands), summer film study in Prague, and course cross registration with the six-member Boston Pro Arts Consortium."

## ADMISSIONS

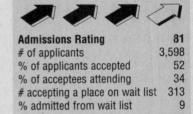

| | |
|---|---|
| Admissions Rating | 81 |
| # of applicants | 3,598 |
| % of applicants accepted | 52 |
| % of acceptees attending | 34 |
| # accepting a place on wait list | 313 |
| % admitted from wait list | 9 |

### FRESHMAN PROFILE

| | |
|---|---|
| Range SAT Verbal | 570-660 |
| Average SAT Verbal | 612 |
| Range SAT Math | 510-630 |
| Average SAT Math | 577 |
| Range ACT Composite | 23-28 |
| Average ACT Composite | 26 |
| Minimum TOEFL | 550 |
| Average HS GPA | 3.3 |
| % graduated top 10% of class | 21 |
| % graduated top 25% of class | 62 |
| % graduated top 50% of class | 94 |

### DEADLINES

| | |
|---|---|
| Regular admission | 2/1 |
| Regular notification | 4/1 |
| Nonfall registration? | yes |

### APPLICANTS ALSO LOOK AT
### AND OFTEN PREFER
Boston U.
NYU
Syracuse
### AND SOMETIMES PREFER
U. Mass-Amherst
Ithaca

## FINANCIAL FACTS

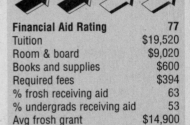

| | |
|---|---|
| Financial Aid Rating | 77 |
| Tuition | $19,520 |
| Room & board | $9,020 |
| Books and supplies | $600 |
| Required fees | $394 |
| % frosh receiving aid | 63 |
| % undergrads receiving aid | 53 |
| Avg frosh grant | $14,900 |
| Avg frosh loan | $3,800 |

# EMORY UNIVERSITY

BOISFEUILLET JONES CENTER, ATLANTA, GA 30322 • ADMISSIONS: 404-727-6036 • FAX: 404-727-4303

## CAMPUS LIFE

**Quality of Life Rating**     **78**
Type of school     private
Affiliation     Methodist
Environment     urban

### STUDENTS

| | |
|---|---|
| Total undergrad enrollment | 6,316 |
| % male/female | 46/54 |
| % from out of state | 71 |
| % from public high school | 70 |
| % live on campus | 65 |
| % in (# of) fraternities | 30 (11) |
| % in (# of) sororities | 35 (9) |
| % African American | 9 |
| % Asian | 16 |
| % Caucasian | 68 |
| % Hispanic | 3 |
| % international | 2 |

### SURVEY SAYS . . .

*Students love Atlanta, GA*
*Frats and sororities dominate social*
*scene*
*Great library*
*Athletic facilities are great*
*Great off-campus food*
*Student publications are popular*

## ACADEMICS

**Academic Rating**     **81**
Calendar     semester
Student/faculty ratio     6:1
Profs interesting rating     92
Profs accessible rating     92
Avg lab size     under 10 students
Avg reg class size     10-19 students

### MOST POPULAR MAJORS
business
biology
psychology

## STUDENTS SPEAK OUT
### Academics

It's the "combination of academics, social life, and real-world experience" that draws students to Emory University, "little brother to the Ivies" located in booming Atlanta, Georgia. In truth, Emory holds its own against venerable "big brothers" like Harvard and Yale. With a "big endowment" and "huge potential for growth," Emory's future—and the future of its academically oriented, competitive student body—looks bright. Notes a first-year, "Students here are smart. Everyone at Emory will go far." Nor is this excellence limited to attendees. "Professors here are leaders in their field[s]," notes a junior. "They wrote the book—literally." Fortunately for Emory undergrads, faculty is accessible and student-focused, as well. Adds another first-year, "My professors have been very good in giving me freedom to learn things in a way that's best for me. Also, professors are always free to help out even when not during office hours. All of my professors have actually cared about my success." A diverse curriculum (especially good in the sciences, say students), "amazing" classroom technology, and "awesome" research facilities and resources complement solid teaching. The administration, too, "works with students" and "doesn't try to weed us out," says a senior. (Though one first-year wonders, "Does all our tuition money go to planting new tulips in the quad every week or is it just me?") And while there is some sentiment that, with such a reputation-conscious administration, "the name associated with the school is its greatest strength," most students would probably say that Emory's reputation is well deserved. A sophomore sums up: "Emory is the embodiment of a great college experience. It has more than lived up to my expectations."

### Life

"Life at Emory has many different possibilities," explains a first-year. "The greatest strength of the school is the balance between a great academic school and a place to explore and have fun." The school's proximity to downtown Atlanta certainly helps—students can do the usual around campus ("hang out with friends, frat parties, bowl, play Frisbee, watch movies"), or they can "head into Atlanta," with its big-city restaurants, plays, films, and other cultural events. Unfortunately, the school is located some distance from the epicenter of activity, so, as a first-year points out, "As a freshman without a car, life is Emory." She continues: "We go to the mall on the free shuttle and take cabs everywhere else. City transport is great, but if you want to get out, you need friends with cars." With many upperclassmen living off campus, students say the school lacks a sense of "community" and "school spirit." They also complain that it's a fairly "materialistic" school. With a beautiful campus, Atlanta at an arm's reach, and a fairly sociable student body, "life is fun—just don't leave home without your Prada bag."

### Student Body

While there might be more than your average amount of "skinny brunettes with capri pants and cell phones," at Emory, there are also a lot of "really nice, down-to-earth people" who get along well—especially in the freshman residence halls. Granted, some of this cohesion is bound to disappear as students move away from campus. A sophomore notes that folks "seemed more friendly at the beginning of school; this has progressively decreased, however, and become somewhat cliquish." But for the most part, Emory's "diverse student body" blends well. We like this junior's take on Emory's student population: "It's a mixed lot."

FINANCIAL AID: 800-727-6039 • E-MAIL: ADMISS@UNIX.CC.EMORY.EDU • WEBSITE: WWW.EMORY.EDU

## ADMISSIONS

*Very important* academic and nonacademic factors considered by the admissions committee include essays, recommendations, and secondary school record. *Important* factors considered include character/personal qualities, class rank, standardized test scores, and talent/ability. *Other* factors considered include alumni/ae relation, extracurricular activities, interview, minority status, volunteer work, and work experience. Factors *not* considered include religious affiliation/commitment, and state residency. SAT I or ACT required; SAT II recommended. High school diploma is required and GED is not accepted. *High school unites required/recommended:* 13 total required.; 4 English required, 3 math required, 2 science required, 1 science lab required, 2 foreign language required, 2 social studies required, 2 history required. *The admissions office says:* "Primarily school achievement record [is considered], with careful examination of program content. Diversity of interests, background, and special talents [are] sought."

### The Inside Word

Applications to Emory have doubled in the last six years. At the same time, the quality of the entering class has risen to record levels. As the South continues to increase its population and presence on the national scene, Emory will continue to increase its selectivity and prestige.

## FINANCIAL AID

The Princeton Review suggests that all financial aid forms be submitted as soon as possible after January 1. Need-based scholarships/grants offered: Pell, SEOG, state scholarships/grants, private scholarships, the school's own gift aid, and Federal Nursing. Loan aid offered: FFEL Subsidized Stafford, FFEL Unsubsidized Stafford, FFEL Plus, Federal Perkins, and Federal Nursing. Institutional employment available. Federal Work-Study Program available. Off-campus job opportunities are good.

## FROM THE ADMISSIONS OFFICE

"The combination Emory offers you is really a rarity in today's college marketplace. As an Emory student, you can still have the benefits of a small liberal arts college while enjoying the wider opportunities found in a major university. Emory college is the four-year undergraduate division of the university and provides a broad, rogorous liberal arts curriculum. At the same time, Emory University, with its nine major divisions, numerous centers for advanced study, and a host of prestigous affiliated institutions, provides the larger context, thus enriching your total college experience "

### ADMISSIONS

| | |
|---|---|
| Admissions Rating | 88 |
| # of applicants | 9,444 |
| % of applicants accepted | 45 |
| % of acceptees attending | 30 |
| # accepting a place on wait list | 400 |
| % admitted from wait list | 5 |
| # of early decision applicants | 767 |
| % accepted early decision | 67 |

### FRESHMAN PROFILE

| | |
|---|---|
| Range SAT Verbal | 640-720 |
| Range SAT Math | 660-740 |
| Range ACT Composite | 28-32 |
| Minimum TOEFL | 600 |
| Average HS GPA | 3.7 |
| % graduated top 10% of class | 88 |
| % graduated top 25% of class | 99 |
| % graduated top 50% of class | 100 |

### DEADLINES

| | |
|---|---|
| Early decision | 11/1 |
| Early decision notification | 12/15 |
| Regular admission | 1/15 |
| Regular notification | 4/1 |

### APPLICANTS ALSO LOOK AT

**AND OFTEN PREFER**
Brown
Northwestern U.
Duke

**AND SOMETIMES PREFER**
Wake Forest
Washington U.
U. Penn

**AND RARELY PREFER**
Rhodes
SMU
Tulane

### FINANCIAL FACTS

| | |
|---|---|
| Financial Aid Rating | 84 |
| Tuition | $24,240 |
| Room & board | $7,868 |
| Books and supplies | $700 |
| Required fees | $292 |
| % frosh receiving aid | 33 |
| Avg frosh grant | $16,219 |
| Avg frosh loan | $3,295 |

# EUGENE LANG COLLEGE

65 WEST 11TH STREET, NEW YORK, NY 10011 • ADMISSIONS: 212-229-5665 • FAX: 212-229-5355

## CAMPUS LIFE

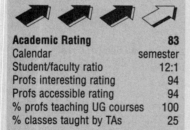

| Quality of Life Rating | 85 |
|---|---|
| Type of school | private |
| Affiliation | none |
| Environment | urban |

### STUDENTS

| | |
|---|---|
| Total undergrad enrollment | 518 |
| % male/female | 32/68 |
| % from out of state | 45 |
| % from public high school | 64 |
| % live on campus | 30 |
| % African American | 7 |
| % Asian | 6 |
| % Caucasian | 53 |
| % Hispanic | 10 |
| % Native American | 1 |
| % international | 4 |

### SURVEY SAYS . . .
Theater is hot
Students love New York, NY
High cost of living
Student publications are ignored
Great off-campus food
Intercollegiate sports unpopular or
nonexistent
No one plays intramural sports
Class discussions encouraged

## ACADEMICS

| Academic Rating | 83 |
|---|---|
| Calendar | semester |
| Student/faculty ratio | 12:1 |
| Profs interesting rating | 94 |
| Profs accessible rating | 94 |
| % profs teaching UG courses | 100 |
| % classes taught by TAs | 25 |

### MOST POPULAR MAJORS
writing/literature
arts/society
social science/cultural studies

## STUDENTS SPEAK OUT

### Academics

Like its parent institution, New School University (formerly known as the New School for Social Research), Eugene Lang College has an air of experimentalism about it. Lang was founded in 1978 to extend the New School's tradition as a bastion of free academic inquiry to the undergraduate level. The school demands a large degree of self-sufficiency from its students, imposing only minimal curricular requirements. As one student explains, "Students are treated with respect; there is almost no supervision, so one must take total responsibility for success." Lang's faculty size is necessarily limited by the small student body, but undergraduates can supplement their curricula with courses at other divisions of New School University, including Parsons School of Design, the Adult Division, and the Graduate Faculty for Social and Political Science. They can also cross register at Cooper Union. Sophomores, juniors, and seniors may also take graduate courses at the New School. Students report that "the professors at Lang really make themselves and their ideas accessible to us. In turn, they allow our ideas to be heard as well. It is a really supportive atmosphere." Adds another, "These teachers are on point. Every time they open their mouths, they hit you with fast-paced, cutting-edge, super-fresh knowledge." The administration "really tries to get on a first-name basis with every student."

### Life

Lang is located at the northern tip of New York's Greenwich Village, a hub of social life for young New Yorkers. The Village is home to numerous funky bars, cheap (and good) ethnic restaurants, and shops, as well as artistic and political communities of nearly every variety. Notes one student (somewhat obliquely), "I cannot complain at all about my life in NYC as a young poet. The school will hand you success if you want it. You have to be hungry, though, really hungry. You can't come to NYC for just a soda." Beyond the Village is a massive city that offers something for everyone. As an added bonus, "internships in all fields (including publishing, teaching, fashion, music and nonprofit organizations) are readily available to Lang students." The city's assets help make up for Lang's lack of a campus or school spirit. Explains one student, "There is very little social interaction between Lang students once they are out of the dorms, which for most students is after freshman year." Students complain that "we need more housing," a problem magnified exponentially by the exorbitant cost of housing in New York. However, the administration has heard their plea and will be opening a new residence hall in fall of 2001.

### Student Body

Lang students are proud of the diversity of their student body, which ranges over ethnicity, race, gender, and lifestyle. Writes one student, "Lang is a special college in that it celebrates differences. That's what my fellow students pride themselves in." Adds another, "From the purple-haired, nose-ringed extremist to the prep—everyone's cool." Students are very similar in one area, however: politics. Students, like the New School's founders, lean hard to the left. Reports one student, "Students here are certainly not politically diverse. The uniformity of political thought is somewhat depressing."

FINANCIAL AID: 212-229-8930 • E-MAIL: LANG@NEWSCHOOL.EDU • WEBSITE: WWW.LANG.EDU

## ADMISSIONS

*Very important* academic and nonacademic factors considered by the admissions committee include secondary school record, standardized test scores, recommendations, essays, and character/personal qualities. *Important* factors include extracurricular activities, interview, talent/ability, volunteer work, and work experience. *Other* factors considered include class rank, geography, and minority status. Factors *not* considered include alumni/ae relation and religious affiliation/commitment. SAT I or ACT required; SAT II recommended. TOEFL required of all international applicants. High school diploma is required and GED is accepted. *High school units required/recommended:* 4 English required, 2 math required, 2 science required, 2 foreign language required, 2 social studies required. *The admissions office says:* "We seek to gain a complete picture of the applicant's ability to succeed in a rigorous and nontraditional liberal arts program by reviewing grade/subject patterns in the transcript, as well as an ability to write and communicate evidence of self-directedness, maturity, and enthusiasm for learning."

### The Inside Word

The college draws a very self-selected and intellectually curious pool, and applications are up. Those who demonstrate little self-motivation will find themselves denied.

## FINANCIAL AID

*Students should submit:* FAFSA. Priority filing deadline is March 1. The Princeton Review suggests that all financial aid forms be submitted as soon as possible after January 1. *Need-based scholarships/grants offered:* Pell, SEOG, state scholarships/grants, private scholarships, and the school's own gift aid. *Loan aid offered:* subsidized Stafford, unsubsidized Stafford, PLUS, federal Perkins, and the school's own loans. Institution employment available. Federal Work-Study Program available. Off-campus job opportunities are good.

## FROM THE ADMISSIONS OFFICE

"Eugene Lang College offers students of diverse backgrounds an innovative and creative approach to a liberal arts education, combining stimulating classroom activity of a small, intimate college with rich resources of a dynamic, urban university—New School University. The curriculum at Lang College is challenging and flexible. Class size, limited to fifteen students, promotes energetic and thoughtful discussions and writing is an essential component of all classes. Students design their own program of study within one of five interdisciplinary concentrations in the Social Sciences and Humanities. They also have the opportunity to pursue a five-year BA/BFA, BA/MA, or BA/MST at one of the university's six other divisions. Our Greenwich Village location means that all the cultural treasures of the city—museums, libraries, music, theater—are literally at your doorstep."

## ADMISSIONS

| | |
|---|---|
| Admissions Rating | 76 |
| # of applicants | 718 |
| % of applicants accepted | 54 |
| % of acceptees attending | 31 |
| # accepting a place on wait list | 50 |
| % admitted from wait list | 24 |
| # of early decision applicants | 19 |
| % accepted early decision | 68 |

### FRESHMAN PROFILE

| | |
|---|---|
| Range SAT Verbal | 590-700 |
| Average SAT Verbal | 610 |
| Range SAT Math | 500-610 |
| Average SAT Math | 570 |
| Range ACT Composite | 18-30 |
| Average ACT Composite | 27 |
| Minimum TOEFL | 550 |
| Average HS GPA | 3.4 |
| % graduated top 10% of class | 24 |
| % graduated top 25% of class | 27 |
| % graduated top 50% of class | 33 |

### DEADLINES

| | |
|---|---|
| Early decision | 11/15 |
| Early decision notification | 12/15 |
| Regular admission | 2/1 |
| Regular notification | 4/1 |
| Nonfall registration? | yes |

### APPLICANTS ALSO LOOK AT
**AND OFTEN PREFER**
Bard
NYU
**AND SOMETIMES PREFER**
Hampshire
Sarah Lawrence
Reed
**AND RARELY PREFER**
St. Johns College
Bennington

## FINANCIAL FACTS

| | |
|---|---|
| Financial Aid Rating | 81 |
| Tuition | $21,530 |
| Room & board | $9,000 |
| Books and supplies | $1,800 |
| Required fees | $670 |
| % frosh receiving aid | 78 |
| % undergrads receiving aid | 81 |
| Avg frosh grant | $10,906 |
| Avg frosh loan | $3,125 |

# THE EVERGREEN STATE COLLEGE

OFFICE OF ADMISSIONS, OLYMPIA, WA 98585 • ADMISSIONS: 360-866-6000 • FAX: 360-866-6680

## CAMPUS LIFE

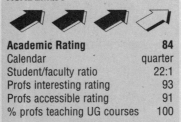

| Quality of Life Rating | 86 |
|---|---|
| Type of school | public |
| Affiliation | none |
| Environment | rural |

### STUDENTS

| | |
|---|---|
| Total undergrad enrollment | 3,901 |
| % male/female | 43/57 |
| % from out of state | 24 |
| % live on campus | 25 |
| % African American | 4 |
| % Asian | 4 |
| % Caucasian | 67 |
| % Hispanic | 4 |
| % Native American | 4 |
| % international | 1 |

### SURVEY SAYS . . .
*Beautiful campus*
*Campus easy to get around*
*Political activism is hot*
*Campus feels safe*
*No one cheats*
*Intercollegiate sports unpopular or
nonexistent*
*Student government is unpopular*
*No one plays intramural sports*
*Theater is unpopular*

## ACADEMICS

| Academic Rating | 84 |
|---|---|
| Calendar | quarter |
| Student/faculty ratio | 22:1 |
| Profs interesting rating | 93 |
| Profs accessible rating | 91 |
| % profs teaching UG courses | 100 |

## STUDENTS SPEAK OUT
### Academics
The Evergreen State College's unique academic program elicits strong reactions from its students, some positive, some negative, and all strongly felt. Instead of enrolling in individual courses, Greeners study in "holistic" and interdisciplinary programs designed to examine major academic topics—often philosophical questions, such as the nature of democracy. Students design their own majors with the guidance of faculty throughout their academic careers. Instead of traditional grades, students receive narrative evaluations. Explains one proponent, "I believe that in 50 years the average university will be structured like Evergreen. Here you frequently get two different professors, e.g., a math and an English professor, in the same class. The interdisciplinary approach lets me learn everything that's connected in a subject. One class taught me how geometry and Camus are related." Writes another, "If you know what you want to get out of this school you can shape it and make the school work for you and study until you drop. I love the contracts and independent study." Some here, however, are not convinced. Complains one, "Evergreen has interdisciplinary education. A lot of people like this. As for me, if I want to learn about filmmaking, I don't want to have to waste my time and money being taught extraneous information about Orissi dance. I've taken two classes now that incorporate Orissi into the lesson, and after the first I already knew that I will never use this Orissi business. Ever." The faculty here received mixed reviews, with students reporting that "the school has some fine professors and some duds."

### Life
"Pretty laid back" describes the social vibe at Evergreen, where an evening's entertainment is more likely to consist of hanging in a friend's dorm room than heading off campus. Life here is "isolated because of the distance between town and campus" and also because "the weather just isn't that accommodating." There is no Greek system and traditional college sports are "nonexistent," so many traditional outlets for undergrad socializing aren't available. Still, it is possible to construct an active social life, and go-getters find plenty to keep them busy. Writes one, "For fun I go mountain biking on the forest trails, practice Tae Kwon Do, have pillow fights, take pajama runs to the Branch (school store) for Ben and Jerry's, play soccer, meditate, sit in the sauna, write, hike, and practice Native American drumming and dancing." The campus is rife with progressive activism. "There are so many student groups here—one for just about anything you could imagine. There is excellent support for gay, lesbian, and bisexual individuals," says a sophomore. Off campus, nearby Portland is "fun," but the school's hometown of Olympia "is boring." Pot is the recreational drug of choice here, and hallucinogens are also popular. Notes one student, "Most people here believe that marijuana should be legal, which explains why it's so popular here."

### Student Body
Evergreen undergrads admit that their ranks are filled primarily by "hippies, hippies, and hippies. Gotta love 'em." Students are "mostly misfits and outcasts from mainstream society, which is to say they are kind, caring, intelligent, completely strange," and "some of the most interesting, funny, and free-thinking people I've met." Students lean toward iconoclasm, a trend reflected in their tonsorial tastes: writes one student, "People at Evergreen have purple hair and nose rings so they can show their kids pictures of themselves in 20 years and say, 'See, your parents were cool back in the '90s.'"One undergrad notes that "at Evergreen, there are two types of students: doers and snoozers. The doers are always on the move, constantly partaking in the Evergreen experience. The snoozers tend to stay in their dorms and watch television."

# THE EVERGREEN STATE COLLEGE

FINANCIAL AID: 360-866-6000 EXT. 6205 • E-MAIL: ADMISSIONS@EVERGREEN.EDU • WEBSITE: WWW.EVERGREEN.EDU

## ADMISSIONS

*Very important* academic factors considered by the admissions committee include secondary school record and standardized test scores. *Important* factors include essay and state residency. *Other* factors considered include recommendations, extracurricular activities, talent/ability, volunteer work, and work experience. Factors *not* considered include class rank, interview, character/personal qualities, alumni/ae relation, geographical residence, religious affiliation/commitment, and minority status. SAT I or ACT required. TOEFL required of all international applications. High school diploma is required and GED is accepted. *High school units required/recommended:* 16 total required; 4 English required, 3 math required, 2 science required (1 lab science required), 2 foreign language required, 3 social studies required, 1 fine/performing arts required, 1 academic elective required. *The admissions office says:* "[Our students] are seriously involved with their education; [each] designs [his or her] own major; making a difference is a widely held objective. [Our students] are interested in the process of learning . . . as opposed to studying for a grade."

### The Inside Word

Evergreen is one of the rare breed of "alternative" colleges—places where intellectual curiosity and a high level of self-motivation are critical factors in the admissions process. Still, candidates must meet minimum academic standards in order to get a closer look from the admissions committee, and those with GPAs below 2.0 won't have a chance. A visit is a good idea for all candidates.

## FINANCIAL AID

The Princeton Review suggests that all financial aid forms be submitted as soon as possible after January 1. *Need-based scholarships/grants offered:* Pell, SEOG, state scholarships/grants, private scholarships, the school's own gift aid. *Loan aid offered:* FFEL Subsidized Stafford, FFEL Unsubsidized Stafford, FFEL PLUS, Federal Perkins, and Federal Nursing. Institutional employment available. Federal Work-Study Program available. Off-campus job opportunities are good.

## FROM THE ADMISSIONS OFFICE

"Evergreen, a public college of arts and sciences, is a national leader in developing full-time interdisciplinary studies programs. Students work closely with faculty (there are no teaching assistants) to study an issue or theme from the perspective of several academic disciplines. They apply what's learned to real-world issues, complete projects in groups, and discuss concepts in seminars that typically involve a faculty member and 22 students. The emphasis on seminars, interdisciplinary problem-solving, and collaboration means students are well prepared for graduate school and the world of work. Our students tend to be politically active, environmentally savvy, and more concerned about social justice than competition and personal gain."

## ADMISSIONS

| | |
|---|---|
| Admissions Rating | 77 |
| # of applicants | 1,453 |
| % of applicants accepted | 87 |
| % of acceptees attending | 26 |

### FRESHMAN PROFILE

| | |
|---|---|
| Range SAT Verbal | 540-640 |
| Average SAT Verbal | 586 |
| Range SAT Math | 480-580 |
| Average SAT Math | 536 |
| Minimum TOEFL | 525 |
| Average HS GPA | 3.1 |

### DEADLINES

| | |
|---|---|
| Priority admission deadline | 3/1 |
| Nonfall registration? | yes |

### APPLICANTS ALSO LOOK AT

**AND OFTEN PREFER**
U. Washington
UC—Santa Cruz

**AND SOMETIMES PREFER**
Western Washington
U. Puget Sound

**AND RARELY PREFER**
U. Oregon

## FINANCIAL FACTS

| | |
|---|---|
| Financial Aid Rating | 74 |
| In-state tuition | $2,856 |
| Out-of-state tuition | $10,110 |
| Room & board | $5,244 |
| Books and supplies | $780 |
| Required fees | $159 |
| % frosh receiving aid | 25 |
| Avg frosh grant | $3,640 |
| Avg frosh loan | $3,890 |

# FAIRFIELD UNIVERSITY

1073 NORTH BENSON ROAD, FAIRFIELD, CT 06430 • ADMISSIONS: 203-254-4100 • FAX: 203-254-4199

## CAMPUS LIFE

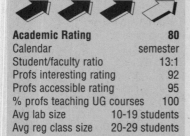

| Quality of Life Rating | 87 |
|---|---|
| Type of school | private |
| Affiliation | Jesuit |
| Environment | suburban |

### STUDENTS

| | |
|---|---|
| Total undergrad enrollment | 4,173 |
| % male/female | 45/55 |
| % from out of state | 75 |
| % from public high school | 64 |
| % live on campus | 75 |
| % African American | 3 |
| % Asian | 2 |
| % Caucasian | 85 |
| % Hispanic | 4 |
| % international | 1 |
| # of countries represented | 37 |

### SURVEY SAYS . . .

*Diversity lacking on campus
Students don't get along with local
community
Classes are small
Student government is popular
Lots of beer drinking
Registration is a pain
Lousy food on campus*

## ACACEMICS

| Academic Rating | 80 |
|---|---|
| Calendar | semester |
| Student/faculty ratio | 13:1 |
| Profs interesting rating | 92 |
| Profs accessible rating | 95 |
| % profs teaching UG courses | 100 |
| Avg lab size | 10-19 students |
| Avg reg class size | 20-29 students |

### MOST POPULAR MAJORS
communication
English
marketing

## STUDENTS SPEAK OUT

### Academics

With five undergraduate divisions, Fairfield University offers an unusually wide range of academic options to its small student body, and like many Jesuit schools, it manages to do so at a price that nonaffiliated private schools rarely match. Our survey shows widespread satisfaction with all the undergraduate schools, with students singling out the Dolan School of Business and the School of Nursing for praise. Of the latter, one student tells us, "My nursing teachers are wonderful. They always make time for you and are willing to take the time until you understand the material. They are easy to talk to and they show so much enthusiasm for the courses." Throughout the university, professors "are extremely accessible," although "teaching abilities are mixed. Some teachers are great, some others aren't, but the good teachers really inspire." Administrative tasks, especially registration, are not so well regarded, however. Complains one typical student, "Forget finals. Registration is the worst part of the semester. Something should be done to improve the process." Those quibbles aside, most Fairfield students proclaim themselves perfectly content with their choice of schools. As one student puts it, "Fairfield has the perfect combination of academics, service, and extracurricular activity to produce well-rounded, highly employable students."

### Life

Students split into two separate camps when discussing social life at Fairfield—those who party hard and those who just say no. The former, and the larger of the two groups, maintains a long-standing student tradition for Long Island Sound beach parties and beer swilling. Explains one student, "There is a very huge off-campus life and we try to balance our time between fun and studying. People work really hard all week and party really hard on weekends. It is a good combination." Adds another, "I think you would have a hard time fitting in and having a good time if you didn't drink." Given students' propensity for rowdy weekend behavior, it is unsurprising that "town relations at the beach are terrible" and that students generally avoid the town of Fairfield, which they describe as "a rich boring town. If you are used to city life, this is not the place for you." A smaller, but reportedly growing, contingent of students abjures the party scene, opting instead for community service, student organizations, and arts excursions to New York City. Writes one such student, "I participate in glee club, volunteering, tour guiding, and telecounseling. For fun, my friends and I attend various campus events like concerts, plays, and movies. We also very much enjoy taking the train into New York for the day." Says another, "Fairfield's community service opportunities are unparalleled. If you want to help, Fairfield's the place for you."

### Student Body

Fairfield has a long and well-earned reputation for attracting a wealthy, preppy student body. One student describes his classmates as "Borgs! If you know one, you know them all. The only difference is in the color of their J.Crew sweaters." Another agrees, "They're all rich and spoiled. That's why they get along so well with each other. They form their own cliques and no outsiders are allowed in." Within these parameters (tight though they may be), "students are very friendly toward each other," according to several respondents. There are "lots of students from New England, especially Massachusetts" and, of course, Fairfield's home state of Connecticut.

# FAIRFIELD UNIVERSITY

FINANCIAL AID: 203-254-4125 • E-MAIL: ADMIS@FAIR1.FAIRFIELD.EDU • WEBSITE: WWW.FAIRFIELD.EDU

## ADMISSIONS

*Very important* academic and nonacademic factors considered by the admissions committee include class rank, extracurricular activities, interview, recommendations, secondary school record, and standardized test scores. *Important* factors considered include alumni/ae relation, character/personal qualities, essays, minority status, talent/ability, and volunteer work. *Other* factors considered include geography and work experience. Factors *not* considered include religious affiliation/commitment and state residency. SAT I or ACT required. TOEFL required of all international applicants. High school diploma is required and GED is not accepted. *High school units required/recommended*: 16 total required; 18 total recommended; 4 English required, 3–4 history/social sciences required, 3 math required, 4 math recommended, 2 science required, 3–4 science recommended, 2 science lab required, 3 science lab recommended, 2 foreign language required. *The admissions office says:* "Students at Fairfield University learn that academic achievement should be coupled with social concerns, so 25 percent of them are involved in serving at area kitchens and shelters for the homeless, working with children whose parents have AIDS, tutoring inner-city children, and volunteering to assist the needy in Appalachia, Ecuador, Haiti, and Mexico."

### The Inside Word

Solid support from Catholic high schools goes a long way toward stocking the applicant pool. Recent successes on the part of both the men's and women's basketball teams in NCAA competition have no doubt helped boost both the applicant pool and public awareness of this solid regional choice, as have the recent openings of the library and campus center.

## FINANCIAL AID

*Students should submit:* FAFSA and CSS/Financial Aid PROFILE. Filing deadline is February 15. The Princeton Review suggests that all financial aid forms be submitted as soon as possible after January 1. *Need-based scholarships/grants offered:* Pell, SEOG, state scholarships/grants, private scholarships, and the school's own gift aid. *Loan aid offered:* Subsidized Stafford, Unsubsidized Stafford, PLUS, Federal Perkins, Federal Nursing, state, and private alternative loans. Institutional employment available. Federal Work-Study Program available. Applicants will be notified of awards on or about April 5. Off-campus job opportunities are good.

## FROM THE ADMISSIONS OFFICE

"Fairfield University's primary objectives are to develop the creative intellectual potential of its students and to foster in them ethical and religious values and a sense of social responsibility. It also seeks to foster in its students a continuing intellectual curiosity and to develop leaders. As the key to the lifelong process of learning, Fairfield has developed a core curriculum (60 credits) to introduce all students to the broad range of liberal learning. Students choose from 33 majors and 19 interdisciplinary minors. They also have outstanding internship opportunities in Fairfield County and New York City. Fairfield grads wishing to continue their education are highly successful in gaining graduate and professional school admission, while others pursue extensive job opportunities throughout the region. Fifteen Fairfield students have been tapped as Fulbright Scholars in just the past three years."

## ADMISSIONS

| | |
|---|---|
| Admissions Rating | 79 |
| # of applicants | 6,499 |
| % of applicants accepted | 63 |
| % of acceptees attending | 25 |
| # accepting a place on wait list | 512 |
| # of early decision applicants | 141 |
| % accepted early decision | 68 |

### FRESHMAN PROFILE

| | |
|---|---|
| Range SAT Verbal | 540-630 |
| Average SAT Verbal | 580 |
| Range SAT Math | 550-630 |
| Average SAT Math | 591 |
| Range ACT Composite | 24-28 |
| Average ACT Composite | 26 |
| Minimum TOEFL | 550 |
| Average HS GPA | 3.6 |
| % graduated top 10% of class | 30 |
| % graduated top 25% of class | 75 |
| % graduated top 50% of class | 96 |

### DEADLINES

| | |
|---|---|
| Early decision | 11/15 |
| Early decision notification | 1/1 |
| Regular admission | 2/1 |
| Regular notification | 4/1 |

### APPLICANTS ALSO LOOK AT

**AND OFTEN PREFER**
Georgetown U.
Holy Cross
Notre Dame
**AND SOMETIMES PREFER**
Villanova
U. Mass—Amherst
Boston Coll.
Providence
**AND RARELY PREFER**
U. Scranton
U. Conn

### FINANCIAL FACTS

| | |
|---|---|
| Financial Aid Rating | 74 |
| Tuition | $21,940 |
| Room & board | $8,000 |
| Books and supplies | $800 |
| Required fees | $435 |
| % frosh receiving aid | 55 |
| % undergrads receiving aid | 50 |
| Avg frosh grant | $9,240 |
| Avg frosh loan | $2,985 |

# FISK UNIVERSITY

1000 17TH AVENUE NORTH, NASHVILLE, TN 37208-3051 • ADMISSIONS: 615-329-8666 • FAX: 615-329-8774

## CAMPUS LIFE

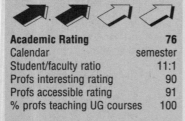

| Quality of Life Rating | 68 |
|---|---|
| Type of school | private |
| Affiliation | none |
| Environment | urban |

### STUDENTS

| | |
|---|---|
| Total undergrad enrollment | 812 |
| % male/female | 28/72 |
| % from out of state | 71 |
| % from public high school | 85 |
| % live on campus | 56 |
| % African American | 100 |
| % international | 2 |
| # of countries represented | 5 |

### SURVEY SAYS . . .

*Frats and sororities dominate social scene*
*Diversity lacking on campus*
*Classes are small*
*Very little drug use*
*Athletic facilities need improving*
*Very little beer drinking*
*Lousy food on campus*
*Lab facilities are great*
*Library needs improving*

## ACACADEMICS

| Academic Rating | 76 |
|---|---|
| Calendar | semester |
| Student/faculty ratio | 11:1 |
| Profs interesting rating | 90 |
| Profs accessible rating | 91 |
| % profs teaching UG courses | 100 |

### MOST POPULAR MAJORS
business administration
biology
psychology

## STUDENTS SPEAK OUT

### Academics

Ask Fisk students what they love about their school and they invariably mention the school's history. W. E. B. DuBois' alma mater was founded in 1866; its first classes convened in a Union army barracks mere months after the conclusion of the Civil War. Notes one student, "It is the history of this school that is its great strength. Most students leave Fisk with a great understanding of the struggle of the black university as a whole and are determined to do their best." From day one Fisk has striven to achieve "the highest standards, not of Negro education, but of American education at its best," succeeding despite a funding crisis and, until relatively recently, a hostile southern environment. Today, Fisk is "a wonderful place to learn" at which "individuals are definitely allowed to excel." Students here appreciate an intimate classroom setting. Explains one, "Since the student population is small, you develop a rapport with your professors. The professors are usually willing to help you with anything you need. Most teachers are challenging. They are very open-minded and caring of students' opinions." Departments in the hard sciences are popular and well respected here, as are pre-business studies and the music school. Students love the "cordial, accessible administration" but "wish Fisk was better funded," complaining that the facilities need a major upgrade. Explains one, "Despite my love for my school, I can't help but feel cheated because of the lack of organization and the lack of educational necessities (e.g. lab equipment, diversity of majors)." Sums up one student, "Fisk is unique. Despite the lack of funding and technology and advances, it produces 'top flight' students. The professors range from terrible to tremendous, but the overall experience creates well-rounded individuals with the ability to compete and succeed ultimately in any environment."

### Life

Students report that "Fisk is a very academic school. Many activities focus around academically oriented activities, like lectures and speakers." Although they enjoy the fact that Fisk is a "very historic, beautiful, and family-oriented school" with a "very peaceful" campus, they also "wish that there were more things to do on campus." Because Fisk is relatively small, "there are very few activities for the average student to partake in. Greek organizations play a big role in providing activities, whether it be a party or some type of community service. Other than that, many students are not as active as they need to be." Campus social life, many say, is also dampened by a paternalistic administration; explains one student, "The university treats students like children and not like young adults. The dorm life for freshmen ladies is awful." Most students end up learning to be satisfied with a quiet lifestyle. Writes one, "For me, a few parties, a good movie, and a seminar or two make up a fun-filled social week. School is what you make it." Food on campus is "awful," but several cheap southern-style restaurants and food stands are close by, including Mary's Bar-B-Q, perhaps Nashville's best. South Nashville, the neighborhood surrounding Fisk, is "a bad area" but one that is gradually improving.

### Student Body

Over and over, the word "family" pops up in students' descriptions of the Fisk community. Writes one, "The weird thing here is people really get along. We are really a family because we are so small. You know people by name." Another offers a slightly different perspective, observing that "because our campus is small, we all tend to feel like a family. Like most family, there are people you love and those whom you despise. But when you are off campus and see someone from Fisk, you look out for them." The typical Fiskite is politically liberal, religious, serious about study, and adamant in the belief that African American students are best served at a predominantly black university.

FINANCIAL AID: 615-329-8735 • E-MAIL: ADMISSIONS@FISK.EDU • WEBSITE: WWW.FISK.EDU

## ADMISSIONS

*Very important* academic and nonacademic factors considered by the admissions committee include class rank. *Important* factors considered include alumni/ae relation, character/personal qualities, essays, extracurricular activities, recommendations, and secondary school record. *Other* factors considered include standardized test scores and talent/ability. Factors *not* considered include geography, interview, minority status, religious affiliation/commitment, state residency, volunteer work, and work experience. TOEFL required of all international applicants. High school diploma is required and GED is accepted. *High school units required/recommended:* 4 English recommended, 4 math recommended, 2 science recommended, 1 science lab recommended, 2 foreign language recommended, 2 history recommended. *The admissions office says:* "Fisk University seeks to enroll men and women who will benefit from a liberal arts experience designed to equip them for intellectual and social leadership. It is the policy of Fisk University to grant admission to applicants showing evidence of adequate preparation and the ability to successfully pursue college studies at Fisk."

### The Inside Word

While a solid academic record is central to getting in, applicants to Fisk should not underestimate the personal side of admissions criteria. A high level of motivation and involvement in your school, church, and/or community goes a long way toward a successful candidacy here.

## FINANCIAL AID

The Princeton Review suggests that all financial aid forms be submitted as soon as possible after January 1. *Need-based scholarships/grants offered:* Pell, SEOG, state scholarships/grants, the school's own gift aid, and United Negro College Fund. *Loan aid offered:* Direct Subsidized Stafford, Direct Unsubsidized Stafford, Direct PLUS, and Federal Perkins. Institutional employment available. Off-campus job opportunities are good.

## FROM THE ADMISSIONS OFFICE

"Founded in 1866, the university is coeducational, private, and one of America's premier historically black universities. The first black college to be granted a chapter of Phi Beta Kappa Honor Society, Fisk serves a national student body, with an enrollment of 900 students. There are residence halls for men and women. The focal point of the 40-acre campus and architectural symbol of the university is Jubilee Hall, the first permanent building for the education of blacks in the South, and named for the internationally renowned Fisk Jubilee Singers, who continue their tradition of singing the Negro spiritual. From its earliest days, Fisk has played a leadership role in the education of African Americans. Faculty and alumni have been among America's intellectual leaders. Among them include Fisk graduates Nikki Giovanni, poet/writer; John Hope Franklin, historian/scholar; David Lewis, professor/recipient of the prestigious Pulitzer Prize; Hazel O'Leary, U.S. Secretary of Energy; John Lewis, U.S. Representative–GA; and W. E. B. DuBois, the great social critic and cofounder of the NAACP. Former Fisk students whose distinguished careers bring color to American culture include Judith Jamison, director of the Alvin Ailey Dance Company, and Johnetta B. Cole, president of Spelman College. In proportion to its size, Fisk continues to contribute more alumni to the ranks of scholars pursuing doctoral degrees than any other institution in the United States."

### ADMISSIONS

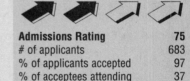

| | |
|---|---|
| Admissions Rating | 75 |
| # of applicants | 683 |
| % of applicants accepted | 97 |
| % of acceptees attending | 37 |

#### FRESHMAN PROFILE

| | |
|---|---|
| Range SAT Verbal | 395-545 |
| Average SAT Verbal | 448 |
| Range SAT Math | 365-540 |
| Average SAT Math | 441 |
| Range ACT Composite | 17-22 |
| Average ACT Composite | 19 |
| Minimum TOEFL | 500 |
| Average HS GPA | 3.0 |
| % graduated top 10% of class | 35 |
| % graduated top 25% of class | 48 |
| % graduated top 50% of class | 73 |

#### DEADLINES

| | |
|---|---|
| Regular admission | 6/15 |
| Nonfall registration? | yes |

#### APPLICANTS ALSO LOOK AT

**AND OFTEN PREFER**
Howard
Morehouse
Spelman

**AND SOMETIMES PREFER**
Vanderbilt
Penn State—Univ. Park

**AND RARELY PREFER**
Clark Atlanta

### FINANCIAL FACTS

| | |
|---|---|
| Financial Aid Rating | 74 |
| Tuition | $8,480 |
| Room & board | $4,930 |
| Books and supplies | $800 |
| Required fees | $290 |
| % frosh receiving aid | 89 |
| % undergrads receiving aid | 90 |
| Avg frosh grant | $2,200 |
| Avg frosh loan | $6,700 |

# FLORIDA A&M UNIVERSITY

SUITE G-9, FOOTE-HILYER ADMINISTRATION CENTER, TALLAHASSEE, FL 32307 • ADMISSIONS: 850-599-3796 • FAX: 850-599-3069

## CAMPUS LIFE

| | |
|---|---|
| **Quality of Life Rating** | **71** |
| Type of school | public |
| Affiliation | none |
| Environment | urban |

### STUDENTS

| | |
|---|---|
| Total undergrad enrollment | 10,691 |
| % male/female | 42/58 |
| % from out of state | 21 |
| % from public high school | 85 |
| % live on campus | 77 |
| % African American | 95 |
| % Asian | 1 |
| % Caucasian | 3 |
| % Hispanic | 1 |
| % international | 1 |

### SURVEY SAYS . . .

*Frats and sororities dominate social scene*
*Student government is popular*
*Very little drug use*
*Everyone loves the Rattlers*
*Diversity lacking on campus*
*Library needs improving*
*Musical organizations are hot*
*(Almost) no one smokes*
*Dorms are like dungeons*

## ACADEMICS

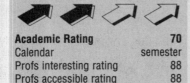

| | |
|---|---|
| **Academic Rating** | **70** |
| Calendar | semester |
| Profs interesting rating | 88 |
| Profs accessible rating | 88 |

### MOST POPULAR MAJORS
business administration
health professions
liberal arts

## STUDENTS SPEAK OUT

### Academics

"You receive an all-around education" at Florida A&M University. "Fine academic programs" available here include pharmacy, architecture, and engineering. Business administration takes the cake, though; over one-third of FAMU grads opt for career-track jobs in commerce. "We have a diverse group of professors at FAMU and they complement each other very well," claims one business major. "They prepare us—as Rattlers [the school mascot]—to strike, strike, and strike again!" Profs "sincerely care about your progress" and "there is a definite opportunity to develop a one-on-one relationship with instructors" at this rather large institution. "They are eager to help if you take the initiative and are an active learner." A senior tells us: "My overall experience has been great." The administration receives considerably lower marks than the faculty. One student comments, "I often wonder what it is that they do" while a senior discloses that "the 'U' in FAMU stands for 'Unorganized.'" Says an English major, "If my major was standing in line, I'd graduate with honors." Students also gripe that "financial aid needs an overhaul." Still, there's little doubt that they're doing something right here; FAMU is one of the leading historically black universities in the nation, and a powerful draw for top students.

### Life

The football team and the Marching 100—"the greatest band in the universe"—are the ties that bind FAMU students. Beyond these entities, "it's basically get in where you fit in." Students "bowl, play cards, table tennis, basketball, watch TV," and hang out at "a central location on campus called 'The Set.'" The Greek system is king when it comes to socializing at FAMU. Raves one student, "There are parties galore. We have our own rendition of the Apollo, called the 'Stoop,' for fun." Some popular student events are Greek Week, Homecoming, and Harambee. Religious and community service events also draw large turnouts. "Also, we don't usually fraternize with Florida State students. They stay over there and we stay over here," explains a sophomore. "Tallahassee is in love with Florida State University, which sucks when you attend FAMU." Just like at crosstown neighbor FSU, though, parking is a serious problem. To complicate matters, "FAMU is located on the highest of Tallahassee's seven hills. So much walking up and down is a pain but you do stay in shape," points out a fit first-year student.

### Student Body

Almost every student is from Florida, so "they all have accents" and "the southern hospitality thing" is big. FAMU is proud of its home-grown student body, which is chock-full of "enormous talent" and many, many National Achievement Scholars (more than any other university). "Black pride and unity" are significant themes in this "strong, positive, intelligent African American community." A pre-med major explains: "People here are mainly concerned with money and their futures. They want to make money now, and they want to make lots of money in their futures." Political awareness is "prevalent on campus" as well. FAMU's homogeneity provides a feeling of comfort and caring, like "one big family."

# FLORIDA A&M UNIVERSITY

FINANCIAL AID: 904-599-3730 • E-MAIL: BCOX2@FAMU.EDU • WEBSITE: WWW.FAMU.EDU

## ADMISSIONS

*Very important* academic and nonacademic factors considered by the admissions committee include religious affiliation/commitment, secondary school record, and standardized test scores. *Important* factors considered include character/personal qualities, essays, extracurricular activities, and recommendations. *Other* factors considered include class rank, volunteer work, and work experience. Factors *not* considered include alumni/ae relation, geography, interview, minority status, state residency, and talent/ability. SAT I or ACT required. TOEFL required of all international applicants. High school diploma is required and GED is accepted. *High school units required/recommended:* 16 total required; 4 English required, 3 math required, 2 science required, 2 science lab required, 2 foreign language required, 2 social studies required, 2 history required, 3 elective required.

### The Inside Word

FAMU's admissions staff does a terrific job. Collectively, they are warm, compassionate, and skilled counselors. This goes a long way toward explaining why the University has enrolled the highest number of National Achievement Scholars of any school in the country. There's a lot to like about the way these guys do business—they never lose sight of the notion that they are educators first and marketers second. Other colleges would do well to study FAMU's approach.

## FINANCIAL AID

The Princeton Review suggests that all financial aid forms be submitted as soon as possible after January 1. *Need-based scholarships/grants offered:* Pell, SEOG, state scholarships/grants, private scholarships, the school's own gift aid, and Federal Nursing. *Loan aid offered:* FFEL Subsidized Stafford, FFEL Unsubsidized Stafford, FFEL PLUS, Federal Perkins, and Federal Nursing. Institutional employment available. Off-campus job opportunities are good.

## FROM THE ADMISSIONS OFFICE

"FAMU encourages applications for admission from qualified applicants regardless of sex, culture, race, religion, ethnic background, age, or disability. We are committed to enrolling the best possible students and we are interested in applicants who have demonstrated superior academic ability and outstanding personal qualities. For more than a century, the primary goals of FAMU have been to promote academic excellence and to improve the quality of life for those individuals it serves and their society. FAMU is located in the capital city of Florida (Tallahassee) and is a four-year public, general purpose, land-grant institution. It offers undergraduate and graduate programs designed to meet the needs of a diverse student population."

## ADMISSIONS

| | |
|---|---|
| Admissions Rating | 79 |
| # of applicants | 5,634 |
| % of applicants accepted | 70 |
| % of acceptees attending | 48 |

### FRESHMAN PROFILE

| | |
|---|---|
| Average ACT Composite | 20 |
| Minimum TOEFL | 500 |
| Average HS GPA | 3.2 |

### DEADLINES

| | |
|---|---|
| Priority admission deadline | 3/1 |
| Regular admission | 5/13 |
| Regular notification | rolling |
| Nonfall registration? | yes |

### APPLICANTS ALSO LOOK AT AND SOMETIMES PREFER

Tuskegee
Spelman
Morehouse
Florida State
Howard

### AND RARELY PREFER

U. South Florida
U. Florida
Hampton

## FINANCIAL FACTS

| | |
|---|---|
| Financial Aid Rating | 75 |
| In-state tuition | $1,777 |
| Out-of-state tuition | $7,368 |
| Room & board | $3,896 |
| Books and supplies | $600 |
| Required fees | $129 |
| Avg frosh grant | $3,031 |

# FLORIDA STATE UNIVERSITY

2500 UNIVERSITY CENTER, TALLAHASSEE, FL 32306-2400 • ADMISSIONS: 850-644-6200 • FAX: 850-644-0197

## CAMPUS LIFE

| Quality of Life Rating | 79 |
|---|---|
| Type of school | public |
| Affiliation | none |
| Environment | suburban |

### STUDENTS

| | |
|---|---|
| Total undergrad enrollment | 27,014 |
| % male/female | 44/56 |
| % from out of state | 14 |
| % from public high school | 88 |
| % live on campus | 16 |
| % in (# of) fraternities | 14 (21) |
| % in (# of) sororities | 13 (14) |
| % African American | 12 |
| % Asian | 3 |
| % Caucasian | 76 |
| % Hispanic | 8 |
| % international | 1 |

### SURVEY SAYS . . .

*Frats and sororities dominate social scene*
*Everyone loves the Seminoles*
*Student publications are popular*
*Hard liquor is popular*
*(Almost) everyone plays intramural sports*
*Athletic facilities need improving*
*Library needs improving*
*Computer facilities need improving*

## ACADEMICS

| Academic Rating | 79 |
|---|---|
| Calendar | semester |
| Student/faculty ratio | 22:1 |
| Profs interesting rating | 70 |
| Profs accessible rating | 68 |
| % profs teaching UG courses | 95 |
| % classes taught by TAs | 32 |
| Avg reg class size | 20-29 students |

### MOST POPULAR MAJORS
criminology
biological sciences
psychology

## STUDENTS SPEAK OUT

### Academics

With its terrific climate and perennially excellent football team, one could excuse Florida State University if its academic reputation was not a strong selling point. Fortunately, it is. Along with an extremely affordable tuition, Florida State is a world-class research institution that offers an excellent education if one can ignore all of the outside distractions. While entry-level classes are extremely large, students laud their "caring" professors for both their quality and accessibility. "Teachers make it as easy as possible for a student to access them," an electrical engineering major comments. And the upper-level professors are considered "enthusiastic and motivated." A junior child development major adds that her professors "are here for us and try to help us to the best of their ability." Because of its auspicious location in Florida's capital, students can take the skills they learn on campus and apply them in a host of internships at federal and state agencies. According to students, the administration is disorganized, and a sophomore international affairs major describes the it as "more bureaucratic than Nixon's." That's just the bigwigs, though, as the campus staff is "extremely friendly" and financial aid is "the bomb." An overjoyed first-year biology major describes FSU as "an excellent school that . . . has made me realize that I made the right decision."

### Life

Students at Florida State aren't fanatical about their studying. An English major tattles that many students skip classes and that the party scene is considered by many to be as important as the academic one. Students recommend living off campus because they aren't fond of the "old and cramped" dorms. Besides, there's a "glut of affordable off-campus housing within walking distance." Tallahassee clubs are "decent," and there are always parties to crash, both at private off-campus houses and at fraternities and sororities. Greek organizations are extremely popular and are known as much for their charitable endeavors as for the parties that they host. Campus organizations are active and plentiful. Students praise the top-notch recreation center and take advantage of the temperate climate to go hiking, camping, and biking. "There are all kinds of things to do for fun," a senior social sciences major explains. "You just have to be creative." The football team is a perennial national championship contender, and students take a great deal of pride ("Seminole Spirit") in their clubs. Students give the food a thumbs-down and say that the university needs to increase the number of available parking spaces because "you have to get to campus by 7:30 [or] 8 A.M. to get a spot."

### Student Body

Though most FSU students are united by their common desire to have fun, they tend to "separate themselves into groups." Consequently, "minorities hang out with minorities and whites hang out with whites," muses one junior. "They all get along, but it's still segregated." Students note the lack of diversity on campus, and most agree that the university needs to work to correct that problem. Accordingly, some students believe that there is a limited sense of community. Neverthless, most students describe their peers as "outgoing" and "friendly" as well as "approachable" and "helpful."

FINANCIAL AID: 850-644-5871 • E-MAIL: ADMISSIONS@ADMIN.FSU.EDU • WEBSITE: WWW.FSU.EDU

## ADMISSIONS

*Very important* academic and nonacademic factors considered by the admissions committee include secondary school record and class rank. *Important* factors considered include standardized test scores, state residency, and talent/ability. *Other* factors considered include alumni/ae relation, extracurricular activities, volunteer work, and work experience. Factors *not* considered include race and religious affiliation. TOEFL required of all international applicants. High school diploma is required and GED is accepted. *High school units required/recommended:* 4 English required, 3 math required, 3 science required, 2 science lab required, 2 foreign language required, 4 elective required. *The admissions office says:* "One of the most unique qualities of Florida State University is that there isn't a typical student. There are as many perspectives as there are FSU students. An ideal of individualism permeates every facet of student life at FSU—academically, culturally, politically, and socially."

### The Inside Word

The high volume of applicants has everything to do with Florida State's selectivity, which continues to increase as budgets hold enrollment fairly level. Non-Floridians will find FSU's selection process to be a bit more welcoming than UF's, but just as impersonal. Performing arts auditions are quite competitive.

## FINANCIAL AID

*Students should submit:* FAFSA. The Princeton Review suggests that all financial aid forms be submitted as soon as possible after January 1. *Need-based scholarships/grants offered:* Pell, SEOG, state scholarships/grants, private scholarships, and the school's own gift aid. *Loan aid offered:* FFEL Subsidized Stafford, FFEL Unsubsidized Stafford, FFEL PLUS, and Federal Perkins. Institutional employment available. Federal Work-Study Program available. Applicants will be notified of awards on a rolling basis beginning on or about March 15. Off-campus job opportunities are excellent.

## FROM THE ADMISSIONS OFFICE

"Established in 1851, Florida State University is seated on the oldest continuous site of higher education in Florida and holds the state's first chapter of Phi Beta Kappa. It enjoys an outstanding reputation for offering a wide range of innovative academic achievements, like our College of Medicine, the first in the nation in 20 years; conducting groundbreaking research; attracting renowned faculty; being one of the "most wired" universities in the U.S.; housing an exceptional Career Center; and producing successful graduates. Seventeen colleges and schools offer nearly 200 undergraduate majors, 198 graduate degrees, and professional degrees in law and medicine. A diverse student body has access to student services that include the University Honors Program, the Center for Academic Retention and Enhancement, Disabled Student Services, the International Center, the Center for Civic Education and Service, and the Undergraduate Academic Advising Center. FSU leads the way in global education with international programs in Costa Rica, the Czech Republic, England, France, Italy, Panama, Russia, Spain, Switzerland, Vietnam, and the West Indies."

## ADMISSIONS

| | |
|---|---|
| Admissions Rating | 83 |
| # of applicants | 22,273 |
| % of applicants accepted | 52 |
| % of acceptees attending | 35 |

### FRESHMAN PROFILE

| | |
|---|---|
| Range SAT Verbal | 540-640 |
| Average SAT Verbal | 593 |
| Range SAT Math | 550-640 |
| Average SAT Math | 595 |
| Range ACT Composite | 23-27 |
| Average ACT Composite | 25 |
| Minimum TOEFL | 550 |
| Average HS GPA | 3.7 |
| % graduated top 10% of class | 57 |
| % graduated top 25% of class | 75 |
| % graduated top 50% of class | 98 |

### DEADLINES

| | |
|---|---|
| Priority admission deadline | 12/31 |
| Regular admission | 3/1 |
| Nonfall registration? | yes |
| Nonfall registration? | yes |

### APPLICANTS ALSO LOOK AT AND SOMETIMES PREFER
Georgia Tech.
Auburn
Florida A&M
U. Central Florida
U. Florida

### AND RARELY PREFER
Wesleyan Coll.
Stetson
U. Colorado—Boulder

## FINANCIAL FACTS

| | |
|---|---|
| Financial Aid Rating | 79 |
| In-state tuition | $2,378 |
| Out-of-state tuition | $9,716 |
| Room & board | $5,610 |
| Books and supplies | $702 |
| Required fees | $739 |
| % frosh receiving aid | 42 |
| % undergrads receiving aid | 37 |
| Avg frosh grant | $2,839 |
| Avg frosh loan | $2,146 |

# FORDHAM UNIVERSITY

441 EAST FORDHAM ROAD, THEBAUD HALL, NEW YORK, NY 10458 • ADMISSIONS: 718-817-4000 • FAX: 718-367-9404

## CAMPUS LIFE

| | |
|---|---|
| **Quality of Life Rating** | **79** |
| Type of school | private |
| Affiliation | Roman Catholic |
| Environment | urban |

### STUDENTS

| | |
|---|---|
| Total undergrad enrollment | 6,989 |
| % male/female | 41/59 |
| % from out of state | 37 |
| % from public high school | 40 |
| % live on campus | 57 |
| % African American | 5 |
| % Asian | 5 |
| % Caucasian | 59 |
| % Hispanic | 12 |
| % international | 1 |
| # of countries represented | 38 |

### SURVEY SAYS . . .

*Students love New York, NY*
*Musical organizations aren't popular*
*Theater is hot*
*Classes are small*
*Dorms are like palaces*
*Intercollegiate sports unpopular or nonexistent*
*Athletic facilities need improving*
*Lousy food on campus*

## ACADEMICS

| | |
|---|---|
| **Academic Rating** | **78** |
| Calendar | semester |
| Student/faculty ratio | 10:1 |
| Profs interesting rating | 90 |
| Profs accessible rating | 91 |
| % profs teaching UG courses | 77 |
| Avg lab size | under 10 students |
| Avg reg class size | 10-19 students |

### MOST POPULAR MAJORS
business administration
psychology
communications

## STUDENTS SPEAK OUT

### Academics

Fordham University has two campuses: Rose Hill in the Bronx and Lincoln Center in Manhattan. Rose Hill remains a traditional liberal arts and sciences program on a traditional "green lawns and Gothic architecture" campus. Lincoln Center, a "concrete campus," offers a wide range of courses but focuses on media studies, visual arts, and theater. At both campuses, students must complete a "great core curriculum" heavy in the liberal arts before proceeding to their major studies. Students appreciate the benefits of their location, explaining that "Fordham University offers a lot because of its diverse surroundings (the Bronx, New York City). Just by living here you are educated by meeting and seeing new places and things." Professors, who earn high marks, are "strict and difficult but good teachers" and also "humorous and easily accessible. Many are jolly ol' Jesuits who never fail to be passionate about what they teach." The administration is a different story: deans and upper administration receive good grades for being "very involved in the students' lives," but lower-level staff, with whom students more regularly interact, "don't answer student questions or lead you [to] where you can get help. Perhaps they don't know themselves." Still, students feel that the occasional administrative hassle is more than offset by small classes, an excellent library, and overall satisfaction with their academic experience here.

### Life

Fordham's two campuses tell a tale of two cities. Rose Hill is located in a working-class Bronx neighborhood. "The boogie-down Bronx is the best," offers one student. "It's a real culture shock for the majority of us who grew up in suburbia." Students are quick to note that both the campus and the immediate area are safe. Among Rose Hill's assets are "a beautiful green campus"; a nearby Little Italy with "great, cheap Italian food"; and easy access to the Botanical Gardens and the Bronx Zoo. Also, the Bronx campus "offers a lot of extracurriculars," writes one student. Reports another, "We have a lot of comedy and music get-togethers. There is always something going on around here." Plus, Rose Hill is only a short subway or bus ride away from Manhattan; many students take advantage of the University Shuttle Service to go between campuses. The other campus is at Lincoln Center, an exclusive area at the heart of Manhattan's West Side. Lincoln Center students have "no real campus." All residential students at Lincoln Center live in a connected campus high-rise and are almost certainly the lowest-income residents of their neighborhood. They report that "New York City provides amazing possibilities. I love to explore Central Park and the Village. Also, the museums are great." The school sits on the south end of the Lincoln Center complex, home to the New York City Opera and the Metropolitan Opera. Nearby Columbus Avenue provides high-end shopping and many restaurants, some of which, pricewise, are very reasonable.

### Student Body

Fordham students "are smart, but they also like to party. Because of the balance most students have, there is a relatively calm atmosphere on campus. Not too much partying, yet not too much stressing over the next exam or paper." Those who choose Fordham "want both a campus community and an independent city life. We all come together for big events, but there can be lulls where nothing seems to be going on." Students are "warm and friendly, but too apathetic" for some, as politics is not a preoccupation of most students here. The student body is "representative of the surrounding population, i.e. Long Island, northern Jersey, and Connecticut." Writes one student, "I feel like the entire population of Long Island goes to school here at times. It's hard to find someone who isn't from New York."

FINANCIAL AID: 718-817-3800 • E-MAIL: ENROLL@FORDHAM.EDU • WEBSITE: WWW.FORDHAM.EDU

## ADMISSIONS

*Very important* academic and nonacademic factors considered by the admissions committee include secondary school record and standardized test scores. *Important* factors considered include character/personal qualities, class rank, recommendations, and talent/ability. *Other* factors considered include alumni/ae relation, essays, extracurricular activities, interview, minority status, volunteer work, and work experience. Factors *not* considered include geography, religious affiliation/commitment, and state residency. SAT I or ACT required; SAT II recommended. TOEFL required of all international applicants. High school diploma is required and GED is accepted. *High school units required/recommended:* 16 total required; 18 total recommended; 4 English required, 3 math required, 4 math recommended, 2 science required, 3 science recommended, 2 science lab required, 3 foreign language required, 4 social studies required. *The admissions office says:* "Interviews and tours are recommended for all applicants." The school catalog states that the admissions committee looks for "personal characteristics such as strength of character, intellectual and extracurricular interests, special talents, and potential for growing and developing within the environment and academic programs offered."

### The Inside Word

Candidates are reviewed by a committee made up of admissions officers, faculty, administrators, and deans. Admission to Fordham isn't as competitive as it once was, but a solid flow of applicants from metropolitan-area Catholic schools keeps their student profile sound.

## FINANCIAL AID

*Students should submit:* FAFSA, CSS/Financial Aid PROFILE, state aid form, noncustodial (divorced/separated) parent's statement, and business/farm supplement. The Princeton Review suggests that all financial aid forms be submitted as soon as possible after January 1. *Need-based scholarships/grants offered:* Pell, SEOG, state scholarships/grants, and the school's own gift aid. *Loan aid offered:* FFEL Subsidized Stafford, FFEL Unsubsidized Stafford, FFEL PLUS, and Federal Perkins. Institutional employment available. Applicants will be notified of awards on or about April 1. Off-campus job opportunities are excellent.

## FROM THE ADMISSIONS OFFICE

"Fordham, an independent institution offering an education based on the Jesuit tradition, has two major campuses in New York City. The Rose Hill campus is a beautiful 85-acre campus located next to the New York Botanical Garden and the Bronx Zoo. The Rose Hill campus is the largest 'green' campus in New York. The Lincoln Center campus, with a new 20-story residence hall, is located in the middle of Manhattan across from one of the world's greatest cultural centers, Lincoln Center for the Performing Arts. Fordham offers its students a variety of majors, concentrations, and programs that can be combined with an extensive internship program. Fordham works with more than 2,000 organizations in the New York metropolitan area to arrange internships for students in fields such as business, communications, medicine, law, and education."

## ADMISSIONS

| | |
|---|---|
| Admissions Rating | 82 |
| # of applicants | 8,979 |
| % of applicants accepted | 63 |
| % of acceptees attending | 30 |
| # accepting a place on wait list | 205 |
| % admitted from wait list | 40 |
| # of early decision applicants | 143 |
| % accepted early decision | 45 |

### FRESHMAN PROFILE

| | |
|---|---|
| Range SAT Verbal | 530-630 |
| Average SAT Verbal | 596 |
| Range SAT Math | 520-620 |
| Average SAT Math | 574 |
| Range ACT Composite | 22-27 |
| Average ACT Composite | 25 |
| Minimum TOEFL | 550 |
| Average HS GPA | 3.6 |
| % graduated top 10% of class | 27 |
| % graduated top 25% of class | 63 |
| % graduated top 50% of class | 92 |

### DEADLINES

| | |
|---|---|
| Early decision | 11/1 |
| Early decision notification | 12/15 |
| Regular admission | 2/1 |
| Regular notification | 4/1 |
| Nonfall registration? | yes |

### APPLICANTS ALSO LOOK AT

**AND OFTEN PREFER**
NYU
Binghamton U.
Columbia
Boston U.
Villanova

**AND SOMETIMES PREFER**
SUNY Albany
SUNY Stony Brook
George Washington
Boston Coll., Siena

**AND RARELY PREFER**
St. John's U. (NY)
Iona, Hofstra

### FINANCIAL FACTS

| | |
|---|---|
| Financial Aid Rating | 79 |
| Tuition | $20,200 |
| Room & board | $8,310 |
| Books and supplies | $640 |
| Required fees | $460 |
| % frosh receiving aid | 73 |
| % undergrads receiving aid | 73 |

# FRANKLIN & MARSHALL COLLEGE

PO Box 3003, Lancaster, PA 17604-3003 • Admissions: 717-291-3953 • Fax: 717-291-4381

## CAMPUS LIFE

**Quality of Life Rating** 80
Type of school private
Affiliation none
Environment suburban

### STUDENTS
Total undergrad enrollment 1,891
% male/female 50/50
% from out of state 57
% from public high school 57
% live on campus 67
% African American 3
% Asian 4
% Caucasian 90
% Hispanic 3
% international 8
# of countries represented 60

### SURVEY SAYS . . .
*Popular college radio*
*Frats and sororities dominate social scene*
*Campus easy to get around*
*Profs teach upper-levels*
*Classes are small*
*Students are cliquish*
*Students don't like Lancaster, PA*
*Lousy food on campus*
*Very little drug use*
*Student publications are ignored*

## ACACADEMICS

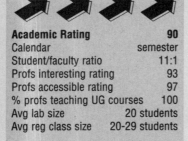

**Academic Rating** 90
Calendar semester
Student/faculty ratio 11:1
Profs interesting rating 93
Profs accessible rating 97
% profs teaching UG courses 100
Avg lab size 20 students
Avg reg class size 20-29 students

### MOST POPULAR MAJORS
government
business admin.—management
biology

## STUDENTS SPEAK OUT

### Academics

Academics at Franklin & Marshall are no joke. One student sighs, "Rigorous, man, rigorous." While many students respond with comments about the demanding workload, most of them in the same breath are praising the efforts of the professors, deans, and the administration for providing them with a cool environment. As one student puts it, "I have had a rich academic experience, and I don't think F & M gets a good enough reputation for the demanding workload of the courses." Another student offers, "My professors are very knowledgeable. They really know what they are talking about—more importantly, they are my friends." A good number of students share anecdotes about professors waking up in the middle of the night to answer a question, hosting laid-back potluck dinners, or attending intramural sporting events. At F & M the majority of the students also feel good about the administration. One student insists, "This is the real reason to come to Franklin & Marshall: the approachability of administration." Another agrees, "The deans and administration are awesome!" So it's not too hard to see why so many students put up with the demands at Franklin & Marshall; most of them feel like they've got a good support group behind them. And with F & M's solid reputation, many students feel like they are bound to succeed after graduation. As one student points out, "Not a liberal arts college, really, but a pre-professional school."

### Life

Greek life is the center of student life at Franklin & Marshall, even though the administration has withdrawn official recognition. Many respondents praise the social scene, while others are less positive. A senior student majoring in psychology admits, "One of the big problems is frat life. It totally consumes the school. Those interested in doing something else will have to search to find it. This is not necessarily bad, just limiting." Another student takes a stronger view: "Life here without fraternities would suck unless you like chilling with the Amish." Still, at least some find other things to do at F & M: "There are the frats, but activist groups (gay rights, human rights, etc.) are gaining in prominence." A junior geology major agrees: "There are so many campus clubs that I wish I had more time to do everything I am interested in." Lancaster receives only passing marks as a college town, but many students pick out the restaurants as a particular bonus: "Lancaster has an excellent variety of restaurants."

### Student Body

Over three-quarters of the students are white, with Asian students being the largest percentage of the minority population. A number of happy students had lots of glowing comments: "supportive," "caring," "friendly." There were some students who remarked about the diversity of the campus ("students from over 40 countries!"), but many more criticize the "cloning" at Franklin & Marshall. One student jokes, "The J.Crew catalog basically sums up the students at F & M." Politically, the school is conservative. According to one student, "The school finds new ways to display its conservatism every day. They all need to lighten up and get the sticks out of their 'beep.'"

FINANCIAL AID: 717-291-3991 • E-MAIL: ADMISSION@FANDM.EDU • WEBSITE: WWW.FANDM.EDU

## ADMISSIONS

*Very important* academic and nonacademic factors considered by the admissions committee include character/personal qualities, class rank, secondary school record, essays, and standardized test scores. *Important* factors considered include alumni/ae relation, essays, extracurricular activities, recommendations, talent/ability, and volunteer work. *Other* factors considered include minority status, religious affiliation/commitment, and work experience. Factors *not* considered include geography, interview, and state residency. TOEFL required of all international applicants. High school diploma is required and GED is accepted. *High school units required/recommended:* 16 total required; 4 English recommended, 4 math recommended, 4 science recommended, 3 science lab recommended, 2 foreign language recommended, 3 social studies recommended. *The admissions office says:* "Graded writing samples are accepted in place of standardized tests from students in the top 10 percent of their high school classes."

### The Inside Word

Applicants who are serious about attending the college should definitely interview; it will also help to make it known that F & M is one of your top choices. The college loses a lot of its admits to competitor colleges and will take notice of a candidate who is likely to enroll.

## FINANCIAL AID

*Students should submit:* FAFSA, CSS/Financial Aid PROFILE, and state aid form. Regular filing deadline is February 1. The Princeton Review suggests that all financial aid forms be submitted as soon as possible after January 1. *Need-based scholarships/grants offered:* Pell, SEOG, state scholarships/grants, private scholarships, and the school's own gift aid. *Loan aid offered:* FFEL Subsidized Stafford, FFEL Unsubsidized Stafford, FFEL PLUS, and Federal Perkins. Institutional employment available. Applicants will be notified of awards on or about April 1. Off-campus job opportunities are excellent.

## FROM THE ADMISSIONS OFFICE

"Franklin & Marshall students choose from a variety of fields of study, traditional and interdisciplinary, that typify liberal learning. Professors in all of these fields are committed to a common purpose, which is to teach students to think, speak, and write with clarity and confidence. Whether the course is in theater or in physics, the class will be small, engagement will be high, and discussion will dominate over lecture. Thus throughout his or her four years, beginning with the First Year Seminar, a student at Franklin & Marshall is repeatedly invited to active participation in intellectual play at a high level. Our graduates consistently testify to the high quality of an F & M education as a mental preparation for life."

## ADMISSIONS

| | |
|---|---:|
| Admissions Rating | 86 |
| # of applicants | 3,534 |
| % of applicants accepted | 56 |
| % of acceptees attending | 26 |
| # accepting a place on wait list | 297 |
| % admitted from wait list | 26 |
| # of early decision applicants | 316 |
| % accepted early decision | 57 |

### FRESHMAN PROFILE

| | |
|---|---:|
| Range SAT Verbal | 580-670 |
| Average SAT Verbal | 627 |
| Range SAT Math | 590-680 |
| Average SAT Math | 638 |
| Minimum TOEFL | 600 |
| % graduated top 10% of class | 56 |
| % graduated top 50% of class | 97 |

### DEADLINES

| | |
|---|---:|
| Early decision 1 | 11/15 |
| Early decision 1 notification | 12/15 |
| Early decision 2 | 1/15 |
| Early decision 2 notification | 2/15 |
| Regular admission | 2/1 |
| Regular notification | 4/1 |
| Nonfall registration? | yes |

### APPLICANTS ALSO LOOK AT

**AND OFTEN PREFER**
U. Penn
Hamilton
Cornell U.
Haverford, Lafayette
**AND SOMETIMES PREFER**
Lehigh
Bucknell
Dickinson
Colgate, Skidmore
**AND RARELY PREFER**
Gettysburg
Boston U., Tufts

## FINANCIAL FACTS

| | |
|---|---:|
| Financial Aid Rating | 77 |
| Tuition | $26,060 |
| Room & board | $6,300 |
| Books and supplies | $700 |
| Required fees | $50 |
| % frosh receiving aid | 49 |
| % undergrads receiving aid | 50 |
| Avg frosh grant | $13,704 |
| Avg frosh loan | $2,664 |

# FURMAN UNIVERSITY

OFFICE OF ADMISSIONS, 3300 POINSETT HIGHWAY, GREENVILLE, SC 29613 • ADMISSIONS: 864-294-2034 • FAX: 864-294-3127

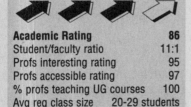
## STUDENTS SPEAK OUT

### Academics

"Furman is the best secret in the nation," writes a sophomore at this conservative, traditional liberal arts school located near the mountains in "beautiful" Greenville, South Carolina. Associated with the South Carolina Baptist Convention until 1992, Furman retains some of its religious feel even though, as students readily point out, the school is "only 25 percent Baptist." Furman's special brand of "engaged learning" as well as its small size (under 3,000) makes for "rigorous classes and good teachers." During their first two years, students fulfill their general education requirements in humanities, social sciences, natural sciences, math, foreign language, health and exercise science, and nonwestern studies before moving on to complete their major. Music, biology, chemistry, business administration, health and exercise science, and political science are among the most popular. It's a "well-balanced and strong" curriculum that yields a "well-balanced individual," notes a senior. Professors are "generally the best part of Furman" since they're "almost always well prepared and challenging." And while "a school whose professors are more liberal than their students is odd, surely, there's a general camaraderie because we—students and teachers—feel in league together against the administration," which is "more in touch with the dead (and Furman's rich Baptist alumni) than with current students." Still, "this campus is not as conservative as people may think," according to a feisty sophomore. "There are protests and demonstrations. . . . Some of my professors influence controversy. We actually discuss issues that affect the world."

### Life

"Life at Furman is definitely privileged," writes a junior; with its "beautiful campus close to mountains and beach, amazing students, great facilities, wonderful education, and solid combination of Greeks, independents, and great student activities," who could ask for more? Not many. Furman students seem, on the whole, genuinely happy with their college experience, noting that "people at Furman are incredibly supportive. Because academics are so strenuous and students are very involved after class, people are busy but willing to be available." One senior admits that "life at Furman is like a Brady Bunch episode; everyone is smiling and friendly, and the problems are solved at the end of each episode." Chalk it up to the "Furman Bubble," says a junior, who wishes that "campus was not so far away from downtown Greenville," with its many restaurants, bars, and small-city cultural scene. Party-wise, Furman is officially a dry campus, though a senior jokes that this is "because all the bottles you see are empty." (It's "damp" rather than dry, argues a second-year. "Administrators just look the other way.") And while the larger-than-average religious population does make for something of a schizophrenic social situation, a senior declares, "Fun is either praise songs or pounding beers. . . . There is no middle ground."

### Student Body

A sophomore sums up: At FU, "regardless of race, ethnicity, and status, everyone gets along." While most students would agree with this assessment, there's also the sense that tolerance and true diversity of opinion often take a backseat to good old-fashioned southern gentility. "Everyone's friendly . . . especially when they want you to go to church," says one we surveyed. Another adds, "Students at Furman are generally friendly and intelligent; however, the lack of diversity and overwhelming presence of Betty BMW and Johnny SUV is a little disconcerting." Still, "we're not all Christians who sit around and pray together," argues a senior, calling Furman's reputation for ultraconservatism "a big misconception."

FINANCIAL AID: 864-294-2204 • E-MAIL: ADMISSIONS@FURMAN.EDU • WEBSITE: WWW.FURMAN.EDU

## ADMISSIONS

*Very important* academic and nonacademic factors considered by the admissions committee include secondary school record. *Important* factors considered include character/personal qualities, essays, extracurricular activities, recommendations, standardized test scores, and talent/ability. *Other* factors considered include alumni/ae relation, class rank, geography, interview, minority status, religious affiliation/commitment, volunteer work, and work experience. Factors *not* considered include state residency. SAT I or ACT required. TOEFL required of all international applicants. High school diploma is required and GED is accepted. *High school units required/recommended:* 20 total recommended; 4 English recommended, 4 math recommended, 3 science recommended, 3 foreign language recommended, 3 social studies recommended. *The admissions office says:* "While our Early Decision process is not binding by application, it does require a response date of January 15."

### The Inside Word

While Furman is selective academically, a high level of self-selection on the part of its applicants. Good students who truly want to be here will encounter little resistance from the admissions committee.

## FINANCIAL AID

*Students should submit:* FAFSA and institution's own financial aid form. The Princeton Review suggests that all financial aid forms be submitted as soon as possible after January 1. *Need-based scholarships/grants offered:* Pell, SEOG, state scholarships/grants, private scholarships, and the school's own gift aid. *Loan aid offered:* FFEL Subsidized Stafford, FFEL Unsubsidized Stafford, FFEL PLUS, Federal Perkins, college/university loans from institutional funds, alternative loans, and TERI loans. Institutional employment available. Federal Work-Study Program available. Applicants will be notified of awards on or about March 15. Off-campus job opportunities are excellent.

## FROM THE ADMISSIONS OFFICE

"Furman University offers an excellent liberal arts education and quality of life. Outside the classroom, the university places a high value on community service. Furman is regularly recognized as one of the nation's top educational values."

## ADMISSIONS

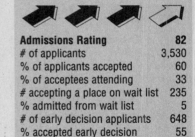

| | |
|---|---|
| Admissions Rating | 82 |
| # of applicants | 3,530 |
| % of applicants accepted | 60 |
| % of acceptees attending | 33 |
| # accepting a place on wait list | 235 |
| % admitted from wait list | 5 |
| # of early decision applicants | 648 |
| % accepted early decision | 55 |

### FRESHMAN PROFILE

| | |
|---|---|
| Range SAT Verbal | 580-680 |
| Range SAT Math | 580-670 |
| Range ACT Composite | 25-29 |
| Minimum TOEFL | 570 |
| Average HS GPA | 3.5 |
| % graduated top 10% of class | 61 |
| % graduated top 25% of class | 87 |
| % graduated top 50% of class | 99 |

### DEADLINES

| | |
|---|---|
| Early decision | 11/15 |
| Early decision notification | 12/15 |
| Regular admission | 1/15 |
| Regular notification | 3/15 |

### APPLICANTS ALSO LOOK AT

**AND OFTEN PREFER**
Wake Forest
Duke
UNC—Chapel Hill
Washington and Lee
Vanderbilt

**AND SOMETIMES PREFER**
Emory
Davidson
U. South Carolina—Columbia
Georgia Tech.
Wofford

**AND RARELY PREFER**
Clemson
Auburn U.

### FINANCIAL FACTS

| | |
|---|---|
| Financial Aid Rating | 75 |
| Tuition | $19,680 |
| Room & board | $5,416 |
| Books and supplies | $650 |
| Required fees | $396 |
| % frosh receiving aid | 45 |
| % undergrads receiving aid | 49 |
| Avg frosh grant | $13,496 |
| Avg frosh loan | $3,110 |

# GEORGE MASON UNIVERSITY

UNDERGRADUATE ADMISSIONS OFFICE, 4400 UNIV. DRIVE MSN 3A4, FAIRFAX, VA 22030-4444 • ADMISSIONS: 703-993-2400

## CAMPUS LIFE

| | |
|---|---|
| **Quality of Life Rating** | **75** |
| Type of school | public |
| Affiliation | none |
| Environment | suburban |

### STUDENTS

| | |
|---|---|
| Total undergrad enrollment | 15,185 |
| % male/female | 44/56 |
| % from out of state | 9 |
| % live on campus | 19 |
| % in (# of) fraternities | 3 (18) |
| % in (# of) sororities | 3 (7) |
| % African American | 10 |
| % Asian | 16 |
| % Caucasian | 66 |
| % Hispanic | 8 |
| % international | 4 |

### SURVEY SAYS . . .
Theater is hot
(Almost) everyone smokes
Popular college radio
Musical organizations aren't popular
Students love Fairfax, VA
Ethnic diversity on campus
Large classes
Intercollegiate sports unpopular or
nonexistent
Campus difficult to get around

## ACADEMICS

| | |
|---|---|
| **Academic Rating** | **78** |
| Calendar | semester |
| Student/faculty ratio | 16:1 |
| Profs interesting rating | 88 |
| Profs accessible rating | 88 |
| % profs teaching UG courses | 82 |
| % classes taught by TAs | 18 |
| Avg lab size | 10-19 students |
| Avg reg class size | 10-19 students |

### MOST POPULAR MAJORS
psychology
computer science
communications

## STUDENTS SPEAK OUT
### Academics

George Mason undergrads know that they have a good thing going; they just wish the rest of the world would catch on. As one student puts it, "GMU may not get as much recognition as other Virginia state schools, but if students took the time to look at how well renowned many of our professors are, they would see a multitude of opportunities." Says another, "The academic atmosphere at GMU generally gets a bad reputation. Yet my classes are challenging, my professors are very knowledgeable of their subjects, and my workload is just about right." At state university prices, GMU is a great bargain for Virginia residents, providing "an easygoing and helpful atmosphere and a spirit of innovation." An extremely heterogeneous student body, in terms of economic background, race, and nationality, means that "classes here are made interesting by the wide variety of ethnicity, age, and origin of students." Professors, when compared with teachers at other schools, receive average marks for teaching ability and accessibility. While many students voice the opinion that "like most schools we have some good and some bad professors," others note that "if you are an enthusiastic student who makes even the slightest effort to get to know your professors, they will instantly reward you with special attention and help with internships and career plans." An honors program affords enrollees "even more interesting classes and small class size." For the motivated self-starter at GMU, "the sky's the limit. This school has lots of potential in many areas."

### Life

With a relatively small portion of the student body living on campus, "GMU is largely a commuter school. There are very few people on campus on weekends. Consequently, student activities are only available Monday through Thursday." One resident explains, "The fact that this is a huge commuter school made it somewhat hard at first, but with Washington, D.C., so close, and Baltimore right up the road, there are many options for a social life. Also, this area is so rich in new jobs that going to school here gives you such a jump on finding a job right out of school." D.C. draws kudos from most students, both for the career opportunities it presents and its hopping night life. "Easy access by Metro and Cue Bus to the city" provides "alternative means of transportation, allowing those of us without cars to enjoy Washington." Although on-campus weekend activities are "neither as organized or as frequent" as students would like, "they certainly are increasing" at this "young university." GMU was founded in 1957 as a branch of UVA, and was granted its independence in 1972. On the plus side, students report that "the school itself is extremely aesthetically pleasing" and that "the new Aquatics Center (a swimming and fitness facility) is amazing."

### Student Body

GMU undergrads are justly proud of their "incredibly diverse" student body. Writes one, "The people here changed my outlook on life. The students are incredibly diverse ethnically and ideologically, but very open-minded, friendly, and positive. The high number of nontraditional students makes GMU feel like part of the real world, not a disengaged campus of 18- to 22-year-olds." Another offers a slight caveat: "I really enjoy the social and ethnic diversity at my university, but I feel like there could be less segregation. Students of different groups interact well in the classroom setting, but socially some groups are rather exclusive."

Fax: 703-993-2392 • Financial Aid: 703-993-2353 • E-mail: ADMISSIONS@GMU.EDU • Website: WWW.GMU.EDU

## ADMISSIONS

*Very important* academic and nonacademic factors considered by the admissions committee include secondary school record. *Important* factors considered include character/personal qualities, class rank, essays, extracurricular activities, recommendations, standardized test scores, talent/ability, volunteer work, and work experience. *Other* factors considered include alumni/ae relation, geography, interview, and state residency. Factors *not* considered include religious affiliation/commitment. SAT I or ACT required. TOEFL required of all international applicants. High school diploma is required and GED is accepted. *High school units required/recommended:* 18 total required; 4 English required, 3 math required, 4 math recommended, 2 science required, 2 science lab required, 2 foreign language required, 3 foreign language recommended, 2 social studies required, 3 social studies recommended, 1 history required, 2 elective required. *The admissions office says:* "We have a strong matriculation agreement with Northern Virginia Community College. Students denied admission are encouraged to contact an admissions officer to discuss plans for future enrollment possibilities at Mason."

### The Inside Word

George Mason is a popular destination for college for two key reasons: its proximity to Washington, D.C., and the fact that it is not nearly as difficult to gain admission at Mason as it is at UVA or William and Mary, the two flagships of the Virginia state system. The university's quality faculty and impressive facilities make it worth taking a look if low-cost, solid programs in the D.C. area are high on your list.

## FINANCIAL AID

*Students should submit:* FAFSA. Priority filing deadline is March 1. The Princeton Review suggests that all financial aid forms be submitted as soon as possible after January 1. *Loan aid offered:* Direct Subsidized Stafford, Direct Unsubsidized Stafford, Direct PLUS, Federal Perkins, state, and college/university loans from institutional funds. Institutional employment available. Federal Work-Study Program available. Applicants will be notified of awards on a rolling basis beginning on or about April 1. Off-campus job opportunities are excellent.

## FROM THE ADMISSIONS OFFICE

"Great minds don't think alike, and at George Mason University, we don't expect them to. From creative writing to systems engineering, Mason programs offer cutting-edge curricula and facilities along with the best that technology has to offer. Our visionary outlook has attracted a faculty of renowned scholars and teachers, while our business and community partnerships provide students with practical experience and career opportunities."

## ADMISSIONS

| Admissions Rating | 82 |
|---|---|
| # of applicants | 7,406 |
| % of applicants accepted | 61 |
| % of acceptees attending | 48 |
| # accepting a place on wait list | 233 |
| % admitted from wait list | 41 |

### FRESHMAN PROFILE

| | |
|---|---|
| Range SAT Verbal | 480-590 |
| Average SAT Verbal | 534 |
| Range SAT Math | 490-590 |
| Average SAT Math | 532 |
| Range ACT Composite | 19-24 |
| Minimum TOEFL | 570 |
| Average HS GPA | 3.2 |

### DEADLINES

| | |
|---|---|
| Regular admission | 2/1 |
| Regular notification | 4/1 |
| Nonfall registration? | yes |

### APPLICANTS ALSO LOOK AT AND OFTEN PREFER

U. Virginia
Georgetown U.
William and Mary
James Madison
Virginia Tech

### AND SOMETIMES PREFER

George Washington

## FINANCIAL FACTS

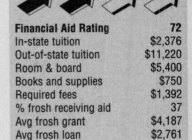

| Financial Aid Rating | 72 |
|---|---|
| In-state tuition | $2,376 |
| Out-of-state tuition | $11,220 |
| Room & board | $5,400 |
| Books and supplies | $750 |
| Required fees | $1,392 |
| % frosh receiving aid | 37 |
| Avg frosh grant | $4,187 |
| Avg frosh loan | $2,761 |

# GEORGE WASHINGTON UNIVERSITY

2121 I STREET NW, SUITE 201, WASHINGTON, DC 20052 • ADMISSIONS: 202-994-6040 • FAX: 202-994-0325

## CAMPUS LIFE

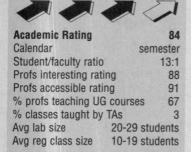

| Quality of Life Rating | **89** |
|---|---|
| Type of school | private |
| Affiliation | Roman Catholic |
| Environment | urban |

### STUDENTS

| | |
|---|---|
| Total undergrad enrollment | 6,418 |
| % male/female | 46/54 |
| % from out of state | 99 |
| % from public high school | 42 |
| % live on campus | 67 |
| % African American | 6 |
| % Asian | 10 |
| % Caucasian | 75 |
| % Hispanic | 6 |
| % international | 6 |

### SURVEY SAYS . . .

Students love Washington, D.C.
Political activism is hot
Dorms are like palaces
Students don't get along with local community
High cost of living
Unattractive campus
Ethnic diversity on campus
Lots of long lines and red tape
Athletic facilities need improving
No one plays intramural sports

## ACADEMICS

| Academic Rating | **84** |
|---|---|
| Calendar | semester |
| Student/faculty ratio | 13:1 |
| Profs interesting rating | 88 |
| Profs accessible rating | 91 |
| % profs teaching UG courses | 67 |
| % classes taught by TAs | 3 |
| Avg lab size | 20-29 students |
| Avg reg class size | 10-19 students |

### MOST POPULAR MAJORS

international affairs
business administration
psychology

## STUDENTS SPEAK OUT

### Academics

Few schools exploit their location as fully as George Washington University, a school whose faculty and programs are deeply entrenched in the goings-on of Washington, D.C. "Being in D.C., GW takes advantage of the resources and personnel found here," notes one approving student. "Much of the faculty are experts in political science and criminal justice." Writes another, "It's all about location. Whatever teachers can't give you in the classroom, they send you out to get." A few caution that "GW's profs are part of D.C., not GW. That has benefits and drawbacks," but most agree that the pluses outweigh the minuses. Nearly one-quarter of the students here are engaged in international studies, and many others pursue such government-related majors as political science, political communication, and criminal justice. Other strong programs include biology, psychology, and English. Professors here "are what make or break the course. Some are excellent and some are horrible." Lecture courses, especially those at the intro level, "can be rather large," and some suggest that "there is never a need to attend large lecture classes. By attending only the discussion sections you gain all the information necessary for the course plus a couple of extra hours sleep." However, things improve with upper-level courses. GW's administration earns low marks, with students complaining that "there's a lot of administrative bureaucratic red tape to get through for certain things" and that "the administration tends not to listen to students until they raise a big public ruckus. Making appointments to meet with upper-level administrators can be very difficult." Students give props to the Honors Program and excellent marks to the library.

### Life

GW, like New York University and Boston University, lacks a traditional campus, instead occupying buildings scattered throughout an urban neighborhood. As at other such schools, the sense of community here is weak and the social scene is fragmented. Fortunately, D.C. picks up the slack, offering students some of the nation's finest museums and monuments, beautiful public spaces, limitless shopping, a thriving nightlife, and a boatload of internship and networking opportunities. "D.C. rocks!" writes one student. "There is so much to do here, you literally could do something different every night of the week. A lot of bars and clubs turn into GW parties, which is cool." Also, "we do a lot of shopping because Georgetown is so close," explains another. On-campus activity centers on "over 300 student organizations on campus, so whatever your lifestyle is, there should be a group for you." Students complain that, due to an increase in admissions, classrooms and dining halls are growing uncomfortably overcrowded. Greek life is slight but students feel it "could be an important and positive part of this school except for the administration's vendetta against it."

### Student Body

Students come to GW to be in the nation's capital, and accordingly "it's not a school for someone who isn't into politics. Everyone here is glued to CNN." On the political spectrum, "it's a very Democratic and liberal school," writes one student. "If you want to protest, this school's for you!" Students also tend to be reformed slackers. Explains one, "This school is for everyone who could have been accepted to an Ivy League school and could have afforded it, but never applied themselves to that extent." A huge international contingent contributes to "the diversity—ethnically, politically, geographically, and intellectually—that breeds so many wonderful relationships."

# GEORGE WASHINGTON UNIVERSITY

FINANCIAL AID: 202-994-6620 • E-MAIL: GWADM@GWIS2.CIRC.GWU.EDU • WEBSITE: WWW.GWU.EDU

## ADMISSIONS

*Very important* academic and nonacademic factors considered by the admissions committee include class rank, essays, secondary school record, and talent/ability. *Important* factors considered include character/personal qualities, extracurricular activities, recommendations, standardized test scores, volunteer work, and work experience. *Other* factors considered include interview. Factors *not* considered include alumni/ae relation, geography, minority status, religious affiliation/commitment, and state residency. SAT I or ACT required, SAT I preferred. TOEFL required of all international applicants. High school diploma is required and GED is not accepted. *High school units required/recommended:* 18 total required; 4 English required, 3 math required, 2 science required, 3 science recommended, 2 science lab required, 3 foreign language recommended, 1 social studies required, 1 history required, 3 elective required.

### The Inside Word

The low percentage of admitted students who enroll at GW works to keep the admit rate relatively high. For strong students, this is definitely a low-stress admissions process. The university's location and access to faculty with impressive credentials are the main reasons for GW's sound freshman profile.

## FINANCIAL AID

*Students should submit:* FAFSA and CSS/Financial Aid PROFILE. The Princeton Review suggests that all financial aid forms be submitted as soon as possible after January 1. *Need-based scholarships/grants offered:* Pell, SEOG, state scholarships/grants, and the school's own gift aid. *Loan aid offered:* FFEL Subsidized Stafford, FFEL Unsubsidized Stafford, FFEL PLUS, and Federal Perkins. Institutional employment available. Federal Work-Study Program available. Applicants will be notified of awards on or about March 20. Off-campus job opportunities are excellent.

## FROM THE ADMISSIONS OFFICE

"At GW, we welcome students who show a measure of impatience with the limitations of traditional education. At many universities, the edge of campus is the real world, but not at GW, where our campus and Washington, D.C., are seamless. We look for bold, bright students who are ambitious, energetic, and self-motivated. Here, where we are so close to the centers of thought and action in every field we offer, we easily integrate our outstanding academic tradition and faculty connections with the best internship and job opportunities of Washington, D.C. A generous scholarship and financial assistance program attracts top students from all parts of the country and the world."

## ADMISSIONS

| | |
|---|---|
| Admissions Rating | 89 |
| # of applicants | 14,767 |
| % of applicants accepted | 49 |
| % of acceptees attending | 29 |
| # of early decision applicants | 692 |
| % accepted early decision | 62 |

### FRESHMAN PROFILE

| | |
|---|---|
| Range SAT Verbal | 570-660 |
| Average SAT Verbal | 620 |
| Range SAT Math | 580-660 |
| Average SAT Math | 620 |
| Range ACT Composite | 24-28 |
| Average ACT Composite | 26 |
| Minimum TOEFL | 550 |
| % graduated top 10% of class | 45 |
| % graduated top 25% of class | 85 |
| % graduated top 50% of class | 99 |

### DEADLINES

| | |
|---|---|
| Early decision | 12/1 |
| Early decision notification | 12/15 |
| Regular admission | 1/15 |
| Regular notification | 3/15 |
| Nonfall registration? | yes |

### APPLICANTS ALSO LOOK AT
### AND OFTEN PREFER
Georgetown U.
U. Virginia
Boston U.
Emory
NYU

### AND SOMETIMES PREFER
Tufts
U. Vermont
U. Maryland—Coll. Park
American
Catholic

### FINANCIAL FACTS

| | |
|---|---|
| Financial Aid Rating | 74 |
| Tuition | $23,396 |
| Room & board | $8,538 |
| Books and supplies | $850 |
| Required fees | $1,035 |
| % frosh receiving aid | 42 |
| % undergrads receiving aid | 41 |
| Avg frosh grant | $11,800 |
| Avg frosh loan | $3,000 |

# GEORGETOWN UNIVERSITY

37TH AND P STREETS, NW, WASHINGTON, DC 20057 • ADMISSIONS: 202-687-3600 • FAX: 202-687-5084

## CAMPUS LIFE

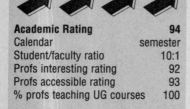

| Quality of Life Rating | 89 |
|---|---|
| Type of school | private |
| Affiliation | Roman Catholic |
| Environment | urban |

### STUDENTS

| | |
|---|---|
| Total undergrad enrollment | 6,418 |
| % male/female | 46/54 |
| % from out of state | 99 |
| % from public high school | 42 |
| % live on campus | 67 |
| % African American | 6 |
| % Asian | 9 |
| % Caucasian | 68 |
| % Hispanic | 5 |
| % international | 9 |

### SURVEY SAYS . . .

Students love Washington, D.C.
Political activism is hot
High cost of living
Great off-campus food
Lots of beer drinking
Student publications are popular
Computer facilities need improving
(Almost) no one listens to college radio
Lab facilities are great

## ACADEMICS

| Academic Rating | 94 |
|---|---|
| Calendar | semester |
| Student/faculty ratio | 10:1 |
| Profs interesting rating | 92 |
| Profs accessible rating | 93 |
| % profs teaching UG courses | 100 |

### MOST POPULAR MAJORS
English
finance
international politics

## STUDENTS SPEAK OUT

### Academics

Georgetown University is the leader among the nation's 28 Jesuit colleges and universities. Undergrads study within four self-contained schools: Arts and Sciences, Business Administration, Nursing, and the School of Foreign Service ("known worldwide"). No matter which of the schools you're in, get ready to hit the books ("We enjoy studying!"), because "Georgetown students work hard." Every student is required to take core requirements, including courses in the liberal arts and religious studies. "Georgetown is the best of a small school's atmosphere and a large school's opportunities (big-name professors and reputation)." The profs do indeed receive high grades from the students. One first-year student writes, "I am impressed by every teacher." Another adds, "It's nice to go to a school where professors are always being consulted by the media and politicians." She follows with a warning about celebrity faculty: "It is a rare occurrence to actually get [those] professors for a class." The few gripes the student body has about Georgetown are best put into perspective by one student's comment that "I couldn't be happier anywhere else, but I could be happier here." The bursar receives poor reviews; as one student told us, "The overall university administration is very bureaucratic and not student-friendly." "Classes should be easier for underclassmen to get into." But some students point out other positive aspects of the administration. "The deans are extremely accessible." Another big plus is abundant "internship opportunities, etc." to be found in the nation's capital. "More on-campus housing" would make many students happier. So would a more significant "commitment to the arts."

### Life

"Location, location, location." Georgetown's Washington, D.C., location "really makes the experience. There is no excuse to ever say 'there's nothing to do.'" "Students work hard, but always can make time to go out and have a great time." "Georgetown's social life is one of the best in the nation." The university "offers a diverse atmosphere that gives people a chance to do things—from museums and theater to sessions of Congress." All federal museums, most notably the many facilities that comprise the Smithsonian Institution, have no admission charge—your tax dollars at work. But bring your cash card, because much of the rest of the fun in D.C. doesn't come cheap. One student responds, "Everything here costs something—the school will drain you for all you are worth." There's a "big bar scene [and the university's] sizable Euro population frequents D.C. clubs." "The Jesuits have banned frats," but you can always find "lots of parties on the weekends, most of which feature kegs." For some students there's "a little too much beer and basketball," though the legendary John Thompson has departed the scene and Georgetown's once omnipotent Hoyas are no longer dominant in the Big East. Intramural sports are also very popular, as are campus clubs.

### Student Body

Take it from a senior who should know: "Georgetown is great, if you don't mind dealing with a bunch of kids who think they're future presidents of the U.S. But then you think, 'what the hell, maybe they are!'" Georgetown students tend to be very serious about their academics, and there's "a very goal-oriented, pre-professional attitude that is pervasive." Most place a high priority on landing a job once they are finished with college. While that's not necessarily uncommon as we approach the next millenium, it can make it hard to associate on a more down-to-earth level. As one sophomore points out: "I find it difficult to get anyone to participate in something that isn't going to enhance a resume." As far as diversity goes, there are many foreign nationals, and minority groups, though small, are not invisible. Although "everyone gets along well—different ethnic groups do not intermingle in social circles."

FINANCIAL AID: 202-687-4547 • WEBSITE: WWW.GEORGETOWN.EDU

## ADMISSIONS

*Very important* academic and nonacademic factors considered by the admissions committee include class rank and essays. *Important* factors considered include secondary school record and standardized test scores. *Other* factors considered include alumni/ae relation, character/personal qualities, extracurricular activities, interview, recommendations, talent/ability, volunteer work, and work experience. Factors *not* considered include geography, minority status, religious affiliation/commitment, and state residency. SAT I or ACT required, SAT I preferred; SAT II also recommended. TOEFL required of all international applicants. High school diploma is required and GED is accepted. *High school units required/recommended:* 16 total required; 3 English required, 4 English recommended, 3 math required, 4 math recommended, 1 science required, 1 science lab required, 2 science lab recommended, 2 foreign language recommended, 2 social studies required, 3 social studies recommended, 2 history recommended. *The admissions office says:* "Students who plan a program in mathematics or science should include four years of math and at least three years of science. Candidates for the nursing program [are recommended to include] one year of biology, one year of chemistry, and one year of physics."

### The Inside Word

It was always tough to get admitted to Georgetown, but in the early 1980s Patrick Ewing and the Hoyas created a basketball sensation that catapulted the place into position as one of the most selective universities in the nation. There has been no turning back since. GU gets almost 10 applications for every space in the entering class, and the academic strength of the pool is impressive. Virtually 50 percent of the entire student body took AP courses in high school. Candidates who are waitlisted here should hold little hope for an offer of admission; over the past several years Georgetown has taken very few off their lists.

## FINANCIAL AID

*Students should submit:* FAFSA, CSS/Financial Aid PROFILE, noncustodial (divorced/separated) parent's statement, business/farm supplement, and most recent federal tax return and W-2 forms. The Princeton Review suggests that all financial aid forms be submitted as soon as possible after January 1. *Need-based scholarships/grants offered:* Pell, SEOG, state scholarships/grants, private scholarships, the school's own gift aid, and Federal Nursing. *Loan aid offered:* FFEL Subsidized Stafford, FFEL Unsubsidized Stafford, FFEL PLUS, Federal Perkins, and Federal Nursing. Institutional employment available. Federal Work-Study Program available. Applicants will be notified of awards on or about April 1. Off-campus job opportunities are excellent.

## FROM THE ADMISSIONS OFFICE

"Georgetown was founded in 1789 by John Carroll, who concurred with his contemporaries Benjamin Franklin and Thomas Jefferson in believing that the success of the young democracy depended upon an educated and virtuous citizenry. Carroll founded the school with the dynamic, Jesuit tradition of education, characterized by humanism and committed to the assumption of responsibility and action. Georgetown is a national and international university, enrolling students from all 50 states and over 100 foreign countries. Undergraduate students are enrolled in one of four undergraduate schools: the College of Arts and Sciences, School of Foreign Service, Georgetown School of Business, and Georgetown School of Nursing. All students share a common liberal arts core and have access to the entire university curriculum."

### ADMISSIONS

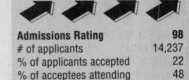

| Admissions Rating | 98 |
| --- | --- |
| # of applicants | 14,237 |
| % of applicants accepted | 22 |
| % of acceptees attending | 48 |

#### FRESHMAN PROFILE

| | |
| --- | --- |
| Range SAT Verbal | 640-720 |
| Range SAT Math | 640-730 |
| Range ACT Composite | 28-32 |
| Minimum TOEFL | 550 |
| % graduated top 10% of class | 78 |
| % graduated top 25% of class | 94 |
| % graduated top 50% of class | 98 |

#### DEADLINES

| | |
| --- | --- |
| Regular admission | 1/10 |
| Regular notification | 4/1 |

#### APPLICANTS ALSO LOOK AT

**AND OFTEN PREFER**
Duke
Harvard
U. Virginia
Yale
Stanford

**AND SOMETIMES PREFER**
U. Penn
U. Chicago
Cornell U.
Boston Coll.

**AND RARELY PREFER**
Syracuse
Tulane
Emory

### FINANCIAL FACTS

| Financial Aid Rating | 80 |
| --- | --- |
| Tuition | $23,952 |
| Room & board | $9,103 |
| Books and supplies | $900 |
| Required fees | $216 |
| % frosh receiving aid | 39 |
| % undergrads receiving aid | 41 |
| Avg frosh grant | $15,094 |
| Avg frosh loan | $2,625 |

# GEORGIA INSTITUTE OF TECHNOLOGY

225 NORTH AVENUE, ATLANTA, GA 30332-0320 • ADMISSIONS: 404-894-4154 • FAX: 404-894-9511

## CAMPUS LIFE

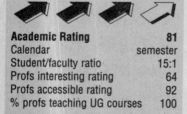

**Quality of Life Rating**    **87**
Type of school    public
Affiliation    none
Environment    urban

### STUDENTS
Total undergrad enrollment    10,745
% male/female    71/29
% from out of state    31
% from public high school    82
% live on campus    58
% in (# of) fraternities    29 (32)
% in (# of) sororities    20 (9)
% African American    8
% Asian    13
% Caucasian    71
% Hispanic    3
% international    5

### SURVEY SAYS . . .
Great computer facilities
Great off-campus food
Students love Atlanta, GA
Athletic facilities are great
Lab facilities are great
Ethnic diversity on campus
Unattractive campus
Library needs improving
Campus difficult to get around
Students aren't religious
Everyone loves the Yellow Jackets

## ACADEMICS

**Academic Rating**    **81**
Calendar    semester
Student/faculty ratio    15:1
Profs interesting rating    64
Profs accessible rating    92
% profs teaching UG courses    100

### MOST POPULAR MAJORS
computer science
mechanical engineering
management

## STUDENTS SPEAK OUT
### Academics

"It seems like every class has a website and no class has more than five girls" at the Georgia Institute of Technology, a "damn hard" public school that is always "very demanding" and "at times very humbling." "Make no mistake; unless you're Albert Einstein, Georgia Tech can be very intimidating," warns an aerospace engineering major. "This is a school that challenges any 'straight A' student a high school can spit out," and a historically low, but improving percentage of first-year students never graduate. The faculty here is generally "brilliant." "Every now and then you come across a professor who is monotonous or hard to understand" but, for the most part, "our professors are more than happy to help. Tech professors will do whatever they can to help you succeed." Georgia Tech also boasts "tons of research opportunities," traditionally strong relations with regional industry, and "fantastic cooperative education programs." The "student-focused" administration is "very approachable," and the top brass "cultivates as many opportunities as possible for students to succeed." However, bureaucracy reigns supreme here. In fact, there is so much "red tape" on campus that students have a special name for it: "the Tech Shaft." On the whole, though, Tech students are more or less happy with their lot in life. "They work you hard but I know for certain that I will be prepared for anything when I leave," concludes a chemical engineering major. "True, it is difficult, but who wants a degree that says, 'hey, look, I accomplished jack in four years'?"

### Life

Undergraduates on this urban, downtown campus "study excessively" but, overall, "Tech has an awesome mix of sports, social life, and academics" that "balances really well." Georgia Tech's location in the "vibrant" "party city" of Atlanta—a place where "it is extremely rare to be bored"—is a substantial perk. "There are lots of places to go off campus" to see movies, go to concerts, and eat (a plus because on-campus cuisine isn't so appealing). "Thrashers and Braves games" are also big draws and students frequent local clubs and bars. On campus, "people play on computers," "design Web pages," and indulge in hours of video gaming. If you get bored, the university sponsors more than 300 clubs and organizations. Sports are big as well (especially games against the hated University of Georgia) and there is "amazing school spirit" on campus. With almost one-fourth of all undergrads pledging, though, most on-campus life is "centered around" frat parties. Students tell us "there is a lot of drinking on the weekends." If you are a female, you'll love "The Ratio (3:1 guys to girls)," which guarantees women "their pick of events." Of course, guys here aren't too happy about "The Ratio." No one seems too happy about the parking situation, and though "the facilities are awesome," a lot of buildings are less than spectacular. The athletic facilities—"redone in 1996 for the Olympics"—are an exception.

### Students

"People who go to Tech start early on career planning." Luckily for them, graduates from this august university have tremendous opportunities "to work with major companies" and "make lots of money." The students here are "competitive," "motivated, organized, and willing to work hard." "Some of the people at Tech are a little shy and reserved." There is a notable contingent of "computer nerds that play Quake all day" and many students are "a little dorky." Then again, "it takes a little dorkiness to succeed in this high-tech world." As a general rule, "all students—Greek or non-Greek, computer science or management, blonde or brunette —have that engineering aura that screams: 'What do you mean you can't program in Java?'" Georgia Tech is "wonderfully diverse"; about 25 percent of the students here represent minorities. Everyone is "extremely friendly" and there is "surprisingly little friction" on campus. "Cliques form" mostly around various majors and the Greek system. "I think we're all too busy trying to survive and defeat the monster that is Tech to spend time disliking one another," speculates a first-year engineering student. "The fact that all Tech students have endured extremely difficult classes creates a certain bond."

# GEORGIA INSTITUTE OF TECHNOLOGY

FINANCIAL AID: 404-894-4160 • E-MAIL: ADMISSIONS@SUCCESS.GATECH.EDU • WEBSITE: WWW.GATECH.EDU

## ADMISSIONS

*Very important* academic and nonacademic factors considered by the admissions committee include secondary school record, standardized test scores, and essay. *Important* factors considered include extracurricular activities, talent/ability, volunteer work, and work experience. *Other* factors considered include alumni/ae relation, state residency, and character/personal qualities. Factors *not* considered include class rank, interview, geography, religious affiliation/commitment, and minority status. SAT I or ACT required, SAT I preferred. TOEFL required of all international applicants. High school diploma is required and GED is accepted. *High school units required/recommended:* 4 English required, 4 math required, 3 science required, 4 science recommended, 2 science lab required, 2 foreign language required, 4 foreign language recommended, 3 social sciences required, 4 additional academic courses required. *The admissions office says:* "Qualified Georgia residents and children/relatives of alumni receive extra consideration."

### The Inside Word

Tech has made significant changes in its admissions requirements over the past four years, which by their nature have resulted in a somewhat more personal and well-rounded approach to selecting the entering class. Still, candidates must have solid grades and test scores in order to be competitive.

## FINANCIAL AID

*Students should submit:* FAFSA and institution's own financial aid form. Regular filing deadline is March 1. The Princeton Review suggests that all financial aid forms be submitted as soon as possible after January 1. *Need-based scholarships/grants offered:* Pell, SEOG, state scholarships/grants, private scholarships, the school's own gift aid, and Georgia HOPE Scholarship. *Loan aid offered:* FFEL Subsidized Stafford, FFEL Unsubsidized Stafford, FFEL PLUS, Federal Perkins, and college/university loans from institutional funds. Institutional employment available. Federal Work-Study Program available. Applicants will be notified of awards on or about April 1. Off-campus job opportunities are excellent.

## FROM THE ADMISSIONS OFFICE

"Georgia Tech consistently ranks among the nation's leaders in engineering, computing, management, architecture, and the sciences while remaining one of the best college buys in the country. The 330-acre campus of red brick buildings and green rolling hills is nestled in the heart of the fun, dynamic, and progressive city of Atlanta in the shadows of a majestic skyline dominated by the work of Georgia Tech-trained architects and designers. During the past decade, over $400 million invested in campus improvements has yielded new state-of-the-art academic and research buildings, apartment-style housing, enhanced social and recreational facilities, and the most extensive fiber-optic cable system on any college campus. Georgia Tech's combined commitment to technologically focused hands-on educational experiences, teamwork, great teaching, innovation, leadership development, and community service make it unique. Great things are happening at Georgia Tech. We hope you will join us, become a part of our community, and help us create the future."

## ADMISSIONS

| | |
|---|---|
| Admissions Rating | 89 |
| # of applicants | 7,579 |
| % of applicants accepted | 69 |

### FRESHMAN PROFILE

| | |
|---|---|
| Range SAT Verbal | 590-690 |
| Average SAT Verbal | 642 |
| Range SAT Math | 630-725 |
| Average SAT Math | 687 |
| Minimum TOEFL | 600 |
| Average HS GPA | 3.8 |
| % graduated top 10% of class | 60 |
| % graduated top 25% of class | 87 |
| % graduated top 50% of class | 100 |

### DEADLINES

| | |
|---|---|
| Regular admission | 1/15 |
| Regular notification | 3/15 |
| Nonfall registration? | yes |

### APPLICANTS ALSO LOOK AT
**AND OFTEN PREFER**
UC—Berkeley
Duke
MIT
UNC—Chapel Hill
**AND SOMETIMES PREFER**
Florida State
U. Florida
U. Georgia
Clemson
**AND RARELY PREFER**
Carnegie Mellon
Auburn U.
Emory
Virginia Tech

### FINANCIAL FACTS

| | |
|---|---|
| Financial Aid Rating | 82 |
| In-state tuition | $2,506 |
| Out-of-state tuition | $10,024 |
| Room & board | $5,234 |
| Books and supplies | $1,278 |
| Required fees | $802 |
| % frosh receiving aid | 29 |
| % undergrads receiving aid | 32 |
| Avg frosh grant | $5,400 |
| Avg frosh loan | $2,800 |

# GETTYSBURG COLLEGE

ADMISSIONS OFFICE, EISENHOWER HOUSE, GETTYSBURG COLLEGE, GETTYSBURG, PA 17325-1484 • ADMISSIONS: 717-337-6100

## CAMPUS LIFE

| | |
|---|---|
| **Quality of Life Rating** | **84** |
| Type of school | private |
| Affiliation | Lutheran |
| Environment | suburban |

### STUDENTS

| | |
|---|---|
| Total undergrad enrollment | 2,218 |
| % male/female | 48/52 |
| % from out of state | 70 |
| % from public high school | 70 |
| % live on campus | 93 |
| % in (# of) fraternities | 46 (11) |
| % in (# of) sororities | 27 (4) |
| % African American | 2 |
| % Asian | 1 |
| % Caucasian | 96 |
| % Hispanic | 1 |
| % international | 2 |

### SURVEY SAYS . . .

*Great food on campus*
*Frats and sororities dominate social scene*
*Diversity lacking on campus*
*Beautiful campus*
*Campus easy to get around*
*Theater is unpopular*
*Low cost of living*

## ACADEMICS

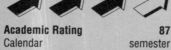

| | |
|---|---|
| **Academic Rating** | **87** |
| Calendar | semester |
| Student/faculty ratio | 11:1 |
| Profs interesting rating | 94 |
| Profs accessible rating | 97 |
| % profs teaching UG courses | 100 |
| Avg reg class size | 10-19 students |

### MOST POPULAR MAJORS
business administration/management
psychology
political science

## STUDENTS SPEAK OUT

### Academics

At Gettysburg, "academics are challenging and stimulating without being overbearingly stressful," a situation appreciated by most undergraduates. "The work is difficult," warns one student, "but with concentration, balance, and help from a great faculty, anyone can succeed." The small campus allows for plenty of personal attention. Writes one respondent, "At Gettysburg, I am pushed to do my best because professors will not let you slip through the cracks. We have to attend classes because they are so small. If you don't show up, you can expect a phone call." Faculty members earn high praise for being "friendly and acting as equals rather than authority figures" and for their helpfulness. They are "always willing to meet with students, [and] they offer help in obtaining internships and expose us to experiences outside the classroom." A "good advising system [that's] very personalized" helps students navigate curricular requirements, including a liberal arts core curriculum (really a set of distribution requirements covering the humanities, natural and social sciences, mathematics, foreign language, writing skills, and nonwestern civilization) geared toward introducing underclassmen to a broad spectrum of academics. Upperclassmen focus on their majors, among which history, political science, and the hard sciences are generally regarded as "top-notch." Students also applaud the computer facilities and the Honor Code, the latter "an undeniable part of campus. You're truly treated like an adult."

### Life

Greek life, most undergrads concede, holds center court at Gettysburg College. Warns one student, "The administration wants prospectives to think that Greek life isn't essential, but don't let them fool you. A lot of people end up unhappy when they are left out." Says another, "Gettysburg does offer a lot of activities; it's just that so many of them are geared toward the Greek system. There's something for most people, but a lot of times the good events aren't publicized." Drinking, not surprisingly, is big here. Writes one student, "Beer is life. Even if you don't know what Natty Ice is before you get here, your fridge will be stocked by the second week." There are other options, among them intramural sports, community service, and events organized by the Student Activities Council and the Student Senate, but many still see the 'Burg as a one-horse town. As one student puts it, "Good luck if you aren't in Greek life. The frat doormen look you up and down and decide whether you are 'good enough' to enter their frat. If you are a girl in a skirt you can get in. If you're a guy, bring a girl in a skirt." Students speak highly of the Center for Public Service, which provides opportunities for "tutoring, clean-ups, and service-related trips all over the world." The campus is "beautiful and comfortable," and the food is "among the school's greatest strengths." Students give the "lame" town of Gettysburg a thumb's-down: "It's isolated, and there are no buses to other towns," gripes one. Students list a local diner, Wal-Mart, an outlet mall, and the tour of the famous local battlefield as the best off-campus attractions.

### Student Body

Gettysburg undergrads are "very homogeneous, mostly upper- and middle-class white students." However, "although there is diversity lacking," reports one student, "the college has been doing better in recent years to change that." Politically, "many kids are very conservative. You have to search for liberals." The same goes for intellectuals; while kids here are bright, they are not bookish. Points out one frustrated egghead, "The classic term for girls here is 'eye candy,' and it goes for a lot of the guys too. They're fun to look at but don't talk about anything past next Friday night. My solution is to travel a lot and keep in touch with friends from home."

FAX: 717-337-6145 • FINANCIAL AID: 717-337-6611 • E-MAIL: ADMISS@GETTYSBURG.EDU • WEBSITE: WWW.GETTYSBURG.EDU

## ADMISSIONS

*Very important* academic and nonacademic factors considered by the admissions committee include class rank and secondary school record. *Important* factors considered include recommendations and standardized test scores. *Other* factors considered include alumni/ae relation, character/personal qualities, essays, extracurricular activities, minority status, talent/ability, volunteer work, and work experience. Factors *not* considered include geography, interview, religious affiliation/commitment, and state residency. SAT I or ACT required. TOEFL required of all international applicants. High school diploma is required and GED is accepted. *High school units required/recommended:* 20 total recommended; 4 English recommended, 4 math recommended, 4 science recommended, 4 foreign language recommended, 4 social studies recommended. *The admissions office says:* "Students can expect a careful, individual review of their applications. We particularly value: (1) high school achievement, including the choice of challenging courses; (2) personal qualities and talents which will contribute to the community. Evidence of leadership, creativity, integrity, commitment, and service to community is strongly considered."

### The Inside Word

Gettysburg's small size definitely allows for a more personal approach to admission. The admissions committee puts a lot of energy into matchmaking, and last year it paid off with its largest freshman class in its history. Most Gettysburg types are good students and also match up well with competitor colleges, which makes this accomplishment even more laudable. Look for a somewhat more selective profile as a result.

## FINANCIAL AID

*Students should submit:* FAFSA, CSS/Financial Aid PROFILE, noncustodial (divorced/separated) parent's statement, and business/farm supplement. Regular filing deadline is March 15. The Princeton Review suggests that all financial aid forms be submitted as soon as possible after January 1. *Need-based scholarships/grants offered:* Pell, SEOG, state scholarships/grants, private scholarships, and the school's own gift aid. *Loan aid offered:* FFEL Subsidized Stafford, FFEL Unsubsidized Stafford, FFEL PLUS, Federal Perkins, and college/university loans from institutional funds. Institutional employment available. Federal Work-Study Program available. Applicants will be notified of awards on or about March 30. Off-campus job opportunities are good.

## FROM THE ADMISSIONS OFFICE

"Four major goals of Gettysburg College, to best prepare students to enter the 21st century, include: first, to accelerate the intellectual development of our first-year students by integrating them more quickly into the intellectual life of the campus; second, to use interdisciplinary courses combining the intellectual approaches of various fields; third, to encourage students to develop an international perspective through course work, study abroad, association with international faculty, and a variety of extracurricular activities; and fourth, to encourage students to develop (1) a capacity for independent study by ensuring that all students work closely with individual faculty members on an extensive project during their undergraduate years and (2) the ability to work with their peers by making the small group a central feature in college life."

## ADMISSIONS

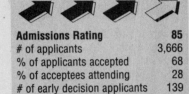

| | |
|---|---|
| Admissions Rating | 85 |
| # of applicants | 3,666 |
| % of applicants accepted | 68 |
| % of acceptees attending | 28 |
| # of early decision applicants | 139 |
| % accepted early decision | 11 |

### FRESHMAN PROFILE

| | |
|---|---|
| Range SAT Verbal | 560-630 |
| Average SAT Verbal | 595 |
| Range SAT Math | 570-640 |
| Average SAT Math | 600 |
| Average ACT Composite | 25 |
| Minimum TOEFL | 550 |
| % graduated top 10% of class | 42 |
| % graduated top 25% of class | 75 |
| % graduated top 50% of class | 99 |

### DEADLINES

| | |
|---|---|
| Priority admission deadline | 2/15 |
| Early decision | 2/1 |
| Early decision notification | 12/15 |
| Nonfall registration? | yes |

### APPLICANTS ALSO LOOK AT
#### AND OFTEN PREFER
William and Mary
James Madison
Lafayette
Lehigh
Bucknell
#### AND SOMETIMES PREFER
Dickinson
Franklin & Marshall
U. of Richmond
#### AND RARELY PREFER
Penn State—Univ. Park
Muhlenberg

### FINANCIAL FACTS

| | |
|---|---|
| Financial Aid Rating | 83 |
| Tuition | $24,761 |
| Room & board | $5,956 |
| Books and supplies | $500 |
| Required fees | $114 |
| % frosh receiving aid | 58 |
| % undergrads receiving aid | 56 |
| Avg frosh grant | $15,300 |
| Avg frosh loan | $3,000 |

# GODDARD COLLEGE

123 PITKIN ROAD, PLAINFIELD, VT 05667 • ADMISSIONS: 802-454-8311 • FAX: 802-454-1029

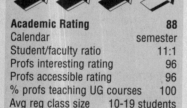
## STUDENTS SPEAK OUT
### Academics

If you loathe the idea of a "traditional school," check out Goddard College, an "artsy, eccentric," "alternative, progressive" school located in rural Vermont where "academic freedom" reigns supreme. At Goddard you can "design" an individual curriculum—"a self-directed, experimental education" if you will—tailored to your own "specific needs." But be warned: "There's no handholding here." The program is "independent, self-directed, and focused." Essentially, "your education is all on you." Classes (called "group studies" in Goddard-speak) are "intriguing and thought-provoking" discussion sessions with "hardly ever more than 10 people." The "open-minded, hip, intellectual" "facilitators"—translation: professors—are "warm and caring and very much a part of the community." There are "no grades or exams, as they interfere with the business of learning." Instead, students receive written evaluations. Also, all students "are a part of the decision making and governance here" and attend "community-based meetings with students/faculty/staff." Suffice it to say, "Goddard is not for everyone" and it has its flaws even for students who thrive in this kind of environment. "The facilities blow," for example, and "the administration is a joke." Nevertheless, students happily declare that Goddard provides a "wonderful, creative, free" atmosphere. "My academic experience has been nothing short of incredible, " boasts a satisfied junior. "I truly love this school."

### Life

"Activism, art, punk rock, philosophy, and sex" are all the rage on this tiny campus. Because Goddard is so small, each student has a "tremendous opportunity" to get involved in various activities, including the popular school newspaper, radio station, and Women's Center. Students "go to musical events on campus, hang out in dorms, and spend a lot of time in discussion and debate" as well. Not surprisingly, religious activity is not popular here, although "spiritual" and "pagan clubs" are widely embraced. Community action is vital as well, and each student must work for the college in some constructive way several hours per week. Much campus life is of the "spontaneous" variety. "We held our own Olympics which included streaking, an egg toss, a three-legged race, and other events, followed after dinner by a drag show and lip synch," relates a first-year student. "Parties at Goddard consist of everyone on campus gathering together and getting really drunk." Drug use (especially pot) is profoundly high as well. Skiing trails and plenty of places to hike are nearby, and the quiet and secluded campus feels somewhat disconnected from reality—perhaps too disconnected. Goddard students report that when they "go back to the real world," they have a difficult time assimilating.

### Student Body

"The student body consists of all the kids in high school who were alienated because they were weird," making Goddard a leftist paradise which is no doubt "an uncomfortable place for a person with a conservative background." While students at Goddard admit they're "not rocket scientists," they say their campus "is filled with creative, intelligent, and artistic" students "who love life on this planet too much to abandon themselves to the materialism of the modern world." Students call themselves "amazingly unique and creative" and they swear there "is always the potential for enlightening conversations, and connections." The "eclectic" students also say there is "intense diversity of thought" here, as well as "collective ecstasy and depression," but the limited outward diversity ranges "from dirty hippies to even dirtier hippies," as a junior quips.

FINANCIAL AID: 802-454-8311 • E-MAIL: ADMISSIONS@EARTH.GODDARD.EDU • WEBSITE: WWW.GODDARD.EDU

## ADMISSIONS

*Very important* academic and nonacademic factors considered by the admissions committee include secondary school record. *Important* factors considered include class rank, minority status, standardized test scores, state residency, and talent/ability. *Other* factors considered include alumni/ae relation, character/personal qualities, essays, extracurricular activities, geography, recommendations, and volunteer work. Factors *not* considered include interview, religious affiliation/commitment, and work experience. TOEFL required of all international applicants. High school diploma is required and GED is accepted. *High school units required/recommended:* 15 total required; 19 total recommended; 4 English required, 3 math required, 4 math recommended, 2 science required, 3 science recommended, 2 science lab required, 3 science lab recommended, 2 foreign language required, 3 foreign language recommended, 2 history required, 2 elective required. *The admissions office says:* "Goddard aims to bring students into the college, not keep them out. Admissions criteria have to do with an applicant's interest in attending Goddard, readiness to do so, and willingness to embrace the evolving Goddard educational program fully. Underlying these must be a thorough understanding of what Goddard is and is not, what the curriculum and programs can and cannot offer."

### The Inside Word

A small applicant pool, the need to have an entering class each year, and a high level of self-selection among candidates makes for Goddard's high acceptance rate. Even though students are not banging down the doors to get into the college, applicants should prepare themselves for a fairly demanding experience. The committee here wants to know a lot about the people who apply, none of which can be supplied in the clean and neat form of transcripts or score reports. This place is not for everyone, and careful self-assessment is the toughest part of the admissions process.

## FINANCIAL AID

*Students should submit:* FAFSA. There is no regular filing deadline. The Princeton Review suggests that all financial aid forms be submitted as soon as possible after January 1. *Need-based scholarships/grants offered:* Pell, SEOG, state scholarships/grants, private scholarships, and the school's own gift aid. *Loan aid offered:* FFEL Subsidized Stafford, FFEL Unsubsidized Stafford, FFEL PLUS, Federal Perkins, and college/university loans from institutional funds. Institutional employment available. Applicants will be notified of awards on a rolling basis. Off-campus job opportunities are fair.

## FROM THE ADMISSIONS OFFICE

"Goddard is a small, coeducational liberal arts college that has an international reputation for appealing to the creative, independent student. Its commitment is to adventurous, capable persons who want to make their own educational decisions and work closely with the faculty. Individually designed programs can be pursued on or off campus."

## ADMISSIONS

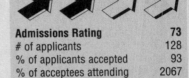

| | |
|---|---|
| Admissions Rating | 73 |
| # of applicants | 128 |
| % of applicants accepted | 93 |
| % of acceptees attending | 2067 |

### FRESHMAN PROFILE

| | |
|---|---|
| Range SAT Verbal | 530-660 |
| Average SAT Verbal | 511 |
| Range SAT Math | 480-580 |
| Average SAT Math | 489 |
| Range ACT Composite | 19-26 |
| Minimum TOEFL | 550 |
| Average HS GPA | 2.5 |
| % graduated top 10% of class | 9 |
| % graduated top 25% of class | 27 |
| % graduated top 50% of class | 57 |

### DEADLINES

| | |
|---|---|
| Regular notification | rolling |
| Nonfall registration? | yes |
| Nonfall registration? | yes |

### APPLICANTS ALSO LOOK AT AND OFTEN PREFER

New College
Reed
Oberlin
Hampshire
Bennington

### AND SOMETIMES PREFER

Antioch
Marlboro
Coll. of the Atlantic

## FINANCIAL FACTS

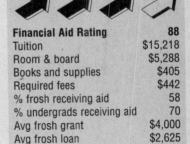

| | |
|---|---|
| Financial Aid Rating | 88 |
| Tuition | $15,218 |
| Room & board | $5,288 |
| Books and supplies | $405 |
| Required fees | $442 |
| % frosh receiving aid | 58 |
| % undergrads receiving aid | 70 |
| Avg frosh grant | $4,000 |
| Avg frosh loan | $2,625 |

# GOLDEN GATE UNIVERSITY

536 MISSION STREET, SAN FRANCISCO, CA 94105 • ADMISSIONS: 415-442-7800 • FAX: 415-442-7807

## CAMPUS LIFE

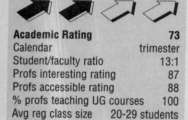

| Quality of Life Rating | 70 |
|---|---|
| Type of school | private |
| Affiliation | none |
| Environment | urban |

### STUDENTS

| | |
|---|---|
| Total undergrad enrollment | 1,215 |
| % male/female | 42/58 |
| % from out of state | 5 |
| % African American | 13 |
| % Asian | 17 |
| % Caucasian | 52 |
| % Hispanic | 11 |
| % international | 17 |
| # of countries represented | 60 |

### SURVEY SAYS . . .

*Musical organizations aren't popular*
*Theater is hot*
*High cost of living*
*Students love San Francisco, CA*
*Very little hard liquor*
*No one plays intramural sports*
*Intercollegiate sports unpopular or*
*nonexistent*

## ACADEMICS

| Academic Rating | 73 |
|---|---|
| Calendar | trimester |
| Student/faculty ratio | 13:1 |
| Profs interesting rating | 87 |
| Profs accessible rating | 88 |
| % profs teaching UG courses | 100 |
| Avg reg class size | 20-29 students |

### MOST POPULAR MAJORS
management
information systems

## STUDENTS SPEAK OUT

### Academics

Golden Gate University "offers its students a unique experience that most universities don't. It's practical, up-to-date, and has a very rich and diverse culture as a community." In nearly every respect, GGU is atypical. Most of its undergraduates study part time, and many were out of high school for several years before entering college. It has no real campus or campus life to speak of, and it is decidedly orientated toward graduate, not undergraduate, study. Still, Golden Gate has many excellent qualities. The university offers fine undergraduate business programs and attracts a bright, motivated, and unusually diverse student body. And it is located in downtown San Francisco, an exceptional place to spend one's college years. "Class size is small"—the vast majority of students indicate that their lectures have fewer than 50 students— "and most instructors are accessible." Students praise their "small classes and the opportunity to be taught by business professionals rather than professional teachers" whose "frequent use of case studies . . . will be very useful when we graduate and start our careers." Students also laud the fact that "the school allows the motivated student to get a good degree quickly." Another bonus is that there are "no student teachers." Golden Gate's cooperative education and internship programs allow students to study and work concurrently in the San Francisco business community.

### Life

If you're bound to get an education at a university where "extracurricular activities are nonexistent," it might as well be in San Francisco. The city gets raves from students at GGU. Not surprisingly, town/gown relations are solid between the City by the Bay and these "focused students." Most of the mainstays of typical college life—dormitories, parties, drinking, sports, and clubs—simply aren't to be found. As one Golden Gate student puts it: "Don't come here for the football team because we don't have one. We come here to learn and eventually to become prominent figures in our society." Efforts to boost extracurricular options have been undertaken, and "the club/organization activities are improving, especially student government." A "new student newspaper is doing well," although most students would like to see an improvement in recreational facilities. Given the low-key free time options afforded by Golden Gate U., most students "gather their coworkers and classmates for private activities" on their own. Students only gripe: "Food is cheap in San Francisco, but rent is too expensive. We need dorms!"

### Student Body

Golden Gate boasts a high level of diversity among its student body, including a large number of international students. In fact, to some it seems as though "there are almost no American students. It seems like everyone is an international." Students report that interaction among undergraduates of different ethnicity and backgrounds is frequent, despite the rarity of university-supported venues in which students can congregate. GGU students report themselves to be moderate politically, but not particularly aware of political issues. Perhaps that's because while they're "very friendly," they are also "focused." They clearly admire one another for their tenacity: "My fellow students are good people, hardworking, and ambitious," says one. In general, they're pretty happy, too.

FINANCIAL AID: 415-442-7270 • E-MAIL: INFO@GGU.EDU • WEBSITE: WWW.GGU.EDU

## ADMISSIONS

*Very important* academic and nonacademic factors considered by the admissions committee include secondary school record. *Other* factors considered include class rank, essays, recommendations, standardized test scores, minority status, volunteer work, and work experience. Factors *not* considered include alumni/ae relation, character/personal qualities, extracurricular activities, geography, interview, religious affiliation/commitment, state residency, and talent/ability. SAT I recommended. TOEFL required of all international applicants. High school diploma is required and GED is accepted. *High school units required/recommended:* 4 English required, 3 math required, 4 math recommended, 2 science required, 3 science recommended, 2 science lab required, 3 science lab recommended, 2 foreign language required, 3 foreign language recommended, 1 social studies required, 2 history required, 3 history recommended.

### The Inside Word

Golden Gate's focus is unique and requires a high level of independence, self-discipline, and motivation. Grades may be the most important factor in admission, but candidates who are lacking in the aforementioned personal qualities stand the greatest likelihood of denial.

## FINANCIAL AID

The Princeton Review suggests that all financial aid forms be submitted as soon as possible after January 1. Institutional employment available. Federal Work-Study Program available. Off-campus job opportunities are good.

## FROM THE ADMISSIONS OFFICE

"Golden Gate University is an ideal choice for men and women who are serious about their careers. Here, students work together with faculty who are leaders in their fields to build foundations for achievement in the world today and in the years ahead. Convenience, practical education, and personalized attention are the norm. Classes are small to encourage interaction between students and instructors. A full range of graduate and undergraduate courses are offered during the day, evenings, or on weekends to accommodate the needs of working adults as well as full-time students. Located in the financial district of San Francisco, Golden Gate's largest campus is convenient to business and social opportunities and has just completed a major renovation of classrooms and library. The university also has campuses and programs throughout California. Golden Gate remains one of the most affordable private universities in northern California. A full range of financial aid and scholarships, including full-tuition scholarships for transfer students and underrepresented minorities, are available for those who need financial assistance to pursue their studies. Golden Gate is a multicultural institution. The university celebrates its diverse student body and seeks staff and faculty members reflective of the community."

### ADMISSIONS

| Admissions Rating | 68 |
|---|---|

#### FRESHMAN PROFILE

| Minimum TOEFL | 525 |
|---|---|
| Average HS GPA | 2.7 |

#### DEADLINES

| Priority admission deadline | 7/1 |
|---|---|
| Nonfall registration? | yes |

#### APPLICANTS ALSO LOOK AT AND SOMETIMES PREFER

San Francisco State

### FINANCIAL FACTS

| Financial Aid Rating | 74 |
|---|---|
| Tuition | $9,192 |
| Books and supplies | $1,000 |
| Avg frosh grant | $4,304 |
| Avg frosh loan | $4,824 |

# GONZAGA UNIVERSITY

502 E. BOONE AVENUE, SPOKANE, WA 99258 • ADMISSIONS: 509-323-6572 • FAX: 509-324-5780

## CAMPUS LIFE

| | |
|---|---|
| **Quality of Life Rating** | **86** |
| Type of school | private |
| Affiliation | Roman Catholic |
| Environment | urban |

### STUDENTS

| | |
|---|---|
| Total undergrad enrollment | 2,852 |
| % male/female | 45/55 |
| % from out of state | 48 |
| % from public high school | 65 |
| % live on campus | 47 |
| % African American | 1 |
| % Asian | 5 |
| % Caucasian | 76 |
| % Hispanic | 3 |
| % Native American | 2 |
| % international | 3 |

### SURVEY SAYS . . .
*Diversity lacking on campus*
*Theater is hot*
*Classes are small*
*Everyone loves the Bulldogs*
*Very little drug use*
*(Almost) no one smokes*
*Students are very religious*
*Students get along with local community*

## ACADEMICS

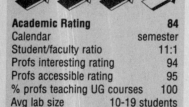

| | |
|---|---|
| **Academic Rating** | **84** |
| Calendar | semester |
| Student/faculty ratio | 11:1 |
| Profs interesting rating | 94 |
| Profs accessible rating | 95 |
| % profs teaching UG courses | 100 |
| Avg lab size | 10-19 students |
| Avg reg class size | 10-19 students |

### MOST POPULAR MAJORS
business administration
social sciences
engineering

## STUDENTS SPEAK OUT
### Academics

Gonzaga University softens the blow of its rigorous academic programs by placing them within the context of a comfortable and caring academic community. Explains one student, "Gonzaga is a happy place. Over my four years here, I've made many friends with other students, but more so with professors and administrators. They are willing to listen to students and develop real relationships. It's a very comforting feeling." Another student elaborates, "At Gonzaga, learning is enjoyable. The Jesuit education aims at developing the person as a whole, and I have felt this development personally. I've grown and changed on the spiritual, intellectual, and physical levels." Students' high levels of satisfaction are attributable primarily to a dedicated faculty. Professors "are excited and love what they are doing, which makes learning fun as well as easy and exciting." One student offers this anecdote: "As a freshman, one of the first classes I had to take was a business computer class. Considering myself a fairly computer-literate person, I thought the class would be a piece of cake. Countless hours of frustration quickly changed my mind. I went to my professor, who put the keyboard in my lap and spent three hours reviewing with me. Professors here really do more." Students also warn that "Gonzaga's professors are almost all PhDs. This means they pay us back for all the work they had to go through when they were in school. They really teach us a lot and care, but this is not an easy school." A wide-ranging integrated core curriculum ensures that students in all majors graduate with a well-rounded education.

### Life

Students report that "life at Gonzaga is very much campus-focused. Much of our social life revolves around campus activities and near-campus parties." While some perceive Gonzaga as a "study-hard, party-hard school," others write that tales of wild parties are exaggerated. Explains one, "Parties happen every weekend, but it is no worse than any other school." Spare time is relatively scarce at Gonzaga: "People are studying at all hours of the day. Academics are highly stressed here." In their spare time, most respondents pursue outdoor activities and campus-sponsored events, not parties, as their prime source of recreation. "The school offers a lot of activities on weekends for people who don't want to go to parties," writes one student, enumerating among those options skiing, rock climbing, mountain biking, golf, bowling, and on-campus movies. "It is easy to get involved if you want to," notes another. "This school is full of activities outside of academics. From intramural sports to academic clubs to diversity clubs, there's something for everyone." Others point out that the campus ministry "is terrific for providing opportunities to meet students and faculty through retreats." Downtown Spokane "is only a 10-minute walk from campus and has some fun things to do. There are lots of good restaurants in town and also in Coeur d'Alene, Idaho, which is a 30-minute drive away."

### Student Body

Gonzaga undergrads concede that "everyone is basically the same here: white, conservative, well-off Catholics. Those people get along pretty well, but tolerance of anyone else does not seem a priority." Those who focus on superficial details will quickly notice that "Gonzaga is a walking, talking Abercrombie and Fitch ad." Others might observe, as one student does, that "people here are a little preppier than at most schools." While "the lack of diversity is a drawback . . . it is slowly changing."

FINANCIAL AID: 800-793-1716 • E-MAIL: BALLINGER@GU.GONZAGA.EDU • WEBSITE: WWW.GONZAGA.EDU

## ADMISSIONS

*Very important* academic and nonacademic factors considered by the admissions committee include character/personal qualities and secondary school record. *Important* factors considered include class rank, extracurricular activities, recommendations, and standardized test scores. *Other* factors considered include alumni/ae relation, essays, geography, interview, minority status, talent/ability, volunteer work, and work experience. Factors *not* considered include religious affiliation/commitment and state residency. SAT I or ACT required. TOEFL required of all international applicants. High school diploma is required and GED is accepted. *High school units required/recommended:* 16 total recommended; 4 English required, 3 math required, 3 science required, 2 science lab required, 2 foreign language recommended, 3 social studies required, 2 history recommended. *The admissions office says:* "We are real people with whom applicants can talk. We want to 'meet' them by phone if not in person. It helps us if they take the time to become 'real' to us."

### The Inside Word

As with many religiously affiliated universities, getting into Gonzaga is much more a matter of making a good match philosophically than having high grades and test scores. An above-average academic record should be more than adequate to gain admission.

## FINANCIAL AID

*Students should submit:* FAFSA. The Gonzaga University Financial Aid Office recommends that students submit all financial aid forms by February 1 of each year to be considered for priority funding. *Need-based scholarships/grants offered:* Pell, SEOG, state scholarships/grants, private scholarships, the school's own gift aid, and Federal Nursing. *Loan aid offered:* FFEL Subsidized Stafford, FFEL Unsubsidized Stafford, FFEL PLUS, Federal Perkins, Federal Nursing, and college/university loans from institutional funds. Institutional employment available. Federal Work-Study Program available. Applicants will be notified of awards on a rolling basis beginning on or about March 1. Off-campus job opportunities are good.

## FROM THE ADMISSIONS OFFICE

"We at Gonzaga wish you the very best as you enter your college years. Take your applications and admissions process with a grain of salt. Humor is of the essence. If they are interested, let the college folks get to know you a bit. Let them see you in a way not afforded by their applications. Finally, don't be a wallflower. Ask questions—you might get answers! Good luck!"

### ADMISSIONS

| | |
|---|---|
| Admissions Rating | 79 |
| # of applicants | 2,730 |
| % of applicants accepted | 82 |
| % of acceptees attending | 35 |
| # accepting a place on wait list | 67 |
| % admitted from wait list | 15 |

#### FRESHMAN PROFILE

| | |
|---|---|
| Range SAT Verbal | 500-800 |
| Average SAT Verbal | 578 |
| Range SAT Math | 500-800 |
| Average SAT Math | 586 |
| Range ACT Composite | 23-28 |
| Average ACT Composite | 26 |
| Minimum TOEFL | 530 |
| Average HS GPA | 3.6 |
| % graduated top 10% of class | 38 |
| % graduated top 25% of class | 75 |
| % graduated top 50% of class | 91 |

#### DEADLINES

| | |
|---|---|
| Regular admission | 3/1 |
| Nonfall registration? | yes |

#### APPLICANTS ALSO LOOK AT
**AND OFTEN PREFER**
Notre Dame
U. San Diego
Marquette
**AND SOMETIMES PREFER**
Santa Clara
U. Puget Sound
U. Washington
Lewis & Clark Coll.
Washington State
**AND RARELY PREFER**
Loyola Marymount
Central Washington

### FINANCIAL FACTS

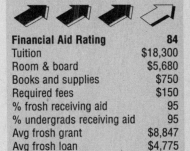

| | |
|---|---|
| Financial Aid Rating | 84 |
| Tuition | $18,300 |
| Room & board | $5,680 |
| Books and supplies | $750 |
| Required fees | $150 |
| % frosh receiving aid | 95 |
| % undergrads receiving aid | 95 |
| Avg frosh grant | $8,847 |
| Avg frosh loan | $4,775 |

# GOUCHER COLLEGE

1021 DULANEY VALLEY ROAD, BALTIMORE, MD 21204-2794 • ADMISSIONS: 410-337-6100 • FAX: 410-337-6354

## CAMPUS LIFE

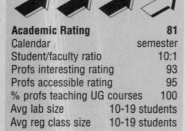

| Quality of Life Rating | 78 |
|---|---|
| Type of school | private |
| Affiliation | none |
| Environment | suburban |

### STUDENTS

| | |
|---|---|
| Total undergrad enrollment | 1,195 |
| % male/female | 27/73 |
| % from out of state | 60 |
| % from public high school | 64 |
| % live on campus | 70 |
| % African American | 8 |
| % Asian | 3 |
| % Caucasian | 70 |
| % Hispanic | 3 |
| % international | 1 |

### SURVEY SAYS . . .
*Theater is hot*
*Students love Baltimore, MD*
*Great off-campus food*
*(Almost) everyone smokes*
*Student government is popular*
*Class discussions encouraged*
*Library needs improving*

## ACADEMICS

| Academic Rating | 81 |
|---|---|
| Calendar | semester |
| Student/faculty ratio | 10:1 |
| Profs interesting rating | 93 |
| Profs accessible rating | 95 |
| % profs teaching UG courses | 100 |
| Avg lab size | 10-19 students |
| Avg reg class size | 10-19 students |

### MOST POPULAR MAJORS
psychology
communications
biology

## STUDENTS SPEAK OUT
### Academics
"Many opportunities in a little school" makes the academically challenging Goucher College a popular choice for students looking for personal attention, top-quality professors, and a left-of-center social and political environment. With both a strong science program and a solid emphasis on writing proficiency, Goucher manages to offer "creative and exceptional" classes in many disciplines, with professors who "go out of their way" to help students succeed. A first-year provides an example: "When teachers know what mode of transportation you use in coming to class (i.e., scooter), and they draw a 'scooter parking meter' on the board of the classroom, you know you're at a place where people care about your well-being and academic achievement." And though you wouldn't expect it from such a tiny school, it's Goucher's bureaucracy that gets the thumbs-down from students: "The administration process is lengthy and tedious at best," says a sophomore. Perhaps too much attention can be a bad thing? A junior notes that "student input is really used in the selection and hiring of professors. They're willing to do independent studies with you for whatever topic you want. Lots of paperwork, red tape, hoops to jump through, though." Still, with a "good reputation, great location, and generous scholarships" (the average frosh grant is about $13,500), a little paper pushing might not be such a bad thing. And though Goucher could "clean up their dorms," improve the library, and "get a T3," major renovation during the last few years should put Goucher back on track facilities-wise.

### Life
Situated in an upscale suburb a few miles north of Baltimore, Goucher's "beautiful" campus is "close to D.C. and Baltimore but outside of the city"— important for students who consider themselves "politically aware" and "care about what's going on in the world," and also for those who like to go to Baltimore's "movies, concerts, clubs, and bars." Though Goucher's "warm environment," small size, and "active students" guarantee the "opportunity to get involved in the campus community," some students complain that "there needs to be more to do on campus. It's dead on the weekends." Some of it may have to do with Goucher's men-to-women ratio (about 70 percent of the former women's college are female). What does Goucher College need? A senior jokes, "cuter, smarter boys with better bodies who are sensitive to my needs." Or, as a first- year puts it, "The odds are good but the goods are odd." Baltimore, however, "is a 'college town,' so the lack of men is compensated by the large amount of Johns Hopkins boys." In terms of partying, although one sophomore claims that "we are all pot-smoking, fun-loving, intellectually curious, caring people," a been-there-done-that senior argues that "Goucher's once easy-going social atmosphere has been threatened by a heightened presence of policing/weekly pot busts and a new lockdown policy aimed to keep everyone in their respective houses." Maybe she's just tired of Goucher's "incredible one-on-one attention: professors, administration . . . even security."

### Student Body
While "men are somewhat fishbowled at Goucher," notes a first-year, "everyone is really relaxed, and there is no real campus strife—except maybe the parking tickets." Adds a senior, "People here are politically aware, intelligent, and love class discussion. There are lots of weirdos but I love them anyway, and I know I'm one of them." Love—and lots of it—seems to be a theme at Goucher. Writes another freshman: "I love the majority of our students. They are very caring, loving, curious, optimistic, and out-to-get-the-world people, more conscious than most of our peers." And though there are your "superficial" types ("dancers & equestrians = snobs," writes a junior), a sophomore points out that "there are a lot of interesting people at Goucher. You just have to take the time to get to know them, which isn't hard at such a small school. I can't go anywhere on campus without seeing someone I can smile at."

FINANCIAL AID: 410-337-6141 • E-MAIL: ADMISSIONS@GOUCHER.EDU • WEBSITE: WWW.GOUCHER.EDU

## ADMISSIONS

*Very important* academic and nonacademic factors considered by the admissions committee include recommendations and secondary school record. *Important* factors considered include essays, extracurricular activities, standardized test scores, and talent/ability. *Other* factors considered include alumni/ae relation, character/personal qualities, class rank, interview, volunteer work, and work experience. Factors *not* considered include geography, minority status, religious affiliation/commitment, and state residency. SAT I or ACT required. TOEFL required of all international applicants. High school diploma is required and GED is accepted. *High school units required/recommended:* 15 total required; 4 English required, 3 math required, 3 science required, 2 science lab required, 2 foreign language required, 3 social studies required. *The admissions office says:* "We [try to make the admissions process] as personal as possible, meeting students' individual needs. We accomplish this through individually tailored visits to campus, personalized mailings, and consistent follow-through by staff. Our application reading and decision making are very humane; we keep in mind that each file represents a person."

### The Inside Word

Goucher is in serious battle for the students to which it is best-suited, and often fills the role of safety to some of the region's strongest colleges. Though the College is a solid choice in its own right, its admissions profile reflects modest competitiveness as a result of these circumstances.

## FINANCIAL AID

*Students should submit:* FAFSA and CSS/Financial Aid PROFILE. Regular filing deadline is February 15. The Princeton Review suggests that all financial aid forms be submitted as soon as possible after January 1. *Need-based scholarships/grants offered:* Pell, SEOG, state scholarships/grants, private scholarships, and the school's own gift aid. *Loan aid offered:* FFEL Subsidized Stafford, FFEL Unsubsidized Stafford, FFEL PLUS, Federal Perkins, and college/university loans from institutional funds. Institutional employment available. Federal Work-Study Program available. Applicants will be notified of awards on or about April 1. Off-campus job opportunities are good.

## FROM THE ADMISSIONS OFFICE

"A Goucher liberal arts education aims to prepare students for the real world. The college integrates thought and action, combining a strong liberal arts curriculum with hands-on learning in off-campus settings through internships, field work, study abroad, and independent projects. Students can choose majors in 18 departments and four interdisciplinary areas, or they may design their own individualized program of study. Small classes taught by skilled faculty, strong international studies programs, and research with faculty are other key characteristics. Goucher has impressive resources in technology, including a campus fully wired for access to the Internet and the World Wide Web. Goucher's merit scholarship program is one of the top programs in the nation, offering strong students awards ranging from partial tuition to full tuition plus room and board."

## ADMISSIONS

| | |
|---|---|
| Admissions Rating | 79 |
| # of applicants | 2,171 |
| % of applicants accepted | 82 |
| % of acceptees attending | 21 |
| # accepting a place on wait list | 96 |

### FRESHMAN PROFILE

| | |
|---|---|
| Range SAT Verbal | 550-660 |
| Average SAT Verbal | 610 |
| Range SAT Math | 520-630 |
| Average SAT Math | 570 |
| Range ACT Composite | 21-28 |
| Average ACT Composite | 26 |
| Minimum TOEFL | 550 |
| Average HS GPA | 3.1 |
| % graduated top 10% of class | 30 |
| % graduated top 25% of class | 60 |
| % graduated top 50% of class | 90 |

### DEADLINES

| | |
|---|---|
| Early decision | 11/15 |
| Early decision notification | 12/15 |
| Regular admission | 2/1 |
| Regular notification | 4/1 |
| Nonfall registration? | yes |

### APPLICANTS ALSO LOOK AT AND OFTEN PREFER
Skidmore
U. of Maryland—College Park
Bard
Cornell U.
Mount Holyoke
### AND SOMETIMES PREFER
Trinity College
NYU
American U.
Franklin & Marshall U.
George Washington U.
### AND RARELY PREFER
Mary Washington College

## FINANCIAL FACTS

| | |
|---|---|
| Financial Aid Rating | 84 |
| Tuition | $22,000 |
| Room & board | $7,800 |
| Books and supplies | $800 |
| Required fees | $300 |
| % undergrads receiving aid | 59 |
| Avg frosh grant | $13,398 |
| Avg frosh loan | $2,389 |

# GRINNELL COLLEGE

GRINNELL, IA 50112-1690 • ADMISSIONS: 800-247-0113 • FAX: 641-269-4800

## CAMPUS LIFE

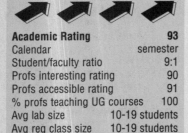

| Quality of Life Rating | 78 |
| --- | --- |
| Type of school | private |
| Affiliation | none |
| Environment | rural |

### STUDENTS

| | |
| --- | --- |
| Total undergrad enrollment | 1.464 |
| % male/female | 44/56 |
| % from out of state | 89 |
| % from public high school | 81 |
| % live on campus | 90 |
| % African American | 5 |
| % Asian | 5 |
| % Caucasian | 74 |
| % Hispanic | 5 |
| % international | 10 |
| # of countries represented | 42 |

### SURVEY SAYS . . .

*Political activism is hot*
*Students are very religious*
*Popular college radio*
*Theater is hot*
*Students get along with local community*
*Campus difficult to get around*
*Library needs improving*
*Unattractive campus*

## ACACEMICS

| Academic Rating | 93 |
| --- | --- |
| Calendar | semester |
| Student/faculty ratio | 9:1 |
| Profs interesting rating | 90 |
| Profs accessible rating | 91 |
| % profs teaching UG courses | 100 |
| Avg lab size | 10-19 students |
| Avg reg class size | 10-19 students |

### MOST POPULAR MAJORS
biology
English
anthropolgy

## STUDENTS SPEAK OUT

### Academics

"No one competes" at "intense" Grinnell College, "a small liberal arts school" with no core curriculum and "a high level of academic freedom." Of course, nobody really has time to compete, thanks to the "rigorous academics" and "depressing academic workload" here (Grinnellians normally clock about four hours of studying every day). Indeed, Grinnell is definitely an "academic pressure cooker," complete with "tons of work" but "after all the pain and frustration, it's rewarding," a senior assures us. The "amazing, intelligent, interesting, and engaging" professors are "very personable" and "very good" at what they do. "Classes require a lot of work but the professors are very accommodating," says a first-year student. "They want us to learn and it is evident that they enjoy teaching." Faculty members are "practically begging for student contact" as well, and many students tell us that it is ordinary for students and even entire classes to dine in professors' homes. Criticism of the top brass is rare at Grinnell because the student population is basically self-governing. "Things get done" because students "run the show." Facilities are excellent as well, and so is financial aid. In a nutshell, there aren't many negatives about the academics at this "extraordinary place."

### Life

Grinnell is a small college that shares its name with a "small" town "in the middle" of "podunk Iowa." Students say "crime does not happen" on this "very comfortable and welcoming" campus, which is home to "a lot of activism," and "free movies and cultural stuff" galore. There are "exciting performers," "renowned speakers," and popular dances like "the Cross-Dressers Ball" and the "annual disco party." Other diversions of varying popularity include such things as "dancing, playing music," and "buying local foods at farmers' markets." Also, "late night philosophical discussions until 4:00 in the morning are common." Dating is "nearly nonexistent" here and there are no fraternities or sororities at Grinnell, which is a blessing according to students. "It's an added bonus that we don't have a Greek system," reflects a junior. "Everyone belongs." Parties "are big on the weekends," and they range from "pretty low-key" to "out-of-control." The way we hear it, "you can drink all you want and never get in trouble," and "from Friday to Sunday, you can smell pot everywhere you go." For nature lovers, the abundance of squirrels on campus provides "an endless source of amusement," and "nakedness" is a Big Deal around campus. "Streaking" is a regular occurrence, as are "other incredibly naked activities." "For example," swears a junior, "some guys just set the school shower record with seven hours of continuous showering."

### Student Body

At Grinnell, "the perennial complaint is that every year the first-year students are too homogenous." We aren't sure why this is. While Grinnellians are mostly "white, progressive liberals," they're definitely "not a bunch of career-focused bores." They are, instead, "long-haired, tree-hugging, commie, pinko, queer, hippie freaks" who are "politically aware" and "unquestionably weird." Grinnell is also reportedly "great for gays." Students here "work hard," "think too much," and are entirely "overextended." They also "tend to get worked up over odd issues." Of course, "there is always petty drama" on campus, as "living in close quarters with 1,300 people for four years can be trying." But the "nonjudgmental," "warm and fuzzy" folks here are "good-hearted and pretty funny," and they report few serious problems. The only real tension on campus is felt between the north side of campus ("jocks") and the south side ("intellectuals and drug users").

FINANCIAL AID: 515-269-3250 • E-MAIL: ASKGRIN@GRINNELL.EDU • WEBSITE: WWW.GRINNELL.EDU

## ADMISSIONS

*Very important* academic and nonacademic factors considered by the admissions committee include secondary school record and standardized test scores. *Important* factors considered include essays, recommendations, extracurricular activities, interview, and volunteer work. *Other* factors considered include alumni/ae relation, character/personal qualities, class rank, geography, minority status, religious affiliation/commitment, talent/ability, and work experience. Factors *not* considered include state residency and financial need. SAT I or ACT required. TOEFL required of all international applicants. High school diploma is required and GED is accepted. *High school units required/recommended:* 16 total required; 4 English recommended, 3 math recommended, 3 science recommended, 2 foreign language recommended, 3 social studies recommended, 1 elective recommended. *The admissions office says:* "Intellectual curiosity, motivation, and depth and breadth of out-of-class involvement are stressed."

### The Inside Word

Grinnell has plenty of academically talented applicants. This enables the admissions committee to put a lot of energy into matchmaking, and gives candidates who have devoted time and energy to thought about themselves, their future, and Grinnell the opportunity to rise to the top. All applicants should consider interviewing; you're likely to leave with a positive impression.

## FINANCIAL AID

*Students should submit:* FAFSA, institution's own financial aid form, and non-custodial (divorced/separated) parent's statement. Regular filing deadline is February 1. The Princeton Review suggests that all financial aid forms be submitted as soon as possible after January 1. *Need-based scholarships/grants offered:* Pell, SEOG, state scholarships/grants, private scholarships, and the school's own gift aid. *Loan aid offered:* FFEL Subsidized Stafford, FFEL Unsubsidized Stafford, FFEL PLUS, Federal Perkins, and college/university loans from institutional funds. Institutional employment available. Federal Work-Study Program available. Applicants will be notified of awards on or about April 1. Off-campus job opportunities are fair.

## FROM THE ADMISSIONS OFFICE

"Grinnell students are involved and committed to academic work and involved in community and volunteer service. Students are independent and can exercise that independence in Grinnell's open curriculum. Grinnell hopes to produce individualism, social commitment, and intellectual self-awareness in its graduates."

### ADMISSIONS

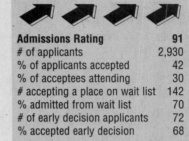

| | |
|---|---|
| Admissions Rating | 91 |
| # of applicants | 2,930 |
| % of applicants accepted | 42 |
| % of acceptees attending | 30 |
| # accepting a place on wait list | 142 |
| % admitted from wait list | 70 |
| # of early decision applicants | 72 |
| % accepted early decision | 68 |

#### FRESHMAN PROFILE

| | |
|---|---|
| Range SAT Verbal | 630-740 |
| Average SAT Verbal | 678 |
| Range SAT Math | 640-730 |
| Average SAT Math | 678 |
| Range ACT Composite | 28-32 |
| Average ACT Composite | 30 |
| Minimum TOEFL | 550 |
| % graduated top 10% of class | 70 |
| % graduated top 25% of class | 96 |
| % graduated top 50% of class | 99 |

#### DEADLINES

| | |
|---|---|
| Early decision | 11/20 |
| Early decision notification | 12/20 |
| Regular admission | 1/20 |
| Regular notification | 4/1 |

#### APPLICANTS ALSO LOOK AT AND SOMETIMES PREFER

Carleton
Macalester
Washington U.
Oberlin
Swarthmore
Brown

#### AND RARELY PREFER

Kenyon
Colorado College
Denison

### FINANCIAL FACTS

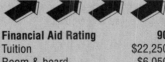

| | |
|---|---|
| Financial Aid Rating | 90 |
| Tuition | $22,250 |
| Room & board | $6,050 |
| Books and supplies | $400 |
| Required fees | $550 |
| % frosh receiving aid | 59 |
| % undergrads receiving aid | 59 |
| Avg frosh grant | $12,062 |
| Avg frosh loan | $3,471 |

# GROVE CITY COLLEGE

100 CAMPUS DRIVE, GROVE CITY, PA 16127-2104 • ADMISSIONS: 724-458-2100 • FAX: 724-458-3395

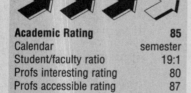
## STUDENTS SPEAK OUT
### Academics

If you are looking for a "conservative" and "affordable" private school with "strong Christian values" and "rigorous academic standards," check out Grove City College, where "chapel requirements," "challenging academics," and a host of required courses unquestionably keep students on their toes. GCC also boasts "small classes," a "free laptop for every student," and one of the best all-around bargains in higher education. As a matter of fact, tuition at Grove City is less than half of the national average for private colleges. Students here love their "friendly, patient," and "very approachable" professors. "They go out of their way to be involved in students' lives outside the classroom," beams a senior. "They are here to teach" and they "are very excited about what they teach and want to pass that passion on to you." Professors "often think their class is the only class," though—"Most students cannot loaf and get a B"—and the faculty in engineering and in some of the science departments leave much to be desired. Grove City's administration gets a thumbs-up from many students for being "very personable and responsive to student concerns," even if it does "heavily censor the newspaper."

### Life

GCC is "definitely a study school." "People study on Saturday night for Pete's sake." Students also abide by a mega-structured code of conduct that, among other things, forbids alcohol and premarital sex on Grove City's "beautiful campus," and there are strict intervisitation rules, which govern when men can visit women's dorms and vice versa. "For fun," jokes one GCC junior, "I pretend I am at Penn State." Not surprisingly, "drinking is not a big thing here." Instead, Grovers "have fun in clean ways." They "go to Bible studies," campus dances, "movies, ice skating, nearby restaurants," and "the wonderful outlet mall" not too far away. "Intramural sports are really big" as well, and "the Coffee Grove, a coffee shop downtown," is a popular hangout. Sororities and fraternities provide off-campus parties and other social activities. When all else fails, Grovers "sing Christian songs" or roadtrip to Pittsburgh, "only 45 minutes away." Getting married is a Big Deal, too, and GCC "is proud of the fact that most Grovers marry other Grovers." One academic affairs staffer is "obsessed" with helping students find spouses-to-be. "'Look to your left, look to your right, your future mate might be in sight' is one of her more memorable quotes." On the whole, you'll find "an atmosphere of safety, tradition, and family values" here, but all-night keggers are pretty much out of the question. "Grove City is not for everybody and doesn't pretend to be," declares a sophomore. "If you like to party or if you don't like to study and pray, don't come here."

### Student Body

"The average Grover" has "a sincere desire to live the Christian life" and is glad to be around people with similar goals. Political liberals are few and far between at Grove City—a bastion of conservatism if ever there was one. The "very goal-oriented" students here are either "spiritually arrogant" or overflowing with "genuine faith," depending on your point of view. "Many students feel like it is their job to judge the heathens," while others just want to maintain "a warm Christian environment." Grovers describe themselves as "kindred spirits" who are career-oriented and looking to get hitched in the not-too-distant future. "The naivete of students" is reportedly "amusing at times," and Grovers are definitely a "homogenous" bunch. Minority students? "We have no minority students," scoffs a junior. That's not far from the truth; GCC is as "diverse as a box of nails." Despite their outward similarities, "there's a pretty wide rift between some groups of people (Christians and non-Christians, Greeks and independents, etc.)."

FINANCIAL AID: 724-458-2163 • E-MAIL: ADMISSIONS@GCC.EDU • WEBSITE: WWW.GCC.EDU

## ADMISSIONS

*Very important* academic and nonacademic factors considered by the admissions committee include secondary school record. *Important* factors considered include class rank, essays, recommendations, and standardized test scores. *Other* factors considered include alumni/ae relation, character/personal qualities, extracurricular activities, geography, interview, minority status, talent/ability, volunteer work, and work experience. Factors *not* considered include religious affiliation/commitment and state residency. SAT I or ACT required. TOEFL required of all international applicants. High school diploma is required and GED is accepted. *High school units required/recommended:* 22 total required; 25 total recommended; 4 English required, 3 math required, 4 math recommended, 3 science required, 4 science recommended, 2 science lab required, 1 foreign language required, 2 foreign language recommended, 3 social studies required, 1 history required, 5 elective required.

### The Inside Word

If you're looking for a northeastern college with a Christian orientation, Grove City is a pretty good choice, but it's getting tougher to get in as we speak. Applications and standards are on the rise, and the college is fast becoming the newest addition to the lofty realm of the highly selective. Minorities are in short supply, and will encounter a somewhat friendlier admissions process. All students should definitely follow the college's recommendation and interview.

## FINANCIAL AID

*Students should submit:* institution's own financial aid form. Regular filing deadline is April 15. The Princeton Review suggests that all financial aid forms be submitted as soon as possible after January 1. *Need-based scholarships/grants offered:* state scholarships/grants and the school's own gift aid. *Loan aid offered:* College Loan Program funded by PNC Bank. Applicants will be notified of awards on or about June 1. Off-campus job opportunities are good.

## FROM THE ADMISSIONS OFFICE

"A good college education doesn't have to cost a fortune. For decades, Grove City College has offered a quality education at costs among the lowest nationally. The 1990s have brought increased national academic acclaim to Grove City College. In the 1997 issue of *Money Guide*, 'Best College Buys Now' ranked GCC 3rd in the mid-Atlantic region and 12th in their top 100 honor roll of public and private four-year colleges across the country. Grove City College is a place where professors teach. You will not see graduate assistants or teacher's aides in the classroom. Our professors are also active in the total life of the campus. More than 100 student organizations on campus afford opportunity for a wide variety of co-curricular activities. Outstanding scholars and leaders in education, science, and international affairs visit the campus each year. The environment at GCC is friendly, secure, and dedicated to high standards. Character-building is emphasized and traditional Christian values are supported."

### ADMISSIONS

| | |
|---|---:|
| **Admissions Rating** | 90 |
| # of applicants | 1,906 |
| % of applicants accepted | 51 |
| % of acceptees attending | 65 |
| # accepting a place on wait list | 125 |
| # of early decision applicants | 619 |
| % accepted early decision | 51 |

| FRESHMAN PROFILE | |
|---|---:|
| Range SAT Verbal | 560-680 |
| Average SAT Verbal | 629 |
| Range SAT Math | 600-690 |
| Average SAT Math | 629 |
| Range ACT Composite | 24-29 |
| Average ACT Composite | 27 |
| Minimum TOEFL | 550 |
| Average HS GPA | 3.7 |
| % graduated top 10% of class | 57 |
| % graduated top 25% of class | 85 |
| % graduated top 50% of class | 98 |

| DEADLINES | |
|---|---:|
| Early decision | 11/15 |
| Early decision notification | 12/15 |
| Priority admission deadline | 11/15 |
| Regular admission | 2/15 |
| Regular notification | 3/15 |
| Nonfall registration? | yes |

**APPLICANTS ALSO LOOK AT
AND SOMETIMES PREFER**
Penn State—U. Park
Allegheny
Wheaton (IL)
Westminster (PA)
Hillsdale
**AND RARELY PREFER**
Slippery Rock
Indiana U. (PA)

### FINANCIAL FACTS

| | |
|---|---:|
| **Financial Aid Rating** | 81 |
| Tuition | $7,870 |
| Room & board | $4,410 |
| Books and supplies | $900 |
| % frosh receiving aid | 38 |
| % undergrads receiving aid | 28 |
| Avg frosh grant | $4,135 |
| Avg frosh loan | $5,355 |

# GUILFORD COLLEGE

5800 WEST FRIENDLY AVENUE, GREENSBORO, NC 27410 • ADMISSIONS: 800-992-7759 • FAX: 336-316-2954

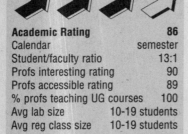
## STUDENTS SPEAK OUT

### Academics

Guilford College, a small Quaker liberal arts school in central North Carolina, offers its students a unique brand of chaperoned academic independence. The school makes few core or distribution requirements of its students, allowing them the freedom to fashion their own curricula and even to design their own majors. Administrators, advisors, and faculty play a key role, however, in supervising and supporting this degree of liberty. "Guilford encourages you to find and know yourself," explains one student. The linchpin in the Guilford experience is the school's dedicated faculty. Professors "really care about the students and are available a lot. Many will also chat with you outside the academic environment, whether it's catching a smoke on the steps, going for coffee, or having a class over to their home for a meal." Notes one student, "The teachers are intelligent, sensitive, and excited about each student. There are a lot of opportunities for outside experience and jobs." Small classes reinforce Guilford's support network, allowing "tremendous intellectual intimacy for students and professors." The administration's "extreme liberal stance on a vast majority of issues has caused it to lose some common sense in its politics," claims a junior. "You always get a real person to talk to instead of a machine," though, and overall impressions of the administration are excellent. "I had been waiting in line to congratulate our new president, Don, on his inauguration ceremony, and realized it would take forever before I'd reach him," recounts a geology major. "So I slipped out of the line and began to cross the lawn in the center of campus. I soon heard my name, and looked back to see Don running to me! He took my hand and thanked me for being there, while all the visiting dignitaries looked on."

### Life

Students enjoy the "beautiful" campus and "idyllic" climate that come part and parcel with a Guilford education. As for their hometown, they say that "Greensboro is not the most exciting place, but it is a small city so there are a few decent bars, clubs, and a decent variety of restaurants. Not too much big social stuff on campus, but we all have fun, usually in small group parties." Winston-Salem is close by, and Chapel Hill and Durham are also within reasonable driving distance, providing those who own cars with a reasonable array of urban options. On campus, some complain that "social life has a lot of improving to do," while others reproach a "rather whiny, apathetic student body" that is "too lazy to find or create" its own entertainment. "There are usually a lot of events (plays, poetry readings, coffeehouse conversations)" and "panel discussions happening on campus, on topics from homosexuality to Buddhism. Students are encouraged to think and question, not just absorb like a sponge." "You need not drink and party, but that aspect is here," says a sophomore. "Roller-skating, putt-putt golf," and hanging out at "Harris Teeter—the 24-hour grocery store across the street" all provide nonalcoholic social outlets for those so inclined.

### Student Body

The students of Guilford "generally stick to their comfort groups and are wary of other 'types.' I wish there was more interaction, particularly with people of color, outside of set groups." Within these parameters, however, the largely liberal-minded students here see themselves as "friendly, educated, active, and open-minded." Notes one equivocal undergrad, "Students are selfish, rich, spoiled hippies. Still, some are cool and it's a friendly environment overall. Everyone says 'hi' to each other." Students are "strongly opinionated"—"there always seems to be someone protesting something"—and "definitely unusual" but "at ease." Everyone here "believes in something, and that makes Guilford an incredible place." One student qualifies this characterization, explaining that "the people at Guilford all have their hearts in the right place. We like to think of ourselves as socially aware and active. Although many times action gives way to just talking about taking action, Guilford tries really hard to be politically active."

FINANCIAL AID: 336-316-2354 • E-MAIL: ADMISSION@GUILFORD.EDU • WEBSITE: WWW.GUILFORD.EDU

## ADMISSIONS

*Very important* academic and nonacademic factors considered by the admissions committee include secondary school record and interview. *Important* factors considered include class rank, essays, recommendations, and standardized test scores. *Other* factors considered include alumni/ae relation, character/personal qualities, extracurricular activities, interview, talent/ability, volunteer work, and work experience. Factors *not* considered include geography, minority status, religious affiliation/commitment, and state residency. SAT I or ACT are optional. If not submitted, creative project must be presented. TOEFL required of all international applicants. High school diploma is required and GED is accepted. *High school units required/recommended:* 17 total required; 4 English required, 3 math required, 3 science required, 2 foreign language required, 3 social studies required, 2 elective required.

### The Inside Word

Guilford is indeed a sleeper, and is likely to become more selective as it becomes better known. Its current acceptance rate is high mainly because the competition includes many of the best colleges and universities east of the Mississippi.

## FINANCIAL AID

*Students should submit:* FAFSA, institution's own financial aid form, noncustodial (divorced/separated) parent's statement, and business/farm supplement. The Princeton Review suggests that all financial aid forms be submitted as soon as possible after January 1. *Need-based scholarships/grants offered:* Pell, SEOG, state scholarships/grants, private scholarships, and the school's own gift aid. *Loan aid offered:* FFEL Subsidized Stafford, FFEL Unsubsidized Stafford, FFEL PLUS, Federal Perkins, and college/university loans from institutional funds. Institutional employment available. Federal Work-Study Program available. Applicants will be notified of awards on a rolling basis beginning on or about February 15. Off-campus job opportunities are good.

## FROM THE ADMISSIONS OFFICE

"At Guilford we take pride in the fact that we strive to empower our enrolled students to exercise some influence in what happens on campus day to day. We encourage prospective students to do no less. Show some active interest in your application for admission and make sure that we know the unique ways you will contribute to Guilford. Although academic achievement and preparation are extremely important as we review applicants' files, we truly want to look beyond those factors to find men and women with broad perspectives, social concerns, untapped potential, and a love for learning."

### ADMISSIONS

| | |
|---|---|
| Admissions Rating | 73 |
| # of applicants | 1,419 |
| % of applicants accepted | 78 |
| % of acceptees attending | 29 |
| # accepting a place on wait list | 17 |
| % admitted from wait list | 35 |
| # of early decision applicants | 52 |
| % accepted early decision | 88 |

### FRESHMAN PROFILE

| | |
|---|---|
| Range SAT Verbal | 650-510 |
| Average SAT Verbal | 579 |
| Range SAT Math | 620-490 |
| Average SAT Math | 557 |
| Range ACT Composite | 28-20 |
| Average ACT Composite | 24 |
| Minimum TOEFL | 550 |
| Average HS GPA | 3.1 |
| % graduated top 10% of class | 18 |
| % graduated top 25% of class | 42 |
| % graduated top 50% of class | 82 |

### DEADLINES

| | |
|---|---|
| Early decision | 11/1 |
| Early decision notification | 12/15 |
| Priority admission deadline | 1/15 |
| Regular admission | 2/15 |
| Regular notification | 4/1 |
| Nonfall registration? | yes |

### APPLICANTS ALSO LOOK AT

**AND OFTEN PREFER**
UNC—Chapel Hill
Davidson, Oberlin, Duke, U. Virginia

**AND SOMETIMES PREFER**
Earlham, UNC—Greensboro
Swarthmore, Wake Forest
Warren Wilson

**AND RARELY PREFER**
U. Richmond, Elon
Randolph-Macon

### FINANCIAL FACTS

| | |
|---|---|
| Financial Aid Rating | 88 |
| Tuition | $17,200 |
| Room & board | $5,610 |
| Books and supplies | $700 |
| Required fees | $270 |
| % frosh receiving aid | 88 |
| % undergrads receiving aid | 90 |
| Avg frosh grant | $7,120 |
| Avg frosh loan | $4,691 |

# Gustavus Adolphus College

800 West College Avenue; Saint Peter, MN 56082 • Admissions: 507-933-7676 • Fax: 507-933-7474

## CAMPUS LIFE

**Quality of Life Rating**    **78**
Type of school    private
Affiliation    Lutheran
Environment    suburban

### STUDENTS

| | |
|---|---|
| Total undergrad enrollment | 2,560 |
| % male/female | 43/57 |
| % from out of state | 22 |
| % from public high school | 92 |
| % live on campus | 85 |
| % in (# of) fraternities | 26 (7) |
| % in (# of) sororities | 20 (5) |
| % African American | 1 |
| % Asian | 3 |
| % Caucasian | 95 |
| % Hispanic | 1 |
| % international | 1 |
| # of countries represented | 19 |

### SURVEY SAYS . . .

*Athletic facilities are great*
*Diversity lacking on campus*
*Everyone loves the Golden Gusties*
*(Almost) everyone plays intramural*
*sports*
*Student publications are popular*
*Campus difficult to get around*
*Computer facilities need improving*
*Unattractive campus*
*Students are cliquish*

## ACADEMICS

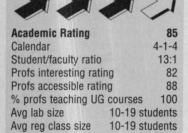

**Academic Rating**    **85**
Calendar    4-1-4
Student/faculty ratio    13:1
Profs interesting rating    82
Profs accessible rating    88
% profs teaching UG courses    100
Avg lab size    10-19 students
Avg reg class size    10-19 students

### MOST POPULAR MAJORS

biology
psychology
communication studies

## STUDENTS SPEAK OUT

### Academics

Students at Gustavus Adolphus College report that theirs is a "challenging and interesting" academic program tempered with ample opportunities for community service, religious life, and just plain fun. "Academics are a major portion of my life here, but not so much that I don't have time for extracurriculars and friends," happily reports one student. Professors here "are exceptionally great with being available to students"; brags one Gustie (the name by which students refer to themselves), "My professor in a lecture knew my name. Another gets called weekly by CNN for his input." Students looking for a school with that personal touch should be most at home at Gustavus, where "it is not uncommon for professors to include their home phone number on their class syllabus. If you are looking for a school where you don't participate in class discussions and the teacher does not know your name, then Gustavus is NOT for you." Those expecting the rigors of an Ivy-wannabe, however, might be disappointed; "Overall," assesses one student, "the academic environment at Gustavus has not been as rigorous as I hoped or expected it to be." Undergraduates here can choose one of two required cores. Curriculum I resembles distribution requirements; students in this program spend approximately one-third of their academic careers taking courses in different liberal arts areas. Curriculum II, open to only 60 first-year students each year, offers fewer courses but presents material in a sequence designed to help students "develop a comprehensive understanding of global society." Neither curriculum interferes with a student's ability to study abroad (as more than 40 percent reportedly do).

### Life

Gustavus undergrads agree that their campus is home to a bustling extracurricular life where "there's always something fun for everyone on or off campus. The school provides many alternatives to partying every weekend. But if you want to party, you'll find some good ones here." For freshman in particular, socializing means "a lot of partying, but not all is mass drunkenness. Sophomore year and on tends to move to smaller groups. People become more creative with activities once they are comfortable and find out what's available in the area. Having a car helps, too!" Notes one student, "I think Gustavus does an excellent job of providing activities for us. It seems like there is at least one activity a week, be it a movie, concert, comedian, games, or a short trip to see a show in the Minneapolis–Saint Paul area." On-campus clubs and intramural sports are very popular, and Gustavus's Division III sports teams are well supported, especially football, women's tennis, and gymnastics. While some love the "small-town, small-community atmosphere" of Gustavus's surroundings, others warn that "there is not much to do in Saint Peter. Still, Mankato [home to a bigger university] is close by and is a nice retreat."

### Student Body

"The Midwest is best!" writes one student, summing up the cordial vibe that pervades this campus. "It is so great to go to a school with many friendly, outgoing people," reports another. "I could honestly approach any member of the Gustavus campus and start a conversation with them." Others, however, warn that the friendliness is "very superficial" and that students "tend to be cliquish" and "very religious and close-minded due to their beliefs." A "strong Swedish heritage" is evident on campus—you can major in Scandinavian studies here—and students tend to be white, Nordic, Lutheran, and from Minnesota. There's "a definite social split" between opposing camps on the north and south sides of campus. "Northsiders" are "the athletes and the preppy kinds of people," while Southsiders "study more and party less" and tend to be a bit "more friendly and open-minded."

FINANCIAL AID: 507-933-7527 • E-MAIL: ADMISSION@GUSTAVUS.EDU • WEBSITE: WWW.GUSTAVUS.EDU

## ADMISSIONS

*Very important* academic and nonacademic factors considered by the admissions committee include essays, interview, secondary school record, and standardized test scores. *Important* factors considered include character/personal qualities, class rank, extracurricular activities, and recommendations. *Other* factors considered include alumni/ae relation, geography, minority status, talent/ability, volunteer work, and work experience. Factors *not* considered include religious affiliation/commitment and state residency. SAT I or ACT required. TOEFL required of all international applicants. High school diploma is required and GED is accepted. *High school units required/recommended:* 4 English recommended, 3 math recommended, 3 science recommended, 3 foreign language recommended, 2 social studies recommended, 2 history recommended. *The admissions office says:* "We encourage all students to visit the campus, and will meet students flying into the Minneapolis–Saint Paul airport and transport them to and from the campus. Many applicants have self-selected Gustavus with 20 percent not applying to another college. We are interested in recruiting more students from the West and the South. Relatives/children of alumni receive extra consideration, and are 'especially encouraged' to apply. Minorities also receive extra consideration."

### The Inside Word

While the college refers to itself as a national liberal arts college, the applicant pool is decidedly regional and mostly from Minnesota. The pool is also small and highly self-selected, which explains the high acceptance rate and solid freshman profile. Minorities and those who hail from far afield will find their applications met with enthusiasm by the admissions committee.

## FINANCIAL AID

*Students should submit:* FAFSA, institution's own financial aid form, noncustodial (divorced/separated) parent's statement, and business/farm supplement. Regular filing deadline is April 15. The Princeton Review suggests that all financial aid forms be submitted as soon as possible after January 1. *Need-based scholarships/grants offered:* Pell, SEOG, state scholarships/grants, private scholarships, and the school's own gift aid. *Loan aid offered:* Direct Subsidized Stafford, Direct Unsubsidized Stafford, Federal Perkins, Federal Nursing, and college/university loans from institutional funds. Institutional employment available. Federal Work-Study Program available. Applicants will be notified of awards on a rolling basis beginning on or about March 1. Off-campus job opportunities are fair.

## FROM THE ADMISSIONS OFFICE

"Gustavus Adolphus, a national liberal arts college with a strong tradition of quality teaching, is committed to the liberal arts and sciences; to its Lutheran history; to innovation as evidenced by the 4-1-4 calendar, Curriculum I and II, and the writing program; and to affordable costs with its unique Guaranteed Cost Plan and Partners in Scholarship Program. The most recent additions to its excellent facilities are Olin Hall for physics and mathematics; Confer Hall for the humanities; Lund Center for physical education, athletics, and health; International Center for residential living and international education; and Jackson Campus Center."

## ADMISSIONS

| | |
|---|---|
| Admissions Rating | 83 |
| # of applicants | 2,091 |
| % of applicants accepted | 76 |
| % of acceptees attending | 42 |
| # accepting a place on wait list | 40 |
| % admitted from wait list | 10 |
| # of early decision applicants | 137 |
| % accepted early decision | 79 |

### FRESHMAN PROFILE

| | |
|---|---|
| Range SAT Verbal | 540-670 |
| Average SAT Verbal | 610 |
| Range SAT Math | 560-680 |
| Average SAT Math | 613 |
| Range ACT Composite | 23-29 |
| Average ACT Composite | 26 |
| Minimum TOEFL | 550 |
| Average HS GPA | 3.6 |
| % graduated top 10% of class | 36 |
| % graduated top 25% of class | 71 |
| % graduated top 50% of class | 95 |

### DEADLINES

| | |
|---|---|
| Early decision | 11/15 |
| Early decision notification | 12/1 |
| Priority admission deadline | 2/15 |
| Regular admission | 4/1 |
| Nonfall registration? | yes |

### APPLICANTS ALSO LOOK AT AND SOMETIMES PREFER

Carleton
St. Olaf
U. Minnesota
U. Wisconsin—Madison
Macalester

## FINANCIAL FACTS

| | |
|---|---|
| Financial Aid Rating | 89 |
| Tuition | $18,940 |
| Room & board | $4,900 |
| Books and supplies | $700 |
| Required fees | $360 |
| % frosh receiving aid | 61 |
| % undergrads receiving aid | 65 |
| Avg frosh grant | $6,500 |
| Avg frosh loan | $4,500 |

# HAMILTON COLLEGE

198 COLLEGE HILL ROAD, CLINTON, NY 13323 • ADMISSIONS: 315-859-4421 • FAX: 315-859-4457

## STUDENTS SPEAK OUT

### Academics

Students offer overwhelming praise for the "intimate" academic atmosphere at Hamilton College. "It is unusual to have a class larger than 30 students," writes one Hamilton undergrad. "This allows teachers to learn the name of every student in class, which, whether they like it or not, creates a better, more intimate atmosphere for students to learn in." The faculty and administration here "are very connected with the students. Many teachers will attend sporting events and school activities. Most students find adults in the community who they bond with. Babysitting, going out for lunch or dinner, and attending events together are typical 'bonding' experiences." Hamilton professors earn high marks for their teaching, with students frequently citing their commitment to the student body. Reports one student, "In the first week of my freshman year, my professor called on me by name in an 80-person class! Last semester my professor invited my class to her house for dinner and we sat by the fireside and discussed our final projects." Add the availability of "a wide variety of classes" and well-received academic facilities (especially the library, labs, and Career Center), and you start to wonder what students here don't like. Answer: "The registration process: it's from the Stone Age." With so many positives going for the school, it's no wonder students are convinced that "Hamilton College is genuinely committed to being one of the finest liberal arts colleges in the country."

### Life

"Well, we're up in the cornfields of central New York," notes one student asked to describe life on the Hamilton campus. Fortunately, "social life on campus makes up for the absence of life after dark in Clinton." Explains one student, "Although Hamilton is located in the middle of nowhere, there is always something to do. Each weekend night movies are played, concerts or comedians perform, and there is always a party in one of our four 'social spaces.' A lot of students drink for fun, but it isn't the only option." Others point out, however, that for the majority of students, "Life on campus is focused around drinking. However, the college has become much stricter in its enforcement of its alcohol policy. Because of the tougher laws, students have begun to move to the bars instead of the fraternity/sorority parties." As a result, "The number of parties has been steadily and significantly decreasing since my freshman year." Partiers and teetotalers alike agree that the school "does an excellent job of bringing outside groups and speakers to campus—the Capitol Steps, James Carville and Mary Matalin, B.B. King, the Dave Matthews Band, [and] Margaret Thatcher have all left a lasting impression." They also report that "students are very eager and willing to get involved in organizations and groups on campus" and that "there are many extracurricular activities available," including varsity and intramural sports, arts and cultural programs, and fraternity-sponsored social events.

### Student Body

If you are searching for Hamilton students among the residents in the idyllic town of Clinton, New York, try this sophomore's litmus test: "If they don't wear khakis, they're probably townies." Students here are "very preppy," friendly, and politically moderate, although many are "apathetic and uninvolved." Students note that "Hamilton is very diverse socially but perhaps not so much ethnically. Students get along and interact well with one another for the most part, although students with similar interests, beliefs, and backgrounds often interact with one another more frequently or exclusively." Several point out, though, that "there is increasing diversity here. The more diverse Hamilton gets, the better students get along. Going away are the days of mass Greek life and social inequality." Many students "hail from mostly rich, white, suburban towns and have never had to deal with anything tragic in their lives. Despite all this, I like them because they are remarkably friendly."

FINANCIAL AID: 800-859-4413 • E-MAIL: ADMISSION@HAMILTON.EDU • WEBSITE: WWW.HAMILTON.EDU

## ADMISSIONS

*Very important* academic and nonacademic factors considered by the admissions committee include secondary school record, class rank, and recommendations. *Important* factors considered include standardized test scores, essays, interview, extracurricular activities, alumni/ae relation, minority status, and volunteer work. *Other* factors considered include talent/ability, character/personal qualities, geographical residence. Factors *not* considered include state residency and religious affiliation/commitment. SAT I or ACT required; SAT II recommended. TOEFL required of all international applicants. *High school units required/recommended:* 16 total required; 4 English required, 3 math required, 3 science required, 3 foreign language required, 3 social studies required. *The office of admissions says:* "We place most of our emphasis on the high school record when judging academic potential."

### The Inside Word

Gaining admission to Hamilton is difficult, and would be more so if the college didn't lose many of its shared applicants to competitor schools. The college's position as a popular safety for the top tier of northeastern colleges has always benefited the quality of its applicant pool, but it translates into a tough fight when it comes to getting admits to enroll. Although selectivity has risen significantly of late, Hamilton remains in the position of losing many of its best candidates to other, more prestigious schools. Students who view Hamilton as their first-choice college should definitely make it plain to the admissions committee—such news can often be influential, especially under circumstances like those mentioned here.

## FINANCIAL AID

*Students should submit:* FAFSA, CSS/Financial Aid PROFILE, noncustodial (divorced/separated) parent's statement and business/farm supplement. The Princeton Review suggests that all financial aid forms be submitted as soon as possible after January 1. *Need-based scholarships/grants offered:* Pell, SEOG, private scholarships, and the school's own gift aid. *Loan aid offered:* FFEL Subsidized Stafford, FFEL Unsubsidized Stafford, FFEL PLUS, Federal Perkins, and college/university loans from institutional funds. Institutional employment available. Federal Work-Study Program available. Applicants will be notified of awards on or about April 1. Off-campus job opportunities are fair.

## FROM THE ADMISSIONS OFFICE

"One of Hamilton's most important characteristics is the exceptional interaction that takes place between students and faculty members. Whether in class or out, they work together, challenging one another to excel. Academic life at Hamilton is rigorous, and emerging from that rigor is a community spirit based on common commitment. It binds together student and teacher, and stimulates self-motivation, thus making the learning process not only more productive but also more enjoyable and satisfying. Hamilton's Bristol Scholars program is merit-based, offering six to eight awards of up to $10,000 for each of the student's four years at Hamilton. Both the Bristol and the need-based Schambach Scholars program also offer special research opportunities with faculty on campus."

## ADMISSIONS

| | |
|---|---|
| Admissions Rating | 91 |
| # of applicants | 3,811 |
| % of applicants accepted | 39 |
| % of acceptees attending | 31 |
| # of early decision applicants | 294 |
| % accepted early decision | 72 |

### FRESHMAN PROFILE

| | |
|---|---|
| Range SAT Verbal | 580-670 |
| Range SAT Math | 580-670 |
| Minimum TOEFL | 600 |
| % graduated top 10% of class | 55 |
| % graduated top 25% of class | 85 |
| % graduated top 50% of class | 99 |

### DEADLINES

| | |
|---|---|
| Early decision | 11/15 |
| Early decision notification | 12/15 |
| Regular admission | 1/15 |
| Regular notification | 4/1 |
| Nonfall registration? | yes |

### APPLICANTS ALSO LOOK AT AND OFTEN PREFER

Dartmouth
Bowdoin
Cornell U.
Middlebury
Williams

### AND SOMETIMES PREFER

Trinity Coll. (CT)
Colby
Bucknell
Colgate
Bates

### AND RARELY PREFER

Hobart & William Smith
Skidmore

## FINANCIAL FACTS

| | |
|---|---|
| Financial Aid Rating | 75 |
| Tuition | $27,350 |
| Room & board | $6,800 |
| Books and supplies | $900 |
| Required fees | $100 |
| % frosh receiving aid | 54 |
| % undergrads receiving aid | 55 |
| Avg frosh grant | $17,767 |
| Avg frosh loan | $2,502 |

# HAMPDEN-SYDNEY COLLEGE

PO Box 667, HAMPDEN-SYDNEY, VA 23943 • ADMISSIONS: 804-223-6120 • FAX: 804-223-6346

## CAMPUS LIFE

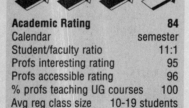

| Quality of Life Rating | 82 |
|---|---|
| Type of school | private |
| Affiliation | Presbyterian |
| Environment | rural |

### STUDENTS

| | |
|---|---|
| Total undergrad enrollment | 997 |
| % male/female | 100/0 |
| % from out of state | 40 |
| % from public high school | 62 |
| % live on campus | 94 |
| % in (# of) fraternities | 37 (11) |
| % African American | 3 |
| % Caucasian | 95 |
| % Hispanic | 1 |
| # of countries represented | 2 |

### SURVEY SAYS . . .

*Musical organizations aren't popular*
*Frats dominate social scene*
*Diversity lacking on campus*
*No one cheats*
*Lots of conservatives on campus*
*Students don't like Hampden-Sydney, VA*
*Students get along with local community*
*Computer facilities need improving*
*Class discussions encouraged*

## ACADEMICS

| Academic Rating | 84 |
|---|---|
| Calendar | semester |
| Student/faculty ratio | 11:1 |
| Profs interesting rating | 95 |
| Profs accessible rating | 96 |
| % profs teaching UG courses | 100 |
| Avg reg class size | 10-19 students |

### MOST POPULAR MAJORS

economics
history
political science

## STUDENTS SPEAK OUT

### Academics

If you've been searching for "a great atmosphere to reach your highest academic potential" or a rich southern heritage, or if you just want to hang out with a bunch of guys for four years, all-male Hampden-Sydney may be the place for you. Since 1776, H-SC has been churning out "good men and good citizens in an atmosphere of sound learning." The administration "goes out of its way to interact with students" and the "well-rounded" professors "challenge you all the time." According to a political science major, "You cannot hide if you didn't do your homework and you are forced to be vocal and express your ideas." Professors also "go out of their way to help" and often develop friendships with students. "It is not uncommon to eat dinner at a professor's house." As for classes that aren't taught by professors, there aren't any. "Zero percent of all classes are taught by teaching assistants." What's more, "only one classroom is large enough to hold 50 students, and it is never full." In class, "the all-male atmosphere allows for more concentration" and "permits 'politically-not-so-correct' discussions" that might not occur in a coed environment. H-SC also boasts an "excellent curriculum" and students laud its principled and earnest reverence for tradition, honor, and character embodied in the Honor Code. On the negative side, many H-SC men tell us "the facilities could use improvement." As things stand, the campus is a little drab and "the library and the computers" aren't technologically up to snuff. Overall, though, the academic environment here is tremendous. "In a nutshell," concludes a junior, "Hampden-Sydney is the best kept secret in Virginia."

### Life

"The workload isn't easy" at H-SC, and students spend a significant chunk of every weekday studying on this "rural," "traditional" campus in southeastern Virginia. Beginning on Thursday or Friday, though, this all-male bastion transforms into a southern *Animal House*–like country club" where "drugs and alcohol play a dominant role in the social scene." The Greek system here is definitely "the main thing socially" and "fraternity parties are the primary outlet for fun on campus." "The 'all-male thing' is not bad," explains a senior, "because we're coed Friday through Sunday." There are five prestigious women's colleges nearby and H-SC students either travel in packs to their parties or let the women flock to H-SC on the weekends. As a student puts it, "We are a small, all-male liberal arts college during the week and a large, coed college on the weekends." Outside of fraternity and academic life, many students here are community-minded and the majority are "involved in athletic and outdoor activities." Plenty of "biking, running, backpacking, climbing," and "fishing" can be had in the "surrounding countryside." In the fall, football games are big, as alumni come back to visit the campus and "lavish tailgate spreads abound."

### Student Body

The first thing you are likely to notice on Hampden-Sydney's small campus is that students are "uncommonly friendly" and are as "laid back" as "yawning young leopards." They are "very goal-oriented," are very serious about school, and "will be successful when they leave college." Many follow in the footsteps of fathers and brothers who came to H-SC before them, and they "care deeply about their school." They are also remarkably "white," "wealthy," and predominately southern. Without a doubt, "conformity is in" at H-SC, and "there is a stereotypical Hampden-Sydney model." As numerous students point out, H-SC students "get along because they are such a homogenous group." "Liberal attitudes are shunned" as "conservatism rules the roost." Students are very "supportive" of each other, and they "develop friendship bonds here that will never be broken." Claims a senior, "A brotherhood emerges out of the shared experience." Among H-SC's alumni are one U.S. president and 13 senators, and nearly 10 percent have become president, owner, or CEO of a company. One last thing: If you are gay, this is probably not the school for you.

FINANCIAL AID: 804-223-6119 • E-MAIL: HSAPP@TIGER.HSC.EDU • WEBSITE: WWW.HSC.EDU

## ADMISSIONS

*Very important* academic and nonacademic factors considered by the admissions committee include secondary school record. *Important* factors considered include essays and extracurricular activities. *Other* factors considered include alumni/ae relation, character/personal qualities, class rank, geography, interview, recommendations, standardized test scores, talent/ability, volunteer work, and work experience. Factors *not* considered include minority status, religious affiliation/commitment, and state residency. SAT I or ACT required; SAT II recommended. TOEFL required of all international applicants. High school diploma is required and GED is accepted. *High school units required/recommended:* 16 total required; 4 English required, 3 math required, 2 science required, 2 foreign language recommended, 2 social studies required, 2 history recommended, 5 elective required. *The admissions office says:* "We are in written contact with our prospects throughout the latter part of their junior year and senior year. We strongly encourage campus visits, personal interviews, conferences with professors and coaches, and overnight stays when possible."

### The Inside Word

Hampden-Sydney is one of the last of its kind. Understandably, the applicant pool is heavily self-selected, and a fairly significant percentage of those who are admitted choose to enroll. This enables the admissions committee to be more selective, which in turn requires candidates to take the process more seriously than might otherwise be necessary. Students with consistently sound academic records should have little to worry about nonetheless.

## FINANCIAL AID

*Students should submit:* FAFSA and CSS/Financial Aid PROFILE. The Princeton Review suggests that all financial aid forms be submitted as soon as possible after January 1. *Need-based scholarships/grants offered:* Pell, SEOG, state scholarships/grants, private scholarships, and the school's own gift aid. *Loan aid offered:* FFEL Subsidized Stafford, FFEL Unsubsidized Stafford, FFEL PLUS, Federal Perkins, college loans from institutional funds, Edvantage, Excel, and Nellie Mae. Institutional employment available. Federal Work-Study Program available. Applicants will be notified of awards on a rolling basis beginning on or about March 1. Off-campus job opportunities are fair.

## FROM THE ADMISSIONS OFFICE

"The spirit of Hampden-Sydney is its sense of community. As one of only 996 students, you will be in small classes and find it easy to get extra help or inspiration from professors when you want it. Many of our professors live on campus and enjoy being with students in the snack bar as well as in the classroom. They give you the best, most personal education as possible. A big bonus of small-college life is that everybody is invited to go out for everything, and you can be as much of a leader as you want to be. From athletics to debating to publications to fraternity life, this is part of the process that produces a well-rounded Hampden-Sydney graduate."

### ADMISSIONS

| | |
|---|---|
| Admissions Rating | 77 |
| # of applicants | 998 |
| % of applicants accepted | 72 |
| % of acceptees attending | 41 |
| # accepting a place on wait list | 27 |
| % admitted from wait list | 81 |
| # of early decision applicants | 86 |
| % accepted early decision | 78 |

#### FRESHMAN PROFILE

| | |
|---|---|
| Range SAT Verbal | 500-610 |
| Average SAT Verbal | 563 |
| Range SAT Math | 500-610 |
| Average SAT Math | 561 |
| Range ACT Composite | 19-25 |
| Average ACT Composite | 23 |
| Minimum TOEFL | 570 |
| Average HS GPA | 3.1 |
| % graduated top 10% of class | 14 |
| % graduated top 25% of class | 37 |
| % graduated top 50% of class | 72 |

#### DEADLINES

| | |
|---|---|
| Early decision | 11/15 |
| Early decision notification | 12/15 |
| Regular admission | 3/1 |
| Regular notification | 4/15 |
| Nonfall registration? | yes |

#### APPLICANTS ALSO LOOK AT

**AND OFTEN PREFER**
William and Mary
U. Virginia

**AND SOMETIMES PREFER**
Washington and Lee
James Madison
Vanderbilt
UNC—Chapel Hill

**AND RARELY PREFER**
Randolph-Macon

### FINANCIAL FACTS

| | |
|---|---|
| Financial Aid Rating | 89 |
| Tuition | $16,690 |
| Room & board | $6,110 |
| Books and supplies | $800 |
| Required fees | $499 |
| % frosh receiving aid | 49 |
| % undergrads receiving aid | 57 |
| Avg frosh grant | $6,980 |
| Avg frosh loan | $2,727 |

# SHIRE COLLEGE

FICE, 893 WEST STREET, AMHERST, MA 01002 • ADMISSIONS: 413-559-5471 • FAX: 413-559-5631

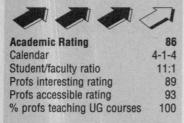
## STUDENTS SPEAK OUT
### Academics

Those seeking a progressive approach to undergraduate education should seriously consider Hampshire College, a small, reputable liberal arts school in western Massachusetts. As one student explains, "Hampshire gives you a grad school experience as an undergrad. Classes are about learning and doing, not getting a grade. In fact, we don't have grades, and this makes it much easier to focus on really understanding the material rather than just memorizing it long enough to pass a test (which we also don't have!)." Adds another, "What is unique and blessed about Hampshire is that my academic life cannot be separated from my social life, my intellectual life, my spiritual life. There is a unified collectiveness to my days and my thoughts and my work." Academic freedom is the name of the game at Hampshire, where "a student recently developed a program called EPEC (Experimental Program in Education and Community) for his Div. III project (similar to a senior thesis). There are now a number of student-run classes being offered. These are amazing and empowering classes." This freedom can be "very exciting. As a student, you have the power to help in the growing of a progressive, alternative institution. These are important lessons we're learning." However, it also means that "the academic experience here varies. Some courses are magnificent; for example, my philosophy and law courses here have been better than at Amherst! Other areas can be too pretentious or touchy-feely. Any class with the word 'race,' 'class,' 'gender,' 'postmodern,' or 'social construct' in the title is suspect. But if you're dissatisfied, there's always four other schools!" Some warn that "class discussions can sometimes be redundant and pointless because there isn't enough structure." Even so, Hampshire students ultimately praise the school, extolling the benefits of profs who "are extremely approachable," opportunities "to do a lot of research and real work," and "a five-college library system that makes it next to impossible not to have enough sources."

### Life

Amherst, Massachusetts, is the quintessential New England college town, and with several similar towns nearby (among them Northampton, home to Smith College), Hampshire students enjoy a setting that is very amenable to the student lifestyle. "As far as 'things to do' go, the Five College area provides a huge array of theatrical, cultural, social, and other events and groups," reports one undergrad. On campus, "A pretty chill atmosphere of small parties in dorm rooms or Mods (on-campus apartments)" predominates the social scene, although some also indulge in such activities as "the knitting circle and the *Twin Peaks* [David Lynch's oddball television series of the late 80s] showings at Ash lecture hall." In short, "anyone can find their niche" because "if you want a group or activity at Hampshire, you start it! I've run a movie group here since my first year, and I make all the decisions independent of school or faculty pressures. However, the school funds me. Having my own organization is very rewarding." Casual drug use is not uncommon on campus; in fact, according to one student, "A professor was stopped by a tour group. A mother asked him about the drug problem at Hampshire. His reply: 'I don't think anyone ever had problems getting drugs here.'"

### Student Body

Hampshire undergrads come pretty close to fitting the stereotype of alt-students: "If you get past the hippies, skaters, windbags, and druggies, this is the best school in the country," writes one student. To those who fit the mold, it seems that "students at Hampshire will accept anyone and everyone. It's hard to be disliked here—you have to go out of your way. There are cliques, but it's easy to find nice, helpful, friendly people." To those with a more mainstream aspect, however, "too many of them have become leftist parrots (and no, I'm not a conservative)." Even those who dis the majority of their peers, however, are quick to add that "I've also found many more students here that are multi-talented and passionate about what they do than I've seen at other schools."

FINANCIAL AID: 413-559-5484 • E-MAIL: ADMISSIONS@HAMPSHIRE.EDU • WEBSITE: WWW.HAMPSHIRE.EDU

## ADMISSIONS

*Very important* academic and nonacademic factors considered by the admissions committee include secondary school record. *Important* factors considered include essays, recommendations, and class rank. *Other* factors considered include extracurricular activities, talent/ability, standardized test scores (optional), interview, and work experience. TOEFL required of all international applicants. *High school units required/recommended:* 19 total recommended; 4 English recommended, 4 math recommended, 4 science recommended, 4 foreign language recommended. *The admissions office says:* "We require every applicant to submit an analytical writing sample in addition to the personal statement."

### The Inside Word

Don Quixote would be a fairly solid candidate for admission to Hampshire. The admissions committee (and it really is one, unlike at many colleges) looks to identify thinkers, dreamers, and the generally intellectually curious. It is important to have a solid record from high school, but high grades only go so far toward impressing the committee. Those who are denied usually lack self-awareness and are fairly poor communicators. Candidates should expect their essays to come under close scrutiny.

## FINANCIAL AID

*Students should submit:* CSS/Financial Aid PROFILE, FAFSA, institution's own financial aid form, noncustodial (divorced/separated) parent's statement, and business/farm supplement. Regular filing deadline is February 1. The Princeton Review suggests that all financial aid forms be submitted as soon as possible after January 1. *Need-based scholarships/grants offered:* Pell, SEOG, state scholarships/grants, private scholarships, and the school's own gift aid. *Merit-based aid*: Hampshire is a National Merit College Sponsor (renewable $1,000 scholarships) and offers other merit scholarships of up to $7,500, renewable. No seperate application required. *Loan aid offered:* Direct Subsidized Stafford, Direct Unsubsidized Stafford, and FFEL PLUS. Institutional employment available. Federal Work-Study Program available. Applicants will be notified of awards on or about April 1. Off-campus job opportunities are good.

## FROM THE ADMISSIONS OFFICE

"Students tell us they like our application. It is less derivative and more open-ended than most. Rather than assigning an essay topic, we ask to learn more about you as an individual and invite your ideas. Instead of just asking for lists of activities, we ask you how those activities (and academic or other endeavors) have shown some of the traits that lead to success at Hampshire (initiative, independence, persistence, for example). This approach parallels the work you will do at Hampshire, defining the questions you will ask and the courses and experiences that will help you to answer them, and integrating your interests."

## ADMISSIONS

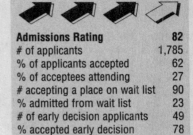

| | |
|---|---|
| Admissions Rating | 82 |
| # of applicants | 1,785 |
| % of applicants accepted | 62 |
| % of acceptees attending | 27 |
| # accepting a place on wait list | 90 |
| % admitted from wait list | 23 |
| # of early decision applicants | 49 |
| % accepted early decision | 78 |

### FRESHMAN PROFILE

| | |
|---|---|
| Range SAT Verbal | 600-700 |
| Average SAT Verbal | 648 |
| Range SAT Math | 550-650 |
| Average SAT Math | 597 |
| Range ACT Composite | 21-29 |
| Minimum TOEFL | 577 |
| Average HS GPA | 3.4 |
| % graduated top 10% of class | 36 |
| % graduated top 25% of class | 69 |
| % graduated top 50% of class | 90 |

### DEADLINES

| | |
|---|---|
| Early decision | 11/15 |
| Early decision notification | 12/15 |
| Regular admission | 2/1 |
| Regular notification | 4/1 |
| Nonfall registration? | yes |

### APPLICANTS ALSO LOOK AT

**AND OFTEN PREFER**
Brown
Vassar
Smith
New College, Oberlin

**AND SOMETIMES PREFER**
Reed
Sarah Lawrence
Bard
Skidmore, NYU

**AND RARELY PREFER**
Antioch
Goddard
Marlboro

## FINANCIAL FACTS

| | |
|---|---|
| Financial Aid Rating | 83 |
| Tuition | $26,455 |
| Room & board | $7,010 |
| Required fees | $416 |
| % frosh receiving aid | 55 |
| % undergrads receiving aid | 60 |
| Avg frosh grant | $14,900 |
| Avg frosh loan | $2,625 |

# HAMPTON UNIVERSITY

OFFICE OF ADMISSIONS, HAMPTON UNIVERSITY, HAMPTON, VA 23668 • ADMISSIONS: 804-727-5328 • FAX: 757-727-5084

## CAMPUS LIFE

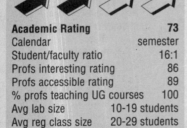

| | |
|---|---|
| **Quality of Life Rating** | **65** |
| Type of school | private |
| Affiliation | none |
| Environment | urban |

### STUDENTS

| | |
|---|---|
| Total undergrad enrollment | 4,891 |
| % male/female | 39/61 |
| % from out of state | 38 |
| % from public high school | 90 |
| % live on campus | 59 |
| % in (# of) fraternities | 5 (5) |
| % in (# of) sororities | 5 (3) |
| % African American | 96 |
| % Caucasian | 3 |
| % Hispanic | 1 |
| % international | 1 |

### SURVEY SAYS . . .

*Very little drug use*
*Frats and sororities dominate social scene*
*Diversity lacking on campus*
*Classes are small*
*Students are cliquish*
*Registration is a pain*
*Library needs improving*
*Lots of long lines and red tape*
*Athletic facilities need improving*

## ACADEMICS

| | |
|---|---|
| **Academic Rating** | **73** |
| Calendar | semester |
| Student/faculty ratio | 16:1 |
| Profs interesting rating | 86 |
| Profs accessible rating | 89 |
| % profs teaching UG courses | 100 |
| Avg lab size | 10-19 students |
| Avg reg class size | 20-29 students |

### MOST POPULAR MAJORS
biology
psychology
mass media

## STUDENTS SPEAK OUT

### Academics

Hampton University, a historically black school founded in the wake of Reconstruction, makes no bones about its approach to undergraduate education. School promotional literature announces Hampton's commitment to "rigorous academics" that stress "scientific and professional [subjects] with a strong liberal arts undergirding" and an "emphasis on the development of character" through a strict code of conduct. In short: Get ready to work hard and toe the line if you choose Hampton. This approach yields ample benefits, according to students. Writes one, "Hampton University is a school of great educational opportunity. There is always room for academic, social, and personal growth. One must only take advantage of those opportunities." Adds a psychology/education double major, "Overall, the academic experience here is very fulfilling and educational. There are superior programs offered here at Hampton University." Professors "range from very articulate and understanding in their teachings to having a heavy accent and just lecturing the whole time, not answering students' questions." Students in business departments were most sanguine about their profs, while those in mathematics and computer science complained most about unintelligible instructors. Student opinion of the administration is more uniform—students agree it is "unorganized" because "the business office and administration do not communicate with each other."

### Life

Life at Hampton involves conforming to an unusual number of rules, including an 11 P.M. curfew for freshmen, a schoolwide dress code, and strict visitation restrictions at dormitories, all of which are single-sex. Writes one student, "The school is very strict, too strict maybe. We are all adults, aren't we?" Freshmen and sophomores are not allowed to have cars, and "without a car or friends with cars you are stuck on campus, which sucks. There is nothing on campus, not to mention anything on or off campus open after 11 P.M." Sub-par dorms and dining services further undermine on-campus life. As a result, "Life at school can be boring. On weekends there are parties, but they are wack, and you get tired of seeing the same faces and the same parties ending at 2 A.M. Sororities and fraternities are stressed too much." Explains one student, "You must go off campus or to neighboring schools to find creative, stimulating, educational, and open-minded entertainment." Campus is not totally devoid of entertainment, though, as "Greeks are involved in a lot of fun yet educational opportunities. They provide a support group not only for themselves but for every student here." Furthermore, sports teams, especially the football team, provide a rallying point for most students. Despite the shortcomings of life here, students have a great deal of school spirit. Reports one, "Before freshmen even start class, they are taught a whole bunch of cheers and dances to do at sporting events. That's why I love Hampton: I can be the cheerleader I've always wanted to be."

### Student Body

There is little racial diversity at Hampton, but there is a great deal of regional diversity. Explains one student, "We have students from all over the world. To attend a mostly black institution where I am able to learn alongside people who look and act like me is a very powerful experience." Students are generally "friendly but high maintenance." While they "always have smiles on their faces, and the upperclassmen are very helpful with orienting freshmen to campus," some complain that superficiality pervades the student body. One student comments, "My fellow students are sometimes shallow and pretentious. Although I enjoy fashion, too much emphasis is placed on it by students attending HU; there seems to be a judgment of one's character based on what one wears." Some see an upside, noting that "many of the students here are arrogant, but arrogance sparks competition and encourages students to do as well as they possibly can."

# HAMPTON UNIVERSITY

FINANCIAL AID: 800-624-3341 • E-MAIL: ADMIT@HAMPTONU.EDU • WEBSITE: WWW.HAMPTONU.EDU

## MISSIONS

*Very important* academic and nonacademic factors considered by the admissions committee include secondary school record. *Important* factors considered include class rank and standardized test scores. *Other* factors considered include alumni/ae relation, character/personal qualities, essays, extracurricular activities, interview, minority status, recommendations, talent/ability, volunteer work, and work experience. Factors *not* considered include geography, religious affiliation/commitment, and state residency. SAT I or ACT required, SAT I preferred. TOEFL required of all international applicants. High school diploma is required and GED is accepted. *High school units required/recommended:* 18 total required; 24 total recommended; 4 English required, 3 math required, 4 math recommended, 3 science required, 4 science recommended, 3 science lab required, 4 science lab recommended, 2 foreign language required, 3 foreign language recommended, 3 social studies required, 4 social studies recommended, 3 elective required, 5 elective recommended.

### The Inside Word

Hampton has less general visibility than such better-known historically black colleges as Morehouse, Spelman, and Howard, but it has just as much of a tradition of academic quality. In recent years the university's profile has been boosted by hosting national workshops on counseling minority students in the college admissions process. Candidates can expect a personal and caring experience in the admissions process.

## FINANCIAL AID

*Students should submit:* FAFSA and state aid form; Virginia residents apply for Tuition Assistance Grants (TAG). Regular filing deadline is March 31. The Princeton Review suggests that all financial aid forms be submitted as soon as possible after January 1. *Need-based scholarships/grants offered:* Pell, SEOG, state scholarships/grants, private scholarships, and Federal Nursing. *Loan aid offered:* Direct Subsidized Stafford, Direct Unsubsidized Stafford, Direct PLUS, and Federal Perkins. Institutional employment available. Applicants will be notified of awards on a rolling basis. Off-campus job opportunities are excellent.

## FROM THE ADMISSIONS OFFICE

"Hampton attempts to provide the environment and structures most conducive to the intellectual, emotional, and aesthetic enlargement of the lives of its members. The university gives priority to effective teaching and scholarly research while placing the student at the center of its planning. Hampton will ask you to look inwardly at your own history and culture and examine your relationship to the aspirations and development of the world."

## ADMISSIONS

| Admissions Rating | 78 |
|---|---|
| # of applicants | 6,107 |
| % of applicants accepted | 48 |
| % of acceptees attending | 32 |

### FRESHMAN PROFILE

| | |
|---|---|
| Range SAT Verbal | 470-550 |
| Average SAT Verbal | 510 |
| Range SAT Math | 450-540 |
| Average SAT Math | 500 |
| Range ACT Composite | 17-21 |
| Average ACT Composite | 19 |
| Minimum TOEFL | 550 |
| Average HS GPA | 3.0 |
| % graduated top 10% of class | 24 |
| % graduated top 25% of class | 49 |
| % graduated top 50% of class | 99 |

### DEADLINES

| | |
|---|---|
| Regular admission | 3/15 |
| Regular notification | rolling |
| Nonfall registration? | yes |

### APPLICANTS ALSO LOOK AT
### AND OFTEN PREFER
Florida A&M
Tuskegee
Spelman
### AND SOMETIMES PREFER
U. Maryland—Coll. Park
Howard
Virginia Tech

## FINANCIAL FACTS

| Financial Aid Rating | 65 |
|---|---|
| Tuition | $9,966 |
| Room & board | $5,090 |
| Books and supplies | $662 |
| Required fees | $1,090 |
| % frosh receiving aid | 60 |
| % undergrads receiving aid | 89 |
| Avg frosh grant | $2,885 |
| Avg frosh loan | $2,254 |

# HANOVER COLLEGE

PO BOX 108, HANOVER, IN 47243-0108 • ADMISSIONS: 812-866-7021 • FAX: 812-866-7098

## CAMPUS LIFE

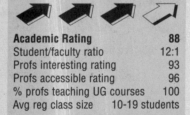

| | |
|---|---|
| **Quality of Life Rating** | **78** |
| Type of school | private |
| Affiliation | Presbyterian |
| Environment | rural |

### STUDENTS

| | |
|---|---|
| Total undergrad enrollment | 1,142 |
| % male/female | 45/55 |
| % from out of state | 35 |
| % live on campus | 92 |
| % in (# of) fraternities | 44 (4) |
| % in (# of) sororities | 43 (4) |
| % African American | 1 |
| % Asian | 2 |
| % Caucasian | 93 |
| % Hispanic | 1 |
| % international | 3 |

### SURVEY SAYS . . .

*Frats and sororities dominate social
scene
Theater is hot
Very little drug use
Athletic facilities are great
Diversity lacking on campus
Library needs improving
Students don't like Hanover, IN
Political activism is (almost)
nonexistent
Lousy off-campus food
Lab facilities are great*

## ACACEMICS

| | |
|---|---|
| **Academic Rating** | **88** |
| Student/faculty ratio | 12:1 |
| Profs interesting rating | 93 |
| Profs accessible rating | 96 |
| % profs teaching UG courses | 100 |
| Avg reg class size | 10-19 students |

### MOST POPULAR MAJORS
business administration
sociolgy
elementary education

## STUDENTS SPEAK OUT

### Academics

Among small liberal arts schools, Hanover College scores high on the "quality-to-price ratio" scale. Hanover is a very affordable private school made even more so by a large endowment, which finances the school's generous aid packages. A Hanover education comes with a few caveats, however. Those attending must be comfortable in an extremely homogenous population, as the vast majority of students are white, midwestern, and Christian. Students must also be willing to live under an extremely—many say excessively—paternalistic administration. Complains one typical student, "The administration does not treat us like the adults we are. They are unreasonably strict. I feel like I'm back in kindergarten." Within those parameters, however, lies an excellent, well-rounded liberal arts education. Students here must complete a wide range of distribution requirements, including courses in philosophy, theology, literature, science, and nonwestern society. Approves one student, "This liberal arts school truly captures all that liberal arts means as far as linking completely different courses to one another." Professors, by all accounts, are top-notch. Writes one undergrad, "The professors really care that you learn and understand the concepts being taught. There is a strong emphasis on open-minded learning, in which, by discussion and research, the student draws the conclusion. The professor is more like a coach." Another reports that "the professors are very knowledgeable and . . . always open to one-on-one conversation."

### Life

Two factors strongly influence the quality of life at Hanover. The first is the administration, which strictly enforces drinking and visitation rules. Explains one student, "Our administration's social policies are up-to-date with the 90s . . . the 1890s! The campuswide prohibition on alcohol and restrictions on times males are allowed in female rooms and vice versa are oppressive and out of date." The other is the town of Hanover and the area immediately surrounding it. Says one student, "There is not much in the way of cultural attractions in southern Indiana." Students quickly resign themselves to the fact that "since we are in the sticks, there is nothing much to do except grab a movie and/or drink." Many gravitate toward the Greeks, who "run the campus socially." Reports one senior, "If you aren't in a fraternity you're kind of screwed as far as a partying social life goes. Many upperclassmen go to the local bars to get away from campus. The social life revolves around fraternities/sororities and maybe venturing to Louisville, Indy, or Cincy." Otherwise, "for fun we have fire pits, late night Wal-Mart trips, dinner at 3 A.M., Nerf wars, and . . . the occasional band." The Hanover football program has recently made a name for itself nationally, but not all students are pleased. Writes one dissident, "Our school used to be excellent academically. Then, our football team got really good, so the school seemed to think we need[ed] more football players. It's like half the freshman class is the football team," for whom it seems the administration "lowered the standards to attract more boys. Just what we need: bigger, dumber boys!"

### Student Body

The "very conservative, religious, not very open-minded, Republican majority" that makes up Hanover's student body recognize that they are "all from the same socioeconomic status. There's no diversity, and they are somewhat snobby." Writes one student, "Unless you are totally at ease living with kids from small-town Indiana, you will get an uncomfortable feeling from the total lack of diversity here." Adds another, "The administration is making extreme attempts to make the campus diverse. Hanover, Indiana, though, isn't the most appealing place for a minority because of its size and location." Students note that there are divisions among the student body and that "our differences arise from Greek affiliation rather than other factors."

FINANCIAL AID: 812-866-7030 • E-MAIL: ADMISSIONS@HANOVER.EDU • WEBSITE: WWW.HANOVER.EDU

## ADMISSIONS

*Very important* academic and nonacademic factors considered by the admissions committee include secondary school record and standardized test scores. *Important* factors considered include class rank, extracurricular activities, minority status, state residency, talent/ability, volunteer work, and work experience. *Other* factors considered include character/personal qualities, essays, geography, and recommendations. Factors *not* considered include alumni/ae relation, interview, and religious affiliation/commitment. SAT I or ACT required, SAT I preferred. TOEFL required of all international applicants. High school diploma is required and GED is accepted. *High school units required/recommended:* 22 total recommended; 4 English recommended, 3 math recommended, 3 science recommended, 3 foreign language recommended, 3 social studies recommended, 3 history recommended, 3 elective recommended. *The admissions office says:* "Alumni children receive some special consideration."

### The Inside Word

Despite significant national publicity in recent years, Hanover still has a relatively small applicant pool. There is no doubt that these candidates are capable academically—few schools have as impressive a graduation rate or percentage of its alums going on to grad school. It pays to put some energy into the completion of the application process, especially given the sizable percentage of students awarded academic scholarships.

## FINANCIAL AID

*Students should submit:* FAFSA. Regular filing deadline is March 1. The Princeton Review suggests that all financial aid forms be submitted as soon as possible after January 1. *Need-based scholarships/grants offered:* Pell, state scholarships/grants, private scholarships, and the school's own gift aid. *Loan aid offered:* FFEL Subsidized Stafford, FFEL Unsubsidized Stafford, FFEL PLUS, and Shell Loan. Federal Work-Study Program available. Applicants will be notified of awards on a rolling basis beginning on or about April 15. Off-campus job opportunities are fair.

## FROM THE ADMISSIONS OFFICE

"Hanover College offers a unique community to all who live here. With 95 percent of our students and over 50 percent of our faculty and staff residing on campus, the pursuit of academic excellence extends well beyond the confines of the classroom. This is enhanced by a caring faculty, 90 percent of whom hold earned doctoral degrees. The desire to meet academic challenges and the strong sense of community may be the two greatest contributors to the 86 percent retention rate of which Hanover is quite proud. These contributions are also apparent in that over the past five years more than 65 percent of our graduates have advanced their educational degrees. Hanover's total cost qualifies the college as one of the best values in the nation, and its sizable endowment, on a dollar-per-student ratio, places it in the top 10 percent nationally."

## ADMISSIONS

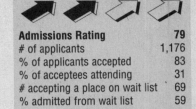

| | |
|---|---|
| Admissions Rating | 79 |
| # of applicants | 1,176 |
| % of applicants accepted | 83 |
| % of acceptees attending | 31 |
| # accepting a place on wait list | 69 |
| % admitted from wait list | 59 |

### FRESHMAN PROFILE

| | |
|---|---|
| Range SAT Verbal | 510-620 |
| Average SAT Verbal | 568 |
| Range SAT Math | 530-630 |
| Average SAT Math | 579 |
| Range ACT Composite | 23-28 |
| Average ACT Composite | 25 |
| Minimum TOEFL | 550 |
| % graduated top 10% of class | 39 |
| % graduated top 25% of class | 72 |
| % graduated top 50% of class | 94 |

### DEADLINES

| | |
|---|---|
| Priority admission deadline | 12/1 |
| Regular admission | 3/1 |
| Nonfall registration? | yes |

### APPLICANTS ALSO LOOK AT
#### AND SOMETIMES PREFER
Indiana U.—Bloomington
DePauw
Centre
Butler
Franklin Coll.
#### AND RARELY PREFER
Ball State
Purdue U.—West Lafayette
Wittenberg
Indiana State

## FINANCIAL FACTS

| | |
|---|---|
| Financial Aid Rating | 81 |
| Tuition | $11,425 |
| Room & board | $4,930 |
| Books and supplies | $600 |
| Required fees | $345 |
| % frosh receiving aid | 56 |
| % undergrads receiving aid | 51 |
| Avg frosh grant | $7,891 |
| Avg frosh loan | $2,467 |

# HARVARD COLLEGE

BYERLY HALL, 8 GARDEN STREET, CAMBRIDGE, MA 02318 • ADMISSIONS: 617-495-1551 • FAX: 617-495-8821

## CAMPUS LIFE

| Quality of Life Rating | 93 |
| Type of school | private |
| Affiliation | none |
| Environment | urban |

### STUDENTS

| Total undergrad enrollment | 6,684 |
| % male/female | 54/46 |
| % from out of state | 84 |
| % from public high school | 65 |
| % live on campus | 96 |
| % African American | 8 |
| % Asian | 19 |
| % Caucasian | 45 |
| % Hispanic | 8 |
| % Native American | 1 |
| % international | 7 |

### SURVEY SAYS . . .
Great library
High cost of living
Registration is a breeze
Students love Cambridge
Great computer facilities
Lots of TAs teach upper-level courses
Student government is unpopular
Ethnic diversity on campus
Large classes

## ACADEMICS

| Academic Rating | 93 |
| Calendar | semester |
| Student/faculty ratio | 8:1 |
| Profs interesting rating | 90 |
| Profs accessible rating | 89 |
| % profs teaching UG courses | 100 |
| Avg lab size | under 10 students |
| Avg reg class size | 10-19 students |

### MOST POPULAR MAJORS
government
economics
biology

## STUDENTS SPEAK OUT
### Academics
Harvard College's "academic reputation" precedes it. Home to a distinguished faculty and phenomenal world-class research facilities, Harvard is the perhaps the most prestigious hub of intellectual activity in America and is certainly one of the best academic universities on the planet. Students lucky and talented enough to gain admission have the opportunity to pursue virtually any academic interest under the tutelage of some of the finest minds ever. Not surprisingly, though, "there's not much hand-holding here," as the "really challenging" professors are the college faculty equivalent of rock stars. Harvard profs are, however, "more approachable than some people think." "One of my professors took Polaroids of his 200-person lecture so that he could learn our names," reports an awed sophomore. "We all thought it was great until he started cold-calling us in lecture by name." And another professor "gives milk and cookies to students who come to his office hours." There are, however, a considerable number of TAs who teach undergraduate courses, a situation that causes students to give the faculty only average marks. Overall, the administration runs Harvard College like butter.

### Life
Every school in the Ivy League is great, but one area in which Harvard has a leg up on all of its fellow Ivies is its safe, attractive, and entertaining location in Cambridge, just minutes from "the great city" of Boston. During the week, "Harvard makes students work very hard" and intense studying is commonplace. "We all study hard," relates a sophomore, "but we all play just as hard." There are "some people who don't go out so much, but there's always a party if you want to find one." On the weekends (and, actually, during the week as well) "there is always so much happening on campus"—"concerts, plays, games, lectures, movies," you name it. As a result, students "rarely leave" campus. It helps that Harvard's community-like dorms are great. When Harvard students must venture into the world, the sights, sounds, and bars of Boston are usually the destination. Also, "everyone loves to get dressed up in black-tie" duds, and students tell us they find many excuses to don the highbrow look. There is no Greek system here, but there are several exclusive, upper-crust, fancy-schmancy social clubs (membership by invitation only) "similar to a combination of fraternities and Princeton's eating clubs" that provide some social life, though they are not affiliated with the college. Clubs and activities abound as well, including *The Harvard Lampoon*, Harvard's hilarious and satirical magazine.

### Student Body
Harvard students generally perceive themselves as "bright, motivated, fun, and interesting" souls who are "extremely civil and polite and easy to get along with." The school does, however, have its share of "huge" egos and "people who could stand to balance work and play a bit better." The admissions staff here definitely makes it a point to seek out "a very diverse student body in all ways," and many students laud Harvard for attracting "a wide variety of backgrounds and personalities" to campus. Interpersonal skills "are sometimes lacking" in certain super-genius circles, but many students are "preppy" types who "try very hard to look 'pulled together' in all respects, no matter how they are really doing." And, given that they got into Harvard, you've got to think that most students here are doing pretty well. "The single greatest strength Harvard has to offer is its students," beams a sophomore, "the most incredibly talented group of people I've ever met."

FINANCIAL AID: 617-495-1581 • E-MAIL: COLLEGE@FAS.HARVARD.EDU • WEBSITE: WWW.FAS.HARVARD.EDU

## ADMISSIONS

*Very important* academic and nonacademic factors considered by the admissions committee include character/personal qualities, essays, recommendations, and secondary school record. *Important* factors considered include class rank, extracurricular activities, standardized test scores, and talent/ability. *Other* factors considered include alumni/ae relation, interview, minority status, volunteer work, and work experience. Factors *not* considered include geography, religious affiliation/commitment, and state residency. SAT I or ACT required; SAT II also required. *High school units required/recommended:* 17 total recommended; 4 English recommended, 3 math recommended, 3 science recommended, 2 science lab recommended, 2 foreign language recommended, 3 social studies recommended, 2 history recommended.

### The Inside Word

It just doesn't get any tougher than this. Candidates to Harvard face dual obstacles—an awe-inspiring applicant pool and, as a result, admissions standards that defy explanation in quantifiable terms. Harvard denies admission to the vast majority, and virtually all of them are top students. It all boils down to splitting hairs, which is quite hard to explain and even harder for candidates to understand. Rather than being as detailed and direct as possible about the selection process and criteria, Harvard keeps things close to the vest—before, during, and after. They even refuse to admit that being from South Dakota is an advantage. Thus the admissions process does more to intimidate candidates than to empower them. Moving to a common application seemed to be a small step in the right direction, but with the current explosion of early decision applicants and a super-high yield of enrollees, things are not likely to change dramatically.

## FINANCIAL AID

*Students should submit:* FAFSA, CSS/Financial Aid PROFILE, noncustodial (divorced/separated) parent's statement, business/farm supplement, and tax returns. There is no regular filing deadline. The Princeton Review suggests that all financial aid forms be submitted as soon as possible after January 1. *Need-based scholarships/grants offered:* Pell, SEOG, state scholarships/grants, private scholarships, and the school's own gift aid. *Loan aid offered:* Direct Subsidized Stafford, Direct Unsubsidized Stafford, Direct PLUS, Federal Perkins, state, and college/university loans from institutional funds. Institutional employment available. Federal Work-Study Program available. Applicants will be notified of awards on or about April 1. Off-campus job opportunities are excellent.

## FROM THE ADMISSIONS OFFICE

"The admissions committee looks for energy, ambition, and the capacity to make the most of opportunities. Academic ability and preparation are important, and so is intellectual curiosity—but many of the strongest applicants have significant nonacademic interests and accomplishments as well. There is no formula for admission and applicants are considered carefully, with attention to future promise."

## ADMISSIONS

| | |
|---|---|
| Admissions Rating | 99 |
| # of applicants | 18,161 |
| % of applicants accepted | 11 |
| % of acceptees attending | 79 |

### FRESHMAN PROFILE

| | |
|---|---|
| Range SAT Verbal | 700–800 |
| Range SAT Math | 700–790 |
| Range ACT Composite | 30–34 |
| % graduated top 10% of class | 90 |
| % graduated top 25% of class | 98 |
| % graduated top 50% of class | 100 |

### DEADLINES

| | |
|---|---|
| Priority admission deadline | 12/15 |
| Regular admission | 1/1 |
| Regular notification | 4/1 |

### APPLICANTS ALSO LOOK AT AND SOMETIMES PREFER

Princeton
Stanford
Yale
Swarthmore

**AND RARELY PREFER**

Northwestern U.
Georgetown U.
Amherst
Williams
U. Penn

## FINANCIAL FACTS

| | |
|---|---|
| Financial Aid Rating | 74 |
| Tuition | $22,694 |
| Room & board | $7,982 |
| Books and supplies | $800 |
| Required fees | $2,434 |
| % frosh receiving aid | 52 |
| % undergrads receiving aid | 50 |
| Avg frosh grant | $18,828 |
| Avg frosh loan | $2,556 |

# HARVEY MUDD COLLEGE

301 EAST 12TH STREET, CLAREMONT, CA 91711-5990 • ADMISSIONS: 909-621-8011 • FAX: 909-621-8360

## CAMPUS LIFE

| Quality of Life Rating | 82 |
|---|---|
| Type of school | private |
| Affiliation | none |
| Environment | suburban |

### STUDENTS

| | |
|---|---|
| Total undergrad enrollment | 717 |
| % male/female | 71/29 |
| % from out of state | 61 |
| % live on campus | 96 |
| % African American | 1 |
| % Asian | 22 |
| % Caucasian | 68 |
| % Hispanic | 4 |
| % Native American | 1 |
| % international | 3 |
| # of countries represented | 13 |

### SURVEY SAYS . . .

*Student publications are ignored*
*Great computer facilities*
*Popular college radio*
*No one cheats*
*Lab facilities need improving*
*Very small frat/sorority scene*
*Intercollegiate sports unpopular or nonexistent*
*Unattractive campus*
*Lousy food on campus*

## ACADEMICS

| Academic Rating | 94 |
|---|---|
| Calendar | semester |
| Student/faculty ratio | 9:1 |
| Profs interesting rating | 95 |
| Profs accessible rating | 98 |
| % profs teaching UG courses | 100 |
| Avg lab size | 10-19 students |
| Avg reg class size | 10-19 students |

### MOST POPULAR MAJORS

engineering
computer science
physics

## STUDENTS SPEAK OUT

### Academics

The Claremont Colleges are five small undergraduate schools and two graduate schools sharing a central location and facilities. Each school has its own personality; Harvey Mudd College is defined by its focus on engineering, mathematics, and science. The school's mission is to create technologically gifted graduates who are also "well versed . . . in the humanities and the social sciences," a goal it achieves through an unusually demanding set of nonscience core requirements. Students describe the regimen as extremely difficult. Writes one, "This is a hardcore school. Day in, day out, we get our butts worked. Ninety-five percent of us come from the top 10 percent of our class and have to deal with becoming a part of the other faction." Adds another, "Grades, social life, sleep: pick any two of three." Why put yourself through this? Great professors, unparalleled access to top facilities, and the knowledge that, when it's all over, an interesting and high-paying job probably awaits you. The professors here "are the best part. They're intelligent, understanding, dedicated, respectful, funny, laid-back, kind, and always there for you." Similarly, administrators are "hardworking and approachable. They're always there to help; I should know." While these amenities soften the blow of Mudd's demanding program, students still warn that "Mudd is like a bottle of vodka. Some people like it, some people hate it, but either way it hits you hard the next morning."

### Life

With one of the heaviest workloads in the country, Mudd students have very little time for anything but classes and studying. As one student tells us, "Life is hard in a school like this for people who aren't used to the great amount of studying this place requires." Elaborates another, "Life at Mudd is pretty much academic. Sure we have a close relation with the other colleges on the five-campus spread, but we generally don't have time for them. Generally, we just do our work. Of course, we work hard and play hard, just like at other schools. On weekends we throw heavy-duty parties." When they can make the time, students indulge in such Mudd traditions as "Five Class Competition (a huge, stupid relay race) and the Doughnut Rally (we drive around town in a race and eat lots of doughnuts). Traditions like this make Mudd fun!" Los Angeles and San Diego are relatively close to the surrounding town of Claremont. Students say the town is "nice, but there is nothing of interest here"—except, of course, the many doughnut shops.

### Student Body

Like most schools of engineering and science, Mudd attracts a student body that can be, at times, a little strange. Students describe themselves as "weird nerds who never take showers and are always picking things off their feet. The 'different' habits of a large portion of the population here take some getting used to." Once acclimated, students discover a level of comfort few had known before: "When you spend high school as an intellectual outcast, it's nice to come to a place like Mudd and see that you're not alone. Still, all of us are unique." The student body is neither homogeneous nor heterogeneous; it is, rather, bigeneric, consisting almost entirely of whites and Asians. Students report that "there are no well-defined cliques or outcasts." In fact, "Everyone's willing to help everyone else both on school and personal levels."

FINANCIAL AID: 909-621-8055 • E-MAIL: ADMISSION@HMC.EDU • WEBSITE: WWW.HMC.EDU

## ADMISSIONS

*Very important* academic and nonacademic factors considered by the admissions committee include secondary school record. *Important* factors include character/personal qualities, class rank, essays, recommendations, and standardized test scores. *Other* factors considered include alumni/ae relation, extracurricular activities, geography, minority status, state residency, interview, talent/ability, volunteer work, and work experience. Factors *not* considered include religious affiliation/commitment. SAT I and three SAT IIs required. TOEFL recommended of all international applicants. GED is accepted. High school curriculum must include 1 year each of calculus, physics, and chemistry. (Students may substitute one semester of college-level work in these subjects.) *The admissions office says:* "HMC students get the best of both worlds academically and socially: high-powered math, science, and engineering as well as the opportunities presented by the Claremont College Consortium. Over 2,500 classes and hundreds of extracurricular activities (including athletics, music, performing arts, and more) combine with the abundance of cultural opportunities to make Harvey Mudd one of the most unique institutions in the country."

### The Inside Word

Harvey Mudd is a place for serious students, and its admissions process expects excellence from all candidates. Not to say that they don't have a sense of humor out there in Claremont. The college attracted national attention in the past by mailing recruitment literature that poked fun at the overly serious world of college admissions while at the same time showcasing the school's academic quality. Any admissions staff that contributes to the lessening of student stress in the college search and admissions process is to be commended.

## FINANCIAL AID

*Students should submit:* FAFSA, CSS/Financial Aid PROFILE, state aid form, noncustodial (divorced/separated) parent's statement, and business/farm supplement. Regular filing deadline is February 1. The Princeton Review suggests that all financial aid forms be submitted as soon as possible after January 1. *Need-based scholarships/grants offered:* Pell, SEOG, state scholarships/grants, private scholarships, and the school's own gift aid. *Loan aid offered:* FFEL Subsidized Stafford, FFEL Unsubsidized Stafford, FFEL PLUS, Federal Perkins, and college/university loans from institutional funds. Institutional employment available. Federal Work-Study Program available. Applicants will be notified of awards on a rolling basis beginning on or about April 1. Off-campus job opportunities are fair.

## FROM THE ADMISSIONS OFFICE

"Students interested in HMC must have a talent and passion for science and mathematics. The college offers majors in mathematics, physics, engineering, chemistry, biology, and computer science. 'Mudders' have very diverse interests. Because nearly one-third of the course work at HMC is in the humanities and social sciences, HMC students also enjoy studying economics, psychology, philosophy, history, the fine arts, and literature."

## ADMISSIONS

| | |
|---|---|
| Admissions Rating | 94 |
| # of applicants | 1,647 |
| % of applicants accepted | 35 |
| % of acceptees attending | 33 |
| # accepting a place on wait list | 157 |
| % admitted from wait list | 0 |
| # of early decision applicants | 85 |
| % accepted early decision | 54 |

### FRESHMAN PROFILE

| | |
|---|---|
| Range SAT Verbal | 670-760 |
| Average SAT Verbal | 710 |
| Range SAT Math | 740-790 |
| Average SAT Math | 760 |
| Minimum TOEFL | 600 |
| % graduated top 10% of class | 94 |
| % graduated top 25% of class | 100 |

### DEADLINES

| | |
|---|---|
| Early decision | 11/15 |
| Early decision notification | 12/15 |
| Regular admission | 1/15 |
| Regular notification | 4/1 |

### APPLICANTS ALSO LOOK AT AND OFTEN PREFER
Stanford
MIT
**AND SOMETIMES PREFER**
Cornell U.
Rice
**AND RARELY PREFER**
Worcester Poly.
Virginia Tech

### FINANCIAL FACTS

| | |
|---|---|
| Financial Aid Rating | 82 |
| Tuition | $22,663 |
| Room & board | $8,418 |
| Books and supplies | $800 |
| Required fees | $524 |
| % frosh receiving aid | 61 |
| % undergrads receiving aid | 60 |

# HAVERFORD COLLEGE

370 LANCASTER AVENUE, HAVERFORD, PA 19041 • ADMISSIONS: 610-896-1350 • FAX: 610-896-1338

## CAMPUS LIFE

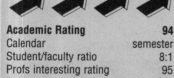

| Quality of Life Rating | 87 |
|---|---|
| Type of school | private |
| Affiliation | none |
| Environment | suburban |

### STUDENTS

| | |
|---|---|
| Total undergrad enrollment | 1,135 |
| % from out of state | 79 |
| % from public high school | 58 |
| % live on campus | 97 |
| % African American | 6 |
| % Asian | 10 |
| % Caucasian | 75 |
| % Hispanic | 6 |
| % international | 3 |

### SURVEY SAYS . . .
*Beautiful campus*
*Campus easy to get around*
*Campus feels safe*
*No one cheats*
*Great library*
*Musical organizations are hot*
*(Almost) no one smokes*
*Lousy food on campus*
*Very little hard liquor*
*Registration is a pain*
*Very little beer drinking*
*Student publications are popular*

## ACADEMICS

| Academic Rating | 94 |
|---|---|
| Calendar | semester |
| Student/faculty ratio | 8:1 |
| Profs interesting rating | 95 |
| Profs accessible rating | 98 |
| % profs teaching UG courses | 100 |
| Avg lab size | under 10 students |
| Avg reg class size | 10-19 students |

### MOST POPULAR MAJORS
biology
English
history

## STUDENTS SPEAK OUT
### Academics

At prestigious Haverford College, a small school with a big reputation in the liberal arts and premedical sciences, "The professors aren't concerned with teaching you to think like the renowned critics and authors that we read in class. Instead, they teach us to think for ourselves." This approach is just one of the reasons why students remain steadfastly devoted to this school despite the backbreaking workload it often heaps upon them. Warns one psychology major, "Sometimes the amount of work makes us feel as though we're being hit by a tsunami. At least we know that we're all in the same boat." Other reasons include a faculty that is "amazing—passionate, accommodating, and extremely dedicated," and a much-loved, student-enforced Honor Code that governs not only academic activity but social activity as well. Explains one student, "The Honor Code affects so many aspects of academics and relationships. The Quaker heritage is prevalent here." Says another, "Picture yourself during finals week. Your professor hands you your test. You go to the library, put a blanket on your shoulders, take the test, and return it at your convenience. This is the essential Haverford: learning for the sheer joy of it." Small classes also contribute to the air of conviviality here; an academic partnership with Bryn Mawr College, which allows students to cross-register for courses and provides each campus access to the others' libraries, helps to mitigate the shortcomings of Haverford's small-school status.

### Life

The scenic, parklike Haverford campus "is pleasing to the eye," "the kind of place where impromptu Frisbee games break out without warning on a sunny spring day." It also provides "a lot of fun, free entertainment," a necessary diversion for the school's hardworking undergrads. Reports one student, "I love all the activities and clubs on campus, from cultural organizations to comedy troupes. I joined the hockey club this fall, even though I barely know how to skate. Chasing a puck around an ice rink at 9:00 on a Sunday night is a great stress reliever!" Students speak highly of campus housing accommodations, but have few kind words for food service. The school is located on the Main Line, a suburban area outside Philadelphia described as "safe but boring." Notes one sophomore, "Haverford is a place where you don't worry about leaving your wallet lying around. Unfortunately, staying on campus is about as fun as watching a submarine race." Says another, "Although there are five colleges and universities in the area, this is not a college town. Fortunately, Philly is close by, and that gives us much to do: Fringe Festival, plays, restaurants, First Friday, community service."

### Student Body

Haverford students "run the gamut from earthy tree-huggers to frat-boy wannabes, and from science genius to your classic boy- or girl-next-door type. Yet everyone you meet is incredibly nice." They all have one other thing in common: "Everyone here is at least a closet nerd. It's great!" Students are typically "conservative, shy, socially rather inept, but nice, polite, and friendly," and, by their own accounts, not the most physically attractive lot ("We may not be the best-looking, but we certainly are interesting!" is a typical comment from a Haverford survey, respondent). The Honor Code rules social as well as academic aspects of the 'Ford. Some point out that the Honor Code tends to limit some discussion of tensions on campus. As one sophomore explains, "The Honor Code fosters respect for all students, regardless of race, class, and sexual orientation. Because of this, people are rarely hostile or even unkind to each other."

FINANCIAL AID: 610-896-1350 • E-MAIL: ADMITME@HAVERFORD.EDU • WEBSITE: WWW.HAVERFORD.EDU

## ADMISSIONS

*Very important* academic and nonacademic factors considered by the admissions committee include alumni/ae relation, minority status, and secondary school record. *Important* factors considered include character/personal qualities, class rank, essays, extracurricular activities, interview, recommendations, standardized test scores, talent/ability, and volunteer work. *Other* factors considered include geography, state residency, and work experience. Factors *not* considered include religious affiliation/commitment. SAT I or ACT required; SAT II also required. High school diploma is required and GED is accepted. *High school units required/recommended:* 20 total recommended; 4 English recommended, 3 math recommended, 3 science recommended, 3 foreign language recommended, 1 social studies recommended.

### The Inside Word

Candidate evaluation at Haverford is quite thorough, and the applicant pool is sizable and strong. Applicants who are successful through the initial academic review are then carefully considered for the match they make with the college. This part of the process is especially important at small schools like Haverford, and students should definitely spend some time assessing the reasons for their interest in attending before responding to essays and interviewing. Interviewing is a must.

## FINANCIAL AID

*Students should submit:* FAFSA, CSS/Financial Aid PROFILE, state aid form, noncustodial (divorced/separated) parent's statement, and business/farm supplement. Regular filing deadline is January 31. The Princeton Review suggests that all financial aid forms be submitted as soon as possible after January 1. *Need-based scholarships/grants offered:* Pell, SEOG, state scholarships/grants, private scholarships, and the school's own gift aid. *Loan aid offered:* FFEL Subsidized Stafford, FFEL Unsubsidized Stafford, FFEL PLUS, and Federal Perkins. Institutional employment available. Federal Work-Study Program available. Applicants will be notified of awards on or about April 15. Off-campus job opportunities are good.

## FROM THE ADMISSIONS OFFICE

"Haverford strives to be a college in which integrity, honesty, and concern for others are dominant forces. The college does not have many formal rules; rather, it offers an opportunity for students to govern their affairs and conduct themselves with respect and concern for others. Each student is expected to adhere to the Honor Code as it is adopted each year by the Students' Association. Haverford's Quaker roots show most clearly in the relationship of faculty and students, in the emphasis on integrity, in the interaction of the individual and the community, and through the college's concern for the uses to which its students put their expanding knowledge. Haverford's 1,100 students represent a wide diversity of interests, backgrounds, and talents. They come from public, parochial, and independent schools across the United States, Puerto Rico, and 27 foreign countries. Students of color are an important part of the Haverford community. The Minority Coalition, which includes Asian, black, and Hispanic students' associations, works with faculty and administration on matters directly concerned with the quality of life at the college."

## ADMISSIONS

| | |
|---|---:|
| Admissions Rating | 97 |
| # of applicants | 2,683 |
| % of applicants accepted | 32 |
| % of acceptees attending | 39 |
| # accepting a place on wait list | 157 |
| % admitted from wait list | 1 |
| # of early decision applicants | 174 |
| % accepted early decision | 47 |

### FRESHMAN PROFILE

| | |
|---|---:|
| Range SAT Verbal | 630-730 |
| Range SAT Math | 630-720 |
| % graduated top 10% of class | 83 |
| % graduated top 25% of class | 99 |
| % graduated top 50% of class | 100 |

### DEADLINES

| | |
|---|---:|
| Early decision | 11/15 |
| Early decision notification | 12/15 |
| Regular admission | 1/15 |
| Regular notification | 4/15 |

### APPLICANTS ALSO LOOK AT

**AND OFTEN PREFER**
Princeton
Harvard
Yale
Brown
Wellesley

**AND SOMETIMES PREFER**
Amherst
Swarthmore
Williams
U.Penn
Bryn Mawr

**AND RARELY PREFER**
Vassar
Middlebury
Earlham

## FINANCIAL FACTS

| | |
|---|---:|
| Financial Aid Rating | 82 |
| Tuition | $25,826 |
| Room & board | $8,230 |
| Required fees | $244 |
| % frosh receiving aid | 41 |
| % undergrads receiving aid | 44 |
| Avg frosh grant | $19,407 |
| Avg frosh loan | $2,992 |

# HENDRIX COLLEGE

1600 WASHINGTON AVENUE, CONWAY, AR 72032 • ADMISSIONS: 501-450-1362 • FAX: 501-450-3843

## CAMPUS LIFE

| Quality of Life Rating | 84 |
|---|---|
| Type of school | private |
| Affiliation | Methodist |
| Environment | suburban |

### STUDENTS

| | |
|---|---|
| Total undergrad enrollment | 1,130 |
| % male/female | 46/54 |
| % from out of state | 33 |
| % live on campus | 80 |
| % African American | 5 |
| % Asian | 3 |
| % Caucasian | 82 |
| % Hispanic | 1 |
| % Native American | 1 |
| % international | 1 |

### SURVEY SAYS . . .
*Political activism is hot
Student government is popular
(Almost) everyone smokes
Campus easy to get around
Great library
Diverse students interact*

## ACADEMICS

| Academic Rating | 88 |
|---|---|
| Calendar | trimester |
| Student/faculty ratio | 13:1 |
| Profs interesting rating | 95 |
| Profs accessible rating | 97 |
| % profs teaching UG courses | 100 |
| Avg lab size | 10-19 students |
| Avg reg class size | 10-19 students |

### MOST POPULAR MAJORS
psychology
biology
history

## STUDENTS SPEAK OUT

### Academics

"I never cease to be amazed by my professors," says an awed chemistry major at "fast-paced" Hendrix College. "One of the main reasons I decided to attend was the amount of involvement between professors [and students] in and out of the classroom. At Hendrix, even the most boring subjects come alive through the professors' spunk, wit, and love of the material." There are "a few tenured sticks in the mud" here, but the vast majority of professors are "wonderfully gifted and insightful." Students also like the fact that "Hendrix is small enough that professors can recognize you in and out of class yet large enough to make you feel like it's okay to miss a day and you won't be shot for it." The curriculum includes a host of flexible but demanding general education requirements in the humanities, social sciences, natural sciences, and a foreign language. "Western Intellectual Traditions is required for all freshmen, and it's a good foundation," declares a religion major. "'Unto the whole person' is our whole motto and I think we live up to it. This college makes you think. It makes you think about things you don't want to think about." Students like the "fairly accessible" administration because there is "no red tape to stumble through" and "they try," though "there is one particular dean who seems to believe it is her duty to take some of the fun out of being a college kid." A jaded senior reflects that Hendrix "has been a learning experience that parallels real life—one that I don't regret and will never forget."

### Life

"Hendrix is a happy place with happy people" and there is "a real balance between academics and partying" on this "beautiful" and "safe" campus. "During the week everyone studies every night, but on the weekends the parties are wild." Dorm parties are reportedly "very popular" and, as Hendrix has "no sororities or fraternities," "everyone parties together." However, "the food has gone downhill," all the campus construction "sucks," and "alcohol runs are the worst. Being in a dry county, it's not like we can just run around the corner. It's a good 20-minute ride." Beyond partying, students here often "study outside" or "sit in the pecan groves and talk about life." The school brings "bands, dances, movies, and other entertainment" to campus, and "there is a lot of involvement in volunteer work, activist groups, and the arts," according to a sophomore. "Everyone here volunteers." Intramural athletics are also very popular, "because everyone can participate," and "basketball games are a big source of fun." After hours, "midnight runs to Taco Bell and Waffle House" are common. "A large percentage of the students are from Arkansas" and "too many students go home on the weekends, leaving the campus dead." Certainly, "there is nothing to do off campus" in Conway, by all accounts "a pretty boring town." Students looking for urban pursuits can take "road trips to Little Rock and Memphis."

### Student Body

"Part of what makes Hendrix a great school is the fact that it is such a close-knit community," explains a first-year student. "Everyone knows everyone else without the negative and petty stuff from high school. Everyone has a genuine chance to become the person they want to become." The "very open-minded and accepting" students here describe themselves as "generally helpful, good-natured," and "very friendly"—"an easygoing bunch of kids." As one student explains, "Anyone who enjoys sitting down with a good cup of coffee, listening to original music, and having some interesting conversation would be happy here." The "gay population" on campus "is extremely high," and Hendrix students are also "pacifistic" and "very liberal," not to mention "self-absorbed." "We all want to change the world," says one student. "They are also very outspoken" and "it totally looks like everybody smokes." Hendrix attracts "bright" students who long to become "worldly and educated." "Dumb-dumbs don't hack it at this school" and "the close-minded, shallow, and inept seem to be weeded out freshman year."

FINANCIAL AID: 501-450-1368 • E-MAIL: ADM@HENDRIX.EDU • WEBSITE: WWW.HENDRIX.EDU

## ADMISSIONS

*Very important* academic and nonacademic factors considered by the admissions committee include secondary school record and standardized test scores. *Important* factors considered include class rank, extracurricular activities, talent/ability, volunteer work, and work experience. *Other* factors considered include alumni/ae relation, character/personal qualities, essays, interview, minority status, and recommendations. Factors *not* considered include geography, religious affiliation/commitment, and state residency. SAT I or ACT required. TOEFL required of all international applicants. High school diploma is required and GED is accepted. *High school units required/recommended:* 4 English required, 3 math required, 3 science required, 2 science lab required, 2 foreign language required, 2 social studies required, 1 history required, 2 elective required.

### The Inside Word

Hendrix has a small but well-qualified applicant pool. The college is a sleeper, and is an especially good bet for students with strong grades who lack the test scores usually necessary for admission to colleges on a higher level of selectivity. Look for Hendrix to get tougher as they continue to garner attention from national publications. This place has been making the lists, and it is solid.

## FINANCIAL AID

*Students should submit:* FAFSA, institution's own financial aid form, and state aid form. The Princeton Review suggests that all financial aid forms be submitted as soon as possible after January 1. *Need-based scholarships/grants offered:* Pell, SEOG, state scholarships/grants, private scholarships and the school's own gift aid. *Loan aid offered:* FFEL Subsidized Stafford, FFEL Unsubsidized Stafford, FFEL PLUS, Federal Perkins, and Methodist Loan. Institutional employment available. Federal Work-Study Program available. Applicants will be notified of awards on a rolling basis beginning on or about March 1. Off-campus job opportunities are excellent.

## FROM THE ADMISSIONS OFFICE

"Students who choose Hendrix are bright, eager learners. They have high aspirations; many go on to pursue advanced degrees in graduate and professional schools. Each year the average ACT and College Board scores of the incoming class are in the 85th to 90th percentile range nationally. But Hendrix students expect more from the school than academic challenge. For most, there is a desire to balance their schedules with other kinds of activity—from ensemble practice to a game of intramural racquetball. Everyone fits in; the small campus engenders a sense of openness and belonging. Among the recent graduating class, 200 seniors are recipients of offers to study biochemistry at Yale, English at the University of Virginia, electrical engineering at Duke, business administration at Harvard, medicine at Johns Hopkins, theology at Claremont, and law at Georgetown."

### ADMISSIONS

| | |
|---|---|
| Admissions Rating | 82 |
| # of applicants | 929 |
| % of applicants accepted | 87 |
| % of acceptees attending | 40 |

### FRESHMAN PROFILE

| | |
|---|---|
| Range SAT Verbal | 590-690 |
| Average SAT Verbal | 643 |
| Range SAT Math | 550-670 |
| Average SAT Math | 615 |
| Range ACT Composite | 25-31 |
| Average ACT Composite | 27 |
| Minimum TOEFL | 550 |
| Average HS GPA | 3.7 |
| % graduated top 10% of class | 46 |
| % graduated top 25% of class | 75 |
| % graduated top 50% of class | 94 |

### DEADLINES

| | |
|---|---|
| Priority admission deadline | 1/15 |
| Nonfall registration? | yes |

### APPLICANTS ALSO LOOK AT AND OFTEN PREFER

Tulane
Vanderbilt
Wash. U
Millsaps

### AND SOMETIMES PREFER

U. of the South
Rhodes
U. Arkansas
SMU

### FINANCIAL FACTS

| | |
|---|---|
| Financial Aid Rating | 75 |
| Tuition | $12,340 |
| Room & board | $4,625 |
| Books and supplies | $700 |
| Required fees | $325 |
| % frosh receiving aid | 52 |
| % undergrads receiving aid | 55 |
| Avg frosh grant | $8,927 |
| Avg frosh loan | $3,137 |

# HIRAM COLLEGE

PO Box 67, Hiram, OH 44234 • Admissions: 800-362-5280 • Fax: 330-569-5944

## CAMPUS LIFE

| | |
|---|---|
| **Quality of Life Rating** | **82** |
| Type of school | private |
| Affiliation | Disciples of Christ |
| Environment | rural |

### STUDENTS

| | |
|---|---|
| Total undergrad enrollment | 1,204 |
| % male/female | 45/55 |
| % from out of state | 17 |
| % from public high school | 93 |
| % live on campus | 92 |
| % African American | 9 |
| % Asian | 1 |
| % Caucasian | 88 |
| % Hispanic | 2 |
| % international | 2 |

### SURVEY SAYS . . .

*Campus easy to get around
Campus feels safe
Beautiful campus
Great library
Diversity lacking on campus
Students don't get along with local
community
Lousy food on campus
Students are cliquish*

## ACADEMICS

| | |
|---|---|
| **Academic Rating** | **83** |
| Calendar | semester |
| Student/faculty ratio | 12:1 |
| Profs interesting rating | 93 |
| Profs accessible rating | 96 |
| % profs teaching UG courses | 100 |
| Avg lab size | under 10 students |
| Avg reg class size | 10-19 students |

### MOST POPULAR MAJORS

management
biology
communication

## STUDENTS SPEAK OUT

### Academics

Strength across the board in natural sciences and a unique "12-3" academic calendar help set Hiram apart from the nation's many small colleges. The school's innovative calendar, called "the Hiram Plan," divides each semester into two sessions that last 12 and 3 weeks, respectively. The three-week sessions take the form of hands-on learning experiences like study abroad, research, internships, and field trips. Reports one student, "I love the 12-3 semester. Where else can a three-week trip be taken like that? We've had people in Soviet Moscow, in Turkey right before the earthquake, and in Berlin two weeks before the Wall came down!" In most other areas, Hiram closely resembles other small private schools. Classes are "small and challenging" and require "a lot of studying." Professors "are completely dedicated to education and to the students here at Hiram. They are like students themselves; they're easy to talk to, fun to hang out with, and generally good teachers. They do everything in their power to help us be successful." Overall, "The small-school atmosphere helps each individual shine as their own person." As one student puts it, "Academically, Hiram might not have the breadth of larger colleges, but the attention that each individual student receives makes up for it." As an added bonus, "Our college is currently in the process of dramatically improving the lacking areas . . . we have opened a new Science Building, and also selecting a campuswide computer system that will aid in many things, including class registration."

### Life

Adjusting to life at Hiram requires most students to slow things down a bit: "Since we are located so far away from everything, it takes a little while to get used to life here. At first it is boring, but then everyone usually adjusts and learns to entertain themselves. Stupid games you played when you were younger come back, such as Jenga. Friends are the key to having fun here." Hiram is isolated enough that "on Friday nights we walk along pitch-black streets, avoiding roadkill and speeding cars the best we can. Then we watch *The Muppet Movie*. Hiram is not exactly a happenin' town." Others point out, however, that "people will always say there is nothing to do, but when there is something to do or some event, they will not show up." Also, "Cleveland and Kent are close enough that we go out there. If I went to a big school, I would never get anything done." Hiram has no Greek system, but it does have "social clubs," which are fairly popular and which serve the same function as fraternities and sororities do elsewhere. Intramural athletics are popular, as are "watching movies and making Taco Bell runs." On Friday afternoons, the campus becomes somewhat desolate because, as one student puts it, Hiram "has a weekend migration problem." During the week, students occupy themselves with study and community service: "Many Hiram students think and care deeply for many social causes and tend to be activists. I'm not sure what brings them all here to a school in the middle of nowhere, but I think it is one of the greatest resources among the student body." In fact, "One day each semester, classes are cancelled and students plan community service and community building activities. Everyone from the housekeepers to the students to the president of the college participates."

### Student Body

The atmosphere at this "mostly white, middle-class college" tends to be "relaxed," but "everyone knows everything about everyone," which "can be a problem." While "most people get along with everybody else" and "the boundaries between cliques is blurred here," there is some friction between students of different sociopolitical outlooks, especially between religious students and liberals. The former warn that "this is a very liberal college, but if you don't share quite the same beliefs as others, watch out! Some of the most 'liberal' students here are the most close-minded," while the latter accuse religious students of intolerance. Most feel that the school would benefit from a more diverse student population.

FINANCIAL AID: 330-569-5107 • E-MAIL: ADMISSION@HIRAM.EDU • WEBSITE: WWW.HIRAM.EDU

## ADMISSIONS

*Very important* academic and nonacademic factors considered by the admissions committee include secondary school record. *Important* factors considered include character/personal qualities, class rank, essays, interview, recommendations, and standardized test scores. *Other* factors considered include alumni/ae relation, extracurricular activities, geography, minority status, talent/ability, volunteer work, and work experience. Factors *not* considered include religious affiliation/commitment and state residency. SAT I or ACT required. TOEFL required of all international applicants. High school diploma is required and GED is accepted. *High school units required/recommended:* 17 total recommended; 4 English recommended, 3 math recommended, 3 science recommended, 2 foreign language recommended, 2 social studies recommended, 3 elective recommended. *The admissions office says:* "Minority students and alumni relations receive special consideration." All applicants are considered for merit-based scholarships.

### The Inside Word

Students with consistent academic records will find little difficulty in gaining admission. The applicant pool is decidedly local; out-of-state candidates benefit from their scarcity.

## FINANCIAL AID

*Students should submit:* FAFSA. The Princeton Review suggests that all financial aid forms be submitted as soon as possible after January 1. *Need-based scholarships/grants offered:* Pell, SEOG, state scholarships/grants, private scholarships, and the school's own gift aid. *Loan aid offered:* FFEL Subsidized Stafford, FFEL Unsubsidized Stafford, FFEL PLUS, Federal Perkins, and college/university loans from institutional funds. Institutional employment available. Applicants will be notified of awards on a rolling basis beginning on or about February 15. Off-campus job opportunities are fair.

## FROM THE ADMISSIONS OFFICE

"Hiram College offers several distinctive programs that set us apart from other small, private liberal arts colleges. Over half of Hiram's students participate in our nationally recognized study abroad program at some point during their four years here. In 2001–2002, Hiram faculty will lead trips to England, France, Costa Rica, Pakistan, Greece, and Turkey; in 2002–2003, we will visit Australia, Germany, Denmark, Zimbabwe, Israel, Guatemala, and Mexico. Because Hiram students receive credits for the courses taught by faculty on these trips, studying abroad will not impede progress in their majors or delay graduation. Another unique aspect of a Hiram education is our academic calendar, known as the Hiram Plan. Our semesters are divided into 12-week and 3-week periods. Students usually enroll in three courses during each 12-week period, and one intensive course during the 3-week periods. Many students spend the 3-week periods on study abroad trips or taking unusual courses not typically offered during the 12-week periods. In addition to numerous study abroad options and the Hiram Plan, our small classes (the average class size is 15) encourage interaction between students and their professors, both in and out of the classroom. Students can work with professors on original research projects, and often participate in musical groups and intramural sports teams alongside faculty members."

## ADMISSIONS

| | |
|---|---:|
| Admissions Rating | 79 |
| # of applicants | 799 |
| % of applicants accepted | 80 |
| % of acceptees attending | 37 |

### FRESHMAN PROFILE

| | |
|---|---:|
| Range SAT Verbal | 520-630 |
| Average SAT Verbal | 573 |
| Range SAT Math | 510-630 |
| Average SAT Math | 566 |
| Range ACT Composite | 21-27 |
| Average ACT Composite | 24 |
| Minimum TOEFL | 550 |
| Average HS GPA | 3.5 |
| % graduated top 10% of class | 33 |
| % graduated top 25% of class | 64 |
| % graduated top 50% of class | 89 |

### DEADLINES

| | |
|---|---:|
| Priority admission deadline | 12/1 |
| Regular admission | 2/1 |
| Nonfall registration? | yes |

### APPLICANTS ALSO LOOK AT

**AND OFTEN PREFER**
Miami U.
Kenyon
Wooster

**AND SOMETIMES PREFER**
Wittenberg
Ohio Wesleyan

**AND RARELY PREFER**
Ohio State U.—Columbus
Mount Union
Kent State

## FINANCIAL FACTS

| | |
|---|---:|
| Financial Aid Rating | 84 |
| Tuition | $1 |
| Room & board | $6,514 |
| Books and supplies | $600 |
| Required fees | $576 |
| % frosh receiving aid | 86 |
| % undergrads receiving aid | 85 |
| Avg frosh grant | $10,998 |
| Avg frosh loan | $5,176 |

# HOBART AND WILLIAM SMITH COLLEGES

639 SOUTH MAIN STREET, GENEVA, NY 14456 • ADMISSIONS: 315-781-3472 • FAX: 315-781-3471

## CAMPUS LIFE

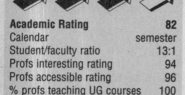

| Quality of Life Rating | 80 |
|---|---|
| Type of school | private |
| Affiliation | none |
| Environment | rural |

### STUDENTS

| | |
|---|---|
| Total undergrad enrollment | 1,854 |
| % male/female | 47/53 |
| % from out of state | 49 |
| % from public high school | 65 |
| % live on campus | 90 |
| % in (# of) fraternities | 20 (5) |
| % African American | 6 |
| % Asian | 2 |
| % Caucasian | 86 |
| % Hispanic | 4 |
| % international | 1 |
| # of countries represented | 21 |

### SURVEY SAYS . . .

*Great food on campus*
*Everyone loves the Statesmen*
*Beautiful campus*
*Athletic facilities are great*
*Students don't like Geneva, NY*
*Theater is unpopular*
*Class discussions encouraged*

## ACACEMICS

| Academic Rating | 82 |
|---|---|
| Calendar | semester |
| Student/faculty ratio | 13:1 |
| Profs interesting rating | 94 |
| Profs accessible rating | 96 |
| % profs teaching UG courses | 100 |
| Avg reg class size | 10-19 students |

### MOST POPULAR MAJORS
individual major
English
economics

## STUDENTS SPEAK OUT

### Academics

Hobart and William Smith Colleges are separate, single-sex institutions sharing the same campus and classes. In an effort to combine the best aspects of single-sex and coeducational instruction, the schools share classes and even a common faculty, yet maintain separate traditions and coordinate priorities. The effect of this "coordinate education" is particularly prominent at William Smith, the women's school. Acknowledging that women often take a "back seat" at "traditionally male-dominated coeducational colleges," William Smith co-opts the most successful attributes of all-women's colleges, such as self-government and an emphasis on gender studies. According to students at both schools, HWS' chief assets include "small classes and discussion groups" and professors who "are always around to help the students out, giving out e-mail addresses and even home phone numbers and encouraging us to call. They seem to care about the students and want them to do well." Writes one student, "The interaction I've had with the faculty has been extremely helpful and constructive. There is a high expectation in the courses, but the profs are very willing to meet with you [to] help you meet those expectations." Administrators are regarded more ambivalently. While one freshman gushes that "we have administrators who make sure you are adjusting to school easily. They are willing to help if you have any problems," many upperclassmen complain about the administration. "The rushed conversion from the trimester to semester system was done quite poorly and screwed a lot of people over," reports one. Most students, however, feel it's worth enduring these complications to be "recognized as an individual, which to me is extremely important. At a large university, I would be recognized as merely a number."

### Life

The social scene at HWS runs the whole spectrum from "hanging down town with all the sweet townies to getting drunk or stoned." According to one respondent, "There are two bars that let everyone in. So everyone goes, which means you have to wait 20 minutes before you can get a drink. Either the school should think of better things for us to do or they should build more bars." Plenty of students offered another solution to the situation: "For myself and everyone on campus," writes a typical undergrad, "we have one word for you: fraternities!!! Bring them back on campus [proper]. To its credit, "the school is trying to increase the number of on-campus activities." It isn't all doldrums here: HWS boasts a "beautiful campus, which is enjoyed by students. People really like the outdoors and will do the craziest things just to have an excuse to be outdoors, like sled downhill on trays from the dining hall." Besides traying, lots of students are involved in athletics, especially lacrosse.

### Student Body

Don't come to HWS looking for a melting pot. As one student points out, "I really like a lot of people who go here, but they are all carbon copies of one another." Writes one, "Going to class is like going to a J.Crew fashion show and the parking lot is a SAAB dealership." There is "noticeable segregation of the races, particularly in the dining hall. It's a little disturbing." Students also subdivide into "cliques structured along socioeconomic lines, but this does not mean that these groups don't interact with each other." It is clear that cliques, though friendly, are king.

FINANCIAL AID: 315-781-3315 • E-MAIL: HOADM@HWS.EDU • WEBSITE: WWW.HWS.EDU

## ADMISSIONS

*Very important* academic and nonacademic factors considered by the admissions committee include class rank and secondary school record. *Important* factors considered include standardized test scores. *Other* factors considered include alumni/ae relation, character/personal qualities, essays, extracurricular activities, geography, interview, recommendations, state residency, talent/ability, volunteer work, and work experience. Factors *not* considered include minority status and religious affiliation/commitment. SAT I or ACT required, SAT I preferred. TOEFL required of all international applicants. High school diploma is required and GED is accepted. *High school units required/recommended:* 16 total recommended; 4 English recommended, 3 math recommended, 3 science recommended, 3 foreign language recommended, 2 social studies recommended, 1 history recommended. *The admissions office says:* "The admissions process tends to be highly individualized, even more so than at other small liberal arts colleges, we've been told by prospective students. We encourage students to spend at least a day on campus with a student host in order to observe the colleges in action. This is a place where students do a lot of exploring and experience a number of interesting intellectual collisions with other students and faculty. Our students tend to be pretty daring and adventurous, whether it's a matter of swimming in the lake in March, arguing politics with a dean, or taking a nontraditional course."

### The Inside Word

Hobart and William Smith lose a lot of students to their competitors, who are many and strong. This helps open up the gates a bit for more candidates. However, the schools' location, right on Seneca Lake, offers students a great place to study.

## FINANCIAL AID

The Princeton Review suggests that all financial aid forms be submitted as soon as possible after January 1. *Need-based scholarships/grants offered:* Pell, SEOG, state scholarships/grants, private scholarships, the school's own gift aid, and Federal Nursing. *Loan aid offered:* Subsidized Stafford, Unsubsidized Stafford, PLUS, Federal Perkins, and Federal Nursing. Applicants will be notified of awards on or about April 1. Institutional employment available. Federal Work-Study Program available. Off-campus job opportunities are fair.

## FROM THE ADMISSIONS OFFICE

"Hobart and William Smith Colleges seek students with a sense of adventure and a commitment to the life of the mind. Inside the classroom, students find the academic climate to be rigorous, with a faculty that is deeply involved in teaching and working with them. Outside, they discover a supportive community that helps to cultivate a balance and hopes to foster an integration among academics, extracurricular activities, and social life. Hobart and William Smith, as coordinate colleges, have an awareness of gender differences and equality and are committed to respect and a celebration of diversity."

### ADMISSIONS

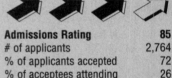

| Admissions Rating | 85 |
|---|---|
| # of applicants | 2,764 |
| % of applicants accepted | 72 |
| % of acceptees attending | 26 |
| # accepting a place on wait list | 113 |
| % admitted from wait list | 14 |
| # of early decision applicants | 118 |
| % accepted early decision | 86 |

#### FRESHMAN PROFILE

| | |
|---|---|
| Range SAT Verbal | 540-620 |
| Average SAT Verbal | 550 |
| Range SAT Math | 540-620 |
| Average SAT Math | 600 |
| Minimum TOEFL | 550 |
| Average HS GPA | 3.2 |
| % graduated top 10% of class | 28 |
| % graduated top 25% of class | 60 |

#### DEADLINES

| | |
|---|---|
| Early decision | 11/15 |
| Early decision notification | 12/15 |
| Regular admission | 2/1 |
| Regular notification | 4/1 |

#### APPLICANTS ALSO LOOK AT AND OFTEN PREFER

Colgate
Trinity Coll. (CT)
Connecticut Coll.
Hamilton
Union Coll. (NY)

#### AND SOMETIMES PREFER

Skidmore
Kenyon
Gettysburg
St. Lawrence
Dickinson

### FINANCIAL FACTS

| Financial Aid Rating | 77 |
|---|---|
| Tuition | $24,700 |
| Room & board | $6,808 |
| Books and supplies | $750 |
| Required fees | $492 |
| % frosh receiving aid | 61 |
| % undergrads receiving aid | 87 |
| Avg frosh grant | $19,267 |
| Avg frosh loan | $2,863 |

# HOFSTRA UNIVERSITY

ADMISSIONS CENTER, BERNON HALL, HEMPSTEAD, NY 11549 • ADMISSIONS: 516-463-6700 • FAX: 516-560-7660

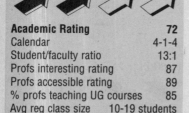
## STUDENTS SPEAK OUT

### Academics

Students in the New York metropolitan area looking for a school where they can have the same professors for both their undergraduate and graduate business education should consider Hofstra University. The quality of the professors varies throughout the university. A common complaint among students is that professors tend to forsake classroom discussion for "boring" lectures that "often put students to sleep." A sophomore communications major claims "the teachers in the communications department are some of the most knowledgeable in the entertainment industry," while a senior psychology majors answers the question about her overall academic experience at Hofstra by asking, "Academic experience? What academic experience?" Overall, a junior psychology major says, "the quality of professors ranges from poor to excellent." Students note that the university needs to offer more classes at more convenient times. Sometimes it seems that "no classes are ever available," a senior marketing major laments. Advisors also get really low marks. Students also note that the computer graphics lab needs improvement. Students universally abhor Hofstra's administration. "Administration treats students like furniture," a senior psychology major writes. "Our needs are not important," and "it is commonplace for students to be given the run around until they give up" on whatever they're trying to get accomplished. A sophomore political science major adds, "I wish every department was as efficient as the billing department."

### Life

Though life in Hempstead is far from exciting (the hometown New York Islanders have been bad for a long time), students are about an hour away from all that New York City has to offer. Hofstra students support the school's Division I basketball and football programs, programs whose graduates include New York Jets wide receiver Wayne Chrebet. The "beautiful" campus is an arboretum, and students look forward to the spring when "one million tulips" bloom. Students complain that more dormitory space is needed and the campus needs much more parking, though they note that "you can get away with anything" in the dorms. While many whine that there isn't much to do on a campus where the food "is expensive" and "sucks," a sophomore accounting major notes, "life here is good, but only if you are involved with an organization." A drama major adds, "there are more opportunities offered to the Greek community." The one social activity in which many Hofstra students participate is going out "and getting hammered." Hofstra students begin partying on Wednesday or Thursday and, one cynical student notes, "they drink themselves into comas and brag about [how] they threw up to their friends."

### Student Body

Hofstra is working hard to change its reputation as a commuter school. Fewer than half of the university's students live on campus, and many say that the splintered nature of the student body does not improve relations between students who are already "unfriendly." One sophomore says, "People tend to stick with their own cliques," and Hofstra's Pride (which also happens to be the name of the university's sports teams) is rarely in evidence. Many of the students come from middle- to upper-class backgrounds "without much care for academics," and, as one finance major notes, "people are stuck up and won't give you the time of day." A communications major adds, "all the spoiled, rich, look-what-Daddy-just-bought-me kids make the college experience a bit duller than it should be." Independents believe that those associated with fraternities and sororities are treated better by the administration, a perception that those involved in Greek life agree to be true.

FINANCIAL AID: 516-463-6680 • E-MAIL: HOFSTRA@HOFSTRA.EDU • WEBSITE: WWW.HOFSTRA.EDU

## ADMISSIONS

*Very important* academic and nonacademic factors considered by the admissions committee include secondary school record, standardized test scores, and state residency. *Important* factors considered include class rank, essays, extracurricular activities, recommendations, volunteer work, and work experience. *Other* factors considered include alumni/ae relation, character/personal qualities, minority status, and talent/ability. Factors *not* considered include geography, interview, and religious affiliation/commitment. SAT I or ACT required. TOEFL required of all international applicants. High school diploma is required and GED is accepted. *High school units required/recommended:* 16 total required; 20 total recommended; 4 English required, 3 math required, 3 science required, 3 foreign language required, 3 social studies required, 4 elective required. *The admissions office says:* "Applicants who do not meet high school curricular standards will be given careful consideration by the admissions committee to determine from achievements and from assessment of abilities and maturity the probability of [their] success."

### The Inside Word

Hofstra wants to be national, and has positioned itself very well with impressive facilities, appealing program offerings, solid athletic teams, and an effective national ad campaign. However, the current student profile just isn't strong enough academically to draw top students on a national level: Too many of Hofstra's best applicants choose to go to school elsewhere. This makes the university a good choice for students who would not be strong candidates at some of its competitors.

## FINANCIAL AID

*Students should submit:* FAFSA and state aid form. The Princeton Review suggests that all financial aid forms be submitted as soon as possible after January 1. Institutional employment available. Federal Work-Study Program available. Applicants will be notified of awards on a rolling basis beginning on or about March 1. Off-campus job opportunities are excellent.

## FROM THE ADMISSIONS OFFICE

"Founded in 1935, Hofstra University has grown to be recognized both nationally and internationally for its resources, academic offerings, accreditations, conferences, and cultural events. Academically Hofstra is comprised of six schools: College of Liberal Arts and Sciences, School of Education, Frank G. Zarb School of Business, School of Communication, New College, and Hofstra Law School. Focused on undergraduate education, Hofstra places great emphasis on the role of the student in the life of the university. Students come from 45 states and 72 countries. Hofstra also offers graduate programs in business, education, liberal arts, and law. Students have easy access to the theater and cultural life of New York City, yet have a learning environment on Long Island on a 238-acre campus that is also a registered arboretum and accredited museum. Admission information sessions are offered daily at 10:15 A.M. and 2 P.M. Please call the Admissions Center for an appointment at 1-800-HOFSTRA."

## ADMISSIONS

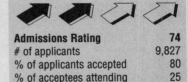

| | |
|---|---:|
| Admissions Rating | 74 |
| # of applicants | 9,827 |
| % of applicants accepted | 80 |
| % of acceptees attending | 25 |
| # of early decision applicants | 111 |
| % accepted early decision | 80 |

### FRESHMAN PROFILE

| | |
|---|---:|
| Range SAT Verbal | 500-590 |
| Average SAT Verbal | 548 |
| Range SAT Math | 510-590 |
| Average SAT Math | 555 |
| Range ACT Composite | 21-26 |
| Average ACT Composite | 24 |
| Minimum TOEFL | 550 |
| Average HS GPA | 2.8 |
| % graduated top 10% of class | 12 |
| % graduated top 25% of class | 50 |
| % graduated top 50% of class | 94 |

### DEADLINES

| | |
|---|---:|
| Priority admission deadline | 2/15 |
| Early decision | 12/1 |
| Early decision notification | 12/15 |
| Nonfall registration? | yes |

### APPLICANTS ALSO LOOK AT
**AND OFTEN PREFER**
NYU
Cornell U.
Binghamton U.
Syracuse
Boston U.
**AND SOMETIMES PREFER**
Fordham
Rutgers U.
SUNY Stony Brook
SUNY Albany
Siena

### FINANCIAL FACTS

| | |
|---|---:|
| Financial Aid Rating | 73 |
| Tuition | $14,280 |
| Room & board | $7,240 |
| Books and supplies | $600 |
| Required fees | $762 |
| % frosh receiving aid | 74 |
| % undergrads receiving aid | 70 |
| Avg frosh grant | $2,300 |
| Avg frosh loan | $4,300 |

# HOLLINS UNIVERSITY

PO BOX 9707, ROANOKE, VA 24020-1707 • ADMISSIONS: 540-362-6401 • FAX: 540-362-6218

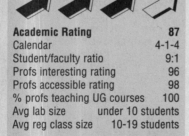
## STUDENTS SPEAK OUT

### Academics

Tiny Hollins University is an all-women's liberal arts school with a "great creative writing program" that "encourages personal growth and discovery." Students say the one-of-a-kind traditions here and the honor code—which allows exams to be scheduled by the student and taken without a teacher present—"make the school stand out from any other in the world." Small classes mean "they know when you skip" but the intimate atmosphere also allows for heaps of "individual attention" from "awesome and wonderful" professors who "really care about students" and share "a real commitment to teaching." At Hollins, "access to profs is super-amazingly-wonderfully-easy," and faculty members are "passionate about their subjects and really try to relate it to their students." Students also say they are able to work "hand-in-hand" with administrators to get things done, though "the administration often runs like a bad episode of *COPS*." "Too much tough-guy bureaucracy," declares a senior. Facilities-wise, the labs and computers on campus are adequate but not earth-shattering, and a "new library" has replaced the "pitiful" one that came before it. "Hollins is a wonderful community and much like your second family," says a junior. "It's great to go to a school where everyone knows your name, where your professors care about whether you enjoy your classes and whether you do well, where there are always people willing to help you, and where womanhood and academics bring people together."

### Life

Being at Hollins means men are an hour away, which sends some students "in search of a livelier social life" when the weekend comes. "We road trip! It's not a suitcase school, but a road trip school," explains a sophomore. "We visit friends at area schools and go to their parties on weekends." Typical weekend destinations include Washington and Lee University or all-male Hampden-Sydney. As a result, some students contend that "although it is a women's college, we never have a problem socializing with men." Others lament that "it's very hard to meet guys." Back on the "beautiful" antebellum campus, located at the foot of the Blue Ridge Mountains, the dorms (where almost everyone lives) are roomy and comfortable, but "the food could be better." For the most part, students are "very creative" but "social life is nonexistent," unless "a big slumber party" is your idea of a rollicking good time. Hollins does sponsor "bands twice a month" in addition to "lectures, films, and readings." "Horseback riding is big here" as well. The surrounding town of Roanoke offers "great coffee shops, a fantastic farmer's market, and some good clubs," and the countryside provides opportunities for "hiking, climbing, and biking." There is no Greek system, but the campus certainly does not lack its share of festive traditions. Examples include "Tinker Day," when classes are cancelled and students hike Tinker Mountain dressed in nutty costumes, and "Passing of the Robes," when seniors pass on "decorated robes" to juniors.

### Student Body

The "bright and motivated," "cliquish" women of Hollins describe themselves as "open and friendly" folks who "need to gossip." "We're all pretty much the same which, personally, I like a lot," says one student. This "sisterly community" of "white, upper-class, conservative, southern" republicans "is changing," though, and it is becoming "easier to find your niche if you are not 'typical.'" The Hollins campus is "divided between southern girls full of Daddy's girl sweetness and Old South bigotry, and young, gifted women full of creativity and spirit," further elucidates a senior. "They mix like cats and koalas in a eucalyptus patch," which we suspect means not very well. At any rate, though there is definitely "some racial tension," "money," not race, "is the biggest dividing factor" here. There is also a visible gay contingent; one student describes Hollins as "very diverse sexually." Upon graduation, "Hollins alums are legendary" for helping recent grads get started on their careers and into graduate and professional schools.

FINANCIAL AID: 540-362-6332 • E-MAIL: HUADM@HOLLINS.EDU • WEBSITE: WWW.HOLLINS.EDU

## ADMISSIONS

*Very important* academic and nonacademic factors considered by the admissions committee include secondary school record. *Important* factors considered include alumni/ae relation, class rank, essays, minority status, recommendations, standardized test scores, and talent/ability. *Other* factors considered include character/personal qualities, extracurricular activities, interview, volunteer work, and work experience. Factors *not* considered include geography, religious affiliation/commitment, and state residency. SAT I or ACT required; SAT II recommended. TOEFL required of all international applicants. High school diploma is required and GED is accepted. *High school units required/recommended:* 19 total required; 20 total recommended; 4 English required, 3 math required, 3 science required, 2 science lab required, 2 foreign language required, 3 social studies required, 4 elective required, 5 elective recommended. *The admissions office says:* "Alumni relations are taken into consideration."

### The Inside Word

Only candidates who overtly display their lack of compatibility with the Hollins milieu are likely to encounter difficulty in gaining admission. A high level of self-selection and its weak, but improving, freshman profile allow most candidates to relax.

## FINANCIAL AID

*Students should submit:* FAFSA and state aid form. Regular filing deadline is February 15. The Princeton Review suggests that all financial aid forms be submitted as soon as possible after January 1. *Need-based scholarships/grants offered:* Pell, SEOG, state scholarships/grants, private scholarships, and the school's own gift aid. *Loan aid offered:* Direct Subsidized Stafford, Direct Unsubsidized Stafford, Direct PLUS, Federal Perkins, CitiAssist, Key, Gate, and Plato. Institutional employment available. Federal Work-Study Program available. Applicants will be notified of awards on or about March 15. Off-campus job opportunities are good.

## FROM THE ADMISSIONS OFFICE

"As a liberal arts college dedicated to high achievement for women, Hollins celebrates and encourages the success—whether in the classroom, in the laboratory, on stage, or on the athletic field—of each student. A spirit of independent inquiry, the free exchange of ideas, and a love for learning characterize life on campus. At Hollins, creativity and imaginative thinking are applauded with the same vigor that rewards academic achievement.

"The Hollins Experience. Personal. Practical. Powerful"

## ADMISSIONS

| | |
|---|---|
| Admissions Rating | 78 |
| # of applicants | 624 |
| % of applicants accepted | 81 |
| % of acceptees attending | 38 |
| # accepting a place on wait list | 29 |
| % admitted from wait list | 31 |
| # of early decision applicants | 57 |
| % accepted early decision | 88 |

### FRESHMAN PROFILE

| | |
|---|---|
| Range SAT Verbal | 520-650 |
| Average SAT Verbal | 591 |
| Range SAT Math | 490-600 |
| Average SAT Math | 543 |
| Range ACT Composite | 21-28 |
| Average ACT Composite | 24 |
| Minimum TOEFL | 550 |
| Average HS GPA | 3.3 |
| % graduated top 10% of class | 25 |
| % graduated top 25% of class | 62 |
| % graduated top 50% of class | 89 |

### DEADLINES

| | |
|---|---|
| Priority admission deadline | 2/15 |
| Early decision | 12/1 |
| Early decision notification | 12/15 |
| Nonfall registration? | yes |

### APPLICANTS ALSO LOOK AT AND OFTEN PREFER

U. Virginia
William and Mary
James Madison
Smith
Vanderbilt

### AND SOMETIMES PREFER

UNC—Chapel Hill
Randolph-Macon Woman's
Sweet Briar
Mount Holyoke

## FINANCIAL FACTS

| | |
|---|---|
| Financial Aid Rating | 90 |
| Tuition | $16,960 |
| Room & board | $6,415 |
| Books and supplies | $600 |
| Required fees | $250 |
| % frosh receiving aid | 61 |
| % undergrads receiving aid | 60 |
| Avg frosh grant | $8,947 |
| Avg frosh loan | $3,678 |

# HOWARD UNIVERSITY

2400 SIXTH STREET, NW, WASHINGTON, DC 20059 • ADMISSIONS: 202-806-2700 • FAX: 202-806-4465

## CAMPUS LIFE

**Quality of Life Rating**    **78**
Type of school    private
Affiliation    none
Environment    urban

### STUDENTS
Total undergrad enrollment    6,099
% male/female    37/63
% from out of state    90
% from public high school    80
% live on campus    53
% African American    80
% Asian    1
% Hispanic    1
% international    2
# of countries represented    102

### SURVEY SAYS . . .
*Frats and sororities dominate social scene*
*Very little drug use*
*Political activism is hot*
*Student government is popular*
*Students don't get along with local community*
*Registration is a pain*
*Theater is unpopular*
*Very little beer drinking*
*Lots of long lines and red tape*
*Student publications are popular*

## ACADEMICS

**Academic Rating**    **75**
Calendar    semester
Student/faculty ratio    7:1
Profs interesting rating    89
Profs accessible rating    90
Avg lab size    under 10 students
Avg reg class size    10-19 students

### MOST POPULAR MAJORS
biology
psychology
radio, TV, & film

## STUDENTS SPEAK OUT

### Academics

"Prestigious" Howard University is arguably "the best" historically African American university in the nation and, as the school points out, it is "the largest community of African American scholars in the world." "There's only one Howard," according to students, who tell us it's "a special place" with "a rich history" and cultural legacy. In addition to the abundant "heritage and reputation" available here, there is plenty of "real-world" training. The "very caring" faculty gets solid reviews, and "the majority of the professors are excellent and care about the students," says a math major. Unfortunately, though, "customer service" seems to be perennially lousy on this campus. Staff members are often "very rude," and "there needs to be more communication in the different departments" to avoid hassles with registration, financial aid, maintenance, and housing. On a positive note, the campus boasts computer labs in every residence hall, a new 24-hour tech lab, and a pretty respectable library. Popular programs here include biology; psychology; radio, television, and film; and international business. Howard also offers a bang-up array of pre-med courses to prep would-be doctors for its exceptional medical school.

### Life

Academics can be "very stressful" at Howard. The active social life and prime location in Washington, D.C., don't make things any easier. To be sure, there's plenty to do in the nation's capital, and life off campus gets two thumbs up for entertainment from the students; museums, malls, clubs, concerts, bars, and restaurants keep Howardites well occupied. Howard's hometown also provides great opportunities for social activism as well as internships and, after graduation, stellar employment opportunities. School spirit shows up in full force on campus. Intramural and intercollegiate sports, lectures, singing, clubs, and student government are all integral parts of the Howard experience. Fraternities and sororities also play a huge though not overpowering role. Dating—the real, live, time-honored variety—is frequent, too. The party scene is also healthy and thriving in some quarters but, for the most part, Howard students favor hitting the books over carousing. Howard also has a tremendous campus newspaper and a significant number of religious organizations.

### Student Body

Obviously, the vast majority of students at Howard are African American, but they are by no means all the same. "Diverse attitudes, philosophies, and styles" permeate this place, and Howard attracts a good number of international students, which gives the campus something of an international flair. Sometimes, students here are "overly fashion conscious, which can be both entertaining and obnoxious" and there are "so many cliques" at Howard, it can feel "like a super-sized high school." These qualms aside, though, the "friendly," "bright, lively, and creative" students at Howard say they are mostly "well-rounded," "extremely gifted, and talented." They are also a "proud" and seriously ambitious bunch "who want to improve their communities" and who "all seem to be working toward a common goal": to "change the world."

FINANCIAL AID: 202-806-2800 • E-MAIL: ADMISSION@HOWARD.EDU • WEBSITE: WWW.HOWARD.EDU

## ADMISSIONS

*Very important* academic and nonacademic factors considered by the admissions committee include class rank, extracurricular activities, secondary school record, standardized test scores, and talent/ability. *Important* factors considered include character/personal qualities, essays, interview, recommendations, and volunteer work. *Other* factors considered include alumni/ae relation, geography, state residency, and work experience. Factors *not* considered include minority status and religious affiliation/commitment. SAT I or ACT required. TOEFL required of all international applicants. High school diploma is required and GED is accepted. *High school units required/recommended:* 17 total required; 4 English required, 3 math required, 2 science required, 2 foreign language recommended, 2 history required, 6 elective required. *The admissions office says:* "For admission to most majors, a student should have a combined SAT I score of 800 or above or ACT composite of 20, rank in the top half of his/her graduation class, or have a C+ average."

### The Inside Word

A large applicant pool and solid yield of acceptees who enroll is a combination that adds up to selectivity for Howard. Pay strict attention to the formula.

## FINANCIAL AID

The Princeton Review suggests that all financial aid forms be submitted as soon as possible after January 1. *Need-based scholarships/grants offered:* Pell, SEOG, state scholarships/grants, private scholarships, the school's own gift aid, and Federal Nursing. *Loan aid offered:* FFEL Subsidized Stafford, FFEL Unsubsidized Stafford, FFEL PLUS, Federal Perkins, and Federal Nursing. Institutional employment available. Federal Work-Study Program available. Off-campus job opportunities are good.

## FROM THE ADMISSIONS OFFICE

"Since its founding, Howard has stood among the few institutions of higher learning where African Americans and other minorities have participated freely in a truly comprehensive university experience. Thus, Howard has assumed a special responsibility to prepare its students to exercise leadership wherever their interest and commitments take them. Howard has issued approximately 90,785 degrees, diplomas, and certificates to men and women in the professions, the arts and sciences, and the humanities. The university has produced and continues to produce a high percentage of the nation's African American professionals in the fields of medicine, dentistry, pharmacy, engineering, nursing, architecture, religion, law, music, social work, education, and business. There are more than 8,200 students from across the nation and approximately 104 countries and territories attending the university. Their varied customs, cultures, ideas, and interests contribute to Howard's international character and vitality. More than 1,300 faculty members represent the largest concentration of African American scholars in any single institution of higher education."

## ADMISSIONS

| | |
|---|---|
| Admissions Rating | 74 |
| # of applicants | 6,664 |
| % of applicants accepted | 56 |
| % of acceptees attending | 27 |

### FRESHMAN PROFILE

| | |
|---|---|
| Range SAT Verbal | 450-670 |
| Average SAT Verbal | 533 |
| Range SAT Math | 420-670 |
| Average SAT Math | 517 |
| Range ACT Composite | 17-28 |
| Minimum TOEFL | 500 |

### DEADLINES

| | |
|---|---|
| Priority admission deadline | 11/30 |
| Early decision | 11/30 |
| Early decision notification | 12/25 |
| Regular admission | 4/1 |
| Nonfall registration? | yes |

### APPLICANTS ALSO LOOK AT

**AND OFTEN PREFER**
Morehouse
Spelman
Hampton

**AND SOMETIMES PREFER**
George Washington
U. Maryland—Coll. Park
Florida A&M

**AND RARELY PREFER**
Morgan State

## FINANCIAL FACTS

| | |
|---|---|
| Financial Aid Rating | 71 |
| Tuition | $8,750 |
| Room & board | $5,250 |
| Books and supplies | $800 |
| Required fees | $405 |
| % frosh receiving aid | 67 |
| Avg frosh grant | $4,475 |
| Avg frosh loan | $9,457 |

# ILLINOIS INSTITUTE OF TECHNOLOGY

10 WEST 33RD STREET, CHICAGO, IL 60616 • ADMISSIONS: 312-567-3025 • FAX: 312-567-6939

## CAMPUS LIFE

**Quality of Life Rating** 68
Type of school private
Affiliation none
Environment urban

### STUDENTS
Total undergrad enrollment 1,736
% male/female 75/25
% from out of state 35
% from public high school 82
% live on campus 58
% in (# of) fraternities 12 (7)
% in (# of) sororities 16 (3)
% African American 8
% Asian 18
% Caucasian 64
% Hispanic 8
% Native American 1
% international 13

### SURVEY SAYS . . .
*Ethnic diversity on campus*
*Different students interact*
*Everyone loves Chicago, IL*
*Low cost of living*
*Great off-campus food*
*Unattractive campus*
*Very little drug use*
*Musical organizations aren't popular*
*Students are not very happy*
*No one plays intramural sports*

## ACADEMICS

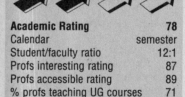

**Academic Rating** 78
Calendar semester
Student/faculty ratio 12:1
Profs interesting rating 87
Profs accessible rating 89
% profs teaching UG courses 71
Avg lab size 10-19 students
Avg reg class size 10-19 students

### MOST POPULAR MAJORS
computer engineering
architecture
computer science

## STUDENTS SPEAK OUT
### Academics

Like most engineering institutions, the Illinois Institute of Technology "is an intense school." Undergrads appreciate the fact that studies "are very good and career-oriented" and that "even though we are small and [aren't] that well known, we have a very challenging and strong engineering curriculum." Hoping to give its student body a leg up in the working world, IIT requires undergraduates to complete two Interprofessional Projects before graduation. IPROs, as they're known at IIT, bring together undergraduate and graduate students from different academic disciplines to complete a task as a team. Recent IPROs have ranged from designing a new football stadium for the Chicago Bears to improving automated patient monitoring and diagnosis systems. In its efforts to create well-rounded students, IIT requires a wide array of courses in the humanities, writing, and social and behavioral sciences. Do students appreciate these efforts on their behalf? Well, some of the students we spoke to didn't think so. Although they appreciate the value of their academic programs, students find fault with several aspects of the school. They complain that "most professors don't utilize the small class sizes for discussions—they seem to enjoy lecturing too much," and that the administration could do more to involve students and their opinions. Most of all, they gripe about the advising system: "There is no proper guidance to choose the right courses pertaining to the interest of each student," writes a typical student.

### Life

Academic demands encroach a lot on social life at IIT, to the dissatisfaction of many. Writes one typically disgruntled student: "Homework dominates our lives. We do homework all the time, including weekends." Adds another, "You really have to work in order to get involved. Classes require a lot of time and leave little left to do fun stuff." Of the campus itself, parts of which were designed by legendary architect Ludwig Mies Van der Rohe, making it one of the 100 top travel destinations of the new millenium by *Travel & Leisure Magazine*. As one student explains life on campus, "Being involved in a fraternity has been pretty fun for me. There are also a lot of opportunities to participate in a variety of student organizations. IIT has attracted some big-name entertainment for its size . . . which is cool." Adds another, "Life in the dorms is quite fun. On weekends we [usually] have movies in the lounge." Most students try to get off campus as often as possible. The El, Chicago's version of a subway system, "runs through campus, so we have access to everything that Chicago has to offer."

### Student Body

The "very diverse and intelligent" students of IIT inhabit "a very international campus," prompting one student to exclaim that "I've made friends with people from all over the world!" Some students report, however, that "to some degree cultures split off into their own groups," making interaction somewhat more difficult. Exacerbating the situation is the fact that "this school doesn't have enough facilities to get together. It makes it hard to get to know other students." Men and women alike agree that "more women are needed at this school!"

FINANCIAL AID: 312-567-3025 • E-MAIL: ADMISSION@IIT.EDU • WEBSITE: WWW.IIT.EDU

## ADMISSIONS

*Very important* academic and nonacademic factors considered by the admissions committee include character/personal qualities, class rank, secondary school record, and volunteer work. *Important* factors considered include essays, extracurricular activities, interview, minority status, recommendations, religious affiliation/commitment, standardized test scores, and talent/ability. *Other* factors considered include alumni/ae relation, geography, and work experience. Factors *not* considered include state residency. SAT I or ACT required. TOEFL required of all international applicants. High school diploma is required and GED is accepted. *High school units required/recommended:* 4 English recommended, 3 math recommended, 3 science recommended, 2 foreign language recommended, 2 social studies recommended, 2 history recommended. *The admissions office says:* "The admissions office considers each application on its individual merits, always looking for superior ability as determined through previous academic records, recommendations, statements by the student, leadership experiences, aptitudes, and goals. The student's record of achievement in high school, however, most often provides the best prediction of success at IIT."

### The Inside Word

IIT's applicant pool is small and includes a strong element of self-selection. This means the majority get in, but not without solid academic preparation. While the committee evaluates other criteria, the bottom line is that candidates need fairly solid grades and better than average test scores in order to get admitted.

## FINANCIAL AID

*Students should submit:* FAFSA. The Princeton Review suggests that all financial aid forms be submitted as soon as possible after January 1. *Need-based scholarships/grants offered:* Pell, SEOG, state scholarships/grants, private scholarships, and the school's own gift aid. *Loan aid offered:* FFEL Subsidized Stafford, FFEL Unsubsidized Stafford, FFEL PLUS, Federal Perkins, and college/university loans from institutional funds. Institutional employment available. Federal Work-Study Program available. Applicants will be notified of awards on a rolling basis. Off-campus job opportunities are excellent.

## FROM THE ADMISSIONS OFFICE

"IIT is committed to providing undergraduate education of the highest quality. We believe that every one of our students has the ability to make significant contributions to society. Our goal is to help you attain the knowledge, skills, ethical perspective, and motivation you will need to realize that potential. Our university is especially well suited to prepare you to seize the opportunities and address the real problems of a rapidly changing, increasingly complex world. The IIT scholars with whom you will study contribute to the nation's intellectual wealth in areas ranging from ethics and management to design processes, mathematical problems, and theoretical physics. Our multicultural student body and our location in the heart of one of America's most ethnically diverse cities make the undergraduate experience an ideal way to prepare for tomorrow's global society."

## ADMISSIONS

| | |
|---|---|
| Admissions Rating | 83 |
| # of applicants | 2,726 |
| % of applicants accepted | 65 |
| % of acceptees attending | 23 |

### FRESHMAN PROFILE

| | |
|---|---|
| Range SAT Verbal | 560-680 |
| Average SAT Verbal | 613 |
| Range SAT Math | 630-730 |
| Average SAT Math | 679 |
| Range ACT Composite | 25-30 |
| Average ACT Composite | 28 |
| Minimum TOEFL | 550 |
| Average HS GPA | 3.8 |
| % graduated top 10% of class | 53 |
| % graduated top 25% of class | 80 |
| % graduated top 50% of class | 98 |

### DEADLINES

| | |
|---|---|
| Priority admission deadline | 3/1 |
| Regular notification | rolling |
| Nonfall registration? | yes |

### APPLICANTS ALSO LOOK AT AND OFTEN PREFER

UC—Berkeley
U. Illinois—Urbana-Champaign
Northwestern U.
Abilene Christian

### AND SOMETIMES PREFER

Purdue U.—West Lafayette
Case Western Reserve
Southern Illinois U.
Marquette

## FINANCIAL FACTS

| | |
|---|---|
| Financial Aid Rating | 73 |
| Tuition | $18,600 |
| Room & board | $5,592 |
| Books and supplies | $1,000 |
| Required fees | $160 |
| % frosh receiving aid | 69 |
| % undergrads receiving aid | 66 |
| Avg frosh grant | $14,694 |
| Avg frosh loan | $7,241 |

# ILLINOIS WESLEYAN UNIVERSITY

PO Box 2900, BLOOMINGTON, IL 61720 • ADMISSIONS: 309-556-3031 • FAX: 309-556-3411

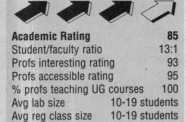

## CAMPUS LIFE

**Quality of Life Rating**     **73**
Type of school     private
Affiliation     independent
Environment     suburban

### STUDENTS

| | |
|---|---|
| Total undergrad enrollment | 2,027 |
| % male/female | 43/57 |
| % from out of state | 10 |
| % from public high school | 84 |
| % live on campus | 86 |
| % in (# of) fraternities | 36 (6) |
| % in (# of) sororities | 29 (5) |
| % African American | 3 |
| % Asian | 3 |
| % Caucasian | 89 |
| % Hispanic | 2 |
| % international | 2 |

### SURVEY SAYS . . .

*Athletic facilities are great
Frats and sororities dominate social scene
Very little drug use
Everyone loves the Titans
Theater is hot
Library needs improving
Musical organizations are hot
(Almost) no one listens to college radio
Students get along with local community*

## ACADEMICS

**Academic Rating**     **85**
Student/faculty ratio     13:1
Profs interesting rating     93
Profs accessible rating     95
% profs teaching UG courses     100
Avg lab size     10-19 students
Avg reg class size     10-19 students

### MOST POPULAR MAJORS
business administration
biology
English

## STUDENTS SPEAK OUT

### Academics

Through aggressive expansion of its facilities, the "constantly building and improving" Illinois Wesleyan has transformed itself in the last decade from a well-respected regional school to a nationally renowned university; the newest additions include a library and campus center. At the same time, IWU has remained committed to maintaining a moderate-size student body, and as a result, students here feel they get the best of both worlds. "It's just the right size: enough people but small enough that the personal attention and benefits are huge," explains one undergrad. Says another, "The reason I decided to go to this school is because I knew that I could participate in a variety of activities, and that I could work first-hand with professors." Facilities "are incredible. For a school of its size, Wesleyan has one of the best science/academic facilities in the nation." Professors "are generally really cool: interesting, knowledgeable, and real. They remember their students, even from 25 years ago. I get teased by one professor because he had my dad and recognized the name." Reports one student, "Profs have stayed past midnight in study groups when we needed help. One even came back after a tuxedo dinner and was helping us in full attire!" Students gripe that "grading is way too tough. It is extremely hard at this school to get an A," but concede that "academically, Illinois Wesleyan challenges you to be the best and does it in a way that isn't discouraging. Smaller class sizes and more attention from the professors help students become more excited about their work." Among the school's innovative offerings is May Term, which one student describes as "the best part of our academic program. It provides amazing experiential learning opportunities. Through May Term, I have traveled to eastern Europe, the Democratic National Convention, and backpacked in the Appalachians."

### Life

IWU students describe a low-key but enjoyable social scene, reporting that "people at this school are hard workers and put a lot into their studies. Naturally, however, the weekends are filled with parties and dances, mostly involving fraternities and sororities. There are a lot of really good co-curricular programs, too." Agrees one undergrad, "During the week, studying is the social life, in between trips to Denny's. It's not bad, though; everyone here wants to learn, but is laid-back enough that we can still do crazy stuff like steal someone's mattress and put it outside." Intercollegiate sports "are big here: our basketball games are always packed (we won the Division III championship a few years ago)." So too are student clubs and organizations and guest lectures. Writes one student, "There is always something going on, from speakers to workshops to athletics to parties. We know how to have fun." Because "the town of Bloomington-Normal is very boring," students soon discover that "most people stay on campus for activities and entertainment." When they leave, they "either go to Chicago or to ISU, which is right down the street."

### Student Body

IWU students enjoy a "highly friendly atmosphere on campus," although students are also "very cliquey between Greek houses and theater, music, and other groups." The small minority populations here benefit from a support network that includes the Black Student Union, the Council of Latin American Student Enrichment, and an on-campus Multicultural Center. Still, minority students report that "being a minority student here is like you're always under someone's microscope." Agrees a white student, "Most of the students, myself included, are spoiled white middle-class suburbia. The real downfall is their narrow-minded prejudices due to a lack of exposure to diversity." Students' similarity in background fosters the "Wesleyan bubble," a sense that life begins and ends at the campus gates.

FINANCIAL AID: 309-556-3096 • E-MAIL: IWUADMIT@TITAN.IWU.EDU • WEBSITE: WWW.IWU.EDU

## ADMISSIONS

*Very important* academic and nonacademic factors considered by the admissions committee include recommendations, secondary school record, and standardized test scores. *Important* factors considered include class rank and essays. *Other* factors considered include alumni/ae relation, extracurricular activities, geography, interview, character/personal qualities, minority status, talent/ability, and volunteer work. Factors *not* considered include, religious affiliation/commitment, state residency, and work experience. SAT I or ACT required. TOEFL required of all international applicants. High school diploma is required and GED is accepted. *High school units required/recommended:* 16 total required; 4 English required, 3 math required, 4 math recommended, 3 science required, 1 science lab required, 2 science lab recommended, 2 foreign language required, 3 foreign language recommended, 3 social studies required, 4 social studies recommended.

### The Inside Word

Illinois Wesleyan is selective enough that serious candidates should exceed the suggested curriculum requirements in order to improve their chances for admission.

## FINANCIAL AID

*Students should submit:* FAFSA, institution's own financial aid form, CSS/Financial Aid PROFILE, and business/farm supplement. Regular filing deadline is March 1. The Princeton Review suggests that all financial aid forms be submitted as soon as possible after January 1. *Need-based scholarships/grants offered:* Pell, SEOG, state scholarships/grants, private scholarships, and the school's own gift aid. *Loan aid offered:* FFEL Subsidized Stafford, FFEL Unsubsidized Stafford, FFEL PLUS, Federal Perkins, Federal Nursing, and college/university loans from institutional funds. Institutional employment available. Federal Work-Study Program available. Applicants will be notified of awards on a rolling basis beginning on or about January 1. Off-campus job opportunities are good.

## FROM THE ADMISSIONS OFFICE

"Illinois Wesleyan University attracts a wide array of multitalented students—students interested in pursuing diverse fields like vocal performance and biology, psychology and German, or physics and business administration. At IWU, students are not forced into 'either/or' choices. Rather, they are encouraged to pursue multiple interests simultaneously—a philosophy in keeping with the spirit and value of a liberal arts education. The distinctive 4-4-1 calendar allows students to follow their interests each school year in two semesters followed by an optional month-long class in May. May Term opportunities include classes on campus; research collaboration with faculty; travel and study in such places as Australia, China, South Africa, and Europe; as well as local, national, and international internships.

"At Illinois Wesleyan, we assume the mind is the key to an educated person; thus, we hope to foster during the college years the knowledge, values, and skills that will sustain a lifetime of learning. We prepare our students for responsible citizenship and leadership in a democratic society and global community. Above all, whatever their course of studies, we wish to enable Illinois Wesleyan University graduates to lead useful, creative, fully realized lives."

## ADMISSIONS

| | |
|---|---|
| Admissions Rating | 90 |
| # of applicants | 2,570 |
| % of applicants accepted | 61 |
| % of acceptees attending | 34 |
| # accepting a place on wait list | 381 |
| % admitted from wait list | 1 |

### FRESHMAN PROFILE

| | |
|---|---|
| Range SAT Verbal | 580-670 |
| Average SAT Verbal | 630 |
| Range SAT Math | 580-680 |
| Average SAT Math | 630 |
| Range ACT Composite | 26-30 |
| Average ACT Composite | 28 |
| Minimum TOEFL | 550 |
| % graduated top 10% of class | 46 |
| % graduated top 25% of class | 81 |
| % graduated top 50% of class | 100 |

### DEADLINES

| | |
|---|---|
| Priority admission deadline | 11/1 |
| Regular admission | 2/15 |
| Nonfall registration? | yes |

### APPLICANTS ALSO LOOK AT
**AND OFTEN PREFER**
U. Illinois—Urbana-Champaign
Northwestern U.
U. Chicago
Notre Dame
Indiana U.—Bloomington
**AND SOMETIMES PREFER**
DePauw
Northern Illinois
Southern Illinois—Edwardsville
Illinois State
**AND RARELY PREFER**
Eastern Illinois
Bradley

## FINANCIAL FACTS

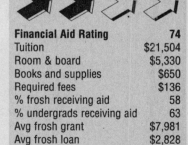

| | |
|---|---|
| Financial Aid Rating | 74 |
| Tuition | $21,504 |
| Room & board | $5,330 |
| Books and supplies | $650 |
| Required fees | $136 |
| % frosh receiving aid | 58 |
| % undergrads receiving aid | 63 |
| Avg frosh grant | $7,981 |
| Avg frosh loan | $2,828 |

# INDIANA UNIVERSITY—BLOOMINGTON

300 NORTH JORDAN AVENUE, BLOOMINGTON, IN 47405-1106 • ADMISSIONS: 812-855-0661 • FAX: 812-855-5102

## CAMPUS LIFE

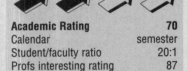

| Quality of Life Rating | 86 |
|---|---|
| Type of school | public |
| Affiliation | none |
| Environment | suburban |

### STUDENTS

| | |
|---|---|
| Total undergrad enrollment | 29,383 |
| % male/female | 47/53 |
| % from out of state | 27 |
| % from public high school | 87 |
| % live on campus | 39 |
| % in (# of) fraternities | 16 (31) |
| % in (# of) sororities | 17 (25) |
| % African American | 4 |
| % Asian | 3 |
| % Caucasian | 86 |
| % Hispanic | 2 |
| % international | 4 |

### SURVEY SAYS . . .

*Everyone loves the Hoosiers*
*Students are happy*
*Frats and sororities dominate social scene*
*Campus is beautiful*
*Lots of beer drinking*
*Students are cliquish*
*Lousy food on campus*
*(Almost) no one listens to college radio*
*Student publications are ignored*

## ACADEMICS

| Academic Rating | 70 |
|---|---|
| Calendar | semester |
| Student/faculty ratio | 20:1 |
| Profs interesting rating | 87 |
| Profs accessible rating | 90 |
| Avg lab size | 20-29 students |
| Avg reg class size | 10-19 students |

### MOST POPULAR MAJORS
business
elementary education
psychology

## STUDENTS SPEAK OUT

### Academics

Indiana University's national reputation may rest on its killer athletic teams, but Indiana residents and students know, and others are beginning to learn, that IU is a fine academic university. Students particularly praise the top-notch business and journalism schools, the excellent psychology departments, and the competitive School of Music. A journalism student characterizes his department as "not excessively competitive, while still maintaining academic excellence." In all departments, students agree that "the opportunities are there, but size is a big deterrent." Indeed, as at most state schools, classes can be less than intimate. Most agree that professors must be sought for help but are excellent teachers. One student notes, "My professors are witty, memorable, and accurate." New registration procedures seem to have sped up the process considerably, putting to rest an age-old gripe of IU students. But as always, assertiveness is the key to success at IU; as one student sums up, "IU is big only if you make it that way! Administrators and professors are more than willing to help if you take the initiative. Success is yours if you seek it." Once you learn the ropes, you can find "the big-school opportunities with the experience of a small campus."

### Life

Bloomington, home of Indiana University, is "the perfect college town, not a big city but always open to students," according to our respondents. The campus itself, according to one junior, is "one of the most beautiful places I've ever seen," where, as another mentions, "there are a million and one things to do . . . , which was nice before I turned 21." But now, "I love hangin' out at Sports—the bar scene is a pretty good one around here and it's made my senior year a great one." Athletics, as the bar's name suggests, are a very important part of nonacademic life. Intercollegiate sports are universally popular—men's basketball, however, is the big draw—and intramural programs are also well attended. Day-to-day social life basically revolves around fraternities and sororities, acceptance to which can be brutally competitive. Students also "go camping, we go to musicals, free jazz at the Encore Cafe, [and] hang out on this awesome campus." Our survey shows that IU has earned its reputation as a party school: alcohol and drugs (particularly hallucinogens) are on-campus favorites.

### Student Body

Around three-fifths of IU students are from in state, which translates to a relatively high percentage of out-of-staters for a state school. The percentage of minorities in the student body is low, but since the school is large, the minority population is as well. Some undergrads find the students to be an interesting mix: "This campus is incredibly diverse. You have your beer-drinking crazy partiers and your snobby (not so snobby) intellectuals, your realists, your idealists, and some people who just don't know who they are." But most report that "there is not an honest outreach to unite different types of students," particularly along racial lines, in this conservative school. Although people get along superficially, "everyone knows their boundaries," because, as one student reports, "racial hate still resides on our campus." Racial tension became more publicly painful to African American students during and after the O.J. Simpson trial.

# INDIANA UNIVERSITY—BLOOMINGTON

FINANCIAL AID: 812-855-0321 • E-MAIL: IUADMIT@INDIANA.EDU • WEBSITE: WWW.INDIANA.EDU

## ADMISSIONS

*Very important* academic and nonacademic factors considered by the admissions committee include secondary school record. *Important* factors considered include standardized test scores and recommendations. *Other* factors considered include alumni/ae relation, extracurricular activities, talent/ability, and volunteer work. Factors *not* considered include geography, interview, minority status, religious affiliation/commitment, state residency, and work experience. SAT I or ACT required; SAT II recommended. TOEFL required of international applicants who intend to major in music or wish to be considered for merit awards or for the Honors College. High school diploma is required and GED is accepted. *High school units required/recommended:* 19 total required; 4 English required, 3 math required, 3 science required, 2 science lab required, 2 foreign language required, 4 elective required. *The admissions office says:* "University-bound students should establish a solid foundation at the high school level in English (the school requires four years), laboratory sciences (one year), and social sciences (two years) if they intend to compete in any academic program offered by Indiana University. Society's increasing demands for mathematical analysis and computing make a broad background in mathematics, including algebra and trigonometry (three years total required), essential for many fields of study. The study of a foreign language is desirable but not required for admission."

### The Inside Word

A high volume of applicants makes Indiana's individual admissions review process relatively selective for a university of its size. Candidates to the School of Music face a highly selective audition process.

## FINANCIAL AID

*Students should submit:* FAFSA and institution's own financial aid form. The Princeton Review suggests that all financial aid forms be submitted as soon as possible after January 1. *Need-based scholarships/grants offered:* Pell, SEOG, state scholarships/grants, private scholarships, and the school's own gift aid. *Loan aid offered:* Direct Subsidized Stafford, Direct Unsubsidized Stafford, Direct PLUS, Federal Perkins, Federal Nursing, and college/university loans from institutional funds. Institutional employment available. Federal Work-Study Program available. Applicants will be notified of awards on a rolling basis beginning on or about May 1. Off-campus job opportunities are excellent.

## FROM THE ADMISSIONS OFFICE

"Indiana University is a traditional university located in Bloomington, Indiana. The campus is known for its spacious, wooded beauty, classic limestone buildings, and wide variety of trees and flowers. Bloomington is a wonderful college town. The liberal arts curriculum offers students a wide range of academic options combined with built-in flexibility."

## ADMISSIONS

| | |
|---|---|
| **Admissions Rating** | 74 |
| # of applicants | 19,896 |
| % of applicants accepted | 82 |
| % of acceptees attending | 42 |

### FRESHMAN PROFILE

| | |
|---|---|
| Range SAT Verbal | 480-600 |
| Average SAT Verbal | 543 |
| Range SAT Math | 490-620 |
| Average SAT Math | 554 |
| Range ACT Composite | 21-27 |
| Average ACT Composite | 24 |
| Minimum TOEFL | 550 |
| % graduated top 10% of class | 21 |
| % graduated top 25% of class | 53 |
| % graduated top 50% of class | 91 |

### DEADLINES

| | |
|---|---|
| Priority admission deadline | 2/1 |
| Nonfall registration? | yes |

### APPLICANTS ALSO LOOK AT
**AND OFTEN PREFER**
Notre Dame
U. Illinois—Urbana-Champaign
**AND SOMETIMES PREFER**
U. Wisconsin—Madison
U. Iowa
Ohio State—Columbus
Purdue U.—West Lafayette
**AND RARELY PREFER**
Wabash
Bellarmine
SUNY Buffalo

### FINANCIAL FACTS

| | |
|---|---|
| **Financial Aid Rating** | 74 |
| In-state tuition | $3,902 |
| Out-of-state tuition | $12,958 |
| Room & board | $5,608 |
| Books and supplies | $712 |
| Required fees | $503 |
| % frosh receiving aid | 38 |
| % undergrads receiving aid | 36 |

# INDIANA UNIVERSITY OF PENNSYLVANIA

216 PRATT HALL, INDIANA, PA 15705 • ADMISSIONS: 724-357-2230 • FAX: 724-357-6281

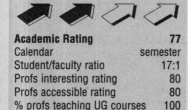
## STUDENTS SPEAK OUT

### Academics

Indiana University of Pennsylvania is an "inexpensive," career-oriented, "rural school" with "small class sizes" and a "thought-provoking" Honors College. "All classes" at IUP "are taught by professors," as just about every student here will eagerly tell you. Most of the instructors here "really challenge you" and "really care." Professors are also "knowledgeable in their fields," "enthusiastic about teaching," and "very willing to spend extra time with students when necessary." Students in the vaunted Robert E. Cook Honors College receive especially excellent academic perks including priority registration and classes limited to 20 students. "Almost all of my professors have been in the 'good' to 'great' category," beams one. However, "multiple-choice tests" are not uncommon at IUP, and non-Honors students say some professors here definitely fall in the "not very good" category. In fact, "some of the professors are awful." The administration receives mixed reviews as well. Some students say administrators are "accessible, helpful, quick," and "congenial." Others gripe about IUP's "red tape," which can be "an overall pain" to navigate. Students are united in their aversion toward IUP's less-than-perfect library. Perhaps, forecasts one forlorn student, "a prophet will emerge to tell these people what a real library is." Their complaints notwithstanding, though, students at IUP admit that they've got it pretty good, especially for students at a public university. "If you're looking for a great undergraduate program, come to IUP," exhorts a junior. "You get bang for your buck here."

### Life

IUP's western Pennsylvania campus has a really cool "Oak Grove" where students love to hang out, weather permitting. Also, the campus has "plays, speakers, concerts," and other events "nearly every day." In the fall, the highly successful Division II football team is a pretty big draw. Leisure opportunities include a large recreational park, a driving range, a university sailing base, and a cross-country ski area complete with lodge and ski hut. The Greek scene on IUP's campus is noticeable but "frats don't run rampant." Instead, "social life is broken down into two groups," helpfully explains a sophomore, "those who are 21 and those who aren't. This is nice because once the frat and house party scene gets redundant, you turn 21 and go uptown." Besides "bars and small parties," though, "there isn't much to do unless you have a car" and, for many students, IUP "tends to be a suitcase school." Off campus, even though the surrounding town is the birthplace of Jimmy Stewart and the Christmas tree capital of the world, "there isn't too much to do" once you get bored "racing carts through Wal-Mart." Fortunately, IUP is "fairly close to" the cultural mecca of Pittsburgh, "where there are"—among other things—"real restaurants."

### Student Body

Among the predominantly white student population on this campus of about 12,000, there are "definite cliques." There is also "a lot of competition between different fraternities and different sororities" and IUP is home to "a few groups of brainless lemmings." Then again, there are "no suburbanite, pseudo-radicals wearing Goodwill clothes," which these salt-of-the-earth students view as a generally blessed thing. A high percentage of IUP students "come to this university from small towns" and, while some are overly "closed-minded," most are simply "amazingly friendly" folks who "get along" extremely well. However, international and Asian students tell us they feel like they are often "not respected" by others.

FINANCIAL AID: 415-357-2218  E-MAIL: ADMISSIONS_INQUIRY@GROVE.IUP.EDU  WEBSITE: WWW.IUP.EDU

## ADMISSIONS

*Very important* academic and nonacademic factors considered by the admissions committee include secondary school record, class rank, and standardized test scores. *Important* factors considered include talent/ability, essay, and recommendations. *Other* factors considered include volunteer work, work experience, extracurricular activities, and alumni/ae relation. Factors *not* considered include religious affiliation/commitment and minority status. High school diploma is required and GED is accepted. *High school units required/recommended:* 4 English recommended, 4 math recommended, 3 science recommended, 2 science lab recommended, 2 foreign language recommended, 4 social studies recommended. *The admissions office says:* "Applicants to the Robert E. Cook Honors College or those seeking early decision should apply by November 15."

## FINANCIAL AID

*Students should submit:* FAFSA. The Princeton Review suggests that all financial aid forms be submitted as soon as possible after January 1. *Need-based scholarships/grants offered:* Pell, SEOG, state scholarships/grants, private scholarships, and the school's own gift aid. *Loan aid offered:* Direct Subsidized Stafford, Direct Unsubsidized Stafford, Direct PLUS, Federal Perkins, state, and college/univeristy loans from institutional funds. Institution employment available. Federal Work-Study Program available. Off-campus job opportunities are fair.

## ADMISSIONS

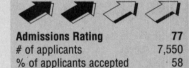

| | |
|---|---|
| **Admissions Rating** | **77** |
| # of applicants | 7,550 |
| % of applicants accepted | 58 |
| % of acceptees attending | 65 |

### FRESHMAN PROFILE

| | |
|---|---|
| Range SAT Verbal | 490-580 |
| Average SAT Verbal | 536 |
| Range SAT Math | 480-560 |
| Average SAT Math | 524 |
| Minimum TOEFL | 500 |
| % graduated top 10% of class | 20 |
| % graduated top 25% of class | 48 |
| % graduated top 50% of class | 81 |

### DEADLINES

| | |
|---|---|
| Priority admission deadline | 12/31 |
| Nonfall registration? | yes |

## FINANCIAL FACTS

| | |
|---|---|
| **Financial Aid Rating** | **80** |
| In-state tuition | $3,792 |
| Out-of-state tuition | $9,480 |
| Room & board | $3,966 |
| Books and supplies | $600 |
| Required fees | $825 |
| % frosh receiving aid | 70 |
| Avg frosh grant | $2,650 |
| Avg frosh loan | $2,625 |

# IOWA STATE UNIVERSITY

100 ALUMNI HALL, AMES, IA 50011-2011 • ADMISSIONS: 515-294-5836 • FAX: 515-294-2592

## CAMPUS LIFE

| | |
|---|---|
| **Quality of Life Rating** | **78** |
| Type of school | public |
| Affiliation | none |
| Environment | suburban |

### STUDENTS

| | |
|---|---|
| Total undergrad enrollment | 21,503 |
| % male/female | 55/45 |
| % from out of state | 17 |
| % from public high school | 93 |
| % live on campus | 35 |
| % in (# of) fraternities | 16 (32) |
| % in (# of) sororities | 16 (18) |
| % African American | 3 |
| % Asian | 3 |
| % Caucasian | 89 |
| % Hispanic | 1 |
| % international | 5 |

### SURVEY SAYS . . .

*Student publications are popular*
*Frats and sororities dominate social scene*
*Diverse students interact*
*Lots of liberals*
*(Almost) everyone plays intramural sports*
*Campus is beautiful*
*Athletic facilities need improving*
*Campus easy to get around*
*Library needs improving*
*Computer facilities need improving*

## ACADEMICS

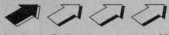

| | |
|---|---|
| **Academic Rating** | **68** |
| Calendar | semester |
| Student/faculty ratio | 14:1 |
| Profs interesting rating | 66 |
| Profs accessible rating | 71 |
| % profs teaching UG courses | 74 |
| % classes taught by TAs | 24 |
| Avg lab size | 20-29 students |
| Avg reg class size | 20-29 students |

### MOST POPULAR MAJORS

management information systems
exercise and sport science
elementary education

## STUDENTS SPEAK OUT

### Academics

As you might expect of a land-grant school smack-dab in the middle of corn country, Iowa State University is among the nation's leading agricultural schools. According to students, though, ISU is more than that; reports one, "When I first came to Iowa State I thought it would be all about farming and agriculture, but there is a lot of diversity here and I think overall it's a really good school." Academic rigor here is "about as challenging as you want it to be," with some students opting for demanding courseloads and others merely coasting through. The determined student who makes the most of an ISU education should find an "abundance" of research opportunities and an astonishing array of academic specialties, but is less likely to find consistent, high-quality instruction. The professors "are OK, but some seem to not care about teaching. They just want to do research." Students point out that "if you really go out of your way to make a point to be known, professors are easy to get to know, but if you want to, it is really easy to slip between the cracks." The administration receives reasonable marks for a school of this size, but does not escape criticism for having "little regard for undergraduates" and "not listening to the wants and needs of students." One final note: There is a large population of older adult students here, and "Iowa State makes a big effort to include non-traditional students."

### Life

"Life on campus is pretty relaxed," writes a typical undergrad, "and students are fine with that." Most students in our survey remarked on the "easygoing" mood here, reporting approvingly that, at ISU, there are "no big-city pressures (like crappy traffic), but there are big-city services." Because "there is no true metropolitan area close . . . we come up with our own fun. The campus/town area is fun, but lacking some cultural opportunities of large cities." Fortunately, opportunities abound on Iowa State's gigantic, "well-thought-out campus," which is "absolutely beautiful" and easy to navigate thanks to a "good transportation system." Students enjoy "concerts, intercollegiate sports, intramural sports, music performances, swing dancing, ballroom dancing, art exhibits," "rock climbing, biking, working out at the gym," and "free Friday flicks." Much of the social life here "is run by the Greeks." On the weekends, "the social scene is mainly fraternity parties if you are underage." For the 21-and-over crowd, a hopping bar scene is immensely popular. "Meeting new people is very hard at this university, especially for individuals who do not do the bar scene," notes one lonely student. The malls and nightlife of the more exciting Des Moines are about 30 miles south.

### Student Body

A "very conservative" small-town vibe permeates this "remarkably diverse campus [considering the fact that it's in] central Iowa." Students agree that "as a whole, it is really easy to find someone like you; however, we are pretty segregated in who we hang out with. I would say minorities of all groups tend to stick together and isolate themselves." Many do, no doubt, because they feel alienated from the ISU majority; as one Latina student notes, "I've heard too many racial remarks at ISU. There needs to be more interaction between the races." A few students complain of their peers' "general lack of ability to consider different viewpoints." Still others see no problems, simply characterizing ISU as "a place full of friendly, ambitious students."

## ADMISSIONS

*Very important* academic and nonacademic factors considered by the admissions committee include class rank, secondary school record, and standardized test scores. *Other* factors considered include character/personal qualities, essays, extracurricular activities, geography, interview, recommendations, state residency, talent/ability, volunteer work, and work experience. Factors *not* considered include alumni/ae relation, minority status, and religious affiliation/commitment. SAT I or ACT required. TOEFL required of all international applicants. High school diploma is required and GED is accepted. *High school units required/recommended:* 16 total recommended; 4 English recommended, 3 math recommended, 2 science recommended, 2 science lab recommended, 2 foreign language recommended, 4 social studies recommended, 3 elective recommended.

### The Inside Word

With a decided lack of mystery in the admissions process and a super-high acceptance rate, Iowa State still attracts a solid student body. What we have here is living proof of the value of a good reputation and a little national press.

## FINANCIAL AID

*Students should submit:* FAFSA. There is no regular filing deadline. The Princeton Review suggests that all financial aid forms be submitted as soon as possible after January 1. *Need-based scholarships/grants offered:* Pell, SEOG, state scholarships/grants, private scholarships, and the school's own gift aid. *Loan aid offered:* Direct Subsidized Stafford, Direct Unsubsidized Stafford, Direct PLUS, Federal Perkins, state, college/university loans from institutional funds, and private alternative loans. Institutional employment available. Federal Work-Study Program available. Applicants will be notified of awards on a rolling basis beginning on or about April 1. Off-campus job opportunities are excellent.

## FROM THE ADMISSIONS OFFICE

"Iowa State University offers all the advantages of a major university along with the friendliness and warmth of a residential campus. There are more than 100 undergraduate programs of study in the Colleges of Agriculture, Business, Design, Education, Engineering, Family and Consumer Sciences, Liberal Arts and Sciences, and Veterinary Medicine. Our 1,700 faculty members include Rhodes Scholars, Fulbright Scholars, and National Academy of Sciences and National Academy of Engineering members. Recognized for its high quality of life, Iowa State has taken practical steps to make the university a place where students feel like they belong. Iowa State has been recognized for the high quality of campus life and the exemplary out-of-class experiences offered to its students. Along with a strong academic experience, students also have opportunities for further developing their leadership skills and interpersonal relationships through any of the more than 500 student organizations, 60 intramural sports, and a multitude of arts and recreational activities. All residence hall rooms are wired for Internet connections and all students have the opportunity to create their own World Wide Web pages."

### ADMISSIONS

| | |
|---|---|
| Admissions Rating | 75 |
| # of applicants | 12,172 |
| % of applicants accepted | 88 |
| % of acceptees attending | 38 |

#### FRESHMAN PROFILE

| | |
|---|---|
| Range SAT Verbal | 520-660 |
| Average SAT Verbal | 590 |
| Range SAT Math | 550-690 |
| Average SAT Math | 610 |
| Range ACT Composite | 21-27 |
| Average ACT Composite | 24 |
| Minimum TOEFL | 500 |
| Average HS GPA | 3.5 |
| % graduated top 10% of class | 25 |
| % graduated top 25% of class | 56 |
| % graduated top 50% of class | 91 |

#### DEADLINES

| | |
|---|---|
| Regular admission | 8/21 |
| Nonfall registration? | yes |

#### APPLICANTS ALSO LOOK AT

**AND OFTEN PREFER**
U. Iowa
U. Kansas
U. Northern Iowa

**AND SOMETIMES PREFER**
U. Wisconsin—Madison
U. Michigan—Ann Arbor
Purdue U.—West Lafayette
U. Minnesota

**AND RARELY PREFER**
Kansas State
Illinois State
Creighton

#### FINANCIAL FACTS

| | |
|---|---|
| Financial Aid Rating | 82 |
| In-state tuition | $2,906 |
| Out-of-state tuition | $9,748 |
| Room & board | $4,171 |
| Books and supplies | $684 |
| % frosh receiving aid | 63 |
| % undergrads receiving aid | 55 |
| Avg frosh grant | $3,049 |
| Avg frosh loan | $5,283 |

# ITHACA COLLEGE

100 JOB HALL, ITHACA, NY 14850-7020 • ADMISSIONS: 607-274-3124 • FAX: 607-274-1900

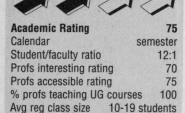

## CAMPUS LIFE

**Quality of Life Rating** **75**
Type of school                     private
Affiliation                         none
Environment                        rural

### STUDENTS
Total undergrad enrollment         5,906
% male/female                      44/56
% from out of state                51
% from public high school          76
% live on campus                   70
% African American                 2
% Asian                            2
% Caucasian                        88
% Hispanic                         3
% international                     2
# of countries represented         77

### SURVEY SAYS . . .
*Diversity lacking on campus*
*Students love Ithaca, NY*
*Student government is popular*
*Lab facilities need improving*
*Great off-campus food*
*Very small frat/sorority scene*
*Musical organizations are hot*
*Student publications are popular*

## ACADEMICS

**Academic Rating** **75**
Calendar                           semester
Student/faculty ratio              12:1
Profs interesting rating           70
Profs accessible rating            75
% profs teaching UG courses        100
Avg reg class size       10-19 students

### MOST POPULAR MAJORS
television-radio
music
physical therapy

## STUDENTS SPEAK OUT
### Academics
The "other" college in Ithaca, New York, is Ithaca College, "a wonderful institution" that originated as a conservatory of music and has grown into a nationally renowned pre-professional college with a "highly diverse curriculum." Students flock to this upstate New York school for "one of the best" physical therapy programs "on the East Coast" and the highly respected School of Communications (which boasts an extension program in Los Angeles). IC offers "small classes" and a promise that full-fledged professors teach virtually every class. Students say many professors are "committed" teachers who "care about your personal goals," "love what they are teaching, and enjoy teaching it." These professors are also "very approachable," "enthusiastic," and "energetic." Unfortunately, not all of Ithaca's faculty members are created equal. Some profs at IC are by no means "incredible"; they are "not very good at all." Overall, though some administrators are "friendly and helpful," IC's "bureaucracy" gets low marks as well. There is "a lot of red tape" here—especially for a reasonably small school. One ray of hope: "The president is always available and extremely social," but "problems never get solved and a lot is swept under the royal college carpet," remarks a senior.

### Life
In the 1960s, IC abandoned its campus in the downtown area of "absolutely gorgeous" Ithaca for a hillside overlooking Cayuga Lake. The result is a modern and relatively new campus (though "residence halls need improvement big-time") in a "beautiful" area. "If you like hiking and spending time in the outdoors, this is the place for you," promises a senior. "You couldn't ask for a better setting." The stunning scenery includes "many waterfalls and parks" and, for the adventurer in you, opportunities for "cliff jumping." And "a five-minute car ride takes you into town, over to Cornell, to a state park, or into the countryside." There is, however, more to life at Ithaca College than its lovely landscape. For starters, there are "many activities on and off campus" including "movie nights," "plays," "concerts," "festivals, arts and crafts, volunteer organizations," and watching football games while "looking over Lake Cayuga." Also, "you get the small-school attention with the big-school atmosphere" of nearby Cornell. As a result, "there is an excellent mix of academics, activities, and social life." As one student sums up, IC is a "big drinking college" in "a huge college town" with "lots of entertainment and educational opportunities." Many students frequent local bars and attend "plenty" of parties. "There's tons of fun stuff to do even if you don't drink alcohol." But if you do, "you can't beat 25-cent drafts" at "happy hour" and "a lenient ID checking policy."

### Student Body
There are plenty of "closed-minded, rich kids" at "predominantly white" Ithaca. The typical IC student "has money and dresses well" and comes from an "upper-middle-class background" in New York, Connecticut, or New Jersey. IC's "sociable, upbeat, and friendly" students describe themselves as "outgoing, career-minded, and self-motivated," and since they are all so much alike, they all get along really well. They are also "friendly, involved, and committed to having a great four years" and "very intelligent." Students also say that, despite the unmistakable lack of ethnic diversity on campus, there are many "unique" individuals here.

FINANCIAL AID: 607-274-3131 • E-MAIL: ADMISSION@ITHACA.EDU • WEBSITE: WWW.ITHACA.EDU

## ADMISSIONS

*Very important* academic and nonacademic factors considered by the admissions committee include secondary school record and standardized test scores. *Important factors* considered include character/personal qualities, class rank, essays, extracurricular activities, interview, recommendations, and talent/ability. *Other factors* considered include alumni/ae relation, volunteer work, and work experience. Factors *not* considered include minority status, religious affiliation/commitment, geography, and state residency. SAT I or ACT required. TOEFL required of all international applicants. High school diploma is required and GED is accepted. *High school units required/recommended:* 16 total required; 4 English required, 3 math required, 3 science required, 2 foreign language required, 3 social studies required, 1 elective required.

### The Inside Word

Ithaca has enjoyed a renaissance of interest from prospective students of late, and its moderately competitive admissions profile has been bolstered as a result. In addition to a thorough review of academic accomplishments, candidates are always given close consideration of their personal background, talents, and achievements. Programs requiring an audition or portfolio review are among the college's most demanding for admission; the arts have always been particularly strong here.

## FINANCIAL AID

*Students should submit:* FAFSA required of all applicants. CSS/Financial Aid PROFILE required of Early Decision applicants. Priority filing deadline is February 1. The Princeton Review suggests that all financial aid forms be submitted as soon as possible after January 1. *Need-based scholarships/grants offered:* Pell, SEOG, state scholarships/grants, private scholarships, and the school's own gift aid. *Loan aid offered:* Subsidized Stafford, Unsubsidized Stafford, PLUS, and Federal Perkins. Institutional employment available. Federal Work-Study Program available. Applicants will be notified of awards on a rolling basis beginning on or about March 15. Off-campus job opportunities are good.

## FROM THE ADMISSIONS OFFICE

"Ithaca College was founded in 1892 as a music conservatory and today continues that commitment to performance and excellence. Its modern, residential, 750-acre campus, equipped with state-of-the-art facilities, is home to the Schools of Business, Communications, Health Sciences and Human Performance, Humanities and Sciences, and Music. With more than 100 majors—from biochemistry to business administration, journalism to jazz, philosophy to physical therapy, and with upper-division programs in Rochester, Los Angeles, and London—students get the curricular opportunities of a large university in a personalized smaller college environment. Ithaca's students benefit from an education that emphasizes hands-on learning, collaborative student-faculty research, and development of the whole student. Located in central New York's spectacular Finger Lakes region in what many consider the classic college town, Ithaca College offers 25 highly competitive varsity teams, more than 130 campus clubs, and two radio stations and a television station, as well as hundreds of concerts, recitals, and theater performances annually."

### ADMISSIONS

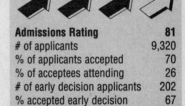

| | |
|---|---|
| Admissions Rating | 81 |
| # of applicants | 9,320 |
| % of applicants accepted | 70 |
| % of acceptees attending | 26 |
| # of early decision applicants | 202 |
| % accepted early decision | 67 |

#### FRESHMAN PROFILE

| | |
|---|---|
| Range SAT Verbal | 520-620 |
| Range SAT Math | 530-630 |
| Minimum TOEFL | 550 |
| % graduated top 10% of class | 30 |
| % graduated top 25% of class | 64 |
| % graduated top 50% of class | 92 |

#### DEADLINES

| | |
|---|---|
| Early decision | 11/1 |
| Early decision notification | 12/15 |
| Priority admission deadline | 3/1 |
| Regular notification | 4/15 |
| Nonfall registration? | yes |

### FINANCIAL FACTS

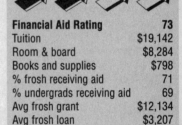

| | |
|---|---|
| Financial Aid Rating | 73 |
| Tuition | $19,142 |
| Room & board | $8,284 |
| Books and supplies | $798 |
| % frosh receiving aid | 71 |
| % undergrads receiving aid | 69 |
| Avg frosh grant | $12,134 |
| Avg frosh loan | $3,207 |

# JAMES MADISON UNIVERSITY

UNDERGRADUATE ADMISSION, SONNER HALL MSC 0101, HARRISONBURG, VA 22807 • ADMISSIONS: 540-568-6147

## CAMPUS LIFE

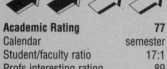

**Quality of Life Rating**    **84**
Type of school    public
Affiliation    none
Environment    rural

### STUDENTS

| | |
|---|---|
| Total undergrad enrollment | 14,280 |
| % male/female | 42/58 |
| % from out of state | 30 |
| % from public high school | 95 |
| % live on campus | 41 |
| % in (# of) fraternities | 12 (18) |
| % in (# of) sororities | 15 (10) |
| % African American | 4 |
| % Asian | 4 |
| % Caucasian | 85 |
| % Hispanic | 2 |
| % international | 1 |
| # of countries represented | 64 |

### SURVEY SAYS . . .

Great food on campus
Campus feels safe
Student publications are popular
Lots of beer drinking
Everyone watches the Dukes
Students are cliquish
Students don't like Harrisonburg, VA
Student government is unpopular
Very little drug use
Students are not very happy

## ACADEMICS

| | |
|---|---|
| **Academic Rating** | **77** |
| Calendar | semester |
| Student/faculty ratio | 17:1 |
| Profs interesting rating | 89 |
| Profs accessible rating | 91 |
| % profs teaching UG courses | 100 |
| % classes taught by TAs | 9 |
| Avg lab size | 20-29 students |
| Avg reg class size | 20-29 students |

### MOST POPULAR MAJORS
marketing
psychology
computer information systems

## STUDENTS SPEAK OUT

### Academics

With "topnotch facilities," affordable tuition for both in-state and out-of-state students, and standout programs in music and business, James Madison University has a lot going for it. JMU also boasts an "innovative" Integrated Science and Technology (ISAT) program that offers degree programs in health sciences, computer science, and other technology-based fields. However, while some students praise ISAT to the heavens, others complain that it drains resources away from every other program. Students tell us that the "unbelievably good" professors here are "very knowledgeable in their fields." What's more, JMU's "very, very approachable" profs are "genuinely concerned about students," and they maintain the kind of "open-door policy" that you find almost exclusively at small liberal arts colleges. Advising is only "okay," though; students warn "you are mostly on your own" when it comes to selecting classes. Also, a "lack of faculty in some majors" cramps students' style, as JMU continues to grow "without a proportional increase in teachers and staff." Though the administration receives glowing praise from some, most students here are not impressed. The top brass is "not polite" and "tinkers" too much with policies and student life. Also, red tape abounds. "Basically, if there is an easy way of doing something, it is not practiced here," observes an anthropology major.

### Life

James Madison is located in Virginia's "beautiful and historic" Shenandoah Valley, a fact not lost on students. "Our campus is beautiful," chortles a senior, "especially in the spring when all the flowers bloom and in fall when the leaves turn." Harrisonburg is "a nice town" as well, though nightlife "is lacking." Nevertheless, "a lot of people like to party" and "live their lives for the weekends, which coincidentally start on Wednesday." Fraternities and students who live in apartments throw bang-up parties and, for a significant chunk of JMU's student population, alcohol is a big part of their social life. "You don't have to party for fun" though. "The university does a good job of providing lots of activities for different people." There are "many clubs and organizations in which to get involved," including "very strong and active" Christian groups, an "outstanding marching band," and "experimental theater" on campus. "On sunny days, people are playing Frisbee everywhere, playing guitars, walking dogs," and generally cavorting about the JMU campus. The local area surrounding campus provides outdoor activities galore—"camping and hiking in the mountains" as well as skiing, snowboarding, canoeing, and horseback riding. When students get tired of the "cow pasture community" that is Harrisonburg, they usually head off to Richmond or Washington, D.C., both within driving distance. Think twice before leaving campus, though: the food at James Madison is "a great strength," according to a junior. "It's practically like home cooking" and students call it "the best food in the Northeast."

### Student Body

"The general friendliness on this campus is super," according to one student. There are "smiles everywhere" and "southern hospitality abounds." In fact, students tell us that JMU is the "door-opening school because everyone is so friendly." JMU students call themselves "stereotypical college kids." "Everyone looks the same" (though many are apparently "gorgeous"). You'll find a fair share of "holy rollers" here and a lot of students who are "crazy, but in a good, laugh-all-night kind of way," according to a giddy first-year student. "My friends are my family and I want to be a student here until I am 30!" On the downside, racial interaction could stand to be improved on JMU's largely whitebread campus. Students hail primarily from Virginia.

Fax: 540-568-3332 • Financial Aid: 540-568-7820 • E-mail: gotojmu@jmu.edu • Website: www.jmu.edu

## ADMISSIONS

*Very important* academic and nonacademic factors considered by the admissions committee include class rank, secondary school record, and standardized test scores. *Important* factors considered include essays and extracurricular activities. *Other* factors considered include alumni/ae relation, character/personal qualities, geography, minority status, recommendations, state residency, talent/ability, volunteer work, and work experience. Factors *not* considered include interview and religious affiliation/commitment. SAT I or ACT required; SAT I preferred. TOEFL required of all international applicants. High school diploma is required and GED is accepted. *High school units required/recommended:* 14 total required; 18 total recommended; 4 English required, 3 math required, 3 science required, 4 science recommended, 2 foreign language required, 4 foreign language recommended, 2 social studies required, 3 social studies recommended.

### The Inside Word

James Madison has prospered from the applications of students faced with severe competition for admission to UVA and William and Mary. Third place on the Virginia public university totem pole is not a bad spot to be, as JMU's admissions committee will attest. Pay attention when they stress that your high school schedule should be chock-full of challenging academic courses.

## FINANCIAL AID

*Students should submit:* FAFSA. Priority filing deadline is March 1. The Princeton Review suggests that all financial aid forms be submitted as soon as possible after January 1. *Need-based scholarships/grants offered:* Pell, SEOG, state scholarships/grants, private scholarships, and the school's own gift aid. *Loan aid offered:* FFEL Subsidized Stafford, FFEL Unsubsidized Stafford, FFEL PLUS, Federal Perkins, and college/university loans from institutional funds. Institutional employment available. Federal Work-Study Program available. Applicants will be notified of awards on or about April 15. Off-campus job opportunities are good.

## FROM THE ADMISSIONS OFFICE

"James Madison University's philosophy of inclusiveness—known as 'all together one'—means that students become a part of a real community that nurtures its own to learn, grow, and succeed. Our professors, many of whom have a wealth of real-world experience, pride themselves on making teaching their top priority. We take seriously the responsibility to maintain an environment that fosters learning and encourages students to excel in and out of the classroom. Our rich variety of educational, social, and extracurricular activities include more than 100 innovative and traditional undergraduate majors and programs, a well-established study abroad program, a cutting-edge information security program, more than 250 student clubs and organizations, and a 147,000-square-foot, state-of-the-art recreation center. The university's picturesque, self-contained campus is located in the heart of the Shenandoah Valley, a four-season area that's easy to call home. Great food, fun times, exciting intercollegiate athletics, and rigorous academics all combine to create the unique James Madison experience. From the library to the residence halls and from our understanding honors program to our highly successful career placement program, the university is committed to equipping our students with the tools they need to achieve their dreams."

## ADMISSIONS

| | |
|---|---|
| Admissions Rating | 83 |
| # of applicants | 13,573 |
| % of applicants accepted | 64 |
| % of acceptees attending | 37 |
| # accepting a place on wait list | 600 |

### FRESHMAN PROFILE

| | |
|---|---|
| Range SAT Verbal | 540-620 |
| Average SAT Verbal | 582 |
| Range SAT Math | 550-630 |
| Average SAT Math | 589 |
| Minimum TOEFL | 570 |
| Average HS GPA | 3.5 |

### DEADLINES

| | |
|---|---|
| Priority admission deadline | 11/1 |
| Regular admission | 1/15 |
| Regular notification | 4/1 |

### APPLICANTS ALSO LOOK AT

**AND OFTEN PREFER**
U. Virginia
William and Mary
UNC—Chapel Hill
Duke

**AND SOMETIMES PREFER**
Virginia Tech
George Mason
American
Mary Washington

**AND RARELY PREFER**
West Virginia U.
Clemson
Hampden-Sydney
Dickinson

### FINANCIAL FACTS

| | |
|---|---|
| Financial Aid Rating | 76 |
| In-state tuition | $4,094 |
| Out-of-state tuition | $10,606 |
| Room & board | $5,968 |
| Books and supplies | $750 |
| % frosh receiving aid | 34 |
| % undergrads receiving aid | 30 |
| Avg frosh grant | $4,002 |
| Avg frosh loan | $5,037 |

# JOHNS HOPKINS UNIVERSITY

3400 NORTH CHARLES STREET/140 GARLAND, BALTIMORE, MD 21218 • ADMISSIONS: 410-516-8171 • FAX: 410-516-6025

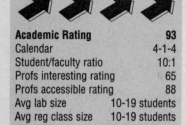

## CAMPUS LIFE

**Quality of Life Rating** 83
Type of school | private
Affiliation | none
Environment | urban

### STUDENTS
Total undergrad enrollment | 3,910
% male/female | 58/42
% from out of state | 78
% from public high school | 67
% live on campus | 54
% in (# of) fraternities | 18 (13)
% in (# of) sororities | 19 (7)
% African American | 6
% Asian | 18
% Caucasian | 66
% Hispanic | 2
% international | 8

### SURVEY SAYS . . .
*Great library*
*Campus easy to get around*
*Beautiful campus*
*Lab facilities are great*
*Theater is hot*
*Ethnic diversity on campus*
*Athletic facilities need improving*
*Lousy food on campus*
*No one plays intramural sports*
*Student publications are ignored*

## ACADEMICS

**Academic Rating** 93
Calendar | 4-1-4
Student/faculty ratio | 10:1
Profs interesting rating | 65
Profs accessible rating | 88
Avg lab size | 10-19 students
Avg reg class size | 10-19 students

### MOST POPULAR MAJORS
biomedical engineering
biology
international studies

## STUDENTS SPEAK OUT
### Academics

Prospective Johns Hopkins students, beware: A JHU education is not for the faint of heart. There's little of the hand-holding and kindly mentoring that characterizes small, undergrad-oriented colleges here. Students don't come to JHU for a warm, fuzzy experience, though; they come for the prestige of graduating from one of the nation's top schools, one with a particularly stellar reputation in English, international studies, business, the sciences, and pre-medicine. Writes one student, "It's damn hard. But if it doesn't kill you, it will make you stronger." Says another, "Hopkins is a meat-grinder, but the post-graduate opportunities make it worth it. Hopkins has a strong alumni network that is a tremendous asset to students. Hopkins is much more than a pre-med mecca; the alumni network makes it especially valuable to anyone interested in business or Wall Street." Because of the school's focus on the sciences, "perhaps Hopkins' most valuable asset is its profound commitment to research, which paradoxically is also its most deplorable characteristic. A consequence of this commitment is that either top-notch researchers with abhorrent teaching skills, or else faculty who are completely uninterested in teaching students, are faced with the duty of engaging students in the material, with disastrous results." Agrees another student, "The science professors are rather wrapped up in their research, so [they] don't make office hours for students. Basically it's up to you and your book to learn the material. The liberal arts professors, however, are more enthusiastic about helping their students." Making the JHU experience more arduous still is a "big-school bureaucracy surrounded by small-school facilities." All the same, most agree that "there is a tremendous upside to attending JHU, so long as you are willing to actively pursue your interests."

### Life

The academic demands of a JHU education mean that "you can have a social life if you try, but you have to face the fact that in classes we work harder than students at other schools. Hopefully, it'll pay off at some point." The ungodly workload is one handicap to a normal social life; the school's location, in the quiet residential Homewood section of Baltimore, is another. Explains one student, Hopkins lacks "college-y surroundings directly off campus. It needs restaurants, shops, and things to do." Greater Baltimore offers the amenities of big-city life, but most are a car ride's distance from campus, leaving those who lack transport with the feeling that "Baltimore is a totally dead city. Even when you don't have any work, which doesn't happen all that often, there's nothing to do." For the transportation-challenged, Hopkins offers an active Greek organization along with a panoply of student activities. On-campus movies are plentiful and well attended; among sports, lacrosse is a student favorite. For those who can get away from campus, social opportunities expand appreciably. Downtown Baltimore offers a variety of decent restaurants and bars as well as the ever-popular Inner Harbor and cultural and sports events. Many students note with appreciation that Baltimore is "very close to D.C."

### Student Body

Hopkins students are among the nation's brightest, a group of "passionate, academically minded people with interesting opinions and tons of different talents." Notes one student, "A few could use a shower now and again, but most are so funny and intelligent that you'll hardly notice. Hardly." There are downsides to having all this brainpower around, however; some believe there are "too many people here with book smarts but no common sense." Hopkins undergrads, especially those in the prestigious pre-med program, are driven individuals "enormously concerned with grades and careers." Many "can't think about anything but work. If you look for the cool people, though, there are sooo many great people here." A fifth of the population is Asian, and students note that there is some tendency for the Asians to segment themselves from the others.

FINANCIAL AID: 410-516-8028 • E-MAIL: GOTOJHU@JHU.EDU • WEBSITE: WWW.JHU.EDU

## ADMISSIONS

*Very important* academic and nonacademic factors considered by the admissions committee include secondary school record, standardized test scores, and extracurricular activities. *Important* factors considered include class rank, recommendations, essays, talent/ability, character/personal qualities, minority status, and volunteer work. *Other* factors considered include interview, alumni/ae relations, and work experience. Factors *not* considered include geographical residence, state residency, and religious affiliation/commitment. TOEFL required of all international applicants. High school diploma is required and GED is accepted. *High school units required/recommended:* 16 total required; 17 total recommended; 4 English required, 3 math required, 4 math recommended, 2 science required, 2 science lab required, 2 foreign language required, 3 social studies required.

### The Inside Word

The admissions process at Hopkins demands to be taken seriously. Competition with the best colleges and universities in the country keeps the acceptance rate artificially high. Make certain that your personal credentials—essays, recommendations, and extracurricular activities—are impressive.

## FINANCIAL AID

*Students should submit:* FAFSA, institution's own financial aid form, state aid form, noncustodial (divorced/separated) parent's statement, business/farm supplement, and federal income tax forms. Regular filing deadline is February 15. The Princeton Review suggests that all financial aid forms be submitted as soon as possible after January 1. *Need-based scholarships/grants offered:* Pell, SEOG, state scholarships/grants, private scholarships, and the school's own gift aid. *Loan aid offered:* Direct Subsidized Stafford, Direct Unsubsidized Stafford, Direct PLUS, FFEL PLUS, Federal Perkins, and college/university loans from institutional funds. Institutional employment available. Federal Work-Study Program available. Applicants will be notified of awards on or about April 1. Off-campus job opportunities are excellent.

## FROM THE ADMISSIONS OFFICE

"The admissions process at Johns Hopkins is a highly competitive one, but also a highly personal process. Our staff gets to know you through your application essays and extracurricular activities. We would also like to know you personally through one of a variety of campus programs we offer, including individual interviews, overnight visits with current students, and open houses. We are not a huge university and we seek to build a true 'community' of scholars; as we get to know each other we hope you will sense this and seek to be a part of it."

## ADMISSIONS

| | |
|---|---|
| Admissions Rating | 97 |
| # of applicants | 9,445 |
| % of applicants accepted | 32 |
| % of acceptees attending | 33 |
| # accepting a place on wait list | 982 |
| # of early decision applicants | 554 |
| % accepted early decision | 41 |

### FRESHMAN PROFILE

| | |
|---|---|
| Range SAT Verbal | 630-720 |
| Average SAT Verbal | 670 |
| Range SAT Math | 670-760 |
| Average SAT Math | 711 |
| Range ACT Composite | 28-32 |
| Average ACT Composite | 30 |
| Minimum TOEFL | 600 |
| Average HS GPA | 3.9 |
| % graduated top 10% of class | 70 |
| % graduated top 25% of class | 93 |
| % graduated top 50% of class | 98 |

### DEADLINES

| | |
|---|---|
| Early decision | 11/15 |
| Early decision notification | 12/15 |
| Regular admission | 1/1 |
| Regular notification | 4/1 |

### APPLICANTS ALSO LOOK AT
**AND OFTEN PREFER**
Harvard
Stanford
MIT
U. Virginia
Princeton
**AND SOMETIMES PREFER**
Yale
Brown
Duke
Columbia
**AND RARELY PREFER**
Cornell U.
Georgetown U.
UC—Berkeley
U. Maryland—Coll. Park

### FINANCIAL FACTS

| | |
|---|---|
| Financial Aid Rating | 75 |
| Tuition | $26,220 |
| Room & board | $8,580 |
| Books and supplies | $800 |
| % frosh receiving aid | 47 |
| % undergrads receiving aid | 42 |

# KALAMAZOO COLLEGE

1200 ACADEMY STREET, KALAMAZOO, MI 49006 • ADMISSIONS: 616-337-7166 • FAX: 616-337-7390

## STUDENTS SPEAK OUT
### Academics
Kalamazoo College's unique K Plan provides students a well-rounded education through a combination of classroom instruction, study abroad, a senior thesis project, and internships. This "diverse, yet rigorous" plan "is geared toward preparing you for your future endeavors." The approach, one human development major explains, is that "here, education is a process." An enthusiastic sophomore gushes, "Last quarter, I had an internship at the Philadelphia District Attorney's office. . . . Next year, I'll be studying in Thailand for five months." Though the quality of professors varies from "great" to "terrible," students believe that their professors are always accessible and incredibly dedicated. "I wholeheartedly believe that some of them never leave their offices," an English major writes. Professors expect a similar level of dedication from their students. "The work can be overwhelming," warns one sophomore, and others complain about the "ridiculous amount" of "busy work assigned." Students rave about the small class sizes, even in lower-level courses. "I expected large lectures in college and found only seven other students in my class," one first-year English major explains. "I was shocked and impressed to find that such classes are the rule, not the exception." The administration is open, friendly, and "interested in helping each and every one of their students succeed." Offers a senior biology major, "I have shown up at the president's home unannounced and [was] welcomed in with open arms." Despite its small size, Kalamazoo offers students "an amazing amount of options." Writes a sophomore, "The academics are rigorous, but extremely rewarding." Students believe that the heavy academic workload prepares them well for graduate school.

### Life
Ask a student about his or her choice to attend Kalamazoo College, and a standard response might be, "I can't imagine having a more intellectually and socially stimulating environment." Students "spend way too much time studying" but still have time to participate in many extracurricular activities. Bowling and the three formal dances held every year are among students' favorite amusements. The campus improvisational group, Monkapult, is another popular diversion. Students say that the food needs to be improved. Most first-year students are not allowed to have cars on campus, which seriously curtails their off-campus activities. There are no fraternities on campus, and students often go to small house parties or fiestas thrown at Western Michigan University. The onerous workload means that most students restrict their partying to Friday and Saturday nights. "Study is the key word around here," a senior Spanish major advises. "Academics are by far the most important [priority]." Of course, this means that students will use words like "dull" and "boring" to describe on-campus life.

### Student Body
Kalamazoo College attracts a "disparate and not entirely meshing group of students." Which is cool. The dearth of fraternities adds to the "family atmosphere" and eliminates some of the associated cliques, but "it's easy to feel inadequate with so many overachievers." Students like their peers and believe that they are genuinely friendly, "compassionate," and always willing to help. Students agree, however, that they "do not have enough ethnic diversity." Most students come from upper-middle-class backgrounds. Still, "there are lots of different people here who are respectful and tolerant," according to one sophomore biology major. Social activism could use a jump-start, too.

FINANCIAL AID: 616-337-7192 • E-MAIL: ADMISSION@KZOO.EDU • WEBSITE: WWW.KZOO.EDU

## ADMISSIONS

*Very important* academic and nonacademic factors considered by the admissions committee include extracurricular activities, secondary school record, standardized test scores, and talent/ability. *Important* factors considered include character/personal qualities, class rank, essays, recommendations, volunteer work, and work experience. *Other* factors considered include alumni/ae relation, geography, interview, minority status, and state residency. Factors *not* considered include religious affiliation/commitment. SAT I or ACT required. TOEFL required of all international applicants. High school diploma is required and GED is accepted. *High school units required/recommended:* 4 English required, 2 math required, 3 math recommended, 2 science required, 3 science recommended, 2 foreign language required, 2 social studies recommended, 2 history recommended, 1 elective recommended.

### The Inside Word

K-Zoo's applicant pool is small and self-selected academically, which leads to the unusual combination of a very high acceptance rate and an impressive freshman profile. The admissions committee expects candidates to show evidence of serious academic intent, suitability for the college, and a willingness to contribute to the life of the college. Those who underestimate the evaluation process risk denial.

## FINANCIAL AID

*Students should submit:* FAFSA and institution's own financial aid form. The Princeton Review suggests that all financial aid forms be submitted as soon as possible after January 1. *Need-based scholarships/grants offered:* Pell, SEOG, state scholarships/grants, private scholarships, and the school's own gift aid. *Loan aid offered:* Direct Subsidized Stafford, Direct Unsubsidized Stafford, Direct PLUS, Federal Perkins, and state. Institutional employment available. Federal Work-Study Program available. Applicants will be notified of awards on or about March 31. Off-campus job opportunities are good.

## FROM THE ADMISSIONS OFFICE

"The educational program offered by Kalamazoo College combines traditional classroom instruction with experiential education. During their four years, students move freely from working and learning in groups to pursuing individual academic and artistic projects. The Kalamazoo Plan, or K Plan, enables every student to participate in four different educational experiences: on-campus learning, a career development internship, overseas study, and a senior project. The Career Development internship is typically done during the sophomore year summer allowing students to 'try on' a career. Eighty percent of all Kalamazoo College students choose to participate in this valuable experience. The Senior Individualized Project provides students with the opportunity to make use of all their experiences at the college. They may choose to do research, a thesis, creative or artistic work, or other work related to their major. All students complete a Senior Individualized Project prior to graduation."

## ADMISSIONS

| | |
|---|---|
| Admissions Rating | 81 |
| # of applicants | 1,422 |
| % of applicants accepted | 70 |
| % of acceptees attending | 32 |
| # of early decision applicants | 38 |
| % accepted early decision | 76 |

### FRESHMAN PROFILE

| | |
|---|---|
| Range SAT Verbal | 590-700 |
| Average SAT Verbal | 641 |
| Range SAT Math | 600-690 |
| Average SAT Math | 641 |
| Range ACT Composite | 26-30 |
| Average ACT Composite | 28 |
| Minimum TOEFL | 550 |
| Average HS GPA | 3.7 |
| % graduated top 10% of class | 47 |
| % graduated top 25% of class | 83 |
| % graduated top 50% of class | 97 |

### DEADLINES

| | |
|---|---|
| Early decision | 11/15 |
| Early decision notification | 12/1 |
| Regular admission | 2/15 |

### APPLICANTS ALSO LOOK AT

**AND OFTEN PREFER**
U. Michigan—Ann Arbor
Northwestern U.
Georgetown U.
Dartmouth

**AND SOMETIMES PREFER**
Notre Dame
Oberlin
Earlham
Macalester
Michigan State

**AND RARELY PREFER**
Albion, Alma
Hope, Wooster
DePauw

### FINANCIAL FACTS

| | |
|---|---|
| Financial Aid Rating | 80 |
| Tuition | $19,188 |
| Room & board | $5,787 |
| Books and supplies | $750 |
| Required fees | $70 |
| % frosh receiving aid | 48 |
| % undergrads receiving aid | 55 |
| Avg frosh grant | $10,870 |
| Avg frosh loan | $3,628 |

# KANSAS STATE UNIVERSITY

119 ANDERSON HALL, MANHATTAN, KS 66506 • ADMISSIONS: 785-532-6250 • FAX: 785-532-6393

## CAMPUS LIFE

| Quality of Life Rating | **75** |
|---|---|
| Type of school | public |
| Affiliation | none |
| Environment | suburban |

### STUDENTS

| | |
|---|---|
| Total undergrad enrollment | 18,252 |
| % male/female | 53/47 |
| % from out of state | 7 |
| % from public high school | 90 |
| % live on campus | 30 |
| % in (# of) fraternities | 20 (28) |
| % in (# of) sororities | 20 (15) |
| % African American | 3 |
| % Asian | 1 |
| % Caucasian | 90 |
| % Hispanic | 2 |
| % Native American | 1 |
| % international | 1 |
| # of countries represented | 70 |

### SURVEY SAYS . . .

*Frats and sororities dominate social scene*
*Everyone loves the Wildcats*
*Athletic facilities are great*
*(Almost) everyone plays intramural sports*
*Students love Manhattan, KS*
*Large classes*
*Students get along with local community*
*Student publications are popular*
*Students are very religious*
*Library needs improving*

## ACADEMICS

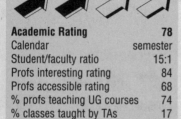

| Academic Rating | **78** |
|---|---|
| Calendar | semester |
| Student/faculty ratio | 15:1 |
| Profs interesting rating | 84 |
| Profs accessible rating | 68 |
| % profs teaching UG courses | 74 |
| % classes taught by TAs | 17 |
| Avg reg class size | 10-19 students |

### MOST POPULAR MAJORS
animal science
journalism
mechanical engineering

## STUDENTS SPEAK OUT

### Academics

A bargain-basement tuition and a staggering array of courses (the curriculum offers approximately 3,000 courses each semester) draw undergraduates to Kansas State University. Once there, many students are pleasantly surprised to discover that K-State offers many of the advantages of smaller school. Writes one student, "Many of our professors give home phone numbers and don't mind if they receive calls at home, but most of all they are dedicated to do anything to help us reach our goals and succeed." Adds an agricultural economics/pre-law double major, "I feel my professors are nearly as accessible here as they were in my high school of 100 students." Similarly, the administration "is very approachable and willing to spend time with students." Student complaints center on required general education classes. "They're real bad. It seems like international instructors who are difficult to understand teach all my general classes. But once you're a sophomore the instructors are great." Also, as at some other large universities, "the school doesn't offer enough sections of certain classes, making it almost impossible to graduate in four years."

### Life

The mainstay of K-State social life is football, pure and simple. No other activity has the power to draw K-State's student body and thousands of alumni so close together. "Fall Saturday afternoons at K-State are awesome. People tailgate for hours before the game—students, alumni, faculty, and staff interacting and having a great time. There is enormous school spirit." Another student adds, "K-State football has kept our campus buzzing with excitement! It's pretty remarkable!" The Greek system attracts a considerable portion of the student body, providing another social hub for students. Other student activities filter through the student government, which "is given a lot of power, allowing us to represent the students and give our opinions to the administrators, and they listen." Students also enjoy outdoor activities, reporting that "For fun we go to Tuttle Creek or the Konza Prairie (when it's warm). Aggieville is a very popular area for shopping and nighttime fun." K-State has "a smaller campus than many large schools, and that's a good thing," because of its blend of "small-town atmosphere with, at the same time, larger-city resources." Some students might find the setting too confining: life at K-State is "fun, enjoyable, but not terribly exciting. Not as much to do as bigger towns and cities have, but the small, enclosed atmosphere is nice." Topeka, roughly three times the size of hometown Manhattan (a.k.a. the Little Apple), is about an hour away by car. Wichita, the largest city in Kansas, is a two-hour drive.

### Student Body

K-State's 17,000-plus undergraduates are drawn mostly from within Kansas, which is reflected in its overwhelmingly white and rural student body. Students admit, "We're a bunch of hicks. Nice hicks, but hicks all the same." While student relations are mostly copacetic, several respondents note that "it seems like there are a lot of cliques on campus. Greeks hang out with Greeks, etc. I love the social aspect, but I feel like I interact with the same people over and over again." A large commuter population translates into a weaker sense of campuswide community, especially in the spring (nonfootball) semester.

# KANSAS STATE UNIVERSITY

FINANCIAL AID: 785-532-6420 • E-MAIL: KSTATE@KSU.EDU • WEBSITE: WWW.KSU.EDU

## ADMISSIONS

*Very important* academic and nonacademic factors considered by the admissions committee include class rank, secondary school record, standardized test scores, and state residency. *Other* factors considered include minority status. Factors *not* considered include alumni/ae relation, character/personal qualities, essays, extracurricular activities, geography, interview, recommendations, religious affiliation/commitment, talent/ability, volunteer work, and work experience. ACT required. TOEFL required of all international applicants. High school diploma is required and GED is accepted. *High school units required/recommended:* 16 total recommended; 4 English recommended, 3 math recommended, 3 science recommended, 1 science lab recommended, 2 foreign language recommended.

### The Inside Word

As at most public universities, the admissions process is about as straightforward as it can get. Kansas high school grads are automatically admitted; out-of-state students are expected to be in the top half of their graduating class and to show evidence of academic potential via ACT scores. (SAT scores are acceptable, but if you haven't taken the ACT you'll have to do so once you enroll. Ouch!) Don't be deceived by the seeming lack of rigor in admissions standards—K-State is chock full of strong students. Heightened national visibility for its athletic teams over the past few years will no doubt attract more applicants.

## FINANCIAL AID

*Students should submit:* FAFSA and institution's own financial aid form. Priority filing deadline is March 1. The Princeton Review suggests that all financial aid forms be submitted as soon as possible after January 1. *Need-based scholarships/grants offered:* Pell, SEOG, state scholarships/grants, and private scholarships. *Loan aid offered:* Direct Subsidized Stafford, Direct Unsubsidized Stafford, PLUS, Federal Perkins, and the school's own loans. Institution employment available. Federal Work-Study Program available. Applicants will be notified of awards on a rolling basis beginning on or about August 15. Off-campus job opportunities are good.

## FROM THE ADMISSIONS OFFICE

"Kansas State University offers strong academic programs, a lively intellectual atmosphere, a friendly campus community, and an environment where students achieve: K-State's total of Rhodes, Marshall, Truman, and Goldwater scholars since 1986 ranks first in the nation among state universities. In the Goldwater competition, only Princeton and Harvard have produced more winners. K-State's student government was named best in the nation in 1997 and 1995. The debate and forensics squads finished their current seasons ranked seventh and eighth in the country. Research facilities include the Konza Prairie, the world's largest tall grass prairie preserve, and the Macdonald Lab, the only university accelerator devoted primarily to atomic physics. Open House, held each April, is a great way to explore K-State's more than 200 majors and options and 370 student organizations."

## ADMISSIONS

| | |
|---|---|
| Admissions Rating | 82 |
| # of applicants | 8,417 |
| % of applicants accepted | 61 |
| % of acceptees attending | 70 |

### FRESHMAN PROFILE

| | |
|---|---|
| Range ACT Composite | 19-23 |
| Average ACT Composite | 23 |
| Minimum TOEFL | 550 |
| Average HS GPA | 3.4 |
| % graduated top 10% of class | 24 |
| % graduated top 25% of class | 60 |
| % graduated top 50% of class | 89 |

### DEADLINES

| | |
|---|---|
| Nonfall registration? | yes |

## FINANCIAL FACTS

| | |
|---|---|
| Financial Aid Rating | 82 |
| In-state tuition | $2,333 |
| Out-of-state tuition | $9,260 |
| Room & board | $4,240 |
| Books and supplies | $684 |
| Required fees | $514 |
| % frosh receiving aid | 47 |
| % undergrads receiving aid | 49 |
| Avg frosh grant | $2,000 |
| Avg frosh loan | $1,098 |

# KENYON COLLEGE

Admissions Office, Ransom Hall, Gambier, OH 43022-9623 • Admissions: 800-848-2468 • Fax: 740-427-5770

## CAMPUS LIFE

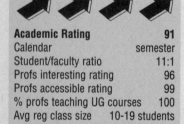

**Quality of Life Rating**    **88**
Type of school    private
Affiliation    Episcopal
Environment    rural

### STUDENTS

| | |
|---|---|
| Total undergrad enrollment | 1,599 |
| % male/female | 45/55 |
| % from out of state | 80 |
| % from public high school | 58 |
| % live on campus | 98 |
| % in (# of) fraternities | 35 (8) |
| % in (# of) sororities | 3 (1) |
| % African American | 4 |
| % Asian | 3 |
| % Caucasian | 88 |
| % Hispanic | 3 |
| % international | 1 |
| # of countries represented | 23 |

### SURVEY SAYS . . .

*Diversity lacking on campus*
*Beautiful campus*
*Classes are small*
*Students aren't religious*
*(Almost) everyone smokes*
*Lousy off-campus food*
*(Almost) no one listens to college*
*radio*
*Athletic facilities need improving*
*Musical organizations are hot*

## ACADEMICS

**Academic Rating**    **91**
Calendar    semester
Student/faculty ratio    11:1
Profs interesting rating    96
Profs accessible rating    99
% profs teaching UG courses    100
Avg reg class size    10-19 students

### MOST POPULAR MAJORS

English
history
biology

## STUDENTS SPEAK OUT

### Academics

With its small classes, dedicated teachers, and sharp student body, Kenyon College is a classic example of a small liberal arts college. Perhaps most paradigmatic is the close relationship students enjoy with the faculty; writes one undergrad, "Professors are amazing. They are a huge part of the family known as Kenyon. We have dinner at their houses, babysit their kids, and look to many of them as mentors." Adds another, "Professors here are completely approachable. We often know their spouses, their children, their dogs, and their houses. As a result, it's extremely easy to find them and to ask them questions, etc." The community atmosphere helps students deal with the considerable rigors of a Kenyon education. Explains one student, "It's not easy here, but it's satisfying in every way when you do well. I feel quite lucky to be surrounded by such a select group of intelligent students and faculty." Says another, "Kenyon is very academic in atmosphere, but it doesn't have a competitive slant to it. We have lots of interesting, specialized classes and very much focus on knowing things in depth rather than simply what you need to know to get by." Students enjoy a surprisingly wide variety of courses considering the size of the school. Says one, "Often students are heard saying there are so many courses they want to take they don't know if they'll have time to take all the ones they want in the four years they have." The administration, though it is "too politically correct," receives praise as well for its willingness "to listen and discuss anything" at practically any time.

### Life

The Greek system, student organizations, and a full slate of school-sponsored events attempt to offset the relative lack of activity in Gambier, Kenyon's small hometown. Students report that "there are a TON of student organizations and activities to get involved in on campus and opportunities to create new ones each year." Writes one student, "Life at Kenyon is busy. . . . With over 90 student organizations from fencing to Zen meditation there is simply not enough time." Still, "Kenyon can be a bit boring at times. It's just such a small place that if you're not into the frat party scene, you don't have many other party environment options. But the school does try to provide other opportunities for students to have fun. There is almost always a movie showing, a musical performance, or a comedian somewhere on campus! And the college also provides shuttles to go into the little town that is near us in case we need anything. Once or twice a month there is even a shuttle that goes into Columbus." Many students don't mind the slow pace and seclusion of Kenyon life. Notes one, "It's pretty much true that as one of those colleges "on top of the hill," Kenyon is closed off from the rest of society. If World War III were going on, I probably wouldn't know about it."

### Student Body

As at many private colleges, diversity at Kenyon is primarily geographic. Writes one student, "Students come here from all over the U.S. They are some of the brightest and friendliest scholars in the country. As a freshman, I was humbled by my peers. In high school, I was the valedictorian, but at Kenyon I discovered that there are so many people that are more talented and intelligent." Students acknowledge that "Kenyon has a problem with the fact that so many of its students come from well-off, two-parent households that sent them to private school. Many people led sheltered lives and continue to do that here. But not everyone is that way, and there is diversity, just not as much as there ideally would be." Students enjoy the fact that "people generally get along," which makes the "strong" community here "more close-knit than most." Undergrads are usually so absorbed in their studies that they "tend to be somewhat apathetic politically."

FINANCIAL AID: 740-427-5430 • E-MAIL: ADMISSIONS@KENYON.EDU • WEBSITE: WWW.KENYON.EDU

## ADMISSIONS

*Very important* academic and nonacademic factors considered by the admissions committee include secondary school report (grades, class rank, and difficulty of courses), standardized tests, and recommendations. *Important* factors include essay, extracurricular activities, talent or ability (e.g., music, drama, athletics etc.), and character. *Other* factors considered include interview, alumni connection, minority status, geography (state of the country of residence), and work experience. Factors *not* considered include religious affiliation. SAT I or ACT required. TOEFL required of all international applicants. High school diploma is required and GED is accepted. *High school units required/recommended:*18 units required; 22 units recommended; 4 English required, 3 math required, 4 math recommended, 3 science required, 4 science recommended, 3 foreign language required, 4 foreign language recommended, 2 social science required, 3 social science recommended, 3 electives required, 3 electives recommended. *The admissions office says:* "We look for students who have taken AP or honors courses in two or more subjects. Students who have outstanding achievement in activities, e.g., athletics, drama, music, community service, and leadership, and sound academic records are given preference."

### The Inside Word

Kenyon pays close attention to matchmaking in the course of candidate selection, and personal accomplishments are just as significant as academic ones. Applicants who rank the college high among their choices should definitely interview.

## FINANCIAL AID

*Students should submit:* FAFSA and CSS/Financial Aid PROFILE. The Princeton Review suggests that all financial aid forms be submitted as soon as possible after January 1. *Need-based scholarships/grants offered:* Pell, SEOG, state scholarships/grants, private scholarships, and the school's own gift aid. *Loan aid offered:* FFEL Subsidized Stafford, FFEL Unsubsidized Stafford, FFEL PLUS, Federal Perkins, and college/university loans from institutional funds. Institutional employment available. Federal Work-Study Program available. Applicants will be notified of awards on or about April 1. Off-campus job opportunities are fair. Academic scholarships, including national merit scholarships, are offered.

## FROM THE ADMISSIONS OFFICE

"Kenyon's president describes the college as 'learning in the company of friends,' a phrase he coined on his first day on campus. While faculty expectations are rigorous and the work challenging, the academic atmosphere is cooperative, not competitive. Indications of intellectual curiosity and passion for learning, more than just high grades and test scores, are what we look for in applications. Important as well are demonstrated interests in nonacademic pursuits, whether in athletics, the arts, writing, or another passion. Life in this small college community is fueled by the talents and enthusiasm of our students, so the admission staff seeks students who have a range of talents and interests."

## ADMISSIONS

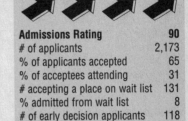

| | |
|---|---|
| Admissions Rating | 90 |
| # of applicants | 2,173 |
| % of applicants accepted | 65 |
| % of acceptees attending | 31 |
| # accepting a place on wait list | 131 |
| % admitted from wait list | 8 |
| # of early decision applicants | 118 |
| % accepted early decision | 92 |

### FRESHMAN PROFILE

| | |
|---|---|
| Range SAT Verbal | 610-710 |
| Average SAT Verbal | 656 |
| Range SAT Math | 590-670 |
| Average SAT Math | 635 |
| Range ACT Composite | 27-31 |
| Average ACT Composite | 29 |
| Minimum TOEFL | 570/230 |
| Average HS GPA | 3.7 |
| % graduated top 10% of class | 58 |
| % graduated top 25% of class | 84 |
| % graduated top 50% of class | 99 |

### DEADLINES

| | |
|---|---|
| Early decision | 12/1 |
| Early decision notification | 12/15 |
| Regular admission | 1/15 |
| Regular notification | 4/1 |

### APPLICANTS ALSO LOOK AT

**AND OFTEN PREFER**
Brown
Northwestern U.
Williams
Middlebury, Oberlin

**AND SOMETIMES PREFER**
Bowdoin
Bates, Carleton
Colgate, Dartmouth

**AND RARELY PREFER**
Colby, Denison
Hobart & William Smith
Skidmore, Hamilton

### FINANCIAL FACTS

| | |
|---|---|
| Financial Aid Rating | 76 |
| Tuition | $25,370 |
| Room & board | $4,370 |
| Books and supplies | $920 |
| Required fees | $710 |
| % frosh receiving aid | 48 |
| % undergrads receiving aid | 50 |
| Avg frosh grant | $15,658 |
| Avg frosh loan | $3,519 |

# KNOX COLLEGE

BOX K-148, GALESBURG, IL 61401 • ADMISSIONS: 309-341-7100 • FAX: 309-341-7070

## CAMPUS LIFE

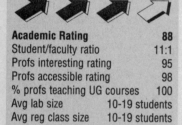

| Quality of Life Rating | **84** |
|---|---|
| Type of school | private |
| Affiliation | none |
| Environment | rural |

### STUDENTS

| | |
|---|---|
| Total undergrad enrollment | 1,199 |
| % male/female | 43/57 |
| % from out of state | 46 |
| % live on campus | 93 |
| % in (# of) fraternities | 24 (5) |
| % in (# of) sororities | 12 (2) |
| % African American | 4 |
| % Asian | 5 |
| % Caucasian | 79 |
| % Hispanic | 4 |
| % international | 10 |
| # of countries represented | 32 |

### SURVEY SAYS . . .

Campus easy to get around
Beautiful campus
Great library
Great computer facilities
Athletic facilities are great
Ethnic diversity on campus
Popular college radio
Student publications are popular
Students don't like Galesburg, IL
Students are cliquish

## ACADEMICS

| Academic Rating | **88** |
|---|---|
| Student/faculty ratio | 11:1 |
| Profs interesting rating | 95 |
| Profs accessible rating | 98 |
| % profs teaching UG courses | 100 |
| Avg lab size | 10-19 students |
| Avg reg class size | 10-19 students |

### MOST POPULAR MAJORS

educational studies
biology
economics

## STUDENTS SPEAK OUT

### Academics

"Freedom to Flourish" is the motto of Knox College, a "fabulous," "extremely competitive" school located very close to the middle of nowhere. The motto "is kind of corny," admits a senior, "but it's true." A junior agrees: "You are an individual to Knox's faculty and staff, worthy of respect and trust." Professors expect a lot from students. "This school is very hard. I've never been challenged like this before," reports one undergrad. "But, there are always people to help you." Profs also offer a lot in return for the hard work; they are "genuinely interested in our academic and social well-being. They are always available to make time for us." And although "there is not a wide variety of courses offered . . . the classes that are offered are made interesting and fun by the professors." Students are also satisfied with their "very accessible," if sometimes slow, administration system. "It's nice to be treated as a person instead of a number," says a junior. Knox students also report receiving extremely generous financial aid packages. The highly praised trimester system allows students to "concentrate more on classes" and take advantage of "nice, long breaks" in between sessions. Forty percent of Knox grads go directly to graduate and professional programs. "If you are ambitious," asserts a chemistry major, "Knox is the place to be." No wonder students offer this unofficial motto for their school: "Knox rocks!"

### Life

Knox's hometown of Galesburg is "your average small Illinois town," explains a computer science major. It "closes at five, but it's safe, pleasant, and pretty." Warns one student, "The area we are located in is extremely boring. There is really no point leaving campus to find activities unless you're prepared for an hour drive or more." Students report that they remain busy during the week with both curricular and extracurricular responsibilities; especially popular are theater groups, the student newspaper, and the college radio station. "I can never understand how people can get bored here. There is always something going on," contends a sophomore. "You're either studying your butt off, or you're doing something with a group of people and trying to keep your mind off how much studying you should be doing." On weekends, however, "there's nothing much to do. Fun on the weekends usually consists of a movie (when they change the movies) and drinking before frat parties." Students agree that "this is a big drinking school. People here like to have a good time. We get our work done, but we also do our fair share of partying," leading some wishing that "at some point . . . the administration [would] have activities during weekend nights. On weekends, activities at night are run by Anheuser Busch, Jack Daniels, and Jim Beam." When students lay down to sleep, the rooms that spin around them are first-rate; the large suites at Knox are among the most luxurious in the nation.

### Student Body

The tiny Knox student body draws heavily from the Chicago area. "We have our share of cliques of preps, internationals, grunge, etc.," writes one student, "but they all seem interwoven to some degree." Divisions do exist between the school's liberal and conservative factions; reports a member of the latter group, "Students have a tendency to proclaim themselves so open-minded that they refuse to see the perspective of students with certain convictions, especially religious convictions. Ironic, isn't it?" Others, pointing to Latino and African American populations of about 40 students each, complain that "Knox isn't as diverse and open as it likes to think it is. Having a few token minority students who don't challenge the majority doesn't make us diverse."

# KNOX COLLEGE

## ADMISSIONS

*Very important* academic and nonacademic factors considered by the admissions committee include essays, recommendations, secondary school record, and talent/ability. *Important* factors considered include character/personal qualities, class rank, extracurricular activities, and standardized test scores. *Other* factors considered include alumni/ae relation, interview, minority status, state residency, volunteer work, and work experience. Factors *not* considered include geography and religious affiliation/commitment. SAT I or ACT required. TOEFL required of all international applicants. High school diploma is required and GED is accepted. *High school units required/recommended:* 17 total required; 4 English required, 2 math required, 4 math recommended, 2 science required, 4 science recommended, 2 foreign language recommended, 2 social studies required, 4 social studies recommended. *The admissions office says:* "[Approximately two-thirds of our consideration] is placed upon the difficulty of the applicant's academic program combined with his/her performance. We review each application and accompanying documents thoroughly. The key to admissibility is for a student to have successfully completed his/her school's most challenging curriculum and demonstrate integrity, initiative, and leadership."

### The Inside Word

A small applicant pool necessitates Knox's high acceptance rate. The student body is nonetheless well qualified, and candidates should show solid academic accomplishment.

## FINANCIAL AID

*Students should submit:* FAFSA, institution's own financial aid form, and income tax return. The Princeton Review suggests that all financial aid forms be submitted as soon as possible after January 1. *Need-based scholarships/grants offered:* Pell, SEOG, state scholarships/grants, private scholarships, and the school's own gift aid. *Loan aid offered:* Direct Subsidized Stafford, Direct Unsubsidized Stafford, Direct PLUS, Federal Perkins, and college/university loans from institutional funds. Institutional employment available. Federal Work-Study Program available. Applicants will be notified of awards on or about April 15. Off-campus job opportunities are fair.

## FROM THE ADMISSIONS OFFICE

"Economists talk about the importance of finding your niche—knowing that one special thing you do better than anyone else. At Knox, we specialize in changing people's lives. Knox isn't an elitist school with mile-high hoops for applicants to jump through. We work hard at finding those students who will flourish here and giving them the freedom to do so. The result is a top-notch academic school with a remarkably unpretentious sense of itself."

## ADMISSIONS

| | |
|---|---|
| **Admissions Rating** | **81** |
| # of applicants | 1,423 |
| % of applicants accepted | 72 |
| % of acceptees attending | 29 |

### FRESHMAN PROFILE

| | |
|---|---|
| Range SAT Verbal | 540-690 |
| Range SAT Math | 560-660 |
| Range ACT Composite | 24-29 |
| Minimum TOEFL | 550 |
| % graduated top 10% of class | 46 |
| % graduated top 25% of class | 75 |
| % graduated top 50% of class | 96 |

### DEADLINES

| | |
|---|---|
| Regular admission | 2/1 |
| Regular notification | 3/31 |
| Nonfall registration? | yes |

### APPLICANTS ALSO LOOK AT AND OFTEN PREFER

Northwestern U.
Grinell
U. Illinois—Urbana-Champaign

### AND SOMETIMES PREFER

Bradley
Lawrence U.
Beloit

## FINANCIAL FACTS

| | |
|---|---|
| **Financial Aid Rating** | **91** |
| Tuition | $22,380 |
| Room & board | $5,610 |
| Books and supplies | $600 |
| Required fees | $240 |
| % frosh receiving aid | 72 |
| % undergrads receiving aid | 74 |
| Avg frosh grant | $15,343 |
| Avg frosh loan | $3,566 |

# LAFAYETTE COLLEGE

118 MARKLE HALL, EASTON, PA 18042 • ADMISSIONS: 610-330-5100 • FAX: 610-330-5355

## STUDENTS SPEAK OUT

### Academics

"Lafayette's greatest strength," opines one astute undergraduate, "is giving its students the resources and opportunities of a large school in a nice smaller-school environment." Indeed, Lafayette students enjoy many of the perks usually associated with larger universities, including "opportunities for research," but without the inconvenience of graduate students monopolizing professors' time or teaching intro classes. "With an entire student body of undergraduates, the primary focus of the faculty is classroom teaching. This means that faculty are always accessible to students," explains one student. Adds another, "The small-school setting means that relations with faculty and administrators are very intimate and welcomed." The engineering department is the school's star attraction, and students agree that "academics in the engineering department are exceptional." Warns one engineer, "You learn how to work, and you learn how to solve problems, but you also learn that you can't do it all by yourself." Other students point out that "the business program is really good" and that many liberal arts departments are standouts as well. Professors "are fantastic! They genuinely care whether their students learn. It is great to have such a personable group of people to learn from." Writes one student, "Our professors are not Ivy Tower stiffs; they are our peers and our colleagues on many things that we do. I know most of my profs on a first-name basis, and have even gone golfing with two or three of them." A thorough core curriculum means that, for many, "Lafayette can be a little boring academically until you reach the upper-level courses. However, I feel well prepared for my career and believe that my education has been as good as at anywhere else."

### Life

Lafayette has a long-standing reputation as a huge Greek school, and despite the administration's best efforts to scale down the Greek scene, "Greek life is still very big" here, proving the adage that old habits sometimes do die hard. When asked about the social scene, few students fail to mention the Greeks, noting that "the Greek culture either sucks you in or drives you away." Most weigh in on the side of Frat Row; complains one typical student, "The school is trying very hard to discourage underage drinking and like many schools they are targeting frats and sororities. It sucks. The town of Easton has little to offer 18- to 22-year-olds." Another concurs, "For fun at Lafayette we go to fraternity parties. There really isn't that much to do on campus, except for the occasional interesting cultural event." Others, however, disagree, reporting that "there are so many things to do here that it surprised me, considering what a small campus it is. We have many popular groups come for concerts, etc. There are dance parties at the fraternities as well." Writes one student approvingly, "Although Lafayette has the comforts of small school academics, the social life has a large-school feel, with Division I athletics . . . and major cities within driving distance." Philadelphia and New York City are the most frequent destinations for those desperate to get away from campus.

### Student Body

The Lafayette student body "is very homogeneous: white and upper-middle-class, with minorities very segregated." Notes one local wisecracker, "This campus is made up of about 2,000 students who are pretty much exactly alike. All the girls wear black pants. Everyone wears Abercrombie and has a North Face backpack." While some report that "people seem to get along well," many detect the presence of "huge cliques that don't always interact well with each other. Maybe it's the small size or maybe it's the 'rich school' mentality." While nearly all aggressively pursue academic success, not everyone at Lafayette can be described as "bookish"; writes one undergrad, "Intellectual pursuits outside of the classroom are supported by some and looked down upon by others." Agrees another, "Many here are concerned with what I consider superficial things: clothes, money, appearance, and social status. There are great people here, too. The trick is to find them!"

FINANCIAL AID: 610-330-5055 • E-MAIL: ADMISSIONS@LAFAYETTE.EDU • WEBSITE: WWW.LAFAYETTE.EDU

## ADMISSIONS

*Very important* academic and nonacademic factors considered by the admissions committee include secondary school record and standardized test scores. *Important* factors considered include character/personal qualities, class rank, essays, extracurricular activities, interview, recommendations, and talent/ability. *Other* factors considered include alumni/ae relation, geography, volunteer work, and work experience. Factors *not* considered include minority status, religious affiliation/commitment, and state residency. SAT I or ACT required; SAT II recommended. TOEFL required of all international applicants. High school diploma is required and GED is accepted. *High school units required/recommended:* 15 total required; 4 English required, 2 math required, 4 math recommended, 1 science required, 2 science recommended, 4 foreign language recommended, 1 social studies required, 3 social studies recommended. *The admissions office says:* "Lafayette looks for the student who tries to stretch in secondary school. Honors courses, advanced placement work, a range of serious electives, and evidence of willingness to take risks will always count for more than spectacular marks in 'soft' subjects."

### The Inside Word

Applications are reviewed three to five times and evaluated by as many as nine different committee members. In all cases, students who continually seek challenges and are willing to take risks academically win out over those who play it safe in order to maintain a high GPA.

## FINANCIAL AID

*Students should submit:* FAFSA, CSS/Financial Aid PROFILE, noncustodial (divorced/separated) parent's statement, business/farm supplement, and prior-year tax returns along with all schedules and W-2s for student and parent(s). Regular filing deadline is February 1. The Princeton Review suggests that all financial aid forms be submitted as soon as possible after January 1. *Need-based scholarships/grants offered:* Pell, SEOG, state scholarships/grants, private scholarships, and the school's own gift aid. *Loan aid offered:* FFEL Subsidized Stafford, FFEL Unsubsidized Stafford, FFEL PLUS, Federal Perkins, state, college/university loans from institutional funds, and HELP loans to parents. Institutional employment available. Federal Work-Study Program available. Applicants will be notified of awards on or about April 1. Off-campus job opportunities are good.

## FROM THE ADMISSIONS OFFICE

"We choose students individually, one by one, and we hope that the ones we choose will approach their education the same way, as a highly individual enterprise. Our first-year seminars have enrollments limited to 15 or 16 students each in order to introduce the concept of learning not as passive receipt of information but as an active, participatory process. Our low average class size and 11:1 student/teacher ratio reflect that same philosophy. We also devote substantial resources to our Marquis Scholars Program, to one-on-one faculty-student mentoring relationships, and to other programs in engineering within a liberal arts context, giving Lafayette its distinctive character, articulated in our second-year seminars exploring values in science and technology. Lafayette provides an environment in which its students can discover their own personal capacity for learning, personal growth, and leadership."

## ADMISSIONS

| | |
|---|---|
| Admissions Rating | 82 |
| # of applicants | 5,038 |
| % of applicants accepted | 40 |
| % of acceptees attending | 28 |
| # accepting a place on wait list | 621 |
| % admitted from wait list | 1 |
| # of early decision applicants | 247 |
| % accepted early decision | 62 |

### FRESHMAN PROFILE

| | |
|---|---|
| Range SAT Verbal | 560-650 |
| Average SAT Verbal | 610 |
| Range SAT Math | 590-680 |
| Average SAT Math | 645 |
| Range ACT Composite | 24-30 |
| Average ACT Composite | 26 |
| Minimum TOEFL | 550 |
| % graduated top 10% of class | 55 |
| % graduated top 25% of class | 87 |
| % graduated top 50% of class | 99 |

### DEADLINES

| | |
|---|---|
| Early decision | 12/1 |
| Early decision notification | 2/15 |
| Priority admission deadline | 1/1 |
| Regular notification | 4/1 |
| Nonfall registration? | yes |

### APPLICANTS ALSO LOOK AT

**AND OFTEN PREFER**
U. Penn, Tufts
Boston Coll., Cornell U.

**AND SOMETIMES PREFER**
Gettysburg, Bucknell
Lehigh, Colgate, Hamilton

**AND RARELY PREFER**
Dickinson
Franklin & Marshall
Penn State—Univ. Park

### FINANCIAL FACTS

| | |
|---|---|
| Financial Aid Rating | 75 |
| Tuition | $24,828 |
| Room & board | $7,734 |
| Books and supplies | $600 |
| Required fees | $93 |
| % frosh receiving aid | 56 |
| % undergrads receiving aid | 47 |
| Avg frosh grant | $20,552 |
| Avg frosh loan | $3,500 |

# LAKE FOREST COLLEGE

555 NORTH SHERIDAN ROAD, LAKE FOREST, IL 60045 • ADMISSIONS: 847-735-5000 • FAX: 847-735-6291

## CAMPUS LIFE

| Quality of Life Rating | 83 |
| --- | --- |
| Type of school | private |
| Affiliation | Presbyterian |
| Environment | suburban |

### STUDENTS

| | |
| --- | --- |
| Total undergrad enrollment | 1,251 |
| % male/female | 40/60 |
| % from out of state | 51 |
| % from public high school | 63 |
| % live on campus | 85 |
| % in (# of) fraternities | 18 (4) |
| % in (# of) sororities | 14 (3) |
| % African American | 6 |
| % Asian | 5 |
| % Caucasian | 85 |
| % Hispanic | 3 |
| % international | 7 |
| # of countries represented | 44 |

### SURVEY SAYS . . .

Great food on campus
Student publications are ignored
Classes are small
Campus feels safe
Students love Lake Forest, IL
Computer facilities need improving
Lousy off-campus food
Class discussions encouraged

## ACADEMICS

| Academic Rating | 87 |
| --- | --- |
| Calendar | semester |
| Student/faculty ratio | 13:1 |
| Profs interesting rating | 96 |
| Profs accessible rating | 98 |
| % profs teaching UG courses | 100 |
| Avg lab size | 10-19 students |
| Avg reg class size | 10-19 students |

### MOST POPULAR MAJORS

business/economics
psychology
communications

## STUDENTS SPEAK OUT

### Academics

An "excellent combination" of "strongly challenging" academics, "competitive Division III sports," "great financial aid," and a choice location sets this "small liberal arts college" apart from the pack. Of special note is the Richter Apprentice Scholars Program, which allows first-year students to "conduct independent, individual research" under the direct guidance of Lake Forest College faculty. LFC's General Education Curriculum requires students to take classes in a broad set of electives, and though some students admittedly slide by, the school offers "stimulating class discussions and interesting lectures." As a rule, the "teacher-student relationship is very tight" on this campus. The "very kind" and "usually entertaining" professors here are "genuinely impassioned about their respective subject matters," according to one student. "They are always willing to help outside the classroom." What's more, "the administrators are not faceless names in offices" but "people" who "know the students personally and care about their well-being." The top brass is also "responsive to demands of students." Students say their school is just dandy in virtually every academic facet. About the only thing that needs changing is the rather large amount of administrative "red tape" on this small campus. Also, students say campus technology "could use improvement," even though they are more satisfied with their computer labs than the national average.

### Life

Lake Forest boasts a "gorgeous campus," and despite some old dorms, soon to be replaced by palace-like digs, the school is known for good grub and a "safe" suburban location on the well-to-do North Shore of Chicago. The "boring" surrounding area "does not offer much to college students," though. "Our town is not a college town and therefore it is difficult to find a restaurant or grocery store open late," explains a sophomore. Both intramural and intercollegiate athletics enjoy widespread popularity. As for the romantic scene, "students 'hook up' but rarely date other students." The Greek system is active, but not all-encompassing in this "close-knit community." Students can also "spend time looking out on the lake" or "just relaxing with friends in the dorm," but they say social options are somewhat limited. Administration efforts to curtail the once-rampant partying seem to have toned things down a bit, but students nevertheless "booze a lot," mostly at the "fraternity parties" which provide "the weekend highlights" around campus. Luckily, "if you get sick of the school scene, you can easily hop on a train to the city" as "downtown Chicago" is "a short" and convenient train ride away. Students report that "Chicago is a great resource." There are "great internship opportunities," clubs, bars, museums—"something for every mood."

### Student Body

Once a getaway for snobby underachievers who went to boarding schools on the East Coast, this "preppy" and "friendly" little college has made phenomenal strides in terms of diversity and national prestige, but it's still "kind of like high school with ashtrays and nicer cars." Though students "can be cliquish," they "greet you with a smile and a 'hello'" on campus, and "treat each other with respect for the most part." To hear them tell it, the "bright, interested in learning, active" students here also "like to have fun." On the minus side, Lake Forest is "a bit segregated when it comes to race." In addition, the politically "apathetic" students here are "mostly rich, white, and drunk on Friday and Saturday nights." Upon graduation, though, even the most wayward students can take advantage of an immense and loyal alumni network.

# LAKE FOREST COLLEGE

FINANCIAL AID: 847-735-5103 • E-MAIL: ADMISSIONS@LFC.EDU • WEBSITE: WWW.LAKEFOREST.EDU

## ADMISSIONS

*Very important* academic and nonacademic factors considered by the admissions committee include secondary school record. *Important* factors considered include essays and extracurricular activities. *Other* factors considered include alumni/ae relation, character/personal qualities, class rank, geography, interview, recommendations, standardized test scores, talent/ability, volunteer work, and work experience. Factors *not* considered include minority status, religious affiliation/commitment, and state residency. SAT I or ACT required. TOEFL required of all international applicants. High school diploma is required and GED is accepted. *High school units required/recommended:* 4 English required, 3 math required, 2 science required, 2 foreign language required, 3 social studies required.

### The Inside Word

Candidates with good grades will meet with little resistance on the road to acceptance. But remember that Lake Forest definitely has a prep-school-at-the-college-level feel. It pays to keep the admissions committee's eagerness to assess the whole person in mind when completing the application.

## FINANCIAL AID

*Students should submit:* FAFSA and CSS/Financial Aid PROFILE. The Princeton Review suggests that all financial aid forms be submitted as soon as possible after January 1. *Need-based scholarships/grants offered:* Pell, SEOG, state scholarships/grants, private scholarships, and the school's own gift aid. *Loan aid offered:* Direct Subsidized Stafford, Direct Unsubsidized Stafford, Direct PLUS, Federal Perkins, and college/university loans from institutional funds. Institutional employment available. Federal Work-Study Program available. Applicants will be notified of awards on a rolling basis beginning on or about March 15. Off-campus job opportunities are good.

## FROM THE ADMISSIONS OFFICE

Where you go to college can have everything to do with what you get out of college. As you consider the overall experience that you want—and the learning adventure that you should expect—think about the resources Lake Forest has to offer you. Location: Lake Forest is the leading national liberal arts college near Chicago. Our campus is located 30 miles north of Chicago, a half-mile from Lake Michigan, and in a town of about 18,000 that is on record as the safest city in Illinois. The Company: Our 1,250 students represent 47 states and 44 other countries. Lake Forest's nationally and internationally recognized faculty is just as diverse as our student body and enjoys and excels at teaching undergraduates. In fact, professors (94 percent holding a PhD) do all the teaching at Lake Forest, not teaching assistants. Our average class size is 17, and our student/faculty ratio is 12.5:1. The Curriculum: Lake Forest's broad curriculum emphasizes learning and teaching; includes 19 departmental and 8 interdisciplinary majors; and encourages internships, international study, and faculty-student research. Outside the Classroom: College should be demanding, but not a relentless grind. Part of the adventure is exploring the diversions, like Lake Forest's more than 100 student-run organizations and clubs and 17 varsity NCAA Division III teams. Plus the nation's third-largest city, Chicago, and all it's academic, cultural, and social resources, is only a short train ride away. After Lake Forest: Our Career Development Center and alumni mentors provide all kinds of resources for job searches or graduate education. Ultimately, Lake Forest endeavors to help individuals develop themselves for the lives of leadership, service, and personal fulfillment."

## ADMISSIONS

| | |
|---|---|
| Admissions Rating | 78 |
| # of applicants | 1,438 |
| % of applicants accepted | 71 |
| % of acceptees attending | 33 |
| # accepting a place on wait list | 17 |
| % admitted from wait list | 65 |
| # of early decision applicants | 38 |
| % accepted early decision | 66 |

### FRESHMAN PROFILE

| | |
|---|---|
| Range SAT Verbal | 520-630 |
| Average SAT Verbal | 570 |
| Range SAT Math | 510-620 |
| Average SAT Math | 570 |
| Range ACT Composite | 23-27 |
| Average ACT Composite | 25 |
| Minimum TOEFL | 550 |
| Average HS GPA | 3.4 |
| % graduated top 10% of class | 26 |
| % graduated top 25% of class | 51 |
| % graduated top 50% of class | 83 |

### DEADLINES

| | |
|---|---|
| Early decision | 1/1 |
| Early decision notification | 1/21 |
| Priority admission deadline | 3/1 |
| Regular admission | 7/1 |
| Regular notification | 4/1 |
| Nonfall registration? | yes |

### APPLICANTS ALSO LOOK AT

**AND OFTEN PREFER**
Kenyon
Connecticut Coll.
DePauw

**AND SOMETIMES PREFER**
U. Illinois—Urbana-Champaign
Bradley, Valparaiso
Cornell Coll.
U. Iowa

**AND RARELY PREFER**
Hollins

### FINANCIAL FACTS

| | |
|---|---|
| Financial Aid Rating | 92 |
| Tuition | $21,896 |
| Room & board | $5,254 |
| Books and supplies | $500 |
| Required fees | $310 |
| % frosh receiving aid | 68 |
| % undergrads receiving aid | 74 |
| Avg frosh grant | $15,197 |
| Avg frosh loan | $2,541 |

# LAWRENCE UNIVERSITY

PO Box 599, Appleton, WI 54912-0599 • Admissions: 920-832-6500 • Fax: 920-832-6782

## CAMPUS LIFE

| **Quality of Life Rating** | **78** |
| --- | --- |
| Type of school | private |
| Affiliation | none |
| Environment | suburban |

### STUDENTS

| | |
| --- | --- |
| Total undergrad enrollment | 1,285 |
| % male/female | 46/54 |
| % from out of state | 54 |
| % from public high school | 81 |
| % live on campus | 98 |
| % in (# of) fraternities | 35 (5) |
| % in (# of) sororities | 15 (3) |
| % African American | 1 |
| % Asian | 3 |
| % Caucasian | 90 |
| % Hispanic | 2 |
| % Native American | 1 |
| % international | 7 |

### SURVEY SAYS . . .
No one cheats
Student publications are ignored
Classes are small
Campus feels safe
Students aren't religious
Musical organizations are hot
Low cost of living
Diverse students interact
No one plays intramural sports

## ACADEMICS

| **Academic Rating** | **91** |
| --- | --- |
| Calendar | trimester |
| Student/faculty ratio | 11:1 |
| Profs interesting rating | 95 |
| Profs accessible rating | 97 |
| % profs teaching UG courses | 100 |
| Avg reg class size | 10-19 students |

### MOST POPULAR MAJORS
biology
English
music performance

## STUDENTS SPEAK OUT

### Academics

Students at "demanding" Lawrence University would very much like to "dispel the myth that Lawrence is just a music school." Of course, the music program is excellent, but so is the strong biology program and other departments as well. This little liberal arts college boasts "small classes" and "dedicated" professors who are "always willing to help the students." The profs are "very tough graders," though, and they place a great deal of emphasis on writing. While students seem to appreciate the level of difficulty, a few complain that intro classes can become stale pretty quickly, especially those taught by the few stodgy, "old school" professors. Regardless of what classes you take, it appears to be a requirement that you "work hard" and "study a lot." The "very bureaucratic" administration at Lawrence leaves a bit to be desired. Several students speculate that Lawrence is admitting "too many students each year," which causes serious registration problems as well as some congestion in the music program. "Perhaps this should improve," suggests a senior. Despite the morass that is registration, other students contend that "administrators really care about the students and want us to be happy, healthy, and stimulated." Many students agree that the "new, modern-looking buildings" are nowhere near as stunning as the "lovely" older buildings on campus.

### Life

Not only is it an "isolated" little burg, but "Appleton can be boring" as well. To make matters worse, a "smelly" paper mill sits across the river from the largely "student-run" campus "but that's not Lawrence's fault," points out a junior. "We were here first." Despite these nuisances, students at Lawrence manage to have a good time on a pretty consistent basis. "Opportunities to get involved" are plentiful. "Almost every student at Lawrence is involved in some kind of extracurricular activity," explains a sophomore. "There's usually 60 things going on at once," and there is "always something to do or go see." "Most students participate in sports" and because so many students are into music and the arts, there are "continuous performances, recitals, plays, [and] movies." In addition, "there is something going on virtually every weekend, from a showing of a film series to an art opening to a concert to a musical to a student recital to intramural sports," according to a junior. "The list is never ending." When students are not attending these events, they often "play cards" or "sled down Union Hill on cafeteria trays" during the long Wisconsin winter. On the weekends (mostly), "Greek life and drinking" become the focal point of Lawrence social life. "Campuswide" fraternity parties—which often have themes—are "a big deal here" and are "what the majority of people do for fun" on the weekends. Students who aren't in the mood for the frat scene often "leave town for fun."

### Student Body

The "academically motivated" and "liberal" students at Lawrence call themselves "original, creative, and intelligent" as well as "hardworking" and "serious about their studies." The conservatory attracts many earnestly music-minded students "from all over" and there is a visible international contingent on campus. Consequently, the student body is "extremely diverse" given its "small midwestern town" location (though nearly "everyone pronounces Wisconsin with a g instead of a c"). Lawrence often seems like "like one gigantic family" although "rivalries between fraternities" occasionally flare up. Also, "gossip is intense" and "people at Lawrence aren't afraid to disagree with each other." Students here reportedly separate themselves into "many cliques" pretty quickly. The general consensus, though, seems to be that "everyone gets along great for the most part," and "a very friendly atmosphere" permeates the campus.

# LAWRENCE UNIVERSITY

FINANCIAL AID: 920-832-6583 • E-MAIL: EXCEL@LAWRENCE.EDU • WEBSITE: WWW.LAWRENCE.EDU

## ADMISSIONS

*Very important* academic and nonacademic factors considered by the admissions committee include secondary school record. *Important* factors considered include alumni/ae relation, class rank, essays, minority status, recommendations, standardized test scores, and talent/ability. *Other* factors considered include character/personal qualities, extracurricular activities, interview, volunteer work, and work experience. Factors *not* considered include geography, religious affiliation/commitment, and state residency. SAT I or ACT required. TOEFL required of all international applicants. High school diploma is required and GED is not accepted. *High school units required/recommended:* 16 total required; 23 total recommended; 4 English required, 3 math required, 4 math recommended, 2 science required, 4 science recommended, 2 foreign language required, 4 foreign language recommended, 2 social studies required, 4 social studies recommended, 3 elective required.

### The Inside Word

Although the admit rate is fairly high, getting into Lawrence demands an above-average academic record. Students who are serious about the university should stick with a very challenging high school courseload straight through senior year, put significant energy into their application essays, and definitely interview.

## FINANCIAL AID

*Students should submit:* FAFSA and institution's own financial aid form. Regular filing deadline is March 15. The Princeton Review suggests that all financial aid forms be submitted as soon as possible after January 1. *Need-based scholarships/grants offered:* Pell, SEOG, state scholarships/grants, private scholarships, and the school's own gift aid. *Loan aid offered:* Direct Subsidized Stafford, Direct Unsubsidized Stafford, Direct PLUS, and Federal Perkins. Institutional employment available. Federal Work-Study Program available. Applicants will be notified of awards on or about April 15. Off-campus job opportunities are excellent.

## FROM THE ADMISSIONS OFFICE

"Lawrence students are characterized by their energy, commitment to community service, respect for each other, and desire to achieve their full potential. Campus activities are abundant, off-campus study programs are popular (more than half of the students take advantage of them), small classes are the norm (65 percent of the classes have 10 or fewer students in them), and, yes, winters are for the hardy! But the diversity of interests and experiences, the drive to excel, the wealth of cultural opportunities presented by the art, theater, and music departments, the quality of research students undertake alongside PhD faculty, and the general friendly attitude of everyone at the university contribute to an excitement that more than outweighs the challenge of winter."

## ADMISSIONS

| | |
|---|---|
| Admissions Rating | 85 |
| # of applicants | 1,585 |
| % of applicants accepted | 73 |
| % of acceptees attending | 31 |
| # accepting a place on wait list | 45 |
| % admitted from wait list | 29 |
| # of early decision applicants | 26 |
| % accepted early decision | 88 |

### FRESHMAN PROFILE

| | |
|---|---|
| Range SAT Verbal | 560-690 |
| Average SAT Verbal | 615 |
| Range SAT Math | 580-680 |
| Average SAT Math | 626 |
| Range ACT Composite | 25-30 |
| Average ACT Composite | 27 |
| Minimum TOEFL | 575 |
| Average HS GPA | 3.7 |
| % graduated top 10% of class | 43 |
| % graduated top 25% of class | 79 |
| % graduated top 50% of class | 97 |

### DEADLINES

| | |
|---|---|
| Early decision | 11/15 |
| Early decision notification | 12/1 |
| Regular admission | 1/15 |
| Regular notification | 4/1 |

### APPLICANTS ALSO LOOK AT

**AND OFTEN PREFER**
Carleton
**AND SOMETIMES PREFER**
Grinnell
Oberlin
**AND RARELY PREFER**
Ripon

## FINANCIAL FACTS

| | |
|---|---|
| Financial Aid Rating | 90 |
| Tuition | $22,584 |
| Room & board | $4,983 |
| Books and supplies | $450 |
| Required fees | $144 |
| % frosh receiving aid | 72 |
| % undergrads receiving aid | 68 |
| Avg frosh grant | $12,934 |
| Avg frosh loan | $2,101 |

# LEHIGH UNIVERSITY

27 MEMORIAL DRIVE WEST, BETHLEHEM, PA 18015 • ADMISSIONS: 610-758-3100 • FAX: 610-758-4361

## CAMPUS LIFE

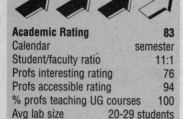

| | |
|---|---|
| **Quality of Life Rating** | **85** |
| Type of school | private |
| Affiliation | none |
| Environment | small city |

### STUDENTS

| | |
|---|---|
| Total undergrad enrollment | 4,722 |
| % male/female | 59/41 |
| % from out of state | 70 |
| % from public high school | 69 |
| % live on campus | 67 |
| % in (# of) fraternities | 41 (26) |
| % in (# of) sororities | 42 (9) |
| % African American | 3 |
| % Asian | 6 |
| % Caucasian | 75 |
| % Hispanic | 4 |
| % international | 3 |
| # of countries represented | 45 |

### SURVEY SAYS . . .

*Beautiful campus*
*Great library*
*Great computer facilities*
*Athletic facilities are great*
*Frats and sororities dominate social scene*
*Students don't like Bethlehem, PA*
*Political activism is (almost) nonexistent*
*Lousy off-campus food*

## ACADEMICS

| | |
|---|---|
| **Academic Rating** | **83** |
| Calendar | semester |
| Student/faculty ratio | 11:1 |
| Profs interesting rating | 76 |
| Profs accessible rating | 94 |
| % profs teaching UG courses | 100 |
| Avg lab size | 20-29 students |
| Avg reg class size | 10-19 students |

### MOST POPULAR MAJORS
finance
mechanical engineering
industrial engineering

## STUDENTS SPEAK OUT

### Academics

Lehigh University is "large enough to be powerful yet still small enough to be personal," explains a molecular biology major. Traditionally, Lehigh has been noted for its distinguished engineering school and strong College of Business and Economics. A push in recent years to improve the reputation and quality of the liberal arts programs—highlighted by a new performing arts facility—has really paid off. The newly opened Zoellner Arts Center has a 1,000-seat theater, a two-story art gallery, and practice rooms. Some still complain, however, that "liberal arts takes a back seat to engineering and business. Liberal arts students really get the shaft." In the sciences and business, facilities and research resources are top-notch and universally appreciated. "Very tough" courses here are "a lot of work," and it's "hard to get good grades on tests." While "you tend to learn tons, your grades don't necessarily show it." Professors' teaching abilities "vary from class to class. You are always taking your chances and keeping your fingers crossed." Profs are, however, "always available, which makes life at Lehigh a lot easier." The administration "is full of sweethearts. They know how to make you feel comfortable and make sure that you get what you need." In addition, the university gets high marks for its new online registration. In the final analysis, students feel that they get what they expect from this venerable university. Concludes one, "Lehigh prepares you for a career. I'm confident that I'll make the transition to the real world easily."

### Life

Somewhere on its steep, rolling hills, "Lehigh's philosophy" of "work hard/party hard" must be etched in stone. It's not just a hackneyed cliché here; it's a way of life. Even a recently imposed strict alcohol policy has done little to dampen the party scene; writes one undergrad, "We used to work hard and party hard. Now we simply work hard and try to get around the new alcohol policy to party hard." The Greek system "rules the social life on campus" with "at least three frat parties every night between Wednesday and Sunday. Life gets very repetitive." However, there are campus activities that do not center around Greek life. Sporting events are great, though." Undergrads warn that "if you don't drink, the things to do on weekends are pretty limited." The "work hard" part of the equation is just as important as the "party hard" component, though. Academic demands here result in a "hectic" and "stress-filled" existence "with occasional bursts of free time." Nearly as demanding is the campus' gorgeous terrain; observes one student, "There are very few fat people on campus because of all the hills we must walk up." Hometown Bethlehem offers little in the way of entertainment, but provides a "good location to Philly and NYC." Both on and off campus activities are listed on lehighlive.com.

### Student Body

Lehigh draws its "friendly but competitive" and very career-oriented student body primarily from Pennsylvania, New Jersey, and the rest of the eastern seaboard. For outsiders, this eastern bias takes some getting used to; writes one, "I almost transferred my freshman year because I am from the South and I had about 10 guys on my hall from New York City and northern New Jersey. Needless to say, it took a few months to adjust, but I made some great friends and I'll be graduating next spring." Lehigh "is a rich kids' school, predominantly white, upper-middle to upper-class" where "everyone is very conservative." Consequently, some feel that "people are nice but monotonous. Everybody acts and dresses the same. Our school would benefit from more diversity, not among genders but minorities." Students "don't see much interaction between minorities and others. The campus is pretty racially divided."

FINANCIAL AID: 610-758-3181 • E-MAIL: ADMISSIONS@LEHIGH.EDU • WEBSITE: WWW.LEHIGH.EDU

## ADMISSIONS

*Very important* academic and nonacademic factors considered by the admissions committee include class rank, standardized test scores, character/personal qualities, extracurricular activities, secondary school record, and talent/ability. *Important* factors considered include essays, recommendations, interviews, alumni/ae relation, and geography. *Other* factors considered include minority status, volunteer work, and work experience. Factors *not* considered include religious affiliation/commitment, and state residency. SAT I or ACT required; SAT II required. TOEFL required of all international applicants. *High school units required/recommended:* 16 total recommended; 4 English recommended, 3 math recommended, 2 science recommended, 2 science lab recommended, 2 foreign language recommended, 3 elective recommended.

### The Inside Word

Lots of work at bolstering Lehigh's public recognition for overall academic quality has paid off—liberal arts candidates will now find the admissions process to be as selective as it is for engineering and business applicants. Students without solidly impressive academic credentials will have a rough time getting in regardless of their choice of programs. So will unenthusiastic but academically strong candidates who have clearly chosen Lehigh as a safety.

## FINANCIAL AID

*Students should submit:* FAFSA, CSS/Financial Aid PROFILE, noncustodial (divorced/separated) parent's statement, state aid form, and business/farm supplement. Regular filing deadline is February 1. The Princeton Review suggests that all financial aid forms be submitted as soon as possible after January 1. *Need-based scholarships/grants offered:* Pell, SEOG, state scholarships/grants, private scholarships, and the school's own gift aid. *Loan aid offered:* FFEL Subsidized Stafford, FFEL Unsubsidized Stafford, FFEL PLUS, Federal Perkins, and college/university loans from institutional funds. Institutional employment available. Federal Work-Study Program available. Applicants will be notified of awards on or about April 1. Off-campus job opportunities are fair.

## FROM THE ADMISSIONS OFFICE

"Lehigh is a comprehensive, national university located in Bethlehem, which is 50 miles north of Philadelphia and 75 miles southwest of Manhattan. It offers a wide range of degree programs (more than 70 majors) in arts and science, business and economics, and engineering and applied science. Lehigh has always prided itself on preparing students for a rewarding and useful life. Our philosophy has always been that the most effective way to learn is to do. We encourage you to pursue your college career to its fullest potential. The best way to find out if Lehigh is right for you is to come visit our campus and talk to some of our students and faculty."

## ADMISSIONS

| | |
|---|---|
| Admissions Rating | 88 |
| # of applicants | 9,248 |
| % of applicants accepted | 46 |
| % of acceptees attending | 27 |
| # accepting a place on wait list | 1,394 |
| % admitted from wait list | 3 |
| # of early decision applicants | 361 |
| % accepted early decision | 66 |

### FRESHMAN PROFILE

| | |
|---|---|
| Range SAT Verbal | 569-662 |
| Average SAT Verbal | 616 |
| Range SAT Math | 614-703 |
| Average SAT Math | 659 |
| Minimum TOEFL | 570 |
| Average HS GPA | 3.8 |
| % graduated top 10% of class | 52 |
| % graduated top 25% of class | 88 |
| % graduated top 50% of class | 99 |

### DEADLINES

| | |
|---|---|
| Early decision | 11/15 |
| Early decision notification | 12/23 |
| Regular admission | 1/1 |
| Regular notification | 4/1 |
| Nonfall registration? | yes |

### APPLICANTS ALSO LOOK AT

**AND OFTEN PREFER**
U. Penn
Cornell U.

**AND SOMETIMES PREFER**
Lafayette
Penn State—Univ. Park
Bucknell
Union (NY)
Colgate

**AND RARELY PREFER**
Boston U.
Boston Coll.
Villanova, Syracuse
Gettysburg

## FINANCIAL FACTS

| | |
|---|---|
| Financial Aid Rating | 81 |
| Tuition | $24,900 |
| Room & board | $6,720 |
| Books and supplies | $1,900 |
| Required fees | $280 |
| % frosh receiving aid | 52 |
| % undergrads receiving aid | 51 |
| Avg frosh grant | $13,676 |
| Avg frosh loan | $4,424 |

# LEWIS & CLARK COLLEGE

0615 SW PALATINE HILL ROAD, PORTLAND, OR 97219-7899 • ADMISSIONS: 800-444-4111 • FAX: 503-768-7055

## CAMPUS LIFE

| | |
|---|---|
| **Quality of Life Rating** | **82** |
| Type of school | private |
| Affiliation | none |
| Environment | suburban |

### STUDENTS

| | |
|---|---|
| Total undergrad enrollment | 1,709 |
| % male/female | 40/60 |
| % from out of state | 74 |
| % from public high school | 71 |
| % live on campus | 52 |
| % African American | 1 |
| % Asian | 8 |
| % Caucasian | 66 |
| % Hispanic | 3 |
| % Native American | 1 |
| % international | 5 |
| # of countries represented | 34 |

### SURVEY SAYS . . .

*Students love Portland, OR*
*Students aren't religious*
*Great off-campus food*
*Political activism is hot*
*Theater is unpopular*
*Intercollegiate sports unpopular or*
*nonexistent*
*Student government is unpopular*

## ACADEMICS

| | |
|---|---|
| **Academic Rating** | **84** |
| Calendar | semester |
| Student/faculty ratio | 12:1 |
| Profs interesting rating | 93 |
| Profs accessible rating | 95 |
| % profs teaching UG courses | 100 |
| Avg lab size | 20-29 students |
| Avg reg class size | 10-19 students |

### MOST POPULAR MAJORS
international affairs
English
psychology

## STUDENTS SPEAK OUT

### Academics

"If you are looking for a great liberal arts education in the Northwest," writes one undergraduate, "Lewis & Clark is it!!" Indeed, with its small classes, caring faculty, and emphasis on overseas study, Lewis & Clark falls squarely in the tradition of "novel, high-energy undergraduate liberal arts studies." Reports one student, "Professors are always accessible and will bend over backward for you!" Notes another, "Students and teachers are what make this school. There is a close relationship, whether a class is being taken to a WTO protest in Seattle or are having a potluck at a professor's house." Don't know who the WTO is or why students would protest its meeting? Perhaps you should consider a different school; students here are politically aware and very active. Writes a typical undergrad, "My academic experience has been wonderful. I have learned so much, not just from class, but from the political activism in which I am involved. The high level of political awareness has been a powerful force in my educational experience. Students have fewer kind words for "the man," i.e., the administration. Red tape, top-down decision making, and general inaccessibility alienate the administration from the students. However, one Hispanic Studies major notes, "If you are willing to go beyond normal means, you can shape your education." Lewis & Clark offers strong programs in foreign languages, English, and international affairs. More than half the students take advantage of the school-subsidized overseas studies program, which sends students virtually everywhere in the world.

### Life

Like many big-city campuses, Lewis & Clark benefits from the cultural cornucopia that lies just beyond the campus gates. Explains one student, "Portland is an incredible city to explore. There's always something to do and it's all very accessible. Concerts, cultural events, social events, shopping, exploring, snowboarding, hiking, and climbing are all options." Close to the coast and mountain ski slopes, Portland offers a variety of settings in which students can enjoy leisure time. Students don't have to venture far to enjoy a park-like environment, however; the LC campus is "gorgeous. You can just go out and wander around the woods, ravine, or rose garden. The grass is lush and relaxing." As previously noted, many students fill their spare time serving activist causes. Writes one undergrad, "Being a highly politically active school, students enjoy going to political rallies . . . smoking up, and of course playing some Ultimate Frisbee while listening to some Dylan." Ahh, yes, "smoking up" . . . as one student explains, "Many people use marijuana. I think it may even be possible to get high just by walking down the hall."

### Student Body

LC students describe themselves as a mixture of "many distinct cliques: hippies, jocks, preps, and those caught in the middle." The predominant group, however, is "rich hippies. I know this sounds like an oxymoron but it is true." Home backgrounds tend to be upper-middle-class and liberal, and students believe that diversity stems from the broad spectrum of interests and personalities at LC. The growing contingent of leftist activists think you should know "People care! We take action against injustice and make our voices heard." So don't say you weren't warned.

FINANCIAL AID: 503-768-7090 • E-MAIL: ADMISSIONS@LCLARK.EDU • WEBSITE: WWW.LCLARK.EDU

## ADMISSIONS

*Very important* academic and nonacademic factors considered by the admissions committee include character/personal qualities, class rank, essays, recommendations, secondary school record, standardized test scores, and talent/ability. *Important* factors considered include extracurricular activities, volunteer work, and work experience. *Other* factors considered include alumni/ae relation, geography, interview, minority status, and state residency. Factors *not* considered include religious affiliation/commitment. TOEFL required of all international applicants. SAT I or ACT required unless applying via the Portfolio Path Option. GED is accepted. *High school units required/recommended:* 4 English recommended, 3 math recommended, 3 science recommended, 2 science lab recommended, 2 foreign language recommended, 1 fine arts recommended.

### The Inside Word

Admissions evaluations are thorough, and the Portfolio Path is an intriguing option that guarantees a purely personal evaluation. Few colleges of Lewis & Clark's quality are as accommodating to students.

## FINANCIAL AID

*Students should submit:* FAFSA. The Princeton Review suggests that all financial aid forms be submitted as soon as possible after January 1. *Need-based scholarships/grants offered:* Pell, SEOG, state scholarships/grants, private scholarships, and the school's own gift aid. *Loan aid offered:* FFEL Subsidized Stafford, FFEL Unsubsidized Stafford, Federal Perkins, and state. Institutional employment available. Federal Work-Study Program available. Applicants will be notified of awards on or about April 1. Off-campus job opportunities are good.

## FROM THE ADMISSIONS OFFICE

"A record number of applicants in recent years cited a variety of reasons they were drawn to Lewis & Clark. Many had to do with the multiple environments experienced by our students, including (1) a small arts and sciences college with a 12:1 student/faculty ratio; (2) a location only six miles from downtown Portland (metropolitan population 1.6 million); (3) a setting in the heart of the Pacific Northwest, making more than 80 trips per year possible for our College Outdoors Program; and (4) the rest of the world—more than 55 percent of our graduates included an overseas program in their curriculum. Since 1962, more than 8,000 students and 170 faculty members have participated in 468 programs in 65 countries on 6 continents. Our international curriculum has undergone a total review to better prepare graduates going into the 21st century."

## ADMISSIONS

| | |
|---|---|
| Admissions Rating | 83 |
| # of applicants | 2,859 |
| % of applicants accepted | 68 |
| % of acceptees attending | 22 |
| # accepting a place on wait list | 136 |
| % admitted from wait list | 21 |

### FRESHMAN PROFILE

| | |
|---|---|
| Range SAT Verbal | 590-670 |
| Range SAT Math | 570-660 |
| Range ACT Composite | 25-29 |
| Minimum TOEFL | 550 |
| % graduated top 10% of class | 35 |
| % graduated top 25% of class | 69 |
| % graduated top 50% of class | 97 |

### DEADLINES

| | |
|---|---|
| Regular admission | 2/1 |
| Regular notification | 4/1 |
| Nonfall registration? | yes |

### APPLICANTS ALSO LOOK AT

**AND OFTEN PREFER**
Colorado Coll.
Stanford
Pomona

**AND SOMETIMES PREFER**
U. Puget Sound
Willamette
Whitman
U. Colorado—Boulder
Reed

**AND RARELY PREFER**
UC—Santa Cruz
U. Oregon
Pacific U.

### FINANCIAL FACTS

| | |
|---|---|
| Financial Aid Rating | 78 |
| Tuition | $21,870 |
| Room & board | $6,650 |
| Books and supplies | $1,800 |
| Required fees | $740 |
| % frosh receiving aid | 55 |
| % undergrads receiving aid | 54 |
| Avg frosh grant | $13,701 |
| Avg frosh loan | $3,914 |

# LOUISIANA STATE UNIVERSITY—BATON ROUGE

110 THOMAS BOYD HALL, BATON ROUGE, LA 70803 • ADMISSIONS: 225-388-1175 • FAX: 225-388-4433

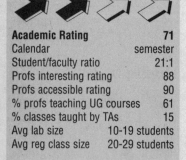

## CAMPUS LIFE

| Quality of Life Rating | 87 |
|---|---|
| Type of school | public |
| Affiliation | none |
| Environment | urban |

### STUDENTS

| | |
|---|---|
| Total undergrad enrollment | 26,121 |
| % male/female | 47/53 |
| % from out of state | 8 |
| % live on campus | 23 |
| % in (# of) fraternities | 11 (22) |
| % in (# of) sororities | 15 (15) |
| % African American | 10 |
| % Asian | 4 |
| % Caucasian | 79 |
| % Hispanic | 2 |
| % international | 3 |

### SURVEY SAYS . . .

Frats and sororities dominate social scene
Everyone loves the Tigers
Athletic facilities are great
Great food on campus
Great off-campus food
Large classes
Ethnic diversity on campus
Student publications are popular
Dorms are like dungeons

## ACADEMICS

| Academic Rating | 71 |
|---|---|
| Calendar | semester |
| Student/faculty ratio | 21:1 |
| Profs interesting rating | 88 |
| Profs accessible rating | 90 |
| % profs teaching UG courses | 61 |
| % classes taught by TAs | 15 |
| Avg lab size | 10-19 students |
| Avg reg class size | 20-29 students |

### MOST POPULAR MAJORS
general studies
elementary education
mass communication

## STUDENTS SPEAK OUT
### Academics

Typical of the Louisiana spirit and sense of priorities, students at LSU boast that their school "is a wonderful place to learn, meet people, and actually have fun." A "tough school in some areas, but pretty laid-back in general," LSU offers "a huge variety of subjects to study," including well-regarded programs in engineering, business and management, and basic science. Students here enjoy a more personable atmosphere than is found at most large state schools. Reports one undergrad, "At a big school like LSU, it is easy to assume that professors and other officials do not care about students, but that is not true. I will never forget my first English professor, who brought the entire class [out] for ice cream on a hot day and let us write a paper comparing the two flavors he bought for [each of] us." Another agrees, "I was genuinely surprised by the accessibility of administrators and professors at LSU. Everyone seems to want their students to both learn and perform well academically." On the whole, however, professors here receive mixed grades. "Most professors are average," says one student. "Only a few are memorable, both on the great end and the terrible end." Writes another, "Overall, most professors know what they're talking about. However, there are a few who don't and need to consult other professors about every question asked. Students appreciate the "great internships and research opportunities" the university affords them.

### Life

"Students reacted with mixed emotions to their school's ranking in 2000 as the "Number One Party School" in a certain college guide. Though the ranking was based entirely on information LSU students reported about campus life there, some students responded with skepticism. Said a sophomore accounting major, "They don't really have parties on campus or anything like that." But a freshman called the ranking "a source of pride" and a senior said it was "pretty much accurate," adding, "It doesn't have to mean it's a bad thing. I party, but I do well in school, and that goes for most of my friends." Everyone agrees, however, that this is a fun place to go to school." According to LSU's student newspaper, *The Daily Reveille*, even the school's Chancellor, Mark Emmert, agrees, saying before a group of fraternity leaders, "Being ranked the number one party school is fine with me if it means this is a fun place to study." The LSU experience is enhanced by "great school spirit," as well as "beautiful surroundings, an excellent learning environment," and a plethora of extracurricular activities that include "local bands, trips to New Orleans, community service, social gatherings at apartments, drinking games, flirting, etc." Athletic events, of course, are number one. Writes one undergrad, "Student life is great, especially during football season when the students tailgate before and after the game." Baseball and basketball also attract large crowds here, and students appreciate the "300-plus student organizations on campus, giving us many ways to get involved." Hometown Baton Rouge "is fantastic! The city also offers plenty in the way of live music and "really good restaurants (Louisiana cuisine is great!)" Students have few complaints here but do point out that "parking is pretty bad, and several buildings could stand a serious renovation."

### Student Body

The student population at LSU is composed of about 30,000 students from every state and from more than 100 countries. Students here run the gamut from "shallow sorority girls" to "righteous Catholics to everyday pot heads." Though students say their campus is a warm, "friendly," and close-knit place full of "southern hospitality," some warn that "people whose ideas and lifestyles differ from the norm stand out in the crowd." Student life at LSU is marked by "strong social distinctions between blacks and whites, gays and straights, Greeks and GDIs," says one student. About the only time all students rally together is during football games. For reasons that sociologists don't completely understand, "everyone loves each other at football games" at LSU.

# LOUISIANA STATE UNIVERSITY—BATON ROUGE

FINANCIAL AID: 225-388-3103 • E-MAIL: LSUADMIT@LSU.EDU • WEBSITE: WWW.LSU.EDU

## ADMISSIONS

*Very important* academic and nonacademic factors considered by the admissions committee include secondary school record and standardized test scores. *Important* factors considered include class rank. *Other* factors considered include extracurricular activities, talent/ability, alumni relations, geography, minority status, state residency, volunteer work, and work experience. Factors not considered include religious affiliation/commitment. ACT or SAT I scores are required; ACT preferred. TOEFL is required of all international applicants. *High school units required:* 17.5 total required; 4 English required, 3 math required, 3 science required, 2 foreign language required, 3 social studies required, .5 unit computer studies required, 2 elective required. *The admissions office says:* "Applicants not meeting course units and/or grades or test score minimums may be considered by the admissions committee."

### The Inside Word

LSU's admissions process is a straight numbers game. The university is rare among formula-driven institutions in recognizing that some good students fall through the cracks in such systems. It is commendable that LSU's admissions committee is also willing to take a closer, more personal look if circumstances warrant.

## FINANCIAL AID

The Princeton Review suggests that all financial aid forms be submitted as soon as possible after January 1. *Need-based scholarships/grants offered:* Pell, SEOG, state scholarships/grants, private scholarships, the school's own gift aid, and Federal Nursing. *Loan aid offered:* FFEL Subsidized Stafford, FFEL Unsubsidized Stafford, FFEL PLUS, and Federal Perkins. Institutional employment available. Federal Work-Study Program available. Off-campus job opportunities are excellent.

## FROM THE ADMISSIONS OFFICE

"LSU is the most prestigious and comprehensive public institution of higher learning in Louisiana. We are a leader in higher education with a world-renowned reputation for preparing students for future educational and professional success. Louisiana State University offers the southern hospitality of a small community while providing the benefits of a large, technologically advanced institution. Throughout its history, LSU has served the people of Louisiana, the region, the nation, and the world through extensive, multipurpose programs encompassing instruction, research, and public service."

---

### ADMISSIONS

| | |
|---|---|
| Admissions Rating | 76 |
| # of applicants | 9,789 |
| % of applicants accepted | 78 |
| % of acceptees attending | 67 |

### FRESHMAN PROFILE

| | |
|---|---|
| Range ACT Composite | 21-26 |
| Average ACT Composite | 24 |
| Minimum TOEFL | 500 |
| Average HS GPA | 3.2 |
| % graduated top 10% of class | 26 |
| % graduated top 25% of class | 56 |
| % graduated top 50% of class | 85 |

### DEADLINES

| | |
|---|---|
| Regular admission | 5/1 |
| Nonfall registration? | yes |

### APPLICANTS ALSO LOOK AT
**AND SOMETIMES PREFER**
Centenary
Florida State
U. Florida
**AND RARELY PREFER**
SMU
TCU
Spring Hill

### FINANCIAL FACTS

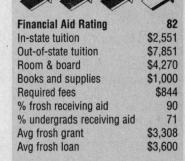

| | |
|---|---|
| Financial Aid Rating | 82 |
| In-state tuition | $2,551 |
| Out-of-state tuition | $7,851 |
| Room & board | $4,270 |
| Books and supplies | $1,000 |
| Required fees | $844 |
| % frosh receiving aid | 90 |
| % undergrads receiving aid | 71 |
| Avg frosh grant | $3,308 |
| Avg frosh loan | $3,600 |

# LOYOLA COLLEGE

4501 NORTH CHARLES STREET, BALTIMORE, MD 21210 • ADMISSIONS: 410-617-5012 • FAX: 410-617-2176

## STUDENTS SPEAK OUT

### Academics

"Most professors are great. None are TAs." That's a good summation of students' positive comments about their academic experience at Loyola. Fills in another, "All of my professors have been genuinely concerned about my current and future success. They push me to my full potential." Classes are small at Loyola, and the academic burden can be tough. There is a core curriculum that must be completed in the first two years. "The course load can be unbearable," says a senior studying political science. Adds a freshman, "The accelerated and high standards of teaching don't allow for catching up. You must be able to do the materials immediately." Along the same lines, "The honors program here is awesome!" The administration gets similar praise: "The administration is friendly and understanding." Indeed, registration procedures, lab facilities, computer facilities, and the bursar are all given high marks by students, leaving just a few harsh comments like this one: "When it comes to getting something done with finances or academics, no one knows anything and everyone sends you to everybody else." Students as a whole concur with this junior: "Loyola College is teaching me to be academically, socially, and spiritually advanced. I love it."

### Life

Located in the beautiful city of Baltimore, Loyola boasts a student body that loves to frequent their fair city's many bars. Of Baltimore's diversity of opportunity, "Baltimore is great. They have a bar for every kind of student." Another tries valiantly to promote Baltimore's other fine features, "There is a lot to do . . . including museums, parks, clubs, bars, concerts, [and] large malls," but it is a vain attempt. Alcohol, especially beer, reigns supreme with Loyola undergrads, especially on the weekends. Those who go against the grain (pun intended) report mixed feelings. "Even though Loyola is a bar school my friends and I don't drink [and] there is [still] a lot to do!" Warns one junior, though, "I am among the minority on this campus who doesn't drink, for which I find myself condemned." While "the school has implemented many alternatives" to off-campus carousing, and promotes a fairly strict drug and alcohol policy, you get the picture. Otherwise, Loyola dorms get high marks but "the food plan is horrendous." There are no sororities or frats at Loyola (perhaps another factor contributing to the huge bar scene), and student government is popular and active on campus.

### Student Body

"Everyone looks and dresses the same, but everyone is happy and nice." Yes, Loyola's student body is very white, and interaction between the white majority and minorities is lacking, but that doesn't seem to bother the students. Explains an Asian male, "Unfortunately, the school is lily white. But minority students don't have anything to worry about. They're very nice here." Wisecracks one of the college's J.Crew contingent, "Loyola has the highest concentration of plaid on the East Coast." Another comedian notes, "About three-fourths of the students here were cloned off the same . . . prototype, heavy-drinking frat boys without frats to live in so they trash the freshman dorm." Perhaps the only students that should worry about open discrimination are gays. Explains a sophomore studying psychology, "Generally we all get along. This campus is pretty homophobic though." Adds another, "Remember that no matter what the administration says—this is a Catholic school!" There is a real commitment to public service at Loyola: "Community service is an integral part of my life and most students' lives," and undergrads describe themselves as very sexually active. A Catholic school? Are these kids married?

FINANCIAL AID: 410-617-2576 • WEBSITE: WWW.LOYOLA.EDU

## ADMISSIONS

*Very important* academic and nonacademic factors considered by the admissions committee include secondary school record and standardized test scores. *Important* factors considered include class rank. *Other* factors considered include essays, extracurricular activities, minority status, volunteer work, work experience, recommendations and talent/ability. Factors *not* considered include alumni/ae relation, character/personal qualities, geography, interview, religious affiliation/commitment, and state residency. SAT I required. TOEFL required of all international applicants. High school diploma is required and GED is accepted. *High school units required/recommended:* 18 total recommended; 4 English recommended, 4 math recommended, 4 science recommended, 3 foreign language recommended, 3 social studies recommended.

### The Inside Word

Loyola is to be commended for notifying outstanding candidates of acceptance early in the applicant review cycle without demanding an early commitment in return. Traditional Early Decision plans are confusing, archaic, and unreasonable to students. A binding commitment is a huge price to pay to get a decision four months sooner. This is obviously one place that cares.

## FINANCIAL AID

*Students should submit:* FAFSA and CSS/Financial Aid PROFILE. Regular filing deadline is February 1. The Princeton Review suggests that all financial aid forms be submitted as soon as possible after January 1. Institutional employment available. Federal Work-Study Program available. Applicants will be notified of awards in April. Off-campus job opportunities are good.

## FROM THE ADMISSIONS OFFICE

"To make a wise choice about your college plans, you will need to find out more. We extend to you these invitations. Question-and-answer periods with an admissions counselor are helpful to prospective students. An appointment should be made in advance. Admissions office hours are 9 A.M. to 5 P.M., Monday through Friday. College day programs and Saturday information programs are scheduled during the academic year. These programs include a film about Loyola, a general information session, a discussion of various majors, a campus tour, and lunch. Summer information programs can help high school juniors to get a head start on investigating colleges. These programs feature an introductory presentation about the college and a campus tour."

---

### ADMISSIONS

| | |
|---|---:|
| Admissions Rating | 81 |
| # of applicants | 6,536 |
| % of applicants accepted | 61 |
| % of acceptees attending | 23 |
| # accepting a place on wait list | 647 |

### FRESHMAN PROFILE

| | |
|---|---:|
| Range SAT Verbal | 570-640 |
| Average SAT Verbal | 606 |
| Range SAT Math | 580-640 |
| Average SAT Math | 608 |
| Minimum TOEFL | 550 |
| Average HS GPA | 3.4 |
| % graduated top 25% of class | 77 |
| % graduated top 50% of class | 94 |

### DEADLINES

| | |
|---|---:|
| Regular admission | 1/15 |
| Regular notification | 4/15 |

### APPLICANTS ALSO LOOK AT
**AND OFTEN PREFER**
Boston Coll.
Villanova
**AND SOMETIMES PREFER**
James Madison
U. Richmond
Fairfield
Lafayette
St. Joseph's U.
**AND RARELY PREFER**
U. Scranton
Fordham
Rutgers U.
Catholic
Penn State—Univ. Park

### FINANCIAL FACTS

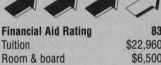

| | |
|---|---:|
| Financial Aid Rating | 83 |
| Tuition | $22,960 |
| Room & board | $6,500 |
| Books and supplies | $720 |
| Required fees | $570 |
| % frosh receiving aid | 44 |
| % undergrads receiving aid | 28 |
| Avg frosh grant | $10,540 |
| Avg frosh loan | $3,500 |

# LOYOLA MARYMOUNT UNIVERSITY

7900 LOYOLA BOULEVARD, LOS ANGELES, CA 90045 • ADMISSIONS: 310-338-2750 • FAX: 310-338-2797

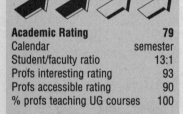
## STUDENTS SPEAK OUT

### Academics

Strongly Catholic Loyola Marymount University offers "small class sizes," a "rewarding and challenging academic experience," and the only "Jesuit education" in the southwestern United States. In order to graduate, all students must complete a thorough, "integrated" core curriculum emphasizing humanities, sciences, math, philosophy, and Catholic theology courses. Beyond the core curriculum, LMU offers four undergraduate colleges (business administration, liberal arts, communication and fine arts, and science and engineering) and a broad array of liberal arts and engineering majors from which students may choose. Popular majors here include film and music production—not surprising given the school's "media capital" locale—and business administration. Future software moguls take note: LMU boasts one of the top entrepreneur programs in the nation. A high-quality theatre program also draws several raves from students. The generally "good" professors here are "always available and ready to help whenever necessary," and "seem to be concerned with" the welfare of students. "Like Superman, they can often be found in students' time of need," marvels a sophomore. "Students shout, 'Aaargh! I need help!' and there they are." The engineering professors are notably "awesome." However, these same profs can be "misinformed and useless" when it comes to advising. "Registering with the little man in the phone who never sleeps is really fun," but it can also be problematic at times, and the library and research facilities could use some refurbishing.

### Life

A number of students tell us they chose this "small school in the big city" because of its "beautiful campus" and relatively "small size." One student describes LMU as "a comfortable scene where students can have fun and study," and most agree that its "smallness" gives it "a family-type atmosphere." Asserts one student, "I can't walk from one side of campus to the other without seeing at least one person I know." There are "lots of activities" on campus, ranging from "Greeks and sports" to "theatre clubs" to "the greatest college newspaper in the nation," according to a scoop-getting sophomore. The healthy and popular Greek system keeps social life buzzing along nicely. Nevertheless, weekends on campus "are kind of dull," especially if you don't like to "drink and smoke." Luckily, "off-campus activities are just as popular as on-campus activities." There is always the vibrant, "exciting," 24-hour city of Los Angeles, where students can "see lots of movies and plays," go to clubs, go shopping at the malls, and eat at restaurants. "There's the beach," too, and students say "everything is in pretty close range" because LMU is somehow "close to anything in L.A."

### Student Body

The "pretty hep cats" here, if they may say so themselves, are "nice, helpful, and friendly" folks. Sure, there are "some real jerks" here and there, and "cliques do tend to form," but most students are "easy to get along with." They promise you'll see "smiles everywhere you go" at LMU. You'll also see a great deal of diversity on campus. Thanks to solid recruiting by the administration, nearly half of the student population is made up of minorities. One very distinctive characteristic that makes Loyola Marymount unique is the prevalence of religious belief and observance among its student population. In fact, LMU students are more religious than students at most other schools, which is not surprising given the fact that the university maintains a vigorous affiliation with the Roman Catholic Church.

# LOYOLA MARYMOUNT UNIVERSITY

FINANCIAL AID: 310-338-2753 • E-MAIL: ADMISSNS@LMUMAIL.LMU.EDU • WEBSITE: WWW.LMU.EDU

## ADMISSIONS

*Very important* academic and nonacademic factors considered by the admissions committee include secondary school record and standardized test scores. *Important* factors considered include character/personal qualities, class rank, essays, and recommendations. *Other* factors considered include alumni/ae relation, extracurricular activities, interview, talent/ability, volunteer work, and work experience. Factors *not* considered include geography, minority status, religious affiliation/commitment, and state residency. SAT I or ACT required. TOEFL required of all international applicants. High school diploma is required and GED is accepted. *High school units required/recommended:* 14 total required; 4 English required, 3 math required, 2 science required, 1 science lab recommended, 2 foreign language required, 3 social studies required.

### The Inside Word

Loyola Marymount's admissions committee is particular about candidate evaluation, but a large applicant pool has more to do with the university's moderate acceptance rate than does academic selectivity. Even so, underachievers will have difficulty getting in.

## FINANCIAL AID

*Students should submit:* FAFSA and CSS/Financial Aid PROFILE. Regular filing deadline is February 15. The Princeton Review suggests that all financial aid forms be submitted as soon as possible after January 1. *Need-based scholarships/grants offered:* Pell, state scholarships/grants, private scholarships, and the school's own gift aid. *Loan aid offered:* Direct Subsidized Stafford, Direct Unsubsidized Stafford, Federal Perkins, state, and college/university loans from institutional funds. Institutional employment available. Federal Work-Study Program available. Off-campus job opportunities are excellent.

## FROM THE ADMISSIONS OFFICE

"Loyola Marymount University is a dynamic, student-centered university. We are medium sized (4,500 undergraduates), and we are the only Jesuit University in the southwestern United States.

"Our campus is located in Westchester, a friendly, residential neighborhood that is removed from the hustle and bustle of Los Angeles yet offers easy access to all the richnesss of our most cosmopolitan environment. One mile from the ocean, our students enjoy ocean and mountain vistas as well as the moderate climate and crisp breezes characteristic of a coastal location.

"Loyola Marymount is committed to the ideals of Jesuit and Marymount education. We are a student-centered university, dedicated to the education of the whole person and to the preparation of our students for lives of service to their families, communities, and professions. Breadth and rigor are the hallmarks of the curriculum.

"Taken together, our academic program, our Jesuit and Marymount heritage, and our terrific campus environment enable our students unparalleled opportunity to prepare for life and leadership in the 21st century."

## ADMISSIONS

| | |
|---|---|
| Admissions Rating | 71 |

### FRESHMAN PROFILE

| | |
|---|---|
| Range SAT Verbal | 510-610 |
| Average SAT Verbal | 562 |
| Range SAT Math | 530-620 |
| Average SAT Math | 571 |
| Minimum TOEFL | 550 |
| Average HS GPA | 3.3 |

### DEADLINES

| | |
|---|---|
| Regular admission | rolling |
| Priority admission deadline | 2/1 |
| Nonfall registration? | yes |

### APPLICANTS ALSO LOOK AT

**AND OFTEN PREFER**
UC—Davis
Stanford
UCLA

**AND SOMETIMES PREFER**
UC—Irvine
UC—San Diego
UC—Santa Barbara

**AND RARELY PREFER**
Santa Clara
UC—Riverside
Pepperdine

## FINANCIAL FACTS

| | |
|---|---|
| Financial Aid Rating | 82 |
| Tuition | $19,100 |
| Room & board | $6,828 |
| Books and supplies | $846 |
| Required fees | $307 |
| % frosh receiving aid | 53 |
| % undergrads receiving aid | 60 |

# LOYOLA UNIVERSITY CHICAGO

820 NORTH MICHIGAN AVENUE, CHICAGO, IL 60611 • ADMISSIONS: 800-262-2373 • FAX: 312-915-6449

## CAMPUS LIFE

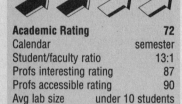

**Quality of Life Rating**            **70**
Type of school                      private
Affiliation                Roman Catholic
Environment                         urban

### STUDENTS

| | |
|---|---|
| Total undergrad enrollment | 7,141 |
| % male/female | 36/64 |
| % from out of state | 24 |
| % from public high school | 57 |
| % live on campus | 29 |
| % in (# of) fraternities | 7 (6) |
| % in (# of) sororities | 5 (5) |
| % African American | 9 |
| % Asian | 12 |
| % Caucasian | 59 |
| % Hispanic | 9 |
| % international | 1 |

### SURVEY SAYS . . .

Musical organizations aren't popular
Classes are small
Class discussions are rare
Students don't get along with local community
Unattractive campus
Students are not very happy
Ethnic diversity on campus
Intercollegiate sports unpopular or nonexistent
Lots of long lines and red tape

## ACADEMICS

**Academic Rating**                   **72**
| | |
|---|---|
| Calendar | semester |
| Student/faculty ratio | 13:1 |
| Profs interesting rating | 87 |
| Profs accessible rating | 90 |
| Avg lab size | under 10 students |
| Avg reg class size | 10-19 students |

### MOST POPULAR MAJORS

biology
business
psychology

## STUDENTS SPEAK OUT

### Academics

Top four reasons to attend this mid-sized Roman Catholic institution perched at the edge of "beautiful" Lake Michigan on Chicago's North Shore: "academic reputation, diverse student body, small class size, and great location." Many students, religious and nonreligious, still consider the school's "Jesuit character" one of its biggest draws. "Loyola's greatest strength is its commitment to providing students" with a "whole-person education," the mark of the Jesuits. Most students agree that "Loyola's professors are dedicated to their research, to their students (by being approachable), and to the Loyola mission—which is to provide a good education and guide to [becoming] a balanced, independent thinker." The historical Jesuit commitment to providing education for all has another benefit: true cultural, economic, and ethnic diversity amongst its faculty, staff, and student body. This diversity is enhanced by the school's division into several different campuses—one in downtown Chicago, another uptown, and the medical center (Loyola has a popular pre-med program) in the western suburbs. Notes a sophomore, "The diverse atmosphere at the different campuses is great. Where else can you be a frat boy on Monday, Wednesday, Friday, and a corporate guru on Tuesday and Thursday?" And while some point out that Loyola has had some rough times in recent years with lack of funds, long-tenured professors, substandard facilities, and an out-of-touch administration ("Trying to talk to the administration is like trying to contact Elvis," writes a junior), a sophomore points out that "Loyola is in a transition period" and that the mood is very hopeful about the school's new president.

### Life

A senior sums up the scene: "Loyola isn't your 'typical' college campus. If you are looking for big frat parties or keggers this isn't the place to be. However, if you are into smaller parties, cultural events, and the fun of Chicago, this place ROCKS!" Whether it's going down to Clarke & Belmont (a nexus for the Alternation); taking in an improv show right down the street from the uptown campus; or "heading downtown to grab some famous Chicago-style pizza," the city is "just a short El ride away," as a junior puts it, "and there's never a shortage of fun things to do." Indeed, as one first-year writes, "Life at Loyola is living in Chicago with a side of school." And while this situation suits most Loyola undergrads fine, "a lot of people don't like it and transfer," notes a second year. An international student from Ireland gives the down-low: "So far the social activities organized have been as exciting as knitting with my mum." What's needed? More sports events, a better newspaper, more funding for student events, and the renovation of key facilities are high on students' wish lists. Still, proximity to the city has its upside—"social justice and volunteer opportunities" abound, and, as a senior points out, "despite the high percentage of commuters [students], attendance at on-campus events is on the rise."

### Student Body

"Choose Loyola if you're comfortable enough with yourself to handle serious diversity," writes a frank first-year, though most rave about Loyola's unique mix of people from all around the nation and the world. "I enjoy my fellow students," remarks a senior. "I have learned a lot about other cultures and religions because of them." Adds another, "If you have an open mind, you can make friends from almost every ethnic group." With such a heterogeneous community, there's bound to be cliques and divisions, which some Loyola undergrads complain can be "closed off and unapproachable."

FINANCIAL AID: 312-915-6639 • E-MAIL: ADMISSION@LUC.EDU • WEBSITE: WWW.LUC.EDU

## ADMISSIONS

*Very important* academic and nonacademic factors considered by the admissions committee include character/personal qualities, recommendations, secondary school record, and standardized test scores. *Important* factors considered include class rank, essays, extracurricular activities, and volunteer work. *Other* factors considered include alumni/ae relation, geography, interview, minority status, talent/ability, and work experience. Factors *not* considered include religious affiliation/commitment and state residency. TOEFL required of all international applicants. High school diploma is required and GED is accepted. *High school units required/recommended:* 15 total required; 18 total recommended; 4 English recommended, 4 math recommended, 3 science recommended, 1 science lab recommended, 3 foreign language recommended, 2 social studies recommended, 2 history recommended. *The admissions office says:* "We review student files on a rolling basis once they are complete with an application for admission, official transcripts, and ACT or SAT I scores."

### The Inside Word

The admissions process is fairly formulaic, and the standards aren't too demanding for most candidates.

## FINANCIAL AID

The Princeton Review suggests that all financial aid forms be submitted as soon as possible after January 1. *Need-based scholarships/grants offered:* Pell, SEOG, state scholarships/grants, private scholarships, the school's own gift aid, and Federal Nursing. *Loan aid offered:* FFEL Subsidized Stafford, FFEL Unsubsidized Stafford, FFEL PLUS, Federal Perkins, and Federal Nursing. Institutional employment available. Federal Work-Study Program available. Off-campus job opportunities are excellent.

## FROM THE ADMISSIONS OFFICE

"As a national research university, Loyola provides a superb academic program that is distinctive because of its personal approach. Nationally and internationally renowned scholars teach introductory freshman-level courses in classes that average 21 students. A special emphasis in our curriculum is placed on the examination of ethics and values as well as a commitment to instill intensive writing skills that will benefit the student throughout his/her life. Despite its large population, Loyola is committed to the individual student, and its programs and policies reflect the importance of community. Students from throughout the nation are attracted to Loyola for the opportunities offered by the university as well as the benefits of studying in Chicago, a world-class city."

## ADMISSIONS

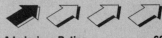

| | |
|---|---|
| Admissions Rating | 68 |
| # of applicants | 4,001 |
| % of applicants accepted | 81 |
| % of acceptees attending | 28 |

### FRESHMAN PROFILE

| | |
|---|---|
| Range SAT Verbal | 520-640 |
| Average SAT Verbal | 577 |
| Range SAT Math | 520-630 |
| Average SAT Math | 570 |
| Range ACT Composite | 22-27 |
| Average ACT Composite | 25 |
| Average HS GPA | 3.0 |
| % graduated top 10% of class | 29 |
| % graduated top 25% of class | 62 |
| % graduated top 50% of class | 93 |

### DEADLINES

| | |
|---|---|
| Regular notification | rolling |
| Nonfall registration? | yes |

### APPLICANTS ALSO LOOK AT
### AND OFTEN PREFER
De Paul
U. Illinois—Urbana-Champaign
Illinois—Chicago
Northwestern
Marquette
### AND SOMETIMES PREFER
Northern Illinois
Notre Dame
U. Chicago
Indiana U.—Bloomington
### AND RARELY PREFER
Saint Louis

## FINANCIAL FACTS

| | |
|---|---|
| Financial Aid Rating | 74 |
| Tuition | $18,814 |
| Room & board | $7,266 |
| Books and supplies | $700 |
| Required fees | $460 |
| % frosh receiving aid | 66 |
| Avg frosh grant | $12,209 |
| Avg frosh loan | $3,284 |

# LOYOLA UNIVERSITY NEW ORLEANS

6363 St. Charles Avenue, Box 18, New Orleans, LA 70118 • Admissions: 504-865-3240 • Fax: 504-865-3383

## CAMPUS LIFE

| Quality of Life Rating | 79 |
|---|---|
| Type of school | private |
| Affiliation | Roman Catholic |
| Environment | urban |

### STUDENTS

| | |
|---|---|
| Total undergrad enrollment | 3,733 |
| % male/female | 36/64 |
| % from out of state | 43 |
| % from public high school | 44 |
| % live on campus | 36 |
| % in (# of) fraternities | 17 (6) |
| % in (# of) sororities | 17 (6) |
| % African American | 12 |
| % Asian | 4 |
| % Caucasian | 67 |
| % Hispanic | 10 |
| % international | 4 |

### SURVEY SAYS . . .

Student publications are popular
Lots of liberals
Hard liquor is popular
Student government
(Almost) everyone smokes
Students love New Orleans, LA
Theater is unpopular
Great off-campus food
Lousy food on campus

## ACADEMICS

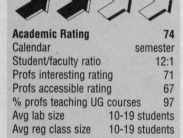

| Academic Rating | 74 |
|---|---|
| Calendar | semester |
| Student/faculty ratio | 12:1 |
| Profs interesting rating | 71 |
| Profs accessible rating | 67 |
| % profs teaching UG courses | 97 |
| Avg lab size | 10-19 students |
| Avg reg class size | 10-19 students |

### MOST POPULAR MAJORS
communications
biology
psychology

## STUDENTS SPEAK OUT

### Academics

The Jesuits and New Orleans—a match made in heaven? The students at Loyola University apparently think so. "Loyola captures the spirit and liberal essence of New Orleans." It also personifies the caring nature of a Jesuit education. One grateful student tells us that "the great thing about Loyola is that it accepts students who may not have shown their true academic capabilities in high school and gives them a second chance." Its small size and personal attention also rate as big pluses with those we surveyed. The university "gives you the opportunity to be more than just a number. The professors know you on a first-name basis and they are available in and out of class for anything that you may need." Many students described the faculty they work with as "very friendly, helpful, accessible, and good at what they do." "Teachers are like friends, although we know that they expect a lot from us. Some of them are kind of weird, but we are in New Orleans." The school's strengths include business, music, and communications (housed in a $13 million complex, complete with TV and radio studios and production facilities). Coursework in religion and philosophy is mandatory, as is a 16-course Common Curriculum. The administration is regarded positively; students feel the university is smoothly run and well maintained, though labs and computer facilities could use an upgrade. A brand-new library was opened last year; it houses one of only three centers in the nation dedicated to combating adult illiteracy.

### Life

"Two words—New Orleans." "There is so much potential social life here it blows my mind." "This city knows how to party." "All the art and music you want, fabulous architecture, an amazing zoo and aquarium, some of the best food I've ever tasted . . . " Loyola students love "the Big Easy," a vibrant city world-renowned for its glorification of good times. Campus life may pale in direct comparison to this carnival by the mighty Mississippi, but there's a sense of community that many students value and appreciate. "There are always activities going on at the residence halls." "Student reps sit on most university committees and are involved in running everything, every aspect" of the school. Dorms get decent marks, as do off-campus frats and sororities, which are popular but not dominant on the social scene. Many simply like the fact that "you can concentrate on your studies" and enjoy life, too. "Since I am an honors student . . . I may not get to participate because of my academic obligations as often as I like, but when I do I have a blast!" Often that "blast" has something to do with drinking beer, rated "extremely" or "very" popular by more than 90 percent of students we surveyed; liquor was not far behind. We've got to wonder how the student who writes "they drink too much and completely violate all that is proper and sacred" wound up in New Orleans.

### Student Body

"Loyola is small, so everyone knows each other." "There is a real sense of community." The student body is "very diverse, friendly, and laid back" "with many people from different cultures and ethnic backgrounds." An international student writes, "During my first few months at Loyola, I received a lot of support from my peers." It seems that almost everyone gets along pretty well; they report little discrimination or bad blood. Viewed overall, at Loyola "they're smart but also like to have a good time." "Most of us take our work seriously, but we don't take ourselves too seriously," though in the eyes of some there's a "high school" element at the U that "needs to grow up."

FINANCIAL AID: 504-865-3231 • E-MAIL: ADMIT@LOYNO.EDU • WEBSITE: WWW.LOYNO.EDU

## ADMISSIONS

*Very important* academic and nonacademic factors considered by the admissions committee include secondary school record and standardized test scores. *Important* factors considered include class rank, extracurricular activities, and interview. *Other* factors considered include alumni/ae relation, character/personal qualities, essays, recommendations, talent/ability, volunteer work, and work experience. Factors *not* considered include geography, minority status, religious affiliation/commitment, and state residency. SAT I or ACT required. TOEFL required of all international applicants. High school diploma is required and GED is accepted. *High school units required/recommended:* 4 English required, 3 math required, 4 math recommended, 3 science required, 4 science recommended, 3 science lab required, 4 science lab recommended, 2 foreign language recommended, 3 social studies required, 3 history required. *The admissions office says:* "Because of the diversity of high school curricula, cultural influences on test results, the various abilities required in collegiate programs, and the unique background of applicants, each applicant's admissions portfolio is reviewed individually."

### The Inside Word

Students with a solid academic record can expect smooth sailing to admission at Loyola. The majority of the University's applicants are admitted. The admissions process is truly personal, and many of the weaker applicants benefit from Loyola's willingness to consider more than just numbers.

## FINANCIAL AID

*Students should submit:* FAFSA. Regular filing deadline is February 15. The Princeton Review suggests that all financial aid forms be submitted as soon as possible after January 1. *Need-based scholarships/grants offered:* Pell, SEOG, and the school's own gift aid. *Loan aid offered:* Direct Subsidized Stafford, Direct Unsubsidized Stafford, Direct PLUS, and Federal Perkins. Institutional employment available. Federal Work-Study Program available. Applicants will be notified of awards on a rolling basis beginning on or about March 15. Off-campus job opportunities are good.

## FROM THE ADMISSIONS OFFICE

"Loyola University New Orleans is a Jesuit university founded by the Society of Jesus and chartered on April 15, 1912, with ownership vested in the Loyola community of Jesuit fathers. The university was authorized to grant degrees by the General Assembly of Louisiana for the year 1912. Today, Loyola University New Orleans still operates under its founding purpose of offering a liberal arts education on the undergraduate level to all who seek knowledge and truth . . . Fronting on tree-lined St. Charles Avenue where streetcars are the mode of public transportation, Loyola's main campus faces Audubon Park directly across the avenue. The 22-acre campus is a collection of Tudor-Gothic and contemporary architecture, set off by broad expanses of green space and walkways. Two blocks up St. Charles Avenue is the four-acre Broadway Campus, location of historic Greenville Hall, Cabra Residence Hall, the Department of Visual Arts, and the School of Law."

## ADMISSIONS

| | |
|---|---|
| Admissions Rating | 76 |
| # of applicants | 2,863 |
| % of applicants accepted | 74 |
| % of acceptees attending | 40 |

### FRESHMAN PROFILE

| | |
|---|---|
| Range SAT Verbal | 540-650 |
| Average SAT Verbal | 598 |
| Range SAT Math | 530-630 |
| Average SAT Math | 575 |
| Range ACT Composite | 22-28 |
| Average ACT Composite | 25 |
| Minimum TOEFL | 550 |
| Average HS GPA | 3.6 |
| % graduated top 10% of class | 29 |
| % graduated top 25% of class | 57 |
| % graduated top 50% of class | 84 |

### DEADLINES

| | |
|---|---|
| Priority admission deadline | 12/1 |
| Regular admission | 5/1 |
| Nonfall registration? | yes |

### APPLICANTS ALSO LOOK AT

**AND OFTEN PREFER**
LSU—Baton Rouge
Tulane
U. New Orleans

**AND SOMETIMES PREFER**
Xavier U. (LA)
Texas Christian U.
U. Texas
U. Florida
Florida State

**AND RARELY PREFER**
NYU

## FINANCIAL FACTS

| | |
|---|---|
| Financial Aid Rating | 84 |
| Tuition | $16,188 |
| Room & board | $6,806 |
| Books and supplies | $650 |
| Required fees | $677 |
| % frosh receiving aid | 60 |
| % undergrads receiving aid | 57 |
| Avg frosh grant | $5,299 |
| Avg frosh loan | $2,306 |

# MACALESTER COLLEGE

1600 GRAND AVENUE, ST. PAUL, MN 55105 • ADMISSIONS: 651-696-6357 • FAX: 651-696-6724

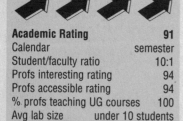
## STUDENTS SPEAK OUT
### Academics

"Academically, Macalester College is second to none and I love it here," exclaims a senior at this "rigorous" college in the Twin City of St. Paul. In the classic liberal arts tradition, students must fulfill a wide array of distribution requirements and, as the finale of the "amazing experience" here, complete a research project, seminar, performance, or other original work during senior year. Classes are generally small, and despite the high academic caliber of entering students, "it isn't so cutthroat in terms of competition." The "always available" and "brilliant" professors at Macalaster challenge students to "talk about things that really matter" and "to think in creative ways." Macalester's facilities are also exceptional—from "beautiful" buildings and well-manicured lawns to "great scientific equipment" and computer labs. The administration, previously labeled as conservative, has scored new high marks due to the college's new president: "He is amazingly open to students." Current students also give glowing reports about financial aid.

### Life

"Minnesota gets cold," warns a Washington, D.C., native, and the winter takes up a pretty solid chunk of the academic year here. Some students spend "very much time" completing the routinely "massive" amounts of homework. Others don't. "Macalester is the only college I know where the slackers can afford to slack while the studious can study all the time," observes a junior. For students with free time, the culturally diverse Twin Cities of St. Paul and Minneapolis offer "everything you could hope for if you're 21" and have a car. As a member of the underage crowd, you can "spend your time complaining about the weather and lack of sex," as some students do, or you can get involved. Annual schoolwide affairs include the Spring Fest (an all-day concert party) and the popular Scottish Country Fair, one of many Macalester events at which you can hear bagpipes being played. Macalester students are also "very big on panel discussions and roundtables," explains a junior, and they involve themselves with "a lot of political and activist issues," as well as volunteer and internship programs. "There are a few campus parties" throughout the week but many "get busted early." They're "fun" while they last, though, "because all the students know each other." Students say they enjoy life here, but not because there is nonstop campus excitement. Instead, most everyone manages to find entertaining ways to amuse themselves. "Once someone stole a milk machine and hooked it up in a dormitory bathroom and all weekend the residents had access to free milk," claims a senior. "I admire the creativity on this campus."

### Student Body

"Diversity and internationalism" are all the rage at Macalester. "I can't provide a generalization of what we are all like, because we are all different," declares a sophomore. Numerous international students "add a lot to campus life," and "Macalester's student body is diverse and exciting," at least "on paper." "In real life," contends a sarcastic senior, "they are a collection of good test scores and different countries." There are plenty of "freaks and weirdos" and "neo-hippy fake activists" on this "progressive" and "eclectic" campus, including a large contingent of pot smokers. The "very competent," "well-rounded individuals" here are "very open to discussion and debate" and "accepting and open" as well. Many admit to being "not very sporty," though. Politically, Macalester is "a liberal's haven" with "very active and aware" students. Some, however, "tend to search for a cause of the week," then complain about it "without considering the overall circumstances, and then move on to the next cause," jeers a skeptical senior. Upon graduation, a lot of alumni seek advanced degrees within a few years.

FINANCIAL AID: 651-696-6214 • E-MAIL: ADMISSIONS@MACALESTER.EDU • WEBSITE: WWW.MACALESTER.EDU

## ADMISSIONS

*Very important* academic and nonacademic factors considered by the admissions committee include secondary school record. *Important* factors considered include character/personal qualities, class rank, essays, extracurricular activities, interview, recommendations, standardized test scores, and talent/ability. *Other* factors considered include alumni/ae relation, minority status, and volunteer work. Factors *not* considered include geography, religious affiliation/commitment, state residency, and work experience. SAT I or ACT required. TOEFL or ELPTrequired of all international applicants. High school diploma is required and GED is not accepted. *High school units required/recommended:* 4 English required, 3 math required, 4 math recommended, 2 science required, 3 science recommended, 2 science lab required, 2 foreign language required, 3 foreign language recommended, 2 social studies required, 3 social studies recommended, 1 elective required. *The admissions office says:* "[We make an] active effort to reach students personally, including interviews with admissions staff offered in 14 to 15 cities a year. Students report we're somewhat friendlier than other options."

### The Inside Word

Macalester is just a breath away from moving into the highest echelon of American colleges; a gift of *Reader's Digest* stock several years ago has recently translated into over $500 million in endowment. As the college has reaped the benefits of this generous gift, the applicant pool has grown dramatically. Macalester is already among the 25 or so most selective colleges in the country. An interview is a good idea: even though they are offered across the country, we also encourage you to visit the campus.

## FINANCIAL AID

The Princeton Review suggests that all financial aid forms be submitted as soon as possible after January 1. *Need-based scholarships/grants offered:* Pell, SEOG, state scholarships/grants, private scholarships, the school's own gift aid, and Federal Nursing. *Loan aid offered:* FFEL Subsidized Stafford, FFEL Unsubsidized Stafford, FFEL PLUS, Federal Perkins, and Federal Nursing. Institutional employment available. Federal Work-Study Program available. Off-campus job opportunities are excellent.

## FROM THE ADMISSIONS OFFICE

"Recent news about Macalester (Spring 2001): Macalester students come from all 50 states and 86 other countries. Before graduating, half of them will study abroad, going to more than 70 countries in any given year. For over 30 years, Macalester's debate program has been ranked among the top 10 in the nation. A Macalester team has qualified for the International Collegiate Programming Contest in four of the past seven years, and recently the team tied with Stanford, Columbia, Carnegie-Mellon, and Harvard. The women's soccer team won the 1998 NCAA Division III national championship. A new campus center opened in 2001. Each year Macalester students win an impressive number of post-graduate awards, including Fulbright Scholarships, National Science Foundation Graduate Fellowships, Truman Scholarships, and more. Recent graduates fare well in the job market and graduate programs. One reports that she was 'accepted into top med school choices: Mayo, Stanford, UCLA and Minnesota' and another that he had a 'striking advantage over many other candidates' and is now enrolled in a PhD program in economics at Princeton University."

## ADMISSIONS

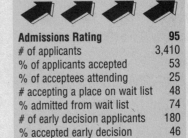

| | |
|---|---|
| Admissions Rating | 95 |
| # of applicants | 3,410 |
| % of applicants accepted | 53 |
| % of acceptees attending | 25 |
| # accepting a place on wait list | 48 |
| % admitted from wait list | 74 |
| # of early decision applicants | 180 |
| % accepted early decision | 46 |

### FRESHMAN PROFILE

| | |
|---|---|
| Range SAT Verbal | 630-730 |
| Average SAT Verbal | 664 |
| Range SAT Math | 610-700 |
| Average SAT Math | 650 |
| Range ACT Composite | 27-31 |
| Average ACT Composite | 29 |
| Minimum TOEFL | 570 |
| % graduated top 10% of class | 67 |
| % graduated top 25% of class | 94 |
| % graduated top 50% of class | 100 |

### DEADLINES

| | |
|---|---|
| Early decision | 11/15 |
| Early decision notification | 12/15 |
| Regular admission | 1/15 |
| Regular notification | 4/1 |

### APPLICANTS ALSO LOOK AT

**AND OFTEN PREFER**
Rice
Middlebury
Swarthmore
**AND SOMETIMES PREFER**
Carleton
Colorado Coll.
**AND RARELY PREFER**
Oberlin
U. Wisconsin—Madison
Earlham

## FINANCIAL FACTS

| | |
|---|---|
| Financial Aid Rating | 90 |
| Tuition | $21,486 |
| Room & board | $5,932 |
| Books and supplies | $700 |
| Required fees | $128 |
| % frosh receiving aid | 77 |
| % undergrads receiving aid | 79 |
| Avg frosh grant | $11,068 |
| Avg frosh loan | $2,142 |

# MARLBORO COLLEGE

PO BOX A, SOUTH ROAD, MARLBORO, VT 05344 • ADMISSIONS: 802-258-9236 • FAX: 802-257-4154

## CAMPUS LIFE

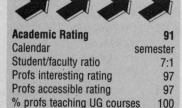

| | |
|---|---|
| **Quality of Life Rating** | **91** |
| Type of school | private |
| Affiliation | none |
| Environment | rural |

### STUDENTS

| | |
|---|---|
| Total undergrad enrollment | 290 |
| % male/female | 41/59 |
| % from out of state | 82 |
| % from public high school | 65 |
| % live on campus | 78 |
| % African American | 1 |
| % Asian | 1 |
| % Caucasian | 87 |
| % Hispanic | 2 |
| % Native American | 1 |
| % international | 2 |
| # of countries represented | 6 |

### SURVEY SAYS . . .
*Theater is hot*
*Student government is popular*
*No one cheats*
*Registration is a breeze*
*Campus feels safe*
*Class discussions encouraged*
*Intercollegiate sports unpopular or nonexistent*
*Lab facilities are great*

## ACADEMICS

| | |
|---|---|
| **Academic Rating** | **91** |
| Calendar | semester |
| Student/faculty ratio | 7:1 |
| Profs interesting rating | 97 |
| Profs accessible rating | 97 |
| % profs teaching UG courses | 100 |

### MOST POPULAR MAJORS
literature
biology
sociology

## STUDENTS SPEAK OUT

### Academics

"Academically, socially, and politically," Marlboro College is "intense." This unusual and intimate school "in the woods" is "a dream" for academic and social self-starters, but it's not for everyone. "You have to be serious about studying" if you are going to succeed here. Marlboro College offers its students the unique opportunity of designing their own individual programs of study. Under "The Plan" (short for Plan of Concentration), students spend their last two years pursuing a self-devised curriculum that culminates in a senior research paper "analogous to a master's thesis." Marlboro requires each student to pass a clear writing requirement, but otherwise, juniors and seniors work "one-on-one" with professors to design and follow their own in-depth academic investigations. The process requires "tons of writing homework" ("Abandon sleep, all who enter," quips a first-year student) but students here unanimously agree that it's a remarkable experience. Though the faculty is quite small, students praise the "wildy entertaining" and "brilliant" teachers for their "dedication, hard work, and knowledge." They are "committed to helping students learn and communicate effectively," explains one student. The "accessible" administration—its offices "packed into an old farmhouse"—is also well respected for its efforts to "involve students at every major decision" by way of regular "town meeting"–style gatherings. A "small" library draws a smattering of complaints, although the "quality librarians" receive much praise.

### Life

While it's an exaggeration to say that there is "no life at this school besides academics, alcohol, and cigarettes," it is most definitely true that "because Marlboro is so isolated, you have to be creative." Popular pastimes on "the Hill" include "sledding, hiking, playing music," and "creative hanging out." Students are also into "gossiping, renting movies, taking road trips," and, thanks to the choice location, a plethora of "great" outdoor activities including "skiing and mountain biking." "Almost everyone here is involved in theater" or the arts. "Oh, and there's a lot of drug and alcohol consumption." While "there aren't huge, raging parties here," there are "lots of events to attend" and students assure us that they "know how to get funky," albeit in a mellow, brainy way. "Marlboro is the only place I've been where your biggest concern at a party is guessing how much alcohol you can drink and still be able to contribute intellectually to the in-depth, philosophical conversation going on," relates one student. The "fishbowl-like setting" that is Marlboro's campus occasionally causes students to "wish that Boston could be moved closer to Brattleboro." These "claustrophobic" impulses are the inevitable result of the constant "spotlight" of the closed environment. As a senior explains, "you must live with the results of your actions. And, believe me, everyone will know, if, when, and how you have acted."

### Student Body

The "strange and intelligent" students that make up Marlboro's "big, dysfunctional, incestuous family" are "all originals," so they "don't always get along," but the sheer magnitude of human diversity "sure makes for an interesting and fruitful environment." You have to be "abnormal by definition to fit in at Marlboro," explains a sophomore. Another student explains: "Essentially, we were all nonconforming rejects in high school and, because of this, can understand and relate to each other on a basic level." Students further describe themselves as "articulate, committed," and "very political." Because of the academic program here, it takes a "committed" person to attend Marlboro. Because of the social life, "Marlboro is only fun for a person who is willing to be creative and adventurous. For the average, mall-walking jock, this is not the college to come to."

FINANCIAL AID: 802-257-4333 • E-MAIL: ADMISSIONS@MARLBORO.EDU • WEBSITE: WWW.MARLBORO.EDU

## ADMISSIONS

*Very important* academic and nonacademic factors considered by the admissions committee include extracurricular activities and secondary school record. *Important* factors considered include character/personal qualities, class rank, recommendations, standardized test scores, and talent/ability. *Other* factors considered include alumni/ae relation, essays, interview, minority status, volunteer work, and work experience. Factors *not* considered include geography, religious affiliation/commitment, and state residency. SAT I or ACT required; SAT II recommended. TOEFL required of all international applicants. High school diploma is required and GED is accepted. *High school units required/recommended:* 16 total required; 20 total recommended; 4 English required, 3 math required, 3 science required, 1 science lab required, 2 foreign language required, 3 social studies required.

### The Inside Word

Don't be misled by Marlboro's high acceptance rate; the College's applicant pool consists mainly of candidates who are sincerely interested in a nontraditional path to their BA. They also possess sincere intellectual curiosity, and students who don't should not bother applying. The admissions process here is driven by matchmaking and a search for those who truly want to learn. For the right kind of person, Marlboro can be a terrific college choice.

## FINANCIAL AID

*Students should submit:* FAFSA, CSS/Financial Aid PROFILE, and noncustodial (divorced/separated) parent's statement. Regular filing deadline is March 1. The Princeton Review suggests that all financial aid forms be submitted as soon as possible after January 1. *Need-based scholarships/grants offered:* Pell, SEOG, state scholarships/grants, private scholarships, and the school's own gift aid. *Loan aid offered:* FFEL Subsidized Stafford, FFEL Unsubsidized Stafford, FFEL PLUS, and college/university loans from institutional funds. Institutional employment available. Federal Work-Study Program available. Applicants will be notified of awards on a rolling basis beginning on or about April 1. Off-campus job opportunities are fair.

## FROM THE ADMISSIONS OFFICE

"Marlboro College is unlike any other college in the United States. It is distinguished by its curriculum, praised in higher education circles as unique; it is known for its self-governing philosophy, in which each student, faculty, and staff has an equal vote on many issues affecting the community; and it is recognized for its 50-year history of offering a rigorous, exciting, self-designed course of study taught in very small classes and individual tutorials. Marlboro's size also distinguishes it from most other schools. With 290 students and a student/faculty ratio of 7 to 1, it is one of the nation's smallest liberal arts colleges. Few other schools offer a program where students have such close interaction with faculty, and where community life is inseparable from academic life. The result, the self-designed, self-directed Plan of Concentration, allows students to develop their own unique academic work by defining a problem, setting clear limits on an area of inquiry, and analyzing, evaluating, and reporting on the outcome of a significant project. A Marlboro education teaches you to think for yourself, articulate your thoughts, express your ideas, believe in yourself, and do it all with the clarity, confidence and self-reliance necessary for later success, no matter what postgraduate path you take."

## ADMISSIONS

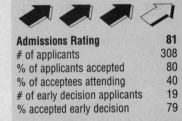

| | |
|---|---|
| Admissions Rating | 81 |
| # of applicants | 308 |
| % of applicants accepted | 80 |
| % of acceptees attending | 40 |
| # of early decision applicants | 19 |
| % accepted early decision | 79 |

### FRESHMAN PROFILE

| | |
|---|---|
| Range SAT Verbal | 580-680 |
| Average SAT Verbal | 610 |
| Range SAT Math | 500-620 |
| Average SAT Math | 580 |
| Minimum TOEFL | 550 |
| Average HS GPA | 3.2 |
| % graduated top 10% of class | 31 |
| % graduated top 25% of class | 51 |
| % graduated top 50% of class | 79 |

### DEADLINES

| | |
|---|---|
| Early decision | 11/15 |
| Early decision notification | 12/15 |
| Regular admission | 3/1 |
| Nonfall registration? | yes |

### APPLICANTS ALSO LOOK AT

**AND OFTEN PREFER**
Sarah Lawrence
Bard
Hampshire

**AND SOMETIMES PREFER**
Bennington
Evergreen State
Antioch

**AND RARELY PREFER**
Goddard
U. Vermont

### FINANCIAL FACTS

| | |
|---|---|
| Financial Aid Rating | 88 |
| Tuition | $18,800 |
| Room & board | $6,750 |
| Books and supplies | $600 |
| Required fees | $760 |
| % frosh receiving aid | 81 |
| % undergrads receiving aid | 76 |
| Avg frosh grant | $12,007 |
| Avg frosh loan | $2,619 |

# MARQUETTE UNIVERSITY

PO Box 1881, MILWAUKEE, WI 53201-1881 • ADMISSIONS: 414-288-7302 • FAX: 414-288-3764

## CAMPUS LIFE

| Quality of Life Rating | 80 |
| --- | --- |
| Type of school | private |
| Affiliation | Roman Catholic |
| Environment | urban |

### STUDENTS

| | |
| --- | --- |
| Total undergrad enrollment | 7,496 |
| % male/female | 45/55 |
| % from out of state | 52 |
| % from public high school | 57 |
| % live on campus | 34 |
| % in (# of) fraternities | 8 (4) |
| % in (# of) sororities | 8 (8) |
| % African American | 5 |
| % Asian | 4 |
| % Caucasian | 85 |
| % Hispanic | 4 |
| % international | 2 |
| # of countries represented | 80 |

### SURVEY SAYS . . .
*Student publications are popular*
*Ethnic diversity on campus*
*Students get along with local community*
*Lots of liberals*
*Diverse students interact*
*Athletic facilities need improving*
*Campus difficult to get around*
*Library needs improving*
*Computer facilities need improving*
*Very small frat/sorority scene*

## ACADEMICS

| Academic Rating | 72 |
| --- | --- |
| Calendar | semester |
| Student/faculty ratio | 15:1 |
| Profs interesting rating | 70 |
| Profs accessible rating | 71 |
| Avg lab size | 10-19 students |
| Avg reg class size | 10-19 students |

### MOST POPULAR MAJORS
business administration
biomedical science
nursing

## STUDENTS SPEAK OUT
### Academics

Because of Marquette University's fame as a legendary "basketball school," you might expect its academics to be easy. Of course, you'd be dead wrong. Educating the whole person is a major principle at Marquette, and the "challenging" core curriculum here includes rigorous course work in mathematics, theology, science, and liberal arts. The result is a "very, very rewarding" experience that makes students "well rounded" and causes them to "grow socially, mentally, physically, and religiously all at once." According to students, "the actual professors" at Marquette are "available for help whenever necessary" and "really approachable." What's more, they "make you want to learn" and "take a sincere interest in their students' needs and dreams." Unfortunately, there are also a lot of teaching assistants at Marquette who "don't have a clue." Equally unfortunately, "variances in grading scales" among different professors is a real concern among students. The "personable" and "very organized" administration at Marquette is "extremely easy to contact." "If you absolutely need a class in a particular semester, they will find a way to get you in," says a senior. "Marquette is not trying to rope you in for another year for more money." That said, however, "class registration is terrible." On the plus side, Marquette is definitely connected in the Milwaukee area, and internships are readily available for students at awesome companies like Arthur Andersen, IBM, Harley-Davidson, and—of course—Miller Brewing.

### Life

They "know it sounds cheesy," but most of Marquette students "love life" on this "drab," "urban campus" in downtown Milwaukee. The city of "cheese, beer, and *Laverne and Shirley*" boasts "jazz and blues festivals," great concerts and restaurants, and a wide array of cultural activities. Milwaukee is an especially "fun town if you are over 21 or have a fake ID." In the downtown area, "there are 15 bars in one area of two blocks." Not surprisingly, "drinking is big" and "there are a lot of house parties." Frat parties are popular, too, though the Greek system doesn't have an overwhelming presence. "Marquette does a lot on campus, too," according to a senior. "Every Friday, there are cheap—good!—movies at the theater," and "student involvement" in extracurricular activities "is pretty high." Men's basketball games are well attended, and students "participate in intramurals and attend Mass regularly." During Winter Flurry, an annual celebration that happens "the week after winter break," "the entire university shows up and it's a blast." Of course, Marquette isn't all fun and games. "Don't come here if you think you'll be drinking every night," advises a sophomore. "Classes are tough here. Studying is a necessity." Also, as Marquette is a decidedly Catholic institution, the "Jesuit work ethic" is alive and well. Community service is a Big Thing here, and students say the Jesuit priests "have an active role on campus and include some of the most humorous, caring, and involved faculty members on campus."

### Student Body

Though a lot of the students here wish it weren't so, they admit that their school is pretty "homogenous"; most everyone at Marquette comes from a midwestern, white, "upper-class," Roman Catholic background. Marquette would be "yuppie hell for someone who isn't a yuppie," according to one student. Students here are "kind midwesterners," though, who are "very polite." These "intelligent, personable, free-thinking men and women" also describe themselves as "extremely friendly, caring, and fun." There are "lots of stuck-up, rich children" on this campus and, perhaps, "too many damn cliques" as well but, overall, Marquette exudes "a strong sense of community." It's a "family environment," explains a junior. "Students pull for each other."

FINANCIAL AID: 414-288-7390 • E-MAIL: ADMISSIONS@MARQUETTE.EDU • WEBSITE: WWW.MARQUETTE.EDU

## ADMISSIONS

*Very important* academic factors considered by the admission committee include secondary school record and standardized test scores. *Important* factors considered include class rank. *Other* factors considered include recommendations, essays, interview, talent/ability, character/personal qualities, extracurricular activities, alumni/ae relations, work experience, character, geographical residence, minority status, and religious affiliation. SAT or ACT required. TOEFL required of all international students. High school diploma is required and GED is accepted. *High school units required/recommended:* 16 total recommended; 4 English recommended, 3 math recommended, 3 science recommended, 2 foreign language recommended, 1 social studies recommended, 4 electives recommended.

### The Inside Word

Class rank may be important to the admissions office as a required criterion, but not to worry—in practice, a little less than a tenth of Marquette's freshmen ranked in the bottom half of their graduating class. The university's low level of selectivity makes it a no-sweat proposition for most candidates.

## FINANCIAL AID

*Students should submit:* FAFSA. There is no regular filing deadline. The Princeton Review suggests that all financial aid forms be submitted as soon as possible after January 1. *Need-based scholarships/grants offered:* Pell, SEOG, state scholarships/grants, private scholarships, and the school's own gift aid. *Loan aid offered:* Direct Subsidized Stafford, Direct Unsubsidized Stafford, Direct PLUS, Federal Perkins, Federal Nursing, and college/university loans from institutional funds. Institutional employment available. Federal Work-Study Program available. Applicants will be notified of awards on or about March 15. Off-campus job opportunities are excellent.

## FROM THE ADMISSIONS OFFICE

"Since 1881, Marquette has been noted for its commitment to educational excellence in the 450-year-old Jesuit, Catholic tradition. Marquette embraces the philosophy that true education should be more than an acquisition of knowledge. Marquette seeks to develop your intellect as well as your moral and spiritual character. This all-encompassing education will challenge you to develop the goals and values that will shape the rest of your life. Each of Marquette's 7,500 undergraduates are admitted as freshman to one of six colleges: Arts and Sciences, Business Administration, Communication, Engineering, Health Sciences, or Nursing. Many co-enroll in the School of Education. The faculty within these colleges are prolific writers and researchers, but more important, they all teach and advise students. Marquette is nestled in the financial center of Milwaukee, the nation's eighteenth largest city, allowing you to take full advantage of the city's cultural, professional, and governmental opportunities. Marquette's urban experience is unique; an 80-acre campus (with real grass and trees), an outdoor athletic complex, and an internationally diverse student body (85 percent of which live on campus) all make Marquette a close-knit community in which you can learn and live."

## ADMISSIONS

| | |
|---|---|
| **Admissions Rating** | 77 |

### FRESHMAN PROFILE

| | |
|---|---|
| Range SAT Verbal | 520-630 |
| Average SAT Verbal | 576 |
| Range SAT Math | 530-640 |
| Average SAT Math | 582 |
| Range ACT Composite | 23-28 |
| Average ACT Composite | 25 |
| Minimum TOEFL | 525 |
| % graduated top 10% of class | 34 |
| % graduated top 25% of class | 66 |
| % graduated top 50% of class | 92 |

### DEADLINES

| | |
|---|---|
| Priority admission deadline | 2/1 |
| Regular admission | rolling |
| Nonfall registration? | yes |

### APPLICANTS ALSO LOOK AT
**AND OFTEN PREFER**
U. Wisconsin—Madison
U. Wisconsin—Milwaukee
U. Illinois—Urbana-Champaign
Notre Dame
Miami U.
**AND SOMETIMES PREFER**
St. Louis
Purdue U.—West Lafayette
Case Western Reserve
**AND RARELY PREFER**
Vanderbilt
Villanova
U. Oklahoma

### FINANCIAL FACTS

| | |
|---|---|
| **Financial Aid Rating** | 75 |
| Tuition | $18,180 |
| Room & board | $6,362 |
| Books and supplies | $900 |
| Required fees | $302 |
| % frosh receiving aid | 61 |
| % undergrads receiving aid | 60 |
| Avg frosh grant | $10,250 |
| Avg frosh loan | $4,625 |

# MARY WASHINGTON COLLEGE

1301 COLLEGE AVENUE, FREDERICKSBURG, VA 22401 • ADMISSIONS: 540-654-2000 • FAX: 540-654-1857

## CAMPUS LIFE

| **Quality of Life Rating** | **82** |
|---|---|
| Type of school | public |
| Affiliation | none |
| Environment | suburban |

### STUDENTS

| | |
|---|---|
| Total undergrad enrollment | 3,965 |
| % male/female | 31/69 |
| % from out of state | 30 |
| % from public high school | 76 |
| % live on campus | 70 |
| % African American | 4 |
| % Asian | 3 |
| % Caucasian | 90 |
| % Hispanic | 2 |
| # of countries represented | 34 |

### SURVEY SAYS . . .

*Diversity lacking on campus*
*Very little drug use*
*No one cheats*
*Classes are small*
*Very small frat/sorority scene*
*Athletic facilities need improving*
*Registration is a pain*
*Students are very religious*
*Low cost of living*

## ACADEMICS

| **Academic Rating** | **80** |
|---|---|
| Calendar | semester |
| Student/faculty ratio | 18:1 |
| Profs interesting rating | 92 |
| Profs accessible rating | 95 |
| % profs teaching UG courses | 100 |
| Avg lab size | 20-29 students |
| Avg reg class size | 20-29 students |

### MOST POPULAR MAJORS
business administration
English
psychology

## STUDENTS SPEAK OUT

### Academics

Students seeking the intimacy of a small-school education without the usual accompanying outrageous price tag should consider Mary Washington College, a small liberal arts–oriented public college in Virginia. While most well known state schools are jumbo-size universities, Mary Washington is a "strong academic school on the rise" that also happens to be "the perfect size. I'm always meeting new people at parties, but I can't walk across campus without running into someone I know." Students report that "academics are hard. Most people find them very challenging, but they are manageable." The difficulty level is abated by teachers who "are exceptional, extremely intelligent, and accessible. . . . Though my education is very challenging, it is also very fulfilling." Adds another undergrad, "The professors are great. You can call most of them at home almost any time. They really treat us like adults, not just some kids passing through." Students are less fervent about the administrators, whom they regard as somewhat "uptight and old-fashioned. Although they run the school efficiently, they won't let us live the lives of college students." Administrative duties aren't helped by an infrastructure that is "20 years behind technologically. Very slow, too much red tape." The school is showing signs of improvement in this area, recently adding "America's newest science facility" to its academic resources. Perhaps an administrative upgrade will follow.

### Life

Those with an independent streak will be most happy with the social life at Mary Washington. Explains one student, "While the school tries hard to have activities on weekends, people really do make their own fun here, whether it be dancing in D.C., taking in a movie, or going for a swim in the fountain." Many of the mainstays of college life are missing here. As one student notes, "The absence of a Greek society puts a damper on those who would wish to participate. Also, I wish we had a football team. That might help campus unity." MWC's proximity to two great towns tempts many undergrads; writes one student, "Campus empties out on weekends . . . because we are right between Richmond and D.C. Still, I usually stay here and so do my friends, and we always find stuff to do, whether we go to parties, go out to dinner, or just stay in the dorm." Those who stick around enjoy a wonderful environment. Says one undergrad, "The dorms are beautiful and very comfortable. Campus is gorgeous and historic, with all the buildings in the same style, not that ugly mishmash of decades so many campuses have." Hometown Fredricksburg is "a quaint little city with a lot of historical, southern character. It's not what you would call a college town, but I enjoy it. My friends and I can spend hours in the antique stores downtown."

### Student Body

In part because of its southern location and in part because it has always done so, Mary Washington attracts an unusually conservative and religious student body. Complains one undergrad, "Some have a 'holier than thou' attitude. Many are very intrusive and imposing with their religious beliefs." Most others, however, agree that "everyone gets along pretty well. However, that is partly because the student body is very homogeneous in nature." Most students "come from middle- and upper-class families, and they are intelligent, academically oriented students. You won't find too many 24/7 drunks and party animals here." As in previous surveys, students here complain that there are "many cliques on campus. . . . It is easier for a freshman to make friends here than it is for someone who has been here longer."

FINANCIAL AID: 800-468-5614 • E-MAIL: ADMIT@MWC.EDU • WEBSITE: WWW.MWC.EDU

## ADMISSIONS

*Very important* academic and nonacademic factors considered by the admissions committee include secondary school record. *Important* factors considered include character/personal qualities, class rank, essays, extracurricular activities, recommendations, standardized test scores, and talent/ability. *Other* factors considered include alumni/ae relation, minority status, religious affiliation/commitment, volunteer work, and work experience. Factors *not* considered include geography, interview, and state residency. SAT I or ACT required, SAT I preferred; SAT II also recommended. TOEFL required of all international applicants. High school diploma is required and GED is accepted. *High school units required/recommended:* 10 total required; 15 total recommended; 4 English required, 2 math required, 3 math recommended, 2 science required, 3 science recommended, 2 foreign language recommended, 2 social studies required, 3 social studies recommended.

### The Inside Word

It's hard to beat small, selective public colleges like Mary Washington for quality and cost, and more and more students are discovering this. The admissions process is very selective and, with the exception of preferential treatment for Virginia residents, functions in virtually the same manner as small private college admissions committees do. Students who are interested need to focus on putting their best into all aspects of the application.

## FINANCIAL AID

*Students should submit:* FAFSA. Regular filing deadline is March 1. The Princeton Review suggests that all financial aid forms be submitted as soon as possible after January 1. *Need-based scholarships/grants offered:* Pell, SEOG, state scholarships/grants, private scholarships, and the school's own gift aid. *Loan aid offered:* FFEL Subsidized Stafford, FFEL Unsubsidized Stafford, FFEL PLUS, and Federal Perkins. Institutional employment available. Federal Work-Study Program available. Off-campus job opportunities are excellent.

## FROM THE ADMISSIONS OFFICE

"Among institutions of higher learning in Virginia, Mary Washington College stands alone. The college is a unique blend of talented, inquisitive students and an exceptional faculty, brought together on a beautiful campus and served by superb facilities. The students come from all over the country and the world, and are instructed by a faculty that considers teaching its primary objective—research and publishing come second. The college is developing an innovative global awareness program that incorporates international perspectives into the academic curriculum. At the same time, the college offers its students exceptional opportunities for conducting and presenting undergraduate research. Through a program that provides more than $100,000 in research grant funds, undergraduates work individually with faculty members and can travel across the country to present their projects to a variety of conferences. The college recently completed a new telecommunications project that provides state-of-the-art facilities for computer service. Additionally, the college built the Jepson Science Center, which opened in 1998."

## ADMISSIONS

| | |
|---|---|
| Admissions Rating | 84 |
| # of early decision applicants | 244 |
| % accepted early decision | 65 |

### FRESHMAN PROFILE

| | |
|---|---|
| Range SAT Verbal | 560-650 |
| Average SAT Verbal | 612 |
| Range SAT Math | 550-630 |
| Average SAT Math | 596 |
| Average ACT Composite | 27 |
| % graduated top 10% of class | 44 |
| % graduated top 25% of class | 82 |
| % graduated top 50% of class | 99 |

### DEADLINES

| | |
|---|---|
| Early decision | 11/01 |
| Early decision notification | 12/15 |
| Priority admission deadline | 1/15 |
| Regular admission | 2/1 |
| Regular notification | 4/1 |
| Nonfall registration? | yes |

### APPLICANTS ALSO LOOK AT

**AND OFTEN PREFER**
William and Mary
U. Virginia

**AND SOMETIMES PREFER**
James Madison
U. Richmond

**AND RARELY PREFER**
George Mason
Longwood
Virginia Tech

### FINANCIAL FACTS

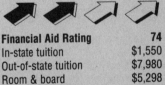

| | |
|---|---|
| Financial Aid Rating | 74 |
| In-state tuition | $1,550 |
| Out-of-state tuition | $7,980 |
| Room & board | $5,298 |
| Books and supplies | $720 |
| Required fees | $1,654 |
| % frosh receiving aid | |
| % undergrads receiving aid | |
| Avg frosh grant | |
| Avg frosh loan | |

# MASSACHUSETTS INSTITUTE OF TECHNOLOGY

77 MASSACHUSETTS AVENUE, CAMBRIDGE, MA 02139 • ADMISSIONS: 617-253-4791 • FAX: 617-253-1986

## CAMPUS LIFE

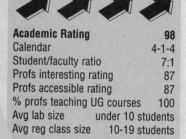

| Quality of Life Rating | 79 |
|---|---|
| Type of school | private |
| Affiliation | none |
| Environment | urban |

### STUDENTS

| | |
|---|---|
| Total undergrad enrollment | 4,300 |
| % male/female | 59/41 |
| % from out of state | 91 |
| % from public high school | 78 |
| % live on campus | 96 |
| % in (# of) fraternities | 45 (28) |
| % in (# of) sororities | 30 (5) |
| % African American | 7 |
| % Asian | 30 |
| % Caucasian | 37 |
| % Hispanic | 11 |
| % Native American | 2 |
| % international | 8 |

### SURVEY SAYS . . .

*Frats and sororities dominate social scene*
*Great computer facilities*
*Students love Cambridge, MA*
*(Almost) everyone plays intramural sports*
*Lab facilities need improving*
*Unattractive campus*
*Large classes*
*Intercollegiate sports unpopular or nonexistent*
*(Almost) no one smokes*

## ACADEMICS

| Academic Rating | 98 |
|---|---|
| Calendar | 4-1-4 |
| Student/faculty ratio | 7:1 |
| Profs interesting rating | 87 |
| Profs accessible rating | 87 |
| % profs teaching UG courses | 100 |
| Avg lab size | under 10 students |
| Avg reg class size | 10-19 students |

### MOST POPULAR MAJORS
electrical engineering
computer science
biology

## STUDENTS SPEAK OUT

### Academics

How intense is an MIT education? "Say you like Pez candy," posits one MIT undergrad. "MIT, then, is like being forced to eat $1 \times 10^9$ Pez candies." Indeed, "the workload is heavy" here, but the crunch is mitigated by an atmosphere of teamwork and a sense that students are getting the very best education money can buy. They study directly under "Nobel Prize–winning faculty, even as freshmen" and enjoy access to "superior labs and outstanding opportunities for undergraduate research." Time management, students point out, is critical. "Tech is hell if you want to attend every lecture, read everything twice, do the homework perfectly, and ace every test," explains one student. "If you understand what does and does not help you learn, life here becomes much more manageable." Material "is taught extremely fast. It takes a few weeks to get used to, but it makes everything so much more interesting and motivating." Most classes consist of "lectures taught by a full professor and recitations taught by TAs." According to several students, "Usually, recitations by undergraduate and graduate TAs, not the classes taught by distinguished faculty, are the most helpful [in learning] the material." MIT's "world-renowned" profs are, for the most part, "excellent teachers as well as researchers. Some are not good at teaching. Many are famous and offer cutting-edge information." Students appreciate the fact that "freshman year is pass/no record, and that was awesome in helping me adjust," and also that "the administration has gone through a lot of work sorting us out and choosing whom to select. They really hate to see students flunk out or transfer."

### Life

Students at MIT warn that their studies leave little time for socializing. They also note, however, that because they are located in Cambridge with so many undergraduate institutions nearby, they are well-situated to make the most of their few free hours. Explains one undergrad, "There are always concerts and events on campus, but when we want to get off campus, Boston is a beautiful, cultural city. Walking down Newbury Street, rollerblading along the Charles River, or eating in the North End Italian district are just a few favorites." The Greek scene "is huge, especially on the weekends," and "guest lectures and movies are always available." Also, students always seem to find some time for "hacking," the time-honored school tradition one student defines as "the act of pulling off elaborate, skillful practical jokes. It requires teamwork and reflects the student body's sense of humor." Among the school's most celebrated hacks are placing a replica of a campus police cruiser atop the Great Dome; the creation of a water fountain–fire plug hybrid (because learning at MIT is "like drinking water from a fire hose"); and the distribution of "Buzzword Bingo" cards during Al Gore's 1996 commencement address. On the downside, the campus "is different shades of ugly." Reports one student, "It seems like all the green patches are being taken away because of new building projects."

### Student Body

The "very diverse" MIT student body lacks variety in one area only: brains. "People here range from the really smart to the insanely smart," writes one student, although some note that their peers have "plenty of book sense but hardly any common sense." Because "students don't compete with each other as much as with themselves, everyone is willing to help everyone else out." MIT undergrads regard each other as "awesome people, although a bit nerdy. They will go out of their way to help, but some of them don't shower enough." Some are overly introverted (warns one student, "Too many people are happy to lock themselves in their rooms and study all day. If you come to MIT do not become one of these people"), but mostly this is a happy, sociable group. Notes one student, "When you come to MIT, the real you comes out. Everyone here is unique and not afraid to show it. That's because we're all tolerant of each other's differences."

FINANCIAL AID: 617-253-4971 • E-MAIL: ADMISSIONS@MIT.EDU • WEBSITE: WWW.MIT.EDU

## ADMISSIONS

*Very important* academic and nonacademic factors considered by the admissions committee include interview, secondary school record, and standardized test scores. *Important* factors considered include character/personal qualities, class rank, essays, and recommendations. *Other* factors considered include alumni/ae relation, extracurricular activities, minority status, talent/ability, volunteer work, and work experience. Factors *not* considered include geography, religious affiliation/commitment, and state residency. SAT I or ACT required; SAT II also required. TOEFL required of all international applicants. *High school units required/recommended:* 16 total required; 4 English required, 3 math required, 3 science required, 2 science lab required, 2 foreign language required, 2 social studies required, 2 elective required.

### The Inside Word

High academic achievement, lofty test scores, and the most rigorous high school courseload possible are prerequisites for a successful candidacy. Among the most selective institutions in the country, MIT's admissions operation is easily one of the most down-to-earth and accessible. Over the years they have shown both a sense of humor in admissions literature and an awareness that applying to such a prestigious and demanding place creates a high level of anxiety in students. Their relaxed and helpful approach does much to temper such stress.

## FINANCIAL AID

*Students should submit:* FAFSA, institution's own financial aid form, CSS/Financial Aid PROFILE, noncustodial (divorced/separated) parent's statement, and business/farm supplement. Regular filing deadline is January 11. The Princeton Review suggests that all financial aid forms be submitted as soon as possible after January 1. *Need-based scholarships/grants offered:* Pell, SEOG, state scholarships/grants, private scholarships, and the school's own gift aid. *Loan aid offered:* Direct Subsidized Stafford, Direct Unsubsidized Stafford, FFEL PLUS, Federal Perkins, state, and college/university loans from institutional funds. Institutional employment available. Federal Work-Study Program available. Applicants will be notified of awards on or about March 10. Off-campus job opportunities are excellent.

## FROM THE ADMISSIONS OFFICE

"The students who come to the Massachusetts Institute of Technology are some of America's—and the world's—best and most creative. As graduates, they leave here to make real contributions—in science, technology, business, education, politics, architecture, and the arts. From any class, a handful will go on to do work that is historically significant. These young men and women are leaders, achievers, producers. Helping such students make the most of their talents and dreams would challenge any educational institution. MIT gives them its best advantages: a world-class faculty, unparalleled facilities, remarkable opportunities. In turn, these students help to make the Institute the vital place it is. They bring fresh viewpoints to faculty research: More than three-quarters participate in the Undergraduate Research Opportunities Program. They play on MIT's 41 intercollegiate teams as well as in its 15 musical ensembles. To their classes and to their out-of-class activities, they bring enthusiasm, energy, and individual style."

## ADMISSIONS

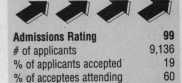

| | |
|---|---|
| Admissions Rating | 99 |
| # of applicants | 9,136 |
| % of applicants accepted | 19 |
| % of acceptees attending | 60 |
| # accepting a place on wait list | 547 |
| % admitted from wait list | 3 |

### FRESHMAN PROFILE

| | |
|---|---|
| Range SAT Verbal | 660-760 |
| Average SAT Verbal | 702 |
| Range SAT Math | 730-800 |
| Average SAT Math | 752 |
| Range ACT Composite | 30-33 |
| Average ACT Composite | 31 |
| Minimum TOEFL | 577 |
| % graduated top 10% of class | 94 |
| % graduated top 25% of class | 100 |
| % graduated top 50% of class | 100 |

### DEADLINES

| | |
|---|---|
| Priority admission deadline | 12/15 |
| Regular admission | 1/1 |
| Regular notification | 4/1 |

### APPLICANTS ALSO LOOK AT
### AND SOMETIMES PREFER

Harvard
Yale
Stanford
Caltech
Brown

### AND RARELY PREFER

Princeton
U. Virginia
Cornell U.
Columbia
RPI

## FINANCIAL FACTS

| | |
|---|---|
| Financial Aid Rating | 74 |
| Tuition | $26,050 |
| Room & board | $7,175 |
| Books and supplies | $1,000 |
| Required fees | $696 |
| % frosh receiving aid | 61 |
| % undergrads receiving aid | 65 |
| Avg frosh grant | $17,053 |
| Avg frosh loan | $4,583 |

# McGill University

845 Sherbrooke Street West, Montreal, PQ H3A 2T5 • Admissions: 514-398-3910 • Fax: 514-398-4193

## CAMPUS LIFE

**Quality of Life Rating**     **88**
Type of school     public
Affiliation     none
Environment     urban

### STUDENTS
Total undergrad enrollment    20,631
% male/female     40/60
% from out of state     28
% live on campus     9
% international     17

### SURVEY SAYS . . .
*Students love Montreal*
*Great off-campus food*
*Ethnic diversity on campus*
*Different students interact*
*Registration is a breeze*
*Computer lab facilities need*
*improving*
*Very small frat/sorority scene*
*Theater is unpopular*
*Student government is unpopular*
*Musical organizations aren't popular*

## ACADEMICS

**Academic Rating**     **90**
Calendar     semester
Student/faculty ratio     8:1
Profs interesting rating     86
Profs accessible rating     87
% profs teaching UG courses    100
Avg lab size    20-29 students
Avg reg class size    100+ students

### MOST POPULAR MAJORS
psychology
English
political science

## STUDENTS SPEAK OUT

### Academics

McGill University has a "great reputation." It is one of Canada's most "renowned" and "prestigious" schools (its alumni rolls read like a Who's Who in Canadian art, literature, and politics), and just about everyone here will gladly tell you it offers "good libraries" and "challenging" and "interesting" academic programs. What's more, courses are really "tough" (expect to study about four hours a day) and the undergraduate experience is reportedly top-notch. Nevertheless, students at McGill spend a considerable amount of their time complaining. "I have been disappointed in the overall quality of the professors," declares one. "The good ones are very good," though, and they are "generally friendly and approachable." However, lectures are sometimes gargantuan and there is "very little interaction with professors if you are a first- or second-year student. There is also "very little guidance in choosing courses" and there are "too many multiple-choice exams." Students save their most serious criticism for the "sometimes very chaotic and disagreeable" administration.

### Life

Nice architecture abounds on McGill's "beautiful" campus, but "school spirit is low" and students don't spend a lot of time engaged in campus activities. Nothing against McGill, you see; it's just that "there are a lot of better things to do" in "historic, multicultural, and safe" Montreal, "the most amazing city in the world," and one of the coldest as well. Winter weather notwithstanding, it's "easy to have fun" in Montreal: a "scenic," happening, and "cosmopolitan" "city of festivals." "It is the Party Central of Canada and McGill is located right in the middle of it all," explains one student. "Everybody smokes cigarettes" at McGill, and the drug and alcohol policies seem lenient. As an added bonus, "the drinking age is 18" and "the beer is great, cold, and cheap." Montreal is also "rich in cultural diversity" and there is "lots of cultural stuff" to experience. There's also "live music, clubs, bars, beer," and "fantastic" coffee (even in the cafeterias). The off-campus food is incredible as well (don't miss the "great smoked meat"). In fact, the whole undergraduate experience here is reportedly "excessively fun" and "unforgettable."

### Student Body

Students at "multi-ethnic" McGill describe themselves as "open," "charming," "respectful and tolerant," "very friendly," and "independent," and they say diversity is a Big Deal. There are "tons" of international students here, about one-fifth of students speak French as their first language, and the student body as a whole is "very eclectic." Nevertheless, "everyone gets along just fine" and discrimination against minority groups is virtually nonexistent. "There are so many different groups of students here that, depending on whom you surround yourself with, you will have a completely different experience," explains a junior. At the same time, "there is a unity among the students" thanks in no small part to the fact that everyone has to "deal with the hardships of Montreal winters." Politics lean left, yet most are "quite apathetic" when it comes to political or social causes: "Most people want to get their degree and get out."

# McGILL UNIVERSITY

FINANCIAL AID: 514-398-6013 • E-MAIL: ADMISSIONS@ARO.LAN.MCGILL.CA • WEBSITE: WWW.MCGILL.CA

## ADMISSIONS

*Very important* academic and nonacademic factors considered by the admissions committee include class rank, secondary school record, and standardized test scores. *Other* factors considered include essays, and recommendations. Factors considered only for scholarship include talent/ability, character/personal qualities, extracurricular activities, interview, religious affiliation/commitment, volunteer work, and work experience. TOEFL required of most international applicants. High school diploma is required and GED is not accepted. *High school units required/recommended:* 12 total required; 17 total recommended; 3 English required, 4 English recommended, 3 math required, 2 science required, 1 science lab recommended, 2 foreign language recommended, 2 social studies required, 3 social studies recommended, 3 elective required. *The admissions office says:* "Admissions requirements vary from faculty to faculty (there are 12 faculties, 10 schools, and 4 institutes at McGill, each specializing in a specific discipline) and are very demanding. Students should have taken the most challenging courses in their chosen field; that is, engineers, nursing students, science students, etc., should have taken the maximum number of science and math courses available to them. American students with Advanced Placement grades of 4 or better will be granted some advanced standing."

### The Inside Word

McGill is as tough as it comes in Canadian higher education; the university is provincially funded. As there are no geographic quotas, competition from applicants around the world is intense. The admissions process is thorough and demanding, and high SAT I and II scores just don't have the same clout across the border. Students who are serious about McGill should put extra energy into French classes. While English is the language of instruction, French is the language of Montreal, and those who speak it fare much better than those who do not in everyday life.

## FINANCIAL AID

*Students should submit:* FAFSA, institution's own financial aid form, and CSS/PROFILE required of some students for entrance awards. The Princeton Review suggests that all financial aid forms be submitted as soon as possible after January 1. Federal Work-Study Program available. Applicants will be notified of awards on a rolling basis. Off-campus job opportunities are fair.

## FROM THE ADMISSIONS OFFICE

"McGill processes over 18,000 new applications for the September and January sessions."

---

### ADMISSIONS

| Admissions Rating | 93 |
|---|---|
| # of applicants | 13,886 |
| % of applicants accepted | 62 |
| % of acceptees attending | 49 |

### FRESHMAN PROFILE

| | |
|---|---|
| Minimum TOEFL | 577 |
| Average HS GPA | 3.5 |
| % graduated top 10% of class | 90 |

### DEADLINES

| | |
|---|---|
| Regular admission | 1/15 |
| Nonfall registration? | yes |

### FINANCIAL FACTS

| Financial Aid Rating | 81 |
|---|---|
| Tuition (in-province) | $1,668 |
| Tuition (international) | $8,268-$15,000 |
| Room & board | $6,024 |
| Books and supplies | $800 |
| Required fees | $837 |
| Avg frosh grant | $3,000 |
| Avg frosh loan | $2,625 |

*Figures in Canadian dollars

# MIAMI UNIVERSITY

301 SOUTH CAMPUS AVENUE BUILDING, OXFORD, OH 45056 • ADMISSIONS: 513-529-2531 • FAX: 513-529-1550

## CAMPUS LIFE

**Quality of Life Rating**     **83**
Type of school     public
Affiliation     none
Environment     suburban

### STUDENTS
Total undergrad enrollment   14,914
% male/female     45/55
% from out of state     27
% live on campus     45
% in (# of) fraternities     24 (28)
% in (# of) sororities     27 (20)
% African American     4
% Asian     2
% Caucasian     90
% Hispanic     2
% international     1
# of countries represented     76

### SURVEY SAYS . . .
*Frats and sororities dominate social scene*
*Athletic facilities are great*
*Student publications are popular*
*Very little drug use*
*Beautiful campus*
*Library needs improving*
*Great food on campus*
*Campus difficult to get around*
*Lots of conservatives*

## ACADEMICS

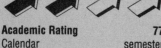

**Academic Rating**     **77**
Calendar     semester
Student/faculty ratio     18:1
Profs interesting rating     69
Profs accessible rating     66
% profs teaching UG courses     100
% classes taught by TAs     25
Avg lab size     20-29 students
Avg reg class size     20-29 students

### MOST POPULAR MAJORS
marketing
elementary education
zoology

## STUDENTS SPEAK OUT
### Academics
Students tell us that "prestigious" Miami University—the "Harvard of Ohio"—"forces you to work hard" and "embodies what college should be like." Miami of Ohio is also a "big school with a small-school feel," and it has a national reputation for offering top-rate programs in combination with state-school affordability. "Some classes" here "have 15 people and some have 115," and there are "a lot of great professors" with "different quirks" who "would be seen as crazy in normal society," speculates a first-year student. "It's what makes them good teachers, though." The professors "bend over backward" regularly and are "eager to help students." It seems like everybody here has a story about a professor going above and beyond the call of duty. One student beams, "My botany professor drove to my dorm in the rain the night before a test to give me a study sheet that I forgot to pick up." Says a finance major: "I went to a professor's office the day before an exam. He stayed two hours late and helped me with practice quizzes for three hours." And "there's nothing like a home-cooked meal at a professor's house," emphasizes a sophomore. Miami's administration "is well organized," except when it comes to class registration. It's such a "big pain" that some students suspect a sinister plot. "I've noticed a subliminal push to try to get us to stay here longer by making classes difficult to get into, or adding more requirements," charges a conspiracy-minded political science major. Also, "Miami cuts costs for everything from toilet paper to sub buns." These grievances aside, students here say they are "getting a better education at Miami than friends at other colleges." In the end, "it'll hurt to leave," predicts an already-nostalgic senior.

### Life
"Slackers will not be successful" at Miami of Ohio, warns a sophomore. "Students work very hard." They "think foremost about schoolwork" and, of course, about "how to get good grades without studying." The weekends "start on Thursdays," though, and students are "never bored" thanks to a "fun social atmosphere." Greek life absolutely "rules the social scene" on campus and "it rocks," at least according to students who pledge, which is about half the student body. There are "great parties" every week and "the uptown area"—"that's where the bars are—is a great time," says a junior. "Everyone gets drunk and goes dancing." Football and basketball games are "very popular," as are intramural sports, especially broomball. Miami also boasts "one of the largest Campus Crusade for Christ organizations in the world, with over 800 members." However, "fun is basically drinking" here and "there's not much to do besides go to parties or hang out at bars." Students say their extremely safe, red brick–covered campus is one of the "most naturally beautiful in the nation," and "the food is unbelievable," but the "parking situation" leaves a lot to be desired (ticketing is one of the "major pains" of student life). Complaints are few, though. On the whole, this medium-size public university in the small town of Oxford, Ohio, is "a great break from the real world for four or five years."

### Student Body
The more or less conservative students at Miami "have their own cliques and agendas," and they readily admit that they are only "average when it comes to friendliness." Also, "it is hard to fit in if you are not rich, thin, and white" and students note that looks (body image, cars, and clothing) are extremely important. Divulges one student: "Sometimes, I think most girls come here to find a rich, good-looking man to marry, not" to get an education. In many ways, "Miami is just a huge frat." "We talk, dress, and look the same," observes a first-year student. "The most exciting event in some people's lives is the arrival of the new J.Crew catalog." Students also realize that their "fantasy-world" lives on campus are "far from reality." Minorities are truly rare here and "ethnic mingling" leaves much to be desired. However, many students aren't much interested in ethnic interaction. "They shove diversity down our throats and it's completely overkill," complains one.

FINANCIAL AID: 513-529-8734 • E-MAIL: ADMISSION@MUOHIO.EDU • WEBSITE: WWW.MUOHIO.EDU

## ADMISSIONS

*Very important* academic and nonacademic factors considered by the admissions committee include extracurricular activities, minority status, secondary school record, talent/ability, and volunteer work. *Important* factors considered include alumni/ae relation, class rank, recommendations, standardized test scores, and work experience. *Other* factors considered include character/personal qualities, essays, geography, interview, and state residency. Factors *not* considered include religious affiliation/commitment. SAT I or ACT required. TOEFL required of all international applicants. High school diploma is required and GED is accepted. *High school units required/recommended:* 16 total required; 4 English recommended, 4 math recommended, 3 science recommended, 3 science lab recommended, 3 foreign language recommended, 3 social studies recommended.

### The Inside Word

Miami is one of the few selective public universities with an admissions process similar to those at highly selective private colleges. The university takes into account a variety of institutional needs as well as the qualifications of individual candidates when making admissions decisions. Don't be deceived by a high acceptance rate; the academic requirements for admission are quite high.

## FINANCIAL AID

*Students should submit:* FAFSA. There is no regular filing deadline. The Princeton Review suggests that all financial aid forms be submitted as soon as possible after January 1. *Need-based scholarships/grants offered:* Pell, SEOG, state scholarships/grants, private scholarships, and the school's own gift aid. *Loan aid offered:* Direct Subsidized Stafford, Direct Unsubsidized Stafford, Direct PLUS, Federal Perkins, Federal Nursing, state, college/university loans from institutional funds, and Bank Alternative Loans. Institutional employment available. Federal Work-Study Program available. Applicants will be notified of awards on a rolling basis beginning on or about March 31. Off-campus job opportunities are good.

## FROM THE ADMISSIONS OFFICE

"Miami's primary concern is its students. This concern is reflected in a broad array of efforts to develop the potential of each student. The university endeavors to individualize the educational experience. It provides personal and professional guidance, and it offers opportunities for its students to achieve understanding and appreciation not only of their own culture but of the cultures of others as well. Selected undergraduate, graduate, and professional programs of quality should be offered with the expectation of students achieving a high level of competence and understanding and developing a personal value system. Since the legislation creating Miami University stated that a leading mission of the university was to promote 'good education, virtue, religion, and morality,' the university has been striving to emphasize the supreme importance of dealing with problems relating to values."

## ADMISSIONS

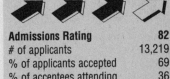

| | |
|---|---|
| Admissions Rating | 82 |
| # of applicants | 13,219 |
| % of applicants accepted | 69 |
| % of acceptees attending | 36 |
| # accepting a place on wait list | 315 |
| % admitted from wait list | 20 |
| # of early decision applicants | 880 |
| % accepted early decision | 70 |

### FRESHMAN PROFILE

| | |
|---|---|
| Range SAT Verbal | 550-640 |
| Range SAT Math | 570-660 |
| Range ACT Composite | 24-28 |
| Average ACT Composite | 26 |
| Minimum TOEFL | 530 |
| % graduated top 10% of class | 38 |
| % graduated top 25% of class | 79 |
| % graduated top 50% of class | 97 |

### DEADLINES

| | |
|---|---|
| Early decision | 11/1 |
| Early decision notification | 12/15 |
| Regular admission | 1/31 |
| Regular notification | 3/15 |
| Nonfall registration? | yes |

### APPLICANTS ALSO LOOK AT
**AND OFTEN PREFER**
Northwestern U.
U. Michigan—Ann Arbor
Indiana U—Bloomington
**AND SOMETIMES PREFER**
Ohio U.
Ohio State U.—Columbus
Dayton
**AND RARELY PREFER**
Dickinson

### FINANCIAL FACTS

| | |
|---|---|
| Financial Aid Rating | 78 |
| In-state tuition | $5,358 |
| Out-of-state tuition | $12,398 |
| Room & board | $5,830 |
| Books and supplies | $704 |
| Required fees | $1,045 |
| % frosh receiving aid | 42 |
| % undergrads receiving aid | 38 |

# MICHIGAN STATE UNIVERSITY

250 ADMINISTRATION BUILDING, EAST LANSING, MI 48824-1046 • ADMISSIONS: 517-355-8332 • FAX: 517-353-1647

## CAMPUS LIFE

**Quality of Life Rating** 76
Type of school public
Affiliation none
Environment suburban

### STUDENTS
Total undergrad enrollment 33,966
% male/female 47/53
% from out of state 9
% live on campus 44
% in (# of) fraternities 7 (35)
% in (# of) sororities 7 (19)
% African American 9
% Asian 5
% Caucasian 83
% Hispanic 2
% Native American 1
% international 2
# of countries represented 85

### SURVEY SAYS . . .
*Everyone loves the Spartans*
*Musical organizations aren't popular*
*Students aren't religious*
*Popular college radio*
*Students don't get along with local community*
*Large classes*
*Student publications are popular*
*Campus difficult to get around*
*Ethnic diversity on campus*
*Lots of TAs teach upper-level courses*

## ACADEMICS

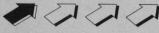

**Academic Rating** 67
Calendar semester
Student/faculty ratio 18:1
Profs interesting rating 84
Profs accessible rating 86
Avg lab size 20-29 students
Avg reg class size 20-29 students

### MOST POPULAR MAJORS
business marketing, general
psychology
finance

## STUDENTS SPEAK OUT

### Academics

Michigan State is a large school, a fact that offers requisite advantages and disadvantages. Students at MSU can choose from over 150 majors, and those who can't find a major they like can design their own. Agriculture and natural resource studies, along with the physiology department, are among Michigan State's academic strengths. The university also boasts extensive international connections, offering students the opportunity to study at 76 universities around the world. One downside of MSU's size is a lack of personal attention—most introductory classes are huge lectures, and a few classes are even taught via television. "MSU is a huge school, so I expected large classes, but I was very disappointed by how many general education classes were overseen by TAs." As a result, students enjoy the opportunities that they do have for contact with their professors. "They don't act like the big school that they teach at; generally, they would love to get to know you on a first-name basis." But "it is hard for professors and students to really get to know each other," even if "they do not look at you as just a number." Despite these difficulties, students still believe that their "professors are great." Large school or not, the administration "is one of the best around," and "helpful and hardworking." They'd be an even bigger help if they would just "get rid of dot matrix printers in our computer lab." Once they've successfully made it through an academic career at Michigan State, seniors can take great comfort in the knowledge that "great companies interview on campus."

### Life

At Michigan State University, home of the 2000 NCAA Basketball Champs and the 1999 Citrus Bowl Champs, "Spartan spirit is very strong." "Socially, you'll never beat this place." "I don't know how anyone could ever get depressed going to school here. I love it." There's no doubt that students here are enthusiastic about their social lives, but we do wonder about the manner in which many choose to express it. "There's not much to do in East Lansing except go to the bars. There needs to be alcohol education before students get hurt or in trouble." It may be a bit too late. In 1996, MSU had 574 alcohol arrests, the most in the country. In 1998, the Chronicle of Higher Education reported that "2,000 students rioted after administrators announced a ban on alcohol at a popular spot for tailgate parties during football games," and "that the violence eclipsed news that two Michigan State professors had just been elected to the National Academy of Sciences." And again last spring, the Chronicle reported that "as many as 5,000 students and others set fires, overturned cars, smashed windows, and threw bottles . . . follow[ing] Michigan State's loss to Duke University in a semi-final game of the National Collegiate Athletic Association's basketball championships." The university has formed a committee to search for solutions—an alcohol-free dormitory was established last year. Obviously, the miscreants in no way speak for the entire student body. There is certainly a diversity of opinions as to what really makes up MSU life. Many students note the fanatical frenzy of the sports program and student spirit for the Michigan State Spartans. Amazingly, over 45 percent of MSU students participate in intramural sports.

### Student Body

MSU has a mostly in-state population and the majority of the undergraduate student body is white. One junior comments that MSU has "much racial tension." But others see it as a true melting pot because of the intense desire for an education. Some students go as far as to say, "This place is very diverse—it seems most are accepting of others that are different. And if they aren't, they hide it pretty well."

FINANCIAL AID: 517-353-5940 • E-MAIL: ADMIS@MSU.EDU • WEBSITE: WWW.MSU.EDU

## ADMISSIONS

*Very important* academic and nonacademic factors considered by the admissions committee include secondary school record and standardized test scores. *Important* factors considered include class rank and minority status. *Other* factors considered include alumni/ae relation, extracurricular activities, recommendations, and talent/ability. Factors *not* considered include essays, interview, religious affiliation/commitment, state residency, and work experience. SAT I or ACT required. TOEFL required of all international applicants. High school diploma is required and GED is accepted. *High school units required:* 4 English required, 3 math required, 2 science required, 2 science lab required, 2 foreign language required, 3 social studies required.

### The Inside Word

Gaining admission to MSU is a matter of following the formulas. Grades, tests, and rank—numbers, numbers, numbers. Solid extracurricular involvement and recommendations may help borderline candidates.

## FINANCIAL AID

*Students should submit:* FAFSA and institution's own financial aid form. Regular filing deadline is June 30. The Princeton Review suggests that all financial aid forms be submitted as soon as possible after January 1. *Need-based scholarships/grants offered:* Pell, SEOG, state scholarships/grants, private scholarships, and the school's own gift aid. *Loan aid offered:* Direct Subsidized Stafford, Direct Unsubsidized Stafford, Direct PLUS, Federal Perkins, state, and college/university loans from institutional funds. Institutional employment available. Federal Work-Study Program available. Applicants will be notified of awards on a rolling basis beginning on or about March 15. Off-campus job opportunities are excellent.

## FROM THE ADMISSIONS OFFICE

"Although Michigan State University is a graduate and research institution of international stature and acclaim, your undergraduate education is our highest priority. More than 2,000 faculty members (95 percent of whom hold the highest degree in their fields) are dedicated to providing academic instruction, guidance, and assistance to our undergraduate students. Our 34,000 undergraduate students are a select group of academically motivated men and women. The diversity of ethnic, racial, religious, and socioeconomic heritage makes the student body a microcosm of the state, national, and international community."

### ADMISSIONS

| | |
|---|---|
| Admissions Rating | 73 |
| # of applicants | 22,709 |
| % of applicants accepted | 69 |
| % of acceptees attending | 43 |

### FRESHMAN PROFILE

| | |
|---|---|
| Range SAT Verbal | 490-610 |
| Average SAT Verbal | 551 |
| Range SAT Math | 510-640 |
| Average SAT Math | 572 |
| Range ACT Composite | 21-26 |
| Average ACT Composite | 24 |
| Minimum TOEFL | 550 |
| Average HS GPA | 3.5 |
| % graduated top 10% of class | 24 |
| % graduated top 25% of class | 60 |
| % graduated top 50% of class | 92 |

### DEADLINES

| | |
|---|---|
| Regular admission | 7/30 |
| Regular notification | rolling |
| Nonfall registration? | yes |

### APPLICANTS ALSO LOOK AT

**AND OFTEN PREFER**
U. Michigan—Ann Arbor
Kalamazoo
Eastern Michigan
Central Michigan
Western Michigan

**AND SOMETIMES PREFER**
U. Illinois—Urbana-Champaign
Indiana U.—Bloomington
U. Wisconsin—Madison
Oakland

**AND RARELY PREFER**
Wayne State U.

### FINANCIAL FACTS

| | |
|---|---|
| Financial Aid Rating | 75 |
| In-state tuition | $5,093 |
| Out-of-state tuition | $12,675 |
| Room & board | $4,472 |
| Books and supplies | $752 |
| Required fees | $602 |
| % frosh receiving aid | 38 |
| % undergrads receiving aid | 40 |

# MICHIGAN TECHNOLOGICAL UNIVERSITY

1400 TOWNSEND DRIVE, HOUGHTON, MI 49931 • ADMISSIONS: 906-487-2335 • FAX: 906-487-2125

## CAMPUS LIFE

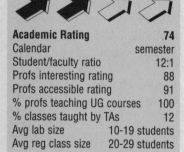

| Quality of Life Rating | 75 |
|---|---|
| Type of school | public |
| Affiliation | none |
| Environment | rural |

### STUDENTS

| | |
|---|---|
| Total undergrad enrollment | 5,666 |
| % male/female | 74/26 |
| % from out of state | 18 |
| % live on campus | 43 |
| % in (# of) fraternities | 9 (16) |
| % in (# of) sororities | 15 (8) |
| % African American | 2 |
| % Asian | 1 |
| % Caucasian | 88 |
| % Hispanic | 1 |
| % Native American | 1 |
| % international | 5 |

### SURVEY SAYS . . .

Frats and sororities dominate social scene
Popular college radio
Hard liquor is popular
Class discussions are rare
(Almost) everyone plays intramural sports
Registration is a pain
Library needs improving
Large classes
Theater is unpopular
Political activism is (almost) nonexistent

## ACADEMICS

| Academic Rating | 74 |
|---|---|
| Calendar | semester |
| Student/faculty ratio | 12:1 |
| Profs interesting rating | 88 |
| Profs accessible rating | 91 |
| % profs teaching UG courses | 100 |
| % classes taught by TAs | 12 |
| Avg lab size | 10-19 students |
| Avg reg class size | 20-29 students |

### MOST POPULAR MAJORS
mechanical engineering
electrical engineering
civil engineering

## STUDENTS SPEAK OUT

### Academics

Founded over 100 years ago to train area metallurgists and mining engineers, Michigan Technological University continues to be a leader in the fields of research and education in the mineral sciences. But MTU long ago expanded its curriculum to encompass all other aspects of engineering, as well as business, forestry, and science. Coursework here is demanding, both on the conceptual level and in terms of sheer quantity. "I really think that MTU should focus more on 'real world' skills and 'actual' learning," writes one student. "There is too much emphasis and taking in tons of data and regurgitating it profusely for tests." Another agrees, "[Teachers] try to weed you out with hard grading." However, the university is introducing a program to increase the amount of hands-on engineering experience for its students. Currently, instruction at MTU is a mixed bag. On the downside, there are the oversize lectures that are "too often taught by TAs who don't speak fluent English." In the plus column, however, is the senior faculty, of whom "most . . . are excellent. They make you feel like learning is a priority." Even more importantly, "the professors here are easily accessible." Also, the University now offers online registration, praised by lots of students.

### Life

A student jokes that there is a sign outside Tech's hometown of Houghton reads: "Houghton, 2 miles; End of the World, 4 miles." Such is life on Michigan's Upper Peninsula, home to copper mines, Indian reservations, and a few very, very small towns. "If you love small-town life and the great outdoors, you will love Tech," writes one student. Adds a detractor, "About the only thing to do in God's country is go four-wheeling and then fix your truck." Winters on the UP are "six months long" and "damn cold!" As a result, students stay indoors as much as possible. On campus, "the standards are all here: movies, parties, and sporting events," and "Greek life is very popular." Tech holds one big annual blowout appropriately named Winter Carnival, a weekend-long "social time that is a nice break right before the end of the winter term crunch." Still, many students feel that "there's a lot of studying up here because it's the only thing to do." A dearth of female students eliminates yet another social option for most Tech men. Bored and stressed out, some students "drink and do drugs because they don't learn to cope with their problems in any other way."

### Student Body

The Tech student body is predominantly male, white, and both socially and politically conservative. Did we forget anything? Oh, yes . . . as one student succinctly puts it, "This is a very nerdy school. If you aren't a nerd and you come here, this school will turn you into one." Writes another, "Students seem too caught up in their technical selves. Students here who avoid eye contact are plentiful. I think this is mainly because they have too much technical attachment to attach their minds to anything but school." Agrees one engineer, "Students are either really gregarious, or lock themselves in their rooms. Very little in between." The relatively scarce female population get to "date frequently," but as for the men . . . well, as one student reports, "Since MTU is all guys, all we think about is women. For fun, we talk about women, drink a lot and fantasize about women, and try to hit on women. It's tough being a guy in the UP!"

# MICHIGAN TECHNOLOGICAL UNIVERSITY

FINANCIAL AID: 906-487-2622 • E-MAIL: MTU4U@MTU.EDU • WEBSITE: WWW.MTU.EDU

## ADMISSIONS

*Very important* academic and nonacademic factors considered by the admissions committee include class rank, standardized test scores, and secondary school record. *Other* factors considered include alumni/ae relation, character/personal qualities, essays, extracurricular activities, interview, recommendations, talent/ability, volunteer work, and work experience. Factors *not* considered include geography, minority status, religious affiliation/commitment, and state residency. SAT I or ACT required, TOEFL required of all international applicants. High school diploma is required and GED is accepted. *High school units required/recommended:* 15 total required; 3 English required, 4 English recommended, 3 math required, 4 math recommended, 1 science required, 3 science recommended, 1 or more foreign language recommended, 1 or more social studies recommended, 1 or more history recommended, 1 or more electives recommended.

### The Inside Word

Michigan Tech has a pretty good reputation and a highly self-selected applicant pool. In light of this, students who are interested should not be deceived by the high admit rate and should spend a little time on self-assessment of their ability to handle an engineering curriculum. There's nothing gained by getting yourself into a program that you can't get out of successfully.

## FINANCIAL AID

*Students should submit:* FAFSA. The Princeton Review suggests that all financial aid forms be submitted as soon as possible after January 1. *Need-based scholarships/grants offered:* Pell, SEOG, state scholarships/grants, private scholarships, and the school's own gift aid. *Loan aid offered:* Direct Subsidized Stafford, Direct Unsubsidized Stafford, Direct PLUS, Federal Perkins, state, college/university loans from institutional funds, and external. Institutional employment available. Federal Work-Study Program available. Applicants will be notified of awards on a rolling basis beginning on or about February 28. Off-campus job opportunities are good.

## FROM THE ADMISSIONS OFFICE

"Michigan Tech is recognized as one of the nation's leading univesities for undergraduate and graduate education in science and engineering. Its state-of-the-art campus is located near Lake Superior in Michigan's beautiful Upper Peninsula. The university owns and operates a downhill ski area and 18-hole golf course. . . . MTU is one of Michigan's four nationally recognized research universities."

## ADMISSIONS

| | |
|---|---|
| **Admissions Rating** | **81** |
| # of applicants | 3,111 |
| % of applicants accepted | 94 |
| % of acceptees attending | 43 |

### FRESHMAN PROFILE

| | |
|---|---|
| Range SAT Verbal | 510-630 |
| Average SAT Verbal | 567 |
| Range SAT Math | 570-690 |
| Average SAT Math | 624 |
| Range ACT Composite | 23-28 |
| Average ACT Composite | 25 |
| Minimum TOEFL | 500 |
| Average HS GPA | 3.5 |
| % graduated top 10% of class | 31 |
| % graduated top 25% of class | 61 |
| % graduated top 50% of class | 88 |

### DEADLINES

| | |
|---|---|
| Priority admission deadline | 1/1 |
| Nonfall registration? | yes |

### APPLICANTS ALSO LOOK AT
### AND SOMETIMES PREFER
Michigan State
U. Michigan—Ann Arbor
U. of Wisconsin—Madison
### AND RARELY PREFER
Kettering Univ.
Lawrence
Milwaukee School of Engineering

## FINANCIAL FACTS

| | |
|---|---|
| **Financial Aid Rating** | **81** |
| In-state tuition | $4,530 |
| Out-of-state tuition | $11,086 |
| Room & board | $4,917 |
| Books and supplies | $900 |
| Required fees | $136 |
| % frosh receiving aid | 46 |
| % undergrads receiving aid | 49 |
| Avg frosh grant | $4,322 |
| Avg frosh loan | $3,268 |

# MIDDLEBURY COLLEGE

THE EMMA WILLARD HOUSE, MIDDLEBURY, VT 05753-6002 • ADMISSIONS: 802-443-3000 • FAX: 802-443-2056

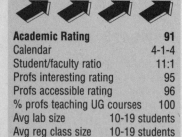
## STUDENTS SPEAK OUT

### Academics

Academically one of the most rigorous programs in the country, "top-rate" Middlebury College, tucked away in rural Vermont (about four hours' drive to Boston, two hours to Burlington) manages to offer the resources, facilities, and faculty excellence of a much larger school—while keeping enrollment for undergrads at around 2,300. Nationally recognized language, writing, and theater programs share the spotlight with a top-notch science curriculum—which has benefited in recent years from the construction of a new science center. One student is thrilled that "professors here actually teach. They manage classes, advising, and research demands seamlessly." Despite "tons of homework" and tough classes, students say there's little of the "cutthroat competition" that might characterize other schools of Middlebury's caliber. It might have something to do with the pristine location of "Club Midd," their "laid-back" atmosphere, and an excellent alumni network that makes finding a job after graduation a whole lot easier. Or it might be the result of a bit of grade inflation (some kids complain that "if you're smart, you can get A's and B's hardly doing any work"). But most likely, it's just Middlebury's special blend of a quality program, personal attention, and something a little more nebulous one student calls "attitude." In any case, Middlebury's got it. Sums up a senior, "Academically, I've been challenged, but also have had time to breathe and have fun."

### Life

You'd think that at a place that gets "so cold your nostrils freeze together" folks would be spending most of their time inside. Not so at Club Midd! "We own our own ski mountain," notes a junior, one of the reasons why, come winter, most students head outside for fun. With skiing, hiking, rock climbing, mountain biking, kayaking, and fishing right in the college's backyard, you can see why "year round people are involved in outdoor activities." "Almost everyone is athletic one way or another," adds another senior. The school's facilities say as much—students can choose between a hockey rink, fitness center, pool, golf course, and "snow bowl" for fun. It's no surprise, then, that "sports are a major preoccupation here." The "work hard, play hard" ethos extends into socializing, too. A senior explains: "As opportunities for nightlife are virtually nonexistent, we drink. While fun, this does take its toll on one's health." And though there doesn't seem to be a shortage of school-sponsored activities and clubs (social houses and a "commons"-style freshman dorm system provide social opportunities for underclassmen), some students complain that the Middlebury experience "varies between having amazing times to wanting to get the hell out of here." What's more, besides the professed lack of academic competition, "life can be very stressful," notes a junior; "everyone around is an overachiever, star athlete, talented musician, and very attractive."

### Student Body

"Students here come from every corner of the world . . . and every New England prep school," jokes a first-year on the subject of Middlebury's fairly homogenous student body (80 percent of its undergrads self-identify as "Caucasian"). A junior gives his take on the situation: "They're cool but the same. This is what I heard before I got here, and this is definitely true. . . . [M]ost are rich and white" and from somewhere "just outside of Boston." Still, it's the people that most students say make the Middlebury experience what it is. Take it from this sophomore: "The main reason I fell in love with Midd was the students. At no other school did I see so many happy, outgoing students." Concludes a classmate, "The majority of the students are really smart and really cool, which makes a small school not feel that way."

FINANCIAL AID: 802-443-5158 • E-MAIL: ADMISSIONS@MIDDLEBURY.EDU • WEBSITE: WWW.MIDDLEBURY.EDU

## ADMISSIONS

*Very important* academic and nonacademic factors considered by the admissions committee include secondary school record. *Important* factors considered include class rank, extracurricular activities, recommendations, and standardized test scores. *Other* factors considered include alumni/ae relation, character/personal qualities, essays, geography, minority status, talent/ability, volunteer work, and work experience. Factors *not* considered include religious affiliation/commitment, and state residency. ACT or three SAT IIs or three APs or three IB tests required. International students for whom English is not their first language must submit a test of English proficiency (TOEFL or SAT I or SAT II: Writing or APIEL). High school diploma is required and GED is accepted. *High school units required/recommended:* 16 total required; 4 English required, 3 math recommended, 2 science recommended, 2 science lab recommended, 2 foreign language recommended, 2 social studies recommended, 1 history recommended, 3 elective recommended.

### The Inside Word

While Middlebury benefits tremendously from its age-old position as an Ivy League safety, it is nonetheless a very strong and demanding place in its own right. Middlebury has a broad national applicant pool and sees more ACT scores than most eastern colleges, so submitting ACT scores to Middlebury is a more comfortable option than at most eastern schools.

## FINANCIAL AID

*Students should submit:* FAFSA, CSS/Financial Aid PROFILE, noncustodial (divorced/separated) parent's statement, business/farm supplement, and federal income tax forms. The Princeton Review suggests that all financial aid forms be submitted as soon as possible after January 1. *Need-based scholarships/grants offered:* Pell, SEOG, state scholarships/grants, private scholarships, and the school's own gift aid. *Loan aid offered:* Direct Subsidized Stafford, Direct Unsubsidized Stafford, Direct PLUS, Federal Perkins, and college/university loans from institutional funds. Institutional employment available. Federal Work-Study Program available. Applicants will be notified of awards on or about April 1. Off-campus job opportunities are limited.

## FROM THE ADMISSIONS OFFICE

"The successful Middlebury candidate excels in a variety of areas including academics, athletics, the arts, leadership, and service to others. These strengths and interests permit students to grow beyond their traditional 'comfort zones' and conventional limits. Our classrooms are as varied as the Green Mountains, the Metropolitan Museum of Art, or the great cities Russia and Japan. Outside the classroom, students informally interact with professors in activities such as intramural basketball games and community service. At Middlebury, students develop critical thinking skills, enduring bonds of friendship, and the ability to challenge themselves."

## ADMISSIONS

| | |
|---|---|
| Admissions Rating | 97 |
| # of applicants | 5,410 |
| % of applicants accepted | 23 |
| % of acceptees attending | 43 |
| # accepting a place on wait list | 625 |
| % admitted from wait list | 5 |
| # of early decision applicants | 822 |
| % accepted early decision | 47 |

### FRESHMAN PROFILE

| | |
|---|---|
| Range SAT Verbal | 680-730 |
| Average SAT Verbal | 710 |
| Range SAT Math | 670-740 |
| Average SAT Math | 700 |
| Range ACT Composite | 29-32 |
| Average ACT Composite | 30 |
| % graduated top 10% of class | 73 |
| % graduated top 25% of class | 92 |
| % graduated top 50% of class | 99 |

### DEADLINES

| | |
|---|---|
| Early decision | 11/15 |
| Early decision notification | 12/15 |
| Regular admission | 12/15 |
| Regular notification | 4/1 |
| Nonfall registration? | yes |

### APPLICANTS ALSO LOOK AT

**AND OFTEN PREFER**
Dartmouth
Harvard
Williams
Amherst
Princeton

**AND SOMETIMES PREFER**
Brown
Yale

**AND RARELY PREFER**
Bowdoin
Hamilton
Skidmore
St. Lawrence

### FINANCIAL FACTS

| | |
|---|---|
| Financial Aid Rating | 70 |
| Books and supplies | $750 |
| % frosh receiving aid | 36 |
| % undergrads receiving aid | 36 |
| Avg frosh grant | $15,427 |
| Avg frosh loan | $3,392 |

# MILLSAPS COLLEGE

1701 NORTH STATE STREET, JACKSON, MS 39210 • ADMISSIONS: 601-974-1050 • FAX: 601-974-1059

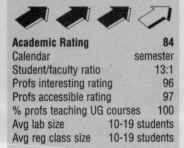
## STUDENTS SPEAK OUT
### Academics

Most people don't associate the image of a small, personalized liberal arts and sciences college with the Deep South, but Mississippi's Millsaps College is working hard to change that. Here, highly rated lab, computer, and classroom facilities complement standout departments in the pre-medical sciences, political science, English, music, and history. And for those hardy few seeking the equivalent of a liberal arts boot camp, the interdisciplinary Heritage Program (a year-long Western Civilization survey) is reportedly both very difficult and very rewarding. As at most small schools, the faculty is the make-or-break point; at Millsaps, teachers make the educational experience. Writes one student, "It's really easy to get to know the teachers here. They're one of our best assets. Classes are small and centered around student involvement. I don't feel like I'm just a number here." Profs "don't hesitate to tell you what they expect from you, and they have no problem in helping you achieve those goals." The administration "is very cognizant of the student body's wants and needs," but "sometimes has a hard time distinguishing between being the authority and being well liked. Still, they get the job done." These academic amenities help soften the blow of "intense written and oral comprehensive exams before graduation." Student complaints often mention the library, which "is not even worthy of that title. 'Old, useless, obsolete book storage facility' would be more appropriate." Yet all and all, most here agree that "Millsaps has been incredible in broadening my learning and enhancing my education. I cannot think of a better total academic experience."

### Life

For many students at Millsaps, the social scene begins and ends with the school's imposing Frat Row. "Does the movie *Animal House* ring a bell?" asks one student. "'Nuff said." To its adherents, "Greek life here is great. It helps everyone get involved in campus life without excluding people who are not Greek." Others note that "fraternity houses are a hot social spot, but you grow out of that. Like most places, it's the people who make it worthwhile." Because so much of the social life here is centered in one area, "If you live off campus, it's really tough to be part of the student mentality." Alternatives to frat parties are available to those willing to break from the pack; a new student center "is a cross between a student center and the Hilton. The imported Italian marble is beautiful. It's great!" The Student Body Association brings entertainment to campus, providing yet other choices. And then there's Jackson, Mississippi, the town immortalized in song by Johnny Cash. As one student told us, "I like to shop and go out to eat in my free time. Jackson is a great city for these activities. I go out to bars or fraternity houses about twice a week." Others disagree, reporting that "Jackson is not a hip-hop happenin' town, but campus life sometimes makes up for it, or it used to before the administration cracked down on partying on Frat Row."

### Student Body

"Students at Millsaps," explains one undergrad here, "are much like most southerners, friendly and interested in meeting new people. This made the transition to college much easier for me." At a school this small, "you have the chance to get to know everyone" and may feel as though you know them all after you've met only a few, since most students seem to have been cut from the same mold. The population consists mostly of "conservative kids who are really into the Greek scene, but luckily most have been raised well enough to be decent and courteous to the small minority segment we have." As for inter-Greek rivalries, "the fraternities pretty much stick together, but many of the sorority girls are friendly with each other." Politically, "the profs and much of the administration are very far to the left in their thinking. The student body makes Ronald Reagan appear moderate. What unfolds is a unique academic experience."

FINANCIAL AID: 601-974-1220 • E-MAIL: ADMISSIONS@MILLSAPS.EDU • WEBSITE: WWW.MILLSAPS.EDU

## ADMISSIONS

*Very important* academic and nonacademic factors considered by the admissions committee include secondary school record. *Important* factors considered include character/personal qualities, class rank, essays, interview, standardized test scores, and talent/ability. *Other* factors considered include alumni/ae relation, extracurricular activities, geography, minority status, recommendations, volunteer work, and work experience. Factors *not* considered include religious affiliation/commitment and state residency. SAT I or ACT required. TOEFL required of all international applicants. High school diploma is required and GED is accepted. *High school units required/recommended:* 4 English required, 3 math required, 2 science required, 2 foreign language required, 1 social studies required, 1 history required. *The admissions office says:* "Applicants must furnish evidence of: (1) good moral character; (2) sound physical and mental health; (3) adequate scholastic preparation; (4) intellectual maturity. Applicants are advised to apply for admission well in advance of the date on which they wish to enter, particularly if housing accommodations on the campus are desired."

### The Inside Word

Despite the college's seemingly deep-probing evaluation process, candidates with a solid track record in high school encounter little resistance in gaining admission. In reality, there is little room for extensive matchmaking by the admissions staff. The high percentage of acceptees who choose to enroll, comparatively, makes getting in less than definite for candidates with weak academic credentials.

## FINANCIAL AID

*Students should submit:* FAFSA, institution's own financial aid form, and state aid form. Recommended filing deadline is March 1. The Princeton Review suggests that all financial aid forms be submitted as soon as possible after January 1. *Need-based scholarships/grants offered:* Pell, SEOG, state scholarships/grants, private scholarships, and the school's own gift aid. *Loan aid offered:* FFEL Subsidized Stafford, FFEL Unsubsidized Stafford, FFEL PLUS, Federal Perkins, and college/university loans from institutional funds. Institutional employment available. Federal Work-Study Program available. Applicants will be notified of awards on a rolling basis beginning on or about March 10. Off-campus job opportunities are good.

## FROM THE ADMISSIONS OFFICE

"Your academic experience at Millsaps begins with Introduction to Liberal Studies, a comprehensive freshman experience. You will be encouraged to develop critical thinking skills, analytical reasoning, and independence of thought as preparation for study in your major. The interdisciplinary Heritage Program offers a unique approach to the culture and development of society through lectures and small group discussions by a team of faculty who represent a cross-section of the humanities. Entering freshmen are primarily taught by full-time PhD professors. The close relationship between faculty and students encourages classroom participation and enables students to explore their options as they choose a major field of study. Coursework in the major may begin as early as the freshman year."

## ADMISSIONS

| | |
|---|---:|
| Admissions Rating | 80 |
| # of applicants | 877 |
| % of applicants accepted | 88 |
| % of acceptees attending | 38 |

### FRESHMAN PROFILE

| | |
|---|---:|
| Range SAT Verbal | 540-640 |
| Average SAT Verbal | 600 |
| Range SAT Math | 560-630 |
| Average SAT Math | 580 |
| Range ACT Composite | 23-29 |
| Average ACT Composite | 26 |
| Minimum TOEFL | 550 |
| Average HS GPA | 3.5 |
| % graduated top 10% of class | 38 |
| % graduated top 25% of class | 65 |
| % graduated top 50% of class | 91 |

### DEADLINES

| | |
|---|---:|
| Regular admission | 2/1 |
| Nonfall registration? | yes |

### APPLICANTS ALSO LOOK AT

**AND OFTEN PREFER**
Duke
Emory

**AND SOMETIMES PREFER**
Vanderbilt
Tulane
Rhodes

**AND RARELY PREFER**
Hendrix

## FINANCIAL FACTS

| | |
|---|---:|
| Financial Aid Rating | 86 |
| Tuition | $15,586 |
| Room & board | $6,580 |
| Books and supplies | $550 |
| Required fees | $960 |
| % frosh receiving aid | 55 |
| % undergrads receiving aid | 60 |
| Avg frosh grant | $12,000 |
| Avg frosh loan | $3,500 |

# MONTANA TECH OF THE UNIVERSITY OF MONTANA

1300 WEST PARK STREET, BUTTE, MT 59701 • ADMISSIONS: 406-496-4178 • FAX: 406-496-4710

## CAMPUS LIFE

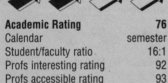

**Quality of Life Rating**          **82**
Type of school                      public
Affiliation                         none
Environment                         suburban

### STUDENTS
Total undergrad enrollment          1,978
% male/female                       55/45
% from out of state                 12
% live on campus                    15
% Asian                             1
% Caucasian                         89
% Hispanic                          1
% Native American                   2
% international                     2

### SURVEY SAYS . . .
*Popular college radio*
*Musical organizations aren't popular*
*(Almost) everyone plays intramural*
*sports*
*Low cost of living*
*Class discussions are rare*
*Very small frat/sorority scene*
*Political activism is (almost)*
*nonexistent*
*(Almost) no one smokes*
*Students get along with local*
*community*

## ACADEMICS

**Academic Rating**                 **76**
Calendar                            semester
Student/faculty ratio               16:1
Profs interesting rating            92
Profs accessible rating             93
% profs teaching UG courses         100
Avg lab size                        10-19 students
Avg reg class size                  10-19 students

### MOST POPULAR MAJORS
general engineering
business and information technology
petroleum engineering

## STUDENTS SPEAK OUT
### Academics
In at least two respects, Montana Tech is a pleasing anomaly. It is a state school at which students rave about small classes, and it is an engineering and technology school at which professors are admired for their teaching ability and expertise. At bargain-basement rates—especially for native Montanans—who could ask for more? Students report that "the student-instructor relationship at this school is extremely conducive to learning" because "pretty much the entire faculty and staff is great, easy to get to, and more than willing to help." Students report that petroleum engineering, geology, mining, environmental engineering, and geophysical engineering are among Tech's strongest suits. The completion of $20 million in renovations should quell student complaints that the facilities "aren't so hot." The Montana Tech curriculum includes a number of distribution requirements (including communications, social sciences, and the humanities), an emphasis on the practical applications of engineering and mining, and plenty of opportunities for cooperative education (working at a major-related job for credit during the school year). Of the last of these, one student boasts that "Montana Tech's placement co-op offices work very hard to coordinate major employers' on-campus interviews. This is a major reason why I chose Montana Tech. I've interviewed with an average of five companies a year, and I've had an internship two of the four summers I've been here." Student satisfaction with Tech is best summed up by the student who writes, "As one teacher told us, 'You will get a job because you graduated from Montana Tech. They know what it takes to get a degree here.'"

### Life
According to most, "Life [at Montana Tech] is centered around school. Students have to spend a great deal of time on classes to succeed." When they can find free time, students enjoy the many outdoor activities available in the Butte area. "There are lots of recreational opportunities here: mountain biking, skiing, hiking," writes one student. Says another, "Schoolwork is typical, but on the downtime I enjoy fly fishing and hiking, camping, and climbing in the mountains nearby." The heavy workload, coupled with the small student body, means that there aren't many extracurricular campus activities. This is fine by most students, who appreciate the fact that campus life is "fairly laid-back and calm." Students indulge in the occasional blowout, such as the campuswide parties on St. Patrick's Day, M-Days (a weekend party during which students repaint a giant stone 'M'), and Homecoming. Of their hometown, students report that "Butte is not a budding metropolis, but it has enough to keep people busy."

### Student Body
Tech undergraduates enjoy a collegial rapport with their classmates. Writes one, "There's a real family atmosphere in the school. Upperclassmen care about and tease underclassmen." Warns another, "Don't come to Montana Tech if you want to be anonymous. The small campus size pretty much guarantees you'll meet just about everyone here during your four years. Everyone is very laid back and cordial." The largely native Montanan student body "dresses like and has the attitude of being rednecks—very conservative, bar-type individuals who will help out at the drop of a hat." Tech students tend to be more religious than most of their counterparts at other engineering schools.

FINANCIAL AID: 406-496-4212 • E-MAIL: ADMISSIONS@MTECH.EDU • WEBSITE: WWW.MTECH.EDU

## ADMISSIONS

*Very important* academic and nonacademic factors considered by the admissions committee include character/personal qualities, class rank, secondary school record, and standardized test scores. *Important* factors considered include essays, extracurricular activities, recommendations, and talent/ability. *Other* factors considered include alumni/ae relation, geography, interview, minority status, volunteer work, and work experience. Factors *not* considered include religious affiliation/commitment and state residency. SAT I or ACT required. TOEFL required of all international applicants. High school diploma is required and GED is accepted. *High school units required/recommended:* 17 total required; 4 English required, 3 math required, 3 science required, 1 science lab required, 2 foreign language required, 3 social studies required, 2 elective required. *The admissions office says:* "We admit students on a rolling basis. We also admit engineering students into their designated area of interest upon admission to Montana Tech; we do not make them wait until their sophomore or junior year."

### The Inside Word

Underrecognized schools like Montana Tech can be a godsend for students who are strong academically but not likely to be offered admission to nationally renowned technical institutes. In fact, because of its small size and relatively remote location, Montana Tech is a good choice for anyone leaning toward a technical career. You'd be hard-pressed to find many other places that are as low-key and personal in this realm of academe.

## FINANCIAL AID

*Students should submit:* FAFSA. There is no regular filing deadline. The Princeton Review suggests that all financial aid forms be submitted as soon as possible after January 1. *Need-based scholarships/grants offered:* Pell, SEOG, state scholarships/grants, private scholarships, and the school's own gift aid. *Loan aid offered:* FFEL Subsidized Stafford, FFEL Unsubsidized Stafford, FFEL PLUS, Federal Perkins, and college/university loans from institutional funds. Institutional employment available. Federal Work-Study Program available. Applicants will be notified of awards on a rolling basis. Off-campus job opportunities are good.

## FROM THE ADMISSIONS OFFICE

"Surrounded by the ore-rich mountains that gave Butte, Montana the name 'the richest hill on earth,' Montana Tech opened its doors in 1900 as the Montana School of Mines. One hundred years later, the school remains one of the most respected mining and engineering schools in the country. Montana Tech's original minerals curriculum has evolved to include programs on the technological edge of resource recovery, environmental protection, business management, and computer science. These programs attract hardworking, practical students from all over the country and many parts of the world. Curriculums designed for hands-on learning support the overall job placement rate of 98 percent in 1995. Montana Tech offers a proven curriculum along with the outdoor adventure of the rugged Rocky Mountains."

## ADMISSIONS

| | |
|---|---|
| Admissions Rating | 73 |
| # of applicants | 585 |
| % of applicants accepted | 97 |
| % of acceptees attending | 71 |

### FRESHMAN PROFILE

| | |
|---|---|
| Range SAT Verbal | 490-590 |
| Average SAT Verbal | 532 |
| Range SAT Math | 480-620 |
| Average SAT Math | 552 |
| Range ACT Composite | 19-25 |
| Average ACT Composite | 22 |
| Minimum TOEFL | 525 |
| Average HS GPA | 3.5 |
| % graduated top 10% of class | 20 |
| % graduated top 25% of class | 47 |
| % graduated top 50% of class | 78 |

### DEADLINES

| | |
|---|---|
| Priority admission deadline | 3/1 |
| Nonfall registration? | yes |

### APPLICANTS ALSO LOOK AT
### AND SOMETIMES PREFER
U. Montana
Montana State—Bozeman
Colorado Mines
U. Washington
Western Montana
### AND RARELY PREFER
Carroll (MT)

## FINANCIAL FACTS

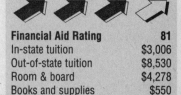

| | |
|---|---|
| Financial Aid Rating | 81 |
| In-state tuition | $3,006 |
| Out-of-state tuition | $8,530 |
| Room & board | $4,278 |
| Books and supplies | $550 |
| % frosh receiving aid | 44 |
| % undergrads receiving aid | 73 |
| Avg frosh grant | $1,000 |
| Avg frosh loan | $2,000 |

# MOREHOUSE COLLEGE

830 WESTVIEW DRIVE, SW, ATLANTA, GA 30314 • ADMISSIONS: 404-215-2632 • FAX: 404-524-5635

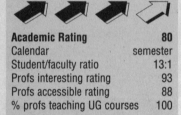
## STUDENTS SPEAK OUT

### Academics

Morehouse College is a star among the nation's historically black colleges and one of America's three remaining all-male institutions. The place is all about a tradition of excellence and commitment. To paraphrase one oft-expressed sentiment, "Give them a boy, they'll give you back a Morehouse man." Distinguished alumni run far and wide, including Dr. Martin Luther King, Jr., Julian Bond, Spike Lee, and Lerone Bennett, to name a few. Morehouse has been a continual source of leaders; half of all recent Morehouse graduates went on to pursue a graduate degree. The college "has excellent science, math, and business programs." Business and management, pre-medical sciences, engineering, and pre-law studies enroll well over half the students. A well-rounded liberal arts, sciences, and ethnic studies background is paramount within every major. Because Morehouse is a member of the Atlanta University Center, a consortium of six predominantly black schools, students have an even greater variety of course offerings to choose from. Students report that their professors are excellent teachers but do not always make themselves readily available outside the classroom. "This school requires a dedication on the part of the student in order to work closely with the faculty." "My overall academic experience is great because I have made it that way." Administrative chores can be difficult. One frustrated sophomore exclaims that "it seems as if the administrative faculty comes from Mars." While recognizing problems, students report satisfaction with Morehouse; the arrival of Dr. Massey as president has them even more pleased—he's been seen serving on the chow line in the cafeteria and eliminating a separate faculty dining room so that "professors now sit down and eat with us." Concludes one student, "There is a true spirit of pride that flows through here. The school's positive effects can be seen in the attitudes of students and faculty. This school teaches you to know yourself." Morehouse's endowment, nearly $95 million, is one of the largest among all such colleges and universities, and has enabled the school to make a $4.5 million investment in technology, wiring the entire campus with computer access to e-mail and the Internet. Next on tap is a new Leadership Development Center.

### Life

Atlanta consistently ranks among the most popular college towns in our annual surveys. It's chock-full of college students, and is a spring-break destination for those at HBCUs. Greek life is popular—although black Greek organizations have many of the same issues to deal with as other national frats do, they can also be very rewarding lifelong affiliations that facilitate career networking. Morehouse's participation in the Atlanta University Center is not solely academic; it gives students the opportunity for social interaction with coeds from Spelman and other member colleges. As a result, social life here is much more lively than at most single-sex institutions. The college's historic campus, while undergoing much needed renovations, still elicits the comment that "Morehouse is by no means a country club."

### Student Body

Morehouse draws students from all over the country. Outside the South, the Eastern Seaboard is the most prolific source of its undergrads. Students are politically progressive but also fairly religious, and therefore socially a little conservative. The typical Morehouse attitude is summed up by the student who writes, "Adversity builds character and the hotter the fire, the tougher the steel. If you come to Morehouse, you will either become a man or you will leave, plain and simple."

FINANCIAL AID: 404-681-2800 EXT. 2638 • E-MAIL: APATTILLO@MOREHOUSE.EDU • WEBSITE: WWW.MOREHOUSE.EDU

## ADMISSIONS

*Very important* academic and nonacademic factors considered by the admissions committee include recommendations, secondary school record, and standardized test scores. *Important* factors considered include character/personal qualities, essays, extracurricular activities, minority status, and talent/ability. *Other* factors considered include alumni/ae relation, class rank, interview, volunteer work, and work experience. Factors *not* considered include geography, religious affiliation/commitment, and state residency. SAT I or ACT required, SAT I preferred. TOEFL required of all international applicants. High school diploma is required and GED is accepted. *High school units required/recommended:* 16 total required; 4 English required, 3 math required, 2 science required, 2 foreign language recommended, 2 social studies required, 2 history recommended, 5 elective required, 5 elective recommended. *The admissions office says:* "Half of the college's current undergraduates (all four years) have graduated in the top 20 percent of their respective high school class."

### The Inside Word

Morehouse is one of the most selective historically black colleges in the country. Applicants should prepare themselves for a rigorous candidate review process. Much more than a solid academic profile is necessary to gain admission; expect to devote significant energy toward demonstrating that you make a good match with the college.

## FINANCIAL AID

*Students should submit:* FAFSA, institution's own financial aid form, and CSS/Financial Aid PROFILE. Regular filing deadline is April 1. The Princeton Review suggests that all financial aid forms be submitted as soon as possible after January 1. *Need-based scholarships/grants offered:* Pell, SEOG, state scholarships/grants, private scholarships, the school's own gift aid, and United Negro College Fund. *Loan aid offered:* Direct Subsidized Stafford, Direct Unsubsidized Stafford, Direct PLUS, Federal Perkins, and state. Institutional employment available. Federal Work-Study Program available. Off-campus job opportunities are good.

## FROM THE ADMISSIONS OFFICE

"Morehouse College is the nation's only predominantly black, all-male, four-year liberal arts college. It is an independent institution located on a 61-acre campus in Atlanta, Georgia. The college was founded in 1867 as the Augusta Institute in Augusta, Georgia. The college was relocated to Atlanta in 1879 as the Atlanta Baptist College and was renamed Morehouse College in 1913. Morehouse is committed to educating and developing strong black leaders who will be dedicated to addressing the problems of society. The Morehouse education is designed to serve the three basic aspects of a well-rounded man: the personal, the social, and the professional."

## ADMISSIONS

| | |
|---|---|
| Admissions Rating | 85 |
| # of applicants | 2,079 |
| % of applicants accepted | 75 |
| % of acceptees attending | 46 |

### FRESHMAN PROFILE

| | |
|---|---|
| Range SAT Verbal | 440-680 |
| Average SAT Verbal | 523 |
| Range SAT Math | 470-680 |
| Average SAT Math | 527 |
| Range ACT Composite | 19-32 |
| Average ACT Composite | 22 |
| Minimum TOEFL | 500 |
| Average HS GPA | 3.1 |
| % graduated top 10% of class | 42 |
| % graduated top 25% of class | 67 |
| % graduated top 50% of class | 99 |

### DEADLINES

| | |
|---|---|
| Early decision | 10/15 |
| Regular admission | 2/15 |
| Regular notification | 4/1 |

### APPLICANTS ALSO LOOK AT
**AND OFTEN PREFER**
Georgia Tech.
**AND SOMETIMES PREFER**
Fisk
Clark Atlanta
U. Maryland—Coll. Park
U. Georgia
Hampton
Howard
**AND RARELY PREFER**
Emory

### FINANCIAL FACTS

| | |
|---|---|
| Financial Aid Rating | 80 |
| Tuition | $9,510 |
| Room & board | $7,382 |
| Books and supplies | $750 |
| Required fees | $2,034 |

# MOUNT HOLYOKE COLLEGE

50 COLLEGE STREET, SOUTH HADLEY, MA 01075 • ADMISSIONS: 413-538-2023 • FAX: 413-538-2409

## CAMPUS LIFE

| Quality of Life Rating | 86 |
|---|---|
| Type of school | private |
| Affiliation | none |
| Environment | suburban |

### STUDENTS

| | |
|---|---|
| Total undergrad enrollment | 2,065 |
| % male/female | 0/100 |
| % from out of state | 74 |
| % from public high school | 64 |
| % live on campus | 92 |
| % African American | 5 |
| % Asian | 9 |
| % Caucasian | 64 |
| % Hispanic | 4 |
| % Native American | 1 |
| % international | 15 |
| # of countries represented | 74 |

### SURVEY SAYS . . .
*Political activism is hot*
*Student publications are popular*
*Student government is popular*
*Students aren't religious*
*Great library*
*Campus difficult to get around*
*Very little beer drinking*
*Musical organizations are hot*

## ACADEMICS

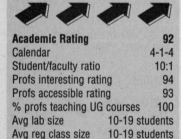

| Academic Rating | 92 |
|---|---|
| Calendar | 4-1-4 |
| Student/faculty ratio | 10:1 |
| Profs interesting rating | 94 |
| Profs accessible rating | 93 |
| % profs teaching UG courses | 100 |
| Avg lab size | 10-19 students |
| Avg reg class size | 10-19 students |

### MOST POPULAR MAJORS
biology
English
psychology

## STUDENTS SPEAK OUT
### Academics

Rigorous academics in a nurturing environment distinguish the Mount Holyoke undergraduate experience. As one student simply puts it, "Mount Holyoke is an extremely tough school. Students enrolled need to learn to separate their 'fun' time from their study time. If they do not, they will sink like rocks." Mount Holyoke demands a lot from its students, but the school also strives to ensure that undergrads have every chance to succeed. Explains one, "At times you feel like you are drowning in work. But there are plenty of lifeguards to help you. By the end of your first semester, not only are you learning to swim, but you're beginning to feel more confident in the water." "The courses are rigorous but not impossible," notes another. Easing the academic burden is a faculty that students universally praise. Writes one typical student, "The professors are unbelievable. I find out every day something new that they have done. They are the top of the line, the most accomplished and most understanding teachers I have ever had. They genuinely care about you and how you are doing, and will make sure that you are performing up to your potential." The administration, "although not as good as the professors, are helpful and cordial." Membership in the Five College Consortium, which also includes UMass—Amherst, Smith, Amherst, and Hampshire, provides access to top profs at other area schools. The MHC Honor Code, which every student signs during their first year and "which the campus takes very seriously," is another plus; it allows ample academic freedom, including "self-scheduled exams." About the only thing the students here really pine for is more "name recognition." As a biology major points out, "No one knows how cool we are."

### Life

Hard work means less play for the women of Mount Holyoke. "This is not the school for a stereotypical college social life," explains one undergrad. "However, if you enjoy Friday night study sessions, come on down." Adds another, "Unfortunately, although there are four other colleges in the area, it is very hard to find anything on the weekend besides the general frat parties of UMass and TAP (the Amherst party) at Amherst College." The administration, to its credit, works hard to provide activities such as "improv comedy, free dances, movie showings, and music performances." Students also point out that "if you can't find something to do on campus, hop on the free bus to the neighboring towns with diverse restaurants, fun shopping, and great bars/clubs. The school provides weekly transportation to the mall and the grocery store (one mile down the road)." But don't hang out in South Hadley. Cautions one undergrad, "Mount Holyoke College is located in a very small town called South Hadley, Massachusetts, which we refer to it as 'How Sadly.' The town hates us." Students conclude that "If you want a social life, you can get it. It's just a little more [of an] effort to find."

### Student Body

The typical Mount Holyoke woman, students report, "seems to be one that believes that she can single-handedly change the world. Most of the students are exceptionally friendly—many, however, are overly p.c." A large and vocal lesbian community makes Mount Holyoke home, prompting one student to write, "If you're gay, you've entered your heaven." Others add, "We have a few major subcultures, like the athletes, the party girls, the queer community, some religious groups, but most people have diverse groups of friends from all over campus. It is easy to make new friends in classes, in clubs, or over a meal in one of our cafeterias (there is one in every dorm). The friends you make here will last a good long time." Be forewarned, though. "There are a lot of opinionated women, which means that there tend to be arguments and debates in classes, in the dorms, in online forums, in the newspaper, etc."

FINANCIAL AID: 413-538-2291 • E-MAIL: ADMISSIONS@MTHOLYOKE.EDU • WEBSITE: WWW.MTHOLYOKE.EDU

## ADMISSIONS

*Very important* academic and nonacademic factors considered by the admissions committee include secondary school record and class rank. *Important* factors considered include character/personal qualities, essays, interview, recommendations, standardized test scores, and volunteer work. *Other* factors considered include alumni/ae relation, extracurricular activities, talent/ability, and work experience. Factors *not* considered include religious affiliation and state residency. SAT I or ACT considered if submitted. TOEFL required of all international applicants. High school diploma is required and GED is accepted. *High school units required/recommended:* 16 total recommended; 4 English recommended, 3 math recommended, 2 science recommended, 2 foreign language recommended, 5 elective recommended.

### The Inside Word

Mount Holyoke has benefited well from the renaissance of interest in women's colleges; selectivity and academic quality are on the rise. Considering that the college was already fairly selective, candidates are well advised to take the admissions process seriously. Matchmaking is a significant factor here; strong academic performance, well-written essays, and an understanding of and appreciation for "the Mount Holyoke experience" will usually carry the day.

## FINANCIAL AID

*Students should submit:* FAFSA, CSS/Financial Aid PROFILE, noncustodial (divorced/separated) parent's statement, business/farm supplement, and parents' and student's most recent tax returns. Regular filing deadline is January 15. The Princeton Review suggests that all financial aid forms be submitted as soon as possible after January 1. *Need-based scholarships/grants offered:* Pell, SEOG, state scholarships/grants, private scholarships, and the school's own gift aid. *Loan aid offered:* Direct Subsidized Stafford, Direct Unsubsidized Stafford, Direct PLUS, Federal Perkins, state, and college/university loans from institutional funds. Institutional employment available. Federal Work-Study Program available. Applicants will be notified of awards on or about April 1. Off-campus job opportunities are excellent.

## FROM THE ADMISSIONS OFFICE

"Did you know that the majority of students who choose Mount Holyoke do so in spite of the fact that it is a women's college? After a semester or two, however, they start to appreciate Mount Holyoke because it is a women's college. They talk about having 'space' to really figure out who they are. They speak of the absence of gender stereotypes, which empowers them to excel in traditionally male subjects, such as science and technology. They talk about the amazingly international community and the pervasive sense on campus that you can do absolutely anything. They talk about the remarkable array of opportunities—for academic achievement, career exploration, and leadership—and the impressive, creative accomplishments of their peers. If you're looking for a college that will challenge you to be your best, most powerful self and to fulfill potential, Mount Holyoke should be at the top of your list."

## ADMISSIONS

| | |
|---|---|
| Admissions Rating | 86 |
| # of applicants | 2,614 |
| % of applicants accepted | 55 |
| % of acceptees attending | 37 |
| # accepting a place on wait list | 174 |
| % admitted from wait list | 10 |
| # of early decision applicants | 212 |
| % accepted early decision | 74 |

### FRESHMAN PROFILE

| | |
|---|---|
| Range SAT Verbal | 600-700 |
| Average SAT Verbal | 647 |
| Range SAT Math | 570-660 |
| Average SAT Math | 612 |
| Range ACT Composite | 26-30 |
| Average ACT Composite | 27 |
| Minimum TOEFL | 600 |
| Average HS GPA | 3.9 |
| % graduated top 10% of class | 54 |
| % graduated top 25% of class | 83 |
| % graduated top 50% of class | 98 |

### DEADLINES

| | |
|---|---|
| Early decision | 11/15 |
| Early decision notification | 1/1 |
| Regular admission | 1/15 |
| Regular notification | 4/1 |

### APPLICANTS ALSO LOOK AT

**AND OFTEN PREFER**
Dartmouth
Bryn Mawr
Trinity Coll. (CT)

**AND SOMETIMES PREFER**
Wellesley
Smith
Vassar

**AND RARELY PREFER**
Skidmore
U. Mass—Amherst

### FINANCIAL FACTS

| | |
|---|---|
| Financial Aid Rating | 90 |
| Tuition | $26,250 |
| Room & board | $7,720 |
| Books and supplies | $1,500 |
| Required fees | $168 |
| % frosh receiving aid | 64 |
| % undergrads receiving aid | 72 |
| Avg frosh grant | $20,846 |
| Avg frosh loan | $4,330 |

# MUHLENBERG COLLEGE

2400 WEST CHEW STREET, ALLENTOWN, PA 18104-5596 • ADMISSIONS: 484-664-3200 • FAX: 484-664-3234

## CAMPUS LIFE

| Quality of Life Rating | 78 |
| --- | --- |
| Type of school | private |
| Affiliation | Lutheran |
| Environment | suburban |

### STUDENTS

| | |
| --- | --- |
| Total undergrad enrollment | 2,470 |
| % male/female | 42/58 |
| % from out of state | 67 |
| % from public high school | 70 |
| % live on campus | 94 |
| % in (# of) fraternities | 27 (5) |
| % in (# of) sororities | 27 (4) |
| % African American | 2 |
| % Asian | 3 |
| % Caucasian | 90 |
| % Hispanic | 2 |
| # of countries represented | 12 |

### SURVEY SAYS . . .

*Popular college radio*
*Frats and sororities dominate social scene*
*Student publications are popular*
*Students get along with local community*
*Lab facilities need improving*
*Campus difficult to get around*
*Library needs improving*
*Athletic facilities need improving*
*Diversity lacking on campus*

## ACADEMICS

| Academic Rating | 84 |
| --- | --- |
| Calendar | semester |
| Student/faculty ratio | 13:1 |
| Profs interesting rating | 85 |
| Profs accessible rating | 88 |
| % profs teaching UG courses | 100 |
| Avg lab size | 10-19 students |
| Avg reg class size | 10-19 students |

### MOST POPULAR MAJORS
business
psychology
biology

## STUDENTS SPEAK OUT
### Academics

The academics are at once "phenomenal" and "difficult" at Muhlenberg College, a fairly small liberal arts school in eastern Pennsylvania with a "comfortable feeling" and "a one-of-a-kind college experience." Besides rigorous major requirements, Muhlenberg students must also complete a battery of liberal arts–oriented requirements designed to guarantee a well-rounded, traditional education. "With the exception of a few bad apples (like any school)," Muhlenberg has "wickedly smart," "compassionate," and "extremely approachable" professors who are "very, very personable" and "understanding" about issues like "extensions, illness," and the like. "They love their jobs, which makes the learning experience enjoyable." Most of the "down-to-earth" faculty here is "even schooled in e-mail," which is "a rarity for a lot of adults," as a political science major observes. The "pompous, hypocritical" administration is composed of "fairly typical bureaucrats" who, although they "remember students' names and faces," are sometimes "anal" and too often "against fun." The availability of classes also leaves something to be desired and, "for as much money as this school has," claims a sophomore, "all of our facilities should be better." Nearly a tenth of all Muhlenberg College graduates proceed to medical school—thanks to a "well-respected" pre-med program—and Muhlenberg maintains "fine" programs in business and management and theater as well.

### Life

Muhlenberg students tell us that, for the most part, living in Allentown is pretty swell. There is a "great atmosphere" on the "beautiful campus," which is home to a wildlife preserve. Some students say there are hordes of activities as well. "The walls of the Union are constantly covered with advertisements for things to do," says one busy student. "They also have a shuttle running every half hour to the movies and malls on the weekends," and Muhlenberg regularly sponsors movies, comedians, and bands. Intramural and intercollegiate sports are also competitive and popular. "Sometimes I wish there was less going on during the weekends," admits a senior. "I'd get more work done and more sleep." Other students disagree. "It would be nice if there were more to do on campus on the weekends besides drinking, seeing three-month-old movies, or seeing some lame hypnotist," contends a first-year student. Another student suggests that "the administration tries to get students to attend nonalcoholic events, but everyone just goes out and gets wasted every weekend." Whatever the case, the Greek system is without a doubt the bedrock of Muhlenberg's "frat-dominated social life." The fraternities are "hopping" all weekend long, and freshmen and sophomores generally flock to them even though campus safety reportedly continues in its quest to "really crack down on the fun."

### Student Body

While "the minority population is slowly increasing," Muhlenberg is "not culturally diverse" and many of the happiest students here seem to fit a certain mold: white and from New Jersey. "Generally," these "very homogenous" students "are concerned with studying and having a good time on the weekends." Just about everyone is "welcoming," "social," and "very friendly," and the "honest, friendly, talented, and ambitious" students here promise that "you are guaranteed several smiles every time you walk down Academic Row." Many students involve themselves in community service activities, ranging from working with Muhlenberg's own Habitat for Humanity chapter to volunteering in local schools. Still, students here are often "blissfully ignorant." There is a large contingent of "Abercrombie models obsessed with alcohol and fraternities" who "get really dressed up on the weekends," and most students "wear the same clothes from the same expensive stores." Cautions a senior, "Life at the Berg is not a hippy's life." Finally, cliques are unavoidable at Muhlenberg. It's easy to "get stuck hanging out with the same people" for four years—not that there's anything wrong with that.

FINANCIAL AID: 484-664-3175 • E-MAIL: ADMISSION@MUHLENBERG.EDU • WEBSITE: WWW.MUHLENBERG.EDU

## ADMISSIONS

*Very important* academic and nonacademic factors considered by the admissions committee include secondary school record. *Important* factors considered include character/personal qualities, class rank, extracurricular activities, standardized test scores, talent/ability, volunteer work, and work experience. *Other* factors considered include alumni/ae relation, essays, geography, interview, and recommendations. Factors *not* considered include minority status, religious affiliation/commitment, and state residency. TOEFL required of all international applicants. High school diploma is required and GED is accepted. *High school units required/recommended:* 16 total required; 4 English required, 4 math required, 3 science required, 3 science lab required, 2 foreign language recommended, 2 social studies required, 2 history recommended, 3 elective required.

### The Inside Word

Muhlenberg's inquiries and applications continue to increase, which serves to reinforce its selectivity despite the relatively low yield of acceptees who enroll. Competition for students among small Pennsylvania liberal arts colleges is quite heated, and the college is among the more competitive of the lot.

## FINANCIAL AID

*Students should submit:* institution's own financial aid form and noncustodial (divorced/separated) parent's statement. Regular filing deadline is February 15. The Princeton Review suggests that all financial aid forms be submitted as soon as possible after January 1. *Need-based scholarships/grants offered:* Pell, SEOG, state scholarships/grants, private scholarships, and the school's own gift aid. *Loan aid offered:* FFEL Subsidized Stafford, FFEL Unsubsidized Stafford, FFEL PLUS, and Federal Perkins. Institutional employment available. Federal Work-Study Program available. Applicants will be notified of awards on or about April 1. Off-campus job opportunities are good.

## FROM THE ADMISSIONS OFFICE

"Listening to our own students, we've learned that most picked Muhlenberg mainly because it has a long-standing reputation for being academically demanding on one hand, but personally supportive on the other. We expect a lot from our students, but we also expect a lot from ourselves in providing the challenge and support they need to stretch, grow, and succeed. It's not unusual for professors to put their home phone numbers on the course syllabus and encourage students to call them at home with questions. Upperclassmen are helpful to underclassmen. 'We really know about collegiality here,' says an alumna who now works at Muhlenberg. 'It's that kind of place.' The supportive atmosphere and strong work ethic produce lots of successes. The pre-med and pre-law programs are very strong, as are programs in theater arts, English, psychology, the sciences, business, and accounting. 'When I was a student here,' recalls Dr. Walter Loy, now a professor emeritus of physics, 'we were encouraged to live life to its fullest, to do our best, to be honest, to deal openly with others, and to treat everyone as an individual. Those are important things, and they haven't changed at Muhlenberg.'"

## ADMISSIONS

| | |
|---|---|
| **Admissions Rating** | **82** |
| # of applicants | 3,501 |
| % of applicants accepted | 44 |
| % of acceptees attending | 37 |
| # accepting a place on wait list | 398 |
| % admitted from wait list | 2 |
| # of early decision applicants | 412 |
| % accepted early decision | 69 |

### FRESHMAN PROFILE

| | |
|---|---|
| Range SAT Verbal | 547-637 |
| Average SAT Verbal | 593 |
| Range SAT Math | 556-646 |
| Average SAT Math | 601 |
| Minimum TOEFL | 550 |
| Average HS GPA | 3.7 |
| % graduated top 10% of class | 37 |
| % graduated top 25% of class | 74 |
| % graduated top 50% of class | 96 |

### DEADLINES

| | |
|---|---|
| Early decision | 1/15 |
| Early decision notification | 2/1 |
| Regular admission | 2/15 |
| Regular notification | 3/15 |
| Nonfall registration? | yes |

### APPLICANTS ALSO LOOK AT
**AND OFTEN PREFER**
Skidmore
Lafayette
Lehigh
**AND SOMETIMES PREFER**
Franklin & Marshall
Bucknell
Gettysburg
Dickinson
Villanova
**AND RARELY PREFER**
Penn State—Univ. Park
Susquehanna

## FINANCIAL FACTS

| | |
|---|---|
| **Financial Aid Rating** | **81** |
| Tuition | $20,865 |
| Room & board | $5,650 |
| Books and supplies | $600 |
| Required fees | $185 |
| % frosh receiving aid | 56 |
| Avg frosh grant | $10,598 |
| Avg frosh loan | $2,990 |

# NEW COLLEGE OF THE UNIVERSITY OF SOUTH FLORIDA

5700 NORTH TAMIAMI TRAIL, SARASOTA, FL 34243-2197 • ADMISSIONS: 941-359-4269 • FAX: 941-359-4435

## CAMPUS LIFE

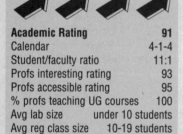

| | |
|---|---|
| **Quality of Life Rating** | **77** |
| Type of school | public |
| Affiliation | none |
| Environment | rural |

### STUDENTS

| | |
|---|---|
| Total undergrad enrollment | 649 |
| % male/female | 37/63 |
| % from out of state | 30 |
| % from public high school | 83 |
| % live on campus | 69 |
| % African American | 3 |
| % Asian | 3 |
| % Caucasian | 85 |
| % Hispanic | 6 |
| % international | 2 |

### SURVEY SAYS . . .

Theater is hot
Political activism is hot
No one cheats
Diversity lacking on campus
Registration is a breeze
No one plays intramural sports
Computer facilities need improving

## ACADEMICS

| | |
|---|---|
| **Academic Rating** | **91** |
| Calendar | 4-1-4 |
| Student/faculty ratio | 11:1 |
| Profs interesting rating | 93 |
| Profs accessible rating | 95 |
| % profs teaching UG courses | 100 |
| Avg lab size | under 10 students |
| Avg reg class size | 10-19 students |

### MOST POPULAR MAJORS

social sciences/history
biology
psychology

## STUDENTS SPEAK OUT

### Academics

For those capable of handling an unusual degree of academic freedom, tiny New College offers the opportunity for a private-school education at a public-school price. Central to the New College experience is the "contract" system, under which "each student receives a written evaluation, along with a pass/fail specification at the end of the semester." While the contract system prevents "grade-grubbing competition" and "encourages learning and experimentation," it's definitely not for everyone. The academic environment is largely "devoid of structure" and self-motivation is crucial—along with the flexibility come high expectations and rigorous workloads. Advocates report that "it's all about doing what you want when you want to do it. If a course is not offered in something you are interested in, you can design your own course. Professors will accommodate you and do anything to help you get the most out of a course." Others warn that you must "make sure you like the contract system. You have to be able to deal with very little direction, even in the more traditional classes." The size of the program presents a further obstacle to some students. Writes one, "Course selection is very slim. Make sure the faculty has similar interests to what you want to do or else you won't learn anything." Others, however, feel that "the personal attention available here more than makes up for the limited classes and resources." They also report a vibrant, genial classroom atmosphere, telling us that "the class discussions are just that—discussions—and since we don't require core curricula, you know that all the students are there because they choose to be. It makes a wonderful difference in classroom atmosphere." Students concur that the faculty is outstanding, "extremely dedicated, and accessible."

### Life

Despite their school's connection to the University of South Florida, New College students tend to keep to themselves, interacting rarely with USF students or the "mostly elderly" residents of surrounding Sarasota. New College lacks most of the trappings of conventional college life, a fact its students appreciate. "No frats, no football, and none of the BS that you normally associate with most big universities," reports one student approvingly. To fill the social void, "New College has a variety of good parties—the Queer Formal, the Fetish Ball, the Halloween Palm Court party, and Walls ["freeform, free-for-all parties" outdoors] every weekend. It's so small that everyone knows each other, and everyone goes to every party. It's sort of nice and sort of incestuous." Students also enjoy recreations on a smaller scale; writes one, "New College is full of people who love to talk about anything. It is not unusual to wander around campus at 2 A.M. and find discussions on research ethics, the latest movies, and ancient civilizations." Outdoor activities such as "camping, hiking, and mountain biking are popular" and are facilitated by the "gorgeous" surroundings. Explains one undergrad, "The campus is beautiful. Sunsets over the bay are postcard-quality every night. The beaches are lovely." As an added bonus, "Local international cuisine is exquisite."

### Student Body

New College students pride themselves on their nonconformity, describing the campus as "a tiny utopia for leftists, liberals, gays, hippies, punks, radical self-educators, pagans, and other weirdoes who care about learning a lot in a friendly place." Jokes one, "We are weird and that is good. Just don't be normal and you'll be OK." The student body is typical in at least one respect: "There is really not that much diversity on campus. Just about everyone is white and hyper-liberal from sheltered suburban communities." A sizable contingent "do a lot of drugs, mon," but "contrary to popular belief, this is NOT a school full of drug-addicted hippies and freaks." On the downside, students "tend to take themselves too seriously. Everybody thinks they're a revolutionary or something."

# NEW COLLEGE OF THE UNIVERSITY OF SOUTH FLORIDA

FINANCIAL AID: 941-359-4255 • E-MAIL: NCADMISSONS@SAR.USF.EDU • WEBSITE: WWW.NEWCOLLEGE.USF.EDU

## ADMISSIONS

*Very important* academic and nonacademic factors considered by the admissions committee include essays and secondary school record. *Important* factors considered include character/personal qualities, recommendations, and standardized test scores. *Other* factors considered include alumni/ae relation, class rank, extracurricular activities, geography, interview, minority status, state residency, talent/ability, volunteer work, and work experience. Factors *not* considered include religious affiliation/commitment. SAT I or ACT required. TOEFL required of all international applicants. High school diploma is required and GED is accepted. *High school units required/recommended:* 19 total required; 4 English required, 3 math required, 3 science required, 2 science lab required, 2 foreign language required, 2 social studies required, 1 history required, 4 elective required. *The admissions office says:* "Decisions are made on a rolling basis beginning in September."

### The Inside Word

Applications keep rolling in to New College like the evening tide on Sarasota Bay. Increases in the academic quality of entering students are virtually perpetual, as is recognition by the media. Perhaps the biggest drawback is a high attrition rate for a college of this caliber—just as the admissions committee strives to choose wisely, so should prospective students. Don't apply simply because it's a great buy; make sure that it's what you're seeking. In order to be successful, candidates must demonstrate a high level of intellectual curiosity, self-awareness, and maturity. It also helps to be a strong writer, given that the application process requires candidates to submit three short essays, a long essay, and a graded paper from school. Did we forget to mention high grades and test scores? They'll help, too, but if you're someone with lots of "potential" as opposed to "credentials," the admissions committee might still vote you in provided you've put together some very convincing evidence that you make a match and deserve a shot.

## FINANCIAL AID

*Students should submit:* FAFSA. The Princeton Review suggests that all financial aid forms be submitted as soon as possible after January 1. *Need-based scholarships/grants offered:* Pell, SEOG, state scholarships/grants, and the school's own gift aid. *Loan aid offered:* FFEL Subsidized Stafford, FFEL Unsubsidized Stafford, FFEL PLUS, Federal Perkins, and college/university loans from institutional funds. Institutional employment available. Federal Work-Study Program available. Applicants will be notified of awards on a rolling basis. Off-campus job opportunities are excellent.

## FROM THE ADMISSIONS OFFICE

"New College provides the opportunity to obtain a very high-quality education at a low state tuition. Students work in close consultation with faculty to develop individualized programs of seminars, tutorials, independent research, and off-campus experiences. The student who will do best at New College is one who is independent, broad-minded, self-confident, and capable of rigorous academic work. The very nature of New College requires one to be dedicated to education and the pursuit of individual growth."

### ADMISSIONS

| | |
|---|---|
| Admissions Rating | 95 |
| # of applicants | 405 |
| % of applicants accepted | 70 |
| % of acceptees attending | 57 |
| # accepting a place on wait list | 21 |
| % admitted from wait list | 29 |

**FRESHMAN PROFILE**

| | |
|---|---|
| Range SAT Verbal | 630-720 |
| Average SAT Verbal | 676 |
| Range SAT Math | 590-670 |
| Average SAT Math | 632 |
| Range ACT Composite | 26-30 |
| Average ACT Composite | 28 |
| Minimum TOEFL | 560 |
| Average HS GPA | 3.9 |
| % graduated top 10% of class | 57 |
| % graduated top 25% of class | 87 |
| % graduated top 50% of class | 98 |

**DEADLINES**

| | |
|---|---|
| Priority admission deadline | 2/1 |
| Regular admission | 5/1 |

**APPLICANTS ALSO LOOK AT
AND OFTEN PREFER**
Emory
Oberlin
Brown
U. Florida
**AND SOMETIMES PREFER**
Rice
UC—Santa Cruz
**AND RARELY PREFER**
Evergreen State
Eckerd
Florida State
Grinnell
Antioch

### FINANCIAL FACTS

| | |
|---|---|
| Financial Aid Rating | 79 |
| In-state tuition | $2,663 |
| Out-of-state tuition | $11,464 |
| Room & board | $4,877 |
| Books and supplies | $700 |
| % frosh receiving aid | 51 |
| % undergrads receiving aid | 36 |
| Avg frosh grant | $8,119 |
| Avg frosh loan | $4,054 |

# NEW JERSEY INSTITUTE OF TECHNOLOGY

UNIVERSITY HEIGHTS, NEWARK, NJ 07102 • ADMISSIONS: 973-596-3300 • FAX: 973-596-3461

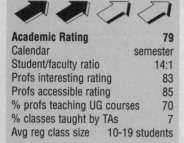

## CAMPUS LIFE

| | |
|---|---|
| **Quality of Life Rating** | **62** |
| Type of school | public |
| Affiliation | none |
| Environment | urban |

### STUDENTS

| | |
|---|---|
| Total undergrad enrollment | 5,639 |
| % male/female | 77/23 |
| % from out of state | 7 |
| % from public high school | 80 |
| % live on campus | 50 |
| % in (# of) fraternities | 7 (19) |
| % in (# of) sororities | 5 (8) |
| % African American | 13 |
| % Asian | 24 |
| % Caucasian | 38 |
| % Hispanic | 13 |
| % international | 6 |

### SURVEY SAYS . . .
Musical organizations aren't
popular
Popular college radio
High cost of living
Very little drug use
Unattractive campus
Very little beer drinking
Very little hard liquor

## ACADEMICS

| | |
|---|---|
| **Academic Rating** | **79** |
| Calendar | semester |
| Student/faculty ratio | 14:1 |
| Profs interesting rating | 83 |
| Profs accessible rating | 85 |
| % profs teaching UG courses | 70 |
| % classes taught by TAs | 7 |
| Avg reg class size | 10-19 students |

### MOST POPULAR MAJORS
computer science
computer engineering
architecture

## STUDENTS SPEAK OUT
### Academics
Those looking for "great 'bang for the buck'" in the world of engineering would do well to consider the New Jersey Institute of Technology. While the school also maintains divisions of architecture, management, and arts and sciences, the low-cost, high-return College of Engineering is the undisputed star of the show. According to NJIT, graduates make up one-fourth of all engineers currently working in the Garden State. Important to note, the university is opening the College of Computing Sciences in fall 2001. Students warn "this school is easy to get into, but when it comes to sticking through it and getting a degree from here, life is 'hell.' The professors love to challenge you, and I can say that when I graduate I know I am going to be very well off." NJIT's curriculum is "extremely vigorous and challenging" and "helps provide you with the proper learning skills that are needed in order for you to make it in the world." Professors receive mixed reviews; some "go above and beyond for 'positive and eager-to-learn' students," while others "tend to read from slides instead of using them as aids" and "are rarely available beyond class hours." The administration "is slow to enact changes desired by students" and could use more "financial advisors and otherwise more help for registration, particularly for freshmen!" Students also gripe about the condition of lecture halls, dorms, and other facilities. Even so, most agree that the NJIT experience is an enriching one. Writes one, "It feels like you're in the United Nations school, as there are so many international students and professors. Great cultural experience if nothing else; sometimes, though, it makes it hard to understand what's going on."

### Life
Hmm . . . a tech school in Newark, New Jersey. Not exactly the formula for a swinging campus, you have to admit. NJIT has other hurdles to overcome as well. As one student explains, "Because we are so diverse and a large percentage of our students are commuters, it is really hard to form any kind of school unity, whether it be in clubs, student government, or athletics." All the same, "While our school is extremely technology-oriented, we do know how to have fun, regardless of how busy we are." As for NJIT's reputation as a dead campus, several students note that "contrary to popular belief, there is plenty to do on campus. More often than not, it is the lack of student participation that creates the perception of a nonexistent social life on campus." Many students report participating in such sports as bowling, swimming, volleyball, lifting weights, and track and field, while some insist that "pool is the biggest 'sport' on campus. Everyone owns a pool cue." Downtown Newark is enjoying a renaissance with the recent addition of a new performing arts center that draws major international artists in music, dance, and theater. And of course, New York City is only a PATH train ride away.

### Student Body
NJIT boasts "good ethnic diversity and individual acceptance," and although "students tend to self-segregate into ethnic/gender/major-related groups," most agree that the atmosphere here is congenial. Writes one student, "I actually often brag about how friendly our campus is. Maybe that's just reflecting the desperation of the male population in [light of] the male-female ratio of 10:1." Students wish there "was more interaction between residents and commuters." Commuters "often come to class and just leave. It's hard to meet non-dormers."

# NEW JERSEY INSTITUTE OF TECHNOLOGY

FINANCIAL AID: 973-596-3480 • E-MAIL: ADMISSIONS@NJIT.EDU • WEBSITE: WWW.NJIT.EDU

## ADMISSIONS

*Very important* academic and nonacademic factors considered by the admissions committee include class rank, secondary school record, and standardized test scores. *Other* factors considered include character/personal qualities, essays, extracurricular activities, interview, recommendations, talent/ability, volunteer work, and work experience. Factors *not* considered include alumni/ae relation, geography, minority status, religious affiliation/commitment, and state residency. SAT I or ACT required, SAT I preferred. TOEFL required of all international applicants. High school diploma is required and GED is accepted. *High school units required/recommended:* 19 total recommended; 4 English recommended, 4 math recommended, 2 science recommended, 2 science lab recommended, 2 foreign language recommended, 3 social studies recommended, 1 history recommended, 3 elective recommended. *The admissions office says:* "Management applicants and Science Technology and Society applicants are required to take only 3 years of mathematics."

### The Inside Word

NJIT is a great choice for students who aspire to technical careers but don't meet the requirements for better known and more selective universities. To top it off, it's a pretty good buy.

## FINANCIAL AID

The Princeton Review suggests that all financial aid forms be submitted as soon as possible after January 1. *Need-based scholarships/grants offered:* Pell, SEOG, state scholarships/grants, private scholarships, and the school's own gift aid. *Loan aid offered:* Direct Subsidized Stafford, Direct Unsubsidized Stafford, Direct PLUS, FFEL Subsidized Stafford, FFEL Unsubsidized Stafford, FFEL PLUS, Federal Perkins, state, and college/university loans from institutional funds. Institutional employment available. Federal Work-Study Program available. Off-campus job opportunities are good.

## FROM THE ADMISSIONS OFFICE

"Talented high school graduates from across the nation come to NJIT to prepare for leadership roles in architecture, business, engineering, medical, legal, science, and technological fields. Students experience a public research university conducting over $43 million in research that maintains a small-college atmosphere at a modest cost. Our attractive 48-acre campus is just minutes from New York City and less than an hour from the Jersey shore. Students find an outstanding faculty and a safe, diverse, caring learning and residential community. All dormitory rooms have sprinklers. NJIT's academic environment challenges and prepares students for rewarding careers and full-time advanced study after graduation. The campus is computing-intensive and all full-time freshmen are given a personal computer for use in their studies. For three consecutive years, *Yahoo! Internet Life* has ranked NJIT as America's Most Wired Public University. No other college or university in the nation has ranked in Yahoo!'s top five in each of the last three years."

## ADMISSIONS

| | |
|---|---|
| Admissions Rating | 80 |
| # of applicants | 2,420 |
| % of applicants accepted | 62 |
| % of acceptees attending | 47 |

### FRESHMAN PROFILE

| | |
|---|---|
| Range SAT Verbal | 480-580 |
| Average SAT Verbal | 534 |
| Range SAT Math | 550-650 |
| Average SAT Math | 600 |
| Minimum TOEFL | 550 |
| % graduated top 10% of class | 22 |
| % graduated top 25% of class | 54 |
| % graduated top 50% of class | 85 |

### DEADLINES

| | |
|---|---|
| Priority admission deadline | 4/1 |
| Nonfall registration? | yes |

### APPLICANTS ALSO LOOK AT AND OFTEN PREFER
Rutgers U.
Coll. of NJ
Stevens Tech

### AND SOMETIMES PREFER
Worcester Poly.
Montclair State
Penn State—Univ. Park
Virginia Tech

## FINANCIAL FACTS

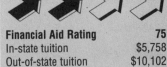

| | |
|---|---|
| Financial Aid Rating | 75 |
| In-state tuition | $5,758 |
| Out-of-state tuition | $10,102 |
| Room & board | $7,500 |
| Books and supplies | $900 |
| Required fees | $972 |
| % frosh receiving aid | 64 |
| % undergrads receiving aid | 60 |
| Avg frosh grant | $4,400 |
| Avg frosh loan | $2,500 |

# NEW MEXICO INSTITUTE OF MINING & TECHNOLOGY

CAMPUS STATION, 801 LEROY PLACE, SOCORRO, NM 87801 • ADMISSIONS: 505-835-5424 • FAX: 505-835-5989

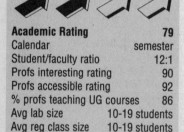
## STUDENTS SPEAK OUT

### Academics

New Mexico Tech, as this "very affordable" state university is commonly called, is "a great research school" with "tremendous research opportunities for undergraduates," "difficult courses," "small classes," and a "good reputation for academics." Although "the liberal arts program is weak," the "cutting edge" engineering programs offer "a rewarding experience for those willing to work hard." NMT's "extremely intelligent" professors are a mixed bag. "Some are vicious jerks" who "just give assignments" and are "busy with their own research." Others "are very kind" and "dedicated" souls who "challenge your ability to think concretely as well as abstractly" and offer "lots of personal attention." As at many engineering school across the country, the profs "wear jeans and T-shirts" but "their teaching skills could use some work." The graduate assistants here are "very helpful and supportive," even "better than the professors" at times. Although the "grading policies are fair" at NMT, good grades are hard to come by; "a 2.5 GPA is nothing to be shocked at" and "a 3.0 will get you a job anywhere" because, students say, companies understand just how hard it is to do well here. Still, "only the dedicated make it through," as is evidenced by the high dropout rate. Students say "the sheer smallness of the school makes the red tape much more manageable than it might otherwise be." Unfortunately, though, registration is a colossal pain. Students suggest that it "would be easier if done over the Internet to avoid long lines." On the plus side, "financial aid is great," according to a satisfied Washington State native. "It was cheaper for me to come here than to go to a state school."

### Life

"Fairly dull" Socorro is a "small town in the middle of the desert." It offers "serenity" and a "quiet, relaxed place to learn," but little else. Luckily, "studying is a major part of college life" in this occasionally "stressful" environment because "School is The Most Important Thing." During the "small amount of free time" they are able to carve out each day, many NMT students are "dorm dwellers" who "play on their computers 24/7" and "emerge only to eat." Speaking of eating, despite the administration's best efforts, several students continue to tell us that "the food sucks" at NMT. For activities away from dorms and cafeterias, "camping, mountain biking, [and] caving" as well as "Frisbee, racquetball," and "stargazing" are common diversions. Paintball is also very popular, and "rugby provides a good release for those who are athletically inclined." For those who are not athletically inclined, "Dungeons and Dragons is a popular weekend pastime." Other students snowboard and climb in the nearby mountains, and many "sleep for fun." While students here do manage to amuse themselves when they aren't cracking the books, drinking is not a big deal here. NMT "is definitely not one of the top ten party schools." There "are parties," swears a sophomore; "you just have to look for them." Students highly recommend that you bring your car here, "to get a glimpse of civilization in Albuquerque and other such places."

### Student Body

Let's face it: This is a technical school. There are few women and many men, and the "brainy," "weird," sometimes "pretentious" students here spend a significant amount of time studying. "If you want to feel like you are not a nerd compared to your peers, this is the place," suggests a first-year student. Many of the "pretty friendly" NMT students are "shy and insecure" "loners" who are "afraid to make eye contact," at least at first glance. But "once you get to know them," New Mexico Tech students are "outspoken and funny." This "diverse group of American misfits and foreigners" is also "open-minded, accepting, unique" and, though "laid back," "very motivated to succeed." A sophomore brags that "half the students here could rob Fort Knox without leaving their dorm rooms," and students often "blow stuff up and sneak around causing mischief." Also, thanks to the stress and their own free spirits, "most skip class once in a while."

FINANCIAL AID: 505-835-5333 • E-MAIL: ADMISSION@ADMIN.NMT.EDU • WEBSITE: WWW.NMT.EDU

## ADMISSIONS

*Very important* academic and nonacademic factors considered by the admissions committee include character/personal qualities, essays, extracurricular activities, minority status, recommendations, secondary school record, talent/ability, and volunteer work. *Important* factors considered include class rank, geography, interview, standardized test scores, and work experience. *Other* factors considered include alumni/ae relation. Factors *not* considered include religious affiliation/commitment and state residency. SAT I or ACT required, ACT preferred. TOEFL required of all international applicants. High school diploma is required and GED is accepted. *High school units required/recommended:* 19 total recommended; 4 English recommended, 4 math recommended, 4 science recommended, 2 foreign language recommended, 3 social studies recommended.

### The Inside Word

A 2.5 GPA and a 21 ACT score is far from stringent. This is one of those situations that call for serious self-examination. Are you really ready to take on the demands of a fairly solid technical institute? If you aren't sure, you should probably pass, even if you're admissible.

## FINANCIAL AID

*Students should submit:* FAFSA and institution's own financial aid form. The Princeton Review suggests that all financial aid forms be submitted as soon as possible after January 1. *Need-based scholarships/grants offered:* Pell, SEOG, state scholarships/grants, private scholarships, and the school's own gift aid. *Loan aid offered:* Direct Subsidized Stafford, Direct Unsubsidized Stafford, Direct PLUS, Federal Perkins, state, and college/university loans from institutional funds. Institutional employment available. Federal Work-Study Program available. Applicants will be notified of awards on a rolling basis beginning on or about April 1. Off-campus job opportunities are fair.

## FROM THE ADMISSIONS OFFICE

"Over a century old, Tech has internationally known programs in the areas of physics, geology, hydrology, and explosives research. At New Mexico Tech, we pride ourselves on the high quality of education we give to our students, in small classes where the professor will know you personally and take the time to help you. New Mexico Tech is also the parent body of several research organizations. These organizations and the many faculty research projects offer students the opportunity for hands-on research work. Many professors have research projects that students work on. Lanngmuir Laboratory for Atmospheric Research, for example, is one of the nation's foremost research organizations for areas such as the physics of clouds and thunderstorms and electrification of clouds. The lab often employs physics majors. The average Tech undergraduate graduating with a BS degree has the equivalent of seven months of full-time technical job experience. That's important when you're looking for a job."

## ADMISSIONS

| | |
|---|---|
| Admissions Rating | 81 |
| # of applicants | 963 |
| % of applicants accepted | 68 |
| % of acceptees attending | 39 |

### FRESHMAN PROFILE

| | |
|---|---|
| Average SAT Verbal | 587 |
| Average SAT Math | 620 |
| Range ACT Composite | 23-29 |
| Average ACT Composite | 26 |
| Minimum TOEFL | 540 |
| Average HS GPA | 3.6 |
| % graduated top 10% of class | 41 |
| % graduated top 25% of class | 74 |
| % graduated top 50% of class | 91 |

### DEADLINES

| | |
|---|---|
| Priority admission deadline | 3/1 |
| Regular admission | 8/1 |
| Regular notification | rolling |
| Nonfall registration? | yes |

### APPLICANTS ALSO LOOK AT AND SOMETIMES PREFER

MIT
Colorado Mines
U. New Mexico

### AND RARELY PREFER

New Mexico State

## FINANCIAL FACTS

| | |
|---|---|
| Financial Aid Rating | 86 |
| In-state tuition | $1,704 |
| Out-of-state tuition | $7,030 |
| Room & board | $3,704 |
| Books and supplies | $700 |
| Required fees | $795 |
| % frosh receiving aid | 48 |
| % undergrads receiving aid | 54 |
| Avg frosh grant | $4,600 |
| Avg frosh loan | $2,412 |

# NEW YORK UNIVERSITY

22 WASHINGTON SQUARE NORTH, NEW YORK, NY 10011 • ADMISSIONS: 212-998-4500 • FAX: 212-995-4902

## CAMPUS LIFE

| | |
|---|---|
| **Quality of Life Rating** | **88** |
| Type of school | private |
| Affiliation | none |
| Environment | urban |

### STUDENTS

| | |
|---|---|
| Total undergrad enrollment | 18,628 |
| % male/female | 40/60 |
| % from out of state | 49 |
| % from public high school | 72 |
| % live on campus | 50 |
| % in (# of) fraternities | 4 (14) |
| % in (# of) sororities | 2 (12) |
| % African American | 7 |
| % Asian | 15 |
| % Caucasian | 40 |
| % Hispanic | 7 |
| % international | 5 |
| # of countries represented | 120 |

### SURVEY SAYS . . .

*Great off-campus food*
*Students love New York, NY*
*Campus feels safe*
*Great library*
*Campus easy to get around*
*Intercollegiate sports unpopular or*
*nonexistent*
*Very small frat/sorority scene*
*No one plays intramural sports*

## ACADEMICS

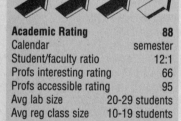

| | |
|---|---|
| **Academic Rating** | **88** |
| Calendar | semester |
| Student/faculty ratio | 12:1 |
| Profs interesting rating | 66 |
| Profs accessible rating | 95 |
| Avg lab size | 20-29 students |
| Avg reg class size | 10-19 students |

### MOST POPULAR MAJORS
business finance
individualized studies
theatre

## STUDENTS SPEAK OUT

### Academics

Most colleges would be honored to have a single world-renowned academic department. Then again, most aren't New York University. The programs at NYU's Stern School of Business and the Tisch School of the Arts are among the best undergraduate programs in the country. NYU professors are "very intelligent, informed, and open-minded." They are both "witty" and "well-prepared" and, considering that many of them live in the city, "tend to be very accessible," though some students complain that, because of the university's size, profs occasionally get "lost in the crowd." Explains one student, "They are helpful in guiding students . . . to careers, internships, grad school programs, good restaurants, movies, hairdressers, and all the best deals that New York City has to offer." Undergrads also appreciate the fact that professors are often the authors of the textbooks used in class. A senior broadcast journalism major writes that though he harbors "a lifelong hatred towards school and education, I've enjoyed learning here." Students not interested in an academic culture need not apply since, according to one junior, "as a freshman, I began doing work people don't touch until grad school." Students get practice as the vociferous liberals they are when dealing with the administration, as they must be "persistent and demanding" in order to get things done. Students rave about online registration, though some complain that upper-level classes close too quickly, "often with the speed of Japan's bullet train."

### Life

"What do we do for fun?" a senior theater major asks. "We do New York." While studies are undeniably important, NYU is located in the heart of downtown Manhattan's Greenwich Village, within shouting distance of hundreds of restaurants, theaters, clubs, and other cultural opportunities. Guess what that means. "Life here is never dull or routine," a junior politics major writes, and "no student can say that she is bored." Students who wish to commune with nature spend time bike riding or inline skating in Central Park. Sports fans not only attend college basketball games on campus (the university's Division III women's basketball team is among the best in the nation), but can also choose from any of the city's professional baseball, basketball, football, and hockey teams. Numerous museums and theaters provide more cultural stimulation than a student can possibly absorb in four years. The city's extensive concert scene assures that both local and national acts can be found somewhere every night of the year. Though there are plenty of on-campus activities, students downplay their importance because of the numerous off-campus opportunities. The lack of a defined campus allows the school to become a part of the city, which, in turn, allows students to smoothly coexist with fellow city dwellers. The tension between towns and campuses that are evident at other universities are nowhere to be found at NYU. While on-campus housing is expensive, the "apartment-style dorms" are often looked upon wistfully by those who end up in almost-as-costly off-campus housing.

### Student Body

New York is one of the most diverse cities in the world and that doesn't exclude the student body of NYU. "Everyone here is very unique—some you love, some you hate." Students are individualistic and passionate, "but somehow this manages to bond us all," and students create close friendships, writes one senior musical theater. "People are cool and unique," adds a sophomore. Students are "tolerant and open-minded" and develop neighborly relationships. Students see their peers as adventurous and focused, which "makes for some really interesting people." A junior English major advises, "If you're looking for an accepting community, this is it." If students have any complaints, it is that their peers are sometimes apathetic about campus life, and "as a result, school spirit is negligible." Still, it's unlikely that anyone looking for a diverse educational experience will easily find one that surpasses the one found at NYU.

FINANCIAL AID: 212-998-4444 • E-MAIL: ADMISSIONS@NYU.EDU • WEBSITE: WWW.NYU.EDU

## ADMISSIONS

*Very important* academic and nonacademic factors considered by the admissions committee include standardized test scores and secondary school record. *Important* factors considered include class rank, recommendations. *Other* factors considered include alumni/ae relation, character/personal qualities, essays, extracurricular activities, interview, minority status, talent/ability, volunteer work, and work experience. Factors *not* considered include geography, religious affiliation/commitment, and state residency. SAT I or ACT required, SAT II recommended. TOEFL required of all international applicants. High school diploma is required and GED is accepted. *High school units required/recommended:* 16 total recommended; 4 English recommended, 3 math recommended, 1 science recommended, 1 science lab recommended, 3 foreign language recommended, 1 history recommended, 4 elective recommended.

### The Inside Word

NYU is more selective than most large private universities but, except for a few particularly choosy programs, no more personal in its evaluation of candidates. A solid GPA and test scores go further toward getting in than anything else. Still, the university is very serious about projecting a highly selective image and it's dangerous to take your application too lightly. Since the completion of several major dormitories in the late 1980s, NYU has turned its attention to increasing the national profile of its student body. Applications have increased by more than half over the past four years.

## FINANCIAL AID

*Students should submit:* FAFSA and state aid form. Regular filing deadline is February 15. The Princeton Review suggests that all financial aid forms be submitted as soon as possible after January 1. *Need-based scholarships/grants offered:* Pell, SEOG, state scholarships/grants, private scholarships, the school's own gift aid, and Federal Nursing. *Loan aid offered:* FFEL Subsidized Stafford, FFEL Unsubsidized Stafford, FFEL PLUS, Federal Perkins, and Federal Nursing. Institutional employment available. Federal Work-Study Program available. Applicants will be notified of awards on a rolling basis beginning on or about April 1. Off-campus job opportunities are excellent.

## FROM THE ADMISSIONS OFFICE

"NYU is distinctive both in the quality of education we provide and in the exhilarating atmosphere in which our students study and learn. As an undergraduate in one of our seven small- to medium-size colleges, you will enjoy a small faculty/student ratio and a dynamic, challenging learning environment that encourages lively interaction between students and professors. At the same time, you will have available to you all the resources of a distinguished university dedicated to research and scholarship at the highest levels, including a curriculum that offers over 2,500 courses and 160 programs of study and a faculty that includes some of the most highly regarded scholars, scientists, and artists in the country. New York University is a vital, vibrant community. There is an aura of energy and excitement here, a sense that possibilities and opportunities are limited only by the number of hours in a day. The educational experience at NYU is intense, but varied and richly satisfying. You will be actively engaged in your own education, both in the classroom and beyond."

## ADMISSIONS

| | |
|---|---|
| Admissions Rating | 89 |
| # of applicants | 30,857 |
| % of applicants accepted | 29 |
| % of acceptees attending | 40 |
| # accepting a place on wait list | 628 |
| % admitted from wait list | 2 |
| # of early decision applicants | 2718 |
| % accepted early decision | 31 |

### FRESHMAN PROFILE

| | |
|---|---|
| Range SAT Verbal | 620-710 |
| Average SAT Verbal | 667 |
| Range SAT Math | 630-710 |
| Average SAT Math | 667 |
| Range ACT Composite | 27-31 |
| Minimum TOEFL | 600 |
| Average HS GPA | 3.6 |
| % graduated top 10% of class | 70 |
| % graduated top 25% of class | 93 |
| % graduated top 50% of class | 100 |

### DEADLINES

| | |
|---|---|
| Early decision | 11/15 |
| ED notification | 12/15-1/15 |
| Regular admission | 1/15 |
| Regular notification | 4/1 |
| Nonfall registration? | yes |

### APPLICANTS ALSO LOOK AT

**AND OFTEN PREFER**
Columbia
Barnard, U. Penn
Cornell U., Boston U.

**AND SOMETIMES PREFER**
UCLA
UC—Berkeley
U. Michigan
U. Chicago, Yale

**AND RARELY PREFER**
Hofstra, Rutgers U.

### FINANCIAL FACTS

| | |
|---|---|
| Financial Aid Rating | 74 |
| Tuition & Fees | $25,380 |
| Room & board | $9,820 |
| Books and supplies | $450 |
| Required fees | $24,336 |
| % frosh receiving aid | 59 |
| % undergrads receiving aid | 57 |
| Avg frosh grant | $16,818 |
| Avg frosh loan | $3,950 |

# NORTH CAROLINA STATE UNIVERSITY

Box 7103, Raleigh, NC 27695 • Admissions: 919-515-2434 • Fax: 919-515-5039

## CAMPUS LIFE

**Quality of Life Rating** **81**

| | |
|---|---|
| Type of school | public |
| Affiliation | none |
| Environment | suburban |

### STUDENTS

| | |
|---|---|
| Total undergrad enrollment | 21,990 |
| % male/female | 58/42 |
| % from out of state | 8 |
| % from public high school | 91 |
| % live on campus | 33 |
| % in (# of) fraternities | 11 (28) |
| % in (# of) sororities | 11 (12) |
| % African American | 10 |
| % Asian | 5 |
| % Caucasian | 82 |
| % Hispanic | 2 |
| % Native American | 1 |
| % international | 1 |

### SURVEY SAYS . . .

*High cost of living*
*Everyone loves the Wolfpack*
*Students love Raleigh, NC*
*Class discussions are rare*
*Athletic facilities are great*
*Ethnic diversity on campus*
*Large classes*
*Dorms are like dungeons*

## ACADEMICS

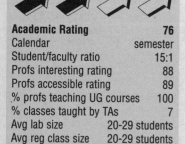

**Academic Rating** **76**

| | |
|---|---|
| Calendar | semester |
| Student/faculty ratio | 15:1 |
| Profs interesting rating | 88 |
| Profs accessible rating | 89 |
| % profs teaching UG courses | 100 |
| % classes taught by TAs | 7 |
| Avg lab size | 20-29 students |
| Avg reg class size | 20-29 students |

### MOST POPULAR MAJORS
business management
communications
electrical engineering

## STUDENTS SPEAK OUT

### Academics

North Carolina State is revamping its academic image after years of media focus on the university's athletic programs. Students confirm that the university's efforts are succeeding. One sophomore biology major gushes, "NC State is a great school. The faculty and professors are well prepared and outgoing." Overall, the students hold their professors in high regard. A first-year business major tells us that the professors are "very helpful and not bothered by student e-mails." Another freshman writes, "My math professor is a genius. He was actually able to explain everything so I understand." Most students (even those who are not engineering majors) cite the strength of the engineering program. However, one junior communications major admonishes that when it comes to the administration's concern for students, "if you aren't engineering, they don't care." A number of students applaud the "first-year college," a program that helps students with undeclared majors . . . well . . . select a major. Comments one sophomore, "The first-year college offered here at State is a great thing for freshmen coming in with an undecided major. It helped me a lot." Students praise the library and the overall beauty of the campus, but complain that many of the academic buildings need improvement. A majority of NC State students live off campus, and many of these commuter students complain about a lack of on-campus parking.

### Life

NC State is a member of the Atlantic Coast Conference, one of the most renowned athletic conferences in Division I sports. Accordingly, sports are a major part of life on campus. Unfortunately, the programs have not been very successful lately. On-campus social activities are limited, and most students go off-campus to find their fun. As one sophomore engineering major writes, "Work is tough, but we cut loose on the weekends by drinking excessive amounts of alcohol at parties and bars." Many students echo that sentiment, adding that beer and hard liquor are their drinks of choice. The bars on Hillsborough Street are very popular, and local bands play in Raleigh. Students rate the on-campus food and dormitories as poor. The majority of students, however, live off-campus, where they enjoy a respectable array of dining opportunities.

### Student Body

The student body at NC State is "very open and friendly." Students who live on campus agree that "people always make eye contact and say 'hi.'" A sophomore history major attests, "NC State students are some of the most friendly and helpful people." Those who don't live on campus agree but warn that it's harder for commuters to meet their fellow students, no matter how amiable. "I live off campus, so besides friends I've previously made, I don't really get to know people," complains one. Students who live on campus agree that the campus is "tight-knit" and "very friendly," and "everyone seems to get along." Though racial and ethnic distinctions don't impede this initial friendliness, relations between different groups don't go much deeper than that. Still, a sophomore history major succinctly summarizes students on this diverse and friendly campus: "I have only met two people I dislike, and in a school this big, that's great."

# NORTH CAROLINA STATE UNIVERSITY

FINANCIAL AID: 919-515-2421 • E-MAIL: UNDERGRAD_ADMISSIONS@NCSU.EDU • WEBSITE: WWW.NCSU.EDU

## ADMISSIONS

*Very important* academic and nonacademic factors considered by the admissions committee include class rank, secondary school record, and standardized test scores. *Other* factors considered include alumni/ae relation, character/personal qualities, essays, extracurricular activities, geography, minority status, recommendations, state residency, talent/ability, volunteer work, and work experience. Factors *not* considered include interview and religious affiliation/commitment. SAT I or ACT required. TOEFL required of all international applicants. High school diploma is required and GED is not accepted. *High school units required/recommended:* 16 total required; 22 total recommended; 4 English required, 3 math required, 4 math recommended, 3 science required, 4 science recommended, 1 science lab required, 2 foreign language required, additional foreign language recommended, 1 social studies required, additional social studies recommended, U.S. history required. *The admissions office says:* "When students are accepted for admission at NC State University, they are admitted directly into the college of their choice, or if undecided, admitted into First Year College. NCSU is divided into nine colleges: Agriculture and Life Sciences, Design, Education and Psychology, Engineering, Forest Resources, Humanities and Social Sciences, Management, Physical and Mathematical Sciences, and Textiles. Students who are interested in a particular college but unsure about a major may elect to apply for the undecided option in that college. NCSU's First Year College program allows students a year to explore their options before choosing a college or major."

### The Inside Word

Prospective students should be certain to investigate additional requirements for the college they wish to enter; universities that admit students to specific programs often vary standards significantly. Nonresidents will find it dramatically easier to get into NC State than to UNC, but application totals have gone up at State and eventually selectivity will follow.

## FINANCIAL AID

*Students should submit:* FAFSA, institution's own financial aid form, and PROFILE recommended but not required. There is no regular filing deadline. The Princeton Review suggests that all financial aid forms be submitted as soon as possible after January 1. *Need-based scholarships/grants offered:* Pell, SEOG, state scholarships/grants, private scholarships, and the school's own gift aid. *Loan aid offered:* FFEL Subsidized Stafford, FFEL Unsubsidized Stafford, FFEL PLUS, Federal Perkins, state, and college/university loans from institutional funds. Institutional employment available. Federal Work-Study Program available. Applicants will be notified of awards on a rolling basis beginning on or about March 15. Off-campus job opportunities are excellent.

## FROM THE ADMISSIONS OFFICE

"NC State is arguably the most popular university in the state, with more NC students seeking admission than at any other college or university. Over 12,000 students from across the nation seek one of the 3,600 available freshman spaces. Students choose NC State for its strong and varied academic programs (approximately 90), national reputation for excellence, low cost, location in Raleigh and the Research Triangle Park area, and very friendly atmosphere. Our students like the excitement of a large campus and the many opportunities it offers, such as Cooperative Education, Study Abroad, extensive honors programming, and theme residence halls. Each year, hundreds of NC State graduates are accepted into medical or law schools or other areas of advanced professional study. More corporate and government entities recruit graduates from NC State than from any other university in the United States. In 1999, IBM hired more graduates from NC State than from any other university in the United States."

## ADMISSIONS

| | |
|---|---|
| **Admissions Rating** | **82** |
| # of applicants | 12,040 |
| % of applicants accepted | 65 |
| % of acceptees attending | 48 |

### FRESHMAN PROFILE

| | |
|---|---|
| Range SAT Verbal | 530-630 |
| Average SAT Verbal | 578 |
| Range SAT Math | 550-660 |
| Average SAT Math | 607 |
| Range ACT Composite | 22-27 |
| Average ACT Composite | 25 |
| Minimum TOEFL | 550 |
| Average HS GPA | 3.9 |
| % graduated top 10% of class | 37 |
| % graduated top 25% of class | 78 |
| % graduated top 50% of class | 98 |

### DEADLINES

| | |
|---|---|
| Priority admission deadline | 11/25 |
| Regular admission | 2/1 |
| Nonfall registration? | yes |

### APPLICANTS ALSO LOOK AT
**AND OFTEN PREFER**
U. Tennessee—Knoxville
UNC—Chapel Hill
**AND SOMETIMES PREFER**
Wake Forest
UNC—Charlotte
Catawba
**AND RARELY PREFER**
Clemson
U. South Carolina—Columbia
Auburn
Georgia Tech.
Virginia Tech.

## FINANCIAL FACTS

| | |
|---|---|
| **Financial Aid Rating** | **73** |
| In-state tuition | $1,860 |
| Out-of-state tuition | $11,026 |
| Room & board | $5,274 |
| Books and supplies | $700 |
| Required fees | $954 |
| % frosh receiving aid | 32 |
| % undergrads receiving aid | 44 |
| Avg frosh grant | $4,208 |
| Avg frosh loan | $3,793 |

# NORTHEASTERN UNIVERSITY

360 HUNTINGTON AVENUE, 150 RICHARDS HALL, BOSTON, MA 02115 • ADMISSIONS: 617-373-2200 • FAX: 617-373-8780

## CAMPUS LIFE

**Quality of Life Rating**    **74**
Type of school    private
Affiliation    none
Environment    urban

### STUDENTS
Total undergrad enrollment    13,671
% male/female    51/49
% from out of state    56
% live on campus    87
% in (# of) fraternities    4
% in (# of) sororities    4
% African American    6
% Asian    9
% Caucasian    75
% Hispanic    4
% international    7
# of countries represented    123

### SURVEY SAYS . . .
*Students love Boston, MA*
*High cost of living*
*Athletic facilities are great*
*Popular college radio*
*Very little drug use*
*Diversity lacking on campus*

## ACADEMICS

**Academic Rating**    **74**
Calendar    quarter
Student/faculty ratio    16:1
Profs interesting rating    88
Profs accessible rating    88
Avg lab size    10-19 students
Avg reg class size    10-19 students

### MOST POPULAR MAJORS
business
engineering
health professions

## STUDENTS SPEAK OUT

### Academics

Northeastern University's major claim to fame is its cooperative education program. It's a major draw for NU's "very career-focused" students. It's a five-year BA program that enables students at the sophomore level and above to spend two of four quarters each year working in a job related to their major. Thousands of employers participate in the program, predominantly in the New England area, but there are also co-op students in training throughout the country and overseas. Studies at the university are geared predominantly toward the professions: business, engineering, criminal justice, and the health sciences are popular programs. "Northeastern is great for career advancement but many times the education feels like a vocational school [rather] than a college," according to a junior journalism major, who nonetheless believes that NU's greatest strength is its "practical nature." "Overall . . . most professors are interested in teaching for learning's sake." "Most are approachable and listen well, but in introductory classes, this is difficult—lectures, too. Some profs make lectures into small discussion groups to enhance understanding." "If you're an independent student with goals, you'll succeed here." You'll need to be persistent, too: Many students describe to us "what you call the NU Shuffle. All incoming freshmen are warned about the process that happens during registration each quarter. The bursar's line usually takes five hours or more to get through. You make a lot of friends while waiting."

### Life

NU social life is directly influenced by the co-op plan. Despite changes designed to put students who are in the same classes on and off campus during the same quarters, many still complain that "it can be difficult to make friends" while in the program. "Life at NU is fun, but also very school-oriented." Simply put by one student, "life is great. With over 180 organizations, there's bound to be one for newcomers." "Hockey . . . the big sport on campus," does rally student interest, but not as much as Boston itself does. "Boston is a great town. NU is in the center of a fast-moving, fun, and respectable city." Clubs, bars, record stores and bookstores, and Fenway Park are just a stone's throw away. According to the impression our survey respondents leave us with, whatever NU students decide to do, "weekend activities usually involve high alcohol intake." "Alcohol and weekends go together here."

### Student Body

"One word to describe NU is diverse, and I mean in all aspects of the word. You will definitely meet some interesting characters here. All good, of course." "Most students are busy, which sometimes creates a cold atmosphere." To be sure, students here are more focused and conservative than the average college student. "Students here are hard workers—many are attending full-time classes and working at full- or part-time jobs." "Generally, they are friendly." Northeastern is yet another school with a good ethnic mix where, sadly, most groups simply don't, or don't get the chance to, interact.

FINANCIAL AID: 617-373-3190 • E-MAIL: ADMISSIONS@NEU.EDU • WEBSITE: WWW.NEU.EDU

## ADMISSIONS

*Very important* academic and nonacademic factors considered by the admissions committee include secondary school record. *Important* factors considered include class rank, extracurricular activities, recommendations, and standardized test scores. *Other* factors considered include character/personal qualities, essays, interview, minority status, talent/ability, volunteer work, work experience, and alumni/ae relations. Factors *not* considered include geography, religious affiliation/commitment, and state residency. SAT I or ACT required, SAT II recommended. TOEFL required of all international applicants. High school diploma is required and GED is accepted. *High school units required/recommended:* 17 total recommended, 4 English recommended, 3 math recommended, 3 science recommended, 2 science lab recommended, 2 foreign language recommended, 3 social studies recommended, 2 history recommended. *The admissions office says:* "We make every effort to recruit qualified minority students. One senior staff member is dedicated to recruiting international students."

### The Inside Word

Northeastern is one of the moderately selective of Boston's mélange of colleges and universities, which makes it a popular safety for students who must go to school in Beantown. This translates into a large applicant pool and a lower acceptance rate than might otherwise be the case. The source of any true selectivity in NU's admissions process is a heavy reliance on the numbers: GPA, rank, and tests.

## FINANCIAL AID

*Students should submit:* FAFSA and CSS/Financial Aid PROFILE. Priority filing deadline is February 15. The Princeton Review suggests that all financial aid forms be submitted as soon as possible after January 1. *Need-based scholarships/grants offered:* Pell, SEOG, state scholarships/grants, private scholarships, the school's own gift aid, and Federal Nursing. *Loan aid offered:* Subsidized Stafford, Unsubsidized Stafford, PLUS, Federal Perkins, Federal Nursing, state, MassPlan, TERI, Signature, and Mass No Interest Loan (NIL). Institutional employment is available. Federal Work-Study Program is available. Applicants will be notified of awards on a rolling basis beginning on or about March 15. Off-campus job opportunities are excellent

## FROM THE ADMISSIONS OFFICE

"Northeastern University's energy comes from its bright, ambitious students and their sense of purpose. In the classroom, in campus activities, and in the city of Boston, they make things happen. Backed by the three components of a Northeastern education—a solid liberal arts foundation, professional knowledge and skills, and on-the-job experience—they're ready to take on any challenge, anywhere. Through Northeastern's cooperative education (co-op) program, students alternate classroom learning with periods of full-time paid work related to their majors or interests. Northeastern students try out different jobs, build their résumés, earn money, and understand the connection between work and classes all before they graduate. And they do it in the heart of an exciting city, where culture, commerce, civic pride, and college students from around the globe are all a part of the mix."

### ADMISSIONS

| Admissions Rating | 76 |
|---|---|
| # of applicants | 14,760 |
| % of applicants accepted | 70 |
| % of acceptees attending | 23 |

#### FRESHMAN PROFILE

| | |
|---|---|
| Range SAT Verbal | 500-610 |
| Average SAT Verbal | 556 |
| Range SAT Math | 520-620 |
| Average SAT Math | 574 |
| Range ACT Composite | 21-26 |
| Average ACT Composite | 23 |
| Minimum TOEFL | 550 |
| Average HS GPA | 3.0 |
| % graduated top 10% of class | 16 |
| % graduated top 25% of class | 46 |
| % graduated top 50% of class | 80 |

#### DEADLINES

| | |
|---|---|
| Priority admission deadline | 2/15 |
| Nonfall registration? | yes |

#### APPLICANTS ALSO LOOK AT AND OFTEN PREFER
MIT
Drexel
Boston Coll.
Boston U.
#### AND SOMETIMES PREFER
U. Mass—Amherst
Syracuse
U. Conn

### FINANCIAL FACTS

| Financial Aid Rating | 74 |
|---|---|
| Tuition (undergraduate) | $16,320 |
| Tuition (freshman) | $19,395 |
| Room & board | $9,135 |
| Books and supplies | $900 |
| Required fees | $195 |
| % frosh receiving aid | 67 |
| % undergrads receiving aid | 62 |
| Avg frosh grant | $8,774 |
| Avg frosh loan | $3,148 |

# NORTHWESTERN UNIVERSITY

PO Box 3060, 1801 Hinman Avenue, Evanston, IL 60208-3060 • Admissions: 847-491-7271

## CAMPUS LIFE

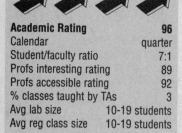

| Quality of Life Rating | 87 |
|---|---|
| Type of school | private |
| Affiliation | none |
| Environment | suburban |

### STUDENTS

| Total undergrad enrollment | 7,724 |
|---|---|
| % male/female | 48/52 |
| % from out of state | 75 |
| % from public high school | 75 |
| % live on campus | 70 |
| % in (# of) fraternities | 31 (21) |
| % in (# of) sororities | 27 (14) |
| % African American | 6 |
| % Asian | 17 |
| % Caucasian | 63 |
| % Hispanic | 4 |
| % international | 4 |

### SURVEY SAYS . . .

*Frats and sororities dominate social scene*
*Athletic facilities are great*
*Class discussions are rare*
*Great library*
*Everyone loves the Wildcats*
*Large classes*
*Student publications are popular*
*(Almost) no one listens to college radio*
*Campus difficult to get around*

## ACADEMICS

| Academic Rating | 96 |
|---|---|
| Calendar | quarter |
| Student/faculty ratio | 7:1 |
| Profs interesting rating | 89 |
| Profs accessible rating | 92 |
| % classes taught by TAs | 3 |
| Avg lab size | 10-19 students |
| Avg reg class size | 10-19 students |

### MOST POPULAR MAJORS

engineering
economics
communications

## STUDENTS SPEAK OUT

### Academics

Considered by many an Ivy of the Midwest, Northwestern University is unarguably "an academically rigorous school" with an "awesome reputation" that "expects hard work from its students." Students warn that "academics here are very challenging, especially with the quarter system," which "makes the pace extremely hectic." Engineering, journalism, pre-medical studies, and the liberal arts departments are all well regarded, as is the "great theater program"—which, according to many, is "essentially a pre-professional program" that is uncommonly rigorous. Students caution that most of the professors here are among the "most important researchers in their fields" and that, while many are "genuinely interested in their students' performance" and "very generous with their time," others are "very research-oriented and lack teaching skills." During a given quarter, "it's likely that you'll take a class with the most enthusiastic and interesting person you've ever met and also one with a professor far inferior to your worst high school teacher." Fortunately, "the teacher evaluation information is excellent. There are so many classes to take here. Like anywhere, there are good and bad professors, but the evaluation system makes it easy to differentiate between them, and it's all online."

### Life

There are two schools of thought about the Northwestern social scene. The first, subscribed to by those who rarely venture off campus or outside Evanston, say that life at Northwestern is pleasant but unexceptional. They report that the Greeks occupy a central position on campus. The Greek system caters to every kind of student—even the ones who would never even consider joining a fraternity or sorority." These students also enjoy the school's "great theater program. . . . There are shows going up all the time. People here are amazingly talented, and I've seen a really diverse range of shows—from mainstage musical productions to small, no-budget plays, all for pretty cheap." Finally, they commend NU's "gorgeous" campus. The second school of thought, championed by those who simply cannot wait to get off campus and into Chicago, holds that Northwestern offers the best of all possible worlds. Not only does the school boast all the above-mentioned benefits, explains one student, but "going into Chicago is a popular weekend activity. Public transportation (the 'EL') is only a block from campus and takes you directly to some of the best shopping in the world," as well as to excellent museums, restaurants, and night life. Adds another, "In Evanston," there are "great restaurants within walking distance but not much in the way of entertainment, which is why you need Chicago!" Both groups agree that "studying is a large part of student life" and also that "people here are very busy. Everyone I know has a TON on their plate, i.e. work, very difficult classes, one to five clubs/organizations, executive board positions, volunteering, sports (varsity, club, or intramural) . . ."

### Student Body

Northwestern students admit that they are probably not America's coolest college kids. "It's a dork school—be forewarned," writes one student. "But it's not cutthroat or pretentious like our neighbors on the East." Even so, "there is so much pressure to succeed at everything and be involved in everything, and everyone here is so good at everything already. Because we were all overachievers and at the top of our classes in high school, we're bound to be disappointed when we realize that there are so many smarter people around us here at college." Many here are "pretty upper-, middle-class conservative," "Greek-loving, country-club types, generally talented, and lots of princess and booksmart dummies, with a few intellectual giants and truly outstanding human beings thrown in the bunch." Despite their sometimes hypercritical reviews of their peers, most students ultimately concede that their classmates are "great. They are all interesting, smart, and fun to talk to."

FINANCIAL AID: 847-491-7400 • E-MAIL: UG-ADMISSION@NORTHWESTERN.EDU • WEBSITE: WWW.NORTHWESTERN.EDU

## ADMISSIONS

*Very important* academic and nonacademic factors considered by the admissions committee include class rank, secondary school record, essays, and test scores. *Important* factors considered include ability/talent, character/personal qualities, extracurricular activities, and recommendations. *Other* factors considered are volunteer work, work experience, interview, minority status, and alumni/ae relation. Factors *not* considered include geography, religious affiliation/commitment, and state residency. SAT I or ACT required; SAT II required for some and recommended for all. TOEFL required of all international applicants. *High school units required/recommended:* 3–4 math recommended, 2 science recommended, 2 foreign language recommended, 4 English recommended, 2–4 social studies recommended, and 1–3 elective recommended.

### The Inside Word

Northwestern's applicant pool is easily among the best in the country. Candidates face both a rigorous evaluation by the admissions committee and serious competition from within the pool. The best approach (besides top grades and a strong personal background) is to take the committee up on their recommendations to visit the campus or interview with an alumnus/a and submit SAT II scores. The effort it takes to get in is well worth it.

## FINANCIAL AID

*Students should submit:* FAFSA, CSS/Financial Aid PROFILE, noncustodial (divorced/separated) parent's statement, and business/farm supplement. The Princeton Review suggests that all financial aid forms be submitted as soon as possible after January 1. *Need-based scholarships/grants offered:* Pell, SEOG, state scholarships/grants, private scholarships, and the school's own gift aid. *Loan aid offered:* FFEL Subsidized Stafford, FFEL Unsubsidized Stafford, FFEL PLUS, Federal Perkins, and college/university loans from institutional funds. Institutional employment available. Federal Work-Study Program available. Applicants will be notified of awards on or soon after April 1. Off-campus job opportunities are excellent.

## FROM THE ADMISSIONS OFFICE

"Consistent with its dedication to excellence, Northwestern provides both an educational and an extracurricular environment that enable its undergraduate students to become accomplished individuals and informed and responsible citizens. To the students in all its undergraduate schools, Northwestern offers liberal learning and professional education to help them gain the depth of knowledge that will empower them to become leaders in their professions and communities. Furthermore, Northwestern fosters in its students a broad understanding of the world in which we live as well as excellence in the competencies that transcend any particular field of study: writing and oral communication, analytical and creative thinking and expression, quantitative and qualitative methods of thinking."

## ADMISSIONS

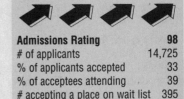

| | |
|---|---|
| Admissions Rating | 98 |
| # of applicants | 14,725 |
| % of applicants accepted | 33 |
| % of acceptees attending | 39 |
| # accepting a place on wait list | 395 |
| % admitted from wait list | 1 |
| # of early decision applicants | 801 |
| % accepted early decision | 50 |

### FRESHMAN PROFILE

| | |
|---|---|
| Range SAT Verbal | 630-720 |
| Average SAT Verbal | 676 |
| Range SAT Math | 660-750 |
| Average SAT Math | 699 |
| Range ACT Composite | 29-32 |
| Average ACT Composite | 30 |
| Minimum TOEFL | 600 |
| % graduated top 10% of class | 84 |
| % graduated top 25% of class | 96 |
| % graduated top 50% of class | 100 |

### DEADLINES

| | |
|---|---|
| Early decision | 11/1 |
| Early decision notification | 12/15 |
| Regular admission | 1/1 |
| Regular notification | 4/15 |
| Nonfall registration? | yes |

### APPLICANTS ALSO LOOK AT
**AND OFTEN PREFER**
Yale
Harvard
**AND SOMETIMES PREFER**
U. Chicago
Stanford
Princeton
Columbia
**AND RARELY PREFER**
DePaul
Marquette
Purdue U.—West Lafayette

### FINANCIAL FACTS

| | |
|---|---|
| Financial Aid Rating | 74 |
| Tuition | $25,839 |
| Room & board | $7,776 |
| Books and supplies | $1,206 |
| % frosh receiving aid | 44 |
| % undergrads receiving aid | 46 |
| Avg frosh grant | $17,587 |
| Avg frosh loan | $3,024 |

# OBERLIN COLLEGE

101 NORTH PROFESSOR STREET, OBERLIN, OH 44074 • ADMISSIONS: 440-775-8411 • FAX: 440-775-6905

## CAMPUS LIFE

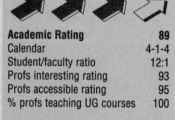

| Quality of Life Rating | 72 |
| --- | --- |
| Type of school | private |
| Affiliation | none |
| Environment | rural |

### STUDENTS

| | |
| --- | --- |
| Total undergrad enrollment | 2,951 |
| % male/female | 41/59 |
| % from out of state | 89 |
| % from public high school | 66 |
| % live on campus | 70 |
| % African American | 8 |
| % Asian | 8 |
| % Caucasian | 80 |
| % Hispanic | 3 |
| % Native American | 1 |
| % international | 6 |

### SURVEY SAYS . . .

*Political activism is hot*
*Great library*
*Students don't get along with local community*
*Students aren't religious*
*Musical organizations are hot*
*Intercollegiate sports unpopular or nonexistent*
*Theater is popular*

## ACADEMICS

| Academic Rating | 89 |
| --- | --- |
| Calendar | 4-1-4 |
| Student/faculty ratio | 12:1 |
| Profs interesting rating | 93 |
| Profs accessible rating | 95 |
| % profs teaching UG courses | 100 |

### MOST POPULAR MAJORS
English
history
biology

## STUDENTS SPEAK OUT

### Academics

With a "culture unlike any other" and a "commitment to developing well-rounded, free-thinking individuals," Oberlin College consistently ranks high among college students looking for a small, politically progressive, and academically challenging liberal arts school. Its highly respected music conservatory is a major draw, as are its "great double degree program," EXCO (Experimental College, where students teach courses for credit), and strong curriculum in both the arts and sciences. In a place where "students are smart and interesting, work is challenging," and there's "no red tape," it's no wonder Oberlin undergrads are so positive about their choice of college. Notes a senior, "The learning community is great, teachers are accessible, and there are great resources." The "fantastic" and "totally available" professors who "love teaching" play a big part in creating Oberlin's reputation of academic excellence. As for administration, though some claim that "the administration hates us," a senior takes the long view: "There is a lot of administration-student interaction. Students are very much involved in the politics on campus and way into creating the environment in which we learn. The administration tries to be responsive."

### Life

At a place where "most learning takes place at formal and informal discussions outside of class," it's not surprising that Oberlin undergrads have a lot to say on the subject of life at this tiny college in a "two-block" town. Writes a junior, "People think about everything, and basically, that's what we do for fun." Students are, for the most part, "aware and involved" so, as a senior points out, there's "lots of activism and challenges to the status quo." A first-year sees the typical "Obie" philosophizing a little differently, however, noting that "people spend a lot of time dwelling in the saturation of their white liberalism and patting themselves on the back for their guilt." All that and a BA too? Of course, not everyone at the school is so, well, cerebral. One fun-loving senior describes her Oberlin experience this way: "I run through the quad naked when it rains, do a running belly flop, and slide 30 feet on my stomach. These things are normal here. Nothing will ever shock me again." As for more mundane pursuits (maybe a movie once in a while?), Cleveland's only 45 minutes away, but most students' social lives revolve around campus with its myriad free or inexpensive "films, lectures, speakers, recitals, performances, art openings, and theme parties" (The Drag Ball and Safer Sex parties headline the year). There aren't any frats at ultra-lefty Oberlin, but the OSCA co-ops "are a great alternative for food and living." As for letting off all that steam built up discussing identity politics and "overdramatic interpersonal dramas," there is a "substantial party and drug scene but no pressure to do either."

### Student Body

The "eclectic" and "diverse" as well as "friendly" people—"definitely the people," notes a first-year—make Oberlin what it is, say students. "Oberlin's like the dumpster where all the weirdos of high school were tossed," says a senior. Weirdos, yes. But in the very best way. Notes a junior, "They're weirdos. That's why I'm here. Good weirdos, smart weirdos—weirdos everyone should go to college with. . . . they're amazing, aggravating, intimidating, and intimate all at the same time. They help me to grow . . . ." And while these "open-minded" and "liberal-thinking" kids are well known for their left-of-center politics, just how left is left? A first-year explains, "The political affiliation bubble on your survey is not comprehensive enough. To the left of the 'left wing' option, there should be a bubble that says either 'radically leftist' or just 'Oberlin.'" Of course, all that intense political discussion can lead to a few "closed-minded people unwilling to listen to others' points of view," but still, most like it that way. A senior sums up: "We're all a bunch of post–New Age left-wing hippies bent on saving/destroying the world. I dig it."

FINANCIAL AID: 440-775-8142 • E-MAIL: COLLEGE.ADMISSIONS@OBERLIN.EDU • WEBSITE: WWW.OBERLIN.EDU

## ADMISSIONS

*Very important* academic and nonacademic factors considered by the admissions committee include recommendations, secondary school record, and standardized test scores. *Important* factors considered include character/personal qualities, essays, extracurricular activities, minority status, and talent/ability. *Other* factors considered include alumni/ae relation, class rank, interview, volunteer work, and work experience. Factors *not* considered include geography, religious affiliation/commitment, and state residency. SAT I or ACT required; SAT II recommended. TOEFL required of all international applicants. High school diploma is required and GED is accepted. *High school units required/recommended:* 16 total required; 22 total recommended; 4 English required, 2 math required, 4 math recommended, 2 science required, 3 science recommended, 2 science lab required, 2 foreign language recommended, 2 social studies required, 3 social studies recommended, 2 history required, 4 elective required.

### The Inside Word

The admissions process at Oberlin is especially demanding for candidates to the Conservatory of Music, which seeks only the best-prepared musicians for its excellent program. All applicants to the college face a thorough and rigorous review of their credentials by the admissions committee regardless of their choice of major. Take our advice—visit the campus to interview, and put extra effort into admissions essays.

## FINANCIAL AID

*Students should submit:* FAFSA, CSS/Financial Aid PROFILE, and noncustodial (divorced/separated) parent's statement. Regular filing deadline is February 15. The Princeton Review suggests that all financial aid forms be submitted as soon as possible after January 1. *Need-based scholarships/grants offered:* Pell, state scholarships/grants, and the school's own gift aid. *Loan aid offered:* Direct Subsidized Stafford, Direct Unsubsidized Stafford, Direct PLUS, Federal Perkins, and college/university loans from institutional funds. Institutional employment available. Federal Work-Study Program available. Applicants will be notified of awards on or about April 1. Off-campus job opportunities are good.

## FROM THE ADMISSIONS OFFICE

"Oberlin College is an independent, coeducational, liberal arts college. It comprises two divisions, the College of Arts and Sciences, with roughly 2,300 students enrolled, and the Conservatory of Music, with about 500 students. Students in both divisions share one campus; they also share residence and dining halls as part of one academic community. Many students take courses in both divisions. Oberlin awards the Bachelor of Arts and the Bachelor of Music degrees; a five-year program leads to both degrees. Selected master's degrees are offered in the Conservatory. Oberlin is located 35 miles southwest of Cleveland. Founded in 1833, Oberlin College is highly selective and dedicated to recruiting students from diverse backgrounds. Oberlin was the first coeducational college in the United States, as well as a historic leader in educating black students. Oberlin's 440-acre campus provides outstanding facilities, modern scientific laboratories, a large computing center, a library unexcelled by other college libraries for the depth and range of its resources, and the Allen Memorial Art Museum."

## ADMISSIONS

| | |
|---|---|
| Admissions Rating | 90 |
| # of applicants | 4,855 |
| % of applicants accepted | 50 |
| % of acceptees attending | 30 |
| # accepting a place on wait list | 410 |
| % admitted from wait list | 7 |
| # of early decision applicants | 145 |
| % accepted early decision | 84 |

### FRESHMAN PROFILE

| | |
|---|---|
| Range SAT Verbal | 630-730 |
| Average SAT Verbal | 685 |
| Range SAT Math | 590-700 |
| Average SAT Math | 644 |
| Range ACT Composite | 26-30 |
| Average ACT Composite | 28 |
| Minimum TOEFL | 600 |
| Average HS GPA | 3.6 |
| % graduated top 10% of class | 59 |
| % graduated top 25% of class | 87 |
| % graduated top 50% of class | 99 |

### DEADLINES

| | |
|---|---|
| Early decision | 11/15 |
| Early decision notification | 12/15 |
| Regular admission | 1/15 |
| Regular notification | 4/1 |
| Nonfall registration? | yes |

### APPLICANTS ALSO LOOK AT
### AND OFTEN PREFER
Yale
Swarthmore
Wesleyan U.
Stanford, Brown
### AND SOMETIMES PREFER
Carleton
Haverford
Tufts
Grinnell, Williams
### AND RARELY PREFER
Connecticut Coll.

### FINANCIAL FACTS

| | |
|---|---|
| Financial Aid Rating | 74 |
| Tuition | $24,096 |
| Room & board | $6,178 |
| Books and supplies | $575 |
| Required fees | $168 |
| % frosh receiving aid | 52 |
| % undergrads receiving aid | 53 |
| Avg frosh grant | $16,715 |
| Avg frosh loan | $4,000 |

# OCCIDENTAL COLLEGE

1600 CAMPUS ROAD, OFFICE OF ADMISSION, LOS ANGELES, CA 90041 • ADMISSIONS: 323-259-2700 • FAX: 323-341-4875

## CAMPUS LIFE

**Quality of Life Rating**    **80**

| | |
|---|---|
| Type of school | private |
| Affiliation | none |
| Environment | suburban |

### STUDENTS

| | |
|---|---|
| Total undergrad enrollment | 1,700 |
| % male/female | 44/56 |
| % from out of state | 50 |
| % from public high school | 57 |
| % live on campus | 79 |
| % in (# of) fraternities | 15 (2) |
| % in (# of) sororities | 15 (3) |
| % African American | 7 |
| % Asian | 18 |
| % Caucasian | 55 |
| % Hispanic | 16 |
| % Native American | 1 |
| % international | 4 |
| # of countries represented | 45 |

### SURVEY SAYS . . .

*Theater is hot*
*Student publications are ignored*
*Classes are small*
*No one cheats*
*Political activism is hot*
*Ethnic diversity on campus*
*Athletic facilities need improving*
*Diverse students interact*

## ACADEMICS

**Academic Rating**    **89**

| | |
|---|---|
| Calendar | semester |
| Student/faculty ratio | 11:1 |
| Profs interesting rating | 93 |
| Profs accessible rating | 96 |
| % profs teaching UG courses | 100 |
| Avg lab size | 10-19 students |
| Avg reg class size | 10-19 students |

### MOST POPULAR MAJORS

English/comparative
psychology
economics

## STUDENTS SPEAK OUT

### Academics

Students love the intimate learning environment provided by Occidental College, a small liberal arts school on the outskirts of Los Angeles. As one student tells us, "Occidental reflects the essence of a true community. The administration, the professors, staff, and students alike mesh together into one happy family." Adds another, "Because Oxy is so small, professors make an effort to remember your name and administrators are always available. Personally, my overall experience has been great!" Oxy makes tough academic demands of its students, requiring a core curriculum so extensive that most students take a full two years to complete it. Things get no easier during senior year: each student must complete an independent project or take a comprehensive exam as part of their major studies. Students don't bristle at the hard work, though, largely because "most of the professors are brilliant and really spark interest where there was none. The overall academic experience is very fulfilling." Students warn that while "the level of excellence in education is high, the grade inflation is frustratingly low." Administrators "are just part of the community, like the cleaning ladies and the gardeners. We all know each other," making it much easier for students to handle administrative tasks.

### Life

For most Oxy undergrads, extracurricular life centers on their places of residence. Explains one, "Here on campus, our living areas are called halls, not dorms. The reason for this is that halls are not only a place for living but also a learning environment. The hall director and residence assistants have not only social events but also educational ones on a daily basis. To keep from excluding profs from the experience, halls have a faculty advisor who helps out and hangs in the hall as well." Social opportunities, while available, take a back seat to Oxy's "very strong academic feel. Students study fairly hard, but at the same time there are numerous opportunities to relieve stress at social events, parties, or college trips. There are many speakers and groups brought to campus as well." The Greek scene "is one option, but it seems out of place at a school this small." Eagle Rock, the L.A. neighborhood that is home to Oxy, offers "nothing to do," but Burbank and Old Town Pasadena ("a strip of restaurants, shopping, and movies") are 15 minutes away by car. Notes one student, "If you don't have a car, it's hard to recreate, so parties, etc., are rather well attended. Those with cars and IDs frequent the club scene." Campus shuttle buses take students to the Old Town on Friday and Saturday nights.

### Student Body

Because of its large Asian and Hispanic populations, "Oxy is known for its diversity." Students take pride in their sensitivity to Oxy's various communities. "Everyone here is interested in multiculturalism," an admirable attitude which, when taken to unfortunate extremes, transforms itself into inflexible political correctness. Complains one student, "The student body is overly concerned with political correctness—not the goals, but the restraints. Many people exploit the concept to alienate others." Still, students are happy overall with their classmates. As one explains, "Oxy is like a big dysfunctional family: we all know each other since the school is so small. On one hand, I love them, but at the same time they drive me up the wall."

# OCCIDENTAL COLLEGE

FINANCIAL AID: 323-259-2548 • E-MAIL: ADMISSION@OXY.EDU • WEBSITE: WWW.OXY.EDU

## ADMISSIONS

*Very important* academic and nonacademic factors considered by the admissions committee include secondary school record. *Important* factors considered include class rank, essays, recommendations, standardized test scores, and state residency. *Other* factors considered include alumni/ae relation, character/personal qualities, extracurricular activities, geography, interview, minority status, talent/ability, volunteer work, and work experience. Factors *not* considered include religious affiliation/commitment. SAT I or ACT required; SAT II recommended. TOEFL required of all international applicants. High school diploma is required and GED is accepted. *High school units required/recommended:* 13 total required; 4 English required, 3 math required, 3 science required, 3 social studies required. *The admissions office says:* "The Committee on Admissions looks for students with very strong academic and personal qualifications who demonstrate motivation, accomplishment, involvement, and commitment. The majority of students admitted to the college rank in the upper 5 to 10 percent of their high school classes. Because the individual characteristics of each candidate are considered, no specific formula of grades and scores guarantees admission. Rigor of course work, grades, test scores [SAT I and ACT accepted, SAT I preferred], recommendations, and extracurricular activities are all taken into consideration when the freshman class is selected."

### The Inside Word

Students who are considering Occidental, or any other college with a rigorous core curriculum, should take five full academic courses a year straight through to graduation from high school. Such work not only gives the admissions committee solid evidence of your ability to handle Oxy's core requirements; it will make completing them much less painful as well.

## FINANCIAL AID

*Students should submit:* FAFSA, CSS/Financial Aid PROFILE, state aid form, noncustodial (divorced/separated) parent's statement, business/farm supplement, and parents' and students' income tax and W-2 forms. Regular filing deadline is February 1. The Princeton Review suggests that all financial aid forms be submitted as soon as possible after January 1. Institutional employment available. Federal Work-Study Program available. Applicants will be notified of awards on or about April 1. Off-campus job opportunities are excellent.

## FROM THE ADMISSIONS OFFICE

"The college is committed to a philosophy of total education. Intellectual capability is a dominant component, but is conceived of as one dimension in a process that includes and stresses personal, ethical, social, and political growth toward maturation as well. The high percentage of students in residence at the college work toward the achievement of this objective. Successful Occidental students are self-motivated, independent-minded, and intellectually talented people. They base their judgments upon respect for evidence, ideas, and a deep concern for values, both private and public. They are alert to the possibilities of betterment in themselves, their college, and their society."

## ADMISSIONS

| | |
|---|---|
| **Admissions Rating** | **87** |
| # of applicants | 3,275 |
| % of applicants accepted | 57 |
| % of acceptees attending | 27 |
| # accepting a place on wait list | 218 |
| % admitted from wait list | 4 |

### FRESHMAN PROFILE

| | |
|---|---|
| Range SAT Verbal | 550-660 |
| Average SAT Verbal | 610 |
| Range SAT Math | 550-660 |
| Average SAT Math | 610 |
| Average ACT Composite | 27 |
| Minimum TOEFL | 600 |
| Average HS GPA | 3.8 |
| % graduated top 10% of class | 60 |
| % graduated top 25% of class | 89 |
| % graduated top 50% of class | 99 |

### DEADLINES

| | |
|---|---|
| Early decision | 11/15 |
| Early decision notification | 12/15 |
| Regular admission | 1/15 |
| Regular notification | 4/1 |

### APPLICANTS ALSO LOOK AT
### AND OFTEN PREFER
Yale
Columbia
Pomona
Stanford
### AND SOMETIMES PREFER
UC—Berkeley
UCLA
UC—Davis
U. Southern Cal
Pitzer

### FINANCIAL FACTS

| | |
|---|---|
| **Financial Aid Rating** | **84** |
| Tuition | $23,532 |
| Room & board | $6,880 |
| Books and supplies | $810 |
| Required fees | $498 |
| % frosh receiving aid | 57 |
| % undergrads receiving aid | 65 |
| Avg frosh grant | $21,000 |
| Avg frosh loan | $3,000 |

# OGLETHORPE UNIVERSITY

4484 PEACHTREE ROAD, NE, ATLANTA, GA 30319 • ADMISSIONS: 404-364-8307 • FAX: 404-364-8491

## CAMPUS LIFE

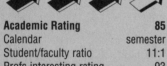

| | |
|---|---|
| **Quality of Life Rating** | **82** |
| Type of school | private |
| Affiliation | none |
| Environment | suburban |

### STUDENTS

| | |
|---|---|
| Total undergrad enrollment | 1,169 |
| % male/female | 34/66 |
| % from out of state | 38 |
| % from public high school | 76 |
| % live on campus | 68 |
| % in (# of) fraternities | 33 (4) |
| % in (# of) sororities | 28 (3) |
| % African American | 19 |
| % Asian | 4 |
| % Caucasian | 68 |
| % Hispanic | 3 |
| % international | 2 |
| # of countries represented | 28 |

### SURVEY SAYS . . .

*Students love Atlanta, GA*
*Theater is hot*
*Frats and sororities dominate social scene*
*Classes are small*
*Great off-campus food*
*Lousy food on campus*
*Library needs improving*
*Political activism is (almost) nonexistent*

## ACADEMICS

| | |
|---|---|
| **Academic Rating** | **85** |
| Calendar | semester |
| Student/faculty ratio | 11:1 |
| Profs interesting rating | 93 |
| Profs accessible rating | 95 |
| % profs teaching UG courses | 100 |
| Avg reg class size | 10-19 students |

### MOST POPULAR MAJORS
business administration
English
psychology

## STUDENTS SPEAK OUT

### Academics

"You are an individual, not a Social Security number" at Oglethorpe University, an "exceptional liberal arts school" located on the outskirts of Atlanta. Features that separate OU from the pack include "fantastic scholarships" and an unusually demanding and broad-based core curriculum. No one, regardless of major, receives a diploma here without a well-versed knowledge of western civilization, world literature, and the physical sciences. "The core curriculum is great," gushes a first-year student. "It's the world's best kept secret." Oglethorpe's "incredibly knowledgeable, friendly," and "enthusiastic" professors also receive high marks. They "make you think," "teach well," and "are willing to help you with most anything." Classes can be time-consuming, though, and professors expect students to engage in classroom dialogue—so much so that one student sarcastically calls OU "the Land of Discussion." Oglethorpe's "very friendly" administration is "wonderfully supportive," at least "until something goes wrong." However, "registration is a pain," according to a sophomore. "You have to get up at 5:00 A.M. to make sure you get your core classes." On the whole, students here speak very fondly of the "very good, competitive experience" and "many weird traditions" of this "kitschy, unique kind of place." "If you want a true liberal arts education," concludes an art history major, "this is the place you should go."

### Life

Though a few crotchety students contend that "they need to improve the social atmosphere around here," most students say Oglethorpe is "a fun school in a great city." "Everything is close" to campus and Buckhead—"the place to be in Atlanta for students"—is just "down the street." Students here can take in "the art museum, concerts, great shopping, and hot dance clubs," "go to a new restaurant every weekend," or "listen to live music" in a local pub without driving anywhere. "Once," swears a sophomore, "I didn't drive for a whole month." Back on the "beautiful and secure" campus, "you can participate in just about anything." Though the athletic facilities are "poor" (and Oglethorpe's "mascot is a Stormy Petrel"), "people like to go to sporting events." They also play "Ultimate Frisbee on the Quad" and enjoy "academic discussions at dinner." On weekends, "frat parties on Greek Row" are all the rage. We're told that "most people walk up to Greek Row to drink and dance at whichever fraternity house they have the most friends in." Some students absolutely love the arrangement; others tell us "it gets old fast." The "deteriorating" but "large and comfy" dorms here are a hit with students. The cafeteria grub could definitely use "vast improvement," though. Students say they will do about anything "to get away from campus to get real food."

### Student Body

"Nowhere will you find more doors open for you" than at Oglethorpe, a little school chock full of "eccentric," politically moderate, "true southerners" with "bizarre lifestyles" and very ambitious professional aspirations. The "cultural variety" is extensive; you'll find "lots of nerdy, happy types," "a lot of ignorant Cult Christians," "apathetic" frat guys, and everything in between. "There are no clear divisions between Greeks, jocks, Jesus freaks, etc.," explains a senior. "This school is so small that everyone basically hangs out with everyone else." The most animosity—and it's not very much—is probably felt between "Greeks and non-Greeks." The "smart" and "open-minded" students here describe themselves as "quite unique," and "pretty accepting and mostly democratic." There is little ethnic diversity on campus. Also, although Oglethorpe pioneered the admission of black students to non-black universities in the South, the current African American population is relatively low.

FINANCIAL AID: 404-364-8356 • E-MAIL: ADMISSIONS@OGLETHORPE.EDU • WEBSITE: WWW.OGLETHORPE.EDU

## ADMISSIONS

*Very important* academic and nonacademic factors considered by the admissions committee include essays and secondary school record. *Important* factors considered include interview and standardized test scores. *Other* factors considered include alumni/ae relation, character/personal qualities, class rank, extracurricular activities, recommendations, talent/ability, volunteer work, and work experience. Factors *not* considered include geography, minority status, religious affiliation/commitment, and state residency. SAT I or ACT required. High school diploma is required and GED is accepted. *High school units required/recommended:* 4 English required, 3 math required, 4 math recommended, 2 science required, 3 science recommended, 2 foreign language recommended, 3 social studies required, 4 social studies recommended.

### The Inside Word

With rising national interest in the South, it won't be long before the academic strength found at Oglethorpe attracts wider attention and more applicants. At present, it's much easier to gain admission here than at many universities of similar quality. Go to Atlanta for a campus interview—you'll leave impressed.

## FINANCIAL AID

*Students should submit:* FAFSA, institution's own financial aid form, and state aid form. There is no regular filing deadline. The Princeton Review suggests that all financial aid forms be submitted as soon as possible after January 1. *Need-based scholarships/grants offered:* Pell, SEOG, state scholarships/grants, private scholarships, and the school's own gift aid. *Loan aid offered:* Direct Subsidized Stafford, Direct Unsubsidized Stafford, Direct PLUS, FFEL Subsidized Stafford, FFEL Unsubsidized Stafford, FFEL PLUS, and Federal Perkins, plus a wide range of merit scholarships. Institutional employment available. Federal Work-Study Program available. Applicants will be notified of awards on a rolling basis beginning on or about January 1. Off-campus job opportunities are excellent.

## FROM THE ADMISSIONS OFFICE

"Promising students and outstanding teachers come together at Oglethorpe University in an acclaimed program of liberal arts and sciences. Here you'll find an active intellectual community on a beautiful English Gothic campus just 10 miles from the center of Atlanta, capital of the Southeast, site of the 1996 Summer Olympics, and home to 4 million people. If you want challenging academics, the opportunity to work closely with your professors, and the stimulation of a great metropolitan area, consider Oglethorpe, a national liberal arts college in a world-class city."

### ADMISSIONS

| | |
|---|---|
| Admissions Rating | 84 |
| # of applicants | 761 |
| % of applicants accepted | 70 |
| % of acceptees attending | 36 |

### FRESHMAN PROFILE

| | |
|---|---|
| Range SAT Verbal | 550-680 |
| Average SAT Verbal | 615 |
| Range SAT Math | 550-630 |
| Average SAT Math | 602 |
| Average ACT Composite | 27 |
| Minimum TOEFL | 550 |
| Average HS GPA | 3.7 |
| % graduated top 10% of class | 36 |
| % graduated top 25% of class | 68 |
| % graduated top 50% of class | 97 |

### DEADLINES

| | |
|---|---|
| Regular notification | 1/15 |
| Nonfall registration? | yes |

### APPLICANTS ALSO LOOK AT

**AND OFTEN PREFER**
Emory
Florida State

**AND SOMETIMES PREFER**
U. Georgia
U. of the South
Furman
Georgia Tech.
Vanderbilt

**AND RARELY PREFER**
Mercer
Berry

### FINANCIAL FACTS

| | |
|---|---|
| Financial Aid Rating | 87 |
| Tuition | $18,790 |
| Room & board | $6,060 |
| Books and supplies | $600 |
| Required fees | $310 |
| % frosh receiving aid | 66 |
| % undergrads receiving aid | 62 |
| Avg frosh grant | $16,359 |
| Avg frosh loan | $2,855 |

# OHIO NORTHERN UNIVERSITY

525 SOUTH MAIN STREET, ADA, OH 45810 • ADMISSIONS: 419-772-2260 • FAX: 419-772-2313

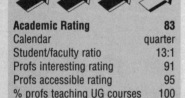
## STUDENTS SPEAK OUT

### Academics

"The atmosphere is comfortable" and "the personal contacts with faculty and staff are excellent" at "small, prestigious" Ohio Northern University, "a premier private university" with a good regional reputation and academics that are "challenging" but not oppressive. Along with engineering and health sciences, ONU's big-ticket programs include an "excellent pharmacy program" as well as a reputable business school. A healthy serving of general education requirements prevents ONU from being merely a professional training ground, however, and ample interaction between professors and students gives ONU a traditional liberal arts feel. Students say their "professors really care about whether or not you succeed" and "go out of their way to make sure you understand the material they are presenting." Most faculty members are "extremely easy to talk to and get help from," although some "are very hard to reach outside of class." Also, while many professors here "are amazing, inspiring, and wonderful," a few are "out-of-touch" and "couldn't teach to save their lives," according to a sophomore. Academic perks include 1,000 on-campus personal computers and a free tutoring system for students who fall behind. Though numerous students say ONU is run smoothly and efficiently, others contend that "the administration likes to see students jump through hoops."

### Life

Thanks to its location in a rural, "small town" of about 5,000 people with "one bar and six fast-food restaurants," ONU's "pretty campus" is "a very great place to be." This is especially true if you crave "a friendly atmosphere" and a "laid-back" college lifestyle that is "not much different from high school." However, life here is sometimes "rather dull," admits a sophomore. "If you don't have a car, you are stuck in the cornfields." Bowling is unusually big here, and the $3 movie theater is often packed. "Though there isn't really all that much to do, we somehow always find something to do," explains a first-year student. "It draws us together, really." The Greek system is strong and weekend frat parties at which "people party and drink for fun" are well attended. An unusual aspect of student life at ONU is that "the Greeks are involved with independents and other Greeks," which keeps the campus "unified." But, "if it weren't for the Greeks, this school would be dead," ventures a sophomore. "Student groups try to plan activities to make up for the small-town atmosphere" as well. There are "many activities and organizations" at ONU, as well as intramural sports and numerous theater events. An annual Fall Mud Volleyball tournament and a spring festival called "Tunes on the Tundra," which features live music of all types, are big draws. Students who need a taste of the city head for the bright lights of Lima, a short drive away.

### Student Body

Here's an interesting statistic: One out of every nine students at ONU is a valedictorian or salutatorian. There are "lots of friendly people" here, and "warm greetings" abound as students walk across campus. However, many students tell us that "stereotypes" are also quite common. "People need to open their minds," explains one student. Until they do, many ONU students will remain "scared of others who come from different ethnic backgrounds." Additionally, "ONU needs more diversity," clamors a junior. The mostly "upper-class and middle-class" white people who constitute the student population just aren't a very diverse bunch. Finally, "some students" at this Methodist-affiliated school "are very religious."

FINANCIAL AID: 419-772-2272 • E-MAIL: ADMISSIONS-UG@ONU.EDU • WEBSITE: WWW.ONU.EDU

## ADMISSIONS

*Very important* academic and nonacademic factors considered by the admissions committee include secondary school record and standardized test scores. *Important* factors considered include class rank and extracurricular activities. *Other* factors considered include interview, alumni/ae relation, character/personal qualities, essays, recommendations, talent/ability, volunteer work, and work experience. Factors *not* considered include geography, minority status, religious affiliation/commitment, and state residency. SAT I or ACT required. TOEFL required of all international applicants. High school diploma is required and GED is accepted.

### The Inside Word

Solid grades from high school are a pretty sure ticket for admission to Ohio Northern. Students who are above average academically are in good positions to take advantage of a very large number of no-need scholarships.

## FINANCIAL AID

*Students should submit:* FAFSA and institution's own financial aid form. There is no regular filing deadline. The Princeton Review suggests that all financial aid forms be submitted as soon as possible after January 1. *Need-based scholarships/grants offered:* Pell, SEOG, state scholarships/grants, private scholarships, and the school's own gift aid. *Loan aid offered:* FFEL Subsidized Stafford, FFEL Unsubsidized Stafford, FFEL PLUS, Federal Perkins, state, college/university loans from institutional funds, alternative loans, and Federal Health Professions Loan. Institutional employment available. Federal Work-Study Program available. Applicants will be notified of awards on a rolling basis beginning on or about March 1. Off-campus job opportunities are good.

## FROM THE ADMISSIONS OFFICE

"Ohio Northern's purpose is to help students develop into self-reliant, mature men and women capable of clear and logical thinking and sensitive to the higher values of truth, beauty, and goodness. ONU selects its student body from among those students possessing characteristics congruent with the institution's objectives. Generally, a student must be prepared to use the resources of the institution to achieve personal and educational goals."

### ADMISSIONS

| | |
|---|---|
| Admissions Rating | 77 |
| # of applicants | 2,268 |
| % of applicants accepted | 95 |
| % of acceptees attending | 28 |

#### FRESHMAN PROFILE

| | |
|---|---|
| Range ACT Composite | 21-28 |
| Average ACT Composite | 24 |
| Minimum TOEFL | 550 |
| Average HS GPA | 3.5 |
| % graduated top 10% of class | 39 |
| % graduated top 25% of class | 66 |
| % graduated top 50% of class | 90 |

#### DEADLINES

| | |
|---|---|
| Priority admission deadline | 12/15 |
| Regular admission | 8/15 |
| Regular notification | rolling |
| Nonfall registration? | yes |

#### APPLICANTS ALSO LOOK AT AND SOMETIMES PREFER

Miami U.
Ohio State U.—Columbus
Whittenberg
Bowling Green State
Toledo

### FINANCIAL FACTS

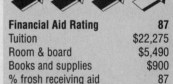

| | |
|---|---|
| Financial Aid Rating | 87 |
| Tuition | $22,275 |
| Room & board | $5,490 |
| Books and supplies | $900 |
| % frosh receiving aid | 87 |
| % undergrads receiving aid | 81 |
| Avg frosh grant | $14,670 |
| Avg frosh loan | $3,693 |

# OHIO STATE UNIVERSITY—COLUMBUS

THIRD FLOOR, LINCOLN TOWER, 1800 CANNON DRIVE, COLUMBUS, OH 43210 • ADMISSIONS: 614-292-3980 • FAX: 614-292-4818

## CAMPUS LIFE

| Quality of Life Rating | 76 |
|---|---|
| Type of school | public |
| Affiliation | none |
| Environment | urban |

### STUDENTS

| | |
|---|---|
| Total undergrad enrollment | 35,749 |
| % male/female | 51/49 |
| % from out of state | 8 |
| % from public high school | 84 |
| % live on campus | 24 |
| % in (# of) fraternities | 6 (33) |
| % in (# of) sororities | 7 (22) |
| % African American | 8 |
| % Asian | 6 |
| % Caucasian | 80 |
| % Hispanic | 2 |
| % international | 4 |

### SURVEY SAYS . . .

*Everyone loves the Buckeyes*
*Students love Columbus, OH*
*Lots of conservatives on campus*
*(Almost) everyone smokes*
*(Almost) everyone plays intramural*
*sports*
*Large classes*
*Lots of TAs teach upper-level*
*courses*
*Ethnic diversity on campus*
*Student publications are popular*
*Lab facilities are great*

## ACADEMICS

| Academic Rating | 67 |
|---|---|
| Calendar | quarter |
| Student/faculty ratio | 13:1 |
| Profs interesting rating | 87 |
| Profs accessible rating | 88 |
| Avg lab size | 20-29 students |
| Avg reg class size | 10-19 students |

### MOST POPULAR MAJORS
psychology
communications
English

## STUDENTS SPEAK OUT

### Academics

Ohio State University "has anything and everything both academically and socially" for those with the patience and tenacity to go after it. With one of the largest undergraduate enrollments in the country, OSU is like a small city, complete with a massive, sometimes-frustrating bureaucracy. For those who can handle this drawback—and for those lucky enough to be admitted to the high-prestige, low-hassle Honors Program—OSU is a bargain hunter's paradise. Career-oriented programs—accounting, nursing, engineering, etc.—are among the university's strongest, as is the school's journalism program. Engineering and business are among other popular majors. "Class size can be too large," warns one student. "Too many people need five years to graduate." Another tempers this observation, noting that "classes are large but professors are very friendly and willing to help." Honors students truly reap the benefits of OSU, receiving "first priority in registration," and sometimes getting into classes with as few as six students taught by "well-known and well-published" professors. Unfortunately, quite a few respondents—even Honors students—feel that graduate students teach too many of the undergraduate courses and that "too many . . . are extremely difficult to understand."

### Life

As with the academic realm, satisfaction with the Ohio State social world requires students' initiative. "This is a big place with lots of great things going, but they won't find you," explains one undergrad. "You must search them out. In order to take advantage of all the opportunities here, you have to be outgoing." Adds another, "No matter what, never pass up the opportunity to get involved in one of the 550 student organizations." The core of OSU life is Buckeye football: "If you don't like football before coming here," warns one student, "you will learn to." Students also love to party ("Pot and Jack Daniels are popular, even in the bleacher during football games"), reporting that "a major part of the OSU lifestyle is the party scene," with plenty of mind-altering substances and other forms of "youthful expression" available. There are also other, legal things to do as well. "This campus is so big, it's tough to categorize anything, except that OSU is justifiably famous for its lines." Sums up one philosophical undergrad, "To attend this school is to have infinite control over your destiny. You can crouch in your room like Gregor Samsa transformed into a dung beetle, or you can plunge into the infinite sea of faces that each year flood OSU like a tidal wave."

### Student Body

"The students make OSU a home rather than just another college," writes one student. "For such a large school, there is a great sense of spirit and community between different kinds of people." Students "of many nationalities, religions, and economic backgrounds" make for a vibrant community. In addition, "There is every social group here, from frat rats to progressives to punks to Deadheads to snobs." And don't forget that "because of OSU's size and diversity, you can always find another person like you." Students are generally politically conservative, and interaction between ethnic groups is reported to be minimal.

# OHIO STATE UNIVERSITY—COLUMBUS

FINANCIAL AID: 614-292-0300 • E-MAIL: ASKABUCKEYE@OSU.EDU • WEBSITE: WWW.OSU.EDU

## ADMISSIONS

*Very important* academic and nonacademic factors considered by the admissions committee include class rank, secondary school record, and standardized test scores. *Important* factors considered include extracurricular activities, minority status, talent/ability, volunteer work, and work experience. *Other* factors considered include essays, geography, recommendations, and state residency. Factors *not* considered include alumni/ae relation, character/personal qualities, interview, and religious affiliation/commitment. SAT I or ACT required. TOEFL required of all international applicants. High school diploma is required and GED is accepted. *High school units required/recommended:* 15 total required; 4 English required, 3 math required, 2 science required, 2 science lab required, 2 foreign language required, 1 visual or performing art and 1 additional unit of above.

### The Inside Word

Although admissions officers consider extracurriculars and other personal characteristics of candidates, there is a heavy emphasis on numbers—grades, rank, and test scores. Although admissions standards have become increasingly competitive in recent years, OSU is still worth a shot for the average student. The university's great reputation and affordable cost make it a good choice for anyone looking at large schools.

## FINANCIAL AID

*Students should submit:* FAFSA. The Princeton Review suggests that all financial aid forms be submitted as soon as possible after January 1. *Need-based scholarships/grants offered:* Pell, SEOG, state scholarships/grants, private scholarships, the school's own gift aid, and United Negro College Fund. *Loan aid offered:* Direct Subsidized Stafford, Direct Unsubsidized Stafford, Direct PLUS, Federal Perkins, Federal Nursing, and college/university loans from institutional funds. Institutional employment available. Federal Work-Study Program available. Applicants will be notified of awards on or about April 1. Off-campus job opportunities are good.

## FROM THE ADMISSIONS OFFICE

"The Ohio State University is Ohio's leading center for teaching, research, and public service. Our exceptional faculty, innovative programs, supportive services, and extremely competitive tuition costs make Ohio State one of higher education's best values. Our central campus is in Columbus, Ohio, the state's largest city. About 48,000 students from every county in Ohio, every state in the nation, and over 87 foreign nations are enrolled at Ohio state. Our faculty include Nobel Prize winners, Rhodes Scholars, members of the National Academy of Sciences, widely published writers, and noted artists and musicians. Our campus boasts world-class facilities like the Wexner Center for the Arts, the nation's largest medical teaching facility, and the new, multibuilding Fisher College of Business. From classes and residence halls to concerts and seminars to clubs and sports and honoraries to Frisbee games on the Oval, Ohio State offers opportunities to develop talents and skills while meeting a variety of people. At Ohio State, you're sure to find a place to call your own."

## ADMISSIONS

| | |
|---|---|
| Admissions Rating | 72 |
| # of applicants | 19,973 |
| % of applicants accepted | 72 |
| % of acceptees attending | 41 |
| # accepting a place on wait list | 149 |
| % admitted from wait list | 36 |

### FRESHMAN PROFILE

| | |
|---|---|
| Range SAT Verbal | 510-630 |
| Average SAT Verbal | 570 |
| Range SAT Math | 530-650 |
| Average SAT Math | 588 |
| Range ACT Composite | 22-28 |
| Average ACT Composite | 25 |
| Minimum TOEFL | 500 |
| % graduated top 10% of class | 32 |
| % graduated top 25% of class | 68 |
| % graduated top 50% of class | 95 |

### DEADLINES

| | |
|---|---|
| Regular admission | 2/15 |
| Nonfall registration? | yes |

### APPLICANTS ALSO LOOK AT
**AND OFTEN PREFER**
Miami U.
Ohio U.
U. Pittsburgh
Bowling Green State
Kent State
U. Cincinnati

**AND RARELY PREFER**
Bellarmine

## FINANCIAL FACTS

| | |
|---|---|
| Financial Aid Rating | 74 |
| In-state tuition | $4,383 |
| Out-of-state tuition | $12,732 |
| Room & board | $5,807 |
| Books and supplies | $888 |
| % frosh receiving aid | 47 |
| % undergrads receiving aid | 43 |
| Avg frosh grant | $3,410 |
| Avg frosh loan | $2,702 |

# OHIO UNIVERSITY—ATHENS

120 Chubb Hall, Athens, OH 45701 • Admissions: 740-593-4100 • Fax: 740-593-0560

## CAMPUS LIFE

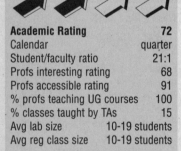

| Quality of Life Rating | 84 |
|---|---|
| Type of school | public |
| Affiliation | none |
| Environment | rural |

### STUDENTS

| | |
|---|---|
| Total undergrad enrollment | 16,712 |
| % male/female | 45/55 |
| % from out of state | 10 |
| % from public high school | 84 |
| % live on campus | 42 |
| % in (# of) fraternities | 13 (20) |
| % in (# of) sororities | 15 (13) |
| % African American | 3 |
| % Asian | 1 |
| % Caucasian | 93 |
| % Hispanic | 1 |
| % international | 2 |
| # of countries represented | 100 |

### SURVEY SAYS . . .
Beautiful campus
Athletic facilities are great
Campus easy to get around
Great library
Great computer facilities
Student publications are ignored
Lousy food on campus
Registration is a pain
Student publications are popular

## ACADEMICS

| Academic Rating | 72 |
|---|---|
| Calendar | quarter |
| Student/faculty ratio | 21:1 |
| Profs interesting rating | 68 |
| Profs accessible rating | 91 |
| % profs teaching UG courses | 100 |
| % classes taught by TAs | 15 |
| Avg lab size | 10-19 students |
| Avg reg class size | 10-19 students |

### MOST POPULAR MAJORS
biological science
journalism
elementary education

## STUDENTS SPEAK OUT
### Academics

Students believe that the academic level at Ohio University is underrated ("Classes are definitely not as easy as some believe") and uniformly praise their education. "It's a wonderful school with great professors who are genuinely interested in the concepts they are teaching us." The journalism program earns especially high praise, though some journalism students complain that they have a difficult time getting into classes within the major. Most professors are held in high regard and "are very nice and accessible outside of class." Ohio operates on a quarterly calendar, and many students laud the system. Though there are few teaching assistants, students complain that the few who are present are difficult to understand because their command of the English language is weak. Students have similar complaints about many of their math professors. First-year students speak of an excellent academic support system. "I was scared that I would get lost in classes, but the teachers were right there to help me find my way." The administration is also appreciated. The advisors are "great," and the dean of students is "personable." The university has attempted to improve the class registration system by implementing online registration. Students agree that while it is still "horrible," online registration is "a step in the right direction."

### Life

Ohio University students describe themselves as "low maintenance" when it comes to having fun. Those who are of age go to the downtown bars for dancing and partying. Weekends usually start on Wednesday night and "you always hear someone talking about how trashed they or their friends were over the weekend." The annual Halloween celebration is legendary. Students "party for an entire weekend," and although mounted police oversee the festivities, "that doesn't stop the girls from [exposing themselves] out a window overlooking the street." While "drinking is the most popular pastime," one student says, "that is not all we do." Students appreciate the "beautiful" campus and because "there really are not a lot of things to do in Athens," students take advantage of the 300-plus on-campus clubs and organizations. Many are associated with the Greek system, and they believe that fraternities and sororities improve campus life. Students support the athletic programs and laud the "new and huge" rec center. Movies are also a popular diversion. Many say that they spend most of their weeknights studying because it is easy to fall behind in a quarterly system if one is not diligent. The campus food needs improvement. "I gave up meat at the first glimpse of what they served me," mutters one journalism major. Students also want the parking situation upgraded.

### Student Body

Nearly 95 percent of Ohio's "laid-back" students are Caucasian, and a majority of the students are "middle class, so . . . everyone seems to be on an even financial level and out to actually get an education, while at the same time enjoying the freedom and experience of college." Students say that their peers are friendly, and only a few are bothered by the lack of on-campus diversity. "There aren't enough minorities, and the minorities that do attend OU assume every white person is racist." Students feel safe on campus.

# OHIO UNIVERSITY—ATHENS

FINANCIAL AID: 740-593-4141 • E-MAIL: ADMISSIONS@OHIOU.EDU • WEBSITE: WWW.OHIOU.EDU

## ADMISSIONS

*Very important* academic and nonacademic factors considered by the admissions committee include secondary school record. *Important* factors considered include class rank, essays, extracurricular activities, interview, recommendations, standardized test scores, talent/ability, and volunteer work. *Other* factors considered include alumni/ae relation, character/personal qualities, geography, minority status, and work experience. Factors *not* considered include religious affiliation/commitment and state residency. SAT I or ACT required, ACT preferred. TOEFL required of all international applicants. High school diploma is required and GED is accepted. *High school units required/recommended:* 4 English recommended, 3 math recommended, 3 science recommended, 2 foreign language recommended, 3 social studies recommended. *The admissions office says:* "Because of the varied backgrounds of the students, the climate of the campus is much more tolerant of people with differences than most competitive schools. Although an essay is optional, applicants are encouraged to submit personal statements and/or a resume."

### The Inside Word

There's little mystery in applying to Ohio U. The admissions process follows the formula approach very closely, and those whose numbers plug in well will get good news.

## FINANCIAL AID

*Students should submit:* FAFSA. The Princeton Review suggests that all financial aid forms be submitted as soon as possible after January 1. *Need-based scholarships/grants offered:* Pell, SEOG, state scholarships/grants, private scholarships, and the school's own gift aid. *Loan aid offered:* Direct Subsidized Stafford, Direct Unsubsidized Stafford, Direct PLUS, Federal Perkins, and college/university loans from institutional funds. Institutional employment available. Federal Work-Study Program available. Applicants will be notified of awards on or about April 1. Off-campus job opportunities are good.

## FROM THE ADMISSIONS OFFICE

"Chartered in 1804, Ohio University symbolizes America's early commitment to higher education. Its historic campus provides a setting matched by only a handful of other universities in the country. Students choose Ohio University mainly because of its academic strength, but the beautiful setting and college-town atmosphere are also factors in their decision. Ohio University is the central focus of Athens, Ohio, located approximately 75 miles southeast of Columbus. We encourage prospective students to come for a visit and experience the beauty and academic excellence of Ohio University."

## ADMISSIONS

| | |
|---|---|
| Admissions Rating | 78 |
| # of applicants | 12,295 |
| % of applicants accepted | 77 |
| % of acceptees attending | 39 |

### FRESHMAN PROFILE

| | |
|---|---|
| Range SAT Verbal | 490-600 |
| Average SAT Verbal | 550 |
| Range SAT Math | 490-600 |
| Average SAT Math | 550 |
| Range ACT Composite | 21-26 |
| Average ACT Composite | 23 |
| Minimum TOEFL | 550 |
| Average HS GPA | 3.4 |
| % graduated top 10% of class | 17 |
| % graduated top 25% of class | 46 |
| % graduated top 50% of class | 87 |

### DEADLINES

| | |
|---|---|
| Regular admission | 2/1 |
| Nonfall registration? | yes |

### APPLICANTS ALSO LOOK AT
**AND OFTEN PREFER**
Oberlin
Miami U.
**AND SOMETIMES PREFER**
Ohio State—Columbus
Michigan State
Penn State—Univ. Park
Wittenberg
U. Cincinnati
**AND RARELY PREFER**
Bowling Green State
Kent State
Purdue U.—West Lafayette
Indiana U.—Bloomington
Dayton

### FINANCIAL FACTS

| | |
|---|---|
| Financial Aid Rating | 76 |
| In-state tuition | $5,085 |
| Out-of-state tuition | $10,704 |
| Room & board | $5,922 |
| Books and supplies | $774 |
| % frosh receiving aid | 43 |
| % undergrads receiving aid | 41 |
| Avg frosh grant | $2,647 |

# OHIO WESLEYAN UNIVERSITY

61 SOUTH SANDUSKY STREET, DELAWARE, OH 43015 • ADMISSIONS: 740-368-3020 • FAX: 740-368-3314

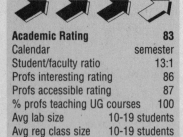

## CAMPUS LIFE

**Quality of Life Rating**   **81**
Type of school   private
Affiliation   Methodist
Environment   suburban

### STUDENTS
Total undergrad enrollment   1,880
% male/female   48/52
% from out of state   40
% from public high school   75
% live on campus   78
% in (# of) fraternities   42 (13)
% in (# of) sororities   36 (8)
% African American   5
% Asian   2
% Caucasian   79
% Hispanic   2
% international   12
# of countries represented   52

### SURVEY SAYS . . .
*Students get along with local community*
*Frats and sororities dominate social scene*
*Registration is a breeze*
*Great food on campus*
*Diverse students interact*
*Ethnic diversity on campus*
*(Almost) no one listens to college radio*

## ACADEMICS

**Academic Rating**   **83**
Calendar   semester
Student/faculty ratio   13:1
Profs interesting rating   86
Profs accessible rating   87
% profs teaching UG courses   100
Avg lab size   10-19 students
Avg reg class size   10-19 students

### MOST POPULAR MAJORS
economics/management
psychology
zoology

## STUDENTS SPEAK OUT
### Academics

At Ohio Wesleyan University, "the atmosphere is comforting, the people are friendly, and the staff is very accessible and caring. I couldn't imagine being anywhere else." To borrow a phrase from Ira Gershwin, who could ask for anything more? In recent years this small midwestern university has grown increasingly well known outside its immediate area, thanks in part to its strength in pre-business studies, English, psychology, and zoology. The school's success in catapulting students into graduate programs—nearly one-third of all graduates proceed directly to grad school—has also played a role in establishing OWU's reputation. Students here enjoy their school's ascending prominence, which they attribute to a faculty that is "very intelligent and passionate about their specialized areas of interest, which transfers into the classroom well." They also appreciate the fact that "the teachers are readily accessible whenever needed, even going to the point of giving out their home phone numbers." Small class and lab sizes help to foster these relationships, and an honors program is available to top students who want a more challenging curriculum. The administration seems to be pulling its weight as well, with solid marks in such categories as accessibility and ease of class registration. Research resources and library and lab facilities are also given the thumbs-up.

### Life

With more than 40 percent of its students active in the Greek scene, OWU hosts one of the stronger fraternity and sorority systems in the country. The situation leaves some students feeling that "if you aren't involved with the Greek system, it's hard to find things to do on weekends," but others point out that "fraternity parties are the primary source of entertainment on the weekends—but not the only possibility. OWU plans a lot of free movies and other activities, and dorms and organizations also put on special events." Relations among frats and between Greeks and independents are peaceful: "The Hill (frats in a cul-de-sac) provides a fun yet safe environment, with no prejudices against independents. Everyone is welcome to walk the Hill and safely walk home." Elsewhere, OWU's Division III intercollegiate sports teams are popular, particularly those in lacrosse and soccer, and "intramural sports like basketball and soccer" also draw enthusiastic crowds. "Community service opportunities abound," with "lots of involvement in the community—tutoring, Big Pal/Little Pal, Patchwork Theater Troupe, and Christian Fellowship groups." As far as college towns go, "Delaware is pretty sleepy, but there are a couple of cool bars." Columbus, Ohio's state capital and the home to Ohio State, is only a short car ride away.

### Student Body

Students at OWU give the school good marks for diversity, primarily the result of a sizable international population. "I love the diversity of our campus! It is truly global and multicultural," writes one student. Remove internationals from the mix and "you've got your midwestern dorks, scholarship geeks, and snobby easterners." Campus relations are good, leading one student to report that "our school has a unique sense of community that is not felt on other campuses. People on the campus genuinely care about and look after each other."

FINANCIAL AID: 740-368-3050 • E-MAIL: OWUADMIT@CC.OWU.EDU • WEBSITE: WWW.OWU.EDU

## ADMISSIONS

*Very important* academic and nonacademic factors considered by the admissions committee include recommendations, character/personal qualities, interview, secondary school record and standardized test scores. *Important* factors considered include talent/ability. *Other* factors considered include alumni/ae relation, essays, extracurricular activities, minority status, volunteer work, and work experience. Factors *not* considered include geography, and religious affiliation/commitment. SAT I or ACT required; SAT II recommended. TOEFL required of all international applicants. High school diploma is required and GED is accepted. *High school units required/recommended:* 4 English required, 3 math required, 3 science required, 1 science lab required, 3 foreign language recommended, 3 social studies required. *The admissions office says:* "We use the SAT I/ACT less and we concentrate more on the students' personal contributions to their school and community. We also look at their personality and creativity. OWU is well known for enrolling students who are independent and individuals who seek a friendly and yet highly diverse environment."

### The Inside Word

OWU's high admit rate garners them both a competetive admit pool, as well as a high yield of those students. Students won't encounter super-selective academic standards for admission, but they will have to put some thought into the completion of their applications. The university's thorough admissions process definitely emphasizes the personal side of candidate evaluation.

## FINANCIAL AID

*Students should submit:* FAFSA and institution's own financial aid form. Regular filing deadline is March 15. The Princeton Review suggests that all financial aid forms be submitted as soon as possible after January 1. *Need-based scholarships/grants offered:* Pell, SEOG, state scholarships/grants, private scholarships, and the school's own gift aid. *Loan aid offered:* Direct Subsidized Stafford, Direct Unsubsidized Stafford, Direct PLUS, Federal Perkins, state, college/university loans from institutional funds, and Private Alternative Loans. Institutional employment available. Federal Work-Study Program available. Applicants will be notified of awards on a rolling basis beginning on or about February 15. Off-campus job opportunities are excellent.

## FROM THE ADMISSIONS OFFICE

"Balance is the key word that describes Ohio Wesleyan. For example: 50 percent male, 50 percent female; 40 percent members of Greek life, 60 percent not; National Colloquium Program; Top Division III sports program; small-town setting of 24,000, near the 16th largest city in U.S. (Columbus, Ohio); excellent faculty/student ratio; outstanding fine and performance arts programs."

## ADMISSIONS

| | |
|---|---:|
| Admissions Rating | 79 |
| # of applicants | 2,016 |
| % of applicants accepted | 81 |
| % of acceptees attending | 33 |
| # accepting a place on wait list | 1 |
| % admitted from wait list | 100 |
| # of early decision applicants | 23 |
| % accepted early decision | 100 |

### FRESHMAN PROFILE

| | |
|---|---:|
| Range SAT Verbal | 540-650 |
| Average SAT Verbal | 600 |
| Range SAT Math | 550-650 |
| Average SAT Math | 598 |
| Range ACT Composite | 23-28 |
| Average ACT Composite | 26 |
| Minimum TOEFL | 550 |
| Average HS GPA | 3.3 |
| % graduated top 10% of class | 30 |
| % graduated top 25% of class | 55 |
| % graduated top 50% of class | 79 |

### DEADLINES

| | |
|---|---:|
| Early decision | 12/1 |
| Early decision notification | 12/30 |
| Priority admission deadline | 3/1 |
| Nonfall registration? | yes |

### APPLICANTS ALSO LOOK AT
**AND OFTEN PREFER**
Miami U.
Ohio State—Columbus
DePauw, Oberlin
U. Vermont
**AND SOMETIMES PREFER**
Wittenberg, Denison
Penn State—Univ. Park
Wooster, Dickinson
**AND RARELY PREFER**
Kenyon
Gettysburg
St. Lawrence, Skidmore
Hobart & William Smith

## FINANCIAL FACTS

| | |
|---|---:|
| Financial Aid Rating | 84 |
| Tuition | $21,880 |
| Room & board | $6,610 |
| Books and supplies | $550 |
| % frosh receiving aid | 62 |
| % undergrads receiving aid | 58 |
| Avg frosh grant | $12,323 |
| Avg frosh loan | $3,850 |

# PENNSYLVANIA STATE UNIVERSITY—UNIVERSITY PARK

201 SHIELDS BUILDING, UNIVERSITY PARK, PA 16802-3000 • ADMISSIONS: 814-865-5471 • FAX: 814-863-7590

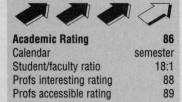
## STUDENTS SPEAK OUT

### Academics

At a helluva big school like Pennsylvania State University, "you can find anything to do academically. If you want a school that will hold your hand, go to Swarthmore. If you're an independent, self-motivated person, come here." The school's main branch offers its students a mind-boggling array of majors, from turfgrass science to ancient Mediterranean studies to aerospace engineering. Engineering at PSU "is a fantastic bargain, provided that you are willing to put in the work." Programs in business, education, and computer science are also excellent. Students warn that "in order to thrive within this gigantic university, you must be able to create your own little world in which to exist. Otherwise, you are not only liable but guaranteed to get lost in the crowd." Several survey respondents offer strategies for coping with PSU's vastness. Writes one, "The longer you are at PSU, the more tricks you learn, and the better and easier it becomes. Here's one: Schedule 24 credits at the beginning of the semester, then pick the five or six classes with the best professors and drop the rest." Offers another, "If you sit in front of classes, you can't tell that there are 150 people behind you." Professors "are very smart and know their stuff, but they are poor communicators." Notes one student, "How good professors are basically depends on two things: your interest in the subject and, more importantly, [whether] they can teach. You can tell some professors are here just to do research, while others can actually teach." While some feel that "TAs are depended on too much" here, others argue that "everyone has negative comments about TAs, but some are actually better, more down-to-earth, and easier to get in touch with than the professors." Administration of the school is unsurprisingly sluggish; recounts one student, "I'm in my fourth semester and I've had two classes cancelled for the semester and one class had a day/time shift. "

### Life

With a student population the size of many American towns, Penn State can offer a wide variety of social options. "Anything you want to do on a weekend," explains one student, "you can find a group of people to do it with. It's not just about drinking. There are concerts, arts, club activities, everything." While it may not be just about drinking, most agree that "Penn State is a party school no matter what anyone says. We throw a party for any reason." Adds another student, "People drink a lot because all there [are] in this town are bars." When students tire of drinking in bars, they . . . drum roll please . . . drink at fraternities! The biggest thing on campus, however, is Nittany Lion football. Reports one student, "Kids go two or three hours early for front-row seats." Students approve of the "beautiful" campus but warn that "it is a pain in the ass to get around campus. Buses are always packed and the campus is huge." They appreciate the school's rural setting, however, which "allows easy access to lots of outdoors activities, like biking, hiking, skiing, canoeing, and boating." As an added bonus, University Park is a "good location for access to major cities (D.C., Baltimore, Philadelphia, Pittsburgh), all three to four hours away." The town itself, however, "is overpriced and pretentious."

### Student Body

The 35,000-plus "very sociable, kind, and easy to talk to" undergraduates of Penn State represent a wide array of attitudes and backgrounds. Writes one student, "A wonderful thing about a large school is that you can find people and opinions from across the board." Geographically, though, "diversity is in short supply, with a large majority of students coming from Pennsylvania." Even though the minority population is proportionally small, they are still 3,000. Unfortunately, "races at PSU segregate themselves. There is no built-in racism; it's all by personal choice." The pragmatic, nonintellectual approach of the majority here doesn't appeal to everyone. To detractors, "the students are all right, but they're like high school students, just a little older."

# PENNSYLVANIA STATE UNIVERSITY—UNIVERSITY PARK

FINANCIAL AID: 814-865-6301 • E-MAIL: ADMISSIONS@PSU.EDU • WEBSITE: WWW.PSU.EDU

## ADMISSIONS

*Very important* academic factors considered by the admissions office include secondary school record and standardized test scores. *Other* factors considered include class rank, extracurricular activities, personal statement, and talent/ability. Factors *not* considered include state residency and religious affiliation. SAT I or ACT required; TOEFL required of international applicants. High school diploma or GED is required. *High school units required/recommended:* 4 English, 3 math, 3 science, 3 social studies, 2 foreign language. *The admissions office says:* "Students are strongly encouraged to apply by our recommended application date of November 30."

### The Inside Word

Penn State is deluged with applicants (they claim to receive more SAT score reports than any other college in the country), which makes it especially important for candidates to have better than average grades and test scores. Although a personal essay and information on extracurricular activities are requested, the university's formula focuses on the numbers. At schools this large it's hard for the admissions process to be more individualized.

## FINANCIAL AID

The Princeton Review suggests that all financial aid forms be submitted as soon as possible after January 1. *Need-based scholarships/grants offered:* Pell, SEOG, state scholarships/grants, private scholarships, the school's own gift aid, and Federal Nursing. *Loan aid offered:* FFEL Subsidized Stafford, FFEL Unsubsidized Stafford, FFEL PLUS, Federal Perkins, and Federal Nursing. Institutional employment available. Off-campus job opportunities are good.

## FROM THE ADMISSIONS OFFICE

"Unique among large public universities, Penn State combines the nearly 35,000-student setting of its University Park campus with 20 academically and administratively integrated undergraduate locations—small-college settings ranging in size from 600 to more than 3,400 students. Each year, over 60 percent of incoming freshman begin their studies at the residential and commuter campuses of the Commonwealth Education System or at Penn State—Erie, the Behrend College, while nearly 40 percent begin at the University Park Campus. The largest number of freshmen begin at the 17 Commonwealth campuses. These locations focus on the needs of new students, offering the first two years of most Penn State baccalaureate degrees in settings that stress close interaction with faculty. Depending on the major selected, students complete their degree at other Penn State locations such as Penn State—Behrend, Penn State—Harrisburg (a junior, senior, and graduate student location), or at the University Park campus. Your application to Penn State qualifies you for review for any of our locations. Your three choices of location are reviewed in the order given. Entrance difficulty is based, in part, on the demand. Due to its popularity, the University Park campus is the most competitive for admission."

## ADMISSIONS

| | |
|---|---|
| Admissions Rating | 85 |
| # of applicants | 28,862 |
| % of applicants accepted | 48 |
| % of acceptees attending | 40 |

### FRESHMAN PROFILE

| | |
|---|---|
| Range SAT Verbal | 530-630 |
| Average SAT Verbal | 593 |
| Range SAT Math | 550-660 |
| Average SAT Math | 617 |
| Minimum TOEFL | 550 |
| Average HS GPA | 3.5 |
| % graduated top 10% of class | 44 |
| % graduated top 25% of class | 80 |
| % graduated top 50% of class | 96 |

### DEADLINES

| | |
|---|---|
| Nonfall registration? | yes |

### APPLICANTS ALSO LOOK AT
### AND OFTEN PREFER
Carnegie Mellon
Georgia Tech.
Muhlenberg
U. Virginia
Lehigh

### AND SOMETIMES PREFER
Bucknell
Miami U.

### AND RARELY PREFER
U. Maryland—College Park

## FINANCIAL FACTS

| | |
|---|---|
| Financial Aid Rating | 84 |
| In-state tuition | $6,546 |
| Out-of-state tuition | $14,088 |
| Room & board | $4,910 |
| Books and supplies | $752 |
| Required fees | $306 |
| % frosh receiving aid | 44 |
| Avg frosh grant | $2,800 |
| Avg frosh loan | $3,193 |

# PEPPERDINE UNIVERSITY

24255 PACIFIC COAST HIGHWAY, MALIBU, CA 90263 • ADMISSIONS: 310-456-4392 • FAX: 310-456-4861

## CAMPUS LIFE

| Quality of Life Rating | 85 |
|---|---|
| Type of school | private |
| Affiliation | Church of Jesus Christ |
| Environment | suburban |

### STUDENTS

| | |
|---|---|
| Total undergrad enrollment | 3,068 |
| % male/female | 42/58 |
| % from out of state | 50 |
| % live on campus | 48 |
| % in (# of) fraternities | 27 (6) |
| % in (# of) sororities | 27 (8) |
| % African American | 7 |
| % Asian | 7 |
| % Caucasian | 55 |
| % Hispanic | 10 |
| % Native American | 1 |
| % international | 7 |
| # of countries represented | 70 |

### SURVEY SAYS . . .
*Very little drug use*
*Frats and sororities dominate social scene*
*Students love Malibu, CA*
*Great food on campus*
*Dorms are like palaces*
*Students are very religious*
*Very little beer drinking*
*Library needs improving*
*Very little hard liquor*
*Computer facilities need improving*

## ACADEMICS

| Academic Rating | 79 |
|---|---|
| Calendar | semester |
| Student/faculty ratio | 12:1 |
| Profs interesting rating | 92 |
| Profs accessible rating | 92 |
| % profs teaching UG courses | 100 |
| Avg lab size | 10-19 students |
| Avg reg class size | 10-19 students |

### MOST POPULAR MAJORS
business administration
telecommunications
sports medicine

## STUDENTS SPEAK OUT
### Academics
To the uninitiated, Pepperdine's spectacular location on the cliffs of Malibu acts almost as a siren bent on deceit—its sybaritic setting belies its conservative bent and affiliation with the Church of Christ. Unless, of course, you happen to notice the 125-foot-tall white stucco cross on campus. The university's stated purpose is "to pursue the very highest academic standards within a context that celebrates and extends the spiritual and ethical ideals of the Christian faith." And they're serious: A weekly assembly is mandatory, the core curriculum contains three religion surveys, and all courses emphasize "Christian values." Many students choose Pepperdine specifically because of its identity; those who are a good fit for such a school are rewarded with excellent academic programs, particularly in pre-professional areas such as communications, business, and computer science. Others feel that "the academics are great but the rules get to be too much at times." Classes "are really small, which is good and bad. The teachers know if you're there, but they can also see if you're sleeping." Speaking of professors, students "love their commitment to students, their dedication to the school, and their enthusiasm about teaching." Not to mention their "personal attention and honest concern." Administrators "are very personable and approachable," and do "a great job of making . . . students feel like people rather than numbers." "The year-in-Europe program is a must. It is the most incredible opportunity of a Pepperdine education."

### Life
"Every day is another day living in paradise." Pepperdine University's campus and location are among the nation's best—where else can you get a dorm room that is "very spacious, and proffers an ocean view?" "Life is great in Malibu. We have a gorgeous beach, great restaurants, and beautiful people all around us." On the other hand, it "sucks as a college town," despite the abundance of "famous people." "You need a car here," because "L.A. provides more than there is time to do." "Peace and serenity" characterize life on campus. The school's religious affiliation results in tough regulations; drinking is prohibited and hanging out in your dorm room with members of the opposite sex is restricted. These rules lead one student to comment, "For a university dedicated to higher learning, it would be nice to get out of the Middle Ages." Those who are not members of the C of C may also find that "religiously, this school is not open-minded. It's affiliated with the Church of Christ and therefore doesn't allow any other religious clubs on campus. Students of different faiths have to leave campus if they want to worship; it's a bit unfair." What campus life there is "revolves completely around fraternities and sororities." Sums up one student: "The frat/sorority scene happens—sports, too—but that's about it."

### Student Body
"Much of the student population comes from a very affluent background, and therefore there is a large gap between those with money and those without." Several Pepperdine students offered similar comments, also describing their classmates as "elitist and materialistic." The student body is divided between devout Christians and all the rest; those who are of the faith "find solace in their similarities" and describe the university community as "a family," while others often feel constricted. Minority enrollment here is high; Asians, Pacific Islanders, and Hispanics are well represented.

# PEPPERDINE UNIVERSITY

FINANCIAL AID: 310-456-4301 • E-MAIL: ADMISSION-SEAVER@PEPPERDINE.EDU • WEBSITE: WWW.PEPPERDINE.EDU

## ADMISSIONS

*Very important* academic and nonacademic factors considered by the admissions committee include character/personal qualities, essays, recommendations, and secondary school record. *Important* factors considered include extracurricular activities, and talent/ability. *Other* factors considered include alumni/ae relation, interview, minority status, standardized test scores, volunteer work, and work experience. Factors *not* considered include geography, religious affiliation/commitment, and state residency. SAT I or ACT required. TOEFL required of all international applicants. High school diploma is required and GED is accepted. *High school units required/recommended:* 4 English required, 3 math required, 2 science required, 3 science recommended, 1 science lab required, 2 science lab recommended, 2 foreign language required, 3 foreign language recommended, 2 social studies required, 2 history recommended. *The admissions office says:* "Academic improvement, triumph over circumstance, and a student's character go a long way in Pepperdine's admissions process. These subjective factors allow us to find the best and brightest students among those who have not excelled in the areas of cumulative GPA or standardized tests. Relation to alumni or membership in the Church of Christ 'may have a positive effect' for marginal candidates."

### The Inside Word

A stunning physical location enables the admissions office to produce beautiful catalogs and viewbooks, which, when combined with the university's reputation for academic quality, help to attract a large applicant pool. In addition to solid grades and test scores, successful applicants typically have well-rounded extracurricular backgrounds. Involvement in school, church, and community is an overused cliché in the world of college admissions, but at Pepperdine it's definitely one of the ingredients in successful applications.

## FINANCIAL AID

*Students should submit:* institution's own financial aid form. The Princeton Review suggests that all financial aid forms be submitted as soon as possible after January 1. *Need-based scholarships/grants offered:* Pell, SEOG, state scholarships/grants, private scholarships, and the school's own gift aid. *Loan aid offered:* FFEL Subsidized Stafford, FFEL Unsubsidized Stafford, FFEL PLUS, Federal Perkins, state, and college/university loans from institutional funds. Institutional employment available. Federal Work-Study Program available. Applicants will be notified of awards on a rolling basis. Off-campus job opportunities are excellent.

## FROM THE ADMISSIONS OFFICE

"As a selective university, Pepperdine seeks students who show promise of academic achievement at the collegiate level. However, we also seek students who are committed to serving the university community, as well as others with whom they come into contact. We look for community service activities, volunteer efforts, and strong leadership qualities, as well as a demonstrated commitment to academic studies and an interest in the liberal arts."

### ADMISSIONS

| | |
|---|---|
| **Admissions Rating** | **85** |
| # of applicants | 5,393 |
| % of applicants accepted | 36 |
| % of acceptees attending | 35 |
| # accepting a place on wait list | 546 |

### FRESHMAN PROFILE

| | |
|---|---|
| Range SAT Verbal | 570-670 |
| Average SAT Verbal | 622 |
| Range SAT Math | 580-680 |
| Average SAT Math | 630 |
| Range ACT Composite | 25-29 |
| Average ACT Composite | 27 |
| Minimum TOEFL | 550 |
| Average HS GPA | 3.75 |

### DEADLINES

| | |
|---|---|
| Regular admission | 1/15 |
| Regular notification | 4/1 |
| Nonfall registration? | yes |

### APPLICANTS ALSO LOOK AT

**AND OFTEN PREFER**
UC—Berkeley
Stanford
UC—Irvine
U. Southern Cal
Loyola Marymount

**AND SOMETIMES PREFER**
UC—Santa Cruz
UC—San Diego
UC—Santa Barbara
U. Colorado—Boulder
Claremont McKenna

**AND RARELY PREFER**
Notre Dame
Vanderbilt
Boston Coll.
BYU

### FINANCIAL FACTS

| | |
|---|---|
| **Financial Aid Rating** | **80** |
| Tuition | $25,180 |
| Room & board | $7,580 |
| Books and supplies | $800 |
| Required fees | $70 |
| % frosh receiving aid | 58 |
| Avg frosh grant | $24,235 |
| Avg frosh loan | $5,363 |

# PITZER COLLEGE

1050 NORTH MILLS AVENUE, CLAREMONT, CA 91711-6101 • ADMISSIONS: 909-621-8129 • FAX: 909-621-8770

## CAMPUS LIFE

**Quality of Life Rating**      **83**
Type of school      private
Affiliation      none
Environment      suburban

### STUDENTS
Total undergrad enrollment    924
% male/female    38/62
% from out of state    48
% live on campus    67
% African American    5
% Asian    12
% Caucasian    56
% Hispanic    14
% Native American    1
% international    4

### SURVEY SAYS . . .
*Political activism is hot*
*Registration is a breeze*
*Great food on campus*
*Great computer facilities*
*Students aren't religious*
*Very small frat/sorority scene*
*No one plays intramural sports*
*Intercollegiate sports unpopular or nonexistent*
*Very little beer drinking*
*Diverse students interact*

## ACADEMICS

**Academic Rating**      **85**
Calendar      semester
Student/faculty ratio      12:1
Profs interesting rating      95
Profs accessible rating      96
% profs teaching UG courses    100
Avg reg class size    15–20 students

### MOST POPULAR MAJORS
psychology
sociology
political studies

## STUDENTS SPEAK OUT

### Academics

"Pitzer is a place for individuals," declares a biology and art major at Pitzer, the most "flexible" and by far the most liberal of the five Claremont Colleges (Claremont McKenna, Harvey Mudd, Pitzer, Pomona, and Scripps). Each Claremont school serves a distinct purpose and maintains its own faculty and campus. Cross-registration among colleges is encouraged. "What is different about Pitzer is that there are very few restraints on your education," explains a double major in English and politics. "You as a student determine how much or how little you learn. With fewer requirements, you are able to decide what kind of education you receive." The curriculum "emphasizes the social and behavioral sciences, particularly psychology, sociology, anthropology, and political science." Pitzer's "fab" and "stupendous" professors are "enthusiastic, knowledgeable, exciting, highly approachable, and generally outrageous." They are also willing to experiment with "nontraditional approaches" to teaching and learning, and many are "very involved in the community outside the classroom." "My friends at large universities gape in awe and say, 'I don't even know who my professors are.'" Students report that the administration is "very eager to please" but "cross-registration among all of the Five Colleges is not what it could be." All in all, "the academic experience is quite challenging and stimulating," says a sophomore. "Pitzer is an eclectic, eccentric institution. It is the perfect place for 'thinkers' and people who want to learn for their own enrichment."

### Life

"This school is somewhere between a country club and a summer camp with some crazy classes on the side," explains a first-year student. "The architecture is a 1960s prison inmate's wet dream," and the "not-exactly-gorgeous" campus is dotted with "student murals and the occasional hammock." Studying tends to be "moderate," and academic stress levels are a lot lower at Pitzer than they are at other Claremont Colleges. "We strive to find the meaning of life through books, drugs, music, sex, conversation, video games, and sleep," explains one student. Students also "host room parties," "ponder stupid questions," "eat lots of pizza," and sample the "good restaurants and variety of shops" around campus. Dorms are "laid back." On and around campus, "the theater is quite decent" and, on weekends, the Five Colleges party scene is usually pretty happening. "If you get bored," you can "flee to the glamour and club life of Los Angeles," only "a half hour away." However, students warn, "L.A. might as well be 20 million miles away if you don't have a car."

### Student Body

Pitzer does have its share of "circus freaks" and there are "lots of piercings," but its days as "a hippie school" are evidently no more. There's still "too much bad hippie music," but Pitzer "has changed in the last few years and now there is a better mix of students and interests." "I was surprised," admits a first-year student. "I was expecting a school running rampant with barefoot, unshaven Ani [DiFranco]-worshipers but this has not been the case. There is actually a shockingly large number of Abercrombie-clad jocks and most everyone else looks like the girl or boy next door." Students say their "very mellow" school is "the friendliest of the five colleges." Pitzer's campus is filled with "a mix of self-righteous individuals, people passionate about what they are doing, and people just enjoying the ride." The "interesting and complicated" students here are "very rich," "very diverse," and "willing to fight for what they believe." "They all seem to have some kind of uniqueness to them that I find intriguing," observes a sophomore. Politically, there is "a strong liberal current, with little tolerance for nonliberal viewpoints." One student describes Pitzer as "a haven for the hypocritically politically correct."

FINANCIAL AID: 909-621-8208 • E-MAIL: ADMISSION@PITZER.EDU • WEBSITE: WWW.PITZER.EDU

## ADMISSIONS

*Very important* academic and nonacademic factors considered by the admissions committee include secondary school record and minority status. *Important* factors considered include geography, character/personal qualities, extracurricular activities, standardized test scores, and talent/ability. *Other* factors considered include class rank, alumni/ae relation, essays, interview, recommendations, volunteer work, and work experience. Factors *not* considered include religious affiliation/commitment and state residency. SAT I or ACT required; SAT II recommended. TOEFL required of all international applicants. High school diploma is required and GED is accepted. *High school units required/recommended:* 20 total recommended; 4 English recommended, 3 math recommended, 3 science recommended, 3 foreign language recommended, 3 social studies recommended. *The admissions office says:* "We are less [standardized] test oriented than most selective colleges. [We look] for students that are socially and politically aware and concerned. We attract more liberal-oriented students, both socially and politically. We also tend to get very creative and unconventional students as well as students that are very traditional but choose to attend a more liberal school."

### The Inside Word

This is a place where applicants can feel confident in letting their thoughts flow freely on admissions essays. Not only does the committee read them (a circumstance more rare in college admissions than one is led to believe), but they've set up the process to emphasize them! Thus, what you have to say for yourself will go much further than numbers in determining your suitability for Pitzer. Paying greater attention to essays also helps Pitzer create a dynamic and engaging freshman class each year.

## FINANCIAL AID

*Students should submit:* FAFSA, CSS/Financial Aid PROFILE, state aid form, noncustodial (divorced/separated) parent's statement, and business/farm supplement. Regular filing deadline is February 1. The Princeton Review suggests that all financial aid forms be submitted as soon as possible after January 1. *Need-based scholarships/grants offered:* Pell, SEOG, state scholarships/grants, private scholarships, and the school's own gift aid. *Loan aid offered:* FFEL Subsidized Stafford, FFEL Unsubsidized Stafford, FFEL PLUS, Federal Perkins, and college/university loans from institutional funds. Institutional employment available. Federal Work-Study Program available. Applicants will be notified of awards on or about April 1. Off-campus job opportunities are good.

## FROM THE ADMISSIONS OFFICE

"Pitzer is about opportunities. It's about possibilities. The students who come here are looking for something different from the usual 'take two courses from column A, two courses from column B, and two courses from column C.' That kind of arbitrary selection doesn't make a satisfying education at Pitzer. So we look for students who want to have an impact on their own education, who want the chief responsibility—with help from their faculty advisors—in designing their own futures."

## ADMISSIONS

| | |
|---|---|
| Admissions Rating | 82 |
| # of applicants | 2,088 |
| % of applicants accepted | 56 |
| % of acceptees attending | 19 |

### FRESHMAN PROFILE

| | |
|---|---|
| Range SAT Verbal | 570-670 |
| Average SAT Verbal | 594 |
| Range SAT Math | 560-650 |
| Average SAT Math | 577 |
| Range ACT Composite | 24-29 |
| Minimum TOEFL | 587 |
| Average HS GPA | 3.5 |
| % graduated top 10% of class | 26 |
| % graduated top 50% of class | 95 |

### DEADLINES

| | |
|---|---|
| Regular admission | 2/1 |
| Regular notification | 4/1 |

### APPLICANTS ALSO LOOK AT
#### AND OFTEN PREFER
UC—Berkeley
Stanford
Pomona
Oberlin
Reed
#### AND SOMETIMES PREFER
Occidental
UCLA
Colorado Coll.
Scripps
UC—Santa Cruz
#### AND RARELY PREFER
U—Davis
UC—San Diego
Middlebury
Grinnell
Sarah Lawrence

### FINANCIAL FACTS

| | |
|---|---|
| Financial Aid Rating | 84 |
| Tuition | $24,260 |
| Room & board | $6,900 |
| Books and supplies | $800 |
| Required fees | $2,770 |
| % frosh receiving aid | 38 |
| % undergrads receiving aid | 52 |
| Avg frosh grant | $17,305 |
| Avg frosh loan | $3,460 |

# POMONA COLLEGE

333 NORTH COLLEGE WAY, CLAREMONT, CA 91711-6312 • ADMISSIONS: 909-621-8134 • FAX: 909-621-8952

## CAMPUS LIFE

| | |
|---|---|
| **Quality of Life Rating** | **87** |
| Type of school | private |
| Affiliation | none |
| Environment | suburban |

### STUDENTS

| | |
|---|---|
| Total undergrad enrollment | 1,565 |
| % male/female | 51/49 |
| % from out of state | 63 |
| % from public high school | 64 |
| % live on campus | 95 |
| % in (# of) fraternities | 8 (4) |
| % African American | 5 |
| % Asian | 16 |
| % Caucasian | 58 |
| % Hispanic | 9 |
| % Native American | 1 |
| % international | 2 |

### SURVEY SAYS . . .
*No one cheats*
*School is well run*
*Athletic facilities are great*
*Great library*
*Dorms are like palaces*
*(Almost) no one smokes*
*Very small frat/sorority scene*
*No one plays intramural sports*
*Musical organizations are hot*

## ACADEMICS

| | |
|---|---|
| **Academic Rating** | **94** |
| Calendar | semester |
| Student/faculty ratio | 9:1 |
| Profs interesting rating | 95 |
| Profs accessible rating | 97 |
| % profs teaching UG courses | 100 |
| Avg lab size | under 10 students |
| Avg reg class size | 10-19 students |

### MOST POPULAR MAJORS
economics
English
biology

## STUDENTS SPEAK OUT

### Academics

"The overall environment is very conducive to learning" at Pomona College, the most distinguished school in the Claremont cluster (which includes Claremont McKenna, Harvey Mudd, Pitzer, and Scripps). Students laud the "traditional liberal arts program" here as well as the "very thought-provoking" and "discussion-oriented" classes. They also like the "the combined resources of the Claremont Colleges" and the fact that they can cross-register at any of the "Five Colleges." However, a degree from Pomona is a long haul. Students must fulfill 10 general education requirements that can take up a lot of time. Then, they concentrate in one field, finishing up with a required comprehensive exam or senior project. Professors are "extremely likable" for the most part. "A few suck, but most are dedicated and truly interested in the subject matter," explains a politics major. The "involved and caring" (though "cheesy") administration receives raves as well. "They roll in so much money that they don't have a choice but to spoil us," explains a sophomore. "Study-break snacks in the dining halls every night at 10:30 P.M.? Done. A $14 million renovation to an already air-conditioned dorm? Done. A new campus center with a bar? Done." In a nutshell, students here live in something of an academic paradise, and they know it.

### Life

"Oftentimes I feel like I live in a utopia," says one of the many happy students at Pomona. For starters, there's an outdoor pool where students can "go swimming in December." The school hosts "incredible visiting speakers" and "there are lots of college-sponsored activities compared to other schools. These range from trips to go shopping on Rodeo Drive to chocolate-and-champagne end-of-semester parties." Students here spend an inordinate amount of time on campus, especially in the residence halls, which are very friendly thanks to "sponsor groups," "15 to 20 freshmen and two sophomores who live next to each other." Sponsor groups are similar to fraternities and sororities, and members participate in planned activities and "eat, sleep, talk, watch movies," and "play sports" together in the dorms. On weekends, the school provides "tons of dough" "for parties" and "alcohol flows like water." "Partying is widely accepted" here and while there is little pressure to join the revelry, Pomona "can be dull at times for nondrinkers." Students report that there is "no dating, just party hookups and full-on relationships." The surrounding town "blows" and "there is a lot of smog," but nearby "Los Angeles has everything you ever dreamed of; you just need to figure out how to get there." Unfortunately, "the L.A. public transportation system is remarkably inefficient." Just like in high school, "people with cars" somehow "have more friends." For students with wheels, "sunny" southern California offers "rock climbing," "mountains, and beaches."

### Student Body

The "very smart and friendly, although somewhat dorky" students at Pomona describe themselves as a "creative, individualistic, motivated," and "cool" bunch. There are "a few knobs" here and a good-size contingent of genuine "nerds." There are also "self-righteous jocks; antisocial, guitar-playing cynics; and workaholics" who "tend to take things too seriously" but most students are "open to new ideas" and they seem to sincerely like each other. "I get the feeling that there's a moratorium on expressing negative feelings," speculates a sophomore. "The campus is high on personality and diversity." "Diversity is not only present; it is like a presidential scandal," analogizes a sophomore; "no one will shut up about it." Politically, Pomona students lean to the left but they are "not politically active." Nevertheless, "when anyone gets upset, the school has a march, holds candlelight vigils, and paints Walker Wall," explains a sophomore. During idle time, there is "a lot of intellectually stimulating conversation" on campus."

FINANCIAL AID: 909-621-8205 • E-MAIL: ADMISSIONS@POMONA.EDU • WEBSITE: WWW.POMONA.EDU

## ADMISSIONS

*Very important* academic and nonacademic factors considered by the admissions committee include character/personal qualities, class rank, essays, extracurricular activities, interview, recommendations, secondary school record, standardized test scores, and talent/ability. *Other* factors considered include alumni/ae relation, geography, minority status, volunteer work, and work experience. Factors *not* considered include religious affiliation/commitment and state residency. SAT II recommended. TOEFL required of all international applicants. *High school units required/recommended:* 18 total recommended; 4 English recommended, 4 math recommended, 3 science recommended, 3 science lab recommended, 2 foreign language recommended, 3 social studies recommended, 3 history recommended.

### The Inside Word

Even though it is tough to get admitted to Pomona, students will find the admissions staff to be accessible and engaging. An applicant pool full of such well-qualified students as those who typically apply, in combination with the college's small size, necessitates that candidates undergo as personal an admissions evaluation as possible. This is how solid matches are made and how Pomona does a commendable job of keeping an edge on the competition.

## FINANCIAL AID

*Students should submit:* FAFSA, CSS/Financial Aid PROFILE, state aid form, noncustodial (divorced/separated) parent's statement, business/farm supplement, and tax returns for both student and parents. Regular filing deadline is February 1. The Princeton Review suggests that all financial aid forms be submitted as soon as possible after January 1. *Need-based scholarships/grants offered:* Pell, SEOG, state scholarships/grants, private scholarships, and the school's own gift aid. *Loan aid offered:* FFEL Subsidized Stafford, FFEL Unsubsidized Stafford, FFEL PLUS, Federal Perkins, and college/university loans from institutional funds. Institutional employment available. Federal Work-Study Program available. Applicants will be notified of awards on or about April 1. Off-campus job opportunities are good.

## FROM THE ADMISSIONS OFFICE

"Perhaps the most important thing to know about Pomona College is that we are what we say we are. There is enormous integrity between the statements of mission and philosophy governing the college and the reality that students, faculty, and administrators experience. The balance in the curriculum is unusual. Sciences, social sciences, humanities, and the arts receive equal attention, support, and emphasis. Most importantly, the commitment to undergraduate education is absolute. Teaching awards remain the highest honor the trustees can bestow upon faculty. The typical method of instruction is the seminar and the average class size of 14 offers students the opportunity to become full partners in the learning process. Our location in the Los Angeles basin and in Claremont, with five other colleges, provides a remarkable community."

### ADMISSIONS

| | |
|---|---|
| Admissions Rating | 95 |
| # of applicants | 3,804 |
| % of applicants accepted | 29.4 |
| % of acceptees attending | 35 |
| # of early decision applicants | 270 |
| % accepted early decision | 43 |

### FRESHMAN PROFILE

| | |
|---|---|
| Range SAT Verbal | 680-760 |
| Average SAT Verbal | 720 |
| Range SAT Math | 680-750 |
| Average SAT Math | 710 |
| Range ACT Composite | 29-32 |
| Average ACT Composite | 32 |
| Minimum TOEFL | 600 |
| % graduated top 10% of class | 83 |
| % graduated top 25% of class | 99 |
| % graduated top 50% of class | 100 |

### DEADLINES

| | |
|---|---|
| Early decision | 11/15 |
| Early decision notification | 12/15 |
| Regular admission | 1/2 |
| Regular notification | 4/10 |

### APPLICANTS ALSO LOOK AT AND OFTEN PREFER
Harvard
UC—Berkeley
Stanford
Yale
Princeton

### AND SOMETIMES PREFER
UCLA
Dartmouth
Williams
Wesleyan U.
Claremont McKenna

### AND RARELY PREFER
UC—Davis
Pitzer

### FINANCIAL FACTS

| | |
|---|---|
| Financial Aid Rating | 88 |
| Tuition | $24,750 |
| Room & board | $8,950 |
| Books and supplies | $850 |
| Required fees | $260 |
| % frosh receiving aid | 50 |
| % undergrads receiving aid | 55 |
| Avg frosh grant | $18,500 |
| Avg frosh loan | $2,000 |

# PRINCETON UNIVERSITY

PO BOX 430, ADMISSION OFFICE, PRINCETON, NJ 08544-0430 • ADMISSIONS: 609-258-3060 • FAX: 609-258-6743

## CAMPUS LIFE

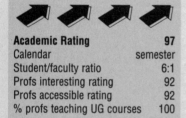

**Quality of Life Rating**    **83**
Type of school    private
Affiliation    none
Environment    suburban

### STUDENTS

| | |
|---|---|
| Total undergrad enrollment | 4,663 |
| % male/female | 53/47 |
| % from out of state | 85 |
| % from public high school | 60 |
| % live on campus | 97 |
| % African American | 8 |
| % Asian | 13 |
| % Caucasian | 72 |
| % Hispanic | 6 |
| % Native American | 1 |
| % international | 6 |

### SURVEY SAYS . . .

*Lots of classroom discussion*
*Registration is a breeze*
*Diverse students interact*
*No one cheats*
*(Almost) everyone smokes*
*Very small frat/sorority scene*
*Computer lab facilities need improving*
*Intercollegiate sports unpopular or nonexistent*
*Lousy food on campus*
*No one plays intramural sports*

## ACADEMICS

**Academic Rating**    **97**
Calendar    semester
Student/faculty ratio    6:1
Profs interesting rating    92
Profs accessible rating    92
% profs teaching UG courses    100

### MOST POPULAR MAJORS
economics
politics
history

## STUDENTS SPEAK OUT

### Academics

Princeton University is arguably the most undergraduate-friendly member of the Ivy League. Its peers and other institutions at a similar level of prestige often feature prominent and powerful professional schools in business, law, and/or medicine, but not Princeton. Over the years, the students we've surveyed here are consistently among the nation's most satisfied with their overall academic experience. A sophomore sums it up as "my dream come true." Academic offerings are excellent; particularly noteworthy are engineering ("It has a friendly 'we're in this together' atmosphere—no 'cutthroat, kill-the-curve-breaker' competition like at MIT," writes one engineer), political science, history, religion, and English. Core distribution requirements guarantee that all students are schooled in the classic academic disciplines (math, natural and social sciences, humanities). A series of independent projects that culminates in a senior thesis gives upperclassmen an unusual amount of responsibility for their own education. "Precepts," once-a-week small-group discussion meetings with each class's professor or TA, offer the opportunity for more personal attention. Professors get solid reviews, ranging from the enthusiastic "brilliant," to the more down-to-earth "good and very accessible." TAs "deserve their much-maligned status" according to a sophomore, but a freshman opines that they're "often better teachers than professors." The amount of work here is "difficult but not overbearing"; Princeton students study no more than the average student surveyed for *Best Colleges*.

### Life

"Princeton inspires love in 90 percent of its undergrads, and hate in 10 percent—it's very insular [and] clubby, but beautiful, charmed, and almost magical," according to one student. Social life centers on the beautiful Gothic campus: "The town and the university are like a divorced couple no longer on speaking terms. They ignore each other. The town offers no student-oriented cafés or amusements within a student's budget. Off-campus housing is exorbitant." Underclassmen live in groups of residential "colleges," each of which provides meals and sponsors a roster of extracurricular activities. For upperclassmen, one of the key elements of life here is "eating clubs," which are a lot like Greek organzations; they provide meals, host parties, and place students in a "sub-community." Most students join one of the 13 eating clubs during sophomore year. Eight of the clubs choose members by lottery; the other five hand-pick members through a process called "bicker." Students report a "big gulf between residential college underclassmen and upperclassmen in eating clubs." Fraternities exist but are not officially sanctioned and have limited memberships. Parties here tend to be "orgies of beer"; "If you're not into the drinking scene, your social life could be a bit mundane." Students actively support Tiger athletic teams, which are particularly strong in basketball and lacrosse.

### Student Body

One student reports that "Princeton today is like Princeton of the last century—it fully deserves its preppy/boarding school reputation." An apparently satisfied and encouraging Hispanic student writes that "if you are a minority, you must come here." Though nearly a quarter of the student body is comprised of minority students, some still feel that the university is "not very diverse." A few call for "more . . . socioeconomic diversity," while others have of late expressed concern about the dwindling percentage of Jewish students in the campus population. Several students seem surprised that their classmates are not nerds, but others characterize their classmates as "anti-intellectual: it's not considered cool to talk about your work or seem passionately committed to it." F. Scott "Fitzgerald described his peers [here] as capricious, and we still are. It can be frustrating, but also fun."

FINANCIAL AID: 609-258-3330 • WEBSITE: WWW.PRINCETON.EDU

## ADMISSIONS

*Very important* academic and nonacademic factors considered by the admissions committee include secondary school record. *Important* factors considered include class rank, recommendations, and standardized test scores. *Other* factors considered include alumni/ae relation, character/personal qualities, essays, minority status, extracurricular activities, geography, talent/ability, volunteer work, and work experience. Factors *not* considered include interview, religious affiliation/commitment, and state residency. SAT I or ACT required, SAT I preferred; SAT II also required. TOEFL required of all international applicants. *High school units required/recommended:* 20 total recommended; 4 English recommended, 4 math recommended, 2 science recommended, 2 science lab recommended, 4 foreign language recommended, 2 history recommended.

### The Inside Word

Princeton is much more open about the admissions process than the rest of their Ivy compatriots. The admissions staff evaluates candidates' credentials using a 1–5 rating scale, common among highly selective colleges. In the initial screening of applicants, admissions staff members assigned to particular regions of the country eliminate weaker students before the admissions committee makes its evaluation. Princeton's recommendation to interview should be considered a requirement, given the ultra-competitive nature of the applicant pool. In addition, three SAT IIs are required; no joke, indeed.

## FINANCIAL AID

*Students should submit:* FAFSA, institution's own financial aid form, CSS/Financial Aid PROFILE, state aid form, noncustodial (divorced/separated) parent's statement, and business/farm supplement. Regular filing deadline is February 1. The Princeton Review suggests that all financial aid forms be submitted as soon as possible after January 1. *Need-based scholarships/grants offered:* Pell, SEOG, private scholarships, and the school's own gift aid. *Loan aid offered:* Direct Subsidized Stafford, Direct Unsubsidized Stafford, Direct PLUS, FFEL Subsidized Stafford, FFEL Unsubsidized Stafford, FFEL PLUS, Federal Perkins, state, and college/university loans from institutional funds. Important to note is Princeton's new no-loan policy whereby all students qualifying for need-based financial aid will accrue no loan debt in their four years at Princeton. Institutional employment available. Federal Work-Study Program available. Applicants will be notified of awards on or about April 1. Off-campus job opportunities are good.

## FROM THE ADMISSIONS OFFICE

"Methods of instruction [at Princeton] vary widely, but common to all areas . . . is a strong emphasis on individual responsibility and the free interchange of ideas. This is displayed most notably in the wide use of preceptorials and seminars, in the provision of independent study for all upperclass students and qualified underclass students, and in the availability of a series of special programs to meet a range of individual interests. The undergraduate college encourages the student to be an independent seeker of information . . . and to assume responsibility for gaining both knowledge and judgment that will strengthen later contributions to society."

### ADMISSIONS

| | |
|---|---|
| Admissions Rating | 99 |
| # of applicants | 13,654 |
| % of applicants accepted | 12 |
| % of acceptees attending | 68 |
| # of early decision applicants | 1669 |
| % accepted early decision | 35 |

#### FRESHMAN PROFILE

| | |
|---|---|
| Range SAT Verbal | 700-780 |
| Average SAT Verbal | 740 |
| Range SAT Math | 710-790 |
| Average SAT Math | 750 |
| Range ACT Composite | 31-35 |
| Average ACT Composite | 33 |
| Minimum TOEFL | 630 |
| % graduated top 10% of class | 92 |
| % graduated top 25% of class | 100 |
| % graduated top 50% of class | 100 |

#### DEADLINES

| | |
|---|---|
| Early decision | 11/1 |
| Early decision notification | 12/15 |
| Regular admission | 1/2 |
| Regular notification | 4/1 |

#### APPLICANTS ALSO LOOK AT AND SOMETIMES PREFER

Harvard
Yale
Stanford
MIT

#### AND RARELY PREFER

Dartmouth
Brown
Duke
Columbia
Williams

### FINANCIAL FACTS

| | |
|---|---|
| Financial Aid Rating | 80 |
| Tuition | $26,160 |
| Room & board | $7,453 |
| Books and supplies | $2,765 |
| % frosh receiving aid | 39 |
| Avg frosh grant | $25,000 |

# PROVIDENCE COLLEGE

RIVER AVENUE AND EATON STREET, PROVIDENCE, RI 02918 • ADMISSIONS: 401-865-2535 • FAX: 401-865-2826

## CAMPUS LIFE

**Quality of Life Rating**    **78**
| | |
|---|---|
| Type of school | private |
| Affiliation | Roman Catholic |
| Environment | suburban |

### STUDENTS
| | |
|---|---|
| Total undergrad enrollment | 4,405 |
| % male/female | 42/58 |
| % from out of state | 76 |
| % from public high school | 58 |
| % live on campus | 66 |
| % African American | 1 |
| % Asian | 2 |
| % Caucasian | 87 |
| % Hispanic | 4 |
| % international | 1 |

### SURVEY SAYS . . .
*Diversity lacking on campus*
*Everyone loves the Friars*
*Hard liquor is popular*
*Students are cliquish*
*(Almost) everyone plays intramural sports*
*Very small frat/sorority scene*
*Students are very religious*
*Registration is a pain*
*Library needs improving*
*Lousy food on campus*

## ACADEMICS

| | |
|---|---|
| **Academic Rating** | **78** |
| Calendar | semester |
| Student/faculty ratio | 13:1 |
| Profs interesting rating | 89 |
| Profs accessible rating | 92 |
| % profs teaching UG courses | 100 |
| Avg lab size | 10-19 students |
| Avg reg class size | 10-19 students |

### MOST POPULAR MAJORS
management/marketing
elementary/special education
biology

## STUDENTS SPEAK OUT

### Academics

Providence College: Welcome to an enjoyable but "demanding" academic experience. Students attend Providence because it is a small Catholic school with a reputation for its strong liberal arts program. The required two-year humanities course, "The Development of Western Civilization," is highly regarded and "comes in handy when watching Jeopardy." Some students complain that it also "lacks perspective outside" of that which is provided by the "white Catholic male" professors. Students appreciate that there are no TAs and that professors are, as one senior political science major puts it, "friendly and easily accessible." Professors "go out of their way to help students—even those not in their classes," a junior communications major brags. Though introductory classes tend to be easy, upper-level classes are "interesting and challenging." The Honors Program is "excellent," and the education program also garners high praise. The administration is "very rigid, keeping in close accordance with traditional Catholic policy," one junior reports, though students admit that the administration is also "very easy to communicate with." Class registration is "frustrating" because some students complain that athletes are provided preferential treatment.

### Life

"Life at Providence College involves working hard during the week and partying on the weekends." Speaking of other entertainment options, one senior management major notes, "there are also many theaters, shows, and intellectually stimulating events in and around the Providence College campus." Downtown Providence is a popular destination. The town's numerous quality restaurants are standard haunts. Students also spend a good deal of time working for various community service organizations. The college's basketball team plays in the powerful Big East conference and often fights its way into the NCAA Tournament. The hockey team is also a popular draw. A political science major speculates that "Friar hockey games [have] become the biggest social event on campus." Students are unhappy with the on-campus food, which one sophomore calls "repulsive," and the dorms. They also complain that the exercise facilities are woefully insufficient and that the school needs an indoor track. Students say that the nearby Indian casinos are a great place to blow off some steam.

### Student Body

A great sense of community pervades Providence College, thanks largely to the fact that students are "very involved on campus, especially through volunteer work." Some students sadly note that their peers "are very likely to conform to the latest styles and social norms." One sophomore admits that her fellow students are "mostly white, Irish-Catholic Republicans, and if you don't fit that mold, you're looked upon as different." Students tend to be "clique-y" and "overly materialistic" as well as "shallow" and "snobbish," and diversity is sorely lacking. "We need more people from different backgrounds, and not just minorities, to open people up to seeing things another way." One biology major affirms, "The lack of diversity is frustrating." Nevertheless, students overwhelmingly admit that their peers are extremely friendly. "There is a familial atmosphere" at Providence College.

FINANCIAL AID: 401-865-2286 • E-MAIL: PCADMISS@PROVIDENCE.EDU • WEBSITE: WWW.PROVIDENCE.EDU

## ADMISSIONS

*Very important* academic and nonacademic factors considered by the admissions committee include class rank, essays, recommendations, and secondary school record. *Important* factors considered include character/personal qualities, extracurricular activities, interview, standardized test scores, and talent/ability. *Other* factors considered include alumni/ae relation, geography, minority status, volunteer work, and work experience. Factors *not* considered include religious affiliation/commitment and state residency. SAT I or ACT required; SAT II recommended. TOEFL required of all international applicants. High school diploma is required and GED is not accepted. *High school units required/recommended:* 18 total required; 4 English required, 3 math required, 2 science required, 3 science recommended, 3 foreign language required, 2 social studies required, 1 history required, 4 elective recommended.

### The Inside Word

Providence's reputation for quality is solidly in place among above-average graduates of northeastern Catholic high schools, who account for almost a quarter of the applicant pool. The strength of these candidates is one of the primary factors that allow the college to be choosy about who gets in. Successful candidates usually project a well-rounded, conservative image. The Friars' surprise appearance in the "elite eight" of the NCAA Division I basketball tournament last March should give applications a boost.

## FINANCIAL AID

*Students should submit:* FAFSA and CSS/Financial Aid PROFILE. Regular filing deadline is February 1. The Princeton Review suggests that all financial aid forms be submitted as soon as possible after January 1. *Need-based scholarships/grants offered:* Pell, SEOG, state scholarships/grants, private scholarships, and the school's own gift aid. *Loan aid offered:* Direct Subsidized Stafford, Direct Unsubsidized Stafford, Direct PLUS, FFEL Subsidized Stafford, FFEL Unsubsidized Stafford, FFEL PLUS, and Federal Perkins. Institutional employment available. Federal Work-Study Program available. Applicants will be notified of awards on or about April 7. Off-campus job opportunities are excellent.

## FROM THE ADMISSIONS OFFICE

"Infused with the history, tradition, and learning of a 700-year-old Catholic teaching order, the Dominican Friars, Providence College offers a value-affirming environment where students are enriched through spiritual, social, physical, and cultural growth as well as through intellectual development. Providence College offers over 36 programs of study leading to baccalaureate degrees in business, education, the sciences, arts, and humanities. Our faculty is noted for a strong commitment to teaching. A close student/faculty relationship allows for in-depth classwork, independent research projects, and detailed career exploration. While noted for the physical facilities and academic opportunities associated with larger universities, Providence also fosters personal growth through a small, spirited, family-like atmosphere that encourages involvement in student activities and athletics."

## ADMISSIONS

| | |
|---|---|
| Admissions Rating | 82 |
| # of applicants | 5,543 |
| % of applicants accepted | 57 |
| % of acceptees attending | 29 |
| # accepting a place on wait list | 426 |
| % admitted from wait list | 47 |

### FRESHMAN PROFILE

| | |
|---|---|
| Range SAT Verbal | 540-630 |
| Average SAT Verbal | 585 |
| Range SAT Math | 550-640 |
| Average SAT Math | 595 |
| Range ACT Composite | 23-28 |
| Average ACT Composite | 25 |
| Minimum TOEFL | 550 |
| Average HS GPA | 3.4 |
| % graduated top 10% of class | 35 |
| % graduated top 25% of class | 71 |
| % graduated top 50% of class | 97 |

### DEADLINES

| | |
|---|---|
| Regular admission | 1/15 |
| Regular notification | 4/1 |
| Nonfall registration? | yes |

### APPLICANTS ALSO LOOK AT

**AND OFTEN PREFER**
Boston Coll.
Holy Cross
Fairfield
Villanova, Stonehill

**AND SOMETIMES PREFER**
U. Scranton
U. Vermont
U. New Hampshire
U. Conn
U. Mass—Amherst

**AND RARELY PREFER**
U. Rhode Island
Bentley
Boston U.
Fordham

### FINANCIAL FACTS

| | |
|---|---|
| Financial Aid Rating | 73 |
| Tuition | $18,440 |
| Room & board | $7,625 |
| Books and supplies | $650 |
| Required fees | $310 |
| % frosh receiving aid | 59 |
| % undergrads receiving aid | 60 |
| Avg frosh grant | $7,636 |
| Avg frosh loan | $4,125 |

# PURDUE UNIVERSITY—WEST LAFAYETTE

1080 SCHLEMAN HALL, WEST LAFAYETTE, IN 47907 • ADMISSIONS: 765-494-1776 • FAX: 765-494-0544

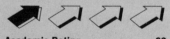
## STUDENTS SPEAK OUT

### Academics

Purdue University is one of the great buys of higher education, especially for in-staters, who make up the vast majority of students. With career-minded undergrads and great programs in business and engineering (one in five pursues an engineering degree), Purdue is run efficiently and effectively. The administration receives above-average marks from students for its accessibility and responsiveness: "The administration at Purdue makes itself extremely accessible. The student body and the school administration offer constructive feedback on a regular basis," reports one respondent. Some groan about long lines ("It's a long wait at the bursar's office") and old systems ("The school needs to automate most processes including registering for classes"), but most feel that the school is smoothly run overall, especially given its size. Classes tend to be rigorous ("The academic program is challenging for all majors. I like the environment here because the pressure keeps me on my feet"), and some students complain of overwork ("I love taking classes where the professors think that the class is the only one I'm enrolled in," as one student sarcastically put it). Professors receive good marks for competence ("Professors are well-known and respected in their fields" and are "really good at getting their points across"), but students feel they need improvement in enthusiasm and accessibility. Facilities receive average marks ("Library needs improvement in its computers"; "Labs are now open later"). But more than one student claims that Purdue is "completely underrated. It's a great academic experience. Purdue is the 'sleeper' education of the U.S.!"

### Life

Purdue students give the campus's surrounding area low-to-average marks. However, activities do exist on campus for those students who make the effort to find them: "You basically make your own fun." An overwhelmingly large number of our respondents cite drinking as a popular activity. "In terms of entertainment, there ain't much," says one. "Most people go to pubs to drink and hang out." Another observes that "the emphasis surrounding Purdue's campus seems to be on alcohol and party-like behavior. Everyone tends to live for the weekends, if only to get away from the humdrum-ness of classes." But Purdue students still take their studies very seriously: "More students are concerned with their grades here than at other schools. I study a lot." Purdue's large Greek system used to dominate the social scene here, but more than one respondent notes that "Greek life isn't as popular as it used to be. It's a very conservative campus, but that's starting to change."

### Student Body

The happiest students in our survey were the ones who were most accepting of Purdue's conservative leanings. "I feel the students of Purdue U are very friendly and typically lean toward the conservative side." One Prairie Village, Kansas, native proclaims, "Very easy-going student body. Most relaxed, clean-cut, crime-free major university in the nation!" Other respondents, while happy with their fellow students, were dissatisfied with the lack of diversity and acceptance they felt was apparent on their campus. "I get along with my fellow students, yet I think, for being such a large campus, that it is very narrow-minded, culturally biased, and dull. There are too many small-town students and too many engineers." Notes another, "Students are friendly in general, but the campus is very segregated. Members of different ethnic groups often socialize with only each other."

FINANCIAL AID: 765-494-5050 • E-MAIL: ADMISSIONS@ADMS.PURDUE.EDU • WEBSITE: WWW.PURDUE.EDU

## ADMISSIONS

*Very important* academic and nonacademic factors considered by the admissions committee include class rank, secondary school record, and standardized test scores. *Other* factors considered include alumni/ae relation, geography, recommendations, and state residency. Factors *not* considered include character/personal qualities, essays, extracurricular activities, interview, minority status, religious affiliation/commitment, talent/ability, volunteer work, and work experience. SAT I or ACT required. TOEFL required of all international applicants. High school diploma is required and GED is accepted. *High school units required/recommended:* 15 total required; 4 English required, 3 math required, 3 science required, 2 foreign language required, 4 foreign language recommended, 3 social studies required.

### The Inside Word

The fact that Purdue holds class rank as one of its most important considerations in the admission of candidates is troublesome. There are far too many inconsistencies in ranking policies and class size among the 25,000-plus high schools in the U.S. to place so much weight on an essentially incomparable number. The university's high admit rate thankfully renders the issue relatively moot, even though applications have increased.

## FINANCIAL AID

*Students should submit:* FAFSA. The Princeton Review suggests that all financial aid forms be submitted as soon as possible after January 1. *Need-based scholarships/grants offered:* Pell, SEOG, state scholarships/grants, private scholarships, and the school's own gift aid. *Loan aid offered:* FFEL Subsidized Stafford, FFEL Unsubsidized Stafford, FFEL PLUS, Federal Perkins, and college/university loans from institutional funds. Institutional employment available. Federal Work-Study Program available. Applicants will be notified of awards on or about April 15. Off-campus job opportunities are good.

## FROM THE ADMISSIONS OFFICE

"Although it is one of America's largest universities, Purdue does not 'feel' big to its students. The main campus in West Lafayette was built around a master plan that keeps walking time between classes to a maximum of 12 minutes. Purdue is a comprehensive university with an international reputation in a wide range of academic fields. A strong work ethic prevails at Purdue. As a member of the Big 10, Purdue has a strong and diverse athletic program. Purdue offers nearly 600 clubs and organizations. The residence halls and Greek community offer many participatory activities for students. Numerous convocations and lectures are presented each year. Purdue is all about people, and allowing students to grow academically as well as socially, preparing them for the real world."

## ADMISSIONS

| | |
|---|---|
| Admissions Rating | 75 |
| # of applicants | 20,405 |
| % of applicants accepted | 78 |
| % of acceptees attending | 40 |

### FRESHMAN PROFILE

| | |
|---|---|
| Range SAT Verbal | 500-600 |
| Average SAT Verbal | 550 |
| Range SAT Math | 520-640 |
| Average SAT Math | 580 |
| Range ACT Composite | 22-28 |
| Average ACT Composite | 25 |
| Minimum TOEFL | 550 |
| % graduated top 10% of class | 27 |
| % graduated top 25% of class | 61 |
| % graduated top 50% of class | 94 |

### DEADLINES

| | |
|---|---|
| Priority admission deadline | 3/1 |
| Nonfall registration? | yes |

### APPLICANTS ALSO LOOK AT

**AND OFTEN PREFER**
Indiana U.—Bloomington
Valparaiso
U. Illinois
Rose—Hulman

**AND SOMETIMES PREFER**
Penn State—U. Park
U. Wisconsin—Madison

**AND RARELY PREFER**
Hanover

### FINANCIAL FACTS

| | |
|---|---|
| Financial Aid Rating | 76 |
| In-state tuition | $3,872 |
| Out-of-state tuition | $12,904 |
| Room & board | $5,800 |
| Books and supplies | $780 |
| % frosh receiving aid | 35 |
| % undergrads receiving aid | 37 |

# RANDOLPH-MACON COLLEGE

BOX 5005-5505, ASHLAND, VA 23005 • ADMISSIONS: 804-752-7305 • FAX: 804-752-4707

## CAMPUS LIFE

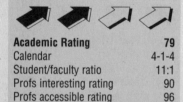

**Quality of Life Rating** **85**
Type of school                private
Affiliation                   Methodist
Environment                   suburban

### STUDENTS
Total undergrad enrollment    1,171
% male/female                 49/51
% from out of state           42
% from public high school     71
% live on campus              90
% in (# of) fraternities      45 (7)
% in (# of) sororities        45 (4)
% African American            5
% Asian                       1
% Caucasian                   91
% Hispanic                    1
% international               2
# of countries represented    9

### SURVEY SAYS . . .
*Campus easy to get around*
*Athletic facilities are great*
*Beautiful campus*
*Great library*
*Great computer facilities*
*Students are cliquish*
*Political activism is (almost)*
*nonexistent*
*Student publications are ignored*
*(Almost) no one listens to college*
*radio*

## ACADEMICS

**Academic Rating**           **79**
Calendar                      4-1-4
Student/faculty ratio         11:1
Profs interesting rating      90
Profs accessible rating       96
% profs teaching UG courses   100

### MOST POPULAR MAJORS
economics/business
English
sociology

## STUDENTS SPEAK OUT

### Academics

"The academic process" at "challenging" Randolph-Macon College "is like Burger King," explains a business major, "your way, right away." Indeed, if R-MC stands for one thing, it appears to be more "personal attention" than you can shake a stick at. R-MC boasts "small classes in which you can get good academic support" and, while it's "not a hard school to get into, R-MC is hard to stay in." Students say "there are few employees on this campus who are unwilling to help students out," and they simply adore the faculty. R-MC professors are "readily available, personable, excellent teachers" who "have a genuine desire to teach" and who are "always there for extra help." The 4-1-4 calendar here includes a January term, during which students explore nontraditional academic themes, undertake field study and internships, or study abroad. Randolph-Macon also offers an extensive internship program where students can gain "real world" experience, and all students are encouraged to participate in original research projects with members of the faculty. In addition, R-MC students may take courses at any of the other schools in the Seven Colleges Consortium of Virginia (Washington and Lee, Hampden-Sydney, Sweet Briar, Mary Baldwin, Hollins, or Randolph-Macon Woman's College). After they graduate, almost two-thirds continue their education within five years.

### Life

Students at Randolph-Macon report that their "beautiful" campus provides a "a safe and comfortable environment." They really like "the smallness" of R-MC. "We never have to leave campus because everything is here and it's so fun," beams a junior. "It's hard for things to go too bad at such a small school. When anything goes wrong, the administration takes care of it quickly and effectively." Few schools in the United States can boast a Greek system more prominent than the one here. "Greek life is huge," and nearly half of the men and women here belong to a fraternity or sorority. Some students go so far as to say that fraternity parties—which are "open to the whole school"—are "the only source of entertainment on campus." Other students beg to differ, citing over 100 clubs and organizations operating outside the Greek system. But with all the parties, there is "lots of drinking." R-MC students are also "very involved" in extracurricular activities, especially "intercollegiate athletics," which are "very important." Students log a lot of hours "as participants and as fans," and "sports and fitness" are generally "a huge part of campus life." There are also "lectures, guest speakers," and a nearby mall and the movie theater. The surrounding suburban hamlet of Ashland is definitely not a metropolis, but students who want a taste of city life can "go to Richmond," which is minutes away. Virginia Beach and Washington, D.C., are not too far, and the Blue Ridge Mountains are about an hour north.

### Student Body

At "friendly" R-MC, "Everyone knows each other and there seems to be a bond between the students," explains a sophomore. "It is really easy to get along with people, but, of course, everyone has their own little groups they hang out with." Students admit that they can be "a little too into the Greek thing" at times. Gossip "travels fast" on campus and there are "a few fraternity and sorority rivalries" as well, but mostly "everyone helps everyone else." The "very homogenous" students themselves are "somewhat cookie-cutter," and they hold "similar ideas, backgrounds, beliefs." They regard themselves as moderate to conservative politically, but most aren't especially active politically. Mostly, R-MC students just "don't react well to change or to anything they don't have a say in," according to a sage senior. The population at R-MC is mostly white, with very small African American and Asian contingents.

# RANDOLPH-MACON COLLEGE

FINANCIAL AID: 804-752-7259 • E-MAIL: ADMISSIONS@RMC.EDU • WEBSITE: WWW.RMC.EDU

## ADMISSIONS

*Very important* academic and nonacademic factors considered by the admissions committee include class rank and secondary school record. *Important* factors considered include recommendations and standardized test scores. *Other* factors considered include alumni/ae relation, character/personal qualities, essays, extracurricular activities, interview, minority status, talent/ability, volunteer work, and work experience. Factors *not* considered include geography, religious affiliation/commitment, and state residency. SAT I or ACT required, SAT I preferred; SAT II also recommended. TOEFL required of all international applicants. High school diploma is required and GED is accepted. *High school units required/recommended:* 16 total required; 22 total recommended; 4 English required, 3 math required, 4 math recommended, 3 science required, 4 science recommended, 2 science lab required, 3 science lab recommended, 2 foreign language required, 4 foreign language recommended, 3 social studies required.

### The Inside Word

Candidates who are above-average students and testers are very likely to receive scholarships at Randolph-Macon. The college has a low yield of admits who enroll, and every strong student who signs on gives the freshman academic profile a boost. If the competition among Virginia colleges weren't so strong, admission to Randolph-Macon would be much tougher.

## FINANCIAL AID

*Students should submit:* FAFSA. The Princeton Review suggests that all financial aid forms be submitted as soon as possible after January 1. *Need-based scholarships/grants offered:* Pell, SEOG, state scholarships/grants, private scholarships, and the school's own gift aid. *Loan aid offered:* FFEL Subsidized Stafford, FFEL Unsubsidized Stafford, FFEL PLUS, Federal Perkins, and college/university loans from institutional funds. Institutional employment available. Federal Work-Study Program available. Applicants will be notified of awards on or about April 1. Off-campus job opportunities are good.

## FROM THE ADMISSIONS OFFICE

"Randolph-Macon is an independent, coeducational college with the broadest liberal arts core curriculum in Virginia. The academic program is designed to allow students considerable freedom in planning their own program, while showing them that they will acquire not only the breadth of knowledge traditionally emphasized in a liberal education but also a sound foundation in a particular field. Students receive solid support from advisors, faculty, and peers. The Counseling and Career Center provides personal and career counseling as well as workshops and seminars. The combination of people, programs, and services prepares students for any future, including success in securing a job or in gaining acceptance to graduate or professional school. The college offers a wide variety of social and recreational opportunities. A full-time student activities director works in conjunction with over 70 campus organizations to ensure that almost every day there are activities and events in which students can participate; 40 percent of the students participate in one or more community service activities; 70 percent play intramural sports; 45 percent join a fraternity or sorority; and everyone has a voice in student government. A new $9.5 million sports and recreation center recently opened and a new performing arts center is now under renovation and is scheduled to open in winter 2000."

## ADMISSIONS

| | |
|---|---|
| Admissions Rating | 76 |
| # of applicants | 2,083 |
| % of applicants accepted | 70 |
| % of acceptees attending | 24 |
| # accepting a place on wait list | 61 |
| # of early decision applicants | 43 |
| % accepted early decision | 70 |

### FRESHMAN PROFILE

| | |
|---|---|
| Range SAT Verbal | 510-600 |
| Average SAT Verbal | 558 |
| Range SAT Math | 510-600 |
| Average SAT Math | 552 |
| Range ACT Composite | 22-27 |
| Minimum TOEFL | 550 |
| Average HS GPA | 3.2 |
| % graduated top 10% of class | 18 |
| % graduated top 25% of class | 49 |
| % graduated top 50% of class | 85 |

### DEADLINES

| | |
|---|---|
| Early decision | 12/1 |
| Early decision notification | 12/20 |
| Priority admission deadline | 2/1 |
| Regular admission | 3/1 |
| Regular notification | 4/1 |
| Nonfall registration? | yes |

### APPLICANTS ALSO LOOK AT

**AND OFTEN PREFER**
U. Virginia

**AND SOMETIMES PREFER**
James Madison
Virginia Tech
Washington and Lee
Hampden-Sydney

**AND RARELY PREFER**
Mary Washington
Roanoke
Sweet Briar
U. Richmond

### FINANCIAL FACTS

| | |
|---|---|
| Financial Aid Rating | 86 |
| Tuition | $17,850 |
| Room & board | $4,905 |
| Books and supplies | $600 |
| Required fees | $500 |
| % frosh receiving aid | 45 |
| % undergrads receiving aid | 47 |
| Avg frosh grant | $7,831 |
| Avg frosh loan | $1,815 |

# RANDOLPH-MACON WOMAN'S COLLEGE

2500 RIVERMONT AVENUE, LYNCHBURG, VA 24503-1526 • ADMISSIONS: 464-947-8100 • FAX: 464-947-8996

## CAMPUS LIFE

**Quality of Life Rating** 86
Type of school private
Affiliation Methodist
Environment suburban

### STUDENTS
| | |
|---|---|
| Total undergrad enrollment | 748 |
| % from out of state | 58 |
| % from public high school | 78 |
| % live on campus | 75 |
| % African American | 7 |
| % Asian | 3 |
| % Caucasian | 75 |
| % Hispanic | 4 |
| % international | 11 |
| # of countries represented | 37 |

### SURVEY SAYS . . .
*Student publications are popular*
*Student government is popular*
*Theater is hot*
*No one cheats*
*Very small frat/sorority scene*
*Beautiful campus*
*Great food on campus*
*Very little beer drinking*
*Dorms are like palaces*

## ACADEMICS

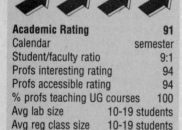

**Academic Rating** 91
Calendar semester
Student/faculty ratio 9:1
Profs interesting rating 94
Profs accessible rating 94
% profs teaching UG courses 100
Avg lab size 10-19 students
Avg reg class size 10-19 students

### MOST POPULAR MAJORS
psychology and English (tied for first)
biology

## STUDENTS SPEAK OUT
### Academics

The women of Randolph-Macon Woman's College want everyone to know that their academic program is challenging. "Our unofficial motto is, 'At any other school, it would have been an A.' While R-MWC may not be a hard college to get accepted to, it can be hard as hell to stay here. While I appreciate the education I am getting, sometimes it's hard to remember why I'm putting myself through this." Students also want prospects to know, however, that an R-MWC education is well worth the effort it requires. Writes one, "In a single-sex environment, you're more than a pretty face. You're seen as an athlete, scholar, leader, learner, and most importantly, a woman. It's a place that nurtures individual growth and promotes intellectualism." Professors are seen as facilitators and friends here; explains one student, "Be prepared to work for your grade, but also be prepared to have professors who are willing to help you make sure you get good grades." Students also crow about small classes that "are a real asset. They promote great discussions that allow for much better learning than would large ones." Most of all, they love the Honor Code, which "requires you to be mature and responsible enough not to steal, cheat, lie, etc. It is held in very high regard. We have our mailboxes unlocked because stealing simply isn't an issue. We have self-scheduled exams where, within limit, you choose when to take your finals during Final Exam Week." Is there anything R-MWC undergrads don't like about their academic experience? Gripes one, "We are not ranked as high academically as we should be. The expectations and standards of the professors and challenging nature of courses are that of an Ivy League institution."

### Life

Students at R-MWC admit that while their single-sex environment can be confining, "R-MWC has a wonderful sense of community and sisterhood. We can all get along even though sometimes we squabble like siblings." Writes one student. "I will say that, while I sometimes feel trapped here, I've learned a lot." School life offers plenty in the way of extracurricular clubs, sports, and traditions, but little in the way of a conventional social life. Sports (horseback riding and soccer are big); secret societies; traditional events like Ring Night, the Tacky Party, and Odd and Even Day (odd- and even-graduating classes are paired up as "sisters"); and classic southern traditions add even more to the sense of community among R-MWC students. To meet men, however, "many students leave campus for the weekends. Hampton-Sydney and VMI are places where many students go." Hometown Lynchburg, Virginia, is no help. The town "is a suburb ideal for middle-aged yuppies with kids. There are several movie theaters and good restaurants, but the town seems dead." Says one student of Lynchburg, "It's boring. My friends and I make our own fun by hanging out, watching movies, driving around and meeting people, etc. There are many colleges here but it is not a college town. To have fun, you must leave the city of Lynchburg." Accordingly, "cars are a necessity." The campus itself, with its large comfortable dorms, receives rave reviews. One student reports, "The elegant dining hall and resident halls make my family wonder if I'm living at a five-star hotel or college."

### Student Body

"Q: How many R-MWC students does it take to screw in a light bulb? A: Two. One to whine about it and the other to call maintenance to fix it." At least students here are able to look in the mirror and laugh at themselves, a redeeming quality to be sure. For majority students, R-MWC offers a "wonderful sense of community and sisterhood." It is less effective at assimilating minorities; writes one, "Most of the students are white, Protestant, straight, and upper-middle class. As a minority student, I feel isolated." The school for the most part seems "conservative," but R-MWC women do represent a respectable range of personalities, from your southern debutante to your Pacific Northwestern grunge goddess, within one end of the color spectrum.

# RANDOLPH-MACON WOMAN'S COLLEGE

FINANCIAL AID: 464-947-8128 • E-MAIL: ADMISSIONS@RMWC.EDU • WEBSITE: WWW.RMWC.EDU

## ADMISSIONS

*Very important* academic and nonacademic factors considered by the admissions committee include character/personal qualities, essays, recommendations, and secondary school record. *Important* factors considered include class rank, extracurricular activities, standardized test scores, and talent/ability. *Other* factors considered include alumni/ae relation, interview, minority status, volunteer work, and work experience. Factors *not* considered include geography, religious affiliation/commitment, and state residency. SAT I or ACT required. TOEFL required of all international applicants. High school diploma is required and GED is accepted. *High school units required/recommended:* 4 English recommended, 3 math recommended, 3 science recommended, 2 science lab recommended, 2 foreign language recommended, 1 social studies recommended, 2 history recommended.

### The Inside Word

The admissions process at Randolph-Macon Woman's College works pretty much as it does at most small liberal arts colleges, with one worthwhile exception: Each candidate is assigned to an admissions staff member who functions as an advocate for the student throughout the process. It's nice to have somewhat regular contact with someone in the admissions office over the course of the cycle. This saves time restating problems, questions, and circumstances every time you call or write. It also helps the college make a strong positive impression on applicants.

## FINANCIAL AID

*Students should submit:* FAFSA and state aid form. Regular filing deadline is March 1. The Princeton Review suggests that all financial aid forms be submitted as soon as possible after January 1. *Need-based scholarships/grants offered:* Pell, SEOG, state scholarships/grants, private scholarships, and the school's own gift aid. *Loan aid offered:* FFEL Subsidized Stafford, FFEL Unsubsidized Stafford, FFEL PLUS, Federal Perkins, and college/university loans from institutional funds. Institutional employment available. Federal Work-Study Program available. Applicants will be notified of awards on a rolling basis beginning on or about March 1. Off-campus job opportunities are good.

## FROM THE ADMISSIONS OFFICE

"At Randolph-Macon Woman's College, our students follow a multitude of career paths—lawyer, psychologist, banker, oceanographer, teacher, artist, physician. But an R-MWC education is much more than course work and skill-building. It's about academic challenges and choices. It's about working closely with your faculty advisor to prepare your individualized, four-year Macon Plan. It's about making friendships that last a lifetime. And ultimately it's about preparing to lead 'the life more abundant', the college motto—*vita abundantior*."

## ADMISSIONS

| | |
|---|---:|
| Admissions Rating | 79 |
| # of applicants | 787 |
| % of applicants accepted | 82 |
| % of acceptees attending | 33 |
| # of early decision applicants | 34 |
| % accepted early decision | 82 |

### FRESHMAN PROFILE

| | |
|---|---:|
| Range SAT Verbal | 560-660 |
| Average SAT Verbal | 608 |
| Range SAT Math | 520-630 |
| Average SAT Math | 577 |
| Range ACT Composite | 24-28 |
| Average ACT Composite | 26 |
| Minimum TOEFL | 550 |
| Average HS GPA | 3.4 |
| % graduated top 10% of class | 44 |
| % graduated top 25% of class | 78 |
| % graduated top 50% of class | 97 |

### DEADLINES

| | |
|---|---:|
| Early decision | 11/15 |
| Early decision notification | 12/15 |
| Priority admission deadline | 2/15 |
| Regular admission | 3/1 |
| Nonfall registration? | yes |

### APPLICANTS ALSO LOOK AT
**AND OFTEN PREFER**
Duke
U. Richmond
U. Virginia
Smith
Mount Holyoke
**AND SOMETIMES PREFER**
Sweet Briar
Hollins
William and Mary
**AND RARELY PREFER**
Washington and Lee
U. South Carolina—Columbia
Virginia Tech, Rhodes

### FINANCIAL FACTS

| | |
|---|---:|
| Financial Aid Rating | 89 |
| Tuition | $18,090 |
| Room & board | $7,350 |
| Books and supplies | $800 |
| Required fees | $380 |
| % frosh receiving aid | 59 |
| % undergrads receiving aid | 59 |
| Avg frosh grant | $13,660 |
| Avg frosh loan | $2,487 |

# REED COLLEGE

3203 SE WOODSTOCK BOULEVARD, PORTLAND, OR 97202-8199 • ADMISSION: 503-777-7511 • FAX: 503-777-7553

## CAMPUS LIFE

| | |
|---|---|
| **Quality of Life Rating** | **87** |
| Type of school | private |
| Affiliation | none |
| Environment | suburban |

### STUDENTS

| | |
|---|---|
| Total undergrad enrollment | 1,366 |
| % male/female | 47/53 |
| % from out of state | 84 |
| % from public high school | 69 |
| % live on campus | 55 |
| % African American | 1 |
| % Asian | 5 |
| % Caucasian | 69 |
| % Hispanic | 4 |
| % Native American | 2 |
| % international | 3 |

### SURVEY SAYS . . .

*Diversity lacking on campus*
*No one cheats*
*Students love Portland, OR*
*(Almost) everyone smokes*
*Registration is a breeze*
*Class discussions encouraged*

## ACADEMICS

| | |
|---|---|
| **Academic Rating** | **94** |
| Calendar | semester |
| Student/faculty ratio | 10:1 |
| Profs interesting rating | 97 |
| Profs accessible rating | 98 |
| % profs teaching UG courses | 100 |
| Avg lab size | 10-19 students |
| Avg reg class size | 10-19 students |

### MOST POPULAR MAJORS

biology
English
psychology

## STUDENTS SPEAK OUT

### Academics

Tucked away in the Pacific Northwest, Reed College is a hidden acorn in the forest of academia. A Reed education combines a traditional classical curriculum with a progressive atmosphere that de-emphasizes grades and encourages intellectual discussion both in and out of class. Classes are intense and the workload is extremely challenging. A sophomore biochemistry major wryly comments, "Choosing to go to Reed was like choosing to go to hell: your work is never completely done and nobody believes in heaven." A junior math major concurs, "Sometimes I do homework for one class as a break from work for another class. But it's a lot of fun and intellectually exciting." Students driven by comparing their grades to those of their peers need not apply. "This school is not for everyone. It is for people who consider themselves intellectuals and are driven to work not out of competition but for the intellectual endeavor," one student counsels. Reed's professors are generally well respected for both their intelligence and accessibility. Professors teach classes; TA's are nonexistent. "Most professors are incredibly accessible and almost all put their students ahead of their research," one junior economics student comments. Still, one senior English major opines that "while lauded for its academic standards, I find many parts of Reed's curriculum to be outdated and Eurocentric." Students agree that the student/administration relationship is much stronger than it is at most universities. To prospective applicants, one junior forewarns, "No matter how smart you are, kiddo, Reed will kick your butt. It's up to you to decide whether that's a good thing or not."

### Life

Students cite Reed's location in rainy Portland, Oregon, as one of the major reasons that they stay inside and study. Recently, Reed's administration has given other good reasons to stay inside, with a new library, sports center, and biology, studio art, and educational technology centers underway. Reed's demanding academic schedule ensures that "one learns a great deal here, but that [obviously] means lots of studying and lots of stress." Accordingly, students don't spend much time having fun. One junior economics major asks, "Fun, what's that? I work, I sometimes eat, and I occasionally sleep and bathe." A sophomore music major adds, "We study, study, and study more. Sometimes we sleep and eat, but not often." According to a freshman, "People like to sit inside and 'expand their minds.' Sometimes this means reading. Often this means other substances," which include alcohol and marijuana. A first-year theater major notes that "the pot is fantastic and relatively cheap." The campus pool hall is a popular destination. When they do venture off campus, students take advantage of the national parks and the Pacific Ocean—both of which are near Portland.

### Student Body

Most students note the lack of on-campus diversity. Reed offers "a diversity of white American subcultures that is really quite amazing." While students regard their classmates as "smart" and "inspiring," they are, at the same time, "a bunch of basket cases. They should put a fence around campus and observe the true definition of anti-social." A senior history major writes, "Reed students are weird, creative, and radical in theory. I find them to be self-centered, cynical, homogeneously rich, [and] white." Still, Reed students are inspired by their classmates' creativity. "I never know when someone might ride by on a flaming bicycle or paint the bathrooms green," notes one biochemistry major. Reed students challenge each other academically but focus on intellectual stimulation instead of on grades. An English major reflects, "Sometimes Reedies derive too much of our identities from our academic abilities, which can feed a dismissive and overly interrogative atmosphere." A first-year theater major sums up the student attitude at Reed: "If academia is a religion, we're retty damned pious."

FINANCIAL AID: 800-547-4750 • E-MAIL: ADMISSION@REED.EDU • WEBSITE: WWW.REED.EDU

## ADMISSIONS

*Very important* academic and nonacademic factors considered by the admissions committee include secondary school record. *Important* factors considered include character/personal qualities, class rank, essays, standardized test scores, talent/ability, and volunteer work. *Other* factors considered include alumni/ae relation, extracurricular activities, geography, interview, minority status, recommendations, and work experience. Factors *not* considered include religious affiliation/commitment and state residency. SAT I or ACT required. SAT II also recommended. TOEFL required of all international applicants. High school diploma is required and GED is accepted. *High school units required/recommended:* 4 English required, 3 math required, 2 science required, 2 science lab required, 3 social studies required, 2 elective required. *The admissions office says:* "The Committee on Admission takes into account many integrated factors, but academic accomplishments and talents are given the greatest weight in the selection process. Strong verbal and qualitative skills and demonstrated writing ability are important considerations. The Committee on Admission may give special consideration to applicants who represent a particular culture, region, or background that will contribute to the diversity of the college. Qualities of character—in particular, motivation, attitude toward learning, and social consciousness—also are important considerations."

### The Inside Word

Despite the progressive nature of the educational attitudes and student body at Reed, the college zealously avoids such labeling in admissions literature, preferring to portray itself in a much more traditional fashion. While a social conscience is definitely an asset, applicants should devote particular attention to discussing their intellectual curiosity and academic interests in essays and/or interviews—Reed seems to like it best when their different side is downplayed.

## FINANCIAL AID

*Students should submit:* FAFSA, institution's own financial aid form and CSS/Financial Aid PROFILE. Regular filing deadline is March 1. The Princeton Review suggests that all financial aid forms be submitted as soon as possible after January 1. *Need-based scholarships/grants offered:* Pell, SEOG, state scholarships/grants, private scholarships, and the school's own gift aid. *Loan aid offered:* FFEL Subsidized Stafford, FFEL Unsubsidized Stafford, FFEL PLUS, Federal Perkins, and college/university loans from institutional funds. Institutional employment available. Federal Work-Study Program available. Applicants will be notified of awards on or about April 1. Off-campus job opportunities are good.

## FROM THE ADMISSIONS OFFICE

"Dedication to the highest standards of academic scholarship is central to a Reed education. A well-structured curriculum and small classes with motivated students and dedicated faculty provide the environment in which a student's quest for learning can be given broad rein. Students most likely to derive maximum benefit from a Reed education are individuals who possess a high degree of self-discipline and a genuine enthusiasm for academic work."

### ADMISSIONS

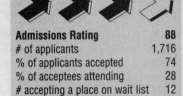

| | |
|---|---|
| Admissions Rating | 88 |
| # of applicants | 1,716 |
| % of applicants accepted | 74 |
| % of acceptees attending | 28 |
| # accepting a place on wait list | 12 |
| # of early decision applicants | 134 |
| % accepted early decision | 63 |

### FRESHMAN PROFILE

| | |
|---|---|
| Range SAT Verbal | 630-730 |
| Average SAT Verbal | 688 |
| Range SAT Math | 590-700 |
| Average SAT Math | 651 |
| Average ACT Composite | 29 |
| Minimum TOEFL | 600 |
| Average HS GPA | 3.7 |
| % graduated top 10% of class | 51 |
| % graduated top 25% of class | 81 |
| % graduated top 50% of class | 97 |

### DEADLINES

| | |
|---|---|
| Early decision | 11/15 |
| Early decision notification | 12/15 |
| Regular admission | 1/15 |
| Regular notification | 4/1 |
| Nonfall registration? | yes |

### APPLICANTS ALSO LOOK AT

**AND OFTEN PREFER**
UC—Berkeley
Oberlin

**AND SOMETIMES PREFER**
Colorado Coll.
Pomona
Grinnell, Carleton

**AND RARELY PREFER**
Hampshire
UC—Santa Cruz
Evergreen State

### FINANCIAL FACTS

| | |
|---|---|
| Financial Aid Rating | 74 |
| Tuition | $26,060 |
| Room & board | $7,090 |
| Books and supplies | $950 |
| Required fees | $200 |
| % frosh receiving aid | 52 |
| % undergrads receiving aid | 42 |
| Avg frosh grant | $20,388 |
| Avg frosh loan | $2,133 |

# RENSSELAER POLYTECHNIC INSTITUTE

110 EIGHTH STREET, TROY, NY 12180-3590 • ADMISSIONS: 518-276-6216 • FAX: 518-276-4072

## STUDENTS SPEAK OUT

### Academics

Rensselaer Polytechnic Institute is an engineering school in transition, and most students here are happy about it. "We are in the middle of a big change in administration," writes one. "Good times are coming with strong, positive leadership." Another concurs, "The new administration seems to have aggressive but achievable goals for improvements. The four-by-four [four courses, four credits each, per semester] curriculum has made many majors much easier. The notebook/studio format for many courses makes them much more enjoyable." A few dissenters worry about standards at the school, which admittedly has ratcheted down the level of academic difficulty from "impossible" to "highly improbable." Says one, "Although Rensselaer's image is mostly hype, it retains its solid technical core despite the administration's best efforts to water it down." Rest assured, students here still spend nearly every waking hour staring at books or computer screens. Of course, all the hard work has a payoff: "As I met and talked with interns from other schools and we compared our courses, I realized that I've already taken classes that the others won't take until their senior year." For students having a hard time keeping up, "professors are usually willing to help you out whenever you need it, but you have to find them." The quality of professorial instruction, alas, leaves something to be desired; explains one student, "Despite the claim that teaching has become a priority recently, the school's insistence that teaching be coupled with research effectively ensures that it will never happen. Until teaching quality becomes a factor in tenure review, professors will not regard it seriously." The problem, according to most, is that "professors often teach at a level much higher than students' understanding."

### Life

"Social life during the week? Where do you think you are, Florida State?!" It's not a surprise that most students at RPI find little time to do anything but study. Still, free campus movies, concerts, "playing at Wal-Mart," the local bars and coffee shops, and "a sea of beer" provide a few diversions. The two most popular activities are sports ("especially the hockey team" and intramurals) and Greek parties; writes one student, "The Greek system is responsible for a significant portion of the social scene. Fraternities are a way of life, and the weekend starts on Thursday. A hard weekend of studying is followed by a hard weekend of partying." Sums up another, "Most people are very stressed from the workload. At RPI, fun = alcohol and frat parties." Hometown Troy offers little to supplement campus life: "The main problem with the RPI experience isn't RPI, it's the town. The old joke is that Troy is a city of urban renewal, except without the renewal." According to students, Troy's only asset is its location, "three hours from Boston and New York, and four hours from Montreal. There are two casinos within four hours." Along this line, many of the students mention that "a car is an absolute necessity, since Albany and Boston aren't too far away." "Nearby state schools offer fun, girls, and political activism," but only to those with the wheels to get there. High on the list of students' other complaints are the fact that "the weather sucks" and the strongly held belief that "eating on campus is strictly at your own risk."

### Student Body

At RPI, "the population is small enough that there are familiar faces everywhere, but large enough that you'll still be meeting new people senior year." While those familiar faces will include students of many races and nationalities, undergrads report that these groups stick pretty much to themselves: quips one, "When saying that the student body is diverse, what I mean is that I can't speak to 75 percent of them because they speak so many different languages." Students also note that "RPI has two communities: a social community and an unsociable, 'play computer games all day,' 'think about Star Trek' community." Typical of engineering schools, "The male/female ratio of three-to-one adds a twist to interaction." As one man pithily puts it, "What's a girl?"

FINANCIAL AID: 518-276-6813 • E-MAIL: ADMISSIONS@RPI.EDU • WEBSITE: WWW.RPI.EDU

## ADMISSIONS

*Very important* academic and nonacademic factors considered by the admissions committee include secondary school record. *Important* factors considered include standardized test scores. *Other* factors considered include alumni/ae relation, character/personal qualities, class rank, essays, extracurricular activities, geography, minority status, recommendations, talent/ability, volunteer work, and work experience. Factors *not* considered include interview, religious affiliation/commitment, and state residency. SAT I or ACT required. TOEFL required of all international applicants. High school diploma is required and GED is accepted. *High school units required/recommended:* 15 total required; 4 English required, 4 math required, 4 science required, 3 social studies required. *The admissions office says:* "Here at Rensselaer, we personally read every application. Our primary concern is a student's ability to handle Rensselaer's demanding curriculum!"

### *The Inside Word*

Although scores and numbers may not be the only consideration of the admissions committee at RPI, it is important to remember that you have to have high ones in order to stay in the running for admission. Here in Troy and at many other highly selective colleges and universities, the first review weeds out those who are academically weak and without any special considerations. Underrepresented minorities and women are high on the list of desirables in the applicant pool here, and go through the admissions process without any hitches if reasonably well qualified.

## FINANCIAL AID

*Students should submit:* FAFSA and state aid form. Regular filing deadline is February 15. The Princeton Review suggests that all financial aid forms be submitted as soon as possible after January 1. *Need-based scholarships/grants offered:* Pell, SEOG, state scholarships/grants, and private scholarships. *Loan aid offered:* Direct Subsidized Stafford, Direct Unsubsidized Stafford, Direct PLUS, Federal Perkins, college/university loans from institutional funds, and private alternative loans. Institutional employment available. Federal Work-Study Program available. Applicants will be notified of awards on a rolling basis beginning on or about March 20. Off-campus job opportunities are good.

## FROM THE ADMISSIONS OFFICE

"Rensselaer emphasizes the study of technology and science, preparing students for today's high-tech world. The university is devoted to the discovery and dissemination of knowledge and its application to the service of humanity. Rensselaer has been in the forefront of scientific and professional education since its founding in 1824, and today its reputation for educational excellence draws students from every state and more than 70 foreign countries. Newly-constructed Barton Hall is state-of-the-art housing with Web and Ethernet access in all rooms and conference rooms, plus a fully wired lounge. Rensselaer has recently completed construction of a $6 million fitness center and a $9.5 million renovation to the student union."

## ADMISSIONS

| | |
|---|---|
| **Admissions Rating** | **82** |
| # of applicants | 5,479 |
| % of applicants accepted | 73 |
| % of acceptees attending | 33 |
| # of early decision applicants | 212 |
| % accepted early decision | 82 |

### FRESHMAN PROFILE

| | |
|---|---|
| Range SAT Verbal | 560-660 |
| Average SAT Verbal | 611 |
| Range SAT Math | 620-710 |
| Average SAT Math | 671 |
| Range ACT Composite | 23-28 |
| Average ACT Composite | 26 |
| Minimum TOEFL | 570 |
| % graduated top 10% of class | 59 |
| % graduated top 25% of class | 87 |
| % graduated top 50% of class | 99 |

### DEADLINES

| | |
|---|---|
| Early decision | 11/15 |
| Early decision notification | 12/21 |
| Regular admission | 1/1 |
| Regular notification | 3/15 |
| Nonfall registration? | yes |

### APPLICANTS ALSO LOOK AT
**AND OFTEN PREFER**
Yale
MIT
Cornell U.
**AND SOMETIMES PREFER**
Carnegie Mellon
Boston U.
Lehigh
Worcester Poly.
U. Rochester
**AND RARELY PREFER**
Binghamton U.
Clarkson
SUNY Buffalo
Syracuse, RIT

## FINANCIAL FACTS

| | |
|---|---|
| **Financial Aid Rating** | **83** |
| Tuition | $24,820 |
| Room & board | $8,308 |
| Books and supplies | $1,470 |
| Required fees | $735 |
| % frosh receiving aid | 74 |
| % undergrads receiving aid | 72 |
| Avg frosh grant | $16,992 |
| Avg frosh loan | $4,800 |

# RHODES COLLEGE

OFFICE OF ADMISSIONS, 2000 NORTH PARKWAY, MEMPHIS, TN 38112 • ADMISSIONS: 901-843-3700 • FAX: 901-843-3631

## CAMPUS LIFE

| Quality of Life Rating | 91 |
|---|---|
| Type of school | private |
| Affiliation | Presbyterian |
| Environment | urban |

### STUDENTS

| | |
|---|---|
| Total undergrad enrollment | 1,546 |
| % male/female | 43/57 |
| % from out of state | 74 |
| % from public high school | 63 |
| % live on campus | 68 |
| % in (# of) fraternities | 54 (6) |
| % in (# of) sororities | 58 (7) |
| % African American | 4 |
| % Asian | 3 |
| % Caucasian | 88 |
| % Hispanic | 2 |
| % international | 1 |
| # of countries represented | 13 |

### SURVEY SAYS . . .
Theater is hot
Frats and sororities dominate social
scene
Athletic facilities are great
No one cheats
Beautiful campus
Lousy food on campus
Students get along with local
community
Class discussions encouraged
Students are very religious
Diverse students interact

## ACADEMICS

| Academic Rating | 89 |
|---|---|
| Calendar | semester |
| Student/faculty ratio | 12:1 |
| Profs interesting rating | 96 |
| Profs accessible rating | 98 |
| % profs teaching UG courses | 100 |
| Avg lab size | 10-19 students |
| Avg reg class size | 10-19 students |

### MOST POPULAR MAJORS
business administration
biology
English

## STUDENTS SPEAK OUT
### Academics
Regarding this private college in the heart of Memphis, a sophomore writes, "Rhodes is the perfect school for those looking for a small, liberal arts school in the urban South." With a solid reputation, a "fortified learning environment," and a "small student-teacher ratio," Rhodes's students are by and large quite pleased with their choice of school. Writes a senior, "If you enroll in college for the right reasons, those being academic reasons, the Rhodes academic standard is second to none. If you plan on going to college with your 'MTV These Are the Best Years of My Life, I'm Here to Find Myself' attitude, stay home." In addition to the well-respected honor code, as well as excellent study abroad and experiential education opportunities (e.g., studying urban planning by working in downtown Memphis), it's a caring, accessible faculty that makes the difference to Rhodes undergrads. A junior art major provides an example: "I am very close to my professors. I have borrowed their clothes, slept in their beds (without them there—I house-sit), shared dinner, brought cookies, swam in their Jacuzzi. We are like family." A benefit of this close personal attention is the fact that students can "write their own majors" and "approach any professor about getting a class started, like Arabic or playwriting." Of course, there's always a down side: "They will hunt you down, however, if you miss a class." Listening to students extends to the administration as well. "You know student input is important when the president of the college knows your name," writes a senior. The result of all this attention? A happy, satisfied student body.

### Life
With its "beautiful" and "serene" neo-Gothic campus (ivied walls and all) and its high incidence of Beautiful People, Rhodes "is like a posh country club," notes a senior. "Everyone is polite, intelligent, wealthy, and good looking—professors and students included." Socially, people do things in large groups, and one sophomore writes of the pack mentality: "The community calls us Rhodents, and the rumor mill here is worse than at a private, boarding, 100-student, all-girl high school in the country." Greek affiliation at the school is over 50 percent, and while the current administration is trying to minimize its influence, many students resist their efforts. There are those who would like Rhodes to widen its horizon a bit—"get more f/n liberal," as one student puts it. Others practice what they preach: "I particularly enjoy writing for the newspaper and [playing] intramural sports," states one senior. "People are very interested in community service and activity in Memphis." Not surprisingly, it's in the city where most non-Rhodents seem to find solace. With a "growing art scene" and "all sorts of entertainment and culture," Memphis provides a nearby haven for independent spirits. "I've left campus and found a niche for myself in Memphis," writes a senior. "There's too much to do off campus to waste time here."

### Student Body
"Not a helluva lot of diversity," quips a sophomore. A senior explains, "Students tend to be southern and rich, and many have a hard time getting past their own background, but [they're] extremely friendly." The friendliness seems genuine, however, and built on a solid foundation of time spent together. Notes a senior, "In a classroom situation there is so much interaction between the students that you build solid friendships. This is the sort of campus where you know everyone and never feel like you're alone. You always can go to someone . . . student, faculty, or staff." As for the lack of diversity, the administration is trying to turn the situation around. What's more, some like the chance to define themselves against the crowd. A heavy metal–loving senior sings the praises of being a fish out of water (or a rat without a pack?): "Abercrombie & Fitch, Birkenstocks, Phish, Widespread, Dave Matthews. This is what to expect. Then again, it's kind of fun to stand out like a sore thumb."

FINANCIAL AID: 901-843-3810 • E-MAIL: ADMINFO@RHODES.EDU • WEBSITE: WWW.RHODES.EDU

## ADMISSIONS

*Very important* academic and nonacademic factors considered by the admissions committee include secondary school record. *Important* factors considered include class rank, essays, recommendations, and standardized test scores. *Other* factors considered include alumni/ae relation, character/personal qualities, extracurricular activities, geography, interview, minority status, talent/ability, volunteer work, and work experience. Factors *not* considered include religious affiliation/commitment and state residency. SAT I or ACT required. TOEFL required of all international applicants. High school diploma is required and GED is accepted. *High school units required/recommended:* 16 total required; 4 English required, 3 math required, 2 science lab required, 2 foreign language required, 2 social studies required, 3 elective required. *The admissions office says:* "Our admissions counseling staff travels and reads by territory with individual attention given to each and every application."

### The Inside Word

Rhodes is one of the best kept secrets in higher education, familiar mainly to those in the Southeast but beginning to develop more national recognition. Its student body is very impressive academically. Only the college's upper-echelon competition—the best universities in the South—prevents the admissions committee from being even more selective. Even so, candidates should be prepared for a thorough review of their academic qualifications and the match they make with Rhodes.

## FINANCIAL AID

*Students should submit:* FAFSA and CSS/Financial Aid PROFILE. The Princeton Review suggests that all financial aid forms be submitted as soon as possible after January 1. *Need-based scholarships/grants offered:* Pell, SEOG, state scholarships/grants, private scholarships, and the school's own gift aid. *Loan aid offered:* FFEL Subsidized Stafford, FFEL Unsubsidized Stafford, FFEL PLUS, and Federal Perkins. Institutional employment available. Federal Work-Study Program available. Applicants will be notified of awards on or about April 1. Off-campus job opportunities are good.

## FROM THE ADMISSIONS OFFICE

"It's not just one characteristic that makes Rhodes different from other colleges, it's a special blend of features that sets us apart. We are a selective liberal arts college, yet without a cutthroat atmosphere; we are a small community, yet located in a major city; we are in a metropolitan area, yet offer one of the most beautiful and serene campuses in the nation. Our students are serious about learning and yet know how to have fun . . . in an atmosphere of trust and respect brought about by adherence to the honor code. And they know that learning at Rhodes doesn't mean sitting in a lecture hall and memorizing the professor's lecture. It means interaction, discussion, and a process of teacher and student discovering knowledge together. Rhodes is a place that welcomes new people and new ideas. It's a place of energy and light, not of apathy and complacency. Everyone who is a part of the Rhodes community is striving to be the best at what she/he does."

## ADMISSIONS

| | |
|---|---|
| Admissions Rating | 80 |
| # of applicants | 2,121 |
| % of applicants accepted | 70 |
| % of acceptees attending | 27 |
| # accepting a place on wait list | 207 |
| % admitted from wait list | 22 |
| # of early decision applicants | 84 |
| % accepted early decision | 83 |

### FRESHMAN PROFILE

| | |
|---|---|
| Range SAT Verbal | 600-690 |
| Average SAT Verbal | 646 |
| Range SAT Math | 590-680 |
| Average SAT Math | 642 |
| Range ACT Composite | 25-30 |
| Average ACT Composite | 28 |
| Minimum TOEFL | 550 |
| Average HS GPA | 3.6 |
| % graduated top 10% of class | 55 |
| % graduated top 25% of class | 82 |
| % graduated top 50% of class | 96 |

### DEADLINES

| | |
|---|---|
| Early decision | 11/1 & 1/1 |
| ED notification | 12/1 & 2/1 |
| Regular admission | 2/1 |
| Regular notification | 4/1 |
| Nonfall registration? | yes |

### APPLICANTS ALSO LOOK AT
#### AND OFTEN PREFER
Duke
Davidson
U. of the South
#### AND SOMETIMES PREFER
Wake Forest
U. Tennessee—Knoxville
Emory
Wesleyan Coll., Vanderbilt
#### AND RARELY PREFER
Centre
Randolph-Macon Woman's

### FINANCIAL FACTS

| | |
|---|---|
| Financial Aid Rating | 84 |
| Tuition | $20,366 |
| Books and supplies | $620 |
| Required fees | $200 |
| % frosh receiving aid | 43 |
| % undergrads receiving aid | 42 |
| Avg frosh grant | $9,717 |
| Avg frosh loan | $3,288 |

# RICE UNIVERSITY

PO Box 1892, Houston, TX 77251-1892 • Admissions: 713-348-7423 • Fax: 713-348-5952

## CAMPUS LIFE

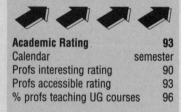

**Quality of Life Rating**    **85**
Type of school    private
Affiliation    none
Environment    urban

### STUDENTS
Total undergrad enrollment    2,658
% male/female    53/47
% from out of state    50
% live on campus    63
% African American    7
% Asian    16
% Caucasian    54
% Hispanic    10
% Native American    1
% international    3

### SURVEY SAYS . . .
No one cheats
(Almost) everyone plays intramural
sports
Registration is a breeze
Great off-campus food
Class discussions are rare
Very small frat/sorority scene
(Almost) no one smokes
Lousy food on campus
Ethnic diversity on campus

## ACADEMICS

**Academic Rating**    **93**
Calendar    semester
Profs interesting rating    90
Profs accessible rating    93
% profs teaching UG courses    96

### MOST POPULAR MAJORS
economics
electrical engineering
English

## STUDENTS SPEAK OUT

### Academics

Justifiably promoted as the "Ivy of the South," Rice boasts a world-renowned faculty that actually enjoys teaching, state-of-the-art research facilities, a rigorous curriculum, and a student body that is up to the challenge. And, through the good graces of a massive endowment, Rice University is also one of the most affordable top-tier undergraduate programs in the country. Students here know how good they have it. Writes one, "Rice provides an intense academic atmosphere that revived the love of learning that high school had sucked out of me." Says another, "My introductory honors chemistry class is taught by a Nobel Prize winner in chemistry. Where else are freshmen taught by Nobel Prize winners?" Undergraduates must complete distribution requirements in the humanities, social sciences, and natural sciences along with all the requirements of their majors. A small student body means that "we always get the classes we want. It's the best thing about Rice." It also provides students with a voice in running the school. As one student tells us, "The administration and professors here are very receptive to the needs and wants of the students." An honor code affords students flexibility; explains one, "Because of the honor code, most professors are helpful in situations that come up when you can't make it to a test." No wonder students tell us "I made one of the best decisions in coming to Rice. The school gives students the opportunity to experiment and try new things with the safety net of a great support system."

### Life

One of the toughest academic workloads in the nation tempers extracurricular life at Rice. As one undergrad puts it, "Fun? What's that? When would I have time to do such a thing?" Still, many students manage to create spare time. As one student explains, "Students are expected to be involved in activities other than classes. Rice offers essentially every activity that an enormous state university does, but since we have a small student body, every student can become actively involved. If you want to act, dance, write for the newspaper, be on the radio, debate, or play sports, go to Rice." Or run naked in the streets, this student might have added; Rice's Baker 13 Club promotes 1970s-ish streaking. Students love Rice's residential college system, which provides student-governed, faculty-supervised housing. The colleges serve the function that the Greek system (absent at Rice) serves on other campuses. Explains one student, "The college system creates a wide array of social activities, from dances to dinners. It also creates a sense of community similar to that of the Greek system, but in the college system, everyone belongs." Students enjoy their hometown of Houston, telling us "Houston is a pretty big town. Anything you want is usually available. You just have to find it."

### Student Body

The typical Rice student is the manifestation of southern geniality to the extreme. Writes one student, "There are many different people from different social backgrounds. Because the school is so small, we learn from and befriend each other." Adds another, "Everyone is really nice and really smart." The prevalent attitude can be disconcerting for some, especially those from more gruff regions. Writes one New Yorker, "Never have I seen a place where people are so eager to be good, to feel a common allegiance through the school. If they were any nicer, they'd explode. Maybe I'm a New York City fish out in Texas waters, but I feel ready to heave at how hard people try."

FINANCIAL AID: 713-348-4958 • E-MAIL: ADMISSION@RICE.EDU • WEBSITE: WWW.RICE.EDU

## ADMISSIONS

*Very important* academic and nonacademic factors considered by the admissions committee include recommendations, secondary school record, class rank, standardized test scores, essays, extracurricular activities, talent/ability, and character/personal qualities. *Other* factors considered include alumni/ae relation, interview, geographical residence, volunteer work, and work experience. Factors *not* considered include minority status and religious affiliation/commitment. SAT I or ACT required; 3 SAT II: Subject Tests also required (writing and two other fields related to the candidate's proposed area of study). *High school units required/recommended:* 16 total required, must include 4 English, 3 math, 2 science lab, 2 foreign language, 2 social studies.

### The Inside Word

Rice has gotten loads of positive publicity over the past few years. As a result, what was already an extremely selective university is even more so. Candidates with less than the most impressive applications are not likely to last long in the admissions process.

## FINANCIAL AID

The Princeton Review suggests that all financial aid forms be submitted as soon as possible after January 1. *Need-based scholarships/grants offered:* Pell, SEOG, state scholarships/grants, private scholarships, the school's own gift aid, and Federal Nursing. *Loan aid offered:* FFEL Subsidized Stafford, FFEL Unsubsidized Stafford, FFEL PLUS, Federal Perkins, and Federal Nursing. Institutional employment available. Federal Work-Study Program available. Off-campus job opportunities are excellent.

## FROM THE ADMISSIONS OFFICE

"Admission committee decisions are based not only on high school grades and test scores but also on such qualities as leadership, participation in extracurricular activities, and personal creativity. Admission is extremely competitive; Rice attempts to seek out and identify those students who have demonstrated exceptional ability and the potential for personal and intellectual growth."

### ADMISSIONS

| | |
|---|---|
| **Admissions Rating** | **97** |
| # of applicants | 6,802 |
| % of applicants accepted | 23 |
| % of acceptees attending | 40 |
| # of early decision applicants | 489 |
| % accepted early decision | 24 |

#### FRESHMAN PROFILE

| | |
|---|---|
| Range SAT Verbal | 650-750 |
| Range SAT Math | 660-760 |
| Range ACT Composite | 28-33 |
| Minimum TOEFL | 550 |

#### DEADLINES

| | |
|---|---|
| Early decision | 11/1 |
| Early decision notification | 12/15 |
| Regular admission | 1/2 |

#### APPLICANTS ALSO LOOK AT
#### AND OFTEN PREFER
Harvard
Stanford
MIT
Princeton
#### AND SOMETIMES PREFER
Columbia
Duke
#### AND RARELY PREFER
Emory
U. Texas—Austin

### FINANCIAL FACTS

| | |
|---|---|
| **Financial Aid Rating** | **84** |
| Tuition | $16,600 |
| Room & board | $7,200 |
| Books and supplies | $600 |
| Required fees | $525 |

# Ripon College

300 Seward Street, PO Box 248, Ripon, WI 54971 • Admissions: 800-947-4766 • Fax: 920-748-8335

## STUDENTS SPEAK OUT

### Academics

Tiny, nationally recognized Ripon College in rural Wisconsin is "a good liberal arts school" with "unbelievable" facilities and a "high-intensity learning environment." Classes are "small and very discussion-oriented," and students tell us that "the overall experience" here is nothing short of "wonderful." "This is my second semester with a class of three people," says a senior. "I love it. It forces us to know what we're talking about." Ripon's "easygoing" and "extremely approachable" professors "know their stuff," and perhaps more importantly, old-fashioned, hands-on "personal attention" is abundantly available. Profs are "visible on campus and easy to talk to" and "actually get to know you," beams a sophomore. "Many encourage students to call them at home if they have questions," says a physics major, and "cookouts at professors' homes" are not uncommon. The administration "actually cares about you and how you do here" as well, and Ripon's top brass receives a great deal of praise for being "ready and willing to talk." For students who itch to see the world beyond Ripon's campus, study abroad is available in over 20 locations on every side of the planet. Ripon also offers an Educational Development Program free of charge to physically impaired and learning-disabled students, which includes tutoring in subject areas, skill-development workshops, and personal advisement. And, finally, it is worth noting that Spencer Tracy and Harrison Ford—Indiana Jones himself!—are Ripon grads.

### Life

While students tend to agree that "learning is the number one priority" at Ripon, most readily admit that drinking isn't too far behind. Students here "like to drink beer" and they "mostly party for fun." Indeed, "in the small" and "very safe" surrounding town, "there isn't much to do if you don't drink," and finding off-campus entertainment is "like trying to find someone in Wisconsin who isn't a Packer fan," explains a first-year student. "Impossible." Fraternities and sororities dominate the Ripon social scene and provide "a great source of entertainment." The frats throw "wildly popular parties," and the Greek system is generally a very "big deal on campus." For students who choose not to participate in the Greek scene (or who tire of it), "there is always something to do" on campus, "and chances are it is free." There's "capture-the-flag," "movies," "speakers who come in," "bowling," "sports, theater, intramurals, clubs," and, of course, "coed drunken sledding." Students often take road trips to "some of the neighboring towns," or to enjoy "snowboarding" or "camping." They also go out to eat when they can, as "the mass-produced institutional food" here could stand serious improvement. Also, "some of the dorms need a little work," while others just "suck" but, "hell, at least the laundry facilities are free."

### Student Body

There are "no unfamiliar faces at all" at Ripon, and the "nifty," "kind and caring," "energetic and driven" students here call their peers "the friendliest in the Midwest." It's a small campus, though, where "news travels fast" among "back-stabbing" gossipmongers. "It's almost as bad as high school." Ethnic diversity is nothing to write home about, though this shouldn't be surprising given Ripon's middle-of-Wisconsin location. The mostly "white, middle- to upper-middle class" students are "a lot alike," remarks a sophomore, "which allows for easy interaction" on the one hand, but "limits exposure to other cultures and backgrounds" on the other. "I wish they would formulate a thought independent of their friends and their Greek comrades," gripes one student. Overall, students say their campus has "very little discrimination," "a good mix of intellectuals, athletes, and activists," and fairly tolerant environment. "Only here can I traipse around wearing bee antennae and still be 'normal,' " beams a sophomore.

FINANCIAL AID: 920-748-8101 • E-MAIL: ADMINFO@RIPON.EDU • WEBSITE: WWW.RIPON.EDU

## ADMISSIONS

*Very important* academic and nonacademic factors considered by the admissions committee include secondary school record and standardized test scores. *Important* factors considered include essays. *Other* factors considered include interview, recommendations and talent/ability. Factors *not* considered include alumni/ae relation, extracurricular activities, minority status, religious affiliation/commitment, and state residency. SAT I or ACT required. TOEFL required of all international applicants. High school diploma is required and GED is accepted. *High school units required/recommended:* 17 total required; 4 English required, 4 math required, 3 science required, 1 science lab required, 2 foreign language required, 3 social studies required.

### The Inside Word

Candidates for admission to Ripon should prepare their applications with the knowledge that they will be subjected to a very thorough and demanding review. Even though the college faces formidable competition from other top midwestern liberal arts colleges and highly selective universities, the admissions staff succeeds at enrolling a very impressive freshman class each year. That doesn't happen without careful matchmaking and a lot of personal attention.

## FINANCIAL AID

*Students should submit:* FAFSA. There is no regular filing deadline. The Princeton Review suggests that all financial aid forms be submitted as soon as possible after January 1. *Need-based scholarships/grants offered:* Pell, SEOG, state scholarships/grants, private scholarships, and the school's own gift aid. *Loan aid offered:* FFEL Subsidized Stafford, FFEL Unsubsidized Stafford, FFEL PLUS, and Federal Perkins. Institutional employment available. Federal Work-Study Program available. Applicants will be notified of awards on a rolling basis beginning on or about March 1. Off-campus job opportunities are good.

## FROM THE ADMISSIONS OFFICE

"Since its founding in 1851, Ripon College has adhered to the philosophy that the liberal arts offer the richest foundation for intellectual, cultural, social, and spiritual growth. Academic strength is a 150-year tradition at Ripon. We attract excellent professors who are dedicated to their disciplines; they in turn attract bright, committed students from 36 states and 19 countries. Ripon has a national reputation for academic excellence as well a friendly, relaxed atmosphere, small class size, and the availability of outstanding facilities. Ripon is also a community. Not only do you see your professors in the classroom, but you can relate to them in a variety of other social situations. Ripon offers a rigorous curriculum in 30 major areas, including unique pre-professional programs. There is also ample opportunity for co-curricular involvement."

## ADMISSIONS

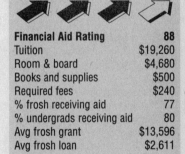

| | |
|---|---|
| Admissions Rating | 79 |
| # of applicants | 810 |
| % of applicants accepted | 83 |
| % of acceptees attending | 42 |

### FRESHMAN PROFILE

| | |
|---|---|
| Range SAT Verbal | 520-560 |
| Average SAT Verbal | 541 |
| Range SAT Math | 540-570 |
| Average SAT Math | 549 |
| Range ACT Composite | 19-29 |
| Average ACT Composite | 24 |
| Minimum TOEFL | 550 |
| Average HS GPA | 3.4 |
| % graduated top 10% of class | 24 |
| % graduated top 25% of class | 57 |
| % graduated top 50% of class | 86 |

### DEADLINES

| | |
|---|---|
| Priority admission deadline | 3/15 |
| Nonfall registration? | yes |

### APPLICANTS ALSO LOOK AT AND SOMETIMES PREFER

Lawrence
U. Wisconsin—Madison
Beloit

### AND RARELY PREFER

U. Wisconsin—Stevens Point
U. Wisconsin—Whitewater

## FINANCIAL FACTS

| | |
|---|---|
| Financial Aid Rating | 88 |
| Tuition | $19,260 |
| Room & board | $4,680 |
| Books and supplies | $500 |
| Required fees | $240 |
| % frosh receiving aid | 77 |
| % undergrads receiving aid | 80 |
| Avg frosh grant | $13,596 |
| Avg frosh loan | $2,611 |

# ROCHESTER INSTITUTE OF TECHNOLOGY

60 LOMB MEMORIAL DRIVE, ROCHESTER, NY 14623 • ADMISSIONS: 716-475-6631 • FAX: 716-475-7424

## CAMPUS LIFE

| Quality of Life Rating | 74 |
|---|---|
| Type of school | private |
| Affiliation | none |
| Environment | suburban |

### STUDENTS

| | |
|---|---|
| Total undergrad enrollment | 11,100 |
| % male/female | 67/33 |
| % from out of state | 40 |
| % from public high school | 85 |
| % live on campus | 60 |
| % in (# of) fraternities | 8 (19) |
| % in (# of) sororities | 8 (10) |
| % African American | 5 |
| % Asian | 6 |
| % Caucasian | 78 |
| % Hispanic | 3 |
| % international | 4 |

### SURVEY SAYS . . .
*Very little drug use*
*Musical organizations aren't popular*
*Great computer facilities*
*Student publications are ignored*
*Popular college radio*
*Unattractive campus*
*Campus difficult to get around*
*Student government is unpopular*
*Intercollegiate sports unpopular or nonexistent*
*Political activism is (almost) nonexistent*

## ACADEMICS

| Academic Rating | 79 |
|---|---|
| Calendar | quarter |
| Student/faculty ratio | 13:1 |
| Profs interesting rating | 88 |
| Profs accessible rating | 90 |
| % profs teaching UG courses | 95 |
| Avg lab size | 10-19 students |
| Avg reg class size | 10-19 students |

### MOST POPULAR MAJORS
business administration
information technology
mechanical engineering

## STUDENTS SPEAK OUT

### Academics

The "very prestigious" Rochester Institute of Technology is a demanding arts and technology school with a humanist approach to academics: the school requires every student, regardless of major, to complete a core curriculum of liberal arts courses. Students love or endure the requirements in order to benefit from RIT's modern classrooms, "exceptional" laboratories, and "state-of-the-art" equipment. Classes, students report, are "difficult and require a lot of work," a situation made more intense by a quarterly academic schedule that causes courses to fly by. "It's impossible to get ahead of your work," writes one student. "The trick is to not fall too far behind." One student sees the upside of quarterly classes: "The quarter system here is great. If you dislike a class or have a bad professor, it's over in 10 to 11 weeks." Alas, "bad" professors are not that uncommon here; while some are very knowledgeable" and "accessible" and are "genuinely concerned with their students' success," others run the gamut from "okay" to "incompetent." Even when the instructors are subpar, students enjoy "classes [that] are small so you can get more individual attention along with the fast pace." All told, students concede that an RIT education is a stressful one, but feel "the stress is worth it" because "graduates are in demand." One reason why grads are able to land prime jobs is RIT's co-op program, which allows students to gain hands-on experience in paid internships. Participating companies include biggies like Xerox, Kodak, and Bausch & Lomb. Each year, over 2,600 RIT co-op students work in more than 1,300 firms around the country. A few students find RIT's cozy relationship with industry a little discomforting; explains one, "RIT's reliance on corporate sponsorships turns students into customers as we 'shop' around for a degree."

### Life

Students don't come to RIT for the social life, which is a good thing, since, according to most, there isn't much of one. "RIT is in no way geared toward the social lives of students," moans a student. "The general setup of the school makes it difficult to meet and interact with those outside your major." Adds another, "Since RIT is such an intense learning environment, there isn't a lot of time left for extracurricular activities." When students do find some time to put their books and laptops away, they "go to movies, work out at the gym, or hang out in somebody's room" playing video games. For more lively entertainment, students often "travel to other schools for parties." Greek life provides a social outlet for some students, though at least as many despise fraternities and sororities. The result is a deeply divided campus, with Greeks complaining of an "anti-frat sentiment" and independents griping that fraternities and sororities act like they own the campus. Though RIT boasts several intercollegiate sports teams, school spirit isn't widespread.

### Student Body

Almost two-thirds of the "hard-working" and "goal-orientated" students of RIT are from New York State, and most of the rest are from the northeastern and midwestern states. And they say that their peers "are very friendly and mix well together no matter what race." The glue that binds them, according to many, is stress. "Camaraderie is often essential to survive the hellish upper-level courses. Having friends in your major really helps to relieve stress and work better." With heavy workloads burdening them, RIT undergrads have little time for and less interest in the outside world. "If I only had one word with which to describe RIT students," notes one student, "it would be 'apathy.'"

FINANCIAL AID: 716-475-2186 • E-MAIL: ADMISSIONS@RIT.EDU • WEBSITE: WWW.RIT.EDU

## ADMISSIONS

*Very important* academic and nonacademic factors considered by the admissions committee include essays, recommendations, secondary school record, and standardized test scores. *Important* factors considered include class rank, extracurricular activities, talent/ability, and volunteer work. *Other* factors considered include alumni/ae relation, character/personal qualities, geography, interview, minority status, state residency, and work experience. Factors *not* considered include religious affiliation/commitment. SAT I or ACT required. TOEFL required of all international applicants. High school diploma is required and GED is accepted. *High school units required/recommended:* 21 total required; 4 English required, 2 math required, 3 math recommended, 2 science required, 3 science recommended, 1 science lab required, 2 science lab recommended, 3 foreign language recommended, 4 social studies required, 9 elective required, 4 elective recommended.

### The Inside Word

RIT is not as competitive as the top tier of technical schools, but its location and contacts with major research corporations make it a top choice for many students. The acceptance rate is deceptively high when considered in conjunction with the student academic profile and the high yield of admitted students who enroll. There is a strong element of self-selection at work in the applicant pool; the successful candidate is one who is solid academically and ready to hit the ground running.

## FINANCIAL AID

*Students should submit:* FAFSA and state aid form. There is no regular filing deadline. The Princeton Review suggests that all financial aid forms be submitted as soon as possible after January 1. *Need-based scholarships/grants offered:* Pell, SEOG, state scholarships/grants, private scholarships, and the school's own gift aid. *Loan aid offered:* Direct Subsidized Stafford, Direct Unsubsidized Stafford, Direct PLUS, Federal Perkins, and private bank loans. Institutional employment available. Federal Work-Study Program available. Applicants will be notified of awards on a rolling basis beginning on or about April 1. Off-campus job opportunities are excellent.

## FROM THE ADMISSIONS OFFICE

"A nationally respected leader in professional and career-oriented education, RIT has been described as one of America's most imitated institutions and has been recognized as one of the nation's leading universities. RIT has also been rated the number one comprehensive university in the East for its scientific and technology programs. RIT's strength lies in its dedication to providing superior career preparation for today's students. This has attracted excellent faculty to RIT and has led to the development of academic programs that combine small classes and an emphasis on undergraduate teaching, modern classroom facilities, and work experience gained through the university's cooperative education program. Few universities provide RIT's variety of career-oriented programs. Our seven colleges offer outstanding programs in business, engineering, art and design, science and mathematics, liberal arts, photography, hotel management, computer science, and other areas. RIT's National Technical Institute for the Deaf (NTID) is the world's largest mainstreamed college program for the deaf and hearing impaired."

### ADMISSIONS

| | |
|---|---|
| Admissions Rating | 84 |
| # of applicants | 8,061 |
| % of applicants accepted | 74 |
| % of acceptees attending | 39 |
| # accepting a place on wait list | 125 |
| % admitted from wait list | 20 |
| # of early decision applicants | 897 |
| % accepted early decision | 67 |

### FRESHMAN PROFILE

| | |
|---|---|
| Range SAT Verbal | 530-630 |
| Range SAT Math | 570-660 |
| Range ACT Composite | 25-29 |
| Minimum TOEFL | 525 |
| Average HS GPA | 3.7 |
| % graduated top 10% of class | 28 |
| % graduated top 25% of class | 60 |
| % graduated top 50% of class | 90 |

### DEADLINES

| | |
|---|---|
| Early decision | 12/15 |
| Early decision notification | 1/15 |
| Priority admission deadline | 2/15 |
| Regular admission | 3/15 |
| Nonfall registration? | yes |

### APPLICANTS ALSO LOOK AT

**AND OFTEN PREFER**
Cornell U.
RPI

**AND SOMETIMES PREFER**
Binghamton U.
SUNY Buffalo
U. Rochester
Carnegie Mellon

**AND RARELY PREFER**
SUNY Albany
Drexel
Syracuse
Boston U.
Clarkson U.

### FINANCIAL FACTS

| | |
|---|---|
| Financial Aid Rating | 79 |
| Tuition | $18,633 |
| Room & board | $7,242 |
| Books and supplies | $600 |
| Required fees | $330 |
| % frosh receiving aid | 75 |
| % undergrads receiving aid | 72 |
| Avg frosh grant | $9,260 |
| Avg frosh loan | $3,900 |

# ROLLINS COLLEGE

CAMPUS BOX 2720, WINTER PARK, FL 32789-4499 • ADMISSIONS: 407-646-2161 • FAX: 407-646-1502

## CAMPUS LIFE

**Quality of Life Rating** 82
Type of school private
Affiliation none
Environment suburban

### STUDENTS

| | |
|---|---|
| Total undergrad enrollment | 1,598 |
| % male/female | 40/60 |
| % from out of state | 52 |
| % from public high school | 57 |
| % live on campus | 75 |
| % in (# of) fraternities | 27 (6) |
| % in (# of) sororities | 27 (6) |
| % African American | 3 |
| % Asian | 3 |
| % Caucasian | 72 |
| % Hispanic | 7 |
| % Native American | 1 |
| % international | 4 |
| # of countries represented | 25 |

### SURVEY SAYS . . .

*Frats and sororities dominate social scene*
*Ethnic diversity on campus*
*Diverse students interact*
*(Almost) everyone smokes*
*Popular college radio*
*Beautiful campus*
*Campus easy to get around*
*Lousy off-campus food*
*(Almost) no one listens to college radio*

## ACADEMICS

**Academic Rating** 82
Calendar semester
Student/faculty ratio 12:1
Profs interesting rating 87
Profs accessible rating 83
% profs teaching UG courses 100
Avg lab size 10-19 students
Avg reg class size 10-19 students

### MOST POPULAR MAJORS
economics
psychology
international business

## STUDENTS SPEAK OUT
### Academics

If you'd rather learn exclusively from "PhD" professors in "small classes" in sunny Florida instead of teaching assistants in dingy, cold lecture halls, consider "small," private Rollins College, home to "great research and lab facilities," a "solid academic reputation," and "connections with grad schools and companies" throughout the Southeast. While students tell us "you receive an excellent education" here, they also say that theirs is "a tough school which requires hard work," and caution that the academic pace is "very hectic and demanding." The "small classes help a lot," in this regard, though. "We are given lots of attention," beams a sophomore. Students appear mostly unperturbed by the fact that course registration "is still run with paper forms." "The school's administration is great," they say, and "for the most part, all of the professors and administrators are always available if you need to talk to them." Almost uniformly, the "excellent" professors at Rollins are "available to see students after class," and they "serve as both teachers and mentors, preparing us not only for exams but for life," according to one happy student here. Music, theater, and business are among the departments that Rollins students cite as noteworthy.

### Life

Rollins boasts an unbeatable location and climate, and "aesthetic beauty" abounds on this immaculate, "small" campus where "every one knows one another." On and around campus, Rollins students "party hard," especially on the weekends. While the students here don't seem to rage the way they once did, Rollins's party-school reputation seems to be at least partially deserved. "Greek life is popular" but not too overwhelming. Sports don't seem to be very popular at all, but there is a wealth of other extracurricular activities to get involved in. Still, "life on campus can be slow at times." When it is, students "just head out to Orlando," land of "clubbing," "shopping," restaurants, and "many opportunities for employment." There are also "popular spots for nightlife," the thrills and spills of Disney World (just minutes away), and several "good places for golf." Of course, you definitely need a car to take advantage of all that burgeoning Orlando has to offer. "A means of transportation is a must or else one feels like they are stuck on Alcatraz," warns one student.

### Student Body

In search of a paradise of ethnic diversity? Look elsewhere. "There is absolutely no diversity here," charges a first-year student. "Everyone is the same." The minority students who do attend Rollins "stick together," and, to be sure, "the majority of the students" on campus are white. There are "rich kids" galore here, and there are reportedly pockets of "extremely affluent and snobby" types. "Some of the frat guys are obnoxious" as well. The "generally nice" students here are, on the whole, "good people," though, and they seem to "get along" just splendidly with one another. "The campus seems to be composed of two groups," observes a junior: "Those who are generally detached and keep to themselves and those who are very friendly and very involved."

FINANCIAL AID: 407-646-2395 • E-MAIL: ADMISSION@ROLLINS.EDU • WEBSITE: WWW.ROLLINS.EDU

## ADMISSIONS

*Very important* academic and nonacademic factors considered by the admissions committee include essays and secondary school record. *Important* factors considered include class rank and interview. *Other* factors considered include alumni/ae relation, character/personal qualities, extracurricular activities, minority status, recommendations, standardized test scores, state residency, talent/ability, volunteer work, and work experience. Factors *not* considered include geography and religious affiliation/commitment. SAT I or ACT required; SAT II recommended. TOEFL required of all international applicants. High school diploma is required and GED is accepted. *High school units required/recommended:* 4 English required, 3 math required, 2 science required, 2 science lab required, 2 foreign language required, 2 social studies required, 2 elective required.

### The Inside Word

It's fairly important to put together a well-rounded candidacy when applying to Rollins. Academic standards are moderate, but the admissions committee puts a great deal of emphasis on the whole package when evaluating candidates. Despite this thorough personal approach, solid numbers will still be enough on their own to get you admitted, provided you don't take the process too lightly.

## FINANCIAL AID

*Students should submit:* FAFSA. Regular filing deadline is March 1. The Princeton Review suggests that all financial aid forms be submitted as soon as possible after January 1. *Need-based scholarships/grants offered:* Pell, SEOG, state scholarships/grants, private scholarships, and the school's own gift aid. *Loan aid offered:* Direct Subsidized Stafford, Direct Unsubsidized Stafford, Direct PLUS, and Federal Perkins. Institutional employment available. Federal Work-Study Program available. Applicants will be notified of awards on or about March 1. Off-campus job opportunities are excellent.

## FROM THE ADMISSIONS OFFICE

"As you begin the college selection process, you should remember that you're in control of your destiny. While the grades you've earned and the scores you've achieved are very important in the college's review of your credentials, places like Rollins pay serious attention to your personal side—your interests, talents, strengths, values, and potential to contribute to college life. Don't sell yourself short in the process. Be proud of what you've accomplished and who you are, and be ready to describe yourself honestly. If you can get an interview at a college, take it. You'll find that we encourage you to talk about yourself and what you do well. If you have a portfolio of your artwork or a scrapbook of your athletic accomplishments, bring it with you. If you play the violin, maybe your interviewer would like to hear you play. Your essay is equally important in describing yourself. Write it in your own voice, and read it aloud when you're finished. It shouldn't sound like an essay, but like a conversation. And most of all, it should be about you! Many colleges appreciate your personal side and look for ways to know you better. Take advantage of that in the college selection process."

## ADMISSIONS

| | |
|---|---|
| Admissions Rating | 81 |
| # of applicants | 2,100 |
| % of applicants accepted | 61 |
| % of acceptees attending | 33 |
| # accepting a place on wait list | 100 |
| % admitted from wait list | 30 |
| # of early decision applicants | 252 |
| % accepted early decision | 72 |

### FRESHMAN PROFILE

| | |
|---|---|
| Range SAT Verbal | 540-630 |
| Average SAT Verbal | 585 |
| Range SAT Math | 540-630 |
| Average SAT Math | 585 |
| Range ACT Composite | 24-28 |
| Average ACT Composite | 26 |
| Minimum TOEFL | 550 |
| % graduated top 10% of class | 39 |
| % graduated top 25% of class | 65 |
| % graduated top 50% of class | 85 |

### DEADLINES

| | |
|---|---|
| Early decision | 11/15 |
| Early decision notification | 12/15 |
| Regular admission | 2/15 |
| Regular notification | 4/1 |
| Nonfall registration? | yes |

### APPLICANTS ALSO LOOK AT
**AND OFTEN PREFER**
U. Richmond
**AND SOMETIMES PREFER**
Emory
Furman
U. Florida
U. Miami
**AND RARELY PREFER**
U. of Central Florida
Stetson
Eckerd

### FINANCIAL FACTS

| | |
|---|---|
| Financial Aid Rating | 82 |
| Tuition | $23,205 |
| Room & board | $7,341 |
| Books and supplies | $520 |
| Required fees | $677 |
| % frosh receiving aid | 46 |
| % undergrads receiving aid | 47 |
| Avg frosh grant | $14,400 |
| Avg frosh loan | $4,625 |

# Rose-Hulman Institute of Technology

5500 Wabash Avenue, CM 1, Terre Haute, IN 47803-3999 • Admissions: 812-877-8213 • Fax: 812-877-8941

## CAMPUS LIFE

| | |
|---|---|
| **Quality of Life Rating** | **77** |
| Type of school | private |
| Affiliation | none |
| Environment | suburban |

### STUDENTS

| | |
|---|---|
| Total undergrad enrollment | 1,581 |
| % male/female | 83/17 |
| % from out of state | 52 |
| % from public high school | 85 |
| % live on campus | 50 |
| % in (# of) fraternities | 45 (8) |
| % in (# of) sororities | 35 (2) |
| % African American | 1 |
| % Asian | 3 |
| % Caucasian | 94 |
| % Hispanic | 1 |
| % international | 1 |

### SURVEY SAYS . . .

*Frats and sororities dominate social scene*
*(Almost) everyone plays intramural sports*
*Student publications are popular*
*Lots of conservatives on campus*
*Classes are small*
*Campus difficult to get around*
*Very little hard liquor*
*Diverse students interact*
*Students don't like Terre Haute, IN*

## ACADEMICS

| | |
|---|---|
| **Academic Rating** | **90** |
| Calendar | quarter |
| Student/faculty ratio | 15:1 |
| Profs interesting rating | 88 |
| Profs accessible rating | 91 |
| % profs teaching UG courses | 100 |
| Avg lab size | under 10 students |
| Avg reg class size | 20-29 students |

### MOST POPULAR MAJORS
mechanical engineering
chemical engineering
electrical engineering

## STUDENTS SPEAK OUT

### Academics

It may not be possible to put a friendly face on the boot camp-like experience of engineering school, but if the Rose-Hulman Institute doesn't get the job done, it comes pretty darn close. Students praise this "technology nerd's paradise" as "the best undergraduate engineering school in the nation," lauding "its small community feeling. It makes people feel at home and prepares students to learn." Students praise professors for their dedication and coherence (not always a given with engineering professors!). Writes one, "I came from a high school which didn't prepare me for college-level courses. The professors immediately saw that I was struggling and helped me until I was up to speed." Adds another, "The professors are very willing to help those students who have questions. They will stay late on Fridays, come in on Sundays, and tell you to call them at home." Students are similarly sanguine about the administration, noting that "the president of our school eats with the students in the cafeteria and teaches one of my classes. He shows up at all sporting events, once in a kilt!" They also appreciate the way that "Rose-Hulman incorporates technology into everything they do. I wouldn't be surprised if we had high-tech meditation courses." Sums up one student, "What you see is what you get at Rose. It is an academically challenging engineering school with professors who are accessible and an administration that does its job well."

### Life

The academic workload at Rose-Hulman is demanding, to say the least. "The big challenge," students say, "is to fit eight hours of class, eight hours of sleep, and eight hours of homework into one day." Still, "most people realize that if they don't have some fun, they'll go crazy," so they somehow manage to carve out a few hours a week for leisure. Students report that "there are always activities on campus to do. Activities are sponsored by all different campus groups, such as comedians on campus, movie nights, talent shows, fine arts series, and drama club productions." Greek life is big ("We hang out at fraternity houses a lot and just have fun"), as are "intramural sports," "hall activities," and "numerous clubs." Role-playing games and science fiction are also "huge." And, "as laptop computers are mandatory, a large part of free time is spent on games or surfing the Internet." Maybe too much time: "The laptops here introvert everybody," complains a junior. All the on-campus activity helps mitigate life in Terre Haute, referred to as "Terrible Hole" by most students. "Terre Haute offers a movie theater but not much more," writes one student.

### Student Body

According to our survey, students at Rose-Hulman enjoy an unusual degree of camaraderie. "All of the students at Rose-Hulman have a common goal (receiving an engineering degree)," explains one student, "so there is a bond between all the students, unlike at most schools with other majors." Despite the end of single-sex education in 1995, students report sadly that "the vast majority of students are still white males" with a bent for the unusual: "If you've always liked academic discussions or oddball talks about life, the universe, and everything," notes one engineer here, "Rose is the place for you." Most students are from Indiana or the Midwest, and are "conservative but apolitical."

FINANCIAL AID: 812-877-8259 • E-MAIL: ADMIS.OFC@ROSE-HULMAN.EDU • WEBSITE: WWW.ROSE-HULMAN.EDU

## ADMISSIONS

*Very important* academic and nonacademic factors considered by the admissions committee include character/personal qualities, interview, religious affiliation/commitment, secondary school record, and standardized test scores. *Important* factors considered include essays, extracurricular activities, minority status, recommendations, and volunteer work. *Other* factors considered include talent/ability and work experience. Factors *not* considered include alumni/ae relation, class rank, geography, and state residency. SAT I or ACT required. TOEFL required of all international applicants. High school diploma is required and GED is not accepted. *High school units required/recommended:* 16 total required; 4 English required, 3 math required, 4 math recommended, 2 science required, 4 science recommended, 2 foreign language required, 4 foreign language recommended.

### The Inside Word

Five years ago, after 100 years as an all-male institution, Rose-Hulman opened its doors to women. The results have been largely successful—each of the last two freshman classes were 20 percent women. The Institute expects to continue at this pace as it builds up the female presence on its campus; thus, for adventurous, ambitious, and technologically-minded women, Rose-Hulman will be a relatively easy admit for the foreseeable future. "Relatively" is the key word here; academic standards are high and so are the expectations of the admissions committee.

## FINANCIAL AID

*Students should submit:* FAFSA. The Princeton Review suggests that all financial aid forms be submitted as soon as possible after January 1. *Need-based scholarships/grants offered:* Pell, SEOG, state scholarships/grants, private scholarships, and the school's own gift aid. *Loan aid offered:* Direct Subsidized Stafford, Direct Unsubsidized Stafford, Direct PLUS, Federal Perkins, and college/university loans from institutional funds. Institutional employment available. Federal Work-Study Program available. Applicants will be notified of awards on a rolling basis beginning on or about March 1. Off-campus job opportunities are good.

## FROM THE ADMISSIONS OFFICE

"Rose-Hulman is generally considered one of the premier undergraduate colleges of engineering and science. We are nationally known as an institution that puts teaching above research and graduate programs. At Rose-Hulman, professors (not graduate students) teach the courses and conduct their own labs. Department chairmen teach freshmen. To enhance the teaching at Rose-Hulman, computers have become a prominent addition to not only our labs but also in our classrooms and residence halls. Additionally, all students are now required to purchase laptop computers."

### ADMISSIONS

| | |
|---|---|
| Admissions Rating | 90 |
| # of applicants | 2,796 |
| % of applicants accepted | 77 |
| % of acceptees attending | 20 |

#### FRESHMAN PROFILE

| | |
|---|---|
| Average SAT Verbal | 650 |
| Average SAT Math | 690 |
| Average ACT Composite | 30 |
| Minimum TOEFL | 550 |
| Average HS GPA | 3.5 |
| % graduated top 10% of class | 70 |
| % graduated top 25% of class | 100 |

#### DEADLINES

| | |
|---|---|
| Priority admission deadline | 12/1 |
| Regular admission | 3/1 |

#### APPLICANTS ALSO LOOK AT
#### AND OFTEN PREFER
MIT
Caltech
Notre Dame
#### AND SOMETIMES PREFER
U. Illinois—Urbana-Champaign
Washington U.
Georgia Tech.
Carnegie Mellon
Lehigh
#### AND RARELY PREFER
Purdue U.—West Lafayette
U. Missouri—Rolla

### FINANCIAL FACTS

| | |
|---|---|
| Financial Aid Rating | 83 |
| Tuition | $21,086 |
| Room & board | $6,039 |
| Books and supplies | $900 |
| Required fees | $435 |
| % frosh receiving aid | 76 |
| % undergrads receiving aid | 78 |
| Avg frosh grant | $5,125 |
| Avg frosh loan | $4,500 |

# RUTGERS UNIVERSITY—RUTGERS COLLEGE

65 DAVIDSON ROAD, PISCATAWAY, NJ 08854-8097 • ADMISSIONS: 732-932-4636 • FAX: 732-445-0237

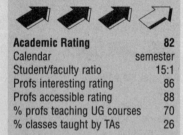
## STUDENTS SPEAK OUT
### Academics

For most undergrads, the choice to come to Rutgers is primarily an economic one; even for out-of-state students, this public university provides a name-brand education at a discount rate. Once they arrive, though, most students are surprised to discover not just a cheap school but also a top-notch university, one that can offer its 35,000 undergraduates academic opportunities in practically every field under the sun. Students report finding RU's size daunting at first ("It is very easy to get lost in the crowd here," warns one sophomore), but eventually they learn to work the system and get the most of their myriad opportunities. Writes one, "As I grew up at this school I learned to like it more, especially as I got into research. Based on my experiences I would rate Rutgers as great for doing research—that is, if you know how to use the school." Agrees another, "Rutgers University promotes education that helps individuals to explore learning in an independent manner. Students are challenged by professors to solve problems and expand their critical thinking skills. When entering the working world, I felt totally prepared. Learning is continuous at this school." Professors are "great but the higher up the ladder you go, the bigger the egos," explains a junior. Teaching assistants, unfortunately, are often "unqualified, unprepared, or just unable to effectively teach classes." Consequently, "Rutgers is basically a do-it-yourself school where you have to occasionally look for help." Don't look to the administration, though, unless you're prepared for the "RU Screw," or, as one student put it—less colorfully and more diplomatically—"some bureaucratic difficulty."

### Life

At Rutgers "there is no lack of activities for the interested, motivated student," says a sophomore. "It's just a matter of keeping your eyes and ears open to take advantage of everything" Rutgers has to offer. Writes another student, "Rutgers has provided a multitude of opportunities for me to grow through community service," as well as clubs and other organizations. Activities "range from the Rutgers Ambulance Service to Model United Nations to one of the best college newspapers in the country." Intercollegiate sports are popular, and students report a decent variety of movies and plays presented on campus. The Greek system is thriving but not overwhelming, and parties of all kinds are "going on practically every night." Even so, some feel that life in New Brunswick leaves something to be desired. "Thank God we are near New York City," writes one. "Otherwise, I hope you like drinking beer in a basement because that is what everyone does until they turn 21." Philadelphia is also an easy train ride away.

### Student Body

As a public university that draws lots of nontraditional students (i.e., part-timers, continuing education students), "RU students are very representative of people in the real world. It takes all kinds." Attests one student, "Few campuses offer the same diversity of lifestyles" or "so many diverse social groups." Students are "friendly, active, and involved. I have made many friendships here that will last an entire lifetime." And while they may not have the time to hang out and grab a beer (since many have families, jobs, and the like), "most are easy to get along with and quite friendly. I do a lot of group work with them and they're just great. . . . Everyone is willing to offer their advice or knowledge."

FINANCIAL AID: 732-932-7057 • E-MAIL: ADMISSIONS@ASB-UGADM.RUTGERS.EDU • WEBSITE: WWW.RUTGERS.EDU

## ADMISSIONS

*Very important* academic and nonacademic factors considered by the admissions committee include secondary school record, class rank, and standardized test scores. *Other* factors considered include extracurricular activities, talent/ability, geography, state residency, minority status, volunteer work, and work experience. Factors *not* considered include recommendations, essay, interview, character/personal qualities, alumni/ae relation, geography, and religious affiliation/commitment. SAT I or ACT required. TOEFL required of all international applicants. High school diploma is required and GED is accepted. *High school units required/recommended:* 16 total required; 4 English required, 3 math required, 4 math recommended, 2 science required, 2 foreign language required, 5 academic electives required.

### The Inside Word

New Jersey residents are finally acknowledging that the flagship of their state university system is among the finest public universities in the nation. As a result, getting in keeps getting tougher every year as more and more New Jersey residents elect to stay home for college.

## FINANCIAL AID

*Students should submit:* FAFSA. There is no regular filing deadline. The Princeton Review suggests that all financial aid forms be submitted as soon as possible after January 1. *Need-based scholarships/grants offered:* Pell, SEOG, state scholarships/grants, and the school's own gift aid. *Loan aid offered:* Direct Subsidized Stafford, Direct Unsubsidized Stafford, Direct PLUS, Federal Perkins, state, college/university loans from institutional funds, and other educational loans. Institutional employment available. Federal Work-Study Program available. Applicants will be notified of awards on a rolling basis beginning on or about February 15. Off-campus job opportunities are good.

## FROM THE ADMISSIONS OFFICE

"Rutgers, The State Universtiy of New Jersey, one of only 61 members of the Association of American Universities, is a research university, which attracts students from across the nation and around the world. What does it take to be accepted for admission to Rutgers University? There's no single answer to that question. Our primary emphasis is on your past academic performance as indicated by your high school grades (particularly in required academic subjects), your class rank, the strength of your academic program, your standardized test scores on the SAT or ACT, any special talents you may have, and your participation in school and community activities. We seek students with a broad diversity of talents, interests, and backgrounds. Above all else, we're looking for students who will get the most out of a Rutgers education—students with the intellect, initiative, and motivation to make full use of the opportunities we have to offer."

### ADMISSIONS

| | |
|---|---|
| **Admissions Rating** | **86** |
| # of applicants | 20,441 |
| % of applicants accepted | 48 |
| % of acceptees attending | 25 |

### FRESHMAN PROFILE

| | |
|---|---|
| Range SAT Verbal | 540-640 |
| Average SAT Verbal | 591 |
| Range SAT Math | 560-670 |
| Average SAT Math | 612 |
| Minimum TOEFL | 550 |
| % graduated top 10% of class | 43 |
| % graduated top 25% of class | 82 |
| % graduated top 50% of class | 99 |

### DEADLINES

| | |
|---|---|
| Priority admission deadline | 12/15 |
| Regular notification | 2/27 |

### APPLICANTS ALSO LOOK AT

**AND OFTEN PREFER**
U. Penn
Cornell U.
Virginia

**AND SOMETIMES PREFER**
Penn State—U. Park
Boston Coll.
New Jersey Tech
Montclair State

**AND RARELY PREFER**
Trenton State
Seton Hall
George Washington

### FINANCIAL FACTS

| | |
|---|---|
| **Financial Aid Rating** | **75** |
| In-state tuition | $4,762 |
| Out-of-state tuition | $9,692 |
| Room & board | $6,098 |
| Books and supplies | $700 |
| Required fees | $1,290 |
| % frosh receiving aid | 48 |
| % undergrads receiving aid | 43 |
| Avg frosh grant | $6,065 |
| Avg frosh loan | $3,923 |

# SAINT BONAVENTURE UNIVERSITY

PO Box D, Saint Bonaventure, NY 14778 • Admissions: 716-375-2400 • Fax: 716-375-4005

## CAMPUS LIFE

**Quality of Life Rating** 82
Type of school private
Affiliation Roman Catholic
Environment rural

### STUDENTS

| | |
|---|---|
| Total undergrad enrollment | 2,202 |
| % male/female | 46/54 |
| % from out of state | 26 |
| % from public high school | 71 |
| % live on campus | 76 |
| % African American | 1 |
| % Caucasian | 49 |
| % Hispanic | 1 |
| % international | 1 |

### SURVEY SAYS . . .
*Beautiful campus*
*Campus easy to get around*
*Great library*
*Athletic facilities are great*
*Great computer facilities*
*Theater is unpopular*
*Students are cliquish*
*Lousy food on campus*

## ACADEMICS

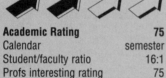

| | |
|---|---|
| **Academic Rating** | **75** |
| Calendar | semester |
| Student/faculty ratio | 16:1 |
| Profs interesting rating | 75 |
| Profs accessible rating | 78 |
| % profs teaching UG courses | 98 |
| Avg lab size | 10-19 students |
| Avg reg class size | 10-19 students |

### MOST POPULAR MAJORS
elementary education
journalism/mass communication
accounting

## STUDENTS SPEAK OUT

### Academics

The fun-loving students at Saint Bonaventure University tell us that their little school in the southwest corner of New York State (about two hours from Buffalo) boasts a "good science program" and a bang-up "reputation for journalism" in the Northeast. Career-minded business and management, communication, and education majors won't be disappointed, and "small class size is a plus as well." Required courses in theology, liberal arts, math, science, and philosophy ensure that everyone here gets a complete undergraduate education. The "generally caring and interesting" faculty is, on the whole, "personable and attentive to students' needs." "Professors are excellent," proclaims a business management major. "They always have time for students." However, there are definitely some "terrible teachers" here that students advise avoiding like the plague. Saint Bonaventure is noticeably Catholic, and Franciscan tradition and influence are prominent. "The friars are always there if you have a problem." Students say the administration does a reasonably good job running the school. At the very least, the top brass at Saint Bonaventure stays out of the way. "I'm a junior and I don't know what the president looks like," claims one student.

### Life

Though Saint Bonaventure's campus is undeniably "gorgeous," "on-campus living sucks." Dormitories are single-sex, and resident hall assistants "walk around like prison guards" to enforce "intervisitation" rules. The school also forbids fraternities or sororities, but luckily, the hopping off-campus party scene here is truly something to behold. To sum it up in three words or less: "Parties, parties, parties." There is a "multitude of bars" nearby, and the students take beer consumption very seriously. "Our school is definitely a party school," explains a senior. "Students are in the bars every night of the week. Everyone smokes cigarettes and lots smoke marijuana. Everyone has a good time, though." Weekends reportedly start "on Wednesday," and "it's typical for students to spend $1,000 on alcohol each semester." Boredom seems to be the the prime mover behind all the carousing. "People drink for fun because there's nothing but trees and cows in Olean" and "the surrounding towns are not too exciting." Saint Bonaventure's Division I basketball team also draws throngs to its games. Students also love the radio station—88.3 "The Buzz"—and there is a "good" newspaper here, but "if you work for the radio or paper," cautions a first-year student, "your life is devoted to them." Students at Bona also "play intramurals with a passion" and spend a great deal of time agonizing over where they will park their cars, as "there is no parking anywhere."

### Student Body

The overwhelming white, Catholic, and middle-class students at Saint Bonaventure "get along" well. The vast majority hail from the Northeast. They range from "exceptionally friendly" to "nice, except when they get drunk and break everything," and they describe themselves as "small town nomads" who "live to party." There are fights on campus from time to time, but there is a great deal of bonding on this somewhat remote campus in upstate New York, and the student population is reportedly "tight" as a whole. Most of the students here know each other, and "people say 'hi' to you on campus even if they don't know you."

# SAINT BONAVENTURE UNIVERSITY

FINANCIAL AID: 716-375-2528 • E-MAIL: ADMISSIONS@SBU.EDU • WEBSITE: WWW.SBU.EDU

## ADMISSIONS

*Very important* academic and nonacademic factors considered by the admissions committee include character/personal qualities, interview, recommendations, and secondary school record. *Important* factors considered include class rank, extracurricular activities, standardized test scores, and talent/ability. *Other* factors considered include alumni/ae relation, essays, geography, minority status, volunteer work, and work experience. Factors *not* considered include religious affiliation/commitment and state residency. SAT I or ACT required. TOEFL required of all international applicants. High school diploma is required and GED is accepted. *High school units required/recommended:* 4 total recommended; 3 English recommended, 3 math recommended, 3 science recommended, 2 foreign language recommended, 4 social studies recommended, 1 history recommended. *The admissions office says:* "[We] highly encourage students to submit a personal essay—it is an excellent opportunity to point out individual uniqueness or experiences, and situations that have affected academic performance."

### The Inside Word

Saint Bonaventure is a safety for many students applying to more selective Catholic universities, but it does a good job of enrolling a sizable percentage of its admits. Most solid students needn't worry about admission; even so, candidates who rank St. Bonnie as a top choice should still submit essays and interview.

## FINANCIAL AID

*Students should submit:* FAFSA, institution's own financial aid form, and state aid form. The Princeton Review suggests that all financial aid forms be submitted as soon as possible after January 1. *Need-based scholarships/grants offered:* Pell, SEOG, state scholarships/grants, private scholarships, and the school's own gift aid. *Loan aid offered:* FFEL Subsidized Stafford, FFEL Unsubsidized Stafford, FFEL PLUS, and Federal Perkins. Institutional employment available. Federal Work-Study Program available. Applicants will be notified of awards on a rolling basis beginning on or about April 1. Off-campus job opportunities are excellent.

## FROM THE ADMISSIONS OFFICE

"The Saint Bonaventure University family has been imparting the Franciscan tradition to men and women of a rich diversity of backgrounds for more than 130 years. This tradition encourages all who become a part of it to face the world confidently, respect the earthly environment, and work for productive change in the world. The charm of our campus and the inspirational beauty of the surrounding hills provide a special place where growth in learning and living is abundantly realized. Academics at Saint Bonaventure are challenging. Small classes and personalized attention encourage individual growth and development for students. Saint Bonaventure's nationally known Schools of Arts and Sciences, Business Administration, Journalism/Mass Communication, and Education offer majors in 31 disciplines. The School of Graduate Studies also offers several programs leading to the master's degree."

## ADMISSIONS

| | |
|---|---|
| **Admissions Rating** | **76** |
| # of applicants | 1,707 |
| % of applicants accepted | 89 |
| % of acceptees attending | 39 |

### FRESHMAN PROFILE

| | |
|---|---|
| Range SAT Verbal | 480-575 |
| Average SAT Verbal | 537 |
| Range SAT Math | 490-585 |
| Average SAT Math | 541 |
| Range ACT Composite | 20-25 |
| Average ACT Composite | 22 |
| Minimum TOEFL | 550 |
| Average HS GPA | 3.2 |
| % graduated top 10% of class | 14 |
| % graduated top 25% of class | 42 |
| % graduated top 50% of class | 76 |

### DEADLINES

| | |
|---|---|
| Priority admission deadline | 2/1 |
| Regular admission | 4/1 |
| Nonfall registration? | yes |

### APPLICANTS ALSO LOOK AT

**AND OFTEN PREFER**
Villanova
Geneseo State
Providence

**AND SOMETIMES PREFER**
LeMoyne
Siena
Ithaca
SUNY Buffalo
Niagara

**AND RARELY PREFER**
Syracuse

## FINANCIAL FACTS

| | |
|---|---|
| **Financial Aid Rating** | **83** |
| Tuition | $13,888 |
| Room & board | $5,800 |
| Books and supplies | $500 |
| Required fees | $550 |
| % frosh receiving aid | 71 |
| % undergrads receiving aid | 71 |
| Avg frosh grant | $8,281 |
| Avg frosh loan | $3,050 |

# ST. JOHN'S COLLEGE (MD)

PO Box 2800, Annapolis, MD 21404 • Admissions: 410-626-2522 • Fax: 410-269-7916

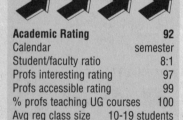
## STUDENTS SPEAK OUT

### Academics

"I believe this school has the most amazingly unique and stimulating curriculum available to college students today," proclaims a student at St. John's College in Annapolis, Maryland. It's unmistakably "not a multiple-choice kind of place." At St. John's, students "read good books." Tons of them. The "unique" Great Books Program requires Johnnies to study a strict four-year curriculum of ancient Greek, French, classical mathematics, science, music, literature, and philosophy—all from the original texts. The "very accessible" professors called "tutors" meet with students each semester to review their progress. In class, Johnnies and their "intelligent, funny, personable" tutors "discuss philosophy" and inquire "into the foundations of things." Outside of class, students must read "rigorous" amounts of material. "Completing all assignments as well as you'd like would be akin to slicing Thanksgiving turkey with a straw," analogizes one student. "To get through you just have to do what you can and be content with that, or you'll go mad." It's an occasionally frustrating process, and it's definitely not for everybody. "If you are looking for something else," suggests one student, "go someplace else," or "you will be very disappointed." "Our tutors have no answers, and our classes only inspire more questions," discloses another student, "but St. John's gives you the greatest means of helping yourself."

### Life

Though the food services and the dorms could both use significant improvement, students at St. John's are some of the most content in the nation. Johnnies call their social atmosphere "explosive, frustrating, enlightening, and mesmerizing." There is "no real division between academics and social life" here. Outside of class, students think and talk (and talk and talk) about the same topics they cover in class: "everything from the existence of God and the meaning of anything that can have meaning, to the distinction between being and becoming." It's pretty heavy stuff. "For fun," students "read books about ancient history," "then get drunk." Though "a tea party is as common as a beer party" at St. John's, "drinking is for many an integral endeavor." This is because "you are constantly confronting the Greatest Works, and you have to drink so you won't get too contemplative about your laundry." However, there is much more to life at St. John's than books and beer. "The college provides the resources for people to do just about anything they want, from pottery to competitive sports," explains a senior. "The key is personal initiative." Social options include a "well-run" intramurals program, a "great" film series, "midnight dodgeball, and swing dancing" ("and we were doing it long before the stupid Gap commercial"). "Waltz parties" are also big, and a long-standing tradition of "playing croquet against the Naval Academy is also a blast."

### Student Body

Though one student asserts that Johnnies are "way too white," another suggests that "St. John's students are not defined as white, straight, gay, or black. Here, you are a Sophist or a Socratic first." These "incredibly articulate" and "abstract and wacky" students are "thoughtful, intense, funny, and rather eccentric." They are "curious" and "intelligent" as well. However, "up to 450 amateur philosophers on a tiny campus can get old fast." Some students are "elitist," "morose WASPS" who are "somewhat lacking in social skills" and have a "pretension that's nearly unbearable." As one student points out, "most of these people were nerds in high school and it shows." Nevertheless, students "share a thirst for knowledge," and most get along pretty well because, with only 450 students, they have little choice. "You will come to hate about 14 percent" of the students here "so much that it will hurt to look at them," one Johnny explains. "Sixty-six percent of the people you will find tolerable and even likable. Twenty percent you will fall for and won't be able to make it a whole summer without seeing.""

FINANCIAL AID: 410-626-2502 • E-MAIL: ADMISSIONS@SJCA.EDU • WEBSITE: WWW.SJCA.EDU

## ADMISSIONS

TOEFL required of all international applicants. High school diploma is required and GED is accepted. *High school units required/recommended:* 16 total required; 20 total recommended; 4 English required, 3 math required, 4 math recommended, 3 science required, 4 science recommended, 2 science lab required, 3 science lab recommended, 2 foreign language required, 4 foreign language recommended, 1 social studies required, 2 social studies recommended, 2 history required.

### The Inside Word

St. John's has one of the most personal admissions processes in the country. The applicant pool is highly self-selected and extremely bright, so don't be fooled by the high acceptance rate—every student who is offered admission deserves to be here. Candidates who don't give serious thought to the kind of match they make with the college and devote serious energy to their essays are not likely to be successful.

## FINANCIAL AID

*Students should submit:* FAFSA, CSS/Financial Aid PROFILE, noncustodial (divorced/separated) parent's statement, and business/farm supplement. Regular filing deadline is February 15. The Princeton Review suggests that all financial aid forms be submitted as soon as possible after January 1. *Need-based scholarships/grants offered:* Pell, SEOG, state scholarships/grants, and the school's own gift aid. *Loan aid offered:* FFEL Subsidized Stafford, FFEL Unsubsidized Stafford, FFEL PLUS, Federal Perkins, and college/university loans from institutional funds. Institutional employment available. Federal Work-Study Program available. Applicants will be notified of awards on a rolling basis beginning on or about March 1. Off-campus job opportunities are excellent.

## FROM THE ADMISSIONS OFFICE

"The purpose of the admission process is to determine whether an applicant has the necessary preparation and ability to complete the St. John's program satisfactorily. The essays are designed to enable applicants to give a full account of themselves. They can tell the committee much more than statistical records reveal. Previous academic records show whether an applicant has the habits of study necessary at St. John's. Letters of reference, particularly those of teachers, are carefully read for indications that the applicant has the maturity, self-discipline, ability, energy, and initiative to succeed in the St. John's program. St. John's attaches little importance to 'objective' test scores, and no applicant is accepted or rejected because of such scores."

### ADMISSIONS

| | |
|---|---|
| Admissions Rating | 83 |
| # of applicants | 499 |
| % of applicants accepted | 79 |
| % of acceptees attending | 35 |

#### FRESHMAN PROFILE

| | |
|---|---|
| Range SAT Verbal | 650-750 |
| Range SAT Math | 590-690 |
| Minimum TOEFL | 600 |
| % graduated top 10% of class | 33 |
| % graduated top 25% of class | 66 |
| % graduated top 50% of class | 96 |

#### DEADLINES

| | |
|---|---|
| Priority admission deadline | 3/1 |
| Nonfall registration? | yes |

#### APPLICANTS ALSO LOOK AT
#### AND OFTEN PREFER
Oberlin
Harvard
Princeton
#### AND SOMETIMES PREFER
Brown
U. Chicago
Reed
#### AND RARELY PREFER
Kenyon
Grinnell
Bard

### FINANCIAL FACTS

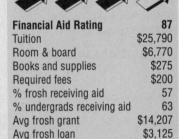

| | |
|---|---|
| Financial Aid Rating | 87 |
| Tuition | $25,790 |
| Room & board | $6,770 |
| Books and supplies | $275 |
| Required fees | $200 |
| % frosh receiving aid | 57 |
| % undergrads receiving aid | 63 |
| Avg frosh grant | $14,207 |
| Avg frosh loan | $3,125 |

# St. John's College (NM)

1160 CAMINO CRUZ BLANCA, SANTA FE, NM 87501 • ADMISSIONS: 505-984-6060 • FAX: 505-984-6162

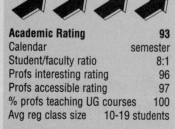

## CAMPUS LIFE

**Quality of Life Rating** **89**
Type of school | private
Affiliation | none
Environment | urban

### STUDENTS
Total undergrad enrollment | 431
% male/female | 55/45
% from out of state | 89
% from public high school | 75
% live on campus | 71
% Asian | 2
% Caucasian | 88
% Hispanic | 7
% Native American | 2
# of countries represented | 8

### SURVEY SAYS . . .
*Students love Santa Fe, NM*
*Great off-campus food*
*Student government is popular*
*Students are happy*
*Student publications are popular*
*(Almost) everyone smokes*

## ACADEMICS

**Academic Rating** **93**
Calendar | semester
Student/faculty ratio | 8:1
Profs interesting rating | 96
Profs accessible rating | 97
% profs teaching UG courses | 100
Avg reg class size | 10-19 students

### MOST POPULAR MAJORS
liberal arts

## STUDENTS SPEAK OUT
### Academics

"Education is the priority," and "academics are extremely intense" at St. John's College in Santa Fe, New Mexico, where "no one is here for job preparation." The 400 or so students on this tiny campus participate in one rigorous and "intensely thoughtful program," composed entirely of requirements in a host of fields, ranging from classical Greek to modern science to music. "St. John's has a set curriculum called the Great Books Program," explains a sophomore. "We read the Classics of mathematics, science, history, philosophy, religion, and Western Civilization." The professors at St. John's are called "tutors" and, despite their PhDs, they serve primarily as guides in the "discussion-based" classes rather than as lecturers. "Tutors" are "perceptive and entertaining in a manner that leads you to wonder what planet they came from," but classes generally take the form of "students and tutors versus the Great Books." For the right kind of student, SJC is nothing short of "academic nirvana." The "basic truths of life" and "the Big Questions face you constantly," relates a "humbled" sophomore. "The program definitely turns your previous religious, moral, and political beliefs into mush, and everyone leaves a changed person." It keeps you very busy as well—Johnnies put in about four hours of studying each day—and it is by no means easy. "Graduating from St. John's will be the hardest thing I have ever accomplished in my life," discloses a senior. While Johnnies say their Great Books program is "definitely worth the stress and money" in the end, they tell us it's no picnic. "Don't bother coming here unless you want to work," warns a junior. "I love my school and my tutors too much to recommend St. John's to lazy people."

### Life

St. John's is a universe unto itself and "a great place to completely lose touch with the modern world." It's also a great place to see "two drunks fighting over Plato." Students tell us that "the academic experience" on this gorgeous, adobe campus "is inextricably connected to the social experience." Students here "read for fun," and "studying flows over into everyday lives." Both in and out of class, "dead authors make for Great Conversation." When students aren't reading or debating, there are "theme dance parties (disco, funk, swing)" and "lots of classic and foreign movies for one dollar." There are also "parties in the dorms," outdoor activities galore (including mountain biking, hiking, rafting, and rock-climbing), and trips to the nearby hot springs. "People here party constantly" as well, explains a sophomore. "One guy was drunk in my hallway screaming 'Forever and Ever, Amen' by Randy Travis at 4:00 A.M. on a Tuesday." However, plentiful as drugs and alcohol may be, "it's not uncommon for people to study instead of party," even on the weekends. Overall, Johnnies tell us they are a happy bunch with few gripes. "There are no weaknesses here," asserts a first-year student, "save for the dining hall food quality."

### Student Body

"Imagine if John Belushi and Plato were genetically spliced together and this new 'Uberman' then had Ayn Rand's love child," posits a sophomore. "That child is St. John's." The "slightly crazy" and "thought-entrenched" students here "tend to be intense and socially odd," and there is a "certain weirdness to all who attend," but "this makes the SJC experience unique and enjoyable." The mostly white, left-leaning, middle-class students here are certainly not at a loss for explaining themselves. "People here are freaks," admits a junior. "We were the people who hated high school. No one in high school liked us, not even our teachers." Johnnies are "mellow," "godless heathens" with "an intense passion for learning" who are "easy to get to know" and who "have great senses of humor." They are "a bunch of philosophers with their heads in the clouds" who "love to hear themselves talk" and who are "just smarter than everyone else." "We are self-involved, ungrateful brats who drink too much, gossip viciously, and analyze everything," observes a junior. "We will eventually grow up to be some of the most interesting people you will ever meet."

# ST. JOHN'S COLLEGE (NM)

FINANCIAL AID: 505-984-6058 • E-MAIL: ADMISSIONS@MAIL.SJCSF.EDU • WEBSITE: WWW.SJCSF.EDU

## ADMISSIONS

TOEFL required of all international applicants. High school diploma is required and GED is accepted. High school units required/recommended: 4 English recommended, 3 math required, 4 math recommended, 3 science recommended, 3 science lab recommended, 2 foreign language required, 4 foreign language recommended, 2 social studies recommended, 2 history recommended. *The admissions office says:* "The Admissions Committee—five tutors and the director of admissions—regards the application as being a question from the applicant: 'Do you think I am ready to profit from the program of studies at St. John's?' In the essays, applicants are asked to discuss their previous education, reasons for choosing St. John's, and their experience with books. Optional topics are also suggested. These can tell the committee much more than statistical records reveal."

### The Inside Word

Self-selection drives this admissions process—over one-half of the entire applicant pool each year indicates that St. John's is their first choice, and half of those admitted send in tuition deposits. Even so, no one in admissions takes things for granted, and neither should any student considering an application. The admissions process is highly personal on both sides of the coin. Only the intellectually curious and highly motivated need apply.

## FINANCIAL AID

*Students should submit:* FAFSA, CSS/Financial Aid PROFILE, and noncustodial (divorced/separated) parent's statement. The Princeton Review suggests that all financial aid forms be submitted as soon as possible after January 1. *Need-based scholarships/grants offered:* Pell, SEOG, state scholarships/grants, private scholarships, and the school's own gift aid. *Loan aid offered:* Direct Subsidized Stafford, Direct Unsubsidized Stafford, Direct PLUS, Federal Perkins, and college/university loans from institutional funds. Institutional employment available. Federal Work-Study Program available. Applicants will be notified of awards on a rolling basis beginning on or about December 1. Off-campus job opportunities are good.

## FROM THE ADMISSIONS OFFICE

"St. John's appeals to students who value good books, love to read, and are passionate about discourse and debate. There are no lectures and virtually no tests or electives. Instead, classes of 20 students occur around conference tables where professors are as likely to be asked to defend their points of view as are students. Great books provide the direction, context, and stimulus for conversation. The entire student body adheres to the same, all-required arts and science curriculum. Someone once said 'A classic is a house we still live in,' and at St. John's, students and professors alike approach each reading on the list as if the ideas it holds were being expressed for the first time—questioning the logic behind a geometrical proof, challenging the premise of a scientific development, or dissecting the progression of modern political theory as it unfolds."

## ADMISSIONS

| | |
|---|---|
| Admissions Rating | 82 |
| # of applicants | 355 |
| % of applicants accepted | 84 |
| % of acceptees attending | 42 |
| # accepting a place on wait list | 20 |
| % admitted from wait list | 25 |

### FRESHMAN PROFILE

| | |
|---|---|
| Range SAT Verbal | 650-710 |
| Range SAT Math | 590-670 |
| Range ACT Composite | 26-30 |
| Minimum TOEFL | 550 |
| % graduated top 10% of class | 29 |
| % graduated top 25% of class | 72 |
| % graduated top 50% of class | 90 |

### DEADLINES

| | |
|---|---|
| Priority admission deadline | 3/1 |
| Regular notification | rolling |
| Nonfall registration? | yes |

### APPLICANTS ALSO LOOK AT AND SOMETIMES PREFER

Colorado Coll.
Reed
Oberlin
UC—Santa Cruz
U. Chicago

## FINANCIAL FACTS

| | |
|---|---|
| Financial Aid Rating | 84 |
| Tuition | $25,790 |
| Room & board | $6,770 |
| Books and supplies | $275 |
| Required fees | $200 |
| % frosh receiving aid | 63 |
| % undergrads receiving aid | 46 |
| Avg frosh grant | $19,953 |
| Avg frosh loan | $2,625 |

# ST. LAWRENCE UNIVERSITY

PAYSON HALL, CANTON, NY 13617 • ADMISSIONS: 315-229-5261 • FAX: 315-229-5818

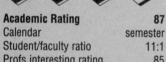
## STUDENTS SPEAK OUT

### Academics

At St. Lawrence University, a distinguished liberal arts enclave in remote, frigid, and rural upstate New York, "the small classes are great," and students can't seem to praise the "extremely knowledgeable," "incredibly accessible and enthusiastic" faculty highly enough. There are a few bad apples here, but the overwhelming majority of professors are "stimulating," "witty, and fun." "You can always set up a time to meet with them to discuss anything," attests a sophomore. Professors are "always willing to go the extra mile" and they are "wonderful people to get to know." The "unbelievably well-run"(and apparently improved) administration "does a great job" as well, especially when it comes to the "excellent financial aid program." At the end of the day, "the administration and the professors really engulf themselves in the St. Lawrence community," observes a math major. "It's great to see them at plays, hockey games, and other campus events. It shows they really care about the students." First-year students seem generally pleased with SLU's "challenging," unique, and year-long first-year program, which "will definitely improve your writing skills." Juniors and seniors laud SLU's "connections to the real world for jobs" and a strong placement rate throughout the Northeast corridor, thanks in part to "a network of alumni always ready to help you." "Going abroad is very popular," too. SLU sponsors a wide variety of highly recommended semester abroad programs.

### Life

The perception of the students we spoke to is clear: "What do we do? Five letters are key," explains one student. "D-R-I-N-K." Without a doubt, St. Lawrence has a rich and well-deserved reputation as a party school of the highest caliber. "I never knew how many beer games there were until I came here," reveals an astonished freshman. "The classes are definitely challenging," adds a sophomore. "It's getting motivated and out of bed for class that serves as the real challenge, though. Students are usually are too tired or hung over to get up." The Greek system is immense, so "fraternity parties are very popular," especially since the surrounding town of Canton offers so little in the way of amusement. "Here in Canton, it is up to the students to entertain themselves," says a senior. "When it warms up outside, we play frisbee, BBQ, and fly kites." Hockey is also enormously popular. ("Whether or not you like hockey before you get here, you will by the time you leave.") "Outdoor excursions" are frequent as well, especially to the nearby Adirondacks. And we hear that "you can see the Aurora Borealis" from campus. When SLU students need a change of scenery, Burlington and Syracuse aren't too far away. And "with Canada so close, it's easy to go over the border for a weekend." Back on campus, "the living arrangements for first-year students are cool because you get to know everyone really well," but the dorms in general "are a little loud" and could stand to be "more enjoyable to live in and more homey."

### Student Body

"Sure, there's the occasional weirdo," explains a senior, but overall, "we're just a happy bunch of 18- to 22-year-olds living in our St. Lawrence bubble." The students on this "tight-knit campus" describe themselves as "a particularly fun and laid back bunch of kids." They're "very outgoing" and "fun to be with and fairly easy to talk to." "Just about anyone will say 'hi' to you when you walk by." Of course, it doesn't hurt that "everyone knows everyone else." "Most students are from prep schools and private high schools," and there are certainly "rich, stuck-up credit-card kids" here, but "because SLU offers large amounts of financial aid, you are not as apt to encounter the snobbish attitudes which are so prevalent at other small, northeastern liberal arts colleges." You will find "pot-smoking, tree-hugging WASPS," though, and a few "loudmouth drunks." SLU students complain that there is "not enough racial diversity on campus," but they also concede that sustaining a diverse population is "difficult in this location."

FINANCIAL AID: 315-229-5265 • E-MAIL: ADMISSIONS@STLAW.EDU • WEBSITE: WWW.STLAWU.EDU

## ADMISSIONS

*Very important* academic and nonacademic factors considered by the admissions committee include recommendations and secondary school record. *Important* factors considered include character/personal qualities, class rank, essays, extracurricular activities, interview, minority status, and standardized test scores. *Other* factors considered include alumni/ae relation, geography, talent/ability, volunteer work, and work experience. Factors *not* considered include religious affiliation/commitment and state residency. SAT I or ACT required. TOEFL required of all international applicants. High school diploma is required and GED is accepted. *High school units required/recommended:* 20 total recommended; 4 English recommended, 4 math recommended, 4 science recommended, 4 foreign language recommended, 2 social studies recommended, 2 history recommended. *The admissions office says:* "We are assured by prospective students that the high level of personal attention they receive distinguishes St. Lawrence's [admissions] process. On average, an inquirer receives information about St. Lawrence every two weeks. Prospective students feel nurtured."

### The Inside Word

St. Lawrence has a rough time convincing students to commit to spending four years in relative isolation. Serious competition from many fine northeastern colleges also causes admissions standards to be less selective than the university would like. This makes St. Lawrence an especially good choice for academically sound but average students who are seeking an excellent small college experience and/or an outdoorsy setting.

## FINANCIAL AID

*Students should submit:* FAFSA, institution's own financial aid form, state aid form, and noncustodial (divorced/separated) parent's statement. Regular filing deadline is February 15. The Princeton Review suggests that all financial aid forms be submitted as soon as possible after January 1. *Need-based scholarships/grants offered:* Pell, SEOG, state scholarships/grants, private scholarships, and the school's own gift aid. *Loan aid offered:* Direct Subsidized Stafford, Direct Unsubsidized Stafford, FFEL Subsidized Stafford, FFEL Unsubsidized Stafford, FFEL PLUS, Federal Perkins, college/university loans from institutional funds, and Gate Student Loan Program. Institutional employment available. Federal Work-Study Program available. Applicants will be notified of awards on or about March 20. Off-campus job opportunities are poor.

## FROM THE ADMISSIONS OFFICE

"St. Lawrence is an independent, nondenominational liberal arts and sciences university, and the oldest coeducational institution in New York State. The campus is composed of 30 buildings, two of which are on the National Historic Register, in a country setting at the edge of the village of Canton, New York, St. Lawrence's 1,000 acres include a golf course, cross-country ski trails, and jogging trails at the outer edges of campus. Canton is a town of 7,000 people who welcome St. Lawrence students into their gift and clothing shops, grocery stores, restaurants, and movie theater. The university is 90 minutes from the capital of Canada, one-half hour from Adirondack Park and the Thousand Islands, and two hours from Montreal, Canada."

## ADMISSIONS

| | |
|---|---|
| Admissions Rating | 85 |
| # of applicants | 2,554 |
| % of applicants accepted | 69 |
| % of acceptees attending | 35 |
| # accepting a place on wait list | 126 |
| % admitted from wait list | 3 |
| # of early decision applicants | 124 |
| % accepted early decision | 84 |

### FRESHMAN PROFILE

| | |
|---|---|
| Range SAT Verbal | 520-620 |
| Average SAT Verbal | 570 |
| Range SAT Math | 520-620 |
| Average SAT Math | 570 |
| Range ACT Composite | 21-26 |
| Average ACT Composite | 24 |
| Minimum TOEFL | 600 |
| Average HS GPA | 3.3 |
| % graduated top 10% of class | 26 |
| % graduated top 25% of class | 60 |
| % graduated top 50% of class | 91 |

### DEADLINES

| | |
|---|---|
| Early decision | 11/15 |
| Early decision notification | 12/15 |
| Regular admission | 2/15 |
| Nonfall registration? | yes |

### APPLICANTS ALSO LOOK AT

**AND OFTEN PREFER**
Middlebury
Colby, Colgate
U. Vermont

**AND SOMETIMES PREFER**
Hamilton
Syracuse
Bates
Skidmore
U. New Hampshire

**AND RARELY PREFER**
Union (NY)
Denison

### FINANCIAL FACTS

| | |
|---|---|
| Financial Aid Rating | 82 |
| Tuition | $23,795 |
| Room & board | $7,475 |
| Books and supplies | $600 |
| Required fees | $190 |
| % frosh receiving aid | 80 |
| % undergrads receiving aid | 65 |
| Avg frosh grant | $16,982 |
| Avg frosh loan | $4,093 |

# SAINT LOUIS UNIVERSITY

221 NORTH GRAND BOULEVARD, SAINT LOUIS, MO 63103 • ADMISSIONS: 314-977-2500 • FAX: 314-977-3079

## CAMPUS LIFE

| Quality of Life Rating | 76 |
|---|---|
| Type of school | private |
| Affiliation | Roman Catholic |
| Environment | urban |

### STUDENTS

| | |
|---|---|
| Total undergrad enrollment | 7,086 |
| % male/female | 45/55 |
| % from out of state | 42 |
| % from public high school | 51 |
| % live on campus | 48 |
| % in (# of) fraternities | 17 (11) |
| % in (# of) sororities | 18 (4) |
| % African American | 8 |
| % Asian | 4 |
| % Caucasian | 69 |
| % Hispanic | 2 |
| % international | 6 |
| # of countries represented | 55 |

### SURVEY SAYS . . .

Student publications are popular
Lots of liberals
Student government is popular
Everyone loves the Billiken
Musical organizations are hot
Lousy off-campus food
Campus difficult to get around
Athletic facilities need improving
Library needs improving

## ACADEMICS

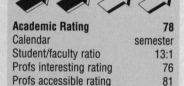

| Academic Rating | 78 |
|---|---|
| Calendar | semester |
| Student/faculty ratio | 13:1 |
| Profs interesting rating | 76 |
| Profs accessible rating | 81 |
| % profs teaching UG courses | 92 |
| % classes taught by TAs | 8 |
| Avg lab size | 10-19 students |
| Avg reg class size | 10-19 students |

### MOST POPULAR MAJORS
biology
physical therapy
pyschology

## STUDENTS SPEAK OUT

### Academics

Pre-professional programs are all the rage at prestigious and "challenging" Saint Louis University, especially physical therapy, education, business, and the med-scholars program. SLU also boasts a strong Jesuit tradition, an "excellent academic environment," a "small, personal atmosphere," and an uncommonly affordable tuition for a private school. Students here can't say enough about their "very knowledgeable," "enthusiastic," and "flexible" faculty. "SLU's professors care about their students." They "not only teach, they mentor, befriend, and genuinely" take "the time to listen." Students also tell us that "discussions in class are wonderful." SLU also has "a great tutoring center with convenient hours" and "nice," "up-to-date" facilities, but there are reportedly "more statues than computers" here. Its "tendency to purchase naked female statues" notwithstanding, the "very well organized" administration receives a great deal of praise from students, not least for realizing "that they wouldn't be here if it wasn't for the students." The top brass also does "a lot financially, verbally, politically, and publicly to promote and support the Jesuit ideals on which SLU is based." "My overall academic experience has been awesome," concludes an elementary education major. "I am very happy with my choice. This school is awesome."

### Life

The way SLU students see it, you'd have to work to be bored here. St. Louis is "a great city to be young in" as well as "a great college city," and "SLU is a fun school." "It's not a party school but we do have a social scene," explains a sophomore. "With six bars within walking distance, we keep the bartenders busy." During the week, "there's very little time to do anything but go to the library and study, but come Friday," beer and liquor are "huge." Students say "dorm life is great" and there's plenty to do on the "beautiful" campus "in the heart of midtown St. Louis." However, there's a lot more to do offcampus. "Life is great if you're 21 or have a good fake I.D." because St. Louis is brimming with "excellent" bars and clubs that are "extremely easy to get into." The hopping St. Louis bar scene stands to reason because, after all, "they brew Bud here." If you are underage, or if the bars aren't your bag, you'll still find plenty to keep you occupied. "St. Louis has so much to do, from sports to malls to downtown parks," says a first-year student, "and it's not so big that it is intimidating." Movies, "formal dances," concerts, "Cardinals games, Blues games, Rams games," and "throwing the disc at Forest Park" are all popular pastimes.

### Student Body

From what we gather, it's hard to be humble when you go to SLU. The "mature and goal-oriented" students here describe themselves as "open," not to mention "generous and conscientious." They say it's "very easy to make friends" here, what with "so many friendly faces walking around" campus. "Many students come from Catholic all-boys or all-girls schools," and "most students come from suburban middle-class" families in the Midwest. "That could be the reason why we get along so well," muses one keenly observant student. Indeed, there's very little in the way of ethnic diversity on campus, though the school and students say they are doing what they can to entice minorities to attend SLU. "We're working on it. We have a strong diversity advocate group that attempts to make the campus aware overall." Meanwhile, the sharpest distinction to speak of here is "a real division between the Greek and non-Greek students," but students are quick to point out that even here there's little actual discord; it's mostly just a difference in where you hang out on the weekends.

# SAINT LOUIS UNIVERSITY

FINANCIAL AID: 314-977-2350 • E-MAIL: ADMITME@SLU.EDU • WEBSITE: WWW.SLU.EDU

## ADMISSIONS

*Very important* academic and nonacademic factors considered by the admissions committee include character/personal qualities, essays, secondary school record, standardized test scores, talent/ability and volunteer work. *Important* factors considered include class rank, extracurricular activities, interview, recommendations, and work experience. *Other* factors considered include alumni/ae relation. Factors *not* considered include geography, minority status, religious affiliation/commitment, and state residency. SAT I or ACT required, ACT preferred. TOEFL required of all international applicants. High school diploma is required and GED is accepted. *High school units required/recommended:* 16 total required; 4 English required, 4 math required, 2 science required, 2 science lab required, 2 foreign language recommended, 1 social studies recommended, 1 history recommended, 2 elective recommended.

### The Inside Word

Students who are ranked in the top half of their graduating class will have a fairly easy path to admission at Saint Louis. Those who are not can find success in the admissions process by being a minority, having a top Catholic school diploma, or possessing a major talent in soccer.

## FINANCIAL AID

*Students should submit:* FAFSA. Regular filing deadline is June 1. The Princeton Review suggests that all financial aid forms be submitted as soon as possible after January 1. *Need-based scholarships/grants offered:* Pell, SEOG, state scholarships/grants, private scholarships, and the school's own gift aid. *Loan aid offered:* FFEL Subsidized Stafford, FFEL Unsubsidized Stafford, FFEL PLUS, Federal Perkins, Federal Nursing, college/university loans from institutional funds, private and non-federal/state alternative loans for students and parents. Institutional employment available. Applicants will be notified of awards on a rolling basis beginning on or about February 1. Off-campus job opportunities are excellent.

## FROM THE ADMISSIONS OFFICE

"Saint Louis University (SLU) is not resting on its 183-year-old reputation for excellence in education. Thanks to a $100 million project that includes academic initiatives and an enhanced campus environment, entering students experience decreasing class sizes, more full-time faculty teaching those classes, better-equipped classrooms, and many more opportunities for scholarships. Students live and learn in a safe and attractive campus environment that has set the standard nationwide for urban campus growth and renewal with extensive outreach opportunities. Even more impressive, though, is that students are experiencing all of these benefits in the framework of a Carnegie research-extensive university. As a leading Catholic, Jesuit university, our goal is to graduate men and women of competence and conscience—individuals who are not only capable of making wise decisions, but who also understand why they made them. Today, we enroll more than 11,000 students earning a broad array of undergraduate, graduate, and professional degrees and dedicated to our long tradition to excel academically, to serve others, and to be leaders in society. Saint Louis University is truly the place where knowledge touches lives."

## ADMISSIONS

| | |
|---|---:|
| Admissions Rating | 76 |
| # of applicants | 5,534 |
| % of applicants accepted | 67 |
| % of acceptees attending | 42 |

### FRESHMAN PROFILE

| | |
|---|---:|
| Average SAT Verbal | 582 |
| Average SAT Math | 594 |
| Range ACT Composite | 23-28 |
| Average ACT Composite | 26 |
| Minimum TOEFL | 500 |
| Average HS GPA | 3.5 |
| % graduated top 10% of class | 36 |
| % graduated top 25% of class | 63 |
| % graduated top 50% of class | 89 |

### DEADLINES

| | |
|---|---:|
| Priority admission deadline | 4/1 |
| Regular admission | 8/1 |
| Nonfall registration? | yes |

### APPLICANTS ALSO LOOK AT

**AND OFTEN PREFER**
Washington U.

**AND SOMETIMES PREFER**
Northeast Missouri State
Marquette
U. Illinois—Urbana-Champaign
U. Wisconsin—Madison
U. Missouri—Columbia

**AND RARELY PREFER**
Creighton
Indiana U.—Bloomington
Kansas State

## FINANCIAL FACTS

| | |
|---|---:|
| Financial Aid Rating | 87 |
| Tuition | $18,400 |
| Room & board | $6,140 |
| Books and supplies | $500 |
| Required fees | $38 |
| % frosh receiving aid | 96 |
| % undergrads receiving aid | 70 |
| Avg frosh grant | $11,392 |
| Avg frosh loan | $5,345 |

# SAINT MARY'S COLLEGE OF CALIFORNIA

PO Box 4800, Moraga, CA 94575-4800 • Admissions: 925-631-4224 • Fax: 925-376-7193

## CAMPUS LIFE

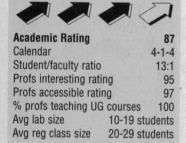

**Quality of Life Rating**                    **89**
Type of school                            private
Affiliation                    Roman Catholic
Environment                          suburban

### STUDENTS
Total undergrad enrollment          2,492
% male/female                          41/59
% from out of state                        11
% from public high school              56
% live on campus                           68
% African American                          6
% Asian                                          8
% Caucasian                                  63
% Hispanic                                    15
% Native American                            1
% international                                2
# of countries represented              14

### SURVEY SAYS . . .
*Classes are small
Beautiful campus
Campus easy to get around
Campus feels safe
Musical organizations aren't popular
Very small frat/sorority scene
Class discussions encouraged
Theater is unpopular
Lousy food on campus
Political activism is (almost)
nonexistent*

## ACADEMICS

**Academic Rating**                            **87**
Calendar                                    4-1-4
Student/faculty ratio                    13:1
Profs interesting rating                    95
Profs accessible rating                    97
% profs teaching UG courses          100
Avg lab size              10-19 students
Avg reg class size    20-29 students

### MOST POPULAR MAJORS
business administration
communications
psychology

## STUDENTS SPEAK OUT
### Academics
With a core curriculum centered on the "one-of-a-kind" Great Books Seminar Program, and a strong affiliation with the Roman Catholic church, this small private college manages to keep one foot firmly planted in tradition, while the other is pointed straight towards the future. The school's "beautiful" campus—located in the heart of the Napa Valley close to San Francisco—"is booming with new buildings, technologies, and media," yet the school's classic approach encourages undergrads to gain a solid liberal arts foundation before they head into one of the school's many pre-professional majors, such as business administration. "I can't think of any other school that allows students to soak up some sun while discussing the dominant 'Amazonian' women and their roles in Lysistrata," writes a sophomore. With a little less than 2,500 undergrads, small "seminar-style discussions" and lots of "personal attention" are guaranteed; and while "no one has a cow if you don't come to class," notes another sophomore, "students here know that missing a class is as bad as not calling Mom back after she's left yet another message." And like Mom, professors are student-focused and very available. Says a junior, "I have been very pleased with my academic experience. My professors have all been extremely accessible and interested in seeing me succeed." Faculty and administration are described as "friendly" and "willing to help." Writes another junior, "They work hard to get to know you as a person." A first-year provides an unusual example of faculty devotion: "Last week, my professor in 'Culture and Community' bought my whole class Round Table Pizza and before that, Starbucks, and before that, Ben & Jerry's. I love my professors here!" And while with all this fussing over the student body may make it hard to leave, SMC encourages students to widen their educational horizons by offering a January term every year during which students pursue nontraditional themes, internships, and travel, as well as study abroad programs at affiliated Catholic institutions in Rome, France, and England.

### Life
Only a short BART ride away from San Francisco, yet far enough away to offer hiking, biking, skating, and climbing just minutes from campus, "gorgeous" Saint Mary's is ideally situated to provide a little something for every type of student. It's also a "community-oriented" school, improved since the inception of a new student union building last year. In terms of campus life, crew and other sports are reasonably popular, as is the Campus Ministry—"a great way to get involved." And while many students mention the lack of a weekend scene at SMC due to the fact that many of its students live in nearby towns, "a new sprouting of on-campus activities makes life here much more exciting." Still, writes one junior, "Moraga is a very upper-class white town, and the students here are those usually with money, so they go home on weekends a lot as there isn't much to do. It sucks for out-of-state students, socially, unless they find friends with cars and generosity." Of course there's always the good old college standby: "meet at students' rooms, listen to music, dance, and drink."

### Student Body
Though SMC students have the reputation of being fairly conservative, Roman Catholic, and career-oriented (and a bit "behind in diversity," notes a first-year), a sophomore notes that "many aren't as serious about academics as I'd expected." She continues, "They're not too spiritual and they like to have fun." One thing is certain: Most students point out that "everyone is very friendly" at SMC, and a senior takes it a step further, saying, "The best thing about this school is the people you meet."

# SAINT MARY'S COLLEGE OF CALIFORNIA

FINANCIAL AID: 925-631-4370 • E-MAIL: SMCADMIT@STMARYS-CA.EDU • WEBSITE: WWW.STMARYS-CA.EDU

## ADMISSIONS

*Very important* academic and nonacademic factors considered by the admissions committee include class rank, secondary school record, and standardized test scores. *Important* factors considered include character/personal qualities, essays, extracurricular activities, recommendations, talent/ability, and volunteer work. *Other* factors considered include alumni/ae relation, interview, minority status, and work experience. Factors *not* considered include geography, religious affiliation/commitment, and state residency. SAT I or ACT required. TOEFL required of all international applicants. High school diploma is required and GED is accepted. *High school units required/recommended:* 15 total required; 19 total recommended; 4 English required, 3 math required, 4 math recommended, 2 science required, 3 science recommended, 1 science lab required, 3 science lab recommended, 1 foreign language required, 3 foreign language recommended, 2 social studies required, 1 history required, 2 history recommended, 3 elective required.

### *The Inside Word*

The typical St. Mary's admit is a better-than-average student who has attending a Catholic college very high on his or her list of preferences. The applicant pool is full of such candidates. Candidates should give serious attention to the application process, as they are guaranteed close scrutiny despite the college's high admit rate.

## FINANCIAL AID

*Students should submit:* FAFSA and state aid form. The Princeton Review suggests that all financial aid forms be submitted as soon as possible after January 1. *Need-based scholarships/grants offered:* Pell, SEOG, state scholarships/grants, and the school's own gift aid. *Loan aid offered:* FFEL Subsidized Stafford, FFEL Unsubsidized Stafford, FFEL PLUS, and Federal Perkins. Institutional employment available. Federal Work-Study Program available. Applicants will be notified of awards on or about April 15. Off-campus job opportunities are excellent.

## FROM THE ADMISSIONS OFFICE

"Today St. Mary's College continues to offer a value-oriented education by providing a classical liberal arts background second to none. The emphasis here is on teaching an individual how to think independently and responsibly, how to analyze information in all situations, and how to make choices based on logical thinking and rational examination. Such a program develops students' ability to ask the right questions and to formulate meaningful answers, not only within their professional careers but also for the rest of their lives. St. Mary's College is committed to preparing young men and women for the challenge of an ever-changing world, while remaining faithful to an enduring academic and spiritual heritage. We believe the purpose of a college experience is to prepare men and women for an unlimited number of opportunities. We believe this is best accomplished by educating the whole person, both intellectually and ethically. We strive to recruit, admit, enroll and graduate students who are generous, faith-filled, and human, and we believe this is reaffirmed in our community of Brothers, in our faculty, and in our personal concern for each student."

## ADMISSIONS

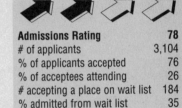

| Admissions Rating | 78 |
| --- | --- |
| # of applicants | 3,104 |
| % of applicants accepted | 76 |
| % of acceptees attending | 26 |
| # accepting a place on wait list | 184 |
| % admitted from wait list | 35 |

### FRESHMAN PROFILE

| Range SAT Verbal | 500-590 |
| --- | --- |
| Average SAT Verbal | 551 |
| Range SAT Math | 510-590 |
| Average SAT Math | 552 |
| Minimum TOEFL | 525 |
| Average HS GPA | 3.4 |

### DEADLINES

| Priority admission deadline | 11/30 |
| --- | --- |
| Regular admission | 2/1 |
| Nonfall registration? | yes |

### APPLICANTS ALSO LOOK AT

**AND OFTEN PREFER**
Notre Dame
UC—Berkeley

**AND SOMETIMES PREFER**
UC—Davis
Villanova
Loyola Marymount
UC—San Diego

**AND RARELY PREFER**
Santa Clara
Gonzaga
UC—Santa Barbara
U. of the Pacific

### FINANCIAL FACTS

| Financial Aid Rating | 78 |
| --- | --- |
| % frosh receiving aid | 59 |
| % undergrads receiving aid | 58 |
| Avg frosh grant | $14,726 |
| Avg frosh loan | $3,116 |

# St. Mary's College of Maryland

Admissions Office, 18952 East Fisher Road, St. Mary's City, MD 20686-3001 • Admissions: 800-492-7181 • Fax: 301-862-0906

## CAMPUS LIFE

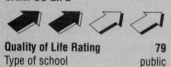

| | |
|---|---|
| **Quality of Life Rating** | **79** |
| Type of school | public |
| Affiliation | none |
| Environment | rural |

### STUDENTS

| | |
|---|---|
| Total undergrad enrollment | 1,547 |
| % male/female | 41/59 |
| % from out of state | 15 |
| % from public high school | 80 |
| % live on campus | 74 |
| % African American | 8 |
| % Asian | 4 |
| % Caucasian | 84 |
| % Hispanic | 2 |
| % international | 1 |
| # of countries represented | 24 |

### SURVEY SAYS . . .

Beautiful campus
Classes are small
Lab facilities need improving
No one cheats
Campus easy to get around
Students don't like St. Mary's
City, MD
Lousy off-campus food
Library needs improving

## ACADEMICS

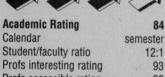

| | |
|---|---|
| **Academic Rating** | **84** |
| Calendar | semester |
| Student/faculty ratio | 12:1 |
| Profs interesting rating | 93 |
| Profs accessible rating | 96 |
| % profs teaching UG courses | 100 |
| Avg lab size | 10-19 students |
| Avg reg class size | 10-19 students |

### MOST POPULAR MAJORS

biology
economics
psychology

## STUDENTS SPEAK OUT

### Academics

Small, highly selective, state-funded, and ultra-affordable St. Mary's College is Maryland's public honors college or, as one student here quips, its "liberal arts school for poor kids." Whatever you want to call it, SMCM is a heck of a deal. You can graduate from St. Mary's, buy yourself a nice Subaru, probably have Puff Daddy play your graduation party, and still not drop the kind of cash you would shell out for four years at a private college of a similar caliber. Students give "two thumbs up" to the academic experience here. Every St. Mary's student must complete an extensive senior project—a "student-initiated, culminating experience" that is "the centerpiece of the honors college curriculum." SMC's "small classes" also receive high marks, as does the "exceptional, beautiful" environment, which is "a great place to learn and live for four years." The "excellent, inspiring," and "very knowledgeable" professors at St. Mary's "are always extremely accessible, and students can get to know them very well." "You run into professors everywhere," observes a senior, "on the paths, at the grocery store, in the bars." They are "like the friends you want to have when you are middle-aged: smart, funny, and cool, if not a little unhip." The "image-obsessed" administration is an altogether different story. Though the top brass plays "an active part of campus life," students complain that they "treat us like babies" at best and are "petty tyrants" at worst. Also, despite "good financial aid" and "great" labs, most campus facilities are only "average."

### Life

The "breathtaking," "beautiful," and otherwise "gorgeous" campus of St. Mary's College is located "out in the boonies," right on the water. It offers its 1,600 or so students "incredible sunsets and quiet evenings," and it reportedly comes complete with "peacocks." The "isolated location" in a "small" town with "nothing around for miles" only "adds to the unique life at St. Mary's." With no Greek system to provide social opportunities, students here must make their own fun. Luckily, there is "tons to do on campus." Basketball games "are major social events, and dances are fairly popular." Intramurals are big as well, and the nationally ranked varsity sailing team travels widely to compete. St. Mary's students also "hang out with friends, watch movies, go hiking," and go "boating, sailing, and kayaking on nice weekends." It seems as though they also play as much or more "frisbee golf" than any other student body in the nation. On the weekends, there is "lots of boozing" here. "Parties generally consist of people standing around and drinking," though there are "huge parties featuring dancing and music" from time to time. "The administration is doing its best to kill the party atmosphere, which is a shame," according to a sophomore. "People work hard during the week and like to break loose and party hard on weekends, but public safety frowns on that, so the party scene is off campus."

### Student Body

"The initial impression I got of SMCM was on my campus tour when random people walking by, said 'hello' and told me to come here," explains a junior. This campus is definitely full of "open-minded, kind," "good-natured," "friendly people." They are "generally very smart," though the occasional "stupid college kids" and "self-absorbed Abercrombie advertisements" slip through the admissions process. Friends are reportedly easy to make at SMCM, and "trust is overwhelming on campus. Books and bags are left wherever, and no one touches them." Students admit that they can be "a bit cliquish," but they are quick to point out that they are "not too exclusive." It's more like "one big," "really tight-knit," "slightly disgruntled family" than anything else. "Most of the people here are from Maryland" and since St. Mary's is such a small school, "you see the same faces every day," advises a junior. "If that isn't your thing, you won't like it." Finally, the lopsided male-female ratio doesn't sit well with the women here. They say sheer numbers make male dates difficult to come by.

FINANCIAL AID: 301-862-0300 • E-MAIL: ADMISSIONS@HONORS.SMCM.EDU • WEBSITE: WWW.SMCM.EDU

## ADMISSIONS

*Very important* academic and nonacademic factors considered by the admissions committee include essays, secondary school record, and standardized test scores. *Important* factors considered include extracurricular activities, recommendations, and talent/ability. *Other* factors considered include alumni/ae relation, character/personal qualities, geography, interview, minority status, state residency, volunteer work, and work experience. Factors *not* considered include class rank and religious affiliation/commitment. SAT I or ACT required, SAT I preferred. TOEFL required of all international applicants. High school diploma is required and GED is accepted. *High school units required/recommended:* 14 total required; 21 total recommended; 4 English required, 3 math required, 3 science required, 4 science recommended, 1 science lab required, 2 science lab recommended, 4 foreign language recommended, 3 social studies required, 1 history recommended. *The admissions office says:* "Very personalized admissions process. Each counselor is responsible for a specific geographic region, particularly with regard to the state of Maryland. This gives the staff an opportunity to meet a given student in a variety of settings. The staff really gives consideration to each student's individual merits."

### The Inside Word

There are few better choices than St. Mary's for better-than-average students who are not likely to get admitted to one of the top 50 or so colleges in the country. It is likely that if funding for public colleges is able to stabilize, or even grow, that this place will soon be joining the ranks of the best. Now is the time to take advantage, before the academic expectations of the admissions committee start to soar.

## FINANCIAL AID

The Princeton Review suggests that all financial aid forms be submitted as soon as possible after January 1. *Need-based scholarships/grants offered:* Pell, SEOG, state scholarships/grants, private scholarships, and the school's own gift aid. *Loan aid offered:* FFEL Subsidized Stafford, FFEL Unsubsidized Stafford, FFEL PLUS, and Federal Perkins. Institutional employment available. Federal Work-Study Program available. Off-campus job opportunities are good.

## FROM THE ADMISSIONS OFFICE

"St. Mary's College of Maryland . . . occupies a distinctive niche and represents a real value in American higher education. It is a public college, dedicated to the ideal of affordable, accessible education but committed to quality teaching and excellent programs for undergraduate students. The result is that St. Mary's offers the small college experience of the same high caliber usually found at prestigious private colleges, but at public college prices. Designated by the state of Maryland as 'A Public Honors College,' one of only two public colleges in the nation to hold that distinction, St. Mary's has become increasingly attractive to high school students. Admission is very selective."

## ADMISSIONS

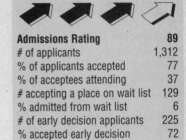

| | |
|---|---|
| Admissions Rating | 89 |
| # of applicants | 1,312 |
| % of applicants accepted | 77 |
| % of acceptees attending | 37 |
| # accepting a place on wait list | 129 |
| % admitted from wait list | 6 |
| # of early decision applicants | 225 |
| % accepted early decision | 72 |

### FRESHMAN PROFILE

| | |
|---|---|
| Range SAT Verbal | 570-660 |
| Average SAT Verbal | 618 |
| Range SAT Math | 560-650 |
| Average SAT Math | 604 |
| Minimum TOEFL | 550 |
| Average HS GPA | 3.4 |
| % graduated top 10% of class | 39 |
| % graduated top 25% of class | 72 |
| % graduated top 50% of class | 96 |

### DEADLINES

| | |
|---|---|
| Early decision | 12/1 |
| Early decision notification | 1/1 |
| Priority admission deadline | 12/1 |
| Regular admission | 1/15 |
| Regular notification | 4/1 |
| Nonfall registration? | yes |

### APPLICANTS ALSO LOOK AT

**AND OFTEN PREFER**
William and Mary
U. Delaware
Lehigh
Bucknell

**AND SOMETIMES PREFER**
Dickinson
James Madison
Loyola Coll. (MD)
U. Maryland—Coll. Park
Towson State

### FINANCIAL FACTS

| | |
|---|---|
| Financial Aid Rating | 80 |
| In-state tuition | $6,474 |
| Out-of-state tuition | $11,459 |
| Room & board | $6,555 |
| Books and supplies | $870 |
| Required fees | $1,075 |
| % frosh receiving aid | 37 |
| Avg frosh grant | $4,388 |
| Avg frosh loan | $2,737 |

# ST. OLAF COLLEGE

1520 ST. OLAF AVENUE, NORTHFIELD, MN 55057-1098 • ADMISSIONS: 507-646-3025 • FAX: 507-646-3832

## CAMPUS LIFE

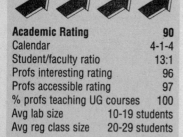

| | |
|---|---|
| **Quality of Life Rating** | **87** |
| Type of school | private |
| Affiliation | Lutheran |
| Environment | rural |

### STUDENTS

| | |
|---|---|
| Total undergrad enrollment | 3,014 |
| % male/female | 43/57 |
| % from out of state | 45 |
| % from public high school | 90 |
| % live on campus | 96 |
| % African American | 1 |
| % Asian | 3 |
| % Caucasian | 90 |
| % Hispanic | 1 |
| % international | 1 |
| # of countries represented | 25 |

### SURVEY SAYS . . .
*Great library*
*No one cheats*
*Campus feels safe*
*Campus is beautiful*
*Dorms are like palaces*
*Very little drug use*
*Lousy food on campus*
*Students are cliquish*
*Student publications are ignored*

## ACADEMICS

| | |
|---|---|
| **Academic Rating** | **90** |
| Calendar | 4-1-4 |
| Student/faculty ratio | 13:1 |
| Profs interesting rating | 96 |
| Profs accessible rating | 97 |
| % profs teaching UG courses | 100 |
| Avg lab size | 10-19 students |
| Avg reg class size | 20-29 students |

### MOST POPULAR MAJORS
biology
economics
English

## STUDENTS SPEAK OUT

### Academics

Few student bodies we survey on campuses around the country are as taken with their academic experience as those at St. Olaf College. "Academically, St. Olaf is tops. . . . I have friends at Ivy League schools, yet feel that I am getting the better education"; "St. Olaf has a wonderful community and a strong academic life." This liberal arts college has "many strong academic departments . . . but the music department is the jewel in the crown," known internationally for its excellence in choral music. Fine arts, economics, and the sciences also garner praise, as do the college's study abroad opportunities. General education requirements are numerous, and include two religion courses. First-year students who apply and are selected for "The Great Conversation" program can take a special intensive five-course sequence in their first two years that covers the equivalent of more than nine required general education areas. It gets raves. Classes are small, challenging, and very personal: St. Olaf's "professors are definitely DAMN smart individuals" who are "full of energy, and most important, love to teach undergraduates"; "This school is extremely dedicated to the success of the student—if you want to do well, the resources are there"; "Part of the reason I came to St. Olaf is I knew I would be a person and not a number on the computer—I received a handwritten message on my acceptance letter." Basically, "The students of St. Olaf are what make this school interesting and fun. The professors' open attitudes and constant willingness to help are what make St. Olaf an ideal learning environment. With this stellar combination, how can you go wrong?"

### Life

Student life "on the hill" above Northfield takes place on a beautiful campus. "Life is busy" and "there is . . . a lot of positive energy on campus." Students report that "the days go by fast and more time seems to be on everyone's wish list" and "Since so many students . . . live on campus, there is always something going on—from bands playing to theater productions to swing dancing to bonfires." "Small parties are far more common than huge house parties"; many students simply "round up a group of friends and have a good conversation." (St. Olaf has no Greek system.) According to one student, "It's kind of funny when you realize that instead of 'hanging out' . . . you can have just as much fun in a small group discussion, study group, or bible study." Campus facilities include a new student center and a "nine-hole Frisbee golf course." Students express a desire for less strict administrative policies "on parking [freshmen aren't allowed to have cars on campus], alcohol [it's a dry campus], and intervisitation"; "Because of the . . . policy about freshmen having cars, and the lack of things to do around Northfield, the hill can get to feeling pretty restrictive." One easterner remarked that "coming from a Philadelphia suburb, [it's] really boring." Northfield may be lacking, but "on the other hand, students are just 45 minutes from all of the life, energy, and entertainment that Minneapolis has to offer." Buses run regularly to the Twin Cities, "a major entertainment resource."

### Student Body

Lots of those we surveyed here feel "the well-rounded students" are one of the greatest strengths of the college: "We have a diverse school in terms of experience, but it is not very diverse in looks"; "I'd like to see more students of color"; "St. Olaf may not win a prize for most ethnically diverse, but this campus is truly a zoo!" As one student describes it, "Socially, we are jocks, preps, alternatives, punks, and study geeks. Everyone seems to get along, amazingly enough!" One gets the sense that anyone would find a welcome here. "I get more homesick on breaks than I do while I'm here because everyone is so nice." "Most students are polite and social, but there are a lot of cliques." There's also "a distinct religious presence on campus." At least one male student took particular note that he "chose to attend St. Olaf not only for its gorgeous vistas, but also because of its . . . attentive and caring professors, . . . focused liberal arts curriculum, and of course, its . . . female to male ratio."

FINANCIAL AID: 507-646-3019 • E-MAIL: ADMISSIONS@STOLAF.EDU • WEBSITE: WWW.STOLAF.EDU

## ADMISSIONS

*Very important* academic and nonacademic factors considered by the admissions committee include secondary school record. *Important* factors considered include character/personal qualities, essays, extracurricular activities, recommendations, standardized test scores, and talent/ability. *Other* factors considered include alumni/ae relation, class rank, geography, interview, minority status, religious affiliation/commitment, volunteer work, and work experience. Factors *not* considered include state residency. SAT I or ACT required. TOEFL required of all international applicants. High school diploma is required and GED is accepted. *High school units required/recommended:* 18 total recommended; 4 English recommended, 3 math recommended, 2 science recommended, 2 foreign language recommended, 3 social studies recommended, 2 elective recommended.

### The Inside Word

St. Olaf truly deserves a more national reputation; the place is a bastion of excellence and has always crossed applications with the best schools in the Midwest. Despite its lack of widespread recognition, it is a great choice. Candidates benefit from the relative anonymity of the college through an admissions process, which, while demanding, isn't as tough as other colleges of St. Olaf's caliber.

## FINANCIAL AID

*Students should submit:* FAFSA and institution's own financial aid form. The Princeton Review suggests that all financial aid forms be submitted as soon as possible after January 1. *Need-based scholarships/grants offered:* Pell, SEOG, state scholarships/grants, private scholarships, and the school's own gift aid. *Loan aid offered:* FFEL Subsidized Stafford, FFEL Unsubsidized Stafford, FFEL PLUS, Federal Perkins, Federal Nursing, state, and college/university loans from institutional funds. Institutional employment available. Federal Work-Study Program available. Applicants will be notified of awards on a rolling basis beginning on or about March 15. Off-campus job opportunities are fair.

## FROM THE ADMISSIONS OFFICE

"St. Olaf College provides an education in the liberal arts that is rooted in the Christian gospel and offered with a global perspective. Sixty-seven percent of each graduating class will have studied overseas during the four years at St. Olaf. The Center for Integrative Studies and Great Conversation programs offer alternatives to the traditional curriculum."

## ADMISSIONS

| | |
|---|---|
| Admissions Rating | 85 |
| # of applicants | 2,505 |
| % of applicants accepted | 74 |
| % of acceptees attending | 41 |
| # accepting a place on wait list | 82 |
| % admitted from wait list | 51 |
| # of early decision applicants | 136 |
| % accepted early decision | 81 |

### FRESHMAN PROFILE

| | |
|---|---|
| Range SAT Verbal | 580-680 |
| Average SAT Verbal | 626 |
| Range SAT Math | 590-680 |
| Average SAT Math | 626 |
| Range ACT Composite | 25-30 |
| Average ACT Composite | 27 |
| Minimum TOEFL | 550 |
| Average HS GPA | 3.7 |
| % graduated top 10% of class | 49 |
| % graduated top 25% of class | 79 |
| % graduated top 50% of class | 97 |

### DEADLINES

| | |
|---|---|
| Early decision | 11/15 |
| Early decision notification | 12/15 |
| Priority admission deadline | 2/1 |
| Nonfall registration? | yes |

### APPLICANTS ALSO LOOK AT

**AND OFTEN PREFER**
Carleton
Northwestern U.

**AND SOMETIMES PREFER**
Gustavus Adolphus

**AND RARELY PREFER**
U. Minnesota—Twin Cities
Luther
Lawrence

### FINANCIAL FACTS

| | |
|---|---|
| Financial Aid Rating | 88 |
| Tuition | $21,280 |
| Room & board | $4,600 |
| Books and supplies | $770 |
| % frosh receiving aid | 61 |
| % undergrads receiving aid | 60 |
| Avg frosh grant | $10,181 |
| Avg frosh loan | $3,805 |

# SALISBURY STATE UNIVERSITY

ADMISSIONS OFFICE, 1101 CAMDEN AVENUE, SALISBURY, MD 21801 • ADMISSIONS: 410-543-6161 • FAX: 410-546-6016

## CAMPUS LIFE

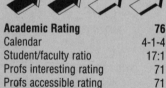

**Quality of Life Rating**     **75**
Type of school     public
Affiliation     none
Environment     rural

### STUDENTS
Total undergrad enrollment     5,883
% male/female     43/57
% from public high school     80
% African American     7
% Asian     2
% Caucasian     84
% Hispanic     1

### SURVEY SAYS . . .
*Great food on campus*
*Classes are small*
*(Almost) everyone smokes*
*Musical organizations aren't popular*
*Lots of conservatives on campus*
*Computer facilities need improving*
*Library needs improving*
*Lab facilities are great*
*Student government is unpopular*

## ACADEMICS

**Academic Rating**     **76**
Calendar     4-1-4
Student/faculty ratio     17:1
Profs interesting rating     71
Profs accessible rating     71
% profs teaching UG courses     100
Avg lab size     10-19 students
Avg reg class size     20-29 students

### MOST POPULAR MAJORS
business administration
elementary education
biology

## STUDENTS SPEAK OUT
### Academics
Career-minded students on and around the Delmarva Peninsula would be hard pressed to find a better bargain than Salisbury State University. The school's super-low tuition is further discounted by an unusually large endowment, funded by such business magnates as Frank Perdue (for whom the business school is named). Salisbury State's greatest strengths are in such meat-and-potato areas as education, business administration, accounting, engineering, and communications; one notable deficiency is in computer sciences, where an antiquated system holds students back. "The computer system on campus constantly crashes and needs some serious work," notes a typically disgruntled student. Although some students complain that "the school is so small that the course choice isn't as broad as we might like," most feel that SSU strikes the right balance between course selection and affordability. Students uniformly praise professors as "very helpful and approachable," explaining that "professors aren't just teachers. Many are valuable friends and mentors, which is important to me." They're similarly sanguine about the "very personable, accessible administration." They also appreciate the fact that "the classes are a nice size." Although nearly all students are satisfied at Salisbury, a few echo this sentiment: "This school is decent without being excellent in any one area. It's like driving a Ford Escort. It will get you from A to B, but not particularly fast or in good style."

### Life
Life on the "really beautiful," "very clean and well-maintained" Salisbury campus is low-key, to say the least. Our survey indicates that "students don't get involved in campus life. Attendance at sports events and other on-campus activities is usually low." According to some students, the situation is partly due to the heavy workload at SSU; others suspect that it stems from "an alcohol policy that is too strict. That is why most weekend fun is found off campus." Others attribute the slow pace to the town of Salisbury, which "does not provide much for the students." None of this matters when the weather is warm, since Salisbury is so close to the resort town of Ocean City, Maryland. OC has long been a party Mecca for area youngsters, and SSU undergrads are no exception. But when the weather turns cold, both Ocean City and Salisbury social life essentially shut down for the season. On the bright side, "the campus is trying to get more activities for students" and already offers numerous clubs and organizations. Explains one student, "Life at school depends on how involved you are in campus organizations and activities. There are many events such as movies, lectures, performances, etc., that are available, and most are free. There is a club for virtually every interest and major. There are also game rooms and a pub on campus."

### Student Body
Salisbury undergrads readily admit the lack of diversity of their student body. Notes one, "Everyone is pretty much the same: white and middle-class. There are very few minorities here." Another elaborates: "When students come to SSU, they fit a mold. If students don't fit the mold, I wonder if they paid attention to what they saw on the [campus] tour. However, there is a small percentage of students that doesn't look or act like everyone else." Quality academic programs combined with the low out-of-state tuition attract an unusually large number of students from Delaware, New Jersey, Pennsylvania, and Virginia.

FINANCIAL AID: 410-543-6165 • E-MAIL: ADMISSIONS@SSU.EDU • WEBSITE: WWW.SSU.EDU

## ADMISSIONS

*Very important* academic and nonacademic factors considered by the admissions committee include secondary school record. *Important* factors considered include class rank and standardized test scores. *Other* factors considered include alumni/ae relation, character/personal qualities, essays, extracurricular activities, geography, interview, minority status, recommendations, state residency, talent/ability, volunteer work, and work experience. Factors *not* considered include religious affiliation/commitment. SAT I or ACT required. TOEFL required of all international applicants. High school diploma is required and GED is accepted. *High school units required/recommended:* 4 English required, 3 math required, 4 math recommended, 3 science required, 4 science recommended, 2 science lab required, 3 science lab recommended, 2 foreign language required, 4 foreign language recommended, 3 social studies required.

### The Inside Word

As a part of the new wave of public institutions of higher learning focusing their energies on undergraduate research, Salisbury State has seen its admissions standards and the quality of its freshman class steadily improve over the past few years. As a result, candidate review is also more personalized than the formula-driven approaches of most public colleges. The admissions committee will pay close attention to the match you make with the University, evaluating your entire background instead of simply your numbers—though most students are strong academically to begin with.

## FINANCIAL AID

*Students should submit:* FAFSA. Regular filing deadline is February 15. The Princeton Review suggests that all financial aid forms be submitted as soon as possible after January 1. *Need-based scholarships/grants offered:* Pell, SEOG, state scholarships/grants, and the school's own gift aid. *Loan aid offered:* Direct Subsidized Stafford, Direct Unsubsidized Stafford, Direct PLUS, and Federal Perkins. Institutional employment available. Federal Work-Study Program available. Applicants will be notified of awards on a rolling basis beginning on or about April 1. Off-campus job opportunities are good.

## FROM THE ADMISSIONS OFFICE

"Location, location, location. Geography and a welcoming environment have long been a major factor in Salisbury State University's popularity with students. Thirty minutes from Ocean City, Maryland, one of the East Coast's most popular resorts, and 45 minutes from Rehoboth Beach, Delaware, one of the trendiest, SSU students enjoy year-round resort social life as well as an inside track on summer jobs. The University uses its proximity to the Chesapeake Bay, North America's largest estuary, for environmental programs, which have developed into some of its most popular majors and extracurricular activities. First explored by Captain John Smith, the Eastern Shore has a rich and well-preserved history attractive to students in American Studies. An easy two-hour drive from Washington, D.C.; Baltimore and Wilmington, Delaware; Norfolk, Virginia; and Philadelphia; and four from New York have made it close enough, but not too close to home."

## ADMISSIONS

| | |
|---|---|
| Admissions Rating | 82 |
| # of applicants | 4,466 |
| % of applicants accepted | 57 |
| % of acceptees attending | 100 |
| # accepting a place on wait list | 653 |
| % admitted from wait list | 4 |
| # of early decision applicants | 448 |
| % accepted early decision | 64 |

### FRESHMAN PROFILE

| | |
|---|---|
| Range SAT Verbal | 510-590 |
| Range SAT Math | 520-610 |
| Minimum TOEFL | 550 |
| % graduated top 10% of class | 19 |
| % graduated top 25% of class | 54 |
| % graduated top 50% of class | 88 |

### DEADLINES

| | |
|---|---|
| Early decision | 12/15 |
| Early decision notification | 1/15 |
| Priority admission deadline | 1/15 |
| Nonfall registration? | yes |

### FINANCIAL FACTS

| | |
|---|---|
| Financial Aid Rating | 81 |
| In-state tuition | $3,216 |
| Out-of-state tuition | $8,672 |
| Room & board | $5,990 |
| Books and supplies | $800 |
| Required fees | $1,270 |
| % frosh receiving aid | 39 |
| % undergrads receiving aid | 39 |

# SAMFORD UNIVERSITY

800 LAKESHORE DRIVE, BIRMINGHAM, AL 35229 • ADMISSIONS: 205-726-3673 • FAX: 205-726-2171

## CAMPUS LIFE

| | |
|---|---|
| **Quality of Life Rating** | **88** |
| Type of school | private |
| Affiliation | Baptist |
| Environment | suburban |

### STUDENTS

| | |
|---|---|
| Total undergrad enrollment | 2,870 |
| % male/female | 38/62 |
| % from out of state | 52 |
| % from public high school | 70 |
| % live on campus | 65 |
| % in (# of) fraternities | 38 (7) |
| % in (# of) sororities | 45 (8) |
| % African American | 6 |
| % Asian | 1 |
| % Caucasian | 92 |
| % Hispanic | 1 |

### SURVEY SAYS . . .

*Frats and sororities dominate social scene*
*Very little drug use*
*Diversity lacking on campus*
*Theater is hot*
*Lots of conservatives on campus*
*Students are very religious*
*Very little beer drinking*
*Political activism is (almost) nonexistent*
*Very little hard liquor*
*(Almost) no one smokes*

## ACADEMICS

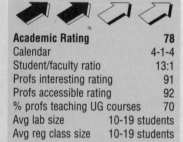

| | |
|---|---|
| **Academic Rating** | **78** |
| Calendar | 4-1-4 |
| Student/faculty ratio | 13:1 |
| Profs interesting rating | 91 |
| Profs accessible rating | 92 |
| % profs teaching UG courses | 70 |
| Avg lab size | 10-19 students |
| Avg reg class size | 10-19 students |

### MOST POPULAR MAJORS
management
biology
early childhood education

## STUDENTS SPEAK OUT

### Academics

As one student tells us, "It takes a special kind of person to enjoy Samford. It has to do with how you are brought up, your morals and values." The predominant values here are those of the Southern Baptist church, a socially and politically conservative faith that infuses all aspects of daily life with religious significance. For those comfortable within this setting, Samford's rewards can be tremendous. Samford combines the affordability and academic diversity of a state university with the small-school atmosphere of a private university. The school, home to 1,600 graduate students as well as its undergraduate population, maintains separate divisions for arts and sciences, business, education, music, nursing, pharmacy, and divinity. Students in all divisions must complete a core curriculum called "coNexus" that requires students not only to read a common syllabus and write traditional papers, but also to participate in e-mail discussion groups, make multimedia presentations, and work through group problem-solving projects. The goal of coNexus is to promote thinking skills in conjunction with communication skills. Students approve, describing Samford as "an incredible institution." Best, they say, are the faculty members, who "are very dedicated and want to help you learn. They usually make themselves available 24/7." Be forewarned, however, that they are "more liberal than the students." Administrators receive lower marks, mostly because "they are inaccessible, and they don't seem to appreciate student input." One student encapsulates the school neatly, telling us that "Samford is academically rigorous and has a great many opportunities for those interested in Christian ministry."

### Life

As you might expect, "Life at Samford is not your typical college life. People here are very focused on their education and their relationship with God." Explains one student, "People are so concerned about their ministry and their religion. It is popular to go on mission trips, but not very much to football games. Intercollegiate sports are just a chance to socialize with fraternity brothers and sorority sisters." Students differ on the impact Greeks have on social life. One student opines that "while fraternities and sororities are big on campus, you don't feel left out if you're not in one." Another, however, counters that "there is a line drawn between the Greeks and the independents. If you're not Greek, you don't have too much of a social life." On-campus regulations are strict: no drinking or drugs, of course, and strict visitation policies in the single-sex dorms. While many students are comfortable and happy with these limitations, others occasionally find them too confining. As a result, "We go home on weekends for fun." Complains one undergrad, "The campus is a ghost town on weekends. Students really need to learn to stay on campus and not go home so much." Hometown Birmingham is "fun and filled with activity."

### Student Body

Samford undergrads "are incredibly nice but lack diversity. Since this school is religiously affiliated, many are sheltered. Still, they are easy to get along with." According to one, "Students here are carbon copies of one another, each molded slightly to fit a specific fraternity or sorority." Agrees another, "Appearance, whether it is physical, intellectual, or religious, is very important to most." Furthermore, anyone considering Samford should know that "if there is anything about you that is even remotely 'different' (race, religion, politics, sexual orientation), you will be ostracized." Concludes one student, "It takes a very special person to be completely happy here. There are students who pretend to be happy here, but they are not."

FINANCIAL AID: 800-888-7245 • E-MAIL: ADMISSION@SAMFORD.EDU • WEBSITE: WWW.SAMFORD.EDU

## ADMISSIONS

*Very important* academic and nonacademic factors considered by the admissions committee include character/personal qualities, essays, extracurricular activities, secondary school record, and standardized test scores. *Important* factors considered include class rank, interview, recommendations, religious affiliation/commitment, and volunteer work. *Other* factors considered include alumni/ae relation, geography, state residency, talent/ability, and work experience. Factors *not* considered include minority status. SAT I or ACT required. TOEFL required of all international applicants. High school diploma is required and GED is accepted. *High school units required/recommended:* 16 total required; 4 English required, 3 math required, 2 science required, 2 science lab required, 2 foreign language required, 2 social studies required, 2 history required. *The admissions office says:* "Samford uses the application credentials as the scholarship application as well (scores, grades, résumés). [Our students typically have a] Christian background, strong leadership skills, [and a] well-developed sense of social consciousness. Alumni relations receive some special consideration."

### The Inside Word

Samford's use of admission credentials in scholarship considerations is something that is quite common at colleges across the country. Students should always complete their applications as if such is the case. Even for universities where you are clearly admissible academically, giving some additional attention to essays and visiting for an interview can make the difference between being a scholarship winner and taking on an additional summer job.

## FINANCIAL AID

*Students should submit:* FAFSA and state aid form. The Princeton Review suggests that all financial aid forms be submitted as soon as possible after January 1. *Need-based scholarships/grants offered:* Pell, SEOG, state scholarships/grants, private scholarships, and the school's own gift aid. *Loan aid offered:* Direct Subsidized Stafford, Direct Unsubsidized Stafford, FFEL Subsidized Stafford, FFEL Unsubsidized Stafford, FFEL PLUS, Federal Perkins, and college/university loans from institutional funds. Institutional employment available. Federal Work-Study Program available. Applicants will be notified of awards on or about April 1. Off-campus job opportunities are excellent.

## FROM THE ADMISSION OFFICE

"Students who are drawn to Samford are well-rounded individuals who not only expect to be challenged, but are excited by the prospect. It is the critical and creative way you think, it is the articulate way you write and speak, it is the joy of learning that stays with you throughout your life, and it is the clarity of decision-making guided by Christian principles."

### ADMISSIONS

| | |
|---|---|
| Admissions Rating | 76 |
| # of applicants | 2,035 |
| % of applicants accepted | 88 |
| % of acceptees attending | 37 |

#### FRESHMAN PROFILE

| | |
|---|---|
| Range SAT Verbal | 510-630 |
| Average SAT Verbal | 573 |
| Range SAT Math | 510-630 |
| Average SAT Math | 573 |
| Range ACT Composite | 22-27 |
| Average ACT Composite | 25 |
| Minimum TOEFL | 550 |
| Average HS GPA | 3.6 |
| % graduated top 10% of class | 34 |
| % graduated top 25% of class | 64 |
| % graduated top 50% of class | 92 |

#### DEADLINES

| | |
|---|---|
| Priority admission deadline | 2/1 |
| Regular admission | 8/1 |
| Nonfall registration? | yes |

#### APPLICANTS ALSO LOOK AT
#### AND OFTEN PREFER
Vanderbilt
Furman
#### AND SOMETIMES PREFER
Baylor
Florida State
U. Georgia
Auburn

### FINANCIAL FACTS

| | |
|---|---|
| Financial Aid Rating | 84 |
| Tuition | $10,738 |
| Room & board | $4,720 |
| Books and supplies | $760 |
| % frosh receiving aid | 39 |
| % undergrads receiving aid | 40 |
| Avg frosh grant | $1,654 |
| Avg frosh loan | $2,299 |

# SANTA CLARA UNIVERSITY

500 EL CAMINO REAL, SANTA CLARA, CA 95053 • ADMISSIONS: 408-554-4700 • FAX: 408-554-5255

## CAMPUS LIFE

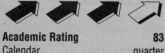

**Quality of Life Rating** **86**
Type of school                         private
Affiliation                   Roman Catholic
Environment                         suburban

### STUDENTS
Total undergrad enrollment      4,308
% male/female                      47/53
% from out of state                   38
% from public high school          51
% live on campus                     58
% in (# of) fraternities           8 (5)
% in (# of) sororities            11 (3)
% African American                    2
% Asian                              19
% Caucasian                          54
% Hispanic                           14
% Native American                     1
% international                       3

### SURVEY SAYS . . .
*Very little drug use*
*Classes are small*
*Musical organizations aren't popular*
*Diversity lacking on campus*
*Popular college radio*
*Athletic facilities need improving*
*Library needs improving*
*Political activism is (almost)*
*nonexistent*
*Student government is unpopular*

## ACADEMICS

**Academic Rating** **83**
Calendar                            quarter
Student/faculty ratio                13:1
Profs interesting rating               92
Profs accessible rating                92
% profs teaching UG courses            74
Avg lab size         10-19 students
Avg reg class size   20-29 students

### MOST POPULAR MAJORS
finance
psychology
marketing

## STUDENTS SPEAK OUT
### Academics
In keeping with the Jesuit educational tradition that "has always emphasized critical thinking and the integration of faith and intellect," Santa Clara University challenges its undergraduates to constantly push the limits of their own expectations and intellectual assumptions. Writes one student, "Receiving a Jesuit education is an educational experience like no other. It is tough and challenging, yet amazingly rewarding. Santa Clara pushes you to be and do your best." Another agrees, "With deep roots in classical thought, Santa Clara forces students to stand up for themselves with a true heart to face the world." As at many Jesuit-run schools, academic requirements are stringent. In addition to their major studies, undergraduates must complete a rigorous and comprehensive curriculum including English, mathematics, social and natural sciences, religion, and ethics; a quarterly academic schedule further intensifies academic pressure. Students appreciate the fact that "smaller classes provide for more personal attention and make it much easier to learn overall" and that professors "are screened for their teaching skills when they are hired. The emphasis here is on learning." With SCU's increased national profile, however, come accompanying growing pains. Students tell us that "registration is a headache. All the courses fill up very quickly. More sections should be added." Notes another wryly, "The beauty of the campus and quality of the education far outweigh the dungeon that is the library." New facilities are currently being added to the campus; check the school's website (address above) for updates on campus renovation. Still, when all is said and done, most students tell us, "I'm actually extremely glad to be attending this school" even though they readily concede "it's damn hard!"

### Life
Santa Clara's quarterly academic schedule means that, for many, "Life at SCU is all study. Quarters go by fast and if you fool around, you will fall behind. There's no time to catch up if you mess up." Accordingly, many students stick close to campus 24/7. Writes one, "At SCU, most people go to fraternity parties on weekends or to the local bars. Soccer and basketball games are the most popular sporting events." There has been a recent school crackdown on drinking and parties, however. As one student cautions, "Don't come here if going to house parties that get broken up by 11 P.M. is going to piss you off. This is no longer the party school it used to be. And no one here dates." These predicaments have sent at least a few students looking further afield for entertainment. Writes one, "The school is extremely small, but San Francisco is an hour away by train. It's a great getaway from the small campus." Another tells us, "For fun, I go sightseeing to Santa Cruz, Monterey, Tahoe, Napa, and San Francisco. There's a lot of shopping around our area. I enjoy outdoor activities such as biking, running, hiking, swimming, and other sports." The town of Santa Clara itself, however, does not rate high with students. "In the area of alternative social activities," explains one student, "Santa Clara has a long way to go."

### Student Body
Santa Clara undergraduates describe a student body that is collegial but fractionalized. "People smile at you and hold doors," but while "students are cool, . . . the various frats, clubs, and groups have become cliques, thus creating social problems." Also, "students gossip like there's no tomorrow. They can be quite cliquish." Large Asian and Latino populations give students access to an unusually diverse undergraduate population.

FINANCIAL AID: 408-554-4505 • E-MAIL: UGADMISSIONS@SCU.EDU • WEBSITE: WWW.SCU.EDU

## ADMISSIONS

*Very important* academic and nonacademic factors considered by the admissions committee include essays and standardized test scores. *Important* factors considered include class rank and secondary school record. *Other* factors considered include character/personal qualities, extracurricular activities, geography, religious affiliation/commitment, talent/ability, volunteer work, and work experience. Factors *not* considered include alumni/ae relation, interview, minority status, recommendations, and state residency. SAT I or ACT required. TOEFL required of all international applicants. High school diploma is required and GED is not accepted. *High school units required/recommended:* 17 total required; 4 English required, 4 math required, 3 science required, 2 science lab required, 2 foreign language required, 2 social studies required, 1 history required, 1 elective required.

### The Inside Word

Santa Clara deserves recognition as a rising star that still manages to be highly personal and accessible. It's always better when an admissions staff regards you as a person, not an enrollment target. Unfortunately, such is not always the case. It would be hard to find a place that is more receptive to minority students. There is a very significant minority presence here because Santa Clara works hard and earnestly to make everyone feel at home. The university's popularity is increasing across the board, which proves that nice guys sometimes finish first.

## FINANCIAL AID

*Students should submit:* FAFSA and CSS/Financial Aid PROFILE. Regular filing deadline is February 1. The Princeton Review suggests that all financial aid forms be submitted as soon as possible after January 1. *Need-based scholarships/grants offered:* Pell, SEOG, state scholarships/grants, private scholarships, and the school's own gift aid. *Loan aid offered:* Direct Subsidized Stafford, Direct Unsubsidized Stafford, Direct PLUS, Federal Perkins, and college/university loans from institutional funds. Institutional employment available. Federal Work-Study Program available. Applicants will be notified of awards on a rolling basis beginning on or about April 15. Off-campus job opportunities are excellent.

## FROM THE ADMISSIONS OFFICE

"Santa Clara University, located one hour south of San Francisco, offers its undergraduates an opportunity to be educated within a challenging, dynamic, and caring community. The university blends a sense of tradition and history (as the oldest college in California) with a vision that values innovation and a deep commitment to social justice. Santa Clara's faculty members are talented scholars who are demanding, supportive, and accessible. The students are serious about academics, are ethnically diverse, and enjoy a full range of athletic, social, community service, religious, and cultural activities—both on campus and through the many options presented by our northern California location. The undergraduate program includes three divisions: the College of Arts and Sciences, the School of Business, and the School of Engineering."

### ADMISSIONS

| | |
|---|---|
| Admissions Rating | 80 |
| # of applicants | 5,910 |
| % of applicants accepted | 61 |
| % of acceptees attending | 29 |

#### FRESHMAN PROFILE

| | |
|---|---|
| Range SAT Verbal | 550-640 |
| Average SAT Verbal | 595 |
| Range SAT Math | 550-670 |
| Average SAT Math | 618 |
| Range ACT Composite | 24-28 |
| Average ACT Composite | 27 |
| Average HS GPA | 3.6 |
| % graduated top 10% of class | 39 |
| % graduated top 25% of class | 77 |
| % graduated top 50% of class | 97 |

#### DEADLINES

| | |
|---|---|
| Regular admission | 1/15 |
| Nonfall registration? | yes |

#### APPLICANTS ALSO LOOK AT
##### AND OFTEN PREFER
UC—Berkeley
UC—Davis
Stanford
Notre Dame
UCLA
##### AND SOMETIMES PREFER
Pomona
UC—Irvine
UC—Santa Barbara
UC—San Diego
Loyola Marymount U.
##### AND RARELY PREFER
U. Oregon
UC—Santa Cruz
U. San Francisco
San Jose State

### FINANCIAL FACTS

| | |
|---|---|
| Financial Aid Rating | 77 |
| Tuition | $22,572 |
| Room & board | $8,436 |
| Books and supplies | $810 |
| Required fees | $240 |
| % frosh receiving aid | 54 |
| % undergrads receiving aid | 64 |
| Avg frosh grant | $7,728 |
| Avg frosh loan | $2,512 |

# SARAH LAWRENCE COLLEGE

ONE MEAD WAY, BRONXVILLE, NY 10708-5999 • ADMISSIONS: 914-395-2510 • FAX: 914-395-2676

## CAMPUS LIFE

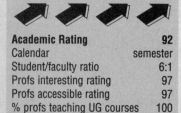

| Quality of Life Rating | 78 |
|---|---|
| Type of school | private |
| Affiliation | none |
| Environment | suburban |

### STUDENTS

| | |
|---|---|
| Total undergrad enrollment | 1,139 |
| % male/female | 25/75 |
| % from out of state | 81 |
| % from public high school | 65 |
| % live on campus | 86 |
| % African American | 6 |
| % Asian | 6 |
| % Caucasian | 76 |
| % Hispanic | 5 |
| % Native American | 1 |
| % international | 1 |
| # of countries represented | 27 |

### SURVEY SAYS . . .
*Theater is hot*
*Students don't get along with local community*
*No one cheats*
*Political activism is hot*
*(Almost) everyone smokes*
*Intercollegiate sports unpopular or nonexistent*
*No one plays intramural sports*
*Class discussions encouraged*

## ACADEMICS

| Academic Rating | 92 |
|---|---|
| Calendar | semester |
| Student/faculty ratio | 6:1 |
| Profs interesting rating | 97 |
| Profs accessible rating | 97 |
| % profs teaching UG courses | 100 |
| Avg reg class size | 10-19 students |

## STUDENTS SPEAK OUT
### Academics

Sarah Lawrence takes an innovative approach to academics. Called the "conference system," the school's approach is universally admired by its undergraduates. Students work with faculty advisors called 'dons' to fashion programs of study unique to their own interests and capabilities. They then take only three courses per semester, all of which involve small classes, seminar-style teaching, and lots of independent study. Explains one enthusiast, "I love the curriculum and general philosophy here. . . . You do independent research projects in each of your courses, which allows you to follow personal passions and interests and to challenge your intellect and curiosity." Adds another, "The conference system forces students to be interested in the course work they are doing. Some students even love their work and ask for more." The system is rigorous. As one student puts it, "Whenever I tell friends that I have only three classes they are envious, until they see the stacks of books I go through each term. Conference work can greatly outweigh class work, so three classes feel like six." Each semester begins with a "shopping" period, during which students can attend courses before committing to registration. Says one student, "Our registration is very unusual, but I couldn't imagine it any other way. It is very helpful, so you don't get stuck in a class you hate, and you get the opportunity to consider classes you might not take otherwise." Professors "treat their students as peers. They are both excited and supportive of your work, and remain friends long after you finish their class." The result is an atmosphere in which academics and intellectualism permeate all facets of life. As one student explains, "Nearly every building on campus contains class space, dorm rooms, AND administrative offices. Life is like that academically here, too—there aren't many boundaries between how you live, what classes you take, and what you can get credit for."

### Life

In many ways, life at Sarah Lawrence is less "collegiate" than at most campuses; it's hard to imagine a Sarah Lawrence pep rally or Homecoming dance. In fact, students' sense of community is generally low-key. Writes one student, "The school tends to attract 'individuals,' which has the tendency to create a noncommunity—cold, noninteractive, impersonal." Individualism is reinforced by the housing system, because "after freshman year, students are provided with single dorm rooms. Although general social space is almost nonexistent, the private rooms are wonderful." Extracurricular life at Sarah Lawrence focuses strongly on the arts, a major component of most students' education. Otherwise, students head for New York City ("There are a million things to do [there] and it's only a train ride away!") when they want to blow off steam.

### Student Body

The combination of extremely selective admissions and a curricular emphasis on the arts attracts an individualistic and precocious student body to Sarah Lawrence. A large majority of students lean strongly to the left politically, a little too self-righteously for some. Says one student, "People here take themselves too seriously." On the flip side, many perceive their peers as "serious, diverse, intelligent, artistic, socially aware students, albeit intermixed with some spoiled rich kids with no sense of social responsibility." The student community as a whole "is extremely accepting of gays. You never even get a double-take from a passerby when holding someone's hand of the same sex." Finally, one student wants the world to know, once and for all: "We are not a hippie school! That is the biggest fallacy!" So there.

# SARAH LAWRENCE COLLEGE

FINANCIAL AID: 914-395-2570 • E-MAIL: SLCADMIT@MAIL.SLC.EDU • WEBSITE: WWW.SLC.EDU

## ADMISSIONS

*Very important* academic and nonacademic factors considered by the admissions committee include essays and secondary school record. *Important* factors considered include character/personal qualities, class rank, extracurricular activities, minority status, recommendations, and talent/ability. *Other* factors considered include alumni/ae relation, geography, interview, standardized test scores, volunteer work, and work experience. Factors *not* considered include religious affiliation/commitment and state residency. SAT I or ACT required. TOEFL required of all international applicants. High school diploma is required and GED is accepted. *High school units required/recommended:* 17 total recommended; 4 English recommended, 3 math recommended, 2 science recommended, 2 foreign language recommended, 3 social studies recommended, 3 history recommended. *The admissions office says:* "The education at Sarah Lawrence demands that a student possess a facility and a desire to work with the written word. The structure of the education requires a student to be self-motivated, comfortable working closely with adults, and interested in an interdisciplinary approach to knowledge. The arts are an integrated part of the curriculum at SLC; many students successfully balance concentrations in both academics and the creative or performing arts."

### The Inside Word

The public generally views Sarah Lawrence as an artsy "alternative" college. The college itself avoids this image, preferring instead to evoke an impression that aligns them with more traditional and prestigious northeastern colleges such as the Ivies, Little Ivies, and former Seven Sisters. The admissions process tends to be more benevolent toward guys, who are in short supply at Sarah Lawrence even though the college has been coed for many years. Both the total number of applicants and the selectivity of the admissions process have increased over the past few years.

## FINANCIAL AID

*Students should submit:* FAFSA, CSS/Financial Aid PROFILE, and noncustodial parent's statement. Regular filing deadline is February 1. Priority filing deadline is February 1. The Princeton Review suggests that all financial aid forms be submitted as soon as possible after January 1. *Need-based scholarships/grants offered:* Pell, SEOG, state scholarships/grants, private scholarships, and the school's own gift aid. *Loan aid offered:* Subsidized Stafford, Unsubsidized Stafford, PLUS, and Federal Perkins. Institution employment available. Federal Work-Study Program available. Applicants will be notified of awards on or about April 1. Off-campus job opportunities are good.

## FROM THE ADMISSIONS OFFICE

"Students who come to Sarah Lawrence are curious about the world, and they have an ardent desire to satisfy that curiosity. Sarah Lawrence offers such students two innovative academic structures: the seminar/conference system and the arts components. Courses in the humanities, social sciences, natural sciences, and mathematics are taught in the seminar/conference style. The seminars enroll an average of 11 students and consist of lecture, discussion, readings, and assigned papers. For each seminar, students also have private tutorials, called conferences, where they conceive of individualized projects and shape them under the direction of professors. Arts components let students combine history and theory with practice. Painters, printmakers, photographers, sculptors and filmmakers, composers, musicians, choreographers, dancers, actors, and directors work in readily available studios, editing facilities, and darkrooms, guided by accomplished professionals. The secure, wooded campus is 30 minutes from New York City, and the diversity of people and ideas at Sarah Lawrence make it an extraordinary educational environment."

## ADMISSIONS

| | |
|---|---|
| Admissions Rating | 89 |
| # of applicants | 2,455 |
| % of applicants accepted | 38 |
| % of acceptees attending | 31 |
| # accepting a place on wait list | 169 |
| % admitted from wait list | 3 |
| # of early decision applicants | 161 |
| % accepted early decision | 48 |

### FRESHMAN PROFILE

| | |
|---|---|
| Range SAT Verbal | 610-700 |
| Average SAT Verbal | 640 |
| Range SAT Math | 540-640 |
| Average SAT Math | 570 |
| Range ACT Composite | 24-28 |
| Average ACT Composite | 25 |
| Minimum TOEFL | 600 |
| Average HS GPA | 3.5 |
| % graduated top 10% of class | 46 |
| % graduated top 25% of class | 77 |
| % graduated top 50% of class | 95 |

### DEADLINES

| | |
|---|---|
| Early decision | 11/15 |
| Early decision notification | 12/15 |
| Regular admission | 1/15 |
| Regular notification | 4/1 |
| Nonfall registration? | yes |

### APPLICANTS ALSO LOOK AT
**AND OFTEN PREFER**
NYU, Smith
Vassar
**AND SOMETIMES PREFER**
Barnard
Bard, Oberlin
Skidmore
**AND RARELY PREFER**
Hampshire
Brown
Bryn Mawr

### FINANCIAL FACTS

| | |
|---|---|
| Financial Aid Rating | 74 |
| Tuition | $26,040 |
| Room & board | $8,460 |
| Books and supplies | $600 |
| Required fees | $628 |
| % frosh receiving aid | 45 |
| % undergrads receiving aid | 62 |
| Avg frosh grant | $19,163 |
| Avg frosh loan | $2,504 |

THE BEST 331 COLLEGES ■ 435

# SCRIPPS COLLEGE

1030 COLUMBIA AVENUE, CLAREMONT, CA 91711 • ADMISSIONS: 909-621-8149 • FAX: 909-607-7508

## CAMPUS LIFE

**Quality of Life Rating**    **77**
Type of school    private
Affiliation    none
Environment    suburban

### STUDENTS

| | |
|---|---|
| Total undergrad enrollment | 787 |
| % from out of state | 53 |
| % from public high school | 59 |
| % live on campus | 88 |
| % African American | 3 |
| % Asian | 14 |
| % Caucasian | 57 |
| % Hispanic | 5 |
| % international | 3 |

### SURVEY SAYS . . .
*Beautiful campus*
*Political activism is hot*
*Students get along with local community*
*Ethnic diversity on campus*
*TAs don't teach upper-level courses*
*Campus easy to get around*
*Very small frat/sorority scene*
*Lab facilities need improving*
*Computer facilities need improving*
*Students aren't religious*
*Very little beer drinking*

## ACADEMICS

**Academic Rating**    **91**
Calendar    semester
Student/faculty ratio    11:1
Profs interesting rating    87
Profs accessible rating    87
% profs teaching UG courses    100
Avg lab size    10-19 students
Avg reg class size    10-19 students

### MOST POPULAR MAJORS
psychology
studio art
English

## STUDENTS SPEAK OUT

### Academics

Scripps College is a "great" place to learn "if you like [a] small, private, all women's, liberal arts" school, says one senior. While the undergraduate population comprises fewer than 800 women, students attending Scripps can take courses at any of the five Claremont Colleges. (Harvey Mudd, Pomona, Claremont McKenna, and Pitzer, are the others.) Good thing the *Academics* paragraph is at the top of this page, because at Scripps "academics are put above everything else here, and it shows." The cross-registration system is "excellent," and the campuses are all near one another. Students agree that "the professors at Scripps are excellent." They are very accessible, "care about every individual in their class, and really mentor the students." Student opinion is obviously regarded, as witnessed to by the fact that one undergrad "recently helped the econ department choose a new professor." The administration is both admired and accessible. ("The college president knows your name and you know her dog's name.") The "huge" library system is a tremendous resource. The main complaint about Scripps' administration is the financial aid system. "Getting money from Scripps is like trying to give birth to a Volvo," one student says. "[It's] painful and not likely to happen."

### Life

While the surrounding town of Claremont doesn't provide Scripps students many social opportunities, the four other Claremont colleges do. "There are always parties and such going on at the other schools, so there's never too much of a dull moment." Another student adds, "While the social life on Scripps' campus can be lacking at times, there is always plenty to do between all of the colleges." The Motley (the college coffeehouse) "is a great place to hang out, meet people, study, or relax." It also hosts live musical acts twice a week. Students spend plenty of time studying during the week, but on the weekends, they "turn to dance parties, lectures, and . . . when all else fails, sex with students from [the other Claremont Colleges] can provide a break from routine." While some students complain that the school "gets too small, there are a lot of people involved in a lot of activities, and they make an effort to have something going on all the time." The campus is lush and "beautiful." Scripps students say that Scripps "is probably the strictest in its [party] policies," but that is also a positive because "you can come home from a party, not come home to a party." Students looking to get off campus are close enough to Los Angeles and Pasadena to take advantage of those cities' cultural and social events. They also take advantage of the region's outdoor opportunities, and ski, hike, and go to the beach whenever possible.

### Student Body

The general undergrad sentiment is that "Scripps women are kick-ass. We're going to rule the world." The student body is very involved in "political/interest/religious organizations or student government." Most are very socially and environmentally conscious and consider themselves politically liberal. Many complain, though, that the student body isn't diverse enough: "It's really hard to discuss racism in a class full of white girls." Students admit "the stereotype of a typical women's college fits to a certain extent—either angry women and lesbians or daddy's girls," and "close-mindedness is everywhere." Despite that, they are "nice people, and a lot of them take interest in their work." Some students complain that "the gossip flies around here like nobody's business and rumors are a part of life." Still, there aren't many cliques and "you can sit and talk to anyone in the dining hall, or eat alone and no one will think the less of you." One Scripps student describes her peers as "an incredible group of women. . . . We treat each other with consideration and watch each other's backs."

# SCRIPPS COLLEGE

FINANCIAL AID: 909-621-8275 • E-MAIL: ADMOFC@AD.SCRIPPSCOL.EDU • WEBSITE: WWW.SCRIPPSCOL.EDU

## ADMISSIONS

*Very important* academic and nonacademic factors considered by the admissions committee include character/personal qualities, secondary school record and volunteer work. *Important* factors considered include essays, interview, extracurricular activities, recommendations, and talent/ability. *Other* factors considered include alumni/ae relation, class rank, geography, minority status, standardized test scores, and work experience. Factors *not* considered include interview, religious affiliation/commitment, and state residency. SAT I or ACT required. TOEFL required of all international applicants. High school diploma is required and GED is accepted. *High school units required/recommended:* 17 total required; 20 total recommended; 4 English required, 3 math required, 4 math recommended, 1 science required, 2 science recommended, 1 science lab required, 2 science lab recommended, 4 foreign language required, 1 social studies required, 2 social studies recommended, 1 history required, 2 history recommended, 2 elective required, 4 elective recommended. "Applicants must submit a graded paper from a junior or senior year academic class."

### The Inside Word

With a graded paper required in addition to application essays, it is safe to say that Scripps is going to take a long, hard look at the writing ability of its candidates. Colleges that require such papers often use them to temper the unnatural aura that sometimes envelops the application essay-writing process; a school paper will usually reflect a student's work under more normal circumstances. Here's a classic case where you should pay little heed to the high admit rate; academic standards are formidable and admissions committee expectations high.

## FINANCIAL AID

*Students should submit:* FAFSA, CSS/Financial Aid PROFILE, noncustodial (divorced/separated) parent's statement, business/farm supplement, verification worksheet, and parent and student federal tax returns and W-2 forms. Regular filing deadline is February 1. The Princeton Review suggests that all financial aid forms be submitted as soon as possible after January 1. *Need-based scholarships/grants offered:* Pell, SEOG, state scholarships/grants, private scholarships, and the school's own gift aid. *Loan aid offered:* FFEL Subsidized Stafford, FFEL Unsubsidized Stafford, FFEL PLUS, Federal Perkins, and college/university loans from institutional funds. Institutional employment available. Federal Work-Study Program available. Applicants will be notified of awards on or about April 1. Off-campus job opportunities are fair.

## FROM THE ADMISSIONS OFFICE

"At Scripps we believe that learning involves much more than amassing information. The truly educated person is one who can think analytically, communicate effectively, and make confident, responsible choices. Scripps classes are small (the average class size is 15) so that they foster an atmosphere where students feel comfortable participating, testing old assumptions, and exploring new ideas. Our curriculum is based on the traditional components of a liberal arts education: a set of general requirements in a wide variety of disciplines including foreign language, natural science, and writing; a multicultural requirement; a major that asks you to study one particular field in depth; and a variety of electives that allows considerable flexibility. What distinguishes Scripps from other liberal arts colleges is an emphasis on interdisciplinary courses."

## ADMISSIONS

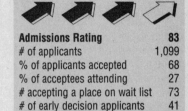

| | |
|---|---|
| Admissions Rating | 83 |
| # of applicants | 1,099 |
| % of applicants accepted | 68 |
| % of acceptees attending | 27 |
| # accepting a place on wait list | 73 |
| # of early decision applicants | 41 |
| % accepted early decision | 63 |

### FRESHMAN PROFILE
| | |
|---|---|
| Range SAT Verbal | 610-700 |
| Average SAT Verbal | 649 |
| Range SAT Math | 580-670 |
| Average SAT Math | 626 |
| Range ACT Composite | 26-30 |
| Average ACT Composite | 26 |
| Minimum TOEFL | 600 |
| Average HS GPA | 3.6 |
| % graduated top 10% of class | 45 |
| % graduated top 25% of class | 76 |
| % graduated top 50% of class | 96 |

### DEADLINES
| | |
|---|---|
| Early decision | 11/1 |
| Early decision notification | 12/15 |
| Regular admission | 2/1 |
| Regular notification | 4/1 |
| Nonfall registration? | yes |

### APPLICANTS ALSO LOOK AT
**AND OFTEN PREFER**
Smith
Wellesley
UC—Berkeley
Occidental
UC—San Diego
**AND SOMETIMES PREFER**
Mount Holyoke
UCLA
Pomona
Bryn Mawr
Claremont McKenna

## FINANCIAL FACTS

| | |
|---|---|
| Financial Aid Rating | 88 |
| Tuition | $22,470 |
| Room & board | $7,800 |
| Books and supplies | $725 |
| Required fees | $130 |
| % frosh receiving aid | 46 |
| % undergrads receiving aid | 50 |
| Avg frosh grant | $16,033 |
| Avg frosh loan | $3,037 |

# SETON HALL UNIVERSITY

400 SOUTH ORANGE AVENUE, SOUTH ORANGE, NJ 07079-2697 • ADMISSIONS: 973-761-9332 • FAX: 973-275-2040

## CAMPUS LIFE

**Quality of Life Rating** | **80**
Type of school | private
Affiliation | Roman Catholic
Environment | suburban

### STUDENTS

| | |
|---|---|
| Total undergrad enrollment | 5,403 |
| % male/female | 49/51 |
| % from out of state | 17 |
| % from public high school | 70 |
| % live on campus | 37 |
| % in (# of) fraternities | 10 (11) |
| % in (# of) sororities | 8 (11) |
| % African American | 11 |
| % Asian | 7 |
| % Caucasian | 54 |
| % Hispanic | 9 |
| % international | 2 |

### SURVEY SAYS . . .
*Theater is hot*
*Student publications are popular*
*Frats and sororities dominate social scene*
*Everyone loves the Pirates*
*Classes are small*
*Ethnic diversity on campus*
*Lab facilities are great*
*Computer facilities are great*
*Campus difficult to get around*
*Lots of conservatives*

## ACADEMICS

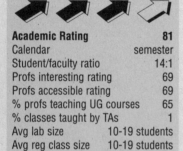

| | |
|---|---|
| **Academic Rating** | **81** |
| Calendar | semester |
| Student/faculty ratio | 14:1 |
| Profs interesting rating | 69 |
| Profs accessible rating | 69 |
| % profs teaching UG courses | 65 |
| % classes taught by TAs | 1 |
| Avg lab size | 10-19 students |
| Avg reg class size | 10-19 students |

### MOST POPULAR MAJORS
communication
biology
criminal justice

## STUDENTS SPEAK OUT
### Academics

Seton Hall is a "major Catholic university" that takes its religious values "seriously." SHU primarily serves students who are looking for an "affordable," pre-professional, and career-specific education. Most of the students here choose criminal justice, communications, biology, and business-related majors. However, curriculum requirements ensure that no student graduates without completing a heavy dose of liberal arts distribution requirements. "Class sizes are small" here and "students receive a lot of attention" from "helpful" professors who "are available outside the classroom." Students say that, on the whole, "teachers know you and are readily available" at SHU, although "the adjunct professors are deplorable." Some of the resources here could stand to be improved. A relatively new library receives rave reviews, and online registration should make students happy. Dealing with the administration is generally hassle-free. "People working at SHU are very cooperative, helpful, and are very easy to associate with," observes one student. Plus, through the university's Mobile Computing Program, full-time students are issued IBM laptops, which are integrated into the curriculumn.

### Life

Seton Hall is "nestled on 58 acres" in the suburban New Jersey hamlet of South Orange. "The Hall" is very much "like a suitcase school." Social life is "great during the week, but everyone goes home on the weekends." During the week, SHU offers a happening social scene. "Thursday nights are big," says a senior. "Everyone hits the bars, but the ones that you can get into without an ID are in a horrible area." The numerous "malls, movies, and restaurants" offer popular diversions as well. In the spring, throngs of students "hang out on The Green in the center of campus." On Friday, though, many students clear out of town, and "there is absolutely nothing to do" in the immediate local area for those who remain. In response to the "nonexistent party scene" on the weekends, many students who live on campus "sit around, drink, and play video games." Others "usually go to bars for fun." Of course, there's always New York City. New Jersey Transit runs a "Midtown Direct" train that takes students from South Orange to Manhattan's Penn Station in 22 minutes. Campus activities and intramural sports are plentiful. Many of the students who live on and near campus—which is less than half of the student population—become very active in fraternities and sororities. If you don't go Greek "it's hard to get involved unless you are an athlete." Seton Hall's basketball team is very big, especially when the team is competing for the Big East championship, and Seton Hall made it to the Sweet Sixteen in 2000.

### Student Body

Despite the best efforts of the administration, racial tension runs pretty high among some factions at Seton Hall. The student population here is "very diverse" but "somewhat segregated," with Caucasians, African Americans, and Hispanics sticking mostly to their own groups. While most students are content with this arrangement, there is an unmistakable undercurrent of "racial tension" and even occasional "confrontations." The "friendly but often superficial" students in this "small, closely knit community where everyone knows each other" describe themselves as "easy to get along with." They are politically conservative, very career-oriented folks. New Jersey natives make up a tremendous majority of the student body.

FINANCIAL AID: 973-761-9350 • E-MAIL: THEHALL@SHU.EDU • WEBSITE: WWW.SHU.EDU

## ADMISSIONS

*Very important* academic and nonacademic factors considered by the admissions committee include secondary school record, recommendations, standardized test scores, and essay. *Important* factors considered include extracurricular activities, volunteer work, and work experience. *Other* factors considered include class rank, interview, talent/ability, and character/personal qualities. Factors *not* considered include alumni/ae relation, geography, state residency, religious affiliation/commitment, and minority status. SAT I or ACT required. TOEFL required of all international applicants. High school diploma is required and GED is accepted. *High school units required/recommended:* 16 total required; 4 English required, 3 math required, 1 science required, 1 science lab required, 2 foreign language required, 2 social studies required, 4 elective required. *The admissions office says:* "The personal attention given each application is what makes the admissions process at Seton Hall different. Every prospective student's file is read by two counselors, a committee review is held weekly, and folders are not assigned numeric averages."

### The Inside Word

Getting into Seton Hall shouldn't be too stressful for most average students who have taken a full college-prep curriculum in high school. In the New York metropolitan area there are a lot of schools with similar characteristics, and collectively they take away the large proportion of Seton Hall's admits. Above average students who are serious about the university should be able to parlay their interest into some scholarship dollars, over 300 full scholarships this year.

## FINANCIAL AID

The Princeton Review suggests that all financial aid forms be submitted as soon as possible after January 1. *Need-based scholarships/grants offered:* Pell, SEOG, state scholarships/grants, private scholarships, the school's own gift aid, and Federal Nursing. *Loan aid offered:* Direct Subsidized Stafford, Direct Unsubsidized Stafford, Direct PLUS, Federal Perkins, and Federal Nursing. Institutional employment available. Federal Work-Study Program available. Off-campus job opportunities are excellent.

## FROM THE ADMISSIONS OFFICE

"As the oldest and largest diocesan university in the United States, Seton Hall University is committed to providing its students with a diverse environment focusing on academic excellence and ethical development. Outstanding faculty, a technologically advanced campus, and a values-centered curriculum challenge Seton Hall students. Through these things and the personal attention students receive, they are prepared to be leaders in their professional and community lives in a global society. Seton Hall's campus offers students up-to-date facilities, including an award-winning library facility opened in 1994 and the state-of-the art Kozlowski Hall, which opened in 1997. The university has invested more than $25 million in the past five years to provide its students and faculty with leading edge information technology. The Mobile Computing Program is widely recognized as one of the nation's best. In 1999 and 2000, Seton Hall was ranked as one of the nation's Most Wired universities by *Yahoo! Internet Life* magazine. Recent additions to Seton Hall's academic offerings include the School of Diplomacy and International Relations and a number of dual-degree health sciences programs, including physical therapy, physician assistant, and occupational therapy."

## ADMISSIONS

| Admissions Rating | 76 |
| --- | --- |
| # of applicants | 4.264 |
| % of applicants accepted | 88 |
| % of acceptees attending | 30 |
| # accepting a place on wait list | 579 |
| % admitted from wait list | 85 |

### FRESHMAN PROFILE

| | |
| --- | --- |
| Range SAT Verbal | 470-570 |
| Average SAT Verbal | 525 |
| Range SAT Math | 480-590 |
| Average SAT Math | 533 |
| Minimum TOEFL | 550 |
| % graduated top 10% of class | 15 |
| % graduated top 25% of class | 38 |
| % graduated top 50% of class | 71 |

### DEADLINES

| | |
| --- | --- |
| Priority admission deadline | 3/1 |
| Nonfall registration? | yes |

### APPLICANTS ALSO LOOK AT

**AND OFTEN PREFER**
Rutgers U.
NYU
Villanova

**AND SOMETIMES PREFER**
Montclair State
Trenton State
Providence
U. Conn

**AND RARELY PREFER**
St. Bonaventure
Fairfield
Hofstra

## FINANCIAL FACTS

| Financial Aid Rating | 76 |
| --- | --- |
| Tuition | $17,400 |
| Room & board | $8,060 |
| Books and supplies | $950 |
| Required fees | $2,000 |
| % frosh receiving aid | 72 |
| % undergrads receiving aid | 71 |
| Avg frosh grant | $8,250 |
| Avg frosh loan | $4,310 |

# SIENA COLLEGE

515 Loudon Road, Loudonville, NY 12211 • Admissions: 518-783-2423 • Fax: 518-783-2436

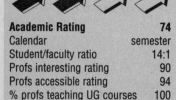
## STUDENTS SPEAK OUT

### Academics

Students at Siena College have very mixed feelings about their education. They praise their favorite professors because they are "always available and willing to help with anything." And they're "creative and open-minded" to boot. The history program gets especially high marks. Professors "not only know what they are talking about, [but] they [also] know how to relay the information to students in a user-friendly way," writes a senior psychology major. Despite the small classes, "some professors tend to lecture too much and don't get the students involved." While the professors are "nice," some "really don't seem like they want to be" here. A disgruntled sophomore believes, "If one were coming here for academic reasons, community colleges do just as well and are much cheaper." Students also complain that they have a difficult time registering for the most desired classes, which therefore makes "the good teachers impossible to get." The administration also gets mixed reviews. While a sophomore English major believes, "Those who don't look at the administration as the enemy from day one get listened to with relative seriousness," most students say that the lack of communication between the administration and themselves is a major problem. One senior history major describes the administration as "a bunch of bureaucrats on valium who are underpaid and consequently don't care." She adds that the various administrative offices "treat students like juvenile delinquents."

### Life

Although Loudonville is not far from the bars of Albany, the lack of transportation is a problem—one that encourages many students to stay in town, where entertainment options are seriously limited. Party days at Siena are "any day that ends in the letter 'y,'" quips one senior. Some students "get all dolled up in their party best and pile 12 to a taxi"; however, because taxis are expensive, which makes it difficult to get off campus, many students go to the upperclassmen's townhouses to pour a few down the hatch. "Students love to drink," one sophomore admits. A psychology major adds, "The weekend is time to put down the books and pick up a drink or 10 or 20." The "alcohol and drug policies are strict but not strongly enforced." One biology major that "loves" Siena notes that the school "would be better without classes." Students attend movies, and a number enjoy their association with a medieval history club—the Society for Creative Anachronism. The gym is well used, the dorms are overcrowded, and students go out to dinner as often as they can because the on-campus food leaves much to be desired.

### Student Body

Siena's students are primarily Catholic and conservative. Some believe that the "upper-middle-class Catholic students are unacquainted with reality." An English major describes his fellows as "good people who do very stupid things." Students complain about the evident lack of diversity on campus; this is not surprising considering that over 90 percent of the students are Caucasian. "There is some diversity," a chemistry major says, "but it's primarily Abercrombie-wearing Dave Matthews fans." A senior history major decries the "bigotry and closed-mindedness" that she observes among her schoolmates. Students describe their peers as "friendly" but "cliquey." Overall, "students here . . . are nice and usually show respect for you," a business major writes. "They are able to get along together pretty well."

FINANCIAL AID: 518-783-2427 • E-MAIL: ADMIT@SIENA.EDU • WEBSITE: WWW.SIENA.EDU

## ADMISSIONS

*Very important* academic and nonacademic factors considered by the admissions committee include secondary school record. *Important* factors considered include character/personal qualities, essays, extracurricular activities, recommendations, standardized test scores, talent/ability, volunteer work, and work experience. *Other* factors considered include alumni/ae relation, class rank, interview, and minority status. Factors *not* considered include geography, religious affiliation/commitment, and state residency. SAT I or ACT required. TOEFL required of all international applicants. High school diploma is required and GED is accepted. *High school units required/recommended:* 15 total required; 19 total recommended; 4 English required, 3 math required, 4 math recommended, 3 science required, 4 science recommended, 3 science lab required, 2 foreign language required, 3 foreign language recommended, 1 social studies required, 1 social studies recommended, 2 history required, 3 history recommended.

### The Inside Word

Students who have consistently solid grades should have no trouble getting admitted. There is hot competition for students between colleges in New York State; Siena has to admit the large majority of its applicants in order to meet freshman class enrollment targets.

## FINANCIAL AID

The Princeton Review suggests that all financial aid forms be submitted as soon as possible after January 1. Institutional employment available. Federal Work-Study Program available. Off-campus job opportunities are good.

## FROM THE ADMISSIONS OFFICE

"Siena is a coeducational, independent liberal arts college with a Franciscan tradition. It is a community where the intellectual, personal, and social growth of all students is paramount. Siena's faculty calls forth the best Siena students have to give—and the students do the same for them. Students are competitive, but not at each other's expense. Siena's curriculum includes 23 majors in three schools—liberal arts, science, and business. In addition, there are over a dozen pre-professional and special academic programs. With a student-faculty ratio of 14:1, class size ranges between 15 and 35 students. Siena's 152-acre campus is located in Loudonville, a suburban community within two miles of the New York State seat of government in Albany. With 15 colleges in the area, there is a wide variety of activities on weekends. Regional theater, performances by major concert artists, and professional sports events compete with the activities on the campus. Within 50 miles are the Adirondacks, the Berkshires, and the Catskills, providing outdoor recreation throughout the year. Because the capital region's easy, friendly lifestyle is so appealing, many Siena graduates try to find their first jobs in upstate New York."

## ADMISSIONS

| | |
|---|---|
| Admissions Rating | 73 |
| # of applicants | 3,121 |
| % of applicants accepted | 73 |
| % of acceptees attending | 31 |
| # accepting a place on wait list | 92 |
| % admitted from wait list | 59 |
| # of early decision applicants | 62 |
| % accepted early decision | 65 |

### FRESHMAN PROFILE

| | |
|---|---|
| Range SAT Verbal | 500-590 |
| Average SAT Verbal | 546 |
| Range SAT Math | 520-620 |
| Average SAT Math | 565 |
| Range ACT Composite | 23-27 |
| Average ACT Composite | 24 |
| Minimum TOEFL | 550 |
| % graduated top 10% of class | 20 |
| % graduated top 25% of class | 56 |
| % graduated top 50% of class | 88 |

### DEADLINES

| | |
|---|---|
| Early decision | 12/1 |
| Early decision notification | 12/15 |
| Regular admission | 3/1 |
| Regular notification | 3/15 |
| Nonfall registration? | yes |

### APPLICANTS ALSO LOOK AT
**AND OFTEN PREFER**
Villanova
Providence
**AND SOMETIMES PREFER**
Fairfield
Marist
SUNY Albany
U. Scranton
Loyola Coll. (MD)
**AND RARELY PREFER**
Oswego State
Fredonia State
LeMoyne
Syracuse
U. Conn

### FINANCIAL FACTS

| | |
|---|---|
| Financial Aid Rating | 79 |
| Tuition | $15,330 |
| Room & board | $7,430 |
| Books and supplies | $675 |
| Required fees | $470 |
| % frosh receiving aid | 72 |

# SIMMONS COLLEGE

300 THE FENWAY, BOSTON, MA 02115 • ADMISSIONS: 617-521-2051 • FAX: 617-521-3190

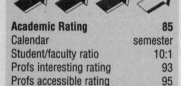
## STUDENTS SPEAK OUT

### Academics

Boston's Simmons College may not be the flashiest, most modern school on the block. That hardly matters, however, to the 1,200-plus women who chose to attend the school. Explains one, "Although Simmons is not the most up-to-date technology-wise, it is a place where you can get a great education. The professors are easily accessible and patient." Students come here to take advantage of the school's formidable pre-professional programs in nursing, physical therapy, management, and other career-oriented areas, as well as to capitalize on internship and work opportunities in Boston. The demanding Simmons curriculum requires hard work; graduation requirements include 40 hours of core courses, another 20 to 40 hours of major courses, and about a dozen hours of independent study. Notes one student, "Everyone who attends this college is really in it for the challenge." Professors "are amazing and try to spark interest in their students." Reports one undergrad, "I transferred to Simmons as a sophomore and felt right at home immediately. I noticed how willing my professors were not only to treat you as an adult, but also to treat you as an equal. I really feel that I have been able to connect with my professors and classmates in a way I wasn't able to at my old school." Students also enjoy "the small classroom environment. It makes me feel comfortable to ask questions and to be asked." Overall, students tell us they are satisfied with their education here. "I have been challenged, pushed, and encouraged," beams an English major. "Simmons is a great school, where women become leaders."

### Life

Simmons undergrads brag that they enjoy the best of both worlds: "At Simmons, there is a small college environment inside the gated fence, but outside is the entire city of Boston. Going to Simmons offers a nice contrast to the big city life." Writes one student, "Simmons is in a great location. You have total safety yet all the advantages of the city. It is a women's college, so we focus on our studies during the week and have fun in the city during the weekend." Because "exploring Boston is the best part" of life here, Simmons "is not a social school, and very few students are thoroughly involved with events outside of the classroom. Many students are here only for class." Explains one student, "For fun people leave campus. They go into Boston or to other colleges in the area. People find the school to be very safe but a little boring due to the all-girl campus." They go "shopping at the Prudential Center and Copley. . . . Jillian's and Fanneuil Hall are also really fun places to take in all Boston has to offer." Also, "students here do the same thing that every other college student does. That means they go to bars to drink beer and meet guys." Once back on campus, students appreciate the fact that "Simmons dorms are very quiet, which is great because if you want to party you go off campus and have a good time, but it's always nice and quiet when you get back." On the downside, "the rules for living in the dorms are ridiculous" and "the food on campus is awful."

### Student Body

You've got to hand it to the women of Simmons: they definitely score points for sarcasm. As one mordant undergrad notes, "Simmons offers a wide variety of Caucasian upper-middle-class women from Maine and Massachusetts." Others offer more direct criticism of their "snobby, unfriendly" classmates: "People here aren't extremely friendly. Most people keep to themselves, but they are generally polite and respectful." Get past the "spoiled, rich girls who have never worked a day in their lives" and those who "are way too serious about school, themselves, and life in general," however, and you'll find some "mature, smart women, with open minds and a good sense of humor." Furthermore, those who fit the majority mold are usually perfectly happy here, finding the community "very supportive, encouraging, and inspiring."

FINANCIAL AID: 617-521-2036 • E-MAIL: UGADM@SIMMONS.EDU • WEBSITE: WWW.SIMMONS.EDU

## ADMISSIONS

*Very important* academic and nonacademic factors considered by the admissions committee include secondary school record. *Important* factors considered include character/personal qualities, essays, interview, recommendations, and standardized test scores. *Other* factors considered include alumni/ae relation, class rank, extracurricular activities, minority status, talent/ability, volunteer work, and work experience. Factors *not* considered include geography, religious affiliation/commitment, and state residency. SAT I or ACT required. TOEFL required of all international applicants. High school diploma is required and GED is accepted. *High school units required/recommended:* 15 total required; 4 English required, 3 math required, 3 science required, 2 foreign language required, 3 social studies required. *The admissions office says:* "To retain [Simmons's] diversity means its policies must be flexible, focusing on each applicant's qualities of scholarship and character."

### The Inside Word

Most of the best women's colleges in the country are in the Northeast, including those Seven Sister schools (roughly the female equivalent of the formerly all-male Ivies) that remain women's colleges. The competition for students is intense, and although Simmons is a strong attraction for many women, there are at least a half-dozen competitors who draw the better students away. For the majority of applicants there is little need for anxiety while awaiting a decision. Its solid academics, Boston location, and bountiful scholarship program make Simmons well worth considering for any student opting for a women's college.

## FINANCIAL AID

The Princeton Review suggests that all financial aid forms be submitted as soon as possible after January 1. Institutional employment available. Federal Work-Study Program available. Off-campus job opportunities are good.

## FROM THE ADMISSIONS OFFICE

"The Simmons idea is not novel today; indeed, its time has come. Since the early 1900s there have been dramatic changes in society's attitudes toward women and in women's perception of themselves and what they contribute in every field of activity. Simmons College has not only kept pace with these changes, it also has helped to shape them in its classrooms and by the example of its graduates in the careers they have undertaken and the leadership they have provided."

## ADMISSIONS

| | |
|---|---|
| Admissions Rating | 76 |
| # of applicants | 1,772 |
| % of applicants accepted | 65 |
| % of acceptees attending | 22 |
| # accepting a place on wait list | 34 |
| % admitted from wait list | 76 |

### FRESHMAN PROFILE

| | |
|---|---|
| Range SAT Verbal | 510-590 |
| Range SAT Math | 500-540 |
| Range ACT Composite | 21-28 |
| Minimum TOEFL | 550 |
| % graduated top 10% of class | 22 |
| % graduated top 25% of class | 58 |
| % graduated top 50% of class | 92 |

### DEADLINES

| | |
|---|---|
| Regular admission | 2/1 |
| Regular notification | 4/15 |
| Nonfall registration? | yes |

### APPLICANTS ALSO LOOK AT
### AND OFTEN PREFER
Boston Coll.
Boston U.
Mount Holyoke
Wellesley
Bryn Mawr
### AND SOMETIMES PREFER
Wheaton (MA)
Northeastern U.
Smith
### AND RARELY PREFER
U. Mass—Amherst
U. New Hampshire

## FINANCIAL FACTS

| | |
|---|---|
| Financial Aid Rating | 79 |
| Tuition | $20,260 |
| Room & board | $8,410 |
| Books and supplies | $600 |
| Required fees | $630 |
| % frosh receiving aid | 76 |

# SIMON'S ROCK COLLEGE OF BARD

84 ALFORD ROAD, GREAT BARRINGTON, MA 01230 • ADMISSIONS: 413-528-7312 • FAX: 413-528-7334

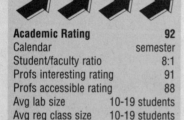
## STUDENTS SPEAK OUT

### Academics

Let's face it: For a lot of kids, high school just plain sucks. Bright oddballs often have the worst time of it in these youth-oriented conformity factories, where mediocrity is often the norm to which most aspire. For many such misfits, Simon's Rock of Bard plays the role of Superman, swooping down to rescue them from at least a couple of years of torture, humiliation, and boredom. Simon's Rock offers college-level instruction for high school juniors and seniors, allowing a lucky few to both escape high school *and* get a jump-start on their college education. Explains one student, "This is a dream school for a kid who is too smart for high school." Although most undergrads transfer out after the second year, about 40 stay on each year to participate in the school's recently revamped four-year BA program. Reports one student, "Simon's Rock used to be seen as an inflated community college. Now people are staying in droves to get the benefit of our four-year BA, even though the senior thesis [a prerequisite for graduation] is hell." The educational philosophy of Simon's Rock stresses both independence and rigor. Notes one student, "Most classes are discussion-based, which is very effective . . . Assignments are generally open-ended, which allows for much creativity." The school gives students considerable leeway but expects a lot in return; as one student puts it, "The difficulty of the work can be summed up by what one professor said: 'C for you, B for me, A for God or Shakespeare.'" Students appreciate the mentoring relationships provided by faculty and administrators. Some of "the faculty and administration live on campus," writes one student. "This isn't just a job for them; it's something they care about." All this, and nobody tries to shove your head into your gym locker. What more could you ask for?

### Life

It is a testament to students' satisfaction with the academics here that most stay at Simon's Rock despite a near-lifeless extracurricular scene both on and around campus. Explains one student, "The college attracts bright 16-year-olds but does not offer alternatives to the 'life of the mind,' which would explain the high levels of apathy and alienation among the students. Faculty and staff do not support the development or maintenance of student organizations, whether it be debate club or a music group." Hometown Great Barrington—dubbed "Great Borrington" by students—does little to supplement the on-campus austerity. To make matters worse, "Students without cars have virtually no access to theater performances, music concerts, or other socio-cultural events" in nearby Berkshire communities. As a result, "People here talk to each other all the time because there's not much else to do but sit around, have great conversations, and 'be creative.'" Summing up the situation, one student describes a typical Simon's Rock weekend as "truly sad. If you come here you will find yourself reading a lot to get through them. Don't be surprised to find yourself hanging out in the library on a Saturday night." On the bright side, the campus, set in the woods of Massachusetts, is beautiful and relaxing, according to students. As one puts it, "The school is a clean mountain place. Being from the city, I see how here things just flow. It's a strange utopia of sorts, and highly enjoyable."

### Student Body

The Simon's Rock student body is a mix of "ambitious and dedicated students for whom high school was truly inadequate, [as well as] a fair number of apathetic junky-types who probably relish earning their freedom from parental supervision two years early. The trend, though, is toward the former type, as the college is trying to live up to its epithet: 'The College For Younger Scholars.'" Nearly all here chose Simon's Rock because they could not bear the traditional high school experience. Explains one, "Knowing what it's like to be outcast and alienated from traditional high school stereotypes, students are free to be themselves and to be appreciated for it." Primarily left-leaning in political orientation, students pride themselves on being "individual thinkers" with "pleasantly bizarre" personalities.

# SIMON'S ROCK COLLEGE OF BARD

FINANCIAL AID: 413-528-7297 • E-MAIL: ADMIT@SIMONS-ROCK.EDU • WEBSITE: WWW.SIMONS-ROCK.EDU

## ADMISSIONS

*Very important* academic and nonacademic factors considered by the admissions committee include essays, interview, recommendations, and secondary school record. *Important* factors considered include character/personal qualities and standardized test scores. *Other* factors considered include alumni/ae relation, extracurricular activities, minority status, talent/ability and volunteer work. Factors *not* considered include class rank, geography, religious affiliation/commitment, state residency, and work experience. SAT I or ACT required. TOEFL required of all international applicants. *High school units required/recommended:* 2 English recommended, 2 math recommended, 2 science recommended, 1 science lab recommended, 2 foreign language recommended, 2 social studies recommended, 2 history recommended, 2 elective recommended. *The admissions office says:* "Simon's Rock seeks students who demonstrated the intellectual ability, motivation, and self-discipline to pursue college studies at high school age."

### The Inside Word

There is no other college like Simon's Rock in the country, and no other similar admissions process. Applying to college doesn't get any more personal, and thus any more demanding, than it does here. If you're not ready to tap your potential as a thinker in college beginning with completion of the application, avoid Simon's Rock. Simply hating high school isn't going to get you in. Self-awareness, intellectual curiosity, and a desire for more formidable academic challenges than those typically found in high school will.

## FINANCIAL AID

*Students should submit:* FAFSA, CSS/Financial Aid PROFILE, state aid form, and noncustodial (divorced/separated) parent's statement. Regular filing deadline is June 15. The Princeton Review suggests that all financial aid forms be submitted as soon as possible after January 1. *Need-based scholarships/grants offered:* Pell, SEOG, state scholarships/grants, private scholarships, and the school's own gift aid. *Loan aid offered:* Direct Subsidized Stafford, Direct Unsubsidized Stafford, Direct PLUS, FFEL Subsidized Stafford, FFEL Unsubsidized Stafford, FFEL PLUS, Federal Perkins, and state. Institutional employment available. Federal Work-Study Program available. Applicants will be notified of awards on a rolling basis beginning on or about April 15. Off-campus job opportunities are good.

## FROM THE ADMISSIONS OFFICE

"Simon's Rock is dedicated to one thing: to allow bright highly motivated students the opportunity to pursue college work leading to the AA and BA degrees at an age earlier than our national norm."

## ADMISSIONS

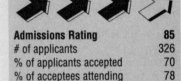

| | |
|---|---|
| Admissions Rating | 85 |
| # of applicants | 326 |
| % of applicants accepted | 70 |
| % of acceptees attending | 78 |
| # accepting a place on wait list | 9 |
| % admitted from wait list | 67 |

### FRESHMAN PROFILE

| | |
|---|---|
| Range SAT Verbal | 500-640 |
| Average SAT Verbal | 640 |
| Range SAT Math | 500-610 |
| Average SAT Math | 610 |
| Average ACT Composite | 25 |
| Minimum TOEFL | 550 |

### DEADLINES

| | |
|---|---|
| Regular admission | 7/1 |
| Regular notification | rolling |
| Nonfall registration? | yes |

## FINANCIAL FACTS

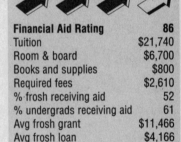

| | |
|---|---|
| Financial Aid Rating | 86 |
| Tuition | $21,740 |
| Room & board | $6,700 |
| Books and supplies | $800 |
| Required fees | $2,610 |
| % frosh receiving aid | 52 |
| % undergrads receiving aid | 61 |
| Avg frosh grant | $11,466 |
| Avg frosh loan | $4,166 |

# SKIDMORE COLLEGE

815 NORTH BROADWAY, SARATOGA SPRINGS, NY 12866-1632 • ADMISSIONS: 518-580-5570 • FAX: 518-580-5584

## CAMPUS LIFE

| | |
|---|---|
| **Quality of Life Rating** | **92** |
| Type of school | private |
| Affiliation | none |
| Environment | suburban |

### STUDENTS

| | |
|---|---|
| Total undergrad enrollment | 2,451 |
| % male/female | 39/61 |
| % from out of state | 72 |
| % from public high school | 57 |
| % live on campus | 78 |
| % African American | 2 |
| % Asian | 4 |
| % Caucasian | 78 |
| % Hispanic | 5 |
| % international | 1 |

### SURVEY SAYS . . .
*Great library*
*Students love Saratoga Springs, NY*
*Great computer facilities*
*Dorms are like palaces*
*Diversity lacking on campus*
*No one plays intramural sports*
*Class discussions encouraged*

## ACADEMICS

| | |
|---|---|
| **Academic Rating** | **82** |
| Calendar | semester |
| Student/faculty ratio | 11:1 |
| Profs interesting rating | 93 |
| Profs accessible rating | 95 |
| % profs teaching UG courses | 100 |
| Avg lab size | 10-19 students |
| Avg reg class size | 10-19 students |

### MOST POPULAR MAJORS
business
English
art

## STUDENTS SPEAK OUT

### Academics

Skidmore College, a small liberal arts school in upstate New York, boasts strengths in the "liberal arts, fine arts, and performing arts." In addition, Skidmore offers excellent pre-professional programs and programs in education and social work. A core curriculum—the Liberal Studies sequence—exposes students to the "greatest hits" of western arts and sciences and provides "a valuable supplement to a solid liberal arts education." Says one student of the curriculum, "Skidmore embraces versatility. It's the training ground for modern Leonardo da Vincis, Aristotles, and tap-dancing brain surgeons." Students at Skidmore enjoy a relaxed but rigorous academic atmosphere in which "academics are challenging yet manageable" and the workload is "just right. I think I was well prepared for the academic atmosphere here. Just when things seem too easy, something challenging comes along, and vice versa." Professors are "fun and interesting. They seem to love what they do." Writes an undergrad, "Professors are always available to talk to. They are so helpful and friendly. Not only can you talk to them about academics but you can get advice on life in general." About the only beef students have with the faculty is that "we need more professors in order to expand the number of courses offered." Undergrads are more circumspect about the administration, complaining that "students have very little input in what happens on this campus. Decisions are made behind closed doors." For a select group of "highly motivated and talented students," Skidmore offers the Honors Forum, "an enriched combination of academic and co-curricular opportunities."

### Life

For those who enjoy crisp autumns, beautiful campuses, and lovely small cities, Skidmore offers an excellent quality of life. "The campus is beautiful, dorms are awesome, and Saratoga Springs is great!" gushes one student. "It's a 30,000-person town with the facilities and entertainment of a town three times its size. Wonderful coffee shops [and a] great night life" are among the most popular amenities. Students are quick to point out that "for the outdoorsy types, the Adirondacks are an hour drive away" and that "Lake George is beautiful and less than 30 minutes away." One student remarks that there's "lots of stuff to do here with nature. Mad nice parks. We usually do outdoor activities for fun (hiking, biking, Frisbee, etc.) until the sun goes down, then we usually consume a lot of alcohol and do a variety of drugs." Students also note that "big cities [New York, Boston] are four hours away . . . a little too far, but there are buses and trains." Albany is close by for students needing an instant fix of urban style. On campus, "students are highly involved in clubs and other extracurriculars," but "sports and school spirit are lacking." Offers one undergrad, "There is always something going on: lectures, bands, plays, free movies on weekends, bowling, laser tag. . . . I think this may account for the low support of sports." Skidmore has no Greek scene, which many here see as "a plus. Off-campus parties are fun, relaxed environments."

### Student Body

"Skidmore students," explains one undergrad, "are generally considered wealthy, spoiled, privileged people. To a certain extent, it's true. But at the same time, you can surround yourself with people who do not fit the stereotype. There are many hard-working, down-to-earth people here." Comments another, "Skidmore is, unfortunately, a pretty homogeneous place. The administration works hard to give financial aid. Without it, the cost of tuition would make this place completely exclusive. All issues of diversity directly relate to money." Some report that "all the different types of people—jocks, thespians, artists, hippies, and preps—all interact well together. It isn't uncommon to have friends in all circles." Others complain that students are very cliquey. One woman warns prospective female applicants that "the students at Skidmore are mostly women. The ratio of men to women is about 2:3, which is really good if you're a straight guy because a lot of the men here are gay."

FINANCIAL AID: 518-580-5750 • E-MAIL: ADMISSIONS@SKIDMORE.EDU • WEBSITE: WWW.SKIDMORE.EDU

## ADMISSIONS

*Very important* academic and nonacademic factors considered by the admissions committee include character/personal qualities, essays, extracurricular activities, recommendations, secondary school record, and talent/ability. *Important* factors considered include class rank, interview, minority status, standardized test scores, and volunteer work. *Other* factors considered include alumni/ae relation, geography, state residency, and work experience. Factors *not* considered include religious affiliation/commitment. SAT I or ACT required; SAT II recommended. TOEFL required of all international applicants. High school diploma is required and GED is accepted. *High school units required/recommended:* 20 total recommended; 4 English recommended, 4 math recommended, 4 science recommended, 3 science lab recommended, 4 foreign language recommended, 4 social studies recommended. *The admissions office says:* "We seek students who demonstrate intellectual curiosity, open-mindedness, an energetic commitment to learning, and a concern for others. The admissions committee's primary emphasis is on the strength of the candidate's academic record, personal qualities, accomplishments, interests, and capacity for growth. Although a personal interview is not required, it is strongly recommended."

### The Inside Word

Although Skidmore overlaps applicants with some of the best colleges and universities in the Northeast, it's mainly viewed as a safety. Still, this makes for a strong applicant pool, and those students who do enroll give the college a better-than-average freshman academic profile. The entire admissions operation at Skidmore is impressive and efficient, proof that number two does indeed try harder.

## FINANCIAL AID

*Students should submit:* FAFSA, state aid form, noncustodial (divorced/separated) parent's statement, business/farm supplement, and CSS/Financial Aid PROFILE required for all students applying for need-based financial aid. Regular filing deadline is January 15. The Princeton Review suggests that all financial aid forms be submitted as soon as possible after January 1. *Need-based scholarships/grants offered:* Pell, SEOG, state scholarships/grants, and the school's own gift aid. *Loan aid offered:* FFEL Subsidized Stafford, FFEL Unsubsidized Stafford, and FFEL PLUS. Institutional employment available. Federal Work-Study Program available. Applicants will be notified of awards on or about April 1. Off-campus job opportunities are good.

## FROM THE ADMISSIONS OFFICE

"Skidmore's Liberal Studies Curriculum is a highly interdisciplinary core curriculum that enriches a student's first two years of study. Students take one course in each of four liberal studies areas, beginning that Liberal Studies I: The Human Experience. This is a cornerstone course that is team-taught to all freshmen by 28 professors from virtually every department in the college. It involves lectures, performances, films, and regular small group discussions. Students then take one liberal studies course in each of the three succeeding semesters in the following areas: Cultural Traditions and Social Change; Artistic Forms and Critical Concepts; and Science, Society, and Human Values. The purpose of this constellation of courses is to show the important academic interrelationships across disciplines, across cultures, and across time. The result is that our students learn to look for connections among the disciplines rather than see them in isolation. With this interdisciplinary foundation under their belts by the end of the sophomore year, students are better prepared to then select a major (or combination of majors) that matches their interests."

## ADMISSIONS

| | |
|---|---:|
| Admissions Rating | 82 |
| # of applicants | 5,471 |
| % of applicants accepted | 43 |
| % of acceptees attending | 26 |
| # accepting a place on wait list | 485 |
| % admitted from wait list | 8 |
| # of early decision applicants | 357 |
| % accepted early decision | 67 |

### FRESHMAN PROFILE

| | |
|---|---:|
| Range SAT Verbal | 570-660 |
| Average SAT Verbal | 610 |
| Range SAT Math | 570-650 |
| Average SAT Math | 610 |
| Range ACT Composite | 24-29 |
| Average ACT Composite | 28 |
| Minimum TOEFL | 580 |
| Average HS GPA | 3.5 |
| % graduated top 10% of class | 29 |
| % graduated top 50% of class | 93 |

### DEADLINES

| | |
|---|---:|
| Early decision | 12/1 |
| Early decision notification | 1/1 |
| Regular admission | 1/15 |
| Regular notification | 4/1 |
| Nonfall registration? | yes |

### APPLICANTS ALSO LOOK AT
#### AND OFTEN PREFER
Trinity (CT)
Middlebury
Vassar
#### AND SOMETIMES PREFER
American
Syracuse
Boston U.
#### AND RARELY PREFER
Clark

## FINANCIAL FACTS

| | |
|---|---:|
| Financial Aid Rating | 78 |
| Tuition | $25,190 |
| Room & board | $7,260 |
| Books and supplies | $700 |
| Required fees | $269 |
| % frosh receiving aid | 41 |
| % undergrads receiving aid | 42 |
| Avg frosh grant | $14,847 |
| Avg frosh loan | $2,412 |

# SMITH COLLEGE

7 COLLEGE LANE, NORTHAMPTON, MA 01063 • ADMISSIONS: 413-585-2500 • FAX: 413-585-2527

## CAMPUS LIFE

**Quality of Life Rating**    **92**
Type of school    private
Affiliation    none
Environment    suburban

### STUDENTS
Total undergrad enrollment    2,630
% female    100
% from out of state    78
% from public high school    65
% live on campus    91
% African American    5
% Asian    10
% Caucasian    60
% Hispanic    4
% Native American    1
% international    6
# of countries represented    53

### SURVEY SAYS . . .
*Dorms are like palaces*
*Political activism is hot*
*Campus feels safe*
*No one cheats*
*Great library*
*Musical organizations are hot*
*Theater is unpopular*
*Very little beer drinking*
*Very little hard liquor*

## ACADEMICS

**Academic Rating**    **94**
Calendar    semester
Student/faculty ratio    10:1
Profs interesting rating    96
Profs accessible rating    97
% profs teaching UG courses    100
Avg lab size    10-19 students
Avg reg class size    10-19 students

### MOST POPULAR MAJORS
government
psychology
English

## STUDENTS SPEAK OUT

### Academics
There is no core curriculum at all-women's Smith College; instead, students fulfill the requirements of their chosen major and are free to take whatever other courses they chooses outside their major, a feature that encourages "independent work" and requires self-motivation. Although "there are some professors that only care about research," most of the "inspiring," "exuberant," and "very accessible" profs here "go above and beyond the call of duty to help their students." "They encourage us to improve and always respect our opinions," states a sophomore. Also, "the faculty is at least 50 percent women," and students say "it's nice to be able to learn not only with women but from women." The "nightmare" workload is "incredibly demanding," though, according to a senior. "If you attend, prepare to work hard." Students say the "intense" academic pressure is largely "self-induced," but there's no denying its existence at this "competitive" school. "The workload in the lower level classes isn't too bad," explains an astronomy and physics major, "but once you hit the upper-level—woosh!— there goes any hope of having a life this semester." Financial aid is "good" and "because this is a small liberal arts college, the administration runs smoothly," says a senior. Other students see ample room for improvement on the administrative front, especially when it comes to registration. Relatively large introductory classes can be a problem as well.

### Life
"It's really inspiring to see so many women in such a supportive atmosphere," says a junior here. Smith's "beautiful," safe campus offers a strong "sense of community," good grub, and terrific dorms (which are actually large houses). "The houses are like sororities," complete with "living rooms with grand pianos, an in-house dining room," and "the option to live in the same house all four years." About the only downside is the difficulty in "making a friend outside of one's house." On campus, "there is a wide range of things to do, and it's easy to get involved in clubs and activities even if you just want to experiment," explains a first-year student. "You can go from pianist to fencer to actor to astronomer." Also, "gay rights activism is very big" at Smith, and "the lesbian social scene" is buzzing. The "low key" social scene involves "going to coffee shops and doing things in town with friends," explains a sophomore. Off campus, Northampton is "a really cool college town." On weekends, "you can catch the bus to Amherst or U Mass and party with the boys," or "play Nintendo all night." Smith's all-female arrangement can be both a blessing and a curse: "My friends and I fondly refer to it as 'Girl Town.' We are all sort of stuck in a bubble here, and sometimes we forget how to interact with men." A sophomore counters: "People think that because the school is not coed, we miss out on a 'normal' college experience. What they don't realize is that while we may miss part of the 'normal' college experience, we get to experience things they will miss at a coed school."

### Student Body
"The world as a whole seems to think that everyone who goes to Smith is a radical, lesbian, feminist, pagan, warrior girl," speculates a sophomore. "This is not the case." However, "everyone has a cause," and "people with conservative views may feel or may be made to feel uncomfortable here." A left winger confesses that "elitist attitudes" often prevail on campus, and students criticize their peers for being "far too politically correct." Beyond politics, Smithees describe themselves as "fabulous, extremely intelligent, confident, beautiful," "open-minded young women" who have a "tendency to complain about how much work they have to do" as well as "the lack of guys." They are also "very grade-oriented and very perfectionistic" and "busy to a fault." The women here are also "very diverse," though "students from different races don't interact much" and cliques are commonplace. "People at Smith suck until you find your groove, but when you find it, life becomes bliss." Upon graduation, an "incredible alumni network" awaits new grads in virtually every field.

FINANCIAL AID: 413-585-2530 • E-MAIL: ADMISSIONS@SMITH.EDU • WEBSITE: WWW.SMITH.EDU

## ADMISSIONS

*Very important* academic and nonacademic factors considered by the admissions committee include secondary school record. *Important* factors considered include; standardized test scores, recommendations, character/personal qualities, class rank, extracurricular activities, interview, and talent/ability. *Other* factors considered include alumni/ae relation, essays, volunteer work, and work experience. Factors *not* considered include geography, minority status, religious affiliation/commitment, and state residency. SAT I or ACT required; SAT II recommended. TOEFL required of all international applicants. *High school units required/recommended:* 15 total recommended; 4 English recommended, 3 math recommended, 3 science recommended, 3 science lab recommended, 3 foreign language recommended, 2 history recommended.

### The Inside Word

Don't be fooled by the relatively high acceptance rate at Smith (or at other top women's colleges). The applicant pool here is small and highly self-selected, and it's fairly tough to get admitted. Only women who have taken the most challenging course loads in high school and achieved at a superior level will be competitive.

## FINANCIAL AID

*Students should submit:* FAFSA, institution's own financial aid form, CSS/Financial Aid PROFILE, state aid form, noncustodial (divorced/separated) parent's statement, and business/farm supplement. Regular filing deadline is February 1. The Princeton Review suggests that all financial aid forms be submitted as soon as possible after January 1. *Need-based scholarships/grants offered:* Pell, SEOG, state scholarships/grants, and the school's own gift aid. *Loan aid offered:* Direct Subsidized Stafford, Direct Unsubsidized Stafford, FFEL PLUS, Federal Perkins, and college/university loans from institutional funds. Institutional employment available. Federal Work-Study Program available. Applicants will be notified of awards with their decision letter. Off-campus job opportunities are excellent.

## FROM THE ADMISSIONS OFFICE

"Smith students choose from 1,000 courses in more than 50 areas of study. There are no specific course requirements outside the major; students meet individually with faculty advisers to plan a balanced curriculum. Smith programs offer unique opportunities, including the chance to study abroad, or at another college in the United States, and to learn firsthand about the federal government. The Ada Comstock Scholars Program encourages women beyond the traditional age to return to college and complete their undergraduate studies. Smith is located in the scenic Connecticut River valley of western Massachusetts near a number of other outstanding educational institutions. Through the Five College Consortium, Smith, Amherst, Hampshire, and Mount Holyoke colleges and the University of Massachusetts enrich their academic, social, and cultural offerings by means of joint faculty appointments, joint courses, student and faculty exchanges, shared facilities, and other cooperative arrangements."

### ADMISSIONS

| | |
|---|---:|
| **Admissions Rating** | **95** |
| # of applicants | 3,017 |
| % of applicants accepted | 53 |
| % of acceptees attending | 39 |
| # accepting a place on wait list | 331 |
| # of early decision applicants | 190 |
| % accepted early decision | 71 |

#### FRESHMAN PROFILE

| | |
|---|---:|
| Range SAT Verbal | 580-710 |
| Average SAT Verbal | 650 |
| Range SAT Math | 570-668 |
| Average SAT Math | 620 |
| Range ACT Composite | 25-30 |
| Minimum TOEFL | 600 |
| Average HS GPA | 3.8 |
| % graduated top 10% of class | 59 |
| % graduated top 25% of class | 90 |
| % graduated top 50% of class | 99 |

#### DEADLINES

| | |
|---|---:|
| Early decision | 11/15 & 1/1 |
| ED notification | 12/15 & 1/26 |
| Regular admission | 1/15 |
| Regular notification | 4/1 |
| Nonfall registration? | yes |
| | (not for first year) |

#### APPLICANTS ALSO LOOK AT

**AND OFTEN PREFER**
Wellesley, Brown
Swarthmore
Amherst

**AND SOMETIMES PREFER**
Bryn Mawr
Vassar, Barnard
Wesleyan U.

**AND RARELY PREFER**
Tufts
Mount Holyoke
Boston U.

### FINANCIAL FACTS

| | |
|---|---:|
| **Financial Aid Rating** | **74** |
| Tuition | $24,550 |
| Room & board | $8,560 |
| Books and supplies | $1,550 |
| Required fees | $192 |
| % frosh receiving aid | 57 |
| % undergrads receiving aid | 59 |
| Avg frosh grant | $19,750 |
| Avg frosh loan | $2,732 |

# SONOMA STATE UNIVERSITY

1801 EAST COTATI AVENUE, ROHNERT PARK, CA 94928 • ADMISSIONS: 707-664-2778 • FAX: 707-664-2060

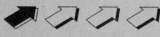
## STUDENTS SPEAK OUT

### Academics

Like other state universities, Sonoma State University offers students a broad and challenging education at a bargain rate. Unlike most state schools, however, Sonoma also provides an intimate setting, complete with small classes and attentive, accessible professors. Students describe Sonoma State as "a small school that is personable. If you want to be involved, there are great opportunities to do so." Its six divisions—the Schools of Arts and Humanities, Business and Economics, Extended Education, Natural Sciences, and Social Sciences—each benefit from what one student describes as "professors who are very willing to meet with the students outside of class. "To me this is especially helpful. I've been able to get to know some professors as people instead of just the student/teacher relationship." Adds another student, "Your professors are always there for you, and since classes are smaller, you get a better understanding of the topics you are studying." Although undergraduates complain that "the administrators are not as student-oriented as they should be," they also are quite happy with most administrative aspects of the school, reporting that "having phone registration makes everyone's life easier" and that "the computer labs and all the offices have excellent Macs. There is a lot of focus on computers here." Business and psychology are the most popular majors here; the departments of environmental studies, English, and the Hutchins School of Liberal Studies are also big draws.

### Life

Sonoma State is primarily a commuter campus, and like most such schools, "there is never anything to do on weekends because everybody leaves for home." However, Sonoma's administration has put in place a clear housing initiative, accomodating freshmen and most sophomores this year. Nevertheless, on-campus parties are curtailed not only by the lack of resident upperclassmen but also by tough administration regulations. Complains one student, "The administration is too strict about drinking on campus. Lighten up!" Apartments near campus are difficult to find; those lucky few who have found them report that "life improves once you turn 21. Greek life provides lots of entertainment." However, in fall 2000, new apartments opened, providing housing for 2,000 students and an opportunity to make a more cohesive community. Intramural sports are popular with a number of students, as are Sonoma's intercollegiate sports teams; the five men's and seven women's varsity teams compete in Division II of the NCAA. Outdoor activities such as hiking are also popular. Students give their hometown poor grades, telling us that "I wish the town of Rohnert Park would be more accepting of the fact that it's a college town." With San Francisco about 50 miles away, undergrads with cars and gas money can head for the big city when they need to blow off steam.

### Student Body

Sonoma State is a mixed bag of part-timers and commuters, nontraditional and traditional students. But one student writes, "It's hard to meet students if you're a commuter and don't live in the dorms, although joining clubs helps." On the bright side, students are "very friendly. Almost everybody that walks by smiles and says 'hi' to you." They are, unfortunately, too busy to stop or say much else. Sonoma attracts large Asian American, Chicano, and Latino populations.

FINANCIAL AID: 707-664-2389 • E-MAIL: ADMITME@SONOMA.EDU • WEBSITE: WWW.SONOMA.EDU

## ADMISSIONS

*Very important* academic and nonacademic factors considered by the admissions committee include secondary school record and standardized test scores. *Other* factors considered include geography, talent/ability, family educational and economic background, and state residency. Factors *not* considered include alumni/ae relation, character/personal qualities, essays, extracurricular activities, interview, recommendations, religious affiliation/commitment, volunteer work, and work experience. SAT I or ACT required. TOEFL required of all international applicants. High school diploma is required and GED is accepted. *High school units required/recommended:* 16 total required; 4 English required, 3 math required, 2 science required, 1 science lab required, 2 foreign language required, 1 history required, 3 elective required.

### The Inside Word

Admission by formula is the rule at Sonoma State, consistent with its role in the Cal State system. Plug in to the formula and sign up for class—there's no mystery to candidate selection here. Solid courses, grades, and test scores lead the way into the freshman class.

## FINANCIAL AID

*Students must submit:* FAFSA. The Princeton Review suggests that all financial aid forms be submitted as soon as possible after January 1. *Need- and merit-based scholarships/grants offered:* Pell, SEOG, state scholarships/grants, private scholarships, and the school's own gift aid. *Loan aid offered:* Direct Subsidized Stafford, Direct Unsubsidized Stafford, Direct PLUS, and Federal Perkins. Institutional employment available. Federal Work-Study Program available. Applicants will be notified of awards on a rolling basis beginning on or about April 15. Off-campus job opportunities are good.

## FROM THE ADMISSIONS OFFICE

"Sonoma State University occupies 275 acres in the beautiful wine country of Sonoma County, in northern California. Located at the foot of the Sonoma hills, the campus is an hour's drive north of San Francisco and centrally located between the Pacific Ocean to the west and the wine country to the north and east. SSU is deeply committed to the teaching of the liberal arts and sciences. The campus has earned a national reputation as a leader in integrating the use of technology into its curriculum. Within its 32 academic departments, SSU awards bachelor's degrees in 66 areas of specialization and master's degrees in 22 areas. In addition, the university offers a joint master's degree in mathematics with San Francisco State University. The campus ushered in the 21st century with the opening of a new library and technology center, the Jean and Charles Schulz Information Center."

### ADMISSIONS

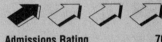

| | |
|---|---|
| Admissions Rating | 70 |
| # of applicants | 4,504 |
| % of applicants accepted | 92 |
| % of acceptees attending | 27 |

#### FRESHMAN PROFILE

| | |
|---|---|
| Range SAT Verbal | 460-570 |
| Average SAT Verbal | 513 |
| Range SAT Math | 460-570 |
| Average SAT Math | 514 |
| Minimum TOEFL | 500 |
| Average HS GPA | 3.2 |
| % graduated top 10% of class | 10 |
| % graduated top 25% of class | 40 |
| % graduated top 50% of class | 78 |

#### DEADLINES

| | |
|---|---|
| Priority admission deadline | 12/31 |
| Regular admission | 1/31 |
| Nonfall registration? | yes |

### FINANCIAL FACTS

| | |
|---|---|
| Financial Aid Rating | 78 |
| Out-of-state tuition | $7,910 |
| Room & board | $7,011 |
| Books and supplies | $846 |
| Required fees | $2,006 |
| % frosh receiving aid | 47 |
| % undergrads receiving aid | 43 |
| Avg frosh grant | $1,500 |
| Avg frosh loan | $2,500 |

# SOUTHERN METHODIST UNIVERSITY

PO Box 750296, Dallas, TX 75275-0296 • Admissions: 214-768-2058 • Fax: 214-768-2507

## CAMPUS LIFE

| Quality of Life Rating | 87 |
|---|---|
| Type of school | private |
| Affiliation | Methodist |
| Environment | suburban |

### STUDENTS

| | |
|---|---|
| Total undergrad enrollment | 5,662 |
| % male/female | 45/55 |
| % from out of state | 35 |
| % from public high school | 71 |
| % live on campus | 48 |
| % in (# of) fraternities | 37 (13) |
| % in (# of) sororities | 38 (12) |
| % African American | 7 |
| % Asian | 6 |
| % Caucasian | 73 |
| % Hispanic | 8 |
| % Native American | 1 |
| % international | 3 |
| # of countries represented | 100 |

### SURVEY SAYS . . .

*Beautiful campus*
*Students love Dallas, TX*
*Great off-campus food*
*Campus easy to get around*
*Great computer facilities*
*Student publications are ignored*
*Students aren't religious*
*Lousy food on campus*

## ACADEMICS

| Academic Rating | 81 |
|---|---|
| Calendar | semester |
| Student/faculty ratio | 11:1 |
| Profs interesting rating | 86 |
| Profs accessible rating | 93 |
| Avg lab size | 10-19 students |
| Avg reg class size | 10-19 students |

### MOST POPULAR MAJORS
finance
psychology
advertising

## STUDENTS SPEAK OUT

### Academics

Many students tell us they chose Southern Methodist because of its "prestigious academics." SMU's strong suits are business and management, as well as other pre-professional degrees. The nationally renowned performing arts programs in the Meadows School (crows one acting student, "In the theater school, we are taught by professionals who are usually full-time theater pros") and liberal arts studies are also very well regarded. For many, SMU's faculty is the biggest draw. Explains one undergrad, "SMU profs bend over backwards to help out their students. SMU is not so big, but it's not so small to become a gossip mill either. It's just the right size." Students agree that, at SMU, "you make your academic life as hard as you want it to be—you can coast through four years and party hard, or make it a stressful, intense experience." Most seem to opt for the former—despite the first-rate academic programs, more than half of the students we surveyed report that they spend fewer than three hours a day studying outside of class. For those wishing to broaden their experience in foreign lands, "SMU . . . has an amazing program for studying abroad."

### Life

Sure, "Dallas is a great town," with lots of "athletic events, movies, clubs, and great restaurants," but "Greek life is a big thing" at SMU. A freshman artist says that "if you don't want to be in a frat/sorority, don't bother coming to this school. You would likely be miserable." As at most frat-dominated universities (and college in general), drinking is extremely popular. Notes one student, "People party . . . and they party. If there isn't alcohol there, there aren't any students, either." Fortunately, peer pressure is not a problem; as one student puts it, "There is a lot of heavy drinking here and heavy partying. However, people are not looked down upon for not drinking or partaking in any vices." Points out one student, "You can always find a group to hang out with that shares common interests." Also, "there are more activities, guest speakers, and seminars available (on campus) than I can attend." Volunteerism is one of the most popular constructive pursuits among SMU students; almost half are involved in a variety of activities that provide support for their less fortunate neighbors in urban Dallas and throughout the United States. Students look forward to game day even though "the football is awful" because "more people tailgate than actually go to games."

### Student Body

The popular stereotype of SMU undergrads is that "SMU = Southern Millionaire's University." Students agree that "there is a definite upper-class-Dallas face, and with the similar makeup, clothing, and hair, the students all look the same. The minority students are definitely marginalized." They are also quick to point out, however, that "there are many who fit the stereotype . . . but there are also many who don't, so unless you're allergic to those who do, you can find your own niche and be yourself." Finding your niche is the key to happiness here: "There are bubbles: the Greek bubble, the arts bubble, the minority bubble, etc. They rarely interact and yet things are comfortable. You find your niche and stick to it." In general, the "student body is apathetic . . . anything that does not pertain to the Greek scene or Dallas life is foreign on campus." However, "there are tiny numbers of politically active people and intellectuals, but the school environment stifles that type of thing."

FINANCIAL AID: 214-768-3417 • E-MAIL: UGADMISSION@SMU.EDU • WEBSITE: WWW.SMU.EDU

## ADMISSIONS

*Very important* academic and nonacademic factors considered by the admissions committee include secondary school record. *Important* factors considered include class rank, extracurricular activities, recommendations, and standardized test scores. *Other* factors considered include character/personal qualities, essays, interview, minority status, talent/ability, volunteer work, and work experience. Factors *not* considered include minority status, alumni/ae relation, geography, religious affiliation/commitment, and state residency. SAT I or ACT required. TOEFL required of all international applicants. High school diploma is required and GED is accepted. *High school units required/recommended:* 15 total recommended; 4 English recommended, 3 math recommended, 3 science recommended, 2 science lab recommended, 2 foreign language recommended, 3 social studies recommended. *The admissions office says:* "No one item is given precedence over another. The entire application package is considered for acceptance at Southern Methodist University. Though an interview is optional, it is always recommended."

### The Inside Word

SMU's School of the Arts is one of the best in the country, and applicants face a very competitive admissions process. The university in general is not quite as selective, but the expectations are high enough so that average students with academic inconsistencies or weak test scores can expect to encounter a rocky road to admission.

## FINANCIAL AID

*Students should submit:* FAFSA. The Princeton Review suggests that all financial aid forms be submitted as soon as possible after January 1. *Need-based scholarships/grants offered:* Pell, SEOG, state scholarships/grants, private scholarships, and the school's own gift aid. *Loan aid offered:* Direct Subsidized Stafford, Direct Unsubsidized Stafford, Direct PLUS, Federal Perkins, state, and college/university loans from institutional funds. Institutional employment available. Federal Work-Study Program available. Applicants will be notified of awards on a rolling basis beginning on or about March 15. Off-campus job opportunities are excellent.

## FROM THE ADMISSIONS OFFICE

"As a private, comprehensive university enriched by its United Methodist heritage and its partnership with the Dallas Metroplex, SMU seeks to enhance the intellectual, cultural, technical, ethical, and social development of a diverse student body. SMU offers undergraduate programs centered on the liberal arts; excellent graduate, professional, and continuing education programs; and abundant opportunities for access to faculty in small classes, research experience, international study, leadership development, and off-campus service and internships. SMU comprises six degree-granting schools: Dedman College of Humanities and Sciences, Meadows School of the Arts, Edwin L. Cox School of Business, the School of Engineering and Applied Science, the School of Law, and Perkins School of Theology. SMU is nonsectarian in its teaching and committed to the values of academic freedom and open inquiry."

## ADMISSIONS

| | |
|---|---|
| **Admissions Rating** | **81** |
| # of applicants | 4,577 |
| % of applicants accepted | 82 |
| % of acceptees attending | 34 |
| # accepting a place on wait list | 107 |
| % admitted from wait list | 32 |

### FRESHMAN PROFILE

| | |
|---|---|
| Range SAT Verbal | 520-630 |
| Range SAT Math | 530-640 |
| Range ACT Composite | 22-27 |
| Minimum TOEFL | 550 |
| Average HS GPA | 3.2 |
| % graduated top 10% of class | 31 |
| % graduated top 25% of class | 61 |
| % graduated top 50% of class | 88 |

### DEADLINES

| | |
|---|---|
| Regular admission | 1/15 |
| Regular notification | 3/15 |
| Nonfall registration? | yes |

### APPLICANTS ALSO LOOK AT
**AND OFTEN PREFER**
Northwestern U.
Georgetown U.
**AND SOMETIMES PREFER**
Tulane
Emory
U. Texas—Austin
Rhodes
Vanderbilt
**AND RARELY PREFER**
TCU
Pepperdine
Baylor
U. Southern Cal

### FINANCIAL FACTS

| | |
|---|---|
| **Financial Aid Rating** | **86** |
| Tuition | $17,406 |
| Room & board | $7,177 |
| Books and supplies | $576 |
| Required fees | $2,214 |
| % frosh receiving aid | 35 |
| % undergrads receiving aid | 47 |
| Avg frosh grant | $12,870 |
| Avg frosh loan | $3,768 |

# SOUTHWESTERN UNIVERSITY

ADMISSIONS OFFICE, PO BOX 770, GEORGETOWN, TX 78627-0770 • ADMISSIONS: 512-863-1200 • FAX: 512-863-9601

## CAMPUS LIFE

| Quality of Life Rating | 78 |
| --- | --- |
| Type of school | private |
| Affiliation | Methodist |
| Environment | suburban |

### STUDENTS

| | |
| --- | --- |
| Total undergrad enrollment | 1,309 |
| % male/female | 42/58 |
| % from out of state | 7 |
| % from public high school | 83 |
| % live on campus | 81 |
| % in (# of) fraternities | 34 (4) |
| % in (# of) sororities | 36 (4) |
| % African American | 2 |
| % Asian | 3 |
| % Caucasian | 82 |
| % Hispanic | 13 |
| # of countries represented | 10 |

### SURVEY SAYS . . .
Theater is hot
Frats and sororities dominate social
scene
No one cheats
Athletic facilities are great
Registration is a pain
Intercollegiate sports unpopular or
nonexistent
Class discussions encouraged
Lousy off-campus food

## ACADEMICS

| Academic Rating | 84 |
| --- | --- |
| Calendar | semester |
| Student/faculty ratio | 11:1 |
| Profs interesting rating | 88 |
| Profs accessible rating | 88 |
| % profs teaching UG courses | 100 |
| Avg lab size | under 10 students |
| Avg reg class size | 10-19 students |

### MOST POPULAR MAJORS
biology
business
psychology

## STUDENTS SPEAK OUT

### Academics

Here's "something you wouldn't expect in a little Texas town: A well-rounded liberal arts school" with "demanding" academics, a "very writing intensive" core curriculum, and "an excellent opportunity to get" a "fabulous education." That's Southwestern University in a nutshell, where "small classes and a lot of one-on-one attention" are the norm. Students praise SU's "excellent" study-abroad programs (nearly a third of the students here spend time overseas) and the Brown Symposium, a two-day series of seminars during spring semester for which classes are suspended and scholars from around the world deliver lectures and lead discussions. But SU students save their greatest praise for their teachers, whom they rank among the most "incredible" in the nation. The "exceptional" and "very approachable" profs at SU are "delighted to be here and bend over backwards to make their subject areas interesting." There are no teaching assistants at SU, and "unlike at big schools, our professors can teach," trumpets a senior. "They are concerned about you at your core—where you are, where you have been, and where you want to go." Unfortunately, the "barbaric" registration system is not nearly as "personable" as the faculty. The administration does a pretty good job otherwise, though it can be somewhat "too paternal" at times, and "you're never quite sure what horrors they're concocting" beneath "their really big smiles."

### Life

"Social life revolves around Greek life," explains one student. "Frats throw cool parties on weekends," and "drinking, drugs, and other rebellious activities" are the highlights of these soirees. After fraternity parties, the most popular activity is "rolling," a.k.a. "driving down the Georgetown country roads very slowly and drinking lots." We're not kidding. Thankfully, drivers remain sober. On campus, the "beautiful" facilities are very reminiscent of "a country club." The "dorms could use improvement," but "the sofas are nice and the fireplace" in the new campus center "adds that special touch of home." Students say life here is "really laid-back," but it can be "routine" and "predictable" at times. "There's pretty much a student organization for everyone," though, and "Student Activities sponsors a lot of activities" from "swing dancing" to "kick boxing." "Dances, bands, comedy shows," and "frequent" trips to Wal-Mart also keep students entertained. There are "lots of opportunities for intellectual, informal, enlightening, and interesting" discussions, too. Intramurals and "outdoor activities are popular" as well, but school spirit is somewhat lacking. When "weekends here are slow and empty," students with cars—highly recommended!—often head to the great American college town of Austin for "partying," "concerts," and entertainment. It's anywhere from 15 to 30 minutes away, depending on whom you talk to.

### Student Body

SU students are "welcoming" and "certainly friendly." They are "very intelligent people" who "have a lot to offer" and are "overachievers in academics and usually highly involved in organizations." They "all mesh well." They are, however, "often given to complaining." They are also "rich, inconsiderate," and "sheltered," and "too many cannot function outside of the classroom." "When we leave campus, things like culture and policemen frighten us," reports a sophomore. "Southwestern is a Never-Never Land where nothing is real." Also on a negative note, a noticeable contingent of SU students "take refuge in the comforting arms of recreational drug use," especially "when confronted with academic pressures." Politically, some are "too conservative" while others are "too damn liberal." Most seem to be middle-of-the-road, which probably makes them liberal by Texas standards, but in any case, "both radicals and moderates" seem to "coexist happily." There is a "a general sense of camaraderie," even though it is slightly of the "elitist" variety. "We all like our tight community and want it to stay that way," says a sophomore.

FINANCIAL AID: 512-863-1259 • E-MAIL: ADMISSION@SOUTHWESTERN.EDU • WEBSITE: WWW.SOUTHWESTERN.EDU

## ADMISSIONS

*Very important* academic and nonacademic factors considered by the admissions committee include secondary school record. *Important* factors considered include character/personal qualities, class rank, essays, recommendations, standardized test scores, and talent/ability. *Other* factors considered include alumni/ae relation, extracurricular activities, geography, interview, volunteer work, and work experience. Factors *not* considered include religious affiliation/commitment and state residency. SAT I or ACT required. TOEFL required of all international applicants. High school diploma is required and GED is accepted. *High school units required/recommended:* 16 total required; 4 English required, 4 math required, 2 science required, 3 science recommended, 2 foreign language required, 3 foreign language recommended, 3 social studies required, 2 elective required. *The admissions office says:* "[Our admissions process includes] a participatory and democratic review process. All decisions involve agreement from at least two readers."

### The Inside Word

Southwestern is one of the best "sleepers" in the nation. Admissions standards are high, but they would be even more so if more people knew of this place. Academic excellence abounds, the administration is earnest and helpful, and the school is beginning to attract national recognition. If you could thrive in a small-town, close-knit environment, Southwestern definitely deserves a look.

## FINANCIAL AID

The Princeton Review suggests that all financial aid forms be submitted as soon as possible after January 1. Institutional employment available. Federal Work-Study Program available. Off-campus job opportunities are good.

## FROM THE ADMISSIONS OFFICE

"On the outskirts of Texas's vibrant capital city of Austin in historic Georgetown lies Southwestern University, the state's oldest national liberal arts college. At Southwestern, we are committed to helping you achieve success in whatever way you define it. Students work closely with professors to envision their greatest goals and together find out the best ways to reach their intellectual, professional, and personal dreams. Experimental learning, Internships, study abroad, and a recommended four-year career development track lead to high acceptance rates in prestigious graduate and professional schools and careers right out of college. Southwestern professors not only know their students' names but students know each other too, and the result is a place that is intellectually rigorous but always friendly and nurturing. Southwestern is today what it always has been: a small liberal arts college with a Texas accent, dedicated to giving its students the strengths they need to develop fulfilling lives."

## ADMISSIONS

| | |
|---|---|
| Admissions Rating | 83 |
| # of applicants | 1,562 |
| % of applicants accepted | 59 |
| % of acceptees attending | 39 |
| # accepting a place on wait list | 48 |
| % admitted from wait list | 8 |
| # of early decision applicants | 177 |
| % accepted early decision | 72 |

### FRESHMAN PROFILE

| | |
|---|---|
| Range SAT Verbal | 570-660 |
| Average SAT Verbal | 617 |
| Range SAT Math | 570-670 |
| Average SAT Math | 619 |
| Range ACT Composite | 24-29 |
| Average ACT Composite | 26 |
| Minimum TOEFL | 570 |
| Average HS GPA | 3.5 |
| % graduated top 10% of class | 56 |
| % graduated top 25% of class | 86 |
| % graduated top 50% of class | 99 |

### DEADLINES

| | |
|---|---|
| Early decision | 11/1 |
| Early decision notification | 12/1 |
| Priority admission deadline | 1/15 |
| Regular admission | 2/15 |
| Regular notification | 4/1 |

### APPLICANTS ALSO LOOK AT

**AND OFTEN PREFER**
Rice
Trinity U.

**AND SOMETIMES PREFER**
Texas A&M
U. Texas—Austin
Rhodes
Tulane
Vanderbilt

**AND RARELY PREFER**
Austin, Baylor
SMU, TCU

### FINANCIAL FACTS

| | |
|---|---|
| Financial Aid Rating | 83 |
| Tuition | $15,750 |
| Room & board | $5,560 |
| Books and supplies | $700 |
| % frosh receiving aid | 55 |
| % undergrads receiving aid | 55 |
| Avg frosh grant | $13,754 |
| Avg frosh loan | $3,255 |

# Spelman College

350 SPELMAN LANE, SOUTH WEST, ATLANTA, GA 30314 • ADMISSIONS: 800-982-2411 • FAX: 404-215-7788

## CAMPUS LIFE

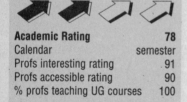

**Quality of Life Rating** **80**
Type of school | private
Affiliation | none
Environment | urban

### STUDENTS
Total undergrad enrollment | 1,899
% from out of state | 75
% from public high school | 84
% live on campus | 62
% in (# of) sororities | 1 (4)
% African American | 100
% international | 3
# of countries represented | 29

### SURVEY SAYS . . .
*Theater is hot*
*Student publications are ignored*
*Students don't get along with local community*
*Class discussions are rare*
*High cost of living*
*Very little beer drinking*
*Lab facilities are great*
*Library needs improving*
*Very little hard liquor*
*Athletic facilities need improving*

## ACADEMICS

**Academic Rating** **78**
Calendar | semester
Profs interesting rating | 91
Profs accessible rating | 90
% profs teaching UG courses | 100

### MOST POPULAR MAJORS
psychology
biology
English

## STUDENTS SPEAK OUT
### Academics

One of the nation's preeminent historically black colleges, Spelman College is also one of the two remaining all-women's HBCUs in the country. This place is steeped in tradition, with long legacies of family members among the alumnae; many of the women we surveyed express sentiments similar to the sophomore who tells us she "wanted to go since she was five years old." Virtually all the students who choose Spelman do so for the opportunity to be surrounded by others like themselves: female, black, bright, and highly motivated. "Spelman is a wonderful academic environment. There is a standard of excellence." Pre-professional majors—computer science, pre-med, pre-law, and pre-business—are most popular with Spelman women, but all students receive a well-rounded education in communication skills, science, math, social science, fine arts, and literature because of a rigorous core curriculum. Of their professors, students note that "most here have thorough command of their disciplines and are concerned with the students having a good grasp of information presented in the classroom. The academic experience is a humbling one for the average student here—you have to get beyond 'making the grade.'" "I love the fact that I have many brilliant black professors. It does wonders for your self-esteem when your professors look just like you." Academics and facilities at the college have been given a boost by a recent capital campaign that raised $114 million, the most successful fund-raising effort by an HBCU, and the Southern Education Foundation's Gateway 21 Project to improve technology, which will insure that students are wired to the information superhighway. "Future students have a lot to look forward to." Academic options also include the ability to take courses at all-male Morehouse College, just across the street. "The administration is very friendly and personable" and "nurturing." Spelman is also among the best buys in the nation.

### Life

"Atlanta is a great city for young black people," "a cultural center." This not only sums up the attitudes of students at Spelman, but also of those at every area HBCU. Another Spelman student reports that "Atlanta is a big city and there is always something to do. "A drawback common to many urban campuses is that "any weirdo can get on our campus far too easily," though students are of mixed opinions in this regard: "The AUC is a safe haven of sorts. In the Atlanta University Center [a shared higher education complex that encompasses Spelman and five other colleges, including Morehouse, Clark Atlanta University, and Morris Brown College], there are so many students that many different activities are provided for our entertainment and fun." Most students feel that the "social atmosphere is very inviting." "Many people enjoy going over to Morehouse, an all-male school just across the street." Greek parties at Spelman and Morehouse are generally big events. Also popular are extracurricular clubs, particularly those involved with community service and leadership organizations. Students complain that athletic facilities are poor, which might explain students' lack of interest in intercollegiate and intramural sports. Concludes one woman: "I would recommend Spelman College to any young lady who wants to get the full experience of college life."

### Student Body

"The girls at Spelman are like a family," one student explained. "I feel like I have 1,000 sisters." "There are good people here"; and "students get along with each other remarkably well" and "are very supportive of each other." The typical Spelman student is dedicated to career success. She is also religious (church services are a regular part of most students' lives), socially conservative, and politically liberal but not activist. Explains one senior: "It has been my experience that Spelman students are not very politically minded, i.e., not concerned with the ramifications of their actions and beliefs outside the microcosm of Spelman."

FINANCIAL AID: 404-681-3643 • E-MAIL: ADMISS@SPELMAN.EDU • WEBSITE: WWW.SPELMAN.EDU

## ADMISSIONS

SAT I or ACT required. High school diploma is required and GED is accepted. *High school units required/recommended:* 17 total required; 24 total recommended; 4 English required, 2 math required, 4 math recommended, 2 science required, 3 science recommended, 1 science lab required, 2 foreign language required, 4 foreign language recommended, 1 social studies required, 2 social studies recommended, 2 history required, 3 elective required. *The admissions office says:* "Alumnae relations receive special consideration."

### The Inside Word

No historically black college in the country has a more competitive admissions process than Spelman, and on top of this, application totals were up 25 percent last season. Successful candidates show strong academic records with challenging course loads and solid grades. Applicant evaluation here is very personal; it is quite important to show depth of character and social consciousness.

## FINANCIAL AID

The Princeton Review suggests that all financial aid forms be submitted as soon as possible after January 1. *Need-based scholarships/grants offered:* Pell, SEOG, state scholarships/grants, private scholarships, the school's own gift aid, and Federal Nursing. *Loan aid offered:* FFEL Subsidized Stafford, FFEL Unsubsidized Stafford, FFEL PLUS, Federal Perkins, and Federal Nursing. Institutional employment available. Federal Work-Study Program available. Off-campus job opportunities are fair.

## FROM THE ADMISSIONS OFFICE

"As an outstanding historically black college for women, Spelman strives for academic excellence in liberal education. This predominantly residential private college provides students with an academic climate conducive to the full development of their intellectual and leadership potential. The college is a member of the Atlanta University Center consortium, and Spelman students enjoy the benefits of a small college while having access to the resources of the other five participating institutions. The purpose extends beyond intellectual development and professional career preparation of students. It seeks to develop the total person. The college provides an academic and social environment that strengthens those qualities that enable women to be self-confident as well as culturally and spiritually enriched. This environment attempts to instill in students both an appreciation for the multicultural communities of the world and a sense of responsibility for bringing about positive change in those communities."

## ADMISSIONS

| Admissions Rating | 82 |
|---|---|

### FRESHMAN PROFILE

| | |
|---|---|
| Range SAT Verbal | 500-600 |
| Average SAT Verbal | 549 |
| Range SAT Math | 500-599 |
| Average SAT Math | 524 |
| Range ACT Composite | 21-24 |
| Average ACT Composite | 22 |
| Minimum TOEFL | 500 |
| Average HS GPA | 3.1 |

### DEADLINES

| | |
|---|---|
| Early decision | 11/15 |
| Early decision notification | 12/31 |
| Regular admission | 2/1 |
| Regular notification | 4/1 |
| Nonfall registration? | yes |

### APPLICANTS ALSO LOOK AT
**AND OFTEN PREFER**
Georgia Tech.
**AND SOMETIMES PREFER**
Howard
Hampton
Clark Atlanta
Tuskegee
Florida A&M
**AND RARELY PREFER**
U. Maryland—College Park
Emory
U. Georgia

### FINANCIAL FACTS

| Financial Aid Rating | 74 |
|---|---|
| Tuition | $9,250 |
| Room & board | $6,560 |
| Books and supplies | $750 |
| Required fees | $1,600 |

# STANFORD UNIVERSITY

520 LASUEN MALL, OLD UNION 232, STANFORD, CA 94305-3005 • ADMISSIONS: 650-723-2091 • FAX: 650-723-6050

## CAMPUS LIFE

**Quality of Life Rating** 87
Type of school private
Affiliation none
Environment suburban

### STUDENTS
Total undergrad enrollment 7,886
% male/female 48/52
% from out of state 51
% from public high school 65
% live on campus 91
% in (# of) fraternities 17 (15)
% in (# of) sororities 12 (8)
% African American 9
% Asian 26
% Caucasian 52
% Hispanic 11
% Native American 2
% international 4

### SURVEY SAYS . . .
*Registration is a breeze*
*Political activism is hot*
*Everyone loves the Cardinals*
*Student publications are popular*
*Ethnic diversity on campus*
*Students don't like Stanford, CA*
*(Almost) no one listens to college radio*
*Very little drug use*
*Students are cliquish*

## ACADEMICS

**Academic Rating** 91
Calendar quarter
Student/faculty ratio 7:1
Profs interesting rating 90
Profs accessible rating 89
Avg lab size 10-19 students
Avg reg class size 10-19 students

### MOST POPULAR MAJORS
biology
economics
computer science

## STUDENTS SPEAK OUT
### Academics
There are perhaps a half-dozen universities in the United States with *de facto* Ivy League status. Though not actually members of the vaunted Ivy League, these schools are recognized as equal in stature to Dartmouth, Princeton, and Yale; without question, Stanford University is among this elite group. Stanford students, however, enjoy several perks unknown to Ivy undergrads: a nationally ranked intercollegiate athletic program, an "almost carefree" atmosphere, and the truly hospitable California climate. Engineering, biology, physical science, and liberal arts programs are standouts among the uniformly strong academic disciplines here. Entering students encounter a mix of crowded required lecture classes ("You've got to be brave or a brown-noser to get to know your freshman-year profs," writes one student) and small seminars (through the recently added Freshman Seminars series), all of which rush by due to the quarterly academic schedule. Beyond freshman year, "the upper-division profs are more accessible and interested in getting to know you." Students tell us that "teaching is generally good" but deride the administration as "very image-oriented and politically conservative" and decry its fondness for "lots of bureaucracy and red tape." Overall, however, students are pleased with the academic experience here. Says one student, "You get what you pay (a lot) for."

### Life
When it comes to college living, Stanford students enjoy the best of both worlds: a sprawling, beautiful campus, and a world-class city (San Francisco) close by. Stanford's well-tended grounds are spectacular and expansive ("You definitely need a bike"), and its dorms are homey and attractive. Student complaints about the dorms center not on the buildings themselves but on many students' unwillingness to leave them. "Dorm life is central to a lot of people,"writes one student. Says another, "Social life is too campus-oriented." Undergrads also warn that "students are very busy all the time, which does make getting to know people more difficult. School comes before friends too often." On-campus activities include frequent guest speakers, an active Greek system, and plenty of sports, both intramural and intercollegiate (Stanford's tennis, football, basketball, and baseball programs, for example, have yielded a surprising number of professional athletes, and most of the school's Division I teams are competitive). They do not, however, include much dating; says one frustrated student, "My only complaints are that there's not much formal dating and it's hard to get off campus on the weekends without a car." Those with cars (or friends with cars) "sometimes go to San Francisco to experience a real atmosphere" and "to get away from the suburban snobbiness." Food on-campus is okay—off-campus is better ("there are great restaurants nearby") but pricey.

### Student Body
Stanford's status as a premier undergraduate institution, combined with the school's sizeable endowment, allow the university to draw from a wider range of applicants than can other similarly priced private schools. The result is an unusually diverse student body, although one in which minority students tend to keep to themselves. "I am comfortable with other students. I feel as if we are all on the same level, but most ethnic groups tend to stick together," reports one undergrad. Stanford's high-powered reputation also attracts "too many self-centered pre-professionals" derided by the large alternative/leftist undergrad population as "shallow." While complaining about one on-campus clique or another, many students are quick to add that "there are also some of the most amazing people I've met, and many are genuinely interesting in working for social change."

FINANCIAL AID: 650-723-3058 • E-MAIL: UNDERGRAD.ADMISSIONS@FORSYTHE.STANFORD.EDU • WEBSITE: WWW.STANFORD.EDU

## ADMISSIONS

*Very important* academic and nonacademic factors considered by the admissions committee include secondary school record, standardized test scores, and state residency. *Important* factors considered include geography. *Other* factors considered include alumni/ae relation, character/personal qualities, essays, extracurricular activities, minority status, recommendations, talent/ability, volunteer work, and work experience. Factors *not* considered include class rank, interview, and religious affiliation/commitment. SAT I or ACT required; SAT II recommended. TOEFL required of all international applicants. High school diploma is required and GED is accepted. *High school units required/recommended:* 16 total required; 4 English required, 3 math required, 3 science recommended, 3 science lab recommended, 3 foreign language recommended, 3 social studies recommended.

### The Inside Word

Not only is Stanford a pinnacle of academic excellence, but among the nation's ultra-selective universities it is one of the most compassionate toward students, both those who attend and those who aspire to attend. It isn't easy for an admissions staff to be warm and caring when your reputation is based in part on how many candidates you say "no" to. In our opinion, Stanford is the best of the best in this regard. Students who haven't devoted themselves to excellence in the same fashion that Stanford itself has are not likely to meet with success in gaining admission.

## FINANCIAL AID

*Students should submit:* FAFSA, CSS/Financial Aid PROFILE, and noncustodial (divorced/separated) parent's statement. The Princeton Review suggests that all financial aid forms be submitted as soon as possible after January 1. *Need-based scholarships/grants offered:* Pell, SEOG, state scholarships/grants, private scholarships, and the school's own gift aid. *Loan aid offered:* FFEL Subsidized Stafford, FFEL Unsubsidized Stafford, FFEL PLUS, Federal Perkins, and college/university loans from institutional funds. Institutional employment available. Federal Work-Study Program available. Applicants will be notified of awards on or about April 1. Off-campus job opportunities are good.

## FROM THE ADMISSIONS OFFICE

"Stanford University is an independent, coeducational, nondenominational, residential institution with goals of practicality, humanism, and excellence. It provides students an abundant and challenging environment and much personal and academic freedom. Located in a residential area, 40 minutes from San Francisco and the Pacific and four hours from the Sierra, Stanford's 8,800 acres consist of a central cluster of academic and residence buildings surrounded by rolling foothills and open space. The setting promotes an informal atmosphere and encourages use of the extensive academic, athletic, and fine arts facilities, which include an 85,000-seat football stadium, golf course, riding stables, and intimate theater, and one of the largest Rodin sculpture collections in the U.S. Academic facilities and features include a faculty of 1,600, more than 60 majors, many interdepartmental and innovative programs, advanced scientific equipment, a network of 25 libraries, plus the opportunity for all students to study at one of the nine Overseas Studies Centers."

### ADMISSIONS

| | |
|---|---|
| Admissions Rating | 98 |
| # of applicants | 18,363 |
| % of applicants accepted | 13 |
| % of acceptees attending | 66 |
| # accepting a place on wait list | 533 |
| % admitted from wait list | 6 |
| # of early decision applicants | 2087 |
| % accepted early decision | 23 |

### FRESHMAN PROFILE

| | |
|---|---|
| Range SAT Verbal | 670-770 |
| Average SAT Verbal | 715 |
| Range SAT Math | 690-790 |
| Average SAT Math | 717 |
| Range ACT Composite | 29-33 |
| Average ACT Composite | 31 |
| Minimum TOEFL | 600 |
| Average HS GPA | 3.9 |
| % graduated top 10% of class | 89 |
| % graduated top 25% of class | 98 |
| % graduated top 50% of class | 100 |

### DEADLINES

| | |
|---|---|
| Early decision | 11/1 |
| Early decision notification | 12/15 |
| Regular admission | 12/15 |

### APPLICANTS ALSO LOOK AT
**AND OFTEN PREFER**
Harvard
**AND SOMETIMES PREFER**
Duke
MIT
Caltech
Yale
Princeton
**AND RARELY PREFER**
UC—Berkeley
UCLA
Gonzaga
U. Virginia
Northwestern U.

### FINANCIAL FACTS

| | |
|---|---|
| Financial Aid Rating | 76 |
| Tuition | $24,441 |
| Room & board | $8,030 |
| Books and supplies | $1,080 |
| % frosh receiving aid | 42 |
| % undergrads receiving aid | 45 |

# STATE UNIVERSITY OF NEW YORK AT ALBANY

1400 WASHINGTON AVENUE, ALBANY, NY 12222 • ADMISSIONS: 518-442-5435 • FAX: 518-442-5383

## CAMPUS LIFE

**Quality of Life Rating**    **74**
Type of school    public
Affiliation    none
Environment    suburban

### STUDENTS

Total undergrad enrollment    11,780
% male/female    51/49
% from out of state    4
% live on campus    58
% in (# of) fraternities    15 (19)
% in (# of) sororities    15 (15)
% African American    9
% Asian    7
% Caucasian    66
% Hispanic    7
% international    1

### SURVEY SAYS . . .

*Class discussions are rare*
*Students don't get along with local community*
*Students are cliquish*
*Ethnic diversity on campus*
*Large classes*
*Unattractive campus*

## ACADEMICS

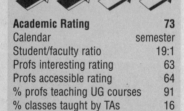

**Academic Rating**    **73**
Calendar    semester
Student/faculty ratio    19:1
Profs interesting rating    63
Profs accessible rating    64
% profs teaching UG courses    91
% classes taught by TAs    16
Avg lab size    10-19 students
Avg reg class size    20-29 students

### MOST POPULAR MAJORS
psychology
biology
English

## STUDENTS SPEAK OUT

### Academics

SUNY—Albany lures students with an affordable, quality education—an uncommon combination these days. The psychology, business, and English programs are popular. Unfortunately, these departments are often very large, which causes a number of problems. A senior business administration major voices, "Many of the professors are disinterested and lack substance. It just seems as though a substantial portion of the faculty doesn't care about the student body." SUNY—Albany is a research university. Accordingly, professors "don't want to teach and quite a few don't even know how to teach." Students also complain that classes are impersonal. "My name is my social security number," one junior writes, and in popular majors, class sizes do not decrease in upper-level courses. One senior theater major points out that "the [classes] tend to be different from department to department. Some are huge, cold, and impersonal, while others are small and extremely good about giving attention to the individual." Science students love the new research library, and many students rave about the design of the campus. "Everything is in a rectangular area so it's easy to get from class to class," writes one. The administration takes some serious lumps. "Class registration is preposterous. There are too many students and not enough classes or room in classes," one junior psychology major writes. Advisors do not fare well either. A disappointed psychology major comments, "It is nearly impossible to get an appointment with my advisor. He's always too busy." Another adds, "I don't know my advisor's name. I have never met [him] because I've always seen grad students or associates." Despite those disillusioned by little student-faculty interaction, for many students Albany "is a good school if you like big schools."

### Life

Students at SUNY—Albany know that studying is only one ingredient in the smorgasbord that is a rewarding college experience. "We're not a party school. We just have lots of parties, drinking, and drugs. Okay, I guess we are a party school," one senior psychology major admits. "Students care more about partying than studying. If they have to choose between studying or going out and getting drunk, the latter usually prevails." Another senior adds that students only make an effort "when it comes to getting drunk. They spend all night trying to accomplish that." On the upside, downtown Albany, though "always cold and gray," provides "many entertainment opportunities." The area contains numerous inexpensive bars and clubs, and "anyone with a library card could get into [them]." Thursday, Friday, and Saturday are popular party nights, though students agree, "there are parties almost every night." Students complain about the cafeteria food and the lack of parking. "If you have a class after 9 A.M., it's difficult to find a spot." The school also needs to improve a few facilities. One senior math major writes, "Many of the classrooms are disgusting. Walls are dirty, desks are small, and the blackboards don't erase."

### Student Body

SUNY—Albany is a diverse campus where students "all get along like pigs in a blanket." The university is popular among students who reside in the Northeast because of its central location. A junior criminal justice major writes that "SUNY—Albany is one of the few schools where you can walk around campus and feel like you're in Beverly Hills, then in a minute feel like you're in Flatbush." GDIs do not hold the Greek system in high regard. While students are generally friendly, many of them form cliques "like in high school," leading to some campus tension. Nevertheless, one junior psychology major writes, "Everyone has a generally friendly attitude."

# STATE UNIVERSITY OF NEW YORK AT ALBANY

FINANCIAL AID: 518-442-5757 • E-MAIL: UGADMISSIONS@ALBANY.EDU • WEBSITE: WWW.ALBANY.EDU

## ADMISSIONS

*Very important* academic and nonacademic factors considered by the admissions committee include secondary school record, standardized test scores, class rank, recommendations, and essay. *Other* factors considered include volunteer work and work experience. Factors *not* considered include geography, religious affiliation/commitment, and state residency. *High school units required/recommended:* 18 total required; 4 English required, 2 math required, 4 math recommended, 2 science required, 3 science recommended, 2 science lab recommended, 3 foreign language recommended, 3 social studies required, 5 elective required.

### The Inside Word

While the SUNY system's budgetary woes have abated to a degree, funding uncertainties continue to be a problem. Applications and standards are on the rise. Albany is the third most selective SUNY campus. Perhaps the university's status as the training camp site for the New York Giants will bring both revenue and facilities to aid a turnaround. Without increased private funding, Albany is likely to remain a relatively easy path into a SUNY university center.

## FINANCIAL AID

*Students should submit:* FAFSA. The Princeton Review suggests that all financial aid forms be submitted as soon as possible after January 1. *Need-based scholarships/grants offered:* Pell, SEOG, state scholarships/grants, private scholarships, and the school's own gift aid. Merit scholarships are available to in-state and out-of-state students. *Loan aid offered:* FFEL Subsidized Stafford, FFEL Unsubsidized Stafford, FFEL PLUS, Federal Perkins, and college/university loans from institutional funds. Institutional employment available. Federal Work-Study Program available. Applicants will be notified of awards on a rolling basis beginning on or about April 1. Off-campus job opportunities are excellent.

## FROM THE ADMISSIONS OFFICE

"Albany has attracted more applicants than any other SUNY school for the past two years. As a result, Albany has been increasingly selective with an admission rate of just above 50 percent. Out-of-state and international enrollments are also increasing as Albany seeks greater national visibility and greater geographic representation of students. The Presidential Scholars Program for top-achieving students increased this year by 35 percent, and Project Renaissance, the unique freshman-year experience, also remains a very popular option for students interested in a high-quality, affordable college experience."

## ADMISSIONS

| Admissions Rating | 77 |
|---|---|
| # of applicants | 16,448 |
| % of applicants accepted | 58 |
| % of acceptees attending | 23 |

### FRESHMAN PROFILE

| | |
|---|---|
| Range SAT Verbal | 510-610 |
| Range SAT Math | 530-620 |
| Minimum TOEFL | 550 |
| % graduated top 10% of class | 15 |
| % graduated top 25% of class | 49 |
| % graduated top 50% of class | 90 |

### DEADLINES

| | |
|---|---|
| Priority admission deadline | 11/15 |
| Regular admission | 3/1 |
| Regular notification | rolling |
| Nonfall registration? | yes |

### APPLICANTS ALSO LOOK AT
**AND OFTEN PREFER**
Cornell U.
Binghamton U.
**AND SOMETIMES PREFER**
U. Rochester
Fordham
Syracuse
Siena
U. Mass—Amherst
**AND RARELY PREFER**
Hofstra

## FINANCIAL FACTS

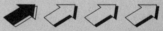

| Financial Aid Rating | 69 |
|---|---|
| In-state tuition | $3,400 |
| Out-of-state tuition | $8,300 |
| Room & board | $5,550 |
| Books and supplies | $700 |
| Required fees | $1,225 |
| % frosh receiving aid | 52 |
| % undergrads receiving aid | 55 |
| Avg frosh grant | $3,763 |
| Avg frosh loan | $3,306 |

# STATE UNIVERSITY OF NY—BINGHAMTON

PO BOX 6000, BINGHAMTON, NY 13902-6001 • ADMISSIONS: 607-777-2171 • FAX: 607-777-4445

## CAMPUS LIFE

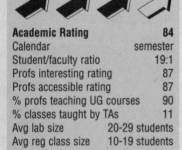

| | |
|---|---|
| **Quality of Life Rating** | **73** |
| Type of school | public |
| Affiliation | none |
| Environment | suburban |

### STUDENTS

| | |
|---|---|
| Total undergrad enrollment | 9,858 |
| % male/female | 46/54 |
| % from out of state | 4 |
| % from public high school | 87 |
| % live on campus | 56 |
| % in (# of) fraternities | 12 (19) |
| % in (# of) sororities | 11 (16) |
| % African American | 6 |
| % Asian | 18 |
| % Caucasian | 56 |
| % Hispanic | 5 |
| % international | 2 |
| # of countries represented | 93 |

### SURVEY SAYS . . .

*Class discussions are rare*
*Students don't get along with local community*
*Students are cliquish*
*Ethnic diversity on campus*
*Large classes*
*Unattractive campus*

## ACACEMICS

| | |
|---|---|
| **Academic Rating** | **84** |
| Calendar | semester |
| Student/faculty ratio | 19:1 |
| Profs interesting rating | 87 |
| Profs accessible rating | 87 |
| % profs teaching UG courses | 90 |
| % classes taught by TAs | 11 |
| Avg lab size | 20-29 students |
| Avg reg class size | 10-19 students |

### MOST POPULAR MAJORS
psychology
English
business

## STUDENTS SPEAK OUT

### Academics

Binghamton University, "the Ivy of the SUNYs" as its students like to call it, is "an academically competitive" public school with a decidedly pre-profession-al bent. Students are rightfully proud of the "great education" they get here for the price tag many consider to be "the buy of a lifetime." Students do counsel, however, that you will get out of your Binghamton education what you put into it: "You can get by doing very little work," cautions one. While lectures here can be "large," upper-level courses are generally smaller and "very informative." The faculty is large and individual professors "range from real-ly good and really caring to only concerned about research." Students say the "luck of the draw" determines which teachers you might end up with. The good professors are "extremely inspiring" and "the nicest people you'd ever want to meet." Bad professors certainly "know their subjects, but not how to relate to their students." Students at Binghamton take great pains to point out, though, that most professors "make themselves accessible" and work hard to be "extremely approachable" both "in and out of the classroom." Just plain luck will also determine the quality of your advisor. The administration is not great, but it's surprisingly efficient and hassle-free for a big school, although "getting the classes you need" can be "very difficult."

### Life

Binghamton students tend to have a "study-based mentality" ("the library is always packed on weekdays") on their "cloudy and gloomy" campus in upstate New York. They tell us that "campus comes alive when spring comes," or even when "it is over 40 degrees." Also, "the student clubs on campus are terrific," claims one student, "namely because the students get to run them completely." For students who "get involved," life is "fantastic" and "there is always something to do." Many students go Greek—there is "great pressure" to do so—and, for them, social life "consists of frat parties, frat parties, and frat parties." The campus has a "beautiful" nature preserve, but off campus there's not much else. "The town is barren" and "boring" and "Binghamton townies hate us," discloses a junior. There is "good shuttle bus service to malls and free city bus admission," but "it is hard to do anything here without a car." Students also gripe that Binghamtom "needs a football team" and a massive injection of school spirit. "Everyone wears T-shirts that sport other schools," complains a sophomore. "How lame is that?"

### Student Body

Although a very large percentage of Binghamton's student body comes from New York State, the school offers a "refreshing" amount of diversity. In general, students are "extremely friendly," "highly creative," and "down-to-earth." Some students complain, however, that students of different ethnicities "don't interact with other groups of people except in rare instances." There is a notice-able "tension between up staters and Long Islanders" and a "clique" mentali-ty. According to one frustrated student, "a lot of people come along with 50 or so members of their senior class," which "makes it harder to find good friends." Another notes that there are plenty of sorority girls who "all dress alike" and "frat boys trying to discover their manhood" here, as well as students who are "very serious about their career goals." Nevertheless, students overall describe their community as "welcoming."

# STATE UNIVERSITY OF NEW YORK—BINGHAMTON

FINANCIAL AID: 607-777-2428 • E-MAIL: ADMIT@BINGHAMTON.EDU • WEBSITE: WWW.BINGHAMTON.EDU

## ADMISSIONS

*Very important* academic and nonacademic factors considered by the admissions committee include secondary school record. *Important* factors considered include class rank, essays, extracurricular activities, recommendations, and standardized test scores. *Other* factors considered include alumni/ae relation, interview, minority status, talent/ability, and volunteer work. Factors *not* considered include geography, religious affiliation/commitment, state residency, and work experience. SAT I or ACT required. TOEFL required of all international applicants. High school diploma is required and GED is accepted. *High school units required/recommended:* 19 total required; 4 English required, 3 math required, 4 math recommended, 2 science required, 3 science recommended, 3 foreign language required, 4 foreign language recommended, 2 social studies required, 2 history recommended.

### The Inside Word

Binghamton's admissions process is highly selective, but fairly simple. Candidates go through a process that first considers academic qualifications, primarily through numbers, and then takes a relatively brief look at other components of the application. Binghamton hasn't been hurt by New York's budget problems as much as the rest of the SUNY system has, and may escape relatively free from harm. Out-of-state enrollment is miniscule for a public university of Binghamton's reputation, but the University's enrollment management strategy includes enhancing efforts to recruit students from further afield.

## FINANCIAL AID

*Students should submit:* FAFSA, CSS/Financial Aid PROFILE, and noncustodial (divorced/separated) parent's statement. The Princeton Review suggests that all financial aid forms be submitted as soon as possible after January 1. *Need-based scholarships/grants offered:* Pell, SEOG, state scholarships/grants, private scholarships, the school's own gift aid, and Federal Nursing. *Loan aid offered:* Direct Subsidized Stafford, Direct Unsubsidized Stafford, Direct PLUS, Federal Perkins, and Federal Nursing. Institutional employment available. Federal Work-Study Program available. Off-campus job opportunities are excellent.

## FROM THE ADMISSIONS OFFICE

"Binghamton University prides itself on excellent teaching and solid research from a faculty remarkably accessible to students. Students have the opportunity to engage in research with faculty and, together, they have designed projects and coauthored papers. Teaching and mentoring by faculty builds students' confidence and competence, encouraging them to become independent learners. Binghamton University welcomes serious students interested in working toward a productive future in our dynamic academic community."

## ADMISSIONS

| Admissions Rating | 89 |
| --- | --- |
| # of applicants | 16,506 |
| % of applicants accepted | 42 |
| % of acceptees attending | 28 |
| # accepting a place on wait list | 433 |
| % admitted from wait list | 42 |

### FRESHMAN PROFILE

| | |
| --- | --- |
| Range SAT Verbal | 540-640 |
| Average SAT Verbal | 586 |
| Range SAT Math | 570-670 |
| Average SAT Math | 622 |
| Range ACT Composite | 24-29 |
| Minimum TOEFL | 550 |
| Average HS GPA | 3.4 |
| % graduated top 10% of class | 53 |
| % graduated top 25% of class | 94 |
| % graduated top 50% of class | 100 |

### DEADLINES

| | |
| --- | --- |
| Priority admission deadline | 1/15 |
| Nonfall registration? | yes |

### APPLICANTS ALSO LOOK AT
#### AND OFTEN PREFER
Cornell U.
NYU
U. Penn
#### AND SOMETIMES PREFER
Univ. of Michigan
Clarkson U.
Penn State
#### AND RARELY PREFER
SUNY—Genedeo
SUNY—Buffalo
SUNY—Albany

## FINANCIAL FACTS

| Financial Aid Rating | 70 |
| --- | --- |
| In-state tuition | $3,400 |
| Out-of-state tuition | $8,300 |
| Room & board | $5,772 |
| Books and supplies | $750 |
| Required fees | $1,063 |
| % frosh receiving aid | 49 |
| % undergrads receiving aid | 50 |
| Avg frosh grant | $12,325 |
| Avg frosh loan | $12,482 |

# STATE UNIVERSITY OF NEW YORK AT BUFFALO

17 CAPEN HALL, BUFFALO, NY 14260 • ADMISSIONS: 716-645-6900 • FAX: 716-645-6411

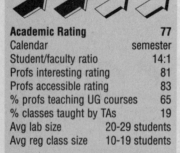
## STUDENTS SPEAK OUT

### Academics

A "wonderful variety of majors" and an "inexpensive" education await those willing to brave the frosty winters of New York State's northwestern academic outpost, SUNY—Buffalo. Engineering, business, and pre-med are the major draws here, but other disciplines (especially communications and the liberal arts and sciences) also offer competitive programs. Students report that "classes are big, which kind of sucks." Instruction in large lectures, many feel, is "not very easy. They expect you to understand right away what they understand. Also, they need to get more experienced instructors instead of using TAs to teach courses." Classes improve, though, at the upper levels, where "professors relate well to students, are accessible, and overall, keep learning interesting." Buffalo's administration "communicates very poorly with students," not a very unusual situation at a large state university. Even so, students cheerfully acknowledge Buffalo's many assets, which include "great computer facilities," as well as "wonderful" research opportunities, a great library, and "an [excellent] Honors Program."

### Life

SUNY—Buffalo is situated on two distinct campuses, a "south urban" campus within the city limits of the city and a "north rural (or suburban)" campus just outside of town. South Campus is home to departments related to the medical sciences, while most other departments are headquartered to the north. Other offices and facilities are split between the two campuses. Students feel that the university is relatively easy to get around. From South Campus "it's very easy to go out and do stuff. We're close to the theater district." Downtown is also home to "the bars of Main Street or Chippewa Street," music venues, and a bevy of great pizzerias. At the northern campus, however, "either you go to frats and dance clubs and get wasted or you don't. If you don't, there's really nothing else for you to do here. If you want a life, you need a car." Adds one student, "Greeks make up only 2 percent of the population but are so evident around North Campus. They don't have a good reputation at all! " For those desirous of more constructive pursuits, "there's something for everyone"; the student newspaper, minority student organizations, student government, and sports are all popular. A sophomore tells us that "getting involved is easy, and it makes a big school like UB feel smaller." Students give parking and campus food an adamant thumbs down and warn all upstate neophytes that "UB lives up to the isolated tundra stereotype of Buffalo."

### Student Body

The student body at UB "is broad and diverse, enabling students to gain valuable cultural insight." And therefore, "we treat each other with respect," notes one white student, a sentiment apparently confirmed by an African American student who feels "Buffalo has a great deal to offer minority students." Leaning to the left-of-center politically, most UB students we surveyed don't consider themselves particularly politically active. As a whole, they're a "generally friendly" lot who rate themselves as pretty happy, if lacking a little "school spirit" and a strong sense of community. Writes one, "It's hard to make a lot of friends with such a large commuter population."

# STATE UNIVERSITY OF NEW YORK AT BUFFALO

FINANCIAL AID: 716-829-3724 • E-MAIL: UB-ADMISSIONS@ADMISSIONS.BUFFALO.EDU • WEBSITE: WWW.BUFFALO.EDU

## ADMISSIONS

*Very important* academic and nonacademic factors considered by the admissions committee include secondary school record. *Important* factors considered include class rank, minority status, and standardized test scores. *Other* factors considered include alumni/ae relation, character/personal qualities, essays, extracurricular activities, geography, interview, recommendations, talent/ability, volunteer work, and work experience. Factors *not* considered include religious affiliation/commitment and state residency. SAT I or ACT required. TOEFL required of all international applicants. High school diploma is required and GED is accepted. *High school units required/recommended:* 17 total recommended; 4 English recommended, 3 math recommended, 3 science recommended, 3 foreign language recommended, 4 social studies recommended. *The admissions office says:* "Competition for available places is keen. Mean combined SAT I scores for accepted students are typically above 1100 and mean high school averages are above 90. A limited number of freshmen may be offered admission to the university based upon evidence of special talents [such as] exceptional creative talent in art, media study, music, theater, writing, special academic achievement, demonstrated leadership, outstanding athletic ability, and community service."

### The Inside Word

Buffalo was formerly a private university and was absorbed into the SUNY system. Its admissions process reflects this private heritage to the extent possible (applications are centrally processed for the entire system in Albany). It's one of the few SUNY schools with a freshman academic profile higher than its published admissions standards. Although Binghamton is academically the most selective of the SUNY University Centers, Buffalo is in many ways closer to what other states refer to as the flagship of the state system.

## FINANCIAL AID

*Students should submit:* FAFSA. Regular filing deadline is March 1. The Princeton Review suggests that all financial aid forms be submitted as soon as possible after January 1. *Need-based scholarships/grants offered:* Pell, SEOG, state scholarships/grants, private scholarships, the school's own gift aid, and Federal Nursing. *Loan aid offered:* Direct Subsidized Stafford, Direct Unsubsidized Stafford, Direct PLUS, Federal Perkins, Federal Nursing, and college/university loans from institutional funds. Institutional employment available. Applicants will be notified of awards on a rolling basis beginning on or about February 1. Off-campus job opportunities are good.

## FROM THE ADMISSIONS OFFICE

"Steeped in tradition, modern in focus, large in concept, and personal in form, the State University of New York at Buffalo (UB) is a university in the richest sense. Important in graduate and professional education, it displays also remarkable breadth, diversity, and quality in undergraduate programs in the humanities, natural sciences, social sciences, and fine arts. In short, New York State's major public university provides unparalleled opportunities for learning, for career preparation, for developing a rewarding way of life. On the cutting edge of technology, UB offers its students electronic mail and a campus-wide electronic information service that provides a direct gateway to the internet's World Wide Web. Prospective transfer students receive a transfer credit evaluation report, and UB students can take advantage of touch-tone registration and an automated degree audit system to monitor their progress toward a degree. We encourage students and their families to visit the University at Buffalo and to feel the many textures of the campus—its personalities, paths, and facilities. Campus tours and presentations are offered year-round."

## ADMISSIONS

| | |
|---|---|
| Admissions Rating | 81 |
| # of applicants | 15,511 |
| % of applicants accepted | 68 |
| % of acceptees attending | 29 |
| # accepting a place on wait list | 66 |
| % admitted from wait list | 326 |
| # of early decision applicants | 440 |
| % accepted early decision | 61 |

### FRESHMAN PROFILE

| | |
|---|---|
| Range SAT Verbal | 490-600 |
| Average SAT Verbal | 563 |
| Range SAT Math | 520-630 |
| Average SAT Math | 587 |
| Range ACT Composite | 21-27 |
| Average ACT Composite | 24 |
| Minimum TOEFL | 550 |
| Average HS GPA | 3.0 |
| % graduated top 10% of class | 22 |
| % graduated top 25% of class | 55 |
| % graduated top 50% of class | 92 |

### DEADLINES

| | |
|---|---|
| Early decision | 11/1 |
| Early decision notification | 12/1 |
| Priority admission deadline | 11/1 |
| Regular notification | rolling |
| Nonfall registration? | yes |

### APPLICANTS ALSO LOOK AT
**AND OFTEN PREFER**
SUNY Albany, Binghamton U.
Cornell U., NYU
**AND SOMETIMES PREFER**
Syracuse, Alfred
U. Rochester, SUNY Stony Brook
Boston U.
**AND RARELY PREFER**
U. Mass—Amherst
Penn State—Univ. Park, U. Conn.

### FINANCIAL FACTS

| | |
|---|---|
| Financial Aid Rating | 74 |
| In-state tuition | $3,400 |
| Out-of-state tuition | $8,300 |
| Room & board | $6,054 |
| Books and supplies | $750 |
| Required fees | $1,315 |
| % frosh receiving aid | 56 |
| % undergrads receiving aid | 52 |
| Avg frosh grant | $5,196 |
| Avg frosh loan | $3,999 |

# STATE UNIVERSITY OF NEW YORK COLLEGE AT GENESEO

1 COLLEGE CIRCLE, GENESEO, NY 14454-1401 • ADMISSIONS: 716-245-5571 • FAX: 716-245-5550

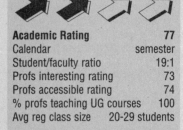

## CAMPUS LIFE

**Quality of Life Rating**    **74**
Type of school    public
Affiliation    none
Environment    rural

### STUDENTS
Total undergrad enrollment    5,197
% male/female    34/66
% from out of state    2
% from public high school    92
% live on campus    53
% in (# of) fraternities    12 (10)
% in (# of) sororities    9 (10)
% African American    2
% Asian    4
% Caucasian    91
% Hispanic    3

### SURVEY SAYS . . .
*Diversity lacking on campus*
*Class discussions are rare*
*Lots of beer drinking*
*Students are cliquish*
*Registration is a pain*
*Student government is unpopular*
*Lousy food on campus*
*Low cost of living*

## ACADEMICS

**Academic Rating**    **77**
Calendar    semester
Student/faculty ratio    19:1
Profs interesting rating    73
Profs accessible rating    74
% profs teaching UG courses    100
Avg reg class size    20-29 students

### MOST POPULAR MAJORS
special education
biology
business management

## STUDENTS SPEAK OUT

### Academics

Darwinian academics—"survival of the fittest"—is the standard at "challenging" SUNY College at Geneseo, one of the most selective schools in the Empire State and the "Harvard of the SUNY system," according to a senior here. This "professionally focused" public liberal arts college has much to recommend it: "a very rigorous academic program," an "affordable price," and several good majors including "excellent" dance and theatre programs, a "great" School of Business, and popular psychology and biology departments. Also, much to students' liking, it's "not too big." The "small campus and small size enable professors to get to know students, which enhances the Geneseo experience," explains a first-year student. The "extremely diverse faculty" is a mostly "very accessible and friendly" bunch who strive to "really make class interesting." Some professors are "not-so-hot" and "show very little interest in students' progress." Others are "tyrannical," but "bad experiences are few and far between." Overall, "the professors are kind, intelligent people" who "love to work with students" and "convey lots of excitement through lectures." A junior suggests that "most departments could use more faculty members," and "the registration process could be better." Also, the people in the financial aid office are "extremely difficult, rude, and unapproachable." Good grades are seriously hard to come by here. "At my former college, I was on the Dean's List," explains a transfer student. "My first semester here, I failed a midterm and had a 2.5 GPA. To put it mildly, Geneseo is a difficult school. You have to work extremely hard to do well."

### Life

Geneseo is located in a "quaint and wonderful village" in the hinterlands of upstate New York where "they decorate Main Street for the holidays." Students call it "a picture-postcard place." The residence halls here are "wired for the Internet and e-mail," and the entire campus is seriously plugged in to technology. "Life is stressful and busy due to academics" for Geneseo students. "People tend to work very hard during the week, then go out on weekends." Students still manage to have a good time, though. The trick is that "weekends start" on "Thursday and sometimes Wednesday," according to a sophomore. "Greek parties, house parties," and trips to the local bars "are the main weekend activities." Apparently, "the local bar in the big red barn" is especially hip. "Mini-golf, cart racing, bowling, movies," "broomball, working out," and "watching hockey" are also big draws. Extracurricular clubs and activities on campus are popular as well. "You'll be bored out of your mind if you don't belong to anything," warns a senior. Somewhat ironically, though, "no one really cares about the school itself," and there is a serious dearth of school spirit here. When Geneseo's smallness becomes overwhelming (or when students are overcome by the miserable campus chow), "shopping, concerts" and good restaurant food can be had in the veritable metropolis of Rochester, "about 30 minutes away." "Road trips to Canada" are also common.

### Student Body

"There are four types of people at Geneseo," helpfully explains a sophomore. "There are those in fraternities and sororities, those who are varsity athletes, those that stay in all the time, and those who people see but no one really knows." There are also "lots of preps" as well as a sizeable contingent of "hippies and weirdos." And practically everybody is white. The "competitive" students here describe themselves as a "personable" and "friendly bunch" of "great, down-to-earth people." Many are "too concerned with how they look." They are "often rude and elitist," too, and "sort of clique-like." For a significant chunk of the population, "your worth is measured by what Greek letters you wear," and there is "separation among Greek and non-Greek students as well as of people from different ethnic backgrounds." Many of the female students here also lament the "ridiculous" male-to-female ratio. Geneseo "needs more boys," asserts one.

FINANCIAL AID: 716-245-5731 • E-MAIL: ADMISSIONS@GENESEO.EDU • WEBSITE: WWW.GENESEO.EDU

## ADMISSIONS

*Very important* academic and nonacademic factors considered by the admissions committee include secondary school record. *Important* factors considered include class rank, essays, extracurricular activities, recommendations, and standardized test scores. *Other* factors considered include alumni/ae relation, character/personal qualities, minority status, talent/ability, volunteer work, and work experience. Factors *not* considered include geography, interview, religious affiliation/commitment, and state residency. SAT I or ACT required. TOEFL required of all international applicants. High school diploma is required and GED is accepted. *High school units required/recommended:* 19 total recommended; 4 English recommended, 4 math recommended, 4 science recommended, 3 foreign language recommended, 4 social studies recommended.

### The Inside Word

Geneseo is the most selective of SUNY's 13 undergraduate colleges and more selective than three of SUNY's university centers. No formula approach is used here. Expect a thorough review of both your academic accomplishments (virtually everyone here graduated in the top half of their high school classes) and your extracurricular/personal side. Admissions standards are tempered only by a somewhat low yield of admits who enroll; this keeps the admit rate higher than it might otherwise be.

## FINANCIAL AID

*Students should submit:* FAFSA and state aid form. The Princeton Review suggests that all financial aid forms be submitted as soon as possible after January 1. *Need-based scholarships/grants offered:* Pell, SEOG, state scholarships/grants, private scholarships, and the school's own gift aid. *Loan aid offered:* FFEL Subsidized Stafford, FFEL Unsubsidized Stafford, FFEL PLUS, Federal Perkins, and state. Institutional employment available. Federal Work-Study Program available. Applicants will be notified of awards on a rolling basis. Off-campus job opportunities are fair.

## FROM THE ADMISSIONS OFFICE

"Geneseo has carved a distinctive niche among the nation's premier public liberal arts colleges. Founded in 1871, the college occupies a 220-acre hillside campus in the historic Village of Geneseo, overlooking the scenic Genesee Valley. As a residential campus—with nearly two-thirds of the students living in college residence halls—it provides a rich and varied program of social, cultural, recreational, and scholarly activities. Geneseo is noted for its distinctive core curriculum and the extraordinary opportunities it offers undergraduates to pursue independent study and research with faculty who value close working relationships with talented students. Equally impressive is the remarkable success of its graduates, nearly one-third of whom study at leading graduate and professional schools immediately following graduation."

## ADMISSIONS

| | |
|---|---|
| Admissions Rating | 88 |
| # of applicants | 7,944 |
| % of applicants accepted | 50 |
| % of acceptees attending | 27 |
| # accepting a place on wait list | 587 |
| % admitted from wait list | 5 |
| # of early decision applicants | 223 |
| % accepted early decision | 57 |

### FRESHMAN PROFILE

| | |
|---|---|
| Range SAT Verbal | 570-650 |
| Average SAT Verbal | 609 |
| Range SAT Math | 580-650 |
| Average SAT Math | 612 |
| Range ACT Composite | 24-28 |
| Average ACT Composite | 26 |
| Minimum TOEFL | 525 |
| Average HS GPA | 3.6 |
| % graduated top 10% of class | 48 |
| % graduated top 25% of class | 91 |
| % graduated top 50% of class | 100 |

### DEADLINES

| | |
|---|---|
| Early decision | 11/15 |
| Early decision notification | 12/15 |
| Regular admission | 1/15 |
| Nonfall registration? | yes |

### APPLICANTS ALSO LOOK AT

**AND OFTEN PREFER**
Binghamton U.
Cornell U.

**AND SOMETIMES PREFER**
U. Rochester
SUNY—Buffalo
Boston College
SUNY—Albany
Colgate

**AND RARELY PREFER**
Hamilton
Ithaca
St. Bonaventure

### FINANCIAL FACTS

| | |
|---|---|
| Financial Aid Rating | 77 |
| In-state tuition | $3,400 |
| Out-of-state tuition | $8,300 |
| Room & board | $4,890 |
| Books and supplies | $600 |
| Required fees | $821 |
| % frosh receiving aid | 52 |
| % undergrads receiving aid | 63 |

# STEPHENS COLLEGE

1200 EAST BROADWAY, BOX 2121, COLUMBIA, MO 65215 • ADMISSIONS: 573-876-7207 • FAX: 573-876-7237

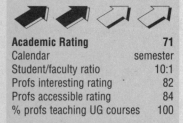
## STUDENTS SPEAK OUT

### Academics

Although it accepts a handful of men to its prestigious theater program, Stephens College is essentially an all-women's school for students on serious career tracks. Aside from the "wonderful" theater program, business administration, equestrian business, education, and fashion all receive high marks (although some students warn that "sometimes you feel left out if you're not a theater or dance student"). "Stephens is about instilling confidence in women soon to enter the work force," says one sophomore, reflecting student satisfaction with the college's highly supported and recommended internship programs. Students are similarly sanguine about the faculty, reporting that "the professors here are wonderful. They really like us to learn and like to know that we are doing okay in every other aspect of our life." Profs are "willing to stay late and give up their weekends to help students prepare for exams or grasp concepts." SC undergrads are less satisfied with the administration, complaining about "poor communication skills" and noting that "the politics here have gone from mite-bit annoyances to 'killer-bee sting' annoyances." Some feel that "the administration is getting better about listing to students, but it still needs work."

### Life

For Stephens' performing artists, life revolves around the stage. "To echo the words of Stephens graduate actress Annie Potts," writes one such undergrad, "'I live, drink, and breathe theater at Stephens.'" For others there is time for fun, but "you have to get off campus. But that's good: on campus, work; off campus, fun!" You don't have to get too far off-campus, however, because there are "three colleges in a mile stretch that make this College Town, USA. Lots of great restaurants, movie theaters, etc." Explains one student, "I was worried about attending an all-woman's college, but you know what? There's life outside of campus . . . and a whole university of boys only a few blocks away." On campus, students enjoy a gorgeous 11-acre lake and riding stables, among other amenities. Most love the small college atmosphere, especially with the University of Missouri just down the street. Explains one student, "We get the best of both worlds. It's a small school with lots to do, but you can find many places to study. Columbia is such a college town. So many frat parties and bars to go to. So many great places to eat and great shopping. The sorority life is great." Some note that a car is a definite plus for getting around, but others say that the campus itself has a good deal to offer—active sororities, sports, and a respectable variety of student-run cultural, political, and social clubs. Observes one undergrad, "The students that are involved are extremely involved. The others aren't at all." Another points out an often-overlooked advantage of attending a small school: "We are NCAA, but we are not really competitive. I like that if you want to participate in sports, you can."

### Student Body

Most students find the all-women atmosphere at Stephens liberating: "You can go to class just after waking up because we're all women and no one has to impress anyone." "For the most part," writes one undergrad, "we're women who are going somewhere, women who have goals and expect to achieve them." Students here appreciate the fact that "people treat each other with a great deal of respect" at SC and generally speak very highly of their classmates, although a few note traces of class animus. "[Fellow students] come across as kind of snobby," explains one undergrad. "They have a lot of money. Once you get to know them, some of them are okay." Offers another, "Well, the sorority girls are annoying, but there are a lot of really down-to-earth people." Minority student associations have a visible presence on campus, and students make it clear that differences are welcome.

FINANCIAL AID: 573-876-7106 • E-MAIL: APPLY@SC.STEPHENS.EDU • WEBSITE: WWW.STEPHENS.EDU

## ADMISSIONS

*Very important* academic and nonacademic factors considered by the admissions committee include character/personal qualities, essays, extracurricular activities, secondary school record, and standardized test scores. *Important* factors considered include alumni/ae relation, class rank, interview, recommendations, talent/ability, and volunteer work. *Other* factors considered include work experience. Factors *not* considered include geography, minority status, religious affiliation/commitment, and state residency. SAT I or ACT required. TOEFL required of all international applicants. High school diploma is required and GED is accepted. *High school units required/recommended:* 16 total required; 19 total recommended; 4 English required, 4 English recommended, 3 math required, 4 math recommended, 2 science required, 3 science recommended, 2 science lab required, 3 science lab recommended, 2 foreign language required, 4 foreign language recommended, 1 social studies required, 2 social studies recommended, 1 history required, 2 history recommended, 3 elective required. "Women at Stephens College never hear the words, 'You can't do that because you're a woman.' Their self-confidence, self-esteem, and self-concept grow in an accelerated manner."

### The Inside Word

Each candidate's application is read by three members of the admissions committee, and essays carry much more significance than test scores. You'll get a lot of personal attention from the admissions staff here; with the kind of competition Stephens faces for students, they have to work pretty hard here to bring in the freshman class. Their success is a testament to the quality of the college.

## FINANCIAL AID

*Students should submit:* FAFSA. There is no regular filing deadline. The Princeton Review suggests that all financial aid forms be submitted as soon as possible after January 1. *Need-based scholarships/grants offered:* Pell, SEOG, state scholarships/grants, private scholarships, and the school's own gift aid. *Loan aid offered:* Direct Subsidized Stafford, Direct Unsubsidized Stafford, Direct PLUS, and Federal Perkins. Institutional employment available. Federal Work-Study Program available. Off-campus job opportunities are excellent.

## FROM THE ADMISSIONS OFFICE

"Stephens College encourages applications from women who are interested in developing their self-confidence and 'voice.' As a women's college, Stephens works with women who are independent, inquisitive, intelligent, and creative—be sure your application demonstrates this when you apply."

### ADMISSIONS

| | |
|---|---|
| Admissions Rating | 72 |
| # of applicants | 327 |
| % of applicants accepted | 80 |
| % of acceptees attending | 64 |

#### FRESHMAN PROFILE

| | |
|---|---|
| Range SAT Verbal | 470-610 |
| Average SAT Verbal | 560 |
| Range SAT Math | 460-550 |
| Average SAT Math | 525 |
| Range ACT Composite | 20-25 |
| Average ACT Composite | 24 |
| Minimum TOEFL | 550 |
| Average HS GPA | 3.4 |
| % graduated top 10% of class | 37 |
| % graduated top 25% of class | 57 |
| % graduated top 50% of class | 80 |

#### DEADLINES

| | |
|---|---|
| Early decision | 12/1 |
| Priority admission deadline | 12/2 |
| Regular admission | 7/31 |
| Regular notification | rolling |
| Nonfall registration? | yes |

#### APPLICANTS ALSO LOOK AT AND SOMETIMES PREFER
U. Missouri—Columbia
William Woods
**AND RARELY PREFER**
Butler

### FINANCIAL FACTS

| | |
|---|---|
| Financial Aid Rating | 82 |
| Tuition | $16,245 |
| Room & board | $6,050 |
| Books and supplies | $500 |
| % frosh receiving aid | 45 |
| % undergrads receiving aid | 80 |
| Avg frosh grant | $9,500 |
| Avg frosh loan | $2,500 |

# STETSON UNIVERSITY

421 N. WOODLAND BOULEVARD, UNIT 8378, DELAND, FL 32720 • ADMISSIONS: 800-688-0101 • FAX: 386-822-7112

## CAMPUS LIFE

**Quality of Life Rating** 75
Type of school private
Affiliation none
Environment suburban

### STUDENTS

Total undergrad enrollment 2,155
% male/female 43/57
% from out of state 20
% from public high school 75
% live on campus 66
% in (# of) fraternities 32 (7)
% in (# of) sororities 29 (6)
% African American 4
% Asian 2
% Caucasian 87
% Hispanic 6
% international 4
# of countries represented 61

### SURVEY SAYS . . .

*Frats and sororities dominate social
scene
Theater is hot
Classes are small
Lots of conservatives on campus
Athletic facilities are great
Political activism is (almost)
nonexistent
Musical organizations are hot
Students don't like DeLand, FL
Lousy food on campus
Dorms are like dungeons*

## ACADEMICS

**Academic Rating** 78
Calendar semester
Student/faculty ratio 10:1
Profs interesting rating 71
Profs accessible rating 72
% profs teaching UG courses 98
Avg lab size 10-19 students
Avg reg class size 10-19 students

### MOST POPULAR MAJORS
business
education
psychology

## STUDENTS SPEAK OUT

### Academics

Students interested in business, music, and education have found a welcome home at Stetson University. Nearly half of Stetson students major in one of these three fields; pre-medical sciences and psychology are also popular. Some students warn that "academically, the school is definitely like butter. If you are not in music, education, or business, do not come here!" Others report that both academics and teaching are strong throughout the university. Writes one student: "The courses at Stetson are challenging and fun. The teachers are fan-diddily-tastic. They are really special people who care about their students." Another agrees, "The teachers are accessible and embrace technology. Students are encouraged to join on-campus activities. For the most part, students are expected to maintain and change, for the positive, the campus environment." Our respondents speak especially highly of Stetson's honors program, an add-on to students' undergraduate majors rather than a separate program. Honors graduation requires students to write a personal credo and pass oral examinations in addition to meeting all other graduation requirements. Sums up one satisfied undergrad: "What a difference from high school. This school really makes you think, and professors actually care about your opinions."

### Life

Campus life at Stetson is hampered by the school's proximity to Orlando and Daytona, both excellent party towns. Unfortunately, the same cannot be said of hometown DeLand. Charitable students describe the town as "small and quaint"; blunter students report that "we call DeLand DeadLand. The most exciting thing to do in town is go to the Wal-Mart." With paradise a short drive away, most students don't see the need to foster an active campus scene. This upsets those who yearn for a more conventional college experience, as well as those who simply don't have access to a car. "Students here need to become more enthusiastic about their college experience by becoming actively involved in extracurriculars and showing that they are proud of their school." The situation is exacerbated by the fact that "many people go home on weekends. That's bad for social life." Still, those students willing to make the effort say that a fine time can be found on the Stetson campus. Students note that "Greek life is big" and add that "like any school, some students invariably make weekend excursions, but there are many students who stay on campus and have similar interests. That creates a scene." Those who stick around can enjoy the great weather, midnight "Capture the Flag" contests, and the fact that "the campus is one of the best looking places on Earth."

### Student Body

Although it is not affiliated with any church, Stetson's heritage is steeped in Christianity. How well the school still fits its image as a southern Christian school is open to debate. One student reports that "Stetson is having a hard time shedding its religious/traditional heritage. Diversity is only achieved kicking and screaming." Conversely, a more religious student complains, "I came here in anticipation of religiously involved students, but this wasn't the case, and this is my only knock on the school." About 20 percent of students are Catholic; the school also hosts large Baptist and Methodist populations. Overall students "are friendly. You see a smiling face no matter where you are going." However, they are also "fairly cliquish. But, because Stetson is so small, you get to know lots of people."

FINANCIAL AID: 386-822-7120 • E-MAIL: ADMISSIONS@STETSON.EDU • WEBSITE: WWW.STETSON.EDU

## ADMISSIONS

*Very important* academic and nonacademic factors considered by the admissions committee include secondary school record. *Important* factors considered include character/personal qualities, class rank, essays, extracurricular activities, interview, recommendations, standardized test scores, talent/ability, volunteer work, and work experience. *Other* factors considered include alumni/ae relation, geography, minority status, and state residency. Factors *not* considered include religious affiliation/commitment. SAT I or ACT required, SAT I preferred. TOEFL required of all international applicants. High school diploma is required and GED is accepted. *High school units required/recommended:* 4 English required, 3 math required, 4 math recommended, 3 science required, 4 science recommended, 2 foreign language required, 3 foreign language recommended, 3 social studies required, 4 social studies recommended, 2 elective required.

### The Inside Word

Stetson is a university with strong academic offerings, yet moderate admissions standards. Solid B students with slightly-above-average test scores should encounter few obstacles to admission. What sort of fit a candidate makes with the university is in many ways more important than numbers, and the admissions committee closely evaluates applicants' personal sides.

## FINANCIAL AID

*Students should submit:* FAFSA and institution's own financial aid form. The Princeton Review suggests that all financial aid forms be submitted as soon as possible after January 1. *Need-based scholarships/grants offered:* Pell, SEOG, state scholarships/grants, private scholarships, and the school's own gift aid. *Loan aid offered:* FFEL Subsidized Stafford, FFEL Unsubsidized Stafford, FFEL PLUS, Federal Perkins, state, and college/university loans from institutional funds. Institutional employment available. Federal Work-Study Program available. Applicants will be notified of awards on a rolling basis. Off-campus job opportunities are good.

## FROM THE ADMISSIONS OFFICE

"As Florida's first private university, Stetson University sets a high standard for quality teaching and innovative, superior programs. Stetson maintains a more-than century-old commitment to values and social responsibility for its students. Perhaps most important of all, Stetson is committed to making top quality, private education affordable to a diverse group of qualified students. Stetson offers a personalized education from professors who are experts in their fields using the latest in classroom technology. Whether managing a $2 million investment portfolio or conducting biology research with pygmy rattlesnakes in a nearby wildlife preserve, Stetson students learn by doing. The campus is both historic and high tech. The University has just begun a $12 million renovation of its Business School. And, thanks to a $9.5 million donor-funded construction program, Stetson has added three new facilities and renovated a fourth on the beautiful, historic DeLand campus in Central Florida."

## ADMISSIONS

| | |
|---|---|
| **Admissions Rating** | **79** |
| # of applicants | 1,940 |
| % of applicants accepted | 75 |
| % of acceptees attending | 36 |
| # of early decision applicants | 67 |
| % accepted early decision | 91 |

### FRESHMAN PROFILE

| | |
|---|---|
| Range SAT Verbal | 500-610 |
| Average SAT Verbal | 562 |
| Range SAT Math | 503-620 |
| Average SAT Math | 560 |
| Range ACT Composite | 21-27 |
| Average ACT Composite | 24 |
| Minimum TOEFL | 550 |
| Average HS GPA | 3.5 |
| % graduated top 10% of class | 30 |
| % graduated top 25% of class | 59 |
| % graduated top 50% of class | 89 |

### DEADLINES

| | |
|---|---|
| Early decision | 11/1 |
| Early decision notification | 11/15 |
| Priority admission deadline | 1/1 |
| Regular admission | 3/15 |
| Nonfall registration? | yes |

## FINANCIAL FACTS

| | |
|---|---|
| **Financial Aid Rating** | **81** |
| Tuition | $18,350 |
| Room & board | $6,170 |
| Books and supplies | $600 |
| Required fees | $960 |
| % frosh receiving aid | 64 |
| % undergrads receiving aid | 59 |

# STEVENS INSTITUTE OF TECHNOLOGY

CASTLE POINT ON HUDSON, HOBOKEN, NJ 07030 • ADMISSIONS: 800-458-5323 • FAX: 201-216-8348

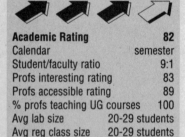
## STUDENTS SPEAK OUT

### Academics

Students looking for a highly regarded engineering school near a major city need look no further than Stevens Institute of Technology in Hoboken, New Jersey. Of course, some students point out that Stevens is one of those techie schools that "tries to be broad-based, but isn't." Students don't come to Stevens for the humanities. Professors are "brilliant" but also "often too smart for their own good." They sometimes forget that students are not yet experts in their field and accordingly, "their expectations are quite high." They "need to stop reading the text to us." Many believe that their professors "are basically just here to do research and write books." Also, many of the TAs for labs and recitations are not native speakers of English. "Half the time, you have to guess what the professor is saying," a junior electrical engineering major says. First- and second-year students find the school's mandatory course load a relief—one less thing for them to worry about. Of course, the workload is significant, and many students worry as much about the grading curve as they do about passing classes that they consider superfluous. Nevertheless, the "engineering department and comp-sci programs are great." Students also tell us that the co-op programs are very strong, and the school's career services center is very helpful. The school also reportedly does an excellent job supporting students with any extra tutoring they might need.

### Life

Stevens students love the campus because it is located in Hoboken, a town with numerous bars and restaurants across the Hudson from New York City. "It is the best view of New York you could ever get," one student writes. New York offers numerous opportunities for diversion, and students often go to the movies in Greenwich Village. The campus itself is small and "park-like," which makes it "easy to get to classes from the dorms." Students, especially those who are underage, go to parties at the fraternities and sororities. While Stevens is not a commuter school, a large number of students go home on the weekend. However, athletics is a big draw, with over 70 percent of undergraduates participating. Studying is a must on week nights if one is to keep up with the workload. Students also report a dislike for on-campus fare, and all agree that parking is difficult in Hoboken. Also, students wish clubs and student organizations had better support from the school's administration.

### Student Body

It's not surprising on a campus whose male population is greater than 75 percent that the primary complaint is that there aren't enough female students. While most students are friendly and noncompetitive, there is a good percentage of "anti-social types who just sit at their computers all day." Those not involved with the Greek community tend to form cliques based on their ethnicity. Students feel like they know everyone because the campus and the student body are so small. While there are many students "who'd rather stay in on a Saturday night and play network games rather than go out and enjoy Manhattan or Hoboken," there are very bright people at Stevens, "so you're bound to come across some interesting characters." In general, Stevens's students get along because they are united by a common goal: "To get a great education that will put us out in the world with a very good salary."

FINANCIAL AID: 201-216-5194 • E-MAIL: ADMISSIONS@STEVENS-TECH.EDU • WEBSITE: WWW.STEVENS-TECH.EDU

## ADMISSIONS

*Very important* academic and nonacademic factors considered by the admissions committee include secondary school record and standardized test scores. *Important* factors considered include essays, recommendations, character/personal qualities and class rank. *Other* factors considered include extracurricular activities, work experience, minority status, talent/ability, and volunteer work. Factors *not* considered include alumni/ae relation, geography, interview, religious affiliation/commitment, and state residency. SAT I or ACT required, SAT I preferred; SAT II also recommended. TOEFL required of all international applicants who score less than a 550 on the Verbal SAT. High school diploma is required and GED is not accepted. *High school units required/recommended:* 4 English required, 4 math required, 4 science required, 4 science lab required, 2 foreign language recommended, 2 social studies recommended, 2 history recommended, 4 elective recommended. *The admissions office says:* "Our applicants give high marks to one-on-one admission interviews and personalized communication flow"

### The Inside Word

Stevens is indeed impressive and legitimately near the top of the "second tier" of technical schools. Above-average students who would run into difficulty trying to gain admission to the MITs and Caltechs of the world will find a much more receptive admissions process here. Given its solid reputation and metropolitan New York location, it's an excellent choice for techies who want to establish their careers in the area.

## FINANCIAL AID

*Students should submit:* FAFSA. Priority (recommended) filing deadline is February 15. The Princeton Review suggests that all financial aid forms be submitted as soon as possible after January 1. *Need-based scholarships/grants offered:* Pell, SEOG, state scholarships/grants, private scholarships, and the school's own gift aid. *Loan aid offered:* Direct Subsidized Stafford, Direct Unsubsidized Stafford, Direct PLUS, Federal Perkins, state, Signature Loans, and TERI Loans. Institutional employment available. Federal Work-Study Program available. Applicants will be notified of awards on a rolling basis beginning on or about March 15. Off-campus job opportunities are excellent.

## FROM THE ADMISSIONS OFFICE

"The quality and achievements of our graduates are the greatest hallmarks of the Stevens education. Approximately 100 percent have had technical, pre-professional experience outside the classroom during their undergraduate years. Among other benefits, this enables them to be the finest candidates for prestigious graduate schools or positions of employment in industry. Striking indications of this are that all students seeking a full-time position receive a job offer prior to graduation from the institute, and Stevens ranks 11th among the Top 550 institutions that produce presidents, vice presidents, and directors of U.S. companies. However, outstanding academic excellence needs to be balanced with an outstanding campus life, and at Stevens students will find 70 student organizations and NCAA Division III athletics. Plus, the Hoboken location overlooking the Hudson River and New York City skyline offers a campus environment like no other."

## ADMISSIONS

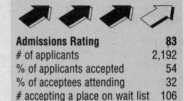

| | |
|---|---:|
| **Admissions Rating** | **83** |
| # of applicants | 2,192 |
| % of applicants accepted | 54 |
| % of acceptees attending | 32 |
| # accepting a place on wait list | 106 |
| # of early decision applicants | 74 |
| % accepted early decision | 45 |

### FRESHMAN PROFILE

| | |
|---|---:|
| Range SAT Verbal | 570-660 |
| Average SAT Verbal | 630 |
| Range SAT Math | 630-710 |
| Average SAT Math | 710 |
| Minimum TOEFL | 550 |
| Average HS GPA | 3.8 |
| % graduated top 10% of class | 53 |
| % graduated top 25% of class | 83 |
| % graduated top 50% of class | 100 |

### DEADLINES

| | |
|---|---:|
| Early decision | 11/15 |
| Early decision notification | 12/15 |
| Regular admission | 2/15 |

### APPLICANTS ALSO LOOK AT AND OFTEN PREFER

RPI
Carnegie Mellon
Lehigh
Cornell U.

### AND SOMETIMES PREFER

New Jersey Tech
Rutgers U.

## FINANCIAL FACTS

| | |
|---|---:|
| **Financial Aid Rating** | **74** |
| Tuition | $22,980 |
| Room & board | $7,730 |
| Books and supplies | $900 |
| Required fees | $250 |
| % frosh receiving aid | 89 |
| % undergrads receiving aid | 78 |
| Avg frosh grant | $19,140 |
| Avg frosh loan | $2,500 |

# STONY BROOK UNIVERSITY (SUNY)

OFFICE OF ADMISSIONS, STONY BROOK, NY 11794-1901 • ADMISSIONS: 631-632-9898 • FAX: 631-632-9898

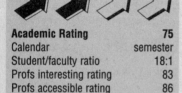
## STUDENTS SPEAK OUT

### Academics

The State University of New York at Stony Brook "is what you make it. You can take a rigorous, challenging curriculum or you can take Basketweaving 101." Most choose the former route, attending Stony Brook in hopes of earning a valuable degree in the sciences and engineering at public-school prices. A nationally renowned graduate research center ("Our research facilities are awesome!!"), Stony Brook comes complete with all of the advantages and drawbacks one would expect to find in a large university. Students "are very much on their own here." Professors "are usually too into lecturing as opposed to making sure students understand what they are being taught. There are few excellent professors, a large sum of nonchalant professors, and a few no-care professors." Notes one student, "Studying electrical engineering at Stony Brook is one of the most brutal and crushing experiences a person can have. The required work is voluminous and extremely challenging and there is almost no support whatsoever: TAs don't speak English and the professors are, for the most part, unhelpful. On the plus side, the professors are extremely knowledgeable." Upperclassmen have access to better teachers and smaller classes and are accordingly more positive about the school. Writes one, "My upperdivision professors are fabulous. They do all their own research and have developed their own views on their subjects. The lack of real professors during freshman and sophomore year was awful, but these past two years have made up for it." Students in the Honors College also laud the "priority registration, close-knit group of students," and the fact that the program "encourages students to question everything and to think freely." As for the administration, a typical student asks, "Administration? It's a state school, the people who bring you the DMV. Sadly, the civil-service taint is felt here at the school big time."

### Life

Several factors conspire to make Stony Brook's campus one of the nation's least active socially. First, many students are deeply immersed in science and engineering and thus have little time for socializing. "Most people here," explains one student, "think about chemistry. Once they're done with that, they think about chemistry some more. Then they go home for the weekend." Second, many undergrads commute to Stony Brook for classes only. The parking situation, it should be noted, does little to encourage commuters to stick around: it is "a major crisis for most commuter students" because so few spaces are available. Of those who reside on campus, many go home nearly every weekend. Third, "Port Jefferson and Stony Brook aren't great college towns, although they're getting better" as they add "shopping, entertainment, and many local bars and clubs with a young crowd." As a result, many feel that "there is nothing to do for fun. On weekends this place is dead, a ghost campus until Monday morning." A small but vocal minority protest that "some people feel that there is nothing to do on this campus because our campus is portrayed as a suitcase college . . . but by being part of a group or team, your life on campus is a lot more fun, with parties, mixers, etc." With "Campus Recreation making small improvements every year," perhaps Stony Brook is growing closer to a more typical undergraduate social environment.

### Student Body

The diversity of SUNY SB's student body "is a great asset to the campus because it allows students to get to know other cultures, races, etc., and to become more tolerant and understanding of human beings as a whole." Students "generally keep to their own ethnic groups but also get along with other students." While "some students seem exceptionally smart, interesting, etc., others fall into the basic Long Island 'big hair and muscle car' category. And many, of course, are science geeks." Because the many commuters here usually come only for classes and study sessions, "it's hard to meet people."

# STONY BROOK UNIVERSITY (SUNY)

FINANCIAL AID: 631-632-6840 • E-MAIL: UGADMISSIONS@NOTES.CC.SUNYSB.EDU • WEBSITE: WWW.STONYBROOK.EDU

## ADMISSIONS

*Very important* academic and nonacademic factors considered by the admissions committee include character/personal qualities, essays, recommendations, and secondary school record. *Important* factors considered include extracurricular activities, interview, talent/ability, and volunteer work. *Other* factors considered include alumni/ae relation, class rank, standardized test scores, and work experience. Factors *not* considered include geography, minority status, religious affiliation/commitment, and state residency. SAT I or ACT required; SAT II recommended. TOEFL required of all international applicants. High school diploma is required and GED is accepted. *High school units required/recommended:* 14 total required; 19 total recommended; 4 English required, 3 math required, 4 math recommended, 3 science required, 4 science recommended, 3 foreign language recommended, 4 social studies required.

### The Inside Word

Like Albany, Stony Brook has also felt significant effects from years of SUNY cuts. But its graduate programs continue to receive national accolades, and the New York State legislature has been somewhat kinder to SUNY of late. Stony Brook's athletic programs have moved to NCAA Division I, America East Conference, in hopes of generating greater visibility and increases in applications. For the near future, admission will remain relatively easy for solid students.

## FINANCIAL AID

The Princeton Review suggests that all financial aid forms be submitted as soon as possible after January 1. *Need-based scholarships/grants offered:* Pell, SEOG, and state scholarships/grants. Institutional employment available. Federal Work-Study Program available. Off-campus job opportunities are excellent.

## FROM THE ADMISSIONS OFFICE

"Stony Brook has exceptional strength in the sciences, mathematics, humanities, fine arts, social sciences, engineering, and health professions. Stony Brook's undergraduate degree programs are augmented by a number of special academic opportunities. Among them are living/learning centers that integrate academic pursuits with residential life; the Honors College for outstanding students, which offers a four-year sequence of interdisciplinary seminars taught by some of Stony Brook's most respected faculty; and Federated Learning Communities, a nationally acclaimed 'experiment' in interdisciplinary education that brings a small group of students together with a faculty 'master learner' in six courses centered on a common theme. Stony Brook is quickly becoming the national model for undergraduate education at a research university."

## ADMISSIONS

| | |
|---|---|
| Admissions Rating | 79 |
| # of applicants | 15,458 |
| % of applicants accepted | 56 |
| % of acceptees attending | 27 |

### FRESHMAN PROFILE

| | |
|---|---|
| Range SAT Verbal | 490-600 |
| Average SAT Verbal | 545 |
| Range SAT Math | 530-640 |
| Average SAT Math | 588 |
| Minimum TOEFL | 550 |
| Average HS GPA | 3.2 |
| % graduated top 10% of class | 25 |
| % graduated top 25% of class | 63 |
| % graduated top 50% of class | 98 |

### DEADLINES

| | |
|---|---|
| Regular admission | 7/10 |
| Regular notification | rolling |
| Nonfall registration? | yes |

### APPLICANTS ALSO LOOK AT
**AND OFTEN PREFER**
Yale
Columbia
U. Penn
Brown
Cornell U.

**AND SOMETIMES PREFER**
Wesleyan U.
Williams
NYU
Cooper Union
Binghamton U.

**AND RARELY PREFER**
St. John's U. (NY)
Vassar

## FINANCIAL FACTS

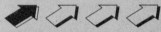

| | |
|---|---|
| Financial Aid Rating | 69 |
| In-state tuition | $3,400 |
| Out-of-state tuition | $8,300 |
| Room & board | $6,524 |
| Books and supplies | $750 |
| Required fees | $828 |
| % frosh receiving aid | 62 |
| Avg frosh loan | $7,157 |

# SUSQUEHANNA UNIVERSITY

514 UNIVERSITY AVENUE, SELINSGROVE, PA 17870 • ADMISSIONS: 570-372-4260 • FAX: 570-372-2722

## CAMPUS LIFE

| | |
|---|---|
| **Quality of Life Rating** | **85** |
| Type of school | private |
| Affiliation | Lutheran |
| Environment | rural |

### STUDENTS

| | |
|---|---|
| Total undergrad enrollment | 1,829 |
| % male/female | 42/58 |
| % from out of state | 37 |
| % from public high school | 86 |
| % live on campus | 80 |
| % in (# of) fraternities | 26 (4) |
| % in (# of) sororities | 27 (4) |
| % African American | 2 |
| % Asian | 2 |
| % Caucasian | 94 |
| % Hispanic | 2 |

### SURVEY SAYS . . .

*Diversity lacking on campus*
*Frats and sororities dominate social scene*
*Classes are small*
*Beautiful campus*
*Campus easy to get around*
*Musical organizations are hot*
*Theater is hot*
*Library needs improving*
*Political activism is (almost) nonexistent*
*(Almost) no one listens to college radio*

## ACADEMICS

| | |
|---|---|
| **Academic Rating** | **81** |
| Calendar | semester |
| Student/faculty ratio | 14:1 |
| Profs interesting rating | 92 |
| Profs accessible rating | 94 |
| % profs teaching UG courses | 100 |
| Avg lab size | 10-19 students |
| Avg reg class size | 10-19 students |

### MOST POPULAR MAJORS

business administration
communication
biology

## STUDENTS SPEAK OUT

### Academics

Susquehanna University, a small liberal arts college located in a "quaint," rural Pennsylvania town, offers "an excellent education" to its 1,700 or so undergrads. The academic focus here is on "pre-professional and career preparation." English, business, communications, and environmental science are some of the most popular majors. SU boasts "small classes" taught by "brilliant" professors who are "very friendly and open" as well as "interested in helping" students. "My academic experience has been pure heaven," raves a psychology major. "The professors give you as much extra help and attention as you want." Every SU undergraduate must complete a broad and sufficiently rigorous core curriculum, which is spread out over all four years. While "the core" includes the foreign language and writing intensive courses typically required at small liberal arts schools, SU requires courses in computer literacy and career planning as well. Susquehanna also prides itself in its emphasis on internships and the kinds of practical skills that will "help students achieve a competitive advantage" in the workplace. Though students here are all for the competitive advantage, they complain that registration is exceedingly difficult because of the core requirements and limited course availability in the most popular majors. "I have yet to make it through a registration period without having a problem getting the classes I signed up for," charges an irate computer science major. The "patronizing" administration provides little help in this regard.

### Life

About 80 percent of the students at SU live on its "small, friendly," and "beautiful" campus. Many students maintain that, "for a small school," SU provides "a good variety" of on-campus activities. "Sports, theater, music," and "church activities" are "all big." As a result, "it is easy to have leadership roles," and staying busy is a breeze. Also, to its credit, the university dependably provides non-alcoholic entertainment "to those who want to take part in it." However, these events "are not very well attended and are usually over by 10 p.m." Consequently, "fraternity parties are the cornerstone of the social scene here," and large quantities of beer are generally the cornerstone of frat parties. Even though partying is a favorite pastime here, students say the SU fraternity scene "is a lot more laid back than the average Greek scene." Off campus, the "extremely boring" surrounding town offers "nothing to do." Selinsgrove "is cute, but not nearly as good a college town as it could be," laments a senior. How bad is it? "Pizza places close at 11 P.M." For students with cars and free time, there are several state parks in the area, and good skiing is only 90 minutes away. More locally, "shopping with Amish people" can be quite an experience. SU students tell us they are "very community-involved," and the relationship between students and locals is extremely positive.

### Student Body

Approximately 1,700 students attend SU, most of them are white, somewhat wealthy, and from eastern Pennsylvania. What Susquehanna lacks in diversity (and students here say it lacks quite a bit) it makes up in hospitality. Students at SU claim to be "tremendously welcoming," not to mention "very friendly and easy to get along with." The politically conservative and "preppy" students here describe themselves as "funny, intelligent, friendly" as well as "courteous and professional in their academic and social lives." They do suffer from a "lack of ambition," though. Few dream of making their fortunes in global cosmopolitan centers. After graduation, most envision themselves starting a career locally, or going to graduate or professional school nearby. While they are in school, a large number of Susquehanna students pledge fraternities and sororities, but people who do not want to go Greek still fit in. "There aren't a lot of cliques, and there's very little tension between Greeks and independents," explains one student.

FINANCIAL AID: 570-372-4450 • E-MAIL: SUADMISS@SUSQU.EDU • WEBSITE: WWW.SUSQU.EDU

## ADMISSIONS

*Very important* academic and nonacademic factors considered by the admissions committee include class rank and secondary school record. *Important* factors considered include standardized test scores. *Other* factors considered include alumni/ae relation, minority status, character/personal qualities, essays, extracurricular activities, interview, recommendations, talent/ability, volunteer work, and work experience. Factors *not* considered include geography, religious affiliation/commitment, and state residency. SAT II recommended. TOEFL required of all international applicants. High school diploma is required and GED is accepted. *High school units required/recommended:* 18 total required; 22 total recommended; 4 English required, 3 math required, 4 math recommended, 3 science required, 4 science recommended, 2 science lab required, 3 science lab recommended, 2 foreign language required, 3 foreign language recommended, 1 social studies required, 2 social studies recommended, 1 history required, 1 elective required, 2 elective recommended.

### The Inside Word

Susquehanna is about as low profile as universities come in the age of MTV. Getting in is made easier by the serious competition the university faces from numerous like institutions in the region, some with significantly better reputations.

## FINANCIAL AID

*Students should submit:* FAFSA, CSS/Financial Aid PROFILE, state aid form, business/farm supplement, and prior year tax documents. Regular filing deadline is May 1. The Princeton Review suggests that all financial aid forms be submitted as soon as possible after January 1. *Need-based scholarships/grants offered:* Pell, SEOG, state scholarships/grants, private scholarships, and the school's own gift aid. *Loan aid offered:* FFEL Subsidized Stafford, FFEL Unsubsidized Stafford, FFEL PLUS, Federal Perkins, and college/university loans from institutional funds. Institutional employment available. Federal Work-Study Program available. Applicants will be notified of awards on a rolling basis beginning on or about January 15. Off-campus job opportunities are good.

## FROM THE ADMISSIONS OFFICE

"Students tell us they are getting both a first-rate education and practical experience to help them be competitive upon graduation. Faculty, especially in psychology, marketing, and the sciences, regularly encourage students in their research. Students also do internships at such sites as the White House, Continental Insurance, Estee Lauder, State Street Global Advisors, and Cable News Network. About 90 percent of our graduates go on for advanced degrees or get jobs in their chosen field within six months of graduation. Keeping up with the latest in information technology is easy for our students now that all residence hall rooms have connections to the computer network. Even though the university has six micro-computing laboratories, including one open 24 hours a day, many students find it convenient to use their own PCs to 'surf the 'Net' from their rooms. . . . Small classes, the opportunity to work closely with professors, and the sense of campus community all contribute to the educational experience here. . . . More than 100 student organizations provide lots of opportunity for leadership and involvement in campus life."

## ADMISSIONS

| | |
|---|---|
| Admissions Rating | 78 |
| # of applicants | 2,369 |
| % of applicants accepted | 75 |
| % of acceptees attending | 28 |
| # accepting a place on wait list | 42 |
| % admitted from wait list | 17 |
| # of early decision applicants | 120 |
| % accepted early decision | 76 |

### FRESHMAN PROFILE

| | |
|---|---|
| Range SAT Verbal | 520-610 |
| Range SAT Math | 520-620 |
| Minimum TOEFL | 550 |
| % graduated top 10% of class | 29 |
| % graduated top 25% of class | 67 |
| % graduated top 50% of class | 94 |

### DEADLINES

| | |
|---|---|
| Early decision | 12/15 |
| Early decision notification | 1/15 |
| Regular admission | 3/1 |
| Nonfall registration? | yes |

### APPLICANTS ALSO LOOK AT

**AND OFTEN PREFER**
Ithaca
**AND SOMETIMES PREFER**
Franklin & Marshall
Bucknell
Dickinson
Gettysburg
**AND RARELY PREFER**
Penn State—Univ. Park

## FINANCIAL FACTS

| | |
|---|---|
| Financial Aid Rating | 89 |
| Tuition | $20,140 |
| Room & board | $5,770 |
| Books and supplies | $600 |
| Required fees | $300 |
| % frosh receiving aid | 65 |
| % undergrads receiving aid | 69 |
| Avg frosh grant | $10,515 |
| Avg frosh loan | $3,300 |

# SWARTHMORE COLLEGE

500 COLLEGE AVENUE, SWARTHMORE, PA 19081 • ADMISSIONS: 610-328-8300 • FAX: 610-328-8580

## CAMPUS LIFE

| | |
|---|---|
| **Quality of Life Rating** | **85** |
| Type of school | private |
| Affiliation | none |
| Environment | suburban |

### STUDENTS

| | |
|---|---|
| Total undergrad enrollment | 1,428 |
| % male/female | 47/53 |
| % from out of state | 82 |
| % from public high school | 62 |
| % live on campus | 87 |
| % in (# of) fraternities | 6 (2) |
| % African American | 9 |
| % Asian | 14 |
| % Caucasian | 61 |
| % Hispanic | 10 |
| % Native American | 1 |
| % international | 6 |

### SURVEY SAYS . . .
*Beautiful campus*
*Political activism is hot*
*Students get along with local community*
*Popular college radio*
*Students love Swarthmore, PA*
*Very small frat/sorority scene*
*Campus difficult to get around*
*(Almost) no one smokes*
*Library needs improving*
*Students aren't religious*

## ACADEMICS

| | |
|---|---|
| **Academic Rating** | **95** |
| Calendar | semester |
| Student/faculty ratio | 8:1 |
| Profs interesting rating | 91 |
| Profs accessible rating | 93 |
| % profs teaching UG courses | 100 |
| Avg lab size | under 10 students |
| Avg reg class size | 10-19 students |

### MOST POPULAR MAJORS
economics
political science
English literature

## STUDENTS SPEAK OUT

### Academics

A Swarthmore education is definitely not for the weak of heart. Commenting on the legendary workload here, one undergrad explains: "At times I feel like I signed up for married life with the Marquis de Sade—work enjoys beating me down every night. But then I remember that I've learned more in one class than in four years of high school, and that makes it all better." Concurs another, "First you think they [i.e. the faculty] are out to get you. Then you think they're out to get everybody. Finally you realize they're just too damned smart. And from there it's easy—try to be as smart as them. You won't succeed (well, you might) and if you don't, suddenly you realize you've learned more than you ever thought possible." To ease students' transition from high-school academics to the rigors of college, Swarthmore offers all first-semester courses on a pass-fail basis only. "Do not underestimate the value of taking your first semester pass-fail!" notes one student. "It's a great way to adjust." To further facilitate success, the faculty provides a substantial support network to the school's budding scholars. "One of my profs has four hours a day of office hours, sometimes including weekends," explains one undergrad. Says another, "My professors have always been more than willing to help me in my academic ventures, even if the project I am working on is not specifically for his/her class." The end result is a student body confident of and competent in its skills. Recounts one student, "Last week, no lie, one of my professors asked me to proofread her latest journal submission because she wanted to know if it was understandable to the world at large. By the time you're a senior, you start to feel like a colleague more than just a student."

### Life

Because of the sizable workload, "academic thinking tends to invade private spaces—a strength and weakness," according to one senior. Students carry classroom discussions into social settings; the fave activity at Swarthmore is "talking into the wee hours of the morning." Study breaks at PACES, the student-run coffeehouse, keep Swatties caffeinated and in contact with each other, and one sophomore notes, "It is surprising how social a place the library is." Although "there's lots of self-imposed guilt about homework and other obligations," students do get involved in all sorts of campus activities. Students definitely dig intramural sports, movies, coffee, and even the low-key party scene. One student remarks, "Swat is one of those places where you can attend an open mike, comedy improv group, a pterodactyl hunt, a frat party, and a movie all in one night." All events are free or extremely inexpensive, and if the beautiful campus gets a little claustrophobic after a while, the nearby commuter rail offers access to Philadelphia's nightlife and cultural scene.

### Student Body

Swatties cannot sing each other's praises enough. Comments such as the following are typical here: "Being surrounded by 1,400 extremely bright people is one of the great experiences of my life. The people here are smart, funny, and incredibly friendly. I don't know anyone I don't like." The typical Swattie is liberal, and upper-middle-class. Students with varying ethnic, political, and sexual orientations definitely have a place at Swarthmore, though. As one sophomore notes, "Everyone here is more or less an opinionated weirdo. It's rather comforting." Most students believe that the student body is diverse; some, however, feel that minorities are underrepresented.

FINANCIAL AID: 610-328-8358 • E-MAIL: ADMISSIONS@SWARTHMORE.EDU • WEBSITE: WWW.SWARTHMORE.EDU

## ADMISSIONS

*Very important* academic and nonacademic factors considered by the admissions committee include secondary school record, standardized test scores, class rank, essays, character/personal qualities, and recommendations. *Important* factors include extracurricular activities. *Other* factors considered include talent/ability, alumni/ae relation, minority status, volunteer work, work experience, geography, and interview. Factors *not* considered include religious affiliation/commitment and state residency. SAT I or ACT required, SAT I preferred; SAT II also required. *High school units required/recommended:* 4 English recommended, 3 math recommended, 3 science recommended, the study of one or two foreign languages recommended, 3 social studies recommended. Course work in art and music is also recommended.

### The Inside Word

Swarthmore is as good as they come; among liberal arts colleges there is none better. Candidates face an admissions process that is appropriately demanding and thorough. Even the best qualified of students need to complete their applications with a meticulous approach—during candidate evaluation, serious competition is just another file away. Those who are fortunate enough to be offered admission usually have shown the committee that they have a high level of intellectual curiosity, self-confidence, and motivation.

## FINANCIAL AID

*Students should submit:* FAFSA, institution's own financial aid form, CSS/Financial Aid PROFILE, noncustodial (divorced/separated) parent's statement, business/farm supplement, federal tax return, W-2 statements, and year-end paycheck stub. Regular filing deadline is February 10. The Princeton Review suggests that all financial aid forms be submitted as soon as possible after January 1. *Need-based scholarships/grants offered:* Pell, SEOG, state scholarships/grants, private scholarships, and the school's own gift aid. *Loan aid offered:* FFEL Subsidized Stafford, FFEL Unsubsidized Stafford, FFEL PLUS, Federal Perkins, state, and college/university loans from institutional funds. Institutional employment available. Federal Work-Study Program available. Applicants will be notified of awards on or about April 1. Off-campus job opportunities are fair.

## FROM THE ADMISSIONS OFFICE

"The purpose of Swarthmore College is to make its students more valuable human beings and more useful members of society. While it shares this purpose with other educational institutions, each school, college, and university seeks to realize that purpose in its own way. Each must select those tasks it can do best. By such selection it contributes to the diversity and richness of educational opportunity that is part of the American heritage. Swarthmore seeks to help its students realize their fullest intellectual and personal potential combined with a deep sense of ethical and social concern."

## ADMISSIONS

| | |
|---|---|
| Admissions Rating | 97 |
| # of applicants | 3,956 |
| % of applicants accepted | 24 |
| % of acceptees attending | 39 |
| # of early decision applicants | 283 |
| % accepted early decision | 45 |

### FRESHMAN PROFILE

| | |
|---|---|
| Range SAT Verbal | 680-770 |
| Average SAT Verbal | 718 |
| Range SAT Math | 660-760 |
| Average SAT Math | 706 |
| % graduated top 10% of class | 88 |
| % graduated top 25% of class | 98 |
| % graduated top 50% of class | 100 |

### DEADLINES

| | |
|---|---|
| Early decision | 11/15 |
| Early decision notification | 12/15 |
| Regular admission | 1/1 |
| Regular notification | 4/1 |

### APPLICANTS ALSO LOOK AT
**AND OFTEN PREFER**
Harvard
Princeton
Yale
Stanford
Dartmouth
**AND SOMETIMES PREFER**
Amherst
Wesleyan U.
Columbia
Brown
Williams
**AND RARELY PREFER**
Vassar
Haverford
U. Chicago
U. Penn

### FINANCIAL FACTS

| | |
|---|---|
| Financial Aid Rating | 82 |
| Tuition | $26,098 |
| Room & board | $8,162 |
| Books and supplies | $920 |
| Required fees | $278 |
| % frosh receiving aid | 49 |
| % undergrads receiving aid | 48 |
| Avg frosh grant | $20,084 |
| Avg frosh loan | $1,917 |

# SWEET BRIAR COLLEGE

PO BOX B, SWEET BRIAR, VA 24595 • ADMISSIONS: 434-381-6142 • FAX: 434-381-6152

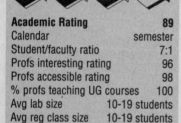
## STUDENTS SPEAK OUT
### Academics

Nestled in the foothills of Virginia's Blue Ridge Mountains, Sweet Briar's romantic name and distinctly southern location might lead the uninitiated to think its ladies are receiving instruction in the fine arts of swooning, eyelash batting, and fork placement. Not so. One African American junior puts it quite bluntly: "The general public mistakenly thinks this is a rich white girls' school. That's a load of crap." So where's the real SBC? In "cutting-edge" programs like Law & Society, the Center for Civic Renewal, and an environmental science program that includes, as one junior puts it, 3,300 acres of outdoor campus—woods, lakes, mountains—like having your own personal ecology laboratory." Sweet Briar's strengths also include highly focused instruction, a well-designed advisor program, and excellent professor-student dynamics: "Sweet Briar prides itself on small classes, individual attention, and a supportive environment," writes one student. "In a class of seven people, the professors won't let you fail." One sophomore remarks, "It's not just easy to find your professors here, it's hard to avoid them." Plus, everyone could use a little protection once they get out into the big bad world. Notes a sophomore: "The alumnae network is incredible."

### Life

While there's certainly no shortage of enthusiasm for life at Sweet Briar (one student warns, "if I loved it any more than I already do, I would buy it up and keep it")—there are varying opinions about the ups and downs of socializing on and off campus. Writes a senior, "Life at Sweet Briar can get pretty dull with no men around, and the college has been characterized as a 'suitcase school' as many leave during the weekend to visit neighboring colleges"—which include Hampden-Sydney College, University of Virginia, and Washington and Lee. Fairly strict alcohol policies also "force people to go off campus to have fun," though there have been concerted efforts by the administration in the last few years to improve SBC's social programming, which now includes "feature films, musicians, lectures, theater, 'Dell Parties,' casino nights, and formals throughout the year." Though there are the occasional trips to movies, the Wal-Mart, and a local country-and-western bar, a junior complains that "the town is much like Deliverance, and I just want to escape." Despite the negatives, SBC women manage to make the best of the situation, citing the school's stunning location on "a really beautiful campus with lots of great trails for running, hiking, mountain biking, and horseback riding."

### Student Body

Here's a motto for you: "SBC: Where women are leaders and men are guests!" While this might not accurately describe all of the school's population, one gets a sense that Sweet Briar women are, in general, happy, active, involved, and mutually supportive. As one sophomore puts it, "The goals they have set for themselves are high and challenging." Adds another, "Living with 600 women changes the way you interact with women overall. Women respect women here." Of course, there are always your slightly irritating overachievers (e.g., "I sing in choir, am a class officer, am the chair of the Saturday Enrichment Program, ride on the fall team, have two campus jobs and a boyfriend!"), but on the whole SBC seems to offer students a noncompetitive, friendly atmosphere in which to pursue their studies. One student lauds "the encouragement of the women here to be all they can and to do whatever [they] want [with their] futures." And though a few students remarked on the ethnic and economic homogeneity of the student body, others disagreed. "Some people think we're a lily-white country club," writes a junior. "They've never been here. I have made friends from a wide variety of countries, cultures, races, and lifestyles. We're friends not because of some phony diversity movement, but because we're united by our academic pursuits." You go girl!

FINANCIAL AID: 434-381-6156 • E-MAIL: ADMISSIONS@SBC.EDU • WEBSITE: WWW.SBC.EDU

## ADMISSIONS

*Very important* academic and nonacademic factors considered by the admissions committee include secondary school record. *Important* factors considered include essays, recommendations, and standardized test scores. *Other* factors considered include alumni/ae relation, character/personal qualities, class rank, extracurricular activities, interview, minority status, talent/ability, volunteer work, and work experience. Factors *not* considered include geography, religious affiliation/commitment, and state residency. SAT I or ACT required, SAT II recommended. TOEFL required of all international applicants. High school diploma is required and GED is not accepted except for adult students. *High school units required/recommended:* 4 English required, 3 math required, 4 math recommended, 3 science required, 2 science lab required, 2 foreign language required, 3 foreign language recommended, 2 social studies required, 3 social studies recommended. *The admissions office says:* "Faculty are highly involved in our admissions process. We encourage prospective students to work closely with their Sweet Briar admissions counselor, particularly if there are extenuating circumstances in regard to the academic record."

### The Inside Word

An extremely small applicant pool tempers selectivity greatly but also allows the admissions committee to take a longer look at most candidates than is typical in college admission. Despite the small applicant pool, candidates are usually well-qualified academically. A lackadaisical application can spell denial.

## FINANCIAL AID

*Students should submit:* FAFSA, institution's own financial aid form, noncustodial (divorced/separated) parent's statement, and business/farm supplement. The Princeton Review suggests that all financial aid forms be submitted as soon as possible after January 1. *Need-based scholarships/grants offered:* Pell, SEOG, state scholarships/grants, private scholarships, and the school's own gift aid. *Loan aid offered:* Direct Subsidized Stafford, Direct Unsubsidized Stafford, Direct PLUS, FFEL Subsidized Stafford, FFEL Unsubsidized Stafford, FFEL PLUS, Federal Perkins, and college/university loans from institutional funds. Institutional employment available. Federal Work-Study Program available. Applicants will be notified of awards on a rolling basis beginning on or about March 1. Off-campus job opportunities are poor.

## FROM THE ADMISSIONS OFFICE

"The woman who applies to Sweet Briar is mature and far-sighted enough to know what she wants from her college experience. She is intellectually adventuresome, more willing to explore new fields, and more open to challenging her boundaries. Sweet Briar attracts the ambitious, confident woman who enjoys being immersed not only in a first-rate academic program, but in a variety of meaningful activities outside the classroom. Our students take charge and revel in their accomplishments. This attitude follows graduates, enabling them to compete confidently in the corporate world and in graduate school."

## ADMISSIONS

| | |
|---|---|
| Admissions Rating | 80 |
| # of applicants | 415 |
| % of applicants accepted | 89 |
| % of acceptees attending | 45 |
| # of early decision applicants | 30 |
| % accepted early decision | 93 |

### FRESHMAN PROFILE

| | |
|---|---|
| Range SAT Verbal | 530-650 |
| Average SAT Verbal | 592 |
| Range SAT Math | 490-600 |
| Average SAT Math | 547 |
| Range ACT Composite | 23-28 |
| Average ACT Composite | 25 |
| Minimum TOEFL | 580 |
| Average HS GPA | 3.5 |
| % graduated top 10% of class | 30 |
| % graduated top 25% of class | 62 |
| % graduated top 50% of class | 96 |

### DEADLINES

| | |
|---|---|
| Early decision | 12/1 |
| Early decision notification | 12/15 |
| Regular admission | 2/15 |
| Nonfall registration? | yes |

### APPLICANTS ALSO LOOK AT

**AND OFTEN PREFER**
William & Mary
Mount Holyoke
Randolph-Macon Woman's
**AND SOMETIMES PREFER**
Hollins
Vanderbilt
U. Richmond

### FINANCIAL FACTS

| | |
|---|---|
| Financial Aid Rating | 90 |
| Tuition | $17,860 |
| Room & board | $7,300 |
| Books and supplies | $600 |
| Required fees | $150 |
| % frosh receiving aid | 64 |
| % undergrads receiving aid | 55 |
| Avg frosh grant | $10,820 |
| Avg frosh loan | $1,902 |

# SYRACUSE UNIVERSITY

201 TOLLEY, ADMINISTRATION BUILDING, SYRACUSE, NY 13244 • ADMISSIONS: 315-443-3611

## CAMPUS LIFE

**Quality of Life Rating**     **81**
Type of school     private
Affiliation     none
Environment     urban

### STUDENTS

| | |
|---|---|
| Total undergrad enrollment | 10,740 |
| % male/female | 46/54 |
| % from out of state | 53 |
| % from public high school | 83 |
| % live on campus | 72 |
| % in (# of) fraternities | 20 (21) |
| % in (# of) sororities | 30 (19) |
| % African American | 8 |
| % Asian | 5 |
| % Caucasian | 72 |
| % Hispanic | 4 |
| % international | 4 |
| # of countries represented | 70 |

### SURVEY SAYS . . .

*Student publications are popular*
*Diverse students interact*
*Everyone loves the Orangemen*
*Frats and sororities dominate social scene*
*Students are cliquish*
*Athletic facilities are great*
*Lousy off-campus food*
*Lab facilities need improving*
*Students aren't religious*

## ACADEMICS

**Academic Rating**     **83**

| | |
|---|---|
| Calendar | semester |
| Student/faculty ratio | 12:1 |
| Profs interesting rating | 72 |
| Profs accessible rating | 71 |
| % profs teaching UG courses | 95 |
| % classes taught by TAs | 7 |
| Avg lab size | 20-29 students |
| Avg reg class size | 10-19 students |

### MOST POPULAR MAJORS
psychology
information management
and technology
political science

## STUDENTS SPEAK OUT

### Academics

Students choose Syracuse University for the tremendous scope of its offerings, its excellent resources (including "a fantastic library!") and of course, its national reputation. Among its 21 academic divisions, SU boasts notable programs in business, engineering, visual and performing arts, and natural sciences. It is probably best known, however, for the "amazing" Newhouse School of Communications, which is universally thought to be "one of the best in the country" and includes one of the nation's top broadcast journalism programs. Like most universities, "this school is very research oriented." Warns one student, "Syracuse University is supposedly a student-centered research campus; however, if the students don't know and act upon that, they'll get lost in the crowd." Instruction varies markedly from one division to the next, with journalism profs earning the highest marks. Notes one sophomore, "Some professors are captivating and others are awful. The TAs, in my experience, are uninformed, dull, and disinterested. The class sizes usually prevent individual interaction between students and teachers." Complains one math education major, "There is no doubt in my mind that the professors know their stuff, but a large portion of them don't know how to present the material in a beneficial manner." The administration generally receives favorable reviews; writes one student, "The school's administration is very accessible . . . many of them go to great lengths to accommodate your needs as a student. This helps reduce the stress of the whole academic experience." Many students, however, complain that the administration nickels-and-dimes them with "lots of extra charges on top of the very expensive tuition."

### Life

Students are split in their assessment of the social scene at Syracuse. Detractors badmouth the town ("dull and depressing . . . the local establishments—stores, shops, etc.—could use some restoration"), the weather ("This is the third most overcast city in the U.S.—lots of rain"), and the variety of available entertainment ("A car is needed to go anywhere that has culture," writes one student; says another, "No one leaves campus except to go to the mall. Culture in Syracuse is nonexistent"). Others disagree, pointing out that "there's more to do in Syracuse than people give it credit for. Many people go to the campus bars for entertainment. By far they are the most popular, but there are other things to do, like bowling, dancing, coffee houses, etc." They also point to a moderately active Greek system that "provides more stuff to do, especially since there isn't much to do in local areas. Bars are big here, as are casual drugs like marijuana. This could be a very depressing place or the best time ever." All students agree that drinking is a popular pastime, explaining that "SU is a drinking school, not a party school." They also agree that intercollegiate sports, especially football, basketball, and lacrosse, are huge. Sums up one student, "If you like sports, snow, and beer, this is a great school for you."

### Student Body

"People think that the only type of people that come here are rich spoiled kids from Long Island," writes one SU student. "In reality, those are the ones that stick out the most, but there are many different types of people here." Indeed, undergrads at SU represent "a diverse student population with diverse interests." However, according to most students, different populations rarely intermingle. "I would love to believe that we all get along," writes one African American junior, "but we segregate from each other based on Greek life, race, religion, class, etc. It's rather sad: some just live in a bubble and think SU is A-OK. We have some work to do."

FINANCIAL AID: 315-443-1513 • E-MAIL: ORANGE@SYR.EDU • WEBSITE: WWW.SYRACUSE.EDU

## ADMISSIONS

*Very important* academic and nonacademic factors considered by the admissions committee include class rank, secondary school record, and standardized test scores. *Important* factors considered include character/personal qualities, essays, and recommendations. *Other* factors considered include alumni/ae relation, extracurricular activities, geography, interview, minority status, talent/ability, volunteer work, and work experience. Factors *not* considered include religious affiliation/commitment. SAT I or ACT required. TOEFL required of all international applicants. High school diploma is required and GED is accepted. *High school units required:* 17 total required; 18 total recommended; 4 English required, 4 math required, 3 science required, 2 foreign language required, 3 foreign language recommended, 3 social studies required.

### The Inside Word

Thanks to nationally competitive athletic teams and the Newhouse School of Communications, Syracuse draws a large applicant pool. At the same time, it has reduced the size of the freshman class, so the university has gotten more selective over the past few years. Most above-average students should still be strong candidates; though many weaker students are also able to benefit from Syracuse's individualized admissions process, they must show true promise in order to have a shot. Candidates for the Newhouse School will encounter even greater competition for admission.

## FINANCIAL AID

*Students should submit:* FAFSA. The Princeton Review suggests that all financial aid forms be submitted as soon as possible after January 1. *Need-based scholarships/grants offered:* Pell, SEOG, state scholarships/grants, and the school's own gift aid. *Loan aid offered:* FFEL Subsidized Stafford, FFEL Unsubsidized Stafford, FFEL PLUS, Federal Perkins, and Federal Nursing. Institutional employment available. Federal Work-Study Program available. Applicants will be notified of awards on or about April 1. Off-campus job opportunities are good.

## FROM THE ADMISSIONS OFFICE

"Syracuse University offers students a world of opportunities. Opportunities to explore over 200 majors or to design majors of their own; to actively participate in real-world research assisting faculty; to participate in extracurricular clubs and organizations (there are nearly 300). Because Syracuse has one of the most formidable lists of celebrated alumni in American higher education, there are events that provide the chance to hear the experiences of such alumni as U.S. Secretary of Health and Human Services Donna Shalala, entertainer and production executive Dick Clark, ABC News anchor Ted Koppel, Broadway and film star Vanessa Williams, sports legend Jim Brown, New York Times columnist William Safire, U.S. Senators Joseph Biden and Alfonse D'Amato, retired U.S. Senator and Concord Coalition co-founder Warren Rudman, "60 Minutes" correspondent Steve Kroft, NBC sportscaster Bob Costas, Estee Lauder CEO and president Robin Burns, and astronauts Eileen Collins and Story Musgrave. Other academic opportunities include participation in the Honors Program, internships and programs abroad in England, France, Italy, Spain, Hong Kong, and Zimbabwe, Africa. Syracuse University combines the best characteristics of a research institution with a traditional focus on the highest quality teaching, advising, and mentoring. It is a student-centered research university, and is committed to giving students the very best educational experience available."

## ADMISSIONS

| | |
|---|---|
| Admissions Rating | 87 |
| # of applicants | 12,637 |
| % of applicants accepted | 58 |
| % of acceptees attending | 38 |
| # of early decision applicants | 577 |
| % accepted early decision | 81 |

### FRESHMAN PROFILE

| | |
|---|---|
| Range SAT Verbal | 540-640 |
| Range SAT Math | 570-660 |
| Minimum TOEFL | 550 |
| Average HS GPA | 3.5 |
| % graduated top 10% of class | 40 |
| % graduated top 25% of class | 77 |
| % graduated top 50% of class | 98 |

### DEADLINES

| | |
|---|---|
| Early decision | 11/15 |
| Early decision notification | 12/31 |
| Regular admission | 1/15 |
| Nonfall registration? | yes |

### APPLICANTS ALSO LOOK AT

**AND OFTEN PREFER**
Cornell U.
Union (NY)
Lehigh
Boston U.
NYU

**AND SOMETIMES PREFER**
Penn State—U. Park
Ithaca
Lafayette
Bucknell
Geneseo State

**AND RARELY PREFER**
Hobart & William Smith
Siena
Northeastern U.

## FINANCIAL FACTS

| | |
|---|---|
| Financial Aid Rating | 75 |
| Tuition | $21,500 |
| Room & board | $9,130 |
| Books and supplies | $1,050 |
| Required fees | $454 |
| % frosh receiving aid | 56 |
| % undergrads receiving aid | 61 |
| Avg frosh grant | $11,100 |
| Avg frosh loan | $3,400 |

# TCU

OFFICE OF ADMISSIONS, TCU BOX 297013, FORT WORTH, TX 76129 • ADMISSIONS: 817-257-7490 • FAX: 817-257-7268

## CAMPUS LIFE

**Quality of Life Rating**    **86**
Type of school    private
Affiliation    Disciples of Christ
Environment    suburban

### STUDENTS
Total undergrad enrollment    6,675
% male/female    41/59
% from out of state    24
% from public high school    91
% live on campus    48
% in (# of) fraternities    26 (14)
% in (# of) sororities    35 (16)
% African American    5
% Asian    2
% Caucasian    84
% Hispanic    6
% Native American    1
% international    4
# of countries represented    75

### SURVEY SAYS . . .
*Beautiful campus*
*Campus easy to get around*
*Frats and sororities dominate social scene*
*Great library*
*Students love Fort Worth, TX*
*Student publications are ignored*
*Students don't get along with local community*
*Students aren't religious*
*Political activism is (almost) nonexistent*
*(Almost) no one listens to college radio*

## ACADEMICS

**Academic Rating**    **78**
Calendar    semester
Student/faculty ratio    15:1
Profs interesting rating    79
Profs accessible rating    96
% profs teaching UG courses    97
% classes taught by TAs    2
Avg lab size    10-19 students
Avg reg class size    10-19 students

### MOST POPULAR MAJORS
finance
marketing
psychology

## STUDENTS SPEAK OUT
### Academics

Everything is big in Texas except, we suppose, TCU. Students say it is the "ideal size" because it offers world-class research resources and facilities that rival those at enormous state universities as well as "small classes" and a personalized learning environment. The "very challenging" classes are just the right size, too, according to students. They are "small enough so that teachers know your name, but big enough that you are not constantly singled out." Some of TCU's professors "aren't good," but most are "wonderful" and "profoundly interesting" teachers who "go out of their way to make a personal connection with students." "If they don' know your name," advises an accounting major, "you are doing something wrong." Faculty members are not bashful about giving extra help, either. "I once approached a professor to ask who the best tutor was for her course," explains a junior. "She responded, 'Here's my phone number. I'm the best tutor for my course.'" Students have few qualms with the "accessible and involved" administration. "I doubt that at many universities the chancellor urges the students to e-mail him with concerns," speculates a junior. As far as majors at TCU, many students recommend the "very good" business school. Popular, too, are education, journalism, and the health sciences. "TCU's spiel since I was a freshman has been 'It's all about you.' Throughout my four years, it has truly been about me," says a satisfied senior. "I have truly enjoyed my years at TCU and it has been a great asset to say, 'I attend Texas Christian University.'"

### Life

On Texas Christian's "gorgeous campus," there is a notably "Christian atmosphere" and religious groups "are especially important" to student life. Intramural sports are also pretty big, not least because they provide "a great chance to meet people and stay active." Beyond these diversions, fraternities and sororities "dominate" TCU's social scene, and most social life for Greeks and non-Greeks reportedly takes place off campus. On the weekends, students "go to parties" or head out to the bright lights of Fort Worth, "a cool town with lots of stuff to do" and "great nightlife." Students promise that, so long as "you don't mind spending the money," there are "many different things to do in the Metroplex," as the student-friendly Dallas–Fort Worth region is generally known. "Dancing and drinking" top the list of off-campus social activities. The bars and clubs of downtown Fort Worth are especially popular, but "you need a car" to get there. Although many students cite a lack of school spirit for—we kid you not—Horned Frog athletics, TCU students nevertheless eternally cherish their sports. This is Texas, after all. In the fall, football games are widely attended "social events."

### Student Body

We are here to tell you: Greek life is nothing short of huge at TCU, and most students seem to like it that way. Members of fraternities and sororities do, anyway. Students who choose not to pledge complain that TCU is "too Greek." Consider yourself warned: "If you have no interest in Greek life, you can be very annoyed by the way they seem to take over the school" and "you have to work to find your niche." Also, there is a somewhat lopsided "girl-to-guy ratio" here (far fewer men than women). The "super-friendly," "outgoing," and "attractive" students here are "welcoming" but "sometimes superficial" and "cliquish to extremes." "TCU should change its name to Texas Christian High School," suggests a senior. In the future, most of these "quality people" expect to land good jobs in the professional world. TCU actively seeks to recruit under-represented minorities, but they have yet to enroll in droves. Those minority students who do come sometimes find it difficult to break into the dominant social scene.

FINANCIAL AID: 817-257-7858 • E-MAIL: FROGMAIL@TCU.EDU • WEBSITE: WWW.TCU.EDU

## ADMISSIONS

*Very important* academic and nonacademic factors considered by the admissions committee include secondary school record. *Important* factors considered include standardized test scores and state residency. *Other* factors considered include alumni/ae relation, character/personal qualities, interview, recommendations, religous affiliation/commitment, class rank, essays, extracurricular activities, talent/ability, volunteer work, and work experience. Factors *not* considered include geography and minority status. SAT I or ACT required, SAT I preferred. TOEFL required of all international applicants. High school diploma is required and GED is not accepted. *High school units required/recommended:* 4 English required, 3 math required, 3 science required, 2 science lab required, 2 foreign language required. *The admissions office says:* "Students who wish to be considered for academic scholarship awards and students who would like to be evaluated on their transcript through junior year only should apply by December 31."

### The Inside Word

The most important element of the admissions process at TCU for most candidates is deciding whether they want to be here. Most applicants are admitted, notwithstanding TCU's challenging academic standards.

## FINANCIAL AID

The Princeton Review suggests that all financial aid forms be submitted as soon as possible after January 1. *Need-based scholarships/grants offered:* Pell, SEOG, state scholarships/grants, private scholarships, the school's own gift aid, Federal Nursing. *Loan aid offered:* FFEL Subsidized Stafford, FFEL Unsubsidized Stafford, FFEL PLUS, Federal Perkins, and Federal Nursing. Institutional employment available. Federal Work-Study Program available. Off-campus job opportunities are excellent.

## FROM THE ADMISSIONS OFFICE

"TCU is a major teaching and research university with the feel of a small college. You will find it is large enough to challenge and small enough to care. An affordable, private university, TCU offers new students The Freshman Commitment, seven opportunities on which you can depend: Frog Camp, an invitation to friends and Horned Frog traditions; freshman seminars, small classes with great professors; TCU Leadership Center, because leaders are made, not born; writing enhancement, in classes of 25 or less; technology, with each residence hall room connected to the Internet and lots of computer labs; on-campus housing, only a short walk from your classes; and globalism, study abroad opportunities, international ideas, and events. We are historically related to, but not governed by, the Christian Church (Disciples of Christ), a mainstream Protestant denomination that encourages understanding among the world's religions. That means we have people with all kinds of values and viewpoints on our campus. From National Merit Scholars to those just now realizing their academic potential, TCU attracts and serves those who want to lead and learn."

### ADMISSIONS

| | |
|---|---|
| Admissions Rating | 80 |
| # of applicants | 5,055 |
| % of applicants accepted | 76 |
| % of acceptees attending | 39 |
| # accepting a place on wait list | 80 |

#### FRESHMAN PROFILE

| | |
|---|---|
| Range SAT Verbal | 520-620 |
| Range SAT Math | 530-630 |
| Range ACT Composite | 22-28 |
| Minimum TOEFL | 550 |
| % graduated top 10% of class | 34 |
| % graduated top 25% of class | 66 |
| % graduated top 50% of class | 94 |

#### DEADLINES

| | |
|---|---|
| Priority admission deadline | 11/15 |
| Regular admission | 2/15 |
| Regular notification | 4/1 |
| Nonfall registration? | yes |

#### APPLICANTS ALSO LOOK AT
#### AND SOMETIMES PREFER
U. Texas—Austin
Trinity U.
Texas A&M
Rice
#### AND RARELY PREFER
SMU
Austin Coll.
Southwestern

### FINANCIAL FACTS

| | |
|---|---|
| Financial Aid Rating | 83 |
| Tuition | $15,000 |
| Room & board | $4,870 |
| Books and supplies | $720 |
| % frosh receiving aid | 37 |
| % undergrads receiving aid | 39 |

# TEMPLE UNIVERSITY

1801 NORTH BROAD STREET, PHILADELPHIA, PA 19122-6096 • ADMISSIONS: 215-204-7200 • FAX: 215-204-5694

## CAMPUS LIFE

| | |
|---|---|
| **Quality of Life Rating** | **85** |
| Type of school | public |
| Affiliation | none |
| Environment | urban |

### STUDENTS

| | |
|---|---|
| Total undergrad enrollment | 18,394 |
| % male/female | 42/58 |
| % from out of state | 22 |
| % from public high school | 80 |
| % live on campus | 22 |
| % in (# of) fraternities | 1 (13) |
| % in (# of) sororities | 1 (12) |
| % African American | 28 |
| % Asian | 9 |
| % Caucasian | 59 |
| % Hispanic | 4 |
| % international | 3 |
| # of countries represented | 117 |

### SURVEY SAYS . . .

Athletic facilities are great
Great computer facilities
Campus feels safe
Campus easy to get around
Great library
Ethnic diversity on campus
Students are cliquish
Student publications are ignored
Students aren't religious
(Almost) no one listens to college
radio
Lots of TAs teach upper-level
courses

## ACADEMICS

| | |
|---|---|
| **Academic Rating** | **72** |
| Calendar | semester |
| Student/faculty ratio | 15:1 |
| Profs interesting rating | 65 |
| Profs accessible rating | 92 |
| Avg lab size | 10-19 students |
| Avg reg class size | 10-19 students |

### MOST POPULAR MAJORS

early childhood/elementary education
computer and information sciences
psychology

## STUDENTS SPEAK OUT
### Academics

The "highly regarded" School of Communications at "inexpensive" Temple University is "easily one of the best in the country," and the music, art, and pre-professional programs certainly aren't too shabby. Students at this "fine urban institution" tell us you'll "get a good, solid education" regardless of major and "a dose of the real world" as well. To be sure, "you're not treated like a child." Everyone here must complete Temple's Core Curriculum, a cross-section of courses taught mostly by full-time faculty members that "provides an intellectual foundation for understanding the world." The core includes courses in composition, mathematics, American culture, international studies, science and technology, the arts, and studies in race and racism. Students in Temple's Honors Program seem especially pleased; they contend that their professors are "comparable to" those "at elite schools around the country." The rest of the "highly educated and knowledgeable" professors are generally "pretty approachable and reasonable," but the actual teaching ability of some is a little suspect. Teaching assistants are reportedly "helpful," and Temple also boasts "excellent" technology and "nice lab facilities." Financial aid "can be tough" to navigate, though, and the administration, while "very well-organized" and "open to suggestion," has "little or no contact with the actual student population." On the whole, "Temple does have its ebbs and flows, like any school," concludes a public relations major, but the "overall experience is great."

### Life

Temple's distinctly urban campus is located in North Philadelphia—not the warmest and fuzziest area of the City of Brotherly Love—and safety can be a concern for some students. However, most students insist that the neighborhood isn't a big deal because "a subway ride gets you directly to a nearby area of Philadelphia called Center City," which provides "a multitude of recreational resources," as well as entertainment and nightlife. Though the campus buzzes with activity during the week, "a large proportion of the students leave on the weekends." While some head home, many Temple students "go to the city and hang out" in droves. This is because "Philly is awesome." "It's whatever you want," promises a junior. Off-campus, house parties and "frat parties" are abundant. Back on campus, it's "not too noisy," which makes for "a good study atmosphere." Students can take in "a play, an ensemble performance, or even a movie" at the campus movie theater, where shows are only "75 cents and they show good movies." Many students participate in intramural sports, and men's basketball is "huge." Games at the Liacouras Center (formerly known as the Apollo of Temple) "get us out," according to a junior.

### Student Body

Some students at Temple "go out of their way to be friendly while others keep to themselves and would rather not be bothered." Almost all are "nice and easy to get along with," though. The "very diverse" and "open" student population is "a real melting pot of ethnicities," and it ranges from "frat rats to those who live for Philadelphia Orchestra performances," explains one student. "Everyone has something to offer," asserts a junior. "It's amazing." "I really don't think there is any other school quite like Temple with so many different people," agrees a senior. The largely blue-collar and "very business-like" undergraduates here are "politically aware" and "very politically correct." "Career preparation is important." Students also describe themselves as "very personable," "easy to talk to," and "weird but in a cool way."

FINANCIAL AID: 215-204-8760 • E-MAIL: TUADM@MAIL.TEMPLE.EDU • WEBSITE: WWW.TEMPLE.EDU

## ADMISSIONS

*Very important* academic and nonacademic factors considered by the admissions committee include secondary school record. *Important* factors considered include class rank, essays, extracurricular activities, interview, and recommendations. *Other* factors considered include alumni/ae relation, character/personal qualities, standardized test scores, and talent/ability. Factors *not* considered include geography, minority status, religious affiliation/commitment, state residency, volunteer work, and work experience. SAT I or ACT required. TOEFL required of all international applicants. High school diploma is required and GED is accepted. *High school units required/recommended:* 20 total recommended; 4 English recommended, 4 math recommended, 4 science recommended, 3 science lab recommended, 4 foreign language recommended, 4 social studies recommended.

### The Inside Word

Applicants to Temple are overwhelmingly local and very eager to attend the university. Admissions standards are lenient in general, but candidates for the College of Music, in particular, face a rigorous review.

## FINANCIAL AID

*Students should submit:* FAFSA. The Princeton Review suggests that all financial aid forms be submitted as soon as possible after January 1. *Need-based scholarships/grants offered:* Pell, SEOG, state scholarships/grants, private scholarships, the school's own gift aid, and Federal Nursing. *Loan aid offered:* FFEL Subsidized Stafford, FFEL Unsubsidized Stafford, FFEL PLUS, Federal Perkins, Federal Nursing, and college/university loans from institutional funds. Institutional employment available. Federal Work-Study Program available. Applicants will be notified of awards on a rolling basis beginning on or about February 15. Off-campus job opportunities are excellent.

## FROM THE ADMISSIONS OFFICE

"Temple combines the academic resources and intellectual stimulation of a large research university with the intimacy of a small college. The university experienced record growth in attracting new students from all 50 states and over 125 countries: up 44 percent in two years. Students choose from 125 undergraduate majors. Special academic programs include honors, learning communities for first-year undergraduates, co-op education, and study abroad. Temple has seven regional campuses, including Main Campus and the Health Sciences Center in historic Philadelphia, suburban Temple University, Ambler, and overseas campuses in Tokyo and Rome. Main Campus is home to the new Tuttleman Learning Center, with 1,000 computer stations linked to Paley Library. The Center is a hub for emerging learning technologies, and is designed for the high-tech students of today and tomorrow. The Liacouras Center is a state-of-the-art entertainment, recreation, and sports complex that hosts concerts, plays, trade shows, and college and professional athletics. It also includes the Independence Blue Cross Student Recreation Center, a major fitness facility for students now and in the future. Students can also take advantage of the brand new Student Fieldhouse. The university has constructed two new dorms, built to meet an unprecedented demand for main campus housing, and added yet another 1,000-bed residence hall in fall 2001."

## ADMISSIONS

| | |
|---|---|
| Admissions Rating | 78 |
| # of applicants | 13,995 |
| % of applicants accepted | 70 |
| % of acceptees attending | 37 |

### FRESHMAN PROFILE

| | |
|---|---|
| Range SAT Verbal | 460-570 |
| Average SAT Verbal | 520 |
| Range SAT Math | 460-570 |
| Average SAT Math | 516 |
| Range ACT Composite | 18-23 |
| Minimum TOEFL | 525 |
| Average HS GPA | 3.1 |
| % graduated top 10% of class | 17 |
| % graduated top 25% of class | 44 |
| % graduated top 50% of class | 81 |

### DEADLINES

| | |
|---|---|
| Regular admission | April 1 |
| Nonfall registration? | yes |

### APPLICANTS ALSO LOOK AT

**AND OFTEN PREFER**
U. Pittsburgh
Penn State—Univ. Park

**AND SOMETIMES PREFER**
Villanova
Rutgers U.
LaSalle
Drexel
Lehigh

**AND RARELY PREFER**
Gettysburg
St. Joseph's U.
NYU

## FINANCIAL FACTS

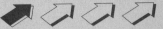

| | |
|---|---|
| Financial Aid Rating | 69 |
| In-state tuition | $6,648 |
| Out-of-state tuition | $12,022 |
| Room & board | $6,482 |
| Books and supplies | $800 |
| Required fees | $300 |
| % frosh receiving aid | 72 |
| % undergrads receiving aid | 66 |
| Avg frosh grant | $9,200 |
| Avg frosh loan | $2,249 |

# TEXAS A&M UNIVERSITY—COLLEGE STATION

ADMISSIONS COUNSELING, COLLEGE STATION, TX 77843-1265 • ADMISSIONS: 409-845-3741 • FAX: 409-847-8737

## CAMPUS LIFE

| Quality of Life Rating | 88 |
| --- | --- |
| Type of school | public |
| Affiliation | none |
| Environment | suburban |

### STUDENTS

| Total undergrad enrollment | 36,229 |
| --- | --- |
| % male/female | 51/49 |
| % from out of state | 4 |
| % live on campus | 27 |
| % in (# of) fraternities | 6 (26) |
| % in (# of) sororities | 14 (20) |
| % African American | 2 |
| % Asian | 3 |
| % Caucasian | 83 |
| % Hispanic | 9 |
| % international | 1 |
| # of countries represented | 115 |

### SURVEY SAYS . . .

*Everyone loves the Aggies*
*Athletic facilities are great*
*(Almost) everyone plays intramural*
*sports*
*Class discussions are rare*
*Political activism is hot*
*Large classes*
*Students are very religious*
*Students get along with local*
*community*
*Campus difficult to get around*
*(Almost) no one smokes*

## ACADEMICS

| Academic Rating | 79 |
| --- | --- |
| Calendar | semester |
| Student/faculty ratio | 21:1 |
| Profs interesting rating | 86 |
| Profs accessible rating | 89 |
| % profs teaching UG courses | 75 |
| % classes taught by TAs | 25 |
| Avg lab size | 10-19 students |
| Avg reg class size | 10-19 students |

### MOST POPULAR MAJORS

information & operations management
interdisciplinary studies (education)
biomedical science

## STUDENTS SPEAK OUT

### Academics

Tradition-laden Texas A&M neatly divides its student body in two: those who live, breathe, and die A&M maroon, and those who can't figure out what all the fuss is about. Explains one student, "A&M has tradition, tradition, and some more tradition. If you get involved, it will sweep you along (sometimes to the detriment of your studies), but if you aren't the type to buy into it, it can take longer to find friends with similar interests." Not surprisingly, those who get swept up love the place; those who don't usually exit before their four years are up. To its champions, "Texas A&M is a great place. It's very big and has lots of students, so it can be very overwhelming for a first-semester freshman, but once you learn the ropes and how to do things" things get a lot better. Detractors warn that "at times, I feel like I am only a number to a lot of my professors. My advisor is not always available either." They also complain that "Texas A&M is so concerned about research and money and the prestige that accompanies both that they feel a great researcher equals [a] great instructor." Aggie boosters disagree, saying that "A&M's obvious focus is on research, but not to the overall detriment of undergraduates." All agree that A&M has superior schools of engineering, veterinary science, and business, and also that the vast alumni network is an invaluable resource to graduates.

### Life

Attending A&M is not just an academic decision; for most, it is a lifestyle choice. "Aggies are fanatical about being Aggies" and "share a fabulous heritage." If you love school spirit and want to be a part of some of the greatest college traditions offered by humankind, this is the place for you. Leading the way is A&M's military training program, the Corps of Cadets. A member boasts, "It is the best leadership training in the nation. We are known as 'keepers of the spirit' and 'founders of tradition.'" Another tradition is "saying 'Howdy' to everyone that you pass. That is just one of the many things I like about the Aggies. We get along very well." With more than 700 student organizations, a first-class student union, and a thriving Greek community, A&M offers just about anything for the student who feels at home in College Station. For those few who don't, life can get pretty monotonous. Writes one such student, "Nightlife consists of either going to a country bar, some smoked-filled bar teeming with other guys, going to a party (more beer and guys), or just hauling ass to Austin, Houston, or even [Dallas/Fort Worth]. For fun I like to dream about this upcoming August when I shall graduate and never set foot here again." P.S.: Football is HUGE here.

### Student Body

Because of A&M's many cherished traditions, students here "are strongly bonded by the fact that we are all Aggies. There is a deep camaraderie that extends long after you graduate. No matter where you are later in life, if you see an Aggie ring, you have an instant bond with that person. Many students are here because of that camaraderie, and that's what makes A&M such an amazing place." Those who don't fit in, however, have a difficult time. Explains one Aggie, "The first thing I will admit about A&M is that it is very conservative. While most of the students are open-minded about the differences between us, there is a small yet visible group of students who are very close-minded. The one flaw I can point out about A&M is that people of minorities—whether a religious minority, a racial minority, or a minority based on sexual orientation—are not necessarily encouraged to come here by what they see. . . . Honestly, we are a school of white, heterosexual, Christian students."

FINANCIAL AID: 409-845-3236 • E-MAIL: ADMISSIONS@TAMU.EDU • WEBSITE: WWW.TAMU.EDU

## ADMISSIONS

*Very important* academic and nonacademic factors considered by the admissions committee include class rank, secondary school record, and state residency. *Important* factors considered include essays, standardized test scores, extracurricular activities, and talent/ability. *Other* factors considered include recommendations, alumni/ae relations, character/personal qualities, geography, volunteer work, and work experience. Factors *not* considered include interview, minority status, and religion. SAT I or ACT is required and GED is accepted. *High school units recommended:* 4 English recommended, 3.5 math recommended, 3 science recommended, 2 science lab required, 2 foreign language recommended, 2 social studies recommended, 1 history recommended, 2 computer course recommended.

### The Inside Word

Texas A&M has a very impressive record of enrolling strong students. A superhigh percentage of these admits enroll, which, when combined with the university's impressive graduation rate, is probably the best testament to A&M's reputation. Don't be deceived by the fairly high admit rate, however—for it to be significantly lower, there would have to be a huge increase in the size of the already enormous applicant pool. African American and Hispanic applicants may find it somewhat easier going, as applications from those groups declined last season. Affirmative action issues in Texas ultimately cloud the picture for out-of-state minority applicants, at least until it becomes more clear what steps will or will not be taken in the admissions processes at Texas schools. The current approach guarantees admission for those Texas students graduating in the top 10 percent of their high school class.

## FINANCIAL AID

*Students should submit:* FAFSA, institution's own financial aid form, and financial aid transcripts (for transfers). The Princeton Review suggests that all financial aid forms be submitted as soon as possible after January 1. *Need-based scholarships/grants offered:* Pell, SEOG, state scholarships/grants, private scholarships, and the school's own gift aid. *Loan aid offered:* FFEL Subsidized Stafford, FFEL Unsubsidized Stafford, FFEL PLUS, Federal Perkins, state, and college/university loans from institutional funds. Institutional employment available. Federal Work-Study Program available. Applicants will be notified of awards on a rolling basis beginning on or about April 5. Off-campus job opportunities are good.

## FROM THE ADMISSIONS OFFICE

"Established in 1876 as the first public college in the state, Texas A&M University today has become a world leader in teaching, research, and public service. Located in College Station in the heart of Texas, it is centrally situated among three of the country's 10 largest cities—Dallas, Houston, and San Antonio. Texas A&M is the only university to be ranked nationally among the top 10 in these four areas: enrollment (fall 1997 enrollment was 41,461), enrollment of top students (7th in number of new National Merit Scholars for fall 1997), value of research (7th with $367 million in 1997), and endowment (10th in endowment with $2.4 billion as of 1997)."

## ADMISSIONS

| | |
|---|---:|
| Admissions Rating | 83 |
| # of applicants | 16,776 |
| % of applicants accepted | 66 |
| % of acceptees attending | 60 |

### FRESHMAN PROFILE

| | |
|---|---:|
| Range SAT Verbal | 520-630 |
| Average SAT Verbal | 577 |
| Range SAT Math | 550-660 |
| Average SAT Math | 603 |
| Range ACT Composite | 23-28 |
| Average ACT Composite | 25 |
| Minimum TOEFL | 550 |
| % graduated top 10% of class | 53 |
| % graduated top 25% of class | 87 |
| % graduated top 50% of class | 99 |

### DEADLINES

| | |
|---|---:|
| Regular admission | 2/15 |
| Nonfall registration? | yes |

### APPLICANTS ALSO LOOK AT

**AND OFTEN PREFER**
Rice

**AND SOMETIMES PREFER**
U. Texas—Austin
Texas Tech
LSU—Baton Rouge
Baylor

**AND RARELY PREFER**
SMU
Stephen F. Austin
Southwest Texas

## FINANCIAL FACTS

| | |
|---|---:|
| Financial Aid Rating | 82 |
| In-state tuition | $2,400 |
| Out-of-state tuition | $8,850 |
| Room & board | $5,164 |
| Books and supplies | $788 |
| Required fees | $974 |
| % frosh receiving aid | 26 |
| % undergrads receiving aid | 32 |
| Avg frosh grant | $3,280 |
| Avg frosh loan | $4,350 |

# TRINITY COLLEGE

300 SUMMIT STREET, HARTFORD, CT 06016 • ADMISSIONS: 860-297-2180 • FAX: 860-297-2287

## CAMPUS LIFE

**Quality of Life Rating** **80**
Type of school          private
Affiliation             none
Environment             urban

### STUDENTS
Total undergrad enrollment    2,100
% male/female                 50/50
% from out of state           73
% from public high school     45
% live on campus              86
% in (# of) fraternities      9 (7)
% in (# of) sororities        10 (7)
% African American            6
% Asian                       5
% Caucasian                   72
% Hispanic                    5
% international               3
# of countries represented    50

### SURVEY SAYS . . .
*Diversity lacking on campus*
*Everyone loves the Bantams*
*Great computer facilities*
*Great food on campus*
*Class discussions encouraged*

## ACADEMICS

**Academic Rating**          **89**
Calendar                    semester
Student/faculty ratio       9:1
Profs interesting rating    94
Profs accessible rating     96
% profs teaching UG courses 100
Avg lab size          10-19 students
Avg reg class size    10-19 students

### MOST POPULAR MAJORS
sociology and history (tie)
English
biology

## STUDENTS SPEAK OUT
### Academics

Students at Trinity College enjoy an uncommon degree of academic intimacy and comfort. Notes one, "Trinity is a small school where it is easy to form strong relationships with professors, administration, and even the buildings and grounds staff." Agrees another, "There is no line between faculty, administration, and students. We work hard together; we play hard together. We are a proud campus!" While students appreciate the bond they form with faculty, they also enjoy the degree of autonomy Trinity's academic approach grants them. Even the curricular requirements here provide opportunities for independence, as students are allowed to choose from a number of courses to fulfill each requirement and to design their own "integration of knowledge" sequence. One engineering major boasts, "Trinity has given me educational opportunities not normally available to undergraduates. I've been involved in graduate-level research since freshman year, have the ability to take graduate courses through the consortium, have an internship through Hartford Hospital, and have presented research at a conference." Profs here earn high marks both for teaching ability ("professors allow the make-up of the class to direct what type of class it is: discussion, group work, field trips, visual aids, lecture, etc.") and accessibility ("I have had some absolutely amazing professors who are accessible outside the classroom and go out of their way to know students"). Students save their highest praise, though, for the school president, who "is really involved. He's even called our room before regarding a question."

### Life

"Trinity is a party school!" proudly exclaim students, who hasten to add that it's not all play here. "People at this school like to have fun," offers one student, "but they know when it's time to buckle down and do some work." A senior qualifies that assessment, opining that "the 'work hard, play hard' ethic still applies here, although profs are sometimes too lenient and students can get away with doing little work or getting extensions." During extracurricular hours, students enjoy theme parties such as the 1980s Dance and the Nastee Greek parties, productions by the school's "strong" theater department, lectures ("We had Cornell West and two descendents of Thomas Jefferson—one black, one white—here recently"), Greek life ("beneficial to all"), and athletic events ("Intercollegiate sports are big here. I can always count on my roommates and friends to show up [at] my games"). They also appreciate the location ("between Boston and New York") of Hartford and report that "Trinity is in a bad neighborhood, but downtown Hartford offers restaurants, theater, and a world-class museum." The lovely campus boasts "the most beautiful chapel on the East Coast."

### Student Body

The students of Trinity are "so friendly, so interesting, everyone gets along." Their harshest critics say they are "rich, shallow, in a bubble. I get along with them, but I wish people cared less about how Daddy didn't put enough money in their checking account." Those looking at the bright side see that "all are passionate about something: a sport, theater, the newspaper, Saturday nights." Minority students are few and far between here. Writes one African American undergrad, "This school needs more support for minority students." Notes a white student, "Black and Hispanic kids are quite noticeably segregated."

FINANCIAL AID: 860-297-2046 • E-MAIL: ADMISSIONS.OFFICE@TRINCOLL.EDU • WEBSITE: WWW.TRINCOLL.EDU

## ADMISSIONS

*Very important* academic and nonacademic factors considered by the admissions committee include class rank, extracurricular activities, and secondary school record. *Important* factors considered include alumni/ae relation, essays, recommendations, standardized test scores, talent/ability, volunteer work, and work experience. *Other* factors considered include character/personal qualities, geography, interview, and minority status. Factors *not* considered include religious affiliation/commitment and state residency. TOEFL required of all international applicants. High school diploma is required and GED is accepted. *High school units required/recommended:* 4 English required, 3 math required, 4 math recommended, 3 science required, 4 science recommended, 2 foreign language required, 3 social studies required, 3 history required. *The admissions office says:* "Trinity College is keenly interested in attracting and admitting candidates who not only give ample proof of academic prowess but also show evidence of such personal qualities as honesty, fairness, compassion, altruism, leadership, and initiative in their high school years."

### The Inside Word

Trinity's Ivy safety status and well-deserved reputation for academic quality enables it to enroll a fairly impressive student body, but many of its best applicants go elsewhere. The price tag is high, and the college's competitors include a large portion of the best schools in the country. Minority candidates with sound academic backgrounds will encounter a most accommodating admissions committee.

## FINANCIAL AID

*Students should submit:* FAFSA, CSS/Financial Aid PROFILE, noncustodial (divorced/separated) parent's statement, and federal tax returns. Regular filing deadline is February 1. The Princeton Review suggests that all financial aid forms be submitted as soon as possible after January 1. *Need-based scholarships/grants offered:* Pell, SEOG, state scholarships/grants, private scholarships, and the school's own gift aid. *Loan aid offered:* Direct Subsidized Stafford, Direct Unsubsidized Stafford, Direct PLUS, FFEL Subsidized Stafford, FFEL Unsubsidized Stafford, FFEL PLUS, Federal Perkins, and college/university loans from institutional funds. Institutional employment available. Applicants will be notified of awards on or about April 1. Off-campus job opportunities are good.

## FROM THE ADMISSIONS OFFICE

"An array of distinctive curricular options—including an interdisciplinary neuroscience major and a professionally accredited engineering degree program, a unique Human Rights Program, a tutorial college for selected sophomores, a Health Fellows Program, and interdisciplinary programs such as the Cities Program, Interdisciplinary Science Program, and InterArts—is one reason record numbers of students are applying to Trinity. In fact, applications are up 80 percent over the past five years. In addition, the college has been recognized for its commitment to diversity; students of color have represented approximately 20 percent of the freshman class for the past four years, setting Trinity apart from many of its peers. Trinity's capital city location offers students unparalleled 'real-world' learning experiences to complement classroom learning. Students take advantage of extensive opportunities for internships for academic credit and community service, and these opportunities extend to Trinity's global learning sites in cities around the world. Trinity's faculty is a devoted and accomplished group of exceptional teacher-scholars; our 100-acre campus is beautiful; Hartford is an educational asset that differentiates Trinity from other liberal arts colleges; our global connections and foreign study opportunities prepare students to be good citizens of the world; and our graduates go on to excel in virtually every field. We invite you to learn more about why Trinity might be the best choice for you."

## ADMISSIONS

| | |
|---|---|
| Admissions Rating | 93 |
| # of applicants | 5,161 |
| % of applicants accepted | 30 |
| % of acceptees attending | 32 |
| # accepting a place on wait list | 337 |
| % admitted from wait list | 12 |
| # of early decision applicants | 444 |
| % accepted early decision | 55 |

### FRESHMAN PROFILE

| | |
|---|---|
| Range SAT Verbal | 590-680 |
| Average SAT Verbal | 636 |
| Range SAT Math | 590-680 |
| Average SAT Math | 636 |
| Range ACT Composite | 24-29 |
| Average ACT Composite | 28 |
| Minimum TOEFL | 550 |
| % graduated top 10% of class | 48 |
| % graduated top 25% of class | 81 |
| % graduated top 50% of class | 98 |

### DEADLINES

| | |
|---|---|
| Early decision | 11/15 |
| Early decision notification | 12/15 |
| Regular admission | 1/15 |
| Regular notification | 4/1 |

### APPLICANTS ALSO LOOK AT
**AND OFTEN PREFER**
Amherst
Yale, Harvard
U. Penn
Tufts
**AND SOMETIMES PREFER**
Middlebury
Wesleyan U.
**AND RARELY PREFER**
Boston U
Colgate
Connecticut Coll.
Fairfield

### FINANCIAL FACTS

| | |
|---|---|
| Financial Aid Rating | 78 |
| Tuition | $24,660 |
| Room & board | $7,160 |
| Books and supplies | $750 |
| Required fees | $780 |
| % frosh receiving aid | 44 |
| % undergrads receiving aid | 47 |
| Avg frosh grant | $24,909 |
| Avg frosh loan | $2,625 |

# TRINITY UNIVERSITY

715 STADIUM DRIVE, SAN ANTONIO, TX 78212 • ADMISSIONS: 210-999-7207 • FAX: 210-999-8164

## CAMPUS LIFE

| | |
|---|---|
| **Quality of Life Rating** | **90** |
| Type of school | private |
| Affiliation | Presbyterian |
| Environment | urban |

### STUDENTS

| | |
|---|---|
| Total undergrad enrollment | 2,356 |
| % male/female | 48/52 |
| % from out of state | 30 |
| % from public high school | 73 |
| % live on campus | 77 |
| % in (# of) fraternities | 26 (8) |
| % in (# of) sororities | 30 (6) |
| % African American | 2 |
| % Asian | 7 |
| % Caucasian | 72 |
| % Hispanic | 9 |
| % international | 2 |

### SURVEY SAYS . . .

*Dorms are like palaces*
*Frats and sororities dominate social scene*
*Great food on campus*
*Athletic facilities are great*
*(Almost) everyone plays intramural sports*
*Registration is a pain*
*Political activism is (almost) nonexistent*
*Student government is unpopular*

## ACADEMICS

| | |
|---|---|
| **Academic Rating** | **89** |
| Calendar | semester |
| Student/faculty ratio | 11:1 |
| Profs interesting rating | 95 |
| Profs accessible rating | 97 |
| % profs teaching UG courses | 100 |
| Avg lab size | 10-19 students |
| Avg reg class size | 25 students |

### MOST POPULAR MAJORS
business administration
computer science
economics

## STUDENTS SPEAK OUT

### Academics

The "well-rounded" liberal arts curriculum at small Trinity University includes a fairly rigorous set of general education courses as well as a writing workshop and a first-year seminar. "I really enjoyed my first-year seminar class," says a freshman. "We discussed ancient literature then watched Monty Python's *Life of Brian*, a parody of the literature." Students love the "very demanding," small classes and the abundance of "career-track majors" here. The "mandatory attendance policy" is somewhat annoying, but Trinity provides a "euphoric academic experience" overall. Trinity has "wonderful" facilities, and the labs, library, computer system, and financial aid packages are all first-rate. However, "tyrannical" administration has a "Big Brother mentality toward students," much "like a council that sits on high and creates ridiculous policies." The top brass does aggressively recruit top professors, though, and Trinity's "amazingly accessible" and "very dedicated" profs are "well-prepared," "flexible," and a big hit with students in just about every way. "The professors here are generally more than well suited to be teachers and scholars—and they know it," observes an English major. "This is fine because a little arrogance here and there makes academia what it is." Trinity is also one of only a handful of small liberal arts colleges to offer an engineering program. A sophomore reports that it's "good for graduate school prep but lacks the specialization and research opportunities of a large university."

### Life

Though there is "plenty of alcohol-related escapism" on this "rather academically oriented" campus, Trinity is "not your typical 'let's party our way through school' university." "For the person involved in intellectual and artistic pursuits like music, theater, and academics," says a sophomore, "it's near utopia." A "three-year residency policy" gives Trinity "a community feel. Some people joke about 'the Trinity Bubble' because the school exists without any interaction with San Antonio, and students often have no knowledge of current events." Though "there seems to be a club or organization for anything you want to participate in," Greek life "is the only real social outlet" for many. A few "neighborhood bars are a big thing" as well, and intramurals are extremely popular. "It's like a religion," reports a spooked first-year student. "Dating on campus is pretty much nonexistent," but there appears to be no shortage of students "hooking up" on the weekends. School spirit is pretty low at Trinity, and monotony does set in occasionally. "Thank God for nearby Austin," where there is a hopping local music scene and a ton of bars. "If you don't have a car, it's really hard to get off campus." For homebodies and the car-impaired, the "Holiday Inn"-like dorms receive glowing reviews as does the "good" campus grub. And get this: Students' rooms "are cleaned every two weeks." Also, a "great student-to-gardener ratio" makes for a perpetually in-bloom campus.

### Student Body

"My only regret is that the campus is not diverse," laments a sophomore. Apart from fairly large Asian and Hispanic populations, this little campus is basically a stomping ground for "white, Republican," "Texas snobs" from "wealthy" and "sheltered backgrounds." Trinity is working hard to buck the homogeneity label attached to many small, private institutions, but it still has a long way to go. In the mean time, students can take solace in the "very diverse selection of expensive cars" in campus parking lots. The "genuine," "mostly intelligent," and somewhat "nerdy" students here are "very easy to get along with." They "have social grace and interact well with each other," despite some notable friction between Greeks and non-Greeks. A sizable contingent of the "stressed" students here also tend to be "stuck up and self-concerned" "lemmings" who "worry too much about how they look" and are "stuck in high school mode." Many Trinity students are also "very Christian and would like to convert you, too."

FINANCIAL AID: 210-999-8315 • E-MAIL: ADMISSIONS@TRINITY.EDU • WEBSITE: WWW.TRINITY.EDU

## ADMISSIONS

*Very important* academic and nonacademic factors considered by the admissions committee include secondary school record and standardized test scores. *Important* factors considered include class rank. *Other* factors considered include alumni/ae relation, character/personal qualities, essays, extracurricular activities, recommendations, talent/ability, volunteer work, and work experience. Factors *not* considered include interview, religious affiliation/commitment, and state residency. SAT I or ACT required. TOEFL required of all international applicants. High school diploma is required and GED is accepted. *High school units required/recommended:* 4 English recommended, 3 math recommended, 3 science recommended, 2 science lab recommended, 3 foreign language recommended, 3 social studies recommended.

### The Inside Word

There is no disputing that Trinity has bought academic excellence in its student body. For this reason alone, above-average students who need significant financial assistance in order to attend college should definitely consider applying. While Trinity's actions may be less than noble, there is no question that it's an extremely capable student body and that there are significant benefits to be derived from attending.

## FINANCIAL AID

*Students should submit:* FAFSA, CSS/Financial Aid PROFILE, and noncustodial (divorced/separated) parent's statement. The Princeton Review suggests that all financial aid forms be submitted as soon as possible after January 1. *Need-based scholarships/grants offered:* Pell, SEOG, state scholarships/grants, private scholarships, and the school's own gift aid. *Loan aid offered:* FFEL Subsidized Stafford, FFEL Unsubsidized Stafford, FFEL PLUS, Federal Perkins, state, and college/university loans from institutional funds. Institutional employment available. Federal Work-Study Program available. Applicants will be notified of awards on or about April 1. Off-campus job opportunities are good.

## FROM THE ADMISSIONS OFFICE

"Three qualities separate Trinity University from other selective, academically challenging institutions around the country. First, Trinity is unusual in the quality and quantity of resources devoted almost exclusively to its undergraduate students. Those resources give rise to a second distinctive aspect of Trinity—its emphasis on undergraduate research. Our students prefer being involved over observing. With superior laboratory facilities and strong, dedicated faculty, our undergraduates fill many of the roles formerly reserved for graduate students. With no graduate assistants, our professors often go to their undergraduates for help with their research. Finally, Trinity stands apart for the attitude of its students. In an atmosphere of academic camaraderie and fellowship, our students work together to stretch their minds and broaden their horizons. For quality of resources, for dedication to undergraduate research, and for the disposition of its student body, Trinity University holds a unique position in American higher education."

## ADMISSIONS

| | |
|---|---|
| Admissions Rating | 83 |
| # of applicants | 2,942 |
| % of applicants accepted | 65 |
| % of acceptees attending | 34 |
| # accepting a place on wait list | 90 |
| % admitted from wait list | 17 |
| # of early decision applicants | 97 |
| % accepted early decision | 88 |

### FRESHMAN PROFILE

| | |
|---|---|
| Range SAT Verbal | 580-680 |
| Average SAT Verbal | 646 |
| Range SAT Math | 610-690 |
| Average SAT Math | 632 |
| Range ACT Composite | 27-30 |
| Average ACT Composite | 29 |
| Minimum TOEFL | 570 |
| Average HS GPA | 3.8 |
| % graduated top 10% of class | 48 |
| % graduated top 25% of class | 81 |
| % graduated top 50% of class | 98 |

### DEADLINES

| | |
|---|---|
| Early action | 11/15 |
| Early action notification | 12/15 |
| Regular admission | 2/1 |
| Regular notification | 4/1 |
| Nonfall registration? | yes |

### APPLICANTS ALSO LOOK AT

**AND OFTEN PREFER**
Rice
Duke
U. Texas—Austin
**AND SOMETIMES PREFER**
TCU, Tulane
Vanderbilt, SMU
Texas A&M
**AND RARELY PREFER**
Rhodes

### FINANCIAL FACTS

| | |
|---|---|
| Financial Aid Rating | 82 |
| Tuition | $16,410 |
| Room & board | $6,560 |
| Books and supplies | $600 |
| Required fees | $144 |
| % frosh receiving aid | 43 |
| % undergrads receiving aid | 45 |
| Avg frosh grant | $10,455 |
| Avg frosh loan | $2,374 |

# TRUMAN STATE UNIVERSITY

McCLAIN HALL 205, 100 EAST NORMAL, KIRKSVILLE, MO 63501 • ADMISSIONS: 660-785-4114 • FAX: 660-785-7456

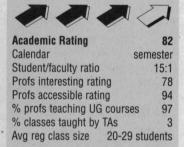
## STUDENTS SPEAK OUT

### Academics

"Highly selective" Truman State University offers small classes, tremendous pre-professional programs, a demanding honors program, and one of the nation's most rigorous liberal arts core curriculums. Every student here is required to take courses in the arts and humanities, communications, science, mathematics, and social science in addition to their majors. TSU is also "priced reasonably"—"cheap," really—and it has a fantastic regional reputation. Students call the academic experience at Truman State "wonderful." The "challenging classes" require "lots of out-of-class work, more so than at other state schools," but the "interesting and caring" professors "truly know their subjects," and they are "very understanding" and "willing to help." It's hard to get lost in the shuffle here. Of course, not everything here is sweetness and light. Though the administration generally "seems to run smoothly," the financial aid office has been known to "seriously mess up" a few accounts. "Getting into classes can be tough" sometimes, too. Overall, though, students here are afforded arguably the premier public liberal arts school in the Midwest and almost certainly the best one in the Show-Me State.

### Life

At Truman State, "people study a lot, but there is also a large party crowd," explains a senior. While a few stout-hearted students here "can be found at the bars any night of the week," life for the overwhelming majority of students here is "serious during the week." "Most people spend their entire week studying, and studying some more, then save the weekend to get wasted," according to a junior. "That's how they unwind." Truman's beautiful, peaceful campus is located in a "small" Missouri town called Kirksville that "offers few distractions" to put it diplomatically. Taco Bell is "open late," and, "on slow nights," students "pack the car full and drive to Wal-Mart." There is also a reasonably lively bar scene here, but "there is really nowhere" else to go. At all. On campus (where parking is reportedly horrendous), there are "tons of clubs," intramural sports galore, and "many extracurricular activities." There are also "a lot of good Christian organizations." Fraternities and sororities at TSU manage to maintain a high profile around campus without dominating social life—an admirable feat pulled off at few other schools. This spring, the women's swimming team brought home the university's first Division II national championship.

### Student Body

One reason a significant percentage of the students here decided to come to Truman State is because it is a "good" school "not too far from home." They also like its size. Truman is "big enough to meet totally new people, but small enough that you don't get lost." There are a few "really superficial" people on campus, but the "intelligent" and "stereotypically midwestern" students who pour into TSU from Missouri and surrounding states are mostly the "extremely friendly and helpful" kind of people "you would want your neighbors to be." They are also mostly white, middle-class, and "concerned about grades." Cliques are common, and there is "little diversity" on this "very segregated" campus. Typical of a smaller, midwestern college, Truman doesn't draw many minorities. It does, for some reason, draw oodles of women, though, and the male-to-female ratio on campus is somewhat skewed.

FINANCIAL AID: 660-785-4130 • E-MAIL: ADMISSIONS@TRUMAN.EDU • WEBSITE: WWW.TRUMAN.EDU

## ADMISSIONS

*Very important* academic and nonacademic factors considered by the admissions committee include secondary school record and standardized test scores. *Important* factors considered include class rank, essays, and extracurricular activities. *Other* factors considered include alumni/ae relation, character/personal qualities, geography, interview, minority status, recommendations, state residency, talent/ability, volunteer work, and work experience. Factors *not* considered include religious affiliation/commitment. SAT I or ACT required, ACT preferred. TOEFL required of all international applicants. High school diploma is required and GED is accepted. *High school units required/recommended:* 16 total required, 17 recommended, 4 English required, 3 math required, 4 math recommended, 3 science required, 2 science lab required, 2 foreign language required, 3 social studies required, 1 fine arts required. *The admissions office says:* "The admissions committee is seeking applicants with varied talents and interests . . . Successful applicants tend to demonstrate significant co-curricular involvement and strong leadership potential."

### The Inside Word

Truman is among the next-in-line among public universities joining the ranks of the highly selective. It's tough to get admitted here, even though application totals declined somewhat last year. Serious students with conservative attitudes make the best match.

## FINANCIAL AID

*Students should submit:* FAFSA and institution's own financial aid form. The Princeton Review suggests that all financial aid forms be submitted as soon as possible after January 1. *Need-based scholarships/grants offered:* Pell, SEOG, state scholarships/grants, private scholarships, and the school's own gift aid. *Loan aid offered:* FFEL Subsidized Stafford, FFEL Unsubsidized Stafford, FFEL PLUS, Federal Perkins, Federal Nursing, state, and college/university loans from institutional funds. Institutional employment available. Federal Work-Study Program available. Applicants will be notified of awards on a rolling basis. Off-campus job opportunities are good.

## FROM THE ADMISSIONS OFFICE

"Truman's talented student body enjoys small classes where undergraduate research and personal interaction with professors are the norm. Truman's commitment to providing an exemplary liberal arts and sciences education with nearly 200 student organizations and outstanding internship and study abroad opportunities allows students to compete in top graduate schools and the job market."

## ADMISSIONS

| | |
|---|---|
| Admissions Rating | 81 |
| # of applicants | 5,268 |
| % of applicants accepted | 79 |
| % of acceptees attending | 34 |

### FRESHMAN PROFILE

| | |
|---|---|
| Range SAT Verbal | 550-670 |
| Average SAT Verbal | 611 |
| Range SAT Math | 560-670 |
| Average SAT Math | 613 |
| Range ACT Composite | 24-30 |
| Average ACT Composite | 27 |
| Minimum TOEFL | 550 |
| Average HS GPA | 3.7 |
| % graduated top 10% of class | 43 |
| % graduated top 25% of class | 79 |
| % graduated top 50% of class | 99 |

### DEADLINES

| | |
|---|---|
| Priority admission deadline | 11/15 |
| Regular admission | 3/1 |
| Nonfall registration? | yes |

### APPLICANTS ALSO LOOK AT

**AND OFTEN PREFER**
Washington U.

**AND SOMETIMES PREFER**
U. Missouri—Columbia
U. Kansas
U. Illinois—Urbana-Champaign
St. Louis

**AND RARELY PREFER**
U. Iowa
Illinois State
Illinois Wesleyan
Purdue U.—West Lafayette

### FINANCIAL FACTS

| | |
|---|---|
| Financial Aid Rating | 84 |
| Tuition | $3,800 |
| Room & board | $4,736 |
| Books and supplies | $600 |
| Required fees | $32 |
| % frosh receiving aid | 31 |
| % undergrads receiving aid | 34 |
| Avg frosh grant | $4,399 |
| Avg frosh loan | $3,198 |

# TUFTS UNIVERSITY

BENDETSON HALL, MEDFORD, MA 02155 • ADMISSIONS: 617-627-3170 • FAX: 617-627-3860

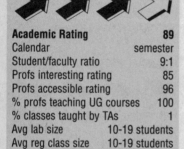

## CAMPUS LIFE

**Quality of Life Rating** — **87**

| | |
|---|---|
| Type of school | private |
| Affiliation | none |
| Environment | suburban |

### STUDENTS

| | |
|---|---|
| Total undergrad enrollment | 4,869 |
| % male/female | 47/53 |
| % from out of state | 77 |
| % from public high school | 60 |
| % live on campus | 80 |
| % in (# of) fraternities | 15 (10) |
| % in (# of) sororities | 3 (3) |
| % African American | 7 |
| % Asian | 14 |
| % Caucasian | 60 |
| % Hispanic | 7 |
| % international | 7 |

### SURVEY SAYS . . .

*Campus feels safe*
*Great library*
*Beautiful campus*
*Campus easy to get around*
*Great off-campus food*
*Student publications are ignored*
*(Almost) no one listens to college radio*
*Students are cliquish*
*(Almost) no one smokes*

## ACADEMICS

**Academic Rating** — **89**

| | |
|---|---|
| Calendar | semester |
| Student/faculty ratio | 9:1 |
| Profs interesting rating | 85 |
| Profs accessible rating | 96 |
| % profs teaching UG courses | 100 |
| % classes taught by TAs | 1 |
| Avg lab size | 10-19 students |
| Avg reg class size | 10-19 students |

### MOST POPULAR MAJORS

international relations
biology
English

## STUDENTS SPEAK OUT

### Academics

Known for stealing the Ivy wait-list population, Tufts University offers rigorous academics that keep the school's hard-working, career-driven students on their toes. With its small class size, ample funding, and noteworthy professors, Tufts offers a wide variety of solid departments. Of particular renown is the international relations major, which draws in students from all over. Notes one student, "The best part of academics at Tufts are the small classes, the accessible faculty and staff, and the fact that NO classes are taught by TAs." Another opines, "Academically Tufts is impressive. The teachers are always available and ready to help, and if you look well, there are some really interesting classes: History of Reggae, Negotiation and Conflict Resolution, and Yoga." Requirements for first-year students are stiff, and some freshmen are hung up on "pointless requirements," but says one older and wiser student, "As an incoming freshman, it was good to have some idea of what to take. The advising program is excellent." Professors are highly regarded: reports one student, "My professors are incredible! From an astronomy professor who was late to class because he was rushing back from a NASA meeting in Houston to a political science professor who accidentally caught Justice Sandra Day O'Connor with food in her teeth, I have had fantastic and knowledgeable professors throughout my Tufts career. They're all open, honest, and enthusiastic educators with whom it is a pleasure to learn." Administrators "are great. . . . The president takes a very personal interest in the lives of the students. He is one of three professors leading a community dialogue/class on Leadership for Active Citizenship." On the downside, "Classrooms are ugly at best. . . . On the outside the buildings are pretty, but our lack of a large endowment has allowed many of them to become somewhat dilapidated on the inside."

### Life

Tufts students describe an active campus life, one cram-packed with both class-related activities and extracurriculars. Writes one, "Even though most people are very focused on academics, most find plenty of time to be active in several of our 150-plus diverse activities. We have fantastic volunteer organizations, for example." Agrees another, "School spirit lies primarily in the 150 student activities groups. Within these groups, the most incredible bonds are formed. From the moment I arrived on campus, I joined everything! The daily newspaper, film series, debate team, tutoring, musical theater, etc. There's so much to do, my parents often question when I do my work." Students report that "everyone at this school is either dating someone here or someone at another school. This is far from a 'frat party and hook up' school." As for the Greeks, students explain that "although the fraternities and sororities make up only a fraction of the student body, they are pretty much the center of freshman life on campus. Once you become an upperclassman, though, you realize there is life beyond the Greek system." That life usually takes students into Boston, fortuitously "nearby to offer an outlet for students to live life. A lot of people go to Boston for fun, movies, dinner, and dance clubs." Then it's back to the beautiful campus, secluded in the suburban hills just a short commuter train ride away.

### Student Body

Assessing his peers, one Tufts undergrad offers these observations: "Tufts students are very intelligent but not extremely competitive, which creates a nice learning environment. People are generally pretty nice and normal. The students are racially diverse, but the vast majority are rich and wear J.Crew." Perhaps it is this last characteristic that leads some students to offer that "The Tufts stereotype is a reality: a lot of nice, average guys from the New York tri-state area named Dave." Overall, Tufts students consider themselves "ambitious" and "energetic." Political personalities vary from the "'cause-of-the-week' types" to the "apathetic." "People often talk about campus politics," writes one student, "but not as much about national or international politics."

FINANCIAL AID: 617-627-3528 • E-MAIL: ADMISSIONS.INQUIRY@ASE.TUFTS.EDU • WEBSITE: WWW.TUFTS.EDU

## ADMISSIONS

*Very important* academic and nonacademic factors considered by the admissions committee include essays, recommendations, and secondary school record. *Important* factors considered include character/personal qualities and extracurricular activities. *Other* factors considered include class rank, interview, standardized test scores, talent/ability, volunteer work, and work experience. Factors *not* considered include alumni/ae relation, geography, minority status, religious affiliation/commitment, and state residency. TOEFL required of all international applicants. High school diploma is required and GED is accepted. *High school units required/recommended:* 16 total required; 24 total recommended; 4 English required, 3 math required, 4 math recommended, 2 science required, 4 science recommended, 2 science lab required, 4 science lab recommended, 2 foreign language required, 4 foreign language recommended, 1 social studies required, 2 social studies recommended, 1 history required, 2 history recommended.

### The Inside Word

Tufts has little visibility outside the Northeast and little personality either. Still it manages to attract and keep an excellent student body, mostly from right inside its own backyard. In order to be successful, candidates must have significant academic accomplishments and submit a thoroughly well-prepared application—the review is rigorous and the standards are high.

## FINANCIAL AID

*Students should submit:* FAFSA, CSS/Financial Aid PROFILE, noncustodial (divorced/separated) parent's statement, business/farm supplement, and parent and student federal income tax forms. Regular filing deadline is February 15. The Princeton Review suggests that all financial aid forms be submitted as soon as possible after January 1. *Need-based scholarships/grants offered:* Pell, SEOG, state scholarships/grants, and private scholarships. *Loan aid offered:* FFEL Subsidized Stafford, FFEL Unsubsidized Stafford, FFEL PLUS, Federal Perkins, state, and college/university loans from institutional funds. Institutional employment available. Federal Work-Study Program available. Applicants will be notified of awards on or about April 10. Off-campus job opportunities are good.

## FROM THE ADMISSIONS OFFICE

"Tufts University, on the boundary between Medford and Somerville, sits on a hill overlooking Boston, five miles northwest of the city. The campus is a tranquil New England setting within easy access by subway and bus to the cultural, social, and entertainment resources of Boston and Cambridge. "Since its founding in 1852 by members of the Universalist church, Tufts has grown from a small liberal arts college into a nonsectarian university of over 7,000 students. By 1900 the college had added a medical school, a dental school, and graduate studies. The University now also includes the Fletcher School of Law and Diplomacy, the Graduate School of Arts and Sciences, the School of Veterinary Medicine, the School of Nutrition, the Sackler School of Graduate Biomedical Sciences, and the Gordon Institute of Engineering Management."

## ADMISSIONS

| | |
|---|---|
| Admissions Rating | 96 |
| # of applicants | 14,192 |
| % of applicants accepted | 26 |
| % of acceptees attending | 33 |
| # of early decision applicants | 1043 |
| % accepted early decision | 42 |

### FRESHMAN PROFILE

| | |
|---|---|
| Range SAT Verbal | 610-700 |
| Range SAT Math | 630-710 |
| Range ACT Composite | 27-31 |
| % graduated top 10% of class | 73 |
| % graduated top 25% of class | 95 |
| % graduated top 50% of class | 99 |

### DEADLINES

| | |
|---|---|
| Early decision | 11/15 |
| Early decision notification | 12/15 |
| Regular admission | 1/1 |
| Regular notification | 4/1 |

### APPLICANTS ALSO LOOK AT

**AND OFTEN PREFER**
Harvard
Duke
Brown
Dartmouth
U. Penn

**AND SOMETIMES PREFER**
Northwestern U.
U. Mass—Amherst

**AND RARELY PREFER**
Boston Coll.
Brandeis

## FINANCIAL FACTS

| | |
|---|---|
| Financial Aid Rating | 77 |
| Tuition | $24,126 |
| Room & board | $7,375 |
| Books and supplies | $700 |
| Required fees | $625 |
| % frosh receiving aid | 40 |
| % undergrads receiving aid | 37 |
| Avg frosh grant | $16,258 |
| Avg frosh loan | $3,400 |

# TULANE UNIVERSITY

6823 St. Charles Avenue, New Orleans, LA 70118-5680 • Admissions: 504-865-5731 • Fax: 504-862-8715

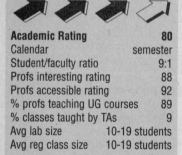
## STUDENTS SPEAK OUT
### Academics

"Every state should have a Tulane," writes a soon-to-be-graduated senior. With "small classes, great financial aid, and a fabulous city" to offer students, private, mid-size Tulane University consistently attracts top-notch students from all around the country and world who are drawn to the school because of its "excellent academic reputation." A second-year is impressed by the "creativity of professors" and their "willingness to teach dynamic and nontraditional material," while a freshman notes that "Tulane is really trying to reach out to the undergraduates, which means you could end up with the president of the university as your professor—I did!" Still, for many Tulane prospectives, it was "location, location, location" that proved to be a deciding factor for attending. The Big Easy's legendary culture, history, and nightlife far outweigh some of Tulane's weaker spots—which, according to those we surveyed, include a few old-guard profs who could "put an entire room of Starbucks customers to sleep" and an administration that's well intentioned but "full of red tape." A junior describes the situation this way: "The administration is more than willing to ask students for input, but they have a little earwax buildup or something, because they aren't the best at *hearing* that input." What's more, with Bourbon Street around the corner, "focusing in a city like New Orleans is not always easy." Thank goodness for 8:00 A.M. calculus; notes a sophomore, "if one actually attends class, there is quite a bit to learn here."

### Life

"During the week we think about classes and homework," writes a freshman. "During the weekends? Yeah, we try to think as little as possible." So goes life at this "mad fun" campus in a "great city" and a "beautiful part of town." Of course, the city that celebrates Mardi Gras with so much, well, alcohol could be a bit tough on the GPA (and the liver), and many an undergrad might ask themselves (as this existentially minded sophomore did), "Do I drink because of poor grades, or do I have poor grades because I drink?" Deep. Fortunately, a first-year offers advice: "After the first few months of school, hanging out with smelly drunk tourists on Bourbon Street gets kind of old. That's when you finally begin to appreciate the rest of New Orleans for what it is—a city with museums and restaurants and history. That's why I love Tulane." Indeed, with N'awlins' "excellent selection of music clubs," parks, industry, nightlife and culture—not to mention "bikini weather in February"—undergrads who don't venture beyond the "Mardi Gras debauchery" are missing much of what the city has to offer. A junior points out, "there are a lot of great groups/programs on campus," and many students consider its facilities unmatched, including a rec center that one sophomore calls "the best I've ever seen."

### Student Body

Summarizes one sanguine student we surveyed, "There is a place for just about every person—and we all fit into the puzzle. I love being here!" Of course, there are those who'd disagree. One senior finds his fellow students "apathetic and drunk," while a junior notes that "most of them are really shallow." Our junior concludes, "There's a saying that you're either a smart kid here on scholarship, or a rich kid looking for the ultimate party school." Is it all scholarship kids and the filthy rich? Not so, argues one undergraduate, "Tulane represents a very diverse montage of students . . . . Students exude the spirit of New Orleans and Tulane, making the social experience encouraging and charming."

FINANCIAL AID: 504-865-5723 • E-MAIL: UNDERGRAD.ADMISSION@TULANE.EDU • WEBSITE: WWW.TULANE.EDU

## ADMISSIONS

*Very important* academic and nonacademic factors considered by the admissions committee include class rank, secondary school record, and standardized test scores. *Important* factors considered include essays and extracurricular activities. *Other* factors considered include alumni/ae relation, character/personal qualities, geography, minority status, recommendations, state residency, talent/ability, volunteer work, and work experience. Factors *not* considered include interview and religious affiliation/commitment. SAT I required; SAT II recommended. TOEFL required of all international applicants. High school diploma is required and GED is accepted. *High school units required/recommended:* 16 total required; 4 English required, 3 math required, 4 math recommended, 1 science required, 4 science recommended, 2 foreign language required, 4 foreign language recommended, 2 social studies required, 4 social studies recommended.

### The Inside Word

Tulane's applicant pool is highly national in origin and very sound academically. The university's competitors include many of the best universities in the country, which tempers its selectivity significantly due to the loss of admitted students. Nonetheless, Tulane is an excellent choice for just about anyone looking for a quality institution that is on the move. Prestige and the value of a Tulane degree stand to increase as the South continues to grow in population and political influence.

## FINANCIAL AID

*Students should submit:* FAFSA, CSS/Financial Aid PROFILE, and noncustodial (divorced/separated) parent's statement. The Princeton Review suggests that all financial aid forms be submitted as soon as possible after January 1. *Need-based scholarships/grants offered:* Pell, SEOG, state scholarships/grants, private scholarships, and the school's own gift aid. *Loan aid offered:* FFEL Subsidized Stafford, FFEL Unsubsidized Stafford, FFEL PLUS, and Federal Perkins. Institutional employment available. Federal Work-Study Program available. Applicants will be notified of awards on a rolling basis beginning on or about March 1. Off-campus job opportunities are good.

## FROM THE ADMISSIONS OFFICE

"With 5,000 full-time undergraduate students in five divisions, Tulane University offers the personal attention and teaching excellence traditionally associated with liberal arts colleges together with the facilities and interdisciplinary resources found only at major research universities—with both complemented by the exciting, historic setting of New Orleans, America's most interesting city. Senior faculty regularly teach introductory and lower-level courses, and 74 percent of the classes have 25 or fewer students. The close student-teacher relationship pays off. Tulane graduates are among the country's most likely to be selected for several prestigious fellowships that support graduate study abroad. Founded in 1834 and reorganized as Tulane University in 1884, Tulane is one of the major private research universities in the South. The Tulane campus offers a traditional collegiate setting in an attractive residential neighborhood."

## ADMISSIONS

| | |
|---|---|
| Admissions Rating | 85 |
| # of applicants | 8,388 |
| % of applicants accepted | 78 |
| % of acceptees attending | 25 |

### FRESHMAN PROFILE

| | |
|---|---|
| Range SAT Verbal | 600-703 |
| Average SAT Verbal | 648 |
| Range SAT Math | 591-690 |
| Average SAT Math | 634 |
| Minimum TOEFL | 550 |
| % graduated top 10% of class | 52 |
| % graduated top 25% of class | 81 |
| % graduated top 50% of class | 97 |

### DEADLINES

| | |
|---|---|
| Early decision | 11/1 |
| Early decision notification | 12/15 |
| Regular admission | 1/15 |
| Regular notification | 4/1 |
| Nonfall registration? | yes |

### APPLICANTS ALSO LOOK AT

**AND OFTEN PREFER**
Duke
Vanderbilt
Emory

**AND SOMETIMES PREFER**
U. Texas—Austin
Northwestern U.
Florida State
Washington U.

**AND RARELY PREFER**
Skidmore
SMU
U. Richmond
Rollins

### FINANCIAL FACTS

| | |
|---|---|
| Financial Aid Rating | 87 |
| Tuition | $23,500 |
| Room & board | $6,908 |
| Books and supplies | $1,000 |
| Required fees | $1,890 |
| Avg frosh grant | $15,700 |
| Avg frosh loan | $3,460 |

# TUSKEGEE UNIVERSITY

OLD ADMINISTRATION BUILDING, SUITE 101, TUSKEGEE, AL 36088 • ADMISSIONS: 334-727-8500 • FAX: 334-724-4402

## CAMPUS LIFE

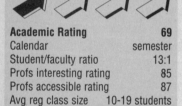

| | |
|---|---|
| **Quality of Life Rating** | **61** |
| Type of school | private |
| Affiliation | none |
| Environment | rural |

### STUDENTS

| | |
|---|---|
| Total undergrad enrollment | 2,467 |
| % male/female | 42/58 |
| % from out of state | 67 |
| % from public high school | 80 |
| % live on campus | 54 |
| % in (# of) fraternities | 6 (5) |
| % in (# of) sororities | 5 (6) |
| % African American | 95 |
| % international | 3 |

### SURVEY SAYS . . .
Popular college radio
Student publications are ignored
Frats and sororities dominate social scene
Theater is hot
Students don't get along with local community
Registration is a pain
Students don't like Tuskegee, AL
Athletic facilities need improving

## ACADEMICS

| | |
|---|---|
| **Academic Rating** | **69** |
| Calendar | semester |
| Student/faculty ratio | 13:1 |
| Profs interesting rating | 85 |
| Profs accessible rating | 87 |
| Avg reg class size | 10-19 students |

### MOST POPULAR MAJORS
biology
veterinary medicine
electrical engineering

## STUDENTS SPEAK OUT
### Academics

Famed agricultural scientist Booker T. Washington founded this "prestigious historically black university" over a century ago. In the intervening years, Tuskegee University has built a "proud" tradition to accompany its "great historical background." Despite several quality liberal arts departments and a great veterinary program (over 70 percent of the African American veterinarians in the world trained here), Tuskegee is proudest of its strong engineering program, which enrolls nearly a quarter of the students. Tuskegee graduates more African American aerospace science engineers than any other school. For the record, it also produces the most African American military officers—including West Point and the Naval Academy. "Extremely caring" professors teach nearly all of the "small," discussion-oriented classes here, a fact not lost on the appreciative students. "I love my professors," beams an English major. They are "great, helpful, nurturing, and always there to help." Also, some professors are "good with one-on-one help." The administration, on the other hand, is universally unpopular for its unhelpful, "negative attitude." Registration is perhaps the biggest problem. Students also complain that "a few buildings could use some work," especially a handful of dilapidated dorms, and the roads on campus are in need of repair. Despite these complaints, students say they would "choose Tuskegee every time." "The Tuskegee experience shapes you as an individual," explains a political science major. "As far as establishing a sound African American foundation for students, it's the best there is."

### Life

For some students here, especially those from metropolitan centers, campus life "takes some getting used to," as one junior reports. Tuskegee, Alabama, is a sleepy southern town "out in the country" where, according to some students, there is "nothing to do" except "visiting friends and renting videos." Other students say their campus is "a lot of fun." Tuskegee has a "great" marching band that is "a way of life" for its members. There is also Greek life. On campus, Greek life is tremendously popular; fraternity and sorority parties are well attended and the festivities of Greek Week are a huge draw. Students also look forward to homecoming ("the best time of the year" because "the campus is overrun by many visitors, alumni, and thrill seekers") and an annual spring festival. When campus is not hopping, nearby Auburn (home to Auburn University) is a popular destination, as is the urban metropolis of Atlanta. "If you don't have a car," though, "you are out of luck." If you do have a car, events that bring Tuskegee students together with students from other historically African American colleges, such as Freaknic in Atlanta and Black College Week in Daytona Beach, are popular road trip destinations.

### Student Body

The "wonderful, cooperative, and encouraging" students at Tuskegee are a "very congenial," generally studious bunch: schoolwork takes up a great deal of the average student's day. When students finally put their books away, though, "it's like one big, beautiful family." Without a doubt, "student unity" prevails on this campus in a way that is truly "unique." It's all part of the Tuskegee experience, to which so many students allude. "Everyone seems to get along with each other," says a senior. "We have our differences, but when it comes down to it, we stick together." The majority of the students come from the South, and they are "extremely socially diverse (geographically, financially, religiously)," but students from all different social strata manage to "interact well, providing a stimulating environment."

FINANCIAL AID: 334-727-8210 • E-MAIL: ADMIS@ACD.TUSK.EDU • WEBSITE: WWW.TUSK.EDU

## ADMISSIONS

*Very important* academic and nonacademic factors considered by the admissions committee include recommendations and secondary school record. *Important* factors considered include essays, extracurricular activities, standardized test scores, and talent/ability. *Other* factors considered include alumni/ae relation, character/personal qualities, class rank, interview, volunteer work, and work experience. Factors *not* considered include geography, minority status, religious affiliation/commitment, and state residency. SAT I or ACT required. TOEFL required of all international applicants. High school diploma is required and GED is accepted. *High school units required/recommended:* 4 English required, 3 math required, 2 science required, 2 science lab required, 2 foreign language recommended, 1 history required.

### The Inside Word

Tuskegee University has a solid reputation and draws a large pool of above-average candidates. Academic accomplishments in high school are first and foremost ingredients of a successful application for admission, but there is no doubt that the committee takes a close look at all aspects of candidate files. Don't downplay the importance of strong essays, recommendations, and a well-rounded extracurricular background.

## FINANCIAL AID

*Students should submit:* FAFSA, institution's own financial aid form, CSS/Financial Aid PROFILE, and noncustodial (divorced/separated) parent's statement. The Princeton Review suggests that all financial aid forms be submitted as soon as possible after January 1. *Need-based scholarships/grants offered:* Pell, SEOG, state scholarships/grants, private scholarships, the school's own gift aid, United Negro College Fund, and Federal Nursing. *Loan aid offered:* Direct Subsidized Stafford, Direct Unsubsidized Stafford, Direct PLUS, FFEL Subsidized Stafford, FFEL Unsubsidized Stafford, FFEL PLUS, Federal Perkins, Federal Nursing, state, and college/university loans from institutional funds. Institutional employment available. Federal Work-Study Program available. Off-campus job opportunities are good.

## FROM THE ADMISSIONS OFFICE

"With distinctive strengths in the sciences, engineering and other professions, the university's basic mission is to provide educational programs of exceptional quality that promote the development of liberally prepared and professionally-oriented people. The university is rooted in a history of successfully educating black Americans to understand themselves against the background of their total heritage and the promise of their individual and collective future. A primary mission has been to prepare them to play effective professional and leadership roles in society and to become productive citizens in the national and world community. Tuskegee University continues to be dedicated to these broad aims."

## ADMISSIONS

| | |
|---|---|
| Admissions Rating | 72 |
| # of applicants | 2,078 |
| % of applicants accepted | 71 |
| % of acceptees attending | 40 |

### FRESHMAN PROFILE

| | |
|---|---|
| Range SAT Verbal | 410-500 |
| Average SAT Verbal | 446 |
| Range SAT Math | 390-500 |
| Average SAT Math | 435 |
| Range ACT Composite | 16-19 |
| Average ACT Composite | 19 |
| Minimum TOEFL | 500 |
| Average HS GPA | 3.0 |
| % graduated top 10% of class | 20 |
| % graduated top 25% of class | 59 |
| % graduated top 50% of class | 100 |

### DEADLINES

| | |
|---|---|
| Regular notification | rolling |
| Nonfall registration? | yes |

### APPLICANTS ALSO LOOK AT AND SOMETIMES PREFER
Florida A&M
Spelman
Howard
Hampton
Alabama A&M
### AND RARELY PREFER
U. Alabama
Auburn
Alabama State

### FINANCIAL FACTS

| | |
|---|---|
| Financial Aid Rating | 82 |
| Tuition | $9,928 |
| Room & board | $5,328 |
| Books and supplies | $815 |
| Required fees | $156 |
| % frosh receiving aid | 68 |
| Avg frosh grant | $2,500 |
| Avg frosh loan | $2,625 |

# UNION COLLEGE

STANLEY R. BECKER HALL, SCHENECTADY, NY 12308 • ADMISSIONS: 518-388-6112 • FAX: 518-388-6986

## CAMPUS LIFE

| Quality of Life Rating | **76** |
| --- | --- |
| Type of school | private |
| Affiliation | none |
| Environment | suburban |

### STUDENTS

| | |
| --- | --- |
| Total undergrad enrollment | 2,124 |
| % male/female | 52/48 |
| % from out of state | 52 |
| % from public high school | 66 |
| % live on campus | 84 |
| % in (# of) fraternities | 30 (14) |
| % in (# of) sororities | 25 (4) |
| % African American | 4 |
| % Asian | 5 |
| % Caucasian | 86 |
| % Hispanic | 4 |
| % international | 2 |

### SURVEY SAYS . . .

*Lots of beer drinking*
*Frats and sororities dominate social scene*
*Popular college radio*
*Profs teach upper-levels*
*Hard liquor is popular*
*Students don't like Schenectady, NY*
*Students are cliquish*

## ACADEMICS

| Academic Rating | **89** |
| --- | --- |
| Calendar | trimester |
| Student/faculty ratio | 11:1 |
| Profs interesting rating | 94 |
| Profs accessible rating | 96 |
| % profs teaching UG courses | 100 |
| Avg lab size | 10-19 students |
| Avg reg class size | 10-19 students |

### MOST POPULAR MAJORS

political science
psychology
economics

## STUDENTS SPEAK OUT

### Academics

Students are attracted to Union College by the great variety of courses available at a school that has fewer than 2,500 undergrads. The enrollment ensures that class sizes are small and that professors have the time to get to know their students. "Academically, Union is great," a senior political science major avers. "Classes are interesting," and professors are, "caring," accessible, and approachable. Professors "go out of their way to . . . get involved on campus," a junior political science major writes, and "many even give you their home numbers." TAs are nowhere to be found. There are a few professors on campus who aren't as highly regarded, and a math major grumbles, "The school puts too much emphasis on selecting professors with good reputations, [instead of] selecting professors who actually can teach and speak English." Students rave about the trimester calendar, according to which they only take three classes at a time. "You never feel too bogged down," one first-year student writes. Students do, however, want to be able to register online. The "conservative" administration is, for the most part, disliked. "The bureaucracy at this school makes the IRS look like a well-oiled machine," a senior history major gripes.

### Life

"Union's a blast," a sophomore beams. "We go to the same two hole-in-the-wall places where we see the same people as always," writes a less enthusiastic classmate. Campus student organizations "work hard to schedule events," but students often forsake those events for frat parties. Still, "the number of clubs we have is great," a senior Spanish major gushes. "There is a club for everything from sign language to ballroom dancing." Theme houses provide an alternative to those not interested in Greek life. Campus sports are popular, as are on-campus movies and concerts. Though students complain that there is little to do in "less-than-desirable" Schenectady, they admit that the area offers much in the way of volunteer opportunities. Many students are involved in the Big Brothers/Big Sisters program. Students are also "within a few hours of New York and Boston, and below the Adirondack Mountains, where prime skiing and hiking" opportunities abound. Students feel that campus security is too strict and that athletic facilities could stand some improvement.

### Student Body

Union's students describe themselves as "apathetic" and "conservative" and "rich snobs." Most come from the East Coast. "If Daddy bought you an SUV and you're from Jersey, you'll fit right in here," a computer engineering major quips. One female student comments that most of her female peers "live by Cosmo," and a junior adds, "There's a division: the Kate Spade, Jeep Grand Cherokee, sorority and frat boy types, versus the rest of the world." Students are "cliquey," and a first-year student marvels, "I have never seen so many North Face Jackets and Kate Spade bags in one place." A sociology major observes, "Many students, especially those involved in the Greek system, view college as one continuous party with the disadvantage of having to take finals at the end of each term to be able to come back." Many students describe their peers as "polite" and "friendly," and people "smile and say 'hi' as they pass between classes." One English major believes, however, that most of her peers view college "as a means to an end—money—[and] not an intellectual adventure."

FINANCIAL AID: 518-388-6123 • E-MAIL: ADMISSIONS@UNION.EDU • WEBSITE: WWW.UNION.EDU

## ADMISSIONS

*Very important* academic and nonacademic factors considered by the admissions committee include secondary school records and class rank. *Important* factors considered include recommendations, essays, interviews, extracurricular activities, talent/ability, character/personal qualities, alumni/ae relation, minority status, and volunteer work. *Other* factors considered include standardized test scores, geographical residence, state residency, and work experience. Factors *not* considered include religious affiliation/commitment. SAT I or SAT II (Writing plus two electives) *or* ACT required. TOEFL required of all international applicants. High school diploma is required and GED is not accepted. *High school units required/recommended:* 16 total required; 24 total recommended; 4 English required, 3 math required, 4 math recommended, 3 science required, 4 science recommended, 2 science lab required, 3 foreign language required, 4 foreign language recommended, 1 history required, 1 social studies required, 2 social studies recommended. *The admissions office says:* "The goal of the admissions process is to bring together [students] who will have general educational impact on each other, in and out of class. A strong academic track record is certainly necessary. We have designed our application process to allow students to highlight their candidacies as 'whole people.'"

### The Inside Word

In this age of MTV-type admissions videos and ultra-glossy promotional literature, Union is decidedly more low-key than most colleges. The college is a bastion of tradition and conservatism and sticks to what it knows best when it comes to recruitment and admission. Students who are thinking about Union need to be prepared with as challenging a high school curriculum as possible and solid grades across the board.

## FINANCIAL AID

*Students should submit:* FAFSA, CSS/Financial Aid PROFILE, state aid form, noncustodial (divorced/separated) parent's statement, and business/farm supplement. Regular filing deadline is February 1. The Princeton Review suggests that all financial aid forms be submitted as soon as possible after January 1. *Need-based scholarships/grants offered:* Pell, SEOG, state scholarships/grants, private scholarships, and the school's own gift aid. *Loan aid offered:* FFEL Subsidized Stafford, FFEL Unsubsidized Stafford, FFEL PLUS, Federal Perkins, and college/university loans from institutional funds. Institutional employment available. Federal Work-Study Program available. Applicants will be notified of awards on or about April 1. Off-campus job opportunities are good.

## FROM THE ADMISSIONS OFFICE

"Union College is an independent, primarily undergraduate, residential college for men and women of high academic promise and strong personal motivation. Throughout its history Union has been distinguished by its commitment to the idea that both experience and reflection are necessary to a proper education. In the past, that commitment was evidenced when Union became the first liberal arts college to offer engineering. Today, that commitment is reflected in our nationally recognized General Education Curriculum, which combines elements of choice within a structure of requirements and incentives; our extensive Terms Abroad program, which attracts 50 percent of our students; and our vigorous encouragement of undergraduate research."

### ADMISSIONS

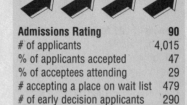

| | |
|---|---|
| Admissions Rating | 90 |
| # of applicants | 4,015 |
| % of applicants accepted | 47 |
| % of acceptees attending | 29 |
| # accepting a place on wait list | 479 |
| # of early decision applicants | 290 |
| % accepted early decision | 71 |

### FRESHMAN PROFILE

| | |
|---|---|
| Range SAT Verbal | 550-640 |
| Average SAT Verbal | 600 |
| Range SAT Math | 580-660 |
| Average SAT Math | 620 |
| Range ACT Composite | 25-29 |
| Average ACT Composite | 27 |
| Minimum TOEFL | 600 |
| Average HS GPA | 3.4 |
| % graduated top 10% of class | 50 |
| % graduated top 25% of class | 76 |
| % graduated top 50% of class | 95 |

### DEADLINES

| | |
|---|---|
| Early decision | 11/15 |
| Early decision notification | 12/15 |
| Regular admission | 2/1 |
| Regular notification | 4/1 |

### APPLICANTS ALSO LOOK AT

**AND OFTEN PREFER**
Brown
Hamilton

**AND SOMETIMES PREFER**
Tufts
SUNY Buffalo
Cornell U.
St. Lawrence
Franklin & Marshall

**AND RARELY PREFER**
Connecticut Coll.
Lehigh

### FINANCIAL FACTS

| | |
|---|---|
| Financial Aid Rating | 77 |
| Tuition | $23,892 |
| Room & board | $6,474 |
| Books and supplies | $450 |
| Required fees | $207 |
| % frosh receiving aid | 58 |
| % undergrads receiving aid | 57 |
| Avg frosh grant | $14,541 |
| Avg frosh loan | $2,781 |

# UNITED STATES AIR FORCE ACADEMY

HQ USAFA/RRS, 2304 CADET DRIVE, SUITE 200, USAF ACADEMY, CO 80840-5025 • ADMISSIONS: 719-333-2520 • FAX: 719-333-3012

## CAMPUS LIFE

| Quality of Life Rating | 86 |
|---|---|
| Type of school | public |
| Affiliation | none |
| Environment | suburban |

### STUDENTS

| | |
|---|---|
| Total undergrad enrollment | 4,325 |
| % from out of state | 95 |
| % live on campus | 100 |
| % African American | 5 |
| % Asian | 4 |
| % Caucasian | 82 |
| % Hispanic | 7 |
| % Native American | 1 |
| % international | 1 |
| # of countries represented | 23 |

### SURVEY SAYS . . .
*Very little drug use*
*Musical organizations aren't popular*
*Everyone loves the Falcons*
*Student publications are ignored*
*Classes are small*
*Athletic facilities need improving*
*Lab facilities are great*
*Library needs improving*

## ACADEMICS

| Academic Rating | 99 |
|---|---|
| Calendar | semester |
| Student/faculty ratio | 8:1 |
| Profs interesting rating | 95 |
| Profs accessible rating | 99 |
| % profs teaching UG courses | 100 |
| Avg lab size | 10-19 students |
| Avg reg class size | 10-19 students |

### MOST POPULAR MAJORS
behavioral science
history-world
space operations

## Students Speak Out
### Academics

"It's not at every college that you can learn how to fight, eat, and fly all on top of academics," but that's the United States Air Force Academy in a nutshell. Every student here receives a full scholarship that includes tuition, room and board, health care, and a monthly living allowance. Cadets also enjoy leadership training that "is second to none," academics "comparable to the Ivy League with more hands-on experience," and a "challenging" physical program. Also, not surprisingly, USAFA is on the cutting edge of technology, which allows cadets access to wind tunnels, shock tubes, rocket engines, and all manner of nifty gadgetry. Classes are "very small," and USAFA's "great" (though often "dry") professors are "always available for extra instruction." Thanks to an "intense" core curriculum, "you have to take classes in every area, no matter what your major is." Some cadets say "it's quite a load, but you get a very well-rounded education," while others gripe that "the core kills you" because it requires "too many classes." Either way, "your schedule is pretty much mapped out for you," as a management major explains. "You're going to get all your classes, and you're going to graduate in four years." On the undeniably bright side, optional courses include soaring, parachuting, and basic flying. In addition to academics, students take great pride in USAFA's strict honor code and, to put it bluntly, "you get the living crap trained out of you" here. From the "strenuous" Basic Cadet Training (called "beast," it begins the summer before first year) to combat, survival, and "escape training" in subsequent summers, vacation time is rare. Immediately upon graduation, a "guaranteed good job" as an Air Force officer (or pilot or medical school) awaits every cadet.

### Life

"This place is about hard work and sacrifice," especially for first-year "doolies," who "march to breakfast and lunch" and generally "don't get to do anything." Life for every cadet on the 18,000-acre campus includes wearing uniforms regularly, plenty of "discipline," and "reasonably short hair." Military activities "take up a large part of your life," and all cadets must participate in intramural, club, or intercollegiate athletics. Intramurals include ordinary sports like basketball and cross-country as well as "flickerball," mountain cycling, team handball, water polo, and boxing. USAFA Falcons intercollegiate athletics include the standard offerings as well as fencing and riflery. When they aren't playing sports or studying (which is "almost all the time"), cadets "watch movies and talk to friends" or "work out." Real fun, though, means "getting off campus," to "ski, hike, fish, and skydive." Cadets also "drive to Denver," or to Boulder or Fort Collins. But free time is a rare commodity. By design, USAFA "takes away all God-given rights and then gives a few back to you as privileges." The payoff, of course, is the exorbitant increase in personal discipline, but it's an "extremist" lifestyle that "either fits or it doesn't," according to a first-year cadet. "You have to want to be here."

### Student Body

Though USAFA unquestionably "produces some of the greatest leaders in the world," one cadet reports that some of these future kahunas are "socially inept," not to mention "very anal and uptight." Also, there are definitely some "very selfish" cadets at USAFA "when it comes to grades and overall academy achievement." However, most of the "dedicated" students here are "outgoing" "good people" who "take a lot of pride" in the academy. They have "high moral and ethical values" and report "unity" and "good camaraderie" in their ranks. Cadets are "a bunch of clowns" off campus (but certainly not on) as well. One cadet says simply, "The friends you meet are the best." "The population of students that are minorities and women is surprisingly low," declares one student, "but you are guaranteed to meet someone from every state." Also, there is some animosity—if not a great divide—between upperclassmen and underclass students, and first-year "doolies" receive pretty harsh treatment.

E-MAIL: NR_WEBMAIL@USAFA.AF.MIL • WEBSITE: WWW.USAFA.AF.MIL

## ADMISSIONS

*Very important* academic and nonacademic factors considered by the admissions committee include character/personal qualities, class rank, interview, secondary school record, and standardized test scores. *Important* factors considered include extracurricular activities, recommendations, talent/ability, volunteer work, and work experience. *Other* factors considered include essays and minority status. Factors *not* considered include alumni/ae relation, geography, religious affiliation/commitment, and state residency. SAT I or ACT required. High school units required/recommended: 4 English recommended, 4 math recommended, 4 science lab recommended, 2 foreign language recommended, 2 social studies recommended, 1 elective recommended.

## The Inside Word

Candidates to the service academies face some of America's most challenging admissions standards. Air Force is no exception in this regard. In addition to a very rigorous academic review, students must first win a nomination from their congressman and pass a demanding physical fitness exam. If you make it through, it's worth the hard work and effort—few students turn down an offer of admission and the chance to join the fold of an elite student body. Admit rates are among the nation's lowest annually.

## FINANCIAL AID

Not applicable as every student receives a full four-year scholarship.

**ADMISSIONS**

| Admissions Rating | 99 |
|---|---|
| # of applicants | 9,548 |
| % of applicants accepted | 18 |
| % of acceptees attending | 79 |

**FRESHMAN PROFILE**

| | |
|---|---|
| Range SAT Verbal | 590-670 |
| Average SAT Verbal | 625 |
| Range SAT Math | 610-690 |
| Average SAT Math | 652 |
| Average HS GPA | 3.8 |
| % graduated top 10% of class | 55 |
| % graduated top 25% of class | 84 |
| % graduated top 50% of class | 97 |

**DEADLINES**

| | |
|---|---|
| Regular admission | 1/31 |
| Regular notification | 4/1 |

**FINANCIAL FACTS**

| Financial Aid Rating | 99 |
|---|---|

# UNITED STATES COAST GUARD ACADEMY

31 MOHEGAN AVENUE, NEW LONDON, CT 06320-8103 • ADMISSIONS: 800-883-8724 • FAX: 860-701-6700

## CAMPUS LIFE

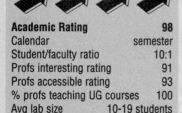

| | |
|---|---|
| **Quality of Life Rating** | **84** |
| Type of school | public |
| Affiliation | none |
| Environment | suburban |

### STUDENTS

| | |
|---|---|
| Total undergrad enrollment | 838 |
| % male/female | 71/29 |
| % from out of state | 93 |
| % from public high school | 80 |
| % live on campus | 100 |
| % African American | 5 |
| % Asian | 5 |
| % Caucasian | 83 |
| % Hispanic | 6 |
| % Native American | 1 |
| % international | 2 |

### SURVEY SAYS . . .
*Student publications are ignored*
*Very little drug use*
*Campus difficult to get around*
*Athletic facilities need improving*
*Lab facilities need improving*

## ACADEMICS

| | |
|---|---|
| **Academic Rating** | **98** |
| Calendar | semester |
| Student/faculty ratio | 10:1 |
| Profs interesting rating | 91 |
| Profs accessible rating | 93 |
| % profs teaching UG courses | 100 |
| Avg lab size | 10-19 students |
| Avg reg class size | 20-29 students |

### MOST POPULAR MAJORS
government
civil engineering
marine science

## STUDENTS SPEAK OUT
### Academics

Looking for a "prestigious" place where students develop "sound bodies, stout hearts, and alert minds," and "a liking for the sea and its lore"? Look no further. The United States Coast Guard Academy is just the place, and it's also one of the best bargains in higher education. Each cadet at USCGA receives a full scholarship complete with a monthly stipend for uniforms, a laptop, and other expenses. After four years, graduates must serve five years as officers in the Coast Guard. The "small classes" here are "very demanding" though some subject matter—like core class requirements in Nautical Science—borders on "vocational." Freshman year begins in July, when new cadets undergo six weeks of physical and military training, then spend a week learning about sailing on "America's Tall Ship," the *Barque Eagle*, a magnificent sailing vessel that serves as a seagoing classroom. Sophomore and junior summers mostly entail a slew of shipboard training. Seniors spend 10 weeks of the summer aboard Coast Guard cutters learning how to be deck watch and engineering officers. During the regular school year, "you choose a major" and "take the classes you are told to take." USCGA's "enthusiastic, caring, and devoted" professors are "very approachable" and "are professional officers. They know how to sail, drive boats, and arrest drug smugglers." However, some "are a little lacking in their ability to convey knowledge." Explains one cadet, "You will learn more about yourself" here "than you could at an 'ordinary' school, and you will accomplish things you never thought you could."

### Life

Just like the other service academies, USCGA is "a great place to be from but not a great place to be at." The "very structured" life "at the academy is nothing like any other college." At most colleges, for example, doors are not required to "remain open at a 90° from 0600 hours to 2200 hours," nor must students "salute almost everyone" on campus. "It's like having 800 brothers and sisters and living in a very small box with really strict parents and not enough hours in the day to do everything," elaborates a sophomore. "We have a bedtime and a wakeup time, semi-daily formations, and meals are mandatory. All classes, lectures, and other military training are required, and sports and study periods are scheduled into our days." Cadets "wear a uniform every day" and "a very strictly enforced honor code" keeps them on the straight and narrow. Not surprisingly, when the weekend comes, cadets are often tuckered out, but raring to get off campus. Problem is, there's "not much to do in the surrounding town" of New London. When the rare opportunity for a genuine weekend pass arises, "popular destinations are New York and Boston." Coast Guard also has "great sports programs for an NCAA Division III school," and both intercollegiate and intramural sports are enormously popular and competitive.

### Student Body

The "small student body" at USCGA is "friendly" or, at the least, "cordial." Cadets "work together to achieve common goals," and "camaraderie" is generally the order of the day. "We're all in the same boat, so to speak," quips a first-year cadet. Though the academy has its share of "back-stabbing social climbers" and "social rejects," most cadets are "all-around good people" who are "very supportive of one another." Over four "disciplined" years here, a real sense of "loyalty" develops, and the "lifelong friendships" between shipmates are "outstanding." Socially, USCGA does tend to be somewhat cliquey. There are "jocks, brains, smokers, and the popular crowd," but they are all "determined to become officers," and most are "just trying to get through the academy." "Most of my fellow students are such a huge part of my life that I don't know how I would survive without them," waxes a sophomore. "They are caring, honest, hardworking, good people."

E-MAIL: ADMISSIONS@CGA.USCG.MIL • WEBSITE: WWW.CGA.EDU

## ADMISSIONS

*Very important* academic and nonacademic factors considered by the admissions committee include class rank, extracurricular activities, secondary school record, and standardized test scores. *Important* factors considered include character/personal qualities, essays, recommendations, and talent/ability. *Other* factors considered include minority status, interview, volunteer work, and work experience. Factors *not* considered include geography, alumni/ae relation, religious affiliation/commitment, and state residency. SAT I or ACT required. TOEFL required of all international applicants. High school diploma is required and GED is accepted. *High school units required/recommended:* 4 English required, 4 math required.

### The Inside Word

Coast Guard is the service academy with the least amount of public recognition. Not that it's any easier to get admitted. Candidates must also go through the rigorous multistep admissions process (though no congressional nomination is required), and can fall short on any of these steps and meet with a roadblock to admission. Those who pass muster join a very proud, if somewhat under-recognized, student body virtually equal in accomplishment to those at the other academies.

## FINANCIAL AID

Not applicable as every student receives a complete four-year scholarship.

## FROM THE ADMISSIONS OFFICE

"Founded in 1876, the United States Coast Guard Academy has a proud tradition as one of the finest colleges in the country. When you've completed the four-year Bachelor of Science program, you're prepared professionally, physically, and mentally for the great challenges of the future. You'll learn from inspiring teachers in small classes, and train in some of the world's most sophisticated labs using equipment as advanced as anything at other top science colleges. You'll have a level of training that will make you stand out from the crowd. Unlike the other federal academies, there are no congressional appointments to our Academy. Acceptance is based solely on annual competition among top students across the nation. The competition evaluates high school performance and standardized test scores—over 95 percent of entering students are in the top 20 percent of their high school class. Just as important is leadership potential and the desire to serve your fellow Americans. Our student body reflects the best of American youth—with all its potential and diversity."

## ADMISSIONS

| | |
|---|---|
| **Admissions Rating** | 97 |
| # of applicants | 5,557 |
| % of applicants accepted | 9 |
| % of acceptees attending | 66 |
| # accepting a place on wait list | 348 |
| % admitted from wait list | 18 |

### FRESHMAN PROFILE

| | |
|---|---|
| Range SAT Verbal | 560-660 |
| Average SAT Verbal | 612 |
| Range SAT Math | 600-680 |
| Average SAT Math | 639 |
| Range ACT Composite | 25-29 |
| Average ACT Composite | 26 |
| Minimum TOEFL | 500 |
| % graduated top 10% of class | 45 |
| % graduated top 25% of class | 79 |
| % graduated top 50% of class | 100 |

### DEADLINES

| | |
|---|---|
| Regular admission | 12/15 |

### FINANCIAL FACTS

| | |
|---|---|
| **Financial Aid Rating** | 99 |
| Required fees | $3,000 |

# UNITED STATES MILITARY ACADEMY

600 THAYER ROAD, WEST POINT, NY 10996-1797 • ADMISSIONS: 914-938-4041 • FAX: 914-938-3021

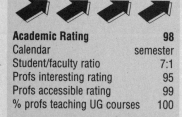
## STUDENTS SPEAK OUT

### Academics

"West Point is unique in many ways: a military institution, a first-class university, and a national landmark all rolled into one," explains one cadet. "Our motto is 'duty, honor, country,' and sometimes duty looms much larger than the rest. Life is hard here, but its difficulty makes it fulfilling." The West Point approach—to cram as much activity into one day as humanly possible—is "very tough. Learn to prioritize. If you procrastinate, you die. Be ready not to sleep." Notes one student, "Academics are tough, but it's the fact that you have no time to study that makes it hard." Life is strictly regimented here, as one would expect. Writes one student, "West Point is similar to high school, at times almost too similar. We start at 7, stop for lunch at 12, and then continue until 3. Classes are small, which means every professor knows your name." For nearly all freshmen and sophomores, "There is no class choice. All classes are required." And even upperclassmen warn that "it's the military: You pick the major, they choose the classes." Fortunately for students, "the professors here, for the most part, are amazing. They understand how rigorous our life is and will tutor you personally every day for hours if you need it." Cadets are the first to admit that this school is not for everyone. "The school is focused toward military development and officership, so if you don't want to be in the Army, don't come!" warns one. Concludes another, "West Point is a machine that takes you in, chews you up, and spits you out—but somehow you are tremendously better person for it." Upon graduation, cadets are commissioned as Second Lieutenants in the U.S. Army and must serve a minimum of five years of active duty.

### Life

As far as extracurricular life is concerned, a student's tenure at West Point is neatly divided in half. Simply put, for their first two years, students have no extracurricular life. Writes one student, "Because I am a sophomore, otherwise known as a 'Yuk,' I have no privileges (like going to the movies or to the mall). I am stuck in the cadet area studying." During their final two years, students are given greater freedom. Explains one upperclassman, "There is not much to do here in the first two years, but once you receive off-post privileges there is more available." The town surrounding the beautiful campus, Highland Falls, is small, so even when cadets do leave campus, they find very little to do unless they have wheels. Writes one student, "If you're not a cow (junior) or a first (senior) with a car, you are hard-pressed to have fun. If you do have a car, New York City and New Jersey aren't so far off. It also helps to be on a sports team." Intercollegiate athletic events are well attended here, even though Army's teams generally lose more often than they win. Army's popular football team, for one, competes in Conference USA, where it is usually overmatched by Tulane, Houston, Louisville, and Southern Mississippi, among others. The lacrosse team is much better, ranking 20th in the nation at the end of the 2000 season. Intramural sports are unusually popular for the simple reason that "all students not on varsity teams must play intramurals here. It's not an option." Mostly, though, life at West Point is defined by study, exercise, and plenty of drilling. "If you don't want to work hard, run, or be in the Army, do not come here," advises a senior.

### Student Body

West Point's undergraduates represent a "great diversity of students and different backgrounds." However, as one cadet pointed out, "Relationships with other students are always filtered through the lens of leadership." As a result, "some get along, and some don't. But one thing about West Point is that I would trust any of [my classmates] with my life—and someday I may have to." Adds another student, "Students here all get along. They are forced to because of our mission in life: to become officers. Teamwork is essential. There are no individuals here." Minority discrimination "does not occur because it is simply not allowed here."

FINANCIAL AID: 914-938-3516 • E-MAIL: 8DAD@EXMAIL.USMA.ARMY.MIL • WEBSITE: WWW.USMA.EDU

## ADMISSIONS

*Very important* academic and nonacademic factors considered by the admissions committee include essays, extracurricular activities, recommendations, secondary school record, and standardized test scores. *Important* factors considered include character/personal qualities, interview, minority status and talent/ability. *Other* factors considered include geography, volunteer work, and work experience. Factors *not* considered include alumni/ae relation, religious affiliation/commitment, and state residency. SAT I or ACT required. TOEFL required of all international applicants. High school diploma is required and GED is accepted. High school units required/recommended: 19 total recommended; 4 English recommended, 4 math recommended, 2 science recommended, 2 science lab recommended, 2 foreign language recommended, 3 social studies recommended, 1 history recommended, 3 elective recommended.

### The Inside Word

Students considering a candidacy at West Point need to hit the ground running in the second half of their junior year. Don't delay initiating the application and nomination processes; together they constitute a long, hard road that includes not one but several highly competitive elements. Successful candidates must demonstrate strength both academically and physically, be solid citizens and contributors to society, and show true fortitude and potential for leadership. Admissions processes at other top schools can seem like a cakewalk compared to this, but those who get a nomination and pass muster through the physical part of the process have made it through the hardest part.

## FINANCIAL AID

Not applicable as every student receives a four-year scholarship.

---

### ADMISSIONS

| | |
|---|---|
| Admissions Rating | 99 |
| # of applicants | 11,473 |
| % of applicants accepted | 13 |
| % of acceptees attending | 74 |

#### FRESHMAN PROFILE

| | |
|---|---|
| Range SAT Verbal | 570-670 |
| Average SAT Verbal | 627 |
| Range SAT Math | 590-680 |
| Average SAT Math | 641 |
| Range ACT Composite | 26-30 |
| Average ACT Composite | 28 |
| Average HS GPA | 3.7 |
| % graduated top 10% of class | 50 |
| % graduated top 25% of class | 81 |
| % graduated top 50% of class | 97 |

#### DEADLINES

| | |
|---|---|
| Priority admission deadline | 12/1 |
| Regular admission | 3/21 |

#### APPLICANTS ALSO LOOK AT
**AND OFTEN PREFER**
U. Rochester
**AND SOMETIMES PREFER**
US Naval Acad.
Notre Dame
Villanova
Tulane U.
U. Oklahoma
**AND RARELY PREFER**
U. Florida
Carnegie Mellon

### FINANCIAL FACTS

| | |
|---|---|
| Financial Aid Rating | 99 |
| Books and supplies | $664 |

# UNITED STATES NAVAL ACADEMY

117 DECATUR ROAD, ANNAPOLIS, MD 21402 • ADMISSIONS: 410-293-4361 • FAX: 410-295-1815

## CAMPUS LIFE

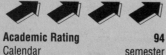

| Quality of Life Rating | **80** |
|---|---|
| Type of school | public |
| Affiliation | none |
| Environment | suburban |

### STUDENTS

| | |
|---|---|
| Total undergrad enrollment | 4,172 |
| % from out of state | 94 |
| % from public high school | 60 |
| % live on campus | 100 |
| % African American | 6 |
| % Asian | 4 |
| % Caucasian | 81 |
| % Hispanic | 8 |
| % Native American | 1 |
| % international | 1 |

### SURVEY SAYS . . .
*Very little drug use
Everyone loves the Midshipmen
(Almost) everyone plays intramural
sports
Classes are small
Popular college radio
Unattractive campus
Campus difficult to get around
Library needs improving
Lab facilities are great
Computer facilities need improving*

## ACADEMICS

| Academic Rating | **94** |
|---|---|
| Calendar | semester |
| Student/faculty ratio | 7:1 |
| Profs interesting rating | 93 |
| Profs accessible rating | 98 |
| Avg reg class size | 10-19 students |

### MOST POPULAR MAJORS
economics
political science
systems engineering

## STUDENTS SPEAK OUT
### Academics

The U.S. Naval Academy offers a great education at a great price—it's free. Midshipmen have one of the "toughest academic programs around," yet the "outstanding" professors are "always willing and ready to help in every way possible." Classes are small and are all taught by full-time military and civilian faculty members. "Tough but rewarding" is how one midshipman sums up his experience here. "If you've never been challenged by academics, get ready for a surprise." Midshipmen must handle a demanding courseload along with naval officer training, and academically they find that "it's a challenge to do well on top of all the military responsibilities." Facilities are absolutely state-of-the-art, and the administration, as might be expected, runs a tight, efficient ship. The innovative core curriculum balances technical and non-technical subjects and has received national acclaim: As one midshipman remarks, "This is the only place I know where history majors are required to take electrical engineering, calculus, and physics courses." All students, regardless of major, are awarded a Bachelor of Science degree upon graduation.

### Life

The U.S. Naval Academy prepares its students (known as midshipmen) for life on the high seas with a rigorous academic and military training program. As a result, the future leaders who attend the academy are extremely busy: "We have about 30 hours' worth of activities in a 24-hour day." No doubt about it, life is very demanding here, but things get better after the first year. Opinion is unanimous that "plebe year (first year) is the hardest." Soon after entering the gate on Induction Day (the first week in July), students don uniforms and commence a "frantic and exhausting" period of summer military training to get ready for the academic year and learn to "think under pressure." Relations with upperclassmen are "tough," and "most freshmen and sophomores go to their sponsor family's home during free time." Students stress that theirs is not the typical college experience: "It's hard to consider this place a school," as one puts it. Midshipmen are encouraged to participate in several intercollegiate and intramural athletics, and to get involved in clubs, bands, and choirs. The historic town of Annapolis gets high marks for its attractiveness and good food. But the bottom line is that students at Annapolis know what they're here for—"service to our country"—and find their training to be the best entertainment: "For fun, we shoot guns, drive ships, jump out of airplanes, and navigate submarines. We practice our future jobs."

### Student Body

Midshipmen form strong bonds with one another. "We're very close because we depend on each other. No one can make it through this school alone." The overall impression is that "students get along extremely well"; one midshipman reports that the academy feels like "the biggest fraternity in the world." The academy boasts that nearly 20 percent of its midshipmen are members of minority groups. And once an all-male bastion, the Naval Academy currently claims well over 600 women within its ranks. Several times, the position of Brigade Commander—the biggest kahuna of all midshipmen—has been held by a woman.

E-MAIL: WEBMAIL@GWMAIL.USNA.COM • WEBSITE: WWW.USNA.EDU

## ADMISSIONS

*Very important* academic and nonacademic factors considered by the admissions committee include character/personal qualities, class rank, essays, extracurricular activities, interview, recommendations, secondary school record, and standardized test scores. *Important* factors considered include talent/ability. *Other* factors considered include alumni/ae relation, geography, state residency, volunteer work, and work experience. SAT I or ACT required. TOEFL required of all international applicants. High school units required/recommended: 4 English required, 4 math through trigonometry required, 1 chemistry with lab required, 1 physics recommended, 2 foreign language recommended, 2 history recommended.

### The Inside Word

It doesn't take a genius to recognize that getting admitted to Annapolis requires true strength of character; simply completing the arduous admissions process is an accomplishment worthy of remembrance. Those who have successful candidacies are strong, motivated students, and leaders in both school and community. Perseverance is an important character trait for anyone considering the life of a midshipman—the application process is only the beginning of a truly challenging and demanding experience.

## FINANCIAL AID

Not applicable as every student receives a four-year scholarship.

## FROM THE ADMISSIONS OFFICE

"The Naval Academy offers you a unique opportunity to associate with a broad cross-section of the country's finest young men and women. You will have the opportunity to pursue a four-year program that develops you mentally, morally, and physically as no civilian college can. As you might expect, this program is demanding, but the opportunities are limitless and more than worth the effort. To receive an appointment to the academy, you need four years of high school preparation to develop the strong academic, athletic, and extracurricular background required to compete successfully for admission. You should begin preparing in your freshman year and apply for admission at the end of your junior year. Selection for appointment to the academy comes as a result of a complete evaluation of your admissions package and completion of the nomination process. Complete admissions guidance may be found at www.usna.edu."

## ADMISSIONS

| | |
|---|---:|
| **Admissions Rating** | 99 |
| # of applicants | 10,296 |
| % of applicants accepted | 15 |
| % of acceptees attending | 81 |

### FRESHMAN PROFILE

| | |
|---|---:|
| Range SAT Verbal | 600-680 |
| Average SAT Verbal | 637 |
| Range SAT Math | 620-700 |
| Average SAT Math | 667 |
| Minimum TOEFL | 500 |
| % graduated top 10% of class | 56 |
| % graduated top 25% of class | 83 |
| % graduated top 50% of class | 97 |

### DEADLINES

| | |
|---|---:|
| Regular admission | 2/28 |

### APPLICANTS ALSO LOOK AT
**AND OFTEN PREFER**
Harvard
Duke
Stanford
U. Virginia
US Air Force Acad.
**AND SOMETIMES PREFER**
US Military Acad.
Georgia Tech.
MIT
Penn State—Univ. Park
U. Michigan—Ann Arbor
**AND RARELY PREFER**
Purdue U.
Boston U.

### FINANCIAL FACTS

| | |
|---|---:|
| **Financial Aid Rating** | 99 |

# UNIVERSITY OF ALABAMA—TUSCALOOSA

Box 870132, Tuscaloosa, AL 35487 • Admissions: 205-348-5666 • Fax: 205-348-9046

## STUDENTS SPEAK OUT

### Academics

Professors at a research university like the University of Alabama often find that it is a delicate balance between focusing on teaching and research. Unfortunately, not all of the professors at 'Bama are able to maintain that balance. According to one student, "Publish or perish takes on a whole new meaning on this campus." Professors are accessible and friendly. "Most professors are cool and are willing to help you out," one student writes. "As long as you go to class, you will pass, and the professor will see to it that you pass." Students in the math department desire professors with a better command of the English language. Undergrads choose from nine educational divisions: commerce and business administration, education, communication, engineering, arts and sciences, nursing, social work, human environmental sciences, and New College—a unique, independent study program. The administration isn't very well regarded. "Every time you need to change a schedule, pay a bill, or buy a book, you can bet on five hours of waiting in line only to be told to take a piece of paper down the hall or up the steps." Students also complain that more class sections need to be made available. Despite these complaints, most students tell us that they "very much enjoyed [their] academic experience at UA."

### Life

School spirit runs wild at Alabama. The Crimson Tide's football program is a celebrated, perennially nationally ranked team with a rich legacy. "Anybody who tries to bad mouth the "Bear" [legendary coach "Bear" Bryant] on campus doesn't stand a chance," one student says. Students go to class and then "just chill" until about 10 P.M., when "everyone goes out, just about every night." The weekend begins in Tuscaloosa on Thursday night, and "on Fridays, everybody goes to happy hour and skips class." Fraternities and sororities are extremely popular (about 20 percent of students pledge), and their parties are all the rage. Independent parties are another social alternative. Testifies on undergrad: "The best parties are thrown by the swim team or the football team because they always have a lot of alcohol and a DJ." Students also go to downtown bars. Nondrinkers find that many of the 250-plus on-campus organizations and groups "have social engagements" that don't involve "getting polluted." Students go to free movies at the theater in the Ferg. One student says that if money is tight, students go to Toys R Us. "It costs nothing and they let you play some of the video games." Students say that the on-campus parking situation needs improvement.

### Student Body

At 'Bama not all students are as academically inclined as they could be. "Some people are academically driven and some aren't." Everyone's very friendly but, outside of the football stadium, students of different races and ethnic backgrounds don't intermingle. "We have diverse students, but when you get a taste of minority life, you wish people were a little open minded." Students "tend to unite for common causes while remaining in their social groups." Because so many students pledge to fraternities and sororities, some students say that "if you're not Greek, it can be tough." Still, one lesbian student says that she and her girlfriend "have encountered no discrimination, other than some sororities making it clear they do not accept gay members." Students say that though they have "never been witness to serious racism or prejudice," the campus could stand some more diversity.

FINANCIAL AID: 205-348-6756 • E-MAIL: UAADMIT@UA.EDU • WEBSITE: WWW.UA.EDU

## ADMISSIONS

*Very important* academic and nonacademic factors considered by the admissions committee include secondary school record and standardized test scores. *Important* factors considered include class rank, essays, recommendations, and interview. *Other* factors considered include talent/ability, volunteer work, and work experience. Factors *not* considered include alumni/ae relations, minority status, state residency, and religious affiliation/commitment. SAT I or ACT required. TOEFL required of all international applicants. High school diploma is required and GED is accepted with a minimum score of 50. *High school units required/recommended:* 16 total required; 4 English required, 3 math required, 4 math recommended, 3 science required, 4 science recommended, 2 science lab required, 4 science lab recommended, 1 foreign language required, 2 foreign language recommended, 4 social studies required (including world history), and additional units in computer science and fine arts recommended.

### The Inside Word

There's no mystery in Alabama's formula-driven approach to admission; any solid "B" student is likely to meet with success. What selectivity there is in the process exists mainly because of the volume of applications. Recommendations are not likely to play a significant role in the admission of applicants unless they are borderline candidates.

## FINANCIAL AID

The Princeton Review suggests that all financial aid forms be submitted as soon as possible after January 1. *Need-based scholarships/grants offered:* Pell, SEOG, state scholarships/grants, private scholarships, the school's own gift aid, Federal Nursing. *Loan aid offered:* FFEL Subsidized Stafford, FFEL Unsubsidized Stafford, FFEL PLUS, Federal Perkins, and Federal Nursing. Institutional employment available. Federal Work-Study Program available. Off-campus job opportunities are good.

## FROM THE ADMISSIONS OFFICE

"Since its founding in 1831 as the first public university in the state, the University of Alabama has been committed to providing the best, most complete education possible for its students. Our commitment to that goal means that as times change, we sharpen our focus and methods to keep our graduates competitive in their fields. By offering outstanding teaching in a solid core curriculum enhanced by multimedia classrooms and campus-wide computer labs, the University of Alabama keeps its focus on the future while maintaining a traditional college atmosphere. Extensive international study opportunities, internship programs, and co-operative education placements help our students prepare for successful futures. Consisting of 14 colleges and schools offering 275 degrees in over 150 fields of study, the university gives its students a wide range of choices and offers courses of study at the bachelor's, master's, specialist, and doctoral levels. The university emphasizes quality and breadth of academic opportunities, and challenging programs for the well-prepared students through the university Honors Program, International Honors Program, and Computer-Based Honors Programs. One-third of undergraduates are from out-of-state providing an enriching social and cultural environment."

## ADMISSIONS

| | |
|---|---|
| Admissions Rating | 79 |
| # of applicants | 8,011 |
| % of applicants accepted | 86 |
| % of acceptees attending | 43 |

### FRESHMAN PROFILE

| | |
|---|---|
| Range SAT Verbal | 490-610 |
| Range SAT Math | 490-610 |
| Range ACT Composite | 20-26 |
| Average ACT Composite | 24 |
| Minimum TOEFL | 500 |
| Average HS GPA | 3.4 |
| % graduated top 10% of class | 28 |
| % graduated top 25% of class | 55 |
| % graduated top 50% of class | 81 |

### DEADLINES

| | |
|---|---|
| Priority admission deadline | 3/1 |
| Regular admission | 7/1 |
| Nonfall registration? | yes |

### APPLICANTS ALSO LOOK AT
#### AND OFTEN PREFER
U. Georgia
Florida State
U. Tennessee
Vanderbilt U.
Birmingham-Southern Coll.
#### AND SOMETIMES PREFER
Auburn U.
Oglethorpe U.
Loyola U. New Orleans
Samford U.
Mississippi State U.

## FINANCIAL FACTS

| | |
|---|---|
| Financial Aid Rating | 79 |
| In-state tuition | $3,014 |
| Out-of-state tuition | $8,162 |
| Room & board | $3,800 |
| Books and supplies | $700 |
| % frosh receiving aid | 35 |
| % undergrads receiving aid | 61 |
| Avg frosh grant | $4,536 |
| Avg frosh loan | $5,012 |

# UNIVERSITY OF ARIZONA

PO BOX 210040, TUCSON, AZ 85721-0040 • ADMISSIONS: 520-621-3237 • FAX: 520-621-9799

## STUDENTS SPEAK OUT

### Academics

Maybe it's all the sunshine in Tucson that makes students so wildly enthusiastic about the University of Arizona, or maybe it's just that this school does a great job making its students a number-one priority. Whatever the cause, students at U of A are nothing short of impassioned about their school, academically and otherwise: "I couldn't imagine attending any other school. Every experience I have had at U of A has been excellent." Says another student, "My experience at U of A has been wonderful! I've had professors and classes I'll never forget." And another reports, "My professors have always been willing to help me outside of class (and always respond to my questioning e-mails!)." The University of Arizona has much to offer students by way of academics, including a demanding engineering program and strong departments in molecular and cellular biology and chemistry, as well as in English and the social sciences. The emphasis on research at this institution offers students the opportunity to work with professors outside of class as well, which "gives students a great opportunity to be part of a published work." The administration receives decent marks from U of A students. One writes, "I have been overly impressed with the administration and professors' availability throughout my experience here." Several students point directly to the new president, Peter Likins, as the source of their smooth relations: "We are really excited. . . . [He] has amply shown that he cares about students."

### Life

It's a virtual love-fest as far as student relations go at U of A. But maybe it's just the sunny weather that puts everyone in such a good mood: "We're all just coolio at U of A!" boasts one enthusiast. "I LOVE the students here. Everyone is very outgoing, active, and friendly and always willing to make new friends." And how could they not? The opportunities to socialize are ever present with all the great outdoor activities available to students in the general area. "Life is a blast! There are always interesting activities, concerts, clubs and such to get involved with. I am always busy . . . never a dull moment," writes one student. Says another active U of Aer, "My friends and I go to the movies, dinner, miniature golfing, go-carting, hiking, back-packing, mountain biking, rollerblading, or just go for coffee for a late night of talking." Sports are extremely popular: "Intramural sports teams are big and very good. People get very involved with teams, especially the NCAA basketball champs." The city of Tucson itself is campus-friendly, and town-gown relations are good: "The town of Tucson is built up around the U of A, so there is a tremendous amount of community spirit and support." Although most agree that a car is necessary, parking can be a problem.

### Student Body

Students at U of A describe each other as "friendly, spirited, and involved in campus life." Greek life is popular, though as one student comments, "Sometimes it's harder to get to know someone who is in the Greek system if you are not in it." Another agrees, "The Greek system tends to be a bit exclusive." Diversity, however, doesn't seem to be a problem. As this student observes, "I'd never met so many people from other cultures until I came to U of A." Says another, "There is a large, diverse population full of interesting people."

FINANCIAL AID: 520-621-1858 • E-MAIL: APPINFO@ARIZONA.EDU • WEBSITE: WWW.ARIZONA.EDU

## ADMISSIONS

*Very important* academic and nonacademic factors considered by the admissions committee include secondary school record. *Important* factors considered include class rank and standardized test scores. *Other* factors considered include essays, recommendations, character/personal qualities, extracurricular activities, interview, state residency, talent/ability, volunteer work, and work experience. Factors *not* considered include alumni/ae relation, geography, minority status, and religious affiliation/commitment. SAT I or ACT required. High school diploma is required and GED is accepted. *High school units required/recommended:* 16 total required, 4 English required, 4 math required, 3 science lab required, 2 foreign language required, 1 social studies required, 1 history required, 1 fine arts required. *The admissions office says:* "Also, all applicants are considered based on student goals and past experiences, so appropriate additional information is considered."

### The Inside Word

Universities like Arizona that use formulas and cutoffs in the admissions process rarely do more than glance at supplementary materials that candidates submit with their applications. Volume processing means that very little time is spent on individual applicants: You either have what is required, or you don't.

## FINANCIAL AID

*Students should submit:* FAFSA. The Princeton Review suggests that all financial aid forms be submitted as soon as possible after January 1. Institutional employment available. Federal Work-Study Program available. Off-campus job opportunities are good.

## FROM THE ADMISSIONS OFFICE

"Surrounded by mountains and the dramatic beauty of the Sonoran Desert, the University of Arizona offers a top-drawer education in a resort-like setting. Some of the nation's highest ranked departments make their homes at this oasis of learning in the desert. In addition to producing cloudless sunshine 350 days per year, the clear Arizona skies provide an ideal setting for one of the country's best astronomy programs. Other nationally rated programs include nursing, sociology, management information systems, anthropology, creative writing, and computer and aerospace engineering. The university balances a strong research component with an emphasis on teaching—faculty rolls include Nobel and Pulitzer Prize winners. Famous Chinese astrophysicist and political dissident Fang Lizhi continues his landmark studies here; he now teaches physics to undergraduates. The wealth of academic choices—the university offers 118 majors—is supplemented by an active, progressive campus atmosphere, conference-winning basketball and football teams, and myriad recreational opportunities."

## ADMISSIONS

| | |
|---|---|
| Admissions Rating | 75 |
| # of applicants | 18,715 |
| % of applicants accepted | 84 |
| % of acceptees attending | 35 |

### FRESHMAN PROFILE

| | |
|---|---|
| Range SAT Verbal | 480-600 |
| Average SAT Verbal | 545 |
| Range SAT Math | 490-620 |
| Average SAT Math | 556 |
| Range ACT Composite | 20-26 |
| Average ACT Composite | 23 |
| Average HS GPA | 3.4 |
| % graduated top 10% of class | 33 |
| % graduated top 25% of class | 61 |
| % graduated top 50% of class | 88 |

### DEADLINES

| | |
|---|---|
| Priority admission deadline | 10/1 |
| Regular admission | 4/1 |
| Nonfall registration? | yes |

### APPLICANTS ALSO LOOK AT

**AND OFTEN PREFER**
UC—Irvine
U. Washington

**AND SOMETIMES PREFER**
U. Colorado—Boulder
UCLA
UC—Santa Barbara
U. Wisconsin—Madison
Ohio U.

**AND RARELY PREFER**
Baylor
Arizona State
Northern Arizona

### FINANCIAL FACTS

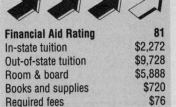

| | |
|---|---|
| Financial Aid Rating | 81 |
| In-state tuition | $2,272 |
| Out-of-state tuition | $9,728 |
| Room & board | $5,888 |
| Books and supplies | $720 |
| Required fees | $76 |
| % frosh receiving aid | 39 |
| % undergrads receiving aid | 52 |

# UNIVERSITY OF ARKANSAS—FAYETTEVILLE

200 SILAS HUNT HALL, FAYETTEVILLE, AR 72701 • ADMISSIONS: 501-575-5346 • FAX: 501-575-7515

## CAMPUS LIFE

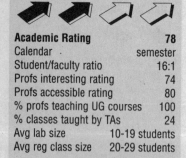

| Quality of Life Rating | 81 |
|---|---|
| Type of school | public |
| Affiliation | none |
| Environment | small city |

### STUDENTS

| | |
|---|---|
| Total undergrad enrollment | 12,502 |
| % male/female | 51/49 |
| % from out of state | 9 |
| % from public high school | 95 |
| % live on campus | 40 |
| % in (# of) fraternities | 17 (11) |
| % in (# of) sororities | 19 (11) |
| % African American | 7 |
| % Asian | 3 |
| % Caucasian | 83 |
| % Hispanic | 1 |
| % Native American | 2 |
| % international | 3 |

### SURVEY SAYS . . .

Great food on campus
Campus easy to get around
No one cheats
(Almost) everyone plays intramural
sports
Everyone loves the Razorbacks
Ethnic diversity on campus
Lots of TAs teach upper-level
courses
Student government is unpopular
Students don't like Fayetteville, AR
Ethnic diversity on campus
Lab facilities are great

## ACADEMICS

| Academic Rating | 78 |
|---|---|
| Calendar | semester |
| Student/faculty ratio | 16:1 |
| Profs interesting rating | 74 |
| Profs accessible rating | 80 |
| % profs teaching UG courses | 100 |
| % classes taught by TAs | 24 |
| Avg lab size | 10-19 students |
| Avg reg class size | 20-29 students |

### MOST POPULAR MAJORS

marketing & transportation
finance
information systems

## STUDENTS SPEAK OUT

### Academics

The flagship campus of the state university system, University of Arkansas—Fayetteville prides itself as a research institute that also provides quality education to undergraduates. Fayetteville's seven undergraduate divisions work hard to prepare the largely pre-professional student body in such areas as agriculture, food sciences, business administration, education, engineering, and pre-law. "Surprisingly, U of A has kept me academically challenged. Coming in, I assumed this was a 'party school,' but all of my teachers have been really superb, and my academic advisor has been great. At the beginning, I was really depressed that I didn't have the funds to attend other schools. But my advisor reached out and helped me to make as challenging a schedule as possible." Faculty receives high marks when compared to profs at other state schools. Explains one student, "The professors I've had have been awesome! They're always willing to go out of their way to help students out." Adds another, "The faculty is readily available out of class. Because professors are generally easy going and understand the needs of students, this has been a very pleasant educational experience." Administrators "recognize that communication between the administration and students has been less than adequate. They are making efforts to improve, and they are making progress." Students particularly recommend Fayetteville's competitive honors program. Writes one participant: "The University of Arkansas' redeeming quality is its honors program. The honors program administration, professors, and classes exceed the level of the university, providing upper-level students an educational opportunity rivaling more acclaimed private universities."

### Life

Students have nothing but praise for their hometown of Fayetteville. Nestled in the western Ozarks, Fayetteville is a haven for those who love the outdoors, including "caving, hiking, ice skating, biking, fishing, boating, and rock climbing." In and around town "there are many things to do such as sports events, coffee shops, ice skating, drive-ins, and hiking." With its temperate climate and laid-back southern vibe, it's no wonder students report that "the atmosphere of Fayetteville is homey and wonderful." Campus life gets a big boost from Greek organizations. "Sororities and fraternities seem to be where the social life of this campus revolves." This situation doesn't sit well with everyone, however; some complain that "those of us who don't choose to go Greek often feel that we are discriminated against." Sports also play a huge role in undergraduate life; many of the Razorbacks' Southeastern Conference (SEC) teams are competitive nationally, and intramurals—especially Ultimate Frisbee and soccer—also attract a large number of participants. Despite all the action, many students head home nearly every weekend, leaving remaining students to ponder, "Where does everyone go on the weekend?" Major and prolonged renovations promise a state-of-the-art campus in the near future, but for the time being students warn that "the campus is usually beautiful, but due to all the construction right now, you would never know it."

### Student Body

Other campuses of the University of Arkansas attract sizable minority populations, but the Fayetteville campus does not. African Americans, for example, make up only 7 percent of the undergraduate student body, hardly representative of the 16 percent of black Arkansans. Other minority populations are even smaller. However, the university is making attempts to improve the situation. Students agree that the school could do more to attract minority students but also point out that students in each community interact easily.

# UNIVERSITY OF ARKANSAS—FAYETTEVILLE

FINANCIAL AID: 501-575-3806 • E-MAIL: UAFADMIS@COMP.UARK.EDU • WEBSITE: WWW.UARK.EDU

## ADMISSIONS

*Very Important* academic and nonacademic factors considered by the admissions committee include secondary school record and standardized test scores. *Important* factors considered include class rank, essays, and recommendations. *Other* factors considered include alumni/ae relation, geography, character/personal qualities, extracurricular activities, talent/ability, work experience, and state residency. Factors *not* considered include religious affiliation/commitment, minority status, and interview. SAT I or ACT required. TOEFL required of all international applicants. High school diploma is required and GED is accepted. *High school units required/recommended:* 16 total required, 4 English required, 3 math required, 3 science required, 2 science lab recommended, 2 foreign language required, 3 social studies required (including history), 3 elective required.

### The Inside Word

Admission is very straightforward here at Arkansas' flagship university campus. Average college prep students (with a 2.75 or better GPA) will encounter a clear path into the freshman class. The university will also consider those with lower grades for possible conditional admission.

## FINANCIAL AID

*Students should submit:* FAFSA. Priority date is March 15. There is no regular filing deadline. The Princeton Review suggests that all financial aid forms be submitted as soon as possible after January 1. *Need-based scholarships/grants offered:* Pell, SEOG, state scholarships/grants, private scholarships, and the school's own gift aid. *Loan aid offered:* FFEL Subsidized Stafford, FFEL Unsubsidized Stafford, FFEL PLUS, Federal Perkins, state, and college/university loans from institutional funds. Institutional employment available. Federal Work-Study Program available. Applicants will be notified of awards on a rolling basis beginning on or about April 15. Off-campus job opportunities are excellent.

## FROM THE ADMISSIONS OFFICE

"In its drive to emerge as one of the nation's top 50 public research universities, the University of Arkansas has bold ambitions for bright students. In fact, the U of A has made some tremendous recent accomplishments that enhance the quality of its nationally competitive education: The ACT scores of the top 500 students in our 1998–1999 freshman class ranked in the 98th percentile nationally; three U of A students received Goldwater scholarships in addition to two Truman Scholars in 1999 alone; and the U of A has expanded its Chancellor's Scholarship program with full tuition, fees, and room and board awarded to almost 500 freshmen in 1998–1999. Among nationally ranked programs would be creative writing—with two Truman Capote Fellows named in both 1998 and 1999; more than $50 million in construction is taking place—including an expanded student union and research facilities; and undergraduates are taught by a world-class faculty such as Cosmochemist Derek Sears, who refuted claims of life on Mars. In addition to tremendous academic opportunities, the U of A prides itself on its friendly atmosphere where students can determine their own identity and find a place to call their own. Located in the Ozark Mountains of northwest Arkansas, the U of A is also a great place for outdoor enthusiasts, with activities such as hiking, canoeing, boating, fishing, biking, and much more."

### ADMISSIONS

| | |
|---|---|
| Admissions Rating | 80 |
| # of applicants | 4,280 |
| % of applicants accepted | 90 |
| % of acceptees attending | 59 |

#### FRESHMAN PROFILE

| | |
|---|---|
| Range SAT Verbal | 510-650 |
| Average SAT Verbal | 575 |
| Range SAT Math | 500-650 |
| Average SAT Math | 573 |
| Range ACT Composite | 22-28 |
| Average ACT Composite | 25 |
| Minimum TOEFL | 550 |
| Average HS GPA | 3.5 |
| % graduated top 10% of class | 33 |
| % graduated top 25% of class | 60 |
| % graduated top 50% of class | 88 |

#### DEADLINES

| | |
|---|---|
| Priority admission deadline | 2/15 |
| Regular admission | rolling |
| Nonfall registration? | yes |

### FINANCIAL FACTS

| | |
|---|---|
| Financial Aid Rating | 89 |
| In-state tuition | $3,116 |
| Out-of-state tuition | $8,674 |
| Room & board | $4,454 |
| Books and supplies | $800 |
| Required fees | $764 |
| % frosh receiving aid | 46 |
| % undergrads receiving aid | 44 |

# University of California, Berkeley

OFFICE OF UNDERGRADUATE ADMISSION AND RELATIONS, 110 SPROUL HALL #5800, BERKELEY, CA 94720-5800 • ADMISSIONS: 510-642-3175

## CAMPUS LIFE

| | |
|---|---|
| **Quality of Life Rating** | **72** |
| Type of school | public |
| Affiliation | none |
| Environment | urban |

### STUDENTS

| | |
|---|---|
| Total undergrad enrollment | 22,593 |
| % male/female | 50/50 |
| % from out of state | 11 |
| % from public high school | 82 |
| % live on campus | 23 |
| % in (# of) fraternities | 10 (31) |
| % in (# of) sororities | 10 (15) |
| % African American | 5 |
| % Asian | 41 |
| % Caucasian | 31 |
| % Hispanic | 12 |
| % Native American | 1 |
| % international | 4 |
| # of countries represented | 88 |

### SURVEY SAYS . . .

*Ethnic diversity on campus*
*Lots of classroom discussion*
*Political activism is hot*
*Everyone loves the Bears*
*Different students interact*
*Campus difficult to get around*
*Lousy food on campus*
*Students are not very happy*
*(Almost) no one listens to college*
*radio*
*Students are cliquish*

## ACADEMICS

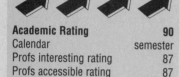

| | |
|---|---|
| **Academic Rating** | **90** |
| Calendar | semester |
| Profs interesting rating | 87 |
| Profs accessible rating | 87 |
| % profs teaching UG courses | 100 |

### MOST POPULAR MAJORS
molecular/cell biology
English
psychology

## STUDENTS SPEAK OUT

### Academics

No matter how you judge academic excellence, UC, Berkeley is the nation's finest public university. "UC, Berkeley offers what I think to be the most challenging and competitive classes in the nation," writes one student, and other's agree. Many of its academic programs are exceptional—particularly noteworthy are the engineering program, all hard sciences, and the English and history departments—and the faculty is internationally recognized as stellar. An overwhelming majority of Berkeley students are bound for some graduate program almost immediately after graduation. The most common complaint is that undergrads are often shortchanged on professor interaction: "The professors are mostly writing books, which leaves the TAs with a lot more time to teach," is a familiar comment. Berkeley's size (more than 30,000 full-time undergraduate and graduate students) can make the bureaucratic hassles a nightmare. One student identifies the typical administrative experience: "Here at UC, Berkeley you have the choice of getting help from every possible office or being ignored on a grand scale." Many students feel that the administration's attitude is one of "indifferent hostility." Berkeley life is big, busy, rigorous, and challenging, but, at least for one student, "Words cannot express how grateful I am for this experience."

### Life

Since the revolutionary days of the 1960s, "Cal" and the surrounding city of Berkeley have been hotbeds of political and social activism. "People take themselves too seriously. Everyone needs to seriously relax, especially about politics," one student notes. Adding to the intensity of emotion is the size of the student body, which alone would mean a diversity of opinions. The campus itself is idyllic, but the neighborhood to the south is not. One student warns that "the homelessness and squalor . . . are difficult for some to get used to." On-campus housing is scarce, so many students live off campus. Some choose to live in the nine student-run co-ops near campus. Others go the way of the Greeks, who are not the center of campus life but an active part. Comments one student: "Life at school is overwhelming; there's too much going on at any one time." For those who need to get away from campus, the city of Berkeley is lively, and a bit farther away, San Francisco is accessible.

### Student Body

Ethnic diversity at Berkeley is "impressive" and includes large Asian and Hispanic populations. People note the large size of the student body encourages students to form small "cliques" based on ethnic groups or social interests, which tend to limit the exposure of each group to others. The gay community is visible and well accepted. Do not let this plurality of students fool you into believing, though, that Berkeley is all about understanding and helping each other. Academically, the student body is very competitive and self-described as "cutthroat."

# UNIVERSITY OF CALIFORNIA, BERKELEY

FAX: 510-642-7333 • FINANCIAL AID: 510-642-6442 • E-MAIL: OUARS@UCLINK.BERKELEY.EDU • WEBSITE: WWW.BERKELEY.EDU

## ADMISSIONS

*Very important* academic and nonacademic factors considered by the admissions committee include character/personal qualities, essays, and secondary school record. *Important* factors considered include, extracurricular activities, standardized test scores, talent/ability, volunteer work, and work experience. *Other* factors considered include state residency and interview. Factors *not* considered include geography, religious affiliation/commitment. SAT I or ACT required, SAT II also required. TOEFL required of all international applicants. High school diploma is required and GED is accepted. *High school units required/recommended:* 16 total required; 4 English required, 4 math required, 3 science required, 3 science lab required, 2 foreign language required, 2 social studies required. *The admissions office says:* "Additional course work in all areas is recommended. Residents must have either a 3.3 GPA or do well on a standardized test to be considered for admission. Nonresidents must earn a 3.4 average (the eligibility index applies to residents only). Any student who fails to meet the academic requirements may gain admission on the basis of test scores alone if (1) his/her SAT I is 1400 or higher (ACT composite: 31 or higher), and (2) his/her combined SAT II: Subject Test scores exceed a minimum score (1760 for residents, 1850 for non-residents), and none is lower than 530."

### The Inside Word

The state of California's discontinuation of affirmative action in the UC admission process has created much uncertainty regarding the future of candidate selection in the system. There is little room for deviation in any applicant's statistical profile, but out-of-state students will find the going even tougher, with available spaces few and far between. Still, minority acceptances remain lower than before the ban. Berkeley is the most selective campus of the university system.

## FINANCIAL AID

The Princeton Review suggests that all financial aid forms be submitted as soon as possible after January 1. *Need-based scholarships/grants offered:* Pell, SEOG, state scholarships/grants, private scholarships, the school's own gift aid, and Federal Nursing. *Loan aid offered:* FFEL Subsidized Stafford, FFEL Unsubsidized Stafford, FFEL PLUS, Federal Perkins, and Federal Nursing. Institutional employment available. Federal Work-Study Program available. Off-campus job opportunities are excellent.

## FROM THE ADMISSIONS OFFICE

"One of the top public universities in the nation and the world, the University of California, Berkeley offers a vast range of courses and a full menu of extracurricular activities. Berkeley's academic programs are internationally recognized for their excellence. Undergraduates can choose one of 100 majors. Or, if they prefer, they can design their own. Many departments are first-rate, including sociology, mathematics, and physics, as are the poets, scholars, and award-winning researchers who comprise Berkeley's faculty. Access to one of the foremost university libraries enriches studies. There are 23 specialized libraries on campus and distinguished museums of anthropology, paleontology, and science."

## ADMISSIONS

| | | |
|---|---|---|
| **Admissions Rating** | | **94** |
| # of applicants | | 31,108 |
| % of applicants accepted | | 27 |

### FRESHMAN PROFILE

| | |
|---|---|
| Range SAT Verbal | 580-710 |
| Average SAT Verbal | 655 |
| Range SAT Math | 620-740 |
| Average SAT Math | 685 |
| Minimum TOEFL | 550 |
| Average HS GPA | 3.9 |
| % graduated top 10% of class | 95 |
| % graduated top 25% of class | 100 |

### DEADLINES

| | |
|---|---|
| Regular admission | 10/30 |
| Regular notification | 3/31 |

### APPLICANTS ALSO LOOK AT
**AND OFTEN PREFER**
Stanford
**AND SOMETIMES PREFER**
UCLA
UC—San Diego
UC—Santa Barbara
UC—Santa Cruz
**AND RARELY PREFER**
UC—Davis
Occidental

## FINANCIAL FACTS

| | |
|---|---|
| **Financial Aid Rating** | **73** |
| Out-of-state tuition | $10,614 |
| Room & board | $8,670 |
| Books and supplies | $1,048 |
| Required fees | $4,048 |
| % frosh receiving aid | 47 |
| % undergrads receiving aid | 55 |
| Avg frosh grant | $6,009 |
| Avg frosh loan | $4,002 |

# UNIVERSITY OF CALIFORNIA—DAVIS

178 MARK HALL, UC DAVIS, DAVIS, CA 95616 • ADMISSIONS: 530-752-2971 • FAX: 530-752-1280

## CAMPUS LIFE

| | |
|---|---|
| **Quality of Life Rating** | **80** |
| Type of school | public |
| Affiliation | none |
| Environment | suburban |

### STUDENTS

| | |
|---|---|
| Total undergrad enrollment | 20,388 |
| % male/female | 44/56 |
| % from out of state | 1 |
| % from public high school | 85 |
| % live on campus | 26 |
| % in (# of) fraternities | 8 (28) |
| % in (# of) sororities | 7 (21) |
| % African American | 3 |
| % Asian | 35 |
| % Caucasian | 44 |
| % Hispanic | 10 |
| % Native American | 1 |
| % international | 1 |

### SURVEY SAYS . . .

*Class discussions are rare*
*Students love Davis, CA*
*Great library*
*Popular college radio*
*High cost of living*
*Large classes*
*(Almost) no one smokes*
*Student publications are popular*
*Unattractive campus*
*Campus difficult to get around*

## ACADEMICS

| | |
|---|---|
| **Academic Rating** | **76** |
| Calendar | quarter |
| Student/faculty ratio | 19:1 |
| Profs interesting rating | 88 |
| Profs accessible rating | 90 |
| Avg lab size | 20-29 students |
| Avg reg class size | 20-29 students |

### MOST POPULAR MAJORS

biological sciences
psychology
engineering

## STUDENTS SPEAK OUT

### Academics

"I like classes and think that they are generally taught well," says one student, "but I believe the problem is with labs and discussion." While students are for the most part happy with their professors ("Excellent professors—very devoted to students") they do have consistent problems with the school's large discussion sections. TA's also teach a decent number of these classes, something that does not sit well with most UC—Davis undergrads. "Most of the time TAs don't know what they are talking about," says one disgruntled sophomore. Getting into the classes you want as a freshman is also often a problem, but as you progress, it gets easier. Dealing with the UC—Davis bureaucracy can be frustrating. Says a senior, "I stood in line for 3-4 hours for financial aid during the fall quarter the last two years only to be sent somewhere else. I hate the system." Indeed, as with most large universities, "help is there, but hard to find." The school's library and computer systems both received stellar marks from students. Adds one, "Davis is on the cutting edge of all technological advancements."

### Life

"The size of Davis can be fairly intimidating [to entering students], but with time it seems to shrink and become more understandable." The campus is big—a bicycle is a help—while the town of Davis is small. A "very relaxed atmosphere in a bike-friendly town" is the majority opinion with a student body that is generally very satisfied with its school. But there can be a dark side to Davis: "For fun I leave. Davis is a rural community in the middle of dullsville." If you like life fast and furious once in awhile, Sacramento is your nearest urban oasis; otherwise, get used to spending time on a campus judged beautiful and safe by its students. UC—Davis also has sports, comfortable dorms, good dorm food, and decent health facilities. Alcohol and drug policies are on the strict side, which might be a problem at times with drinking and pot rated as very popular. Frats are well attended. One reason may be that "there aren't many organizations or clubs to join." Let's hope this computer science major can't be trusted when he says, "When [we] are on the verge of insanity, we listen to 'Mr. Tambourine Man' by William Shatner." That would just not be a good sign.

### Student Body

"Since Davis is so big, any comment would be a huge generalization." This cogent comment by a senior sums up perfectly the varied responses students gave about themselves. Nobody agreed about anything (except one topic that we'll discuss later). Here are a few of the conflicting comments: "Students are friendly and nice—not uptight"; "Most are socially maladjusted dorks, lots of people who really know how to study"; "Most resort to heavy drinking on weekends"; "Students at UC—Davis are very motivated and very tenacious"; "Students are very down to earth and academic but also athletic." See! Davis is obviously big enough for a diversity of students and opinions. The only thing students seem to agree on is that there is an appalling lack of interaction among people with different skin colors. Observes a white female, "For a school that supports ethnic diversity I find it ironic that most races only interact with people of their own race." Actual discrimination on the basis of race, sex, or sexual preference is also a concern with some, but not most UC—Davis undergrads. Most students are sexually active, few are religious. At Davis, there are plenty of niches to choose from; just don't look for the school to be one big happy family.

FINANCIAL AID: 530-752-2390 • E-MAIL: UNDERGRADADMISSIONS@UCDAVIS.EDU • WEBSITE: WWW.UCDAVIS.EDU

## ADMISSIONS

*Very important* academic and nonacademic factors considered by the admissions committee include character/personal qualities, class rank, essays, extracurricular activities, secondary school record, and standardized test scores. *Important* factors considered include alumni/ae relation, recommendations, and talent/ability. *Other* factors considered include geography, interview, minority status, volunteer work, and work experience. Factors *not* considered include religious affiliation/commitment and state residency. SAT I or ACT required, SAT II also required. TOEFL required of all international applicants. High school diploma is required and GED is accepted. *High school units required/recommended:* 15 total required; 4 English required, 3 math required, 3 science required, 1 science lab required, 2 foreign language required. *The admissions office says:* "Residents must have either a 3.3 GPA or do well on a standardized test. Nonresidents must earn a 3.4 average (the eligibility index applies to residents only). Any student who fails to meet the academic requirements may gain admission on the basis of test scores alone if (1) his/her SAT is 1300 or higher (ACT composite: 31 or higher), and (2) his/her combined SAT II: Subject Test scores exceed a minimum score (1760 for residents, 1400 for nonresidents), and none is lower than 530."

### The Inside Word

California's discontinuation of affirmative action in the UC admission process has created much uncertainty regarding the future of candidate selection in the system, and minority admissions have declined. A higher percentage of students are admitted to Davis than to Berkeley or UCLA, but don't forget that the UC system in general is geared toward the best and brightest of California's high school students.

## FINANCIAL AID

*Students should submit:* FAFSA. The Princeton Review suggests that all financial aid forms be submitted as soon as possible after January 1. Institutional employment available. Federal Work-Study Program available. Off-campus job opportunities are good.

## FROM THE ADMISSIONS OFFICE

"The quality of undergraduate instruction is a prime concern of the faculty, students, and administration at Davis. Creative teaching and academic innovation are encouraged by several programs, including the Distinguished Teaching Awards (for which students can nominate outstanding faculty members) and a $25,000 prize for undergraduate teaching and scholarly achievement (believed to be among the largest of its kind in the nation). Student Viewpoint, a student-written and -published evaluation of classes and instructors, is compiled each year from course questionnaires completed by students."

## ADMISSIONS

| | |
|---|---|
| Admissions Rating | 82 |
| # of applicants | 25,224 |
| % of applicants accepted | 63 |
| % of acceptees attending | 27 |

### FRESHMAN PROFILE

| | |
|---|---|
| Range SAT Verbal | 510-630 |
| Average SAT Verbal | 565 |
| Range SAT Math | 550-660 |
| Average SAT Math | 600 |
| Range ACT Composite | 22-27 |
| Average ACT Composite | 24 |
| Minimum TOEFL | 500 |
| Average HS GPA | 3.7 |
| % graduated top 10% of class | 95 |
| % graduated top 25% of class | 100 |
| % graduated top 50% of class | 100 |

### DEADLINES

| | |
|---|---|
| Regular admission | 11/30 |
| Regular notification | 3/31 |
| Nonfall registration? | yes |

### APPLICANTS ALSO LOOK AT AND OFTEN PREFER

UC—Berkeley
UCLA

**AND SOMETIMES PREFER**

UC—Santa Barbara
UC—Santa Cruz
U. Washington

**AND RARELY PREFER**

UC—San Diego
UC—Irvine
UC—Riverside

### FINANCIAL FACTS

| | |
|---|---|
| Financial Aid Rating | 74 |
| Out-of-state tuition | $10,245 |
| Room & board | $6,693 |
| Books and supplies | $1,055 |
| Required fees | $4,072 |
| % frosh receiving aid | 48 |
| % undergrads receiving aid | 50 |
| Avg frosh grant | $5,427 |
| Avg frosh loan | $4,985 |

# UNIVERSITY OF CALIFORNIA—IRVINE

OFFICE OF ADMISSIONS, 204 ADMINISTRATION BLDG., IRVINE, CA 92697-1075 • ADMISSIONS: 949-824-6703 • FAX: 949-824-2711

## CAMPUS LIFE

| | |
|---|---|
| **Quality of Life Rating** | **76** |
| Type of school | public |
| Affiliation | none |
| Environment | suburban |

### STUDENTS

| | |
|---|---|
| Total undergrad enrollment | 16,223 |
| % male/female | 48/52 |
| % from out of state | 3 |
| % from public high school | 70 |
| % live on campus | 30 |
| % African American | 2 |
| % Asian | 54 |
| % Caucasian | 22 |
| % Hispanic | 11 |
| % Native American | 1 |
| % international | 2 |

### SURVEY SAYS . . .

*High cost of living*
*Class discussions are rare*
*Students love Irvine, CA*
*Popular college radio*
*Student publications are ignored*
*Large classes*
*Intercollegiate sports unpopular or nonexistent*
*Lots of TAs teach upper-level courses*
*Students are very religious*
*Athletic facilities need improving*

## ACADEMICS

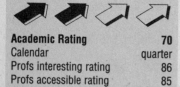

| | |
|---|---|
| **Academic Rating** | **70** |
| Calendar | quarter |
| Profs interesting rating | 86 |
| Profs accessible rating | 85 |

### MOST POPULAR MAJORS
biological sciences
economics

## STUDENTS SPEAK OUT

### Academics

The University of California—Irvine has a strong reputation for excellence as a major scientific research facility. Located on a "small, beautiful campus" smack dab in the heart of affluent, conservative Orange County, UC—Irvine is best known for its biology department. "Very competitive and challenging, but the rewards are great if you're a survivor," says one bio major. "The professors in the biological sciences are excellent." It's no surprise that pre-med is immensely popular, and the university does a great job of preparing students for the challenge of med school. In fact, more than a sixth of its graduates go on to medical school. The ecological sciences department is also popular, and science students in general note excellent facilities and numerous opportunities to participate in research among UC—Irvine's chief advantages. Outside the sciences, academics are less challenging, but still "superior, since the profs take a real interest." Beatle buffs take note: One of UC—Irvine's history profs is a John Lennon expert. Students complain about inaccessible profs and large classes, both common complaints at research-oriented universities like UC—Irvine. Of those departments outside the sciences, economics, English, and political science are the strongest. All UC—Irvine students must complete "breadth requirements," meaning that they must take three courses each in the natural sciences, social sciences, and humanities to graduate. Honors programs are available in most areas of study (although, curiously, not in the natural sciences).

### Life

According to the vast majority of students we surveyed, social life here leaves loads to be desired. Well over half of UC—Irvine students commute, and many others flee on Fridays, which is extremely frustrating to a freshman who vents that "people don't understand this is college, and they go home every weekend." But there are two sides to every story, and "if you live off campus (read: Newport Beach) UC—Irvine is probably one of the most attractive of the UC campuses." "To meet people one must take an active role, joining a club or going Greek," says one student. Says another, "There is little school spirit or unity unless you're in a frat or sorority." About 7 percent of UC—Irvine students go Greek. "People always say UCI is boring or apathetic, but it depends on what you make of it. There are lots of opportunities on campus, you just have to be open minded and willing." If suburban diversions excite you, there's Irvine, but "there isn't much to do in Irvine." The beach is only five miles from campus, a fact that leads one student to assert that UC—Irvine is "a great school if you want to ride some tasty waves and catch a hair-raising buzz." Nighttime parties by the ocean are not uncommon. Excellent skiing is within an hour's drive, as is the sprawling city of Los Angeles.

### Student Body

More than half of UC—Irvine's students are Asian, and about a fifth are caucasian, providing for a uniquely diverse student body. Unfortunately, since there's little in the way of a social scene, "interaction among students from different backgrounds could and should be better." At least on the surface people get along here, but ethnic animosity hovers beneath. Several students remark somewhat bitterly that "Asians dominate the campus;" such feelings have existed for quite some time at UC—Irvine. On the whole Irvine students are pretty conservative but mostly apathetic, reportedly caring little about politics.

FINANCIAL AID: 949-824-6261 • E-MAIL: OARS@UCI.EDU • WEBSITE: WWW.UCI.EDU

## ADMISSIONS

*Very important* academic and nonacademic factors considered by the admissions committee include secondary school record, and standardized test scores. *Important* factors considered include essays, extracurricular activities, talent/ability, volunteer work, and work experience. *Other* factors considered include geography and state residency. Factors *not* considered include alumni/ae relation, interview, minority status and religious affiliation/commitment. TOEFL required of all international applicants. High school diploma is required and GED is accepted. *High school units required/recommended:* 4 English required, 3 math required, 4 math recommended, 1 science required, 4 science recommended, 2 science lab required, 4 science lab recommended, 2 foreign language required, 4 foreign language recommended, 1 social studies required, 2 social studies recommended, 1 history required, 2 history recommended, 6 elective required. *The admissions office says:* "Some majors have limited enrollments and place prerequisites on admission. Also, be aware of the filing periods for applications: November 1–30, fall quarter; July 1–30, winter quarter; October 1–30, spring quarter."

### The Inside Word

The state of California's voter referendum that banned affirmative action in the UC admission process has created much uncertainty regarding the future of candidate selection in the system, and African American and Hispanic admissions have fallen as a result. Few out-of-state students consider Irvine, which lessens the competition among those applicants who are well qualified.

## FINANCIAL AID

*Students should submit:* FAFSA. The Princeton Review suggests that all financial aid forms be submitted as soon as possible after January 1. The deadline for school aid is May 1. *Need-based scholarships/grants offered:* Pell, FSEOG, and the school's own gift aid. *Loan aid offered:* Direct Subsidized Stafford, Direct Unsubsidized Stafford, Direct FPLUS, and Federal Perkins. Institutional employment available. Federal Work-Study Program available. Applicants will be notified of awards on or about May 1. Off-campus job opportunities are excellent.

## FROM THE ADMISSIONS OFFICE

"UCI offers programs designed to provide students with a foundation on which to continue developing their intellectual, aesthetic, and moral capacity. The programs and curricula are based on the belief that a student's collective university experience should provide understanding and insight, which are the bases for an intellectual identity and lifelong learning. An important aspect of the educational approach at UCI is the emphasis placed on student involvement in independent study, research, and the creative process as a complement to classroom study. Independent research in laboratories, field study, involvement in writing workshops, and participation in fine arts productions are normal elements of the UCI experience."

### ADMISSIONS

| | |
|---|---:|
| Admissions Rating | 77 |
| # of applicants | 24,686 |
| % of applicants accepted | 57 |
| % of acceptees attending | 15 |

#### FRESHMAN PROFILE

| | |
|---|---:|
| Range SAT Verbal | 500-620 |
| Range SAT Math | 554-674 |
| Minimum TOEFL | 550 |
| Average HS GPA | 3.7 |

#### DEADLINES

| | |
|---|---:|
| Priority admission deadline | 11/30 |
| Regular notification | 3/30 |
| Nonfall registration? | yes |

#### APPLICANTS ALSO LOOK AT
##### AND OFTEN PREFER
UC—Berkeley
UC—Davis
UCLA
UC—Riverside
Stanford

##### AND SOMETIMES PREFER
U. Southern Cal
UC—San Diego
UC—Santa Cruz
UC—Santa Barbara

### FINANCIAL FACTS

| | |
|---|---:|
| Financial Aid Rating | 72 |
| In-state tuition | $4,057 |
| Out-of-state tuition | $10,244 |
| Room & board | $6,724 |
| Books and supplies | $1,162 |
| Required fees | $2,471 |
| % frosh receiving aid | 46 |
| % undergrads receiving aid | 41 |

# UNIVERSITY OF CALIFORNIA—LOS ANGELES

405 HILGARD AVENUE, LOS ANGELES, CA 90095 • ADMISSIONS: 310-825-3101 • FAX: 310-206-1206

## CAMPUS LIFE

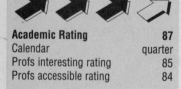

| Quality of Life Rating | 75 |
| --- | --- |
| Type of school | public |
| Affiliation | none |
| Environment | urban |

### STUDENTS

| | |
| --- | --- |
| Total undergrad enrollment | 25,011 |
| % male/female | 45/55 |
| % from out of state | 3 |
| % from public high school | 80 |
| % live on campus | 30 |
| % in (# of) fraternities | 11 (27) |
| % in (# of) sororities | 9 (18) |
| % African American | 4 |
| % Asian | 38 |
| % Caucasian | 35 |
| % Hispanic | 14 |
| % Native American | 1 |
| % international | 3 |
| # of countries represented | 100 |

### SURVEY SAYS . . .

*Everyone loves the Bruins*
*Students love Los Angeles, CA*
*Frats and sororities dominate*
*social scene*
*Great food on campus*
*Great library*
*Large classes*
*Student publications are popular*
*Lots of TAs teach upper-level*
*courses*
*Dorms are like dungeons*
*Campus difficult to get around*
*Computer facilities are great*

## ACADEMICS

| Academic Rating | 87 |
| --- | --- |
| Calendar | quarter |
| Profs interesting rating | 85 |
| Profs accessible rating | 84 |

### MOST POPULAR MAJORS
psychology
economics
political science

## STUDENTS SPEAK OUT

### Academics

To be happy at the UCLA, you have to be a self-starter. No one takes you by the hand and leads you through course selection, registration, and other necessary chores. Fortunately, there are plenty of happy students here; we know because we hear from them in our survey. "I love UCLA! It's big, but if you're savvy and you have the wherewithal to get around, the possibilities for learning and meeting people are endless." Another student tells us, "At first, the bureaucracy of such a large university is extremely intimidating, but once you learn the system it can actually work to your advantage." Students warn that many of the standard big school problems are present at UCLA. "Unfortunately, good researchers are not always good teachers, a big drawback for UCLA as a teaching establishment," writes one student. "Lecture sizes should be made smaller and more personal," complains another. Of course UCLA also offers the standard large-university advantages, including "many opportunities to do research with professors and pursue diverse areas of interest." UCLA's greatest drawing cards are its home city (both an entertaining place to live and an excellent place to search for post-collegiate work) and its "everything-under-one-roof academic offerings." For those who can handle its bureaucracy, UCLA provides excellent opportunities for study in the humanities, arts, architecture, engineering, pre-medical and pre-law studies, film, theater, and television.

### Life

"Talk about diversity. Los Angeles is the epitome of a diverse culture," brags one student. To take advantage of that diversity, however, one needs a car. As one student puts it, "It's pretty fun around here. We are nestled in a great area of town that gives us easy access to Hollywood, the beach . . . well, you name it. However, you must have a car (or a friend who has one!)." As at other schools located in major cities, many students at UCLA tell us that they spend little time on campus after class, preferring instead to enjoy what Los Angeles has to offer. Those who do stay on campus tell us that it's "a great place to get involved. Because of its size, almost anyone can find a particular niche to fit into." Agrees another student, "UCLA's size helps it offer a huge variety of extracurricular activities. There's always something to do here." An active Greek scene attracts over 10 percent of all undergraduates, and the party scene is similarly happening. In addition, over 500 campus clubs provide opportunities for community service and leadership experiences. Finally, there's Bruin sports, the great unifier of this campus. Notes one typical student, "I bleed blue and gold [UCLA's colors]."

### Student Body

UCLA boasts large minority populations, not too surprising considering the tremendous diversity of its home state. African Americans, Asians, Filipinos, and Chicanos are all well represented among undergraduates. While some undergrads report that "students are very friendly and open," many others are "disappointed to find out how segregated the school is." By all accounts, this segregation is self-imposed; students of all backgrounds here, it seems, simply prefer to hang with their own. Nearly all students here are native Californians.

# UNIVERSITY OF CALIFORNIA—LOS ANGELES

FINANCIAL AID: 310-206-0400 • E-MAIL: UGADM@SAONNET.UCLA.EDU • WEBSITE: WWW.UCLA.EDU

## ADMISSIONS

*Very important* academic and nonacademic factors considered by the admissions committee include class rank, extracurricular activities, secondary school record, standardized test scores, talent/ability, volunteer work, and work experience. *Important* factors considered include character/personal qualities, essays, and recommendations. *Other* factors considered include alumni/ae relation, geography, interview, and state residency. Factors *not* considered include religious affiliation/commitment. SAT I or ACT required, SAT II also required. TOEFL required of all international applicants. High school diploma is required and GED is accepted. *High school units required/recommended:* 16 total required; 4 English required, 4 math required, 3 science required, 1 science lab required, 2 foreign language required, 3 social studies required.

### The Inside Word

Now that California's voters have acted to discontinue affirmative action in the UC admission process, there is much uncertainty regarding the future of candidate selection in the system. As a result, African American and Hispanic admissions have plummeted. UCLA is the second most selective university in the UC system. Out-of-state applicants are subject to the same requirements as at Berkeley, but will find their prospects a little better because UCLA accepts a larger freshman class.

## FINANCIAL AID

The Princeton Review suggests that all financial aid forms be submitted as soon as possible after January 1. *Need-based scholarships/grants offered:* Pell, SEOG, state scholarships/grants, private scholarships, the school's own gift aid, Federal Nursing. *Loan aid offered:* FFEL Subsidized Stafford, FFEL Unsubsidized Stafford, FFEL PLUS, Federal Perkins, and Federal Nursing. Institutional employment available. Federal Work-Study Program available. Off-campus job opportunities are good.

## FROM THE ADMISSIONS OFFICE

"Undergraduates arrive at UCLA from throughout California and around the world with exceptional levels of academic preparation. They are attracted by our acclaimed degree programs, distinguished faculty, and the beauty of a park-like campus set amid the dynamism of the nation's second largest city. UCLA's highly ranked undergraduate programs incorporate cutting-edge technology and teaching techniques that hone the critical-thinking skills and the global perspectives necessary for success in our rapidly changing world. The diversity of these programs draws strength from a student body that mirrors the cultural and ethnic vibrancy of Los Angeles. Generally ranked among the nation's top half-dozen universities, UCLA is at once distinguished and dynamic, academically rigorous and responsive."

## ADMISSIONS

| | |
|---|---|
| **Admissions Rating** | **92** |
| # of applicants | 37,794 |
| % of applicants accepted | 29 |
| % of acceptees attending | 38 |

### FRESHMAN PROFILE

| | |
|---|---|
| Range SAT Verbal | 560-680 |
| Average SAT Verbal | 617 |
| Range SAT Math | 610-720 |
| Average SAT Math | 660 |
| Range ACT Composite | 23-29 |
| Average ACT Composite | 26 |
| Minimum TOEFL | 550 |
| % graduated top 10% of class | 97 |

### DEADLINES

| | |
|---|---|
| Regular admission | 11/30 |

### APPLICANTS ALSO LOOK AT
**AND OFTEN PREFER**
UC—Berkeley
**AND SOMETIMES PREFER**
UC—San Diego
**AND RARELY PREFER**
UC—Santa Barbara
UC—Irvine
UC—Davis
UC—Riverside
UC—Santa Cruz

## FINANCIAL FACTS

| | |
|---|---|
| **Financial Aid Rating** | **84** |
| Out-of-state tuition | $10,244 |
| Room & board | $8,565 |
| Books and supplies | $1,116 |
| Required fees | $3,698 |
| Avg frosh grant | $6,492 |
| Avg frosh loan | $2,660 |

# UNIVERSITY OF CALIFORNIA—RIVERSIDE

1120 HINDERAKER HALL, RIVERSIDE, CA 92521 • ADMISSIONS: 909-787-4531 • FAX: 909-787-6344

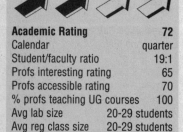
## STUDENTS SPEAK OUT

### Academics

There are a lot of good things about the University of California—Riverside, but it is probably best known for being the most popular second (or third) choice for students who would rather attend another University of California campus. Professors here run the gamut from "really awesome teachers" who are "accessible" and "actually care for your well-being" to inaccessible duds who are "on power trips" and "need to have more office hours." While some UCR professors give "engaging" lectures and are "helpful in making sure we understand what they are teaching," others reportedly "can be downright boring." Teaching assistants "know and seem to enjoy the material they teach," though too many "come from countries where English is" apparently "a novelty." As for the administration, one student states, there is "way too much red tape." On the bright side, UCR is "very challenging when it comes to the sciences" and it boasts a prestigious biomedical program that puts selected students on track for a degree from UCLA medical school (in one year less than it would take otherwise). Liberal arts programs have a solid reputation as well, as does the business program. Also, since UCR is a research center, juniors and seniors often have the chance to participate in cutting-edge research projects.

### Life

"Work hard, play somewhere else" is an apt motto for students at UCR, where school spirit is basically on life support despite a standout sports program that has produced six national championships between the men's and women's karate teams. No matter, according to students, who swear that Riverside is the most boring town in the universe. Not only is UCR "dead," but the "weather sucks" to boot. "The town is the most anti-college town in the United States," claims a jaded first-year student. "If the school was not here, Riverside would be a metropolis of trailers, liquor stores, and fast-food joints." On campus, "the food is kind of nasty," but a "small-school atmosphere" pervades, and there are "excellent recreation facilities." Students who get involved in Greek life seem pretty happy; they say fraternities and sororities throw a lot of parties and alcohol is easily accessible. "Parking is terrible" for everyone, though, and "lots are miles away from classes." Thankfully, Los Angeles is "not far from here." Students who have cars can always drive the hour or so it takes to get to L.A.'s endless array of entertainment options. Students also make frequent pilgrimages to the beaches to the west and the mountains to the east (but they have to leave their prized parking spots to do so).

### Student Body

"Unlike at other schools" filled with students who "have sticks up their behinds," the "unique" students at UCR are "really down to earth"—even "creepily nice." Consequently, it's "not too hard to make friends" on this campus, and there are "no soap operas" among the students. This is not to say that there are no cliques. "Everybody groups according to ethnicities," and "most stay with people in their own groups (sororities, fraternities, sports teams, etc.)" Many students choose UCR because it is "close to home," and many more choose it because it's "the best school" they "got into." At first, anyway, "a lot of students didn't want to come here," reports a sophomore. Though merely "average for SoCal," UCR's campus is pretty diverse. There's "a large Asian population" and a sizable Hispanic contingent. Also, "the number of students who smoke is frightening."

FINANCIAL AID: 909-787-3878 OR 3879 • E-MAIL: DISCOVER@POP.UCR.EDU • WEBSITE: WWW.UCR.EDU

## ADMISSIONS

*Very important* academic and nonacademic factors considered by the admissions committee include secondary school record and standardized test scores. *Important* factors considered include essays. *Other* factors considered include recommendations, extracurricular activities, talent/ability, volunteer work, and work experience. Factors *not* considered include class rank, character/personal qualities, geography, alumni/ae relation, interview, state residency, and minority status. SAT I or ACT required; SAT II also required. TOEFL also required of all international applicants. High school diploma is required and GED is accepted. *High school units required/recommended:* 15 total required; 18 recommended; 4 English required, 3 math required, 4 math recommended, 2 laboratory science required, 3 laboratory science recommended, 2 foreign language required, 3 foreign language recommended, 2 history/social science required, 2 college preparatory electives required. *The admissions office says:* "Supplemental criteria for evaluation include (1) talents and experiences; (2) hardship circumstances; (3) cultural, ethnic, and geographic factors to ensure diversity."

### The Inside Word

The state of California's ban on affirmative action in the UC admission process has created much uncertainty regarding the future of candidate selection in the system. Though African American and Hispanic admissions have dropped system-wide, UC Riverside stands out in its ability to fight this decline—it's one of only two UC schools where minority admissions have grown. Riverside's admit rate is sufficiently high to mean smooth sailing for those who fit into the formulas well.

## FINANCIAL AID

*Students should submit:* FAFSA, state aid form. The Princeton Review suggests that all financial aid forms be submitted as soon as possible after January 1. *Need-based scholarships/grants offered:* Pell, SEOG, state scholarships/grants, private scholarships, and the school's own gift aid. *Loan aid offered:* Direct Subsidized Stafford, Direct Unsubsidized Stafford, Direct PLUS, Federal Perkins, and college/university loans from institutional funds. Institutional employment available. Federal Work-Study Program available. Applicants will be notified of awards on a rolling basis beginning on or about March 1. Off-campus job opportunities are excellent.

## FROM THE ADMISSIONS OFFICE

"The University of California—Riverside offers the quality, rigor, and facilities of a major research institution, while assuring its undergraduates personal attention and a sense of community. Academic programs, teaching, advising, and student services all reflect the supportive attitude that characterizes the campus. Among the exceptional opportunities are the accelerated biomedical sciences program, in which students can earn both the BS and MD degrees in seven years instead of eight; the University Honors Program; a BS degree in business administration; the only UC bachelor's degree in creative writing; and state-of-the-art undergraduate engineering programs. UCR has one of the few internet-based registration systems in the nation, which was recently upgraded to allow greater student access."

## ADMISSIONS

| | |
|---|---|
| Admissions Rating | 79 |
| # of applicants | 18,610 |
| % of applicants accepted | 85 |
| % of acceptees attending | 20 |

### FRESHMAN PROFILE

| | |
|---|---|
| Range SAT Verbal | 450-570 |
| Average SAT Verbal | 506 |
| Range SAT Math | 490-630 |
| Average SAT Math | 554 |
| Range ACT Composite | 18-23 |
| Average ACT Composite | 23 |
| Minimum TOEFL | 550 |
| Average HS GPA | 3.5 |
| % graduated top 10% of class | 94 |
| % graduated top 25% of class | 100 |
| % graduated top 50% of class | 100 |

### DEADLINES

| | |
|---|---|
| Priority admission deadline | 11/1 |
| Regular admission | 11/30 |
| Nonfall registration? | yes |

### APPLICANTS ALSO LOOK AT
#### AND OFTEN PREFER
UC—Berkeley
UCLA
UC—Davis
#### AND SOMETIMES PREFER
UC—Irvine
CalPoly.—San Luis Obispo
Claremont McKenna
UC—Santa Barbara
UC—Santa Cruz
#### AND RARELY PREFER
U. San Diego
U. Southern Cal

### FINANCIAL FACTS

| | |
|---|---|
| Financial Aid Rating | 72 |
| Tuition (out of state) | $10,248 |
| Room & board | $7,200 |
| Books and supplies | $1,200 |
| Required fees | $3,856 |
| % frosh receiving aid | 59 |
| % undergrads receiving aid | 63 |

# UNIVERSITY OF CALIFORNIA—SAN DIEGO

9500 GILMAN DRIVE, 0021, LA JOLLA, CA 92093-0021 • ADMISSIONS: 858-534-4831

## CAMPUS LIFE

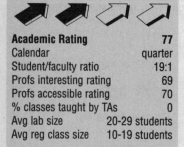

| | |
|---|---|
| **Quality of Life Rating** | **80** |
| Type of school | public |
| Affiliation | none |
| Environment | urban |

### STUDENTS

| | |
|---|---|
| Total undergrad enrollment | 16,496 |
| % male/female | 49/51 |
| % from out of state | 3 |
| % live on campus | 33 |
| % in (# of) fraternities | 10 (19) |
| % in (# of) sororities | 10 (14) |
| % African American | 1 |
| % Asian | 35 |
| % Caucasian | 39 |
| % Hispanic | 10 |
| % Native American | 1 |
| % international | 2 |
| # of countries represented | 70 |

### SURVEY SAYS . . .

Diverse students interact
Students love La Jolla, CA
Student publications are popular
Ethnic diversity on campus
Students get along with local
community
Great off-campus food
Students aren't religious
Dorms are like dungeons
Campus difficult to get around

## ACADEMICS

| | |
|---|---|
| **Academic Rating** | **77** |
| Calendar | quarter |
| Student/faculty ratio | 19:1 |
| Profs interesting rating | 69 |
| Profs accessible rating | 70 |
| % classes taught by TAs | 0 |
| Avg lab size | 20-29 students |
| Avg reg class size | 10-19 students |

### MOST POPULAR MAJORS
biochemistry
psychology
biology

## STUDENTS SPEAK OUT

### Academics

With a growing reputation for being "great in the sciences," UC—San Diego has established itself as one of the rising stars of the UC system. That reputation has been built on a demanding academic program that some students find exhausting: warns one, "Unlike small private schools, UCSD does not care if it is too hard and you flunk out. The difficulty level reflects this view." Another confirms the comparison, reporting that "in many ways, UCSD can be harder than a small, selective private school. You get less attention here, and you have to bust your hump to stand out." In addition to its science offerings, UCSD offers a wide range of liberal arts and social sciences. In its five colleges, each college requires different core courses and each has its own educational philosophy, housing, and social activities. Students agree that, throughout the university, teaching quality can be pretty poor at the introductory level, but improves as students advance to upper-division course work. "Our brilliant professors would often rather be teaching upper-division classes," writes one junior. "The honors classes are wonderful, but many introductory classes don't hold the professors', or the students', interest." TAs, some of whom "could use an attitude adjustment," are responsible for some of the most egregious teaching. As at most large universities, administrative tasks here can be frustrating. Reports one student, "I think there's someone who tries his level best to make sure that all the classes I'd like to take coincide."

### Life

"People confuse us with San Diego State, thereby assuming we are a total 'party' school," writes one undergrad, adding that nothing could be further from the truth. Says another, "Life at school? Study, study, study. Everyone is interested in success and a 4.0 GPA. It's a little intimidating." Social life at UCSD "is lame: movies, parties, TJ [Tijuana]. It's pretty much impossible to get around town without a car unless you're willing to wait long for a bus." On-campus partying is minimal because "UCSD is the 'driest' school probably in the country. Alcohol is served in only two places on campus, and the 'no tolerance' toward alcohol policy is strictly enforced." Not surprisingly, "a lot of people leave on the weekends. Most weekend life happens off campus. It's a real downer." Still, it's not all doldrums here; according to one senior, the school has "made a big effort to have more social life on campus since I started, and it's beginning to pay off. I used to always party off campus, but now there are more festivals, dances, and mixers on campus." Opportunities for outdoor activity also abound, thanks to San Diego's idyllic location and climate; notes one student, "Because UCSD is practically on the beach, the myriad of recreation opportunities, the wonderful people, and comfortable social atmosphere of the dorms, I have a hard time sitting down to study." When students feel the need to let loose, though, they go elsewhere: "Tijuana seems to be the number-one party spot. Aside from that, people really like the beaches nearby, the clubs in downtown San Diego, and the cafes near campus."

### Student Body

UCSD students are determined and career-oriented. They are intelligent but rarely intellectual; most view school as a means to achieve economic goals rather than as an opportunity to question authority. Students come primarily from three ethnic groups: white, Asian, and Latino. As one Latino student remarks, "There's a lot of racial awareness here." However, "people of the same ethnic backgrounds tend to form cliques," closing out those of dissimilar backgrounds. Still, to most students UCSD "feels like a friendly neighborhood. The five-college system makes it easy to get to know each other." As far as nonethnic demographics are concerned, "We have two groups here: the scientists and the surfers. It makes for some interesting interactions."

FINANCIAL AID: 858-534-4480 • E-MAIL: ADMISSIONSINFO@UCSD.EDU • WEBSITE: WWW.UCSD.EDU

## ADMISSIONS

*Very important* academic and nonacademic factors considered by the admissions committee include character/personal qualities, essays, extracurricular activities, secondary school record, and standardized test scores. *Important* factors considered include geography, talent/ability, volunteer work, and work experience. SAT I or ACT required; SAT II also required. TOEFL required and GED is accepted. *High school units required/recommended:* 22 total required; 4 English required, 3 math required, 4 math recommended, 2 science lab required, 3 science lab recommended, 2 foreign language required, 3 foreign language recommended, 2 history/social studies required, 2 elective required. *The admissions office says:* "Residents must either have a 3.3 GPA or do well on a standardized test. Non-residents must have taken the same courses but must earn a 3.4 average (the eligibility index applies to residents only)."

### The Inside Word

The state of California's discontinuance of affirmative action in the UC admission process has created much uncertainty regarding the future of candidate selection in the system, and admissions of African American and Hispanic students have fallen significantly system-wide. Increased national awareness and its reputation for excellence in the sciences is making UCSD more and more popular with high school seniors. Even greater selectivity cannot be far behind.

## FINANCIAL AID

*Students should submit:* FAFSA and state aid form. Regular filing deadline is June 1. The Princeton Review suggests that all financial aid forms be submitted as soon as possible after January 1. *Need-based scholarships/grants offered:* Pell, Cal Grant, state scholarships/grants, private scholarships, and the school's own gift aid. *Loan aid offered:* FFEL Subsidized Stafford, FFEL Unsubsidized Stafford, FFEL PLUS, Federal Perkins, college/university loans from institutional funds, and alternative loans. Institutional employment available. Federal Work-Study Program available. Applicants will be notified of awards on a rolling basis beginning on or about March 15. Off-campus job opportunities are excellent.

## FROM THE ADMISSIONS OFFICE

"UCSD is recognized for the exceptional quality of its academic programs: a recent Johns Hopkins study rated UCSD faculty 1st nationally among public institutions in science; *U.S. News & World Report* rates UCSD 7th in the nation among state-supported colleges and universities; Kiplinger's "100 Best Values in Public Colleges" ranks UCSD 10th in the nation. UCSD ranks 5th in the nation and 1st in the University of California system for the amount of federal research dollars spent on research and development; and the university ranks 10th in the nation in the excellence of its graduate programs and the quality of its faculty, according to the most recent National Research Council college rankings."

## ADMISSIONS

| | |
|---|---|
| **Admissions Rating** | **83** |
| # of applicants | 35,691 |
| % of applicants accepted | 38 |
| % of acceptees attending | 23 |

### FRESHMAN PROFILE

| | |
|---|---|
| Average SAT Verbal | 606 |
| Average SAT Math | 653 |
| Average ACT Composite | 25 |
| Minimum TOEFL | 550 |
| Average HS GPA | 3.99 |
| % graduated top 10% of class | 95 |
| % graduated top 25% of class | 100 |
| % graduated top 50% of class | 100 |

### DEADLINES

| | |
|---|---|
| Regular admission | 11/30 |
| Regular notification | 3/15 |

### APPLICANTS ALSO LOOK AT
**AND OFTEN PREFER**
Stanford
UC—Berkeley
UCLA
**AND SOMETIMES PREFER**
UC—Davis
**AND RARELY PREFER**
UC—Riverside
UC—Irvine
UC—Santa Barbara
UC—Santa Cruz

## FINANCIAL FACTS

| | |
|---|---|
| **Financial Aid Rating** | **73** |
| In-state tuition | $3,848 |
| Out-of-state tuition | $14,552 |
| Room & board | $7,525 |
| Books and supplies | $1,158 |
| Required fees | $3,848 |
| % frosh receiving aid | 58 |
| % undergrads receiving aid | 61 |
| Avg frosh grant | $5,014 |
| Avg frosh loan | $4,668 |

# UNIVERSITY OF CALIFORNIA—SANTA BARBARA

OFFICE OF ADMISSIONS, 1210 CHEADLE HALL, SANTA BARBARA, CA 93106 • ADMISSIONS: 805-893-2881 • FAX: 805-893-2676

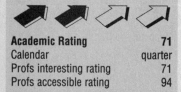

## CAMPUS LIFE

**Quality of Life Rating** — **87**
Type of school — public
Affiliation — none
Environment — suburban

### STUDENTS

| | |
|---|---|
| Total undergrad enrollment | 17,699 |
| % male/female | 46/54 |
| % from out of state | 5 |
| % from public high school | 82 |
| % live on campus | 23 |
| % in (# of) fraternities | 10 (19) |
| % in (# of) sororities | 10 (18) |
| % African American | 2 |
| % Asian | 15 |
| % Caucasian | 58 |
| % Hispanic | 14 |
| % Native American | 1 |
| % international | 1 |

### SURVEY SAYS . . .
*Beautiful campus
Campus easy to get around
Students love Santa Barbara, CA
Great off-campus food
Athletic facilities are great
Student publications are ignored
Students are cliquish
(Almost) no one smokes
Students get along with local
community*

## ACADEMICS

**Academic Rating** — **71**
Calendar — quarter
Profs interesting rating — 71
Profs accessible rating — 94

### MOST POPULAR MAJORS
business economics
biological science
psychology

## STUDENTS SPEAK OUT
### Academics
"I came to this school expecting beer, beaches, and babes," writes a sophomore. "I was thrilled to find exceptional teachers; eager, intellectual students—and beer, beaches, and babes!" While many of its undergrads did choose this "beautiful," "laid-back" state school for reasons not quite academic ("sun," "beach," "girls/guys," and "location" seem to be the decisive factors), the University of California at Santa Barbara, with its "friendly people," "strong liberal faculty" and excellent programs in the sciences and math—as well as in foreign languages, English, theater, and writing—make the school a good choice for the sociable student looking for a solid liberal arts education. Faculty gets high marks all around, and though there's no avoiding a couple of duds once in a while, UCSB students seem to take all things in stride. A first-year explains: "Most of my professors have been interesting, informative, and inspiring. Of course, there have been a few who have lulled me to sleep better than any soft bed I have ever encountered. In general, though, they get an A+—even if I wasn't reciprocated with the same grade." Administrators, too, are well liked—one senior claims that they seem "even stonier than the students"—and work hard to provide resources and services for UCSB's traditional and nontraditional students. (However, the school could stand to improve its academic counseling and computer facilities, say undergrads.) Basically, academic success at UCSB "all depends on your approach," concludes a wise freshman. "If you are motivated and determined, you will get the classes you want and the information and resources you need. If you sit around at the beach and just expect to get into all your classes, you will be 'watching the waves' for a while."

### Life
"UCSB is the greatest place on earth. Nowhere else in the country can you get a college experience like here. Isla Vista is like Disneyland for 20-year-olds." High praise coming from southern California, the land of fun and sun. UCSB has something of a reputation for taking the good life seriously—it's the "University of Casual Sex and Beer," joke undergrads—and the bustling, upscale communities of Isla Vista and Santa Barbara only serve to heighten the experience. "It's a very big party school," writes a second-year, "similar to a Bourbon Street atmosphere." Many students claim that they spend the first few years "trying to find a balance between academics and social life," not an easy task when you've got the beach, surfing, hiking, barbecues, football, Frisbee golf, parties, and downtown S.B. (not to mention L.A. in an hour and a half) luring you away. Of course, not everyone is so enamored of the outdoorsy, party-hearty culture; some students make it their business to get away, to "Vegas, L.A., San Diego," all within a day's drive of campus. Still, it's hard to complain when the only campus improvement one freshman could think of is "moving sidewalks with back massage specialists everywhere."

### Student Body
Students' bodies might be a more apt description of what's on a UCSBer's mind a good portion of the time. "Hot chicks"? Got 'em. "Good looking guys?" That too. This isn't to say students at Santa Barbara don't appreciate their peers' "open-mindedness" and "easy-going, laid-back" personalities, but at UCSB a premium seems to be placed on being nice looking, too. Some students complain about the amount of navel gazing (prettily pierced, of course) that goes on at the U.: "They are largely selfish and unmotivated, except to get what they want," writes a senior; while a junior notes that "many don't want to go outside of their own bubble." Despite some complaints about diversity ("white is over-represented," notes a senior) and substance use ("lots of pot smokers/alcoholics"), many UCSB students remark that their fellow students are "the most open-minded anywhere."

# UNIVERSITY OF CALIFORNIA—SANTA BARBARA

FINANCIAL AID: 805-893-2432 • E-MAIL: APPINFO@SA.UCSB.EDU • WEBSITE: WWW.UCSB.EDU

## ADMISSIONS

*Very important* academic and nonacademic factors considered by the admissions committee include secondary school record and standardized test scores. *Important* factors considered include character/personal qualities, essays, extracurricular activities, volunteer work, work experience, geography, and talent/ability. Factors *not* considered include minority status and religious affiliation/commitment. SAT I or ACT required, and three SAT II exams. TOEFL required of all international applicants. High school diploma is required and GED is accepted. *High school units required/recommended:* 15 total required; 18 total recommended; 4 English required, 4 math recommended, 3 lab science recommended, 3 foreign language recommended, 2 history/social studies required, 2 elective required.

### The Inside Word

Although applications from members of underrepresented minority groups dipped following the 1997 state ban on the use of affirmative action in admissions, the picture has changed dramatically in the past few years. As a result of UC—Santa Barbara's vigorous outreach and recruiting efforts, applications from members of underrepresented minority groups have climbed steadily, as have acceptances. For the fall 2001 entering freshman class, the number of applicants accepted who are members of underrepresented minority groups has returned to pre-1997 levels.

## FINANCIAL AID

*Students should submit:* FAFSA. Regular filing deadline is March 2. The Princeton Review suggests that all financial aid forms be submitted as soon as possible after January 1. *Need-based scholarships/grants offered:* Pell, SEOG, state scholarships/grants, and the school's own gift aid. *Loan aid offered:* Direct PLUS and Federal Perkins. Institutional employment available. Federal Work-Study Program available. Applicants will be notified of awards on a rolling basis beginning on or about March 15. Off-campus job opportunities are fair.

## FROM THE ADMISSIONS OFFICE

"The University of California—Santa Barbara is a major research institution offering undergraduate and graduate education in the arts, humanities, sciences and technology, and social sciences. Large enough to have excellent facilities for study, research, and other creative activities, the campus is also small enough to foster close relationships among faculty and students. The faculty numbers more than 900. A member of the most distinguished system of public higher education in the nation, UC—Santa Barbara is committed equally to excellence in scholarship and instruction. Through the general education program, students acquire good grounding in the skills, perceptions, and methods of a variety of disciplines. In addition, because they study with a research faculty, they not only acquire basic skills and broad knowledge but also are exposed to the imagination, inventiveness, and intense concentration that scholars bring to their work."

## ADMISSIONS

| | |
|---|---|
| **Admissions Rating** | **80** |
| # of applicants | 31,234 |
| % of applicants accepted | 47 |
| % of acceptees attending | 23 |

### FRESHMAN PROFILE

| | |
|---|---|
| Range SAT Verbal | 530-630 |
| Average SAT Verbal | 540 |
| Range SAT Math | 550-660 |
| Average SAT Math | 609 |
| Range ACT Composite | 24-28 |
| Average ACT Composite | 24.5 |
| Minimum TOEFL | 500 |
| Average HS GPA | 3.7 |

### DEADLINES

| | |
|---|---|
| Regular admission | 11/30 |
| Regular notification | 3/15 |
| Nonfall registration? | yes |

### APPLICANTS ALSO LOOK AT

**AND OFTEN PREFER**
UC—Berkeley
UC—San Diego
UC—Irvine
UCLA

**AND SOMETIMES PREFER**
UC—Davis
Pomona
Loyola Marymount

**AND RARELY PREFER**
U. Pacific
UC—Riverside
UC—Santa Cruz

### FINANCIAL FACTS

| | |
|---|---|
| **Financial Aid Rating** | **72** |
| Out-of-state tuition | $10,614 |
| Room & board | $7,577 |
| Books and supplies | $1,101 |
| Required fees | $3,836 |
| Avg frosh grant | $4,651 |
| Avg frosh loan | $2,275 |

# UNIVERSITY OF CALIFORNIA—SANTA CRUZ

OFFICE OF ADMISSIONS, COOK HOUSE, 1156 HIGH STREET, SANTA CRUZ, CA 95064 • ADMISSIONS: 831-459-4008 • FAX: 831-459-4452

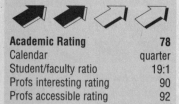
## STUDENTS SPEAK OUT

### Academics

UC Santa Cruz continues to be one of the best deals in California higher education—especially for students looking for a gentler, kinder, more community-oriented college experience. What makes UCSC special? "Natural beauty, small classes, and accessible professors," say students, who seem to appreciate the school's unique blend of big-school resources and small-school liberal arts atmosphere, set along some of the most beautiful coastline in northern California. "It's an excellent college for undergrads," writes a first-year. "All courses are taught by professors, who are generally good teachers." Students say that the school's "fabulous" academics—especially in the natural and computer sciences, language studies, linguistics, film, and digital media studies—are largely a result of the "easygoing," "helpful," and "approachable" faculty. Even UCSC's grading system reflects a concern for the individual student. For the most part, students receive "narrative evaluations"—short summations of performance and progress—as well as traditional letter grades. "I love getting evaluations," writes a first-year. "They are way more helpful than grades. They really increase the sense of community—people are more apt to help each other than compete against each other." And while some students would like to see an increase in the use of letter grades, most seem to like NEs. With such an individually oriented environment, however, it's no wonder that some students complain about a certain amount of administrative inefficiency. Santa Cruz is "not terribly well organized," writes a sophomore, "though I don't think that it's significantly worse than any other large institution." Class scheduling and overcrowding can sometimes be a problem, and there's some concern that the school's current expansion will only worsen the situation. There's something about Santa Cruz that defies the kind of bureaucratic-machine vibe that infuses other large state schools, though. Take it from a wee freshman: "UCSC has done a great job in helping me feel right at home as a Banana Slug!"

### Life

While most students give high marks to Santa Cruz's "secluded" and "gorgeous" location and "laid-back" atmosphere, one sophomore concedes that with so much to do out of doors, the life of the mind can sometimes take a backseat to the life of the mountains and ocean (with a slightly bizarre carney-style boardwalk called "The Strip" in between). With opportunities for mountain biking, surfing, hiking, hot-tubbing, or just hanging out at the beach literally at students' back doors, Santa Cruz is sometimes criticized for being a little too idyllic; yet it's clear that the Banana Slugs wouldn't have it any other way. "Life here at Santa Cruz is so relaxed," says a junior. Of course certain things can get a rise out of this normally mellow crowd. Many UCSCers are politically and environmentally active, and as housing in the area is far beyond most students' budgets, some have joined in a call for better and cheaper residential options. As for social life, Santa Cruz has your standard supply of "bars, restaurants, [and] movie theatres." Frats don't seem particularly overbearing at the school, though they are an option. Basically, kids like to do what they do everywhere (albeit in a hot tub overlooking the Pacific): "Party, party, and party some more."

### Student Body

It probably wouldn't surprise anyone that Santa Cruz students tend to like each other—a lot. "The majority of the students here are open-minded and friendly" is a typical characterization, as are "liberal," "open," "fun," and "unique." Again, the Banana Slug emphasis on community: "You have a voice here and a place to be someone," notes a junior. And while there are bound to be some "stuck up jerks" in any crowd of several thousand, students at UCSC seem to experience a genuine camaraderie with their peers. Still, there's room for improvement: cultural and economic diversity is sorely lacking. With the university's imminent expansion, however, even some of the school's reputed insularity and homogeneity is bound to change for the better.

# UNIVERSITY OF CALIFORNIA—SANTA CRUZ

FINANCIAL AID: 831-459-2963 • E-MAIL: ADMISSIONS@CATS.UCSC.EDU • WEBSITE: WWW.ADMISSIONS.UCSC.EDU

## ADMISSIONS

*Very important* academic and nonacademic factors considered by the admissions committee include secondary school record and standardized test scores. *Important* factors considered include character/personal qualities, essays, recommendations, and talent/ability. *Other* factors considered include alumni/ae relation, extracurricular activities, geography, volunteer work, and work experience. Factors *not* considered include class rank and religious affiliation/commitment. SAT I or ACT and SAT II required. High school diploma is required and GED is accepted. *High school units required/recommended:* 15 total required; 18 total recommended; 4 English required, 3 math required, 4 math recommended, 2 science required, 3 science recommended, 2 foreign language required, 3 foreign language recommended, 2 social studies or history required, 2 electives required. *The admissions office says:* "Residents must either have a 3.30 GPA or higher. A lower GPA (min. 2.82) can be offset by a corresponding test score. Nonresidents must have taken the same courses but must earn a 3.4 average (the eligibility index applies to residents only). Any student who fails to meet the academic requirements may gain admission on the basis of test scores alone if (1) his/her combined SAT is 1400 or higher (ACT composite: 31 or higher), and (2) his/her combined SAT II scores exceed a minimum score (1760 for residents, 1850 for nonresidents), and none is lower than 530."

### The Inside Word

Don't be deceived by the high acceptance rate at Santa Cruz; there are lots of engaging, intellectually motivated students here, and only active learners need apply. The state of California's ban on affirmative action in the UC admission process has created much uncertainty regarding the future of candidate selection in the system, but Santa Cruz is one of only two UC units that have been able to keep minority admission rates from declining precipitously.

## FINANCIAL AID

*Students should submit:* FAFSA and California Student Aid Commission GPA Verification Form for California. Regular filing deadline is March 2. The Princeton Review suggests that all financial aid forms be submitted as soon as possible after January 1. *Need-based scholarships/grants offered:* Pell, SEOG, state scholarships/grants, private scholarships, and the school's own gift aid. *Loan aid offered:* Direct Subsidized Stafford, Direct Unsubsidized Stafford, Direct PLUS, Federal Perkins, and college/university loans from institutional funds. Institutional employment available. Federal Work-Study Program available. Applicants will be notified of awards on a rolling basis beginning on or about June 1. Off-campus job opportunities are good.

## FROM THE ADMISSIONS OFFICE

"Since its founding in 1965, UC Santa Cruz has won a national reputation as a campus devoted to excellence in undergraduate teaching, graduate study and research, and professional education. Its academic plan and physical design combine the advantages of a small-college setting with the research and academic strengths traditional to the University of California. UC Santa Cruz 's activities in undergraduate education is the symbiosis between research and teaching. At UC Santa Cruz, undergraduate courses are taught by the same faculty who conduct cutting-edge research. Over the past five years, UC Santa Cruz has built six major academic research facilities, including a science library, earth and marine sciences building, two social sciences buildings, a visual arts painting studio, and a new music center."

## ADMISSIONS

| | |
|---|---|
| **Admissions Rating** | **79** |
| # of applicants | 16,366 |
| % of applicants accepted | 80 |
| % of acceptees attending | 22 |

### FRESHMAN PROFILE

| | |
|---|---|
| Range SAT Verbal | 510-630 |
| Average SAT Verbal | 570 |
| Range SAT Math | 520-630 |
| Average SAT Math | 575 |
| Range ACT Composite | 21-26 |
| Average ACT Composite | 23 |
| Average HS GPA | 3.5 |

### DEADLINES

| | |
|---|---|
| Regular admission | 11/30 |
| Regular notification | 3/31 |

### APPLICANTS ALSO LOOK AT
**AND OFTEN PREFER**
Stanford
UCLA
UC—Berkeley
**AND SOMETIMES PREFER**
UC—Davis
UC—Riverside
UC—Santa Barbara
**AND RARELY PREFER**
Santa Clara
Scripps
U. Colorado, Boulder

## FINANCIAL FACTS

| | |
|---|---|
| **Financial Aid Rating** | **84** |
| In-state tuition | $4,617 |
| Out-of-state tuition | $10,244 |
| Room & board | $8,106 |
| Books and supplies | $1,047 |
| Required fees | $4,617 |
| % frosh receiving aid | 44 |
| % undergrads receiving aid | 48 |

# UNIVERSITY OF CHICAGO

1116 EAST 59TH STREET, CHICAGO, IL 60637 • ADMISSIONS: 773-702-8650 • FAX: 773-702-4199

## CAMPUS LIFE

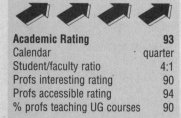

| Quality of Life Rating | 71 |
| --- | --- |
| Type of school | private |
| Affiliation | none |
| Environment | urban |

### STUDENTS

| | |
| --- | --- |
| Total undergrad enrollment | 4,008 |
| % male/female | 51/49 |
| % from out of state | 78 |
| % from public high school | 70 |
| % live on campus | 66 |
| % in (# of) fraternities | 12 (9) |
| % in (# of) sororities | 5 (2) |
| % African American | 5 |
| % Asian | 19 |
| % Caucasian | 69 |
| % Hispanic | 7 |
| % international | 6 |
| # of countries represented | 34 |

### SURVEY SAYS . . .
*Great library*
*Students love Chicago, IL*
*Lab facilities need improving*
*Students don't get along with local community*
*Students aren't religious*
*Athletic facilities need improving*
*Student government is unpopular*
*Campus difficult to get around*

## ACADEMICS

| Academic Rating | 93 |
| --- | --- |
| Calendar | quarter |
| Student/faculty ratio | 4:1 |
| Profs interesting rating | 90 |
| Profs accessible rating | 94 |
| % profs teaching UG courses | 90 |

### MOST POPULAR MAJORS
economics
biological sciences
English

## STUDENTS SPEAK OUT

### Academics

Rigor, reputation, and a world-renowned faculty. The "Three Rs (and a lower case w)"—as well as a common core curriculum—are the reasons why many students choose the University of Chicago, despite Hyde Park's bone-chilling winters, strangely aggressive squirrel population, and what some might see as the school's "elitist, pretentious" attitude. Chances are, you've already heard that at U of C, "academic life is central and very rigorous." Rumor has it that the faculty has racked up more Nobel Prizes than any other university in the world. One junior agrees: "The professors are world-class and know how to teach. Where else can you see a nationally known physicist launch himself out of class to demonstrate nonrelativistic mechanics?" Nor is it just in the sciences that U of C excels. Notes a sophomore, "We have a writing program that actually tries to teach us to write well." Of course, such brilliance requires a sacrifice. "When you come here," warns a first-year, "you become a nerd and the library is your second home." Of course, the school's quarter system and its notable lack of grade inflation can make for a rather pressurized environment at times—"like an axe is ready to drop any minute," writes one student. Still, most wouldn't have it any other way: "Most people, although they wouldn't admit it, like the work that they do." Concludes a second-year, "The University of Chicago is the greatest academic experience of my life. It has introduced me to a world of knowledge I never before knew existed. And the Chicago weather has made me strong."

### Life

On the University of Chicago's reputation as being "the place where fun comes to die," many students choose to look at the bright side: "Learning happens here," quips a glass-is-half-full type. "People go to movies, to coffee, to restaurants, to Math Club." Others aren't so zen: "With all the other core requirements we have to fulfill there should be social skills in there, too. The computer science majors need remedial bathing." A more balanced look at the school is offered by the following senior: "The academic life is the be-all and end-all of U. Chicago. If you're not into your studies and don't enjoy the intellectual life, chances are that you will think U of C is boring. "Of course, the proximity to Chicago makes even the dullest Math Club meeting an opportunity to get out and explore the Windy City, which has "one of the most beautiful skylines in the world" and where "the theatre and restaurant scenes are particularly good." Although campus itself could stand a few more social options, the administration has been trying to upgrade its image in this area over the last few years, making a more concerted effort to address quality-of-life issues such extracurricular activities, student transportation, and safety. Pluses? "Housing is exceptional," according to one student. "Where else can you have a kitchen, living room, and dining room with an excellent view of Lake Michigan?" Then there's the "legendary" Scav Hunt, quintessentially U of C: "Each spring the school nearly shuts down as students rush to answer obscure trivia, party on rooftops on other campuses, and try—successfully—to cobble together nuclear reactors."

### Student Body

"Prospectives be warned," writes a junior. "We are not the stereotypical, boring, academic, nonfun students we are rumored to be!" One student argues, "People here are smart, quick-witted, and aware of the world around them." Sure, "everyone is smart, which means some very interesting people and some who are annoying and egotistical," but look at what's inside, urges a sophomore. "Their sarcasm may make them seem cynical, but it merely masks idealism struggling to exist in a nonideal world. Students here are not friendly, they're honest. You may not feel as 'welcome' or as warm and fuzzy as at other schools, but here at least you know where you stand." But if you're still concerned about the nerd factor, take heart. Writes a junior, "I'm a nerd, and I like it a lot here. So I'm guessing that, if you're a nerd, you'll like it a lot here too."

FINANCIAL AID: 773-702-8666 • E-MAIL: COLLEGE-ADMISSIONS@UCHICAGO.EDU • WEBSITE: WWW.UCHICAGO.EDU

## ADMISSIONS

*Very important* academic and nonacademic factors considered by the admissions committee include class rank, essays, secondary school record, and standardized test scores. *Important* factors considered include character/personal qualities, extracurricular activities, interview, and recommendations. *Other* factors considered include minority status, talent/ability, and volunteer work. Factors *not* considered include alumni/ae relation, geography, religious affiliation/commitment, state residency, and work experience. SAT I or ACT required. TOEFL required of all international applicants. *High school units required/recommended:* 16 total recommended; 4 English recommended, 2 math recommended, 2 science recommended, 2 science lab recommended, 2 social studies recommended, 4 elective recommended.

### The Inside Word

While excellent grades in tough courses and high test scores are the norm for applicants to the university, what really counts is what's on your mind. This is a cerebral institution, and thinkers stand out in the admissions process. Think about yourself, think about what you'd like to know more about, think about why you want to attend the university. Once you have some answers, begin writing your essays. And remember that universities that are this selective and recommend interviews should always be taken up on their recommendation.

## FINANCIAL AID

The Princeton Review suggests that all financial aid forms be submitted as soon as possible after January 1. Institutional employment available. Federal Work-Study Program available. Off-campus job opportunities are good.

## FROM THE ADMISSIONS OFFICE

"Chicago is a place where talented young intellectuals, writers, mathematicians, and scientists come to learn in a setting that rewards hard work and prizes initiative and creativity. It is also a place where collegiate life is urban, yet friendly and open, and free of empty traditionalism and snobbishness. Chicago is the right choice for students who know that they would thrive in an intimate classroom setting. Classes at Chicago are small, emphasizing discussion with faculty members whose research is always testing the limits of their chosen fields. Our students: They take chances; they delight us when they pursue a topic on their own for the fun of it; they display an articulate voice in papers and in discussion; they do not accept our word for everything but respect good argument; they are fanciful or solid at the right time. Most often they are students who choose the best courses available, who take a heavier load than necessary because they are curious and not worried about the consequences, who let curiosity and energy spill over into activities and sports, who are befriended by the best and toughest teachers, and who finish what they set out to do."

## ADMISSIONS

| | |
|---|---|
| Admissions Rating | 95 |
| # of applicants | 7,396 |
| % of applicants accepted | 44 |
| % of acceptees attending | 32 |
| # accepting a place on wait list | 945 |
| % admitted from wait list | 2 |

### FRESHMAN PROFILE

| | |
|---|---|
| Range SAT Verbal | 630-750 |
| Range SAT Math | 650-740 |
| Range ACT Composite | 28-32 |
| % graduated top 10% of class | 82 |
| % graduated top 25% of class | 96 |
| % graduated top 50% of class | 100 |

### DEADLINES

| | |
|---|---|
| Regular admission | 1/1 |
| Regular notification | 4/1 |

### APPLICANTS ALSO LOOK AT
**AND OFTEN PREFER**
Harvard
Yale
Princeton
Columbia
Swarthmore
**AND SOMETIMES PREFER**
Northwestern U.
Johns Hopkins
**AND RARELY PREFER**
Loyola U. Chicago
U. Illinois—Urbana-Champaign
U. Rochester

### FINANCIAL FACTS

| | |
|---|---|
| Financial Aid Rating | 77 |
| Tuition | $23,820 |
| Room & board | $7,835 |
| Books and supplies | $933 |
| Required fees | $553 |
| % frosh receiving aid | 57 |
| % undergrads receiving aid | 56 |
| Avg frosh grant | $16,399 |
| Avg frosh loan | $3,660 |

# UNIVERSITY OF COLORADO—BOULDER

CAMPUS BOX 30, BOULDER, CO 80309-0030 • ADMISSIONS: 303-492-6301 • FAX: 303-492-7115

## CAMPUS LIFE

| | |
|---|---|
| **Quality of Life Rating** | **84** |
| Type of school | public |
| Affiliation | none |
| Environment | suburban |

### STUDENTS

| | |
|---|---|
| Total undergrad enrollment | 23,342 |
| % male/female | 52/48 |
| % from out of state | 32 |
| % live on campus | 26 |
| % in (# of) fraternities | 8 (19) |
| % in (# of) sororities | 12 (13) |
| % African American | 2 |
| % Asian | 6 |
| % Caucasian | 82 |
| % Hispanic | 6 |
| % Native American | 1 |
| % international | 1 |
| # of countries represented | 106 |

### SURVEY SAYS . . .

*Students love Boulder, CO*
*Everyone loves the Buffaloes*
*Athletic facilities are great*
*Diversity lacking on campus*
*Great off-campus food*
*Large classes*
*Lots of TAs teach upper-level*
*courses*

## ACADEMICS

| | |
|---|---|
| **Academic Rating** | **77** |
| Calendar | semester |
| Student/faculty ratio | 14:1 |
| Profs interesting rating | 89 |
| Profs accessible rating | 92 |
| % profs teaching UG courses | 82 |
| % classes taught by TAs | 21 |
| Avg lab size | 20-29 students |
| Avg reg class size | 10-19 students |

### MOST POPULAR MAJORS
psychology
biology
finance

## STUDENTS SPEAK OUT

### Academics

The University of Colorado at Boulder is a large teaching and research (they're not mutually exclusive!) university that offers many academic opportunities and suffers from the same bureaucratic problems often associated with large schools. Students like their upper-level courses. "The more specialized and advanced my classes have become, the more impressed I've been with the caliber of my professors," one senior writes. A classmate concurs, "Overall, I have had a good experience, especially in my upper-level classes, where I feel my professors care about their work and are happy to help their students." Students are not as positive about required courses. "Some required classes are absolute wastes of time, which keeps students from taking courses they would be genuinely interested in," writes one junior accounting major. A sophomore adds, "I have had classes where I could have taught better than the professor." Students also mention the need for more minority professors. Students plainly dislike the administration. Other students dislike the "bureaucratic nonsense." They also believe that "admissions standards could and should be improved" and that they need "a wider variety of classes." The "gorgeous campus" receives rave reviews. The library is "huge," but students say that it still needs improvement: "Books aren't even in the right place." Of a CU—Boulder education, many students comment that "you get what you put into it." One sophomore engineering major admits that CU—Boulder is "a school where an idiot and a scholar can get the education they strive for."

### Life

Students love living in Boulder because "it is full of great restaurants, movie theaters, and shops. So if you can't keep yourself busy with CU concerts, intramural sports, or student groups, there's still plenty to do." The music scene is also strong in Boulder. For lovers of the outdoors, CU—Boulder offers many recreational opportunities: "The outdoor activities are endless—hiking, biking, skiing." According to a journalism major, "The coolest thing about this place [is that] even when everything is getting you down, you can go out and have an awesome night." There are some unhappy students at Colorado. One of them scoffs, "Fun at CU appears to mean getting drunk on the cheapest possible beer, finding you have nowhere good to go, and settling on spending your night making as much noise in the hallway of your apartment building and disturbing as many neighbors as you can." Many admit that they frequently drink, and "people here smoke a lot of pot." If you dig skiing, CU—Boulder "is a four-year break from reality."

### Student Body

The typical CU—Boulder student is white and middle- to upper-class. Though "students at CU are friendly, [they are] not overly passionate or involved in a specific activity." A senior sociology major says, "Going to CU is all about Buffaloes. After the first few weeks you realize it's all just bull. Diversity? What? There is no diversity here." A junior engineering major adds, "This campus is very white. The students are mostly wealthy. What they drive is more important to them than their education." While students claim to be socially active, one wryly notes that they're "outraged at the working conditions in Third World countries—except when their GAP clothes are concerned." A junior admits, "We are supposed to be progressive but are severely lacking in recruitment of students of color."

FINANCIAL AID: 303-492-5091 • E-MAIL: APPLY@COLORADO.EDU • WEBSITE: WWW.COLORADO.EDU

## ADMISSIONS

*Very important* academic and nonacademic factors considered by the admissions committee include class rank, secondary school record, and standardized test scores. *Important* factors considered include essays, geography, minority status, recommendations, and state residency. *Other* factors considered include alumni/ae relation, character/personal qualities, extracurricular activities, talent/ability, volunteer work, and work experience. Factors *not* considered include interview and religious affiliation/commitment. SAT I or ACT required. TOEFL required of all international applicants. High school diploma is required and GED is accepted. *High school units recommended:* 4 English, 3 math, 3 science (includes 2 of lab science), 3 foreign language, 3 social studies. *The admissions office says:* "Our commitment to increasing the ethnic and geographic diversity of our students is considered in admissions decisions."

### The Inside Word

In response to past concerns in Colorado about overly high percentages of out-of-staters being admitted to CU, the out-of-state population has been monitored more carefully than once was the case. Non-Coloradans will definitely find the going a bit tougher than will Colorado residents.

## FINANCIAL AID

*Students should submit:* FAFSA and tax return required. There is no regular filing deadline. The Princeton Review suggests that all financial aid forms be submitted as soon as possible after January 1. *Need-based scholarships/grants offered:* Pell, SEOG, state scholarships/grants, private scholarships, and the school's own gift aid. *Loan aid offered:* Direct Subsidized Stafford, Direct Unsubsidized Stafford, Direct PLUS, Federal Perkins, college/university loans from institutional funds, and private lenders. Institutional employment available. Federal Work-Study Program available. Applicants will be notified of awards on a rolling basis beginning on or about February 1. Off-campus job opportunities are excellent.

## FROM THE ADMISSIONS OFFICE

"The University of Colorado at Boulder, founded in 1876, is a major teaching and research university. Five undergraduate colleges and two schools offer over 2,500 courses in more than 150 fields of study. CU—Boulder offers more than 60 programs that lead to a bachelor's degree. Forty-six percent of all undergraduate course sections enroll no more than 19 students and 86 percent enroll fewer than 50. CU has over 70 research centers and institutes, and has numerous partnerships with businesses. CU—Boulder emphasizes a total learning environment, and many 'academic neighborhoods' tap community resources. Some academic programs allow students to take small classes in their residence halls. In addition, nonresidential programs like FallFEST group new students in courses and small discussion sections of no more than 25 students throughout the fall semester. CU—Boulder has been ranked 17th among all public colleges and universities in Yahoo's list of the 100 most 'wired' colleges and 9th among all public universities in federally funded research. CU—Boulder has traditionally been a leader in the space sciences. Most recently, CU faculty and students designed and built instruments for NASA's Galileo spacecraft now orbiting Jupiter, and a $12 million instrument for the Cassini Mission to Saturn. Faculty members include a Nobel Prize winner in chemistry, 14 members of the National Academy of Sciences, 10 members of the American Academy of Arts and Sciences, and 7 members of the National Academy of Engineering."

## ADMISSIONS

| | |
|---|---|
| Admissions Rating | 83 |
| # of applicants | 15,453 |
| % of applicants accepted | 86 |
| % of acceptees attending | 39 |

### FRESHMAN PROFILE

| | |
|---|---|
| Range SAT Verbal | 520-620 |
| Average SAT Verbal | 569 |
| Range SAT Math | 530-640 |
| Average SAT Math | 584 |
| Range ACT Composite | 22-27 |
| Average ACT Composite | 25 |
| Minimum TOEFL | 500 |
| Average HS GPA | 3.4 |
| % graduated top 10% of class | 21 |
| % graduated top 25% of class | 53 |
| % graduated top 50% of class | 88 |

### DEADLINES

| | |
|---|---|
| Regular admission | 2/15 |
| Nonfall registration? | yes |

### APPLICANTS ALSO LOOK AT
**AND OFTEN PREFER**
UC—Berkeley
Stanford
UC—Santa Cruz
**AND SOMETIMES PREFER**
Northwestern U.
Colorado State
Arizona State
U. Arizona
Oregon State
**AND RARELY PREFER**
U. Oregon
U. Vermont

### FINANCIAL FACTS

| | |
|---|---|
| Financial Aid Rating | 73 |
| In-state tuition | $2,514 |
| Out-of-state tuition | $15,832 |
| Room & board | $5,538 |
| Books and supplies | $720 |
| Required fees | $674 |
| % frosh receiving aid | 24 |
| % undergrads receiving aid | 33 |
| Avg frosh grant | $2,734 |
| Avg frosh loan | $2,649 |

# UNIVERSITY OF CONNECTICUT

2131 HILLSIDE ROAD, U-88, STORRS, CT 06268-3088 • ADMISSIONS: 860-486-3137 • FAX: 860-486-1476

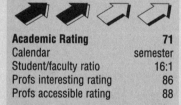
## STUDENTS SPEAK OUT

### Academics

The "highly underrated" University of Connecticut is "a public university with Big University problems and opportunities" where "the workload is challenging but not impossible." UConn has a well-deserved reputation for quality education in a wide variety of academic disciplines; as a large school, it's able to provide courses not only in its strengths (business, education, engineering, and psychology) but also in more specialized areas (pharmacy, marine science, theatre, and psychology). There is "fairly high deviation" in the quality of the faculty here. While more than a few UConn professors are "nationally recognized authors and scientists" and they are all "incredibly talented individuals," students say that "some professors really love their jobs and have a great time enlightening students," but "some are simply horrible" in the classroom. "Language barriers" can also be a "problem," especially with teaching assistants from places far-flung. The top brass is "doing an excellent job improving the University," though much of the campus is under construction. The administration seems to be showing a newfound "willingness to work with students" but "the administrative process could use a little tuning up." Too often, there are "no straight answers" and "bad experiences with touch-tone registration." Also, "the school needs to stop catering to its athletes." As for facilities, students say the gleaming new library, chemistry building, and school of business are top-notch.

### Life

Like many Big State Schools, "your experience is what you make of it" at UConn. If you "make the effort to get involved," there are "lots of organizations to join on campus." There are "University-sponsored trips to Montreal, New York," and "New Hampshire for hiking" as well, and UConn's newspaper, student government, competitive intramural sports, and other activities offer a variety of outlets for student energy and motivation. As one student puts it, at UConn you can see "Dave Mathews one night," and go "whitewater rafting the next." There's also "theatre, movies, local bands, big bands, comedy shows," and the wildly popular men's and women's Huskies basketball squads. "Besides basketball," though, "sports do not draw large crowds." UConn's party scene is pretty thriving, especially among members of fraternities and sororities. Greek life reportedly "offers a lot of opportunities to make friends and hold leadership positions" as well. Some students say life in the quiet, rural town of Storrs is "boring unless you like dancing and frat parties." The town is "too small," complains a senior. It is, apparently, a town with no diners, "few restaurants," and fewer clubs. "It needs to build up some to even come close to other college towns." Students also complain of the "constant construction" on campus, and they say "parking is atrocious." For students who need to get away (or can't find a parking spot), Foxwoods casino and Hartford's urban offerings aren't far.

### Student Body

Most students here hail from the state of Connecticut. Some students say the "very diverse crowd" at UConn is composed of "a lot of different groups that get along fairly well." They say the "down-to-earth and spirited" students here are "extremely friendly (especially for a New England state)" and "willing to help each other out." Others counter that "UConn can be a rather cold environment." Whatever the case, the vast majority of students are white and ethnic groups tend to huddle more or less together. There isn't a ton of animosity between Greeks and non-Greeks, but "Greeks tend to be self-contained." Politically, UConn folk lean to the left, but the school is large and "there's a place for everyone."

FINANCIAL AID: 860-486-2819 • E-MAIL: BEAHUSKY@UCONN.EDU • WEBSITE: WWW.UCONN.EDU

## ADMISSIONS

*Very important* academic and nonacademic factors considered by the admissions committee include secondary school record and standardized test scores. *Important* factors considered include class rank. *Other* factors considered include alumni/ae relation, essays, extracurricular activities, geography, minority status, recommendations, state residency, talent/ability, volunteer work, and work experience. Factors *not* considered include character/personal qualities, interview, and religious affiliation/commitment. SAT I or ACT required. TOEFL required of all international applicants. High school diploma is required and GED is accepted. *High school units required/recommended:* 19 total recommended; 4 English recommended, 4 math recommended, 4 science recommended, 2 science lab recommended, 3 foreign language recommended, 2 social studies recommended, 2 history recommended. *The admissions office says:* "No formulas or cutoffs are used. Every application is read by at least one person."

### The Inside Word

While no formulas or cutoffs may be used at UConn in the admissions process, getting in is still simply a matter of decent courses, grades, and tests. The recent high national profiles of the UConn men's and women's basketball teams has resulted in an increase in applications, and in turn may eventually show a slight increase in selectivity. At present, UConn seems content to bolster its enrollment by admitting more of these eager Huskies-to-be.

## FINANCIAL AID

*Students should submit:* FAFSA. The Princeton Review suggests that all financial aid forms be submitted as soon as possible after January 1. *Need-based scholarships/grants offered:* Pell, SEOG, state scholarships/grants, private scholarships, and the school's own gift aid. *Loan aid offered:* FFEL Subsidized Stafford, FFEL Unsubsidized Stafford, FFEL PLUS, Federal Perkins, and state. Institutional employment available. Federal Work-Study Program available. Applicants will be notified of awards on a rolling basis beginning on or about March 1. Off-campus job opportunities are good.

## FROM THE ADMISSIONS OFFICE

"The University of Connecticut provides students with high quality education, personalized attention, and a wide range of social and cultural opportunities. There are 29 students in the average undergraduate class. From award-winning actors to the federal reserve board chair, fascinating speakers and world leaders have lectured on campus within the past year, while students have taken in shows by premier dance, jazz, and rock performers. Transportation to campus events is convenient and safe; most students walk to class or ride university shuttlebuses. Through UCONN 2000, a landmark 10-year, $1 billion plan to renew, rebuild and enhance UConn's campuses, the university is erecting state-of-the-art academic and residential facilities. Among the projects: A new Center for Undergraduate Education, unifying student support services in one central location and providing speedy answers to student concerns. Because of a variety of innovations like this one, UConn is transforming the undergraduate experience and fast becoming a school of choice for a new generation of achievement-oriented students."

## ADMISSIONS

| | |
|---|---|
| Admissions Rating | 78 |
| # of applicants | 12,120 |
| % of applicants accepted | 67 |
| % of acceptees attending | 35 |
| # accepting a place on wait list | 246 |
| % admitted from wait list | 54 |

### FRESHMAN PROFILE

| | |
|---|---|
| Range SAT Verbal | 510-610 |
| Average SAT Verbal | 562 |
| Range SAT Math | 530-630 |
| Average SAT Math | 573 |
| Minimum TOEFL | 550 |
| % graduated top 10% of class | 23 |
| % graduated top 25% of class | 62 |
| % graduated top 50% of class | 95 |

### DEADLINES

| | |
|---|---|
| Regular admission | 3/1 |
| Regular notification | rolling |
| Nonfall registration? | yes |

### APPLICANTS ALSO LOOK AT

**AND OFTEN PREFER**
Tufts
Boston Coll.
Boston U.

**AND SOMETIMES PREFER**
Villanova
U. Mass—Amherst
Providence
Fairfield
U. Rhode Island

**AND RARELY PREFER**
Central Connecticut State
Siena
Bentley
Clarkson U.
U. Maine—Orono

### FINANCIAL FACTS

| | |
|---|---|
| Financial Aid Rating | 74 |
| In-state tuition | $4,282 |
| Out-of-state tuition | $13,056 |
| Room & board | $6,062 |
| Books and supplies | $725 |
| Required fees | $1,314 |
| % frosh receiving aid | 46 |
| Avg frosh grant | $6,124 |
| Avg frosh loan | $2,962 |

# UNIVERSITY OF DALLAS

1845 EAST NORTHGATE DRIVE, IRVING, TX 75062 • ADMISSIONS: 972-721-5266 • FAX: 972-721-5017

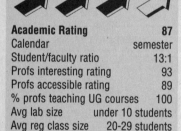
## STUDENTS SPEAK OUT

### Academics

The University of Dallas strives to prepare its students for the future by immersing them in the educational traditions of the past. UD's approach calls for student to attain a thorough grounding in Western classics and to pursue knowledge for its own sake. The result is an academic environment that recalls the agora of ancient Athens: "UD is a place centered around the idea of community and thought," explains one student, "not just a place that caters to those who are career-minded. UD is like the commons area in a city, the marketplace, where all discuss ideas, wander around ancient concepts, and create a colorful atmosphere of love of education, art, and the human spirit." Fundamental to UD's success is a rigorous and demanding core curriculum that stresses classical humanities ("You eat, drink, and sleep Western culture"), a talented and dedicated faculty ("The professors here are genuine. They encourage us and challenge us to live and think in a philosophical manner. I admire the professors' generous time and interest commitment to the students"), and a student body with a truly remarkable enthusiasm for philosophy. Students' work is taken very seriously both by the students and their instructors. "You can disagree with a professor and get an 'A' here if your argument's coherent, intelligent, and informed," says one student. Construction leaves the Irving campus is a constant state of semi-disrepair, but the campus in Rome, where students spend a sophomore semester, "is supposed to be gorgeous!" Besides, students come to UD for the academic experience, not for the ambiance. Sums up one student, "In high school, I had always slacked off and screwed around—why study? I didn't have to in order to get A's. But at UD . . . academically, I feel like my brain is cola, and my profs and fellow students are tossing in handfuls of Pop Rocks every day. The discussions and ideas in and out of class are invigorating!"

### Life

UD's academic approach seeps deeply into the school's social scene. Writes one undergrad, "We discuss academics a lot more than other schools, I would guess. We mainly just sit around and chat, go out to dinner or a movie occasionally, but mostly just enjoy each others' company." Adds another, "Discussions at parties are very philosophical." During the week, "there is always something going on, like Bowling With the Professors, Hawaii UD Pool Parties, and academic forums," but on weekends the campus quiets down. "Life here is typical, lots of studying on weekends," notes one student. "There is a lot of beer drinking and parties. But other than that, there is really nothing else." Most campus activities and policies reflect the University's Catholic affiliation. Grumbles one frosh, "They keep us on campus till we're 21 and expect us not to have members of the opposite sex in our rooms before 6:00 [A.M.] or after 10:00 [P.M.]." Still, "Being near such a big city means there is always something to do": The campus itself is located just outside Dallas. A set of wheels, however, are necessary to access the city's nightlife, shopping, entertainment, sports, and cultural centers.

### Student Body

The "very religious" students at this Roman Catholic university get along extremely well: "There's an aura of family life." Perhaps it's their common background; most UD folk are white, middle-class Catholics. Or perhaps it's their common vision; writes one, "It's amazing how many people are here for the right reasons and are excited about learning, not just getting by." While one non-Catholic student commented that "they want me to be Catholic, and I am a happy pagan," most feel that students who embrace different religious beliefs are sincerely welcomed by the UD community.

FINANCIAL AID: 972-721-5266 • E-MAIL: UNDADMIS@ACAD.UDALLAS.EDU • WEBSITE: WWW.UDALLAS.EDU

## ADMISSIONS

SAT I or ACT required. TOEFL required of all international applicants. High school diploma is required and GED is accepted. *High school units required/recommended:* 24 total recommended; 4 English recommended, 3 math recommended, 3 science recommended, 1 science lab recommended, 2 foreign language recommended, 2 social studies recommended, 2 history recommended. *The admissions office says:* "For over 40 years, the University of Dallas has formed leaders for our time through a finely created Great Books core curriculum that is simply unparalleled. A small, Catholic liberal arts and science institution, UD seeks to educate students who demand excellence of themselves, their teachers, and their college. At the University of Dallas, we actively pursue wisdom, truth, and virtue—all of which lead to excellence in and through every part of collegiate life. The learning process here does not simply consist of attending classes. Rather, it engages every aspect of a student's life: academics, extracurricular activities, even social life. It is the habit of life directed towards excellence, based on a solid, serious curriculum in the liberal arts of the western tradition that allows a UD education to be not only informational, but transformational."

### The Inside Word

The university's conservative nature places significant emphasis on "fit" in the admissions process. Having a solid academic background counts, but what kind of match a candidate makes with Dallas can be even more important.

## FINANCIAL AID

*Students should submit:* FAFSA and institution's own financial aid form. Regular filing deadline is March 1. The Princeton Review suggests that all financial aid forms be submitted as soon as possible after January 1. *Need-based scholarships/grants offered:* Pell, SEOG, state scholarships/grants, private scholarships, and the school's own gift aid. *Loan aid offered:* Direct Subsidized Stafford, Direct Unsubsidized Stafford, Direct PLUS, Federal Perkins, and state. Institutional employment available. Federal Work-Study Program available. Applicants will be notified of awards on a rolling basis beginning on or about March 30. Off-campus job opportunities are good.

## FROM THE ADMISSIONS OFFICE

"Quite unabashedly, the curriculum at the University of Dallas is based on the supposition that truth and virtue exist and are the proper objects of search in an education. The curriculum further supposes that this search is best pursued through an acquisition of philosophical and theological principles on the part of a student and has for its analogical field a vast body of great literature—perhaps more extensive than is likely to be encountered elsewhere—supplemented by a survey of the sweep of history and an introduction to the political and economic principles of society. An understanding of these subjects, along with an introduction to the quantitative and scientific worldview and a mastery of a language, is expected to form a comprehensive and coherent experience, which, in effect, governs the intellect of a student in a manner that develops independence of thought in its most effective mode."

## ADMISSIONS

| | |
|---|---:|
| **Admissions Rating** | **80** |
| # of applicants | 1,213 |
| % of applicants accepted | 76 |
| % of acceptees attending | 33 |

### FRESHMAN PROFILE

| | |
|---|---:|
| Range SAT Verbal | 575-680 |
| Average SAT Verbal | 630 |
| Range SAT Math | 540-650 |
| Average SAT Math | 600 |
| Range ACT Composite | 24-28 |
| Average ACT Composite | 26 |
| Minimum TOEFL | 550 |
| Average HS GPA | 3.4 |
| % graduated top 10% of class | 55 |
| % graduated top 25% of class | 78 |
| % graduated top 50% of class | 93 |

### DEADLINES

| | |
|---|---:|
| Priority admission deadline | 12/1 |
| Regular admission | 2/15 |
| Nonfall registration? | yes |

### APPLICANTS ALSO LOOK AT AND OFTEN PREFER

U. Texas—Austin
U. Texas—Dallas
Trinity U.

### AND SOMETIMES PREFER

Baylor
St. Louis
U. Denver
U. Texas—Arlington
SMU

### FINANCIAL FACTS

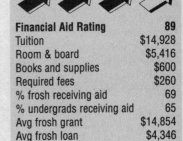

| | |
|---|---:|
| **Financial Aid Rating** | **89** |
| Tuition | $14,928 |
| Room & board | $5,416 |
| Books and supplies | $600 |
| Required fees | $260 |
| % frosh receiving aid | 69 |
| % undergrads receiving aid | 65 |
| Avg frosh grant | $14,854 |
| Avg frosh loan | $4,346 |

# UNIVERSITY OF DAYTON

300 COLLEGE PARK DRIVE, DAYTON, OH 45469-1300 • ADMISSIONS: 937-229-4411 • FAX: 937-229-4729

## CAMPUS LIFE

**Quality of Life Rating**    **85**

| | |
|---|---|
| Type of school | private |
| Affiliation | Roman Catholic |
| Environment | suburban |

### STUDENTS

| | |
|---|---|
| Total undergrad enrollment | 7,132 |
| % male/female | 49/51 |
| % from out of state | 36 |
| % from public high school | 47 |
| % live on campus | 76 |
| % in (# of) fraternities | 14 (14) |
| % in (# of) sororities | 19 (10) |
| % African American | 3 |
| % Asian | 1 |
| % Caucasian | 90 |
| % Hispanic | 2 |
| % international | 1 |
| # of countries represented | 48 |

### SURVEY SAYS . . .

*Student publications are popular
(Almost) everyone plays intramural
sports
Lots of beer drinking
Lots of conservatives on campus
Unattractive campus
Campus difficult to get around
Lots of long lines and red tape
Diversity lacking on campus
Lots of conservatives*

## ACADEMICS

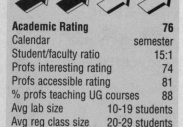

**Academic Rating**    **76**

| | |
|---|---|
| Calendar | semester |
| Student/faculty ratio | 15:1 |
| Profs interesting rating | 74 |
| Profs accessible rating | 81 |
| % profs teaching UG courses | 88 |
| Avg lab size | 10-19 students |
| Avg reg class size | 20-29 students |

### MOST POPULAR MAJORS
communication
marketing
finance

## STUDENTS SPEAK OUT

### Academics

The University of Dayton is one of the nation's 10 largest Catholic universities and Ohio's largest private university, with an enrollment of about 6,500 full-time undergraduates. Students say UD is "the perfect size"—"not too big" and "not too small." Like many Catholic schools, Dayton has a broad set of general education courses. It also offers a challenging University Scholars Program, which offers enrollees special classes, seminars, and symposiums, and an even more rigorous honors program. "Classes are stressful" here, but they are generally small ("very rarely over 30–35 students per session"), and the "energized" and "generally dedicated" professors are "for the most part, outstanding." "I have one professor who, after giving us his phone number, told us, 'call me, call me, call me if you need help, just not on Sunday nights at 10:00 P.M. because that's when *X-Files* is on," claims a math major. "Some profs wear the same outfit every day, but they all seem to have the students as their first priority." Students tell us that "the opportunities here are immense" as well, even though "classes are kind of hard to get into," and registration can be "a horrible experience." Overall, though, UD students aren't complaining. "This is a university predicated on providing students with a quality education," sums up a junior, "while at the same time providing many opportunities to form great friendships with other students and strengthen their faith."

### Life

"There is something to be involved in on campus every day of the week," according to a sophomore at UD. With everything from "guest speakers to service club meetings to intramural games during the week, and movies, retreats, and fun parties on the weekends, there is no excuse for having nothing to do." Nightlife "is especially fun" at UD, even if it is "pretty much limited to house parties and a few bars." Despite a "strict" alcohol policy, "kegs are all over and free, too." The "student neighborhood"—affectionately called "The Ghetto"—"which consists of houses owned by the University, is a place like no other" and a big hit with students. "On weekends," says a junior," you can wander from house to house, following the party, no invitation needed." University-wide functions for "Halloween, St. Patty's Day, and Homecoming" are "tons of fun" as well, and they are "widely" attended. In addition to the hopping party scene, "Christian ideology" and Catholic spirituality "radiate throughout campus." Dayton has one of the largest campus ministries in the country, and "service trips, retreats, and campus Mass" are popular and well attended. Beyond campus, though the city of Dayton isn't much to write home about, nearby metropolises include Cincinnati, Columbus, and Indianapolis. The campus facilities are mostly acceptable, but UD has "a shack for a gym." "My high school has better facilities than UD's rec center," gripes a senior. Perhaps ESPN superstar anchor and UD alumnus Dan Patrick will pull some strings in this regard.

### Student Body

One word to describe "the highly involved" students on this campus is "friendly," according to a UD sophomore. "We party together often and non-selectively." Other words to describe the "fun, easygoing, accepting, and caring" students here include "very outgoing," "unique, and funny." Dayton students are also "service-oriented" and "very well-rounded," and they "balance academics, service, worship, and partying quite well." On the whole, UD is a "huge community," and there is a reportedly a "close-knit family atmosphere" on campus despite "barriers (not visible of course) between social and ethnic groups." Though there are "many people" on UD's campus who are "relatively wealthy," and the student population is largely white, students say that UD is "working hard on improving diversity.

FINANCIAL AID: 937-229-4311 • E-MAIL: ADMISSION@UDAYTON.EDU • WEBSITE: WWW.UDAYTON.EDU

## ADMISSIONS

*Very important* academic and nonacademic factors considered by the admissions committee include secondary school record. *Important* factors considered include class rank and standardized test scores. *Other* factors considered include alumni/ae relation, character/personal qualities, essays, interview, minority status, talent/ability, volunteer work, and work experience. Factors *not* considered include geography, religious affiliation/commitment, and state residency. SAT I or ACT required. TOEFL required of all international applicants. High school diploma is required and GED is accepted. *High school units required/recommended:* 16 total recommended; 4 English recommended, 3 math recommended, 2 science recommended, 4 foreign language recommended, 3 social studies recommended. Two units of foreign language are required for admission to the College of Arts and Sciences. *The admissions office says:* "All applications are reviewed individually with attention given to ALL areas—grades, rank, scores, curriculum, activities, personal statement, recommendations, and counselor feedback. All visitors are given the opportunity for an individual admission interview."

### The Inside Word

While Dayton reviews all applicants individually in regard to their potential for success at the university, its high admit rate means that there's little for all but the weakest applicants to worry about concerning admission.

## FINANCIAL AID

*Students should submit:* FAFSA. The Princeton Review suggests that all financial aid forms be submitted as soon as possible after January 1. *Need-based scholarships/grants offered:* Pell, SEOG, state scholarships/grants, private scholarships, and the school's own gift aid. *Loan aid offered:* FFEL Subsidized Stafford, FFEL Unsubsidized Stafford, FFEL PLUS, Federal Perkins, state, and college/university loans from institutional funds. Institutional employment available. Federal Work-Study Program available. Applicants will be notified of awards on a rolling basis beginning on or about February 20. Off-campus job opportunities are good.

## FROM THE ADMISSIONS OFFICE

"The University of Dayton is respected as one of the nation's leading Catholic universities. We offer the resources and diversity of a comprehensive university and the attention and accessibility of a small college. All university-owned housing is fully wired for direct high-speed connection to the Internet as well as our 78-channel cable system. The technology-enhanced learning and student computer initiative ensures students use of the tools that will prepare them for a technology-dependent workplace. Our programs of study, impressive 110-acre campus, advanced research facilities, NCAA Division I intercollegiate athletics, and international alumni network are big-school advantages. Small class sizes, undergraduate emphasis, student-centered faculty and staff, residential campus life, and friendliness are all attractive small-school qualities. The University of Dayton is committed to student success. Our educational mission is to recognize the talents you bring as an individual and help you reach your potential."

### ADMISSIONS

| | |
|---|---|
| Admissions Rating | 77 |
| # of applicants | 7,494 |
| % of applicants accepted | 79 |
| % of acceptees attending | 30 |
| # accepting a place on wait list | 113 |
| % admitted from wait list | 51 |

#### FRESHMAN PROFILE

| | |
|---|---|
| Range SAT Verbal | 510-610 |
| Average SAT Verbal | 563 |
| Range SAT Math | 520-640 |
| Average SAT Math | 584 |
| Range ACT Composite | 22-28 |
| Average ACT Composite | 25 |
| Minimum TOEFL | 523 |
| % graduated top 10% of class | 22 |
| % graduated top 25% of class | 48 |
| % graduated top 50% of class | 78 |

#### DEADLINES

| | |
|---|---|
| Priority admission deadline | 1/1 |
| Nonfall registration? | yes |

#### APPLICANTS ALSO LOOK AT
**AND OFTEN PREFER**
Miami U.
Notre Dame
**AND SOMETIMES PREFER**
Ohio U.
Ohio State U.—Columbus
Purdue U.—West Lafayette
Indiana U.—Bloomington
**AND RARELY PREFER**
Xavier (OH)
Marquette
John Carroll

### FINANCIAL FACTS

| | |
|---|---|
| Financial Aid Rating | 81 |
| Tuition | $16,320 |
| Room & board | $5,280 |
| Books and supplies | $600 |
| Required fees | $530 |
| % frosh receiving aid | 58 |
| % undergrads receiving aid | 55 |
| Avg frosh grant | $6,632 |
| Avg frosh loan | $4,579 |

# UNIVERSITY OF DELAWARE

116 HULLIHEN HALL, NEWARK, DE 19716 • ADMISSIONS: 302-831-8123 • FAX: 302-831-6905

## CAMPUS LIFE

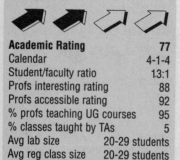

| Quality of Life Rating | 82 |
| --- | --- |
| Type of school | public |
| Affiliation | none |
| Environment | suburban |

### STUDENTS

| | |
| --- | --- |
| Total undergrad enrollment | 17,314 |
| % male/female | 41/59 |
| % from out of state | 59 |
| % from public high school | 80 |
| % live on campus | 53 |
| % in (# of) fraternities | 15 (20) |
| % in (# of) sororities | 15 (14) |
| % African American | 6 |
| % Asian | 3 |
| % Caucasian | 88 |
| % Hispanic | 3 |
| % international | 1 |
| # of countries represented | 100 |

### SURVEY SAYS . . .

Frats and sororities dominate social scene
Class discussions are rare
Hard liquor is popular
(Almost) everyone smokes
Great library
Large classes
Campus difficult to get around
Student government is unpopular
Dorms are like dungeons
Lots of TAs teach upper-level courses

## ACADEMICS

| Academic Rating | 77 |
| --- | --- |
| Calendar | 4-1-4 |
| Student/faculty ratio | 13:1 |
| Profs interesting rating | 88 |
| Profs accessible rating | 92 |
| % profs teaching UG courses | 95 |
| % classes taught by TAs | 5 |
| Avg lab size | 20-29 students |
| Avg reg class size | 20-29 students |

## STUDENTS SPEAK OUT

### Academics

Located at the very center of an urban corridor that stretches from New York City to Washington, D.C., the University of Delaware manages to provide its undergrads with a traditional university education and the opportunity to engage in a meaningful way in today's global society. Besides the old-school virtues of "a beautiful campus, strong academic reputation, and wonderful people," UD was one of the first universities to offer study abroad programs in 19 different countries (as one senior points out, "Who could pass up learning French in Martinique—or economics in Australia—during the winter?"). Additionally, besides being the recipient of a huge influx of funds during the last few years to upgrade their technological capabilities and connectivity, it's also one of the only schools in the country designated a land-grant, sea-grant, urban-grant, and space-grant institution. All that and professors who are "excellent, accessible" and remember students' names too? Yes, writes a junior, "especially when they sense you have a question or concern, or haven't completed an assignment." A top-notch, selective Honors Program and opportunities for undergraduate research "allow for a rigorous academic career," notes one upperclassman—so do the "demanding but fun" classes. And though there are some complaints about "poor teaching style" and an administration that cares more about prospective, rather than currently enrolled, students ("All the construction makes it hard to drive around!" gripes a junior), undergrads realize that the school's many excellent resources, a fairly good financial aid program, and an administration and faculty that are "genuinely interested in students" generally make for a "positive" university experience.

### Life

A UD sophomore waxes philosophical: "Life at the University of Delaware is just that, life! There are tough times and easy times, and all along the way you have so many avenues of help available." In keeping with their take on academics, UD students seem to favor a positive approach to life on this large, "fun," and always interesting college campus. "There is always something to do," claims a junior. Whether it be partying at one of the many different schools that make up the university, going to see an a capella concert, a student play, or an athletic event, or just hanging out at one of the local watering holes, undergrads seem to agree that at UD "there's too much to do and not enough time to do it." (Even "seasonal events like hayrides" get a mention.) As for partying, though one senior makes the case that "instead of using the school to broaden their horizons and think, students use it to get drunk every weekend," another points out that at UD, "you have plenty of options if drinking is not your thing." Newark is a "nice, small" town, after all, and if that's not enough, well, there's always a hayride.

### Student Body

"Extremely friendly" peeps who "say 'hi' just because they're crossing the street towards each other" are just one reason why students love UD. Its "warm environment" and "easygoing atmosphere" are a couple more. "The overall student body is a very accepting group of individuals," adds a sophomore. "It makes such a large school more welcoming and inviting." Some would argue that these "individuals" are really one big "white, Abercrombie, upper-middle-class yuppie." Of course, on a campus that some students feel is slowly becoming more and more Greek, there is the sense that many students are apolitical, self-segregated, and a tad "stuck up." Notes a self-identified "left-wing" senior, "I like my friends, but it took me a while to find progressive activist students on a conservative, apathetic campus like this one."

FINANCIAL AID: 302-831-8761 • E-MAIL: ADMISSIONS@UDEL.EDU • WEBSITE: WWW.UDEL.EDU / VIEWBOOK

## ADMISSIONS

SAT I or ACT required; SAT II recommended. TOEFL required of all international applicants. High school diploma is required and GED is accepted. *High school units required/recommended:* 16 total required; 4 English required, 4 math recommended, 3 science recommended, 2 science lab recommended, 2 foreign language recommended, 3 social studies required. *The admissions office says:* "[In our admissions process] the academic record is weighted more than SATs. A minimum SAT score is not used. Students can be admitted directly to most majors. Engineering, business, and science majors are more competitive."

### The Inside Word

Most students applying to Delaware face a moderately selective admissions process focused mainly on grades and tests with some focus on nonacademic characteristics. Those who seek to enter the university's honors program need to be far more thorough in completing their applications and much better prepared academically in order to gain admission. The honors program has high expectations; from what we know, it appears to be well worth it.

## FINANCIAL AID

The Princeton Review suggests that all financial aid forms be submitted as soon as possible after January 1. *Need-based scholarships/grants offered:* Pell, SEOG, state scholarships/grants, private scholarships, the school's own gift aid, Federal Nursing. *Loan aid offered:* FFEL Subsidized Stafford, FFEL Unsubsidized Stafford, FFEL PLUS, Federal Perkins, and Federal Nursing. Institutional employment available. Federal Work-Study Program available. Off-campus job opportunities are good.

## FROM THE ADMISSIONS OFFICE

"The University of Delaware is a major research university in the nation with a long-standing commitment to teaching and servicing undergraduates. It is one of only a few in the country designated as a land-grant, sea-grant, urban-grant, and space-grant institution. The university received the 1994 CAUSE Award for Excellence in Campus Networking for its use of a campus-wide network to enhance teaching, learning, research, administration, and community service. The University of Delaware offers the wide range of majors and course offerings expected of a university, but in spirit remains a small place where you can interact with your professors and feel at home. The beautiful green campus is ideally located at the very center of the East Coast 'megacity' that stretches from New York City to Washington, D.C. Faculty invite students to participate in their research and scholarship and are especially encouraging to those who want to engage in learning beyond the classroom."

## ADMISSIONS

| | |
|---|---|
| Admissions Rating | 82 |
| # of applicants | 18,165 |
| % of applicants accepted | 49 |
| % of acceptees attending | 36 |
| # accepting a place on wait list | 932 |
| % admitted from wait list | 49 |
| # of early decision applicants | 901 |
| % accepted early decision | 39 |

### FRESHMAN PROFILE

| | |
|---|---|
| Range SAT Verbal | 520-620 |
| Average SAT Verbal | 570 |
| Range SAT Math | 520-640 |
| Average SAT Math | 580 |
| Range ACT Composite | 21-27 |
| Minimum TOEFL | 550 |
| Average HS GPA | 3.5 |
| % graduated top 10% of class | 30 |
| % graduated top 25% of class | 69 |
| % graduated top 50% of class | 95 |

### DEADLINES

| | |
|---|---|
| Early decision | 11/15 |
| Early decision notification | 12/15 |
| Priority admission deadline | 1/15 |
| Regular admission | 2/15 |
| Nonfall registration? | yes |

### APPLICANTS ALSO LOOK AT

**AND OFTEN PREFER**
U. Virginia

**AND SOMETIMES PREFER**
U. Conn.
U. Richmond
Virginia Tech
U. Vermont

**AND RARELY PREFER**
Penn State—Univ. Park
U. Maryland—Coll. Park
Rutgers U.

### FINANCIAL FACTS

| | |
|---|---|
| Financial Aid Rating | 74 |
| In-state tuition | $4,511 |
| Out-of-state tuition | $13,260 |
| Room & board | $5,312 |
| Books and supplies | $800 |
| Required fees | $482 |
| % frosh receiving aid | 36 |
| % undergrads receiving aid | 36 |
| Avg frosh grant | $4,700 |
| Avg frosh loan | $3,500 |

# UNIVERSITY OF DENVER

UNIVERSITY HALL, ROOM 155, 2199 S. UNIVERSITY BLVD., DENVER, CO 80208 • ADMISSIONS: 303-871-2036 • FAX: 303-871-3301

## CAMPUS LIFE

**Quality of Life Rating**    **80**
Type of school    private
Affiliation    Methodist
Environment    suburban

### STUDENTS
Total undergrad enrollment    3,809
% male/female    42/58
% from out of state    56
% live on campus    41
% in (# of) fraternities    15 (9)
% in (# of) sororities    10 (4)
% African American    4
% Asian    5
% Caucasian    81
% Hispanic    6
% Native American    1
% international    6

### SURVEY SAYS . . .
Theater is hot
Frats and sororities dominate social scene
Students love Denver, CO
Student publications are ignored
Unattractive campus
Political activism is (almost) nonexistent

## ACADEMICS

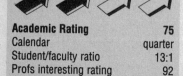

**Academic Rating**    **75**
Calendar    quarter
Student/faculty ratio    13:1
Profs interesting rating    92
Profs accessible rating    93
Avg lab size    10-19 students
Avg reg class size    10-19 students

### MOST POPULAR MAJORS
biology
communication
psychology

## STUDENTS SPEAK OUT

### Academics

Known for its business, mass communications, public relations, and digital media programs ("The Daniels College of Business is an excellent new academic facility"), DU is no slouch academically, though at least one student complains that sometimes "it seems that Denver University is more of a business than a school." This sentiment is echoed in a sophomore's claim that DU "needs more majors," and another's that "arts and humanities need to be treated equally with business." With an administration that's "always available" and "seems to care about students and their success," however, it looks like DU is "definitely becoming more focused on academics"—a welcome sign for those who are interested in seeing the school deepen its traditional liberal arts curriculum. Still, many DU students like its "professionalism," and there are few complaints about classes like "Communication & Popular Culture" and "Human Sexuality." One junior remarks, "I love DU because I always have fun stories about classes to tell my friends back home." Professors are the real gem at the University of Denver; almost across the board, students praise the school's small class sizes, personal attention, and devoted faculty. Writes one sophomore, "My honors courses have all been great, offering me material I never could get anywhere else. How was I to know that during the Black Plague all they thought about was sex?" Of course, there's always a cynic. Comments one senior, "There are enough unmotivated students that don't care about school that the teachers have plenty of time and enthusiasm for those who care." But, hey, when the reigning feeling about the school is that it is "a great academic experience which also guarantees a great time," who's complaining?

### Life

Writes one junior: "DU is the perfect size. It is big enough to offer diversity yet small enough to foster connectedness." A sense of community is clearly important for most DU undergrads, many of whom join the school's flourishing Greek system. "People who are in Greek houses are the most involved," states a sophomore, and there does seem to be a sense amongst the student body that the school could "offer more to non-Greeks." One rather blunt junior describes campus life this way: "Most people don't think much and go to frat parties and get wasted for fun," while another says pretty much the same thing in just three words: "Greek is awesome!" Alternatives? "The best skiing in the country right out the back door" and the obvious draw of Denver, Colorado's biggest city, "which provides a variety of recreational activities," writes a sophomore. Another sings the town's praises by saying, "Being in Denver is great—downtown for clubs, bars, shopping, food. And being in an industrial city is wonderful: internships, jobs, opportunities." Overall, concludes a junior, "There is always something to do and usually people to do it with."

### Student Body

Denver prides itself on a certain brand of individuality; notes a first year: "The students at DU all appear the same on the outside but are anything but the same when you get to know them." One student might be a mom raising a two-year-old while taking classes full time, while another might be one of the school's many international students at DU to study business or management. Writes a junior, "Students at DU are pretty accepting and open-minded. I get along and we get along with each other." And while the school has been accused of being "cliquey" and "comprised of mostly overprivileged rich kids," the majority of the student body are "great friends," writes a sophomore. With a beautiful campus and the mountains an hour-and-a-half away, it shouldn't come as a surprise that "most of the people at DU are pretty laid back and easygoing." And, writes a senior, they're "all smiles." With all that snow and those pearly whites gleaming, just be sure to pack your shades.

# UNIVERSITY OF DENVER

FINANCIAL AID: 303-871-2681 • E-MAIL: ADMISSION@DU.EDU • WEBSITE: WWW.DU.EDU

## ADMISSIONS

*Very important* academic and nonacademic factors considered by the admissions committee include recommendations and secondary school record. *Important* factors considered include character/personal qualities, class rank, essays, extracurricular activities, interview, standardized test scores, and talent/ability. *Other* factors considered include alumni/ae relation, geography, minority status, volunteer work, and work experience. Factors *not* considered include religious affiliation/commitment and state residency. SAT I or ACT required. TOEFL required of all international applicants. High school diploma is required and GED is accepted. *High school units required/recommended:* 15 total required; 4 English required, 2 math required, 3 science required, 1 science lab required, 2 foreign language required, 1 history required, 4 elective required. *The admissions office says:* "The committee on admissions selects students whose backgrounds show that enrollment at the University of Denver will be mutually rewarding. In selecting the freshman class, the committee on admissions considers all available information, including evidence of academic maturity and independence, general contributions to the school and the community, extracurricular activities, and leadership."

### The Inside Word

Any good student will find getting admitted to Denver to be a fairly straightforward process.

## FINANCIAL AID

*Students should submit:* FAFSA. The Princeton Review suggests that all financial aid forms be submitted as soon as possible after January 1. *Need-based scholarships/grants offered:* Pell, SEOG, state scholarships/grants, private scholarships, and the school's own gift aid. *Loan aid offered:* Direct Subsidized Stafford, Direct Unsubsidized Stafford, Direct PLUS, FFEL Subsidized Stafford, FFEL Unsubsidized Stafford, FFEL PLUS, Federal Perkins, and college/university loans from institutional funds. Institutional employment available. Federal Work-Study Program available. Applicants will be notified of awards on or about April 1. Off-campus job opportunities are excellent.

## FROM THE ADMISSIONS OFFICE

"The University of Denver is the oldest independent university in the Rocky Mountain region, founded in 1864 before Colorado became a state. The 125-acre University Park campus is located in a residential neighborhood eight miles southeast of downtown Denver. Reflecting the school mascot, our students tend to be pioneers—congenial, determined, daring individualists with a passion for living and learning. Like the old West pioneers, our students journey from all 50 states and more than 92 countries. That pioneering spirit extends to our academic programs, which begin with a core curriculum recognized for its excellence by the National Endowment for the Humanities. And our students benefit from a new Partners in Scholarship program that offers research grants to undergraduates. The living community includes special residence hall floors focusing on wellness, leadership, honors, and international interests. Denver is a great place to study and launch a career. Denver's robust economy—diversified by tourism, high technology, telecommunications, and government—continues to defy national trends. That's good news for university alumni, half of whom stay in the region to live and work after graduation."

## ADMISSIONS

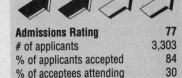

| | |
|---|---|
| **Admissions Rating** | 77 |
| # of applicants | 3,303 |
| % of applicants accepted | 84 |
| % of acceptees attending | 30 |

### FRESHMAN PROFILE

| | |
|---|---|
| Range SAT Verbal | 510-610 |
| Average SAT Verbal | 555 |
| Range SAT Math | 500-610 |
| Average SAT Math | 569 |
| Range ACT Composite | 21-27 |
| Average ACT Composite | 24 |
| Minimum TOEFL | 500 |
| Average HS GPA | 3.4 |
| % graduated top 10% of class | 32 |
| % graduated top 25% of class | 57 |
| % graduated top 50% of class | 85 |

### DEADLINES

| | |
|---|---|
| Nonfall registration? | yes |

### APPLICANTS ALSO LOOK AT
### AND OFTEN PREFER
U. Colorado—Boulder
### AND SOMETIMES PREFER
U. Puget Sound
U. Vermont

### FINANCIAL FACTS

| | |
|---|---|
| **Financial Aid Rating** | 77 |
| Tuition | $18,936 |
| Room & board | $6,165 |
| Required fees | $504 |
| % frosh receiving aid | 52 |
| % undergrads receiving aid | 53 |
| Avg frosh grant | $9,800 |
| Avg frosh loan | $6,500 |

# UNIVERSITY OF FLORIDA

PO Box 114000, 201 Criser Hall, Gainesville, FL 32611-4000 • Admissions: 352-392-1365 • Fax: 352-392-3987

## CAMPUS LIFE

| Quality of Life Rating | 81 |
|---|---|
| Type of school | public |
| Affiliation | none |
| Environment | suburban |

### STUDENTS

| | |
|---|---|
| Total undergrad enrollment | 32,680 |
| % male/female | 47/53 |
| % from out of state | 5 |
| % live on campus | 21 |
| % in (# of) fraternities | 15 (29) |
| % in (# of) sororities | 15 (18) |
| % African American | 8 |
| % Asian | 7 |
| % Caucasian | 73 |
| % Hispanic | 11 |
| % Native American | 1 |
| % international | 1 |

### SURVEY SAYS . . .

Frats and sororities dominate social scene
Everyone loves the Gators
Athletic facilities are great
(Almost) everyone plays intramural sports
Hard liquor is popular
Large classes
Ethnic diversity on campus
Student publications are popular
Campus difficult to get around
Dorms are like dungeons

## ACADEMICS

| Academic Rating | 80 |
|---|---|
| Calendar | semester |
| Student/faculty ratio | 22:1 |
| Profs interesting rating | 88 |
| Profs accessible rating | 90 |
| Avg lab size | 10-19 students |
| Avg reg class size | 20-29 students |

### MOST POPULAR MAJORS
psychology
finance
business administration
and management

## STUDENTS SPEAK OUT

### Academics

University of Florida is regarded by many as the best public university in Florida. Accordingly, in-state students (who are also attracted to Gainesville by the low tuition) abound. Students report that the quality of professors varies dramatically from department to department and even within departments. However, some students don't entirely blame the professors. "Professors tend to look down on their students (rightfully so, since no one here takes their education seriously) and seem to be going through the motions disinterestedly." Another student concurs: "Some professors have something stuck up their butts, but the majority are very good and most are very willing to help you outside of class." Some professors worry too much about the grading curve. The engineering, journalism, and business programs are the most highly regarded, as is the honors program. Unfortunately, the administration is not held in such high regard. "The administration might as well be on another planet; they ignore issues and deny problems by burying their heads in the sand of UF's athletic programs—the only thing that really matters on this campus. The administration's handling of diversity issues—everything from sexual orientation to race—is completely inadequate." Students laud the online registration process.

### Life

Life at UF revolves around sports—specifically, football and basketball—and partying. "A typical UF student's priorities are: beer, football, beer, parties, and beer." The football team is a perennial powerhouse, and the men's basketball team has gone deep into the NCAA Tournament several times over the past few years. Not surprisingly, school spirit runs deep. Homecoming and Gator Growl are very popular. One student says, "Life revolves around Gator football." Many students say that drinking is a "favorite pastime of many students" and that weed is a prevalent recreational drug. Students feel safe on campus, though they complain that they need more parking. Also, the campus bookstore is "overpriced." Students party from Wednesday to Saturday night, and though many consider Gainesville to be a "podunk town," there are plenty of clubs and bars. Also, the university provides a lake where students can sail, canoe, and Jet Ski for free. Students also love the university's proximity to the beach.

### Student Body

"Diverse describes UF," one student crows. According to another, "It's a mixed bag between really amazing people who work hard and have good direction . . . and the spoiled yuppie brats who don't know how lucky they are to be here and what life is all about beyond MTV." Students tend to be cliquey, which bothers many of their peers. "Remember that popular clique of football players and cheerleaders in high school? . . . Now picture an entire university populated by members of that clique." And while minority students say that there is little to no overt racism, one says, "The southern friendliness abounds at UF as long as you're white and middle-class." There is a "pretty strong institutional divide between Greeks and non-Greeks." In general, Gator pride brings these disparate groups together, and they all root for the home team on Saturday afternoons in the fall.

FINANCIAL AID: 352-392-1275 • E-MAIL: FRESHMAN@UFL.EDU • WEBSITE: WWW.UFL.EDU

## ADMISSIONS

*Very important* academic and nonacademic factors considered by the admissions committee include class rank, secondary school record, and standardized test scores. *Important* factors considered include recommendations. *Other* factors considered include alumni/ae relation, essays, geography, minority status, state residency, and talent/ability. Factors *not* considered include character/personal qualities, extracurricular activities, interview, religious affiliation/commitment, volunteer work, and work experience. SAT I or ACT required. High school diploma is required and GED is accepted. *High school units required/recommended:* 14 total required; 4 English required, 3 math required, 2 science required, 2 science lab required, 2 foreign language required, 3 social studies required.

### The Inside Word

Practically every other high school graduate in the state applies to UF, which gives the admissions staff a huge pool of candidates to choose from. The selection process is driven by numbers, with little personal attention afforded anyone but athletes, legacies, minorities, and National Merit Scholars. Out-of-state students will find that getting into this "party school" isn't at all easy. With budget cuts further restricting enrollment, it won't be long before admission to Florida is as difficult for out-of-staters as it is at such top public universities as North Carolina and Virginia.

## FINANCIAL AID

*Students should submit:* FAFSA. The Princeton Review suggests that all financial aid forms be submitted as soon as possible after January 1. *Need-based scholarships/grants offered:* Pell, SEOG, state scholarships/grants, private scholarships, and the school's own gift aid. *Loan aid offered:* Direct Subsidized Stafford, Direct Unsubsidized Stafford, Direct PLUS, Federal Perkins, and college/university loans from institutional funds. Institutional employment available. Federal Work-Study Program available. Applicants will be notified of awards on a rolling basis beginning on or about March 1. Off-campus job opportunities are fair.

## FROM THE ADMISSIONS OFFICE

"University of Florida students come from more than 100 countries, all 50 states, and every one of the 67 counties in Florida. Nineteen percent of the student body is comprised of graduate students. Approximately 2,300 African American students, 3,300 Hispanic students, and 2,200 Asian American students attend UF. Ninety percent of the entering freshmen rank above the national mean of scores on standard entrance exams. UF consistently ranks near the top among public universities in the number of new National Merit and Achievement scholars in attendance."

## ADMISSIONS

| | |
|---|---|
| Admissions Rating | 87 |
| # of applicants | 20,638 |
| % of applicants accepted | 63 |
| % of acceptees attending | 54 |
| # of early decision applicants | 1997 |
| % accepted early decision | 58 |

### FRESHMAN PROFILE

| | |
|---|---|
| Range SAT Verbal | 540-650 |
| Range SAT Math | 560-670 |
| Range ACT Composite | 24-29 |
| Average HS GPA | 3.4 |
| % graduated top 10% of class | 66 |
| % graduated top 25% of class | 89 |
| % graduated top 50% of class | 99 |

### DEADLINES

| | |
|---|---|
| Early decision | 10/13 |
| Early decision notification | 12/1 |
| Regular admission | 1/16 |
| Nonfall registration? | yes |

### APPLICANTS ALSO LOOK AT
**AND OFTEN PREFER**
Georgia Tech.
Tulane
Florida State
**AND SOMETIMES PREFER**
Clemson
West Virginia U.
U. South Florida
Florida A&M
**AND RARELY PREFER**
U. Miami
Howard

### FINANCIAL FACTS

| | |
|---|---|
| Financial Aid Rating | 78 |
| In-state tuition | $2,256 |
| Out-of-state tuition | $9,594 |
| Room & board | $5,440 |
| Books and supplies | $710 |
| % frosh receiving aid | 34 |
| % undergrads receiving aid | 46 |
| Avg frosh grant | $2,950 |
| Avg frosh loan | $3,190 |

# UNIVERSITY OF GEORGIA

Terrell Hall, Athens, GA 30602 • Admissions: 706-542-8776 • Fax: 706-542-1466

## CAMPUS LIFE

| Quality of Life Rating | 86 |
|---|---|
| Type of school | public |
| Affiliation | none |
| Environment | suburban |

### STUDENTS

| | |
|---|---|
| Total undergrad enrollment | 24,213 |
| % male/female | 44/56 |
| % from out of state | 10 |
| % from public high school | 87 |
| % live on campus | 18 |
| % in (# of) fraternities | 15 (25) |
| % in (# of) sororities | 18 (22) |
| % African American | 6 |
| % Asian | 3 |
| % Caucasian | 89 |
| % Hispanic | 1 |
| % international | 1 |

### SURVEY SAYS . . .

*Everyone loves the Bulldogs*
*Students love Athens, GA*
*Athletic facilities are great*
*Frats and sororities dominate social scene*
*Great food on campus*
*Large classes*
*Student publications are popular*
*Theater is unpopular*
*Student government is unpopular*
*Dorms are like dungeons*

## ACADEMICS

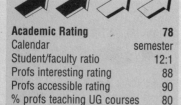

| Academic Rating | 78 |
|---|---|
| Calendar | semester |
| Student/faculty ratio | 12:1 |
| Profs interesting rating | 88 |
| Profs accessible rating | 90 |
| % profs teaching UG courses | 80 |
| % classes taught by TAs | 22 |
| Avg reg class size | 10-19 students |

### MOST POPULAR MAJORS
psychology
biology
pre-journalism

## STUDENTS SPEAK OUT

### Academics

Students seeking a "very good" education at a low cost should consider the University of Georgia. Though a large state school, the 2,000-member honors program is highly regarded. Some honors students believe that it is not as challenging as honors programs at other universities, but they still praise the professors and the small class sizes. They also note that registration is a breeze. The registration process for non-Honors students, however, needs improvement. "There are some fabulous professors in the English department," asserts on student. "I'll go to class even when there isn't an attendance policy." Professors get mixed reviews. One student says, "The professors are very smart, yet their teaching is average." Another notes that upper-level professors "rock," while lower-level professors are nowhere near as good. The major problem is that students often get "discouraged from the start" because the quality of professors in the lower-level classes is significantly lower than the quality of those professors who teach upper-level courses. Students praise the administration and say that the university runs smoothly, though they decry the lack of parking spaces and class availability.

### Life

Look up "college town" in a dictionary and you'll likely find Athens included somewhere in the definition. Its legendary music scene spawned the B-52s and REM, and the town's primary purpose is to cater to the 24,000 students who attend UGA. The town is chock full of terrific clubs, excellent restaurants, and fantastic coffeehouses. There are plenty of bars and pubs as well, and students call the college experience "great." The UGA football team is usually nationally ranked, and the recreational sports facility "is without equal." The other unifying force is the Greek system. Students admit that they party "a lot," but they also study a great deal. There are over 400 student groups, so most students have no problem finding something interesting and fun to do. Obviously, school spirit runs unchecked at UGA.

### Student Body

UGA students are very courteous and friendly once you get to know them. Though this is a bit of a daunting task at first, students find that they assimilate and make friends relatively quickly. "Most people don't socialize in class," points out one first-year. "You get to know people through clubs, Greek life, and stuff like that." Overall, most students get along, though some are not fond of the Greek system and complain, "the emphasis on Greek life and football are out of control." Still, "I have almost never had any problem of any kind with fellow students," a senior history major admits. Diversity is lacking—not surprising on a campus where nearly 90 percent of the students are Caucasian. One student sums up her peers at UGA: "The students here are mostly future-oriented. We like to have fun, but at the same time, we know when it's time to work."

FINANCIAL AID: 706-542-6147 • E-MAIL: UNDER2@ADMISSIONS.UGA.EDU • WEBSITE: WWW.UGA.EDU

## ADMISSIONS

*Very important* academic and nonacademic factors considered by the admissions committee include secondary school record and standardized test scores. *Other* factors considered include essays, extracurricular activities, geography, interview, state residency, talent/ability, volunteer work, and work experience. Factors *not* considered include class rank and religious affiliation/commitment. SAT I or ACT required; SAT II recommended. TOEFL required of all international applicants. High school diploma is required and GED is accepted. *High school units required/recommended:* 20 total recommended; 4 English recommended, 4 math recommended, 3 science recommended, 2 foreign language recommended, 3 social studies recommended, and 4 academic electives.

### The Inside Word

UGA is one of the more popular choices among southern college-bound students. The admissions process is very straightforward, but few large universities have as much success as Georgia in converting admits to enrollees, which makes candidate evaluation fairly selective. So does the fantastically successful Hope Scholarship Program for Georgia residents, now being emulated throughout the United States. Since student satisfaction and interest in the university show no sign of a decline any time soon, look for circumstances to remain the same for the foreseeable future.

## FINANCIAL AID

*Students should submit:* FAFSA. Regular filing deadline is August 1. The Princeton Review suggests that all financial aid forms be submitted as soon as possible after January 1. *Need-based scholarships/grants offered:* Pell, SEOG, state scholarships/grants, private scholarships, and the school's own gift aid. *Loan aid offered:* Direct Subsidized Stafford, Direct Unsubsidized Stafford, Direct PLUS, Federal Perkins, and college/university loans from institutional funds. Institutional employment available. Federal Work-Study Program available. Applicants will be notified of awards on a rolling basis. Off-campus job opportunities are good.

## FROM THE ADMISSIONS OFFICE

"The University of Georgia is a large but friendly campus community in a vibrant but easy-going college town. To more completely understand the wealth of academic and student life possibilities, most prospective students and their families make a visit to Athens, a 90-minute shuttle-van drive northeast of the Atlanta airport. Contact our Visitors Center for tour information and reservations. Contact the admissions office about scheduled weekday information sessions with admission counselors and to receive admissions materials. Applicants for freshman admission should apply early in their senior year. The application for admission also serves as a beginning application for Honors Program membership, merit scholarships, and Regents Waivers of out-of-state tuition, all highly competitive processes."

## ADMISSIONS

| | |
|---|---|
| Admissions Rating | 84 |
| # of applicants | 13,393 |
| % of applicants accepted | 62 |
| % of acceptees attending | 51 |

### FRESHMAN PROFILE

| | |
|---|---|
| Range SAT Verbal | 560-650 |
| Average SAT Verbal | 599 |
| Range SAT Math | 560-650 |
| Average SAT Math | 602 |
| Range ACT Composite | 24-29 |
| Minimum TOEFL | 550 |
| Average HS GPA | 3.6 |
| % graduated top 10% of class | 41 |
| % graduated top 25% of class | 78 |
| % graduated top 50% of class | 97 |

### DEADLINES

| | |
|---|---|
| Regular admission | 1/15 |
| Regular notification | 4/1 |
| Nonfall registration? | yes |

### APPLICANTS ALSO LOOK AT

**AND OFTEN PREFER**
Duke
UNC—Chapel Hill
Georgia Tech.

**AND SOMETIMES PREFER**
Emory
Florida State
U. South Carolina—Columbia
U. Tennessee—Knoxville
Furman

**AND RARELY PREFER**
Clemson
Georgia State
U. Florida

### FINANCIAL FACTS

| | |
|---|---|
| Financial Aid Rating | 84 |
| In-state tuition | $2,632 |
| Out-of-state tuition | $10,528 |
| Room & board | $5,080 |
| Books and supplies | $610 |
| Required fees | $786 |
| % frosh receiving aid | 28 |
| % undergrads receiving aid | 33 |

# UNIVERSITY OF HAWAII—MANOA

2600 CAMPUS ROAD, SSC ROOM 001, HONOLULU, HI 96822 • ADMISSIONS: 808-956-8975 • FAX: 808-956-4148

## CAMPUS LIFE

| | |
|---|---|
| **Quality of Life Rating** | **78** |
| Type of school | public |
| Affiliation | none |
| Environment | urban |

### STUDENTS

| | |
|---|---|
| Total undergrad enrollment | 11,721 |
| % male/female | 45/55 |
| % from out of state | 8 |
| % from public high school | 65 |
| % live on campus | 22 |
| % in (# of) fraternities | 1 (9) |
| % in (# of) sororities | 1 (6) |
| % African American | 1 |
| % Asian | 79 |
| % Caucasian | 18 |
| % Hispanic | 1 |
| % international | 5 |

### SURVEY SAYS . . .

Students love Honolulu, HI
Popular college radio
Musical organizations aren't popular
Class discussions are rare
Great off-campus food
Large classes
Ethnic diversity on campus
Unattractive campus
Political activism is (almost)
nonexistent
TAs teach lower level classes

## ACADEMICS

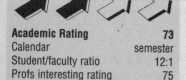

| | |
|---|---|
| **Academic Rating** | **73** |
| Calendar | semester |
| Student/faculty ratio | 12:1 |
| Profs interesting rating | 75 |
| Profs accessible rating | 74 |
| % classes taught by TAs | 7 |
| Avg lab size | 10-19 students |
| Avg reg class size | 10-19 students |

### MOST POPULAR MAJORS
information & computer sciences
psychology
biology

## STUDENTS SPEAK OUT

### Academics

Aloha! The affordable University of Hawaii at Manoa—the flagship campus of the University of Hawaii system—boasts a wide array of strong programs in international business and travel industry management. Its mid-Pacific location also offers unique opportunities for the study of Asian and Pacific cultures and the natural sciences—particularly marine science. The professors here are a mixed bag, though. While many are "friendly," "enthusiastic," "easily accessible, willing to help out," and "inspirational" even, "there is no passion in some teachers." According to students, "some" faculty members "are here just to get paid" and others "are rude and don't teach very well." Classes are often "too big" as well. On the plus side, "registration is super-easy and convenient." "You can be in Japan and still register over the phone or on the Web," beams one happily registered student. The "very professional and friendly staff" also receives praise, but bring a good book when you come to see them because lines are reportedly long, and the right person can be "hard to reach." Students at UHM also tell us they are also none too happy about "budget cuts" and the perpetually rising cost of tuition.

### Life

"Life is pretty good in general" at UHM where—as you might have guessed—"the weather is perfect year-round" and the campus is totally gorgeous. It all makes for "a really relaxing study environment." Volleyball and frequent trips to the beach are popular pastimes among the students. "For fun," students here also go to "movies, parties, clubs" and off-campus bars. "The campus apartments also seem to be pretty busy on Friday nights," and "a lot of drinking goes on" during the weekends. UHM is by no means a party school, though. A large percentage of UHM students are part timers who work full time in addition to attending school. "Many students work two or three jobs while attending college because it is so expensive," according to one. Not too surprisingly, these folks have little time to participate in the party scene. The school's largely nontraditional student body produces a campus social scene typical of many commuter schools: reasonably active during the week but somewhat dead on weekends.

### Student Body

"Aloha Spirit" is alive and well at UHM, where the students are "pretty laid back" and "easy to get along with." "Students are really cool to each other in and out of class," observes a sophomore. They are "very friendly and always willing to help." The campus community here is not particularly tight, though; people are simply too busy working and studying to spend a lot of time socializing. Also, while student diversity is tremendous here, students of various ethnicities "usually stick together" on this remarkably "multi-ethnic" campus. Most of the students are from "The Island," though, and many tell us they chose UHM because it is "close to home."

FINANCIAL AID: 808-956-7251 • E-MAIL: AR-INFO@HAWAII.EDU • WEBSITE: WWW.UHM.HAWAII.EDU

## ADMISSIONS

*Very important* academic and nonacademic factors considered by the admissions committee include secondary school record and standardized test scores. *Other* factors considered include essays. SAT I or ACT required, SAT I preferred. TOEFL required of all international applicants. High school diploma is required and GED is accepted. *High school units required/recommended:* 22 total required; 4 English required, 3 math required, 3 science required, 4 other college prep courses required, 3 social studies required.

### The Inside Word

A 2.8 high school GPA meets the University's minimum standards for admission; out-of-staters are required to have a 3.2. Though preference is given to state residents for admission, in practice there's room for just about any better-than-average student in the freshman class here.

## FINANCIAL AID

*Students should submit:* FAFSA. Priority filing deadline is March 1. The Princeton Review suggests that all financial aid forms be submitted as soon as possible after January 1. *Need-based scholarships/grants offered:* Pell, SEOG, state scholarships/grants, private scholarships, and the school's own gift aid. *Loan aid offered:* Direct Subsidized Stafford, Direct Unsubsidized Stafford, Direct PLUS, Federal Perkins, and the school's own loans. Institutional employment available. Federal Work-Study Program available. Applicants will be notified of awards on a rolling basis. Off-campus job opportunities are good.

### ADMISSIONS

| | |
|---|---|
| Admissions Rating | 80 |
| # of applicants | 4,584 |
| % of applicants accepted | 71 |
| % of acceptees attending | 47 |

#### FRESHMAN PROFILE

| | |
|---|---|
| Range SAT Verbal | 470-570 |
| Average SAT Verbal | 526 |
| Range SAT Math | 510-610 |
| Average SAT Math | 566 |
| Minimum TOEFL | 500 |
| Average HS GPA | 3.3 |
| % graduated top 10% of class | 30 |
| % graduated top 25% of class | 60 |
| % graduated top 50% of class | 91 |

#### DEADLINES

| | |
|---|---|
| Regular admission | 6/1 |
| Nonfall registration? | yes |

### FINANCIAL FACTS

| | |
|---|---|
| Financial Aid Rating | 82 |
| In-state tuition | $3,024 |
| Out-of-state tuition | $9,504 |
| Room & board | $4,933 |
| Books and supplies | $987 |
| Required fees | $133 |
| % frosh receiving aid | 30 |
| % undergrads receiving aid | 30 |
| Avg frosh grant | $2,651 |
| Avg frosh loan | $1,360 |

# UNIVERSITY OF IDAHO

UNIVERSITY OF IDAHO, ADMISSIONS OFFICE, MOSCOW, ID 83844-4264 • ADMISSIONS: 208-885-6326 • FAX: 208-885-9119

## CAMPUS LIFE

| | |
|---|---|
| **Quality of Life Rating** | **84** |
| Type of school | public |
| Affiliation | none |
| Environment | rural |

### STUDENTS

| | |
|---|---|
| Total undergrad enrollment | 8,759 |
| % male/female | 54/46 |
| % from out of state | 31 |
| % from public high school | 97 |
| % live on campus | 45 |
| % in (# of) fraternities | 28 (18) |
| % in (# of) sororities | 21 (8) |
| % African American | 1 |
| % Asian | 2 |
| % Caucasian | 86 |
| % Hispanic | 3 |
| % Native American | 1 |
| % international | 2 |

### SURVEY SAYS . . .

*Beautiful campus*
*Great library*
*Campus easy to get around*
*Athletic facilities are great*
*Campus feels safe*
*Student publications are ignored*
*Political activism is (almost) nonexistent*
*Students are cliquish*
*Students aren't religious*
*Lab facilities are great*

## ACADEMICS

| | |
|---|---|
| **Academic Rating** | **70** |
| Calendar | semester |
| Student/faculty ratio | 17:1 |
| Profs interesting rating | 72 |
| Profs accessible rating | 90 |
| % profs teaching UG courses | 70 |
| % classes taught by TAs | 20 |
| Avg reg class size | 10-19 students |

### MOST POPULAR MAJORS
elementary education
mechanical engineering
psychology

## STUDENTS SPEAK OUT
### Academics

One thing that students love about the "cheap and centrally located" University of Idaho is that it's "very wired for computers." They also love the fact that the campus "has a hometown quality to it." Classes are "small, especially in upper-division courses" as well, and the personalized atmosphere here more than makes up for whatever their school lacks in sheer immensity. UI boasts a "great" environmental sciences program, and the colleges of agriculture and engineering are very strong. Over 90 percent of senior engineers pass the "Fundamentals of Engineering Exam" on the first try to boot (the national rate is much lower). Want more solid programs? Check out business, education, and forestry. Professors at UI can be "opinionated," and some are "difficult to contact outside the classroom." There are "way too many teaching assistants who are not good instructors," too. Most actual professors are "readily available," though. "Teachers here seem to care about the students even though they constantly remind us how little they are paid," observes a junior. As for the "well-organized" administration, it "does what it promises."

### Life

"Outdoor recreation is a very important part of student life," explains a UI junior. "If you love the outdoors but don't really dig rednecks, Moscow is an excellent place" because "outdoor recreation options are almost endless." Students here regularly "mountain bike, backpack, hike, raft, rollerblade, snowboard," and go camping and skiing. Back on campus, rowdy frat parties are common as "Greeks dominate" social life. A popular bar scene keeps the over-21 crowd dancing and drinking as well, and the UI campus is home to "a lot of alcohol and drugs." Beyond keggers, bars, and the Great Outdoors, though, "there's not too much to do" in the "highly educated" college town of Moscow, a place "far away from city life" that primarily caters to its students and faculty. In fact, there is noticeable "animosity from the locals," and "getting the hell out of Dodge" is a priority for some students whenever they get the chance. If you like sports, athletics are definitely "emphasized" here. School spirit is high and support for athletics is intense. The university has an indoor football dome that can get packed for games. Women's volleyball games are also popular—especially the ones against Washington State. Finally, a tradition at Idaho is "Hello Walk," a shaded walkway on which everyone reportedly says "hello" to you, and you say "hello" to everybody you walk past.

### Student Body

The "easily approachable and very friendly" students at the University of Idaho see themselves as "welcoming," individualistic, and "health-conscious." These "relaxed" and "laid-back" students are "pretty mellow" folks who "take things in stride." Politically, "there is a great diversity" on campus. You've got everything from "hard-core leftwingers to Rush Limbaughists." UI "needs to be more ethnically diverse," though. Just about everybody here is white. Students also deride the "adversity" between members of fraternities and sororities and students who choose not to pledge. Many blame the Greeks, who "tend to have an air about them." Most of UI's students hail from the West and Pacific Northwest (Idaho, Washington, Oregon, California, Alaska, Montana, and Nevada, to be specific). A good percentage comes from "rural" communities.

FINANCIAL AID: 208-885-6312 • E-MAIL: NSS@UIDAHO.EDU • WEBSITE: WWW.ITSUIDAHO.EDU/UIHOME/

## ADMISSIONS

*Very important* academic and nonacademic factors considered by the admissions committee include class rank and secondary school record. *Important* factors considered include standardized test scores. Factors *not* considered include interview, minority status, and religious affiliation/commitment. SAT I or ACT required. TOEFL required of all international applicants. High school diploma is required and GED is accepted. *High school units required/recommended:* 16 total required; 4 English required, 3 math required, 2 science required, 1 science lab required, 2 foreign language required, 3 social studies required, 1 elective required.

### The Inside Word

Idaho's admissions process is typical of large universities and easy to deal with—it doesn't get any more straightforward than this. A small number of college-age students in Idaho means out-of-staters face little in the way of any constraints above and beyond in-state standards.

## FINANCIAL AID

*Students should submit:* FAFSA and institution's own financial aid form. The Princeton Review suggests that all financial aid forms be submitted as soon as possible after January 1. *Need-based scholarships/grants offered:* Pell, SEOG, state scholarships/grants, private scholarships, and the school's own gift aid. *Loan aid offered:* Direct Subsidized Stafford, Direct Unsubsidized Stafford, Direct PLUS, Federal Perkins, and college/university loans from institutional funds. Institutional employment available. Federal Work-Study Program available. Applicants will be notified of awards on a rolling basis beginning on or about April 1. Off-campus job opportunities are good.

## FROM THE ADMISSIONS OFFICE

"The University of Idaho combines the best of both worlds. We are the major research university in the state of Idaho, the state's land grant university, and a safe, residential environment. Moscow's small size and the supportive surrounding community provide the ideal atmosphere for a total learning experience."

## ADMISSIONS

| | |
|---|---|
| Admissions Rating | 73 |
| # of applicants | 3,606 |
| % of applicants accepted | 83 |
| % of acceptees attending | 52 |

### FRESHMAN PROFILE

| | |
|---|---|
| Range SAT Verbal | 480-610 |
| Average SAT Verbal | 549 |
| Range SAT Math | 490-630 |
| Average SAT Math | 559 |
| Range ACT Composite | 20-26 |
| Average ACT Composite | 23 |
| Minimum TOEFL | 525 |
| Average HS GPA | 3.4 |
| % graduated top 10% of class | 19 |
| % graduated top 25% of class | 47 |
| % graduated top 50% of class | 77 |

### DEADLINES

| | |
|---|---|
| Regular admission | 8/1 |
| Nonfall registration? | yes |

### APPLICANTS ALSO LOOK AT AND SOMETIMES PREFER

Boise State
Washington State

### FINANCIAL FACTS

| | |
|---|---|
| Financial Aid Rating | 76 |
| Out-of-state tuition | $6,000 |
| Room & board | $4,064 |
| Books and supplies | $1,076 |
| Required fees | $2,476 |

# UNIVERSITY OF ILLINOIS—URBANA-CHAMPAIGN

901 WEST ILLINOIS STREET, URBANA, IL 61801 • ADMISSIONS: 217-333-0302 • FAX: 217-333-9758

## CAMPUS LIFE

| | |
|---|---|
| **Quality of Life Rating** | **75** |
| Type of school | public |
| Affiliation | none |
| Environment | urban |

### STUDENTS

| | |
|---|---|
| Total undergrad enrollment | 27,908 |
| % male/female | 51/49 |
| % from out of state | 7 |
| % live on campus | 32 |
| % in (# of) fraternities | 17 (55) |
| % in (# of) sororities | 22 (30) |
| % African American | 7 |
| % Asian | 14 |
| % Caucasian | 72 |
| % Hispanic | 6 |
| % international | 2 |
| # of countries represented | 52 |

### SURVEY SAYS . . .

*Frats and sororities dominate social scene*
*Everyone loves the Fighting Illini*
*Lots of beer drinking*
*Ethnic diversity on campus*
*Student publications are popular*
*Students are cliquish*
*Students don't like Urbana, IL*
*Students are not very happy*
*Lousy food on campus*
*Very little drug use*

## ACADEMICS

| | |
|---|---|
| **Academic Rating** | **81** |
| Calendar | semester |
| Student/faculty ratio | 20:1 |
| Profs interesting rating | 87 |
| Profs accessible rating | 89 |
| % profs teaching UG courses | 89 |
| Avg lab size | 20-29 students |
| Avg reg class size | 20-29 students |

### MOST POPULAR MAJORS
biological sciences
psychology
electrical and computer engineering

## STUDENTS SPEAK OUT
### Academics

The University of Illinois—Urbana-Champaign is one of America's top research universities, the public flagship institution in a state noted for its excellent educational offerings. Though it's a great deal for out-of-state students, savvy Illinois residents grab most of the available spots, especially because it's "well known nationally" and "esteemed by corporations." The university's greatest strengths are its competitive engineering and business programs, but as is typical of most institutions of its size, there are many other fine programs. ("A few years ago, some computer science students here facilitated our obsession with the World Wide Web when they developed the Mosaic browser, the precursor to Netscape—which later made them very wealthy alums.") A good education is easily within reach for students who don't need to be led by the hand to find it. Some lecture classes can fit the Jumbo-U stereotype, but discussion sections are much smaller. There's "a lot to offer." As one student explains, "I came from a small town and was worried about this school's size, but I wouldn't be happier anywhere else. The possibilities are endless." U of Illinois boasts some of the most studious public university students in the country, perhaps because a major portion of the student body is made up of engineers. Students voice a common complaint we hear at many large schools with a focus on technical programs and research: the flaws of their TAs. "You're lucky if your TA speaks English," writes one disgruntled finance major.

### Life

At a university of this size, one rarely needs to leave campus for entertainment. Students have access to an unbelievable variety of "lectures, seminars, plays, performances, speakers, sports, and other presentations that are readily available for anyone interested." Parties at dorms and off-campus housing are frequent, and fraternities and sororities play a dominant role in the lives of many students at Illinois. "Socially, the university offers an extremely wide variety of . . . bars." Students ardently follow their Big 10 Conference athletic teams, the Fighting Illini—particularly in football and basketball. (An ongoing controversy centers on the team name and mascot, a Native American chief, which some perceive as offensive racial stereotypes.) Students needing a break from the campus scene can access an "excellent transportation system" that makes cars unnecessary for traveling off campus: "Both Champaign and Urbana are accessible with mass transit and offer decent shopping and dining." All in all, "it's about as good as you can have in an area that's completely surrounded by farms."

### Student Body

As one student writes, "For a public school, Illinois students are pretty affluent. Most are seeking a good job and family—the things they were given in their home life." Writes another, "Because this is a large [university], you will find a group to associate with, but you will also have the opportunity to meet people from very diverse backgrounds." Though some students report that their "fellow students are friendly and we all get along," both black and white students report that race relations can be acrimonious. One African American student writes that U of I is "a great school, but the student body and faculty need to be better educated about minorities and their cultures."

# UNIVERSITY OF ILLINOIS—URBANA-CHAMPAIGN

FINANCIAL AID: 217-333-0100 • E-MAIL: ADMISSIONS@OAR.UIUC.EDU • WEBSITE: WWW.UIUC.EDU

## ADMISSIONS

*Very important* academic and nonacademic factors considered by the admissions committee include class rank, secondary school record, and standardized test scores. *Important* factors considered include character/personal qualities, essays, extracurricular activities, interview, recommendations, and talent/ability. *Other* factors considered include alumni/ae relation, geography, minority status, volunteer work, and work experience. Factors *not* considered include religious affiliation/commitment and state residency. SAT I or ACT required. TOEFL required of all international applicants. High school diploma is required and GED is accepted. *High school units required/recommended:* 15 total required; 4 English required, 3 math required, 2 science required, 2 foreign language required, 2 social studies required, 2 elective required.

### The Inside Word

Few candidates are deceived by Illinois' relatively high acceptance rate; the university has a well-deserved reputation for expecting applicants to be strong students, and those who aren't usually don't bother to apply. Despite a jumbo applicant pool, the admissions office reports that every candidate is individually reviewed, which deserves mention as rare in universities of this size.

## FINANCIAL AID

*Students should submit:* FAFSA. Regular filing deadline is March 15. The Princeton Review suggests that all financial aid forms be submitted as soon as possible after January 1. *Need-based scholarships/grants offered:* Pell, SEOG, state scholarships/grants, private scholarships, and the school's own gift aid. *Loan aid offered:* Direct Subsidized Stafford, Direct Unsubsidized Stafford, Direct PLUS, Federal Perkins, and college/university loans from institutional funds. Institutional employment available. Federal Work-Study Program available. Applicants will be notified of awards on or about April 1. Off-campus job opportunities are excellent.

## FROM THE ADMISSIONS OFFICE

"The campus has been aptly described as a collection of neighborhoods constituting a diverse and vibrant city. The neighborhoods are of many types: students and faculty within a department; people sharing a room or house; the members of a professional organization, a service club, or an intramural team; or simply people who, starting out as strangers sharing a class or a study lounge or a fondness for a weekly film series, have become friends. And the city of this description is the university itself—a rich cosmopolitan environment constructed by students and faculty to meet their educational and personal goals. The quality of intellectual life parallels that of other great universities, and many faculty and students who have their choice of top institutions select Illinois over its peers. While such choices are based often on the quality of individual programs of study, another crucial factor is the 'tone' of the campus life that is linked with the virtues of midwestern culture. There is an informality and a near-absence of pretension which, coupled with a tradition of commitment to excellence, creates an atmosphere that is unique among the finest institutions."

## ADMISSIONS

| | |
|---|---|
| Admissions Rating | 85 |
| # of applicants | 18,805 |
| % of applicants accepted | 64 |
| % of acceptees attending | 51 |

### FRESHMAN PROFILE

| | |
|---|---|
| Range SAT Verbal | 550-650 |
| Average SAT Verbal | 608 |
| Range SAT Math | 590-700 |
| Average SAT Math | 652 |
| Range ACT Composite | 24-29 |
| Average ACT Composite | 27 |
| Minimum TOEFL | 550 |
| % graduated top 10% of class | 51 |
| % graduated top 25% of class | 85 |
| % graduated top 50% of class | 99 |

### DEADLINES

| | |
|---|---|
| Regular admission | 1/1 |
| Nonfall registration? | yes |

### APPLICANTS ALSO LOOK AT
**AND OFTEN PREFER**
Northwestern U.
U. Michigan—Ann Arbor
U. Wisconsin—Madison
Purdue
Washington U.
**AND SOMETIMES PREFER**
U. Michigan—Ann Arbor
Northern Illinois
Miami U.
**AND RARELY PREFER**
U. Kentucky
Loyola U. Chicago
Illinois State
Southern Illinois—Edwardsville

### FINANCIAL FACTS

| | |
|---|---|
| Financial Aid Rating | 73 |
| In-state tuition | $3,724 |
| Out-of-state tuition | $11,172 |
| Room & board | $5,844 |
| Books and supplies | $740 |
| Required fees | $1,304 |
| % frosh receiving aid | 38 |
| % undergrads receiving aid | 35 |

# UNIVERSITY OF IOWA

107 CALVIN HALL, IOWA CITY, IA 52242 • ADMISSIONS: 319-335-3847 • FAX: 319-333-1535

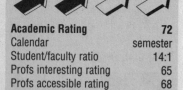
## STUDENTS SPEAK OUT

### Academics

The University of Iowa is a world-class public school that offers "up-to-date technology" and "an excellent education in a comfortable, friendly atmosphere." It is also "not so expensive for out-of-staters," which is good news for the thousands of "Chicago-area" refugees who arrive here annually. Iowa boasts nationally respected creative writing and journalism programs, "a great pharmacy college," and tremendous departments in English, film, and molecular biology. The social sciences are very strong as well, and liberal arts students must complete a massive battery of distribution requirements. The generally "fabulous" professors here are "usually very knowledgeable in their fields" and, for the most part, "easy to reach" and "eager to help." "Some even manage to make classes extremely enjoyable." However, as at any mega-university, there are some professors who "read straight from notes or books." The administrators seem to genuinely "like the students," and they are "down to earth and easily approachable," though "communication to undergraduates" about required courses is "messy and could be greatly improved." The main library could also use "a major facelift." Not everybody here is happy. "Whenever I see high school students touring the campus, I scream, 'Don't do it! Go to a private school,'" reveals a forlorn senior. The vast majority of the students here seem pretty satisfied, though. "I really love Iowa," counters another senior. "I am very pleased with my academic experience and would not trade it for the world."

### Life

The city planners in Iowa City must be very good at what they do. Either that, or they are pros at buying off survey-takers. Students tell us that Iowa City is the "Athens of the Midwest" and, as if that weren't enough, "the greatest college town in the nation." Without a doubt, "there's something for everyone" here; "downtown Iowa City has just about everything a college student needs." There are "live bands" every day and the Ped Mall—an area of shopping and culture closed to traffic—offers choice coffee shops, excellent shopping, and numerous ethnic eating establishments. On campus, there are tons of "cool lectures and films" and many concerts and theatrical productions. There's also "a good arts scene," competitive intramurals, and possibly the best college radio station in the country. Hawkeye sports enjoy "overwhelming" support. "Football is huge here," even though the team has been down lately. Basketball (both women's and men's) and the eternally highly ranked wrestling program are popular, too. Also, there are "many job opportunities on and off campus." To say the least, "life here is fast-paced." And we haven't even gotten to the "very good" nightlife. Frats are big at Iowa, but "life is dominated by the bar scene," perhaps because there are "20 to 25 bars and clubs in a four-block radius." Whatever the reason, it comes as no surprise that Iowa students say they consume massive quantities of beer and liquor. Students gripe that Iowa weather is always "too damn cold or hot" and the on-campus food "could definitely be improved."

### Student Body

"I couldn't have asked for a better group of people," claims a senior at Iowa. Students here tell us that "although the school is large," you "can still get to know many people." Reportedly, "interesting conversations" abound, even "with random people while waiting in line to use the bathroom." Students describe themselves as "pretty intelligent and academically oriented." They are "easygoing," "open-minded," and "really enthusiastic about getting involved," too. Virtually every political faction is represented here, but, on the whole, Iowa's campus is pretty liberal politically. These very career-minded students "tend to stick together in their social classes," especially the "stupid frat guys who all dress the same and major in business." Minority representation is regrettably low, especially for a public school.

FINANCIAL AID: 319-335-1450 • E-MAIL: ADMISSIONS@UIOWA.EDU • WEBSITE: WWW.UIOWA.EDU

## ADMISSIONS

*Very important* academic and nonacademic factors considered by the admissions committee include class rank, secondary school record, and standardized test scores. *Other* factors considered include alumni/ae relation, minority status, state residency, and talent/ability. Factors *not* considered include character/personal qualities, essays, extracurricular activities, geography, interview, recommendations, religious affiliation/commitment, volunteer work, and work experience. SAT I or ACT required. TOEFL required of all international applicants. High school diploma is required and GED is accepted. *High school units required/recommended:* 4 English required, 3 math required, 3 science required, 2 science lab required, 2 foreign language required, 3 social studies required.

### The Inside Word

Iowa's admissions process is none too personal, but on the other hand, candidates know exactly what is necessary to get admitted. The majority of applicants are fairly good students, most get in, and a lot choose to attend. That helps make Iowa the solid academic community it is.

## FINANCIAL AID

*Students should submit:* FAFSA and institution's own financial aid form. The Princeton Review suggests that all financial aid forms be submitted as soon as possible after January 1. *Need-based scholarships/grants offered:* Pell, SEOG, state scholarships/grants, private scholarships, the school's own gift aid, and Federal Nursing Scholarship. *Loan aid offered:* Direct Subsidized Stafford, Direct Unsubsidized Stafford, Direct PLUS, Federal Perkins, Federal Nursing, and college/university loans from institutional funds. Institutional employment available. Federal Work-Study Program available. Applicants will be notified of awards on a rolling basis beginning on or about March 1. Off-campus job opportunities are excellent.

## FROM THE ADMISSIONS OFFICE

"The University of Iowa has strong programs in the creative arts, being the home of the first Writers Workshop and now housing the world-renowned International Writing Program. It also has strong programs in communication studies, journalism, political science, English, and psychology, and was the birthplace of the discipline of speech pathology and audiology. It offers excellent programs in the basic health sciences and health care programs, led by the top-ranked College of Medicine and the closely associated University Hospitals and Clinics."

### ADMISSIONS

| | |
|---|---:|
| Admissions Rating | 79 |
| # of applicants | 11,013 |
| % of applicants accepted | 83 |
| % of acceptees attending | 41 |

#### FRESHMAN PROFILE

| | |
|---|---:|
| Range SAT Verbal | 520-640 |
| Range SAT Math | 530-660 |
| Range ACT Composite | 22-27 |
| Minimum TOEFL | 530 |
| Average HS GPA | 3.5 |
| % graduated top 10% of class | 20 |
| % graduated top 25% of class | 51 |
| % graduated top 50% of class | 90 |

#### DEADLINES

| | |
|---|---:|
| Regular admission | 5/15 |
| Nonfall registration? | yes |

#### APPLICANTS ALSO LOOK AT
##### AND OFTEN PREFER
Northwestern U.
U. Illinois—Urbana-Champaign
##### AND SOMETIMES PREFER
Iowa State
U. Northern Iowa
Indiana U.—Bloomington
Drake
Grinnell
##### AND RARELY PREFER
Illinois State
U. Wisconsin—Madison
Cornell Coll.
U. Missouri—Rolla

### FINANCIAL FACTS

| | |
|---|---:|
| Financial Aid Rating | 73 |
| In-state tuition | $3,116 |
| Out-of-state tuition | $11,544 |
| Room & board | $4,870 |
| Books and supplies | $840 |
| Required fees | $406 |
| % frosh receiving aid | 41 |
| % undergrads receiving aid | 41 |
| Avg frosh grant | $1,200 |
| Avg frosh loan | $2,000 |

# UNIVERSITY OF KANSAS

OFFICE OF AD. AND SCHOLARSHIPS, 1502 IOWA STREET, LAWRENCE, KS 66045 • ADMISSIONS: 785-864-3911 • FAX: 785-864-5006

## CAMPUS LIFE

**Quality of Life Rating**    **85**
Type of school    public
Affiliation    none
Environment    urban

### STUDENTS

| | |
|---|---|
| Total undergrad enrollment | 20,157 |
| % male/female | 47/53 |
| % from out of state | 24 |
| % live on campus | 19 |
| % in (# of) fraternities | 20 (28) |
| % in (# of) sororities | 20 (18) |
| % African American | 3 |
| % Asian | 4 |
| % Caucasian | 88 |
| % Hispanic | 2 |
| % Native American | 1 |
| % international | 3 |
| # of countries represented | 111 |

### SURVEY SAYS . . .

*Everyone loves the Jayhawks*
*Students love Lawrence, KS*
*Frats and sororities dominate social scene*
*Great off-campus food*
*Hard liquor is popular*
*Large classes*
*Registration is a pain*
*Student publications are popular*
*Theater is unpopular*
*Lab facilities are great*

## ACADEMICS

| | |
|---|---|
| **Academic Rating** | **73** |
| Calendar | semester |
| Student/faculty ratio | 14:1 |
| Profs interesting rating | 89 |
| Profs accessible rating | 91 |
| % profs teaching UG courses | 100 |
| % classes taught by TAs | 26 |
| Avg lab size | 10-19 students |
| Avg reg class size | 20-29 students |

### MOST POPULAR MAJORS
business
journalism
biological sciences

## STUDENTS SPEAK OUT

### Academics

The University of Kansas produces students satisfied with their education. Professors are always accessible. According to a biology major, "All professors have office hours and most offer workshops making them accessible to KU students." Professors are "usually at the top of their field," writes one music major. The key to being successful at KU, advises a sophomore, is to "take advantage of the resources available (i.e. TAs, libraries, instructors)." The professors make an excellent impression on first-year students; as one first-year architecture student gushes, "Every teacher I have had or met I want to chill with on the weekends, but sometimes it just doesn't work out." Dangit. While students like their professors, they are less enamored of the administration. Students also disparage KU's technology as a "joke," explaining, "We are the largest school in the state but the only one without online enrollment." Reports are mixed concerning the undergrad academic experience, as one student will gush, "Academically, the University of Kansas exceeded my expectations," while another will declare, "The University of Kansas will always be a good school for average kids from large midwestern cities."

### Life

"Lawrence is a rather alternative, obscure community, typical of a college town. The college students are the number one priority here." Students note that both the campus and the town are beautiful. A senior journalism major happily comments that "the town and university [are] very liberal and open-minded. Anyone is willing to hear you speak your mind as long as you can back it up." Students appreciate the different opportunities that life in Lawrence provides. "If you're going to stay in and do work, that's cool. If you're going to go to the bars, that's cool. If you're going to stay in and party, or go to a house party, everything is cool and fun to do." A sophomore sociology major adds that it isn't difficult to find a party in certain off-campus neighborhoods, as "you can walk down the party streets and smell the alcohol." Some believe that the city can be "a little boring" if one doesn't party. The university's basketball team is a perennial national powerhouse, and students wish that the football team would be as successful.

### Student Body

As would be expected of a large, state university in middle America, students at the University of Kansas are "typical Midwest: middle-class, friendly, laid-back, and white." Most students agree that the university needs more diversity, "both ethnically and from rural areas." There is little mixing between social groups. As one junior history major puts it, "Frat boys hang out with frat boys. Nader lovers hang out with earth-friendly types. Goths chill with goths. It's segregated but united by alcohol." Still, students agree that most of their classmates are "friendly and supportive." One first-year student testifies that his life has been altered by his classmates. "The people here are incredible. I was an edgy person when I came here, but everyone's so courteous that it changes you." A sophomore sums up life at the University of Kansas: "Everyone here is friendly. You can literally just say hi to someone on campus and they will be more than delighted to respond [in a] friendly [manner]."

FINANCIAL AID: 785-864-4700 • E-MAIL: ADM@KU.EDU • WEBSITE: WWW.KU.EDU

## ADMISSIONS

*Very important* academic and nonacademic factors considered by the admissions committee include secondary school record, standardized test scores, and class rank. *Important* factors include state residency and geography. *Other* factors considered include essays, recommendations, alumni/ae relation, character/personal qualities, extracurricular activities, minority status, talent/ability, volunteer work, and work experience. Factors *not* considered include interview and religious affiliation/commitment. SAT I or ACT required. High school diploma is required and GED is accepted. *High school units required/recommended:* 14 total required; 4 English required, 3 math required, 3 science required (1 should be lab), 3 social studies required, 1 computer technology required, 2 foreign language recommended. *The admissions office says:* "New admissions standards that apply to all prospective students went into effect with the fall 2001 entering class. Students are advised to exceed the course distribution requirements, particularly in mathematics."

### The Inside Word

A no-sweat approach to admissions. So who gets denied? Weak out-of-state candidates, who are apparently in large supply in the Kansas applicant pool. But in-state students will have to face the music with new admissions standards starting in 2001.

## FINANCIAL AID

*Students should submit:* FAFSA and state aid form. Regular filing deadline is March 1. The Princeton Review suggests that all financial aid forms be submitted as soon as possible after January 1. *Need-based scholarships/grants offered:* Pell, SEOG, state scholarships/grants, private scholarships, and the school's own gift aid. *Loan aid offered:* Direct Subsidized Stafford, Direct Unsubsidized Stafford, Direct PLUS, Federal Perkins, and college/university loans from institutional funds. Institutional employment available. Federal Work-Study Program available. Applicants will be notified of awards on a rolling basis beginning on or about April 1. Off-campus job opportunities are excellent.

## FROM THE ADMISSIONS OFFICE

"The University of Kansas has a long and distinguished tradition for academic excellence. Outstanding students from Kansas and across the nation are attracted to KU because of its strong academic reputation, beautiful campus, affordable cost of education, and contagious school spirit. KU provides students extraordinary opportunities in honors programs, research, internships, and study abroad. The university is located in Lawrence (40 minutes from Kansas City), a community of 80,000 regarded as one of the nation's best small cities for its arts scene, live music, and historic downtown."

## ADMISSIONS

| | |
|---|---|
| Admissions Rating | 80 |
| # of applicants | 8,479 |
| % of applicants accepted | 69 |
| % of acceptees attending | 65 |

### FRESHMAN PROFILE

| | |
|---|---|
| Range ACT Composite | 22-28 |
| Average ACT Composite | 24 |
| Average HS GPA | 3.4 |
| % graduated top 10% of class | 28 |
| % graduated top 25% of class | 58 |
| % graduated top 50% of class | 89 |

### DEADLINES

| | |
|---|---|
| Regular admission | 4/1 |
| Regular notification | rolling |
| Nonfall registration? | yes |

### APPLICANTS ALSO LOOK AT

**AND OFTEN PREFER**
Notre Dame
U. Colorodo—Boulder

**AND SOMETIMES PREFER**
U. Nebraska
U. Missouri—Coumbia
U. Missouri—Kansas City
Kansas State
Wichita State

**AND RARELY PREFER**
U. Illinois—Urbana-Champaign
Colorodo State

## FINANCIAL FACTS

| | |
|---|---|
| Financial Aid Rating | 74 |
| In-state tuition | $2,333 |
| Out-of-state tuition | $9,260 |
| Room & board | $4,348 |
| Books and supplies | $750 |
| Required fees | $551 |
| % frosh receiving aid | 36 |
| % undergrads receiving aid | 34 |
| Avg frosh grant | $3,750 |
| Avg frosh loan | $2,650 |

# UNIVERSITY OF KENTUCKY

100 FUNKHOUSER BUILDING, LEXINGTON, KY 40506 • ADMISSIONS: 859-257-9000 • FAX: 859-257-3823

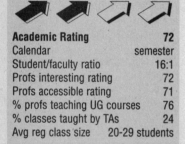
## STUDENTS SPEAK OUT

### Academics

The University of Kentucky "is making a real effort to become a great school. It's a very exciting time to be here," declares an upbeat first-year student. In the mean time, students at UK are happy to settle for what is "probably the best school in the Bluegrass State." "The professors here are a bit of a mixed bag. On one hand, many faculty members are "accessible, helpful," and "concerned about your well-being." "The majority of my instructors have a good knowledge of the subject which they are teaching," says a sophomore. However, UK also has its share of "crappy" professors who are "not flexible" and "know they're getting paid regardless of how well they teach." Just about everyone seems to agree that "the classes are too big" as well. Back on the plus side, there is a "very nice library" on campus, and top high school students can qualify for the highly touted honors program. As you'd expect from a mammoth state university, UK has a wealth of departments. Pre-professional programs are all the rage here, and popular majors also include health sciences, education, engineering, and business and management. UK also requires all students to complete general education requirements, meaning that everyone dabbles at least a little in the liberal arts.

### Life

The "nice, safe," and "middle-sized" city of Lexington ("a short drive" from Louisville) provides a delightful stomping ground for UK students, who say it can hold its own against any college town. The area surrounding the campus boasts a slew of "dance clubs and bars," a hopping live music scene, and really awesome food. Fraternities "tend to thrive" here and off-campus soirees among non-Greeks are "fun" and plentiful as well. In general, "social events are frequently held" and, despite a "strict" and "foolish" alcohol policy, "most students like to drink for fun," according to a junior. "People here tend to follow a pattern of study, drink, study, drink," observes another student. In the winter, the school's (and arguably the entire state's) social calendar is dominated by basketball, which is "almost a religion at UK." Students "like to attend football games and basketball games, tailgate before the games, and party afterwards." Still not satisfied? The Student Activities Board provides even more things to do. "There are so many different kinds of clubs and organizations at UK that there is at least one that can fit everybody," bets a first-year student. Unfortunately, "campus parking is terrible" and the food on campus is, apparently, pretty bad. "I hate the food," gripes a first-year student.

### Student Body

The overwhelming majority of UK's student body hails from the Bluegrass State. Many tell us they chose this school because it is "not too far from home." These "polite and generally kind" students mostly ooze with "southern hospitality," though there are "rude and stuck-up" students to be reckoned with. They are also "very spirited," especially when it comes to men's basketball, and it's not too much of an exaggeration to say that "everybody dresses the same, looks the same, and does the same things" here. Ethnic diversity is not Kentucky's strong suit. The campus is overwhelmingly white, with African Americans forming the largest minority group. While minority discrimination is certainly on the decline here, division "between blacks and whites" is sometimes noticeable, and you my run into the occasional "racist derelict." The "Greek community is very tight," as well, and Greeks "don't mix often with non-Greek students and organizations."

FINANCIAL AID: 859-257-3172 • E-MAIL: ADMISSIO@POP.UKY.EDU • WEBSITE: WWW.UKY.EDU

## ADMISSIONS

*Very important* academic and nonacademic factors considered by the admissions committee include class rank, essays, secondary school record, and standardized test scores. *Important* factors considered include alumni/ae relation, character/personal qualities, extracurricular activities, geography, recommendations, and talent/ability. *Other* factors considered include volunteer work and work experience. Factors *not* considered include minority status, religious affiliation/commitment, and state residency. SAT I or ACT required, ACT preferred. TOEFL required of all international applicants. High school diploma is required and GED is accepted. *High school units required/recommended:* 20 total required; 4 English required, 3 math required, 2 science required, 2 social studies required, 9 elective required. *The admissions office says:* "Apply early. Admission to the University of Kentucky is offered on a competitive basis to students who can demonstrate the ability to succeed in an academically demanding environment. The admissions policy is based on an evaluation of a student's standardized test scores, high school grade point average, and completion of a minimum pre-college curriculum. Students whose scores and grades predict a high probability of achieving a C average or better the freshman year at UK will be accepted automatically."

### The Inside Word

High volume of applications has more to do with Kentucky's selectivity than any other factor. Given the recent successes of the Wildcats in NCAA basketball, more apps are likely to be on the way.

## FINANCIAL AID

*Students should submit:* FAFSA. The Princeton Review suggests that all financial aid forms be submitted as soon as possible after January 1. *Need-based scholarships/grants offered:* Pell, SEOG, state scholarships/grants, private scholarships, and the school's own gift aid. *Loan aid offered:* Federal Perkins and Federal Nursing. Institutional employment available. Federal Work-Study Program available. Applicants will be notified of awards on a rolling basis beginning on or about May 1. Off-campus job opportunities are excellent.

## FROM THE ADMISSIONS OFFICE

"The University of Kentucky offers you an outstanding learning environment and quality instruction through its excellent faculty. Of the 1,892 full-time faculty, 98 percent hold the doctorate degree or the highest degree in their field of study. Many are nationally and internationally known for their research, distinguished teaching, and scholarly service to Kentucky, the nation, and the world. Yet, with a student/teacher ratio of only 16:1, UK faculty are accessible and willing to answer your questions and discuss your interests."

### ADMISSIONS

| | |
|---|---|
| **Admissions Rating** | **79** |
| # of applicants | 8,312 |
| % of applicants accepted | 61 |
| % of acceptees attending | 58 |

### FRESHMAN PROFILE

| | |
|---|---|
| Range ACT Composite | 22-27 |
| Average ACT Composite | 25 |
| Minimum TOEFL | 527 |
| Average HS GPA | 3.4 |
| % graduated top 10% of class | 31 |
| % graduated top 25% of class | 66 |
| % graduated top 50% of class | 97 |

### DEADLINES

| | |
|---|---|
| Regular admission | 2/15 |
| Nonfall registration? | yes |

### APPLICANTS ALSO LOOK AT

**AND OFTEN PREFER**
Centre Coll.
Transylvania
Miami University
Indiana University

**AND SOMETIMES PREFER**
U. Tennessee—Knoxville
Eastern Kentucky
Western Kentucky
Bellarmine

**AND RARELY PREFER**
U. Illinois—Urbana-Champaign
Purdue U.—West Lafayette
Ohio State—Columbus
Florida State
U. Florida

### FINANCIAL FACTS

| | |
|---|---|
| **Financial Aid Rating** | **84** |
| In-state tuition | $3,270 |
| Out-of-state tuition | $9,810 |
| Room & board | $3,980 |
| Books and supplies | $500 |
| Required fees | $465 |
| % frosh receiving aid | 31 |
| % undergrads receiving aid | 34 |
| Avg frosh grant | $3,525 |
| Avg frosh loan | $3,769 |

# THE UNIVERSITY OF MAINE

5713 CHADBOURNE HALL, ORONO, ME 04469-5713 • ADMISSIONS: 207-581-1561 • FAX: 207-581-1213

## CAMPUS LIFE

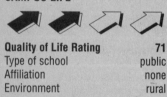

| | |
|---|---|
| **Quality of Life Rating** | **71** |
| Type of school | public |
| Affiliation | none |
| Environment | rural |

### STUDENTS

| | |
|---|---|
| Total undergrad enrollment | 8,229 |
| % male/female | 48/52 |
| % from out of state | 15 |
| % live on campus | 45 |
| % African American | 1 |
| % Asian | 1 |
| % Caucasian | 95 |
| % Hispanic | 1 |
| % Native American | 2 |
| % international | 1 |
| # of countries represented | 71 |

### SURVEY SAYS . . .
*High cost of living*
*Everyone loves the Black Bears*
*Class discussions are rare*
*Students aren't religious*
*Large classes*
*Very little hard liquor*
*Campus difficult to get around*
*Lots of long lines and red tape*
*(Almost) no one smokes*

## ACADEMICS

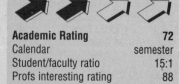

| | |
|---|---|
| **Academic Rating** | **72** |
| Calendar | semester |
| Student/faculty ratio | 15:1 |
| Profs interesting rating | 88 |
| Profs accessible rating | 90 |
| Avg lab size | 10-19 students |
| Avg reg class size | 20-29 students |

### MOST POPULAR MAJORS
engineering
elementary education
business

## STUDENTS SPEAK OUT
### Academics

The University of Maine at Orono—Maine's "premier" public university—boasts "small classes," a tremendous reputation throughout the Northeast, and a swell financial aid program. While UMaine's engineering and forestry programs here are nationally esteemed, students tell us that excellent programs abound in everything from business to agriculture science to journalism to wildlife ecology. Student opinion about the professors here is mixed. Some instructors are "very open to student input" and "easy to contact for help outside of class." "It appears that the professors actually enjoy teaching," remarks an astonished first-year student. However, other faculty members are "preoccupied with research," and "foreign professors" with "thick accents" are too common. There is good news on this front, though: "Many tutors are available to help if students get behind." UMaine's library also gets good grades, and its research facilities are reportedly "first-class." As at any Big School, UMaine unfortunately has its share of bureaucracy, but students say the staff is generally composed of "good people who are willing to help you any way they can." The main complaint about the administration appears to be that it is bent on squelching students' good times.

### Life

At UMaine, the "easy-to-get-around" campus is "beautiful," and "so are the seasons." Much of the focus is on outdoor activities. There's the "on-campus forest." There's also kayaking, canoeing, skiing, biking, and that old standby: ice climbing. Otherwise, though, students say, "Maine is a boring state," and they advise us that Orono is a "secluded, small town." Luckily, "everyone still manages to find things to do." Campus organizations seem to do a decent job of keeping students entertained, and the Onward program provides a much-appreciated "support system" for non-traditional students. Intramural sports are popular, but they pale in comparison to men's hockey and women's basketball. "Cheap movies on the big screen" and, "of course, snowball fights during the longest winter in the world" provide additional cut-rate thrills. UMaine students enjoy partying as much as the next bunch of students, but they gripe that the top brass and the campus police do their best to stop it. "If the university would lighten up and let people have fun, there would be greater campus unity and morale," suggests one student. Also, "the food on campus" could use "a little more taste," and UMaine "desperately needs more student parking." At the least, pleads a first-year student, "students who park really creatively should not be ticketed." When students tire of Orono's humdrum pace, they head to nearby Bangor—Maine's third largest city and home to the state's second largest shopping mall.

### Student Body

UMaine is not a particularly diverse campus; just about everybody here is white, and a great many students tell us they chose UMaine because it is "close to home." Many students consider themselves "open-minded and progressive." Others say there are "too many hippie, tree-hugging students" wandering around campus. Despite these differences, students "generally" get along, though not necessarily right off the bat. "I'm not from Maine and perhaps this is a misconception, but the people here seem reserved and as cold as the weather," observes a native New Yorker. "Under all of that, though, they are normal." Students from Maine—the "Pine Tree State," in case you were wondering—possess a somewhat different view. They fancy themselves as "overall good people" who are "very friendly" and "interact easily." They are "always willing to help" and "funny as hell" to boot. In fact, they say, "the only snobs are the out-of-staters." So there.

FINANCIAL AID: 207-581-1324 • E-MAIL: UM-ADMIT@MAINE.EDU • WEBSITE: WWW.UMAINE.EDU

## ADMISSIONS

*Very important* academic and nonacademic factors considered by the admissions committee include class rank, essays, recommendations, secondary school record, and standardized test scores. *Important* factors considered include character/personal qualities, extracurricular activities, interview, talent/ability, volunteer work, and work experience. *Other* factors considered include alumni/ae relation, geography, minority status, and state residency. Factors *not* considered include religious affiliation/commitment. SAT I or ACT required, SAT I preferred. TOEFL required of all international applicants. High school diploma is required and GED is accepted. *High school units required/recommended:* 17 total required; 4 English required, 3 math required, 4 math recommended, 2 science required, 3 science recommended, 2 science lab required, 2 foreign language required, 2 social studies required, 2 elective required.

### The Inside Word

The University of Maine is much smaller than most public flagship universities, and its admissions process reflects this; it is a much more personal approach than most others use. Candidates are reviewed carefully for fit with their choice of college and major, and the committee will contact students regarding a second choice if the first doesn't seem to be a good match. Prepare your application as if you are applying to a private university.

## FINANCIAL AID

*Students should submit:* FAFSA. The Princeton Review suggests that all financial aid forms be submitted as soon as possible after January 1. *Need-based scholarships/grants offered:* Pell, SEOG, state scholarships/grants, private scholarships, and the school's own gift aid. *Loan aid offered:* FFEL Subsidized Stafford, FFEL Unsubsidized Stafford, FFEL PLUS, Federal Perkins, state, and college/university loans from institutional funds. Institutional employment available. Federal Work-Study Program available. Applicants will be notified of awards on a rolling basis beginning on or about March 15. Off-campus job opportunities are good.

## FROM THE ADMISSIONS OFFICE

"The University of Maine offers students a wide array of academic and social programs, including clubs, organizations, professional societies, and religious groups. We strive to help students feel welcome and to provide opportunities for them to become an integral part of the campus community. Visit our beautiful campus and become better acquainted with this community. Take a guided campus tour and learn about campus history, services and technologies, and living and dining. Our student tour guides give a first-hand view of the UMaine experience. During your visit, meet with faculty and admission staff to learn more about your program of interest and our academic climate. The University of Maine's commitment to educational excellence and community building will be reinforced when you visit our campus!"

### ADMISSIONS

| | |
|---|---|
| **Admissions Rating** | **75** |
| # of applicants | 4,783 |
| % of applicants accepted | 81 |
| % of acceptees attending | 43 |

### FRESHMAN PROFILE

| | |
|---|---|
| Range SAT Verbal | 480-590 |
| Average SAT Verbal | 537 |
| Range SAT Math | 490-600 |
| Average SAT Math | 544 |
| Range ACT Composite | 20-25 |
| Average ACT Composite | 22 |
| Minimum TOEFL | 530 |
| Average HS GPA | 3.1 |
| % graduated top 10% of class | 21 |
| % graduated top 25% of class | 47 |
| % graduated top 50% of class | 82 |

### DEADLINES

| | |
|---|---|
| Nonfall registration? | yes |

### APPLICANTS ALSO LOOK AT

**AND OFTEN PREFER**
U. Vermont

**AND SOMETIMES PREFER**
U. New Hampshire
U. Mass—Amherst
Colby

**AND RARELY PREFER**
U. Rhode Island
U. Conn
U. Maine—Farmington

### FINANCIAL FACTS

| | |
|---|---|
| **Financial Aid Rating** | **75** |
| In-state tuition | $4,200 |
| Out-of-state tuition | $11,940 |
| Room & board | $5,628 |
| Books and supplies | $700 |
| Required fees | $870 |
| % frosh receiving aid | 72 |
| % undergrads receiving aid | 70 |
| Avg frosh grant | $5,326 |
| Avg frosh loan | $3,658 |

# UNIV. OF MARYLAND, BALTIMORE COUNTY

1000 HILLTOP CIRCLE, BALTIMORE, MD 21250 • ADMISSIONS: 410-455-2291 • FAX: 410-455-1094

## CAMPUS LIFE

| Quality of Life Rating | 76 |
| --- | --- |
| Type of school | public |
| Affiliation | none |
| Environment | suburban |

### STUDENTS

| | |
| --- | --- |
| Total undergrad enrollment | 9,101 |
| % male/female | 50/50 |
| % from out of state | 13 |
| % from public high school | 73 |
| % live on campus | 29 |
| % in (# of) fraternities | 3 (8) |
| % in (# of) sororities | 2 (9) |
| % African American | 16 |
| % Asian | 15 |
| % Caucasian | 58 |
| % Hispanic | 3 |
| % Native American | 1 |
| % international | 4 |

### SURVEY SAYS . . .

*Very little drug use*
*(Almost) everyone smokes*
*Class discussions are rare*
*Popular college radio*
*High cost of living*
*Large classes*
*Unattractive campus*
*Ethnic diversity on campus*
*Campus difficult to get around*
*Students are not very happy*

## ACADEMICS

| Academic Rating | 73 |
| --- | --- |
| Calendar | 4-1-4 |
| Student/faculty ratio | 16:1 |
| Profs interesting rating | 75 |
| Profs accessible rating | 75 |
| % profs teaching UG courses | 100 |
| % classes taught by TAs | 2 |
| Avg lab size | 10-19 students |
| Avg reg class size | 20-29 students |

### MOST POPULAR MAJORS

information systems
computer science
chemistry and biochemistry

## STUDENTS SPEAK OUT

### Academics

Once upon a time, University of Maryland, Baltimore County—referred to as UMBC by students and faculty alike—was a school full of bright Maryland kids who had, for one reason or another, not done so well in high school. They'd come, work their tails off, get good grades, and transfer out for their final two years, earning their degrees from "prestige" schools. Somewhere along the way, however, students started realizing what they were leaving behind: a high-quality, low-cost education. Nowadays more students stick around for the full four years, and more out-of-state students are pouring in. As at many schools, professors here receive mixed grades. Complains one student, "Some professors need better attitudes and better teaching assistants, especially if they're going to make us go to discussion and they expect us to get anything out of it." Another points out that "lecture hall instructors aren't as good as smaller classes," but that the situation improves greatly after freshman year, when students gain more access to "professors who really know their material well, and are always willing to offer additional help." Students warn that, despite UMBC's recent surge in popularity, "We still do more work here than my friends at the Ivies do, and we get lower GPAs due to the toughness of the school."

### Life

Although UMBC is increasing in national stature and over 66 percent of freshmen live on campus, it is still home to a large commuter student body. This means "the school is alive with activity four and a half days a week. All through the weekend, the campus is comatose. There are parties during the week, though." Adds one student, "For fun, if you don't have money or a car, this is the University of Maryland Boring Campus." Having transportation opens up a wide range of options in downtown Baltimore or, for those willing to make a slightly longer road trip, Washington, D.C. On-campus activities center around academics, the "great UMBC Gospel Choir," and weekday intramurals. What parties occur on campus are hampered by a "dry campus policy that is too strict." Students also warn, "Campus beauty is a weak point." However, two new dorms will open this year and next, accommodating 500 new residents. With more full-time and out-of-state students arriving, the proportion of upperclassmen living on campus is expected to grow. Student life and campus activity is also building as UMBC's full-time residential population grows. Student affairs staff has initiated a 'Weekend Adventures Team' to promote weekend activities. These include talent shows, dances, performances, movies on campus, and off-campus trips for activities such as rafting, paintball, shopping, and community service. In fall 2002 UMBC plans to open a new University Commons that will include a food court, shops, and a student recreation center.

### Student Body

UMBC's diverse student body is a no-nonsense, goal-oriented group. People "are really focused here. Everyone is here to get an education and a degree, and then it's right on to grad school or a job. People here are very busy." They're easy to get along with because "people tend not to be concerned with what everyone else is doing." However, many do not put a premium on academics and intellectualism for its own sake, meaning that "sometimes it's hard to find people out of class who want to hold intellectually stimulating conversations." Students also complain that "athletes here generally isolate themselves and don't socialize with nonathletes. Athletes make up a big percentage of the residents, so this hurts campus life."

# UNIVERSITY OF MARYLAND, BALTIMORE COUNTY

FINANCIAL AID: 410-455-2387 • E-MAIL: ADMISSIONS@UMBC.EDU • WEBSITE: WWW.UMBC.EDU

## ADMISSIONS

*Very important* academic and nonacademic factors considered by the admissions committee include essays, secondary school record, and standardized test scores. *Important* factors considered include class rank. *Other* factors considered include character/personal qualities, extracurricular activities, interview, minority status, recommendations, talent/ability, and volunteer work. Factors *not* considered include alumni/ae relation, geography, religious affiliation/commitment, state residency, and work experience. SAT I or ACT required, SAT I preferred. TOEFL required of all international applicants. High school diploma is required and GED is accepted. *High school units required/recommended:* 16 total required; 17 total recommended; 4 English required, 3 math required, 4 math recommended, 2 science required, 2 science lab required, 2 foreign language required, 3 social studies required.

### The Inside Word

The State of Maryland seems blessed with several strong, small, public universities in addition to its flagship campus at College Park. UMBC is one of those to watch; its national visibility and admissions standards are on the rise. Strong students are attracted by UMBC's emphasis on academic achievement. As a result, the admissions committee has grown to expect evidence of challenging academic course work throughout high school from its candidates, preferably at the honors or AP level. This competitive path will give you the best shot for admission if you're an eager learner looking for a campus where the academic experience is engaging.

## FINANCIAL AID

*Students should submit:* FAFSA. There is no regular filing deadline. Priority filing deadline is March 1. The Princeton Review suggests that all financial aid forms be submitted as soon as possible after January 1. *Need-based scholarships/grants offered:* Pell, SEOG, state scholarships/grants, private scholarships, and the school's own gift aid. *Loan aid offered:* Subsidized Stafford, Unsubsidized Stafford, PLUS, and Federal Perkins. Institution employment available. Federal Work-Study Program available. Applicants will be notified of awards on a rolling basis beginning on or about March 15. Off-campus job opportunities are good.

## FROM THE ADMISSIONS OFFICE

"UMBC students find out quickly that learning at an honors university takes place in many different ways and in a variety of settings. Students discover an environment with a strong undergraduate liberal arts and sciences focus. A midsize public research university, UMBC provides students with opportunities to work with nationally recognized faculty on research ranging from AIDS prevention and environmental issues affecting Chesapeake Bay to computer graphics and animation. UMBC's academic reputation and industry partnerships help to place students in promising careers and leading graduate programs. In fact, one-third of UMBC students immediately go on to many of the nation's finest graduate or professional schools including Harvard, Johns Hopkins, Yale, and Stanford."

### ADMISSIONS

| | |
|---|---|
| Admissions Rating | 79 |
| # of applicants | 5,411 |
| % of applicants accepted | 65 |
| % of acceptees attending | 38 |
| # accepting a place on wait list | 360 |
| % admitted from wait list | 100 |

#### FRESHMAN PROFILE

| | |
|---|---|
| Range SAT Verbal | 530-630 |
| Average SAT Verbal | 575 |
| Range SAT Math | 550-650 |
| Average SAT Math | 592 |
| Range ACT Composite | 21-27 |
| Average ACT Composite | 24 |
| Minimum TOEFL | 220 |
| Average HS GPA | 3.5 |
| % graduated top 10% of class | 34 |
| % graduated top 25% of class | 63 |
| % graduated top 50% of class | 89 |

#### DEADLINES

| | |
|---|---|
| Priority admission deadline | 12/15 |
| Regular admission | 3/15 |
| Nonfall registration? | yes |

### FINANCIAL FACTS

| | |
|---|---|
| Financial Aid Rating | 76 |
| In-state tuition | $4,206 |
| Out-of-state tuition | $8,974 |
| Room & board | $5,850 |
| Books and supplies | $700 |
| Required fees | $1,284 |
| % frosh receiving aid | 75 |
| % undergrads receiving aid | 70 |
| Avg frosh grant | $6,300 |
| Avg frosh loan | $2,600 |

# UNIVERSITY OF MARYLAND—COLLEGE PARK

MITCHELL BUILDING, COLLEGE PARK, MD 20742-5235 • ADMISSIONS: 301-314-8385 • FAX: 301-314-9693

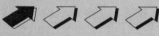

## STUDENTS SPEAK OUT

### Academics

The very affordable University of Maryland is a major research university that offers a "professional atmosphere" and, for those who qualify, an exemplary Honors Program with small classes and lots of personal attention. As at many of the behemoth state universities, though, large lecture classes are the norm for the typical student. Excellent engineering, physics, economics, and business departments provide just a few of the near-limitless choices awaiting the self-starter here. Writes one student, "To the self-directed, enterprising student, Maryland affords immense opportunity. To those with no talent for getting through endless bureaucracy, go somewhere else!" Maryland's core curriculum, usually completed during the first two years, requires students to fulfill a wide range of distribution requirements. During their senior year, undergrads must complete two seminars designed to help integrate these disparate core courses into their major fields of study. Students write that their final two years here are better and more enjoyable than the first two. As one junior explains, "At first you feel like a number, but as you get into your upper-level classes and classes for your major, teachers become more available and there is more individual attention." Professors vary from those who are "interesting, provide humor, and keep me relatively awake" to those who "teach just so they can do research." Of the latter type, one biology major reports that "if you learn to be assertive, professors and staff are more than willing to give you some of their precious time." Students complain that "advising is horrible. There should be someone to advise you not to be advised by an advisor." As for administration, "for a big campus, it runs pretty smoothly."

### Life

Maryland's "huge, largely diverse," and "great campus" has "something for everyone." To some, it's "Party Park," with "lotsa parties and cool bars. You can walk down the street and always find a good party." Others focus on the immensely popular intercollegiate sports teams. Gushes one student, "Men's basketball is huge. Games are so much fun!" Football and lacrosse also pull in big crowds. Intramural sports are big, as are the literally hundreds of clubs and extracurricular activities housed on campus. Fraternities and sororities also exert a "pretty strong" influence on campus life and provide numerous social activities. Writes one undergrad, "There is always something going on on campus and off campus, and if it doesn't suit you, D.C. is only a Metro ride away." The nation's capital has "plenty to do . . . lots of concerts," clubs, and restaurants, while Baltimore, "only 30 minutes away by car," boasts an ever-expanding downtown nightlife. College Park's choice location also provides abundant opportunities for work and "great internships," not only in the two major cities but also in nearby Annapolis, Maryland's capital. Students complain that their hometown, College Park, does not live "up to its potential" and caution that having your own wheels makes city jaunts much easier. Beware though: "We really need more parking spaces. And we need to build more dorms. No one should have to live in a double room with two other roommates. That is torture."

### Student Body

Maryland students are, by and large, a pleasant group. Writes one undergrad, "If you smile at someone, they'll be sure to smile back. Even with a campus of 30,000, you're bound to run into someone you know." Most consider themselves "easy-going" and "apathetic" but "decent people who wish to hold on to their beliefs without criticism." By Maryland state law, "75 percent come from Maryland. Some are nice, some aren't." The majority are "suburban white kids from public schools," but a substantial minority population means that "the diversity at UMCP is great; however, there is little interaction between groups of different cultures."

FINANCIAL AID: 301-314-9000 • E-MAIL: UM-ADMIT@UGA.UMD.EDU • WEBSITE: WWW.MARYLAND.EDU

## ADMISSIONS

*Very important* academic and nonacademic factors considered by the admissions committee include secondary school record. *Important* factors considered include character/personal qualities, class rank, essays, extracurricular activities, interview, recommendations, standardized test scores, and talent/ability. *Other* factors considered include alumni/ae relation, minority status, and volunteer work. Factors *not* considered include geography, religious affiliation/commitment, state residency, and work experience. SAT I or ACT required, SAT I preferred. TOEFL required of all international applicants. High school diploma is required and GED is accepted. *High school units required/recommended:* 14 total required; 4 English required, 3 math required, 2 science required, 2 science lab required, 2 foreign language required, 1 social studies required, 2 history required. *The admissions office says:* "Honors or AP courses are strongly advised for students whose high schools offer them."

### The Inside Word

Maryland's initial candidate review process emphasizes academic credentials and preparedness. Through this first review, roughly 20 percent of the applicant pool is either admitted or denied. The remaining 80 percent are then evaluated in depth by admissions officers and reviewed by an admissions committee of seven, who collectively decide upon each candidate. Don't take essays and the compilation of other personal material that is required of applicants lightly. It's uncommon for a large university to devote this kind of attention to candidate selection. Perhaps this explains why so many of the students here made Maryland their first choice.

## FINANCIAL AID

*Students should submit:* FAFSA. Priority filing deadline is February 15. The Princeton Review suggests that all financial aid forms be submitted as soon as possible after January 1. *Need-based scholarships/grants offered:* Pell, SEOG, state scholarships/grants, private scholarships, and the school's own gift aid. *Loan aid offered:* FFEL Subsidized Stafford, FFEL Unsubsidized Stafford, FFEL PLUS, and Federal Perkins. Institutional employment available. Federal Work-Study Program available. Applicants will be notified of awards on or about April 1. Off-campus job opportunities are excellent.

## FROM THE ADMISSIONS OFFICE

"Commitment to excellence, to diversity, to learning—these are the hallmarks of a Maryland education. As the state's flagship campus and one of the nation's leading public universities, Maryland offers students and faculty the opportunity to come together to explore and create knowledge, to debate and discover our similarities and our differences, and to serve as a model of intellectual and cultural excellence for the state and the nation's capital. With leading programs in engineering, business, journalism, architecture, and the sciences, the university offers an outstanding educational value."

### ADMISSIONS

| Admissions Rating | 80 |
| --- | --- |
| # of applicants | 20,488 |
| % of applicants accepted | 51 |
| % of acceptees attending | 38 |
| # accepting a place on wait list | 1,153 |

### FRESHMAN PROFILE

| | |
| --- | --- |
| Range SAT Verbal | 560-660 |
| Range SAT Math | 590-690 |
| Minimum TOEFL | 575 |
| Average HS GPA | 3.7 |
| % graduated top 10% of class | 52 |
| % graduated top 25% of class | 87 |
| % graduated top 50% of class | 99 |

### DEADLINES

| | |
| --- | --- |
| Priority admission deadline | 12/1 |
| Regular admission | 2/15 |
| Nonfall registration? | yes |

### APPLICANTS ALSO LOOK AT

**AND OFTEN PREFER**
UNC—Chapel Hill

**AND SOMETIMES PREFER**
Howard
Penn State—Univ. Park
Virginia Tech
NYU
U. Delaware

**AND RARELY PREFER**
George Washington
Hampton
Syracuse

### FINANCIAL FACTS

| Financial Aid Rating | 73 |
| --- | --- |
| In-state tuition | $5,136 |
| Out-of-state tuition | $12,688 |
| Room & board | $6,124 |
| Books and supplies | $702 |
| % frosh receiving aid | 46 |
| % undergrads receiving aid | 60 |
| Avg frosh grant | $2,600 |
| Avg frosh loan | $2,625 |

# UNIVERSITY OF MASSACHUSETTS—AMHERST

UNIVERSITY ADMISSIONS CENTER, AMHERST, MA 01003 • ADMISSIONS: 413-545-0222 • FAX: 413-545-4312

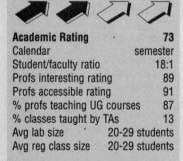
## STUDENTS SPEAK OUT
### Academics

State-run University of Massachusetts at Amherst offers "a great education in a liberal but structured environment," according to its students. Like many large schools, it's "a wonderful university providing countless opportunities to get involved with other students. UMass is fun and active; there is always something going on at UMass every day of the week." The university also suffers from several typical large-school maladies, including a lumbering, inefficient administration ("It would be easier to get an interview with Saddam Hussein than with the dean of undeclared majors here") and a wide range in the quality of instruction. Of profs, opinions range from the positively positive ("All the professors love their work and it shows") to the qualifiedly positive ("The professors are an amalgamation. I've had great teachers I'll never forget and ones I already have forgotten because they were so useless. Overall, this is a good experience, but that's overall"). There are even those who caustically fume that "there are several hundred professors at UMass. By simple law of averages, some of them should be reasonably interesting. Apparently UMass does not know its math." Others complain that "the teachers are OK, but the conditions—in the auditorium-style classrooms—inhibit learning because of external irritations like stuffiness, overheating, small chairs and desks so you can't write comfortably, etc. It's not a good atmosphere for intense concentration." Membership in the Five College Consortium helps to soften some of the griping, as it allows students to use the resources available at the nearby warmer-and-fuzzier campuses of Amherst, Hampshire, Smith, and Mount Holyoke.

### Life

Smack in the middle of the Pioneer Valley, UMass—Amherst is an idyllic setting for collegiate New England–philes. Amherst "is a great little town" with "plenty of things to do," and "good skiing and hiking are nearby." So too are the towns of Northampton, Springfield, and a little further down the line, Albany, New York. Writes one student, "We're close enough to large cities to access them but far enough away to have a small-town feel." The large university, as well as several smaller schools close by, creates an environment in which "there's always something to do no matter what you like." Fraternities and sororities "exist . . . but do not dominate the social scene." University-sponsored clubs are very popular; as one student notes, "There are many groups available to join—hang-gliding club, dance team, animal rights coalition, bridge club, etc." As far as the night scene goes, there's always a good time to be had nearby: "When it comes to having fun, there's everything from parties to dancing to restaurants, movies, or a band playing anywhere at almost any given time." Are there downsides to this little slice o' heaven? The campus itself, for one. "Be prepared to eat, breathe, and live concrete. Bland, uninteresting concrete. UMass is a large slab of gray concrete dropped in the middle of farmland," warns one student. Students also grouse loudly and frequently about the food. Says one, "They really need to improve the food. It's like a poison that kills you a little each time."

### Student Body

UMass undergrads agree that theirs is a diverse population. As one student muses, "UMass is like a big bag of potpourri, made up of a thousand different scents, which, when brought together, create the strongest and sweetest of aromas." Even so, "the students, while pretty cool, are definitely segregated." Undergrads say their fellow students are "friendly, fun, and some are even concerned about real life beyond the UMass community," but they feel they're not as pointy-headed as their neighbors at Amherst College. As one student puts it, "I'd like to think this is a fairly intellectual environment and a good place to learn, but there are still quite a few dumbasses lolling about."

# UNIVERSITY OF MASSACHUSETTS—AMHERST

FINANCIAL AID: 413-545-0801 • E-MAIL: MAIL@ADMISSIONS.UMASS.EDU • WEBSITE: WWW.UMASS.EDU

## ADMISSIONS

*Important* academic and nonacademic factors considered by the admissions committee include secondary school rank, standardized test scores, extracurricular activities, talent/ability, character/personal qualities, and state residency. *Other* factors considered include class rank, recommendation, alumni/ae relation, minority status, volunteer work, and work experience. Factors *not* considered include interview, alumni/ae relation, geography, and religious affiliation/commitment. SAT I or ACT required. TOEFL required of all international applicants. High school diploma is required and GED is accepted. *High school units required/recommended:* 4 English required, 3 math required, 3 science required, (including 2 science lab), 2 foreign language required, 2 social studies required, and 2 electives required.

### The Inside Word

Gaining admission to UMass is generally not particularly difficult, but an increase in applications last year resulted in the University increasing its selectivity. Still, most applicants with solid grades in high school should still be successful. UMass is a great choice for students who might have a tougher time getting in at the other Five College Consortium members.

## FINANCIAL AID

*Students should submit:* FAFSA. The Princeton Review suggests that all financial aid forms be submitted as soon as possible after January 1. *Need-based scholarships/grants offered:* Pell, SEOG, state scholarships/grants, private scholarships, and the school's own gift aid. *Loan aid offered:* Direct Subsidized William D. Ford, Direct William D. Ford, Direct PLUS, Federal Perkins, and state. Institutional employment available. Federal Work-Study Program available. Applicants will be notified of awards on a rolling basis beginning on or about April 1. Off-campus job opportunities are good.

## FROM THE ADMISSIONS OFFICE

"The University of Massachusetts—Amherst is the largest public university in New England, offering its students an almost limitless variety of academic programs and activities. Nearly 100 majors are offered, including a unique program called Bachelor's Degree with Individual Concentration (BDIC) in which students create their own program of study. The outstanding faculty of 1,100 includes novelist John Wideman, Pulitzer Prize winners Madeleine Blais and James Tate, National Medal of Science winner Lynn Margulis, and five members of the prestigious National Academy of Sciences. Students can take courses through the honors program and sample classes at nearby Amherst, Hampshire, Mount Holyoke, and Smith Colleges at no extra charge. Students can take classes in the residence halls with other dorm residents through Residential Academic Programs (RAP), and first-year students may be asked to participate in the Talent Advancement Programs (TAP) in which students with the same majors live and take classes together. And the university's extensive library system is the largest at any public institution in the Northeast. Extracurricular activities include more than 200 clubs and organizations, fraternities and sororities, multicultural and religious centers, and NCAA Division I sports for men and women. Award-winning student-operated businesses, the largest college daily newspaper in the region, and an active student government provide hands-on experiences. About 5,000 students a year participate in the intramural sports program. The picturesque New England town of Amherst offers shopping and dining, and the ski slopes of western Massachusetts and southern Vermont are close by."

## ADMISSIONS

| | |
|---|---|
| Admissions Rating | 74 |
| # of applicants | 19,499 |
| % of applicants accepted | 67 |
| % of acceptees attending | 28 |

### FRESHMAN PROFILE

| | |
|---|---|
| Range SAT Verbal | 500-620 |
| Average SAT Verbal | 558 |
| Range SAT Math | 510-620 |
| Average SAT Math | 569 |
| Minimum TOEFL | 550 |
| Average HS GPA | 3.3 |
| % graduated top 10% of class | 19 |
| % graduated top 25% of class | 52 |
| % graduated top 50% of class | 91 |

### DEADLINES

| | |
|---|---|
| Regular admission | 2/1 |
| Nonfall registration? | yes |

### APPLICANTS ALSO LOOK AT
#### AND OFTEN PREFER
Dartmouth
Boston Coll.
#### AND SOMETIMES PREFER
U. Vermont
U. New Hampshire
U. Conn
Boston U.
Syracuse
#### AND RARELY PREFER
Northeastern U.
U. Rhode Island
SUNY Albany
U. Maine—Orono
Worcester Poly.

## FINANCIAL FACTS

| | |
|---|---|
| Financial Aid Rating | 73 |
| In-state tuition | $1,714 |
| Out-of-state tuition | $9,937 |
| Room & board | $5,115 |
| Books and supplies | $500 |
| Required fees | $3,498 |
| % frosh receiving aid | 46 |
| % undergrads receiving aid | 46 |

# UNIVERSITY OF MIAMI

OFFICE OF ADMISSION, PO BOX 248025, CORAL GABLES, FL 33124-4616 • ADMISSIONS: 305-284-4323 • FAX: 305-284-2507

## CAMPUS LIFE

**Quality of Life Rating**    **87**
| | |
|---|---|
| Type of school | private |
| Affiliation | none |
| Environment | suburban |

### STUDENTS

| | |
|---|---|
| Total undergrad enrollment | 8,955 |
| % male/female | 45/55 |
| % from out of state | 43 |
| % live on campus | 39 |
| % in (# of) fraternities | 12 (14) |
| % in (# of) sororities | 13 (9) |
| % African American | 11 |
| % Asian | 5 |
| % Caucasian | 52 |
| % Hispanic | 29 |
| % international | 8 |

### SURVEY SAYS . . .

*Beautiful campus*
*Athletic facilities are great*
*Campus easy to get around*
*Great off-campus food*
*Great computer facilities*
*Ethnic diversity on campus*
*Students get along with local community*
*Students are cliquish*
*Student publications are ignored*
*Students aren't religious*
*Musical organizations aren't popular*

## ACADEMICS

**Academic Rating**    **81**
| | |
|---|---|
| Calendar | semester |
| Student/faculty ratio | 13:1 |
| Profs interesting rating | 72 |
| Profs accessible rating | 94 |
| Avg lab size | 10-19 students |
| Avg reg class size | 10-19 students |

### MOST POPULAR MAJORS
biology
psychology
finance

## STUDENTS SPEAK OUT

### Academics

"The sun shines nearly every day" on the "beautiful campus" of the University of Miami (which, for the record, is actually located in suburban Coral Gables). Students tell us that UM offers "a first-rate education" and "all the resources of a larger school" despite its relatively "small" size. Plus, "being able to study in paradise is a nice opportunity." Many programs at the University of Miami are top-notch, particularly those in the health sciences, microbiology, and architecture. According to students, though, the nationally renowned marine sciences department takes the cake, offering "the best" programs on campus. The "challenging but enjoyable" classes here "tend to be fairly small" according to a biology major. Some of the faculty members "only care about research" but most are "approachable," "extremely helpful," and "well-prepared." Also, certain departments are home to the "top professors in their fields," and the computer facilities and the labs at UM can hold their own against just about any university in the nation. The main library is fairly nice, too, though a few students gripe that it could use some improvement. Also, like at pretty much every school, UM has its share of administrative red tape and the accompanying stress.

### Life

Did we mention that the University of Miami has a "gorgeous campus" and "great" weather? There's even a "big, smelly lake in the middle of campus." The "totally and completely happy" students here applaud the tremendous recreational and athletic opportunities offered by the Wellness Center and the surrounding area in general. UM, they say, is a lot like "a health spa," and "South Florida is an amazing place to be a student." "Regardless of what your interests are, there is always something to do every minute of the day," promises a senior. "Campus activities are plentiful" and provide tons of opportunities to get involved. "Museums, theater, cinemas, and the occasional reading" provide students with "constructive leisurely activities." However, most students like to drink and dance on the "weekends" (which generally run "Thursday through Sunday" here). Many students frequent "frat parties" and, in the fall, students dedicate themselves to "tailgating" and following the fortunes of Miami's perennially "great" and "exciting" football team. Students also "go to bars, parties, and clubs" pretty regularly. However, "you do need a car" to get to hotspots like "Coconut Grove or South Beach"; "Without one, you are stuck on campus." And if you bring your wheels, be warned: parking is "a mess."

### Student Body

This campus boasts significant ethnic diversity and, in a nutshell, students say they are part of "a receptive and diverse group." "There are people here from everywhere with totally different backgrounds and thought processes," observes a junior. Students at UM describe themselves as "high-energy, fun-loving," "friendly, and outgoing." They are an athletic bunch as well, what with the endless array of "jocks and frat guys and cheerleader types" on campus. They are also "fiercely competitive," and there is a noticeable contingent of "arrogant, self-centered, spoiled rich kids" here. "Some of the less affluent kids resent the wealthier ones," but class antagonism is by no means a serious problem. Life here can be "a constant fashion contest," though, and many students choose to spend their free time getting buff and "working on their appearance."

FINANCIAL AID: 305-284-5212 • E-MAIL: ADMISSION@MIAMI.EDU • WEBSITE: WWW.MIAMI.EDU

## ADMISSIONS

*Very important* academic and nonacademic factors considered by the admissions committee include class rank, essays, and secondary school record. *Important* factors considered include interview, alumni/ae relation, character/personal qualities, extracurricular activities, recommendations, standardized test scores, talent/ability, and volunteer work. *Other* factors considered include minority status, geography and work experience. Factors *not* considered include religious affiliation/commitment and state residency. SAT I or ACT required. TOEFL required of all international applicants. High school diploma is required and GED is accepted. *High school units required/recommended:* 4 English required, 3 math required, 4 math recommended, 2 science required, 3 science recommended, 2 science lab required, 3 science lab recommended, 2 foreign language required, 3 foreign language recommended, 2 history required, 2 history recommended.

### The Inside Word

Over the years Miami has gotten far more national attention for the escapades of the 'Canes on and off the football field than it has for academic excellence. But anyone who takes a closer look will find national-caliber programs in several areas. While in general it is fairly easy for any good student to gain admission, candidates who apply for the schools of music and marine sciences will face lots of competition and rigorous screening from the admissions committee.

## FINANCIAL AID

The Princeton Review suggests that all financial aid forms be submitted as soon as possible after January 1. *Need-based scholarships/grants offered:* Pell, SEOG, state scholarships/grants, private scholarships, the school's own gift aid, Federal Nursing. *Loan aid offered:* FFEL Subsidized Stafford, FFEL Unsubsidized Stafford, FFEL PLUS, Federal Perkins, and Federal Nursing. Institutional employment available. Federal Work-Study Program available. Off-campus job opportunities are excellent.

## FROM THE ADMISSIONS OFFICE

"A private university located in the beautiful, tropical suburb of Coral Gables, the University of Miami is moderate in size for a major research university (8,000 undergraduates), but comprehensive with 130 majors. UM features the intimacy of a small school by virtue of its unique residential college system, where students live with a faculty master and associate masters. Seventy-five percent of all undergraduate classes have 26 or fewer students. Study abroad programs are available in 19 countries. The location of the university in suburban Coral Gables, just a Metrorail ride away from booming metropolitan Miami—a city of the 21st century—offers students a magnificent array of cultural and career opportunities.

## ADMISSIONS

| | |
|---|---|
| **Admissions Rating** | **85** |
| # of applicants | 13,087 |
| % of applicants accepted | 53 |
| % of acceptees attending | 29 |
| # accepting a place on wait list | 254 |
| # of early decision applicants | 644 |
| % accepted early decision | 50 |

### FRESHMAN PROFILE

| | |
|---|---|
| Range SAT Verbal | 530-630 |
| Range SAT Math | 540-650 |
| Range ACT Composite | 22-28 |
| Minimum TOEFL | 550 |
| Average HS GPA | 3.9 |
| % graduated top 10% of class | 45 |
| % graduated top 25% of class | 77 |
| % graduated top 50% of class | 97 |

### DEADLINES

| | |
|---|---|
| Early decision | 11/15 |
| Early decision notification | 12/15 |
| Regular admission | 3/1 |
| Regular notification | 4/15 |
| Nonfall registration? | yes |

### APPLICANTS ALSO LOOK AT
**AND OFTEN PREFER**
Syracuse
**AND SOMETIMES PREFER**
Rollins
Florida International
Penn State—Univ. Park
Duke
Tulane
**AND RARELY PREFER**
Florida State

## FINANCIAL FACTS

| | |
|---|---|
| **Financial Aid Rating** | **82** |
| Tuition | $22,124 |
| Room & board | $7,934 |
| Books and supplies | $734 |
| Required fees | $404 |
| % frosh receiving aid | 54 |
| % undergrads receiving aid | 59 |

# UNIVERSITY OF MICHIGAN—ANN ARBOR

1220 STUDENT ACTIVITIES BUILDING, ANN ARBOR, MI 48109-1316 • ADMISSIONS: 734-764-7433 • FAX: 734-936-0740

## CAMPUS LIFE

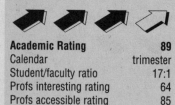

| | |
|---|---|
| **Quality of Life Rating** | **78** |
| Type of school | public |
| Affiliation | none |
| Environment | urban |

### STUDENTS

| | |
|---|---|
| Total undergrad enrollment | 24,412 |
| % male/female | 50/50 |
| % from out of state | 29 |
| % from public high school | 80 |
| % live on campus | 39 |
| % in (# of) fraternities | 17 (36) |
| % in (# of) sororities | 17 (21) |
| % African American | 8 |
| % Asian | 13 |
| % Caucasian | 68 |
| % Hispanic | 4 |
| % Native American | 1 |
| % international | 4 |
| # of countries represented | 75 |

### SURVEY SAYS . . .
*Great library*
*Campus easy to get around*
*Great computer facilities*
*Lab facilities are great*
*(Almost) everyone plays intramural*
*sports*
*Lots of beer drinking*
*Students are not very happy*
*Student government is unpopular*
*Lots of TAs teach upper-level*
*courses*
*Musical organizations aren't popular*

## ACADEMICS

| | |
|---|---|
| **Academic Rating** | **89** |
| Calendar | trimester |
| Student/faculty ratio | 17:1 |
| Profs interesting rating | 64 |
| Profs accessible rating | 85 |

### MOST POPULAR MAJORS
psychology
English
business administration

## STUDENTS SPEAK OUT

### Academics

For many enrolled at the University of Michigan, attending the school has been a lifelong dream: "I've always wanted to come here—since I was a kid," writes one junior. With majors ranging from violin performance and ceramics to aerospace engineering and cellular/molecular biology (and everything in between)—in addition to one of the best faculties in the world—it's no wonder most University of Michigan undergrads are confident in their school's solid reputation of "quality and prestige." The school's a national powerhouse in nearly every aspect: academics (both undergrad and graduate), research, athletics, and student activism, not to mention its thriving social scene and excellent location in Ann Arbor, a town that's "not too big, but has a lot going on." On top of all this, it's a relative bargain for in-state students and still cheaper than comparable private institutions for out-of-staters. Notes another senior, "The academics at U of M are second to none—including the Ivy League." Research opportunities, location near central Michigan industry, "well-qualified" yet "friendly and approachable" professors, as well as the fact that "every department is in the Top 10 list" make Michigan an excellent choice for students looking for a top-quality, large university with unparalleled facilities and staff at a relatively low price. But make sure you like 'em big, because Michigan is, simply put, gigantic. With about 25,000 undergrads packing the lecture halls, you'll probably share this senior's desire for "more personal attention and less GSIs [graduate student instructors]." While you're first starting out you might find, like this first year did, that at Michigan it's "everyone for themselves. . . . you must seek to find your own place."

### Life

Diversity, student activism, and a college town with "piles to do"—one has the sense that things are all good in Ann Arbor. A junior describes the situation this way: "The amount and quality of extracurricular activities here are phenomenal. It almost makes me want to take one class per term so I can use all my time for these activities." And that's just at the university! A classic, just-big-enough "college town," Ann Arbor, too, is known for its "great downtown restaurants and bars, and very diverse culture." U of M is also a "sports heaven," and though an upperclassman warns would-be Michiganers to "avoid our basketball team at all costs," athletics can play a big part in undergraduate life if students are so inclined. "House parties on the weekends" are also an outlet, though one senior complains that "a lot of people drink and use alcohol as a means of escapism. They think it's fun." Her social outlet? "Dancing, working out, reading"—and though finding a "social atmosphere that is moral and healthy" can be tough for chem-free students, at such a big school a kindred soul's bound to turn up sooner rather than later.

### Student Body

"Students here are great," writes a junior. "There's never a shortage of new people to meet." A sophomore elaborates: "As can be expected, social groups form along distinct boundaries, but friendships abound." Sure there are your "elitists" and "spoiled rich kids," but as a senior points out, academics are the ties that bind: "People are pretty friendly," he writes, "very school-oriented." As a result, there's some division according to discipline—English majors hang out with English majors and the like. Jokes a senior, "They are generally friendly in my program. Outside of engineering they aren't friendly." U of M can be "ethnically separated," too, but for the most part, the student vibe seems to be summed up in this junior's statement: "I really like the student atmosphere here. Lots of diversity, and I've learned a lot."

FINANCIAL AID: 734-763-6600 • E-MAIL: UGADMISS@UMICH.EDU • WEBSITE: WWW.UMICH.EDU

## ADMISSIONS

*Very important* academic and nonacademic factors considered by the admissions committee include secondary school record. *Important* factors considered include class rank and standardized test scores. *Other* factors considered include alumni/ae relation, geography, and talent/ability. Factors *not* considered include character/personal qualities, essays, extracurricular activities, interview, minority status, recommendations, religious affiliation/commitment, state residency, volunteer work, and work experience. SAT I or ACT required. TOEFL required of all international applicants. High school diploma is required and GED is accepted. *High school units required/recommended:* 16 total required; 4 English required, 3 math required, 4 math recommended, 2 science required, 1 science lab recommended, 2 foreign language required, 4 foreign language recommended, 3 social studies and history required or 3 elective recommended.

### The Inside Word

Michigan's admissions process combines both formulaic and personal components in its evaluation of candidates. Making the cut is tough—and is getting even tougher for out-of-state applicants, though the university definitely wants them in large numbers. There are simply loads of applicants from outside the state. If being a Wolverine is high on your list of choices, make sure you're well prepared. Michigan establishes an enormous waitlist each year. Controversies surrounding Michigan's approach to affirmative action have resulted in significant changes in the manner in which candidates are evaluated, with greater emphasis now given to aspects of candidates' backgrounds that are not quantified by grades and scores.

## FINANCIAL AID

*Students should submit:* FAFSA and parent and student 1040 form. Regular filing deadline is September 30. The Princeton Review suggests that all financial aid forms be submitted as soon as possible after January 1. *Need-based scholarships/grants offered:* Pell, SEOG, state scholarships/grants, private scholarships, and the school's own gift aid. *Loan aid offered:* Direct Subsidized Stafford, Direct Unsubsidized Stafford, Direct PLUS, Federal Perkins, Federal Nursing, state, college/university loans from institutional funds, Michigan Loan Program, and Health Professional student loans. Institutional employment available. Federal Work-Study Program available. Applicants will be notified of awards on a rolling basis beginning on or about April 30. Off-campus job opportunities are excellent.

## FROM THE ADMISSIONS OFFICE

"The University of Michigan is continuing its dynamic mission into the 21st century—the commitment to diversity. To accomplish our goals, efforts are in place across the campus to meet the challenges of racism, community, and change while preserving the important balance between tradition and preparation for the future. As the university's more than century-old tradition of excellence serves as its foundation, progress toward building a multicultural community is occurring at all levels of the institution. Students and scholars study and work closely together; the residence halls create a living community where lifelong friendships unfold."

---

## ADMISSIONS

| | |
|---|---:|
| **Admissions Rating** | **90** |
| # of applicants | 23,717 |
| % of applicants accepted | 55 |
| % of acceptees attending | 42 |

### FRESHMAN PROFILE

| | |
|---|---:|
| Range SAT Verbal | 570-670 |
| Average SAT Verbal | 615 |
| Range SAT Math | 610-710 |
| Average SAT Math | 654 |
| Range ACT Composite | 25-30 |
| Average ACT Composite | 27 |
| Minimum TOEFL | 560 |
| Average HS GPA | 3.7 |
| % graduated top 10% of class | 63 |
| % graduated top 25% of class | 90 |
| % graduated top 50% of class | 99 |

### DEADLINES

| | |
|---|---:|
| Regular admission | 2/1 |
| Regular notification | rolling |
| Nonfall registration? | yes |

### APPLICANTS ALSO LOOK AT
**AND OFTEN PREFER**
Brown
U. Penn
Dartmouth
**AND SOMETIMES PREFER**
Tufts
Brandeis
U. Chicago
Notre Dame
**AND RARELY PREFER**
Michigan State
Kenyon

### FINANCIAL FACTS

| | |
|---|---:|
| **Financial Aid Rating** | **75** |
| In-state tuition | $6,328 |
| Out-of-state tuition | $20,138 |
| Room & board | $5,780 |
| Books and supplies | $710 |
| Required fees | $185 |
| % frosh receiving aid | 28 |
| % undergrads receiving aid | 36 |
| Avg frosh grant | $5,607 |
| Avg frosh loan | $1,470 |

# UNIVERSITY OF MINNESOTA—TWIN CITIES

231 PILLSBURY DRIVE, SE, 240 WILLIAMSON HALL, MINNEAPOLIS, MN 55455-0115 • ADMISSIONS: 612-625-2008 • FAX: 612-626-1693

## CAMPUS LIFE

| | |
|---|---|
| **Quality of Life Rating** | **74** |
| Type of school | public |
| Affiliation | none |
| Environment | urban |

### STUDENTS

| | |
|---|---|
| Total undergrad enrollment | 31,824 |
| % male/female | 47/53 |
| % from out of state | 25 |
| % live on campus | 20 |
| % African American | 4 |
| % Asian | 9 |
| % Caucasian | 82 |
| % Hispanic | 2 |
| % Native American | 1 |
| % international | 2 |

### SURVEY SAYS . . .

*Students love Minneapolis, MN*
*Athletic facilities are great*
*Class discussions are rare*
*Political activism is hot*
*Students aren't religious*
*Campus difficult to get around*
*Large classes*
*Lots of TAs teach upper-level courses*
*Student publications are popular*
*Unattractive campus*

## ACADEMICS

| | |
|---|---|
| **Academic Rating** | **73** |
| Calendar | semester |
| Student/faculty ratio | 15:1 |
| Profs interesting rating | 86 |
| Profs accessible rating | 87 |
| Avg lab size | under 10 students |
| Avg reg class size | 10-19 students |

### MOST POPULAR MAJORS

psychology
English
engineering

## STUDENTS SPEAK OUT

### Academics

The "good" of most mega-universities is "the breadth of available courses and the number of well-respected departments," while the "bad" is "filling out an eight-page form every semester to prove my whereabouts for in-state tuition." But the University of Minnesota has clawed its way out of the red-tape slough and into the hearts of many of its students. One student relays, "As a first-year, I have noticed how well taken care of we are. They rearrange schedules to help our lives flow more easily." That kind of response to students' needs might be commonplace at a small school, but with around 37,000 students, "the 'U' offers a lot more than its affordable prestige." Still, "coming here fresh from high school with not a clue can be daunting"—"If you know what you want out of life, the 'U' is the best place to pursue it. If you don't know what you want, good luck." With excellent programs to choose from across-the-board, many students concentrate on pre-professional majors like business and management, journalism, psychology, and engineering. Professors get mixed marks for instruction skills ("They know what they're talking about, but a lot of times we don't") but have definitely improved in the accessibility category since our last survey: "All I've ever had to do here is ask, and professors have jumped through rings to help me out." Lab, computer, and library facilities and other research resources get good marks from the students, and the recreational/athletic facilities "rock."

### Life

Located in the heart of the Twin Cities, the University of Minnesota offers "cultural opportunities at every turn." The main campus is located in Minneapolis, where the gentler side of day life ("wonderful outdoor concerts, the world's largest mall, coffee shops, and plays") meets the darker side of night ("clubs, house parties, and bars kickin' it pretty much any day of the week"). Though the vast majority of students live off campus, there are still those who "enjoy hanging with people from the dorm and classes," and at least one sophomore is making a concerted effort to get the most from the "U": "I am active in a national fraternity and Minnesota sports. I really try to be involved with the university by joining school groups, so next year I'm interviewing for orientation leader." Quite a number of students (out-of-staters, most likely) would like to "build a dome over the campus in the winter just so we could feel our toes." Students gripe constantly about the "Campus Connector" buses, which are apparently "very unsafe and never on time (there is a schedule, right?)."

### Student Body

Diversity at the "U" far exceeds diversity in the state of Minnesota, but that's not to say you'll feel transported to UC—Berkeley; more than four-fifths of the student body is white, and a great many of them are from Minnesota. Interaction has reportedly improved, but it still has a ways to go. Perhaps if the school were composed of fewer commuters, or more on-campus activities were taken advantage of, the students "would feel like there was more of a community here. But as it is right now, people just don't want to make this place their true home."

# UNIVERSITY OF MINNESOTA—TWIN CITIES

FINANCIAL AID: 612-624-1665 • E-MAIL: ADMISSIONS@TC.UMN.EDU • WEBSITE: WWW.UMN.EDU/TC/PROSPECTIVE

## ADMISSIONS

*Very important* academic and nonacademic factors considered by the admissions committee include secondary school record. *Important* factors considered include standardized test scores and talent/ability. *Other* factors considered include class rank, essays, and recommendations. Factors *not* considered include alumni/ae relation, character/personal qualities, extracurricular activities, geography, interview, minority status, religious affiliation/commitment, state residency, volunteer work, and work experience. SAT I or ACT required. TOEFL required of all international applicants. High school diploma is required and GED is accepted. *High school units required/recommended:* 16 total required; 4 English required, 3 math required, 4 math recommended, 3 science required, 2 science lab required, 3 social studies required, 2 foreign language required, 1 visual and/or performing arts required. *The admissions office says:* "Minority students, students with special talents, and students active in extracurricular activities may receive special consideration if their admissions indices are not high enough for standard admission."

### The Inside Word

Despite what looks to be a fairly choosy admissions rate, it's the sheer volume of applicants that creates a selective situation at Minnesota. Admission is by formula; only those with weak course selections and inconsistent academic records need to work up a sweat over getting admitted.

## FINANCIAL AID

*Students should submit:* FAFSA. There is no regular filing deadline. The Princeton Review suggests that all financial aid forms be submitted as soon as possible after January 1. *Need-based scholarships/grants offered:* Pell, SEOG, state scholarships/grants, private scholarships, the school's own gift aid, NSS, ROTC scholarships, academic merit scholarships, athletic scholarships, and aid for undergraduate international students. *Loan aid offered:* Direct Subsidized Stafford, Direct Unsubsidized Stafford, state, college/university loans from institutional funds, NSL, Health Professions loans, private loans, and PLUS. Institutional employment available. Federal Work-Study Program available. Off-campus job opportunities are excellent.

## FROM THE ADMISSIONS OFFICE

"Known globally as a leader in teaching, research, and public service, the University of Minnesota ranks among the top 20 public universities in the nation. The classic Big 10 campus, located in the heart of the Minneapolis–St. Paul metropolitan area, provides a world-class setting for lifelong learning. In addition to the top-notch academic programs (and more than 150 undergraduate degrees), the university offers an Undergraduate Research Opportunities Program that is a national model; one of the largest study abroad programs in the country; 20,000 computers available for use in labs across campus; and extraordinary opportunities for internships, employment, and personal enrichment. Students can pursue interests in more than 400 official student organizations. Committed to offering its students an education that is not only outstanding but affordable, the university has been recognized as a 'best value' and 'best buy.' Students from other states may qualify for discounted tuition through one of the university's reciprocity agreements. Plus, the university awards a number of academic scholarships to qualified freshmen. The university community is a broad mix of ethnic backgrounds, interests, and cultures from all 50 states and 110 foreign countries, creating a welcoming feeling on campus. Beyond campus, the dynamic communities of Minneapolis and St. Paul offer something for everyone—a nationally recognized arts and theater community, a thriving entertainment industry, a host of Fortune 500 companies, four glorious seasons of outdoor recreation, exciting professional sports, shopping, and restaurants for every taste."

## ADMISSIONS

| | |
|---|---|
| **Admissions Rating** | **80** |
| # of applicants | 14,467 |
| % of applicants accepted | 75 |
| % of acceptees attending | 45 |

### FRESHMAN PROFILE

| | |
|---|---|
| Range SAT Verbal | 530-650 |
| Average SAT Verbal | 588 |
| Range SAT Math | 550-675 |
| Average SAT Math | 611 |
| Range ACT Composite | 22-28 |
| Average ACT Composite | 25 |
| Minimum TOEFL | 550 |
| % graduated top 10% of class | 30 |
| % graduated top 25% of class | 62 |
| % graduated top 50% of class | 89 |

### DEADLINES

| | |
|---|---|
| Regular admission | 12/15 |
| Nonfall registration? | yes |

### APPLICANTS ALSO LOOK AT
**AND OFTEN PREFER**
St. Olaf
Iowa State
**AND SOMETIMES PREFER**
U. Wisconsin—Madison
U. Iowa
U. Michigan—Ann Arbor
Michigan State
**AND RARELY PREFER**
Syracuse
Case Western

### FINANCIAL FACTS

| | |
|---|---|
| **Financial Aid Rating** | **72** |
| In-state tuition | $4,401 |
| Out-of-state tuition | $12,312 |
| Room & board | $4,914 |
| Books and supplies | $730 |
| Required fees | $476 |
| % frosh receiving aid | 47 |
| % undergrads receiving aid | 51 |
| Avg frosh grant | $4,292 |
| Avg frosh loan | $3,587 |

# UNIVERSITY OF MISSISSIPPI

145 MARTINDALE, UNIVERSITY, MS 38677 • ADMISSIONS: 662-915-7226 • FAX: 662-915-5869

## CAMPUS LIFE

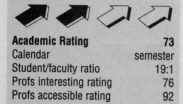

**Quality of Life Rating**    **86**
Type of school    public
Affiliation    none
Environment    rural

### STUDENTS
Total undergrad enrollment    9,608
% male/female    48/52
% from out of state    33
% from public high school    70
% live on campus    37
% in (# of) fraternities    31 (19)
% in (# of) sororities    34 (13)
% African American    12
% Asian    1
% Caucasian    85
% Hispanic    1
% international    1
# of countries represented    68

### SURVEY SAYS . . .
*Beautiful campus*
*Athletic facilities are great*
*Students love Oxford, MS*
*Frats and sororities dominate social*
*scene*
*Great off-campus food*
*Students aren't religious*
*Theater is unpopular*
*Registration is a pain*

## ACADEMICS

**Academic Rating**    **73**
Calendar    semester
Student/faculty ratio    19:1
Profs interesting rating    76
Profs accessible rating    92

### MOST POPULAR MAJORS
general business
accountancy
biological science

## STUDENTS SPEAK OUT
### Academics
"Strong school spirit," a "rich heritage," and a great regional reputation make the "affordable" University of Mississippi "a comfortable learning environment." "Ole Miss" boasts a host of fine programs, among them "great journalism and pharmacy programs" (first-year pharmacy students average an extraordinary high school GPA of 3.8 and an ACT composite of 29). The overall spectrum on this campus of academic programs "ranges from very easy to extremely difficult," and students tell us that "the average class is only somewhat challenging to the average student." The intimate Honors College "has excellent teachers who actually want their students to learn something," according to a junior. "Regular academic classes," on the other hand, can be "boring" because "it's just lecture." Nevertheless, most professors "rate decently" and are "unusually helpful and personable for a school so large," at least the ones "who aren't 80 years old." Many of the profs "really love Ole Miss and care about students' welfare, and they remember your name," beams a senior. Despite a notably exorbitant activity fee and "complex" hoops that students at this big state university must occasionally jump through, the administration receives commendable marks as well. "I am very pleased with the administration, especially the accessibility of our chancellor," says a sophomore. "It's pretty amazing to be walking on campus, pass the chancellor, and hear him say, 'Hi Kara, how are you?' That's cool."

### LIFE
"The campus is majestic, and traditions run deep" at Ole Miss, where the school colors are Red and Blue ("from the crimson of Harvard and the blue of Yale"). Be warned, though: Social life here can be "a culture shock" if you aren't from Mississippi or the Deep South. Fraternities and sororities control much of the social scene. "Just about everything is Greek-oriented," explains a senior. "If you like the frat scene, you will be in heaven." For students who don't equate the Greek system with paradise, the "great" and charming surrounding town of Oxford "offers a number of alternatives." There is "a wonderful local music and art scene," and culture abounds—so much so that *USA Today* named Oxford the "Thriving New South Arts Mecca" and one of the top six college towns in the nation. Students say drug and alcohol policies at Ole Miss are "strict," but "enforcement isn't," and the local bar scene is hopping. "Nearby casinos" provide a nice study break as well, as does simply "hanging out and watching movies with friends." For athletes, "there is a very nice physical fitness facility on campus," and sports are "big" at Ole Miss, "especially" the "festive" football weekends. "I love football season at Ole Miss," says a sophomore. "Students and alumni gather in The Grove and have a great big picnic. Everyone has their tables decorated in red and blue, and the band plays fight songs. Those weekends are the best times at Ole Miss."

### STUDENTS
"That good old 'southern hospitality' that you hear about is actually real and sincere" at the University of Mississippi, at least according to the students here. In fact, if you ask the students here, their "friendliness is unrivaled" across the fruited plain. The "very laid-back" students at Ole Miss also describe themselves as somewhere between "a little elitist" and "way too snobby," though. And students admit that there is "some racism" on campus as well as a notable absence of intermingling across racial lines. On the whole, though, students regard themselves as "pretty agreeable, usually," and they say it's "easy to mix with other people" on campus and in the town of Oxford. Ole Miss also boasts "great alumni relations," which is a real plus because it means that the school gets a lot of money from previous graduates.

FINANCIAL AID: 662-915-7175 • E-MAIL: ADMISSIONS@OLEMISS.EDU • WEBSITE: WWW.OLEMISS.EDU

## ADMISSIONS

*Very important* academic and nonacademic factors considered by the admissions committee include character/personal qualities, essays, secondary school record, standardized test scores, talent/ability, and volunteer work. *Important* factors considered include class rank, extracurricular activities, interview, recommendations, and work experience. *Other* factors considered include alumni/ae relation. Factors *not* considered include geography, minority status, religious affiliation/commitment, and state residency. SAT I or ACT required, ACT preferred. TOEFL required of all international applicants. High school diploma is required and GED is accepted. *High school units required/recommended:* 4 English required, 3 math required, 4 math recommended, 2 science required, 4 science recommended, 2 science lab required, 2 foreign language required, 4 foreign language recommended, 2 social studies required, 2 history required.

### The Inside Word

The admissions process at Ole Miss is relatively stress-free. Solid high school achievement in college-prep courses will open the doors for most applicants.

## FINANCIAL AID

*Students should submit:* FAFSA. There is no regular filing deadline. The Princeton Review suggests that all financial aid forms be submitted as soon as possible after January 1. *Need-based scholarships/grants offered:* Pell, SEOG, state scholarships/grants, private scholarships, and the school's own gift aid. *Loan aid offered:* FFEL Subsidized Stafford, FFEL Unsubsidized Stafford, FFEL PLUS, Federal Perkins, and college/university loans from institutional funds. Institutional employment available. Federal Work-Study Program available. Applicants will be notified of awards on a rolling basis beginning on or about April 1. Off-campus job opportunities are good.

## FROM THE ADMISSIONS OFFICE

"The flagship university of the state, the University of Mississippi offers extraordinary academic opportunities to extraordinary students through such programs as the McDonnell-Barksdale Honors College and the Croft Institute for International Studies. Known around the world as "Ole Miss," the university offers more than 100 academic programs. In the 1998-1999 academic year, the university was one of only 10 schools in the nation whose students garnered both prestigious Rhodes and Truman scholarships. Each residence hall room is hardwired with two connections to the university's computer network, providing 24-hour access to the library, Internet, and more. The first thing most people notice about Ole Miss is its beauty. The Grove and the Circle—broad expanses of shaded lawn at the heart of the campus—are beloved by students, faculty, and alumni."

## ADMISSIONS

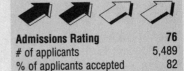

| | |
|---|---|
| Admissions Rating | 76 |
| # of applicants | 5,489 |
| % of applicants accepted | 82 |
| % of acceptees attending | 44 |

### FRESHMAN PROFILE

| | |
|---|---|
| Range ACT Composite | 20-27 |
| Average ACT Composite | 23 |
| Minimum TOEFL | 550 |
| % graduated top 10% of class | 37 |
| % graduated top 25% of class | 52 |
| % graduated top 50% of class | 86 |

### DEADLINES

| | |
|---|---|
| Priority admission deadline | 6/15 |
| Regular admission | 7/20 |
| Nonfall registration? | yes |

### FINANCIAL FACTS

| | |
|---|---|
| Financial Aid Rating | 85 |
| In-state tuition | $3,153 |
| Out-of-state tuition | $7,106 |
| Room & board | $5,060 |
| Books and supplies | $750 |
| % frosh receiving aid | 32 |
| % undergrads receiving aid | 37 |

# UNIVERSITY OF MISSOURI—ROLLA

106 PARKER HALL, ROLLA, MO 65409 • ADMISSIONS: 573-341-4165 • FAX: 573-341-4082

## STUDENTS SPEAK OUT

### Academics

For a bargain in engineering education, it's hard to beat the University of Missouri—Rolla, a "small, very efficient school" with a "solid reputation" throughout the Midwest for "preparing students for industry" and churning out capable, extremely knowledgeable engineers. Rolla grills its students with a "rigid academic program" made up of "two components." "The first two years are the high-stress, flunk-out courses," explains a senior. "The second component kicks in after about half of the people who enrolled run home with their tails between their legs and you start your upper-level classes." Students say that, while these junior- and senior-level courses are much more rewarding, the introductory courses eventually pay big dividends. Still, getting to the upper-level is a real battle; cautions one computer science major, "If you don't plan on studying constantly, there is no reason for you to come here." Rolla's faculty receives mixed reviews. "Great teachers," notes one mechanical engineer. "They can relate, crack jokes, and most of them know everything about their specialty." Counters another student, "I have a class right now where the professor sounds like a teacher from a Charlie Brown cartoon." The final tally? "We have a broad spectrum of students and faculty," writes a typical student. "Some are Ivy League caliber; many are far below that level." Most students agree, however, that a Rolla education is worth putting up with some incomprehensible professors and more than a few all-nighters. "UMR is not for the academically timid," writes one student. "Professors expect a lot out of students. If you apply yourself, you'll get a great education and a solid foundation."

### Life

Reflecting on the gargantuan workload at Rolla, one student concedes that "UMR can drain the life out of you. I like the hard work and the education, but I think socially the students suffer." Neither the UMR campus nor the town of Rolla offers much in the way of diversion. "There is very little to do in Rolla, Missouri," reports one engineer. "There is one movie theater, one bar, and Wal-Mart. We go to the bar, fraternity parties, watch movies, and pray for the day we can leave and move to a real city." Another observes that "you really have to make your own fun because the one bar in town isn't that great and there is no shopping nearby. Lots of drinking and such. The whole thing is comparable to many people's high school experience, I think." Many students pack up and leave as soon as their week's classes are done. Some "go clubbing" in St. Louis; others head for parties at the considerably larger state universities in nearby Columbia and Springfield. Those who don't leave town every weekend agree that "frat life keeps most of us sane." Though UMR won't be vying for any campus beauty awards in the near future, the many national parks and "really pretty countryside" surrounding Rolla "provide a couple of walking trails." Outdoor enthusiasts will find many nearby activities to their liking, including "caving, fishing, camping, and hiking."

### Student Body

Rolla's engineers are predominantly "politically and culturally conservative" small towners who are "extremely intelligent" and "really strange." The extreme male-female ratio here is a source of frustration to many. Writes one, "Women: Can't live with 'em, can't go to a social event without 'em being the center of attention. The four-to-one male-female ratio sucks! Nice guys finish last . . . always!" Another presents a slightly different spin, observing that "the main problem is that women are scarce. However, I think if a guy displays some social skills (which are generally lacking around here) he actually has a chance." Complicating the situation is the fact that "a good percentage of the students here are introverted." Concludes one student, "Social life at this school is not really good for most men, but great for women. Most men don't like it here. I go home for fun most times."

FINANCIAL AID: 800-522-0938 • E-MAIL: UMROLLA@UMR.EDU • WEBSITE: WWW.UMR.EDU

## ADMISSIONS

*Very important* academic and nonacademic factors considered by the admissions committee include secondary school record. *Important* factors considered include alumni/ae relation, character/personal qualities, essays, extracurricular activities, geography, minority status, recommendations, standardized test scores, state residency, talent/ability, volunteer work, and work experience. *Other* factors considered include class rank. Factors *not* considered include interview and religious affiliation/commitment. SAT I or ACT required. TOEFL required of all international applicants. High school diploma is required and GED is accepted. *High school units required/recommended:* 16 total required; 2 English required, 4 English recommended, 2 math required, 3 math recommended, 1 science required, 2 science recommended, 1 science lab required, 2 science lab recommended, 2 foreign language recommended, 4 social studies recommended, 1 elective recommended. *The admissions office says:* "[We] make every attempt to process applications and respond within two weeks."

### The Inside Word

This public university admissions committee functions pretty much the same as most others; admission is based on numbers and course distribution requirements. The applicant pool is small, well-qualified, and self-selected; despite the extremely high admit rate, only strong students are likely to meet with success.

## FINANCIAL AID

*Students should submit:* Institution's own financial aid form. There is no regular filing deadline. The Princeton Review suggests that all financial aid forms be submitted as soon as possible after January 1. *Need-based scholarships/grants offered:* Pell, SEOG, state scholarships/grants, private scholarships, the school's own gift aid, and United Negro College Fund. *Loan aid offered:* Direct Subsidized Stafford, Direct Unsubsidized Stafford, Direct PLUS, and Federal Perkins. Institutional employment available. Federal Work-Study Program available. Applicants will be notified of awards on a rolling basis beginning on or about April 1. Off-campus job opportunities are good.

## FROM THE ADMISSIONS OFFICE

"Students come to the University of Missouri—Rolla because they want a solid education that will prepare them to solve the technical and societal problems of tomorrow. And that's exactly what they get, a top-flight education at an affordable, pulic school price, opportunities for hands-on research, leadership experience on campus and off, and one of the nation's most successful academic-industry partnerships, our cooperative education program. UMR is truly educating tomorrow's leaders."

## ADMISSIONS

| | |
|---|---:|
| **Admissions Rating** | **82** |
| # of applicants | 1,827 |
| % of applicants accepted | 92 |
| % of acceptees attending | 42 |

### FRESHMAN PROFILE

| | |
|---|---:|
| Range SAT Verbal | 530-660 |
| Average SAT Verbal | 597 |
| Range SAT Math | 600-700 |
| Average SAT Math | 646 |
| Range ACT Composite | 26-30 |
| Average ACT Composite | 27 |
| Minimum TOEFL | 550 |
| Average HS GPA | 3.5 |
| % graduated top 10% of class | 46 |
| % graduated top 25% of class | 77 |
| % graduated top 50% of class | 96 |

### DEADLINES

| | |
|---|---:|
| Priority admission deadline | 11/1 |
| Regular admission | 6/1 |
| Nonfall registration? | yes |

### APPLICANTS ALSO LOOK AT AND OFTEN PREFER

U. Missouri—Columbia
U. Illinois—Urbana-Champaign
MIT
Northeast Missouri State
U. Wisconsin—Madison

### AND SOMETIMES PREFER

U. Iowa
Georgia Tech.
Purdue U.—West Lafayette

### FINANCIAL FACTS

| | |
|---|---:|
| **Financial Aid Rating** | **84** |
| In-state tuition | $4,245 |
| Out-of-state tuition | $12,690 |
| Room & board | $5,060 |
| Books and supplies | $850 |
| Required fees | $730 |
| % frosh receiving aid | 54 |
| % undergrads receiving aid | 54 |
| Avg frosh grant | $6,400 |
| Avg frosh loan | $3,400 |

# UNIVERSITY OF MONTANA—MISSOULA

103 LODGE BUILDING, MISSOULA, MT 59812 • ADMISSIONS: 406-243-6266 • FAX: 406-243-5711

## CAMPUS LIFE

| | |
|---|---|
| **Quality of Life Rating** | **78** |
| Type of school | public |
| Affiliation | none |
| Environment | urban |

### STUDENTS

| | |
|---|---|
| Total undergrad enrollment | 10,666 |
| % male/female | 47/53 |
| % from out of state | 26 |
| % from public high school | 56 |
| % live on campus | 21 |
| % in (# of) fraternities | 6 (8) |
| % in (# of) sororities | 5 (4) |
| % Asian | 1 |
| % Caucasian | 89 |
| % Hispanic | 1 |
| % Native American | 3 |
| % international | 2 |

### SURVEY SAYS . . .

Student publications are popular
Students love Missoula, MT
Everyone loves the Grizzlies
Theater is hot
Students aren't religious
Beautiful campus
Lousy off-campus food
Computer facilities need improving
Students aren't religious
Diversity lacking on campus

## ACADEMICS

| | |
|---|---|
| **Academic Rating** | **78** |
| Calendar | semester |
| Student/faculty ratio | 19:1 |
| Profs interesting rating | 72 |
| Profs accessible rating | 70 |
| % profs teaching UG courses | 100 |
| % classes taught by TAs | 7 |
| Avg lab size | 20-29 students |
| Avg reg class size | 20-29 students |

### MOST POPULAR MAJORS
business administration
forestry
education

## STUDENTS SPEAK OUT
### Academics

The University of Montana ranks fourth in the nation among public universities in producing Rhodes Scholars—pretty impressive for a big square-state school. UM offers "a great academic experience," according to the students here. "I have had one positive experience after another," beams a business administration major. Professors are "a hodgepodge, as is common at many universities, some good, some not-so-good." The good ones are "very approachable, and they actually treat you as a person, not just a number." Many are also highly respected and "experienced" in their fields. "When you have a professor miss a class because he has been chosen to be an advisor to NATO, you know you have a good professor," speculates a political science major. Even the most distinguished profs are "extremely nice," though, and can be seen "riding bicycles to school." Teaching assistants, on the other hand, are often "very cocky and don't know how to teach." Some students find the administration "inaccessible" and "rude," while others claim that administrators "have an open-door policy and make an effort to see many different sides of an issue." One student mentions that "the registration system could use some work," and some techies gripe that the computer labs need an upgrade. UM boasts good facilities, including nearby Lubrecht Forest, a huge 29,000-acre "teaching and research forest" located 35 miles northeast of Missoula, and two working ranches.

### Life

"I really enjoy it here in Missoula," exclaims a sophomore. It's difficult not to. This "blue-collar town dominated by liberal university students" offers "great quality of life," and it's generally "an enjoyable place to live." "Missoula has a few dance clubs," and "frequenting the bars downtown is a big draw" as well. On campus, a "relaxed atmosphere" is pervasive, but students say there is "lots of school spirit" and no shortage of extracurricular activities. UM's biggest enticement, though, is the stunning multitude of wilderness areas "within minutes of campus." Western Montana boasts more than 5 million acres of preserved wilderness, "more than 200 miles of floatable river," and some of the best skiing anywhere. "Getting up in the mountains and enjoying life" is a daily possibility. The many, many outdoor activities available to students include, in no particular order, "kayaking, rafting, rock climbing," "snowboarding, and hunting." The environment is also a big deal at UM. "Logging and recycling are big news on our campus," observes a sophomore. "People chain themselves to buildings in protest" from time to time. In the complaints department, students say UM "needs better athletic facilities" and "better lighting on campus for security reasons."

### Student Body

At UM, "there are lots of different types of students," explains a senior, but "they don't all interact with each other." The "individualists" here promise to give you "the opportunity to be yourself," says another senior. "I think that is what's stressed most at U of M." On the other hand, "everybody on this campus has a cause for everything" that "gets tiring," at least according to one pragmatic first-year student. Students describe themselves as generally "nice, open-minded, and accepting." There are a great many in-staters here, and "a lot are paying their own way." Not surprisingly, they tend to take academics "fairly seriously." Others are "very easygoing," nature-loving types.

# UNIVERSITY OF MONTANA—MISSOULA

FINANCIAL AID: 406-243-5373 • E-MAIL: ADMISS@SELWAY.UMT.EDU • WEBSITE: WWW.UMT.EDU

## ADMISSIONS

*Very important* academic and nonacademic factors considered by the admissions committee include secondary school record and standardized test scores. *Important* factors considered include essays. *Other* factors considered include extracurricular activities, recommendations, talent/ability, volunteer work, and work experience. Factors *not* considered include alumni/ae relation, character/personal qualities, class rank, geography, interview, minority status, religious affiliation/commitment, and state residency. SAT I or ACT required. TOEFL required of all international applicants. High school diploma is required and GED is accepted. *High school units required/recommended:* 20 total recommended; 4 English recommended, 4 math recommended, 3 science recommended, 3 science lab recommended, 3 foreign language recommended, 2 social studies recommended, 1 history recommended.

### The Inside Word

Montana's rolling admissions process places few demands on its applicants. Most students with a college-prep curriculum in high school and average grades should encounter no trouble gaining admission.

## FINANCIAL AID

*Students should submit:* FAFSA, institution's own financial aid form, and CSS/Financial Aid PROFILE. The Princeton Review suggests that all financial aid forms be submitted as soon as possible after January 1. *Need-based scholarships/grants offered:* Pell, SEOG, state scholarships/grants, private scholarships, and the school's own gift aid. *Loan aid offered:* FFEL Subsidized Stafford, FFEL Unsubsidized Stafford, FFEL PLUS, and Federal Perkins. Institutional employment available. Federal Work-Study Program available. Applicants will be notified of awards on a rolling basis beginning on or about April 1. Off-campus job opportunities are excellent.

## FROM THE ADMISSIONS OFFICE

"There's something special about this place. It's something different for each person. For some, it's the blend of academic quality and outdoor recreation. For others, it's size. Not too big. Not too little. Just right. Twelve thousand students. A community that could pass for a cozy college town or a bustling big city, depending on your point of view. There's a lot happening, but you won't get lost. There are the people. Friendly. Diverse. They come from all over the world to study and learn and to live a good life. Mostly to live a good life. They come to a place to be inspired. A place where they feel comfortable yet challenged. Some never leave. Most never want to."

## ADMISSIONS

| | |
|---|---|
| Admissions Rating | 76 |
| # of applicants | 3,456 |
| % of applicants accepted | 86 |
| % of acceptees attending | 63 |

### FRESHMAN PROFILE

| | |
|---|---|
| Range SAT Verbal | 450-600 |
| Average SAT Verbal | 550 |
| Range SAT Math | 440-590 |
| Average SAT Math | 540 |
| Range ACT Composite | 19-26 |
| Average ACT Composite | 23 |
| Minimum TOEFL | 500 |
| Average HS GPA | 3.2 |
| % graduated top 10% of class | 13 |
| % graduated top 25% of class | 35 |
| % graduated top 50% of class | 68 |

### DEADLINES

| | |
|---|---|
| Regular notification | rolling |
| Nonfall registration? | yes |

### FINANCIAL FACTS

| | |
|---|---|
| Financial Aid Rating | 85 |
| In-state tuition | $3,064 |
| Out-of-state tuition | $8,311 |
| Room & board | $4,800 |
| Books and supplies | $1,248 |
| % frosh receiving aid | 49 |
| % undergrads receiving aid | 48 |
| Avg frosh grant | $2,500 |
| Avg frosh loan | $2,849 |

# UNIVERSITY OF NEBRASKA—LINCOLN

1410 Q STREET, LINCOLN, NE 68588-0417 • ADMISSIONS: 402-472-2023 • FAX: 402-472-0670

## CAMPUS LIFE

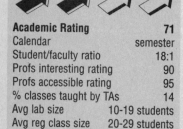

| Quality of Life Rating | 88 |
|---|---|
| Type of school | public |
| Affiliation | none |
| Environment | urban |

### STUDENTS

| | |
|---|---|
| Total undergrad enrollment | 17,968 |
| % male/female | 53/47 |
| % from out of state | 17 |
| % live on campus | 25 |
| % in (# of) fraternities | 11 (25) |
| % in (# of) sororities | 12 (15) |
| % African American | 2 |
| % Asian | 2 |
| % Caucasian | 90 |
| % Hispanic | 2 |
| % Native American | 1 |
| % international | 3 |

### SURVEY SAYS . . .

(Almost) everyone plays intramural sports
Everyone loves the Cornhuskers
Frats and sororities dominate social scene
Students are happy
Student publications are popular
Computer facilities need improving
Library needs improving
Class discussions are rare

## ACADEMICS

| Academic Rating | 71 |
|---|---|
| Calendar | semester |
| Student/faculty ratio | 18:1 |
| Profs interesting rating | 90 |
| Profs accessible rating | 95 |
| % classes taught by TAs | 14 |
| Avg lab size | 10-19 students |
| Avg reg class size | 20-29 students |

### MOST POPULAR MAJORS
psychology
finance
accounting

## STUDENTS SPEAK OUT

### Academics

Although most undergrads are drawn to University of Nebraska at Lincoln by the low in-state tuition, UNL has a lot more to offer students than just an affordable degree. This gargantuan research institute has something for everybody, with 10 undergraduate divisions in the arts, sciences, and pre-professional fields. Business, education, engineering, psychology, and agricultural sciences are huge at UNL, but the school is also home to prospering humanities and fine arts programs. As at many state universities, the scope of the institution can be intimidating. Writes one student, "College life at UNL is like a deli shop in New York: so many options and so many people pushing you to hurry the hell up." Another student notes: "As with any institution, there are many levels of bureaucracy one must traverse to get things done. However, the opportunity to do so exists and, with proper patience, one can have his/her concerns addressed." Faculty members earn mixed grades here, with some described as "highly informed educators that stress the importance of becoming involved in classes," while others "only recite facts and expect students to simply regurgitate information." The key, students say, is to research classes and professors aggressively. Of the school's two campuses, City Campus "is larger and offers more programs for students" than East Campus. Students report that "the unity between the two campuses needs improvement."

### Life

The pillars of Nebraska extracurricular life are intercollegiate sports and the Greek system, in that order. Especially during the fall semester, campus life revolves around the five-time national champion football squad. Explains one student, "Husker football is life on game day Saturdays. Everyone goes to the games. The stadium is unreal; it becomes the third largest city in the state on game days." By comparison, Greek membership is relatively low at 3,000, but students report that the "strong Greek system" serves as the nexus of weekend social life. Even more important, "Outside of Greek houses, no one really knows each other. There aren't that many chances to interact." Students note that "there is a big rift between Greeks, residence hall students, and commuters." Beyond these two mainstays of UNL life, students enjoy an "excellent intramural sports program," a "great recreation center," and "many opportunities for students to get involved in running the school." Hometown Lincoln "is very responsive to UNL students. There are many restaurants, theaters, and other venues for us."

### Student Body

Don't come to Nebraska seeking the company of ivory tower intellectuals. Students here describe their classmates as "solely concerned with grades and jobs for the future." Explains one student, "Students are very focused on 'getting the grade' and minimum requirements for graduation. It is rare that a student will take a class merely for intellectual stimulation. There is a stretch of about 20 bars within two blocks of campus, and they occupy a great deal of students' time." The many part-timers and nontraditional returning students add to the sense that the UNL student body is not one community, but rather a conglomerate of many smaller subcommunities. These groups don't often interact, but when they do, "students at the University of Nebraska reflect midwestern values and tend to represent Nebraska well with their fairly courteous personalities.

## ADMISSIONS

*Very important* academic and nonacademic factors considered by the admissions committee include class rank and secondary school record. *Important* factors considered include alumni/ae relation, essays, extracurricular activities, interview, minority status, recommendations, and standardized test scores. *Other* factors considered include talent/ability. Factors *not* considered include character/personal qualities, geography, religious affiliation/commitment, and state residency. SAT I or ACT required, ACT preferred. TOEFL required of all international applicants. High school diploma is required and GED is accepted. *High school units required/recommended:* 4 English recommended, 3 math recommended, 3 science recommended, 3 science lab recommended, 3 foreign language recommended, 3 social studies recommended.

### The Inside Word

Like most large-scale universities, Nebraska—Lincoln admits a huge freshman class each year. The need for numbers is reflected in an admissions process that concentrates on them—your course selection, GPA, and test scores will be all they need to see. Unless you've had troubles academically, they're likely to welcome you aboard, though some programs have higher expectations than others.

## FINANCIAL AID

*Students should submit:* FAFSA. There is no regular filing deadline. The Princeton Review suggests that all financial aid forms be submitted as soon as possible after January 1. *Need-based scholarships/grants offered:* Pell, SEOG, state scholarships/grants, private scholarships, and the school's own gift aid. *Loan aid offered:* Direct Subsidized Stafford, Direct Unsubsidized Stafford, Direct PLUS, Federal Perkins, and college/university loans from institutional funds. Institutional employment available. Federal Work-Study Program available. Applicants will be notified of awards on a rolling basis beginning on or about April 15. Off-campus job opportunities are excellent.

## FROM THE ADMISSIONS OFFICE

"Chartered in 1869, the University of Nebraska—Lincoln has since grown to become a major international research university, offering 149 undergraduate majors and 118 graduate programs. While 90 percent of the 23,000 students come from Nebraska, students from every state and 110 countries choose the university for its comprehensive programs and reputation for quality. Nebraska is classified as a Carnegie I Research Institution, recognizing the university's commitment to research funding and quality scholarship, and has been a member of the Association of American Universities since 1909—one of only 62 universities to claim this prestigious membership. These affiliations ensure Nebraska students are taught by nationally and internationally recognized faculty who are experts in their fields, bringing the latest discoveries into their classrooms. Lincoln—Nebraska's capital with a population of more than 213,000—offers the comfort and security of a college town with the cultural and entertainment opportunities of a larger city."

## ADMISSIONS

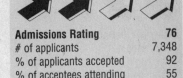

| | |
|---|---|
| **Admissions Rating** | **76** |
| # of applicants | 7,348 |
| % of applicants accepted | 92 |
| % of acceptees attending | 55 |

### FRESHMAN PROFILE

| | |
|---|---|
| Range SAT Verbal | 490-630 |
| Average SAT Verbal | 563 |
| Range SAT Math | 520-650 |
| Average SAT Math | 583 |
| Range ACT Composite | 21-27 |
| Average ACT Composite | 24 |
| Minimum TOEFL | 525 |
| % graduated top 10% of class | 24 |
| % graduated top 25% of class | 54 |
| % graduated top 50% of class | 84 |

### DEADLINES

| | |
|---|---|
| Priority admission deadline | 1/15 |
| Regular admission | 6/30 |
| Nonfall registration? | yes |

## FINANCIAL FACTS

| | |
|---|---|
| **Financial Aid Rating** | **79** |
| In-state tuition | $2,760 |
| Out-of-state tuition | $7,515 |
| Room & board | $4,310 |
| Books and supplies | $700 |
| Required fees | $690 |
| % frosh receiving aid | 42 |
| % undergrads receiving aid | 40 |
| Avg frosh grant | $5,294 |
| Avg frosh loan | $2,801 |

# UNIVERSITY OF NEVADA—LAS VEGAS

4505 MARYLAND PARKWAY, BOX 451021, LAS VEGAS, NV 89154-1021 • ADMISSIONS: 702-895-3443 • FAX: 702-895-1118

## CAMPUS LIFE

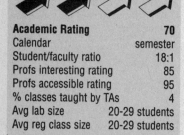

| Quality of Life Rating | 90 |
|---|---|
| Type of school | public |
| Affiliation | none |
| Environment | urban |

### STUDENTS

| | |
|---|---|
| Total undergrad enrollment | 17,327 |
| % male/female | 45/55 |
| % from out of state | 21 |
| % live on campus | 8 |
| % in (# of) fraternities | 7 (14) |
| % in (# of) sororities | 5 (7) |
| % African American | 7 |
| % Asian | 12 |
| % Caucasian | 66 |
| % Hispanic | 9 |
| % Native American | 1 |
| % international | 5 |

### SURVEY SAYS . . .

*(Almost) everyone plays intramural sports*
*Everyone loves the Runnin' Rebels*
*Athletic facilities are great*
*Dorms are like palaces*
*Great off-campus food*
*(Almost) no one listens to college radio*
*Student publications are ignored*

## ACADEMICS

| Academic Rating | 70 |
|---|---|
| Calendar | semester |
| Student/faculty ratio | 18:1 |
| Profs interesting rating | 85 |
| Profs accessible rating | 95 |
| % classes taught by TAs | 4 |
| Avg lab size | 20-29 students |
| Avg reg class size | 20-29 students |

### MOST POPULAR MAJORS
hotel administration
elementary education
communication studies

## STUDENTS SPEAK OUT

### Academics

Perhaps it's the fact that the University of Nevada at Las Vegas is located in America's fun capital. Perhaps it is because UNLV is a sizeable state school. Or, perhaps it's the fame/notoriety of its intercollegiate sports program (see "Campus Life," below). For whatever reason, students fret that "everyone thinks of UNLV as an easy, laid-back, fun kind of school. There's a serious academic side to it as well." UNLV undergrads agree that a rigorous and thorough education can easily be found here, not only in the well-known College of Hotel Administration but also elsewhere. Writes one double major in communications and political science, "UNLV is not just the best hotel school, it also has several other great programs." Students of social work, economics, mathematics, and (of course) hotel management are among those singing UNLV's praise in our survey. Students give UNLV professors and administrators unusually high marks for a state university. Writes one, "The teachers within the Hotel College are very knowledgeable. They have much insight to offer, much more so than from textbooks." Another notes that "the accessibility of faculty and administrators is tremendous. UNLV is truly a student-centered university." Notes one typical respondent, "Most of our professors are cool, except for the ones who are too caught up in research. They have no social skills, but they are smart." For those who can gain admission to UNLV's most selective program, "The best part about UNLV is the Honors College. The dean is awesome! He meets with all of us personally and pulls strings for us. The classes are small, and the professors are very personable."

### Life

There are many notable cities that host universities, but let's face it, there's only one Las Vegas. Understandably, the town that Bugsy Siegal and Frank Sinatra built inspires numerous comments from UNLV undergrads. The town has both supporters and detractors among the student body. Writes one of the former, "Hey, we live in Vegas!! It's the entertainment capital of the world!" Another points out some of the town's lesser-known assets, telling us that "Vegas has great buffets. Also, it's easy to get involved with politics (state, city, or federal)." Others stay away from America's gaming Mecca, writing, "We do not spend a lot of time on The Strip, except for occasions when visitors come from out of town. Vegas is not as much of a party town as the public tends to perceive." Says another, "Fortunately the school offers free, safe alternatives to gambling, drinking, and other inappropriate activities," including movies, club meetings, and guest lectures. Students also note that "the opportunities for student leadership on campus and within the residence halls are outstanding" and praise UNLV's "beautiful campus, young and growing." Points out one student, "The school is very new. The facilities are great." UNLV is host to more than 20 social and service fraternities and sororities. Says one student, "Both students and the school are very active in the community." UNLV's intercollegiate sports program has overcome earlier problems, including a well-publicized recruiting scandal in men's basketball.

### Student Body

UNLV attracts a large nontraditional undergraduate population. Explains one student, "The average age of students here is 25, which goes to show that you are never too old to get your education." UNLV students "have a variety of backgrounds, interests, and goals. Our campus is very nontraditional, which allows for a healthy base of diversity awareness." A minority population of more than one quarter promotes "a lot of multicultural diversity and awareness on campus," although some students complain that "there is sometimes a lack of interaction between cultures." Only about 1,500 students live on campus—"a lot of students commute"—so "lots of people come to school without taking advantage of the opportunities. The upside of the situation is that, for those who do want to get involved, it is very easy to do."

FINANCIAL AID: 702-895-3424 • E-MAIL: UNDRGRADADMISION@CCMAIL.NEVADA.EDU • WEBSITE: WWW.UNLV.EDU

## ADMISSIONS

*Important* academic and nonacademic factors considered by the admissions committee include essays, recommendations, and standardized test scores. Factors *not* considered include alumni/ae relation, character/personal qualities, class rank, extracurricular activities, geography, interview, minority status, religious affiliation/commitment, secondary school record, state residency, talent/ability, volunteer work, and work experience. TOEFL required of all international applicants. High school diploma is required and GED is not accepted. *High school units required/recommended:* 13 total required; 4 English required, 3 math required, 3 science required, 2 science lab required, 3 social studies required.

### The Inside Word

The admissions process at UNLV is pretty direct. The focus is on academic achievement as gauged by your course selection, grades, and test scores. A minimum of a 2.5 cumulative, unweighted GPA is required, which is atypical of more selective universities that factor in weighting for AP and honors courses. Student who fall short of course unit requirements can sometimes get admitted anyway due to a higher GPA or test scores

## FINANCIAL AID

*Students should submit:* FAFSA and institution's own financial aid form. Priority filing deadline is February 1. The Princeton Review suggests that all financial aid forms be submitted as soon as possible after January 1. *Need-based scholarships/grants offered:* Pell, SEOG, state scholarships/grants, private scholarships, and the school's own gift aid. *Loan aid offered:* Direct Subsidized Stafford, Direct Unsubsidized Stafford, Direct PLUS, Federal Perkins, and short-term emergency loans. Institution employment available. Federal Work-Study Program available. Applicants will be notified of awards on a rolling basis beginning on or about March 20. Off-campus job opportunities are excellent.

## FROM THE ADMISSIONS OFFICE

"The University of Nevada—Las Vegas is located in one of the fastest-growing, most exciting areas of the country, in the beautiful desert Southwest. Its distinctive programs include a world-class College of Hotel Administration, with the Las Vegas Strip as its lab; the new William S. Boyd School of Law; a nationally recognized honors college; a community-involved environmental studies program; innovative desert environment programs; international education opportunities; accredited architecture, social work, and business schools; a new physical therapy program; and numerous research centers and interdisciplinary programs. A $50 million library, with a state-of-the-art book retrieval system, opened in 2000. UNLV is also known for its nationally competitive intercollegiate athletics programs."

## ADMISSIONS

| | |
|---|---|
| Admissions Rating | 72 |
| # of applicants | 4,891 |
| % of applicants accepted | 79 |
| % of acceptees attending | 58 |

### FRESHMAN PROFILE

| | |
|---|---|
| Range SAT Verbal | 430-560 |
| Average SAT Verbal | 495 |
| Range SAT Math | 460-580 |
| Average SAT Math | 513 |
| Range ACT Composite | 19-24 |
| Average ACT Composite | 21 |
| Minimum TOEFL | 500 |
| Average HS GPA | 3.2 |
| % graduated top 10% of class | 22 |
| % graduated top 25% of class | 50 |
| % graduated top 50% of class | 87 |

### DEADLINES

| | |
|---|---|
| Priority admission deadline | 5/1 |
| Regular admission | 7/15 |
| Nonfall registration? | yes |

## FINANCIAL FACTS

| | |
|---|---|
| Financial Aid Rating | 80 |
| In-state tuition | $2,340 |
| Out-of-state tuition | $9,320 |
| Room & board | $5,800 |
| Books and supplies | $700 |
| Required fees | $46 |
| % frosh receiving aid | 26 |
| % undergrads receiving aid | 40 |
| Avg frosh grant | $3,806 |
| Avg frosh loan | $2,401 |

# UNIVERSITY OF NEW HAMPSHIRE

4 GARRISON AVENUE, DURHAM, NH 03824 • ADMISSIONS: 603-862-1360 • FAX: 603-862-0077

## CAMPUS LIFE

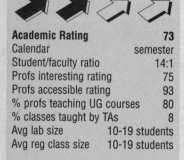

| | |
|---|---|
| **Quality of Life Rating** | **85** |
| Type of school | public |
| Affiliation | none |
| Environment | rural |

### STUDENTS

| | |
|---|---|
| Total undergrad enrollment | 10,927 |
| % male/female | 42/58 |
| % from out of state | 40 |
| % from public high school | 80 |
| % live on campus | 55 |
| % in (# of) fraternities | 5 (11) |
| % in (# of) sororities | 5 (5) |
| % African American | 1 |
| % Asian | 2 |
| % Caucasian | 92 |
| % Hispanic | 1 |
| % international | 1 |
| # of countries represented | 46 |

### SURVEY SAYS . . .

*Beautiful campus*
*Athletic facilities are great*
*Great library*
*Campus easy to get around*
*Great off-campus food*
*Student publications are ignored*
*Students don't get along with local community*
*(Almost) no one listens to college radio*

## ACADEMICS

| | |
|---|---|
| **Academic Rating** | **73** |
| Calendar | semester |
| Student/faculty ratio | 14:1 |
| Profs interesting rating | 75 |
| Profs accessible rating | 93 |
| % profs teaching UG courses | 80 |
| % classes taught by TAs | 8 |
| Avg lab size | 10-19 students |
| Avg reg class size | 10-19 students |

### MOST POPULAR MAJORS

business administration
English
psychology

## STUDENTS SPEAK OUT

### Academics

Students at University of New Hampshire appreciate the way their school offers an opportunity-filled, "well-rounded education" at a reasonable cost, even in the face of state budget cuts. Both "the administration and professors seem very willing and enthusiastic about helping us get the most out of our experience at college," somewhat reducing the effect of "limited funding from the state [that causes] classes and programs to be continually cut. Still, the atmosphere (lots of wool sweaters and trees) and the professors totally make up for it." Despite its funding problems, UNH continues to provide a variety of pre-professional and liberal arts majors, including popular programs in occupational therapy, computer science, nursing, and the sciences as well as an honors program and opportunities for undergraduate research. As at most state schools, getting the most of a UNH education requires independence and perseverance. "Like many other schools, the facilities and programs are somewhat available. It is up to the student to take advantage of such resources," explains one student. Professors, while "very well prepared and organized," are not always the best teachers. Undergrads in the sciences and math warn that "some professors need a reminder that students in introductory classes are not as in tune to the subject as the professors themselves are." Gripes one, "Most of our professors may as well just read textbook chapters aloud in class. I've experimented and found that I do just as well not going to class as I do going to class." Students are much more enthusiastic about campus facilities since the new, "very well-equipped" library opened its doors.

### Life

With an active Greek system, a wide array of on-campus organizations, numerous sporting and entertainment events, and several appealing roadtrip destinations nearby, UNH offers a fairly thorough extracurricular life to undergraduates. "As soon as I walked on this campus, I fell in love with it," writes one satisfied student. Adds another, "We have unbelievable school spirit," most evident at home games for "the awesome hockey team . . . Games are always packed. So are the parties!" Ah, the parties . . . once known as a major party school, UNH has tempered the scene in recent years by offering "tons of activities on campus during the week and weekend to [discourage] students from drinking and partying." According to at least one student, the policy is working; these days, "students balance parties, movies, on-campus events, and work." Add to the mix a "great rec center" and "a nice, attractive campus" that "is very beautiful in autumn" and you begin to understand why so many students are happy with life here. About the only downside is hometown Durham, which students describe as small. Fortunately, Portsmouth ("a nearby funky town"), Boston, and Hampton Beach all provide convenient destinations for those with cars. "I enjoy the ocean, mountains, and Boston nearby," notes one such student.

### Student Body

Given that the minority population of the state of New Hampshire is a meager two percent, it should come as no surprise that the student body at UNH is "very homogeneous." Points out one undergrad, "After all, this is New Hampshire, not Philadelphia." Diversity is found here in students' interests, embodied in the numerous student organizations they join. Students report that "this school is so big and has so many different clubs and organizations that I think it is easy to stick with your own crews, but if we for some reason all got together, I'm sure we'd have a blast." While admitting to being somewhat cliquish, students nonetheless describe themselves as "outgoing" and "friendly," the type of folks who "will smile and say 'hi'" as they pass each other on campus. Political activism is not high on most students' agenda; notes one, "Recycling our campus' cardboard is the sum result of our efforts to change the world."

FINANCIAL AID: 603-862-3600 • E-MAIL: ADMISSIONS@UNH.EDU • WEBSITE: WWW.UNH.EDU

## ADMISSIONS

*Very important* academic and nonacademic factors considered by the admissions committee include essays and secondary school record. *Important* factors considered include class rank and standardized test scores. *Other* factors considered include character/personal qualities, extracurricular activities, recommendations, talent/ability, volunteer work, and work experience. SAT I or ACT required, SAT I preferred. TOEFL required of all international applicants. High school diploma is required and GED is accepted. *High school units required/recommended:* 15 total required; 18 total recommended; 4 English required, 3 math required, 4 math recommended, 2 science required, 4 science recommended, 2 science lab required, 2 foreign language required, 4 foreign language recommended, 3 history required, 4 history recommended, 1 elective required.

### The Inside Word

New Hampshire's emphasis on academic accomplishment in the admissions process makes it clear that the admissions committee is looking for students who have taken high school seriously. Standardized tests take as much of a backseat here as is possible at a large public university.

## FINANCIAL AID

*Students should submit:* FAFSA. The Princeton Review suggests that all financial aid forms be submitted as soon as possible after January 1. *Need-based scholarships/grants offered:* Pell, SEOG, state scholarships/grants, private scholarships, and the school's own gift aid. *Loan aid offered:* FFEL Subsidized Stafford, FFEL Unsubsidized Stafford, FFEL PLUS, Federal Perkins, state, and college/university loans from institutional funds. Institutional employment available. Federal Work-Study Program available. Applicants will be notified of awards on a rolling basis beginning on or about March 15. Off-campus job opportunities are good.

## FROM THE ADMISSIONS OFFICE

"The University of New Hampshire is a public university founded in 1866 with an undergraduate population of 10,900 students. UNH offers an excellent education at a reasonable cost to students with a broad range of interests. Over 100 majors, 2,000 courses, and 150 student clubs and organizations are offered. Programs that provide valuable experience include the honors program, undergraduate research, internships, study abroad, and national exchange. UNH's location also caters to a wide range of interests. The campus itself is in a small town setting, surrounded by woods and farms; within 20 minutes is the Atlantic coastline, and just over an hour away are the White Mountains, Boston, and Portland."

## ADMISSIONS

| | |
|---|---|
| Admissions Rating | 77 |
| # of applicants | 10,057 |
| % of applicants accepted | 76 |
| % of acceptees attending | 34 |
| # accepting a place on wait list | 42 |
| % admitted from wait list | 100 |

### FRESHMAN PROFILE

| | |
|---|---|
| Range SAT Verbal | 500-610 |
| Average SAT Verbal | 560 |
| Range SAT Math | 510-620 |
| Average SAT Math | 560 |
| Minimum TOEFL | 550 |
| % graduated top 10% of class | 19 |
| % graduated top 25% of class | 58 |
| % graduated top 50% of class | 94 |

### DEADLINES

| | |
|---|---|
| Regular admission | 2/1 |
| Regular notification | 4/15 |
| Nonfall registration? | yes |

### APPLICANTS ALSO LOOK AT

**AND OFTEN PREFER**
U. Mass—Amherst
U. Vermont

**AND SOMETIMES PREFER**
U. Conn
Boston Coll.
Syracuse
Northeastern U.

**AND RARELY PREFER**
Providence
U. Rhode Island
Keene State
Stonehill C.

### FINANCIAL FACTS

| | |
|---|---|
| Financial Aid Rating | 80 |
| Books and supplies | $1,000 |
| % frosh receiving aid | 52 |
| % undergrads receiving aid | 54 |
| Avg frosh grant | $3,813 |
| Avg frosh loan | $4,375 |

# UNIVERSITY OF NEW MEXICO

OFFICE OF ADMISSIONS, STUDENT SERVICES CENTER 150, ALBUQUERQUE, NM 87131-2046 • PHONE: 800-225-5866 • FAX: 505-277-6686

## CAMPUS LIFE

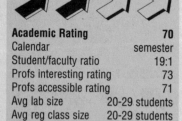

| Quality of Life Rating | 75 |
|---|---|
| Type of school | public |
| Affiliation | none |
| Environment | urban |

### STUDENTS

| | |
|---|---|
| Total undergrad enrollment | 16,414 |
| % male/female | 43/57 |
| % from out of state | 10 |
| % live on campus | 12 |
| % African American | 3 |
| % Asian | 3 |
| % Caucasian | 54 |
| % Hispanic | 32 |
| % Native American | 6 |
| % international | 1 |

### SURVEY SAYS . . .

*Everyone loves the Lobos*
*Very little drug use*
*Popular college radio*
*Great library*
*Class discussions are rare*
*Ethnic diversity on campus*
*Large classes*
*Lots of long lines and red tape*
*Lots of TAs teach upper-level courses*
*Lab facilities are great*

## ACADEMICS

| Academic Rating | 70 |
|---|---|
| Calendar | semester |
| Student/faculty ratio | 19:1 |
| Profs interesting rating | 73 |
| Profs accessible rating | 71 |
| Avg lab size | 20-29 students |
| Avg reg class size | 20-29 students |

### MOST POPULAR MAJORS

university studies
nursing
biology

## STUDENTS SPEAK OUT

### Academics

University of New Mexico at Albuquerque strives to provide for the diverse needs of all its students. Unlike many major state universities, UNM is home to a largely nontraditional student base, with many students taking six years or more to complete their undergraduate degrees. Full-timers and part-timers, students fresh out of high school and returning students, degree and non-degree students, pre-professionals and liberal arts majors all bring their unique demands to campus. Somehow, UNM manages to serve them all, offering 144 majors and concentrations in its 13 undergraduate divisions. Business, education, engineering, and pre-medical sciences are among the most popular offerings here. Students have mixed feelings about the faculty. Some say "the profs are good. They really seem to care about your well-being," but many others are of the opinion that "our teaching standards are pretty low: teachers earn tenure by who they know, not by their teaching effectiveness." Many complain that UNM has "too many TAs teaching classes. The professors are knowledgeable but not good at lecturing and teaching." As at most large state schools, registration and bill paying are often frustrating experiences. Students tell us that "the bureaucracy is a little overwhelming," and "programs change too much and classes tend not to be easily scheduled with times. Too many holds and unnecessary advisements." Still, in the final assessment most of those who stick around to graduate agree that the "overall experience at UNM is positive. What is drawn from the classroom is directly proportional to the effort put into the class."

### Life

With fewer than 1,500 undergraduates in its dormitories, UNM "is pretty much a commuter campus." Most students are on campus only for classes, rushing off afterward to home or jobs, but even they enjoy the "almost always pleasant atmosphere, great overall experience" that the UNM campus provides. Students tell us that "for those few that live here, there are activities," among them a school band, plenty of student-sponsored events and organization meetings (UNM has over 250 student organizations), movies, plays, guest speakers, intramural sports, and 12 intercollegiate athletic teams. The Greek system is popular with residents, providing a nexus of social activity in its four sororities and ten fraternity houses. Beyond the campus is New Mexico's largest city, Albuquerque. Students love it, reporting that "Albuquerque is pretty big. There's all kinds of stuff to do. The mountains are particularly popular for hiking, skiing, and just a great view of the city." Explains another student: "Albuquerque is a bustling city where much can be found to do. I have enjoyed my experience here at UNM and I am glad that I decided to matriculate here rather than at some other, large national university."

### Student Body

UNM is home to a varied, non-traditional student body. The average age of undergraduates here is 24. Many students split time between campus and part- or full-time jobs. "Many of the students at UNM are commuters," detracting further from a sense of typical collegiate unity. All the same, students tell us that "the students at UNM are diverse and reflect a strong sense of community that enables them to interact well." Students appreciate the fact that "the school is very multicultural and it reflects a whole new world that not many usually get to experience."

# UNIVERSITY OF NEW MEXICO

FINANCIAL AID: 505-277-2041 • E-MAIL: APPLY@UNM.EDU • WEBSITE: WWW.UNM.EDU

## ADMISSIONS

*Very important* academic and nonacademic factors considered by the admissions committee include secondary school record. *Important* factors considered include class rank, extracurricular activities, standardized test scores, and talent/ability. *Other* factors considered include alumni/ae relation, character/personal qualities, essays, interview, minority status, recommendations, volunteer work, and work experience. Factors *not* considered include geography, religious affiliation/commitment, and state residency. SAT I or ACT required, ACT preferred. TOEFL required of all international applicants. High school diploma is required and GED is accepted. *High school units required/recommended:* 13 total required; 4 English required, 3 math required, 2 science required, 2 foreign language required, 2 social studies required.

### The Inside Word

UNM's rolling admissions process is quite typical of large public universities. Consideration is based nearly entirely on courses, grades, and test scores, though recommendations can sometimes help a candidate. Solid average students should encounter no difficulty in gaining an offer of admission.

## FINANCIAL AID

*Students should submit:* FAFSA. There is no regular filing deadline. The Princeton Review suggests that all financial aid forms be submitted as soon as possible after January 1. *Need-based scholarships/grants offered:* Pell, SEOG, state scholarships/grants, private scholarships, the school's own gift aid, and Federal Nursing. *Loan aid offered:* Direct Subsidized Stafford, Direct Unsubsidized Stafford, Federal Perkins, Federal Nursing, state, and college/university loans from institutional funds. Institutional employment available. Federal Work-Study Program available. Applicants will be notified of awards on a rolling basis beginning on or about April 15. Off-campus job opportunities are excellent.

## FROM THE ADMISSIONS OFFICE

"The University of New Mexico is a major research institution nestled in the heart of multi-cultural Albuquerque on one of the nation's most beautiful and unique campuses. Students learn in an environment graced by distinctive southwestern architecture, beautiful plazas and fountains, spectacular art and a national arboretum . . . all within view of the 10,000-foot Sandia Mountains. At UNM, diversity is a way of learning with education enriched by a lively mix of students being taught by a world-class research faculty that includes a Nobel laureate, a MacArthur Fellow, and members of several national academies. UNM offers more than 225 degree programs and majors and has earned national recognition in dozens of disciplines, ranging from primary care medicine and clinical law to engineering, photography, Latin American history, and intercultural communications. Research and the quest for new knowledge fuels the university's commitment to an undergraduate education where students work side by side with many of the finest scholars in their fields."

## ADMISSIONS

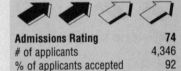

| | |
|---|---|
| **Admissions Rating** | **74** |
| # of applicants | 4,346 |
| % of applicants accepted | 92 |
| % of acceptees attending | 67 |

### FRESHMAN PROFILE

| | |
|---|---|
| Range SAT Verbal | 480-610 |
| Average SAT Verbal | 546 |
| Range SAT Math | 470-600 |
| Average SAT Math | 536 |
| Range ACT Composite | 19-25 |
| Average ACT Composite | 22 |
| Minimum TOEFL | 550 |
| Average HS GPA | 3.3 |
| % graduated top 10% of class | 20 |
| % graduated top 25% of class | 46 |
| % graduated top 50% of class | 80 |

### DEADLINES

| | |
|---|---|
| Regular admission | 6/15 |
| Nonfall registration? | yes |

### FINANCIAL FACTS

| | |
|---|---|
| **Financial Aid Rating** | **80** |
| In-state tuition | $3,026 |
| Out-of-state tuition | $11,424 |
| Room & board | $4,800 |
| Books and supplies | $800 |
| % frosh receiving aid | 39 |
| % undergrads receiving aid | 46 |

# UNIVERSITY OF NEW ORLEANS

OFFICE OF ADMISSIONS-AD 103, LAKEFRONT, NEW ORLEANS, LA 70148 • ADMISSIONS: 504-280-6000 • FAX: 504-280-5522

## CAMPUS LIFE

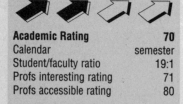

**Quality of Life Rating**    **79**
Type of school    public
Affiliation    none
Environment    urban

### STUDENTS
Total undergrad enrollment    12,260
% male/female    43/57
% from out of state    6
% from public high school    62
% live on campus    5
% in (# of) fraternities    2 (8)
% in (# of) sororities    2 (6)
% African American    22
% Asian    5
% Caucasian    57
% Hispanic    6
% international    3

### SURVEY SAYS . . .
High cost of living
Students love New Orleans, LA
Great food on campus
Class discussions are rare
Popular college radio
Very little hard liquor
Ethnic diversity on campus
Unattractive campus
Very little beer drinking
Dorms are like dungeons

## ACADEMICS

**Academic Rating**    **70**
Calendar    semester
Student/faculty ratio    19:1
Profs interesting rating    71
Profs accessible rating    80

### MOST POPULAR MAJORS
general studies
elementary education
general business

## STUDENTS SPEAK OUT

### Academics

Only one school in the country can claim the best naval architecture program in the United States. That school is the "urban, public" University of New Orleans, "a great commuter school" with "a growing national reputation" that offers "a good education at an affordable price." The "wide range of courses" is "academically challenging." The jazz studies program and "strong engineering school" here are both exceptional. The accounting department is solid, and the business school enjoys "great alumni connections" locally. While some students call the "very informative" and "highly qualified" professors at UNO "the best in Louisiana," others complain about the teaching quality here. Some professors never bother to ask students if their instruction makes any sense. Instead, charges a biology major, "they think students should extrapolate from their 'brilliant' lectures." There's also "the occasional whack-job or airhead" among the faculty, and students gripe that teaching assistants "need more practice before they attempt to teach a class." While student opinion on the faculty is mixed, everyone overwhelmingly agrees that the administration is lousy. Dealing with the "ridiculously slow" administrators here "is comparable" to a visit "to the pits of the hell." An irate first-year student asserts, "I have not found one yet that will say 'thank you,'" and a sophomore calls the registration process "the worst I've ever seen, period." Also, "the chemistry and physics labs suck." On the bright side, the computer facilities at UNO are "excellent."

### Life

The main lakefront campus here "floods during heavy rains," (that's street flooding, not the Biblical kind) but it's "nice" and it's located in a "quiet" residential area just "two miles from the heart of the French Quarter." Though this largely commuter school sponsors "some big events like a free crawfish boil in May," a "lack of school spirit" and campus involvement permeates the atmosphere. "It's mostly go to class and go home" at UNO, as "campus life is too boring to discuss," according to many students. "I feel bad for people who can't go home," says one commuter, "because campus is a ghost town between 1:00 P.M. and 9:00 A.M." Not everyone shares this sentiment. A campus-loving first-year student counters that "people who stay on campus love school so much more than commuters." Either way, most students would probably agree that "fun is mostly off campus" at UNO. "New Orleans is an awesome city" and "a great party area" with "a great music scene, from jazz to rock." Students can "go to the House of Blues on Thursday nights to relieve stress" or "go to Bourbon Street." There is "good food" all over the place as well, and a wealth of "movies, concerts," and theater productions. When they aren't busy enjoying the cultural smorgasbord that is New Orleans, students say they work "extremely hard" on their studies, as good grades are reportedly not easy to come by.

### Student Body

Most students "are from the city" of New Orleans or the surrounding area and do not have to travel far to go to UNO. Many cite "convenience" to home as a reason to come here. Still, the school boasts "great" ethnic diversity and "a mix of different types of students." As at many schools, though, ethnic groups tend to stick together, and students don't often "interact with people outside their peer groups." UNO is home to many single parents and other nontraditional students with a job or two who attend classes during the week and "don't have a lot of free time." The "friendly" and athletic students describe themselves as "blue collar" "serious" types "here to get a degree." Many say they "are not looking for the party scene," despite the numerous diversions New Orleans has to offer. "Most people" are "extremely friendly" and "get along very well," though it's impossible to say what would happen if UNO students commingled more often than they do.

FINANCIAL AID: 504-280-6603 • E-MAIL: ADMISSIONS@UNO.EDU • WEBSITE: WWW.UNO.EDU

## ADMISSIONS

*Very important* academic and nonacademic factors considered by the admissions committee include secondary school record and standardized test scores. *Other* factors considered include alumni/ae relation, character/personal qualities, class rank, essays, extracurricular activities, interview, recommendations, state residency, talent/ability, volunteer work, and work experience. Factors *not* considered include geography, minority status, and religious affiliation/commitment. SAT I or ACT required, ACT preferred. TOEFL required of all international applicants. *High school units required/recommended:* 4 English required, 3 math required, 3 science required, 2 science lab required, 2 foreign language required, 2 social studies required, 1 history required, 2 elective required.

### The Inside Word

It doesn't really get any more direct than the admissions process at UNO. The primary emphasis in candidate evaluation at this public university on the shores of Lake Ponchartrain is on test scores. If you've got a 950 combined SAT or a 20 composite on the ACT, you'll get in with minimal hassle. Course selection and GPA get the rest of the admissions committee's attention.

## FINANCIAL AID

*Students should submit:* FAFSA and institution's own financial aid form. There is no regular filing deadline. The Princeton Review suggests that all financial aid forms be submitted as soon as possible after January 1. *Need-based scholarships/grants offered:* Pell, SEOG, state scholarships/grants, and private scholarships. *Loan aid offered:* Subsidized Stafford, Unsubsidized Stafford, PLUS, Federal Perkins, and the school's own loans. Institution employment available. Federal Work-Study Program available. Off-campus job opportunities are excellent.

## FROM THE ADMISSIONS OFFICE

"Knowledge is perishable and careers inconstant. Corporate and government leaders are looking to higher education for solutions to their immediate needs. The University of New Orleans provides these leaders with graduates who can contribute to the economic, social, and academic growth of their industries now and into the future. UNO embraces its mission by providing the best educational opportunities for undergraduate and graduate students, conducting world-class research, and serving a diverse community in critical areas. The university's general level of excellence is reflected in its students and faculty. Its Centers of Excellence, which address important community needs, are recognized as among the best in the world. UNO's most outstanding offerings include a doctoral program in conservation biology providing training in the most advanced molecular biological techniques; the largest U.S. undergraduate program in naval architecture and marine engineering; one of the top 25 film programs in the country; and the only graduate arts administration program in the Gulf South."

## ADMISSIONS

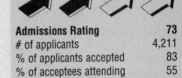

| | |
|---|---|
| **Admissions Rating** | **73** |
| # of applicants | 4,211 |
| % of applicants accepted | 83 |
| % of acceptees attending | 55 |

### FRESHMAN PROFILE

| | |
|---|---|
| Range SAT Verbal | 460-600 |
| Average SAT Verbal | 534 |
| Range SAT Math | 460-600 |
| Average SAT Math | 523 |
| Range ACT Composite | 18-23 |
| Average ACT Composite | 21 |
| Minimum TOEFL | 500 |
| % graduated top 25% of class | 32 |
| % graduated top 50% of class | 73 |

### DEADLINES

| | |
|---|---|
| Priority admission deadline | 7/1 |
| Regular admission | 8/18 |
| Nonfall registration? | yes |

## FINANCIAL FACTS

| | |
|---|---|
| **Financial Aid Rating** | **88** |
| In-state tuition | $2,712 |
| Out-of-state tuition | $9,756 |
| Room & board | $3,300 |
| Avg frosh grant | $3,500 |
| Avg frosh loan | $2,600 |

# UNIV. OF NORTH CAROLINA—ASHEVILLE

CPO #2210, 117 LIPINSKY HALL, ASHEVILLE, NC 28804-8510 • ADMISSIONS: 828-251-6481 • FAX: 828-251-6482

## CAMPUS LIFE

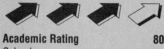

| Quality of Life Rating | 86 |
|---|---|
| Type of school | public |
| Affiliation | none |
| Environment | suburban |

### STUDENTS

| | |
|---|---|
| Total undergrad enrollment | 3,187 |
| % male/female | 43/57 |
| % from out of state | 11 |
| % from public high school | 94 |
| % live on campus | 36 |
| % in (# of) fraternities | 7 (4) |
| % in (# of) sororities | 5 (2) |
| % African American | 3 |
| % Asian | 1 |
| % Caucasian | 93 |
| % Hispanic | 1 |
| % Native American | 1 |
| % international | 1 |
| # of countries represented | 20 |

### SURVEY SAYS . . .

Campus easy to get around
Theater is hot
Beautiful campus
Campus feels safe
(Almost) everyone smokes
Students don't get along with local
community
Students are cliquish
Students aren't religious
Intercollegiate sports unpopular or
nonexistent
Student publications are ignored

## ACADEMICS

| Academic Rating | 80 |
|---|---|
| Calendar | semester |
| Student/faculty ratio | 13:1 |
| Profs interesting rating | 86 |
| Profs accessible rating | 95 |
| % profs teaching UG courses | 100 |
| Avg lab size | 10-19 students |
| Avg reg class size | 10-19 students |

### MOST POPULAR MAJORS

psychology
management
biology

## STUDENTS SPEAK OUT

### Academics

Over and over again, survey respondents at UNC—Asheville brag that they are receiving a private-school-quality education at a public school price. "I really like how UNCA is small and focused enough to seem as if it is a private school," reports one student. Says another, "It's not just the next best thing [to a private school]; this school is better!" Students here enjoy "knowledgeable and challenging professors" teaching in an intimate environment. Explains one undergrad, "Because of the small class size, I have had the opportunity to develop some great relationships with fellow students and professors." Intimacy is the hallmark of relations not just with faculty ("All the professors are extremely approachable inside and outside of class") but also with administrators. Writes one student, "Our chancellor makes personal calls to concerned students. His office (and even his house) is open to the campus community. He has put the student's best interests, not his own, first." Of course, all this attention has a potential downside: Reports one student, "Even though it serves as a double-edged sword sometimes, the faculty is amazingly concerned about students' classroom performance. The classes are so small that teachers really notice if you're not there!" Despite its size, UNC—Asheville provides students with numerous academic options. Departments earning praise include environmental science, English literature, creative writing, philosophy, and engineering. Students are particularly "proud of having started the National Counsel of Undergraduate Research." Concludes one senior, "This school has given me so many choices, opportunities, and new experiences. I think it is great!"

### Life

Asheville undergrads report a high level of satisfaction with their extracurricular lives. "I was here for my first two years without a car and 800 miles from home," explains one student, "and I always found something fun to do, whether it was on campus, in downtown Asheville, or in the wilderness of Appalachia." The "very beautiful and organized campus" is home to about one-third of UNCA's undergrads. The campus housing authority "puts on tons of activities for residents to participate in," while Greek organizations provide a social nexus for many non-residents. Students here engage in such diverse recreations as "discussion groups, Anime fun, weekend camping, traipsing around town, concerts, the arts, UNCA theater, community service, responsible but fun parties—we have just about everything a young adult could want, both relaxing and fun and serious events for intellectual growth." Undergrads are particularly sanguine about the mountain city of Asheville, "an awesome city in a beautiful area!" Explains one, "Asheville's downtown nightlife, including great clubs, theaters, and restaurants, as well as the school's location in the breathtaking Blue Ridge Mountains, makes the location unbeatable." Students also appreciate the fact that "there are many artists and musicians who help make the downtown Asheville scene." The school's mountain setting allows students to "participate in outdoor athletics and go hiking, biking, rock climbing, rafting, and even fly-fishing."

### Student Body

Despite its growing national academic reputation, UNCA remains a well-kept secret from prospects outside the state of North Carolina. Asheville's out-of-state draw remains primarily local, attracting applicants primarily from nearby Georgia and Florida. Students report that the student body has "a good mix for the size of the school" and that classmates are "very friendly and open-minded." Explains one student, "Beside Greek vs. non-Greek, everyone seems to get along. With different groups it might seem hard, but people are very respectful of each other. My friends are the best thing that have happened to me here." Students are also "very intelligent, so stimulating conversation is bound to result anywhere you go."

# UNIVERSITY OF NORTH CAROLINA—ASHEVILLE

FINANCIAL AID: 828-251-6535 • E-MAIL: ADMISSIONS@UNCA.EDU • WEBSITE: WWW.UNCA.EDU

## ADMISSIONS

*Very important* academic and nonacademic factors considered by the admissions committee include class rank and secondary school record. *Important* factors considered include standardized test scores. *Other* factors considered include alumni/ae relation, character/personal qualities, essays, extracurricular activities, geography, interview, recommendations, state residency, talent/ability, volunteer work, and work experience. Factors *not* considered include minority status and religious affiliation/commitment. SAT I or ACT required. TOEFL required of all international applicants. High school diploma is required and GED is not accepted. *High school units required/recommended:* 16 total recommended; 4 English recommended, 3 math recommended, 2 science recommended, 2 science lab recommended, 3 foreign language recommended, 2 history recommended, 2 elective recommended. *The admissions office says:* "Preference given to those students who take additional college preparatory units, i.e., advanced or honors courses."

## The Inside Word

UNC—Asheville is one of those relatively unknown gems in higher education. Recent publicity has fueled increases in applications and in turn boosted selectivity. The university is dynamic and eager to take advantage of this newfound recognition. No doubt admissions will become more and more competitive as the cycle repeats itself. For students who seek a public education in a smaller campus environment than places like Chapel Hill, this is a great choice.

## FINANCIAL AID

*Students should submit:* FAFSA. There is no regular filing deadline. The Princeton Review suggests that all financial aid forms be submitted as soon as possible after January 1. *Need-based scholarships/grants offered:* Pell, SEOG, state scholarships/grants, private scholarships, and the school's own gift aid. *Loan aid offered:* Direct Subsidized Stafford, Direct Unsubsidized Stafford, Direct PLUS, Federal Perkins, state, and college/university loans from institutional funds. Institutional employment available. Federal Work-Study Program available. Applicants will be notified of awards on a rolling basis beginning on or about April 15. Off-campus job opportunities are good.

## FROM THE ADMISSIONS OFFICE

"If you want to learn how to think, how to analyze and solve problems on your own, and how to become your own best teacher, a broad-based liberal arts education is the key. UNC—Asheville focuses on undergraduates, with a core curriculum covering humanities, language and culture, arts and ideas, and health and fitness. Students thrive in small classes, with a faculty dedicated first of all to teaching. The liberal arts emphasis develops discriminating thinkers, expert and creative communicators with a passion for learning. These are qualities you need for today's challenges and the changes of tomorrow."

## ADMISSIONS

| | |
|---|---|
| **Admissions Rating** | **81** |
| # of applicants | 2,050 |
| % of applicants accepted | 64 |
| % of acceptees attending | 38 |

### FRESHMAN PROFILE

| | |
|---|---|
| Range SAT Verbal | 520-640 |
| Average SAT Verbal | 582 |
| Range SAT Math | 520-620 |
| Average SAT Math | 572 |
| Range ACT Composite | 21-27 |
| Average ACT Composite | 24 |
| Minimum TOEFL | 550 |
| Average HS GPA | 3.7 |
| % graduated top 10% of class | 25 |
| % graduated top 25% of class | 64 |
| % graduated top 50% of class | 97 |

### DEADLINES

| | |
|---|---|
| Priority admission deadline | 10/15 |
| Regular admission | 3/15 |
| Nonfall registration? | yes |

### APPLICANTS ALSO LOOK AT

**AND OFTEN PREFER**
Warren Wilson

**AND SOMETIMES PREFER**
UNC—Chapel Hill
North Carolina State
Appalachian State

**AND RARELY PREFER**
UNC—Wilmington
UNC—Greensboro
Western Carolina
UNC—Charlotte

## FINANCIAL FACTS

| | |
|---|---|
| **Financial Aid Rating** | **83** |
| In-state tuition | $1,154 |
| Out-of-state tuition | $8,000 |
| Room & board | $4,440 |
| Books and supplies | $700 |
| Required fees | $1,300 |
| % frosh receiving aid | 37 |
| % undergrads receiving aid | 41 |
| Avg frosh grant | $2,696 |
| Avg frosh loan | $3,697 |

# Univ. of North Carolina—Chapel Hill

Jackson Hall 153A—Campus Box 2200, Chapel Hill, NC 27599 • Admissions: 919-966-3621 • Fax: 919-962-3045

## CAMPUS LIFE

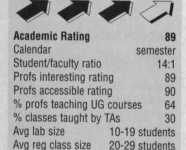

| Quality of Life Rating | 87 |
|---|---|
| Type of school | public |
| Affiliation | none |
| Environment | suburban |

### STUDENTS

| | |
|---|---|
| Total undergrad enrollment | 15,608 |
| % male/female | 39/61 |
| % from out of state | 18 |
| % from public high school | 85 |
| % live on campus | 43 |
| % in (# of) fraternities | 18 (29) |
| % in (# of) sororities | 18 (20) |
| % African American | 11 |
| % Asian | 5 |
| % Caucasian | 81 |
| % Hispanic | 1 |
| % Native American | 1 |
| % international | 1 |

### SURVEY SAYS . . .

*Students love the Tar Heels*
*Students love Chapel Hill, NC*
*Political activism is hot*
*Great library*
*Registration is a pain*
*Large classes*
*Student publications are popular*
*Ethnic diversity on campus*
*Lots of TAs teach upper-level courses*

## ACADEMICS

| Academic Rating | 89 |
|---|---|
| Calendar | semester |
| Student/faculty ratio | 14:1 |
| Profs interesting rating | 89 |
| Profs accessible rating | 90 |
| % profs teaching UG courses | 64 |
| % classes taught by TAs | 30 |
| Avg lab size | 10-19 students |
| Avg reg class size | 20-29 students |

### MOST POPULAR MAJORS

psychology
biology
business

## STUDENTS SPEAK OUT

### Academics

According to undergraduates at Chapel Hill, "The academics at UNC are all about self-motivation. People can definitely find ways to get by taking the easiest classes possible, but there are so many interesting and enriching classes offered. Also, it's really easy to get mediocre grades but almost impossible to get really good grades." Students recognize that, as a large state school, UNC has the capacity to offer tremendous resources. As one undergraduate tells us, "What sets Carolina apart is the opportunities it provides. Opportunities for academic advancement, for social outreach, and for cultural enlightenment." That is not to say that students here are left to fend entirely for themselves. In fact, "administration and professors at this school make themselves very available for students' questions and needs. I don't think enough students take advantage of this opportunity." Students report that "UNC is well-funded in some respects (computers, lab equipment) and poorly funded in many others (classrooms, low number of professors). As one student tells us, the bottom line is that "UNC has a highly accessible faculty with a dedication to teaching, while at the same time having an ability to do research." Students also appreciate the price, especially low for in-state students: "A lot of private schools look down on kids at state schools like Carolina. The truth is that we have more fun, beat them in sports, get just as good an education without going into massive debt, and generally end up just as successful and a lot cooler."

### Life

As one student sums up neatly, "If you want the college experience, there's no better place than here. Chapel Hill—the school and the town—is college. We have everything: the sports, the parties, the diehard alums, the trees blossoming in the spring, the brick buildings with their centuries of history. This place is heaven!" UNC—Chapel Hill offers the perfect combination of settings: a beautiful campus surrounded by a quaint town geared almost entirely toward the school. Writes one student, "Carolina and the town of Chapel Hill offer so much. On a Saturday night, students can hear a speaker on campus, go to a movie on Franklin Street, watch a campus theater performance, go to a frat party, or just chill with hallmates in the dorm." The town of Chapel Hill also offers "great restaurants, bars, movie theaters, coffee houses," and, of course, the pleasant North Carolina climate. Tar Heel intercollegiate sports, especially football and men's basketball, are so central to campus life that "you shouldn't come here if you don't love this school. The whole town literally turns baby blue on game days." The Greek scene, while present, "does not dominate social life." In short, students love life at UNC because "there is always something going on. If you want to go out, people are there. If you want to chill, people are doing that too, and if you want to study, you will probably see half your friends at the library."

### Student Body

"For a southern school," reports one undergrad, "UNC has tons of diversity. People do not all feel the need to dress and act the same way like a lot of places, and no matter what kind of person you are you can find your niche." Agrees another student, "Once you get past the white-bread Greeks, there are some truly incredible and diverse people at this school. Never go on first impressions—you will be surprised." Our survey confirms one student's observation that "for the most part everyone gets along, but campus tends to be self-segregated.

# UNIVERSITY OF NORTH CAROLINA—CHAPEL HILL

FINANCIAL AID: 919-962-8396 • E-MAIL: UADM@EMAIL.UNC.EDU • WEBSITE: WWW.UNC.EDU

## ADMISSIONS

*Very important* academic and nonacademic factors considered by the admissions committee include secondary school record, standardized test scores, and state residency. *Important* factors considered include class rank, essays, extracurricular activities, recommendations, volunteer work, and work experience. *Other* factors considered include alumni/ae relation, character/personal qualities, minority status, and talent/ability. Factors *not* considered include geography, interview, and religious affiliation/commitment. SAT I or ACT required. TOEFL required of all international applicants. High school diploma is required and GED is not accepted for freshmen applicants. *High school units required/recommended:* 16 total required; 4 English required, 3 math required, 4 math recommended, 3 science required, 1 science lab required, 2 foreign language required, 2 social studies required, 2 history required (1 of which must be U.S. history).

### The Inside Word

UNC's admissions process is formula-driven and highly selective. North Carolina students compete against other students from across the state for 82 percent of all spaces available in the freshman class; out-of-state students compete for the remaining 18 percent of the spaces. State residents will find the admissions standards high, and out-of-state applicants will find that it's one of the hardest offers of admission to come by in the country.

## FINANCIAL AID

*Students should submit:* FAFSA and CSS/Financial Aid PROFILE. The Princeton Review suggests that all financial aid forms be submitted as soon as possible after January 1. *Need-based scholarships/grants offered:* Pell, SEOG, state scholarships/grants, and private scholarships. *Loan aid offered:* FFEL Subsidized Stafford, FFEL Unsubsidized Stafford, FFEL PLUS, Federal Perkins, state, college/university loans from institutional funds, and private loans. Institutional employment available. Federal Work-Study Program available. Applicants will be notified of awards on a rolling basis beginning on or about March 1. Off-campus job opportunities are good.

## FROM THE ADMISSIONS OFFICE

"What makes UNC—Chapel Hill different from other institutions? Atmosphere of academic rigor mingled with an unpretentious, friendly lifestyle; planetarium; commitment to vital teaching and cutting-edge research; socioeconomic diversity; classic residential campus; a permeable honors program; study abroad; diversity permeates social life, classes, and curriculum, and paces academic excellence; village-like atmosphere; the university is large enough to grant your individuality yet small enough for you to find your niche; academic quality of highest quality yet inexpensive cost; third among public universities in the production of Rhodes Scholars."

## ADMISSIONS

| | |
|---|---|
| Admissions Rating | 90 |
| # of applicants | 16,569 |
| % of applicants accepted | 37 |
| % of acceptees attending | 56 |
| # accepting a place on wait list | 825 |
| % admitted from wait list | 31 |
| # of early decision applicants | 2,157 |
| % accepted early decision | 46 |

### FRESHMAN PROFILE

| | |
|---|---|
| Range SAT Verbal | 570-670 |
| Average SAT Verbal | 622 |
| Range SAT Math | 580-670 |
| Average SAT Math | 629 |
| Range ACT Composite | 23-29 |
| Minimum TOEFL | 600 |
| Average HS GPA | 4.1 |
| % graduated top 10% of class | 65 |
| % graduated top 25% of class | 92 |
| % graduated top 50% of class | 99 |

### DEADLINES

| | |
|---|---|
| Early decision | 10/15 |
| Early decision notification | 12/1 |
| Priority admission deadline | 10/15 |
| Regular admission | 1/15 |
| Nonfall registration? | yes |

### APPLICANTS ALSO LOOK AT

**AND OFTEN PREFER**
Princeton
Duke

**AND SOMETIMES PREFER**
Harvard, Brown
U.Virginia, Wake Forest
Davidson

**AND RARELY PREFER**
North Carolina State
U. Maryland—Coll. Park
Tulane, Rutgers U.

### FINANCIAL FACTS

| | |
|---|---|
| Financial Aid Rating | 76 |
| In-state tuition | $1,860 |
| Out-of-state tuition | $11,026 |
| Room & board | $5,630 |
| Books and supplies | $700 |
| Required fees | $908 |
| % frosh receiving aid | 27 |
| % undergrads receiving aid | 29 |
| Avg frosh grant | $1,250 |
| Avg frosh loan | $2,200 |

# Univ. of North Carolina—Greensboro

123 Mossman Building, Greensboro, NC 27402-6170 • Admissions: 336-334-5243 • Fax: 336-334-4180

## CAMPUS LIFE

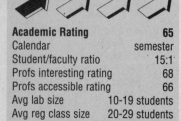

| Quality of Life Rating | **76** |
| --- | --- |
| Type of school | public |
| Affiliation | none |
| Environment | urban |

### STUDENTS

| | |
| --- | --- |
| Total undergrad enrollment | 10,021 |
| % male/female | 33/67 |
| % from out of state | 10 |
| % from public high school | 95 |
| % live on campus | 35 |
| % African American | 19 |
| % Asian | 3 |
| % Caucasian | 75 |
| % Hispanic | 2 |
| % international | 1 |

### SURVEY SAYS . . .

*Frats and sororities dominate social scene*
*Athletic facilities are great*
*Great computer facilities*
*Student publications are ignored*
*Political activism is (almost) nonexistent*
*Ethnic diversity on campus*
*Diverse students interact*

## ACADEMICS

| Academic Rating | **65** |
| --- | --- |
| Calendar | semester |
| Student/faculty ratio | 15:1 |
| Profs interesting rating | 68 |
| Profs accessible rating | 66 |
| Avg lab size | 10-19 students |
| Avg reg class size | 20-29 students |

### MOST POPULAR MAJORS

business administration and management
nursing
elementary education

## STUDENTS SPEAK OUT

### Academics

Despite an undergraduate population of over 10,000, UNC—Greensboro "has a wonderful small-college atmosphere that allows real interaction between students and professors." Students appreciate the fact that "classes are small" and that "the faculty is very responsible and try their best to make UNCG a student-centered university." Liberal arts and social sciences departments are unusually large for a state school, although the school's seven pre-professional programs and two-year pre-engineering program (which prepares students to transfer to a four-year engineering school) are also popular. Ambitious students may apply for the school's honors program, which allows students to pursue independent projects and interdisciplinary study in small team-taught classes. One participant writes: "The faculty in the honors program go out of their way to get to know students, doing things like participating in a weekly discussion over coffee and bagels, hosting a weekly literary hour, and donning wide-brimmed hats and wielding croquet mallets in the annual honors dorm croquet tournament." Throughout all programs, students speak highly of professors. One student says, "The professors are the only thing that have kept me here. They are friendly, accessible, helpful, and genuinely interested in the students. I received such an excellent undergraduate education that I am sticking around for graduate school."

### Life

At a school as large as UNCG, students naturally fall into smaller social groups. Some find their home in the school's active Greek system. "My life is extremely good here. This has a lot to do with my fraternity experience. It has been well-rounded socially, athletically, and definitely been a positive influence on my academics." Others find sanctuary in one of UNCG's two unique residential colleges, modeled on the scholar/student residences at Oxford and Cambridge. Notes one resident, "Our excellent residential college system offers students the chance to socialize with peers and professors. Strong College has truly become a large part of my life." For others, the "over 150 clubs and organizations on campus give us plenty of things to do," as do "lots of coffee shops, clubs, and bars off campus. Also, there's always a party going on somewhere." UNCG also has "a beautiful recreation center." Hometown Greensboro receives high marks; explains one student, "Greensboro is located in the perfect place. The city is wonderful, plus it's only a short drive to Winston-Salem, Charlotte, Raleigh, Durham, and Chapel Hill. It's in the middle of everything. You never run out of things to do." Student complaints focus on parking and the lack of intercollegiate sports teams.

### Student Body

Although UNCG went coed in 1963, the school maintains vestiges of its years as an all-girls' school; in 2000, nearly two-thirds of all students were women. Our respondents rank the student body high in diversity, almost certainly because of a relatively large African American population; out-of-state students are scarce, and other minorities are slightly represented. Interactions among UNCG's communities are "generally friendly, but most stay isolated within their own small social groups and cliques."

# UNIVERSITY OF NORTH CAROLINA—GREENSBORO

FINANCIAL AID: 336-334-5702 • E-MAIL: UNDERGRAD_ADMISSIONS@UNCG.EDU • WEBSITE: WWW.UNCG.EDU

## ADMISSIONS

*Important* factors considered include secondary school record and standardized test scores. *Other* factors considered include class rank. SAT I or ACT required, SAT I preferred. TOEFL required of all international applicants. High school diploma is required and GED is accepted. *High school units required/recommended:* 15 total required; 4 English required, 3 math required, 3 science required, 1 science lab required, 2 foreign language required, 2 social studies required, 1 history required, 1 elective required.

### The Inside Word

UNC—Greensboro has yet to gain much attention outside of regional circles so, at least for the moment, gaining admission is not particularly difficult. The usual public university considerations apply; expect the admissions office to focus on grades and test scores, and not much else. Out-of-staters will find a much smoother path to admission here than at Chapel Hill and will still be within reasonable reach of internship and career possibilities in the Research Triangle.

## FINANCIAL AID

*Students should submit:* FAFSA. There is no regular filing deadline. Priority filing deadline is March 1. The Princeton Review suggests that all financial aid forms be submitted as soon as possible after January 1. *Need-based scholarships/grants offered:* Pell, SEOG, state scholarships/grants, private scholarships, the school's own gift aid, and Federal Nursing. *Merit-based scholarships/grants offered:* State, academic, creative arts/performance, special achievements/activities, special characteristics, athletic, and ROTC. *Loan aid offered:* Subsidized Stafford, Unsubsidized Stafford, PLUS, and Federal Perkins. Institution employment available. Federal Work-Study Program available. Applicants will be notified of awards on a rolling basis beginning on or about April 1. Off-campus job opportunities are good.

## FROM THE ADMISSIONS OFFICE

"For the student who wants more than a small college offers but who would feel lost at a large university, UNC Greensboro is the perfect size. It is a diverse yet close-knit community where its 10,000 undergraduates can flourish as individuals. Students find a healthy balance of academic seriousness and collegiate fun, programs from the BA to the PhD, and charming traditions and cutting-edge scholarship. The UNCG faculty has long been known for exceptional teaching and research, combined with a genuinely caring attitude toward undergraduates. Students choose UNCG for the reputation of its academic programs and faculty, low costs, size, the convenient location in a friendly southern city, and the warm, inviting feeling of its beautiful campus. Students enjoy experiences such as residential colleges, internships, study abroad, small discussion classes, 14 NCAA Division I sports, and more than 150 student organizations."

## ADMISSIONS

| Admissions Rating | 68 |
|---|---|
| # of applicants | 6,726 |
| % of applicants accepted | 74 |
| % of acceptees attending | 38 |

### FRESHMAN PROFILE

| | |
|---|---|
| Range SAT Verbal | 470-570 |
| Average SAT Verbal | 522 |
| Range SAT Math | 460-560 |
| Average SAT Math | 515 |
| Minimum TOEFL | 550 |
| Average HS GPA | 3.4 |
| % graduated top 10% of class | 14 |
| % graduated top 25% of class | 47 |
| % graduated top 50% of class | 86 |

### DEADLINES

| | |
|---|---|
| Priority admission deadline | 3/1 |
| Regular admission | 8/1 |
| Regular notification | rolling |
| Nonfall registration? | yes |

## FINANCIAL FACTS

| Financial Aid Rating | 81 |
|---|---|
| In-state tuition | $1,126 |
| Out-of-state tuition | $9,580 |
| Room & board | $4,742 |
| Books and supplies | $946 |
| Required fees | $1,082 |
| % frosh receiving aid | 44 |
| Avg frosh grant | $5,436 |
| Avg frosh loan | $3,128 |

# UNIVERSITY OF NORTH DAKOTA

Box 8357, Grand Forks, ND 58202 • Admissions: 701-777-4463 • Fax: 701-777-2696

## CAMPUS LIFE

| | |
|---|---|
| **Quality of Life Rating** | **78** |
| Type of school | public |
| Affiliation | none |
| Environment | suburban |

### STUDENTS

| | |
|---|---|
| Total undergrad enrollment | 9,122 |
| % male/female | 52/48 |
| % from out of state | 42 |
| % live on campus | 32 |
| % in (# of) fraternities | 11 (14) |
| % in (# of) sororities | 8 (7) |
| % African American | 1 |
| % Asian | 1 |
| % Caucasian | 94 |
| % Hispanic | 1 |
| % Native American | 3 |
| % international | 2 |
| # of countries represented | 48 |

### SURVEY SAYS . . .

*Student publications are popular*
*Frats and sororities dominate social scene*
*Everyone loves the Fighting Sioux*
*(Almost) everyone plays intramural sports*
*Hard liquor is popular*
*Computer facilities need improving*
*Library needs improving*
*Athletic facilities need improving*
*Lacking diversity on campus*

## ACADEMICS

| | |
|---|---|
| **Academic Rating** | **71** |
| Calendar | semester |
| Student/faculty ratio | 18:1 |
| Profs interesting rating | 69 |
| Profs accessible rating | 69 |
| % profs teaching UG courses | 85 |
| Avg lab size | 20-29 students |
| Avg reg class size | 20-29 students |

### MOST POPULAR MAJORS
psychology
nursing
aeronautical studies

## STUDENTS SPEAK OUT

### Academics

Students at the University of North Dakota commend administrators and faculty as "very approachable and accessible. People take the extra step around here to ensure that the students are as happy as possible." It is just this sort of personalized touch that sets UND apart from many larger, 'assembly line' state universities. Indeed, many students who chose the University of North Dakota do so because "the school offers choices comparable to a large university, but it has the atmosphere of a small close-knit school." The school is large and well-funded enough to offer state-of-the-art facilities in most areas, yet small enough to allow reasonably sized classes ("Since the lectures are not as big as on other campuses, we are not just numbers on a sheet"). That's not to say all is perfect here: "It is hard to get into classes that you would like," and students note the occasional "run around" from administrators, but by the standard set by the nation's state schools, UND does a fine job of serving its students. Aviation is UND's standout department; the John D. Odegard School for Aerospace Science is highly respected throughout the nation and attracts many out-of-state students to the school. Business and management departments are also popular and reputedly top-notch, as are most other pre-professional studies (physical and occupational therapy and education in particular). Students praise the faculty for their teaching skill and accessibility, but some feel that "more of an ethnically and culturally diverse faculty is needed to enhance the quality of education here. There are very few minority faculty members."

### Life

You might expect that life "in the middle of nowhere" would get a little dull (not to mention "cold as a witch's elbow" way up there on top of the states), but a startling number of students mention the plethora of social options: The town is "great if you're 21 because the bar scene rocks," but even still, "there are plenty of good restaurants and movies to go to." If, for some reason, Grand Forks gets a little stale after awhile, "Canada is only an hour-and-a-half's drive, and you only need to be 18 in Winnipeg to drink." The Greek scene has a significant influence party-wise (even though only about 15 percent of the students are in a house), and a few students praised not just their "very excellent taste in beer" but also their "academic, moral, and social standards." Still, a sizeable minority weigh in with the opinion that "life is slightly boring here when there is not homework to do, unless there is a hockey or basketball game (which are free). That's why weekend parties are both popular and frequent."

### Student Body

Students at UND "are pretty much the same since our campus is not diverse racially or politically. We all get along fine—like-minded people attract and work together. That's how life works anywhere." The homogeneity, according to some, creates "a small-town feeling that makes the campus a very friendly, comfortable environment. Most everyone here is very friendly." Agrees one undergrad, "It's freaky how nice people are in North Dakota—it just doesn't seem natural to many people that complete strangers wish them a great day and say 'hi' in passing. I have definitely had a positive experience at UND." Students hail primarily from North Dakota and Minnesota.

FINANCIAL AID: 701-777-3121 • E-MAIL: ENROLSER@SAGE.UND.NODAK.EDU • WEBSITE: WWW.UND.EDU

## ADMISSIONS

*Very important* academic and nonacademic factors considered by the admissions committee include secondary school record. *Important* factors considered include alumni/ae relation, character/personal qualities, class rank, essays, extracurricular activities, minority status, recommendations, standardized test scores, talent/ability, and volunteer work. *Other* factors considered include geography, interview, and work experience. Factors *not* considered include religious affiliation/commitment and state residency. SAT I or ACT required, ACT preferred. TOEFL required of all international applicants. High school diploma is required and GED is accepted. *High school units required/recommended:* 13 total required; 4 English required, 3 math required, 3 science lab required, 3 social studies required.

### The Inside Word

North Dakota shapes up as a low-stress choice with little pressure on applicants. Its sound reputation serves as a reminder that a highly selective admissions profile isn't an indicator of the quality of a university. Who graduates is much more important than who gets admitted or denied.

## FINANCIAL AID

The Princeton Review suggests that all financial aid forms be submitted as soon as possible after January 1. *Need-based scholarships/grants offered:* Pell, SEOG, state scholarships/grants, private scholarships, the school's own gift aid, and Federal Nursing. *Loan aid offered:* FFEL Subsidized Stafford, FFEL Unsubsidized Stafford, FFEL PLUS, Federal Perkins, and Federal Nursing. Institutional employment available. Federal Work-Study Program available. Off-campus job opportunities are excellent.

## FROM THE ADMISSIONS OFFICE

"More than 10,500 students come to the University of North Dakota each year, from every state in the nation and more than 40 countries. They're impressed by our academic excellence, 135 major fields of study, our dedication to the liberal arts mission, and alumni success record. Nearly all of the university's new students rank in the top half of their high school classes, with about half in the top quarter. As the oldest and most diversified institution of higher education in the Dakotas, Montana, Wyoming, and western Minnesota, UND is a comprehensive teaching and research university. Yet the university provides individual attention that may be missing at very large universities. UND graduates are highly regarded among prospective employers. Representatives from more than 200 regional and national companies recruit UND students every year. Our campus is approximately 98 percent accessible."

### ADMISSIONS

| | | |
|---|---|---|
| **Admissions Rating** | | 76 |
| # of applicants | | 3,329 |
| % of applicants accepted | | 59 |
| % of acceptees attending | | 93 |

#### FRESHMAN PROFILE

| | |
|---|---|
| Range SAT Verbal | 490-575 |
| Average SAT Verbal | 539 |
| Range SAT Math | 500-605 |
| Average SAT Math | 552 |
| Range ACT Composite | 20-25 |
| Average ACT Composite | 23 |
| Minimum TOEFL | 525 |
| Average HS GPA | 3.4 |
| % graduated top 10% of class | 17 |
| % graduated top 25% of class | 43 |
| % graduated top 50% of class | 74 |

#### DEADLINES

| | |
|---|---|
| Priority admission deadline | 7/1 |
| Regular admission | rolling |
| Nonfall registration? | yes |

#### APPLICANTS ALSO LOOK AT
##### AND OFTEN PREFER
U. Nebraska—Lincoln
U. Colorado—Boulder
Notre Dame
##### AND SOMETIMES PREFER
Moorhead State
U. Minnesota
Bismarck State
Concordia Coll. (Moorehead, MN)
U. Wisconsin—Madison
##### AND RARELY PREFER
Marquette

### FINANCIAL FACTS

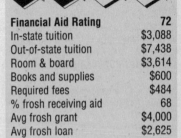

| | |
|---|---|
| **Financial Aid Rating** | 72 |
| In-state tuition | $3,088 |
| Out-of-state tuition | $7,438 |
| Room & board | $3,614 |
| Books and supplies | $600 |
| Required fees | $484 |
| % frosh receiving aid | 68 |
| Avg frosh grant | $4,000 |
| Avg frosh loan | $2,625 |

# UNIVERSITY OF NOTRE DAME

220 MAIN BUILDING, NOTRE DAME, IN 46556 • ADMISSIONS: 219-631-7505 • FAX: 219-631-8865

## CAMPUS LIFE

| Quality of Life Rating | 77 |
|---|---|
| Type of school | private |
| Affiliation | Roman Catholic |
| Environment | suburban |

### STUDENTS

| | |
|---|---|
| Total undergrad enrollment | 8,038 |
| % male/female | 54/46 |
| % from out of state | 90 |
| % from public high school | 56 |
| % live on campus | 79 |
| % African American | 3 |
| % Asian | 4 |
| % Caucasian | 85 |
| % Hispanic | 7 |
| % international | 2 |

### SURVEY SAYS . . .

*Everyone loves the Fighting Irish
(Almost) everyone plays intramural
sports
Diversity lacking on campus
Great library
Great computer facilities
Very small frat/sorority scene
Students are very religious
Students don't like Notre Dame, IN
(Almost) no one smokes
Student publications are popular*

## ACADEMICS

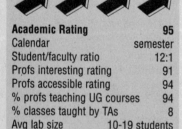

| Academic Rating | 95 |
|---|---|
| Calendar | semester |
| Student/faculty ratio | 12:1 |
| Profs interesting rating | 91 |
| Profs accessible rating | 94 |
| % profs teaching UG courses | 94 |
| % classes taught by TAs | 8 |
| Avg lab size | 10-19 students |
| Avg reg class size | 10-19 students |

### MOST POPULAR MAJORS
business
engineering
pre-medicine studies

## STUDENTS SPEAK OUT
### Academics

Students at Notre Dame don't mince words when it comes to boasting about the education and experiences they've received at their beloved alma mater. Call it Irish Pride. A senior provides a perfect example: "Notre Dame, besides simply BEING college football, is great academically. You are practically guaranteed a job when you leave as long as you kept your grades at decent levels through school. What's more, ND is able to attract not only some of the best students, but also the best teachers." What is it about Notre Dame that engenders such love and devotion? It's the holy trinity of "tradition, faith, and academics" that sets Notre Dame apart, argue undergrads, who also find comfort in ND's "strong sense of community" and "unparalleled school spirit." These last two—and an alumni network that's been called "the biggest fraternity in the world"—are what "make all this studying bearable," notes a sophomore. For the most part, undergrads praise Notre Dame's faculty, curriculum, and resources, noting that the school's strong emphasis on classical liberal arts courses such as theology and philosophy, its top-notch science program, as well as its honor code, exemplify ND's "commitment to instilling quality and character" in its students. Being a big research school, there are the usual complaints about TA's teaching classes (though an honors student points out that she's gotten "the cream of the crop"—"three heads of departments as teachers already, and I'm a freshman!"). This is balanced, however, by the sense that "people really care about you at Notre Dame. You're not another number, but rather, you're respected as an intelligent human. You're expected to treat others in the same way, which creates a wonderful atmosphere."

### Life

A sophomore provides a window onto life at ND: "It's a Catholic university and football is so big that my friends from other schools often ask what we do: pray all the time? Or does everything shut down if the football team loses . . . ." So goes life in Notre Dame-dominated South Bend, Indiana, a few hours drive from anywhere (mostly kids go to Chicago, which is 90 minutes away, for big-city fun). Still, Domers love it: "Life is wonderful!," waxes a junior. "Football games are a little slice of heaven out here—and I am not kidding. Tailgating under a golden dome—what could be better?" Of course not everyone is so smitten with Notre Dame's "tradition of tradition," especially on matters of personal autonomy, choice, and day-to-day life at this conservative religious school. A first-year—living the "painful life of a pagan liberal at Notre Dame"—charges that "it is a sexist campus where women are rarely promoted and sometimes professors are just outright crude to women." Ouch! Yet, despite some distinctly un-twenty-first-century rules and regulations (such as single sex dorms and "parietals"—essentially curfews designed to keep men out of women's rooms and vice versa), most students are okay with Notre Dame's social set up.

### Student Body

A little bit more Irish Pride—this time from a senior: "Notre Dame has the best student body in the country. The students are what make the school." Coming from a Domer, it's probably a bit of an exaggeration; still, students are, for the most part, agreed upon the fact that "the sense of community and the 'Notre Dame Family' are the most valuable part of the university." And while there's a bit of a problem with homogeneity (the typical ND student is "a rich white kid that's Abercrombie and Fitched out wearing a North Face because we do face arctic temperatures out here in Indiana . . ."), a sophomore points out that "the school is trying to become more modern/activist/chic." The problem? "We're dealing with a Catholic institution," notes our wise sophomore, "and the Catholic Church changes about as fast as molasses."

FINANCIAL AID: 219-631-6436 • E-MAIL: ADMISSIO.1@ND.EDU • WEBSITE: WWW.ND.EDU

## ADMISSIONS

*Very important* academic and nonacademic factors considered by the admissions committee include secondary school record. *Important* factors considered include character/personal qualities, class rank, essays, extracurricular activities, recommendations, standardized test scores, and talent/ability. *Other* factors considered include alumni/ae relation, minority status, religious affiliation/commitment, volunteer work, and work experience. Factors *not* considered include geography, interview, and state residency. SAT I or ACT required; SAT I recommended. TOEFL required of all international applicants. High school diploma is required and GED is not accepted. *High school units required/recommended:* 4 English recommended, 4 math recommended, 4 science recommended, 4 foreign language recommended, 4 social studies recommended, 3 electives recommended.

### The Inside Word

For most candidates, getting admitted to Notre Dame is pretty tough. Legacies, however, face some of the most favorable admissions conditions to be found at any highly selective university. Unofficially, athletic talents seem to have some influence on the committee as well: An enormous percentage of the total student body holds at least one varsity letter from high school, and many were team captains. Perhaps it's merely coincidence, but even so, candidates who tap well into the Notre Dame persona are likeliest to succeed.

## FINANCIAL AID

*Students should submit:* FAFSA, CSS/Financial Aid PROFILE, noncustodial (divorced/separated) parent's statement, and business/farm supplement. The Princeton Review suggests that all financial aid forms be submitted as soon as possible after January 1. *Need-based scholarships/grants offered:* Pell, SEOG, state scholarships/grants, private scholarships, and the school's own gift aid. *Loan aid offered:* FFEL Subsidized Stafford, FFEL Unsubsidized Stafford, FFEL PLUS, Federal Perkins, and Notre Dame Undergraduate Loan. Institutional employment available. Federal Work-Study Program available. Applicants will be notified of awards on or about March 31. Off-campus job opportunities are good.

## FROM THE ADMISSIONS OFFICE

"Notre Dame is a Catholic university, which means it offers unique opportunities for academic, ethical, spiritual, and social service development. The First Year of Studies program provides special assistance to our students as they make the adjustment from high school to college. The first-year curriculum includes many core requirements, while allowing students to explore several areas of possible future study. Each residence hall is home to students from all classes; most will live in the same hall for all their years on campus. An average of 93 percent of entering students will graduate within five years."

## ADMISSIONS

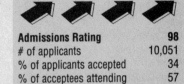

| Admissions Rating | 98 |
|---|---|
| # of applicants | 10,051 |
| % of applicants accepted | 34 |
| % of acceptees attending | 57 |
| # accepting a place on wait list | 284 |
| % admitted from wait list | 13 |

### FRESHMAN PROFILE

| | |
|---|---|
| Range SAT Verbal | 620-710 |
| Average SAT Verbal | 660 |
| Range SAT Math | 650-720 |
| Average SAT Math | 681 |
| Range ACT Composite | 29-32 |
| Average ACT Composite | 31 |
| Minimum TOEFL | 550 |
| % graduated top 10% of class | 84 |
| % graduated top 25% of class | 97 |
| % graduated top 50% of class | 99 |

### DEADLINES

| | |
|---|---|
| Regular admission | 1/9 |
| Regular notification | 4/1 |

### APPLICANTS ALSO LOOK AT

**AND OFTEN PREFER**
Princeton
Stanford

**AND SOMETIMES PREFER**
Georgetown U.
Cornell U.
Duke
Northwestern U.
U.S. Naval Acad.

**AND RARELY PREFER**
U. Michigan—Ann Arbor
Holy Cross
U. Wisconsin—Madison
Boston Coll.

### FINANCIAL FACTS

| Financial Aid Rating | 74 |
|---|---|
| Tuition | $23,180 |
| Room & board | $5,920 |
| Books and supplies | $800 |
| Required fees | $177 |
| % frosh receiving aid | 45 |
| % undergrads receiving aid | 39 |

# UNIVERSITY OF OKLAHOMA

1000 ASP AVENUE, NORMAN, OK 73019-4076 • ADMISSIONS: 405-325-2251 • FAX: 405-325-7124

## CAMPUS LIFE

| Quality of Life Rating | 72 |
|---|---|
| Type of school | public |
| Affiliation | none |
| Environment | suburban |

### STUDENTS

| | |
|---|---|
| Total undergrad enrollment | 18,308 |
| % male/female | 50/50 |
| % from out of state | 17 |
| % live on campus | 20 |
| % in (# of) fraternities | 20 (26) |
| % in (# of) sororities | 23 (15) |
| % African American | 8 |
| % Asian | 6 |
| % Caucasian | 75 |
| % Hispanic | 4 |
| % Native American | 8 |
| % international | 4 |

### SURVEY SAYS . . .

*Frats and sororities dominate social scene*
*Everyone loves the Sooners*
*Great food on campus*
*Theater is hot*
*Students love Norman, OK*
*Large classes*
*Ethnic diversity on campus*
*Students get along with local community*
*Student publications are popular*
*Students are very religious*

## ACADEMICS

| Academic Rating | 71 |
|---|---|
| Calendar | semester |
| Student/faculty ratio | 20:1 |
| Profs interesting rating | 87 |
| Profs accessible rating | 85 |
| % classes taught by TAs | 22 |
| Avg lab size | 20-29 students |
| Avg reg class size | 20-29 students |

### MOST POPULAR MAJORS

management information systems
journalism
psychology

## STUDENTS SPEAK OUT

### Academics

Always a leading research institution, University of Oklahoma has recently set its sites on personalizing the educational experiences of its 16,000-plus undergraduates. The results have been impressive. Past surveys revealed a student body experiencing typical state school blues: inaccessible administrators, professors more concerned with research than teaching, and burdensome administrative tasks. In contrast, our current survey shows that students see, and appreciate, improvement in all areas. Writes one, "President Boren has really made the university an exceptional place since he's held his office. The improvements I've seen here have been incredible." The administration is "extremely accessible and genuinely caring about student experience," and students are pleased to inform us that "before I came to OU, I would have thought I would be a number here. Now I can honestly say that I have been treated like an individual." Things aren't perfect: Classes still fill up too quickly, and "to get something done you have to run all over campus," but most students prefer to focus on the upside of an OU education. Writes one, "the academic selection is out of this world," while another points out that "the opportunities that exist for leadership here at OU are truly outstanding. Students often have the opportunity to work and socialize with top administrators, deans, and even the president. Four years at the University of Oklahoma will give you an excellent education and prepare you for life." The recent addition of an honors college means that OU's top undergrads now regularly enjoy more frequent interaction with professors in classes of 20 or fewer students.

### Life

For many OU undergrads, extracurricular life centers around the school's numerous fraternities and sororities. "This is a pretty Greek-oriented campus," explains one student, "with lots of Greek activities." With over one-fifth of students pledged, the Greek system absorbs the single largest chunk of the OU student body. But for those outside the system, "it isn't hard to find a niche. We have everything from religious groups to a gay and lesbian society." Students inhabit "a great small town atmosphere with a lot of big town amenities" and enjoy "paintball, horseback riding, intramural sports," and going to "the bars around 'Campus Corner' to hang out. Campus Corner is a city block right next to campus with many restaurants, clothing stores, and bars." Football provides the hub of all campus life every autumn, the Sooners' current deficiencies notwithstanding. The basketball team fares better, regularly earning an NCAA tourney invite. OU also boasts "an active campus activities council. They bring in films, comedians, concerts, and speakers. President Boren brings big names to campus: George Bush and Margaret Thatcher, to name a few." Beyond the "beautiful campus" lies Norman, which "isn't huge, but is big enough to do various things like sports, going to the lake, or shopping."

### Student Body

With a student body the size of a small town, OU is home to a varied set of subcommunities. The typical student is practical and goal-oriented ("People think a lot about finding the right job and being happy"). Although some complain that the Greek community holds itself apart from the rest of the student body ("There are a lot of students involved with Greek life who don't like to interact with non-Greeks. They act like they are better than others"), many others brag that "the student body exemplifies an outstanding sense of community. We might not all completely agree with one another all the time, but we have a deep respect for each others' opinions."

# UNIVERSITY OF OKLAHOMA

FINANCIAL AID: 405-325-4521 • E-MAIL: ADMREC@OUWWW.OU.EDU • WEBSITE: WWW.OU.EDU

## ADMISSIONS

*Very important* academic and nonacademic factors considered by the admissions committee include class rank, secondary school record, and standardized test scores. *Important* factors considered include recommendations. *Other* factors considered include essays. Factors *not* considered include alumni/ae relation, character/personal qualities, extracurricular activities, geography, interview, minority status, religious affiliation/commitment, state residency, talent/ability, volunteer work, and work experience. SAT I or ACT required, SAT I preferred. TOEFL required of all international applicants. High school diploma is required and GED is accepted. *High school units required/recommended:* 4 English required, 3 math required, 4 math recommended, 3 science required, 3 science recommended, 2 science lab required, 2 foreign language required, 3 foreign language recommended, 3 social studies required.

### The Inside Word

It's plain from the approach of Oklahoma's evaluation process that candidates needn't put much energy into preparing supporting materials for their applications. This is one place that is going to get you a decision pronto—your numbers will call the shots.

## FINANCIAL AID

*Students should submit:* FAFSA. Regular filing deadline is June 1. The Princeton Review suggests that all financial aid forms be submitted as soon as possible after January 1. *Need-based scholarships/grants offered:* Pell, SEOG, state scholarships/grants, private scholarships, and the school's own gift aid. *Loan aid offered:* FFEL Subsidized Stafford, FFEL Unsubsidized Stafford, FFEL PLUS, Federal Perkins, and college/university loans from institutional funds. Institutional employment available. Federal Work-Study Program available. Applicants will be notified of awards on a rolling basis beginning on or about March 1. Off-campus job opportunities are excellent.

## FROM THE ADMISSIONS OFFICE

"Ask yourself some significant questions. What are your ambitions, goals, and dreams? Do you desire opportunity, and are you ready to accept challenge? What do you hope to gain from your educational experience? Are you looking for a university that will provide you with the tools, resources, and motivation to convert ambitions, opportunities, and challenges into meaningful achievement? To effectively answer these questions you must carefully seek out your options, look for direction, and make the right choice. The University of Oklahoma combines a unique mixture of academic excellence, varied social cultures, and a variety of campus activities to make your educational experience complete. At OU, comprehensive learning is our goal for your life. Not only do you receive a valuable classroom learning experience, but OU is also one of the finest research institutions in the United States. This allows OU students the opportunity to be a part of technology in progress. It's not just learning, it's discovery, invention, and dynamic creativity, a hands-on experience that allows you to be on the cutting edge of knowledge. Make the right choice and consider the University of Oklahoma!"

## ADMISSIONS

| | |
|---|---:|
| **Admissions Rating** | **76** |
| # of applicants | 6,652 |
| % of applicants accepted | 86 |
| % of acceptees attending | 59 |

### FRESHMAN PROFILE

| | |
|---|---:|
| Range ACT Composite | 22-28 |
| Average ACT Composite | 25 |
| Minimum TOEFL | 550 |
| Average HS GPA | 3.5 |
| % graduated top 10% of class | 31 |
| % graduated top 25% of class | 61 |
| % graduated top 50% of class | 89 |

### DEADLINES

| | |
|---|---:|
| Regular admission | 6/1 |
| Nonfall registration? | yes |

### APPLICANTS ALSO LOOK AT AND OFTEN PREFER
Washington U.
Rice
### AND SOMETIMES PREFER
Baylor
U. Texas—Austin
U. Kansas

## FINANCIAL FACTS

| | |
|---|---:|
| **Financial Aid Rating** | **77** |
| In-state tuition | $1,890 |
| Out-of-state tuition | $6,225 |
| Room & board | $4,610 |
| Books and supplies | $869 |
| Required fees | $691 |
| % frosh receiving aid | 49 |
| % undergrads receiving aid | 50 |
| Avg frosh grant | $3,497 |
| Avg frosh loan | $3,464 |

# UNIVERSITY OF OREGON

1217 UNIVERSITY OF OREGON, EUGENE, OR 97403-1217 • ADMISSIONS: 541-346-3201 • FAX: 541-346-5815

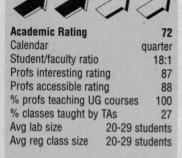
## STUDENTS SPEAK OUT

### Academics

The University of Oregon is full of academic surprises. It's not just research that drives these Eugene intellectuals—UO boasts a nationally renowned writing program and a strong psychology department in addition to typical large university strengths such as pre-professional programs, architecture, journalism, business, and the hard (research) sciences. Many students single out the Honors College as one of the University's best offerings. "At first," says a senior, "I wasn't too ecstatic about UO, but being in the Honors College and getting super involved on campus, I now realize how fortunate I am to have come here. I absolutely love my experiences here—both in and out of the classroom it's been outstanding!" Those not fortunate enough to make the Honors College complain about the number of introductory courses taught by teaching assistants and the overall quality of teaching. Though many professors are "very professional and helpful," it's a common complaint that "some of the professors are unable to bring the material down to our level of comprehension." Auditorium-filling classes and instruction from TAs are the norm for freshmen and sophomores, but "upper division classes vary [in size] from 16 to 60." UO is "run fairly smoothly," and most students find their classes "thought-provoking and stimulating." "Academically, UO offers a quality education and has very competent professors." Although one student's claim that Oregon is "the best school in the best town in the best state with the best people" is probably best taken with a grain of salt, the students who come to Eugene are apparently quite satisfied. Campus computing will no doubt help to continually smooth any remaining rough edges if the university keeps pushing things.

### Life

"Socially, U of O is a 10." Greek life "is not big here"; the social life revolves around "parties, movies, and house dances." Not surprising in the forests of the Pacific Northwest, most mind-alteration is achieved via organic means: "People here are really nice. They are always smiling. Maybe it's just the herb." Some contend that "at night [the] beautiful" city of Eugene "leaves a lot to be desired," while others think "the greatest thing about UO is the nightlife." "Clubs, restaurants, and cafes are abundant and popular." By day, students take advantage of countless outdoor activities, among them climbing, skiing, biking, snowboarding, and rollerblading. "We're an hour from the beach and an hour from the mountains." "For outdoor enthusiasts, you can't get much better." "Especially if you like rain," which hits here with a vengeance (so much so that the university's mascot is a duck). On campus, there are "grassy lawns, quiet walkways, ivy-covered brick buildings, and towering Douglas Fir trees." Dormitory life is safe but uncomfortable, driving many students into off-campus apartments. There's also a major parking problem.

### Student Body

Everyone is "laid back" and "really relaxed" here at UO. "Many students conform to the Eugenian hippie attitude." But "there's no uniform" behavior that students adopt; "people are free to express themselves as they wish." "Our school consists of many subcultures beyond the Greek and hippie lifestyles. It's easy to find your own niche in the multicultural habitat." The "cheerful and friendly" students interact "pretty well; granola types, rural Oregon students, and athletes" all thrive in peaceful coexistence. Oregon "has a veneer of liberalism, but underneath, we live in very conservative territory." Not that this keeps the activist types down: "We have students who protest, and students who protest the protests"; "there's always someone protesting something." Most students hail from "relatively narrow, white, upper-middle class backgrounds." "There is only diversity in the sense that there are various races present. The school is very cliquish-not a lot of mixing." "This is one of the most politically correct places in the universe."

# UNIVERSITY OF OREGON

FINANCIAL AID: 541-346-3211 • E-MAIL: UOADMIT@OREGON.UOREGON.EDU • WEBSITE: WWW.UOREGON.EDU

## ADMISSIONS

*Very important* academic and nonacademic factors considered by the admissions committee include character/personal qualities, class rank, essays, recommendations, secondary school record, and standardized test scores. *Important* factors considered include alumni/ae relation and interview. *Other* factors considered include extracurricular activities, geography, minority status, talent/ability, volunteer work, and work experience. Factors *not* considered include religious affiliation/commitment and state residency. SAT I or ACT required. TOEFL required of all international applicants. High school diploma is required and GED is accepted. *High school units required/recommended:* 4 English required, 3 math required, 4 math recommended, 2 science required, 4 science recommended, 1 science lab required, 2 science lab recommended, 2 foreign language required, 4 foreign language recommended, 3 social studies required, 4 social studies recommended. *The admissions office says:* "A personal essay and two letters of recommendation are required if the applicant does not meet minimum admission requirements."

### The Inside Word

Oregon's admissions process is essentially a formula; it's not likely that anything beyond your grades, rank, and tests will play much of a part in getting you admitted.

## FINANCIAL AID

*Students should submit:* FAFSA. The Princeton Review suggests that all financial aid forms be submitted as soon as possible after January 1. *Need-based scholarships/grants offered:* Pell, SEOG, state scholarships/grants, private scholarships, and the school's own gift aid. *Loan aid offered:* Direct Subsidized Stafford, Direct Unsubsidized Stafford, Direct PLUS, FFEL Subsidized Stafford, FFEL Unsubsidized Stafford, FFEL PLUS, Federal Perkins, and state. Institutional employment available. Federal Work-Study Program available. Applicants will be notified of awards on a rolling basis beginning on or about April 15. Off-campus job opportunities are good.

## FROM THE ADMISSIONS OFFICE

"The University of Oregon is internationally recognized for academic excellence, research opportunities for undergraduates, and commitment to the liberal arts and sciences. The UO's emphasis of 'learning communities'—small, personalized teaching environments—is a national model for undergraduate education. Programs in architecture, literature, journalism, biology, creative writing, physics, and music are nationally competitive. The university's inspiring Northwest location, situated an hour west of the Cascade Mountains and an hour east of the Pacific coast, offers incredible recreation and education options, including field studies in geology and marine biology. The university is currently listed as one of 21 best buys in the country."

## ADMISSIONS

| | |
|---|---|
| Admissions Rating | 79 |
| # of applicants | 8,107 |
| % of applicants accepted | 90 |
| % of acceptees attending | 39 |

### FRESHMAN PROFILE

| | |
|---|---|
| Range SAT Verbal | 498-617 |
| Average SAT Verbal | 557 |
| Range SAT Math | 496-607 |
| Average SAT Math | 552 |
| Minimum TOEFL | 500 |
| Average HS GPA | 3.4 |
| % graduated top 10% of class | 20 |
| % graduated top 25% of class | 49 |
| % graduated top 50% of class | 83 |

### DEADLINES

| | |
|---|---|
| Regular admission | 2/1 |
| Nonfall registration? | yes |

### APPLICANTS ALSO LOOK AT
AND OFTEN PREFER
UC—Berkeley
UC—Davis
AND SOMETIMES PREFER
U. Washington
U. Colorado—Boulder
U. Portland
U. Arizona
UC—Santa Cruz
AND RARELY PREFER
Willamette

### FINANCIAL FACTS

| | |
|---|---|
| Financial Aid Rating | 75 |
| In-state tuition | $2,694 |
| Out-of-state tuition | $12,714 |
| Room & board | $5,564 |
| Books and supplies | $726 |
| Required fees | $1,131 |
| Avg frosh loan | $8,204 |

# UNIVERSITY OF PENNSYLVANIA

1 COLLEGE HALL, PHILADELPHIA, PA 19104 • ADMISSIONS: 215-898-7507 • FAX: 215-898-9670

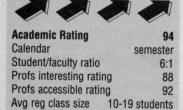
## STUDENTS SPEAK OUT

### Academics

With continuing increases in its popularity with students over the past several years, Penn is clearly a hot ticket. One student explains, "I think Penn's greatest strength is that whatever you decide to major in, you'll find yourself in a strong department, most of which are [among] the best in the country." Students generally agree that the education they receive behind the Ivy-covered walls of this competitive institution is top-notch, especially at the Wharton School. "Being in Wharton means I am getting a wonderful liberal arts education with a very serious focus in business—exactly what I need to enter the real professional world." Not to be overlooked is Penn's College of Arts and Science; history and psychology are also top major choices. Students rave about the variety of opportunities that are available to them at Penn: "The first day of my history class, I went up to my professor and asked if she needed a research assistant, and voila, I had a job." Another adds, "The opportunities are definitely here if you have the drive to take advantage of them." Some find the professors "not focused on the students" and "hard to reach," but past reports of impersonal treatment from profs seem to have ebbed. "Profs here are incredible. They are so accessible and most genuinely want to know their students." The administration receives less glowing compliments, but students are quick to acknowlege that they're trying, noting that they've "encountered red tape, but on the whole, the administration tries really hard to help you."

### Life

"This is really the social Ivy," says one Penn student of life outside of the classroom. "I am happy to be able to get a wonderful education and have a great time doing it." Greek life is reportedly very popular: "there is a strong fraternity/sorority scene." Students do point out that "the range of other cultural and social activities means that there are a lot of different possibilities." Another student adds, "Life at Penn is busy. There is always something to do here; you just have to go out and do it." As for some off-campus fun, "going into center city, Philadelphia, is a very popular thing to do on the weekends." However, safety on campus and in the outside area of West Philadelphia is still an issue. One student claims "all the security measures are a joke. They do nothing to lessen crime on or around campus." On the other hand, the *Daily Pennsylvanian*, the student newspaper, featured an article last year that revealed that most students responding to a survey on the subject indicated that they felt safe or very safe. More than half the students live on campus and most are happy with their digs, though some feel their dorms could be easier on the eyes. Athletic facilities, which have also received their share of complaints in the past, recently got long overdue renovations. Overall, this student's positive attitude seems to prevail: "Penn is an amazing place to grow and learn. We have a great ability to work hard and have a good time concurrently. That's what Penn is all about."

### Student Body

Diversity among the students at Penn is, by and large, decent. Interaction appears to be the big point of contention: "Penn has a lot of diversity, but the different groups engage in self-segregation." There's a noticable New York population. Snipes one, "If you wear black pants and are from Long Island, you'll fit right in." For the most part, Penn students get along along just fine. Sums up this biochemistry major: "Personally, I feel very close to the other students here at Penn. Each person I encounter here has some special talent or attitude, or just some special spark that makes the population at Penn a very exciting and wonderful group of people to be with."

FINANCIAL AID: 215-898-1988 • E-MAIL: INFO@ADMISSIONS.UGAO.UPENN.EDU • WEBSITE: WWW.UPENN.EDU

## ADMISSIONS

*Very important* academic and nonacademic factors considered by the admissions committee include secondary school record. *Important* factors considered include class rank, geography, standardized test scores, state residency, and talent/ability. *Other* factors considered include alumni/ae relation, character/personal qualities, essays, extracurricular activities, minority status, recommendations, volunteer work, and work experience. Factors *not* considered include religious affiliation/commitment. SAT I and SAT II or ACT required. High school diploma is required and GED is accepted. *High school units required/recommended:* 17 total recommended; 4 English recommended, 4 math recommended, 3 science recommended, 3 foreign language recommended, 3 social studies recommended, 2 history recommended.

### The Inside Word

After a small decline three cycles ago, applications are once again climbing at Penn—the fourth increase in five years. The competition in the applicant pool is formidable. Applicants can safely assume that they need to be one of the strongest students in their graduating class in order to be successful.

## FINANCIAL AID

*Students should submit:* CSS/Financial Aid PROFILE, institutional form for financial aid, and FAFSA. The Princeton Review suggests that all financial aid forms be submitted as soon as possible after January 1. *Need-based scholarships/grants offered:* Pell, SEOG, state scholarships/grants, private scholarships, and the school's own gift aid. *Loan aid offered:* Direct Subsidized Stafford, Direct Unsubsidized Stafford, Direct PLUS, FFEL Subsidized Stafford, FFEL Unsubsidized Stafford, FFEL PLUS, Federal Perkins, Federal Nursing, college/university loans from institutional funds, and Penn Guaranteed loan. Institutional employment available. Federal Work-Study Program available. Applicants will be notified of awards with decision letter providing all deadlines are met. Off-campus job opportunities are excellent.

## FROM THE ADMISSIONS OFFICE

"The University of Pennsylvania is the oldest university in the United States and a member of the Ivy League. Penn was founded in 1740 by Benjamin Franklin, a noted visionary and pioneer. Franklin proposed an institution that would fuse a classical education with the modern liberal arts, and from this idea, Penn was born. Complimenting the classics were courses in physics, chemistry, natural history, economics, and modern languages. Today, Penn has 4 undergraduate schools (arts and sciences, business, engineering and applied sciences, and nursing), and 12 graduate professional schools on a traditional campus near the center of Philadelphia. Students are drawn to Penn for the breadth and depth of the academic program, the diversity of the student body, and the extraordinary array of opportunities in and out of the classroom. We hope you will consider Penn."

## ADMISSIONS

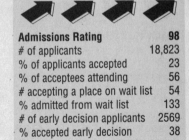

| | |
|---|---|
| Admissions Rating | 98 |
| # of applicants | 18,823 |
| % of applicants accepted | 23 |
| % of acceptees attending | 56 |
| # accepting a place on wait list | 54 |
| % admitted from wait list | 133 |
| # of early decision applicants | 2569 |
| % accepted early decision | 38 |

### FRESHMAN PROFILE

| | |
|---|---|
| Range SAT Verbal | 640-730 |
| Average SAT Verbal | 683 |
| Range SAT Math | 670-760 |
| Average SAT Math | 709 |
| Range ACT Composite | 28-32 |
| Average ACT Composite | 30 |
| Minimum TOEFL | 600 |
| Average HS GPA | 3.9 |
| % graduated top 10% of class | 92 |
| % graduated top 25% of class | 98 |
| % graduated top 50% of class | 100 |

### DEADLINES

| | |
|---|---|
| Early decision | 11/1 |
| Regular admission | 1/1 |
| Regular notification | 4/1 |

### APPLICANTS ALSO LOOK AT
#### AND OFTEN PREFER
Yale
Harvard
Stanford
Princeton, MIT
#### AND SOMETIMES PREFER
Cornell U.
Duke
Brown
Columbia
#### AND RARELY PREFER
Johns Hopkins
Georgetown U.
Northwestern U.
UC—Berkeley

## FINANCIAL FACTS

| | |
|---|---|
| Financial Aid Rating | 74 |
| Tuition | $22,682 |
| Room & board | $7,826 |
| Books and supplies | $730 |
| Required fees | $2,488 |
| % frosh receiving aid | 40 |
| % undergrads receiving aid | 43 |

# SITY OF PITTSBURGH—PITTSBURGH

T FLOOR, PITTSBURGH, PA 15260 • ADMISSIONS: 412-624-7488 • FAX: 412-648-8815

## Quality of Life Rating — 88

| | |
|---|---|
| Type of school | public |
| Affiliation | none |
| Environment | urban |

### STUDENTS

| | |
|---|---|
| Total undergrad enrollment | 17,424 |
| % male/female | 47/53 |
| % from out of state | 14 |
| % live on campus | 35 |
| % in (# of) fraternities | 10 (18) |
| % in (# of) sororities | 6 (11) |
| % African American | 9 |
| % Asian | 4 |
| % Caucasian | 85 |
| % Hispanic | 1 |
| % international | 1 |

### SURVEY SAYS . . .

Campus easy to get around
Campus feels safe
Great library
Great off-campus food
Students love Pittsburgh, PA
Students get along with local
community
Student publications are ignored
Students are cliquish
(Almost) no one listens to college
radio
Registration is a pain
Lots of long lines and red tape

## ACADEMICS

### Academic Rating — 78

| | |
|---|---|
| Calendar | semester |
| Student/faculty ratio | 17:1 |
| Profs interesting rating | 68 |
| Profs accessible rating | 96 |
| Avg lab size | 20-29 students |
| Avg reg class size | 20-29 students |

### MOST POPULAR MAJORS
business
psychology
engineering

## STUDENTS SPEAK OUT

### Academics

"Hail to Pitt!" Such is the general sentiment among most students at the very affordable University of Pittsburgh, "a fantastic place to spend four years of your life" that offers a "plethora of classes" ("most" reportedly "taught by professors") and "the benefits of a small school and a large school." Pitt's wealth of majors include especially strong programs in engineering and health sciences (health information management, pre-med, pre-pharmacy, physical therapy, etc.), and the philosophy department is perhaps the best in the country, if not the world. The "involved and cutting-edge," "wonderfully entertaining and enlightening" professors here "lecture their butts off" and "really enjoy teaching." Outside of class, instructors "really take the time to encourage and support students," and they are "extremely helpful and accessible in their offices and over e-mail." Pitt also boasts "good study-abroad programs," including the nationally renowned Semester at Sea, and computer and research resources get top marks. As far as complaints, the administration could "cut down on the red tape" and "the lines." The staff could also stand to be friendlier. Also, classes are sometimes a bit on the large side. Pitt is a fairly gargantuan, research-oriented public university, though, and students here seem more or less resigned to the fact that big classes come with the territory. "I've had a very good experience here," waxes a history major. "It's a school where you are not left out in the cold, yet also not forced into things. They let you make your own choices but still help you out along the way."

### Life

Pitt is located on a "gorgeous, historic," urban campus that students characterize as "relatively safe." The residence halls are notably "great," and, though we've never considered the words "Pittsburgh" and "culture" to be particularly synonymous, the "incredible" surrounding metropolis is, apparently, a regular Mecca of refinement and civilization. "It's a really clean, safe city" with "great shopping" downtown and in neighborhoods with cool names like "Squirrel Hill and Shadyside," professional sports galore, volunteer opportunities, and plenty to do in nearby Schenley Park, the third largest public park on the eastern seaboard. "In one weekend, you can go see a symphony (for free), see a hockey game, bum around a museum (for free), and window-shop downtown," claims a senior. "If you're bored, it's your own fault." Also, the city of Pittsburgh "has a very homey feel to it," which makes it "a good starter city to live in your first time away from home." On the weekends, Pitt is host to "lots of partying." There are a healthy number of "house parties off campus," and the bar scene is "generally a big one." Greek life is alive and well, but far from excessive. Intramural and intercollegiate sports are significant here, too, and Pitt students definitely exhibit their fair share of "school pride." Football games are well attended—especially against Penn State and West Virginia, two schools students here just love to hate.

### Student Body

Most students at Pitt don't have far to travel when they go home for the holidays; an overwhelming percentage comes from the state of Pennsylvania. And while there's a fair amount of ethnic and social diversity here, different groups don't interact much. Some students tell us they "have a few good friends" but are "not likely to speak with you" unless they know you. Others swear they are "incredibly friendly," and they say they have no problems talking to their "generally nice and easygoing" fellow students. "The school seems big first term," helpfully explains a senior, "but after a semester at Pitt, it begins to feel like a small, rural campus—with the exception of the traffic," of course. Pitt has its share of "awfully weird people" as well. No matter what your interests are, there are reportedly "friends and groups of friends here that would fit just about anyone's personality type."

FINANCIAL AID: 412-624-7488 • E-MAIL: OAFA+@PITT.EDU • WEBSITE: WWW.PITT.EDU

## ADMISSIONS

*Very important* academic and nonacademic factors considered by the admissions committee include secondary school record. *Important* factors considered include character/personal qualities, class rank, standardized test scores, and talent/ability. *Other* factors considered include alumni/ae relation, essays, extracurricular activities, recommendations, volunteer work, and work experience. Factors *not* considered include geography, interview, minority status, religious affiliation/commitment, and state residency. SAT I or ACT required. TOEFL required of all international applicants. High school diploma is required and GED is not accepted except by the College of General Studies. *High school units required/recommended:* 15 total required; 4 English required, 3 math required, 3 science required, 3 science lab required, 1 social studies required, 4 elective required (includes 3 foreign language in a single language).

### The Inside Word

Applicants to Pitt, as at most large public universities, are admitted primarily on the strength of basic qualifiers like grades and test scores. If you are serious about Pitt, rolling admissions allows you to get a decision earlier than most colleges notify their applicants.

## FINANCIAL AID

*Students should submit:* FAFSA and institution's own financial aid form. The Princeton Review suggests that all financial aid forms be submitted as soon as possible after January 1. *Need-based scholarships/grants offered:* Pell, SEOG, state scholarships/grants, the school's own gift aid, and College Work Study Program (CWS). *Loan aid offered:* FFEL Subsidized Stafford, FFEL Unsubsidized Stafford, FFEL PLUS, Federal Perkins, Federal Nursing, VA and HEAL. Institutional employment available. Federal Work-Study Program available. Applicants will be notified of awards on a rolling basis beginning on or about March 15. Off-campus job opportunities are excellent.

## FROM THE ADMISSIONS OFFICE

"The University of Pittsburgh is one of 61 members of the Association of American Universities, a prestigious group whose members include the major research universities of North America. There are nearly 400 degree programs available at the 16 Pittsburgh campus schools (two offering only undergraduate degree programs, four offering graduate degree programs, and ten offering both) and four regional campuses, allowing students a wide latitude of choices, both academically and in setting and style, size and pace of campus. Programs ranked nationally include philosophy, history and philosophy of science, chemistry, economics, English, history, physics, political science, and psychology. The University Center for International Studies is ranked one of the exemplary international programs in the country by the Council on Learning; and the Semester at Sea Program takes students to different ports of call around the world on an ocean liner."

## ADMISSIONS

| | |
|---|---|
| Admissions Rating | 82 |
| # of applicants | 13,565 |
| % of applicants accepted | 62 |
| % of acceptees attending | 35 |

### FRESHMAN PROFILE

| | |
|---|---|
| Range SAT Verbal | 530-630 |
| Average SAT Verbal | 582 |
| Range SAT Math | 530-640 |
| Average SAT Math | 587 |
| Range ACT Composite | 22-29 |
| Average ACT Composite | 25 |
| Minimum TOEFL | 500 |
| % graduated top 10% of class | 32 |
| % graduated top 25% of class | 68 |
| % graduated top 50% of class | 96 |

### DEADLINES

| | |
|---|---|
| Priority admission deadline | 3/1 |
| Nonfall registration? | yes |

### APPLICANTS ALSO LOOK AT AND OFTEN PREFER

Penn State—Univ. Park
Duquesne U.
Temple U.
Indiana U. (PA)
Carnegie Mellon

### AND SOMETIMES PREFER

U. Delaware
Slippery Rock
U. Maryland
West Virginia U.

### AND RARELY PREFER

Villanova

### FINANCIAL FACTS

| | |
|---|---|
| Financial Aid Rating | 76 |
| In-state tuition | $6,422 |
| Out-of-state tuition | $14,104 |
| Room & board | $5,936 |
| Books and supplies | $500 |
| Required fees | $580 |
| % frosh receiving aid | 79 |

# UNIVERSITY OF PUGET SOUND

1500 NORTH WARNER, TACOMA, WA 98416 • ADMISSION: 800-396-7191 • FAX: 253-879-3993

## CAMPUS LIFE

| | |
|---|---|
| **Quality of Life Rating** | **85** |
| Type of school | private |
| Affiliation | none |
| Environment | suburban |

### STUDENTS

| | |
|---|---|
| Total undergrad enrollment | 2,619 |
| % male/female | 39/61 |
| % from out of state | 69 |
| % from public high school | 76 |
| % live on campus | 53 |
| % in (# of) fraternities | 25 (4) |
| % in (# of) sororities | 22 (5) |
| % African American | 2 |
| % Asian | 12 |
| % Caucasian | 77 |
| % Hispanic | 3 |
| % Native American | 1 |
| % international | 1 |
| # of countries represented | 17 |

### SURVEY SAYS . . .

*Ethnic diversity on campus*
*Great food on campus*
*Classes are small*
*Dorms are like palaces*
*Campus easy to get around*
*Intercollegiate sports unpopular or*
*nonexistent*
*Political activism is (almost)*
*nonexistent*
*Musical organizations are hot*
*Students don't like Tacoma, WA*
*Computer facilities need improving*

## ACADEMICS

| | |
|---|---|
| **Academic Rating** | **87** |
| Calendar | semester |
| Student/faculty ratio | 11:1 |
| Profs interesting rating | 94 |
| Profs accessible rating | 96 |
| % profs teaching UG courses | 100 |
| Avg lab size | 10-19 students |
| Avg reg class size | 10-19 students |

### MOST POPULAR MAJORS

business administration
English
psychology

## STUDENTS SPEAK OUT
### Academics

"This school is hard," declares a sophomore. Nevertheless, students at the University of Puget Sound rave that professors with "a passion for their subjects" and a "stimulating, rigorous learning environment" make theirs "the best school in Washington." The "extremely challenging" classes are "small, and people can generally get the classes they want." Although a couple of ancient professors "suck hardcore," students overwhelmingly agree that nearly every prof at UPS is "knowledgeable, humorous," and "extremely accessible." The faculty is not made up of "overbearing know-it-alls; professors "genuinely care" about their students. "They are my instructors, advisors, and friends," reflects a senior. "The best part about this school is being able to run into your prof, drink a beer, and talk about what happened in class that day." The administration is more of a mixed bag. Some are "terrific," "accessible," and "open to comments," while others are "shadows lurking around campus" who are "slow to respond." Overall, the administration receives average to above-average marks. The facilities are solid (some are exceptional), though a few students suggest that UPS could use "better computer labs." Puget Sound offers a unique music business program and a "pioneering multi-disciplinary core requirement" called Science in Context designed to make every graduate "scientifically literate."

### Life

Because "UPS is extremely challenging academically," people "study a lot" in the "large" and "comfortable" dorm rooms on its "aesthetically beautiful" (but dimly lit and rainy) campus. "Classes, homework, and jobs keep people here very busy." That's just as well because "there is absolutely nothing for college-aged kids to do" in Tacoma, a town that "literally stinks." On campus, there are "quite a few fun and free school-sponsored activities such as dinners and dances." The "many fascinating events going on" include "speakers, bands, and political activism." Drinking and getting high are two other favorite pastimes here, and there are "great parties where all kinds of people interact." Greek life "is awesome" at UPS. If you don't go Greek, you might feel "a bit of resentment toward the Greeks," as there is a noticeable "rift between [them] and independents." There is also a "lack of school spirit," and intercollegiate athletics are generally "neglected." And why shouldn't they be? You might neglect watching other people play sports if your wooded campus was located mere minutes away from the waters of Puget Sound and Mount Rainier Park. Not surprisingly, "hiking and backpacking," "skiing, kayaking," and the "outdoors stuff" of the Great Pacific Northwest are seriously in vogue. For more cosmopolitan amusement, Seattle, with its many distractions, is a mere half-hour drive away. In that "great city," students delight in "art exhibits, operas, concerts, shows" great restaurants, bars, coffee houses, and Mariners games.

### Student Body

The "open-minded and self-motivated" students at UPS describe themselves as "well-off white kids" who "respect the differences among themselves and go on their merry way." Although there is a contingent of "snotty" and "pretentious" people, most are "enthusiastic, engaging, extremely friendly," not to mention "totally nice and really laid back socially." However, UPS students "know when to work hard." There are "many good-looking people" here, though several women complain that their gender constitutes an inordinately large percentage of the total population, which can make dates hard to come by. "The school gets to be pretty small by the time you are a senior," but there is "not much interaction between frosh and upperclassmen." Also, there are "lots of conservatives and liberals," but UPS is "not very diverse." Members of different ethnic groups "tend to hang out together" in isolated cliques, "but it is not a hostile atmosphere." Most students seem to genuinely cherish just about every one of their peers. "I like everyone here but the weird guy with the nose rings," discloses a junior. "Four? Four! How does he blow his nose? The fool!"

FINANCIAL AID: 800-396-7192 • E-MAIL: ADMISSION@UPS.EDU • WEBSITE: WWW.UPS.EDU

## ADMISSIONS

*Very important* academic and nonacademic factors considered by the admission committee include secondary school record, recommendations, and standardized test scores. *Important* factors considered include essay, extracurricular activities, minority status, and talent/ability. *Other* factors considered include class rank, character/personal qualities, interview, and volunteer work. Factors *not* considered include geography, religious affiliation/commitment, and state residency. SAT I or ACT required, SAT I preferred. TOEFL required of all international applicants. High school diploma is required and GED is accepted. *High school units recommended:* 19 total recommended, 4 English recommended, 4 math recommended, 4 science lab recommended, 3 foreign language recommended, 3 social studies recommended, 1 elective recommended. *The admissions office says:* "Our admission committee reviews each application carefully. The entire committee will review the files over which there is some question of admissibility. Members of the admission staff will meet with any candidate at any time during the admission process."

### The Inside Word

The University of Puget Sound is on the right track with its willingness to supply students with detailed information about how the selection process works. If universities in general were more forthcoming about candidate evaluation, college admission wouldn't be the angst-ridden exercise that it is for so many students. All students are aware that their academic background is the primary consideration of every admissions committee. How they are considered as individuals remains mysterious. At Puget Sound, it is clear that people mean more to the university than its freshman profile and that candidates can count on a considerate and caring attitude before, during, and after the review process.

## FINANCIAL AID

*Students should submit:* FAFSA. Regular filing deadline is February 1. The Princeton Review suggests that all financial aid forms be submitted as soon as possible after January 1. *Need-based scholarships/grants offered:* Pell, SEOG, state scholarships/grants, private scholarships, and the school's own gift aid. *Loan aid offered:* FFEL Subsidized Stafford, FFEL Unsubsidized Stafford, FFEL PLUS, Federal Perkins, college/university loans from institutional funds, and Alaska Loans. Institutional employment available. Federal Work-Study Program available. Applicants will be notified of awards on a rolling basis beginning on or about March 15. Off-campus job opportunities are excellent.

## FROM THE ADMISSIONS OFFICE

"For over 100 years, students from many locations and backgrounds have chosen to join our community. It is a community committed to excellence—excellence in the classroom and excellence in student organizations and activities. Puget students are serious about rowing and writing, management and music, skiing and sciences, leadership and languages. At Puget Sound you'll be challenged—and helped—to perform at the peak of your ability."

## ADMISSIONS

| | |
|---|---|
| Admissions Rating | 85 |
| # of applicants | 4,124 |
| % of applicants accepted | 72 |
| % of acceptees attending | 22 |
| # of early decision applicants | 186 |
| % accepted early decision | 88 |

### FRESHMAN PROFILE

| | |
|---|---|
| Range SAT Verbal | 580-670 |
| Average SAT Verbal | 624 |
| Range SAT Math | 570-670 |
| Average SAT Math | 619 |
| Range ACT Composite | 24-29 |
| Average ACT Composite | 26 |
| Minimum TOEFL | 550 |
| Average HS GPA | 3.6 |
| % graduated top 10% of class | 44 |
| % graduated top 25% of class | 76 |
| % graduated top 50% of class | 96 |

### DEADLINES

| | |
|---|---|
| Early decision 1 | 11/15 |
| Early decision 1 notification | 12/15 |
| Early decision 2 | 12/15 |
| Early decision 2 notification | 1/15 |
| Regular admission | 2/1 |
| Nonfall registration? | yes |

### APPLICANTS ALSO LOOK AT

**AND OFTEN PREFER**
Stanford
Northwestern U., Pomona

**AND SOMETIMES PREFER**
U. Washington
Whitman
Lewis & Clark
Willamette, Colorado Coll.

**AND RARELY PREFER**
U. Oregon
Gonzaga

## FINANCIAL FACTS

| | |
|---|---|
| Financial Aid Rating | 86 |
| Tuition | $22,350 |
| Room & board | $5,780 |
| Books and supplies | $750 |
| Required fees | $155 |
| % frosh receiving aid | 54 |
| % undergrads receiving aid | 59 |
| Avg frosh grant | $10,092 |
| Avg frosh loan | $5,272 |

# UNIVERSITY OF REDLANDS

PO BOX 3080, REDLANDS, CA 92373-0999 • ADMISSIONS: 909-335-4074 • FAX: 909-335-4089

## CAMPUS LIFE

| | |
|---|---|
| **Quality of Life Rating** | **85** |
| Type of school | private |
| Affiliation | none |
| Environment | suburban |

### STUDENTS

| | |
|---|---|
| Total undergrad enrollment | 1,734 |
| % male/female | 44/56 |
| % from out of state | 29 |
| % from public high school | 75 |
| % live on campus | 74 |
| % in (# of) fraternities | 1 (6) |
| % in (# of) sororities | 3 (5) |
| % African American | 3 |
| % Asian | 6 |
| % Caucasian | 63 |
| % Hispanic | 12 |
| % Native American | 1 |
| % international | 2 |
| # of countries represented | 9 |

### SURVEY SAYS . . .

Frats and sororities dominate social scene
Classes are small
Theater is hot
Everyone loves the Bulldogs
Student publications are ignored
Library needs improving
Musical organizations are hot
Lab facilities are great
Students don't like Redlands, CA
Class discussions encouraged

## ACADEMICS

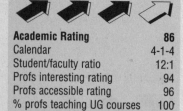

| | |
|---|---|
| **Academic Rating** | **86** |
| Calendar | 4-1-4 |
| Student/faculty ratio | 12:1 |
| Profs interesting rating | 94 |
| Profs accessible rating | 96 |
| % profs teaching UG courses | 100 |

### MOST POPULAR MAJORS

business administration and management
liberal studies
multi/interdisciplinary studies

## STUDENTS SPEAK OUT

### Academics

The Johnson Center for Integrated Studies, which allows students, in association with a professor, to design their own majors, is the major reason that many students attend the University of Redlands. Academically, one can "follow any path one chooses without compromising anything." Students point out that the government and liberal arts programs are exceptional. Professors are not only "eccentric" and "very intelligent" but also "willing to help anytime you need them." To sum up, "the professors rock," enthuses a junior international relations major. "They are the only reason that the 61 percent of us stay." Class sizes are extremely small, which enables students "to be looked at as individual people instead of just numbers." Small class sizes foster conversation and enable students to learn from their peers. While a sophomore asserts that "the courses are rigorous and academically challenging," other students feel the school is "easier than it portrays itself to be." The administration is "supportive," but many complain about the "useless bureaucracy" that seems unnecessary at such a small institution. Students also gripe that they continue to wait for Internet access in their dorm rooms despite assurances that it would be available this year. A junior liberal studies major summarizes the educational experience at UOR: "First year, they hold your hand long enough to allow students to learn what they want out of the University of Redlands. From there on, what you put in is what you walk away with."

### Life

"There's not much to do for fun around here except going to Wal-Mart or Denny's at two in the morning," sighs a sophomore. Redlands, a small town located an hour's drive from both Los Angeles and a number of ski resorts, offers few options for students looking for off-campus entertainment. "Almost everything closes by 9 P.M., and students without cars are stuck on campus." You've had a full night if you catch a flick at the "busy" movie theater in town. "Redlands is quite relaxed," according to one government major. "Sometimes things can be a little boring, but if you make an effort to get out and have a good time, life at Redlands is fun." Students party on campus where fraternities and sororities dominate the social scene, and the university sponsors many on-campus social events. Students agree that the athletic and exercise facilities need improvement. They also decry the limited computer access. Everyone succumbs to an appreciation of the beautiful campus and claims that the quality of life at the University of Redlands is "incredible—sometimes it's like being at school at Club Med."

### Student Body

The students at the University of Redlands are "intelligent" as well as "friendly" and "well-rounded." There are, however, many cliques and the amount of "close-mindedness is irritating." Though nearly a third of the students are members of a minority group, students condemn the lack of diversity on campus and complain about the excess of "petty" and "rich kids" who are still "stuck in high school." Still, as one senior government major says, "the community feeling at the University of Redlands is quite strong."

FINANCIAL AID: 909-335-4047 • E-MAIL: ADMISSIONS@UOR.EDU • WEBSITE: WWW.REDLANDS.EDU

## ADMISSIONS

*Very important* academic and nonacademic factors considered by the admissions committee include essays and secondary school record. *Important* factors considered include character/personal qualities, class rank, extracurricular activities, recommendations, standardized test scores, volunteer work, and work experience. *Other* factors considered include alumni/ae relation, geography, interview, minority status, and talent/ability. Factors *not* considered include religious affiliation/commitment and state residency. SAT I or ACT required. TOEFL required of all international applicants. High school diploma is required and GED is accepted. *High school units required/recommended:* 18 total recommended; 4 English recommended, 3 math required, 4 math recommended, 3 science recommended, 3 science lab recommended, 2 foreign language required, 4 foreign language recommended, 2 social studies recommended, 2 history recommended.

### The Inside Word

The University of Redlands is a solid admit for any student with an above average high school record. Candidates who are interested in pursuing self-designed programs through the University's Johnston Center will find the admissions process to be distinctly more personal than it generally is; the center is interested in intellectually curious, self-motivated students and puts a lot of energy into identifying and recruiting them.

## FINANCIAL AID

*Students should submit:* FAFSA and GPA verification form for California residents. The Princeton Review suggests that all financial aid forms be submitted as soon as possible after January 1. *Need-based scholarships/grants offered:* Pell, SEOG, state scholarships/grants, private scholarships, and the school's own gift aid. *Loan aid offered:* FFEL Subsidized Stafford, FFEL Unsubsidized Stafford, FFEL PLUS, Federal Perkins, college/university loans from institutional funds, and alternative loans. Institutional employment available. Federal Work-Study Program available. Applicants will be notified of awards on a rolling basis beginning on or about March 1. Off-campus job opportunities are good.

## FROM THE ADMISSIONS OFFICE

"We've created an unusually blended curriculum of the liberal arts and pre-professional study because we think education is about learning how to think and learning how to do. For example, our environmental studies students have synthesized their study of computer science, sociology, biology, and economics to develop an actual resource management plan for the local mountain communities. Our creative writing program encourages internships with publishing or television production companies so that when our graduates send off their first novel, they can pay the rent as magazine writers. We educate managers, poets, environmental scientists, teachers, musicians, and speech therapists to be reflective about culture and society so that they can better understand and improve the world they'll enter upon graduation."

## ADMISSIONS

| | |
|---|---|
| Admissions Rating | 73 |
| # of applicants | 2,114 |
| % of applicants accepted | 78 |
| % of acceptees attending | 30 |

### FRESHMAN PROFILE

| | |
|---|---|
| Range SAT Verbal | 510-620 |
| Average SAT Verbal | 562 |
| Range SAT Math | 510-620 |
| Average SAT Math | 566 |
| Range ACT Composite | 20-25 |
| Average ACT Composite | 23 |
| Minimum TOEFL | 550 |
| Average HS GPA | 3.4 |

### DEADLINES

| | |
|---|---|
| Priority admission deadline | 2/1 |
| Regular admission | 7/1 |
| Nonfall registration? | yes |

### APPLICANTS ALSO LOOK AT
**AND OFTEN PREFER**
Occidental
U. Penn
**AND SOMETIMES PREFER**
Pitzer
UC—Irvine
UC—Santa Barbara
U. of the Pacific
U. San Diego
**AND RARELY PREFER**
Whittier
Pepperdine
U. Southern Cal

## FINANCIAL FACTS

| | |
|---|---|
| Financial Aid Rating | 83 |
| Tuition | $21,180 |
| Room & board | $7,840 |
| Books and supplies | $800 |
| Required fees | $576 |
| % frosh receiving aid | 66 |
| % undergrads receiving aid | 70 |
| Avg frosh grant | $14,405 |
| Avg frosh loan | $4,722 |

# SITY OF RHODE ISLAND

KINGSTON, RI 02881-1966 • ADMISSIONS: 401-874-7000 • FAX: 401-874-5523

LANDS

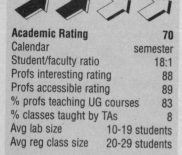

**...ity of Life Rating**    **80**

| | |
|---|---|
| Type of school | public |
| Affiliation | none |
| Environment | rural |

### STUDENTS

| | |
|---|---|
| Total undergrad enrollment | 10,647 |
| % male/female | 44/56 |
| % from out of state | 38 |
| % from public high school | 88 |
| % live on campus | 37 |
| % in (# of) fraternities | 10 (13) |
| % in (# of) sororities | 12 (9) |
| % African American | 4 |
| % Asian | 4 |
| % Caucasian | 75 |
| % Hispanic | 4 |
| % Native American | 1 |
| % international | 1 |
| # of countries represented | 62 |

### SURVEY SAYS . . .

*Frats and sororities dominate social scene*
*Everyone loves the Rams*
*(Almost) everyone smokes*
*High cost of living*
*Large classes*
*Campus difficult to get around*
*Lab facilities are great*

### ACADEMICS

**Academic Rating**    **70**

| | |
|---|---|
| Calendar | semester |
| Student/faculty ratio | 18:1 |
| Profs interesting rating | 88 |
| Profs accessible rating | 89 |
| % profs teaching UG courses | 83 |
| % classes taught by TAs | 8 |
| Avg lab size | 10-19 students |
| Avg reg class size | 20-29 students |

### MOST POPULAR MAJORS

psychology
pharmacology
human development/family studies

## STUDENTS SPEAK OUT

### Academics

The mostly pre-professional students at the University of Rhode Island tell us their school has "respectable academics." Although some classes are huge, well over half of all undergraduate courses have 25 students or less. Student opinion regarding the quality of the professors and teaching assistants who instruct these courses is decidedly mixed. There are professors who "don't care about you at all," and whose "teaching skills leave much to be desired," but "there are also some good, challenging ones." Indeed, a great many profs at URI are "easily accessible" and "dedicated to their students." They are "great teachers" who "really go out of their way to make you feel comfortable." Several electrical engineers single out the faculty in their department as "exceptional." Also, "though there are a lot of graduate assistants and new professors teaching lower level classes, they do a great job," pledges a junior. However, communication breakdowns frequently occur because many teaching assistants don't speak English very well. Students give a thumbs-up to the "good computer labs" here and say the administration is "accommodating." Although "registration by phone" is "a breeze," it is an "uncaring" process, and getting into classes can be a problem, even for juniors and seniors. In addition to a nationally celebrated oceanography program, popular majors at URI include education, business, engineering, nursing, and pharmacy.

### Life

The alcohol policies on this "quintessential New England" campus are strict—"too strict," according to some students. To drink, "we must go off campus, even if we are 21," laments a senior. Still, the parties seem to be making a comeback. There is a "big bar scene" and a happening "off-campus party scene," and many students manage to "get blasted" on a regular basis. A "strong Greek system" provides some of the social life here; for students who do pledge, "Greek Week and Homecoming are the best times of the year." Beyond partying, campus life is "well balanced," and "there are also a lot of things to do to relax." The university's Student Entertainment Committee and the Office of Student Life offer more than 80 organizations for undergrads. But be aware, "This is a big school," declares a junior. "If you feel the need to be pampered, you're in the wrong place. If you are an easily adjustable person, you can find your niche and really fit in." The newly powerful men's basketball team is very popular. Though "Kingston is pretty boring during the winter," there are "many beaches in the area" for when spring arrives. Also, more exciting urban centers such as Providence and Boston are nearby. On campus, "buildings are old," but the "atrocious" parking situation is "the biggest problem" at the school.

### Student Body

Lots of students choose URI because it is "close to home" and "cheap," especially for in-state residents, who make up a majority here. Approximately 50 percent of the students at URI hail from Rhode Island; the next most represented states—New Jersey and Massachusetts—show up a distant second with about 11 percent each. While some students are "snobby," most describe themselves as "easygoing," "polite," and "helpful," and they rate themselves somewhat friendlier than the undergrads at other large state universities. The overall population is reasonably diverse, and "for the most part, everyone gets along," although different ethnic groups "do not mesh well." Students report "quite a bit of racial tension" on campus.

FINANCIAL AID: 401-874-2314 • E-MAIL: URIADMIT@URIACC.URI.EDU • WEBSITE: WWW.URI.EDU

## ADMISSIONS

*Very important* academic and nonacademic factors considered by the admissions committee include secondary school record. *Important* factors considered include class rank, standardized test scores, interview, talent/ability, geography, and state residency. *Other* factors considered include extracurricular activities, character/personal qualities, alumni/ae relation, volunteer work, and work experience. Factors *not* considered include religious affiliation and minority status. SAT I or ACT required. TOEFL required of all international applicants. High school diploma is required and GED is accepted. *High school units required/recommended:* 18 total required; 4 English required, 3 math required, 2 science required, 2 science lab recommended, 2 foreign language required, 2 social studies or history required, 5 electives required. *The admissions office says:* "We have no restriction on the number of out-of-state students, as most public universities do. We recommend interviews and look forward to meeting with as many candidates as possible."

### The Inside Word

Any candidate with solid grades is likely to find the university's admissions committee to be welcoming. The yield of admits who enroll is low and the state's population small. Out-of-state students are attractive to URI because they are sorely needed to fill out the student body. Students who graduate in the top 10 percent of their class are good scholarship bets.

## FINANCIAL AID

*Students should submit:* FAFSA. There is no regular filing deadline. The Princeton Review suggests that all financial aid forms be submitted as soon as possible after January 1. *Need-based scholarships/grants offered:* Pell, SEOG, state scholarships/grants, private scholarships, and the school's own gift aid. *Loan aid offered:* Direct Subsidized Stafford, Direct Unsubsidized Stafford, Direct PLUS, Federal Perkins, Federal Nursing, college/university loans from institutional funds, and health professions loan. Institutional employment available. Federal Work-Study Program available. Applicants will be notified of awards on a rolling basis beginning on or about March 15. Off-campus job opportunities are excellent.

## FROM THE ADMISSIONS OFFICE

"Outstanding freshman candidates with minimum SAT scores of 1120 (1150 for engineering and pharmacy) who rank in the top third of their class are eligible for consideration for a Centennial Scholarship ranging up to full tuition. The scholarships are renewable each semester if the student maintains continuous full-time enrollment and a 3.0 average or better. Eligibility requires a completed admissions application received by our December 15 Early Action deadline. Applications and information received after December 15 cannot be considered. (High School students who present more than 23 college credits are considered transfer applicants and are not eligible for Centennial Scholarships)."Like the permanent granite cornerstones that grace its stately buildings, the University of Rhode Island was founded in the lasting tradition of the land-grant colleges and later became one of the original crop of national sea-grant colleges. Observing its centennial in 1992, the state's largest university prepares its students to meet the challenges of the 21st century."

## ADMISSIONS

| | |
|---|---|
| Admissions Rating | 71 |
| # of applicants | 9,758 |
| % of applicants accepted | 75 |
| % of acceptees attending | 31 |

### FRESHMAN PROFILE

| | |
|---|---|
| Range SAT Verbal | 490-590 |
| Average SAT Verbal | 544 |
| Range SAT Math | 490-600 |
| Average SAT Math | 546 |
| Minimum TOEFL | 550 |
| Average HS GPA | 3.4 |
| % graduated top 10% of class | 17 |
| % graduated top 25% of class | 53 |
| % graduated top 50% of class | 86 |

### DEADLINES

| | |
|---|---|
| Priority admission deadline | 12/14 |
| Regular admission | 3/1 |
| Nonfall registration? | yes |

### APPLICANTS ALSO LOOK AT

**AND OFTEN PREFER**
U. Mass—Amherst
U. Conn

**AND SOMETIMES PREFER**
Boston U.
U. Delaware
U. Vermont
U. New Hampshire

**AND RARELY PREFER**
Providence
U. Maine—Orono

## FINANCIAL FACTS

| | |
|---|---|
| Financial Aid Rating | 76 |
| In-state tuition | $3,464 |
| Out-of-state tuition | $11,906 |
| Room & board | $6,688 |
| Books and supplies | $600 |
| Required fees | $1,690 |
| % frosh receiving aid | 74 |
| % undergrads receiving aid | 73 |

# UNIVERSITY OF RICHMOND

28 WESTHAMPTON WAY, RICHMOND, VA 23173 • ADMISSIONS: 804-289-8640 • FAX: 804-287-6003

## CAMPUS LIFE

| | |
|---|---|
| **Quality of Life Rating** | **96** |
| Type of school | private |
| Affiliation | none |
| Environment | suburban |

### STUDENTS

| | |
|---|---|
| Total undergrad enrollment | 2,910 |
| % male/female | 50/50 |
| % from out of state | 85 |
| % from public high school | 70 |
| % live on campus | 92 |
| % in (# of) fraternities | 30 (8) |
| % in (# of) sororities | 50 (8) |
| % African American | 5 |
| % Asian | 3 |
| % Caucasian | 86 |
| % Hispanic | 2 |
| % international | 3 |
| # of countries represented | 57 |

### SURVEY SAYS . . .

Frats and sororities dominate social scene
Students love Richmond, VA
Diversity lacking on campus
Great food on campus
Athletic facilities are great
Students get along with local community
Class discussions encouraged

## ACADEMICS

| | |
|---|---|
| **Academic Rating** | **87** |
| Calendar | semester |
| Student/faculty ratio | 10:1 |
| Profs interesting rating | 94 |
| Profs accessible rating | 97 |
| % profs teaching UG courses | 100 |
| Avg reg class size | 18 students |

### MOST POPULAR MAJORS
business
social sciences
biology

## STUDENTS SPEAK OUT

### Academics

Most students come to University of Richmond looking for practical instruction dispensed by knowledgeable, caring teachers, and mostly, they find what they're looking for. Writes one typical student, "I couldn't ask for a better quality experience. Administrators, faculty, and staff are very accessible." Education at Richmond "isn't confined to the four walls of the classroom. There is a real effort to integrate class discussions to the real world. A lot of students do research with professors, do independent studies, or hold internships." As for the faculty, they are "friendly, intelligent, and accessible, and they are the ones teaching the classes. Who would want to pay $20,000 a year to go to a school where classes are taught by other students? That doesn't happen here." While many attend Richmond with an eye toward professional graduate programs, students here also appreciate their required studies in the liberal arts; notes one, "The core course that all first-year students must take has been an eye-opening experience." The undergraduate division of the University of Richmond is divided into three coeducational schools: the School of Arts and Sciences, the School of Business, and the School of Leadership Studies. In addition, students are members of a residential college: Richmond College (for men) and Westhampton College (for women). Sums up one happy undergrad, "This school is academically challenging but not at all overwhelming. It is a place where I can be involved in multiple activities on campus and still handle the workload."

### Life

Tidily summarizing life at University of Richmond, one student explains that "students work hard on Monday to Wednesday nights. Many students head to downtown Richmond to bars on Thursday night. Friday and Saturday nights belong to parties, which are usually at the fraternity row or on-campus apartments. Sundays are for relaxing." Most students agree that "social life revolves around the frats," which "provide a good percentage of the activities here." Away from frat row, "students are very involved in extracurricular activities. Through these they meet others and develop friendships. I am involved in club sports, student government, a scholar's social committee, and volunteer organizations." Adds one student, "There are definitely a lot of student organizations to choose from. If you don't drink, there are not many on-campus alternatives on weekends, but there is plenty to do the rest of the time." Students have mixed feelings about Richmond's unique coordinate housing system, which creates "all-guy and all-girl dorms and no coed dorms." Dating and socializing with the other sex, then, is slightly more difficult. There is no disagreement about the campus itself, however, which students describe as "beautiful and easy to get around on by foot." Downtown Richmond, 10 minutes from campus by auto, gets good marks for everything from shops to restaurants to bars, though "it's a shame that we don't get many opportunities to check it all out because there's usually too much happening on campus."

### Student Body

"There is little diversity" on the University of Richmond campus, undergrads concede. "Most students are upper-middle class whites." What heterogeneity exists is mostly regional: "Many students from the North come to our school in the South, creating positive cultural and social interactions," writes one student. Several students note that the "university is really making a concerted effort to draw students here from different classes and races," but some aren't anxious for change. "The student body is very homogeneous," says one student, "but I would not say that is a problem or negative aspect of the school." Others disagree, reporting that the "(lack of) diversity is a huge problem." The student body tends to coagulate into cliques, "especially in the first two years of school, but by the time you're a junior, you just want to meet some new people." In the end, there are many "distinct groups that move around on campus. The challenge is not limiting yourself to only one of them."

# UNIVERSITY OF RICHMOND

FINANCIAL AID: 804-289-8438 • E-MAIL: ADMISSIONS@RICHMOND.EDU • WEBSITE: WWW.RICHMOND.EDU

## ADMISSIONS

*Very important* academic and nonacademic factors considered by the admissions committee include secondary school record. *Important* factors considered include character/personal qualities, class rank, essays, minority status, and standardized test scores. *Other* factors considered include alumni/ae relation, extracurricular activities, geography, recommendations, state residency, talent/ability, volunteer work, and work experience. Factors *not* considered include interview and religious affiliation/commitment. TOEFL required of all international applicants. High school diploma is required and GED is accepted. *High school units required/recommended:* 15 total required; 4 English required, 2 math required, 3 math recommended, 2 science required, 3 science recommended, 2 foreign language required, 3 foreign language recommended, 2 social studies required, 2 elective required.

### The Inside Word

There may not be an admissions formula, but Richmond is very precise about just how much each of the major admissions criteria counts toward a decision. Two SAT II Subject Tests are an important application requirement; we'd advise candidates to prepare thoroughly, since they outweigh the SAT I. When used with a measure of flexibility and a willingness to consider other factors, as Richmond does, there is nothing inherently wrong with such an approach. There does appear to be an effort to look at the candidate's record carefully and thoroughly. Make no mistake: Course of study, high-school performance, and test scores are the most important parts of your application, but Richmond also makes sure that all files are read at least three times before a final decision has been rendered.

## FINANCIAL AID

*Students should submit:* FAFSA and institution's own financial aid form. Regular filing deadline is February 25. The Princeton Review suggests that all financial aid forms be submitted as soon as possible after January 1. *Need-based scholarships/grants offered:* Pell, SEOG, state scholarships/grants, private scholarships, and the school's own gift aid. *Loan aid offered:* Direct Subsidized Stafford, Direct Unsubsidized Stafford, Direct PLUS, and Federal Perkins. Institutional employment available. Federal Work-Study Program available. Applicants will be notified of awards on or about April 1. Off-campus job opportunities are excellent.

## FROM THE ADMISSIONS OFFICE

"The University of Richmond combines the characteristics of a small college with the dynamics of a large university. The unique size, beautiful suburban campus, and world-class facilities offer students an extraordinary mix of opportunities for personal growth and intellectual achievement. At Richmond, students are encouraged to engage themselves in their environment. Discussion and dialogue are the forefront of the academic experience, while research, internships, and international experiences are important components to students' co-curricular lives. The university is committed to providing undergraduate students with a rigorous academic experience, while integrating these studies with opportunities for experiential learning and promoting total individual development."

## ADMISSIONS

| | |
|---|---|
| Admissions Rating | 89 |
| # of applicants | 5,631 |
| % of applicants accepted | 42 |
| % of acceptees attending | 31 |
| # accepting a place on wait list | 639 |
| % admitted from wait list | 6 |
| # of early decision applicants | 369 |
| % accepted early decision | 44 |

### FRESHMAN PROFILE

| | |
|---|---|
| Range SAT Verbal | 610-690 |
| Range SAT Math | 620-700 |
| Range ACT Composite | 27-30 |
| Minimum TOEFL | 550 |
| % graduated top 10% of class | 60 |
| % graduated top 25% of class | 94 |
| % graduated top 50% of class | 99 |

### DEADLINES

| | |
|---|---|
| Early decision 1 | 11/15 |
| Early decision 1 notification | 12/15 |
| Early decision 2 | 1/15 |
| Early decion 2 notification | 2/15 |
| Regular admission | 1/15 |
| Regular notification | 4/1 |

### APPLICANTS ALSO LOOK AT
**AND OFTEN PREFER**
William and Mary
U.Virginia
UNC—Chapel Hill
Duke
**AND SOMETIMES PREFER**
Wake Forest
James Madison
Tulane
Vanderbilt
Washington and Lee
**AND RARELY PREFER**
Lafayette
Lehigh

### FINANCIAL FACTS

| | |
|---|---|
| Financial Aid Rating | 74 |
| Tuition | $22,570 |
| Room & board | $4,730 |
| Books and supplies | $900 |
| % frosh receiving aid | 34 |
| % undergrads receiving aid | 31 |

# UNIVERSITY OF ROCHESTER

Box 270251, Rochester, NY 14627-0251 • Admissions: 716-275-3221 • Fax: 716-461-4595

## CAMPUS LIFE

**Quality of Life Rating**    **80**
Type of school    private
Affiliation    none
Environment    suburban

### STUDENTS

| | |
|---|---|
| Total undergrad enrollment | 4,529 |
| % male/female | 52/48 |
| % from public high school | 88 |
| % African American | 5 |
| % Asian | 12 |
| % Caucasian | 68 |
| % Hispanic | 5 |
| % international | 5 |
| # of countries represented | 45 |

### SURVEY SAYS . . .
*Popular college radio*
*Great library*
*Theater is hot*
*Dorms are like palaces*
*(Almost) everyone plays intramural*
*sports*
*Intercollegiate sports unpopular or*
*nonexistent*
*Athletic facilities need improving*
*Large classes*
*Musical organizations are hot*

## ACADEMICS

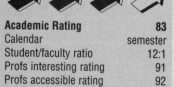

**Academic Rating**    **83**
Calendar    semester
Student/faculty ratio    12:1
Profs interesting rating    91
Profs accessible rating    92

### MOST POPULAR MAJORS
biological sciences
engineering
psychology

## STUDENTS SPEAK OUT

### Academics

The University of Rochester has traditionally been known best for its math and science departments. However, the "home of the Bausch & Lomb scholars and Xerox" has enough diversity in its academic offerings to "dispel the myth that the U of R is solely an engineering/pre-med breeding ground." Although numerous students consider the workload "heavy and tough—they don't mess around!" most also believe their rigorous courses are "extremely rewarding." Rochester has several unique opportunities to offer its students; one is the world-renowned Eastman School of Music (the administration encourages qualified students to take courses there). Distinct to the U of R is a program called "Take Five," an attractive option for students who find themselves unable to fit enough courses of interest into a four-year schedule. One student writes, "As a chemical engineer, I have very little time to take courses outside my major. The U of R has given me the opportunity to stay here for an additional year—tuition-free—to pursue my interest in Japanese history and culture." While some students claim that certain professors "are more interested in their research than they are in undergrads," in general students here are positive and enthusiastic about their academic life; some consider the U of R "better than the Ivies but without the reputation—it's the jewel of upper New York State."

### Life

Cold weather is a given in Rochester: "Siberia for eight months of the year" is a popular description among students we surveyed. It is actually possible to avoid a great deal of winter misery by using the convenient indoor tunnels beneath the campus. Nevertheless, the consensus seems to be that of one student who notes, "I just wish we could take the whole school and place it in California or somewhere where there is no snow." Despite the academic pressures at the U of R (or perhaps because of them), weekends are full of partying opportunities. Fraternities and sororities figure prominently in the social scene, and Greek activities dominate. One student observes, "Many people claim to be anti-Greek, but they tend to show up at frat parties anyway." There are varying degrees of social contentment here; some students have "too many parties to choose from," some contend that "freshman males lead lives of quiet desperation," and some prefer to socialize electronically in the generally comfy and spacious dorms.

### Student Body

The typical student at the University of Rochester is politically moderate, not politically active. A small private school, despite its public-sounding name, the U of R has made an effort to increase student diversity, and minorities account for more than a fifth of the student body. However, some students still feel "the minority population is lacking . . . especially in the black and Hispanic sectors."

FINANCIAL AID: 716-275-3226 • E-MAIL: ADMIT@ADMISSIONS.ROCHESTER.EDU • WEBSITE: WWW.ROCHESTER.EDU

## ADMISSIONS

*Very important* academic and nonacademic factors considered by the admissions committee include character/personal qualities, essays, interview, recommendations, and secondary school record. *Important* factors considered include extracurricular activities, standardized test scores, and talent/ability. *Other* factors considered include alumni/ae relation, class rank, volunteer work, and work experience. Factors *not* considered include geography, minority status, religious affiliation/commitment, and state residency. SAT I or ACT required. TOEFL required of all international applicants. High school diploma is required and GED is accepted. *High school units required/recommended:* 4 English required, 4 math required, 4 science required, 3 science lab required, 3 foreign language required, 4 foreign language recommended, 4 social studies required. *The admissions office says:* "We consider very strongly the demand of course selection. Honors, Regents, or Advanced Placement are expected of students in secondary schools offering these programs. [The admission staff prides] itself on the personalization of the [selection] process."

### The Inside Word

The University of Rochester is definitely a good school, but the competition takes away three-fourths of the university's admits. Many students use Rochester as a safety; this hinders the university's ability to move up among top national institutions in selectivity. It also makes U of R a very solid choice for above-average students who aren't Ivy material.

## FINANCIAL AID

*Students should submit:* FAFSA, CSS/Financial Aid PROFILE, state aid form, and noncustodial and business supplement only if applicable. Regular filing deadline is February 1. The Princeton Review suggests that all financial aid forms be submitted as soon as possible after January 1. *Need-based scholarships/grants offered:* Pell, SEOG, state scholarships/grants, private scholarships, and the school's own gift aid. *Loan aid offered:* Direct Subsidized Stafford, Direct Unsubsidized Stafford, Direct PLUS, and college/university loans from institutional funds. Institutional employment available. Federal Work-Study Program available. Applicants will be notified of awards on or about April 1. Off-campus job opportunities are excellent.

## FROM THE ADMISSIONS OFFICE

"A campus visit can be one of the most important (and most enjoyable) components of a college search. Visiting Rochester can provide you with the opportunity to experience for yourself the traditions and innovations of our university. Whether you visit a class, tour the campus, or meet with a professor or coach, you'll learn a great deal about the power of a Rochester education—with advantages that begin during your undergraduate years and continue after graduation. No other school combines the wealth of academic programs on the personal scale that the University of Rochester offers. Our students achieve academic excellence in a university setting that encourages frequent, informal contact with distinguished faculty. Our faculty-designed 'Rochester Renaissance Curriculum' allows students to spend as much of their time as possible studying subjects they enjoy so much that they stop watching the clock,' says William Scott Green, dean of the undergraduate college. At the heart of the Renaissance Curriculum is the Quest Program. Quest courses are seminar-sized offerings that encourage you to solve problems through investigations and exploration . . . much the same way our faculty do. Working alongside your professor, you will test theories and explore education frontiers on a campus with some of the best resources in the world, driven by a curriculum that is truly unprecedented."

## ADMISSIONS

| | |
|---|---|
| Admissions Rating | 88 |
| # of applicants | 8,652 |
| % of applicants accepted | 66 |
| % of acceptees attending | 19 |
| # accepting a place on wait list | 283 |
| % admitted from wait list | 2 |
| # of early decision applicants | 238 |
| % accepted early decision | 63 |

### FRESHMAN PROFILE

| | |
|---|---|
| Range SAT Verbal | 600-700 |
| Average SAT Verbal | 650 |
| Range SAT Math | 630-710 |
| Average SAT Math | 670 |
| Range ACT Composite | 27-32 |
| Average ACT Composite | 30 |
| Minimum TOEFL | 550 |
| Average HS GPA | 3.6 |
| % graduated top 10% of class | 57 |
| % graduated top 25% of class | 86 |
| % graduated top 50% of class | 99 |

### DEADLINES

| | |
|---|---|
| Early decision | 11/15 |
| Early decision notification | 12/15 |
| Priority admission deadline | 1/31 |
| Regular notification | 4/15 |
| Nonfall registration? | yes |

### APPLICANTS ALSO LOOK AT

**AND OFTEN PREFER**
Cornell U.
Washington U.
Binghamton U.
SUNY Buffalo

**AND SOMETIMES PREFER**
Boston U.
SUNY Albany
U. Vermont
Syracuse
NYU

**AND RARELY PREFER**
Franklin & Marshall

### FINANCIAL FACTS

| | |
|---|---|
| Financial Aid Rating | 78 |
| Tuition | $23,150 |
| Room & board | $7,740 |
| Books and supplies | $575 |
| Required fees | $580 |
| % frosh receiving aid | 65 |
| % undergrads receiving aid | 65 |

# UNIVERSITY OF SAN FRANCISCO

2130 FULTON STREET, SAN FRANCISCO, CA 94117 • ADMISSIONS: 415-422-6563 • FAX: 415-422-2217

## CAMPUS LIFE

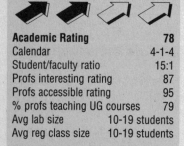

| Quality of Life Rating | 89 |
|---|---|
| Type of school | private |
| Affiliation | Roman Catholic |
| Environment | urban |

### STUDENTS

| | |
|---|---|
| Total undergrad enrollment | 4,572 |
| % male/female | 38/62 |
| % from out of state | 16 |
| % from public high school | 50 |
| % live on campus | 36 |
| % in (# of) fraternities | 2 (4) |
| % in (# of) sororities | 1 (4) |
| % African American | 6 |
| % Asian | 24 |
| % Caucasian | 45 |
| % Hispanic | 12 |
| % Native American | 1 |
| % international | 8 |
| # of countries represented | 78 |

### SURVEY SAYS . . .

*Students love San Francisco, CA*
*Great off-campus food*
*Student government is popular*
*Students are happy*
*Student publicatications are popular*
*Very small frat/sorority scene*
*(Almost) everyone smokes*

## ACADEMICS

| Academic Rating | 78 |
|---|---|
| Calendar | 4-1-4 |
| Student/faculty ratio | 15:1 |
| Profs interesting rating | 87 |
| Profs accessible rating | 95 |
| % profs teaching UG courses | 79 |
| Avg lab size | 10-19 students |
| Avg reg class size | 10-19 students |

### MOST POPULAR MAJORS
nursing
communication
psychology

## STUDENTS SPEAK OUT
### Academics

The University of San Francisco, the Jesuit outpost on the Barbary Coast, is the city's largest private university. "If you're looking for a liberal school in a liberal city, this is it." Set on a "beautiful" 55-acre campus near Golden Gate Park about three miles from the heart of downtown San Francisco, USF offers "small class size, great profs," and a wide variety of undergraduate majors within five schools: the College of Arts & Sciences, School of Education, McLaren School of Business, School of Nursing, and College of Professional Studies. Business, nursing, education, and communications are among the university's most popular majors. All students are required to complete a General Education Curriculum; some have the option of doing so through the Saint Ignatius Institute, a great books program, and one of many special academic enrichment programs offered at USF. The Jesuit influence is felt throughout the campus offerings. "The staff at USF truly care for their students and don't hesitate to show it." "USF challenges you to open your eyes to a global community and find your place in it." "The faculty creates a learning environment anyone can thrive in;" more than 92 percent hold PhDs or other terminal degrees, and "are very dedicated to their students." "The more I speak to students from other universities, [the more] I realize the uniqueness of USF. USF teaches not only the importance of a good education, but of strong communicative skills and community." Speaking of community, don't forget that "the city of San Francisco is one huge classroom. Every moment and every corner offers a new lesson. USF provides a safe haven from the city. It is a strong base."

### Life

"The greatest strength of USF is that it is located in the middle of the best city on Earth." No doubt, as San Francisco's reputation as a first-class cultural city is well deserved, with a fabulous music scene, multinational cuisine, and a spectacular waterfront setting. Golden Gate Park, one of the nation's top city parks, is just down the block from the university. With it comes access to biking and running trails, picnicking, and other typical recreational activities, as well as an occasional free concert event from one of San Francisco's many legends of rock and roll. The on-campus social scene is considerably tamer ("I come here to learn, not to gossip and find my true love"), but there are lots of opportunities to get involved. More than 50 registered clubs and organizations offer activities for students ranging from political groups to an award-winning radio station, movies, and lectures. Many find it important to give something back to the community at large; volunteer service is very popular at USF. Greek life is available here, but doesn't seem to exert a big influence over campus life. School spirit could be better, but USF's athletic teams haven't gotten much more than sporadic attention nationally for quite a while. Multicultural organizations abound, not surprising given the diversity of the student body.

### Student Body

"The University of San Francisco is an eclectic community of races, religions, cultures, and academics." Indeed, students come to USF from all over the United States and throughout the world. Nearly a tenth of the student body consists of international students, but even without leaving the U.S. one finds great diversity within the student body. USF is one of few universities in the country where the enrollment is mostly minority students. Many are Catholic, and over 40 percent come from parochial high schools, but the university is truly a broad mosaic. Though the campus community typically is not overly social, it's not due to any sort of friction among students. "Students at USF generally have a live and let live attitude; they may disagree with your views, but they'll respect your right to have them."

FINANCIAL AID: 415-422-6303 • E-MAIL: ADMISSION@USFCA.EDU • WEBSITE: WWW.USFCA.EDU

## ADMISSIONS

*Very important* academic and nonacademic factors considered by the admissions committee include recommendations, secondary school record, and standardized test scores. *Important* factors considered include class rank and essays. *Other* factors considered include alumni/ae relation, extracurricular activities, geography, interview, minority status, character/personal qualities, volunteer work, and talent/ability. Factors *not* considered include religious affiliation/commitment, state residency, and work experience. SAT I or ACT required, SAT I preferred. *High school units required/recommended:* 20 total recommended; 4 English recommended, 3 math recommended, 2 science recommended, 2 foreign language recommended, 3 social studies recommended, 6 elective recommended.

### The Inside Word

The admissions committee at USF is not purely numbers-focused. They'll evaluate your full picture here, using your academic strengths and weaknesses along with your personal character strengths, essays, and recommendations to assess your suitability for admission. It's matchmaking. If you fit well in the USF community, you'll be welcome

## FINANCIAL AID

*Students should submit:* FAFSA. Regular filing deadline is rolling. The Princeton Review suggests that all financial aid forms be submitted as soon as possible after January 1. *Need-based scholarships/grants offered:* Pell, SEOG, state scholarships/grants, private scholarships, the school's own gift aid, and Federal Nursing. *Loan aid offered:* Direct Subsidized Stafford, Direct Unsubsidized Stafford, Direct PLUS, Subsidized Stafford, Unsubsidized Stafford, Federal Perkins, and Federal Nursing. Institution employment available. Federal Work-Study Program available. Applicants will be notified of awards on a rolling basis beginning on or about April 1. Off-campus job opportunities are excellent.

### ADMISSIONS

| | |
|---|---|
| **Admissions Rating** | **79** |
| # of applicants | 3,504 |
| % of applicants accepted | 80 |
| % of acceptees attending | 27 |

#### FRESHMAN PROFILE

| | |
|---|---|
| Range SAT Verbal | 480-590 |
| Range SAT Math | 480-590 |
| Range ACT Composite | 20-25 |
| Minimum TOEFL | 550 |
| Average HS GPA | 3.3 |
| % graduated top 10% of class | 23 |
| % graduated top 25% of class | 52 |
| % graduated top 50% of class | 82 |

#### DEADLINES

| | |
|---|---|
| Priority admission deadline | 2/1 |
| Nonfall registration? | yes |

### FINANCIAL FACTS

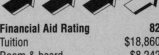

| | |
|---|---|
| **Financial Aid Rating** | **82** |
| Tuition | $18,860 |
| Room & board | $8,242 |
| Books and supplies | $750 |
| Required fees | $200 |
| % frosh receiving aid | 64 |
| % undergrads receiving aid | 54 |
| Avg frosh grant | $6,654 |
| Avg frosh loan | $4,684 |

# UNIVERSITY OF SOUTH CAROLINA—COLUMBIA

OFFICE OF ADMISSIONS, COLUMBIA, SC 29208 • ADMISSIONS: 803-777-7700 • FAX: 803-777-0101

## CAMPUS LIFE

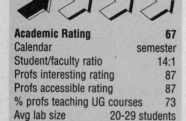

| Quality of Life Rating | 76 |
|---|---|
| Type of school | public |
| Affiliation | none |
| Environment | urban |

### STUDENTS

| | |
|---|---|
| Total undergrad enrollment | 15,266 |
| % male/female | 45/55 |
| % from out of state | 12 |
| % live on campus | 40 |
| % in (# of) fraternities | 17 (18) |
| % in (# of) sororities | 13 (13) |
| % African American | 19 |
| % Asian | 3 |
| % Caucasian | 73 |
| % Hispanic | 1 |
| % international | 2 |
| # of countries represented | 90 |

### SURVEY SAYS . . .

Frats and sororities dominate social
scene
(Almost) everyone smokes
Hard liquor is popular
Lots of beer drinking
Students are cliquish
Campus difficult to get around
Large classes
Unattractive campus
Ethnic diversity on campus
Students get along with local
community

## ACADEMICS

| Academic Rating | 67 |
|---|---|
| Calendar | semester |
| Student/faculty ratio | 14:1 |
| Profs interesting rating | 87 |
| Profs accessible rating | 87 |
| % profs teaching UG courses | 73 |
| Avg lab size | 20-29 students |
| Avg reg class size | 20-29 students |

### MOST POPULAR MAJORS
psychology
biology
engineering

## STUDENTS SPEAK OUT
### Academics

Home of the mighty "Gamecocks" (favored lid of the white-hat crowd), University of South Carolina undergrads don't mince words when it comes to why they chose their school: "Had what I needed at the best price," writes a junior media arts major. "It's in the South, it's in a city, and it has a good journalism school," adds a senior. Offering all the strengths of a traditional liberal arts university—in addition to several pre-professional tracks (popular majors include journalism, business, advertising, and public relations)—this state school is usually the first choice for South Carolina residents who want a solid education, a fun college experience in a big city and the option to go home for mom's grits and sweet potato pie on the weekends. For a big university, USC's "professor accessibility" is second to none—"I was very impressed with the quality and availability of the faculty," declares a sophomore. And though some complain that "a few of the teachers are so old they seem to have no passion for what they're doing," most students are of the opinion that USC's profs are "interesting and intelligent—some even seem like real people sometimes!" On the money front, students are a bit less forgiving. A junior explains the situation like this: "A lack of funding forced USC to make severe budget cuts this year, yet the powers that be still find money to dramatically raise the football coach's salary. It is evident the school's top priority is not academic in nature." While undergrads praise the school's job opportunities and commitment to diversity, as well as its willingness to "keep up with new technology," shoddy maintenance of campus facilities and lax security are considered deficits, as is the aforementioned privileging of athletics over academics. Still, students at South Carolina seem generally happy. Says a sophomore, "It's not bad. There's room for improvement, but I'd say that it's pretty good to be at USC."

### Life

"In general," writes a junior, USC students "go to bars, play sports, and go to frat parties." Columbia's Five Points and The Vista are where most students go to socialize, though for the under-21 crowd, going Greek seems to be the path of least resistance. A strong fraternity/sorority presence on campus isn't to everyone's liking, however. Notes another junior, "There seems to be a lack of individuality among students here. For fun, I get away from campus." A senior agrees: "There's a lot of animosity between Greeks and non-Greeks," she writes. At the same time, students praise the school's "many student organizations" and "awareness of social issues." Writes a sophomore, "I love USC. There is so much to do on and off campus. People are involved in a variety of religious, musical, political, [and] sports-related clubs." And though some USC students might agree with this first-year's words—"College is a lot more boring that I thought it would be"—we like this junior's more positive summation of life at the University of South Carolina: "It's lovely walking through campus. The grass is almost always green."

### Student Body

Perhaps it's a southern stereotype—slow as molasses and all that—but despite their pointed remarks about academics, University of South Carolina students seem to see themselves as a fairly laid-back bunch. "Everyone is friendly and easy to get along with," chirps a junior, while a typically mellow sophomore adds, "Most are easygoing, some are jerks . . . that's life." Diversity seems to be a particular strength of USC's; notes another sophomore, "Most people here are accepting and understanding. I have seen very few, if any, cases of discrimination or bias on campus." Perhaps there is something to the legendary southern hospitality, after all. A junior is only half-joking when she writes, "It's amazing to think that someone opening a door for you is a mentionable event, but so many people do that here. It's a nice addition to my day."

FINANCIAL AID: 803-777-8134 • E-MAIL: ADMISSIONS-UGRAD@SC.EDU • WEBSITE: WWW.SC.EDU

## ADMISSIONS

*Very important* academic and nonacademic factors considered by the admissions committee include secondary school record and standardized test scores. *Other* factors considered include recommendations and talent/ability. Factors *not* considered include alumni/ae relation, character/personal qualities, class rank, essays, extracurricular activities, geography, interview, minority status, religious affiliation/commitment, state residency, volunteer work, and work experience. SAT I or ACT required. TOEFL required of all international applicants. High school diploma is required and GED is accepted. *High school units required/recommended:* 16 total required; 4 English required, 3 math required, 2 science required, 2 foreign language required, 2 social studies required, 1 U.S. history required, 1 elective required, 1 physical education or ROTC required.

### The Inside Word

The admissions process at South Carolina is formula-driven and not particularly demanding. A solid academic performance in high school should do the trick.

## FINANCIAL AID

*Students should submit:* FAFSA. The Princeton Review suggests that all financial aid forms be submitted as soon as possible after January 1. *Need-based scholarships/grants offered:* Pell, SEOG, state scholarships/grants, private scholarships, the school's own gift aid, United Negro College Fund, and Federal Nursing. *Loan aid offered:* FFEL Subsidized Stafford, FFEL Unsubsidized Stafford, FFEL PLUS, Federal Perkins, and Federal Nursing. Institutional employment available. Federal Work-Study Program available. Applicants will be notified of awards on a rolling basis beginning on or about May 1. Off-campus job opportunities are excellent.

## FROM THE ADMISSIONS OFFICE

"The University of South Carolina offers over 80 undergraduate majors and areas of concentration. It has a graduate school, school of law, and professional-degree programs. Fully accredited by the Southern Association of Colleges and Schools, USC awards baccalaureate, master's, and doctoral degrees, and is known for its programs: accounting (United States' top 10), marketing and advertising (top eight), and marine science (number four) are examples. USC's Honors College is one of the nation's best. *The New York Times* calls it a 'thriving undergraduate honors college that operates at Ivy League standards.' Many students decide to attend USC after visiting its campus—one of America's most beautiful—in Columbia, South Carolina. This Sunbelt city offers great entertainment, and cultural and recreational activities, all within walking distance of campus. And South Carolina's world-famous beaches and the Blue Ridge Mountains are less than a three-hour drive away. Growing numbers of students are discovering that the University of South Carolina is the right choice for them."

## ADMISSIONS

| | |
|---|---|
| **Admissions Rating** | **73** |
| # of applicants | 9,959 |
| % of applicants accepted | 69 |
| % of acceptees attending | 37 |

| FRESHMAN PROFILE | |
|---|---|
| Range SAT Verbal | 500-610 |
| Average SAT Verbal | 550 |
| Range SAT Math | 500-610 |
| Average SAT Math | 548 |
| Range ACT Composite | 20-26 |
| Average ACT Composite | 24 |
| Minimum TOEFL | 550 |
| Average HS GPA | 3.5 |
| % graduated top 10% of class | 30 |
| % graduated top 25% of class | 59 |
| % graduated top 50% of class | 90 |

| DEADLINES | |
|---|---|
| Priority admission deadline | 8/1 |
| Regular admission | rolling |
| Nonfall registration? | yes |

**APPLICANTS ALSO LOOK AT**

**AND OFTEN PREFER**
UNC—Chapel Hill
William and Mary
SMU
Duke

**AND SOMETIMES PREFER**
Furman
Clemson
U. Georgia
Coll. of Charleston
Randolph-Macon Woman's

**AND RARELY PREFER**
Francis Marion
Winthrop
Florida State

## FINANCIAL FACTS

| | |
|---|---|
| **Financial Aid Rating** | **73** |
| In-state tuition | $3,768 |
| Out-of-state tuition | $10,054 |
| Room & board | $4,588 |
| Books and supplies | $607 |
| Required fees | $150 |
| % frosh receiving aid | 60 |
| % undergrads receiving aid | 65 |
| Avg frosh grant | $900 |
| Avg frosh loan | $1,900 |

# UNIVERSITY OF SOUTH DAKOTA

414 EAST CLARK, VERMILLION, SD 57069 • ADMISSIONS: 605-677-5434 • FAX: 605-677-6753

## CAMPUS LIFE

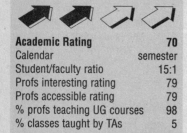

| Quality of Life Rating | 79 |
| --- | --- |
| Type of school | public |
| Affiliation | none |
| Environment | suburban |

### STUDENTS

| | |
| --- | --- |
| Total undergrad enrollment | 5,147 |
| % male/female | 43/57 |
| % from out of state | 20 |
| % from public high school | 92 |
| % live on campus | 28 |
| % in (# of) fraternities | 21 (9) |
| % in (# of) sororities | 11 (5) |
| % African American | 1 |
| % Asian | 1 |
| % Caucasian | 90 |
| % Hispanic | 1 |
| % Native American | 2 |
| % international | 2 |

### SURVEY SAYS . . .

*Diverse students interact
Student government is popular
Student newspaper is popular
Frats and sororities dominate social
scene
Students are happy
Lab facilities need improving
Computer facilities need improving
Athletic facilities need improving*

## ACADEMICS

| Academic Rating | 70 |
| --- | --- |
| Calendar | semester |
| Student/faculty ratio | 15:1 |
| Profs interesting rating | 79 |
| Profs accessible rating | 79 |
| % profs teaching UG courses | 98 |
| % classes taught by TAs | 5 |

### MOST POPULAR MAJORS
biology
psychology
business

## STUDENTS SPEAK OUT

### Academics

The University of South Dakota offers a wide selection of majors—everything from the liberal arts to dental hygiene to mass communication—and many of the degree programs offered here have a pre-professional and practical focus. Students like the choices, and they laud USD's "great" business program. They also say the state's flagship university is blessed with excellent resources and a "good reputation" in the region. Best of all, though, USD is incredibly affordable. In-state residents and residents of Minnesota at USD pay a pittance in tuition compared to private schools and even some state schools. And thanks to the Western Undergraduate Exchange program, residents of pretty much every big, square, western state (as well as Hawaii and Alaska) can attend USD on the cheap. Residents of all other states get a good deal, too. A few glaring exceptions notwithstanding, the "awesome" professors here "involve students in all lectures and class discussions" and receive a general thumbs-up from students. "I am very pleased with the instructors," beams a sophomore. "They are very approachable," and most profs are "genuinely interested in their classes and their students." Unfortunately, and despite the fact that the total undergraduate population at USD is less than 5,000, some students complain that administrative red tape presents occasional hassles. "The different offices have a serious communication problem," gripes a sophomore. And "getting financial aid" resembles "running a gauntlet," though scholarships and aid are abundant. These criticisms aside, students tell us they "feel good about being here."

### Life

USD is located in Vermillion on the wide-open bluffs above the Missouri River—"1,402 miles from New Jersey," according to one student. Actually, Vermillion is more like 1,300 miles from the Garden State, but you get the idea: the lush USD campus is undisturbed by urban hassles and suburban sprawl. The closest urban center is Sioux City, Iowa, which is 25 miles east, and the cozy town of Vermillion "offers the quiet, safe, slow-paced feel of country living." To keep themselves entertained, USD students say they engage in pretty traditional college stuff: "going to movies, dance clubs, etc." There is also a noticeable Greek system here, and a "partying atmosphere" is available, but not overbearing. Students do complain that there is little to do off campus. "We need more commerce," recommends one, not to mention a few businesses "open after 10:00 P.M." Not surprisingly, many students spend a great deal of time on campus. The splendid DakotaDome hosts various athletic events and conventions, and USD sports are often competitive in NCAA Division II. However, "the athletic facilities are horrible if you are an average student instead of an athlete," claims a sophomore. "The equipment is very old," and the good facilities are "not available to the general student population."

### Student Body

Most students tell us they chose USD because it's close to home and because they just couldn't pass up the bargain-basement price. Over 85 percent of the students here hail from South Dakota or the neighboring states of Minnesota and Iowa. Age is probably the biggest factor in campus diversity; over one quarter of USD's students are 24 years and older. There are some students here who are "weird," but nearly all are "friendly," despite a "very cliquish" social atmosphere. "A lot of people seem stuck in their 'groups' and don't let people in," as one junior observes. If you are thinking of launching a political career in South Dakota, we strongly recommend that you attend USD. Ten alums have served as governor, and "all of the state's sitting Supreme Court Justices are USD alumni." In addition, news anchor Tom Brokaw, sports commentator Pat O'Brien, and founder of USA Today Al Neuharth boast USD diplomas.

FINANCIAL AID: 605-677-5446 • E-MAIL: ADMISS@USD.EDU • WEBSITE: WWW.USD.EDU

## ADMISSIONS

*Very important* academic and nonacademic factors considered by the admissions committee include class rank, secondary school record, character/personal qualities, extracurricular activities, and standardized test scores. *Important* factors considered include recommendations. *Other* factors considered include alumni/ae relation, essays, geography, minority status, state residency, and talent/ability. Factors *not* considered include interview, religious affiliation/commitment, volunteer work, and work experience. SAT I or ACT required, ACT preferred. High school diploma is required and GED is accepted. *High school units required/recommended:* 13 total required; 4 English required, 3 math required, 3 science required, 3 social studies required.

### The Inside Word

Given the relatively small numbers of college-bound students coming from South Dakota's high schools each year, the university's rolling admission policy is nearly open admission. Solid college-prep students should encounter no trouble in gaining admission.

## FINANCIAL AID

*Students should submit:* FAFSA. There is no regular filing deadline. Priority filing deadline is March 1. The Princeton Review suggests that all financial aid forms be submitted as soon as possible after January 1. *Need-based scholarships/grants offered:* Pell, SEOG, state scholarships/grants, private scholarships, the school's own gift aid, and federal nursing. *Loan aid offered:* Subsidized Stafford, Unsubsidized Stafford, PLUS, Federal Perkins, Federal Nursing, state, and the school's own loans. Institution employment available. Federal Work-Study Program available. Applicants will be notified of awards on or about May 1. Off-campus job opportunities are good.

## FROM THE ADMISSIONS OFFICE

"USD, a doctorate-granting university with liberal arts emphasis, has a strong academic reputation. Old Main, the campus focal point, houses the Honors Program, high-tech classrooms, and more. Among the many programs on campus are three Centers of Excellence including the center on Ambulatory Medical Student Education. Innovative, this program has a physician-patient approach, which provides learning opportunities in primary care medicine. The Disaster Mental Health Institute, internationally recognized, provides unique programs in disaster mental health response. The W.O. Farber Center for Civic Leadership, which prepares students in leadership, offers academic, enrichment, and community-outreach programs. The center sponsors internationally prominent speakers such as retired U.S. Army General Colin Powell, former President Gerald Ford, NBC News anchor Tom Brokaw, and others. USD's alumni include: NBC's Tom Brokaw, *USA Today* founder Allen Neuharth, motivational speaker Joan Brock, writers Peter Dexter, *Penny Whistle* book author Meredith Auld Brokaw, Pat O'Brien, USD President James W. Abbott, and World War II ace Joe Foss, among others."

## ADMISSIONS

| Admissions Rating | 73 |
| --- | --- |
| # of applicants | 1,165 |
| % of applicants accepted | 97 |
| % of acceptees attending | 91 |

### FRESHMAN PROFILE

| | |
| --- | --- |
| Range ACT Composite | 19-25 |
| Average ACT Composite | 22 |
| Minimum TOEFL | 550 |
| Average HS GPA | 3.2 |
| % graduated top 10% of class | 15 |
| % graduated top 25% of class | 37 |
| % graduated top 50% of class | 65 |

### DEADLINES

| | |
| --- | --- |
| Regular notification | rolling |
| Nonfall registration? | yes |

### FINANCIAL FACTS

| Financial Aid Rating | 78 |
| --- | --- |
| In-state tuition | $1,867 |
| Out-of-state tuition | $5,941 |
| Room & board | $2,946 |
| Books and supplies | $1,000 |
| Required fees | $1,592 |
| % undergrads receiving aid | 85 |
| Avg frosh grant | $1,700 |
| Avg frosh loan | $2,400 |

# UNIVERSITY OF SOUTHERN CALIFORNIA

UNIVERSITY PARK, LOS ANGELES, CA 90089 • ADMISSIONS: 213-740-1111 • FAX: 213-740-6364

## CAMPUS LIFE

| | |
|---|---|
| **Quality of Life Rating** | **78** |
| Type of school | private |
| Affiliation | none |
| Environment | urban |

### STUDENTS

| | |
|---|---|
| Total undergrad enrollment | 15,705 |
| % male/female | 50/50 |
| % from out of state | 30 |
| % from public high school | 64 |
| % live on campus | 35 |
| % in (# of) fraternities | 17 (24) |
| % in (# of) sororities | 18 (12) |
| % African American | 7 |
| % Asian | 23 |
| % Caucasian | 48 |
| % Hispanic | 14 |
| % Native American | 1 |
| % international | 7 |
| # of countries represented | 107 |

### SURVEY SAYS . . .

Frats and sororities dominate social scene
Everyone loves the Trojans
High cost of living
Great computer facilities
Great library
Ethnic diversity on campus
Student publications are popular
Lousy off-campus food

## ACADEMICS

| | |
|---|---|
| **Academic Rating** | **79** |
| Calendar | semester |
| Student/faculty ratio | 11:1 |
| Profs interesting rating | 90 |
| Profs accessible rating | 92 |
| Avg lab size | 20-29 students |
| Avg reg class size | 10-19 students |

### MOST POPULAR MAJORS
business administration
engineering
communication

## STUDENTS SPEAK OUT

### Academics

Students looking for a "cutting-edge" university located in such a heavenly place as the City of Angels ought to turn an eye to the University of Southern California, named School of the Year by *Time/Princeton Review College Guide* in 2000. USC students gush about their "dedicated" faculty, though they note that some professors seem disinterested in teaching lower-level classes. Teaching assistants "sometimes don't teach anything" in their sub-sections, one business major laments, "and you are left to teach yourself." The theater and film departments are (can you believe it?) extremely popular, and journalism students appreciate the fact that many of their classes are taught by real-life journalists. "Where else can . . . you see your teacher in class and then on the 11 o'clock news?" a broadcast journalism major asks. The mathematics and art departments also receive high marks. A little initiative goes a long way here because "everyone wants to help you, but you have to ask first." However, "overpriced" is what many students feel about their tuition bills. The administration is "too bureaucratic" but students believe that, like Big Government with a conscience, it's "committed to ensuring that we receive a top-rate education." A junior business major declares, "I would never want to go to any other school but USC." Graduating students find that being a Trojan has its advantages in the working world/ because USC alumni (approximately 250,000 living) are everywhere and are known to help new alumni find employment.

### Life

USC's location allows u-grads to sample all that Los Angeles has to offer. Specifically, students love the beach (which is only a 10-minute drive away), the clubs, and all aspects of the entertainment industry. Students frequently attend movies (Hello? Hollywood?). Having a car on campus is a major advantage because the public transit system isn't as reliable. Students say that "there's always a party to go to," especially on "The Row"—a legendary group of fraternity houses located near campus. The Greek system is big here, and "Trojan pride" is infectious. Students support the university's football team regardless of its record, and games against cross-town rival UCLA raise school spirit to a fever pitch. The weather in Southern California is usually pretty close to paradisal. With all that the university and the surrounding areas have to offer, a senior theater major editorializes, "You've got to be pretty tough on yourself to go to classes with all the distractions." A sophomore adds, "Coming to USC is like getting a giant dinner plate and having all-access to a world-class buffet. There are so many opportunities, it's almost overwhelming."

### Student Body

USC is one of the more diverse campuses profiled in Best 331. Contrary to what that diversity might imply, however, students of the same ethnic group tend to form "socially segregated" ethnic cliques. Still, students say that their peers are "the school's best asset." Many credit the warm climate (which decreases the necessity for restrictive clothing) for helping them to meet people, and students constantly mention how attractive their peers are, calling them "beautiful" and "awesome" as well as "sexy" and "cute." Of course, some complain that the "'California—beauty-is-everything-mindset' can get tiring sometimes." A senior biology major points out that students are "very competitive" and that "nobody wants to help you or study with you." Despite the cutthroat academics, the "Trojan family" bonds people, no matter what. One enthusiastic sophomore writes, "Whenever you see someone wearing USC clothing around town, you say 'Fight On!'"

FINANCIAL AID: 213-740-1111 • E-MAIL: UGRD@USC.EDU • WEBSITE: WWW.USC.EDU

## ADMISSIONS

*Very important* academic and nonacademic factors considered by the admissions committee include secondary schools record, standardized test scores, and special talent/ability. *Important* factors include recommendations, student essays, interviews, extracurricular activities, and character/personal qualities. *Other* factors considered include alumni relation, minority status, geography, volunteer work, and work experience. Factors *not* considered include religious affiliation/commitment and state residence. SAT I or ACT required. High school diploma is required and GED is not accepted. *High school units required/recommended:* 16 total required; at least 21 total recommended; 4 English required, 3 math required, 4 math recommended, 2 laboratory science required, 3 laboratory science recommended, 2 foreign language required, 3 foreign language recommended, 2 social studies required, 3 social studies recommended, 3 academic electives required, more recommended. *The admissions office says:* "One of the best ways to discover if USC is right for you is to walk around the campus, talk to students, and get a feel for the area both as a place to study and a place to live. If you can't visit, we hold admission information programs around the country. Watch your mailbox for an invitation or send us an e-mail if you're interested."

### The Inside Word

The high national visibility of its athletic teams and glamorous images has long enabled USC to maintain a large applicant pool. Recently, though, this athletic powerhouse has become an academic powerhouse. Admissions is solidly competitive. USC is looking for top students who are motivated and ready to take advantage of all the resources of a large, urban research university.

## FINANCIAL AID

*Students should submit:* FAFSA, CSS/Financial Aid PROFILE; state aid form; parent and student federal income tax forms with all schedules and W-2s; institutional form; single, divorced, and separated parent's form. The Princeton Review suggests that all financial aid forms be submitted as soon as possible after January 1. *Need-based scholarships/grants offered:* Pell, SEOG, state scholarships/grants, and the school's own gift aid. *Loan aid offered:* FFEL Subsidized Stafford, FFEL Unsubsidized Stafford, FFEL PLUS, Federal Perkins, and college/university loans from institutional funds. Institutional employment available. Federal Work-Study Program available. Applicants will be notified of awards on a rolling basis beginning on or about March 1. Off-campus job opportunities are excellent.

## FROM THE ADMISSIONS OFFICE

"USC administers one of the largest financial aid programs in the world. More than 20 percent of USC students receive scholarships based on merit. The scholarship application deadline is December 10."

### ADMISSIONS

| | |
|---|---|
| **Admissions Rating** | 82 |
| # of applicants | 26,351 |
| % of applicants accepted | 34 |
| % of acceptees attending | 32 |

#### FRESHMAN PROFILE

| | |
|---|---|
| Range SAT Verbal | 590-690 |
| Average SAT Verbal | 640 |
| Range SAT Math | 620-710 |
| Average SAT Math | 670 |
| Range ACT Composite | 28-31 |
| Average ACT Composite | 29 |
| Average HS GPA | 3.9 |
| % graduated top 10% of class | 75 |
| % graduated top 25% of class | 90 |
| % graduated top 50% of class | 99 |

#### DEADLINES

| | |
|---|---|
| Priority admission deadline | 12/10 |
| Regular admission | 1/10 |
| Regular notification | 4/1 |
| Nonfall registration? | yes |

#### APPLICANTS ALSO LOOK AT
**AND OFTEN PREFER**
UCLA & UC—Berkley
Georgetown
**AND SOMETIMES PREFER**
Cornell
U. Washington
NYU
Northwestern
UC—San Diego
**AND RARELY PREFER**
UC—Davis
UC—Irvine
UC—Santa Barbara

### FINANCIAL FACTS

| | |
|---|---|
| **Financial Aid Rating** | 75 |
| Tuition | $23,644 |
| Room & board | $7,610 |
| Books and supplies | $650 |
| Required fees | $460 |
| % undergrads receiving aid | 55 |
| Avg frosh grant | $13,061 |
| Avg frosh loan | $3,890 |

# UNIVERSITY OF TENNESSEE—KNOXVILLE

320 STUDENT SERVICE BUILDING, CIRCLE PARK DRIVE, KNOXVILLE, TN 37996 • ADMISSIONS: 865-974-2184 • FAX: 865-974-6341

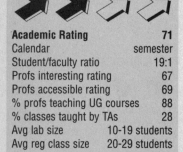
## STUDENTS SPEAK OUT

### Academics

University of Tennessee at Knoxville offers something for everyone, from the diligent scholar to the party animal looking to cruise through four years. For those seeking academic rigor, the opportunities are ample, especially in such prominent programs as engineering, the sciences, education, business, textiles, and advertising. The size of the school is also a major source of frustration, however, creating a massive bureaucracy and a pervading sense of impersonality. As one student puts it, "There are the 'normal' bureaucratic goings-on which, [as] I have witnessed myself, CAN cause freshmen and seniors alike to weep. However, the professors here are incredible. The university gives the instructors space to thrive and play. There are so many interesting classes to take if one can fit it into the schedule, i.e. 'Animal and Human Welfare: Sociological, Philosophical and Medical Aspects.' How cool!!!!!" Not all students are quite so positive about profs, though. In fact, the quality of instructors here is mixed. Reports one student, "The professors are few and far between, and when you do find them, they aren't very good teachers. Most of the classes are taught by teaching assistants, and they are usually first year teachers." Another counters, "Professors try their best to make themselves readily available for help with office hours . . . but it is hard since their classes are so big. This is where the TAs come in, though. I've had awesome TAs." Advising is a sore topic with many; grouses one typical undergrad, "Advisors are not understanding of students' situations. They just tell us to sign up for classes they know are closed and try to get us out of their offices."

### Life

Students agree that "UTK is a social school. Everywhere you go, it's about football or basketball or frat parties." Writes one student, "Well, every week we definitely look forward to the weekend. . . . If it's football season, then it's even better. During football season there are tailgates, pre-game parties, after-game parties, and all the local bars and restaurants are packed. Everyone is drunk enjoying a good ol' game of football. The weekends are still pretty wild, even out of football season; the bars are usually packed, and the parties still go on everywhere." Intercollegiate sports, especially football, are paramount here; reports one undergrad, "Not a day goes by that anyone on this campus, male or female, is not talking about the Big Orange. Whether it be football or basketball, everyone is talking about it all day." Frats and sororities are also huge, as are such diverse organizations and activities as the college ministry, fencing, ballroom dancing, opera, and ballet. The neighborhood surrounding the campus, students say, "is somewhat boring and is only really suited to those students over 21 (or [those] with fake ids) who like to drink and drink and drink . . . while watching sports, of course."

### Student Body

According to most, the vast majority of UT students are cut from the same mold: white, middle-class, southern, conservative, and religious. Writes one student, "This is not the school for you if you want diversity! If you are white, raised in the South, and love football, this is the school for you." Another points out that "the Christians outnumber non-Christians about 20 to 1, but it's somewhat low key." A few, however, see diversity among the monochromatic faces surrounding them: "Some people say there is a lack of diversity on this campus, but I don't look at it that way. Every one of us has something to share from a unique perspective, and that makes for enough diversity in my book." Because UTK is "a big school . . . everyone has their own clique and does their own thing except football—everyone goes to the games!" The Greek system creates the most obvious dividing lines; "A lot of people are 'Greek snobby,' meaning they judge people by what sorority or fraternity they are in. It's a real 'Mine is better than yours' attitude."

FINANCIAL AID: 423-974-3131 • E-MAIL: ADMISSIONS@UTK.EDU • WEBSITE: WWW.UTK.EDU

## ADMISSIONS

*Very important* academic and nonacademic factors considered by the admissions committee include class rank, secondary school record, and standardized test scores. *Important* factors considered include extracurricular activities, minority status, talent/ability, volunteer work, and work experience. *Other* factors considered include essays, geography, recommendations, and state residency. Factors *not* considered include alumni/ae relation, character/personal qualities, interview, and religious affiliation/commitment. SAT I or ACT required, ACT preferred. TOEFL required of all international applicants. High school diploma is required and GED is accepted. *High school units required/recommended:* 16 total required; 4 English required, 4 math required, 5 math recommended, 2 science required, 4 science recommended, 2 foreign language required, 5 foreign language recommended, 1 social studies required, 3 social studies recommended.

### The Inside Word

Don't expect any attention to be given to your essays or extracurriculars at Tennessee unless you are not "automatically admissible." The university takes in a jumbo freshman class and has to use a fairly straightforward approach to getting these kids admitted. Standards are the same for out-of-state applicants as for in-state, but the school's mix of in-state/out-of-state students is firm, since it is set by policy of the Board of Trustees.

## FINANCIAL AID

*Students should submit:* FAFSA, institution's own financial aid form, and Academic College Scholarship Application. There is no regular filing deadline. The Princeton Review suggests that all financial aid forms be submitted as soon as possible after January 1. *Need-based scholarships/grants offered:* Pell, SEOG, state scholarships/grants, private scholarships, and the school's own gift aid. *Loan aid offered:* FFEL Subsidized Stafford, FFEL Unsubsidized Stafford, FFEL PLUS, Federal Perkins, and state. Institutional employment available. Applicants will be notified of awards on a rolling basis beginning on or about April 1. Off-campus job opportunities are good.

## FROM THE ADMISSIONS OFFICE

"The University of Tennessee—Knoxville is the place where you belong if you're interested in outstanding resources and unlimited opportunities to foster your personal and academic growth. Ten colleges offer more than 100 majors to students from all 50 states and 95 foreign countries. More than 300 clubs and organizations on campus offer opportunities for fun, challenge, and service. UTK is a place where students take pride in belonging to a 200-year-old tradition and celebrate the excitement of 'the Volunteer spirit.' We invite you to explore the many advantages UTK has to offer."

---

## ADMISSIONS

| | |
|---|---|
| **Admissions Rating** | **77** |
| # of applicants | 10,171 |
| % of applicants accepted | 62 |
| % of acceptees attending | 60 |

### FRESHMAN PROFILE

| | |
|---|---|
| Range SAT Verbal | 500-610 |
| Average SAT Verbal | 551 |
| Range SAT Math | 500-620 |
| Average SAT Math | 549 |
| Range ACT Composite | 21-26 |
| Average ACT Composite | 24 |
| Minimum TOEFL | 523 |
| Average HS GPA | 3.4 |
| % graduated top 10% of class | 26 |
| % graduated top 25% of class | 53 |
| % graduated top 50% of class | 86 |

### DEADLINES

| | |
|---|---|
| Regular admission | 1/15 |
| Regular notification | rolling |
| Nonfall registration? | yes |

### APPLICANTS ALSO LOOK AT

**AND OFTEN PREFER**
Middle Tennessee State
Auburn
Emory

**AND SOMETIMES PREFER**
U. Florida
Vanderbilt
U. Georgia

**AND RARELY PREFER**
U. Kentucky
East Tennessee State
Clemson
U. of the South

## FINANCIAL FACTS

| | |
|---|---|
| **Financial Aid Rating** | **78** |
| In-state tuition | $2,812 |
| Out-of-state tuition | $9,616 |
| Room & board | $4,490 |
| Books and supplies | $998 |
| Required fees | $550 |
| % frosh receiving aid | 31 |
| % undergrads receiving aid | 33 |
| Avg frosh grant | $5,097 |
| Avg frosh loan | $2,520 |

---

# UNIVERSITY OF TEXAS—AUSTIN

JOHN W. HARGIS HALL, AUSTIN, TX 78712-1111 • ADMISSIONS: 512-475-7440 • FAX: 512-475-7475

## CAMPUS LIFE

| | |
|---|---|
| **Quality of Life Rating** | **84** |
| Type of school | public |
| Affiliation | none |
| Environment | urban |

### STUDENTS

| | |
|---|---|
| Total undergrad enrollment | 38,162 |
| % male/female | 50/50 |
| % from out of state | 5 |
| % live on campus | 16 |
| % in (# of) fraternities | 10 (30) |
| % in (# of) sororities | 12 (18) |
| % African American | 3 |
| % Asian | 15 |
| % Caucasian | 64 |
| % Hispanic | 14 |
| % international | 4 |

### SURVEY SAYS . . .

*Campus easy to get around*
*Theater is hot*
*Campus feels safe*
*School is well run*
*Great computer facilities*
*Ethnic diversity on campus*
*Students get along with local community*
*Students aren't religious*
*Lousy food on campus*
*Students are not very happy*
*(Almost) no one listens to college radio*
*Student publications are ignored*

## ACADEMICS

| | |
|---|---|
| **Academic Rating** | **82** |
| Calendar | semester |
| Student/faculty ratio | 19:1 |
| Profs interesting rating | 69 |
| Profs accessible rating | 96 |
| Avg lab size | 10-19 students |
| Avg reg class size | 10-19 students |

### MOST POPULAR MAJORS
psychology
English
biological sciences

## STUDENTS SPEAK OUT
### Academics

UT—Austin is more than affordable; it is, in the words of one undergraduate, "damn cheap!" Tuition is so low that some out-of-state students pay less than they would to go to public institutions in their own home states. But UT—Austin has more than just price going for it. It also boasts excellent, varied academic programs. The school's huge endowment allows it to recruit scholars aggressively, and it has attracted top professors in many fields. Business-related majors claim a large number of students here; engineering and communications are also popular, and the film school is "up and coming." The only drawback is that UT—Austin is huge. No, it's damn huge! Over 38,000 undergraduates (and almost another 12,000 graduate students) crowd the 300-acre campus. Accordingly, students usually have to assert themselves to get to know their professors (although top students qualify for an honors program with smaller classes). One undergrad cautions, "This is not a teaching school, but rather a research institution." Even so, students occasionally stumble upon a diamond in the rough; writes one, "Individual instructors make the greatest impact on my education. A few very talented teachers made my entire education at UT worthwhile." Also, as you might expect, administering such a large institution is difficult, and the red tape can be a little daunting. Warns one student, "It is very difficult to get the classes you need." Most students know what they're getting into before they arrive and feel that UT—Austin is a "great school with great diversity, even though it has all the bureaucracy associated with large schools."

### Life

No longer the nation's best kept secret, the city of Austin offers almost everything a college student needs for extracurricular bliss: museums, theaters, restaurants, bookstores, and one of America's most vibrant bar/live music scenes. Points out one student, "All Austin needs is a beach." Comments another, "In a city like Austin, there is no need to hang around campus all the time." Those who choose to remain within the confines of UT will find hundreds of clubs and organizations to choose from. Fraternities and sororities are also very popular, but the school is large enough and offers enough in the way of activities that a student could have a full social life without ever attending a frat event. Longhorn football is huge, and other intercollegiate sporting events are also very popular. UT's recreational sports programs and facilities also enjoy a high percentage of student participation. On a campus with the population of a small city, "the very size of this school provides opportunities I would not have found elsewhere. Where else but in UT-Austin can you be in a band, study Sanskrit, star in student films, join a club playing with toy soldiers, and develop web sites, all in one semester?"

### Student Body

It's a cliche, but at a school of 50,000, you're going to find someone who fits just about any description. As one student puts it, "I haven't met the other 49,999 students so I won't try to generalize. It's pretty much been a 'birds of a feather' situation in my experience." Another respondent was bolder, offering this generalization: "People range from sorority and fraternity goers to strong environmentalists to avid Cliff (our campus Christian speaker) watchers." The vast majority of students, nine out of ten undergraduates, are Texans. Although Texas is a conservative state, UT—Austin seems to attract more than its fair share of "alternative" types. Liberal political ideas score surprisingly high, and people are concerned about "discrimination against women and minorities."

FINANCIAL AID: 512-475-6282 • E-MAIL: FRMN@UTS.CC.UTEXAS.EDU • WEBSITE: WWW.UTEXAS.EDU

## ADMISSIONS

*Very important* academic and nonacademic factors considered by the admissions committee include class rank, secondary school record and standardized test scores. *Important* factors considered include essay, extracurricular activities, talent/ability, volunteer work, and work experience. *Other* factors considered include character/personal qualities, geography, recommendations, state residency. Factors *not* considered include alumni/ae relation, interview, minority status, and religious affiliation/commitment. SAT I or ACT required. TOEFL required of all international applicants. High school diploma is required and GED is accepted. *High school units required/recommended:* 16 total required; 4 English required, 3 math required, 2 science required, 2 foreign language required, 3 social studies required, 2 elective required.

### The Inside Word

Top faculty and super facilities draw a mega-sized applicant pool to UT, as does Longhorn football. Texas wants top athletes in each entering class, to be sure. But it also seeks students who are well qualified academically, and it gets loads of them. Both the university and Austin are thriving intellectual communities; Austin has the highest per capita book sales of any city in the United States. Many students continue on to grad school without ever leaving, which is understandable—it's hard to spend any time here without developing an affinity for the school and the city. Legal judgments against affirmative action in the state of Texas (covering the entire fifth circuit of the federal court) have resulted in higher minority applications this year.

## FINANCIAL AID

*Students should submit:* FAFSA; some selected students are also asked to submit documents to verify income or other information. They are notified by the institution if they need to do so. There is no regular filing deadline. The Princeton Review suggests that all financial aid forms be submitted as soon as possible after January 1. *Need-based scholarships/grants offered:* Pell, SEOG, state scholarships/grants, private scholarships, the school's own gift aid, and Federal Nursing. *Loan aid offered:* FFEL Subsidized Stafford, FFEL Unsubsidized Stafford, FFEL Plus Loans, Federal Perkins, state, and college/university loans from institutional funds. Institutional employment available. Federal Work-Study Program available. Applicants will be notified of awards on a rolling basis beginning on or about April 1. Off-campus job opportunities are good.

## FROM THE ADMISSIONS OFFICE

"UT—Austin is a large, research-oriented university located in the capital of Texas, at the edge of the beautiful hill country of Texas. More than 48,000 students representing 50 states and 116 foreign countries live and learn in a competitive academic environment. A strong intercollegiate athletic program for both men and women is supplemented by an intramural athletic program that is available to all students as well as faculty and staff. An undergraduate advising center for undeclared majors, a career choice information center, and college placement centers provide advising, career counseling, and placement. Other student services include an honors center, counseling and student health centers, and a study abroad office. The university serves as a cultural center to the community at large as well as to students, faculty, and staff. A performing arts center is host to Broadway plays, the Austin Civic Opera, the Austin Symphony, and visiting musical and dance groups throughout the year. A strong faculty, fine facilities and student services, and a commitment to undergraduate education make UT—Austin one of the truly great universities in America and in the world."

## ADMISSIONS

| Admissions Rating | 86 |
| --- | --- |
| # of applicants | 21,539 |
| % of applicants accepted | 62 |
| % of acceptees attending | 58 |

### FRESHMAN PROFILE

| | |
| --- | --- |
| Range SAT Verbal | 530-640 |
| Average SAT Verbal | 592 |
| Range SAT Math | 560-670 |
| Average SAT Math | 619 |
| Range ACT Composite | 22-27 |
| Average ACT Composite | 25 |
| Minimum TOEFL | 550 |
| % graduated top 10% of class | 47 |
| % graduated top 25% of class | 79 |
| % graduated top 50% of class | 96 |

### DEADLINES

| | |
| --- | --- |
| Regular admission | 2/1 |
| Nonfall registration? | yes |

### APPLICANTS ALSO LOOK AT

**AND OFTEN PREFER**
Rice
Baylor
**AND SOMETIMES PREFER**
Texas A&M
Texas Tech
U. Houston
**AND RARELY PREFER**
Clemson
Southwest Texas State

### FINANCIAL FACTS

| Financial Aid Rating | 81 |
| --- | --- |
| In-state tuition | $2,400 |
| Out-of-state tuition | $8,850 |
| Room & board | $5,113 |
| Books and supplies | $700 |
| Required fees | $1,175 |
| % frosh receiving aid | 43 |
| % undergrads receiving aid | 47 |
| Avg frosh grant | $4,570 |
| Avg frosh loan | $2,980 |

# UNIVERSITY OF THE PACIFIC

3601 PACIFIC AVENUE, STOCKTON, CA 95211 • ADMISSIONS: 800-959-2867 • FAX: 209-946-2413

## CAMPUS LIFE

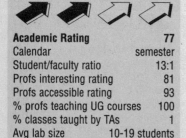

| | |
|---|---|
| **Quality of Life Rating** | **83** |
| Type of school | private |
| Affiliation | Methodist |
| Environment | suburban |

### STUDENTS

| | |
|---|---|
| Total undergrad enrollment | 3,093 |
| % male/female | 42/58 |
| % from out of state | 16 |
| % from public high school | 82 |
| % live on campus | 58 |
| % in (# of) fraternities | 19 (6) |
| % in (# of) sororities | 20 (4) |
| % African American | 3 |
| % Asian | 27 |
| % Caucasian | 56 |
| % Hispanic | 10 |
| % Native American | 1 |
| % international | 4 |

### SURVEY SAYS . . .
*Beautiful campus
Campus easy to get around
Athletic facilities are great
Great off-campus food
Frats and sororities dominate social scene
Ethnic diversity on campus
Student publications are ignored
Students aren't religious
Students are cliquish*

## ACADEMICS

| | |
|---|---|
| **Academic Rating** | **77** |
| Calendar | semester |
| Student/faculty ratio | 13:1 |
| Profs interesting rating | 81 |
| Profs accessible rating | 93 |
| % profs teaching UG courses | 100 |
| % classes taught by TAs | 1 |
| Avg lab size | 10-19 students |
| Avg reg class size | 20-29 students |

### MOST POPULAR MAJORS
business
biological sciences
social sciences & history

## STUDENTS SPEAK OUT

### Academics

The students at the University of the Pacific appreciate the fact that their professors are always there for them. Reports one student, "Academics here are tough, but you can always find your professors. In fact, when I get a break from one of my classes I generally go chat with another professor. Professors I had last year remember my name and still say 'hi' to me!" Enthuses another, "Most of the professors enjoy teaching. It's apparent in their lectures, discussions, and out-of-class availability." UOP's student-centered approach doesn't emanate merely from the faculty, however; administrators also get into the act. Recounts one student, "One semester I had a class with only five students, including myself. I was disappointed because I was certain that the class would be canceled. Well, it wasn't. At UOP, we're offered a great amount of individual attention. The school didn't forget the fact that the five of us wanted to take that course." That kind of concern for the individual student pays off: "Since I transferred from a junior college to UOP, my grades have dramatically improved. I have the professors and myself to thank for that." Health sciences are the school's strongest suit (particularly popular with the students is "the incredible five-year dental program"), although music, engineering, and business-related majors are also well regarded (and reportedly, "excellent"). The administration at this impeccably maintained campus "runs the school well, although sometimes I suspect that they spend more on the lawns than on me."

### Life

How UOP students feel about campus life depends largely on their take on fraternities. For the many who go Greek, campus life can be a blast. Says one such undergrad, "I think that my fraternity is the real reason for the amount of fun I've had here." For those disinclined to pledge a frat or sorority, UOP offers a "boring school life. Everything is all Greek." Complains one woman, "Nobody will shut up about rushing some frat or another. Guys, knock it off, huh?" Hometown Stockton "doesn't have a lot to do. There's a couple of malls and movie theaters, but that's all. Mainly on weekends we either go to frat parties or head to San Francisco or Sacramento." During the week, however, the campus is abuzz with academic and extracurricular activity. "Because there are so many organizations on campus, it gets difficult to choose just one activity to participate in," reports one student. Others note enjoying a variety of "athletic events, plays, concerts, parties, shopping, hanging out in friends' rooms, church and youth groups." Hanging out on Pacific's stunning campus is a student favorite, and for those students with an interest in the great outdoors, "UOP is located in between the mountains and the ocean in the San Joaquin Valley. Biking, hiking, camping, fishing, skiing, whatever you want to do" is readily available—"as long as you or someone you know has a car."

### Student Body

The overriding tone at UOP is one of conservatism, with a strong religious undercurrent. A student describes classmates as "ultra-conservative ultra-Christians who don't care about current issues and aren't open to new and different ideas. The honors students are better." At their best, students are "very worldly, outgoing, intellectual, and involved"; portrayed in a less generous light, they are "somewhat snobby and selfish, coming from wealthy backgrounds." Students are cliquish, in part because of the strong Greek presence on campus. Explains one undergrad, "The fraternities and sororities seem to cause a lot of cliques. But if you can't beat 'em, join 'em! I'm pledging a house next semester!" Warns one student, "Because we have such a small population, gossip makes the rounds in about two seconds."

FINANCIAL AID: 209-946-2421 • E-MAIL: ADMISSIONS@UOP.EDU • WEBSITE: WWW.UOP.EDU

## ADMISSIONS

*Very important* academic and nonacademic factors considered by the admissions committee include character/personal qualities, essays, and secondary school record. *Important* factors considered include alumni/ae relation, extracurricular activities, recommendations, standardized test scores, talent/ability, volunteer work, and work experience. *Other* factors considered include class rank, geography, interview, minority status, and state residency. Factors *not* considered include religious affiliation/commitment. SAT I or ACT required. TOEFL required of all international applicants. High school diploma is required and GED is accepted. *High school units required/recommended:* 16 total required; 4 English recommended, 3 math recommended, 2 lab science recommended, 2 foreign language recommended, 1 history recommended.

### The Inside Word

Pacific's small applicant pool and average yield of admits who enroll results in an admissions profile that is less competitive than the academic quality of the freshmen might predict. Test scores count less than a consistently solid academic performance in high school toward getting admitted. The out-of-state population is small; candidates from far afield can expect this to benefit them to a minor degree.

## FINANCIAL AID

*Students should submit:* FAFSA. The Princeton Review suggests that all financial aid forms be submitted as soon as possible after January 1. *Need-based scholarships/grants offered:* Pell, SEOG, state scholarships/grants, private scholarships, and the school's own gift aid. *Loan aid offered:* Direct Subsidized Stafford, Direct Unsubsidized Stafford, Direct PLUS, Federal Perkins, and state. Institutional employment available. Federal Work-Study Program available. Applicants will be notified of awards on a rolling basis beginning on or about March 15. Off-campus job opportunities are good.

## FROM THE ADMISSIONS OFFICE

"One of the most concise ways of describing the University of the Pacific is that it is 'a major university in a small college package.' Our 3,000 undergraduates get the personal attention that you would expect at a small, residential college. But they also have the kinds of opportunities offered at much larger institutions, including more than 80 majors and programs; 90 student organizations; drama, dance, and musical productions; 16 NCAA Division I athletic teams; and two dozen club and intramural sports. We offer undergraduate major programs in the arts, sciences and humanities, business, education, engineering, international studies, music, pharmacy, and health sciences. Some of the more unique aspects of our academic programs include the following: we have the only independent, coed, nonsectarian liberal arts and sciences college located between Los Angeles and central Oregon; we have the only undergraduate professional school of international studies in California—and it's the only one in the nation that actually requires you to study abroad; we have the only engineering program in the West that requires students to complete a year's worth of paid work experience as part of their degree; our Conservatory of Music focuses on performance but also offers majors in music management, music therapy, and music education; and we offer several accelerated programs in business, dentistry, education, law, and pharmacy. Our beautiful New England–style main campus is located in Stockton (population 250,000) and is within two hours or less of San Francisco, Santa Cruz, Yosemite National Park, and Lake Tahoe."

## ADMISSIONS

| | |
|---|---|
| Admissions Rating | 74 |
| # of applicants | 3,193 |
| % of applicants accepted | 76 |
| % of acceptees attending | 30 |

### FRESHMAN PROFILE

| | |
|---|---|
| Range SAT Verbal | 490-600 |
| Average SAT Verbal | 545 |
| Range SAT Math | 520-630 |
| Average SAT Math | 576 |
| Range ACT Composite | 20-26 |
| Average ACT Composite | 24 |
| Minimum TOEFL | 475 |
| Average HS GPA | 3.5 |
| % graduated top 10% of class | 42 |
| % graduated top 25% of class | 71 |
| % graduated top 50% of class | 91 |

### DEADLINES

| | |
|---|---|
| Priority admission deadline | 2/15 |
| Nonfall registration? | yes |

### APPLICANTS ALSO LOOK AT
### AND OFTEN PREFER
UC—Berkeley
UC—Davis
### AND SOMETIMES PREFER
U. Southern Cal
CalPoly—San Luis Obispo
UCLA
U. Redlands
U. Arizona
### AND RARELY PREFER
Santa Clara

## FINANCIAL FACTS

| | |
|---|---|
| Financial Aid Rating | 87 |
| Tuition | $20,350 |
| Room & board | $6,378 |
| Books and supplies | $810 |
| Required fees | $375 |
| % frosh receiving aid | 64 |
| % undergrads receiving aid | 71 |

# UNIVERSITY OF THE SOUTH

735 UNIVERSITY AVENUE, SEWANEE, TN 37383-1000 • ADMISSIONS: 931-598-1238 • FAX: 931-598-3248

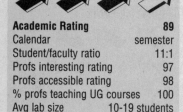
## STUDENTS SPEAK OUT

### Academics

The University of the South (known as "Sewanee") is "a small private school" that offers an "excellent Classical education" in the liberal arts and sciences. "The academics are tough" and "grade inflation is nonexistent," but "Sewanee has an excellent faculty" that "works as hard as the students." Though there are a few "really bad professors," most profs here are "outgoing and approachable." It's common for students at Sewanee to drop by professors' offices "simply to shoot the breeze," or to review before tests "over dessert and coffee at a professor's home." The school abides by a strict honor code, which "is like the Bible" of the campus: "The students' commitment to abstain from lying, cheating, and stealing fosters an overwhelming trust that inspires students to feel safe leaving doors unlocked and backpacks unattended." Though some students tell us that "Sewanee isn't the academic mecca" they read about in promotional materials, the majority contend that the "incredible" academic experience here is tough to beat. "I feel like I've learned more in my 2 years at Sewanee than I did in all 12 years prior to them," beams a French and history major. "I have never been so excited about learning." Complaints center around the administration, which "doesn't take well to student input" and "should stop worrying" so much "about its rankings."

### Life

"Sewanee is magical," exclaims a sophomore. "It is self-sustaining, timeless," and "difficult at times," but "you couldn't live and study in a more beautiful place." The campus is "a great place" to "camp, climb, cave, hike, and bike." It's possible to go "mountain biking and caving on the same day and never leave the campus." For good reason, students on this stunning 10,000-acre campus "on top of a mountain" are some of the happiest in the nation. The University of the South also has a richly deserved "party school" reputation. This doesn't mean that Sewanee is not academically challenging. As one student explains, "you must be ready to work your ass off academically." Come Thursday night, though, "it's time to get wasted." Students drink for fun and to provide a "stress reliever" for the intense and hectic demands of the coursework. "Greek life is a very strong force on campus" and the frats control the social scene. "All parties are open," though. Some students contend that life here is nothing short of awesome. "It's hard not to be active with sports, Greek life, and the outdoors. There is always something to get involved in." Other students argue that "most people just drink and wander around looking for something to do." Though "no one goes home on the weekend," day trips "to get away in Nashville or Chatanooga" are common. Sewanee lacks a dating scene, much to the chagrin of some students, but the "very safe campus" boasts "comfortable" dorms and, generally, "a haven of lush beauty," interrupted only by occasional new construction of "unnecessary monstrosities."

### Student Body

Though the situation is "slowly improving thanks to administrative efforts," Sewanee is "arguably the most homogenous campus in the world." The "southern, alcoholic, white kids" here are conservative politically, and slightly more religious than most. They are also "incredible elitists," but they are hard workers. Ultimately, "despite Sewanee's reputation as a party school, most students are generally concerned about academics; if not, they're not around for very long." There are "a lot of cliques and small groups" on campus but, "as a whole, the students get along." The flip side of the huge lack of diversity is "connectedness" and the existence of "a real community" explains a sophomore. "You've seen everyone on campus at least once by the end of your first year" and "you know everyone well enough to be able to pick out someone who doesn't attend." As is universally the case at small, isolated liberal arts colleges, "everyone knows everyone else's business," too. "Gossip is a way of life" at Sewanee.

FINANCIAL AID: 931-598-1312 • E-MAIL: COLLEGEADMISSION@SEWANEE.EDU • WEBSITE: WWW.SEWANEE.EDU

## ADMISSIONS

SAT I or ACT required. TOEFL required of all international applicants. High school diploma is required and GED is not accepted. *High school units required/recommended:* 17 total required; 20 total recommended; 4 English required, 3 math required, 4 math recommended, 3 science required, 4 science recommended, 2 foreign language required, 3 social studies required, 4 social studies recommended. *The admissions office says:* "We expect students to challenge themselves with advanced classes [in high school], when they are offered."

### The Inside Word

The admissions office at Sewanee is very personable and accessible to students. Its staff includes some of the most well-respected admissions professionals in the South, and it shows in the way they work with students. Despite a fairly high acceptance rate, candidates who take the admissions process here lightly may find themselves disappointed. Applicant evaluation is too personal for a lackadaisical approach to succeed.

## FINANCIAL AID

*Students should submit:* FAFSA and institution's own financial aid form. The Princeton Review suggests that all financial aid forms be submitted as soon as possible after January 1. *Need-based scholarships/grants offered:* Pell, SEOG, state scholarships/grants, private scholarships, and the school's own gift aid. *Loan aid offered:* Direct Subsidized Stafford, Direct Unsubsidized Stafford, Direct PLUS, FFEL Subsidized Stafford, FFEL Unsubsidized Stafford, FFEL PLUS, Federal Perkins, state, and college/university loans from institutional funds. Institutional employment available. Federal Work-Study Program available. Applicants will be notified of awards on or about April 1. Off-campus job opportunities are fair.

## FROM THE ADMISSIONS OFFICE

"The University of the South, popularly known as Sewanee, is consistently ranked among the top tier of national liberal arts universities. Sewanee is committed to an academic curriculum that focuses on the liberal arts as the most enlightening and valuable form of undergraduate education. Founded by leaders of the Episcopal church in 1857, Sewanee continues to be owned by 28 Episcopal dioceses in 12 states. The university is located on a 10,000-acre campus atop Tennessee's Cumberland Plateau between Chattanooga and Nashville. The university has an impressive record of academic achievement—23 Rhodes Scholars and 22 NCAA Postgraduate Scholarship recipients have graduated from Sewanee."

## ADMISSIONS

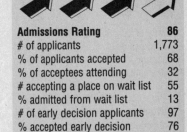

| | |
|---|---|
| Admissions Rating | 86 |
| # of applicants | 1,773 |
| % of applicants accepted | 68 |
| % of acceptees attending | 32 |
| # accepting a place on wait list | 55 |
| % admitted from wait list | 13 |
| # of early decision applicants | 97 |
| % accepted early decision | 76 |

### FRESHMAN PROFILE

| | |
|---|---|
| Range SAT Verbal | 570-670 |
| Range SAT Math | 560-650 |
| Range ACT Composite | 25-29 |
| Minimum TOEFL | 550 |
| Average HS GPA | 3.5 |
| % graduated top 10% of class | 41 |
| % graduated top 25% of class | 75 |
| % graduated top 50% of class | 97 |

### DEADLINES

| | |
|---|---|
| Early decision | 11/15 |
| Early decision notification | 12/15 |
| Regular admission | 2/1 |
| Regular notification | 4/1 |

### APPLICANTS ALSO LOOK AT

**AND OFTEN PREFER**
UNC—Chapel Hill
Washington and Lee
Virginia

**AND SOMETIMES PREFER**
Davidson
Vanderbilt
Wake Forest

**AND RARELY PREFER**
Rhodes
U. Georgia
U. Tennessee—Knoxville

### FINANCIAL FACTS

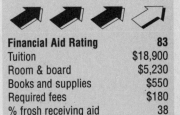

| | |
|---|---|
| Financial Aid Rating | 83 |
| Tuition | $18,900 |
| Room & board | $5,230 |
| Books and supplies | $550 |
| Required fees | $180 |
| % frosh receiving aid | 38 |
| % undergrads receiving aid | 39 |

# UNIVERSITY OF TORONTO

315 BLOOR STREET WEST, TORONTO, ON M5S 1A3 • ADMISSIONS: 416-978-2190 • FAX: 416-978-7022

## STUDENTS SPEAK OUT

### Academics

Looking for a school that offers a major in Slavic languages and literatures? How about metallurgy? Or does theoretical astrophysics float your boat? You can find these majors (and all the traditional ones as well) at the "prestigious" and "well-respected" University of Toronto, one of the finest bastions of higher education in North America. Students say you'll also find classes that are "just too big" and a somewhat "impersonal" atmosphere here, thanks to the U of T's "monolithic size." "There are great resources" on campus, though, and "a really great education" is available "if you take advantage of it." Most students rate the "extremely challenging" but "also extremely rewarding" academics here as "second to none." However, just like at any big research university, the professors aren't always high-quality teachers. While many instructors are "helpful and approachable," "very knowledgable," and "enthusiastic about their material," many others are "boring, abstract, unapproachable," and "sometimes very arrogant." Consequently, it pays to do some research before signing up for classes. Speaking of signing up for classes, quite a number of students also complain about registration, which is apparently a perpetual hassle at U of T. As for the "slow and sometimes unhelpful" administration, it "is like a steamroller," analogizes a political science major. "They do whatever they want, students be damned."

### Life

Students say the experience at U of T is "what you make it." The campus is located in an "amazingly vibrant" and "big" city that boasts "fine cafés, jazz clubs," and a head-spinning array of cultural activities. There's theater, art, professional sports, and it seems "there's always a great restaurant, a movie, or a new club or bar to check out" as well. It all makes for an "exciting environment" "packed with events" and "lots of opportunities to get involved in political, artistic, and social activities." However, "you have to be willing to put something of yourself into it." The vast majority of students at the University of Toronto live off campus, "so the school community isn't as tight-knit as other schools and school spirit isn't as high." Also, there is "lots of work" to do, and "studying is very important to most people." Indeed, though "sex, drugs, and rock and roll" have their place here, U of T is not much of a party school: "Life here is all about academics and growing up. There is a goal to be accomplished and a degree to be gained."

### Student Body

Students are "down-to-earth and easy to get along with" at U of T but, make no mistake, "competition is very strong" within the "huge student population" here and, for most, it's "all about getting a degree and then a job." "U of T is like working for a successful company in a massive office building. You won't know everyone and it's very professional," explains a sophomore. "Some people will be more brilliant than you can imagine, some will be stupid, and some will slack." This campus is definitely "culturally diverse" but ethnic groups often "stick together and speak their own languages" and many students say they decided to come to U of T because it is "close to home." Politically, most students here tend to be left of center, and some gripe that entirely "too much emphasis is placed on political correctness."

FINANCIAL AID: 416-978-2190 • E-MAIL: ASK@ADM.UTORONTO.CA • WEBSITE: WWW.UTORONTO.CA

## ADMISSIONS

*Very important* academic and nonacademic factors considered by the admissions committee include secondary school record and standardized test scores. High school diploma is required and GED is accepted. *High school units required/recommended:* 17 total recommended; 4 English recommended, 4 math recommended, 3 science recommended, 2 science lab recommended, 3 foreign language recommended, 3 social studies recommended. *The admissions office says:* "[Applicants should have completed] Grade 12 in an accredited high school with a high grade point average and good scores on SAT I and three SAT IIs. The ACT and CEEB Advanced Placement tests will also be considered. Transfer credits towards Arts and Science programs are considered for some Advanced Placement tests. Applied Science and Engineering may require completion of a full year of study at an accredited university."

### The Inside Word

The University of Toronto is one of Canada's best, and its admissions process is appropriately selective. American candidates: Give yourself extra time to research and prepare for filing an application You're an international student here, and some additional paperwork is required in order to attend—though the hassles are ultimately minimal, and the financial bargain substantial.

## FINANCIAL AID

The Princeton Review suggests that all financial aid forms be submitted as soon as possible after January 1. Institutional employment available. Off-campus job opportunities are excellent.

## FROM THE ADMISSIONS OFFICE

"The University of Toronto is committed to being an internationally significant research university with undergraduate, graduate, and professional programs of study."

### ADMISSIONS

| Admissions Rating | 79 |
| --- | --- |
| # of applicants | 44,074 |
| % of applicants accepted | 61 |
| % of acceptees attending | 37 |

#### FRESHMAN PROFILE

| Average HS GPA | 3.0 |
| --- | --- |

#### DEADLINES

| Regular admission | 3/1 |
| --- | --- |

### FINANCIAL FACTS

| Financial Aid Rating | 79 |
| --- | --- |
| In-state tuition | $3,951 |
| Out-of-state tuition | $8,755 |
| Room & board | $6,500 |
| Books and supplies | $1,050 |

# UNIVERSITY OF UTAH

201 SOUTH 1460 EAST, ROOM 250S, SALT LAKE CIT, UT 84112-9057 • ADMISSIONS: 801-581-7281 • FAX: 801-585-7864

## CAMPUS LIFE

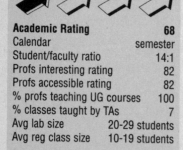

| | |
|---|---|
| **Quality of Life Rating** | **84** |
| Type of school | public |
| Affiliation | none |
| Environment | urban |

### STUDENTS

| | |
|---|---|
| Total undergrad enrollment | 20,963 |
| % male/female | 54/46 |
| % from out of state | 7 |
| % from public high school | 95 |
| % in (# of) fraternities | 2 (8) |
| % in (# of) sororities | 2 (6) |
| % African American | 1 |
| % Asian | 4 |
| % Caucasian | 89 |
| % Hispanic | 3 |
| % Native American | 1 |
| % international | 2 |

### SURVEY SAYS . . .

(Almost) everyone plays intramural sports
Everyone loves the Utes
Dorms are like palaces
Great food on campus
Computer facilities need improving
Library needs improving
Lab facilities need improving

## ACACEMICS

| | |
|---|---|
| **Academic Rating** | **68** |
| Calendar | semester |
| Student/faculty ratio | 14:1 |
| Profs interesting rating | 82 |
| Profs accessible rating | 82 |
| % profs teaching UG courses | 100 |
| % classes taught by TAs | 7 |
| Avg lab size | 20-29 students |
| Avg reg class size | 10-19 students |

### MOST POPULAR MAJORS
psychology
human development and family studies
nursing

## STUDENTS SPEAK OUT

### Academics

For most University of Utah undergrads, about 90 percent of whom come from in state, this large and well-respected public research university offers the best of both worlds—it's "close to home" and less than an hour away from "the best snowboarding in the world." Academics aren't bad either; jokes a junior, "This institution has a highly understated abundance of well-respected tenured professors. They are well-known, serious scholars who could get a Valley Girl interested in any major you can think of." Utah is widely known for its excellent, practically immeasurable resources and facilities, as well as its plethora of programs and majors. In courses that range from pre-med and bioengineering to film studies and modern dance, "top-rate" and "research-focused" professors "really seem like they want to teach the class something beyond general information." And though "classes are big," as a first year points out, "professors are willing to work with students on a personal level." Of course, this isn't always the case; argues a senior, "The faculty are great, but sometimes they become distracted by research and writing and quit focusing heavily on teaching." That's when "students need to be able to take initiative," notes another senior. As for the school's leviathan administration, the vote seems split. A senior waxes about "people willing to help whenever needed with anything from counseling to advising to student involvement or advocacy." But a sophomore disagrees: "It is impossible to get a lot of things done here. They give students the runaround."

### Life

With such a bucolic campus (Utah perches on a long and steep hill that overlooks beautiful downtown Salt Lake City), it's no surprise that most students consider Utah "pretty tame." A senior explains the situation at the fairly quiet, "spread-out" campus: "We are a commuter campus, and so mostly students come here, go to work, and go home. But," she adds, "Salt Lake City has amazing mountains, so people spend a lot of time snowboarding, skiing, hiking, and biking." While some call Utah's "clean, wholesome community" boring and uneventful, others will note "only boring people get bored." Writes a particularly involved first-year, "I'm extremely busy, and the school is full of all kinds of activities—from working and volunteering to studying and playing." Another gets involved in a different way (and we thought Salt Lake was a dry city!): "People in college get drunk and have sex. College is a time for growth and exploration—and yes, this takes place in the classroom but also outside of it." Dorm life seems to provoke a similar split. A junior paints a rosy picture: "The friends you make in the residence halls will be the friends you have all your life." A classmate sees it differently: "The dorms are built and maintained to look nice. They are designed, however, to inhibit any kind of student community." All agree on the meal plans, which are roundly dissed as a "complete rip-off."

### Student Body

Though University of Utah students come from all over the world, the school has a hard time shaking its reputation of being mostly a "religious" school, where "if you're non-Mormon, it seems as if you don't fit." This situation isn't helped by the fairly homogenous student body (about three-quarters of which self-identifies as white). Writes a first-year, "This campus has no diversity, ethnically or religiously. There is a narrow-mindedness here that I did not grow up with." Still, there's hope: "People off campus are way different from those who live on," notes a senior. And though the school's different groups can be "cliquish," a junior points out that "everyone is really friendly and willing to talk to you if you make a little effort to talk to them." A first-year provides a helpful summing up for prospectives: "There are no real in-betweens," he writes. "It's usually a love-hate thing."

FINANCIAL AID: 801-581-6211 • WEBSITE: WWW.UTAH.EDU

## ADMISSIONS

*Very important* academic and nonacademic factors considered by the admissions committee include secondary school record and standardized test scores. *Important* factors considered include talent/ability. *Other* factors considered include class rank, extracurricular activities, interview, and recommendations. Factors *not* considered include alumni/ae relation, character/personal qualities, essays, geography, religious affiliation/commitment, state residency, volunteer work, and work experience. SAT I or ACT required. TOEFL required of all international applicants. High school diploma is required and GED is accepted. *High school units required/recommended:* 15 total required; 4 English required, 2 math required, 3 science required, 1 science lab required, 2 foreign language required, 1 history required, 4 elective required.

### The Inside Word

Utah is another state in which low numbers of high school grads keep selectivity down at its public flagship university. Admission is based primarily on the big three: course selection, grades, and test scores; if you've got a 3.0 GPA or better and average test scores, you're close to a sure bet for admission.

## FINANCIAL AID

*Students should submit:* FAFSA and institution's own financial aid form. Regular filing deadline is February 15. Priority filing deadline is March 15. The Princeton Review suggests that all financial aid forms be submitted as soon as possible after January 1. *Need-based scholarships/grants offered:* Pell, SEOG, state scholarships/grants, private scholarships, and the school's own gift aid. *Loan aid offered:* Subsidized Stafford, Unsubsidized Stafford, PLUS, Federal Perkins, Federal Nursing, and the school's own loans. Institution employment available. Federal Work-Study Program available. Off-campus job opportunities are excellent.

## FROM THE ADMISSIONS OFFICE

"The University of Utah is a distinctive community of learning in the American West. Today's 25,000 students are from every state and 109 foreign countries. The U has research ties worldwide, with national standing among the top comprehensive research institutions. The U offers majors in 73 undergraduate and 94 graduate subjects. Nationally recognized honors and undergraduate research programs stimulate intellectual inquiry. Undergraduates collaborate with faculty on important investigations. The U's intercollegiate athletes compete in the NCAA Division I Mountain West Conference. The men's basketball team has been nationally ranked for several years, as have our women's gymnastics and skiing teams. The U's location in Salt Lake City provides easy access to the arts, theater, Utah Jazz basketball, and hockey. Utah's Great Outdoors—skiing, hiking, and five national parks—are nearby. The university will be the site for the opening and closing ceremonies and the Athletes Village for the 2002 Winter Olympic Games.

"Residential Living has greatly expanded the opportunity for students to live on campus with a new and wide variety of housing. Heritage Commons, located in historic Fort Douglas on campus, consists of 21 newly constructed buildings, including 3 residence hall–style facilities, which accommodate more than 2,500 students."

### ADMISSIONS

| | |
|---|---|
| Admissions Rating | 67 |
| # of applicants | 5,268 |
| % of applicants accepted | 94 |
| % of acceptees attending | 63 |

### FRESHMAN PROFILE

| | |
|---|---|
| Range ACT Composite | 20-26 |
| Average ACT Composite | 24 |
| Minimum TOEFL | 500 |
| Average HS GPA | 3.4 |
| % graduated top 10% of class | 26 |
| % graduated top 25% of class | 52 |
| % graduated top 50% of class | 87 |

### DEADLINES

| | |
|---|---|
| Priority admission deadline | 2/15 |
| Regular admission | 5/1 |
| Nonfall registration? | yes |

### FINANCIAL FACTS

| | |
|---|---|
| Financial Aid Rating | 80 |
| In-state tuition | $2,502 |
| Out-of-state tuition | $8,759 |
| Room & board | $4,700 |
| Books and supplies | $1,086 |
| Required fees | $540 |
| % frosh receiving aid | 25 |
| Avg frosh grant | $2,770 |
| Avg frosh loan | $2,625 |

# UNIVERSITY OF VERMONT

OFFICE OF ADMISSIONS, 194 S. PROSPECT STREET, BURLINGTON, VT 05401-3596 • ADMISSIONS: 802-656-3370 • FAX: 802-656-8611

## CAMPUS LIFE

| Quality of Life Rating | 86 |
| --- | --- |
| Type of school | public |
| Affiliation | none |
| Environment | suburban |

### STUDENTS

| | |
| --- | --- |
| Total undergrad enrollment | 8,618 |
| % male/female | 44/56 |
| % from out of state | 61 |
| % from public high school | 70 |
| % live on campus | 49 |
| % Asian | 1 |
| % Caucasian | 95 |
| % Hispanic | 1 |
| % international | 1 |

### SURVEY SAYS . . .

*Students love Burlington, VT*
*Diversity lacking on campus*
*Great off-campus food*
*Musical organizations aren't popular*
*Students aren't religious*
*Large classes*
*Student government is unpopular*
*Dorms are like dungeons*

## ACADEMICS

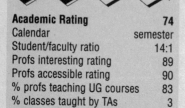

| Academic Rating | 74 |
| --- | --- |
| Calendar | semester |
| Student/faculty ratio | 14:1 |
| Profs interesting rating | 89 |
| Profs accessible rating | 90 |
| % profs teaching UG courses | 83 |
| % classes taught by TAs | 3 |
| Avg lab size | 10-19 students |
| Avg reg class size | 10-19 students |

### MOST POPULAR MAJORS
business administration
English language & literature
psychology

## STUDENTS SPEAK OUT

### Academics

There's no denying that many choose University of Vermont for its lovely ski-resort location and party-school reputation, but that doesn't mean students can't get a first-rate education here as well. Explains one student, "There may be some kids who are here for a good time and a good time only, but many of us are here for a strong education." Others point out that "if you take an active role in your education—if you really believe that no one is going to hand it to you—it is easy to get a great education here." UVM's overall academic reputation is quite solid, and deservedly so. The university is particularly strong in animal science and health- and environment-related areas; students report that psychology, political science, and business and management are also popular majors. Undergrads note that "despite large class sizes, the professors are very dynamic and really get the class involved" and that "the larger classes are intimidating, but most offer helpful discussion groups that are small and more personal." Advises one student, "To get the most out of your tuition, use as many study aids as you can, including study groups, tutors, professors, and supplemental instruction. They will all improve your grades, and they are usually free to students." Professors receive unusually high praise for state-university instructors. Students commend them as "down-to-earth and easy to relate to" and report that they're "open [to] discussions, ideas, and suggestions. A lot of my professors encourage creativity and care about their students and their performance." The administration, on the other hand, "is a nightmare. Getting things done in the UVM bureaucracy is like pulling teeth."

### Life

Just how intense the party scene is at UVM is a matter of some debate. According to many, "Our school is a shameless party school. People here think about where their next beer is coming from." Others take a more nuanced view, explaining that "it's true that UVM is a big party school, but only for those who choose it. There are many students here who study hard, have fun with their friends, participate in athletic activities, and still make the grade." For those who do choose partying, "people smoke a lot of pot, and there are some good hallucinogens floating around, but not quite as much drinking as other colleges. This is good, though—it makes the atmosphere chill instead of drunk and rowdy." That is, until "The Man" shows up. "Police are always in the dorms, and they have little respect for students and our rights," complain several undergrads. Whatever their differences on the topic of partying, nearly all students agree that UVM is ideally located for those who love outdoor winter activities. "What other school has ski mountains 20 minutes away, a lake 5 minutes away, and a beach 10 minutes away?" asks one student. Students also love Burlington, saying it's "an amazing town for its size. There are a ton of things to do, and its location on the lake is beautiful." Town features include "concerts, shows, movies, tons of stores, the waterfront: there's always life downtown." Students work hard during the week, but "on the weekends," notes one student, "most of us go downtown shopping or to the lake during the day. At night, we go to the dance clubs or off-campus parties," though, of course, "always pre-gamed (i.e. drunk or stoned before we arrive)."

### Student Body

Many UVM undergrads feel that their student body provides "a wide variety of social groups. From hippies to jocks, UVM has it all." To these happy undergrads, "the atmosphere up here is real laid-back and relaxed. I noticed when I first came up here that if you smile at someone or say 'hi' to a stranger, they almost always say 'hi' back. People up here are cool." They also note that "the school does an excellent job of making its many out-of-state students feel comfortable, accepted, and appreciated. For us, this truly is a home away from home." Even so, there are more than a few who complain that "sometimes I feel as if I'm surrounded by hippies, extreme environmentalists, and communists. [Though] they aren't that widespread on campus, they're just very vocal."

FINANCIAL AID: 802-656-3156 • E-MAIL: ADMISSIONS@UVM.EDU • WEBSITE: WWW.UVM.EDU

## ADMISSIONS

*Very important* academic and nonacademic factors considered by the admissions committee include the secondary school record. *Important* factors considered include alumni/ae relation, class rank, essays, minority status, standardized test scores, state residency, and character/personal qualities. *Other* factors considered include recommendations, extracurricular activities, geography, interview, talent/ability, volunteer work, and work experience. Factors *not* considered include religious affiliation/commitment. SAT I or ACT required. TOEFL required of all international applicants. High school diploma is required and GED is accepted. *High school units required/recommended:* 16 total required; 4 English required, 3 math required, 2 science required, 1 science lab required, 2 foreign language required, 3 social studies required.

### The Inside Word

UVM is one of the most popular public universities in the country, and its admissions standards are significantly more competitive for out-of-state students. Nonresidents shouldn't get too anxiety-ridden about getting in; more than half of the student body comes from elsewhere. Candidates with above-average academic profiles should be in good shape.

## FINANCIAL AID

*Students should submit:* FAFSA. The Princeton Review suggests that all financial aid forms be submitted as soon as possible after January 1. *Need-based scholarships/grants offered:* Pell, SEOG, state scholarships/grants, private scholarships, and the school's own gift aid. *Loan aid offered:* FFEL Subsidized Stafford, FFEL Unsubsidized Stafford, FFEL PLUS, Federal Perkins, Federal Nursing, and college/university loans from institutional funds. Institutional employment available. Federal Work-Study Program available. Applicants will be notified of awards on a rolling basis beginning on or about March 15. Off-campus job opportunities are excellent.

## FROM THE ADMISSIONS OFFICE

"The University of Vermont blends the close faculty-student relationships most commonly found in a small liberal arts college with the dynamic exchange of knowledge associated with a research university. This is not surprising because UVM is both. A comprehensive research university offering nearly 100 undergraduate majors and extensive offerings through its Graduate College and College of Medicine, UVM has chosen to keep its enrollment relatively small. UVM prides itself on the richness of its undergraduate experience. Distinguished senior faculty teach introductory courses in their fields. They also advise not only juniors and seniors, but also first- and second-year students, and work collaboratively with undergraduates on research initiatives. Students find extensive opportunities to test classroom knowledge in field through practicums, academic internships, and community service. More than 90 student organizations (involving 80 percent of the student body), 26 Division I varsity teams, 18 intercollegiate club and 24 intramural sports programs, and a packed schedule of cultural events fill in where the classroom leaves off."

## ADMISSIONS

| | |
|---|---|
| Admissions Rating | 76 |
| # of applicants | 7,891 |
| % of applicants accepted | 80 |
| % of acceptees attending | 28 |
| # accepting a place on wait list | 254 |
| % admitted from wait list | 17 |
| # of early decision applicants | 205 |
| % accepted early decision | 84 |

### FRESHMAN PROFILE

| | |
|---|---|
| Range SAT Verbal | 520-610 |
| Average SAT Verbal | 565 |
| Range SAT Math | 520-620 |
| Average SAT Math | 570 |
| Range ACT Composite | 21-26 |
| Average ACT Composite | 24 |
| Minimum TOEFL | 550 |
| % graduated top 10% of class | 18 |
| % graduated top 25% of class | 49 |
| % graduated top 50% of class | 87 |

### DEADLINES

| | |
|---|---|
| Early decision | 11/1 |
| Early decision notification | 12/15 |
| Regular admission | 1/15 |
| Regular notification | 3/31 |
| Nonfall registration? | yes |

### APPLICANTS ALSO LOOK AT

**AND OFTEN PREFER**
Dartmouth
U. Colorado—Boulder
Cornell U.
Middlebury, Brown
**AND SOMETIMES PREFER**
Binghamton U.
Boston Coll., Boston U., Tufts, Colby
**AND RARELY PREFER**
Bates, U. Rochester
Skidmore, U. Conn

### FINANCIAL FACTS

| | |
|---|---|
| Financial Aid Rating | 74 |
| In-state tuition | $7,692 |
| Out-of-state tuition | $19,236 |
| Room & board | $5,806 |
| Books and supplies | $647 |
| Required fees | $596 |
| % frosh receiving aid | 53 |
| % undergrads receiving aid | 50 |
| Avg frosh grant | $6,791 |
| Avg frosh loan | $4,442 |

# UNIVERSITY OF VIRGINIA

OFFICE OF ADMISSION, PO BOX 9017, CHARLOTTESVILLE, VA 22906 • ADMISSIONS: 804-982-3200 • FAX: 804-924-3587

## CAMPUS LIFE

**Quality of Life Rating** **87**
Type of school                     public
Affiliation                          none
Environment                      suburban

### STUDENTS
| | |
|---|---|
| Total undergrad enrollment | 13,712 |
| % male/female | 46/54 |
| % from out of state | 30 |
| % from public high school | 71 |
| % live on campus | 48 |
| % in (# of) fraternities | 30 (32) |
| % in (# of) sororities | 30 (22) |
| % African American | 10 |
| % Asian | 11 |
| % Caucasian | 74 |
| % Hispanic | 2 |
| % international | 4 |
| # of countries represented | 106 |

### SURVEY SAYS . . .
*Beautiful campus*
*Athletic facilities are great*
*Great library*
*Great off-campus food*
*Campus easy to get around*
*Ethnic diversity on campus*
*Student publications are ignored*
*Students aren't religious*
*(Almost) no one listens to college radio*
*Students don't get along with local community*

## ACADEMICS

**Academic Rating** **90**
Calendar                        semester
Student/faculty ratio               15:1
Profs interesting rating              73
Profs accessible rating               94
% classes taught by TAs               18
Avg lab size          10-19 students
Avg reg class size    10-19 students

### MOST POPULAR MAJORS
commerce
English
psychology

## STUDENTS SPEAK OUT
### Academics

Why come to the University of Virginia? "The University of Virginia is the finest, most prestigious public school in the nation. I love the faculty, the students, and the tradition," sums up one student, neatly encapsulating the qualities that draw numerous out-of-state undergrads to the venerable institution founded by Thomas Jefferson. English, commerce, religious studies, history, and government are UVA's best-known departments, but serious study in nearly all disciplines is possible here. Of their blue-chip programs, students brag that the "School of Commerce offers the best technology, course offerings, classroom setting, student/faculty interaction, challenge, and reputation," but warn that "the College of Arts and Sciences—especially the math department—likes to employ non-English-speaking professors." Throughout its various departments and schools, UVA strives to keep class sizes as small as possible; reports one American studies major, "For a large university, small classes are unusually common. the majority of my classes have about 15 people in them." Administrative tasks here are surprisingly uncomplicated, leading one student to note that "UVA makes everything—besides the academics—so easy." Students save their highest praise, though, for the faculty: "From resident ex-hippies to former ministers, the UVA faculty has an unusually large range of life experiences to bring to the classroom." Professors here "are enthusiastic. Faculty and students alike are eager to engage in discussion, creating a genuine community and an atmosphere that encourages learning." Furthermore, "professors here don't just teach us the material. They get us excited about the course, and each one seems to try to get us to major in their subject."

### Life

Students love the "great mix of academics and social life here," and as one student claims, "Everyone at UVA, even those with 4.0 GPAs, goes out on weekends." This campus of over 10,000 supports a diverse social scene that includes "movies, plays, football and basketball games," and "lots of clubs—ethnic, athletic, volunteer/service, and musical." The Greeks play a large part in many UVA social orbits, and accordingly, "the Greek scene can be a bit overwhelming when you first get to school. Still, if you know where to look, there are a lot of activities for everyone." Students are split on hometown Charlottesville. Representing the town's proponents, one student tells us that "Charlottesville is a great town. I try to get off-campus as much as I can. There is usually something going on at the university—plays, concerts, sports—but it's nice to get away once in a while." Detractors counter that "Charlottesville isn't exactly the place Alicia Bridges had in mind when she sang 'I love the nightlife,' but we make our own fun here. Fraternity parties and house parties happen every weekend. Plus, there are plenty of cool discount theaters and restaurants here. Richmond isn't far either. If you have a car, life is grand!" If you don't, at least you'll be stuck on one of the nation's loveliest campuses.

### Student Body

UVA undergrads love almost everything about their school, but they see their classmates as the university's potential Achilles' heel. "It's a pretty homogeneous group and rather apathetic," writes one student. Despite a large minority population, "black and white students are somewhat segregated," leading students to give UVA low marks for diversity and overall integration. "The upper-crust southern attitude doesn't help diversity here," observes one student, while others blame cultural organizations like minority support groups and fraternities for the divided population. On other fronts, respondents complain that "the Greek scene is too popular among students here. It tells you something about them." Others warn that "this is the land of the overachievers. Talk about competition—people are friendly, but you have to watch your back." Sheesh! Do these folks have anything nice to say about each other? "The most important thing is that if you are willing to take some time and explain things, usually people will be intelligent and understand," offers one student.

# UNIVERSITY OF VIRGINIA

FINANCIAL AID: 804-982-6000 • E-MAIL: UNDERGRAD-ADMISSION@VIRGINIA.EDU • WEBSITE: WWW.VIRGINIA.EDU

## ADMISSIONS

*Very important* academic and nonacademic factors considered by the admissions committee include secondary school record, alumni/ae relation, state residency, minority status. *Important* factors considered include class rank, recommendation(s), standardized test scores, essay, extracurricular activities, talent/ability, and character/personal qualities. *Other* factors considered include geographical residence, volunteer work, and work experience. Factors *not* considered include religious affiliations/commitment and interview. SAT I or ACT required, SAT I preferred; SAT II also required. TOEFL required of all international applicants. High school diploma is required and GED is accepted. *High school units required/recommended:* 12 total required; 18 total recommended; 4 English required, 4 math required, 2 science required, 2 science lab required, 2 foreign language recommended, 2 social studies required, 1 history required.

### The Inside Word

Even many Virginia residents regard trying to get into UVA as a feeble attempt. The competition doesn't get much more severe, and only the most capable and impressive candidates stand to be offered admission. The volume of out-of-state applications borders on enormous when considered in conjunction with available spots in the entering class.

## FINANCIAL AID

*Students should submit:* FAFSA and institution's own financial aid form. The Princeton Review suggests that all financial aid forms be submitted as soon as possible after January 1. *Need-based scholarships/grants offered:* Pell, SEOG, state scholarships/grants, private scholarships, and the school's own gift aid. *Loan aid offered:* Direct Subsidized Stafford, Direct Unsubsidized Stafford, Direct PLUS, Federal Perkins, Federal Nursing, and college/university loans from institutional funds. Institutional employment available. Federal Work-Study Program available. Applicants will be notified of awards on or about April 5. Off-campus job opportunities are fair.

## FROM THE ADMISSIONS OFFICE

"Admission to competitive schools requires strong academic credentials. Students who stretch themselves and take rigorous courses (honors level and Advanced Placement courses, when offered) are significantly more competitive than those who do not. Experienced admission officers know that most students are capable of presenting superb academic credentials, and the reality is that a very high percentage of those applying do so. Other considerations, then, come into play in important ways for academically strong candidates, as they must be seen as 'selective' as well as academically competitive."

## ADMISSIONS

| | |
|---|---|
| **Admissions Rating** | **94** |
| # of applicants | 14,145 |
| % of applicants accepted | 39 |
| % of acceptees attending | 53 |
| # accepting place on wait list | 1,201 |
| % admitted from wait list | 9 |
| # of early decision applicants | 1847 |
| % accepted early decision | 46 |

### FRESHMAN PROFILE

| | |
|---|---|
| Range SAT Verbal | 590-700 |
| Average SAT Verbal | 643 |
| Range SAT Math | 610-710 |
| Average SAT Math | 661 |
| Range ACT Composite | 25-31 |
| Average ACT Composite | 28 |
| Minimum TOEFL | 550 |
| Average HS GPA | 4.0 |
| % graduated top 10% of class | 83 |
| % graduated top 25% of class | 96 |
| % graduated top 50% of class | 99 |

### DEADLINES

| | |
|---|---|
| Early decision | 11/1 |
| Early decision notification | 12/1 |
| Regular admission | 1/2 |
| Regular notification | 4/1 |

### APPLICANTS ALSO LOOK AT
**AND OFTEN PREFER**
Duke
Georgetown U.
**AND SOMETIMES PREFER**
William and Mary
UNC—Chapel Hill
Virginia Tech
**AND RARELY PREFER**
George Washington
Bucknell
Boston U.

### FINANCIAL FACTS

| | |
|---|---|
| **Financial Aid Rating** | **78** |
| In-state tuition | $3,046 |
| Out-of-state tuition | $16,295 |
| Room & board | $4,767 |
| Books and supplies | $800 |
| Required fees | $1,114 |
| % frosh receiving aid | 23 |
| % undergrads receiving aid | 24 |

# UNIVERSITY OF WASHINGTON

1410 NE Campus Parkway, 320 Schmitz Box 355840, Seattle, WA 98195-5840 • Admissions: 206-543-9686 • Fax: 206-685-3655

## CAMPUS LIFE

| Quality of Life Rating | 85 |
|---|---|
| Type of school | public |
| Affiliation | none |
| Environment | urban |

### STUDENTS

| | |
|---|---|
| Total undergrad enrollment | 25,638 |
| % male/female | 48/52 |
| % from out of state | 11 |
| % live on campus | 17 |
| % in (# of) fraternities | 12 (30) |
| % in (# of) sororities | 11 (18) |
| % African American | 3 |
| % Asian | 23 |
| % Caucasian | 57 |
| % Hispanic | 4 |
| % Native American | 1 |
| % international | 2 |

### SURVEY SAYS . . .

*Students love Seattle, WA*
*Everyone loves the Huskies*
*Theater is hot*
*Class discussions are rare*
*Great off-campus food*
*Large classes*
*Dorms are like dungeons*
*Ethnic diversity on campus*
*Lots of TAs teach upper-level courses*
*Campus difficult to get around*

## ACACDEMICS

| Academic Rating | 77 |
|---|---|
| Calendar | quarter |
| Student/faculty ratio | 11:1 |
| Profs interesting rating | 88 |
| Profs accessible rating | 88 |
| Avg lab size | 20-29 students |
| Avg reg class size | 20-29 students |

### MOST POPULAR MAJORS

business administration
psychology
English

## STUDENTS SPEAK OUT

### Academics

With 17 colleges and over 3,000 professors, the University of Washington offers a mind-boggling array of opportunities to the right type of student. That student must be "self-sufficient and self-motivated in order to get anything done." Students agree that UW (U-dub to the locals) is most overwhelming when they first arrive. Writes one, "The school experience is like navigating through a small country, but once you have a department, you get to see the same people more often." Agrees another, "The higher the level of the class, the more fun I have." As at many large, research-oriented schools, "most professors are not very effective teachers. Students tend to learn more in quiz sections with TAs." Also typical of a large state school, "the school's administration isn't very friendly or helpful." While the school has made efforts to personalize undergraduate education—notably by creating small-class freshmen seminars—our survey shows that the variety of options, opportunities to help with cutting-edge research, and low tuition are the main reasons students choose, and remain happy with UW.

### Life

About the only social quandary for most Washington undergrads concerns whether to take advantage of the many opportunities on campus or to head for another section of Seattle, one of the hippest cities in the United States. Explains one student, "There is always something to do at UW. On campus we offer movie screenings, bowling, game rooms, theatrical performances, musical performances, and athletics. Off campus, Seattle offers anything you could dream of." Another adds, "You can go out for coffee; shop on 'the Avenue'; go to U-Village; go downtown to Westlake Mall or Pacific Place; hang out at friends' houses/rooms; get ice cream at Marbletop; go to Husky football games. That's just the start of it." The area surrounding campus, known as the U-district, "is a little city within the city, with beautiful shops nearby. The school offers plenty of opportunities for sports, exercise, and hanging with friendly people." Many students enthuse over the school's intercollegiate athletic teams although others complain that "too much is spent on athletics, which I think brings the school down. So do the Greeks. They're everywhere and they're a nightmare." Many of the university's hippy-ish undergrads have been known to twist one off on occasion, but students who aren't so inclined report that "if you don't choose to participate in drinking, drugs, etc., you can find lots of others who don't either. There is so much music, theater, hiking, camping, and good restaurants in the Seattle area. It's wonderful." Overall, students are pleased to report that "life here is very laid back. People do whatever they want to do. There is a lot of hanging out in places such as the dorms or in front of libraries."

### Student Body

UW students warn, "In such a big school, people are not as friendly as in a smaller school. Also, many people live off campus and commute." Although "people generally leave you alone, if you want to meet people all you have to do is make the first move. People are generally receptive to that." The university community tends to segregate itself into smaller microcosms. Many of these smaller groups, be they classes, clubs, or cliques, tend to focus their energy inward, which may explain why many respondents mention a lack of school spirit. One student warns us: "There's too much rain here, and it's all the school's fault."

FINANCIAL AID: 206-543-6101 • E-MAIL: ASKUWADM@U.WASHINGTON.EDU • WEBSITE: WWW.WASHINGTON.EDU

## ADMISSIONS

*Very important* academic and nonacademic factors considered by the admissions committee include secondary school record and standardized test scores. *Important* factors considered include character/personal qualities, and recommendations. *Other* factors considered include alumni/ae relation, class rank, extracurricular activities, interview, talent/ability, volunteer work and work experience. Factors *not* considered include geography, religious affiliation/commitment, and state residency. SAT I or ACT required. *High school units required/recommended:* 20 total recommended; 4 English recommended, 4 math recommended, 4 science recommended, 4 foreign language recommended.

### The Inside Word

Admission at UW follows a fairly strict formula that factors the student's combined SAT I or composite ACT scores with GPA to arrive at an admission index (AI). The minimum "AI" changes annually depending on the strength of the applicant pool and is significantly higher for out-of-state students. Those who come close to qualifying for admission based on their AI but still fall short may be considered by the Freshman Review Committee, which evaluates grade trends, course selection, rigor of the candidate's high school, and special talents. In any case, solid numbers will do more to get you in than anything else.

## FINANCIAL AID

*Students should submit:* FAFSA. The Princeton Review suggests that all financial aid forms be submitted as soon as possible after January 1. *Need-based scholarships/grants offered:* Pell, SEOG, state scholarships/grants, private scholarships, and the school's own gift aid. *Loan aid offered:* Direct Subsidized Stafford, Direct Unsubsidized Stafford, Direct PLUS, Federal Perkins, and Federal Nursing. Institutional employment available. Federal Work-Study Program available. Applicants will be notified of awards on or about April 1. Off-campus job opportunities are good.

## FROM THE ADMISSIONS OFFICE

"Undergraduates benefit in special ways by learning from professors who are at the forefront of generating new knowledge."

## ADMISSIONS

| | |
|---|---|
| Admissions Rating | 81 |
| # of applicants | 12,785 |
| % of applicants accepted | 77 |

### FRESHMAN PROFILE

| | |
|---|---|
| Range SAT Verbal | 510-630 |
| Range SAT Math | 530-650 |
| Range ACT Composite | 22-27 |
| Minimum TOEFL | 500 |
| Average HS GPA | 3.6 |
| % graduated top 10% of class | 39 |
| % graduated top 25% of class | 76 |
| % graduated top 50% of class | 97 |

### DEADLINES

| | |
|---|---|
| Regular admission | 1/15 |
| Nonfall registration? | yes |

### APPLICANTS ALSO LOOK AT

**AND OFTEN PREFER**
Washington State
Western Washington
U. Oregon

**AND SOMETIMES PREFER**
U. Puget Sound
UC—Berkeley
UCLA
Stanford

**AND RARELY PREFER**
U. Colorado—Boulder
Central Washington
U. Southern Cal

## FINANCIAL FACTS

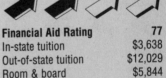

| | |
|---|---|
| Financial Aid Rating | 77 |
| In-state tuition | $3,638 |
| Out-of-state tuition | $12,029 |
| Room & board | $5,844 |
| Books and supplies | $777 |
| % frosh receiving aid | 34 |
| % undergrads receiving aid | 38 |
| Avg frosh loan | $3,376 |

# UNIVERSITY OF WISCONSIN—MADISON

140 PETENSON OFFICE BUILDING, 750 UNIVERSITY AVE., MADISON, WI 53706 • ADMISSIONS: 608-262-3961 • FAX: 608-262-1429

## CAMPUS LIFE

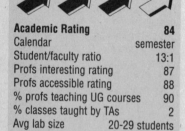

**Quality of Life Rating**    **84**
Type of school    public
Affiliation    none
Environment    urban

### STUDENTS
Total undergrad enrollment    29,336
% male/female    47/53
% from out of state    31
% from public high school    70
% live on campus    24
% in (# of) fraternities    10 (27)
% in (# of) sororities    8 (13)
% African American    2
% Asian    4
% Caucasian    90
% Hispanic    2
% Native American    1
% international    4
# of countries represented    101

### SURVEY SAYS . . .
*Hard liquor is popular*
*Lots of beer drinking*
*Great library*
*Student publications are popular*
*Everyone loves Madison,WI*
*Campus difficult to get around*
*Students are cliquish*
*(Almost) no one listens to college radio*
*Student publications are ignored*
*Everyone loves the Badgers*

## ACADEMICS

**Academic Rating**    **84**
Calendar    semester
Student/faculty ratio    13:1
Profs interesting rating    87
Profs accessible rating    88
% profs teaching UG courses    90
% classes taught by TAs    2
Avg lab size    20-29 students
Avg reg class size    10-19 students

### MOST POPULAR MAJORS
psychology
political science

## STUDENTS SPEAK OUT
### Academics
"Academics can hardly get better for this price!" agree most undergraduates at the University of Wisconsin–Madison, a school that is among the handful of elite state undergraduate programs in the country. College counselors, academics, and perhaps most importantly, employers concur that in business, engineering, pre-medical sciences, journalism, education, and the social sciences, a Madison diploma truly opens doors. Notes one student approvingly, "There are more resources available than I could possibly handle. You can be a number at this school, but if you want to you can also have an impact." Those looking for personal attention and constant guidance, however, might find the school lacking in those areas. "Because this is a research university," writes one student, "some professors spend too little time on students." Others are quick to point out, however, that things improve after one's freshman and sophomore years. Writes one upperclassman, "At the upper levels, I have actually had to go to classes, as classes either take attendance or are small enough that my absence will be noticed." Administrative tasks require tenacity because "this is the 'red tape' school." Advises one student, "The administration can either be your best friend or your worst nightmare. It largely depends on what connections you can forge for yourself and how you use them." All in all, students deal with the bureaucracy as best they can because "the overall experience at UW is incomparable due to its exceptional mix of academic, social, and recreational spheres."

### Life
Madison undergrads report an active, but not overwhelming, party scene on campus. Writes one, "Yes, people party at Madison. There are some that do nothing but, and some who never do. Most, however, find a balance between parties and the thriving cultural scene Madison offers, whether it's Bob Dylan at the Orpheum or an artsy fartsy movie somewhere. The greatest thing about Madison is that whatever you're interested in, someone else is, too." Agrees another, "Although Madison is seen as a party scene, there are many other alternatives that are so much more fun: sliding down [snow covered] hills on lunch trays, running on Lake Shore path, walking down State Street, etc." Students love their hometown, "a great place with so much to do. Everyone finds something." Student life centers on State Street, which "has many restaurants and shops to choose from and offers many job opportunities for students." For a small midwestern city, Madison is truly an oasis of culture. Despite the proximity of the city center, however, most students agree that "you need a car" here. Those who are campus-bound may avail themselves of over 800 campus organizations that sponsor numerous extracurricular events, as well as a plenitude of academic conferences and guest lecturers. Students enjoy Wisconsin—Madison's Big 10 sports teams, especially "Badger hockey and football."

### Student Body
Because of its national prestige, UW—Madison draws a much larger out-of-state population than do most state universities. Still, the predominant feel of the campus is, like its home state, "white and rural." Some students report that "there is great animosity between East Coast students and Wisconsin/Minnesota natives, as well as between fraternity/sorority students and non-Greeks." Others disagree, writing that "students here are all friendly enough in the summer and fall. But come winter, their faces are too frozen to say 'Hello.'" Madison is "a very liberal campus," causing some to comment that "every minor thing is protested."

FINANCIAL AID: 608-262-3060 • E-MAIL: ON.WISCONSIN@MAIL.ADMIN.WISC.EDU • WEBSITE: WWW.WISC.EDU

## ADMISSIONS

*Very important* academic and nonacademic factors considered by the admissions committee include class rank and secondary school record. *Important* factors considered include recommendations, standardized test scores, state residency, and talent/ability. *Other* factors considered include alumni/ae relation, character/personal qualities, essays, extracurricular activities, interview, minority status, volunteer work, and work experience. Factors *not* considered include geography and religious affiliation/commitment. SAT I or ACT required. TOEFL required of all international applicants. High school diploma is required and GED is accepted. *High school units required/recommended:* 12 total recommended; 4 English recommended, 2 math recommended, 2 science recommended, 2 foreign language recommended, 2 social studies recommended.

### The Inside Word

Wisconsin has high expectations of its candidates and virtually all of them relate to numbers. Though not at the top tier of selectivity, this is admissions by formula at its most refined state. Nonresidents will encounter a very selective process.

## FINANCIAL AID

*Students should submit:* FAFSA and institution's own financial aid form. There is no regular filing deadline. The Princeton Review suggests that all financial aid forms be submitted as soon as possible after January 1. *Need-based scholarships/grants offered:* Pell, SEOG, state scholarships/grants, private scholarships, and the school's own gift aid. *Loan aid offered:* FFEL Subsidized Stafford, FFEL Unsubsidized Stafford, FFEL PLUS, Federal Perkins, Federal Nursing, state and college/university loans from institutional funds. Institutional employment available. Federal Work-Study Program available. Applicants will be notified of awards on a rolling basis beginning on or about April 1. Off-campus job opportunities are excellent.

## FROM THE ADMISSIONS OFFICE

"Admission decisions of quality and fairness take time. We don't promise to be the fastest out of the box, but we do guarantee a complete, fair, and thorough decision. We want applicants to provide us with as much information about themselves as they think is necessary for a group of people who don't know them to reach a favorable decision."

## ADMISSIONS

| | |
|---|---|
| Admissions Rating | 90 |
| # of applicants | 17,727 |
| % of applicants accepted | 72 |
| % of acceptees attending | 44 |

### FRESHMAN PROFILE

| | |
|---|---|
| Range SAT Verbal | 550-660 |
| Average SAT Verbal | 611 |
| Range SAT Math | 590-690 |
| Average SAT Math | 638 |
| Range ACT Composite | 25-29 |
| Minimum TOEFL | 550 |
| Average HS GPA | 3.6 |
| % graduated top 10% of class | 48 |
| % graduated top 25% of class | 90 |
| % graduated top 50% of class | 99 |

### DEADLINES

| | |
|---|---|
| Regular admission | 2/1 |
| Nonfall registration? | yes |

### APPLICANTS ALSO LOOK AT

**AND OFTEN PREFER**
Northwestern U.
Miami U.
UC—Berkeley
U. Texas—Austin

**AND SOMETIMES PREFER**
U. Michigan—Ann Arbor
U. Minnesota—Twin Cities
Marquette
Indiana U.—Bloomington

**AND RARELY PREFER**
U. Missouri—Rolla

### FINANCIAL FACTS

| | |
|---|---|
| Financial Aid Rating | 74 |
| In-state tuition | $3,650 |
| Out-of-state tuition | $12,400 |
| Room & board | $5,250 |
| Books and supplies | $660 |
| % frosh receiving aid | 29 |
| % undergrads receiving aid | 31 |
| Avg frosh grant | $2,891 |
| Avg frosh loan | $4,374 |

# UNIVERSITY OF WYOMING

ADMISSIONS OFFICE, PO BOX 3435, LARAMIE, WY 82071 • ADMISSIONS: 307-766-5160 • FAX: 307-766-4042

## CAMPUS LIFE

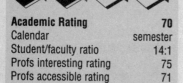

**Quality of Life Rating**    **75**
Type of school    public
Affiliation    none
Environment    rural

### STUDENTS
| | |
|---|---|
| Total undergrad enrollment | 8,490 |
| % male/female | 47/53 |
| % from out of state | 26 |
| % live on campus | 26 |
| % in (# of) fraternities | 9 (9) |
| % in (# of) sororities | 6 (4) |
| % African American | 1 |
| % Asian | 1 |
| % Caucasian | 86 |
| % Hispanic | 4 |
| % Native American | 1 |
| % international | 1 |

### SURVEY SAYS . . .
*Theater is hot*
*Everyone loves the Cowboys*
*Diversity lacking on campus*
*(Almost) everyone plays intramural sports*
*Students get along with local community*
*Lab facilities are great*

## ACADEMICS

**Academic Rating**    **70**
| | |
|---|---|
| Calendar | semester |
| Student/faculty ratio | 14:1 |
| Profs interesting rating | 75 |
| Profs accessible rating | 71 |
| % profs teaching UG courses | 97 |
| % classes taught by TAs | 9 |
| Avg lab size | 20-29 students |
| Avg reg class size | 20-29 students |

### MOST POPULAR MAJORS
elementary education
psychology
business administration

## STUDENTS SPEAK OUT
### Academics
"The key word to describe the University of Wyoming is value," declares a finance major on this "isolated" campus. "Here you can receive an excellent education at an affordable price." UW also offers "great" financial aid, a "small school atmosphere," and a veritable "training ground for future leaders and outstanding people." Upper class students enjoy "small classes" (though some of the actual classrooms "are dumps") and "great opportunities" to gain "hands-on experience" in "well-equipped" research labs. Campus technology and the unique Honors Program are also reportedly "excellent." On the downside, introductory classes can be pretty large, and the "library is pathetic." Wyoming's "very dedicated" and "well-educated" faculty is "easy to contact and similarly easy to talk to when there is a problem," according to a sophomore. "It's easy to build great friendships and working relationships" with profs in each of UW's six colleges. The "nonthreatening" administration "has made an outstanding effort in recent years to provide better access to student services" and to improve registration and records. This is not to say, however, that UW does not have its share of "red tape and paperwork." Elementary education, psychology, and social work are a few of UW's most popular majors.

### Life
UW's "pleasant" home of Laramie is "a great small town" that "caters to its college students." It's "large enough to provide culture" but, students admit, "not much." There are "tons of okay bars," especially if country music is your thing. Drinking is prevalent here; one student tells us, "There is nothing to do out here except abuse substances." In addition, there are "few good jobs" available for students in need of extra cash, and "shopping is restricted to K-Mart and Wal-Mart." With a dearth of good concerts as well, it can get "pretty boring." Luckily, "Cheyenne and Fort Collins, Colorado, aren't far away." When students get the itch for serious civilization, it's "about two hours to Denver." On campus, sports are important but not huge, and "there are lots of organizations and clubs to belong to." A few of the dorms "could use a facelift," but overall the dorms are reasonably livable. Whatever deficiencies the residence halls may have are nothing compared to the serious parking problem on campus. Wyoming's big draw is its "mountain setting," the "beautiful country" surrounding the school in every direction, and the Great Outdoors in general. "The sun shines 320 days each year" here, and there are "a lot of trails and ski resorts in the area." This combo makes for a wealth of "fabulous" outdoor activities including "hiking, hunting, fishing," skiing, mountain biking, and "rock climbing."

### Student Body
For most students, UW is "close to home," but in Wyoming that can apparently mean several hours of driving. The students here are a "friendly and socially active bunch," and something in the campus air "makes it conducive for getting along." There is a remotely "cliquish feel" here, but the "open" students at UW are mostly "just a laid back, easygoing group of individuals who don't care where you came from or how much your parents make." There is a "good mix of city and rural kids" but "not a lot of diversity" on campus. "Our institution is located in the 'Equality State,' and I think it does a remarkable job of providing support services for our minority population," asserts a senior. Still, minority recruitment could use some improvement. The students here seem to "lack diverse social experiences." However, students take great pains to note that they "care about each other's well being" especially in light of the murder of gay UW student Matthew Shepard in an off-campus assault that attracted national attention. Generally, however, the university received high marks for its handling of the tragedy. As one sophomore notes, "Although the incident gave our university a bad reputation, it is important to note that it was an isolated incident." As another student told us, "the majority of our students get along well, regardless of their differences."

FINANCIAL AID: 307-766-2116 • E-MAIL: UNDERGRADUATEADMISSION@UWYO.EDU • WEBSITE: WWW.UWYO.EDU

## ADMISSIONS

*Very important* academic and nonacademic factors considered by the admissions committee include character/personal qualities, class rank, essays, recommendations, secondary school record, and standardized test scores. *Important* factors considered include extracurricular activities and talent/ability. *Other* factors considered include alumni/ae relation, geography, minority status, volunteer work, and work experience. Factors *not* considered include interview, religious affiliation/commitment, and state residency. TOEFL required of all international applicants. High school diploma is required and GED is accepted. *High school units required/recommended:* 13 total required; 4 English required, 3 math required, 3 science required, 3 cultural context required.

### The Inside Word

The admissions process at Wyoming is fairly formula-driven. State residents need a minimum 2.75 high school GPA in order to gain admission. Nonresidents have to have a 3.0 GPA. That and some solid test scores will open the door to Laramie.

## FINANCIAL AID

*Students should submit:* FAFSA and institution's own financial aid form. The Princeton Review suggests that all financial aid forms be submitted as soon as possible after January 1. *Need-based scholarships/grants offered:* Pell, SEOG, state scholarships/grants, private scholarships, the school's own gift aid, and Western Undergraduate Exchange. *Loan aid offered:* FFEL Subsidized Stafford, FFEL Unsubsidized Stafford, FFEL PLUS, and Federal Perkins. Institutional employment available. Federal Work-Study Program available. Applicants will be notified of awards on a rolling basis beginning on or about April 1. Off-campus job opportunities are good.

## FROM THE ADMISSIONS OFFICE

"The entire admission staff have analyzed why we love UW and Laramie. We think it primarily boils down to size and location. The University of Wyoming and Laramie are relatively small, affording students the opportunity to get personal attention and develop a close rapport with their professors. They can easily make friends and find peers with similar interests and values. Over 200 student organizations offer students a great way to get involved and encourage growth and learning. Couple the small size with a great location and you have a winning combination. Laramie sits between the Laramie and the Snowy Range Mountains. There are numerous outdoor activities in which one can participate. Furthermore, the university works hard to attract other great cultural events. Major label recording artists come to UW as well as some of today's great minds. In all, the University of Wyoming is a great place to be because of its wonderful blend of a small town atmosphere with 'big city' activities."

### ADMISSIONS

| | |
|---|---|
| Admissions Rating | 75 |
| # of applicants | 2,560 |
| % of applicants accepted | 97 |
| % of acceptees attending | 55 |

### FRESHMAN PROFILE

| | |
|---|---|
| Range SAT Verbal | 480-600 |
| Range SAT Math | 490-620 |
| Range ACT Composite | 20-26 |
| Average ACT Composite | 23 |
| Minimum TOEFL | 525 |
| Average HS GPA | 3.4 |
| % graduated top 10% of class | 23 |
| % graduated top 25% of class | 48 |
| % graduated top 50% of class | 78 |

### DEADLINES

| | |
|---|---|
| Priority admission deadline | 3/1 |
| Regular admission | 8/10 |
| Nonfall registration? | yes |

### FINANCIAL FACTS

| | |
|---|---|
| Financial Aid Rating | 75 |
| In-state tuition | $2,166 |
| Out-of-state tuition | $7,284 |
| Room & board | $4,568 |
| Books and supplies | $680 |
| Required fees | $409 |
| % frosh receiving aid | 46 |
| % undergrads receiving aid | 45 |
| Avg frosh grant | $1,500 |
| Avg frosh loan | $2,250 |

# URSINUS COLLEGE

URSINUS COLLEGE, ADMISSIONS OFFICE, COLLEGEVILLE, PA 19426 • ADMISSIONS: 610-409-3200 • FAX: 610-409-3662

## CAMPUS LIFE

| | |
|---|---|
| **Quality of Life Rating** | **76** |
| Type of school | private |
| Affiliation | United Church of Christ |
| Environment | suburban |

### STUDENTS

| | |
|---|---|
| Total undergrad enrollment | 1,241 |
| % male/female | 47/53 |
| % from out of state | 35 |
| % from public high school | 68 |
| % live on campus | 88 |
| % in (# of) fraternities | 15 (9) |
| % in (# of) sororities | 25 (5) |
| % African American | 8 |
| % Asian | 4 |
| % Caucasian | 86 |
| % Hispanic | 2 |
| % international | 4 |

### SURVEY SAYS . . .

*Frats and sororities dominate social
scene
Popular college radio
Lots of beer drinking
Political activism is (almost)
nonexistent
Library needs improving
Lousy off-campus food
Low cost of living*

## ACADEMICS

| | |
|---|---|
| **Academic Rating** | **81** |
| Calendar | semester |
| Student/faculty ratio | 11:1 |
| Profs interesting rating | 91 |
| Profs accessible rating | 93 |
| % profs teaching UG courses | 100 |
| Avg lab size | 10-19 students |
| Avg reg class size | 10-19 students |

### MOST POPULAR MAJORS
biology
economics/business
English

## STUDENTS SPEAK OUT
### Academics

Ursinus College is a popular choice among pre-medical students in the Philadelphia area, and for good reason: the school has a proven track record of sending graduates to top medical schools. To ensure that students learn more than biology and organic chemistry, Ursinus recently instituted a liberal studies curriculum encompassing English, math, science, and foreign language. Even with these modifications, humanities students warn of their experiences: "I was a little disappointed at the variety of English and history courses, but then I discovered that most of the students here are pre-med. Still, the professors are very friendly and accessible, and the majority of classes are challenging and entertaining." As at many small schools, teaching is the raison d'être for most faculty members here. Says one student, "Professors and their relationships with students are the heart of Ursinus. I have found mine to be thoroughly knowledgeable, always accessible, and deeply concerned about students." Adds another, "The administration, from deans to the president, can constantly be seen on campus. Also, the administration and department heads have 'round table' discussions with groups of students to deal with improving the school." About the only steady complaint we heard was from students with financial aid. A typical undergrad told us: "It seems that the only glitch in the system is how the employees at the bursar's office treat students in financial need. From their stingy and generally uncooperative attitudes, I sometimes get the feeling that I owe them money instead of the school." Otherwise, students happily report that "the close-knit community encourages very personalized treatment of students and close relationships within the campus community."

### Life

With nearly one-fifth of all undergrads pledging, Greek societies exert a strong influence on Ursinus campus life. One student describes the campus as "heavily Greek. But, as a non-Greek, I can say that the students still interact pretty well, and Greek events are open to independents." Another elaborates: "Sororities or fraternities rent buses and invite the entire campus to attend semi-formal 'dated dances.' We dance and drink until midnight; then the buses return to campus and the party goes on! And on!" As at many frat-heavy schools, alcohol control is a big issue among students. "I don't like the fact that the administration is trying to crack down on alcohol. It's safer to have it on campus than to have drunk students driving off campus." Observes another, "This is probably the most apathetic campus I have seen. Nothing in the world matters to these people except alcohol." Students pan hometown Collegeville, but point out that "it is close enough to Philadelphia and King of Prussia for entertainment. Also, there are plenty of activities on campus." Life at Ursinus requires little adjustment for freshmen, at least according to one student, who writes: "I have come to the conclusion that college is the same as high school, except you do your own laundry and food shopping."

### Student Body

Ursinus undergrads appreciate the fact that their classmates "are generally easygoing and easy to get along with. Upperclassmen do a lot to help out first-year students." They are also quick to acknowledge that theirs is a homogeneous population. The school's diminutive size can also pose problems: "One of the advantages of the school's being so small is that you know everyone. One of the disadvantages of the school's being so small is that you know everyone."

FINANCIAL AID: 610-409-3600 • E-MAIL: ADMISSIONS@URSINUS.EDU • WEBSITE: WWW.URSINUS.EDU

## ADMISSIONS

*Very important* academic and nonacademic factors considered by the admissions committee include essays and secondary school record. *Important* factors considered include character/personal qualities, extracurricular activities, standardized test scores, state residency, and talent/ability. *Other* factors considered include class rank, minority status, recommendations, volunteer work, and work experience. Factors *not* considered include alumni/ae relation, geography, interview, and religious affiliation/commitment. TOEFL required of all international applicants. High school diploma is required and GED is accepted. *High school units required/recommended:* 20 total recommended; 4 English recommended, 4 math recommended, 3 science recommended, 2 science lab recommended, 4 foreign language recommended, 3 social studies recommended, 2 history recommended. *The admissions office says:* "Personality, motivation, and activities are considered. Rank in the top fifth of high school graduating class is preferred."

### The Inside Word

The admission process at Ursinus is very straightforward; about 70 percent of those who apply get in. Grades, test scores, and class rank count for more than anything else, and unless you are academically inconsistent, you'll likely get good news.

## FINANCIAL AID

*Students should submit:* FAFSA, institution's own financial aid form, and CSS/Financial Aid PROFILE. Regular filing deadline is February 15. The Princeton Review suggests that all financial aid forms be submitted as soon as possible after January 1. *Need-based scholarships/grants offered:* Pell, SEOG, state scholarships/grants, private scholarships, and the school's own gift aid. *Loan aid offered:* FFEL Subsidized Stafford, FFEL Unsubsidized Stafford, FFEL PLUS, Federal Perkins, and college/university loans from institutional funds. Institutional employment available. Federal Work-Study Program available. Applicants will be notified of awards on or about April 1. Off-campus job opportunities are excellent.

## FROM THE ADMISSIONS OFFICE

"Located one-half hour from center-city Philadelphia, the college boasts a beautiful 140-acre campus that includes the Residential Village (renovated Victorian-style homes that decorate the Main Street and house our students) and the nationally recognized Berman Museum of Art. Ursinus is a member of the Centennial Conference, competing both in academics and in intercollegiate athletics with institutions such as Dickinson, Franklin and Marshall, Gettysburg, and Muhlenberg. The academic environment is enhanced with such fine programs as a chapter of Phi Beta Kappa, an Early Assurance Program to medical school with the Medical College of Pennsylvania, and myriad student exchanges both at home and abroad. A heavy emphasis is placed on student research—an emphasis that can only be carried out with the one-on-one attention Ursinus students receive from their professors."

## ADMISSIONS

| | |
|---|---|
| Admissions Rating | 79 |
| # of applicants | 1,689 |
| % of applicants accepted | 72 |
| % of acceptees attending | 31 |
| # accepting a place on wait list | 13 |
| # of early decision applicants | 103 |
| % accepted early decision | 75 |

### FRESHMAN PROFILE

| | |
|---|---|
| Range SAT Verbal | 540-640 |
| Average SAT Verbal | 595 |
| Range SAT Math | 550-650 |
| Average SAT Math | 600 |
| Minimum TOEFL | 550 |
| Average HS GPA | 3.5 |
| % graduated top 10% of class | 48 |
| % graduated top 25% of class | 79 |
| % graduated top 50% of class | 95 |

### DEADLINES

| | |
|---|---|
| Early decision | 1/15 |
| Early decision notification | 1/31 |
| Regular admission | 2/15 |
| Regular notification | 4/1 |
| Nonfall registration? | yes |

### APPLICANTS ALSO LOOK AT AND OFTEN PREFER

Swarthmore
Princeton
Brown
Haverford
Johns Hopkins

### AND SOMETIMES PREFER

Villanova
Gettysburg
Dickinson
St. Joseph's U.
Franklin & Marshall

### FINANCIAL FACTS

| | |
|---|---|
| Financial Aid Rating | 89 |
| Tuition | $22,420 |
| Room & board | $6,500 |
| Books and supplies | $600 |
| Required fees | $330 |
| % frosh receiving aid | 78 |
| % undergrads receiving aid | 81 |
| Avg frosh grant | $15,249 |
| Avg frosh loan | $2,625 |

# VALPARAISO UNIVERSITY

OFFICE OF ADMISSION, KRETZMANN HALL, VALPARAISO, IN 46383-9978 • ADMISSIONS: 219-464-5011 • FAX: 219-464-6898

## CAMPUS LIFE

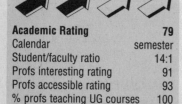

| Quality of Life Rating | **72** |
|---|---|
| Type of school | private |
| Affiliation | Lutheran |
| Environment | rural |

### STUDENTS

| | |
|---|---|
| Total undergrad enrollment | 2,984 |
| % male/female | 46/54 |
| % from out of state | 66 |
| % from public high school | 79 |
| % live on campus | 66 |
| % in (# of) fraternities | 28 (8) |
| % in (# of) sororities | 22 (7) |
| % African American | 3 |
| % Asian | 2 |
| % Caucasian | 89 |
| % Hispanic | 2 |
| % international | 3 |
| # of countries represented | 43 |

### SURVEY SAYS . . .

Frats and sororities dominate social
scene
No one cheats
Musical organizations are hot
Student government is popular
Lots of beer drinking
Library needs improving
Students are cliquish
Students don't like Valparaiso, IN
Very little drug use

## ACACEMICS

| Academic Rating | **79** |
|---|---|
| Calendar | semester |
| Student/faculty ratio | 14:1 |
| Profs interesting rating | 91 |
| Profs accessible rating | 93 |
| % profs teaching UG courses | 100 |
| Avg lab size | 10-19 students |
| Avg reg class size | 10-19 students |

### MOST POPULAR MAJORS
business
engineering
education

## STUDENTS SPEAK OUT

### Academics

Valparaiso's greatest strength lies in its ability to offer a broad variety of majors across four different colleges (arts and sciences, nursing, business, and engineering) while still managing to provide its students with the flexibility, small classes, and personal attention found at small liberal arts colleges. And while Valparaiso definitely caters to career-oriented students, it provides a well-rounded undergraduate education. Nearly all students must complete core freshman courses and a senior seminar, and fulfill an array of liberal arts requirements before graduating. This best-of-both-worlds approach is a hit with students. As far as they are concerned, Valparaiso is a "first rate" and "very prestigious" university that offers a "fabulous academic experience" and "the best education money can buy." What else is the cause of all this student satisfaction? Well, it certainly isn't the library, which students rate dreadfully low. Instead, and without a doubt, the outstanding and dedicated faculty share the credit. "Our professors are extremely helpful; they are here for the students first and the research second," declares one junior. "The faculty here are downright cool and great motivators," explains a senior. And student after student maintains that profs are "always willing to give extra assistance." Unfortunately, however, this fond embrace of authority does not extend so completely to the administration. Although a few students insist that they do "a magnificent job of accommodating students," the administration is generally perceived as "out of touch" and reactionary.

### Life

The Greek system dominates life outside the classroom at Valparaiso University. About one quarter of the students pledge a fraternity or sorority. Indeed, for better or for worse, most students tend to agree that "socially, Greek life is all there is." Strict drug, alcohol, and intervisitation policies, and "lame" campus-sponsored activities don't help matters much. According to one student, "There is nothing to do if you are under 21 unless you go to frat parties." Another confesses, "We go to the frats to have beer." Students who don't enjoy the fraternity scene still keep themselves entertained, though. "Life at Valpo is what you make it. If you want to get involved, you can!" Religious organizations and student government provide two of the most popular extracurricular alternatives. Geographically, the Valparaiso campus receives high marks for safety and ease of navigation. The surrounding town of Valparaiso offers bars, shopping, and "many tasty restaurants." However, as many students are quick to point out, that's about all it offers. Life in rural Indiana can get "boring on the weekends." Several students also complain about the weather, but none of them seem to be doing anything about it. Luckily, the bright lights of Chicago are only about an hour away by car.

### Student Body

Valparaiso is comprised of a "huge majority of Anglo students," most of whom know each other. In general, "a strong sense of community" permeates campus life. The majority of Valpo students are "turtleneck-wearing conservatives." The university is affiliated with the Lutheran church, and religion maintains a noticeable (though by no means predominant) presence on campus. Dating and sexual activity are popular pastimes with the student population. Still, many complain about being inhibited by the overall social atmosphere. As one student so aptly sums up, "Students are too reserved. They need to loosen up. Toga! Toga! Toga!"

# VALPARAISO UNIVERSITY

FINANCIAL AID: 219-464-5015 • E-MAIL: UNDERGRAD.ADMISSIONS@VALPO.EDU • WEBSITE: WWW.VALPO.EDU

## ADMISSIONS

*Very important* academic and nonacademic factors considered by the admissions committee include secondary school record. *Important* factors considered include class rank, extracurricular activities, standardized test scores, and talent/ability. *Other* factors considered include alumni/ae relation, character/personal qualities, essays, interview, minority status, recommendations, and volunteer work. Factors *not* considered include geography, religious affiliation/commitment, state residency, and work experience. SAT I or ACT required. TOEFL required of all international applicants. High school diploma is required and GED is accepted. *High school units required/recommended:* 16 total required; 4 English required, 3 math required, 3 science required, 2 foreign language required, 2 social studies required.

### The Inside Word

Valparaiso admits the vast majority of those who apply, but candidates should not be overconfident. Places like this fill a special niche in higher education and spend a good deal of time assessing the match a candidate makes with the university, even if the expected better-than-average high school record is present. Essays and extracurriculars can help you get admitted if your transcript is weak.

## FINANCIAL AID

*Students should submit:* FAFSA. The Princeton Review suggests that all financial aid forms be submitted as soon as possible after January 1. *Need-based scholarships/grants offered:* Pell, SEOG, state scholarships/grants, private scholarships, and the school's own gift aid. *Loan aid offered:* Direct Subsidized Stafford, Direct Unsubsidized Stafford, Direct PLUS, Federal Perkins, and college/university loans from institutional funds. Institutional employment available. Federal Work-Study Program available. Applicants will be notified of awards on a rolling basis beginning on or about March 1. Off-campus job opportunities are good.

## FROM THE ADMISSIONS OFFICE

"Valpo provides students a blend of academic excellence, social experience, and spiritual exploration. The concern demonstrated by faculty and administration for the total well-being of students reflects a long history as a Lutheran-affiliated university."

## ADMISSIONS

| | |
|---|---|
| Admissions Rating | 79 |
| # of applicants | 3,864 |
| % of applicants accepted | 81 |
| % of acceptees attending | 24 |

### FRESHMAN PROFILE

| | |
|---|---|
| Range SAT Verbal | 540-650 |
| Average SAT Verbal | 598 |
| Range SAT Math | 530-670 |
| Average SAT Math | 600 |
| Range ACT Composite | 24-30 |
| Average ACT Composite | 27 |
| Minimum TOEFL | 550 |
| % graduated top 10% of class | 43 |
| % graduated top 25% of class | 73 |
| % graduated top 50% of class | 93 |

### DEADLINES

| | |
|---|---|
| Priority admission deadline | 1/15 |
| Nonfall registration? | yes |

### APPLICANTS ALSO LOOK AT
#### AND OFTEN PREFER
Indiana U.—Bloomington
Purdue U.—West Lafayette
U. Illinois—Urbana-Champaign
#### AND SOMETIMES PREFER
Marquette
Bradley
Augustana (IL)
Hope
Butler

## FINANCIAL FACTS

| | |
|---|---|
| Financial Aid Rating | 78 |
| Tuition | $17,100 |
| Room & board | $4,660 |
| Books and supplies | $600 |
| Required fees | $536 |
| % frosh receiving aid | 64 |
| % undergrads receiving aid | 64 |
| Avg frosh grant | $9,376 |
| Avg frosh loan | $4,104 |

# VANDERBILT UNIVERSITY

2305 WEST END AVENUE, NASHVILLE, TN 37203 • ADMISSIONS: 615-322-2561 • FAX: 615-343-7765

## CAMPUS LIFE

**Quality of Life Rating**    87
Type of school    private
Affiliation    none
Environment    urban

### STUDENTS

| | |
|---|---|
| Total undergrad enrollment | 5,935 |
| % male/female | 47/53 |
| % from out of state | 81 |
| % from public high school | 60 |
| % live on campus | 84 |
| % in (# of) fraternities | 34 (19) |
| % in (# of) sororities | 50 (12) |
| % African American | 5 |
| % Asian | 6 |
| % Caucasian | 79 |
| % Hispanic | 3 |
| % international | 3 |

### SURVEY SAYS . . .

Frats and sororities dominate social scene
Diversity lacking on campus
Athletic facilities are great
Students are cliquish
Registration is a breeze
Political activism is (almost) nonexistent

## ACACEMICS

**Academic Rating**    91
| | |
|---|---|
| Calendar | semester |
| Student/faculty ratio | 9:1 |
| Profs interesting rating | 90 |
| Profs accessible rating | 93 |
| Avg lab size | 10-19 students |
| Avg reg class size | 10-19 students |

### MOST POPULAR MAJORS

social science, general
engineering
psychology

## STUDENTS SPEAK OUT

### Academics

Smack in the middle of one of the nation's fastest growing regions, venerable Vanderbilt University gives students a taste of both the New and Old South. The school offers "academics on a par with any Ivy League school," which provide a major toehold in the area's high-tech economy. And all in a genteel setting. "There is a sense of academic excellence here," writes one undergraduate, "but without the cutthroat competition." A broad and comprehensive core curriculum covers writing, humanities, mathematics, and natural and social sciences. The "grading standards are stringent," and there is definitely an "adherence to traditional values" at Vandy. There is also an honor code, which students say it is best not to trifle with. Many of the professors here are "outstanding" and "excited about teaching," especially in the liberal arts and sciences. These professors are "so helpful and interested in the students that it's almost overwhelming." Others don't quite rise to their peers' level; reports one student, "The teaching abilities vary widely, from mumbling lecturers to educational gods." The "capable" administration "does a really good job running the university." Student opinion of the administration has improved with the arrival of a new chancellor, who "has made an incredible effort to make the administration open to discussion with students."

### Life

Most undergrads agree that the Greeks dominate the Vandy campus, reporting that "Vanderbilt students' social lives revolve around the Greek system, from football games to week and weekend nights." The Greeks are also active in extracurriculars, "providing ways to get involved in campus and in the Nashville community at large." A few students feel that "although Greek life is a big part of the social scene, it isn't the only thing to do" and point out that "there are a lot of organizations for people interested in every aspect of extracurricular life." Undergrads refer to their environment as "the Vanderbubble," a "sheltered and comfortable" place where students "work hard" during the week and "play hard" during the "almost entirely party-oriented" weekends. Besides frat parties, the bars and clubs and "great nightlife" of Nashville are "just five minutes away." A lot "of variety as far as dining and entertainment" awaits students off campus, and, of course, "great concerts" abound. Nashville is "Music City, after all." However, "cabs are expensive," and "you have to have a car to do any of these cool things." On campus, "the Rites of Spring is a big outdoor party on Alumni Lawn with great music" and "tons of fun." In the fall, "dressing up and taking dates to football games is a great tradition at Vandy." Students rave about the recreation center, which is "120,000 square feet of perfection." The most often cited negative: the weather in Nashville. Don't forget to "bring your umbrella."

### Student Body

As students describe it, the Vanderbilt student body comes straight out of a southern debutante ball. "Prestige matters" to these "conservative" adherents to "a cult of southern gentility and graciousness." Some of these ladies and gentlemen "tend to be somewhat snobbish and cliquish" while others are "very friendly." Students add that "you learn pretty quickly that, even though superficially a lot of people look the same, everyone has had very different experiences and come[s] from a different background." Agrees one student, "There are groups of very different students here: sorority girls, jocks, brains, and people who are a mix." The campus is not as racially diverse as many students would like it to be, though the school has come a long way in the past few years.

# VANDERBILT UNIVERSITY

FINANCIAL AID: 615-322-3591 • E-MAIL: ADMISSIONS@VANDERBILT.EDU • WEBSITE: WWW.VANDERBILT.EDU

## ADMISSIONS

*Very important* academic and nonacademic factors considered by the admissions committee include class rank. *Important* factors considered include alumni/ae relation, character/personal qualities, essays, extracurricular activities, recommendations, and secondary school record. *Other* factors considered include standardized test scores and talent/ability. Factors *not* considered include geography, interview, minority status, religious affiliation/commitment, state residency, volunteer work, and work experience. SAT I or ACT required; SAT II recommended. TOEFL required of all international applicants. *High school units required/recommended:* 16 total required; 4 English required, 3 math required, 1 science required, 3 science recommended, 1 science lab required, 2 foreign language required, 1 social studies required, 1 history required, 4 elective required. "For students who apply to the Blair School of Music, an audition is the primary factor in the application. It is recommended that engineering applicants complete 4 years of math and 2 years of science."

### The Inside Word

Vanderbilt's strong academic reputation has positioned the university among the most selective in the South. Despite an admissions process that is largely formulaic, the applicant pool is competitive enough so that students should not downplay the importance of submitting strong essays and recommendations—they make the difference for some candidates.

## FINANCIAL AID

*Students should submit:* FAFSA and CSS/Financial Aid PROFILE. The Princeton Review suggests that all financial aid forms be submitted as soon as possible after January 1. *Need-based scholarships/grants offered:* Pell, SEOG, state scholarships/grants, private scholarships, and the school's own gift aid. *Loan aid offered:* FFEL Subsidized Stafford, FFEL Unsubsidized Stafford, FFEL PLUS, Federal Perkins, Federal Nursing, and college/university loans from institutional funds. Institutional employment available. Federal Work-Study Program available. Applicants will be notified of awards on a rolling basis beginning on or about April 7. Off-campus job opportunities are excellent.

## FROM THE ADMISSIONS OFFICE

"Exceptional accomplishment and high promise in some field of intellectual endeavor are essential. The student's total academic and nonacademic record is reviewed in conjunction with recommendations and personal essays. For students at Blair School of Music, the audition is a prime consideration."

## ADMISSIONS

| | |
|---|---|
| Admissions Rating | 93 |
| # of applicants | 8,886 |
| % of applicants accepted | 55 |
| % of acceptees attending | 34 |
| # accepting a place on wait list | 537 |
| % admitted from wait list | 3 |
| # of early decision applicants | 742 |
| % accepted early decision | 61 |

### FRESHMAN PROFILE

| | |
|---|---|
| Range SAT Verbal | 600-690 |
| Range SAT Math | 620-710 |
| Range ACT Composite | 26-31 |
| Minimum TOEFL | 570 |
| % graduated top 10% of class | 71 |
| % graduated top 25% of class | 94 |
| % graduated top 50% of class | 100 |

### DEADLINES

| | |
|---|---|
| Early decision | 11/1 |
| Early decision notification | 12/15 |
| Regular admission | 1/4 |
| Regular notification | 4/1 |
| Nonfall registration? | yes |

### APPLICANTS ALSO LOOK AT

**AND OFTEN PREFER**
U. Virginia
Princeton
Notre Dame
Cornell U.
Georgetown U.

**AND SOMETIMES PREFER**
Duke, Emory
Wake Forest
Northwestern U.
Dartmouth

**AND RARELY PREFER**
Tulane
Washington U.
Boston Coll.
SMU, Rhodes

## FINANCIAL FACTS

| | |
|---|---|
| Financial Aid Rating | 74 |
| Tuition | $24,080 |
| Room & board | $8,324 |
| Books and supplies | $870 |
| Required fees | $632 |
| % frosh receiving aid | 39 |
| % undergrads receiving aid | 36 |

# VASSAR COLLEGE

124 RAYMOND AVENUE, POUGHKEEPSIE, NY 12604 • ADMISSIONS: 914-437-7300 • FAX: 914-437-7063

## STUDENTS SPEAK OUT

### Academics

A desire for academic freedom is what attracts most students to Vassar College, a small liberal arts school halfway between New York City and Albany. One of the very few elite schools that requires no core curriculum, Vassar allows students tremendous leeway in selecting courses and even in fashioning their own majors. "I enjoy what I learn here, especially because the requirements are pretty loose. They give you a lot of independence," writes one undergraduate. Says another, "The independent program is a viable option for people like me who want to tailor their education to specific needs." Students also appreciate the opportunity to study in depth, thanks both to university-quality research facilities and an excellent faculty. There are "no grad students to monopolize resources, but the school has the resources of a major university," brags one student. Undergrads agree that "the professors at Vassar are more like friends than anything. They get to know the students and want them to succeed. Plus they're everywhere, from class to the dorms to the concerts and soccer games." History and English are two of Vassar's most popular departments; of the latter, one student warns that "The English department is so popular that it's a little overcrowded. They treat you like a number just because there are so many English majors here." Students have mixed feelings about the administration, praising concerned administrators and generous financial aid packages but also complaining about "a lot of red tape."

### Life

Vassar students report a decided upturn in the quality of on-campus recreation since our last survey here. Says one, "We enjoy anything and everything! A weekend here doesn't consist of frat parties. Every weekend is different, whether I go to an a cappella concert, an on-campus movie, an all-campus party, take a day-trip into New York City, go apple picking, chat in Vassar's coffeehouse, or get pizza and hang out with friends. Usually there is too much to do!" Adds another, "There are always plays, concerts, and other events to attend. Sometimes we go to the Mug (a bar/club on campus) or just chill in someone's room. The senior townhouses throw parties every weekend." For the aesthetically inclined, Vassar provides "a thriving artistic community and outlets for all your creative needs," especially for those interested in theater. Students also appreciate the "beautiful campus" and enjoy playing a large role in governing dorm life (although each residence hall also has "house fellows," faculty residents who are an integral part of the residence hall community). Still, overall student contentment with campus life is only middling when compared to other schools in our survey. Students have few kind words for "grim" and "depressing" Poughkeepsie, their blue-collar hometown on the Hudson. Describing town-gown relations, one students points out that "most people hang out on campus because there is nothing to do off campus in the area." They also complain that "this place dies during the winter." Fortunately, New York City is only an hour and a half away by car, so students can hit the city to blow off steam for a night and still make it back in time to bang out that last paper.

### Student Body

By private college standards, Vassar does an excellent job of recruiting a diverse student body. Students expecting a microcosm of the U.S. population, however, are bound to be disappointed; its fine efforts notwithstanding, Vassar is still a very expensive place to study, a fact that can't help but give the student body an upper-class bias. Perhaps this is why many students observe that the school "is most definitely not as diverse as I was led to believe." Vassar students are typically "fascinating, ambitious, and enthusiastic about their intellectual interest. They can also be somewhat self-absorbed, pretentious, and chilly." The student body here is highly politicized, with "a lot of trust-fund socialists" in the mix. Some students warn, however, that "the student body is moving more and more to that backwards-white-hat-frat-boy image. Yuck!"

FINANCIAL AID: 845-437-5320 • E-MAIL: ADMISSIONS@VASSAR.EDU • WEBSITE: WWW.VASSAR.EDU

## ADMISSIONS

*Very important* academic and nonacademic factors considered by the admissions committee include essays, recommendations, secondary school record, and standardized test scores. *Important* factors considered include character/personal qualities, class rank, and extracurricular activities. *Other* factors considered include alumni/ae relation, geography, interview, minority status, state residency, talent/ability, volunteer work, and work experience. Factors *not* considered include religious affiliation/commitment. TOEFL required of all international applicants. High school diploma is required and GED is accepted. *High school units required/recommended:* 16 total recommended; 4 English recommended, 4 math recommended, 2 science recommended, 1 science lab recommended, 3 foreign language recommended, 2 social studies recommended, 2 history recommended, 2 elective recommended. *The admissions office says:* "There are no rigid requirements as to secondary school programs, and patterns vary, but Vassar expects candidates to have elected the most demanding courses available. Ordinarily, the candidate should have had four years of English, including both literature and continuous practice in writing; at least three years of mathematics; at least two years of laboratory science; three years of social science with a minimum of one year of history; and three years of one ancient or modern foreign language or two years of one language and two of a second. Additional work should be elected in fully credited academic subjects in the humanities, the natural and social sciences, and the arts. Students should take some portion of their work in enriched or honors courses or in the Advanced Placement Program where they are available. Special attention is given to the academic content of the program candidates select in the senior year."

### The Inside Word

Vassar is relatively frank about its standards; you won't get much more direct advice from colleges about how to get admitted. The admissions process here follows very closely the practices of most prestigious northeastern schools. Your personal side—essays, extracurriculars, interview, etc.—is not going to do a lot for you if you don't demonstrate significant academic accomplishments. Multiple applicants from the same high school will be compared against each other as well as the entire applicant pool. Males and minorities are actively courted by the admissions staff, and the college is sincere in its commitment.

## FINANCIAL AID

*Students should submit:* FAFSA, institution's own financial aid form, CSS/Financial Aid PROFILE, state aid form, noncustodial (divorced/separated) parent's statement, and business/farm supplement. Regular filing deadline is January 10. The Princeton Review suggests that all financial aid forms be submitted as soon as possible after January 1. *Need-based scholarships/grants offered:* Pell, SEOG, state scholarships/grants, private scholarships, and the school's own gift aid. *Loan aid offered:* FFEL Subsidized Stafford, FFEL Unsubsidized Stafford, FFEL PLUS, Federal Perkins, and college/university loans from institutional funds. Institutional employment available. Federal Work-Study Program available. Applicants will be notified of awards on or about April 3. Off-campus job opportunities are fair.

## FROM THE ADMISSIONS OFFICE

"Vassar presents a rich variety of social and cultural activities, clubs, sports, living arrangements, and regional attractions. Vassar is a vital, residential college community recognized for its respect for the rights and individuality of others."

## ADMISSIONS

| Admissions Rating | 94 |
|---|---|
| # of applicants | 5,595 |
| % of applicants accepted | 35 |
| % of acceptees attending | 33 |
| # accepting a place on wait list | 300 |
| % admitted from wait list | 3 |
| # of early decision applicants | 400 |
| % accepted early decision | 57 |

### FRESHMAN PROFILE

| | |
|---|---|
| Range SAT Verbal | 640-730 |
| Average SAT Verbal | 681 |
| Range SAT Math | 630-700 |
| Average SAT Math | 660 |
| Range ACT Composite | 28-32 |
| Minimum TOEFL | 600 |
| % graduated top 10% of class | 61 |
| % graduated top 25% of class | 90 |
| % graduated top 50% of class | 99 |

### DEADLINES

| | |
|---|---|
| Early decision | 11/15 |
| Early decision notification | 12/15 |
| Regular admission | 1/1 |
| Regular notification | 4/1 |

### APPLICANTS ALSO LOOK AT
**AND OFTEN PREFER**
Wesleyan U.
Brown
**AND SOMETIMES PREFER**
Barnard
Northwestern U.
Columbia
**AND RARELY PREFER**
Skidmore
Union (NY)

## FINANCIAL FACTS

| Financial Aid Rating | 84 |
|---|---|
| Tuition | $24,600 |
| Room & board | $6,940 |
| Books and supplies | $740 |
| Required fees | $330 |
| % frosh receiving aid | 46 |
| % undergrads receiving aid | 56 |
| Avg frosh grant | $17,800 |
| Avg frosh loan | $1,795 |

# VILLANOVA UNIVERSITY

800 LANCASTER AVENUE, VILLANOVA, PA 19085-1672 • ADMISSIONS: 610-519-4000 • FAX: 610-519-6450

## CAMPUS LIFE

| Quality of Life Rating | 89 |
|---|---|
| Type of school | private |
| Affiliation | Roman Catholic |
| Environment | suburban |

### STUDENTS

| | |
|---|---|
| Total undergrad enrollment | 7,023 |
| % male/female | 50/50 |
| % from out of state | 65 |
| % from public high school | 58 |
| % live on campus | 65 |
| % in (# of) fraternities | 18 (7) |
| % in (# of) sororities | 34 (8) |
| % African American | 3 |
| % Asian | 4 |
| % Caucasian | 87 |
| % Hispanic | 4 |
| % international | 2 |

### SURVEY SAYS . . .
*Beautiful campus*
*Campus feels safe*
*Campus easy to get around*
*Great off-campus food*
*Students love Villanova, PA*
*Students are very religious*
*Student publications are ignored*
*(Almost) no one listens to college radio*
*Students are cliquish*

## ACADEMICS

| Academic Rating | 79 |
|---|---|
| Calendar | semester |
| Student/faculty ratio | 13:1 |
| Profs interesting rating | 82 |
| Profs accessible rating | 97 |
| % profs teaching UG courses | 100 |
| Avg lab size | 10-19 students |
| Avg reg class size | 10-19 students |

### MOST POPULAR MAJORS
finance
communication
accountancy

## STUDENTS SPEAK OUT

### Academics

"Academic reputation, Catholic tradition," and ample opportunities for "personal growth" make Villanova University a hit with its students. The fact that Villanova is "completely committed to undergraduate students" certainly doesn't hurt. The top-notch business school here, the College of Commerce and Finance, is currently the school's finest, but the College of Engineering boasts an 80,000-square-foot engineering laboratory building and is not too far behind. Classes at Nova "are small and never taught by teaching assistants," and, in fact, "a lot of priests teach classes," as the influence of the Augustinian brothers is ever-present, from the well-attended daily Masses to the somewhat strict dorm policies. Students say their "caring," "enthusiastic and concerned" professors are "readily available, willing to help," and downright "talented." They "stress to us that they want us to come to office hours," and "their first priority is students," which is "the way it should be." While the top brass "does some dumb things," and a few student contend that "dealing with the administration is like pulling teeth," most agree that Nova's administration "truly looks out for each and every student" and "actually cares when you have a problem." The "relatively smooth" registration system definitely "sucks" on occasion, at least according to one disappointed sophomore, who grumbles that "if you have a bed time, you are basically screwed" out of the classes you want. Also, the campus shuttle system "never runs on time," and, while nearly all students seem to agree that the technology here is "state-of-the-art," a few naysayers gripe that Nova "needs better computers."

### Life

"Don't have a fake? Now would be the time to invest in one" if you plan to attend Villanova. The students on this suburban campus "study hard during the week" but "have massive amounts of fun on the weekends," and they tell us that, "provided you know where to go," social life here is nothing short of "awesome." Greeks "run the social scene" around campus, and while "you don't need to be part of a Greek organization to have fun," it reportedly "helps a lot." Otherwise, the "bars on the Main Line" are usually hopping all weekend long. Access to "Philadelphia and neighboring towns is provided by a local train that stops on campus." Students often "go out in Philly," or to museums and restaurants in the City of Brotherly Love. The mammoth King of Prussia Mall is not far away, either. Closer to campus, "coffee shops are fun places to spend time," and Nova provides "absolutely amazing" volunteer opportunities." Intercollegiate athletics are extremely popular; Villanova's men's hoops team is widely followed. Complaints abound about parking, and, though "facilities are always improving," students gripe that "everything is under construction."

### Student Body

Just like at practically every Catholic school, there is a "strong sense of community" at Villanova. The "very personable, outgoing, active, and intelligent" students here are "some of the nicest people I've ever met," chirps a happy sophomore. They describe themselves as "motivated to learn," "spirited and very welcoming," and "sincere and kind." Oh, and "gorgeous," too. The "very service-oriented" students at Nova were "brought up in good homes by good families" as well, and a "community service mindset" pervades the campus. Of course, not for nothing is "this school commonly known as 'Vanillanova.'" Campus diversity "is definitely hurting"; almost 90 percent of the students are white. These "very J.Crew" students also "tend to come from more affluent families," discloses one student, and there are "a lot of preppy kids" on campus, not to mention a few "rich, snobby" ones. "The need to wear designer clothes" and to blend in is fairly strong. "If you're a girl and you wear tight black pants and clunky shoes, you'll fit in perfectly."

# VILLANOVA UNIVERSITY

FINANCIAL AID: 610-519-4010 • E-MAIL: GOTOVU@EMAIL.VILLANOVA.EDU • WEBSITE: WWW.VILLANOVA.EDU

## ADMISSIONS

*Important* academic and nonacademic factors considered by the admissions committee include class rank, essays, secondary school record, standardized test scores, and extracurricular activities. *Other* factors considered include alumni/ae relation and minority status. Factors *not* considered include religious affiliation/commitment, state residency, and recommendations. SAT I or ACT required. TOEFL required of all international applicants. High school diploma required. *High school units required/recommended:* 4 English recommended, 4 math recommended, 4 science recommended, 4 foreign language recommended, 4 social studies and history recommended.

## he Inside Word

Villanova has a very solid and growing reputation among Catholic universities nationally, yet is significantly less competitive for admissions than the top tier of schools like Georgetown and Notre Dame. If Villanova is your first choice, be careful. As is the case at many universities, Early Action applicants face higher academic standards than those for the regular pool. This university is a very sound option, whether high on your list of choices or as a safety school.

## FINANCIAL AID

*Students should submit:* FAFSA, institution's own financial aid form, and student and parent W-2 forms and federal income tax forms. The Princeton Review suggests that all financial aid forms be submitted as soon as possible after January 1. *Need-based scholarships/grants offered:* Pell, SEOG, state scholarships/grants, private scholarships, and the school's own gift aid. *Loan aid offered:* FFEL Subsidized Stafford, FFEL Unsubsidized Stafford, FFEL PLUS, Federal Perkins, Federal Nursing, and university loans from outside banking. Institutional employment available. Federal Work-Study Program available. Applicants will be notified of awards on or about April 1. Off-campus job opportunities are excellent.

## FROM THE ADMISSIONS OFFICE

"The University is a community of persons of diverse professional, academic, and personal interests who in a spirit of collegiality cooperate to achieve their common goals and objectives in the transmission, the pursuit, and the discovery of knowledge. . . . Villanova attempts to enroll students with diverse social, geographic, economic, and educational backgrounds. . . . Villanova welcomes students who consider it desirable to study within the philosophical framework of Christian Humanism. . . . Finally, this community seeks to reflect the spirit of St. Augustine by the cultivation of knowledge, by respect for individual differences, and by adherence to the principle that mutual love and respect should animate every aspect of University life."

—*Villanova University Mission Statement*

## ADMISSIONS

| | |
|---|---|
| Admissions Rating | 82 |
| # of applicants | 10,654 |
| % of applicants accepted | 52 |
| % of acceptees attending | 29 |
| # accepting a place on wait list | 1,570 |
| % admitted from wait list | 10 |

### FRESHMAN PROFILE

| | |
|---|---|
| Range SAT Verbal | 570-660 |
| Average SAT Verbal | 615 |
| Range SAT Math | 590-670 |
| Average SAT Math | 630 |
| Average ACT Composite | 28 |
| Minimum TOEFL | 550 |
| % graduated top 10% of class | 46 |
| % graduated top 25% of class | 71 |
| % graduated top 50% of class | 93 |

### DEADLINES

| | |
|---|---|
| Regular admission | 1/7 |
| Regular notification | 4/1 |

### APPLICANTS ALSO LOOK AT

**AND OFTEN PREFER**
Georgetown U.

**AND SOMETIMES PREFER**
Boston Coll.
Fordham
Holy Cross
Dickinson

**AND RARELY PREFER**
Seton Hall
U. Rhode Island
Trenton State
Gettysburg

## FINANCIAL FACTS

| | |
|---|---|
| Financial Aid Rating | 73 |
| Tuition | $20,555 |
| Room & board | $3,040 |
| Books and supplies | $800 |
| Required fees | $300 |
| % frosh receiving aid | 47 |
| % undergrads receiving aid | 49 |
| Avg frosh grant | $11,230 |
| Avg frosh loan | $6,960 |

# VIRGINIA TECH

UNDERGRADUATE ADMISSIONS, 201 BURRUSS HALL, BLACKSBURG, VA 24061 • ADMISSIONS: 540-231-6267 • FAX: 540-231-3242

## CAMPUS LIFE

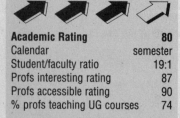

**Quality of Life Rating** **86**
Type of school | public
Affiliation | none
Environment | rural

### STUDENTS

Total undergrad enrollment | 21,419
% male/female | 59/41
% from out of state | 29
% live on campus | 33
% in (# of) fraternities | 13 (33)
% in (# of) sororities | 23 (16)
% African American | 4
% Asian | 7
% Caucasian | 87
% Hispanic | 2
% international | 2

### SURVEY SAYS . . .

*Everyone loves the Hokies*
*Class discussions are rare*
*High cost of living*
*(Almost) everyone smokes*
*Hard liquor is popular*
*Large classes*
*Dorms are like dungeons*
*Political activism is (almost)*
*nonexistent*
*Campus difficult to get around*
*Lots of TAs teach upper-level*
*courses*

## ACADEMICS

**Academic Rating** **80**
Calendar | semester
Student/faculty ratio | 19:1
Profs interesting rating | 87
Profs accessible rating | 90
% profs teaching UG courses | 74

### MOST POPULAR MAJORS
biology
psychology
communication studies

## STUDENTS SPEAK OUT

### Academics

The "research-oriented" Virginia Polytechnic and State University—"Virginia's other great university"—offers over 70 bachelor's degree programs in just about every field of study. Tech boasts "a really strong engineering school," a "surprisingly intense" academic atmosphere, and an "excellent education for the money." The school is definitely "huge," though, which means "rather large" and impersonal classes, especially during the first two years. Writes one undergrad, "Being a big school, you can't expect your professors to come to you and solve all of your problems for you. You have to keep track of what you need to do, when it needs to be done, and seek help if you need it." Agrees another, "Overall the classes tend to be very large. This results in a large percentage of your grades coming from test scores as opposed to daily/weekly assignments. It really isn't practical to ask questions in a class of 300 people but, to account for this, all teachers must have office hours weekly. I find that most of them are readily available even outside of those hours and want to help in anyway possible. . . . Help is always available when you need it." Students warn that "the academic program here is extremely challenging because of Tech's integration of technology with its studies. [It makes] each class you take seem like two different ones: one for the actual theory and written portion, the other for learning the program that goes along with the class. I knew very little about computers when I first came to Tech, and now I know how to run a vast amount of programs." Despite the occasional frustrations of attending a large school, most students are quite pleased with Tech's academic environment. "When it comes to variety of majors, classes, people, activities, almost anything," claims one satisfied student, "you name it, Tech has it."

### Life

For a school so strongly associated with its engineering and technology programs, Virginia Tech has a surprisingly active social scene. "It is a party school. . . . It's a fun place to be," notes one student. Explains another, "Since students work so hard during the week, the partying begins on Thursday night. Most people, however, like to either go downtown or to friends' apartments for parties." Beyond the parties, intercollegiate sports "are a lot of fun, especially in 2000, when the Hokies were in the National Championship Sugar Bowl." Outdoor activities abound as well, including "nature trails, canoeing the New River," and hiking. Gushes one student, "The location is gorgeous with the Blue Ridge Mountains and many trails." The school also "has every club, every organization from concert committee to the kayak club. All of these organizations welcome new members at any time and are for the most part well organized. Whatever it is you like to do, it is offered here. You just have to get up and go." No wonder Tech students rank high in overall happiness. "The longer I'm here, the happier I am that I chose Virginia Tech," reflects a senior. "It's a great school all-around, and it deserves more credit than it gets sometimes."

### Student Body

Students report that "Tech is a very big school, so there is no way to know everyone. But eventually you find your clique and adapt. There are so many different kinds of people here that there is a group for everyone." Do these different groups get along? It depends whom you ask. Some students tell us that "the majority of students are all very similar . . . white, upper-middle-class. The minority students tend to stick together with their respective group: Asians with Asians, etc." Others see things differently; writes one, "I feel that everyone here is friendly and willing to get to know you, but you have to be open to new people and their backgrounds. You have to make the move to introduce yourself or be open with others. Don't expect to make friends by sitting in your room and typing on your computer."

FINANCIAL AID: 540-231-5179 • E-MAIL: VTADMISS@VT.EDU • WEBSITE: WWW.VT.EDU

## ADMISSIONS

*Very important* academic and nonacademic factors considered by the admissions committee include class rank, secondary school record, and standardized test scores. *Important* factors considered include geography, minority status, recommendations, and state residency. *Other* factors considered include character/personal qualities, extracurricular activities, talent/ability, volunteer work, and work experience. Factors *not* considered include interview, essays, alumni/ae relation, and religious affiliation/commitment. SAT I or ACT required, SAT I preferred. TOEFL required of all international applicants. High school diploma is required and GED is accepted. *High school units required/recommended:* 15 total required; 18 total recommended; 4 English required, 3 math required, 4 math recommended, 3 science required, 4 science recommended, 2 science lab required, 3 science lab recommended, 2 foreign language required, 3 foreign language recommended, 3 social studies required, 4 social studies recommended. *The admissions office says:* "Admission to Virginia Tech is selective. We look for a solid B average in college preparatory courses, including English, advanced math, and lab sciences. Students who have challenged themselves in high school are much more likely to receive an offer of admission and to succeed at Virginia Tech."

### The Inside Word

When compared to applying to UVA or William and Mary, getting into Virginia Tech is a cakewalk. Tech has a great reputation, which from a careerist point of view makes it well worth considering.

## FINANCIAL AID

*Students should submit:* FAFSA; some applicants may be requested to submit copies of the most recent federal income tax returns for themselves and their parents. Regular filing deadline is March 1. The Princeton Review suggests that all financial aid forms be submitted as soon as possible after January 1. *Need-based scholarships/grants offered:* Pell, SEOG, state scholarships/grants, and private scholarships. *Loan aid offered:* Direct Subsidized Stafford, Direct Unsubsidized Stafford, Direct PLUS, FFEL PLUS, Federal Perkins, and college/university loans from institutional funds. Institutional employment available. Federal Work-Study Program available. Applicants will be notified of awards on or about April 15. Off-campus job opportunities are good.

## FROM THE ADMISSIONS OFFICE

"Virginia Tech offers the opportunities of a large research university in a small-town setting. Undergraduates choose from 78 majors in 7 colleges, including nationally ranked business, forestry, and engineering schools, as well as excellent computer science, biology, communication studies, and architecture programs. Technology is a key focus, both in classes and in general. All first-year students are required to own a personal computer, each dorm room has Ethernet connections, and every student is provided e-mail and Internet access. Faculty incorporate a wide variety of technology into class, utilizing chat rooms, online lecture notes, and multimedia presentations. The university offers cutting-edge facilities for classes and research, abundant opportunities for advanced study in the Honors Program, undergraduate research opportunities, study abroad, internships, and cooperative education. Students enjoy nearly 500 organizations, which offer something for everyone. Tech offers the best of both worlds—everything a large university can provide and a small-town atmosphere."

## ADMISSIONS

| | |
|---|---|
| Admissions Rating | 83 |
| # of applicants | 18,412 |
| % of applicants accepted | 63 |
| % of acceptees attending | 40 |
| # of early decision applicants | 2300 |
| % accepted early decision | 48 |

### FRESHMAN PROFILE

| | |
|---|---|
| Range SAT Verbal | 530-630 |
| Average SAT Verbal | 573 |
| Range SAT Math | 550-650 |
| Average SAT Math | 594 |
| Minimum TOEFL | 550 |
| Average HS GPA | 3.6 |
| % graduated top 10% of class | 38 |
| % graduated top 25% of class | 81 |
| % graduated top 50% of class | 99 |

### DEADLINES

| | |
|---|---|
| Early decision | 11/1 |
| Early decision notification | 12/15 |
| Regular admission | 1/15 |
| Regular notification | 4/1 |
| Nonfall registration? | yes |

### APPLICANTS ALSO LOOK AT AND OFTEN PREFER

Georgia Tech.
U. Virginia

### AND SOMETIMES PREFER

James Madison
George Mason
William and Mary
Hampton

### AND RARELY PREFER

Radford
Penn State—Univ. Park
U. Tennessee—Knoxville
Randolph-Macon Woman's

### FINANCIAL FACTS

| | |
|---|---|
| Financial Aid Rating | 72 |
| In-state tuition | $2,792 |
| Out-of-state tuition | $11,280 |
| Room & board | $4,776 |
| Books and supplies | $800 |
| Required fees | $848 |
| % frosh receiving aid | 42 |
| % undergrads receiving aid | 45 |
| Avg frosh grant | $3,816 |
| Avg frosh loan | $6,728 |

# WABASH COLLEGE

PO Box 352, 301 W. Wabash Avenue, Crawfordsville, IN 47933 • Admissions: 765-361-6225 • Fax: 765-361-6437

## CAMPUS LIFE

| | |
|---|---|
| **Quality of Life Rating** | **79** |
| Type of school | private |
| Affiliation | none |
| Environment | suburban |

### STUDENTS

| | |
|---|---|
| Total undergrad enrollment | 861 |
| % from out of state | 23 |
| % from public high school | 91 |
| % live on campus | 94 |
| % in (# of) fraternities | 69 (10) |
| % African American | 5 |
| % Asian | 3 |
| % Caucasian | 87 |
| % Hispanic | 5 |
| % international | 5 |

### SURVEY SAYS . . .

*Frats dominate social scene
Everyone loves the Giants
(Almost) everyone plays intramural
sports
No one cheats
Campus feels safe
Students don't like
Crawfordsville, IN
Class discussions encouraged
Student publications are popular*

## ACADEMICS

| | |
|---|---|
| **Academic Rating** | **92** |
| Calendar | semester |
| Student/faculty ratio | 10:1 |
| Profs interesting rating | 97 |
| Profs accessible rating | 98 |
| % profs teaching UG courses | 100 |
| Avg lab size | 10-19 students |
| Avg reg class size | 10-19 students |

### MOST POPULAR MAJORS

English
economics
history

## STUDENTS SPEAK OUT

### Academics

Wabash is one of only three remaining all-male colleges; the others are Hampden-Sydney and Morehouse, also found here among the Best 331. There's good reason why the college continues to succeed without having to alter its reason for being: "The interaction, relationships, and respect among students and between students and faculty are second to none." And "academic excellence is a real goal for all students." "At Wabash we are ardent in our cultivation of the intellect, through expression of our opinions and rigorous study and hard, dedicated work." To put it mildly, "Wabash is a bit more focused and rigorous than most liberal arts institutions." As the college says: "It won't be easy; it will be worth it.'" Students must complete a required core of liberal arts courses, fulfill a major concentration, and pass comprehensive written and oral examinations in order to graduate. Classes are very small, and students heap praise on their professors ("some of the best in the country"), whose attentiveness and caring offset intense academic demands. "My overall experience has been outstanding. I knew of the traditions that were unique to this campus, but I have been able to flourish beyond my wildest dreams. I have been taught by some of the brightest minds in their [respective] fields and feel very lucky." Students also give rave reviews to the library, the computer facilities, the class registration process, and even the administration, which runs the school "like clockwork." It starts at the top: "The president knows me and others by name not as a response to memorization, but [through] interaction with students." "I was fortunate to have the required Cultures and Traditions class with the president; turns out he was a great teacher and a hell of a nice guy."

### Life

At this all-male enclave in rural Indiana, tradition reigns supreme. Students promise to abide by the Gentleman's Rule: "A Wabash man will conduct himself at all times, both on and off campus, as a gentleman and a responsible citizen." "The Sphinx Club, an organization unique to Wabash, promotes continued tradition, campus unity, and philanthropy." "Everyone is extremely involved in campus life, and school spirit is higher than at any other school I have seen. At Wabash you will work your butt off in the classroom and on the athletic field, but you will party your butt off and have a great time on the weekend." A freshman, perhaps still somewhat bewildered by his introduction to this intense new home, almost said the same thing but not quite: "We play hard but only after studying hard. The beer flows like wine, and women flock like the salmon of Kapastruna." [Editor's note: salmon of Kapastruna? We think he meant "like the swallows of Capistrano."] "The social life is very active here. We have bands that range from national acts to local talent. Also, we are centrally located, being close to Purdue, IU, DePauw, Butler, and the University of Illinois." Students gripe that the town of Crawfordsville is ho-hum at best, and relations with "townies" are strained. Wabash is a "big drinking school" with a huge Greek presence (almost three in four undergrads belong to fraternities). "Because of the all-male existence our fun is gained through support of our athletic teams, which includes the consumption of alcoholic beverages. People think about heavy philosophical ideals, yet live like cavemen." "Our culture promotes a lot of competition. It drives us."

### Student Body

"Wabash Men" are "brothers for life." "Students get along very well with each other. The attitude here is one of friendliness and cooperation." Most Wabash men are conservative "good ol' boys" who interact splendidly, provided they aren't "too busy studying or drinking." "There will be a preppy football player living in the same house as a coffee-sipping poet, and they get along. The college does unique things to people." "I had good friends back at home, but the relationships and camaraderie I've experienced here are unparalleled." A network of tightly-knit alums provides grads with "good connections in the business, professional, and graduate school worlds."

FINANCIAL AID: 765-361-6370 • E-MAIL: ADMISSIONS@WABASH.EDU • WEBSITE: WWW.WABASH.EDU

## ADMISSIONS

*Very important* academic and nonacademic factors considered by the admissions committee include class rank, essays, secondary school record, and standardized test scores. *Important* factors considered include character/personal qualities, extracurricular activities, interview, and recommendations. *Other* factors considered include alumni/ae relation, talent/ability, and volunteer work. Factors *not* considered include geography, minority status, religious affiliation/commitment, state residency, and work experience. SAT I or ACT required, SAT I preferred. TOEFL required of all international applicants. High school diploma is required and GED is not accepted. *High school units required/recommended:* 15 total recommended; 4 English recommended, 3 math recommended, 3 science recommended, 2 foreign language recommended, 3 social studies recommended, 3 history recommended. *The admissions office says:* "[T]he selection committee primarily focuses on the four-year academic record. Positive consideration is given to applicants who have sought academic challenge through high school by enrolling in the most advanced level classes."

### The Inside Word

Wabash is one of the few remaining all-male colleges in the country, and like the rest it has a small applicant pool. The vast majority of candidates are offered admission; the pool is highly self-selected, and the academic standards for admission, while selective, are not particularly demanding. However, though not tough to gain admission to, Wabash is tough to graduate from—don't consider it if you aren't prepared to work.

## FINANCIAL AID

*Students should submit:* FAFSA and CSS/Financial Aid PROFILE. Regular filing deadline is March 1. The Princeton Review suggests that all financial aid forms be submitted as soon as possible after January 1. *Need-based scholarships/grants offered:* Pell, state scholarships/grants, private scholarships and the school's own gift aid. *Loan aid offered:* FFEL Subsidized Stafford, FFEL Unsubsidized Stafford, FFEL PLUS, and college/university loans from institutional funds. Federal Work-Study Program available. Applicants will be notified of awards on a rolling basis beginning on or about March 15. Off-campus job opportunities are excellent.

## FROM THE ADMISSIONS OFFICE

"Wabash College is different—and distinctive—from other liberal arts colleges. Different in that Wabash is an outstanding college for men only. Distinctive in the quality and character of the faculty, in the demanding nature of the academic program, in the farsightedness and maturity of the men who enroll, and in the richness of the traditions that have evolved throughout its 168-year history. Wabash is, preeminently, a teaching institution, and fundamental to the learning experience is the way faculty and students talk to each other: with mutual respect for the expression of informed opinion. For example, students who collaborate with faculty on research projects are considered their peers in the research—an esteem not usually extended to undergraduates. The college takes pride in the sense of community that such a learning environment fosters. But perhaps the single most striking aspect of student life at Wabash is personal freedom. The college has only one rule: 'The student is expected to conduct himself at all times, both on and off the campus, as a gentleman and a responsible citizen.' Wabash College treats students as adults, and such treatment attracts responsible freshmen and fosters their independence and maturity."

## ADMISSIONS

| | |
|---|---|
| Admissions Rating | 86 |
| # of applicants | 883 |
| % of applicants accepted | 65 |
| % of acceptees attending | 41 |
| # accepting a place on wait list | 63 |
| % admitted from wait list | 16 |
| # of early decision applicants | 30 |
| % accepted early decision | 87 |

### FRESHMAN PROFILE

| | |
|---|---|
| Range SAT Verbal | 520-630 |
| Average SAT Verbal | 580 |
| Range SAT Math | 540-660 |
| Average SAT Math | 600 |
| Range ACT Composite | 23-29 |
| Average ACT Composite | 25 |
| Minimum TOEFL | 550 |
| Average HS GPA | 3.5 |
| % graduated top 10% of class | 38 |
| % graduated top 25% of class | 73 |
| % graduated top 50% of class | 94 |

### DEADLINES

| | |
|---|---|
| Early decision | 11/15 |
| Early decision notification | 12/15 |
| Priority admission deadline | 12/15 |
| Regular admission | 3/15 |
| Nonfall registration? | yes |

### APPLICANTS ALSO LOOK AT
**AND OFTEN PREFER**
Indiana U.—Bloomington
Notre Dame
**AND SOMETIMES PREFER**
DePaul
Valparaiso
**AND RARELY PREFER**
Purdue U.—West Lafayette

### FINANCIAL FACTS

| | |
|---|---|
| Financial Aid Rating | 88 |
| Tuition | $17,994 |
| Room & board | $5,761 |
| Books and supplies | $600 |
| Required fees | $300 |
| % frosh receiving aid | 76 |
| % undergrads receiving aid | 70 |
| Avg frosh grant | $17,268 |
| Avg frosh loan | $3,140 |

# WAKE FOREST UNIVERSITY

Box 7305 Reynolda Station, Winston-Salem, NC 27109 • Admissions: 336-758-5201 • Fax: 336-758-4324

## STUDENTS SPEAK OUT

### Academics

"Rigorous" Wake Forest University offers a "combination of small classes and great academic opportunities," and a solid, broad-based core curriculum obligates all students to pursue a well-rounded academic program. Wake is also very "wired" and "technology-friendly," and the computers, labs, and research resources on campus are all fabulous. However, students here face a savage workload and a "very tough grading system." Also, while a few students say the "administration has been great," the overwhelming majority gripe that it is "selfish," "very strict," even "ridiculous and fascist." There is "too much red tape and bureaucracy," administrators "waffle on issues like Bill Clinton," and "the administration's push for a better national reputation has caused a division between" the top brass and the students. "I hear we have a president, but I've never seen him," claims a junior, "only his Lexus." On the other hand, "complaints about the administration make for a really entertaining school newspaper," remarks a history major. The "high-caliber" faculty here is "stimulating and challenging," and "generally willing to meet with students outside of class." They are also "here to teach, not just to do research," and "truly interested in helping." Some professors "think their class is the only class you have," though, and Wake profs are apparently somewhat legendary for giving "impossibly hard tests."

### Life

Wake Forest is not "nicknamed 'Work Forest'" for nothing. The "generally horrible" and "outrageous" workload is "heavy," and it often "leads to much stress. This is why parties get wild on the weekends," theorizes a sophomore. As a result, though "this place is like a monastery during the week," on the weekends "everyone turns into a raging alcoholic," despite a "strict drinking policy." Greeks dominate the Wake social scene, and "fun consists of fraternity parties for white or black Greeks . . . and long road trips to other universities for independents." When the frats are throwing parties, there is plenty of "live music and beer." While freshmen and sophomores often feel "trapped on campus," older students "go off campus to bars on the weekends," even though "there are only a handful of off-campus destinations," and the rest of "downtown Winston is dead." Back on the gorgeous "self-supporting and self-contained" campus, "there are tons of organizations to get involved in," including the very popular Volunteer Service Corps. Wake students tell us that "the problem," really, "is juggling them all." Intramural and intercollegiate sports "are a great source of fun," and students support Demon Deacons athletics fairly rabidly. "Dating is nonexistent except for weekend hook-ups." "If you want to have sex," warns a lovelorn sophomore, "don't come to Wake Forest."

### Student Body

"Everybody gets along well at Wake," but "of course, it's not like there's many issues anybody here truly, violently disagrees on. If you are fairly preppy, intelligent, and middle-of-the-road," promises a first-year student, you'll get along fine. The "predominantly white, affluent, clean-cut, and conservative" students here are "anxious and stressed out," and they "like to talk about how busy they are." Normalcy reigns supreme on this "very homogenous" campus; "everyone looks like they walked out of an episode of Dawson's Creek." One student observes that "people fall into strict gender roles and prepare to get married." Wake students are also "smart, down-to-earth," "highly motivated," and "self-reliant." Unfortunately, "race relations on campus are poor," and there is a "definite lack of interracial interaction" among various ethnic and racial groups. There are also "many rifts and divisions between Greek and non-Greek students," and "a very clear division" exists "between socioeconomic groups." Wake regularly admits a throng of "wealthy" students who are "rich and spoiled but polite and likeable." Finally, Wake also boasts "quite a large Christian population" as well.

# WAKE FOREST UNIVERSITY

FINANCIAL AID: 336-758-5154 • E-MAIL: ADMISSIONS@WFU.EDU • WEBSITE: WWW.WFU.EDU

## ADMISSIONS

*Very important* academic and nonacademic factors considered by the admissions committee include secondary school record, class rank, character/personal qualities, and standardized test scores. *Important* factors considered include alumni/ae relation, extracurricular activities, geography, and minority status. *Other* factors considered include religious affiliation/commitment. Factors *not* considered include interview and work experience. SAT I required; SAT II recommended. TOEFL required of all international applicants. High school diploma is required and GED is accepted. *High school units required/recommended:* 4 English recommended, 4 math recommended, 4 science recommended, 3 science lab recommended, 4 foreign language recommended, 4 social studies recommended. *The admissions office says:* "The 'typical' Wake Forest student is characterized by a commitment to personal honor and integrity, a serious and industrious pursuit of academic excellence, and a tradition of service to others within and outside the campus community."

### The Inside Word

An applicant to Wake Forest undergoes very close scrutiny from the admissions committee; many very solid candidates wind up on the wait list. Fortunately, the admissions staff is as friendly and accessible as the university's students rate the whole place. Successful candidates typically show impressive extracurricular accomplishments as well as academic excellence, and are good matches with the university's personality.

## FINANCIAL AID

*Students should submit:* FAFSA, CSS/Financial Aid PROFILE, state aid form and noncustodial (divorced/separated) parent's statement. The Princeton Review suggests that all financial aid forms be submitted as soon as possible after January 1. Institutional employment available. Federal Work-Study Program available. Applicants will be notified of awards on or about April 15. Off-campus job opportunities are excellent.

## FROM THE ADMISSIONS OFFICE

"Wake Forest University has been dedicated to the liberal arts for over a century and a half; this means education in the fundamental fields of human knowledge and achievement. It seeks to encourage habits of mind that ask why, that evaluate evidence, that are open to new ideas, that attempt to understand and appreciate the perspective of others, that accept complexity and grapple with it, that admit error, and that pursue truth. Wake Forest is among a small, elite group of American colleges and universities recognized for their outstanding academic quality. It offers small classes taught by full-time faculty—not graduate assistants—and a commitment to student interaction with those professors. Students are all provided IBM ThinkPads and color printers. Classrooms and residence halls are fully networked. Wake Forest maintains a need-blind admissions policy by which qualified students are admitted regardless of their financial circumstances."

## ADMISSIONS

| | |
|---|---|
| Admissions Rating | 94 |
| # of applicants | 5,079 |
| % of applicants accepted | 49 |
| % of acceptees attending | 41 |
| # of early decision applicants | 490 |
| % accepted early decision | 45 |

### FRESHMAN PROFILE

| | |
|---|---|
| Range SAT Verbal | 600-680 |
| Average SAT Verbal | 639 |
| Range SAT Math | 620-700 |
| Average SAT Math | 652 |
| Minimum TOEFL | 550 |
| % graduated top 10% of class | 67 |
| % graduated top 50% of class | 98 |

### DEADLINES

| | |
|---|---|
| Early decision | 11/15 |
| Early decision notification | 12/15 |
| Regular admission | 1/15 |
| Regular notification | 4/1 |
| Nonfall registration? | yes |

### APPLICANTS ALSO LOOK AT

**AND OFTEN PREFER**
Duke
UNC—Chapel Hill

**AND SOMETIMES PREFER**
Washington and Lee
Vanderbilt
William and Mary
Davidson

**AND RARELY PREFER**
Furman
U. Richmond
North Carolina State

## FINANCIAL FACTS

| | |
|---|---|
| Financial Aid Rating | 82 |
| Tuition | $23,530 |
| Room & board | $6,750 |
| Books and supplies | $700 |
| % frosh receiving aid | 33 |
| % undergrads receiving aid | 33 |
| Avg frosh grant | $13,712 |
| Avg frosh loan | $3,648 |

# WARREN WILSON COLLEGE

PO BOX 9000, ASHEVILLE, NC 28815 • ADMISSIONS: 800-934-3536 • FAX: 828-298-1440

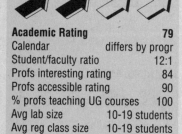
## STUDENTS SPEAK OUT

### Academics

At "small, friendly," and "progressive" Warren Wilson College, "the learning experience is not limited to classroom academics." The unique Triad program here combines academics with a mandatory work-study program and required community service. Students love it. "There is no equal to the interconnectedness of our campus," boasts a senior. "We all spend 15 hours a week working for the school, doing everything from scrubbing toilets and cooking for the food service to working in the library and the organic garden." The "easily approachable," "intelligent and articulate" professors at Wilson "are generally mellow"—many are "old hippies gone New Age"—and they "respect the fact that you have to work 15 hours a week for the school." The quality of the academic experience is a mixed bag, though. Classes are "challenging" for some but "not very challenging" for others, and while "some classes require a lot of work," WWC students "definitely feel spoon-fed at times." In general, the hard sciences are notably harder here, and the pre-veterinary program is "very good." On the administrative front, students are pretty much thrilled. "The best part about this school is the ease in dealing with the dean and other administrators," says a senior. "We call them by their first names, and they are almost always available."

### Life

"I wake up at 4:30 A.M. in the morning and shovel pig crap—just like a real farmer," beams a junior. "It's the best." Another student informs us: "I just came from my job here on campus, where I ran a very high voltage power line to a walk-in cooler. I've got class in 45 minutes, followed by interviews with various people on how to improve our lighting on campus." When WWC students aren't working or studying, there's plenty to do on and around the "beautiful" area, which is home to "cows," "big, old trees, pick up trucks, drag queens, and campus dogs." And let's not forget "veggie co-ops, yoga class, and wellness service." WWC students also participate in several "unusual sports"—"kayaking, white water rafting, Ultimate Frisbee, rock climbing, caving, camping, hiking, etc." - and "outdoor activities" are all the rage. There's also "drumming, meditating," "sewing, poetry," "protesting an injustice somewhere," listening to "bluegrass music," and "drinking beer and hooting and hollering around a fire." Off campus, the surrounding town of Asheville, believe it or not, "is one of the most progressive cities in the nation." "There are no fraternities or sororities" at Wilson (nor any people "who want to be in them"), but that certainly doesn't keep students from drinking and using drugs. Students tell us that marijuana is wildly popular on campus.

### Student Body

This place is a granola paradise, full of "hippies, pseudo-intellectuals"; "liberal non-Christians"; "environmentally aware" rabble rousers; and "white, middle-class suburban kids thinking they can save the world." The "generally friendly and open-minded" students at WWC describe themselves as "very vibrant and energetic," "very activism-motivated," and "shockingly friendly and open." "Five-minute hugs are a common occurrence." WWC is home to "a lot of international students but a clear lack of minority students," and, as one cynic muses, students here are often "trying so hard to be different that we're all the same." Politically, Wilson is somewhere pretty far to the left of Ralph Nader. "I saw a Republican here once," swears a junior, "but no one believed me."

FINANCIAL AID: 828-298-3325 • E-MAIL: ADMIT@WARREN-WILSON.EDU • WEBSITE: WWW.WARREN-WILSON.EDU

## ADMISSIONS

*Very important* academic and nonacademic factors considered by the admission committee include character/personal qualities, essays, and interview. *Important* factors considered include class rank, extracurricular activities, secondary school record, volunteer work, and work experience. *Other* factors considered include minority status, recommendations, religious affiliation/commitment, standardized test scores, and talent/ability. Factors *not* considered include alumni/ae relation, geography, and state residency. SAT I or ACT required, SAT I preferred. TOEFL required of all international applicants. High school diploma is required and GED is accepted. *High school units required/recommended:* 15 total required; 20 total recommended; 4 English required, 3 math required, 4 math recommended, 3 science required, 2 science lab required, 2 foreign language recommended, 1 social studies required, 2 history required, 4 elective recommended.

### The Inside Word

Warren Wilson is a college for thinkers with a deep sense of social commitment. The admissions process clearly reflects the committee's desire for solid academic achievement in successful candidates, but they also take a close and careful look at the person being considered. It isn't supercompetitive to get in here, but only candidates who make good matches with the college are offered admission.

## FINANCIAL AID

*Students should submit:* FAFSA and institution's own financial aid form. The Princeton Review suggests that all financial aid forms be submitted as soon as possible after January 1. *Need-based scholarships/grants offered:* Pell, SEOG, state scholarships/grants, and the school's own gift aid. *Loan aid offered:* FFEL Subsidized Stafford, FFEL Unsubsidized Stafford, FFEL PLUS, Federal Perkins, and college/university loans from institutional funds. Institutional employment available. Federal Work-Study Program available. Applicants will be notified of awards on a rolling basis beginning on or about March 1. Off-campus job opportunities are good.

## FROM THE ADMISSIONS OFFICE

"This book is a 'Guide to the Best 331 Colleges,' but Warren Wilson College may not be the best college for many students. There are 3,500 colleges in the U.S., and there is a best place for everyone. The 'best college' is one that has the right size, location, programs, and above all, the right feel for you, even if it is not listed here. Warren Wilson College may be the best choice if you think and act independently, actively participate in your education, and want a college that provides a sense of community. Your hands will get dirty here, your mind will be stretched, and you'll not be anonymous. If you are looking for the traditional college experience with football and frats, and a campus-on-a-quad, this probably is not the right place. However, if you want to be a part of an academic community that works and serves together, this might be exactly what you are looking for."

## ADMISSIONS

| | |
|---|---:|
| Admissions Rating | 77 |
| # of applicants | 625 |
| % of applicants accepted | 81 |
| % of acceptees attending | 34 |
| # of early decision applicants | 54 |
| % accepted early decision | 63 |

### FRESHMAN PROFILE

| | |
|---|---:|
| Range SAT Verbal | 520-670 |
| Average SAT Verbal | 579 |
| Range SAT Math | 490-620 |
| Average SAT Math | 544 |
| Range ACT Composite | 22-28 |
| Average ACT Composite | 24 |
| Minimum TOEFL | 550 |
| Average HS GPA | 3.3 |
| % graduated top 10% of class | 13 |
| % graduated top 25% of class | 43 |
| % graduated top 50% of class | 77 |

### DEADLINES

| | |
|---|---:|
| Early decision | 11/15 |
| Early decision notification | 12/2 |
| Regular admission | 3/15 |
| Nonfall registration? | yes |

### APPLICANTS ALSO LOOK AT AND SOMETIMES PREFER

UNC—Asheville
UNC—Chapel Hill
Guilford
Earlham

### AND RARELY PREFER

Appalachian State
Antioch

## FINANCIAL FACTS

| | |
|---|---:|
| Financial Aid Rating | 87 |
| Tuition | $15,094 |
| Room & board | $4,874 |
| Books and supplies | $700 |
| Required fees | $200 |
| % frosh receiving aid | 57 |
| % undergrads receiving aid | 50 |
| Avg frosh loan | $2,325 |

# WASHINGTON AND LEE UNIVERSITY

LETCHER AVENUE, LEXINGTON, VA 24450-0303 • ADMISSIONS: 540-463-8710 • FAX: 540-463-8062

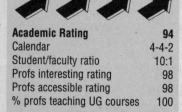
## STUDENTS SPEAK OUT

### Academics

While not the best-known small, traditional, liberal arts school on the East Coast, Washington and Lee may well be the best loved by its students. The school is not for everyone—see *Student Body*, below—but for those who fit the mold, W&L is a "little utopian society" that offers "really small classes" and a "strong sense of community among the students, faculty, and administration." These factors help mitigate the heavy workload here. Writes one student, "Academically, W&L is very challenging, but the small classes and group discussions make it very easy to participate and learn." Students say the faculty is "extremely helpful and always accessible" and appreciate professors who "epitomize southern hospitality. They're amazing!" All classes are taught by full professors; W&L has "no TAs, which is excellent." Undergrads are equally sanguine about the administration, reporting that the "administration and departments bend over backwards to help you out. If you are serious about learning and not just willing but want to work for your education, W&L will present excellent opportunities." The school runs on an unusual academic schedule, featuring two full-length terms (fall and winter) and a mandatory six-week term in the spring, during which students participate in seminars and internships or travel abroad. W&L also has a very popular Honor System that allows students to schedule their own nonproctored exams and leave their dorm rooms unlocked. Take-home, closed-book examinations are not uncommon, and "the buildings are open 24/7" as well. Brags one student, "The Honor System dominates life on campus and is a large part of what makes this university so special."

### Life

Students at W&L really, really want you to know how much they drink. More than a few, in fact, are deeply offended that they dropped in this publication's "Drinking School" ranking last year. We'll let the students set the record straight. Writes one, "W&L allows students to pursue a wide range of academics while maintaining a strong sense of drunkenness." Adds another, "W&L is Utopia, with frat parties and kegs added." Indeed, the W&L social universe revolves around the Greek scene. Comments one student, "We have the greatest fraternity scene in the country. Period. If you like bourbon and Coke or beer flowing like water, there is no place to go but here." Agrees another, "We like to get our drink on." Because "fraternity parties are open to everyone, except for special functions," W&L suffers less from Greek/independent antagonism than do many other Greek-dominated campuses. During nondrinking hours, "club and intramural sports are popular. The opportunities for satisfying extracurricular activities are excellent." Students also love to "go tubing in the river, play Frisbee in the quad, dance all night long," hang out in their "palatial dorms," or walk across their postcard-perfect, ivy-covered campus. But when it comes right down to it, "basically, students study their asses off during the week, then party their asses off on the weekend. 'Work hard, drink hard' is our motto."

### Student Body

"W&L is often described as having a student body like a country club: white, well-off, Republican," explains one student, who, atypical of a Best 331 Colleges respondent, does not follow this unflattering characterization with the word but. Instead, she continues, "Many students here come from families of wealth. My little Neon is parked next to a Lexus, a Saab, and a brand-new SUV—in the freshman lot!" Students concur that the "conservative, clean-cut, red-blooded American boys and girls" who attend W&L are "fun-loving, ambitious, and elitist." Writes one African American undergrad, "You can tell some of them have never even been around minority students before." Those who fit in agree that "never before have I met friendlier people. A lot of our students [approximately 10 percent] are from Texas, so friendliness is an inherent trait." Those who don't fit in either transfer out or endure a long four years.

FINANCIAL AID: 540-463-8715 • E-MAIL: ADMISSIONS@WLU.EDU • WEBSITE: WWW.WLU.EDU

## ADMISSIONS

*Very important* academic and nonacademic factors considered by the admissions committee include essays, extracurricular activities, recommendations, secondary school record, and standardized test scores. *Important* factors considered include character/personal qualities, interview, minority status, and talent/ability. *Other* factors considered include geography, volunteer work, work experience, and alumni/ae relation. Factors *not* considered include religious affiliation/commitment and state residency. SAT I or ACT required; SAT II also required. TOEFL required of all international applicants. High school diploma is required and GED is not accepted. *High school units required/recommended:* 16 total required; 4 English required, 3 math required, 4 math recommended, 1 science required, 3 science recommended, 2 foreign language required, 3 foreign language recommended, 1 history required, 2 history recommended. *The admission office says:* "Individuals are welcome to submit materials that speak of their special talents."

### The Inside Word

If you're looking for a bastion of southern tradition, Washington and Lee is one of the foremost. Its admissions process is appropriately traditional, and highly selective. Under these circumstances, it is always best to take a cautious and conservative approach to preparing your candidacy. Smart applicants have taken the toughest courses available to them in high school—the minimum requirements aren't likely to help you gain admission. Neither will a glib approach to the personal side of the application; a well-written essay is what they're after.

## FINANCIAL AID

*Students should submit:* FAFSA, CSS/Financial Aid PROFILE, noncustodial (divorced/separated) parent's statement, and business/farm supplement. The Princeton Review suggests that all financial aid forms be submitted as soon as possible after January 1. *Need-based scholarships/grants offered:* Pell, SEOG, state scholarships/grants, private scholarships, and the school's own gift aid. *Loan aid offered:* FFEL Subsidized Stafford, FFEL Unsubsidized Stafford, FFEL PLUS, Federal Perkins, and college/university loans from institutional funds. Institutional employment available. Federal Work-Study Program available. Applicants will be notified of awards on or about April 5. Off-campus job opportunities are fair.

## FROM THE ADMISSIONS OFFICE

"W&L, the nation's eighth oldest college, is a small, private, liberal arts school located in the heart of the beautiful Shenandoah Valley. As one might expect, W&L possesses an inordinate amount of history. Quality teaching both in and out of the classroom, and the development of students into well-rounded leaders, summarize the school's primary goals. An average W&L class contains 15 students, and courses are taught by the school's full-time faculty members; no graduate students or teacher assistants are on the faculty. W&L possesses a uniquely broad and deep curriculum, as well as a time-honored, student-run Honor System that allows students a wide range of freedoms. W&L is a highly competitive school, where students will receive a first-rate, personalized education, develop leadership skills, enjoy life outside of the classroom, and reap the innumerable postgraduation benefits of a W&L education."

## ADMISSIONS

| Admissions Rating | 97 |
|---|---|
| # of applicants | 3,057 |
| % of applicants accepted | 35 |
| % of acceptees attending | 42 |
| # accepting a place on wait list | 204 |
| % admitted from wait list | 20 |
| # of early decision applicants | 378 |
| % accepted early decision | 55 |

### FRESHMAN PROFILE

| | |
|---|---|
| Range SAT Verbal | 630-720 |
| Range SAT Math | 640-710 |
| Range ACT Composite | 28-31 |
| Minimum TOEFL | 600 |
| Average HS GPA | 3.9 |
| % graduated top 10% of class | 74 |
| % graduated top 25% of class | 95 |
| % graduated top 50% of class | 100 |

### DEADLINES

| | |
|---|---|
| Early decision | 12/1 |
| Early decision notification | 12/22 |
| Regular admission | 1/15 |
| Regular notification | 4/1 |

**APPLICANTS ALSO LOOK AT**

**AND OFTEN PREFER**
U.Virginia
UNC—Chapel Hill

**AND SOMETIMES PREFER**
Davidson
William and Mary
Vanderbilt
Wake Forest

**AND RARELY PREFER**
Rhodes
SMU
Franklin & Marshall
James Madison
Tulane

## FINANCIAL FACTS

| Financial Aid Rating | 79 |
|---|---|
| Tuition | $19,170 |
| Room & board | $5,750 |
| Books and supplies | $1,040 |
| Required fees | $175 |
| % frosh receiving aid | 26 |
| % undergrads receiving aid | 27 |
| Avg frosh grant | $15,411 |
| Avg frosh loan | $2,598 |

# WASHINGTON STATE UNIVERSITY

342 FRENCH ADMINISTRATION BUILDING, PULLMAN, WA 99164 • ADMISSIONS: 509-335-5586 • FAX: 509-335-4902

## CAMPUS LIFE

**Quality of Life Rating** **75**
Type of school            public
Affiliation               none
Environment               rural

### STUDENTS
Total undergrad enrollment    16,839
% male/female                 48/52
% from out of state           9
% from public high school     96
% live on campus              49
% in (# of) fraternities      17 (24)
% in (# of) sororities        16 (16)
% African American            3
% Asian                       5
% Caucasian                   76
% Hispanic                    3
% Native American             2
% international               3

### SURVEY SAYS . . .
*Frats and sororities dominate social
scene
Everyone loves the Cougars
(Almost) everyone plays intramural
sports
Hard liquor is popular
Registration is a breeze
Large intro classes
Theater is unpopular
Dorms are like dungeons
Student publications are popular*

## ACADEMICS

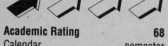

**Academic Rating**          **68**
Calendar                     semester
Student/faculty ratio        16:1
Profs interesting rating     76
Profs accessible rating      69
Avg reg class size    10-19 students

### MOST POPULAR MAJORS
business administration
mass communications
social science

## STUDENTS SPEAK OUT
### Academics
Washington State University is a large state school that offers a wide range of majors and many research opportunities. Professors at the vaunted Edward R. Murrow School of Communications are "very good" and "in touch with their students." A senior communications major writes, "WSU's professors are highly accessible and have a desire to help the students live up to their potential." A psychology major adds, "Overall, my experience has been amazing." Students "leave Washington State prepared for the real world." A "second-to-none" Honors Program also receives rave reviews. "Seriously," counsels a first-year student, "take honors courses over general education if and whenever possible." The school of veterinary medicine also earns high praise. While students adore many of their professors, teaching assistants don't fare so well, as many "do not speak English very well." One senior accounting major muses, "Part of being a teacher is being able to communicate effectively." Advisors are not held in high regard either at WSU. A junior says, "Advisors need to know what they're telling students to take." Relations between students and administrators responsible for student affairs could stand some rehabilitation, an effort the new administration is beginning to undertake. The computer labs, library, and new bookstore receive kudos.

### Life
Pullman is a "small town," approximately 300 miles from Seattle. For students who expect urban entertainment, the location "means there is not a whole lot to do." But for those who enjoy the outdoors, there are "more opportunities than time," including "excellent intramurals and club sports" (such as snowboarding and lacrosse) and "great" athletic facilities. The plush new Student Recreation Center boasts state-of-the-art equipment and the nation's largest free weight and cardio fitness training area. As a Pac-10 school, sports have a major presence on campus. Last year the football team suffered through another losing season and drew the ire of many students: "The bars or sporting events are good [entertainment] options. A good day is when you can combine both." While some students pout that "there is nothing [to do] but school because of [WSU's] location," an upbeat junior advertising major points out "fun is all around you. Just open your eyes and you'll find something exciting to do." Greek life is a popular diversion, and "after you turn 21, going to the bars is a big part of social life."

### Student Body
WSU students are extremely friendly. A senior writes that "her favorite thing about Pullman is the people. If you are walking down the street and you go past a total stranger, they always say hello." An advertising major adds, "I love the students here. It's a lovely place to hang your hat." Students celebrate the campus' diversity, and add with a smirk that Washington State has a "great group of people to spend four, five, or six years with." A senior advertising major complains that "the Greek system is emphasized too much," while a journalism major adds that there is "a little tension between the Greek and individual, non-Greek houses." As for the Greeks themselves, "the fraternity members at WSU are half real good guys and the other half are the worst people" one will meet. Still, most students get along and "are great, down to earth, blossoming adults."

FINANCIAL AID: 509-335-9711 • E-MAIL: ADMISS2@WSU.EDU • WEBSITE: WWW.WSU.EDU

## ADMISSIONS

*Very important* academic and nonacademic factors considered by the admissions committee include secondary school record and standardized test scores. *Other* factors considered include essays, extracurricular activities, recommendations, and talent/ability. Factors *not* considered include alumni/ae relation, character/personal qualities, class rank, geography, interview, minority status, religious affiliation/commitment, state residency, volunteer work, and work experience. SAT I or ACT required. TOEFL required of all international applicants. High school diploma is required and GED is accepted. *High school units required/recommended:* 15 total required; 4 English required, 3 math required, 2 science required, 1 science lab required, 2 foreign language required, 3 social studies required, 1 fine, visual, or performing arts required.

### The Inside Word

It's a large public-U, formula-driven admission at Washington State. Admission is based on the Admissions Index Number (AIN), a weighted combination of high school GPA (75 percent) and standardized test scores (25 percent). The average AIN for admitted students is 57. Check out the AIN calculator on the University website to estimate your admissibility. An appropriate college-prep high school course selection is required ("core requirements" for students in the state of Washington).

## FINANCIAL AID

*Students should submit:* FAFSA. There is no regular filing deadline. Priority filing deadline is March 1. The Princeton Review suggests that all financial aid forms be submitted as soon as possible after January 1. *Need-based scholarships/grants offered:* Pell, SEOG, state scholarships/grants, private scholarships, the school's own gift aid, and United Negro College Fund. *Loan aid offered:* Subsidized Stafford, Unsubsidized Stafford, PLUS, Federal Perkins, Federal Nursing, and Health Profession. Institution employment available. Federal Work-Study Program available. Applicants will be notified of awards on a rolling basis. Off-campus job opportunities are good.

## FROM THE ADMISSIONS OFFICE

"Many of Washington State University's 150 academic programs are ranked among the best in the nation—and in the world. Programs are designed to give you real-world experience through internships, fieldwork, community service, and in-depth labs. The Carnegie Foundation for the Advancement of Teaching ranks Washington State among the top research universities in America. You can take part in faculty research or even conduct your own. Washington State University is one of the largest residential campuses west of the Mississippi. You'll live in the heart of a true college town—a community of faculty and friends who can help you achieve your greatest potential."

## ADMISSIONS

| | |
|---|---|
| **Admissions Rating** | **73** |
| # of applicants | 7,524 |
| % of applicants accepted | 84 |
| % of acceptees attending | 39 |

### FRESHMAN PROFILE

| | |
|---|---|
| Range SAT Verbal | 470-590 |
| Average SAT Verbal | 531 |
| Range SAT Math | 470-590 |
| Average SAT Math | 527 |
| Minimum TOEFL | 520 |
| Average HS GPA | 3.4 |

### DEADLINES

| | |
|---|---|
| Priority admission deadline | 5/1 |
| Nonfall registration? | yes |

## FINANCIAL FACTS

| | |
|---|---|
| **Financial Aid Rating** | **76** |
| In-state tuition | $3,351 |
| Out-of-state tuition | $10,267 |
| Room & board | $4,826 |
| Books and supplies | $698 |
| Required fees | $439 |
| % frosh receiving aid | 54 |
| % undergrads receiving aid | 50 |
| Avg frosh grant | $3,807 |
| Avg frosh loan | $5,655 |

# WASHINGTON UNIVERSITY IN ST. LOUIS

CAMPUS BOX 1089, ONE BROOKINGS DRIVE, SAINT LOUIS, MO 63130-4899 • ADMISSIONS: 800-638-0700 • FAX: 314-935-4290

## CAMPUS LIFE

**Quality of Life Rating** **83**
Type of school                private
Affiliation                      none
Environment                  suburban

### STUDENTS

| | |
|---|---|
| Total undergrad enrollment | 6,695 |
| % male/female | 49/51 |
| % from out of state | 88 |
| % from public high school | 64 |
| % live on campus | 77 |
| % in (# of) fraternities | 21 (12) |
| % in (# of) sororities | 18 (6) |
| % African American | 7 |
| % Asian | 11 |
| % Caucasian | 66 |
| % Hispanic | 2 |
| % international | 5 |
| # of countries represented | 96 |

### SURVEY SAYS . . .

*Students love Saint Louis, MO*
*Registration is a breeze*
*School is well run*
*Great off-campus food*
*Lab facilities need improving*
*Intercollegiate sports unpopular or*
*nonexistent*
*Large classes*
*Ethnic diversity on campus*
*Students get along with local*
*community*

## ACADEMICS

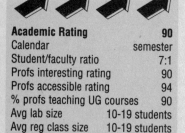

| | |
|---|---|
| **Academic Rating** | **90** |
| Calendar | semester |
| Student/faculty ratio | 7:1 |
| Profs interesting rating | 90 |
| Profs accessible rating | 94 |
| % profs teaching UG courses | 90 |
| Avg lab size | 10-19 students |
| Avg reg class size | 10-19 students |

### MOST POPULAR MAJORS
psychology
biology
finance

## STUDENTS SPEAK OUT

### Academics

With "a great faculty, top caliber students," and "all the resources of the Ivies," Washington University is one of the top universities in the Midwest. Like all universities, Washington requires students to take initiative in order to navigate its sometimes labyrinthine bureaucracy, but students here report fewer hassles than do students at similar-sized schools. "Registration is really easy, although sometimes you have to wait a semester to get into a small, popular class," writes one student. Another happily reports "very little red tape with the administration, so things get done!" Academically it's pretty much the same story: "Once you get past the 200- to 300-person intro classes, the teachers get better and more enjoyable." Students report the typical mix of "some really good professors and also some terrible professors and terrible TAs," but also note that "the professors and staff here actually care about their students both in and out of the classroom, something you don't find at all universities." And because Washington University is a top institution, that caring professor may turn out to be "a Nobel Prize-winning professor teaching your freshman class." Coursework here is "very intense, but it pays off." Indeed, many students pursue graduate study, particularly in medicine (over 10 percent of all Wash U. grads head straight into med programs).

### Life

Describing life on this picturesque campus, one undergrad explains that "Washington U is caught in its own limbo between St. Louis and the surrounding suburbs. While life here is nice, it almost too easy to fall into the 'college bubble' syndrome. Sometimes I have to go downtown or elsewhere to see what's happening out in the world." This sense of estrangement echoes in many students' comments, particularly those stranded on campus without automobiles. "We got to Target for fun! Is that not ridiculous?" asks one student legitimately. "When you don't have a car, life can get really boring." On campus, "Greek life dominates the social scene. Those not interested can have a decent social life . . . if they actively pursue it." Most don't, leaving them to conclude that they'd have to "look hard to find something else to do other than party or study on a Saturday night." In the plus column, right across the street from the university is Forest Park, which "is huge, with a free zoo, art and history museums, bicycle trails, an 18-hole golf course, and a science center." Not much further on is a student-friendly area called "The Loop," which boasts trendy shops, bars, and music venues. Some feel that access to The Loop, however, requires wheels. Public transportation is "not very good," so car-less students must either find friends with cars or learn to love the campus scene.

### Student Body

Tuition at Washington University is high, and "lots of really rich kids" end up here. Even so, "great" financial aid packages ensure that the socioeconomic demographic is not monolithic. Because of its reputation as a top school, Washington draws heavily from outside its region. There is a large East Coast contingent here, but every region of the country is well represented. The campus is also home to "lots of Jewish students" and a considerable Asian population. Students complain that "the lack of true integration is disappointing," pointing out that "it seems that each group secludes itself from the others." Countering this trend is a residence hall system that "throws random students together who become friends with each other although they might not have otherwise," but students agree that the overall situation still needs improvement. While students are "very smart," most are eminently pragmatic about education; notes one junior, "Intellectual students seem few and far between."

# WASHINGTON UNIVERSITY IN ST. LOUIS

FINANCIAL AID: 314-935-5900 • E-MAIL: ADMISSION@WUSTL.EDU • WEBSITE: ADMISSIONS.WUSTL.EDU

## ADMISSIONS

*Very important* academic and nonacademic factors considered by the admissions committee include character/personal qualities, class rank, essays, extracurricular activities, recommendations, secondary school record, standardized test scores, talent/ability, volunteer work, and work experience. *Other* factors considered include alumni/ae relation, interview, and minority status. Factors *not* considered include geography, religious affiliation/commitment, and state residency. SAT I or ACT required. TOEFL required of all international applicants. *High school units required/recommended:* 4 English required, 3 math required, 2 science required, 2 science lab required.

### The Inside Word

The fact that Washington U. doesn't have much play as a nationally respected car-window decal is about all that prevents it from being among the most selective universities. In every other respect—that is, in any way which really matters—this place is hard to beat and easily ranks as one of the best. No other university with as impressive a record of excellence across the board has a more accommodating admissions process. Not that it's easy to get in here, but lack of instant name recognition does affect Washington's admission rate. Students with above-average academic records who are not quite Ivy material are the big winners. Marginal candidates with high financial need may find difficulty; the admissions process at Washington U. is not need-blind and may take into account candidates' ability to pay if they are not strong applicants.

## FINANCIAL AID

*Students should submit:* FAFSA, CSS/Financial Aid PROFILE, and student, and parent 1040 tax return or waiver that there is no tax return. Regular filing deadline is February 15. The Princeton Review suggests that all financial aid forms be submitted as soon as possible after January 1. *Need-based scholarships/grants offered:* Pell, SEOG, state scholarships/grants, private scholarships, the school's own gift aid, United Negro College Fund. *Loan aid offered:* FFEL Subsidized Stafford, FFEL Unsubsidized Stafford, FFEL PLUS, and Federal Perkins. Institutional employment available. Federal Work-Study Program available. Off-campus job opportunities are excellent.

## FROM THE ADMISSIONS OFFICE

"Washington University is a medium-sized research university with world-renowned scholars and professional schools and a commitment to teaching and learning in a friendly supportive community. At Washington University, you are limited by nothing except your imagination and your willingness to take the initiative. Undergraduates choose from the college of arts and sciences and the schools of architecture, art, business, and engineering and applied sience. Whichever undergraduate college or school you choose you can take courses in any other and you can transfer between them. We encourage interdisciplinary work. Our students come from all over the country and the world, and from all manner of social, economic, ethnic, and racial backgrounds. Students are involved in nearly 200 clubs and activities including community service and multicultural groups, fraternities and sororities, intramural sports, student government, and literary groups."

## ADMISSIONS

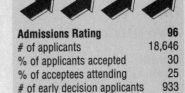

| Admissions Rating | 96 |
|---|---|
| # of applicants | 18,646 |
| % of applicants accepted | 30 |
| % of acceptees attending | 25 |
| # of early decision applicants | 933 |
| % accepted early decision | 34 |

### FRESHMAN PROFILE

| | |
|---|---|
| Range SAT Verbal | 630-710 |
| Range SAT Math | 660-740 |
| Range ACT Composite | 29-32 |
| Minimum TOEFL | 550 |
| % graduated top 10% of class | 85 |
| % graduated top 25% of class | 98 |
| % graduated top 50% of class | 100 |

### DEADLINES

| | |
|---|---|
| Early decision | 11/15 |
| Early decision notification | 12/15 |
| Regular admission | 1/15 |
| Regular notification | 4/1 |

### APPLICANTS ALSO LOOK AT

**AND OFTEN PREFER**
Harvard
Princeton
U. Penn
Yale
Stanford

**AND SOMETIMES PREFER**
Northwestern U.
U. Chicago
Johns Hopkins
Cornell
Duke

**AND RARELY PREFER**
U. Rochester
Boston U.
Tulane
U. Wisconsin—Madison

### FINANCIAL FACTS

| Financial Aid Rating | 74 |
|---|---|
| Tuition | $25,700 |
| Room & board | $8,216 |
| Books and supplies | $900 |
| Required fees | $677 |
| % frosh receiving aid | 41 |
| % undergrads receiving aid | 49 |

# WELLESLEY COLLEGE

BOARD OF ADMISSION, 106 CENTRAL STREET, WELLESLEY, MA 02481-8203 • ADMISSIONS: 781-283-2270 • FAX: 781-283-3678

## CAMPUS LIFE

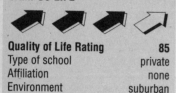

| | |
|---|---|
| **Quality of Life Rating** | **85** |
| Type of school | private |
| Affiliation | none |
| Environment | suburban |

### STUDENTS

| | |
|---|---|
| Total undergrad enrollment | 2,287 |
| % male/female | 0/100 |
| % from out of state | 77 |
| % from public high school | 60 |
| % live on campus | 93 |
| % African American | 6 |
| % Asian | 25 |
| % Caucasian | 55 |
| % Hispanic | 6 |
| % Native American | 1 |
| % international | 6 |
| # of countries represented | 70 |

### SURVEY SAYS . . .

*No one cheats*
*Beautiful campus*
*Dorms are like palaces*
*Student government is popular*
*Political activism is hot*
*Very little beer drinking*
*Very little hard liquor*
*(Almost) no one smokes*
*No one plays intramural sports*

## ACADEMICS

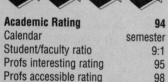

| | |
|---|---|
| **Academic Rating** | **94** |
| Calendar | semester |
| Student/faculty ratio | 9:1 |
| Profs interesting rating | 95 |
| Profs accessible rating | 98 |
| % profs teaching UG courses | 100 |
| Avg lab size | 10-19 students |
| Avg reg class size | 10-19 students |

### MOST POPULAR MAJORS

economics
psychology
English

## STUDENTS SPEAK OUT

### Academics

Wellesley, an all-women's undergraduate institution near Boston, is not just a college; it is also, according to one typical enthusiast, "a community dedicated to developing women of superior intellect, life skills, and savvy. It's simply the best. Wellesley has shown me that it is okay to be a fabulous woman with so much to offer." Most students here simply can't decide what they like most about the school. It could be that classes "are small and well taught. There's good atmosphere for discussion in and out of the classroom." Or, it might be that students have "access to some of the best lecturers and facilities in the world. World-renowned experts give presentations here." Most likely, though, it's the professors. They "are Wellesley's gold. They give individual attention and that's why I'm here," writes one student. Another explains, "The professors are very knowledgeable but also very approachable. It's obvious they love teaching." Faculty and students "are very fond of each other—but not in a way that could get anyone fired." Students probably are less enthusiastic about the brutal workload the school demands, although most accept it as an essential part of the Wellesley experience. "It'll be the hardest four years of your life, but also the most rewarding," sums up one student.

### Life

Despite the rigorous academic requirements of a Wellesley education, most students try to build an active extracurricular life around their studies, a situation that helps to explain the "popular bumper sticker: 'Wellesley—We'll Sleep When We're Dead.'" Writes one student, "Everyone is always busy. Over-programming for activities can be a problem." Many students become involved in some of the "many student organizations, such as Pre-Law Society and Russian Club. There are also many opportunities to volunteer in this area and the greater Boston region." While there are "student groups doing things, as far [as] parties on campus, sporting events, heavy drinking, etc., it's not here. There is no 'college life' per se. If you want fun, you have to go off campus." Explains one student, "People work hard during the week. On weekends, about one-third of the students get dressed up in tube tops and black pants, hop on the Senate Bus, and go to frat parties; one-third watch movies and do laundry or other on-campus events; and the other one-third study all weekend." Hometown Wellesley, Massachusetts, "is a little too upscale—lots of art dealers and people pushing baby strollers past Ann Taylor. But very safe." Writes one student, "Wellesley is not the best town to go out and have a good time. For fun we usually go to Boston," only 30 minutes away by car or bus. For those who simply choose to stay home, "the campus is beautiful and the dorms are fabulous."

### Student Body

Wellesley's "extremely motivated, dedicated, and ambitious" students are "very intelligent. I have great conversations with everyone. I feel so privileged to be around people who have done fantastic things and will have a major impact on the future." Undergrads enjoy a "very strong sense of community" and the fact that there is "no competition here. Eveyone is competing with themselves." Students "are extremely politically conscious. There is a strong tradition of activism and social efficacy," but they are "sometimes too dogmatic. I get tired of the sidewalk telling me what to do and think." Writes one student, "They don't smile enough. People are so stressed that they (myself included) forget to relax and have fun." As for the "typical" Wellesley woman, "everyone jokes about 'Wendy Wellesley,' but in truth there are a dozen different kinds of typical Wellesley students." Concludes one student, "At an all-women's college, people learn to be themselves, whoever that might be. From Wendy Wellesley, Frat Ho, to Wendy Wellesley, Raging Dyke, we're defining who we are daily, and that is awesome!"

FINANCIAL AID: 781-283-2360 • E-MAIL: ADMISSION@WELLESLEY.EDU • WEBSITE: WWW.WELLESLEY.EDU

## ADMISSIONS

*Very important* academic and nonacademic factors considered by the admissions committee include recommendations, secondary school record, and standardized test scores. *Important* factors considered include class rank, extracurricular activities, and talent/ability. *Other* factors considered include alumni/ae relation, character/personal qualities, essays, minority status, volunteer work, and work experience. Factors *not* considered include geography, interview, religious affiliation/commitment, and state residency. *High school units required/recommended:* 20 total required; 21 total recommended; 4 English required, 3 math required, 4 math recommended, 2 science required, 3 science recommended, 2 science lab required, 3 science lab recommended, 3 foreign language required, 4 foreign language recommended, 2 social studies required, 3 social studies recommended, 2 elective required, 3 elective recommended.

### The Inside Word

While the majority of women's colleges have gone coed or even closed over the past two decades, Wellesley has continued with vigor. As a surviving member of the Seven Sisters, the nation's most prestigious women's colleges, Wellesley enjoys even more popularity with students who choose the single-sex option. Admissions standards are rigorous, but among institutions of such high reputation Wellesley's admissions staff is friendlier and more open than the majority. Their willingness to conduct preliminary evaluations for candidates is especially commendable and in some form or another should be the rule rather than an exception at highly selective colleges.

## FINANCIAL AID

*Students should submit:* FAFSA, institution's own financial aid form, CSS/Financial Aid PROFILE, noncustodial (divorced/separated) parent's statement, business/farm supplement, and parents' and student's tax returns and W-2s. The Princeton Review suggests that all financial aid forms be submitted as soon as possible after January 1. *Need-based scholarships/grants offered:* Pell, SEOG, state scholarships/grants, private scholarships, and the school's own gift aid. *Loan aid offered:* FFEL Subsidized Stafford, FFEL Unsubsidized Stafford, FFEL PLUS, Federal Perkins, state, and college/university loans from institutional funds. Institutional employment available. Federal Work-Study Program available. Applicants will be notified of awards on or about April 1. Off-campus job opportunities are excellent.

## FROM THE ADMISSIONS OFFICE

"A student's years at Wellesley are the beginning—not the end—of an education. A Wellesley College degree signifies not that the graduate has memorized certain blocks of material, but that she has acquired the curiosity, the desire, and the ability to seek and assimilate new information. Four years at Wellesley can provide the foundation for the widest possible range of ambitions and the necessary self-confidence to fulfill them. At Wellesley, a student has every educational opportunity. Above all, it is Wellesley's purpose to teach students to apply knowledge wisely and to use the advantages of talent and education to seek new ways to serve the wider community."

## ADMISSIONS

| | |
|---|---|
| Admissions Rating | 97 |
| # of applicants | 3,071 |
| % of applicants accepted | 43 |
| % of acceptees attending | 45 |
| # accepting a place on wait list | 339 |
| % admitted from wait list | 5 |
| # of early decision applicants | 163 |
| % accepted early decision | 70 |

### FRESHMAN PROFILE

| | |
|---|---|
| Range SAT Verbal | 640-730 |
| Average SAT Verbal | 685 |
| Range SAT Math | 630-710 |
| Average SAT Math | 670 |
| Range ACT Composite | 27-31 |
| Average ACT Composite | 29 |
| Minimum TOEFL | 600 |
| % graduated top 10% of class | 67 |
| % graduated top 25% of class | 96 |
| % graduated top 50% of class | 100 |

### DEADLINES

| | |
|---|---|
| Early decision | 11/1 |
| Early decision notification | 12/15 |
| Regular admission | 1/15 |
| Regular notification | 4/1 |

### APPLICANTS ALSO LOOK AT
#### AND OFTEN PREFER
Brown
Swarthmore
#### AND SOMETIMES PREFER
Boston Coll.
Vassar
Barnard
Smith
Cornell U.
#### AND RARELY PREFER
Johns Hopkins
Mount Holyoke

## FINANCIAL FACTS

| | |
|---|---|
| Financial Aid Rating | 74 |
| Tuition | $23,718 |
| Room & board | $7,480 |
| Books and supplies | $800 |
| Required fees | $456 |
| % frosh receiving aid | 47 |
| % undergrads receiving aid | 52 |
| Avg frosh grant | $18,700 |
| Avg frosh loan | $2,414 |

# WELLS COLLEGE

ROUTE 90, AURORA, NY 13026 • ADMISSIONS: 315-364-3264 • FAX: 315-364-3327

## CAMPUS LIFE

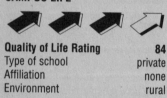

| | |
|---|---|
| **Quality of Life Rating** | **84** |
| Type of school | private |
| Affiliation | none |
| Environment | rural |

### STUDENTS

| | |
|---|---|
| Total undergrad enrollment | 462 |
| % male/female | 0/100 |
| % from out of state | 26 |
| % from public high school | 93 |
| % live on campus | 84 |
| % African American | 5 |
| % Asian | 3 |
| % Caucasian | 74 |
| % Hispanic | 3 |
| % international | 3 |
| # of countries represented | 8 |

### SURVEY SAYS . . .

Theater is hot
Student publications are ignored
No one cheats
Dorms are like palaces
Student government is popular
Very small frat/sorority scene
Class discussions encouraged
Students get along with local
community
Very little beer drinking
Musical organizations are hot

## ACADEMICS

| | |
|---|---|
| **Academic Rating** | **83** |
| Calendar | semester |
| Student/faculty ratio | 8:1 |
| Profs interesting rating | 81 |
| Profs accessible rating | 82 |
| % profs teaching UG courses | 100 |
| Avg lab size | 10-19 students |
| Avg reg class size | 10-19 students |

### MOST POPULAR MAJORS

psychology
English
biological & chemical sciences

## STUDENTS SPEAK OUT

### Academics

Tiny, all-women's Wells College in the Finger Lakes region of upstate New York offers "a writing-intensive" and "exceptionally well-rounded" liberal arts education that is extraordinarily affordable. The reportedly "excellent" academic experience here includes a core curriculum and a required thesis or senior project. "Discussion-oriented" classes are "small" and "women-centered," and "amazing alumnae connections" await students upon graduation. Though students complain that there is "not a huge selection of professors," they commend their modest but "amazing, extremely intelligent, and approachable" faculty. Wells professors show "genuine interest" in students' lives and are legendary for "going above and beyond the call of duty" to "help with personal problems." Many Wells students also applaud the administrators. "Our administration is quite approachable," contends a sophomore. "They take into consideration students' needs and wishes, and they try to change things." Others are tired of "the promise of change" and say the school could be managed better. Student gripes center around the limited number of course offerings, and some dated (but very eye-catching) facilities. "The technical equipment is somewhat lacking," observes a senior. "What we have in the way of computers, scientific equipment, and library resources is adequate but definitely not state-of-the-art." On the whole, though, students at Wells absolutely love their school. "The overall academic experience is fabulous," concludes a biochemistry major. "I don't think I could ask for a better academic environment."

### Life

The women of Wells stay active on their "very isolated" and "beautiful" campus "in the middle of nowhere," and feast on the "many opportunities to become a strong leader." It sure beats feasting on the Wells dining hall food, which "could use some help." Dozens of "traditions" ranging from the truly touching to the kind of nutty also keep students busy. These traditions include the ringing of the bells by juniors and seniors to announce dinner each night, campus serenades, original class songs and skits, a hotly contested annual basketball game, and a senior celebration signifying 100 days until graduation at which seniors wear robes and have a champagne breakfast together. During less traditional moments, students "like to hang out" in their rooms, "watch television and talk," or "play Nintendo." Planned events like "comedians, theme parties, and movie nights keep students occupied" as well, and there is also plenty of impromptu amusement. "Whether it's Ultimate Frisbee in the rain, skinny-dipping, beer-drinking Uno parties, or snowball fights, it's a creative life," explains a senior, "and if we get sick of creating," then "we go to frats, bars, and clubs" in nearby Ithaca to "party, dance, and drink." Though Wells students enjoy a great relationship with the immediately surrounding hamlet of Aurora, they say "regular trips to Ithaca" are "a must."

### Student Body

"Deep friendships" and "a special sort of bond" called "Sisterhood" are very big at Wells. "The best way to describe Wells is as one big sorority," explains a senior. It's "a close-knit community" where the "very understanding and accepting" students describe themselves as "open-minded, friendly, and caring." A junior describes her peers as "the most supportive people I have ever met." Says another student, "Everyone doesn't always get along, but everyone tries to get along." By gosh, "it's like one big, happy family," even if the social life does tend to become a bit "cliquish." Many of the "very goal-oriented" and "very friendly and trustworthy" women here are "strong, creative, ambitious leaders." They are "hard workers," too, who are "very dedicated to their studies" and "spend a lot of time on school work." Not every Wells student is quite so industrious, though. There is a contingent that is "here just to goof off and party."

FINANCIAL AID: 315-364-3289 • E-MAIL: ADMISSIONS@WELLS.EDU • WEBSITE: WWW.WELLS.EDU

## ADMISSIONS

*Very important* academic and nonacademic factors considered by the admissions committee include character/personal qualities, recommendations, secondary school record, and standardized test scores. *Important* factors considered include essays, extracurricular activities, talent/ability, and volunteer work. *Other* factors considered include alumni/ae relation, class rank, geography, interview, minority status, and work experience. Factors *not* considered include religious affiliation/commitment, and state residency. SAT I or ACT required. TOEFL required of all international applicants. High school diploma is required and GED is accepted. *High school units required/recommended:* 4 English required, 3 math required, 2 science required, 2 science lab required, 3 foreign language required, 2 social studies required, 3 elective required, 4 elective recommended.

### The Inside Word

Wells is engaged in that age-old admissions game called matchmaking. There are no minimums or cutoffs in the admissions process here. But don't be fooled by the high admit rate. The admissions committee will look closely at your academic accomplishments, but also gives attention to your essay, recommendations, and extracurricular pursuits. The committee also recommends an interview; we suggest taking them up on it.

## FINANCIAL AID

*Students should submit:* FAFSA; CCS/Finanical Aid PROFILE required only of early decision applicants. There is no regular filing deadline. The Princeton Review suggests that all financial aid forms be submitted as soon as possible after January 1. *Need-based scholarships/grants offered:* Pell, SEOG, state scholarships/grants, private scholarships, and the school's own gift aid. *Loan aid offered:* FFEL Subsidized Stafford, FFEL Unsubsidized Stafford, FFEL PLUS, and Federal Perkins. Institutional employment available. Federal Work-Study Program available. Applicants will be notified of awards on a rolling basis beginning on or about March 1. Off-campus job opportunities are fair.

## FROM THE ADMISSIONS OFFICE

"Seventy percent of Wells's women pursue advanced degrees. Our recent graduates have gained admission to programs at Cornell University, Harvard University, Georgetown University, Duke University, University of California at Berkeley, Yale University, and many others."

## ADMISSIONS

| | |
|---|---|
| Admissions Rating | 79 |
| # of applicants | 375 |
| % of applicants accepted | 89 |
| % of acceptees attending | 37 |
| # of early decision applicants | 19 |
| % accepted early decision | 68 |

### FRESHMAN PROFILE

| | |
|---|---|
| Range SAT Verbal | 530-630 |
| Average SAT Verbal | 570 |
| Range SAT Math | 510-600 |
| Average SAT Math | 550 |
| Range ACT Composite | 22-28 |
| Average ACT Composite | 26 |
| Minimum TOEFL | 550 |
| % graduated top 10% of class | 35 |
| % graduated top 25% of class | 64 |
| % graduated top 50% of class | 90 |

### DEADLINES

| | |
|---|---|
| Early decision | 12/15 |
| Early decision notification | 1/15 |
| Regular admission | 3/1 |
| Regular notification | 4/1 |

## FINANCIAL FACTS

| | |
|---|---|
| Financial Aid Rating | 72 |
| Tuition | $12,200 |
| Room & board | $6,200 |
| Books and supplies | $600 |
| Required fees | $460 |
| % frosh receiving aid | 79 |
| % undergrads receiving aid | 81 |
| Avg frosh grant | $10,246 |
| Avg frosh loan | $2,878 |

# WESLEYAN COLLEGE

4760 FORSYTH ROAD, MACON, GA 31210-4462 • ADMISSIONS: 912-757-5206 • FAX: 912-757-4030

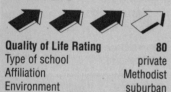
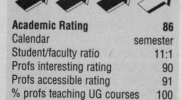
## STUDENTS SPEAK OUT

### Academics

To those comfortable in a small, all-women's academic environment, Georgia's Wesleyan College offers a "wonderful, well-rounded education" in "a unique learning community where the ties of sisterhood push us to make each other our best selves, to demand excellence in every aspect. Discussion-based seminar-style classes give us a forum to engage in 'group thinking,' providing all an opportunity to be heard. The leadership of professors, who truly serve as facilitators of learning, is invaluable." Rigorous academics ("the faculty's standards are tough!" writes one student; adds another, "Professors sometimes assign an unreal amount of work") abated by a caring faculty mark the school's style of instruction. "The professors and the quality of classroom instruction are the college's best assets," agree most students, citing "great student-professor interaction" and professors who "know us personally and are willing to go out of their way to assist us in anything we want to accomplish." Unusual for a small school, "Wesleyan is a great school for those studying the sciences." Students also praise the Computer Focus Program and the curriculum-wide emphasis on writing skills. Administrators receive high marks, although several students complain that "the bursar's office and the financial aid office need to improve communication." As an added benefit to undergrads, "the school's connections to its alumnae and their collaboration with present students is one of the school's great strengths."

### Life

All aspects of campus life at Wesleyan are colored by the school's one-of-a-kind "class system," under which each incoming class "has a name, a set of cheers, and a mascot. Instead of sororities, you bond with your class, your Big Sister class, and the other classes." Most undergrads agree that "Wesleyan's greatest strength is its sister class system. This system brings diverse students together in a way nothing else could." Sisterhood is just one of the "crazy traditions" here; others include "pep rallies, sitting in the middle of the dorm hallway at 3:00 A.M. drinking tea with friends," "midnight dinner hopping," and "random movie fests that are a great way to get away from the academic tension without leaving campus." More conventional activities are also available, among them "hockey games, clubs, restaurants, movies, malls, bowling, regular things." Students crow that "the campus is gorgeous" and that recent renovations are "awesome! The dorms and apartments are great: everything is nice, new, and clean!" Beyond campus lies Macon, a town that is "very diverse. You can usually find something to do there." Macon "is the perfect size for a city. It has a lot to offer but does not present, I think, as much danger and impersonality as larger cities. It maintains a rural feeling." Day trips to Atlanta satisfy those yearning for a big-city experience. Concludes one student, "Personally, I would prefer a larger campus with guys and parties, but going to school here has really helped me concentrate on my grades and my plans for the future." Adds another simply, "It feels like home to me!"

### Student Body

Wesleyan's emphasis on sisterhood fosters a strong, coherent student body. "The women here believe in sisterhood," explains one undergrad, "and it holds a special place in everyone's heart. Wesleyannes care about everyone here." The atmosphere is open and friendly, southern style: "It's so great to be able to make eye contact with everyone and smile without worrying about their being unwelcome to it." The "smart and well-rounded" student body "strives to be diverse. Different types of people interact much more often than just a few years ago." Students observe that "there seems to be more tolerance regarding religion and sexual orientation than a few years ago."

FINANCIAL AID: 800-447-6610 • E-MAIL: ADMISSIONS@WESLEYANCOLLEGE.EDU • WEBSITE: WWW.WESLEYANCOLLEGE.EDU

## ADMISSIONS

*Very important* academic and nonacademic factors considered by the admissions committee include character/personal qualities, class rank, essays, extracurricular activities, interview, recommendations, secondary school record, and standardized test scores. *Important* factors considered include talent/ability. *Other* factors considered include alumni/ae relation, geography, minority status, state residency, volunteer work, and work experience. Factors *not* considered include religious affiliation/commitment. SAT I or ACT required. TOEFL required of all international applicants. High school diploma is required and GED is accepted. *High school units required/recommended:* 15 total required; 4 English required, 3 math required, 3 science required, 4 science recommended, 2 science lab required, 2 foreign language required, 3 foreign language recommended, 2 social studies required, 1 history required, 1 elective required.

### The Inside Word

The college has gotten lots of national publicity of late, but its applicant pool is still primarily southeastern in origin. Candidates from outside the usual sphere of influence of any college draw the attention of admissions officers, and it's no exception here. Recommendations are important at Wesleyan; we'd advise that such letters make at least some reference to your interest in and suitability for a women's college; your own essay won't carry nearly as much weight.

## FINANCIAL AID

*Students should submit:* FAFSA, institution's own financial aid form, state aid form, and noncustodial (divorced/separated) parent's statement. There is no regular filing deadline. The Princeton Review suggests that all financial aid forms be submitted as soon as possible after January 1. *Need-based scholarships/grants offered:* Pell, SEOG, state scholarships/grants, private scholarships, and the school's own gift aid. *Loan aid offered:* Direct Subsidized Stafford, Direct Unsubsidized Stafford, Direct PLUS, Federal Perkins, state, CitiAssist, Wells Fargo, and G.A.T.E. Institutional employment available. Federal Work-Study Program available. Applicants will be notified of awards on a rolling basis beginning on or about March 1. Off-campus job opportunities are good.

## FROM THE ADMISSIONS OFFICE

"Wesleyan College has put women first since 1836. As the world's first college for women, Wesleyan has led the way in curriculum development designed for women. Committed faculty consider students colleagues and collaborate with them on research, papers, internships, or designing interdisciplinary majors. The student/faculty ratio is 11:1, and the average class size is 11. A recent $4 million gift from three alumnae sisters completes funding for an $8 million innovative science center with research laboratories for faculty and students. Construction should begin during 2000–2001 school year."

## ADMISSIONS

| | |
|---|---|
| Admissions Rating | 69 |
| # of applicants | 391 |
| % of applicants accepted | 76 |
| % of acceptees attending | 45 |
| # of early decision applicants | 32 |
| % accepted early decision | 72 |

### FRESHMAN PROFILE

| | |
|---|---|
| Range SAT Verbal | 515-660 |
| Range SAT Math | 480-610 |
| Range ACT Composite | 21-26 |
| Minimum TOEFL | 550 |
| Average HS GPA | 3.5 |
| % graduated top 10% of class | 42 |
| % graduated top 25% of class | 71 |
| % graduated top 50% of class | 95 |

### DEADLINES

| | |
|---|---|
| Early decision | 11/1 |
| Early decision notification | 12/1 |
| Priority admission deadline | 1/15 |
| Regular admission | 3/1 |
| Regular notification | 4/1 |
| Nonfall registration? | yes |

### APPLICANTS ALSO LOOK AT
### AND SOMETIMES PREFER

U. Georgia
Emory
Agnes Scott
Mercer

### AND RARELY PREFER

Berry
Rhodes
U. Florida
Florida State

## FINANCIAL FACTS

| | |
|---|---|
| Financial Aid Rating | 87 |
| Tuition | $8,950 |
| Room & board | $7,150 |
| Books and supplies | $650 |
| Required fees | $850 |
| % undergrads receiving aid | 87 |
| Avg frosh grant | $12,334 |
| Avg frosh loan | $2,522 |

# WESLEYAN UNIVERSITY

The Stewart M. Reid House, 70 Wyllys Avenue, Middletown, CT 06459-0265 • Admissions: 860-685-3000 • Fax: 860-685-3001

## CAMPUS LIFE

| | |
|---|---|
| **Quality of Life Rating** | **78** |
| Type of school | private |
| Affiliation | none |
| Environment | suburban |

### STUDENTS

| | |
|---|---|
| Total undergrad enrollment | 2,722 |
| % male/female | 48/52 |
| % from out of state | 91 |
| % from public high school | 57 |
| % live on campus | 93 |
| % in (# of) fraternities | 4 (9) |
| % in (# of) sororities | 3 (4) |
| % African American | 9 |
| % Asian | 8 |
| % Caucasian | 69 |
| % Hispanic | 6 |
| % international | 5 |

### SURVEY SAYS . . .

*Political activism is hot*
*Great library*
*No one cheats*
*Students aren't religious*
*Athletic facilities are great*
*Students don't like Middletown, CT*
*(Almost) no one listens to college radio*
*Very small frat/sorority scene*

## ACADEMICS

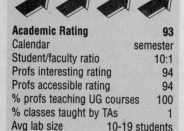

| | |
|---|---|
| **Academic Rating** | **93** |
| Calendar | semester |
| Student/faculty ratio | 10:1 |
| Profs interesting rating | 94 |
| Profs accessible rating | 94 |
| % profs teaching UG courses | 100 |
| % classes taught by TAs | 1 |
| Avg lab size | 10-19 students |
| Avg reg class size | 10-19 students |

### MOST POPULAR MAJORS

English
economics
government

## STUDENTS SPEAK OUT

### Academics

"You live with the coolest people in the world, which is interrupted periodically by instruction from the smartest people on campus," says a sophomore about a Wesleyan education. "There is a serious but noncompetitive academic environment," reports a senior art history major. A junior government major says, "When your government professor is on a first-name basis with the White House and is an excellent teacher [to boot], you can't ask for better academics." A senior chemistry major proclaims, "Our hippie, flower-child reputation overshadows the fact that we have a great science department with opportunities you can't get anywhere else." A sophomore writes, "Professors really care about your opinions, and you're treated as an intellectual equal." Still, one junior dance major laments that "diversity university does not have a diverse faculty." Students enjoy their academic freedom. "Wesleyan's academic requirements give you tremendous freedom to design your own curriculum and to take classes you really want to be in." Learning takes place both in and out of class. Writes a sophomore, "I feel like much of my academic experience occurs outside of class because there is so much political activity and passionate discussion about campus and global issues." While the professors are universally admired, the administration "isn't really in touch with the students' wants and needs. They're like 'independent Ivy,' and we're like 'Can we smoke it?'" A senior neuroscience major adds, "The administration appears to be trying to make us like the schools I didn't want to go to." The registrar's office is the focus of displeasure. The online registration system might be revolutionary, but "online registration is hell; you're basically racing with all the people on the computers next to you," one junior writes.

### Life

A senior East Asian studies major describes life at Wesleyan thusly: "What do people do for fun? Stage a rally during the president's office hours and simultaneously have a knitting bee and discussion about pro-feminist activism." Though some complain that the party policy is getting too strict, a junior English major says, "If you want frat parties, we've got them. If you want naked parties, we've got those too." Others note that while "the beer flows like water if you know where to look, there's not a lot of pressure to drink." Explains one, "Campus life doesn't revolve around drinking because there are always so many other things going on." Students call Middletown "boring" and "like a sketchy ghost town" but love the university's central New England location and its "great sledding hill." Students don't seem too happy that they are required to remain on the meal plan for four years.

### Student Body

Wesleyan "is a school full of very idealistic people who really want to make a significant impact on the world before they even graduate." Though sometimes described as "self-righteous," Wesleyan is home to a "passionate, involved student body. At best, they change the world. At worst, they're entertaining." While the student body is racially mixed, a senior chemistry major notes that "we are diverse and very accepting as long as you've never worn a white hat or had any Republican sympathies." Still, most students overlook the lack of political heterogeneity because they appreciate that "there is no such thing as a typical Wesleyan student. You can meet a lacrosse jock at a fraternity party and then run into him the next day at an Amnesty International meeting or see him later in a theater performance." Another student adds, "My friends are a motley crew of musicians, artists, intellectuals . . . united by good herb." Even the senior art history major who believes that "the school is populated by a lot of whiny left-wing rich kids who have no concept of reality and how an administration must sometimes make unpopular choices," admits that she "like[s] that students are politically active."

FINANCIAL AID: 860-685-2800 • E-MAIL: ADMISSIONS@WESLEYAN.EDU • WEBSITE: WWW.WESLEYAN.EDU

## ADMISSIONS

*Very important* academic and nonacademic factors considered by the admissions committee include character/personal qualities, class rank, essays, and secondary school record. *Important* factors considered include extracurricular activities, minority status, recommendations, standardized test scores, and talent/ability. *Other* factors considered include alumni/ae relation, geography, interview, state residency, volunteer work, and work experience. Factors *not* considered include religious affiliation/commitment. TOEFL required of all international applicants. High school diploma is required and GED is not accepted. *High school units required/recommended:* 19 total recommended; 4 English recommended, 4 math recommended, 4 science recommended, 4 foreign language recommended, 3 social studies recommended.

### The Inside Word

Wesleyan stacks up well against its very formidable competitors academically, yet due to these same competitors the university admits at a fairly high rate for an institution of its high caliber. Candidate evaluation is nonetheless rigorous. If you aren't one of the best students in your graduating class, it isn't likely that you will be very competitive in Wesleyan's applicant pool. Strong communicators can help open the doors by submitting persuasive essays and interviews that clearly demonstrate an effective match with the university.

## FINANCIAL AID

*Students should submit:* FAFSA, CSS/Financial Aid PROFILE, noncustodial (divorced/separated) parent's statement, and business/farm supplement. Regular filing deadline is February 1. The Princeton Review suggests that all financial aid forms be submitted as soon as possible after January 1. *Need-based scholarships/grants offered:* Pell, SEOG, state scholarships/grants, private scholarships, and the school's own gift aid. *Loan aid offered:* FFEL Subsidized Stafford, FFEL Unsubsidized Stafford, FFEL PLUS, Federal Perkins, and college/university loans from institutional funds. Institutional employment available. Federal Work-Study Program available. Applicants will be notified of awards on or about April 1. Off-campus job opportunities are good.

## FROM THE ADMISSIONS OFFICE

"Wesleyan's faculty recently adopted an innovative plan for curricular renewal that reaffirms the individual freedom and flexibility for which Wesleyan is so well known, but also signals a new direction for liberal arts education. The focus of the changes is to help students achieve a coherent education. Wesleyan's Dean of Admission and Financial Aid, Barbara-Ann Wilson, describes the qualities Wesleyan seeks in its students: 'In an admission process as individualized and personalized as Wesleyan's, we evaluate each candidate on academic strength, intellectual curiosity, commitment (or passion!), personal qualitites, and extracurricular talent.'"

## ADMISSIONS

| | |
|---|---|
| Admissions Rating | 97 |
| # of applicants | 6,862 |
| % of applicants accepted | 27 |
| % of acceptees attending | 38 |
| # accepting a place on wait list | 1 |
| % admitted from wait list | 100 |
| # of early decision applicants | 707 |
| % accepted early decision | 41 |

### FRESHMAN PROFILE

| | |
|---|---|
| Range SAT Verbal | 640-730 |
| Average SAT Verbal | 680 |
| Range SAT Math | 640-720 |
| Average SAT Math | 678 |
| Average ACT Composite | 29 |
| Minimum TOEFL | 600 |
| % graduated top 10% of class | 68 |
| % graduated top 25% of class | 92 |
| % graduated top 50% of class | 98 |

### DEADLINES

| | |
|---|---|
| Early decision | 11/15 |
| Early decision notification | 12/15 |
| Regular admission | 1/1 |
| Regular notification | 4/1 |

### APPLICANTS ALSO LOOK AT
**AND OFTEN PREFER**
Harvard
Columbia
Brown
Stanford, Duke
**AND SOMETIMES PREFER**
Amherst
Princeton
Williams
Bowdoin
Swarthmore
**AND RARELY PREFER**
Oberlin
Brandeis
Vassar, Middlebury

## FINANCIAL FACTS

| | |
|---|---|
| Financial Aid Rating | 73 |
| Tuition | $25,380 |
| Room & board | $6,630 |
| Books and supplies | $1,880 |
| Required fees | $800 |
| % frosh receiving aid | 43 |
| % undergrads receiving aid | 47 |
| Avg frosh grant | $19,460 |
| Avg frosh loan | $3,500 |

# WEST VIRGINIA UNIVERSITY

ADMISSIONS OFFICE, PO BOX 6009, MORGANTOWN, WV 26506-6009 • ADMISSIONS: 800-344-9881 • FAX: 304-293-3080

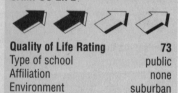
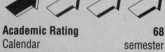
## STUDENTS SPEAK OUT

### Academics

Spread out across three campuses in Morgantown (and several smaller regional campuses), West Virginia University works hard to overcome the usual shortcomings of mammoth undergraduate programs. Operation Jump-Start typifies WVU's efforts to personalize the university. The program groups freshmen in nine residential houses according to academic interest. Faculty couples live close by and serve as mentors for the incoming students, helping them acclimate to the university and quickly achieve a sense of community. Some Jump-Start groups have taken on community service projects, and others have taken trips together. Similarly, "the university Honors Program allows students to have a fulfilling and challenging undergraduate experience" that includes smaller classes and more seminar-style teaching. Professors at WVU run the gamut from wonderful to awful, depending on the department and the individual. Several students in the biological sciences voice such complaints as "I find myself teaching myself through learning centers and excessive studying." Professors in the popular Division of Agriculture and Forestry, however, "run in the good-to-excellent range." The College of Engineering and the College of Human Resources and Education are among the popular and well-regarded options here. According to one dissatisfied student, "Because of problems with the PRT [personnel rapid transit], it usually takes me half an hour to get to class! My advisor has also continually told me wrong information on the classes I need to take."

### Life

Many students love the Morgantown area for its quiet vibe. Explains one, "The town moves at a slow pace when you compare it to some of the larger cities in proximity to Morgantown (i.e., D.C., Pittsburgh, Baltimore, etc.), but that's not a problem. There is always something to do, everything from hiking up to Coopers Rock and taking in the magnificent view from the top, or taking a walk/run along the Monongahela River." They also like its proximity to Pittsburgh, only an hour-and-a-half away by car. Students warn, however, that town-gown relations are extremely strained, except during football games. "WVU students are avid sports fans. Thousands of us go to cheer on our team at each sporting event, be [it] football or basketball." While "WVU was formerly ranked #1 party school in the nation back in 1998 or so . . . now we are nowhere near that ranking. Unfortunately, our president has seen to it that we will never achieve that ranking ever again through [stringent] policies and such." In the place of bleary-eyed beer bashes, "WVU has implemented an alcohol-free program called WVU Up All Night which takes place on Thursday, Friday, and Saturday nights. A lot of free activities and free food are provided during Up All Night. And the turn out is tremendous."

### Student Body

WVU draws students largely from within the state. Maryland, New Jersey, and Pennsylvania also contribute heavily to the student population. Writes one student, "There is a 'country boy meets city boy' situation that occurs for every freshman here at WVU. By this I mean you have a solid in-state population of good ol' West Virginia boys meeting up with the Long Islanders and Jersey boys. Needless to say, if you are from the Bible Belt you haven't seen many New York and New Jersey Jews. I don't want to say there is hostility between these two groups but getting along takes a little effort." Minority populations are tiny, with about 600 African American undergraduates constituting the largest nonwhite group. Complains one black student, "I just wish there were more minorities on campus."

FINANCIAL AID: 304-293-5242 • E-MAIL: WVUADMISSIONS@ARC.WVU.EDU • WEBSITE: WWW.WVU.EDU

## ADMISSIONS

*Very important* academic and nonacademic factors considered by the admissions committee include secondary school record, standardized test scores, and state residency. *Important* factors considered include minority status. *Other* factors considered include alumni/ae relation, character/personal qualities, extracurricular activities, geography, talent/ability, volunteer work, and work experience. Factors *not* considered include class rank, essays, interview, recommendations, and religious affiliation/commitment. SAT I or ACT required. TOEFL required of all international applicants. High school diploma is required and GED is accepted. *High school units required/recommended:* 18 total required; 4 English required, 3 math required, 2 science required, 2 science lab required, 2 foreign language recommended, 3 social studies required, 1 history required, 4 elective required. *The admissions office says:* "Students are urged to focus on meeting required courses, especially math."

### The Inside Word

West Virginia's admissions office made an excellent point about rolling admission in their response to us, which applies to candidates for admission at any university that uses such an approach. As the admissions committee gets closer to its enrollment targets, the admissions process becomes progressively more selective. At West Virginia the early bird usually gets a worm, and there is often another one for a late bird. Still, don't hold off on rolling admission applications just because others have more pressing deadlines. Forget that there's a rolling plan, and complete your application as if it has to be in at the same time as all the rest.

## FINANCIAL AID

*Students should submit:* FAFSA. Regular filing deadline is March 1. Priority filing deadline is February 15. *Need-based scholarships/grants offered:* Pell, SEOG, state scholarships/grants, private scholarships, and the school's own gift aid. *Loan aid offered:* Direct Subsidized Stafford, Direct Unsubsidized Stafford, Direct PLUS, Federal Perkins, Federal Nursing, state, and the school's own loans. Institution employment available. Federal Work-Study Program available. Applicants will be notified of awards on a rolling basis beginning on or about March 30. Off-campus job opportunities are good.

## FROM THE ADMISSIONS OFFICE

"WVU graduates go on to highly successful lives and careers; eight were recently named among the leading Fortune 500 executives by Forbes magazine. WVU has an enviable record of Rhodes (25), Truman (14), Goldwater (19), and Marshall (2) Scholars. In fact WVU was selected in 1996 as a Truman Scholar Honor Institution in the inaugural year. Faculty in the 13 colleges and schools involve students with hands-on research projects, the latest technologies, internships, foreign exchanges, and service learning. The forensics identification program, developed in conjunction with the FBI, is the only such degree program of its kind in the world. The university's unique Career Success Academy pairs students with alumni mentors, contributing to an excellent job placement rate. WVU also boasts a unique Mountaineer Parents Club that currently links more than 8,000 family members around the globe to WVU activities. Other student-centered initiatives that have received national attention include Operation Jump-Start, which has faculty mentors living adjacent to all residence halls; WVUp All Night, with its routine weekend social alternatives like free concerts and activities; and a Festival of Ideas featuring national headline speakers. WVU fields some of the finest Division I sports teams in the nation, and students always get the best seats in the house. The main campus has been touted as being among the safest in the nation, and a national guide has dubbed the city of Morgantown 'Best Small City in the East.' Students travel from campus to campus in a unique personal rapid transport system (PRT) that continually receives high marks."

## ADMISSIONS

| | |
|---|---|
| Admissions Rating | 75 |
| # of applicants | 8,016 |
| % of applicants accepted | 94 |
| % of acceptees attending | 47 |

### FRESHMAN PROFILE

| | |
|---|---|
| Range SAT Verbal | 460-560 |
| Average SAT Verbal | 514 |
| Range SAT Math | 470-570 |
| Average SAT Math | 521 |
| Range ACT Composite | 20-25 |
| Average ACT Composite | 23 |
| Minimum TOEFL | 550 |
| Average HS GPA | 3.2 |
| % graduated top 10% of class | 21 |
| % graduated top 25% of class | 45 |
| % graduated top 50% of class | 77 |

### DEADLINES

| | |
|---|---|
| Priority admission deadline | 3/1 |
| Regular admission | 8/1 |
| Nonfall registration? | yes |

### APPLICANTS ALSO LOOK AT

**AND OFTEN PREFER**
Miami U.
Marquette
Washington U.
James Madison

**AND SOMETIMES PREFER**
U. Pittsburgh
Virginia Tech
U. Maryland—Coll. Park

**AND RARELY PREFER**
Ohio State U.—Columbus
Penn State—Univ. Park

### FINANCIAL FACTS

| | |
|---|---|
| Financial Aid Rating | 73 |
| In-state tuition | $1,994 |
| Out-of-state tuition | $7,520 |
| Room & board | $5,152 |
| Books and supplies | $660 |
| Required fees | $842 |
| % frosh receiving aid | 52 |
| % undergrads receiving aid | 62 |

# WESTMINSTER COLLEGE

319 SOUTH MARKET STREET, NEW WILMINGTON, PA 16172 • ADMISSIONS: 800-942-8033 • FAX: 724-946-7171

## CAMPUS LIFE

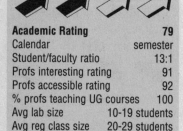

| | |
|---|---|
| **Quality of Life Rating** | **76** |
| Type of school | private |
| Affiliation | Presbyterian |
| Environment | suburban |

### STUDENTS

| | |
|---|---|
| Total undergrad enrollment | 1,451 |
| % male/female | 38/62 |
| % from out of state | 21 |
| % from public high school | 90 |
| % live on campus | 78 |
| % in (# of) fraternities | 50 (5) |
| % in (# of) sororities | 50 (5) |
| % African American | 1 |
| % Asian | 1 |
| % Caucasian | 98 |

### SURVEY SAYS . . .

Frats and sororities dominate social scene
Diversity lacking on campus
Classes are small
(Almost) everyone smokes
Very little drug use
Lousy food on campus
Political activism is (almost) nonexistent
Lousy off-campus food
Students don't like
New Wilmington, PA
Theater is unpopular

## ACADEMICS

| | |
|---|---|
| **Academic Rating** | **79** |
| Calendar | semester |
| Student/faculty ratio | 13:1 |
| Profs interesting rating | 91 |
| Profs accessible rating | 92 |
| % profs teaching UG courses | 100 |
| Avg lab size | 10-19 students |
| Avg reg class size | 20-29 students |

### MOST POPULAR MAJORS
business administration
elementary education
sociology

## STUDENTS SPEAK OUT

### Academics

Tiny Westminster College boasts an "excellent" regional reputation for "very good academics" and plenty of "real world" preparation as well. Students also relish the low tuition (for a high caliber private school, anyway) and very accommodating financial aid. In accordance with the "Westminster Plan," students must complete an exhaustive core curriculum in the sciences, humanities, mathematics, computer science, and religion. The result is that every student graduates with at least two majors—a "common" major in the western liberal arts tradition and a specialized major of the student's choosing. Westminster also boasts "small" and "very challenging" classes in technologically savvy "smart classrooms" that come equipped with Internet connections, laser disc players, and the ability to "audio conference with individuals in remote locations around the world." Although some professors are "downright awful," most here are of the "enthusiastic and eager" variety. "Personal attention" and "close-knit teacher-student relationships" are the norm, and students praise their profs for being "easily accessible" and "willing to help outside of class." The administration is "too strict" and "anal about idiotic rules," but at least it's flexible. "If something needs to be done and no one [in the administration] will listen, students can call the president, and he will change things fast." Popular majors at Westminster include the pre-professional tracks, especially accounting and education.

### Life

The "safe" and "beautiful" campus of Westminster College is located in secluded but "boring" New Wilmington, "a quaint town with a large Amish population" in western Pennsylvania where "the cable sucks." To keep themselves entertained, students "shop at the outlets" nearby, "watch movies," and make "midnight pilgrimages" to Taco Bell and Wal-Mart. "Basically," though, students "drink" for amusement. The Greek system and occasional "apartment parties" are "the source of life on campus," and students go to frats en masse on the weekends to "drink and party" and for a "rip-roaring good time." "People party to escape boredom and frustration," confesses a junior. Students who don't want to drink or who need a break from the frat party scene often go home for the weekend, which is generally not a problem as the majority hail from nearby. Finding a parking place back on campus can be a problem, however. Westminster has a considerable population of religious Christians, many of whom take exception to the rowdy fraternity parties but manage to blend their religious and worldly interests. Westminster presents its students with "opportunities for Christian growth," including optional weekly worship services and Catholic liturgy. Music clubs, an active student government, a radio station, and Bible study groups are also available, and Habitat for Humanity is the largest organization on campus.

### Student Body

The "helpful, nice," and "predominantly Republican" students at Westminster are "easy to get along with" and "fun to be around." Students "talk to each other even if they do not know each other," but on this small campus, it is very rare to pass a stranger who is not visiting campus. On the bright side of this situation, "everyone will stop and ask you how you are" as you walk across campus. As is to be expected in a school of this size, the "rumor mill" can be unpleasant at Westminster, as can "petty gossip" from all quarters. "There are a lot of cliques" as well (in part because "lots of people know each other from high school"). "On the surface, everyone gets along," postulates a sophomore, "but in reality, a lot of people don't like each other and that causes a lot of hidden aggression." Students don't much like the fact that "everyone is white," either, and to make matters worse, "watered down P.C. opinions abound," and "students are afraid to say what they think."

FINANCIAL AID: 724-946-7102 • E-MAIL: ADMIS@WESTMINSTER.EDU • WEBSITE: WWW.WESTMINSTER.EDU

## ADMISSIONS

*Very important* academic and nonacademic factors considered by the admissions committee include recommendations and secondary school record. *Important* factors considered include character/personal qualities, essays, extracurricular activities, standardized test scores, and talent/ability. *Other* factors considered include alumni/ae relation, class rank, geography, minority status, volunteer work, and work experience. Factors *not* considered include interview, religious affiliation/commitment, and state residency. SAT I or ACT required. TOEFL required of all international applicants. High school diploma is required and GED is accepted. *High school units required/recommended:* 16 total recommended; 4 English recommended, 4 math recommended, 2 science recommended, 2 science lab recommended, 4 foreign language recommended, 2 social studies recommended. *The admissions office says:* "Applicants must have a minimum 2.5 GPA in high school."

### The Inside Word

The vast majority of those who apply to Westminster gain admission, but the applicant pool is strong enough to enable the college to weed out those who don't measure up to the solid entering class academic profile. Candidates who are shooting for academic scholarships should play the admissions game all the way and put a solid effort into the completion of their applications.

## FINANCIAL AID

*Students should submit:* FAFSA, institution's own financial aid form, and federal income tax form. The Princeton Review suggests that all financial aid forms be submitted as soon as possible after January 1. *Need-based scholarships/grants offered:* Pell, SEOG, state scholarships/grants, private scholarships, and the school's own gift aid. *Loan aid offered:* FFEL Subsidized Stafford, FFEL Unsubsidized Stafford, and FFEL PLUS. Institutional employment available. Applicants will be notified of awards on a rolling basis. Off-campus job opportunities are good.

## FROM THE ADMISSIONS OFFICE

"Since its founding, Westminster has been dedicated to a solid foundation in today's most crucial social, cultural, and ethical issues. Related to the Presbyterian Church (U.S.A.), Westminster is home to people of many faiths. Our students and faculty, tradition of campus, and small-town setting all contribute to an enlightening educational experience."

### ADMISSIONS

| | |
|---|---|
| Admissions Rating | 74 |
| # of applicants | 975 |
| % of applicants accepted | 89 |
| % of acceptees attending | 41 |

#### FRESHMAN PROFILE

| | |
|---|---|
| Range SAT Verbal | 480-590 |
| Average SAT Verbal | 544 |
| Range SAT Math | 490-590 |
| Average SAT Math | 543 |
| Range ACT Composite | 21-25 |
| Average ACT Composite | 24 |
| Minimum TOEFL | 500 |
| Average HS GPA | 3.3 |
| % graduated top 10% of class | 24 |
| % graduated top 25% of class | 58 |
| % graduated top 50% of class | 90 |

#### DEADLINES

| | |
|---|---|
| Regular admission | 4/15 |

#### APPLICANTS ALSO LOOK AT

**AND OFTEN PREFER**
Miami U.

**AND SOMETIMES PREFER**
Penn State—U. Park
Allegheny

**AND RARELY PREFER**
Duquesne
Indiana U—Bloomington
Washington & Jefferson
Kent State
Slippery Rock

### FINANCIAL FACTS

| | |
|---|---|
| Financial Aid Rating | 85 |
| Tuition | $16,180 |
| Room & board | $4,980 |
| Books and supplies | $600 |
| Required fees | $805 |
| % frosh receiving aid | 81 |
| % undergrads receiving aid | 77 |
| Avg frosh grant | $7,500 |
| Avg frosh loan | $3,100 |

# WHEATON COLLEGE (IL)

501 COLLEGE AVENUE, WHEATON, IL 60187 • ADMISSIONS: 630-752-5005 • FAX: 630-752-5285

## CAMPUS LIFE

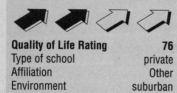

| Quality of Life Rating | 76 |
|---|---|
| Type of school | private |
| Affiliation | Other |
| Environment | suburban |

### STUDENTS

| | |
|---|---|
| Total undergrad enrollment | 2,418 |
| % male/female | 47/53 |
| % from out of state | 79 |
| % from public high school | 63 |
| % live on campus | 88 |
| % African American | 2 |
| % Asian | 4 |
| % Caucasian | 90 |
| % Hispanic | 3 |
| % international | 1 |
| # of countries represented | 13 |

### SURVEY SAYS . . .
*Very little drug use*
*Great food on campus*
*Diversity lacking on campus*
*Lots of conservatives on campus*
*Campus feels safe*
*Very little beer drinking*
*Very little hard liquor*
*(Almost) no one smokes*
*Students are very religious*

## ACADEMICS

| Academic Rating | 88 |
|---|---|
| Calendar | semester |
| Student/faculty ratio | 13:1 |
| Profs interesting rating | 70 |
| Profs accessible rating | 70 |
| % profs teaching UG courses | 90 |
| Avg lab size | 10-19 students |
| Avg reg class size | 10-19 students |

### MOST POPULAR MAJORS
English
business/economics
Christian education & ministry

## STUDENTS SPEAK OUT

### Academics

"It's not every day that you hear about a school that is outwardly devoted to the growth of God's work on Earth and also academically well respected," but that's what you'll find at ultra-religious Wheaton College, "a strong evangelical and academic" school in the far reaches of suburban Chicago. "Christian fellowship and growth in the Lord" are all the rage here. Religion is not only "accepted," it's zealously "applied to life." Students laud Wheaton's "friendly and approachable" professors for going "out of their way to get to know you." Profs are "enthusiastic about their subjects" and "really committed to teaching and mentoring students." They are also deeply religious. Wheaton's administration is "incomprehensible and annoying on occasion," but there is little red tape. Students report that the "responsive" and "very approachable" top brass is "committed to excellence along with serving Christ." The somewhat dated campus technology could use sprucing up, but Wheaton boasts a "strong" and nationally recognized music program in addition to a number of excellent liberal arts programs, and satisfied students say "the academic rigor prepares students" well "for grad school" (though "not so much life in general"). This place is obviously not for everybody, but if "the integration of faith and learning" is what you want out of college, Wheaton is arguably the best school in the nation with a "Christ-based worldview."

### Life

Wheaton students swear off gambling, drugs, dancing on campus, and all manners of social vice. "We all signed a pledge saying we won't drink, smoke, or have sex," explains a junior. Luckily, "the college provides many entertaining events on campus—good, clean fun, if you will." Both intercollegiate sports (especially the perennially strong men's soccer team) and intramurals are big here, and there are plenty of concerts on campus, but there's "not much of a social scene," and life can be "pretty mundane" at times. Off campus, "the town closes down at 9:00 P.M." Some students say the campus is "socially impotent" because of the "unreasonably strict" code of conduct. Others counter that the "no distractions" atmosphere is perfect for the demanding academics that require "tons of studying." "Although some secular college students may have a hard time understanding how we can have fun without partying, we truly have a more fulfilling kind of fun," explains a junior. Students cryptically allude to "an underground" party scene, but no one seems sure who is involved or where the carousing occurs. Most students spend their idle hours "sitting in a room talking until the wee hours of the morning," or in "deep conversations in coffee shops," or "worshiping." For a change of pace, students visit Chicago, "about an hour away by commuter train."

### Student Body

"Everyone gets along pretty well" at Wheaton because the "very driven and focused" students "love Jesus" and "all have a common, Christian-centered bond." Students describe themselves as "really conservative" and "idealistic," as well as "good-humored" and possessing "strong moral character." Some of their peers are described as "socially, sexually, and mentally behind," and some are either "too friendly" or lack "social skills in general." Also, the atmosphere at Wheaton places a "huge amount of pressure" on every student "to become a super-person" who is "super-spiritual, super-athletic," and so on. Students say they are definitely not identical automatons, though. "Because the rules are so strict at Wheaton, you'd almost expect everyone to have the exact same opinion on all political, religious, and social issues," reflects a first-year student. "That's not true, though. Wheaton's population ranges from conservative to liberal, from people who don't think much about God to people who are passionate about their faith, and from people who volunteer for all kinds of service projects to people who just live their own lives."

FINANCIAL AID: 630-752-5021 • E-MAIL: ADMISSIONS@WHEATON.EDU • WEBSITE: WWW.WHEATON.EDU

## ADMISSIONS

*Very important* academic and nonacademic factors considered by the admissions committee include character/personal qualities, religious affiliation/commitment, secondary school record, and standardized test scores. *Important* factors considered include class rank, essays, interview, and recommendations. *Other* factors considered include alumni/ae relation, extracurricular activities, geography, minority status, talent/ability, and volunteer work. Factors *not* considered include state residency and work experience. SAT I or ACT required; SAT II recommended. TOEFL required of all international applicants. High school diploma is required and GED is accepted. *High school units required/recommended:* 18 total required; 4 English recommended, 3 math recommended, 4 science recommended, 3 science lab recommended, 3 foreign language recommended, 4 social studies recommended.

### The Inside Word

The admissions process at Wheaton is quite rigorous. As at most small colleges, the review of candidates focuses on far more than courses, grades, and test scores. The admissions committee will also carefully consider your essays, recommendations, and other indicators of your character as they assess how well suited you are to the campus community. Matchmaking here also includes giving preference to those who are Christian and embrace Christian values.

## FINANCIAL AID

*Students should submit:* FAFSA and Wheaton College Financial Aid Application. Priority filing deadline is February 15. The Princeton Review suggests that all financial aid forms be submitted as soon as possible after January 1. *Need-based scholarships/grants offered:* Pell, SEOG, state scholarships/grants, private scholarships, and the school's own gift aid. *Loan aid offered:* Subsidized Stafford, Unsubsidized Stafford, PLUS, Federal Perkins, and the school's own loans. Institution employment available. Federal Work-Study Program available. Applicants will be notified of awards on a rolling basis beginning on or about March 1. Off-campus job opportunities are excellent.

## FROM THE ADMISSIONS OFFICE

"Wheaton's mission statement emphasizes 'the development of whole and effective Christians.' The college takes seriously its impact on society. The influence of Wheaton is seen in fields ranging from government (the speaker of the house) to sports (two NBA coaches) to business (the CEO of Wal-Mart) to music (Metropolitan Opera National Competition winners) to education (over 40 college presidents) to global ministry (Billy Graham). Wheaton seeks students who want to make a difference and are passionate about their Christian faith and rigorous academic pursuit."

## ADMISSIONS

| | |
|---|---|
| Admissions Rating | 91 |
| # of applicants | 1,846 |
| % of applicants accepted | 58 |
| % of acceptees attending | 54 |
| # accepting a place on wait list | 244 |
| % admitted from wait list | 3 |

### FRESHMAN PROFILE

| | |
|---|---|
| Range SAT Verbal | 610-710 |
| Average SAT Verbal | 660 |
| Range SAT Math | 610-710 |
| Average SAT Math | 660 |
| Range ACT Composite | 27-31 |
| Average ACT Composite | 29 |
| Minimum TOEFL | 550 |
| Average HS GPA | 3.7 |
| % graduated top 10% of class | 58 |
| % graduated top 25% of class | 85 |
| % graduated top 50% of class | 97 |

### DEADLINES

| | |
|---|---|
| Regular admission | 1/15 |
| Regular notification | 4/10 |

### FINANCIAL FACTS

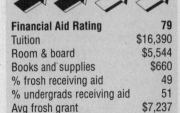

| | |
|---|---|
| Financial Aid Rating | 79 |
| Tuition | $16,390 |
| Room & board | $5,544 |
| Books and supplies | $660 |
| % frosh receiving aid | 49 |
| % undergrads receiving aid | 51 |
| Avg frosh grant | $7,237 |
| Avg frosh loan | $3,587 |

# WHEATON COLLEGE (MA)

OFFICE OF ADMISSION, NORTON, MA 02766 • ADMISSIONS: 508-286-8251 • FAX: 508-286-8271

## CAMPUS LIFE

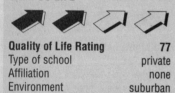

| Quality of Life Rating | 77 |
| --- | --- |
| Type of school | private |
| Affiliation | none |
| Environment | suburban |

### STUDENTS

| | |
| --- | --- |
| Total undergrad enrollment | 1,474 |
| % male/female | 36/64 |
| % from out of state | 64 |
| % from public high school | 61 |
| % live on campus | 99 |
| % African American | 4 |
| % Asian | 3 |
| % Caucasian | 87 |
| % Hispanic | 4 |
| % Native American | 0 |
| % international | 5 |
| # of countries represented | 26 |

### SURVEY SAYS . . .

*Everyone loves the Crusaders
(Almost) everyone smokes
Students don't get along with local
community
Hard liquor is popular
Students aren't religious
Very small frat/sorority scene
Students don't like Norton, MA
Lousy off-campus food
Class discussions encouraged
Low cost of living*

## ACADEMICS

| Academic Rating | 87 |
| --- | --- |
| Calendar | semester |
| Student/faculty ratio | 12:1 |
| Profs interesting rating | 95 |
| Profs accessible rating | 95 |
| % profs teaching UG courses | 100 |
| Avg lab size | 20 students |
| Avg reg class size | 19 students |

### MOST POPULAR MAJORS
psychology
economics
sociology

## STUDENTS SPEAK OUT

### Academics

Small classes and a dedicated faculty are what undergraduates expect, and receive, at Wheaton College of Massachusetts (not to be confused with the conservative religious Wheaton College of Illinois). Writes one typical student, "Individually, professors are amazing. Office hours are almost irrelevant because their doors are always open. Professors know my intellectual potential and push me to exceed all boundaries. The president teaches because she loves students. The deans are always willing to talk and help." Another agrees, "Professors are great. They make the classes enjoyable. They teach with a love for the subject and with lots of enthusiasm and heart." Although "once in a while you get a prof that shouldn't be teaching or shouldn't have been tenured," students note that "it is very easy to find out who the amazing professors are and what classes they teach." Among Wheaton's other assets are a caring administration and a proactive career placement office. "The Filene Center for Work and Learning has been very helpful in providing information regarding internships and jobs." It also helps students write resumes and cover letters. Sums up one student, "Wheaton is what you make of it. You can go with the flow and not do anything, or you can become very active."

### Life

Most Wheaton undergrads identify their hometown of Norton as the school's number one drawback. Explains one, "If you plan on living in a fun town with lots of great places to hang out around campus or cute coffee houses you can take a date to . . . don't pick Wheaton! About the most that happens around town is Wednesday night Bingo at the old folks' home." The "very rural" setting means "not much to do," but fortunately neither Boston nor Providence are far off, and "the school provides rides to the T-station so that Boston is available even to nondrivers." Students report that "there are a lot of events on campus, such as $1 movies, dances, parties, and bands," and that "we have a good mix here. Everyone can usually find their place, whether it be in activities, the classroom, or with friends. It just takes time." Even so, the campus is often too quiet for some students' liking. Writes one, "It can be boring sometimes. People go to bed by midnight on weekends. You have to make your own activities." Another notes, "There are very limited activities. Drinking and other forms of intoxication are common. There is fun if you are willing to reach for it. The viewbook paints a pretty rosy picture of what it's like here." The lack of a Greek system partly accounts for the quiet social scene, although theme houses serve roughly the same function here as the Greeks serve on other campuses. In the plus column, Wheaton has "a beautiful campus" that is "especially nice in the fall, when everybody is outside. Sometimes classes are even held outside."

### Student Body

As at many small liberal arts colleges, students at Wheaton describe the student body and campus atmosphere as insular. Writes one, "The 'Wheaton Bubble' is a common term on campus to describe how disconnected we all are." Also typical of small schools, "word travels faster than it is spoken" at Wheaton. The school's pricey tuition results in a homogeneous cross-section of New England's upper income brackets; "stuck-up yuppie wannabes" is how one student describes her classmates. Adds another, "Students are pretty similar, but they have their own identities." Straight women, beware: "The majority of people here are female, which is not so great when you want to get a date!"

FINANCIAL AID: 508-286-8232 • E-MAIL: ADMISSION@WHEATONCOLLEGE.EDU • WEBSITE: WWW.WHEATONCOLLEGE.EDU

## ADMISSIONS

*Very important* academic and nonacademic factors considered by the admissions committee include secondary school record, essays, and talent/ability. *Important* factors considered include recommendations. *Other* factors considered include character/personal qualities, extracurricular activities, recommendations, volunteer work, and work experience. Factors *not* considered include religious affiliation/commitment and state residency. TOEFL required of all international applicants. High school diploma is required and GED is accepted. *High school units required/recommended:* 4 English recommended, 3 math recommended, 2 science lab recommended, 4 foreign language recommended, 2 social studies recommended.

### The Inside Word

Wheaton is to be applauded for periodically re-examining its admissions process; some colleges use virtually the same application process eternally, never acknowledging the fluid nature of societal attitudes and institutional circumstances. Approaches that emphasize individuals, or even their accomplishments, over their numbers are unfortunately rare in the world of college admission, where GPA and SAT I reign supreme. Wheaton has an easier time than some colleges in taking this step because it isn't particularly selective. Getting in is even easier for men, and will be for the foreseeable future.

## FINANCIAL AID

*Students should submit:* FAFSA, CSS/Financial Aid PROFILE, noncustodial (divorced/separated) parent's statement, business/farm supplement, and parent and student tax returns. Regular filing deadline is February 1. The Princeton Review suggests that all financial aid forms be submitted as soon as possible after January 1. *Need-based scholarships/grants offered:* Pell, SEOG, state scholarships/grants, and the school's own gift aid. *Loan aid offered:* FFEL Subsidized Stafford, FFEL Unsubsidized Stafford, FFEL PLUS, Federal Perkins, state, college/university loans from institutional funds, MEFA and TERI, and other private family education loans. Institutional employment available. Federal Work-Study Program available. Applicants will be notified of awards on or about March 24. Off-campus job opportunities are good.

## FROM THE ADMISSIONS OFFICE

"What makes for a 'best college'? Is it merely the hard-to-define notions of prestige or image? We don't think so. We think what makes college 'best' and best for you is a school that will make you a first-rate thinker and writer, a pragmatic professional in your work, and an ethical practitioner in your life. To get you to all these places, Wheaton takes advantage of its great combinations: a beautiful, secluded New England campus combined with access to Boston and Providence; a high quality, classic liberal arts and sciences curriculum combined with award-winning internship, job, and community service programs; and a campus that respects your individuality in the context of the larger community. What's the 'best' outcome of a Wheaton education? A start on life that combines meaningful work, significant relationships, and a commitment to your local and global community. Far more than for what they've studied or for what they've gone on to do for a living, we're most proud of Wheaton graduates for who they become."

## ADMISSIONS

| | |
|---|---|
| Admissions Rating | 71 |
| # of applicants | 3,137 |
| % of applicants accepted | 65 |
| % of acceptees attending | 25 |
| # accepting a place on wait list | 226 |
| % admitted from wait list | 5 |
| # of early decision applicants | 79 |
| % accepted early decision | 78 |

### FRESHMAN PROFILE

| | |
|---|---|
| Range SAT Verbal | 570-640 |
| Average SAT Verbal | 605 |
| Range SAT Math | 560-630 |
| Average SAT Math | 595 |
| Range ACT Composite | 23-27 |
| Average ACT Composite | 25 |
| Minimum TOEFL | 550 |
| Average HS GPA | 3.4 |
| % graduated top 10% of class | 27 |
| % graduated top 25% of class | 67 |
| % graduated top 50% of class | 92 |

### DEADLINES

| | |
|---|---|
| Early decision 1 | 11/15 |
| Early decision 1 notification | 12/15 |
| Early desision 2 | 1/15 |
| Early decision 2 notification | 2/15 |
| Regular admission | 2/1 |
| Regular notification | 4/1 |
| Nonfall registration? | yes |

### APPLICANTS ALSO LOOK AT
**AND OFTEN PREFER**
Connecticut Coll.
Bates, Skidmore
**AND SOMETIMES PREFER**
Hobart & William Smith
U. Vermont, Brandeis
**AND RARELY PREFER**
Providence
U. Mass—Amherst, Clark

### FINANCIAL FACTS

| | |
|---|---|
| Financial Aid Rating | 83 |
| Tuition | $25,565 |
| Room & board | $7,150 |
| Books and supplies | $940 |
| Required fees | $225 |
| % frosh receiving aid | 57 |
| % undergrads receiving aid | 61 |
| Avg frosh grant | $12,911 |
| Avg frosh loan | $3,300 |

# WHITMAN COLLEGE

345 BOYER AVENUE, WALLA WALLA, WA 99362-2083 • ADMISSIONS: 509-527-5176 • FAX: 509-527-4967

## CAMPUS LIFE

**Quality of Life Rating**    **86**
Type of school    private
Affiliation    none
Environment    suburban

### STUDENTS

| | |
|---|---|
| Total undergrad enrollment | 1,424 |
| % male/female | 42/58 |
| % from out of state | 55 |
| % from public high school | 76 |
| % live on campus | 69 |
| % in (# of) fraternities | 33 (4) |
| % in (# of) sororities | 33 (4) |
| % African American | 1 |
| % Asian | 6 |
| % Caucasian | 85 |
| % Hispanic | 3 |
| % Native American | 1 |
| % international | 2 |
| # of countries represented | 22 |

### SURVEY SAYS . . .

*(Almost) everyone plays intramural sports*
*Dorms are like palaces*
*Diversity lacking on campus*
*Great computer facilities*
*No one cheats*
*Musical organizations are hot*
*(Almost) no one smokes*

## ACADEMICS

**Academic Rating**    **93**
Calendar    semester
Student/faculty ratio    11:1
Profs interesting rating    95
Profs accessible rating    98
% profs teaching UG courses    100
Avg lab size    10-19 students
Avg reg class size    10-19 students

### MOST POPULAR MAJORS
history
biology
English

## STUDENTS SPEAK OUT

### Academics

The teaching staff and administration at Whitman College strive to create a homey atmosphere in which students can learn, and according to our respondents, their efforts are a complete success. Writes one typical student, "My professors are always willing to go the extra mile: approving a thesis for a paper, reading drafts, holding long office hours, and staying home the night before a test to answer our questions over the phone." Another reports, "Our administration has incredible people. They are advisors and mentors, visible on campus, and always making themselves available to students." Students' anecdotes are peppered with stories of professors who invite their classes to their homes for dinner, administrators who regularly eat with students in the dining halls, and a president who walks the library corridors handing out cookies during finals week. This comfort factor softens the blow dealt by Whitman's extremely rigorous academic program. Writes one undergrad, "Whitman is a very challenging school. The common trend I have noticed is that a student has to do decent work to get a 'B,' but must work their you-know-what off to get an 'A.'" Among the greatest challenges are "comprehensive written and oral tests in the major of study in senior year. They provide excellent preparation for grad school." Also helpful in that area is "an excellent advising and counseling resource and career center."

### Life

Whitman hosts a vibrant extracurricular scene replete with social and academic opportunities. Notes one student, "The problem at Whitman is that there is too much to do! Any given night offers five different lectures, movies, presentations, parties, and dances." Greek houses provide a major nexus of social activity for one group of students; student-produced theater and art exhibits serve a different faction. Intramural sports "are really intense here, especially in football. I have not talked to some of my friends for a week after playing against them in a football game!" Outdoor hobbies depend on the weather; says one respondent, "Frisbee golf and Ultimate Frisbee rule the warmer months, with cabin fever and reading tying for winter activities." Finally, a sizable minority dedicates its spare time to political causes. "People care about the environment and specific social issues, such as the death penalty. This is a very politically aware campus, and there are many activities and protest to involve oneself in." All this campus activity helps compensate for the fact that Walla Walla "is mostly devoid of student recreating. The town is anything but a college town; it's more agricultural than anything." The city's deficiencies are accented by the fact that "Walla Walla is a bit isolated from the rest of the world." The nearest large city, Spokane, is more than two hours away by car; trips to Portland and Seattle each require a four-hour drive.

### Student Body

Whitman students are bullish on their classmates. Writes one, "The people are the best part of Whitman. Everyone is super-friendly and down-to-earth. Plus, they're surprisingly open-minded and accepting of new ideas." The glue that binds this group together? "No matter what they say, everyone at Whitman is a nerd in some way. The biggest partiers still care about their grades and are still here to study. This links us all." Students also report that "there is considerably less ethnic diversity at Whitman and in the Pacific Northwest in general than in my hometown of L.A., but Whitman's admissions officers do a great job of finding people with extraordinary backgrounds and experiences. This makes up for our outward appearance of homogeneity."

FINANCIAL AID: 509-527-5178 • E-MAIL: ADMISSION@WHITMAN.EDU • WEBSITE: WWW.WHITMAN.EDU

## ADMISSIONS

*Very important* academic and nonacademic factors considered by the admissions committee include essays and secondary school record. *Important* factors considered include character/personal qualities, recommendations, extracurricular activities, standardized test scores, minority status, and talent/ability. *Other* factors considered include alumni/ae relation, class rank, geography, interview, work experience, state residency, and volunteer work. Factors *not* considered include religious affiliation/commitment. *The admissions office says:* "It is difficult to compare the inner workings of your operation with others you are not privy to. Having said that, several things distinguish us. Our admissions committee is faculty-driven and they meet with us to evaluate over 50 percent of our candidates. Also, our process is highly personalized, and an individual's human qualities (motivation, drive, initiative, concern for others) are given consideration. [Our students are] probably much more concerned about the environment and environmental issues [than average students]. It's a very 'green' student body."

### The Inside Word

Whitman's admissions committee is to be applauded; any admissions process that emphasizes essays and extracurriculars over the SAT I has truly gotten it right. The college cares much more about who you are and what you have to offer if you enroll than it does about what your numbers will do for the freshman academic profile. Whitman is a mega-sleeper. Educators all over the country know it as an excellent institution, and the college's alums support it at one of the highest rates of giving at any college in the nation. Student seeking a top-quality liberal arts college owe it to themselves to take a look.

## FINANCIAL AID

*Students should submit:* FAFSA and CSS/Financial Aid PROFILE. Regular filing deadline is February 1. The Princeton Review suggests that all financial aid forms be submitted as soon as possible after January 1. *Need-based scholarships/grants offered:* Pell, SEOG, state scholarships/grants, private scholarships, and the school's own gift aid. *Loan aid offered:* FFEL Subsidized Stafford, FFEL Unsubsidized Stafford, FFEL PLUS, Federal Perkins, and alternative student loans. Institutional employment available. Federal Work-Study Program available. Applicants will be notified of awards on a rolling basis beginning on or about April 1. Off-campus job opportunities are good.

## FROM THE ADMISSIONS OFFICE

"Whitman is a place that encourages you to explore past the boundaries of disciplines because learning and living don't always fall neatly into tidy little compartments. Many students choose Whitman specifically because they're interested in a particular career such as business or engineering but want the well-rounded preparation that only a liberal arts education provides."

## ADMISSIONS

| | |
|---|---|
| Admissions Rating | 93 |
| # of applicants | 2,167 |
| % of applicants accepted | 50 |
| % of acceptees attending | 32 |
| # accepting a place on wait list | 79 |
| % admitted from wait list | 6 |
| # of early decision applicants | 162 |
| % accepted early decision | 75 |

### FRESHMAN PROFILE

| | |
|---|---|
| Range SAT Verbal | 620-710 |
| Average SAT Verbal | 660 |
| Range SAT Math | 600-690 |
| Average SAT Math | 650 |
| Range ACT Composite | 26-30 |
| Average ACT Composite | 28 |
| Minimum TOEFL | 560 |
| Average HS GPA | 3.8 |
| % graduated top 10% of class | 65 |
| % graduated top 25% of class | 90 |
| % graduated top 50% of class | 100 |

### DEADLINES

| | |
|---|---|
| Early decision | 11/15 |
| Early decision notification | 12/15 |
| Regular admission | 2/1 |
| Regular notification | 4/1 |
| Nonfall registration? | yes |

### APPLICANTS ALSO LOOK AT

**AND OFTEN PREFER**
Stanford

**AND SOMETIMES PREFER**
U. Puget Sound
U. Washington
Willamette
Lewis & Clark
Colorado Coll.

**AND RARELY PREFER**
Western Washington

### FINANCIAL FACTS

| | |
|---|---|
| Financial Aid Rating | 87 |
| Tuition | $22,600 |
| Room & board | $6,290 |
| Books and supplies | $1,000 |
| Required fees | $196 |
| % frosh receiving aid | 51 |
| % undergrads receiving aid | 52 |
| Avg frosh grant | $11,682 |
| Avg frosh loan | $3,331 |

# WHITTIER COLLEGE

13406 East Philadelphia Street, PO Box 634, Whittier, CA 90608 • Admissions: 562-907-4238 • Fax: 562-907-4870

## CAMPUS LIFE

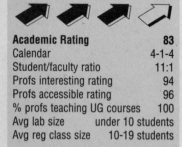

| **Quality of Life Rating** | **79** |
|---|---|
| Type of school | private |
| Affiliation | none |
| Environment | suburban |

### STUDENTS

| | |
|---|---|
| Total undergrad enrollment | 1,297 |
| % male/female | 45/55 |
| % from out of state | 40 |
| % from public high school | 68 |
| % live on campus | 62 |
| % in (# of) fraternities | 15 (4) |
| % in (# of) sororities | 15 (5) |
| % African American | 6 |
| % Asian | 7 |
| % Caucasian | 52 |
| % Hispanic | 27 |
| % Native American | 2 |
| % international | 5 |
| # of countries represented | 12 |

### SURVEY SAYS . . .
*Classes are small*
*Students aren't religious*
*Library needs improving*
*Ethnic diversity on campus*
*Lousy food on campus*
*Diverse students interact*
*No one plays intramural sports*

## ACADEMICS

| **Academic Rating** | **83** |
|---|---|
| Calendar | 4-1-4 |
| Student/faculty ratio | 11:1 |
| Profs interesting rating | 94 |
| Profs accessible rating | 96 |
| % profs teaching UG courses | 100 |
| Avg lab size | under 10 students |
| Avg reg class size | 10-19 students |

### MOST POPULAR MAJORS
business administration
political science
English

## STUDENTS SPEAK OUT

### Academics

Whittier College dropped its affiliation with the Quaker Church over 50 years ago, but, as the school accurately claims, it continues to "uphold [its] founding values, including the love of learning and respect for every individual." Whittier's distinctive curriculum offers students two fundamental choices. Students may choose to pursue the more conventional Liberal Education track, which requires completion of both an integrated core curriculum and a major study. Or, they may select the more adventurous Whittier Scholars Program, in which undergraduates design their own curricula and even their own majors. Either way, students are given a lot of academic independence and are expected, in return, to take advantage of their freedom. Both tracks feature team-taught courses, discussion-intensive seminars that "really get people to think," and an emphasis on interdisciplinary study and the integration of academic disciplines. Students report that, while the curriculum is appealing, the professors are the school's most important asset. Writes one typical undergrad, "If there is one reason to come here, it is because of the excellent professors. For the most part, they are willing to help you and easy to approach." Says another, "The profs are your surrogate parents at this school. They'll be your advisor, mentor, and professor, as well as you counselor, confidante, and cheerleader." All this support helps students negotiate an occasionally overwhelming workload ("It is stressful, stressful, stressful. Teachers give way too much work all at once") and some typical shortcomings of a small college ("I wish a wider variety of courses was offered," complains one student). When all is said and done, students agree that Whittier "is very friendly and warm, family-like, easy to get used to."

### Life

As one student neatly puts it, "Whittier is a good school to come to if you are interested in a quality education. However, if you are looking for a huge social life, Whittier is not the place to be." The lure of nearby Los Angeles, coupled with the administration's vigilant pursuit of drug use and underage drinking, mean that "the school is dead quiet on weekends. Once in a while there is a party on a Friday or Saturday night, but otherwise it's not alive like other college campuses." Campus life consists mostly of life's simple pleasures. "For fun we go to beaches, or hang out in our dorm, or just drive around," explains one student. Adds another, "We go to the movies, go out to eat, shop, hang out in the lounge, play pool and ping pong. The athletic center is always open. There are study groups every night." There are also "fun things in uptown Whittier (which is within walking distance), but mostly you need a car to 'do' something." That something is head for Los Angeles, about 45 minutes away by car.

### Student Body

Undergrads enjoy the fact that "Whittier has a definite community atmosphere. Students and faculty have great relations within their own groups and with each other." Students range "anywhere from super-religious to nonpracticing" and are similarly diverse in race: observes one student, "Despite the stereotype that this is an all rich-white-kid school, the minorities blend in here pretty well." In keeping with the school's past, "We are all individuals and respect one another, which is part of the Quaker heritage." Still, as at nearly all other small schools, the rumor mill grinds quickly and constantly. Complains one student, "I hate the fact that rumors spread around this school like high school."

FINANCIAL AID: 562-907-4285 • E-MAIL: ADMISSION@WHITTIER.EDU • WEBSITE: WWW.WHITTIER.EDU

## ADMISSIONS

*Very important* academic and nonacademic factors considered by the admissions committee include class rank and secondary school record. *Important* factors considered include character/personal qualities, essays, extracurricular activities, recommendations, standardized test scores, talent/ability, volunteer work, and work experience. *Other* factors considered include alumni/ae relation, interview, and minority status. Factors *not* considered include geography, religious affiliation/commitment, and state residency. SAT I or ACT required. TOEFL required of all international applicants. High school diploma is required and GED is not accepted. *High school units required/recommended:* 16 total required; 4 English required, 3 math required, 3 science required, 2 science lab required, 2 foreign language required, 3 foreign language recommended, 2 social studies required, 2 elective required. *The admissions office says:* "What really happens? Picture yourself making a point in a heated class discussion, researching a paper that you and your professor will present together, preparing a senior project that seems to tie in almost everything you've learned. Then imagine yourself feeling more intellectually alive than you've ever felt before. That's what happens to you at Whittier. Want to learn more? Call us, write us, or better yet, visit us and see if we are all we claim to be!"

### The Inside Word

The admissions committee at Whittier subjects each candidate to very close scrutiny. Their academic expectations aren't too high, but their interest in making good solid matches between candidates and the college is paramount. If Whittier is high on your list, make sure you put forth a serious effort to demonstrate what you want out of the college and what you'll bring to the table in return.

## FINANCIAL AID

*Students should submit:* FAFSA and CSS/Financial Aid PROFILE. Regular filing deadline is February 1. The Princeton Review suggests that all financial aid forms be submitted as soon as possible after January 1. *Need-based scholarships/grants offered:* Pell, SEOG, state scholarships/grants, private scholarships, and the school's own gift aid. *Loan aid offered:* FFEL Subsidized Stafford, FFEL Unsubsidized Stafford, FFEL PLUS, Federal Perkins, and college/university loans from institutional funds. Institutional employment available. Federal Work-Study Program available. Applicants will be notified of awards on a rolling basis beginning on or about April 1. Off-campus job opportunities are good.

## FROM THE ADMISSIONS OFFICE

"Faculty and students at Whittier share a love of learning and delight in the life of the mind. They join in understanding the value of the intellectual quest, the use of reason, and a respect for values. They seek knowledge of their own culture and the informed appreciation of other traditions, and they explore the interrelatedness of knowledge and the connections among disciplines. An extraordinary community emerges from teachers and students representing a variety of academic pursuits, individuals who have come together at Whittier in the belief that study within the liberal arts forms the best foundation for rewarding endeavor throughout a lifetime."

## ADMISSIONS

| | |
|---|---|
| Admissions Rating | 74 |
| # of applicants | 1,312 |
| % of applicants accepted | 89 |
| % of acceptees attending | 27 |
| # accepting a place on wait list | 54 |
| % admitted from wait list | 76 |

### FRESHMAN PROFILE

| | |
|---|---|
| Range SAT Verbal | 480-600 |
| Average SAT Verbal | 536 |
| Range SAT Math | 470-590 |
| Average SAT Math | 528 |
| Range ACT Composite | 20-26 |
| Average ACT Composite | 22 |
| Minimum TOEFL | 550 |
| Average HS GPA | 3.1 |
| % graduated top 10% of class | 14 |
| % graduated top 25% of class | 30 |
| % graduated top 50% of class | 52 |

### DEADLINES

| | |
|---|---|
| Priority admission deadline | 2/1 |
| Regular notification | rolling |

### APPLICANTS ALSO LOOK AT

**AND OFTEN PREFER**
Pomona
**AND SOMETIMES PREFER**
Claremont McKenna
UCLA
**AND RARELY PREFER**
U. Redlands
UC—San Diego

## FINANCIAL FACTS

| | |
|---|---|
| Financial Aid Rating | 89 |
| Tuition | $21,036 |
| Room & board | $6,938 |
| Books and supplies | $500 |
| Required fees | $930 |
| % frosh receiving aid | 65 |
| % undergrads receiving aid | 73 |
| Avg frosh grant | $12,412 |
| Avg frosh loan | $5,382 |

# WILLAMETTE UNIVERSITY

900 STATE STREET, SALEM, OR 97301 • ADMISSIONS: 877-LIB-ARTS • FAX: 503-375-5363

## CAMPUS LIFE

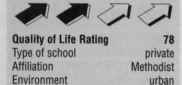

| Quality of Life Rating | 78 |
|---|---|
| Type of school | private |
| Affiliation | Methodist |
| Environment | urban |

### STUDENTS

| | |
|---|---|
| Total undergrad enrollment | 1,749 |
| % male/female | 45/55 |
| % from out of state | 52 |
| % from public high school | 81 |
| % live on campus | 68 |
| % in (# of) fraternities | 25 (5) |
| % in (# of) sororities | 20 (3) |
| % African American | 2 |
| % Asian | 7 |
| % Caucasian | 67 |
| % Hispanic | 5 |
| % Native American | 1 |
| % international | 1 |

### SURVEY SAYS . . .
Classes are small
Great food on campus
Low cost of living
Profs teach upper-levels
Dorms are like palaces
Student publications are ignored
(Almost) no one listens to college radio
Students don't like Salem, OR
Very little drug use

## ACADEMICS

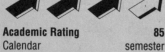

| Academic Rating | 85 |
|---|---|
| Calendar | semester |
| Student/faculty ratio | 10:1 |
| Profs interesting rating | 93 |
| Profs accessible rating | 97 |
| % profs teaching UG courses | 100 |
| Avg lab size | 10-19 students |
| Avg reg class size | 10-19 students |

### MOST POPULAR MAJORS
economics
politics
psychology

## STUDENTS SPEAK OUT

### Academics

It's the personal touches that students at Willamette University appreciate most about their school. "One of the best things about Willamette is that the professors are real people," explains one student. "They eat in the cafeteria with us. We call a lot of them by their first names. Sometimes I forget that Bob, my rhetoric professor, is also a leading rhetorical argumentation theorist." Everyone, from faculty to administration officials, "is very friendly. Even our president has student office hours." Professors here are "highly qualified, intelligent, interesting, hard working, and available outside of class." Writes one student approvingly, "They don't point everything out to us. Instead, they allow us to figure some things out for ourselves through class discussion." Students give WU's distribution requirements, designed to expose all undergraduates to math, literature, social sciences, natural sciences, and fine arts, mixed reviews. Most feel that "the intro classes suck, but most upper-level classes are a kick. They make you work, but it's worth it." All students must also complete a senior project, which can be a major scientific research project, a senior thesis, or a professional internship. Students interested in political science benefit from the school's location, right across the street from the state capitol, as well as an internship program in Washington, D.C. Students also speak highly of the "great study abroad programs" offered here.

### Life

Willamette students describe a peaceful, pleasant atmosphere pervading the gorgeous campus. "Willamette spends a lot on campus beauty," notes one student. It's the kind of place where, one student writes, "if I paid tuition and lived here but didn't have to go to classes, I would [remain] here for the rest of my young adult life." It's "very easy to balance your social and academic life here. There's always something happening on campus," whether its "intramural activities (fun and easy to get involved in)," clubs, or just a free movie. Says one undergrad, "I don't come back to my room from 9 A.M. to 9 P.M. Life is busy, fast-paced, and intense. Everyone here is active in rigorous academics, sports, and clubs." Students appreciate the fact that the area is conducive to "good recreation: skiing, beach, kayaking, and hiking in the mountains are nearby." They also point out that "the rain isn't that bad. Goretex is good." Hometown Salem, unfortunately, "isn't tempting. In fact, I rarely leave campus because there isn't much reason to." But "although Salem sucks, Portland is only 45 minutes away." The weekend party scene revolves around the Greek houses and suffers because "the administration wants an alcohol-free campus. In an attempt to get out the beer, they killed the fun. Saturday nights are very quiet at WU because all the parties are off campus, unless the Greeks are partying." And, warns one GDI, "The Greeks never mix with the rest of the university population." Adds another, "If I could change one thing about WU, I would lessen the focus on drinking and the Greek system."

### Student Body

According to the boosters among their ranks, the "very conservative," as well as "rich and religious" undergraduates of WU each have "something special to offer: artistic ability, leadership, athletics. Everyone has been successful and is interesting! The nicest people I've ever met." At the other end of the spectrum are those who report that many of their fellow students are "very concerned with how they look and what brand names they are wearing. Abercrombie and Fitch is most popular here." They note with consternation that "fellow students seem to be indifferent about academics. They don't study often and skip classes regularly." In the middle are those who see WU students as "generally nice but superficial. Most people are tolerant, yet stuck in their own little world of religious and politically conservative beliefs."

FINANCIAL AID: 503-370-6273 • E-MAIL: UNDERGRAD-ADMISSION@WILLAMETTE.EDU • WEBSITE: WWW.WILLAMETTE.EDU

## ADMISSIONS

*Very important* academic and nonacademic factors considered by the admissions committee include secondary school record. *Important* factors considered include class rank and standardized test scores. *Other* factors considered include character/personal qualities, essays, extracurricular activities, interview, recommendations, state residency, talent/ability, volunteer work, and work experience, alumni/ae relation, geography, and minority status. SAT I or ACT required. TOEFL required of all international applicants. High school diploma is required and GED is accepted. *High school units required/recommended:* 4 total required; 4 English recommended, 3 math recommended, 2 science recommended, 2 science lab recommended, 3 social studies recommended, 3 history recommended.

### The Inside Word

Willamette's admissions process is relatively standard for small liberal arts colleges. Extracurriculars, recommendations, and essays help the admissions committee do some matchmaking, but ultimately it's a candidate's grades that determine admissibility.

## FINANCIAL AID

*Students should submit:* FAFSA. The Princeton Review suggests that all financial aid forms be submitted as soon as possible after January 1. *Need-based scholarships/grants offered:* Pell, SEOG, state scholarships/grants, private scholarships, and the school's own gift aid. *Loan aid offered:* FFEL Subsidized Stafford, FFEL Unsubsidized Stafford, FFEL PLUS, and Federal Perkins. Institutional employment available. Federal Work-Study Program available. Applicants will be notified of awards on or about April 1. Off-campus job opportunities are good.

## FROM THE ADMISSIONS OFFICE

"Two of the primary reasons students choose Willamette are the challenge of the academic experience and the opportunity for significant involvement in co-curricular activities. They see Willamette as a place where they can engage in a rigorous liberal arts and sciences education, and enjoy exceptional, varied, and exciting opportunities outside the classroom. Students are also attracted to Willamette because of its unique location; in particular, they are attracted by the internships and political activity at the adjacent Oregon State Capitol Building, cultural exchange with Willamette's adjacent sister school, the U.S. campus of Tokyo International University, and the fact that Portland, the Oregon Coast, and the Cascade Mountains are within an hour of campus. Some of the words that best describe Willamette: academic, challenging, personal, friendly, well-located, beautiful, balanced, historic."

## ADMISSIONS

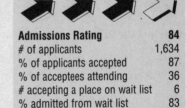

| | |
|---|---|
| Admissions Rating | 84 |
| # of applicants | 1,634 |
| % of applicants accepted | 87 |
| % of acceptees attending | 36 |
| # accepting a place on wait list | 6 |
| % admitted from wait list | 83 |

### FRESHMAN PROFILE

| | |
|---|---|
| Range SAT Verbal | 550-660 |
| Average SAT Verbal | 600 |
| Range SAT Math | 550-660 |
| Average SAT Math | 610 |
| Range ACT Composite | 23-29 |
| Average ACT Composite | 27 |
| Minimum TOEFL | 550/220 |
| Average HS GPA | 3.7 |
| % graduated top 10% of class | 50 |
| % graduated top 25% of class | 81 |
| % graduated top 50% of class | 97 |

### DEADLINES

| | |
|---|---|
| Regular admission | 2/1 |
| Regular notification | 4/1 |
| Nonfall registration? | yes |

### APPLICANTS ALSO LOOK AT
#### AND OFTEN PREFER
Colorado Coll.
Santa Clara
Claremont McKenna
Stanford
#### AND SOMETIMES PREFER
Lewis & Clark
U. Oregon
Oregon State
Whitman
U. Puget Sound
#### AND RARELY PREFER
Portland State

### FINANCIAL FACTS

| | |
|---|---|
| Financial Aid Rating | 87 |
| Tuition | $22,420 |
| Room & board | $5,930 |
| Books and supplies | $1,600 |
| Required fees | $122 |
| % frosh receiving aid | 68 |
| % undergrads receiving aid | 64 |
| Avg frosh grant | $12,000 |
| Avg frosh loan | $4,414 |

# WILLIAMS COLLEGE

988 MAIN STREET, WILLIAMSTOWN, MA 01267 • ADMISSIONS: 413-597-2211 • FAX: 413-597-4052

## CAMPUS LIFE

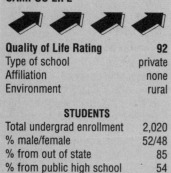

| Quality of Life Rating | 92 |
|---|---|
| Type of school | private |
| Affiliation | none |
| Environment | rural |

### STUDENTS

| | |
|---|---|
| Total undergrad enrollment | 2,020 |
| % male/female | 52/48 |
| % from out of state | 85 |
| % from public high school | 54 |
| % live on campus | 96 |
| % African American | 6 |
| % Asian | 9 |
| % Caucasian | 72 |
| % Hispanic | 6 |
| % international | 6 |
| # of countries represented | 52 |

### SURVEY SAYS . . .

*Everyone loves the Ephs
(Almost) everyone plays intramural
sports
Dorms are like palaces
Registration is a breeze
Campus feels safe
(Almost) no one smokes
Musical organizations are hot*

## ACADEMICS

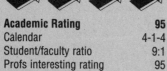

| Academic Rating | 95 |
|---|---|
| Calendar | 4-1-4 |
| Student/faculty ratio | 9:1 |
| Profs interesting rating | 95 |
| Profs accessible rating | 97 |
| % profs teaching UG courses | 100 |
| Avg lab size | 10-19 students |
| Avg reg class size | 10-19 students |

### MOST POPULAR MAJORS
English
economics
biology

## STUDENTS SPEAK OUT

### Academics

Williams is "definitely a tough school." The courses are "very difficult," and the "academic rigor" is pretty stressful. Students must complete a variety of distribution requirements and attend winter session, a month-long term during which students pursue individualized and less traditional areas of academic interest. "I never thought that college would be so much work," says an exasperated first-year student. Still, Williams students are some of the most satisfied in the nation, and the "world-class" and "always accessible" faculty is the overwhelming reason why. They are "eager to teach" and "passionate" about their subjects. Williams professors are also entertaining. "I timidly walked into organic chemistry on the first day of class having heard nightmare stories from my friends at other schools," fondly recalls a junior. "My prof is standing in his underwear and his robe, pretending he is just starting his day. The point is to show that organic chemistry is all around us, from the moment we wake up. Okay, so maybe throwing raw eggs at us was a little much, but I definitely appreciated the attempt at humor." And Williams' "personable" profs are "genuinely concerned about the students' wellness." The administration at Williams is "very accessible as well." To top everything off, "the alumni are well connected and quite helpful to current students."

### Life

The gorgeous "virtual utopia-type oasis" that is Williams College is located in Williamstown, Massachusetts, "a small hole in the middle of nowhere" hemmed in by "purple mountains" and "good skiing." Students here are often "bogged down with work," and "stress is very high." When students have a chance to put away their books, "there isn't much to do off campus," as "sleepy" Williamstown "has failed in its role as a college town." There is no Greek scene, but frat-style parties are nevertheless abundant. There is "definitely a lot of drinking here, but" there is no real pressure to do so because "there are enough people who drink very little or not at all." Students counsel that "you have to be creative." You might go to a "Biore party" or "get into deep discussions about new scientific theories or the meaning of life while standing in the bathroom brushing your teeth." There are "many musical and artistic events happening on campus to relieve tension" as well as a broad range of extracurricular activities. Intercollegiate sports are "very big," and the "sports teams are amazing." The athletic facilities are excellent, and "outdoor activities abound" in the surrounding area. "The only unhappy people I know are those who love city life," says one student. The "high-quality on-campus housing" at Williams ("suites with a common room") is "very comfortable and particularly conducive to forming close groups of friends."

### Student Body

"If you like J.Crew and studying five hours a day," then "you'll love Williams." "Williams has a well-deserved reputation for a preppy New England student body, but with a little work, other students can find their niches." The "very smart" students here are "among the best and the brightest" in the country, and many are "a bit eccentric." The proportion of minority students is considerable, and there is also "a wonderful diversity of experiences, backgrounds, and opinions, which leads to excellent conversations." The "amazingly talented and accepting" students at Williams are "over privileged, but that provides for good connections later on," and they are "moderate to somewhat left-of-center" politically. Some are "very unfriendly" or "excruciatingly polite, but distant in their relationships because of their devotion to their studies," while others are "incredibly friendly and easy to get to know." There is "no cutthroat competition," but the campus "can feel cliquey." Williams students are "so involved in labeling you, they never get a chance to know you," claims a junior. While we're on the subject of labels, students say there are "a large proportion of jocks" here, and "if you fit the Williams student-athlete-investment banker mold, you'll have four paradisiacal years."

FINANCIAL AID: 413-597-4181 • E-MAIL: ADMISSIONS@WILLIAMS.EDU • WEBSITE: WWW.WILLIAMS.EDU

## ADMISSIONS

*Very important* academic and nonacademic factors considered by the admissions committee include secondary school record. *Important* factors considered include class rank and standardized test scores. *Other* factors considered include alumni/ae relation, character/personal qualities, essays, extracurricular activities, interview, recommendations, talent/ability, volunteer work, and work experience. Factors *not* considered include geography, minority status, religious affiliation/commitment, and state residency. SAT I or ACT required; SAT II also required. *High school units required/recommended:* 16 total recommended; 4 English required, 3 math required, 3 science required, 2 science lab required, 2 foreign language required, 2 social studies required, 1 history required.

### The Inside Word

As is typical of highly selective colleges, at Williams high grades and test scores work more as qualifiers than to determine admissibility. Beyond a strong record of achievement, evidence of intellectual curiosity, noteworthy nonacademic talents, and a noncollege family background are some aspects of a candidate's application that might make for an offer of admission. But there are no guarantees—the evaluation process here is rigorous. The admissions committee (the entire admissions staff) discusses each candidate in comparison to the entire applicant pool. The pool is divided alphabetically for individual reading; after weak candidates are eliminated, those who remain undergo additional evaluations by different members of the staff. Admission decisions must be confirmed by the agreement of a plurality of the committee. Such close scrutiny demands a well-prepared candidate and application.

## FINANCIAL AID

*Students should submit:* FAFSA and CSS/Financial Aid PROFILE. Regular filing deadline is March 1. The Princeton Review suggests that all financial aid forms be submitted as soon as possible after January 1. Institutional employment available. Federal Work-Study Program available. Applicants will be notified of awards on a rolling basis. Off-campus job opportunities are fair.

## FROM THE ADMISSIONS OFFICE

"Special course offerings at Williams include Oxford-style tutorials, where students research and defend ideas, engaging in weekly debate with a peer and a faculty tutor. Annually 30 Williams students devote a full year to the tutorial method of study at Oxford; a quarter of Williams students pursue their education overseas. Four weeks of Winter Study each January provide time for individualized projects, research, and novel fields of study. Students compete in 28 Division III athletic teams, perform in 25 musical groups, stage 10 theatrical productions, and volunteer in 30 service organizations. The college receives several million dollars annually for undergraduate science research and equipment. The town offers two distinguished art museums, and 2,200 forest acres—complete with a treetop canopy walkway—for environmental research and recreation."

## ADMISSIONS

| | |
|---|---|
| Admissions Rating | 98 |
| # of applicants | 4,955 |
| % of applicants accepted | 24 |
| % of acceptees attending | 45 |
| # of early decision applicants | 400 |
| % accepted early decision | 45 |

### FRESHMAN PROFILE

| | |
|---|---|
| Range SAT Verbal | 660-760 |
| Average SAT Verbal | 701 |
| Range SAT Math | 650-750 |
| Average SAT Math | 694 |
| Average ACT Composite | 30 |

### DEADLINES

| | |
|---|---|
| Early decision | 11/15 |
| Early decision notification | 12/15 |
| Regular admission | 1/1 |
| Regular notification | 4/8 |

### APPLICANTS ALSO LOOK AT
### AND OFTEN PREFER
Harvard
Princeton
Yale
MIT
Stanford
### AND SOMETIMES PREFER
Brown
Dartmouth
Bowdoin
Amherst
### AND RARELY PREFER
Hamilton
Middlebury
Colgate
Bowdoin
Haverford

### FINANCIAL FACTS

| | |
|---|---|
| Financial Aid Rating | 75 |
| Tuition | $24,619 |
| Room & board | $6,730 |
| Books and supplies | $600 |
| Required fees | $171 |
| % frosh receiving aid | 38 |
| % undergrads receiving aid | 41 |
| Avg frosh grant | $18,187 |
| Avg frosh loan | $2,533 |

# WITTENBERG UNIVERSITY

PO Box 720, Springfield, OH 45501 • Admissions: 800-677-7558 • Fax: 937-327-6379

## CAMPUS LIFE

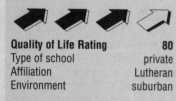

**Quality of Life Rating**    **80**
Type of school    private
Affiliation    Lutheran
Environment    suburban

### STUDENTS

| | |
|---|---|
| Total undergrad enrollment | 2,274 |
| % male/female | 43/57 |
| % from out of state | 46 |
| % from public high school | 78 |
| % live on campus | 90 |
| % in (# of) fraternities | 20 (6) |
| % in (# of) sororities | 35 (7) |
| % African American | 6 |
| % Asian | 1 |
| % Caucasian | 86 |
| % Hispanic | 1 |
| % international | 2 |

### SURVEY SAYS . . .

*Frats and sororities dominate social scene*
*Classes are small*
*Everyone loves the Tigers*
*Athletic facilities are great*
*Students don't get along with local community*
*Students don't like Springfield, OH*
*Theater is unpopular*
*(Almost) no one listens to college radio*
*Diverse students interact*
*Lousy off-campus food*

## ACADEMICS

**Academic Rating**    **85**
Calendar    semester
Student/faculty ratio    14:1
Profs interesting rating    93
Profs accessible rating    96
% profs teaching UG courses    100
Avg reg class size    20-29 students

### MOST POPULAR MAJORS
biology
business administration
education

## STUDENTS SPEAK OUT

### Academics

Home to an ambitious, mostly pre-professional student body, Wittenberg University "is a school where personal relations with instructors and student involvement make a difference." Students responding to our survey report that "the academic experience at Wittenberg is interactive, challenging, and enjoyable." Although the teachers range from "great" to "very dry and boring," students agree that the faculty is largely excellent and that profs take great pains to make themselves accessible to students. Writes one undergrad, "Professors are concerned about providing a quality education and are determined to make it happen. They are more than just faculty. They encourage students to come to them with any questions or problems. They are extremely helpful." Concludes one student, "Wittenberg's teachers, courses, and overall education are like pizza: Even when it's bad, it's good." The administration receives similarly good marks for its ability to "have you in and out with your needs taken care of" and for the fact that "most administrators are quite accessible, even our president. Many know me on a first-name basis."

### Life

Wittenburg is a campus-oriented institution: "Everything involves school activities. At other places, the location (e.g., the city) is part of students' lives. Here the campus is separate from the town." Student opinion differs on the quality and quantity of on-campus offerings. Some write that "we have a lot of things to do besides partying. The school gives many options, from movies to the pool to hypnotists. These activities are very fun. Sororities and fraternities also provide a lot of entertainment like step shows, canoeing, talent shows, card tournaments, and more." Others, especially those outside the Greek system, complain that "Wittenberg does not offer activities for students on weekends. Partying and alcohol are big, and that's it." Even some Greeks admit that "life at Wittenberg is great but a little redundant. The majority of weekends are spent at off-campus parties with the same people. It is fun, but I'd like to have a little more social diversity." Intramural sports and student organizations "keep many students involved," as do "the many colloquia and visiting speakers." Explains one student, "In the winter, students tend to hibernate. But come spring, the campus comes alive. We are a very active group as people can always be seen rollerblading, playing Frisbee golf, or doing some other type of physical activity. It's quite obvious that we love the outdoors." When the campus seems too confining, students make the hour-long trip to Columbus, home to Ohio State and a booming college social scene.

### Student Body

Witt undergrads readily admit that "everyone here is very preppy." The small, homogeneous, largely conservative population of the school leads one student to describe the campus as "a small close-knit mini-community where you see the same faces on a regular basis. This can be great at times and extremely confining at others." Still, "everyone gets along pretty well," a definite plus.

FINANCIAL AID: 800-677-7558 • E-MAIL: ADMISSION@WITTENBERG.EDU • WEBSITE: WWW.WITTENBERG.EDU

## ADMISSIONS

*Very important* academic and nonacademic factors considered by the admissions committee include secondary school record. *Important* factors considered include alumni/ae relation, character/personal qualities, class rank, essays, extracurricular activities, recommendations, standardized test scores, talent/ability, volunteer work, and work experience. *Other* factors considered include interview, minority status, and religious affiliation/commitment. Factors *not* considered include geography and state residency. SAT I or ACT required. TOEFL required of all international applicants. High school diploma is required and GED is accepted. *High school units required/recommended:* 4 English required, 3 math required, 4 math recommended, 2 science required, 3 science recommended, 2 science lab required, 3 science lab recommended, 2 foreign language recommended, 3 social studies required. *The admissions office says:* "The admissions committee evaluates each applicant on individual merit and accomplishment as well as potential for growth. Acceptance to Wittenberg is not based solely on GPA, class rank, or testing data. We want individuals who will contribute to all aspects of the community."

### The Inside Word

Wittenberg's applicant pool is small but quite solid coming off of a couple of strong years. Students who haven't successfully reached an above-average academic level in high school will meet with little success in the admissions process. Candidate evaluation is thorough and personal; applicants should devote serious attention to all aspects of their candidacy.

## FINANCIAL AID

*Students should submit:* FAFSA and institution's own financial aid form. Regular filing deadline is March 15. The Princeton Review suggests that all financial aid forms be submitted as soon as possible after January 1. *Need-based scholarships/grants offered:* Pell, SEOG, state scholarships/grants, private scholarships, and the school's own gift aid. *Loan aid offered:* FFEL Subsidized Stafford, FFEL Unsubsidized Stafford, FFEL PLUS, Federal Perkins, state, and college/university loans from institutional funds. Institutional employment available. Federal Work-Study Program available. Applicants will be notified of awards on a rolling basis beginning on or about March 1. Off-campus job opportunities are good.

## FROM THE ADMISSIONS OFFICE

"At Wittenberg, we believe that helping you to achieve symmetry demands a special environment, a setting where you can refine your definition of self yet gain exposure to the varied kinds of knowledge, people, views, activities, options, and ideas that add richness to our lives. Wittenberg is neither a huge university where students are usually mass produced, nor a very small college with few options, which can provide for the intellectual and personal growth required to achieve balance. Campus life is as diverse as the interests of our students. Wittenberg attracts students from all over the United States and from many other countries. Historically, the university has been committed to geographical, educational, cultural, and religious diversity. With their diverse backgrounds and interests, Wittenberg students have helped initiate many of the more than 100 student organizations that are active on campus. The students will be the first to tell you there's never a lack of things to do on or near the campus any day of the week, if you're willing to get involved."

## ADMISSIONS

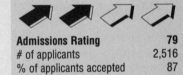

| | |
|---|---|
| **Admissions Rating** | **79** |
| # of applicants | 2,516 |
| % of applicants accepted | 87 |
| % of acceptees attending | 32 |
| # of early decision applicants | 40 |
| % accepted early decision | 83 |

### FRESHMAN PROFILE

| | |
|---|---|
| Range SAT Verbal | 552-652 |
| Average SAT Verbal | 552 |
| Range SAT Math | 554-645 |
| Average SAT Math | 560 |
| Range ACT Composite | 24-27 |
| Average ACT Composite | 25 |
| Minimum TOEFL | 550 |
| Average HS GPA | 3.4 |
| % graduated top 10% of class | 38 |
| % graduated top 25% of class | 68 |
| % graduated top 50% of class | 95 |

### DEADLINES

| | |
|---|---|
| Early decision | 11/15 |
| Early decision notification | 1/1 |
| Priority admission deadline | 12/1 |
| Regular admission | 3/15 |
| Regular notification | rolling |
| Nonfall registration? | yes |

### APPLICANTS ALSO LOOK AT

**AND OFTEN PREFER**
Miami U.
Denison

**AND SOMETIMES PREFER**
Ohio State—Columbus
Ohio Wesleyan
Wooster
DePauw

## FINANCIAL FACTS

| | |
|---|---|
| **Financial Aid Rating** | **84** |
| Tuition | $22,680 |
| Room & board | $5,776 |
| Books and supplies | $500 |
| Required fees | $125 |
| % frosh receiving aid | 74 |
| % undergrads receiving aid | 70 |
| Avg frosh grant | $14,000 |
| Avg frosh loan | $4,400 |

# WOFFORD COLLEGE

429 North Church Street, Spartanburg, SC 29303-3663 • Admissions: 864-597-4130 • Fax: 864-597-4149

## CAMPUS LIFE

**Quality of Life Rating**    **84**
| | |
|---|---|
| Type of school | private |
| Affiliation | Methodist |
| Environment | urban |

### STUDENTS
| | |
|---|---|
| Total undergrad enrollment | 1,087 |
| % male/female | 53/47 |
| % from out of state | 31 |
| % from public high school | 70 |
| % live on campus | 87 |
| % in (# of) fraternities | 53 (8) |
| % in (# of) sororities | 65 (4) |
| % African American | 8 |
| % Asian | 1 |
| % Caucasian | 89 |
| % Hispanic | 1 |
| # of countries represented | 1 |

### SURVEY SAYS . . .
*Frats and sororities dominate social scene*
*Diverse students interact*
*Student government*
*Great computer facilities*
*Classes are small*
*Theater is unpopular*
*Athletic facilities need improving*
*Campus difficult to get around*
*Lots of conservatives*

## ACADEMICS

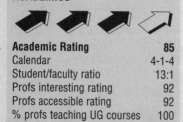

**Academic Rating**    **85**
| | |
|---|---|
| Calendar | 4-1-4 |
| Student/faculty ratio | 13:1 |
| Profs interesting rating | 92 |
| Profs accessible rating | 92 |
| % profs teaching UG courses | 100 |
| Avg reg class size | 10-19 students |

### MOST POPULAR MAJORS
business economics
biology
government

## STUDENTS SPEAK OUT
### Academics
"There is," apparently, "a right way, a wrong way, and a Wofford Way," according to the students at this "prestigious" and "truly unique place" in South Carolina. Students tell us the "Wofford Way" involves traditional liberal arts education, "very challenging," distribution requirements in the sciences and humanities, a Christian emphasis, and exchanging ideas "freely and with great academic zeal." The academic year here is divided into three parts: fall and spring semesters and the much-praised Interim, which occupies a winter month between the two semesters. "Students do not take classes" at Wofford, explains an economics major, "they take professors." The word is that "the Wofford faculty is outstanding." A few are "old," but these "extremely well-qualified, personable," and "seriously committed" professors are "here for the students." They "will bend over backwards" and are "willing to initiate new and inventive projects" with students during Interim. However, a senior cautions: "You cannot skip a class because you know you will see your professor at lunch. It's almost bothersome how available our professors and administrators make themselves." Wofford boasts "great computer facilities," and it is "very well run" (though slightly paternal), but the "archaic" and "awful" registration process is a real hassle. Students say Wofford's strengths are in "government" and "preparing students for a professional career in the South."

### Life
"Classes are extremely rigorous and weekends are extremely vigorous," rhymes a poetic junior at Wofford, where there is reportedly "a good balance" between academics and social life. Social life here typically stays on Wofford's "pretty campus." When Friday comes, "people head down at Fraternity Row for all their entertainment needs." In fact, the social scene here is pretty much confined to "the Row," and the "very important" Greeks seem firmly planted atop Wofford's hierarchy, so much so that "Greek life is a little too involved," and the frat scene can get monotonous. "Students who are not affiliated with a fraternity or sorority often find themselves searching for an outlet on the weekends," observes a sophomore. "This is especially true for students who are not interested in Greek life in general." Sports are probably second to the frat scene. Athletic events are well attended, and Wofford has managed to carve out a competitive place for itself in Division I athletics. "Homecoming is huge and the best weekend of the year." Beyond sports, frats, and religion (a Big Deal to a sizeable percentage of the population), "there's nothing to do in Spartanburg," laments one student. "You have to go to Greenville or Charlotte for fun." You can also go to Hilton Head Island, which is not far off, or spend a semester abroad.

### Student Body
The "basically friendly" and "very cordial" students at Wofford say "true southern hospitality" prevails at this "laid-back school where community is important" and the overwhelming majority of students hail from the Southeast. These students are admittedly "not very diverse economically and racially," but they are "extraordinarily accepting of diverse ideas." The "talented, intelligent" students here are also "high achievers" who spend most of their weekdays in continuous study mode. On the weekends, though, many are "generally determined to have as much fun as they can" in four years. "Guys here think about getting drunk and having sex," says a junior. "Girls think about getting drunk and getting married." The relationship between Greeks and non-Greeks borders on "hostile," and a great animus also exists between students pledged to different houses. While Wofford is home to a large bloc of "SUV-driving" students who "refer to their fathers as 'Daddy,'" most students are simply "conservative, upper-middle-class Caucasians who love fraternities." "If you can fit that mold," advises a junior, "Wofford is great."

FINANCIAL AID: 864-597-4160 • E-MAIL: ADMISSIONS@WOFFORD.EDU • WEBSITE: WWW.WOFFORD.EDU

## ADMISSIONS

*Very important* academic and nonacademic factors considered by the admissions committee include class rank, secondary school record, and standardized test scores. *Important* factors considered include state residency. *Other* factors considered include essays, extracurricular activities, interview, recommendations, and talent/ability. Factors *not* considered include alumni/ae relation, character/personal qualities, geography, minority status, religious affiliation/commitment, volunteer work, and work experience. SAT I or ACT required. TOEFL required of all international applicants. High school diploma is required and GED is accepted. *High school units required/recommended:* 16 total required; 4 English required, 3 math required, 2 science required, 2 science lab required, 2 foreign language required, 2 history required, 2 elective required.

### The Inside Word

Wofford is under-recognized among excellent college options in the South. Matchmaking plays a large part in the decisions of the admissions committee, which means that it takes much more than just above-average grades and solid test scores to get admitted. The admissions staff is friendly and eager to help students put their best foot forward in the process. Wofford is a particularly good choice for those who, while strong academically, are not likely candidates for admission to Duke and other top southern schools.

## FINANCIAL AID

*Students should submit:* FAFSA, institution's own financial aid form, and CSS/Financial Aid PROFILE. The Princeton Review suggests that all financial aid forms be submitted as soon as possible after January 1. *Need-based scholarships/grants offered:* Pell, SEOG, state scholarships/grants, private scholarships, and the school's own gift aid. *Loan aid offered:* Direct Subsidized Stafford, Direct Unsubsidized Stafford, Direct PLUS, and Federal Perkins. Institutional employment available. Federal Work-Study Program available. Applicants will be notified of awards on a rolling basis beginning on or about March 25. Off-campus job opportunities are excellent.

## FROM THE ADMISSIONS OFFICE

"In 1856, Samuel Dibble received the first diploma from Wofford. He went on to serve in the U.S. House of Representatives, becoming the first in a long line of leaders who studied at the college. The list includes five Rhodes Scholars, two U.S. senators, the founder of the National Beta Club, and the leaders of Duke and Vanderbilt as they became great universities. Of about 11,000 living Wofford alumni, 1,160 are presidents or owners of corporations or organizations; 402 are college faculty or staff members; 1,042 practice in medicine, dentistry, or other health care professions; and 560 are attorneys or judges. In 1987, the board of trustees approved a master plan, 'To Improve Quality,' that set some ambitious new goals. Increasing financial support indicates that challenge is being accepted and met. The F. W. Olin Foundation gave the college almost $6 million to build and equip a new high-technology academic building, and Wofford recently received a $12.2 million bequest for the endowment from Mrs. Charles Daniel. Always regarded as one of the South's most respected liberal arts colleges, Wofford today is rapidly earning a national reputation as a college on the move. With almost one of every five students involved, Wofford ranks as the nation's leader in the percentage of its students who each year earn academic credit outside of the United States. Studies abroad range from a full year at universities in Europe, Latin America, and Asia to travel study seminars and independent research during the January Interim term."

## ADMISSIONS

| | |
|---|---|
| **Admissions Rating** | **80** |
| # of applicants | 1,344 |
| % of applicants accepted | 83 |
| % of acceptees attending | 28 |
| # of early decision applicants | 174 |
| % accepted early decision | 90 |

### FRESHMAN PROFILE

| | |
|---|---|
| Range SAT Verbal | 544-640 |
| Average SAT Verbal | 595 |
| Range SAT Math | 516-693 |
| Average SAT Math | 607 |
| Range ACT Composite | 21-26 |
| Average ACT Composite | 24 |
| Minimum TOEFL | 550 |
| Average HS GPA | 3.4 |
| % graduated top 10% of class | 51 |
| % graduated top 25% of class | 79 |
| % graduated top 50% of class | 98 |

### DEADLINES

| | |
|---|---|
| Early decision | 11/15 |
| Early decision notification | 12/15 |
| Regular admission | 2/1 |
| Regular notification | 3/15 |
| Nonfall registration? | yes |

### APPLICANTS ALSO LOOK AT
**AND OFTEN PREFER**
Wake Forest
**AND SOMETIMES PREFER**
U. South Carolina—Columbia
Furman
**AND RARELY PREFER**
Clemson

## FINANCIAL FACTS

| | |
|---|---|
| **Financial Aid Rating** | **89** |
| Tuition | $17,030 |
| Room & board | $5,235 |
| Books and supplies | $850 |
| Required fees | $700 |
| % frosh receiving aid | 56 |
| % undergrads receiving aid | 54 |

# WORCESTER POLYTECHNIC INSTITUTE

100 INSTITUTE ROAD, WORCESTER, MA 01609 • ADMISSIONS: 508-831-5286 • FAX: 508-831-5875

## CAMPUS LIFE

| | |
|---|---|
| **Quality of Life Rating** | **72** |
| Type of school | private |
| Affiliation | none |
| Environment | suburban |

### STUDENTS

| | |
|---|---|
| Total undergrad enrollment | 2,817 |
| % male/female | 77/23 |
| % from public high school | 79 |
| % live on campus | 50 |
| % in (# of) fraternities | 33 (12) |
| % in (# of) sororities | 35 (2) |
| % African American | 1 |
| % Asian | 7 |
| % Caucasian | 86 |
| % Hispanic | 3 |
| % international | 5 |
| # of countries represented | 68 |

### SURVEY SAYS . . .

*Frats and sororities dominate social scene*
*Class discussions are rare*
*Student publications are ignored*
*Students aren't religious*
*Great computer facilities*
*Lousy food on campus*
*Students don't like Worcester, MA*
*Political activism is (almost) nonexistent*
*Athletic facilities need improving*

## ACADEMICS

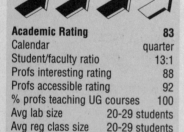

| | |
|---|---|
| **Academic Rating** | **83** |
| Calendar | quarter |
| Student/faculty ratio | 13:1 |
| Profs interesting rating | 88 |
| Profs accessible rating | 92 |
| % profs teaching UG courses | 100 |
| Avg lab size | 20-29 students |
| Avg reg class size | 20-29 students |

### MOST POPULAR MAJORS
mechanical engineering
electrical engineering
computer science

## STUDENTS SPEAK OUT

### Academics

The WPI undergraduate experience centers around the "WPI Plan," a series of required independent projects designed to build research ability and team-work skills. Components of the plan include the "Sufficiency," a five-course sequence outside the student's major that culminates in an independent project; the "Interactive Qualifying Project," which studies the interrelationship of science with social and ethical issues; and the "Major Qualifying Project," a senior research/design project that allows undergraduates to work closely with graduate students, professors, and occasionally, business leaders. Students approve of WPI's unique approach. Writes one, "The projects (IQP, MQP, and Sufficiency) force one to apply knowledge in real life, and they are awesome." Another agrees, "The WPI plan forces real-world experience on college students." Adds a third, "If you put the effort in, there are unparalleled opportunities for innovation in the academic experience." The workload is tough at this science, engineering, and computer science heavyweight, made even tougher by a quarterly academic calendar. Warns one engineering major, "You have to work hard here. The classes seem very fast, but it is better because you don't get bored." WPI professors "are different from class to class and really make the difference in your grade. They're like a Clint Eastwood movie: The Good, The Bad, and the Ugly." While many are "always willing to help if you have any questions," others "do not speak much English, making it hard to understand what they are trying to get across." Administrators "are very friendly. It is not uncommon to find the president or vice president walking around campus or eating in the cafeteria."

### Life

A heavy workload and a lopsided male-female ratio leave little time or opportunity for a social life at WPI. Explains one student, "Life is pretty fast. Classes in the morning and afternoon, and games in the evening along with homework." Weekends offer "not much besides fraternities. If you don't belong to a fraternity or a sports team, I don't know what else people would do except visit friends at liberal arts colleges. There are no girls here!" Parties in student apartments are also popular, if not to everyone's taste. Reports one naysayer, "Fun for most is going to one of the party houses off campus. I, however, personally don't like being crammed into a small room with 50 other people huddled around a keg." Under the circumstances, it is not surprising that "school spirit is low," and students feel that they "need more support for athletics and other campus events. A lot of people get involved, but we need a lot more!" Hometown Worcester offers little help; it's a "small, homogeneous city. There are not many opportunities for fun." Some feel that "the new Student Union being built in Worcester has potential to turn this into a college town," but that, of course, remains to be seen. On the upside, "rooms are spacious and the food is not bad" on campus.

### Student Body

The "international and diverse" students of WPI include "a lot of dorks and weirdoes, but there are also a lot of cool kids." Writes one, "It's a broad range of people from total dorks to total potheads. Frat parties are big with about half the campus. The other half has probably never seen a beer." Students enjoy a spirit of community fostered by a sense that they "have more in common with the students here than I could have at any other school" and because "most people are easygoing and work hard. There is a real sense of helping each other to succeed." On the downside, WPI's "terrible" male-female ratio "causes a strange social scene that most are not used to."

FINANCIAL AID: 508-831-5469 • E-MAIL: ADMISSIONS@WPI.EDU • WEBSITE: WWW.WPI.EDU

## ADMISSIONS

*Very important* academic and nonacademic factors considered by the admissions committee include essays, secondary school record, and standardized test scores. *Important* factors considered include extracurricular activities, state residency, talent/ability, volunteer work, and work experience. *Other* factors considered include geography. Factors *not* considered include alumni/ae relation, character/personal qualities, class rank, interview, minority status, recommendations, and religious affiliation/commitment. SAT I or ACT required. TOEFL required of all international applicants. High school diploma is required and GED is not accepted. *High school units required/recommended:* 16 total required; 19 total recommended; 4 English required, 3 math required, 4 math recommended, 3 science required, 4 science recommended, 2 foreign language required, 3 foreign language recommended, 3 social studies required, 4 social studies recommended.

### The Inside Word

Worcester's applicant pool is small but very well qualified. Its high acceptance rate makes it a good safety choice for those aiming at more difficult tech schools and for those who are solid but aren't MIT material. As is the case at most technical institutes, women will meet with a very receptive admissions committee.

## FINANCIAL AID

The Princeton Review suggests that all financial aid forms be submitted as soon as possible after January 1. *Need-based scholarships/grants offered:* Pell, SEOG, state scholarships/grants, private scholarships, the school's own gift aid, and Federal Nursing. *Loan aid offered:* FFEL Subsidized Stafford, FFEL Unsubsidized Stafford, FFEL PLUS, Federal Perkins, and Federal Nursing. Institutional employment available. Federal Work-Study Program available. Off-campus job opportunities are good.

## FROM THE ADMISSIONS OFFICE

"Projects and research are a distinctive element of the WPI plan. WPI believes that in these times simply passing courses and accumulating theoretical knowledge is not enough to truly educate tomorrow's leaders. Tomorrow's professionals ought to be involved in project work that prepares them today for future challenges. Projects at WPI come as close to professional experience as a college program can possibly achieve. In fact, WPI works with more than 200 companies, government agencies, and private organizations each year. These groups provide project opportunities where students get a chance to work in real, professional settings. Students gain experience in planning, coordinating team efforts, meeting deadlines, writing proposals and reports, making oral presentations, doing cost analyses, and making decisions."

## ADMISSIONS

| | |
|---|---|
| Admissions Rating | 83 |
| # of applicants | 3,501 |
| % of applicants accepted | 71 |
| % of acceptees attending | 28 |
| # of early decision applicants | 253 |
| % accepted early decision | 72 |

### FRESHMAN PROFILE

| | |
|---|---|
| Range SAT Verbal | 560-660 |
| Average SAT Verbal | 620 |
| Range SAT Math | 620-700 |
| Average SAT Math | 660 |
| Minimum TOEFL | 550 |
| % graduated top 10% of class | 45 |
| % graduated top 25% of class | 89 |
| % graduated top 50% of class | 99 |

### DEADLINES

| | |
|---|---|
| Early decision | 11/15 |
| Early decision notification | 12/15 |
| Regular admission | 2/1 |
| Regular notification | 4/1 |
| Nonfall registration? | yes |

### APPLICANTS ALSO LOOK AT

**AND OFTEN PREFER**
MIT
Cornell U.
Caltech

**AND SOMETIMES PREFER**
Rose-Hulman
U. Mass—Amherst
RPI
Case Western Reserve
Carnegie-Mellon

**AND RARELY PREFER**
U. Rhode Island
U. New Hampshire
U. Conn
Clarkson U.
Drexel

## FINANCIAL FACTS

| | |
|---|---|
| Financial Aid Rating | 80 |
| Tuition | $24,278 |
| Room & board | $8,012 |
| Books and supplies | $650 |
| Required fees | $150 |
| % frosh receiving aid | 65 |
| % undergrads receiving aid | 72 |
| Avg frosh grant | $12,121 |
| Avg frosh loan | $4,620 |

# YALE UNIVERSITY

PO Box 208234, New Haven, CT 06520-8234 • Admissions: 203-432-9300 • Fax: 203-432-9392

## CAMPUS LIFE

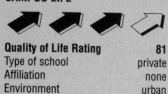

| Quality of Life Rating | 81 |
|---|---|
| Type of school | private |
| Affiliation | none |
| Environment | urban |

### STUDENTS

| | |
|---|---|
| Total undergrad enrollment | 5,351 |
| % male/female | 50/50 |
| % from out of state | 90 |
| % from public high school | 53 |
| % live on campus | 83 |
| % African American | 8 |
| % Asian | 15 |
| % Caucasian | 57 |
| % Hispanic | 6 |
| % Native American | 1 |
| % international | 5 |

### SURVEY SAYS . . .

Registration is a breeze
Ethnic diversity on campus
Students are happy
Lots of classroom discussion
No one cheats
Students don't like New Haven, CT
Very little hard liquor
Very little drug use
(Almost) no one listens to college radio
Very small frat/sorority scene

## ACADEMICS

| Academic Rating | 97 |
|---|---|
| Calendar | semester |
| Student/faculty ratio | 7:1 |
| Profs interesting rating | 90 |
| Profs accessible rating | 92 |
| Avg reg class size | 10-19 students |

### MOST POPULAR MAJORS
history
economics
political science

## STUDENTS SPEAK OUT

### Academics

Yale "is truly one of America's great schools," writes one college counselor. It's an assertion that's hard to debate. As a major national research center, Yale attracts many of the world's great scholars. But unlike other research institutes, Yale also devotes a lot of attention to undergraduates. Reports one student, "There is a genuine focus on undergraduates here. The professors seem genuinely to enjoy teaching, and you really do learn a lot in classes." Students do complain, however, that too many classes at all levels are taught by TAs and that they occasionally encounter professors who are poor teachers. Strife on campus over TAs' demands for higher wages and union representation has also been a cause of concern, heated debate, high anxiety, and student anger at the administration. Indeed, survey respondents consistently cited the administration as the worst aspect of the Yale undergrad experience. As one student puts it, "The administration does its absolute best to squelch student input." Academic departments are "uniformly excellent" here; among the school's many fine departments, standouts include drama, English, history, and the pre-med program. Yale has no core curriculum, instead requiring students to complete a broad range of general education requirements. Students tell us they like the "shopping period" registration system; they don't formally register for classes until two weeks into the semester, so the likelihood of getting stuck with a lousy class is minimized.

### Life

It would be foolish to pass up a chance to attend Yale University for just about any reason—provided you can deal with New Haven. Yale students have survived there for centuries, but they're not thrilled about it. Yalies give their home city extremely low marks. Many who responded to our survey reported that "Yale's worst problem is New Haven. It is dangerous and unreceptive to students. Life on and immediately around campus is great, but otherwise it's a real problem." But one pointed out that "it's a great eye opener to the 'real world,' though." Yale's social scene centers on its residential colleges (groups of students live together for their entire four-year stay): "Our residential college system really improves social life!" There's lots of hanging out, but some students complain that dates are in short supply. Writes one student, "The dating scene here is as much fun as a root canal." Popular student organizations include theater and music groups, the campus newspaper, and numerous political organizations.

### Student Body

Yale is famous enough to attract, and wealthy enough to finance, students from all backgrounds, and the result is a lively, diverse academic atmosphere. Be prepared to enter a fast-paced, very competitive community here: As one student puts it, "'Intense' is definitely the word for Yalies—we get very involved whatever we do here, be it classes, drama, sports, or what have you." Yale students' reputation for being eccentric still holds. One respondent puts it this way: "Everyone here has quirks. Yalies are fascinating people, very self-absorbed, but terrific when they decide to think about others."

FINANCIAL AID: 203-432-0360 • E-MAIL: UNDERGRADUATE.ADMISSIONS@YALE.EDU • WEBSITE: WWW.YALE.EDU

## ADMISSIONS

*Very important* academic and nonacademic factors considered by the admissions committee include class rank, recommendations, secondary school record, and standardized test scores. *Important* factors considered include character/personal qualities, essays, extracurricular activities, interview, and talent/ability. *Other* factors considered include alumni/ae relation, geography, minority status, volunteer work, and work experience. Factors *not* considered include religious affiliation/commitment and state residency. TOEFL required of all international applicants. *High school units required/recommended:* 16 total required; 4 English required, 3 math required, 2 science required, 3 science recommended, 2 science lab required, 2 foreign language required, 3 foreign language recommended, 2 history required, 1 elective required.

### The Inside Word

Yale posted some impressive numbers for the class of 2000, the largest class in 10 years and a result of the highest yield in 25 years of admits who enrolled. After such a fabulous year it was inevitable that apps would drop a bit, and they have. Still, Yale is ultra-selective. And there's nothing to be gained by appealing a denial here—the admissions committee considers virtually all of its decisions final. Yale uses a regional review process that serves as a preliminary screening for all candidates, and only the best-qualified, well-matched candidates actually come before the admissions committee.

## FINANCIAL AID

*Students should submit:* FAFSA, CSS/Financial Aid PROFILE, noncustodial (divorced/separated) parent's statement, and business/farm supplement. Regular filing deadline is February 1. The Princeton Review suggests that all financial aid forms be submitted as soon as possible after January 1. *Need-based scholarships/grants offered:* Pell, SEOG, state scholarships/grants, private scholarships, the school's own gift aid, and Alumni Club Awards. *Loan aid offered:* FFEL Subsidized Stafford, FFEL Unsubsidized Stafford, FFEL PLUS, Federal Perkins, state, and college/university loans from institutional funds. Institutional employment available. Federal Work-Study Program available. Applicants will be notified of awards on or about April 1. Off-campus job opportunities are good.

## FROM THE ADMISSIONS OFFICE

"The most important questions the admissions committee must resolve are 'Who is likely to make the most of Yale's resources?' and 'Who will contribute significantly to the Yale community?' These questions suggest an approach to evaluating applicants that is more complex than whether Yale would rather admit well-rounded people or those with specialized talents. In selecting a class of 1,300 from approximately 11,000 applicants, the admissions committee looks for academic ability and achievement combined with such personal characteristics as motivation, curiosity, energy, and leadership ability. The nature of these qualities is such that there is no simple profile of grades, scores, interests, and activities that will assure admission. Diversity within the student population is important, and the admissions committee selects a class of able and contributing individuals from a variety of backgrounds and with a broad range of interests and skills."

## ADMISSIONS

| Admissions Rating | 99 |
|---|---|
| # of applicants | 12,887 |
| % of applicants accepted | 16 |
| % of acceptees attending | 65 |
| # accepting a place on wait list | 575 |
| % admitted from wait list | 8 |
| # of early decision applicants | 1493 |
| % accepted early decision | 37 |

### FRESHMAN PROFILE

| | |
|---|---|
| Range SAT Verbal | 690-780 |
| Range SAT Math | 690-770 |
| Minimum TOEFL | 600 |
| % graduated top 10% of class | 95 |
| % graduated top 25% of class | 99 |
| % graduated top 50% of class | 100 |

### DEADLINES

| | |
|---|---|
| Early decision | 11/1 |
| Early decision notification | 12/15 |
| Regular admission | 12/31 |
| Regular notification | 4/1 |

### APPLICANTS ALSO LOOK AT AND SOMETIMES PREFER

Harvard
Princeton
Stanford
MIT
Swarthmore

### AND RARELY PREFER

Brown
Amherst
Williams
Wesleyan U.
U. Penn

## FINANCIAL FACTS

| Financial Aid Rating | 78 |
|---|---|
| Tuition | $25,220 |
| Room & board | $7,440 |
| Books and supplies | $720 |
| % frosh receiving aid | 38 |
| % undergrads receiving aid | 46 |

# PART 4

## "MY ROOMMATE'S FEET REALLY STINK."

The questionnaire we distributed to college students closed with a free-form "essay question." We told students that we didn't care *what* they wrote: if it was "witty, informative, or accurate," we'd try to get it into this book. We used all the informative and accurate essays to write the student view boxes; below are excerpts from the wittiest, pithiest, and most outrageous essays.

## LITERARY ALLUSIONS...

"To study at this school is to have infinite control over your destiny: you can crouch in your room like Gregor Samsa transformed into a dung beetle, or you can plunge into the infinite sea of faces that each year flood OSU like a tidal wave."

— A.W., Ohio State University

"Two jokes about St. John's College students:
1. Q: How many Johnnies does it take to change a light bulb?
   A: Let's define 'change' before we go any further.
2. Q: What did the Chorus say to Creon after Oedipus poked out his eyes?
   A: Now that's a face only a mother could love."

— April W., St. John's College

"'Prosperity unbruised cannot endure a single blow, but a man who has been at constant feud with misfortunes develops a skin calloused by time...and even if he falls he can carry the fight upon one knee.' —Seneca on Providence."

— Matthew D., U. of Connecticut

"Very definitely a love/hate relationship here. This is the level of hell that Dante missed."

—Amy P., Caltech

"The Deep Springs Experience is like working in an atrophy factory. Much of what you do in labor and government is fixing, improving, or replacing what came before you. No matter what frame of reference you use—daily, monthly, or yearly—you still feel like Sisyphus. The joy and value comes in building your muscles on so many different rocks."

—Whet M., Deep Springs College

"Lewd quotes on the bathroom walls at least come from great authors."

—Matt J., Simon's Rock College of Bard

"It is a shame that my family pays $12,000 annually for me to eat a different casserole every day."

— S.W., Southwestern University

"The food here is really bad; it's either bland or sickening. You're lucky if they don't screw up the bread."

— Scott P., Bentley College

"When students first arrive, they call the Observatory Hill Dining Facility 'O-Hill.' They soon learn to call it 'O-Hell,' because the food here is beyond revolting."

— Greg F., U. of Virginia

"If I had known that I'd be rooming with roaches and poisoned by the cafeteria staff I would have gone to Wayne State. I really can't complain, though, because I have met my husband here, like my mom did twenty years before."

— M.L.P., Fisk University

"The food here has particularly fancy names, and it seems as though they spend more time thinking of these names than they spend on making decent food."

— Andrew Z., Wheaton College

"If you're looking for gray skies, a gray campus, and gray food, then Albany is the place to be!"

— Michele G., SUNY Albany

"The food isn't that bad, if you don't mind varying shades of brown. On a good day the food on your tray will remind you of the brown paint sampler at your local Sherwin-Williams dealer."

— Rob P., College of the Holy Cross

"You should mention Lil', the lady who has worked in the dining hall for fifty years and who everyone loves. She plays the spoons all the time and runs around."

— Aaron R., Tufts University

"We spend more time at the lunch table than George, Jerry, Elaine, and Kramer, except that our cafeteria workers aren't as good looking."

—Chris D., Wake Forest University

"People ask me, 'Mike Z., why did you come to NYU?' I tell them, 'I didn't come to NYU, I came to New York City.'"

— Mike Z., NYU

"Change the name of UC—Irvine to UC—Newport Beach and we would have more girls."

— Pat M., UC–Irvine

"As this school is located in a tiny Texas town, a favorite activity is called 'rolling.' Rolling entails piling into a car with many drinks and driving the back country roads. Very slowly."

— Anonymous,
Southwestern University

"Connecticut is a cute state. It's a great place to go to school, but I wouldn't want to live here."

— Claire S., NJ native,
Fairfield University

"Binghamton is always gray. The two days a week we have sun, it's beautiful, but otherwise, sunglasses are not a must unless you're an artsy-fartsy pseudo-chic literature and rhetoric/philosophy major."

— Deborah C., SUNY–Binghamton

"Socially, the surrounding area is so dead that the Denny's closes at night."

— Thomas R., UC–Riverside

"The local liquor stores and towing companies make a lot of money."

— Katherine R., U. of Rhode Island

"Last week's major crime was that my left headlight was out, for which the busy Hanover police pulled me over three times."

— Jon K., Dartmouth College

"Davis is boring; you need a lot of drugs."

— Anonymous, UC–Davis

"It is definitely important to have a car, as the population of Canton frequently matches our winter temperature. 'Canton gray,' our perennial sky color, is one Crayola missed."

— Daniel R., St. Lawrence University

"I'm from L.A., and in my opinion Boston sucks. If you're into the frat/Spuds McKenzie crowd, Boston's the place to be. If you ain't, it's a lame social scene."

—Josh M., Emerson College

"Bloomington, Illinois, was recently voted the sixth most normal location in the U.S. Unfortunately, this translates into one of the most boring places. I liken it to New Haven on an overdose of valium."

— Matthew G., Illinois Wesleyan University

"Contrary to popular belief, cow tipping is definitely passé here."

— Anonymous, U. of Connecticut, Storrs

"Life in New Orleans—'And the people sat down to eat and to drink, and rose up to play.'—Exodus 32:6."

— Theresa W., Tulane University

"Fredericksburg is boring if one is not amused by the simple pleasures of existence such as breathing, sleep, and other things."

— Rich W., Mary Washington College

"I love escaping from Claremont. I wish I had a car! Claremont seems to be stuck in a white, bureaucratic, conservative nightmare. I feel cut off from the rest of the world, like I've fallen into Wonderland—the rules of the outside world don't apply here. However, I do feel like I've gotten and am getting a good education."

— Anonymous, Scripps College

## SECURITY...

"Campus security is made up of a bunch of midget high school dropouts with Napoleonic complexes who can spot a beer can from a mile away."

— Anonymous, UC–San Diego

"Public safety here is a joke. The public safety officers are like the Keystone Kops on Thorazine."

— Anonymous, Bryn Mawr College

"For fun we try to ski around campus on the snow, but campus safety must feel that we should be smoking weed because they allow that more than outdoor activities."

—Male Junior, Clarkson University

"No doors are locked here—_none_—but you have to notice the doorknob."

—Female Senior, Simon's Rock College of Bard

"Sure, our campus is diverse if you call diverse a campus full of white kids looking to make thirty to fifty grand after graduation."

— Joseph M. C., Davidson College

"If you're thinking of applying to MIT, go ahead. Because, believe it or not, most people here are at least as stupid as you are."

— Patrick L., MIT

"My 'life' at school revolves around devising new methods in which to escape and to get away from the nagging, 'supportive' women's environment."

—Caitlin B., Mount Holyoke College

"Students here mostly get along and since it is a business school we all have a common goal of being rich."

—Female Sophomore, Babson College

"People who go to school here are all pretty good-looking, especially the women. It should be renamed UKB, the University of Ken and Barbie."

— Tony H., Arizona State University

"Wesleyan is not only the 'diversity university' but also the 'controversy university,' the 'fight adversity university,' and the 'if we keep trying we might have some unity' university. We satisfy all types."

— John P., Wesleyan University

"Mt. Holyoke students are friendly and respectful with the exception of the occasions when the entire campus gets PMS."

—Abigail K., Mount Holyoke College

"Everyone walks too fast around here. You try to say 'hi' to someone, you've got to time it just right 'cause they aren't going to stop to talk to you. Plus, everyone wears the same clothes!"

— Terry B., Wittenberg University

"Girls over 5'8", watch out—for some reason, guys here have munchkin blood in them or something."

— Robyn A., Tufts University

"Life in some dorms can be very distressing. It's amazing how strange some people are."

—Anonymous, Penn State U.

"A school can be defined by its graffiti and its level of cleverness. Three quarters of our school graffiti is pro- or anti- a specific fraternity, with the other one quarter devoted to homophobic or misogynist theories."

— Matthew E., College of William and Mary

"This is a great university if you're not studying sciences involving animal research, politics, teacher education (certification), or anything that offends any long-haired leftist who's a vegetarian."

— Brock M., U. of Oregon

"This school is filled with wealthy, well-dressed egomaniacs who are about as socially conscious as Marie Antoinette."

— Anonymous, Hofstra University

"For self-absorbed artists my peers are all surprisingly good dancers."

—Jackie G., Bennington College

"When you first come here, you think everybody's really strange. Over time, though, you realize everybody is, and so are you. No big deal."

— Josh B., St. John's College

"University of Chicago's reputation is not entirely deserved. It's not true the place is completely full of nerds. It's only partially completely full of nerds."

— David G., U. of Chicago

"Everyone seems to know someone who invented something like Velcro or whose father is a CEO of a corporation."

— William K., Denison University

"I have this really big booger in my nose that I can't quite handle. What do I do? Pick it in public and look like a typical Brown freak, or just deal with it?"

—"Optional," Brown University

"Don't let anyone try to tell you that this is a diverse but close-knit atmosphere. The people here are about as diverse as a box of nails."

— Cari L., College of the Holy Cross

"UNH is about as diverse as the NHL."

— Curtis E., U. of New Hampshire

"We are cheeseballs, but rather enlightened; thus we condescendingly tolerate almost everyone."

—Cache M., Lawrence U.

"Denison has attempted to lose the 'rich kid party school' image and expand the diversity of the student body, but now it is becoming the 'I wish this were still a rich kid party school.' There is an awful lot available here, but students seem unmotivated and lazy."

— Anonymous, Denison University

"Most of my peers are narrow-minded morons who seem to live in the fifties. Because of this constant annoyance, the rest of us have a camaraderie that allows us to see how the other half lives."

—Gary A., LSU

"They say that Harvard students are arrogant, but where else can you find world-class professors and guest lecturers, world-class students, and world-class attitudes?"

— Edward S., Harvard University

"Everyone here is too smart for their [sic] own good. As one upper-level executive in the Houston area put it, 'The students at Rice know how to make it rain, but they don't know to come in out of it.'"

— John B., Rice U.

"My roommate's feet really stink."

— Anonymous, Claremont McKenna

"Kids at Bard are like fish in a fish bowl, no blinking but always hitting the glass."

—Zak V., Bard College

"Sometimes people complain about the lack of student involvement. I think someone should really do something about the apathy at St. Lawrence."

— Bill P., St. Lawrence University

"Bates is so diverse! Yesterday I met somebody from Connecticut!"

— Ellen H., Bates College

"Most are either Bible-thumping, goodie-goodie, white, stuck-up, right-wing, straight-A losers or work hard, play harder and party hardy, willing-to-try-anything cool people."

—Male Sophomore, Colorado School of Mines

"Rose-Hulman is one of the few places where it's safer to leave a $20 bill on your desk than it is to forget to log out of the computer network."

— Zac C., Rose-Hulman Institute of Technology

"The only thing the administration does well is tasks involving what Kenneth Boulding would call 'suboptimization.' Give them something that really doesn't need doing and it will be accomplished efficiently."

— Dana T., U. of Minnesota–Twin Cities

"Our business office may be the smoothest running machine since the Pinto!"

— Robert C., University of Dallas

"Despite the best efforts of the administration to provide TCNJ students with an inefficient, cold-hearted, red-tape infested, snafu-riddled Soviet-style administrative bureaucracy, The College of New Jersey is a pretty decent place to go for a fairly reasonable amount of money."

— Anonymous, The College of New Jersey

"The admissions office tries to make you apply based on, 'Well, we're very old and...and...well, we look nice. We'll do whatever it takes to make you happy! Really! I mean it. See my honest smile?' If you visit the school, ditch the tour and the gimmicks and talk to the professors."

— Anonymous, Southwestern University

"Going to a school as small as Emerson means that instead of saying 'screw you, Mr. 90803,' the administration will say, 'screw you, Joe.'"

— "Joe Bloggs," Emerson College

"The administration runs a wonderful school, and the students and teachers have a wonderful school. Fortunately, these are not the same school."

—Male Freshman/Sophomore, Bard College

"Administration is like the stock market, you invest time and money, sometimes you get a return, other times you don't."

—J.W.R., Albertson College of Idaho

"The bursar's office and financial aid are slightly retarded when it comes to communication. The daily walk between the two offices might have contributed to my not gaining 'The Freshman Fifteen.'"

—Brittany R., Wesleyan College

"Columbia is like a fruit truck. It picks up varied and exotic fruits and deposits them rotten at their destination."

— Paul L., Columbia University

"The U. of Minnesota is a huge black hole of knowledge. It sucks things into it from far and wide, compressing to the essence. Unfortunately, it is very hard to get anything out of a black hole. What I have managed to eke out has been both rewarding and depressing."

— James McDonald, U. of Minnesota

"The strangest incident I've ever had in class was when one of my journalism profs burnt our tests in the microwave. But, he decided to give everyone in the class an A, instead of retesting."

—Ashlea K., Ohio University

"Boulder is the world in a nutshell, served with alfalfa sprouts."

— Glenn H., U. of Colorado, Boulder

"Going to Northwestern is like having a beautiful girlfriend who treats you like crap."

— Jonathan J. G., Northwestern University

"Unless you are totally committed to science, do not come. Caltech has as much breadth as a Russian grocery store."

— Daniel S., Caltech

"Being at Marlboro is like having a recurring bizarre dream. You're not quite sure what it all means, but it happens a lot. If it stopped you'd probably wonder why, but then you'd just eat breakfast."

— Mark L., Marlboro College

"Life at school is an oxymoron."

—Dave G., UC–Davis

"One other thing I LOVE about NYU: online registration! God bless the NYU registrar!"

—Timothy A., New York University

"Vassar is like a sexual disease: once you've accepted it, it's great, but when you realize you've got another three years to put up with it, you go see a medical adviser immediately."

— Henry R., Vassar College

"Vassar is like a big walrus butt: lots of hair but also very moist."

— Calder M., Vassar College

"Attending UC—Riverside is like having your wisdom teeth pulled—not very enjoyable, but necessary."

— David E. Y., UC–Riverside

"I feel that this school is a maze with snakes and bulls. If you live with a raised fist or a raised phallus, it is easy. If you are earthly, bound to do nothing, come."

— Anonymous, U. of Oregon

"Getting an education from MIT is like getting a drink from a firehose."

— Juan G., MIT

"Financial Aid office needs a complete overhaul. An atom bomb would suffice."

—Male Senior, Duquesne University

"Pomona College is a swirling, sucking eddy of despair, filled with small moments of false hope, in an ever-blackening universe."

— Anonymous, Pomona College

"This school is like a tight anus: there's tremendous pressure to come out straight and conformed."

— Stephen J., Washington and Lee University

"My life here is as the torrential rains of Dhamer upon the Yaktong Valley. I bleat like a llama shedding out of season."

— Ronald M., James Madison University

"Intro classes have the consistency of Cheez Whiz: they go down easy, they taste horrible, and they are not good for you."

— Pat T., U. of Vermont

## SEX, DRUGS, ROCK & ROLL...

"This school is no good for people who like art, music, and Sonic Youth. 'Society is a hole.' There's a quote by Sonic Youth."

— Meghan S., Lake Forest College

"William and Mary: where you can drink beer and have sex in the same place your forefathers did."

— Adam L., College of William and Mary

"Montreal is the city of festivals. It is the party-central of Canada. McGill is located right in the middle of it all."

—Female, McGill University

"Yeah, there aren't any guys, but who doesn't like doing homework on a Saturday night?"

— Nicole C., Wellesley College

"The university tries to offer activities as an alternative to alcohol on the weekends. Those are not heavily attended. The weekends are for drinking."

—Maura G., Ohio University

"UCSB is the only place where U Can Study Buzzed and still ace an exam the next day."

— Tracy B., UC–Santa Barbara

"The dances here are a riot because I love watching nerds and intellectuals dance."

—Male Senior, Columbia University

"Beam, Bud, beer, babes—the four essential B's."

— "Jim Beam," Wittenberg University

"When I visited schools, I went to Brown and Northwestern on the same trip. I went to NU on a Wednesday and Thursday night. I partied like a champ. At Brown on Friday I was invited to two parties (I should be psyched) but they were both for NUDE people. AUGH YUCK!"

— Silvy N., Northwestern University

"A Denison student might be quoted as saying, 'Life is a waste of time, and time is a waste of life; so get wasted all the time, and have the time of your life.'"

— Katherine H., Denison University

"We have a Spring party called Mockstock. Fraternities and sororities join together and hire several bands to play throughout a day. Like Woodstock!"

—Anonymous, Hanover College

"This campus is an extremely great place to spend four college years, but it is still plagued, as all other campuses are, including Christian colleges, with sin. Therefore, this campus needs to come under submission to Jesus Christ."

— Laura D., James Madison University

## NEANDERTHALS

"If U R looking to settle down with an unattractive big woman, Hofstra is the place."

— Anonymous, Hofstra University

"There are lots of complaints about the attractiveness of the female students, but we females have our own saying about the guys at CMU—'The odds are good, but the goods are odd.'"

—Beth M., Carnegie Mellon University

"Girls at BYU are like parking spaces: the good ones are taken, the close ones are handicapped or reserved, and the rest are too far out!"

— Todd P., Brigham Young University

"In Rolla, we have tons of women, but not many of them!"

— Todd O., U. of Missouri–Rolla

"The faculty is great, academics are challenging, but the women are liberated and become difficult to live with. To sum it all up, Hendrix is so cool."

— Mike S., Hendrix College

"The students seem to have serious problems in general, perhaps they all need a little Viagra to perk things up a bit."

—Female Freshman, Albertson College

"UCSD rages—NOT! If you like the ocean and the library and have a fear of parties and girls without facial hair, you've hit the jackpot!!!"

— Spencer M., UC–San Diego

"Doesn't matter that we got no women. I'm never in bed anyway."

—Male Sophomore, California Institute of Technology

"There's a saying I've heard around: nine out of ten girls in California look good, the tenth goes to UCSD."

— Michael K., UC–San Diego

"Beer, football, and boobies are what Clemson is all about!"

— Paul S., Clemson University

"U of C is OK if all you want to do is work, but if you are looking for a good social scene or a hot stinkin' babe, go to California, young man!"

—Benjamin D., University of Chicago

"The men here often complain that there are too few women here; if they took a look in the mirror, maybe they'd realize why girls don't come here!"

— Tara L., Stevens Institute of Technology

## SCHOOL VS. THE "REAL WORLD"...

"College is the best time of your life. Never again will you be surrounded by people the same age as you, free from grown-ups and the threat of working in the real world. Your parents give you money when you ask for it, and all you have to do is learn!"

— Jennifer F., Syracuse University

"When we lose a football game to a college with lower academic standards, we console ourselves by saying that one day they will work for us and then we'll get even!"

— Michael J., University of the South, Sewanee

"Real life experience in such concepts—alienation, depression, suppression, isolationism, edge of racial tension, apathy, etc.—before the 'Real World.'"

— Anonymous, NYU

"Going to Chem. review is like masturbating with sandpaper: it's just a bad idea."

—Robby M., California Institute of Technology

## SCHOOLS THAT ARE ALL THAT & A BAG OF CHIPS

*"I like Duquesne because it has a mission beyond just educating students—it tries also to educate the heart and soul—and that makes for better students, a better university and a better world."*

—Female Senior, Duquesne University

*"For the first time in my life I am allowed to think for myself. . . . This is an environment where one can proclaim in class that Socrates is a bastard and, if able to support the statement, be respected for it."*

—Female Freshman, Simon's Rock College of Bard

*"Best ever dude! Nobody complains if I leave the toilet seat up."*

—Derek L., Deep Springs College

*"We're small enough that you'll probably hug a significant portion of the population by the time you graduate."*

—Male Junior, Bard College

*"We play dodgeball at recess and think what it would be like if we could fly."*

—Joseph W., Beloit College

*"The students here are as diverse as their views and backgrounds. My friends are mostly thespians and lesbians, and they rock!"*

—Female Junior, Bennington College

## IN CASE YOU WERE WONDERING...

*"You forgot to ask the most pertinent question, which is: 'Have you ever seen Elvis teach your 100 level courses?'"*

— Adam L., Alfred University

*"I was smart once. I used to sleep. Then I majored in chemical engineering."*

— C. C. Smith, Clemson University

*"There's about 15 too many classes along the lines of 'Talking Heads: The Politics of Cabbage in 19th Century Guam.'"*

—Sarah G., Bennington College

*"About dating, it simply hasn't happened, although there is this one girl—Liz—that's in one of my classes. She's smart, nice, friendly, and pretty, too. But she has a boyfriend—she says she's 'involved'—so I don't know anybody else that I want to date even though there's another girl that likes me."*

—"Joe B," Lawrence U

*"Classes are hard to get. Usually you have to cheat and just add the class, telling them you are a graduating senior. I've done that for the last three years and it works!"*

—Anonymous, UC–Davis

"Syracuse is like a banana. Some of us manage to peel it open easily. Some of us get the peel open after getting the banana all mushy. Sometimes we peel the banana, drop the peel, eat the banana, and then trip on the forgotten skin. At one point or another, we're all upright and eating that banana."

—K.S., Syracuse University

"I am a hermit who enjoys Ramen noodles and skin flicks. In the winter, I sit in a yoga position by a patch of ice on the sidewalk and mock people as they fall. I often bend spoons with my mind."

—Junior, Indiana University of Pennsylvania

"When I'm not trying to free Mumia, experience non-gender orgasm/transgender interpretive dance, contracting any number of venereal diseases, or trying to be hopelessly unique, I obsess to no end in trying to reconcile my existentialist beliefs with paying $30,000 a year to attend this socially legitimizing institution."

—Katherine S., Bard College

"Those who oppose the Dark Lord will be crushed, but those who are its friend will receive rewards beyond the dreams of avarice."

— Anonymous, Sarah Lawrence College

"There is a real problem with moles on this campus; no one is willing to talk about them."

— Alexander D., Bates College

"Bates College is a phallocentric, logocentric, Greco-Roman, linear-rational, ethnocentric, homophobic, patriarchal institution. How's that for a list of catchwords?"

— Stephen H., Bates College

"I think if our generation's parents knew how consumptive, ill-informed, and drug-addicted their children were, they'd suffer a collective nervous breakdown."

— Anonymous, U. of Denver

"Our school is the school of the future and always will be."

— Chuck C., Rhodes College

*"A crust of bread is better than nothing. Nothing is better than true love. Therefore, by the transitive property, a crust of bread is better than true love."*

—Jason G., Gettysburg College

*"Bentley College has fulfilled all and more of my expectations than I ever imagined."*

— Dawn T., Bentley College

*"Everyone seems to be really into political correctness, but in the wake of the recent Supreme Court decision, I don't see that lasting very long."*

—John R., Birmingham Southern College

*"Sarah Lawrence is a haven of unity and acceptance. Every morning at sunrise the entire campus gathers around the flagpole, holds hands, and sings 'We Are The World.' If you're really lucky, you get to be Dionne Warwick or Willie Nelson. If you show up late you have to be Bob Dylan. But everyone gets free doughnuts, and it's the happiest time of the day for most students. One morning I went hung over and threw up in the middle of the circle. I was so ashamed, but then I looked around at the diverse group of smiling faces from all over the country and the world and suddenly I felt better. I went home and threw up some more, thankful to live in the world of love that is Sarah Lawrence."*

— Matt F., Sarah Lawrence College

*(On the Academics/Administration) "They think they know a lot but they actually don't know anything, but some of them know that, so they know everything."*

—Male Junior, College of the Atlantic

# PART 5

# INDEXES

# INDEX OF COLLEGE COUNSELORS

The authors relied heavily on the following independent counselors for their assistance:

## Alabama

Rosalind P. Marie, EdS, CEP
207 Creek Trail
Madison, AL 35758
256-922-1194
consultrm@aol.com

## Arizona

Rusty Haynes, MS, CEP
13610 N. Scottsdale Road #10
Scottsdale, AZ 85254
480-614-8280
rhaynes@collegemasters.org

Ceel Kenny, CEP
182 Sage Drive
Sedona, AZ 86336
520-282-2728
sea@sedona.net

Nancy P. Masland, EdS, CEP
PO Box 32350
Tucson, AZ 85751
520-749-4220
masland@azstarnet.com

Adrianne G. Selbst, MEd, CEP
21826 N. Calle Royale
Scottsdale, AZ 85255
602-585-7993
AdrianneG@juno.com

## Arkansas

Thomas A. Eppley, Jr., EdD, CEP
11219 Financial Centre Parkway #312
Little Rock, AR 72211
501-223-8949

## California

Diane Grant Albrecht, MS, CEP
1255 Post Street, Suite 1001
San Francisco, CA 94109
415-928-1562
DGA84@aol.com

Miriam I. Bodin, MA, CEP
339 S. San Antonio Road, Suite 1-D
Los Altos, CA 94022
650-948-8651
MiriamIB@aol.com

Kay Davison, CEP
2402 Michelson, Suite 250
Irvine, CA 92612
949-833-7867

David Denman, MDiv, CEP
3030 Bridgeway Avenue, Suite 233
Sausalito, CA 94965
415-332-1831

Helen Denne, CEP
PO Box 336
LaCañada Flintridge, CA 91012-0336
818-547-4772
h-denne@pacbell.net

Paula G. Feldman, MS, CEP
4507 Gorham Drive
Corona del Mar, CA 92625
949-759-0330
Paulaedcon@aol.com

Diane Geller, MA, CEP
2300 Westwood Boulevard #104
Los Angeles, CA 90064
310-474-5783

Lynn Hamilton, MA, CEP
PO Box 50724
Santa Barbara, CA 93150
805-969-1177
LHamil3040@aol.com

Ada Horwich, MSW, CEP
9744 Wilshire Boulevard #430
Beverly Hills, CA 90212
310-859-4866
Placement2@aol.com

Amanda Mallory, MA, CEP
200 Lombard at Montgomery
San Francisco, CA 94111
415-421-4177
MMB@creative.net

Patsy J. Palmer, PhD, CEP
9744 Wilshire Boulevard, Suite 430
Beverly Hills, CA 90212
310-859-9866
placement2@aol.com

Jill Q. Porter, MS, CEP
1850 Castellana Road
La Jolla, CA 92037-3840
619-284-7277
porters@electriciti.com

Virginia Reiss, MS
980 Magnolia Avenue, Suite 8
Larkspur, CA 94939
415-461-4788

Paul Vaughn, MSPsy, CEP
15902 Gault Street
Van Nuys, CA 91406
818-787-2610
PaulVaughn@aol.com

## ■ Colorado

Steven R. Antonoff, PhD, CEP
501 South Cherry Street, Suite 490
Denver, CO 80246
303-394-2929
schoolbuff@aol.com

Diane E. Arnold, CEP
2733 Big Horn Circle
Lafayette, CO 80026
303-604-2339
Darnold64@aol.com

Anne W. Carroll, PhD, CEP
1777 S. Bellaire #339
Denver, CO 80222
303-759-8371

Shirley Burr Darling, MA, CEP
1355 S. Colorado Boulevard, Suite 300
Denver, CO 80222
303-757-3010
SBDarling@aol.com

Jana P. Lynn, PhD, CEP
6249 Songbird Circle
Boulder, CO 80303
303-443-7845

Estelle R. Meskin, MA, CEP
282 Monroe Street
Denver, CO 80206
303-394-3291
EMeskin@aol.com

## ■ Connecticut

Peter D. Adams, EdM, CEP
664 Farmington Avenue
Hartford, CT 06105
860-233-6624
padamsec@javanet.com

Camille M. Bertram, CEP
120 Riders Lane
Fairfield, CT 06430
203-255-2577
CMBert@aol.com

Virginia J. Bush, CEP
15 Agawam Avenue, Fenwick
Old Saybrook, CT 06475
860-388-1242

Adrienne A. DuBois, MSEd, CEP
15 E. Putnam Avenue
Greenwich, CT 06830
203-629-2566
AADuBois@aol.com

Donald M. Dunbar, MEd, CEP
191 Elm Street
New Canaan, CT 06840
203-966-5454

Susan Edwards, MA, CEP
10 Pennoyer Street
Rowayton, CT 06853
203-866-2692
SBEEduCon@worldnet.att.net

John Greenwood, CEP
191 Elm Street
New Canaan, CT 06840
203-966-5454

Alan Haas, CEP
191 Main Street
New Canaan, CT 06840
203-966-6993
EduFutures@aol.com

Margaret King, PhD, CEP
1895 Post Road
Fairfield, CT 06430
203-255-5511
mkingec@aol.com

Carol A. Loewith, MA, CEP
191 Fairfield Woods Road
Fairfield, CT 06432
203-372-4222
CALEdCon@aol.com

William M. Morse, PhD, CEP
260 Riverside Avenue
Westport, CT 06880-4804
203-222-1066

Marcia B. Rubinstien, MA, CEP
119 Highwood Road
West Hartford, CT 06117
860-233-3900
edufax@tiac.net

Alison Pedicord Schleifer, MS, CEP
220 Alston Avenue
New Haven, CT 06515
203-387-3454

Susan M. Spain, MA, CEP
126 Leroy Avenue
Darien, CT 06820
203-655-6627
SMSpainEdu@aol.com

Jan M. Traynor, MS, CEP
728 Carter Street
New Canaan, CT 06840
203-972-8730
traynor@concentric.net

Diederik van Renesse, CEP
225 Main Street, Suite 302
Westport, CT 06880
203-227-3190

Susan Wexler, MS
14 Bushy Ridge Road
Westport, CT 06880
203-341-0599
swexler@snet.net

## District of Columbia

Kpakpundu Ezeze, EdD
4545 Connecticut Ave. NW #228
Washington, DC 20008
202-686-6461
kezeze@aol.com

Geraldine C. Fryer, CEP
5125 MacArthur Blvd, Suite 42
Washington, DC 20016-3300
202-333-3230
gcfryer@aol.com

Steven Roy Goodman, MS, JD
Schuyler Arms 705,
1954 Columbia Road NW
Washington, DC 20009
202-986-9431
steve@topcolleges.com

Alexandra Ruttenberg, EdM, CEP
4725 MacArthur Boulevard NW
Washington, DC 20007
202-333-3530
guidance@schoolcounseling.com

Virginia Reynolds Vogel, EdS, CEP
3006 Dent Place, NW
Washington, DC 20007
202-342-1979

## Florida

Robin G. Abedon, MAT, CEP
2200 Corporate Boulevard NW, Suite 406
Boca Raton, FL 33431
561-241-1610
RobinJRA@aol.com

Mary B. Consoli, BSEd, CEP
111 2nd Avenue NE
Saint Petersburg, FL 33701
813-896-5022
mbconsoli@aol.com

Leslie Goldberg, MEd, CEP
Boca Raton, FL 33445
800-696-5684
LSGoldberg@aol.com

Shirley H. Grate, CEP
PO Box 17623
West Palm Beach, FL 33406-7623
561-357-5592
sgrate@aol.com

Janet Greenwood, MA, CEP
310 S. Brevard Avenue
Tampa, FL 33606
813-254-5303
www.GreenwdAssoc.com

Irvin W. Katz, MEd, CEP
8100 SW 81st Drive, Suite 280
Miami, FL 33143
305-274-2711
irvkatzedu@aol.com

Louise Kreiner, CEP
Miami, FL 33181
800-696-5684
KreinerCon@aol.com

Martha Moses, MA, CEP
9655 South Dixie Highway, Suite 300
Miami, FL 33156-2813
305-669-2682
mmoses@icanect.net

Judi Robinovitz, MA, CEP
2200 Corporate Boulevard, Suite 406
Boca Raton, FL 33431
561-241-1610
JudiRobino@aol.com
or
333 17th Street Suite J
Vero Beach, FL 32960
561-778-8001

Joan Tager, MA, CEP
35 Bermuda Lake Drive
Palm Beach Gardens, FL 34180
Phone 561-627-3757
Fax 561-627-4243

## ■ Georgia

Leonard Buccellato, PhD, CEP
3390 Peachtree Road, Suite 1146
Atlanta, GA 30326
404-231-9925
Lenbuccellato@mindspring.com

Carol E. DeLucca, EdD, CEP
235 Lachaize Circle
Atlanta, GA 30327
404-303-0314
cedelucca@aol.com

Mark L. Fisher, CEP
6800 Roswell Road, Suite 2E
Atlanta, GA 30328
770-399-9333
mfisher@mindspring.com

Jean P. Hague, MA, CEP
1201 Peachtree NE #200
Atlanta, GA 30361
404-872-9128
jeanhague@aol.com

B. J. Hopper, MEd, CEP
3400 Peachtree Rd, Suite 1539
Atlanta, GA 30326
404-814-1394
BHopper719@aol.com

George G. Kirkpatrick, MA, CEP
3210 Peachtree Road NE, Suite 12
Atlanta, GA 30305-2400
404-233-3989
kirkeducon@aol.com

## ■ Illinois

Susan J. Bigg, MPH, CEP
1410 Wrightwood Avenue #K
Chicago, IL 60614-1140
773-404-1699
wbyeats@megsinet.net

Harriet R. Gershman, MSEd, CEP
930 North York Road, Suite 10
Hinsdale, IL 60521
630-789-0180
ACSGersh@aol.com
or
1800 Sherman Avenue, Suite 203
Evanston, IL 60201
847-492-3434

Nancy Gore Marcus, MAEd, CEP
560 Green Bay Road
Winnetka, IL 60093
847-446-7557
ngmadvise@aol.com

Jane C. McLagan, EdM, CEP
425 East Seventh Street
Hinsdale, IL 60521
630-325-1079
JaneMcL@aol.com

Jane A. Simmons, PhD, CEP
126 Elmore Avenue
Park Ridge, IL 60068
847-825-3818
JASimCEP@aol.com

Imy F. Wax, MS, CEP
1320 Carol Lane
Deerfield, IL 60015
847-945-0913
ImyWax@aol.com

## Indiana

Robert G. Kindmark, MA, CEP
219 Westchester Avenue
Chesterton, IN 46304
219-926-3131

## Iowa

Phyllis C. Grewell, CEP
924 44th Street
West Des Moines, IA 50265-3030
515-225-1094

## Louisiana

Nancy W. Cadwallader, MFA, CEP
PO Box 66371
Baton Rouge, LA 70896
225-928-1818
cadwallader@worldnet.att.net

Farron G. Peatross, MA, CEP
615 Robert Travis Drive
Shreveport, LA 71106
318-869-0088
farron@iamerica.net

## Maryland

Carol Z. Bloch, MEd, CEP
7 Pinewood Farm Court
Owings Mills, MD 21117
410-252-7565
czbloch@aol.com

Marilyn Colson, MS, CEP
239 Village Square
Baltimore, MD 21210-1694
410-435-6651
marcolson@aol.com

Diane E. Epstein, CEP
6704 Pawtucket Road
Bethesda, MD 20817-4836
301-320-5311
dianecps@erols.com

Shirley Levin, MA, CEP
6809 Breezewood Terrace
Rockville, MD 20852
301-468-6668
lev4advice@aol.com

Lorine Potts-Dupré, PhD, CEP
7010 Westmoreland Avenue, Suite 100
Takoma Park, MD 20912
301-270-2033
LNPD@aol.com

Nancy Rosenberg, MEd, CEP
6412 Kenhowe Drive
Bethesda, MD 20817
301-320-5652
specialcc@yahoo.com

Virginia Reynolds Vogel, EdS, CEP
85 Bay Drive
Annapolis, MD 21403
301-469-6973

## Massachusetts

Lee Askin, CEP
276 Edmands Road
Framingham, MA 01701
508-877-4453
aie@gis.net

Edward L. Bigelow, CEP
20 Chapel Street, #102B
Brookline, MA 02446
617-264-7537

Joan H. Bress, LICSW, CEP
51 A Cedar Street
Worcester, MA 01609
508-757-8920
jbress@aol.com

Christine Jackson Counelis, MEd, CEP
PO Box 2172
Amherst, MA 01004
413-253-4143
cdxine@aol.com

Donald M. Dunbar, MEd, CEP
20 Chapel Street Suite 102B
Brookline, MA 02446
617-734-8632

Marilyn F. Engelman, PhD, CEP
73 Lexington Street, Suite 201
Auburndale, MA 02466
617-964-0440
marilyn171@aol.com
or
57 East Main Street, Suite 224
Westborough, MA 01581
508-870-1515

Carol Gill, MA, CEP
39 Glenoe Road
Chestnut, Hill MA
617-739-6030
carolgill@aol.com

Leslie Goldberg, MEd, CEP
15 Sentinel Road
Hingham, MA 02043
781-749-2074
LSGoldberg@aol.com

Madelaine Hart, CEP
11 Southgate Road
Wellesley, MA 02482-6606
781-431-2550
maddieh@ix.netcom.com

Charlotte Klaar, MS, CEP
9 Laurel Avenue
Northborough, MA 01532-1670
508-393-6730
ccs4college@erols.com

Louise Kreiner, CEP
PO Box 5217
Bradford, MA 01835-0217
978-373-9561
KreinerCon@aol.com

Timothy B. Lee, EdM, CEP
323 Boston Post Road
Sudbury, MA 01776-3022
978-443-0055 x212
tlee@ahpnet.com

Priscilla B. Lewis, EdM, CEP
PO Box 128 (Barnstable)
Cummaquid, MA 02637
508-362-9697

Midge Lipkin, PhD, CEP
127 Marsh Street
Belmont, MA 02478
617-489-5785
mlipkin@schoolsearch.com

Mary Mansfield, MEd, CEP
20 Lincoln Lane
Sudbury, MA 01776
978-443-4404
rsmansfie@aol.com

Benjamin L. Mason, EdM, CEP
323 Boston Post Road
Sudbury, MA
978-443-0055 x221
BEEMASON@aol.com

Sarah M. McGinty, PhD, CEP
322 Marlborough Street
Boston, MA 02116
617-262-3435
http://mcgintyconsulting.com

Jacqueline Mitchell, MSEd, CEP
17 Johnny Cake Hill
Whaling National Park
New Bedford, MA 02740
508-994-8794

Bernice Wilson Munsey, EdD, CEP
**Office open in summer only**
Osterville, MA
508-428-6178
BAnnMunsey@aol.com

Bonny Musinsky, MA, CEP
49 Kendall Common Road
Weston, MA 02493
781-899-5759
musin98@hotmail.com

Laurie H. Nash, EdD, CEP
24 Cross Hill Road
Newton Centre, MA 02459
617-332-2794
NEXTMOVE@aol.com

Cornelia Nicholson, MLS, CEP
44 Fairwinds Drive
Osterville, MA 02655
508-420-3085
www.collegecounselor.com

Stella Christine Oh, CEP
231 Kennedy Drive, Suite 102
Malden, MA 02148
781-397-6701
StellaCOh@aol.com

Michael W. Spence, CEP
262 Beacon Street
Boston, MA 02116
617-536-4319
PHSpence@aol,com

## ■ Michigan

Judith W. Halsted, MS, CEP
934 E. Eighth Street
Traverse City, MI 49686
616-947-4005
jhalsted@traverse.com

Lynn B. Luckenbach, MEd, CEP
111 S. Woodward, Suite 214
Birmingham, MI 48009
248-644-0749
lynnluck@aol.com

## ■ Minnesota

Nicky B. Carpenter, CEP
15500 Wayzata Boulevard
Wayzata, MN 55391
612-475-0330
NCARPEN635@aol.com

## ■ Missouri

James C. Heryer, MA, CEP
705 Brush Creek Boulevard
Kansas City, MO 64110
816-531-2706
jheryer@aol.com

Rosalyn S. Lowenhaupt, MA, CEP
7730 Carondelet, #412
Street Louis, MO 63105
314-727-4909

Jane Schoenfeld, CEP
7730 Carondelet Avenue #412
Street Louis, MO 63105
314-727-4909
isps-jbs@worldnet.att.net

## ■ Nevada

Harriet R. Gershman, MSEd, CEP
Lynn Hamilton, MA, CEP
James A. Nolan, MA, CEP
Access Education International
6879 West Charleston, Suite B
Las Vegas, NV 60201
888-967-5333
WorldEdu@aol.com

## ■ New Hampshire

Mei-Ling Henrichson, CEP
PO Box 138
Winchester, NH 03470
603-239-8189
mlhedcon@ix.netcom.com

Robert M. Kantar, CEP
102 North State Street
Concord, NH 03301
603-228-8442
RKantar@aol.com

## ■ New Jersey

Amy Leib Alexander, MS
170 North Mountain Avenue
Montclair, NJ 07042
973-655-1603
ALAeduc@aol.com

Judith Berg, MA, CEP
257 Monmouth Street, Building B #1
Oakhurst, NJ 07755
732-531-1300
jberg@monmouth.com

Leonard Krivy, PhD, CEP
1765 Fireside Lane
Cherry Hill, NJ 08003
609-428-1282
LPKPHD@aol.com

Ruth Lipka, MA, CEP
13 Jonquil Court
Paramus, NJ 07652
201-447-4477
rlipka@carroll.com

Ronna Morrison, MA, CEP
11 Maple Avenue
Demarest, NJ 07627
201-768-8250
RonnaCEP@aol.com

Helene Reynolds, MAEd, CEP
83 Adams Drive
Princeton, NJ 08540
609-921-1326
hreynolds@helenereynolds.com

Helen Reagan Savage, MA, CEP
3401 Shore Drive
Cape May Beach, NJ 08251
609-889-0560
helsavage@aol.com

Marylou Schaffer, MEd, CEP
17 Hathaway Lane
Verona, NJ 07044
973-857-1251
MLSCROSS@aol.com

Turbi Smilow, MS, CEP
41 Putnam Road
East Brunswick, NJ 08816
732-238-0510
turbismile@aol.com

Donald M. Sykes, MA, CEP
PO Box 457
Rumson, NJ 07760
732-747-2807

Anita Targan, MA, CEP
2 Gloucester Place
Morristown, NJ 7960
973-538-7607

## ■ New Mexico

Alan C. Posich, MA, CEP
4163 Montgomery Boulevard NE
Albuquerque, NM 87109
505-888-1701
Aposich@aol.com

Kim A. Rubin, MA, CEP
3 Altazano Drive
Santa Fe, NM 87505
505-989-8910
ackim@trail.com

## ■ New York

Meryl June Blackman, MS, CEP
3 Birch Grove Drive
Armonk, NY 10504
914-273-9618

Virginia J. Bush, CEP
444 East 86th Street
New York, NY 10028
212-772-3244

Edward T. Custard
CollegeMasters
Educational Consulting Services
PO Box 183
Sugar Loaf, NY 10981-0183
Phone 914-469-9182
Fax 914-469-7601
ecustard@collegemasters.org

Geraldine C. Fryer, CEP
1066 Boston Post Road
Rye, NY 10580-2902
914-967-7952
gcfryer@aol.com

Patricia B. Gildersleeve, MS, CEP
16 Harrogate Road
New Hartford, NY 13413
315-732-9001
pbgilder@aol.com

Carol Gill, MA, CEP
369 Ashford Avenue
Dobbs Ferry, NY 10522
914-693-8200
carolgill@aol.com

Pearl Glassman, PhD, CEP
30 White Birch Road
Pound Ridge, NY 10576
914-764-5153
glassman@cloud9.net

Leslie Goldberg, MEd, CEP
New York, NY 10003
800-696-5684
LSGoldberg@aol.com

Barbara Ann Kenefick, PhD, CEP
County Route 9
Chatham, NY 12037
518-392-4753
bkenefick@berkshireschool.org

Jane Kolber, CEP
142 East 71 Street
New York, NY 10021
212-734-1704
JEKWFK@aol.com

Louise Kreiner, CEP
New York, NY 10003
800-696-5684
KreinerCon@aol.com

Leonard Krivy, PhD, CEP
888 8th Avenue, Suite 18J
New York, NY 10019
609-428-1282
LPKPHD@aol.com

Maryann McCrea, MA, CEP
3 Birch Grove Drive
Armonk, NY 10504
914-273-9618

Mike Musiker, MEd, CEP
1326 Old Northern Boulevard
Roslyn Village, NY 11576
516-621-3713
mike@summerfun.com

Andrea C. O'Hearn, CEP
18 Goodfriend Drive
East Hampton, NY 11937
516-329-5245
acanswers@aol.com

Joan Tager, MA, CEP
577 Old Montauk Highway
Montauk, New York 11954
Phone 516-668-4239
Fax 516-668-7054

Sally M. Ten Eyck, BSEd, CEP
43 Tygert Road
Altamont, NY 12009
518-765-3288
SMTENEYCK@aol.com

Diederik van Renesse, CEP
125 Park Avenue-16th floor
New York, NY 10017
203-227-3190

## ■ North Carolina

Mary Jane Freeman, MAEd, CEP
124 Huntington Lane
Mooresville, NC 28117
704-660-5266
MaryjaneF@aol.com

Renee LeWinter Goldberg, EdD, CEP
9225 Bonnie Briar Circle
Charlotte, NC 28277
704-544-0905
OPTIONSED@aol.com

Linda McMullen, MEd, CEP
PO Box 6278
Kinston, NC 28501
252-523-0998
McMullen@eastlink.net

Marnie Ruskin, MSW, CEP
5 Parkmont Court
Greensboro, NC 27408-3808
336-282-1202
RUSKINM@nr.infi.net

Ann Crandall Sloan, MA, CEP
4072 Barrett Drive
Raleigh, NC 27609
919-783-5555
asloan@mindspring.com

## ■ Ohio

Arline Altman, MAEd, CEP
6050 Cranberry Court
Columbus, OH 43213
614-864-0356

Toni DiPasquale, MSEd, CEP
7353 Old Stable Lane
Centerville, OH 45459-4210
937-435-0621
pepservice@aol.com

Phyllis Kozokoff, MA, CEP
23811 Chagrin Boulevard, Suite 307
Cleveland, OH 44122
216-464-3686
Pkozokoff@aol.com

Thekla Shackelford, MA, CEP
6020 Havens Road
Columbus, OH 43230
614-855-2401

## ■ Oregon

Marilyn Petrequin
2455 NW Marshall Street, Suite 8B
Portland, OR 97210
503-223-4429
petrequin@transport.com

Nancy E. Smith, CEP
1012 SW King, Suite 104
Portland, OR 97205
503-226-0072
dekesmith@aol.com

## ■ Pennsylvania

Laurie Crockett Barclay, EdM, CEP
912 W. Fourth Street
Williamsport, PA 17701
570-322-1313
CPALCB@csrlink.net

Grant Calder, CEP
310 North High Street
West Chester, PA 19380
610-692-9096

Robert Cohen, EdD, CEP
65 E. Elizabeth Avenue Suite 612
Bethlehem, PA 18018
610-867-1818
rdcollege@enter.net

John Granozio, MEd, CEP
Penn Plaza #2, 120 Pennsylvania Ave
Oreland, PA 19075
215-572-1590

Janet Greenwood, MA, CEP
7 Irvine Row
Carlisle, PA 17013
717-249-0101
www.GreenwdAssoc.com

Dodge Johnson, PhD, CEP
547 S. Sugartown Road
Malvern, PA 19355-2643
610-647-6755
djohnson@voicenet.com

Louise Kreiner, CEP
Bucks County, PA 18931
800-696-5684
KreinerCon@aol.com

Leonard Krivy, PhD, CEP
255 South 17th Street
Philadelphia, PA 19103
215-545-1555
LPKPHD@aol.com

Lynne H. Martin, CEP
PO Box 223
Westtown, PA 19395-0223
610-399-6787

James A. Nolan, MA, CEP
1062 Lancaster Avenue #22
Rosemont, PA 19010
610-527-9242
NolEduIntl@aol.com

Lloyd R. Paradiso, CEP
7 Benjamin Franklin Parkway
Philadelphia, PA 19103
215-569-2977
thepyo@erols.com

Patricia Onderdonk Pruett, PhD, CEP
PO Box 1053
Bryn Mawr, PA 19010
610-525-4607
104571.1122@compuserve.com

Suzanne F. Scott, EdM, CEP
1538 Woodland Road
Rydal, PA 19046
215-884-0656
scottaas@aol.com

Barbara Snyderman, PhD, CEP
401 Shady Ave. Suite C107
Pittsburgh, PA 15206
412-361-8887

## ■ Rhode Island

Christopher Covert, CEP
132 George M. Cohan Boulevard
Providence, RI 02903
401-455-0120
CCovert915@aol.com

Andrea C. O'Hearn, CEP
Barrington, RI
401-246-2511
acanswers@aol.com

## ■ South Carolina

William S. Dingledine, Jr., MS, CEP
PO Box 5249
Greenville, SC 29606
864-467-1838
WSDingle@aol.com

Ann Carol Price, MEd, CEP
3104 Devine Street
Columbia, SC 29205
803-252-5777
EdConsultants@msn.com

## ■ Tennessee

Mary B. Consoli, BSEd, CEP
624 Reliability Circle
Knoxville, TN 37932
423-675-1997
mbconsoli@aol.com

Bunny Porter-Shirley, CEP
801 Lynnbrook Road
Nashville, TN 37215
615-269-3322
bunni@usit.net

Anne Thompson, MA, CEP
3978 Central Avenue
Memphis, TN 38111
901-458-6291
athompsn@ixlmemphis.com

## Texas

Carol G. Cohen, CEP
4901 Keller Springs Road, Suite 107
Addison, TX 75001-5930
972-381-9990
cococo@mail.ont.com

Janet Greenwood, MA, CEP
25227 Grogan's Mill Road #125
The Woodlands, TX 77380
281-296-1674
www.GreenwdAssoc.com

Elizabeth Hall, MA, CEP
2509 Hartford Road
Austin, TX 78703
512-476-5082
ehh@xmail.utexas.net

Lindy Kahn, MA, CEP
6717 Vanderbilt
Houston TX 77005
713-668-2609
lindyk23@hotmail.com

Marshall E. Shumsky, PhD, CEP
7887 San Felipe Road, Suite 101
Houston, TX 77063-1620
713-784-6610
shumsky@flash.net

Elissa Sommerfield, MA, CEP
9636 Hollow Way
Dallas, TX 75220
214-363-7043
esom@techrack.com

Rhea M. Wolfram, CEP
13928 Hughes Lane
Dallas, TX 75240-3510
972-233-1115
rwolframsis@airmail.net

## Vermont

Lora K. Block, MA, CEP
McIntosh Lane
Bennington, VT 05201
802-447-0776
lblock@sover.net

Benjamin L. Mason, EdM, CEP
PO Box 59
2687 Greenbush Road
Charlotte, VT 05445
802-425-7600
BEEMASON@aol.com

## Virginia

Bernice Wilson Munsey, EdD, CEP
3623 North 37th Street
Arlington, VA 22207-4821
703-276-8228
BAnnMunsey@aol.com

## Washington

Andrew Bryan, CEP
14655 NE Bel-Red Road, #202
Bellevue, WA 98007-3900
888-385-2877
EdPlan@aol.com

Linda Jacobs, MEd, CEP
2400 East Louisa Street
Seattle, WA 98112
206-323-8902
LinJacobs@aol.com

Sherrill O'Shaughnessy, CEP
14655 NE Bel-Red Road, #202
Bellevue, WA 98007-3900
425-401-6844
EdPlan@aol.com

## Wisconsin

Joanne Hytken, CEP
727 East Daisy Lane
Milwaukee, WI 53217
414-351-2025
educat@execpc.com

## Wyoming

Nicky B. Carpenter, CEP
PO Box 607
Buffalo, WY 82834
307-684-9222
NCARPEN635@aol.com

# INTERNATIONAL

## ■ Canada

Benjamin L. Mason, EdM, CEP
4920 deMaisonneuve Boulevard West, #10
Westmont, Quebec Canada
514-484-3548
BEEMASON@aol.com

## ■ England

Alan Haas, CEP
London, England
44171-266.5716
EduFutures@aol.com

## ■ Germany

Peter D. Adams, EdM, CEP
Gleuler Str. 272
50935 Koln, Germany
0221-463947
padamsec@javanet.com

## ■ Greece

Christine Jackson Counelis, MEd, CEP
61 V. Ipiroo
Vrilissia  152 35 Greece
301-61-31-120
cdxine@aol.com

## ■ South Korea

Ock Kyung Chun, MA, CEP
1003 Korea Business Center
1338-21 Seocho-dong
Seocho-Ku, Seoul  S. Korea 137-070
822-3473-6561

Yung Oh, CEP
Stella Christine Oh, CEP
2nd floor, Jinyoung Building
909-3 Daechidong, Kangnam-ku
Seoul, S. Korea
82-2-561-8191
stellaca@unitel.co.kr

Chang Won Park, MA, CEP
C.PO Box 3561
Seoul, S. Korea  100-635
82-2-777-2211
cfschang@soback.kornet21.net

## ■ Sweden

Josephine M. Griffin, MSEd, CEP
StockholmSweden
468.661.6209
jgriffin@netbox.com

## ■ Switzerland

Alan Haas, CEP
Zurich, Switzerland
411-390-2826
EduFutures@aol.com

## ■ Switzerland

Susan M. Spain, MA, CEP
1005 Lausanne
4121-312-47-41
73021.606@compuserve.com

## ■ Turkey

H. Nazan Kabatepe, CEP
Barbaros Bulvari No: 24/7
Balmumcu-80700
Istanbul, Turkey
90-212-2882826
erka_grp@turk.net

## ■ Zimbabwe

Barbara Stahl, MA, CEP
39 Tunsgate Road
Northwood, Harare,  Zimbabwe
stahls@africaonline.co.zw

# INDEX OF SCHOOLS BY STATE

## Utah

## Vermont

## Virginia

## Washington

## West Virginia

## Wisconsin

## Wyoming

## Canada

**Robert Franek** is a graduate of Drew University and has been a member of The Princeton Review Staff for two years. Robert has assimilated well into TPR Culture and has perma-smile attached to his face when asked about the managing of this project. He is thrilled to be part of this process, and excited to start again this fall. Robert comes to The Princeton Review with an extensive admissions background, most recently at Wagner College in Staten Island, New York. In addition, he owns a walking tour business and leads historically driven, yet not boring, tours of his native city!

**Eric Owens** attended Cornell College, and he is giddy about the fact that it is now in this book. He is a recent graduate of Loyola Chicago School of Law and teaches, writes, and does other stuff for The Princeton Review. He is the voice of Joe Bloggs on a CD-ROM.

**Tom Meltzer** is a graduate of Columbia University. He has taught for The Princeton Review since 1986 and is the author or co-author of seven TPR titles, the most recent of which is *Illustrated Word Smart*, which Tom co-wrote with his wife, Lisa. He is also a professional musician and songwriter. A native of Baltimore, Tom now lives in Durham, North Carolina.

**Roy Opochinski** is a graduate of Drew University and has been a member of The Princeton Review staff since 1990. He has taught courses for TPR for 11 years and has edited several other books for TPR, including *Word Smart II* and *Math Smart*. In addition, Roy is the executive editor at Groovevolt.com, a music website. He now lives in Toms River, New Jersey.

**Tara Bray** is a resident of New York City by way of Hawaii, New Hampshire, Oregon, and Chicago, and is a graduate of Dartmouth College as well as Columbia University's School of the Arts. When she's not writing, Tara likes to spend her time figuring out how to pay the rent. She is also the author of The Princeton Review's guide to life after college, *Why Won't the Landlord Take Visa?*

# NOTES

# NOTES

# NOTES

# NOTES

# Expert Advice

## Talk About It

## Pop Surveys

# Paying for it

## The Princeton Review

# Getting in

## Word du Jour

## Find-O-Rama School & Career Search

# www.review.com

## Best Schools

# Finding it

# HOW CAN THE PRINCETON REVIEW HELP YOU?

# FIND THE RIGHT

## Complete Book of Colleges

There are over 1,500 accredited four year colleges in the U.S. This book devotes a page to each and every one— we've got them all! $26.95

## Student Athlete's Guide to College

A game plan to competing in NCAA sports and a guide to overall college success both on and off the field. $12.00

## The Complete Book of Catholic Colleges

There's more than Notre Dame and St. John's out there! Try 195 schools across the country that are officially recognized as Catholic—and we've got the skinny on all of them. By Edward T. Custard and Dan Saraceno. $21.00

## Visiting College Campuses

Planning on touring one of the 250 most visited colleges? Here's just the thing you need. We help you plan the most efficient and effective trip possible. By Janet Spencer. $20.00

## The Hillel Guide to Jewish Life on Campus

The Hillel organization details the Jewish life, or lack thereof, on over 500 campuses across the country. Whether you're looking for Jewish studies programs or Klezmer music on campus, you'll find it here. Edited by Ruth Fredman Cernea, Ph.D. $18.00

## TIME/The Princeton Review The Best College For You

*Time* magazine, the world's most widely read and respected news source, joins The Princeton Review to deliver the most valuable, up-to-date information on choosing a college, creating a winning application, and finding a way to pay for it all. *The Best College For You* also includes a directory of over 1,500 colleges. Check your newsstand today!

## The K & W Guide to Colleges for Students with Learning Disabilities or A.D.D.

This book features full and comprehensive profiles for over 380 schools—and 800 more are detailed specifically for the LD student's needs. Help yourself find and succeed at the right college for you. By Marybeth Kravets, MA, and Imy Wax, MS. $27.00

## The African American Students Guide to College

Begin the college selection process by learning what to expect once you get there. This book is for first-generation college students as well as those contemplating whether to enroll in a traditional African American college or a traditional Ivy League school. We even detail the 150 best schools for African American students. By Marisa Parham. $18.00

books

# COLLEGE...

## Looking for Colleges Online

The Princeton Review offers a variety of services to help you gather information about colleges and learn more about the college admissions process.

**Search.** Our college search engine is the most sophisticated college search tool available on the Internet. To use it, select the things that are important to you in choosing a college—everything from average SAT scores to our quality of life rating. The result is a list of the schools that match your needs and a wealth of detailed information about each, including, in many cases, the inside word from students on their schools' faculty, workload, social life, sports, and more. Each profile includes links to the colleges' websites.

**College Admissions Discussion.** Share your college admissions experiences and get expert advice from Princeton Review moderators. It's the most popular college admissions discussion area anywhere on the Net.

**Counselor-O-Matic.** Get a sense of your chance of admission at schools you are interested in. You start by completing a profile from which we create three custom lists of schools based on your responses: Safety schools, ballpark schools, and reach schools. You can also use this tool to rate your own statistics against the average for each school. Find out if you're a shoo-in or out of your league.

*APPLY!* Access hundreds of college-specific admissions applications including everything from instructions to financial aid forms, as well as teacher recommendations and counselor reports. *APPLY!* lets you enter personal information just once—common information automatically appears in each application you choose. Complete each application by viewing it on the screen and tabbing through to fill in the blanks. Finally, print and mail applications to the college in the traditional manner or transmit them electronically. It's the easiest and most popular way to complete college applications anywhere!

The Princeton Review can be reached on the World Wide Web at www.review.com.

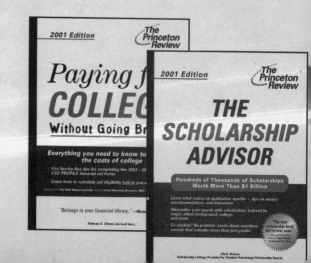

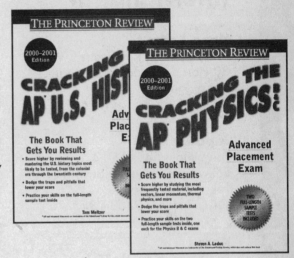
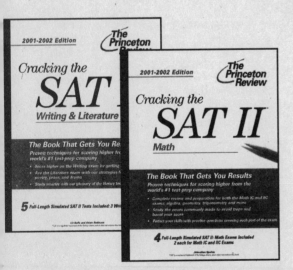

# FIND US...

## International

### Hong Kong
4/F Sun Hung Kai Centre
30 Harbour Road, Wan Chai,
Hong Kong
Tel: (011)85-2-517-3016

### Japan
Fuji Building 40, 15-14
Sakuragaokacho, Shibuya Ku,
Tokyo 150, Japan
Tel: (011)81-3-3463-1343

### Korea
Tae Young Bldg, 944-24,
Daechi- Dong, Kangnam-Ku
The Princeton Review- ANC
Seoul, Korea 135-280,
South Korea
Tel: (011)82-2-554-7763

### Mexico City
PR Mex S De RL De Cv
Guanajuato 228 Col. Roma
06700 Mexico D.F., Mexico
Tel: 525-564-9468

### Montreal
666 Sherbrooke St.
West, Suite 202
Montreal, QC H3A 1E7 Canada
Tel: 514-499-0870

### Pakistan
1 Bawa Park - 90 Upper Mall
Lahore, Pakistan
Tel: (011)92-42-571-2315

### Spain
Pza. Castilla, 3 - 5º A, 28046
Madrid, Spain
Tel: (011)341-323-4212

### Taiwan
155 Chung Hsiao East Road
Section 4 - 4th Floor,
Taipei R.O.C., Taiwan
Tel: (011)886-2-751-1243

### Thailand
Building One, 99 Wireless Road
Bangkok, Thailand 10330
Tel: 662-256-7080

### Toronto
1240 Bay Street, Suite 300
Toronto M5R 2A7 Canada
Tel: 800-495 7737
Tel: 716-839 4391

### Vancouver
4212 University Way NE,
Suite 204
Seattle, WA 98105
Tel: 206-548 1100

## National (U.S.)

We have over 60 offices around the U.S. and run courses in over 400 sites. For courses and locations within the U.S. call 1-800-2-Review and you will be routed to the nearest office.